D0765665

The Cambridge Handbook of the Psychology of Prejudice

The Cambridge Handbook of the Psychology of Prejudice aims to answer the questions: Why is prejudice so persistent? How does it affect people exposed to it? And what can we do about it? Providing a comprehensive examination of prejudice from its evolutionary beginnings and environmental influences through to its manifestations and consequences, this handbook is an essential resource for scholars and students who are passionate about understanding prejudice, social change, collective action, and prejudice reduction. Featuring cutting-edge research from top scholars in the field, the chapters provide an overview of psychological models of prejudice; investigate prejudice in specific domains such as race, religion, gender, and appearance; and develop explicit, evidence-based strategies for disrupting the processes that produce and maintain prejudice. This handbook challenges researchers and readers to move beyond their comfort zone and sets the agenda for future avenues of research, policy, and intervention.

DR. CHRIS G. SIBLEY is a researcher in social psychology and founder of the New Zealand Attitudes and Values Study (NZAVS), a twenty-year longitudinal national probability study of social attitudes, personality, and health outcomes across New Zealand. As an author of over 200 peer-reviewed articles and book chapters, he was identified as a "Rising Star" by the Association for Psychological Science in 2011 and received the Erik Erikson Early Career Award in 2014 from the International Society of Political Psychology. He is a long-time collaborator of Dr. Fiona Kate Barlow and currently holds an Associate Professorship at the University of Auckland, New Zealand.

DR. FIONA KATE BARLOW is a social psychologist specializing in the study of race relations. From 2012 to 2014, she held an Australian Research Council early career fellowship, and in 2016 accepted an Australian Research Council Future Fellowship Award. She is the recipient of the 2013 Society for Australasian Social Psychology Early Career

Researcher Award. During the majority of her role as co-editor of this handbook she was a Senior Lecturer at the School of Applied Psychology and Menzies Health Institute Queensland at Griffith University, Queensland, Australia. She is currently a Senior Research Fellow at the School of Psychology at the University of Queensland.

The Cambridge Handbook
of the Psychology of Prejudice

Edited by

Chris G. Sibley
University of Auckland, New Zealand

Fiona Kate Barlow
University of Queensland, Australia

CAMBRIDGE
UNIVERSITY PRESS

CAMBRIDGE
UNIVERSITY PRESS

University Printing House, Cambridge CB2 8BS, United Kingdom

One Liberty Plaza, 20th Floor, New York, NY 10006, USA

477 Williamstown Road, Port Melbourne, VIC 3207, Australia

4843/24, 2nd Floor, Ansari Road, Daryaganj, Delhi - 110002, India

79 Anson Road, #06-04/06, Singapore 079906

Cambridge University Press is part of the University of Cambridge.

It furthers the University's mission by disseminating knowledge in the pursuit of education, learning and research at the highest international levels of excellence.

www.cambridge.org
Information on this title: www.cambridge.org/9781107098336

© Cambridge University Press 2017

First published 2017

A catalogue record for this publication is available from the British Library

ISBN 978-1-107-09833-6 Hardback
ISBN 978-1-107-48528-0 Paperback

This book is dedicated to Jane Elliott

Contents

List of Figures   *page* x
List of Tables   xii
Notes on the Contributors   xiii

Part I General Theoretical Perspectives   1

1   An Introduction to the Psychology of Prejudice   3
    CHRIS G. SIBLEY AND FIONA KATE BARLOW

2   Evolutionary Approaches to Stereotyping and Prejudice   21
    OLIVER SNG, KEELAH E. G. WILLIAMS, AND STEVEN L. NEUBERG

3   From Prejudice to Social Change: A Social Identity Perspective   47
    KATHERINE J. REYNOLDS, EMINA SUBASIC, LUISA BATALHA, AND
    BENJAMIN M. JONES

4   Ingroup Projection as a Challenge of Diversity: Consensus about
    and Complexity of Superordinate Categories   65
    MICHAEL WENZEL, SVEN WALDZUS, AND MELANIE C. STEFFENS

5   Intergroup Discrimination: Ingroup Love or Outgroup Hate? 90
    MARILYNN B. BREWER

6   Intergroup Emotions Theory: Prejudice and Differentiated
    Emotional Reactions toward Outgroups   111
    ANGELA T. MAITNER, ELIOT R. SMITH, AND DIANE M. MACKIE

7   Intergroup Threats   131
    WALTER G. STEPHAN AND COOKIE WHITE STEPHAN

8   Social Dominance Theory: Explorations in the Psychology of
    Oppression   149
    JIM SIDANIUS, SARAH COTTERILL, JENNIFER
    SHEEHY-SKEFFINGTON, NOUR KTEILY, AND HÉCTOR
    CARVACHO

9   The Dual Process Motivational Model of Ideology and Prejudice   188
    JOHN DUCKITT AND CHRIS G. SIBLEY

10 Is Prejudice Heritable? Evidence from Twin Studies   222
    FIONA KATE BARLOW, JAMES M. SHERLOCK, AND BRENDAN
    P. ZIETSCH

    Part II Prejudice in Specific Domains   239

11 Understanding the Nature, Measurement, and Utility
    of Implicit Intergroup Biases   241
    KUMAR YOGEESWARAN, THIERRY DEVOS, AND KYLE NASH

12 Aversive Racism and Contemporary Bias   267
    JOHN F. DOVIDIO, SAMUEL L. GAERTNER, AND ADAM R. PEARSON

13 Ambivalent Sexism in the Twenty-First Century   295
    RACHEL A. CONNOR, PETER GLICK, AND SUSAN T. FISKE

14 Sexism in Intimate Contexts: How Romantic Relationships
    Help Explain the Origins, Functions, and Consequences of Sexist
    Attitudes   321
    MATTHEW D. HAMMOND AND NICKOLA C. OVERALL

15 Religion and Prejudice   344
    BEN K. L. NG AND WILL M. GERVAIS

16 Sexual Prejudice: Advances in Conceptual and Empirical
    Models   371
    V. PAUL POTEAT AND MICHELLE BIRKETT

17 Weight Bias: Prejudice and Discrimination toward Overweight
    and Obese People   392
    PHILLIPPA C. DIEDRICHS AND REBECCA PUHL

18 Prejudice Against Immigrants in Multicultural Societies   413
    COLLEEN WARD, AGNES SZABO, AND JAIMEE STUART

19 Generalized Prejudice: Old Wisdom and New Perspectives   438
    ROBIN BERGH AND NAZAR AKRAMI

    Part III Prejudice Reduction and Analysis in Applied Contexts   461

20 Recent Developments in Intergroup Contact Research: Affective
    Processes, Group Status, and Contact Valence   463
    LINDA R. TROPP, AGOSTINO MAZZIOTTA, AND STEPHEN C. WRIGHT

21 From Prejudice Reduction to Collective Action: Two Psychological
    Models of Social Change (and How to Reconcile Them)   481
    JOHN DIXON, KEVIN DURRHEIM, CLIFFORD STEVENSON,
    AND HUSEYIN CAKAL

22 Self-Regulation Strategies for Combatting Prejudice   500
    MASON D. BURNS, LAURA RUTH M. PARKER, AND MARGO
    J. MONTEITH

23 Antecedents and Consequences of Evaluative Concerns
    Experienced During Intergroup Interaction: When and
    How Does Group Status Matter?   519
    JACQUIE D. VORAUER AND MATTHEW QUESNEL

24 Stereotypicality Biases and the Criminal Justice System   542
    DANNY OSBORNE, PAUL G. DAVIES, AND SHIRLEY HUTCHINSON

25 Prejudice, Stigma, Bias, Discrimination, and Health   559
    YIN PARADIES, JOÃO LUIZ BASTOS, AND NAOMI PRIEST

26 Development of Delegitimization and Animosity in the
    Context of Intractable Conflict   582
    DANIEL BAR-TAL AND TALIA AVRAHAMZON

27 Interventions in Real-World Settings: Using Media to
    Overcome Prejudice and Promote Intergroup Reconciliation
    in Central Africa   607
    REZARTA BILALI AND ERVIN STAUB

28 Identification with All Humanity: The Antithesis of Prejudice,
    and More   632
    SAM MCFARLAND

29 It's All About Ignorance: Reflections from the
    Blue-eyed/Brown-eyed Exercise   655
    JANE ELLIOTT

    Index   669

Figures

3.1 Classification of social psychological theories of prejudice. *page* 49
4.1 Ingroup projection and perceived projection by outgroups. 71
4.2 Complex representations of the superordinate group. 77
4.3 Schematic map of the ingroup projection model. 81
7.1 Intergroup threat model. 132
8.1 Schematic overview of social dominance theory (from Pratto, Sidanius, & Levin, 2006). 151
9.1 A dual process motivational model of the impact of personality, social environment, and social worldview beliefs on the two ideological attitude dimensions of right-wing authoritarianism (RWA) and social dominance orientation (SDO) and corresponding prejudice-related outcomes. 191
9.2 A dual process motivational model of how intergroup or situational dynamics activate dual motivational goals expressed in the ideological attitudes of RWA and SDO to generate outgroup perceptions that result in outgroup prejudice. 202
10.1 Path diagram demonstrating the degree of resemblance between identical/monozygotic (MZ) and nonidentical/dizygotic (DZ) twins for additive genetic (*A*), shared environmental (*C*), and residual (*E*) influences. Phenotypic variance (equal for each twin pair) is influenced by latent factors *A*, *C*, and *E*. The variance associated with these factors is shared between twin pairs at varying magnitudes based on the zygosity of the twin pair and the characteristics of the factor itself. MZ twins share 100% of the variance caused by *A*, whereas DZ twins share half this influence. *C* is shared equally at 100% between identical and nonidentical twin pairs. By definition, *E* is the remaining unique variance in the phenotype not explained by *A* and *C* combined. 226
11.1 Implicit Association Test procedure. 248
11.2 Priming procedure. 249
11.3 Go/No-Go Association Test procedure. 251
18.1 Acculturation strategies of ethno-cultural groups and the larger society (Berry, 2003). 421

18.2 Multilevel integrative framework for the cross-cultural study of
      prejudice and discrimination against immigrants (adapted from
      Guimond et al., 2014).   427
19.1 A schematic illustration of variance components in prejudice and
      theoretical perspectives explaining them.   447
19.2 A schematic illustration of devaluation of groups perceived as
      symbolically or realistically threatening a societal "order." Alternative
      conceptualizations of the facets are possible (such as security/norms
      and competition/derogation), but the emphasis here is on the
      overarching communalities.   454
22.1 The self-regulation of prejudice model.   505
24.1 Example of variations in perceived stereotypicality. The given
      target's appearance has been digitally altered to appear
      low (a), medium (b), or high (c) in perceived stereotypicality.   546
24.2 Contextual model of eyewitness identification in which the crime
      type affects eyewitness identification via stereotype activation.
      Estimator and system variables moderate this relationship at separate
      stages of the identification process (adapted from Osborne &
      Davies, 2014).   550
25.1 Multiple pathways linking discrimination to ill health (adapted
      from Paradies et al., 2013).   565

Tables

1.1 Historical overview of the major paradigms in the social scientific study of prejudice (from Duckitt, 2010). *page* 5

8.1 Social psychological domains in which social dominance theory has been applied (since 2005). 153

10.1 Variance component estimates for items on the Wilson-Patterson Conservatism scale (Wilson & Patterson, 1968, as reported in Martin et al., 1986). 228

10.2 Variance component estimates for items on the Wilson-Patterson Conservatism scale (Wilson & Patterson, 1968, as reported in Alford et al., 2005). 229

13.1 The Ambivalent Sexism Inventory (ASI). 297

14.1 Summary of key points demonstrating that intimate relationships are central to understanding the emergence, function, and consequences of men's sexist attitudes toward women. 322

14.2 Summary of key points demonstrating that intimate relationships are central to understanding the emergence, function, and consequences of women's sexist attitudes toward women. 323

19.1 Descriptions of generalized prejudice (or ethnocentrism in studies primarily focusing on correlated prejudices, i.e., generalized prejudice). 441

21.1 Two models of social change. 490

23.1 Predictions made by information search model (Vorauer, 2006) regarding pragmatic and self-evaluative importance attached to outgroup's perspective. 523

27.1 Features of the implementation of the intervention. 615

27.2 Summary of research findings assessing the impact of reconciliation radio dramas in Rwanda, Burundi, and the DRC. 618

Notes on the Contributors

NAZAR AKRAMI, Department of Psychology, Uppsala University

TALIA AVRAHAMZON, Research School of Social Science, Australian National University

DANIEL BAR-TAL, School of Education, Tel Aviv University

FIONA KATE BARLOW, School of Applied Psychology and Menzies Health Institute Queensland; Griffith University; and School of Psychology, University of Queensland

JOÃO LUIZ BASTOS, Department of Public Health, Federal University of Santa Catarina

LUISA BATALHA, School of Psychology, Australian Catholic University

ROBIN BERGH, Department of Psychology, Harvard University; and Department of Psychology, Uppsala University

REZARTA BILALI, Department of Applied Psychology, New York University

MICHELLE BIRKETT, School of Medicine, Northwestern University

MARILYNN B. BREWER, Department of Psychology, Ohio State University

MASON D. BURNS, Department of Psychological Sciences, Purdue University

HUSEYIN CAKAL, Department of Psychology, University of Exeter

HÉCTOR CARVACHO, Department of Psychology, Harvard University; and Escuela de Psicología, Pontificia Universidad Católica de Chile

RACHEL A. CONNOR, Department of Psychology, Princeton University

SARAH COTTERILL, Department of Psychology, Harvard University

PAUL G. DAVIES, Department of Psychology, University of British Columbia

THIERRY DEVOS, Department of Psychology, San Diego State University

PHILLIPPA C. DIEDRICHS, Centre for Appearance Research, University of the West of England

JOHN DIXON, Faculty of Social Sciences, Open University

JOHN F. DOVIDIO, Department of Psychology, Yale University

JOHN DUCKITT, School of Psychology, University of Auckland

KEVIN DURRHEIM, Discipline of Psychology, University of KwaZulu-Natal

JANE ELLIOTT, Independent researcher

SUSAN T. FISKE, Department of Psychology, Princeton University

SAMUEL L. GAERTNER, Department of Psychological and Brain Sciences, University of Delaware

WILL M. GERVAIS, Department of Psychology, University of Kentucky

PETER GLICK, Department of Psychology, Lawrence University

MATTHEW D. HAMMOND, School of Psychology, Victoria University of Wellington

SHIRLEY HUTCHINSON, Department of Psychology, University of British Columbia

BENJAMIN M. JONES, Research School of Psychology, Australian National University

NOUR KTEILY, Kellogg School of Management, Northwestern University

DIANE M. MACKIE, Department of Psychological and Brain Sciences, University of California, Santa Barbara

ANGELA T. MAITNER, Department of International Studies, American University of Sharjah

AGOSTINO MAZZIOTTA, Institut für Psychologie, FernUniversität in Hagen

SAM MCFARLAND, Department of Psychology, Western Kentucky University

MARGO J. MONTEITH, Department of Psychological Sciences, Purdue University

KYLE NASH, Department of Psychology, University of Canterbury

STEVEN L. NEUBERG, Department of Psychology, Arizona State University

BEN K. L. NG, Department of Psychology, University of Kentucky

DANNY OSBORNE, School of Psychology, University of Auckland

NICKOLA C. OVERALL, School of Psychology, University of Auckland

YIN PARADIES, Alfred Deakin Institute for Citizenship and Globalization, Deakin University.

LAURA RUTH M. PARKER, Department of Psychological Sciences, Purdue University

ADAM R. PEARSON, Department of Psychology, Pomona College

V. PAUL POTEAT, Lynch School of Education, Boston College

NAOMI PRIEST, Centre for Social Research and Methods, Australian National University

REBECCA PUHL, Rudd Center for Food Policy and Obesity, University of Connecticut

MATTHEW QUESNEL, Department of Psychology, University of Manitoba

KATHERINE J. REYNOLDS, Research School of Psychology, Australian National University

JENNIFER SHEEHY-SKEFFINGTON, Department of Psychology, University of Oslo

JAMES M. SHERLOCK, School of Psychology, University of Queensland.

CHRIS G. SIBLEY, School of Psychology, University of Auckland

JIM SIDANIUS, Department of Psychology, Department of African and African American Studies, Harvard University

ELIOT R. SMITH, Department of Psychological and Brain Sciences, Indiana University

OLIVER SNG, Department of Psychology, Arizona State University

ERVIN STAUB, Department of Psychological and Brain Sciences, University of Massachusetts, Amherst

MELANIE C. STEFFENS, Department of Social and Economic Psychology, University of Koblenz-Landau

COOKIE WHITE STEPHAN, Department of Psychology, New Mexico State University

WALTER G. STEPHAN, Department of Psychology, New Mexico State University

CLIFFORD STEVENSON, Department of Psychology, University of Anglia Ruskin

JAIMEE STUART, Centre for Applied Cross-cultural Research, Victoria University of Wellington

EMINA SUBASIC, School of Psychology, University of Newcastle

AGNES SZABO, Centre for Applied Cross-cultural Research, Victoria University of Wellington

LINDA R. TROPP, Department of Psychological and Brain Sciences, University of Massachusetts, Amherst

JACQUIE D. VORAUER, Department of Psychology, University of Manitoba

SVEN WALDZUS, Departamento de Psicologia Social e das Organizações, Instituto Universitário de Lisboa (ISCTE-IUL)/CIS-IUL

COLLEEN WARD, Centre for Applied Cross-cultural Research, Victoria University of Wellington

MICHAEL WENZEL, School of Psychology, Flinders University

KEELAH E. G. WILLIAMS, Department of Psychology, Arizona State University

STEPHEN C. WRIGHT, Department of Psychology, Simon Fraser University

KUMAR YOGEESWARAN, Department of Psychology, University of Canterbury

BRENDAN P. ZIETSCH, School of Psychology, University of Queensland; and QIMR Berghofer Medical Research Institute

PART I

General Theoretical Perspectives

1 An Introduction to the Psychology of Prejudice

Chris G. Sibley

School of Psychology, University of Auckland

Fiona Kate Barlow

School of Applied Psychology, Griffith University.

What Is Prejudice?

What makes something, say a particular attitude or belief, an expression of prejudice? What defines a particular attitude as racist or sexist? We are often asked these questions by our students, reporters, and sometimes (although perhaps not often enough) by policymakers. The question of "what is prejudice?" is a difficult and extremely important one to answer. According to Gordon Allport (1954, p. 9), and many of the subsequent textbooks in social psychology and related areas, prejudice can be defined as "an antipathy based upon a faulty and inflexible generalization. It may be directed toward a group as a whole, or toward an individual because he [sic] is a member of that group."

Allport's definition of prejudice-as-antipathy, or to use some other synonyms, prejudice-as-overt-dislike, hostility, or aversion, is consistent with many of the types of attitudes that members of the public may tend to naturally think of as being, for example, sexist, racist, homophobic, and so forth. Researchers working in the area of prejudice and intergroup relations owe Gordon Allport a huge intellectual debt for his founding work in the area. However, when it comes to a working definition of prejudice, Allport's was incomplete.

Indeed, in the introduction to *On the Nature of Prejudice: Fifty Years after Allport*, Dovidio, Glick, and Rudman (2005) commented that the definition of prejudice-as-antipathy was "Allport's most fundamental blindspot" (p. 10). We agree, and many of the chapters in this handbook illustrate the point. For example, Connor, Glick, and Fiske (2017) and Hammond and Overall (2017) emphasize that patronizing attitudes that position one group as weaker than the other and in need of protection (such as benevolent sexism) perform remarkably well in maintaining inequality. Similarly, Brewer's (2017) chapter highlights that disparity can arise *not only* as a result from outgroup hate but rather because of ingroup love. Neither of these phenomena fit a definition of prejudice-as-antipathy. However, they may sometimes have a more powerful effect on diffusing resistance to inequality and hierarchy and legitimizing violence and oppression because of the very fact that they seem caring or are focused on ingroup preservation, rather than overt anti-outgroup hostility.

Hence, in our view, asking whether a particular attitude or belief may be defined as prejudice is not necessarily the most important question. Instead, determining whether certain beliefs, attitudes, ideologies, stereotypes, and so forth function to help maintain hierarchy and exploitation may be more productive, at least if the goal is to challenge inequality. It is at this point that we can begin to investigate the factors that disrupt the creation and maintenance of prejudice and inequality. In this sense, we define prejudice as "those ideologies, attitudes, and beliefs that help maintain and legitimize group-based hierarchy and exploitation" (see also Eagly & Diekman, 2005; Jackman, 1994; Sidanius & Pratto, 1999).

Providing concrete answers to questions about the processes that produce and maintain prejudice and explicit, evidence-based, and effective recommendations for how such processes can be disrupted is no easy feat. As we often admit to our students (but sadly, less so to reporters and policymakers), if we had a ready "one size fits all" answer to the question of how the processes that cause – for lack of a better term – prejudice could be disrupted, then the problem of prejudice would probably already be solved.

A Brief Historical Overview

The theoretical lens through which we view prejudice has changed substantially since Allport (1954) penned his seminal work, *The Nature of Prejudice*. To understand current scholarship on the social psychology of prejudice, an understanding of the historical context of our theories and models is needed. Duckitt (2010) argued that the social scientific study of prejudice has undergone eight distinct paradigm shifts since the scientific study of the topic began early last century. Duckitt's (2010) model of these eight historical paradigms begins with a perspective of prejudice as a natural response to so-called "backward" peoples that prevailed up until around the 1920s and leads up to the current zeitgeist, which emerged sometime in the new millennium, where prejudice tends to be viewed as complex, affective, and motivationally driven. Duckitt's (2010) summary of historical paradigms through which prejudice has been studied along with the prevailing definition of prejudice at the time are summarized in Table 1.1.

Duckitt's (2010) analysis of the paradigm shifts in the study of prejudice highlights that such shifts do not necessarily follow a linear progression. That is, the emergence of historical paradigms does not necessarily follow a process in which dominant theories and methods of the time were formally refuted and replaced with more advanced (and more scientifically valid) ones. Certainly this is true to some extent, but as Duckitt (2010) noted, the history of the study of prejudice seems to have also shifted focus in reaction to changing historical circumstances. A good example of this is the development of the theory of authoritarian personality, which

Table 1.1 *Historical overview of the major paradigms in the social scientific study of prejudice (from Duckitt, 2010).*

Social and historical context and issues	Concept of prejudice and dominant theoretical approach	Dominant social policy orientation to prejudice and discrimination
Up to the 1920s: White domination and colonial rule of "backward peoples"	Prejudice as a natural response to the deficiencies of "backward" peoples: race theories	Domination, discrimination, and segregation are natural and justified social policies
The 1920s: The legitimacy of White domination challenged	Prejudice as irrational and unjustified: measuring and describing prejudice	Prejudice will fade as the social sciences clarify how wrong and unjustified it is
The 1930s and 1940s: The ubiquity and tenacity of White racism	Prejudice as an unconscious defense: psychoanalytic and frustration theories	Gradual acceptance as minorities and colonial peoples become assimilated
The 1950s: Nazi racial ideology and the holocaust	Prejudice rooted in antidemocratic ideology and authoritarian personalities	Democracy and liberal values will erode intolerance and prejudice
The 1960s: The problem of institutionalized racism in the American South	Sociocultural explanations: racism rooted in social norms of discriminatory social structures	Desegregation and antidiscriminatory laws will erode and eliminate racism and prejudice
The 1970s: The problem of informal racism and discrimination in the North	Prejudice as an expression of dominant group interests in maintaining intergroup inequality	Reducing intergroup inequality through affirmative action and minority empowerment
The 1980s and 1990s: The stubborn persistence of stereotyping, prejudice, and discrimination	Prejudice as an expression of universal cognitive processes: social categorization and identity	Multicultural policies to provide minorities with esteem and positive identities and to foster tolerance
Post-2000: Confronting a complex world of multiple-based and often irrationally intense intergroup hostilities	Prejudice as complex, affective, and motivationally driven?	Broader approaches with strategies flexibly adapted to varying patterns of prejudice and situational dynamics?

was proposed in the context of understanding Nazi racial ideology and the holocaust (Adorno, Frenkel-Brunswick, Levinson, & Sanford, 1950).

As the chapters in this handbook show beyond contestation, prejudice remains one of the central social problems facing humanity. This is so today, and we expect prejudice and inequality to become more pressing in the future with increased population pressure, diminishing resources, increased globalization, and the growing likelihood of massive population displacement. The problem, or perhaps it would be more apt to say the challenge, of prejudice is also intertwined with the enduring problems of reducing inequality around the globe and solving large-scale human cooperative dilemmas. Such dilemmas are likely to include, for example, how we respond to climate change, how we allocate scarce resources on a global scale, and how we react to massive population displacement, likely the result of climate change and war, in the decades to come. This, we think, is likely to be the sociohistorical context shaping the social scientific study of prejudice in the decades to come.

The sociohistorical context shaping the contemporary study of prejudice also interacts with unprecedented advances in our ability to collect novel forms of data and statistically model the processes involved in the generation and outcomes of prejudice. In our view, the extent to which methodological innovations have influenced past paradigm shifts in the study of prejudice are one aspect of Duckitt's (2010) historical analysis that warrants further elaboration.

In this regard, our current research context is unprecedented with regard to the development of reaction time and neuropsychological, physiological, and genetic measures. It is unprecedented with regard to the ability to collect so-called Big Data, the relative ease of conducting large-scale, cross-national surveys, and the availability of data culled from online activity or automated passive observation. The analysis of data from this latter source is also something of which our field will need to carefully consider the ethics. Our current research context is also unlike any other time in history because of the rapid and exciting development of accessible new methods of statistically analyzing these and many other types of data – and we should add in the open and transparent sharing of data and the growing focus on replication.

Quite simply, the effect of novel methods in data modeling and analysis on consequent theory development cannot be underestimated, neither can developments in our ability to easily and rapidly collect new forms of data and measure new types of processes. To echo Greenwald (2012), who was in turn paraphrasing Lewin (1951), "there is nothing so theoretical as a good method." Greenwald was talking about science in general when he opined this, and it is an observation that the rapid pace of development in methods in the fields of prejudice and intergroup relations corroborate. In short, it is an exciting – and important – time in our history to be involved in the scientific study of prejudice, intergroup relations, and related fields of research.

An Overview of the Handbook

This handbook aims to move us closer toward the goal of understanding the factors that produce prejudice both within individuals and wider groups, as well as the outcomes of prejudice. This handbook also aims to bring us a little closer to the end-goal: that of increasing our understanding of how to go about disrupting the processes that generate or maintain prejudice, inequality, oppression, and their subsequent effects.

The chapters in this handbook represent the cutting edge of the scientific study of prejudice in a variety of domains, and from a variety of perspectives. Their aim as a whole is to provide comprehensive coverage of current theories of prejudice; many, if not all, of the chapters tend to converge on the consensus that prejudice is indeed, as Duckitt (2010) argued, complex, affective, and motivationally driven.

The handbook is organized into three broad parts. The chapters in Part I summarize general theoretical perspectives on prejudice at an overall level. The focus of Part I is thus on reviewing theories that provide the foundation for understanding the psychology of prejudice generally and are relevant for understanding prejudice toward multiple specific target groups and in diverse contexts. Part II contains chapters focusing on prejudice in specific domains, such as sexism and racism; related to this are theories about specific forms of prejudice and how prejudice operates in specific contexts. Finally, the chapters in Part III focus on the study of prejudice in applied domains – its outcomes and how to reduce it.

Part I: General Theoretical Perspectives

In Chapter 2, Sng, Williams and Neuberg (2017) present a broad evolutionary perspective on prejudice, stereotyping, and discrimination. This general evolutionary perspective underpins much of the research on the social scientific study of prejudice, and many of the following chapters in the handbook make explicit assumptions grounded in evolutionary psychology. To paraphrase Dobzhansky's (1973) well-known quote, nothing in the scientific study of prejudice and intergroup relations makes sense except in light of evolution.

Sng et al. begin their chapter by presenting an overview of evolutionary theory and address possible, and sometimes all too common, misconceptions about the theory. The authors then present an overview of the concept of affordance management systems – psychological systems adapted to identify and react to social threats and opportunities – and explain how modern-day expressions of prejudice are a result of such evolved systems. Evolutionary psychology provides a rich theoretical framework for generating novel hypotheses in many domains of psychology. Sng et al. take full advantage of this to review and derive a number of nuanced hypotheses that expand our understanding of the psychological processes that generate prejudice, and the contexts in which specific forms of prejudice will be expressed. This chapter, and the following one on social identity theory provide two of the key overarching meta-theoretical perspectives that anchor the remainder of the handbook.

In Chapter 3, Reynolds, Subasic, Batalha, and Jones (2017) introduce social identity theory and self-categorization theory as theoretical perspectives that explain not only the development and perpetuation of prejudice but also the development of social change and collective action to overcome societal inequality. In taking such an approach, they focus on social, rather than individual, predictors of prejudice. They develop a model in which they categorize theories explaining prejudice on two dimensions: (a) social stability to social change and (b) majority group focused to minority group focused. In particular, they make the case that any theory of prejudice that fails to take into account often rapid social change and challenge is flawed. They draw on multiple studies from within a social identity/ self-categorization framework to challenge old conceptualizations of prejudice, instead looking at factors such as group status, legitimacy, norms, and leadership as core drivers of prejudice versus social change.

In Chapter 4, Wenzel, Waldzus, and Steffens (2017) continue in the tradition of social identity theory with their presentation of the ingroup projection model. Wenzel et al. present a comprehensive review of work on the model to date, and they emphasize the crucial goal of superordinate identity complexity in reducing prejudice and increasing tolerance. Wenzel et al. begin their chapter by discussing an Austrian fable, "When the Crows Were Still Colorful." This fable tells the story of when crows came in myriad hues, with different colorful patterns on their wings. Then one day the crows were asked "what does the real or true crow look like?" and this of course began subgrouping, the creation of group boundaries, and ingroup bias and outgroup hostility. This fable is highly relevant to the ingroup projection model, and indeed to most of the chapters in this book. The handbook cover is a representation of the crows from this fable. We thank Yanshu Huang, who started her PhD in 2016 and is already herself a published researcher in the area of ambivalent sexism, for designing this cover image.

In Chapter 5, Brewer (2017) presents a comprehensive review of ingroup bias and outgroup hostility. Brewer argues that it is critical for research on prejudice and discrimination to differentiate between these two concepts, and further, that ingroup bias (or "love") can account for a substantial portion of the prejudice and discrimination in society. Brewer emphasizes the important point that prejudice and discrimination can readily arise in the absence of outgroup hostility and that ingroup favoritism alone may be enough to produce systemic discrimination and resulting inequality. As in the preceding chapter by Wenzel et al. (2017), Brewer discusses novel ways in which prejudice and discrimination can be ameliorated by reducing group boundaries and creating more inclusive ingroups or a common identity. With regard to the fable of the crows, for instance, this would mean creating a broader definition of crows as being of all colors and patterns (and, of course, this would require considerable crow "buy-in" to work).

In Chapter 6, Maitner, Smith, and Mackie (2017) introduce and review previous research on intergroup emotions theory. This theory extends social identity theory by articulating the mechanisms through which individuals react to and express different types of emotion toward outgroup members. Maitner et al. focus their discussion on three intergroup emotions: fear, anger, and contempt/disgust. These three emotional reactions tend to relate to intergroup conflict. The authors also provide an important discussion of how culture moderates emotional reactions, and they point to new directions for future research on the communication of emotions between groups. In our view, the intergroup communication of emotions provides a promising avenue for interventions aimed at conflict resolution.

In Chapter 7, Stephan and Stephan (2017) update and review their theory of intergroup threats. Intergroup threat theory is a multilevel theory that integrates a diverse array of research findings, including the evolutionary basis of threat perception (see Sng et al., 2017, Chapter 1), Social identity (see Reynolds et al., 2017, Chapter 3), and intergroup emotions (see Maitner et al., 2017, Chapter 6). Here, Stephan and Stephan distinguish between two broad types of threat, those that are realistic and those that are more symbolic in nature. They identify five distinct classes of threat antecedent: individual-based characteristics (such as personality and identity salience), attitudes and cognitions (such as stereotypes), intergroup contact (see also Tropp, Mazziotta, and Wright, 2017, Chapter 20), intergroup relations, and situational factors. The theory synthesizes work within these areas and outlines how the five classes of antecedent can generate realistic and symbolic threats, which in turn shape emotions, cognitions, and behavior.

In Chapter 8, Sidanius, Cotterill, Sheehy-Skeffington, Kteily, and Carvacho (2017) review social dominance theory. As the authors note, this chapter represents the first major review of the theory in a decade (the last being Pratto, Sidanius, & Levin, 2006). Sidanius and colleagues review and discuss research on a number of new and emerging aspects of social dominance theory, including the stability and contingent effects of social dominance orientation, the causal relationship between empathy and social dominance orientation, and a new mechanism through which they propose ideology contributes to the maintenance of inequality. The chapter also contains a comprehensive response to some of the recent criticisms of the theory and notes a number of new promising directions for future research. In addition to all of this, Sidanius et al. provide an exhaustive bibliography of research applying social dominance theory in different domains since 2005. This bibliography should prove invaluable to both students and scholars new to the theory.

In Chapter 9, Duckitt and Sibley (2017) review and update 15 years of research on the dual process model of ideology and prejudice (following the original formulation of the model by Duckitt in 2001). Duckitt's model provides an overall framework identifying *dual processes* that generate individual differences in prejudice and related ideologies. The theory draws on social dominance theory and the identification of social dominance orientation as one of two core motivational goals predicting prejudice. According to the dual process model, the other core motivational goal predicting prejudice is based on a threat-driven motivation for social cohesion, as indexed by right-wing authoritarianism. In this chapter, Duckitt and Sibley expand the dual process model by differentiating between legitimizing myths, group stratifications, targets of prejudice, and support for different policies and leadership styles that should be predicted by social dominance orientation and right-wing authoritarianism.

In Chapter 10, Barlow, Sherlock, and Zietsch (2017) bring the first section of the handbook to a close with their discussion of the heritability of prejudice. They review literature that suggests that individual tendencies to be prejudiced (or not) are genetic. They describe the classic twin study design, which forms the basis of all the research reviewed, before highlighting multiple studies showing that intergroup attitudes, political conservatism, and social dominance orientation (among other things) are often in large part heritable. They end by engaging with the troubled history of genetics and prejudice (with faulty understandings of the former often contributing to the latter) and speculate on how we wed together evidence-based interventions designed to reduce prejudice with the knowledge that some people are going to be more (or less) oriented toward intergroup suspicion and antipathy to begin with. As discussed earlier in this chapter, we believe that the discipline will only continue to grow and improve by taking into account biological as well as psychological determinants of prejudice, as the two are inextricably linked.

Part II: Prejudice in Specific Domains

In Chapter 11, Yogeeswaran, Devos, and Nash (2017) open the second part of the handbook with a review and summary of reaction time and neuropsychological measures of implicit prejudice. The development of such measures is arguably one of the most important advances in the scientific study of prejudice in recent decades. Yogeeswaran et al. provide a comprehensive review of the factors known to shape implicit biases and discuss the strengths and weaknesses of many of the most popular measures in the area. They review the Implicit Association Test, priming designs, the Go/No-Go Association Task, designs using functional magnetic resonance imaging, and electroencephalography. Yogeeswaran et al. also discuss how measures of implicit bias and neuropsychological processes inform our understanding of prejudice in applied domains, such as nonverbal behavior, job hiring, voting decisions, medical decision making, and economic choices. This chapter provides an extensive review of the methods available for assessing implicit prejudice and serves as an excellent starting point for researchers and students new to the field, as well as those wanting to keep abreast of key developments shaping the area.

In Chapter 12, Dovidio, Gaertner, and Pearson (2017) discuss contemporary forms of racism in the United States. Dovidio et al. first describe the development of subtle forms of racism, which came about in response to changing social norms in the post-civil rights era in the United States. The authors then introduce the concepts of symbolic racism, modern racism, ambivalent racism, and aversive racism. It is this latter theory for which Dovidio and colleagues are well known, and they provide a detailed and comprehensive review and update of their theory. A key concept in aversive racism theory is that people can express pro-egalitarian sentiments but simultaneously hold nonconscious or implicit biases.

Dovidio et al. extend the general review of implicit measures provided in the preceding chapter by Yogeeswaran et al. (2017) to focus specifically on measures of implicit or nonconscious racial bias. They also dedicate a substantial part of the chapter to discussing potential interventions informed by research on aversive racism theory. These include designs aiming to reduce implicit bias, correct for unconscious bias, harness egalitarian motives, and redirect the forces of ingroup bias. Aversive racism theory and other theories of contemporary racism form a cornerstone of research on racism more generally, and it is for this reason that we locate the chapter in Part II. However, the informative reflections and discussion of interventions aimed at reducing or eliminating the effects of implicit racial biases mean that this chapter could also easily fit in the third part of the handbook on prejudice reduction in applied contexts.

In Chapter 13, Connor et al. (2017) present a review and update of 20 years of research on ambivalent sexism theory. Since its initial presentation by Glick and Fiske in 1996, ambivalent sexism theory has arguably become the most influential theory of sexism in the field. No handbook on the psychology of prejudice would be complete without a chapter on this topic. The theory describes how two forms of sexism – hostile and benevolent – operate together to provide a powerful and synergistic ideological system that maintains and legitimizes patriarchy. As we alluded to in our opening discussion of the nature of prejudice, a key insight of the theory is that beliefs and attitudes that idealize women and position them as wonderful and caring are a key building block in a larger set of ideologies that justify gender inequality and the oppression of women. Connor et al. review recent research on ambivalent sexism theory and focus specifically on discussing how the theory informs our understanding of physical and sexual violence toward women.

In Chapter 14, Hammond and Overall (2017) follow directly from Connor et al. (2017) and discuss how ambivalent sexism operates in heterosexual romantic relationships. We recommend those new to the area read these two chapters sequentially. The chapter by Hammond and Overall fills an important gap in the literature by bringing together research and perspectives from the study of intimate relationships and the dyadic modeling of relationship processes, with research on ambivalent sexism. Hammond and Overall document and review accumulating evidence that demonstrates that benevolent sexism provides benefits to women *within intimate relationships*. They also provide a comprehensive list and discussion of key points demonstrating why and how intimate relationships are central to understanding the emergence, function, and consequences of women's attitudes toward men, and vice versa. This chapter provides an important bridge between research on interpersonal and intergroup processes relating to sexism, which have, for the most part, developed independently of each other.

In Chapter 15, Ng and Gervais (2017) discuss the links between religion and prejudice. Ng and Gervais turn to evolutionary theorizing to review both adaptationist and by-product accounts of religion. They then present an integrated evolutionary analysis of the role of religion in prejudice. This analysis builds on the more general review of the evolutionary basis of prejudice presented in Chapter 2 by Sng et al. Ng and Gervais identify distinct types of threats to the religious ingroup: threats to belief structures, threats to behaviors and ritual, and threats to belonging. The chapter outlines how reactions to such threats may in turn generate prejudice stratified along religious lines. Writing in 2016, and considering global fears about interreligious terrorism, this is a particularly salient and important chapter. Ng and Gervais apply their model to outline the links between religion and prejudice in three domains: anti-Muslim prejudice, sexual prejudice, and anti-atheist prejudice. According to their model, religious-based prejudice in each of these domains represents specific reactions tailored to deal with adaptive challenges (i.e., types of threat).

In Chapter 16, Poteat and Birkett (2017) review research on sexual prejudice. They begin by describing the different ways in which sexual prejudice has been operationalized over the years, in terms of homophobia, sexual stigma, heterosexism, and the modern definition of sexual prejudice (negative attitudes toward individuals based on their sexual minority group membership). The chapter draws on a wide range of theories and presents a comprehensive review of the individual and intergroup/societal factors associated with sexual prejudice. These include gender ideology, social dominance orientation, right-wing authoritarianism, the salience of sexual identity, levels of intergroup contact, peer socialization, and norms. Poteat and Birkett also discuss the importance of considering sexual prejudice in combination with multiple stigmatized identities and call for future research in this area.

In Chapter 17, Diedrichs and Puhl (2017) discuss the prevalence of weight bias and discrimination, discuss theories about their psychological antecedents, and outline the corrosive effects of this type of prejudice on the people who experience it. Weight bias refers to prejudice and discrimination toward overweight and obese individuals, and as Diedrichs and Puhl argue, represents one of the last socially acceptable or normative expressions of prejudice. The chapter provides a detailed review of the sources of weight bias in children, adolescents, adults, and the media more generally.

Among the many important findings reviewed in the chapter, Diedrichs and Puhl discuss research indicating that those who experience weight bias and body shaming may be more likely to engage in disordered eating and unhealthy weight control and generally show a higher risk of becoming and remaining obese. In our view, weight bias represents an important and potentially growing form of prejudice in many societies, and one that we think deserves more attention from researchers in our field. The chapter by Diedrichs and Puhl provides an excellent overview of current research and thinking in this area, and it makes an urgent call for research developing interventions to reduce this form of prejudice.

In Chapter 18, Ward, Szabo, and Stuart (2017) review theory and research on prejudice and discrimination directed toward immigrants. Immigration is on the rise worldwide, and this has and will continue to increase the cultural diversity of many nations. Ward and colleagues build on Stephan and Stephan's earlier chapter on intergroup threat theory and other related theories to discuss how perceived threats can shape anti-immigrant prejudice. Ward et al. expand this discussion by synthesizing research on intergroup relations with research on acculturation to present a unified multi-level framework for the cross-cultural study of prejudice and discrimination against immigrants. Their model provides a much-needed conduit between the acculturation and intergroup literatures.

In Chapter 19, Bergh and Akrami (2017) close the second part of the handbook with their discussion of generalized prejudice. The other chapters in this part focus on the nuances of prejudice and the diverse causes and consequences of prejudice directed toward specific target groups. Bergh and Akrami balance these perspectives by reviving the discussion of the generalization, or the consistency of individual differences in the expression of prejudice toward multiple targets. The authors argue that prejudice may be operationalized as multi-level framework reflecting different levels of abstraction. This framework contains a higher-order factor reflecting generalized prejudice, a facet-level set of factors, and lower-level factors representing variance in prejudice unique to specific target groups. Bergh and Akrami compile an impressive list of research findings in support of their model, and they argue that operationalizing prejudice as a multi-level phenomenon with varying levels of abstraction may help resolve seemingly inconsistent theoretical predictions in the literature.

Part III: Prejudice Reduction and Analysis in Applied Contexts

In Chapter 20, Tropp et al. (2017) introduce the applied section of the handbook with their comprehensive treatment of recent developments in intergroup contact theory. Intergroup contact is one of the most enduring and widely researched theories for reducing prejudice. The field of intergroup contact is also rapidly expanding in contemporary social psychology, generating many new and exciting developments and innovations in recent years. Tropp and colleagues provide a comprehensive review of contact research and focus on three key emerging areas within the field: the effects of affective processes in both direct and indirect contact, the effects of group status, and the effect of contact valence. This chapter thus provides an excellent review of "classic" contact research, as well as explanations of how contact works to reduce prejudice, while also directing contact researchers toward new avenues of study.

In Chapter 21, Dixon, Durrheim, Stevenson, and Cakal (2017) discuss the difference between models of social change that focus on prejudice reduction (which tend to be the majority of them, as evidenced by the title of this section) and those that focus on collective action. This distinction is something that had been largely overlooked until rather recently, with the emergence of work documenting the so-called ironic effects of contact (Dixon, Durrheim, & Tredoux, 2007) and encapsulated in the pithily titled article on the topic "Let them eat harmony . . ." (Dixon, Tropp, Durrheim, & Tredoux, 2010).

In their chapter, Dixon and colleagues synthesize and formalize their work on the interventions and psychological processes that either (a) may reduce prejudice (in terms of increasing how much groups feel positive toward each other) but not necessarily lead to reductions in inequality or hierarchy or (b) lead to political mobilization and may result in reductions in inequality but not necessarily more liking. Critically, and in their own words, the authors point to how it is inaccurate to think of this distinction in terms of a simple "prejudice reduction *versus* collective action" formulation. In this chapter, Dixon et al. lay the groundwork for future research exploring the strengths of both approaches, and the contexts in which they may be more or less effective for social change more broadly. Dixon et al. make an extremely important point in this regard, and we echo their call for further research on social change that explicitly considers both prejudice reduction and collective action.

In Chapter 22, Burns, Parker, and Monteith (2017) review the self-regulation of prejudice model. This model describes how people may effectively reduce their implicit and sometimes automatic stereotypic biases toward outgroups. This includes many of the types of implicit biases discussed in Chapter 11 by Yogeeswaran et al. The model focuses primarily on methods for reducing bias among individuals who generally hold explicit egalitarian beliefs. These are people who are presumably motivated to regulate their more subtle and automatic biases and are thus open to change (such as might be the general pattern evidenced by aversive racists, as discussed by Dovidio et al. in Chapter 12). Burns and colleagues outline self-regulation strategies that can be used to ameliorate subtle and implicit biases but also caution that such an approach is no silver bullet that will fix the problem (nothing we have seen is). Rather, self-regulation strategies provide an important tool within a broader integrated approach to prejudice reduction involving many lines of intervention.

In Chapter 23, Vorauer and Quesnel (2017) discuss evaluative concerns and review and update the information search model. The model describes the factors that cause people to experience anxiety and concern about how they themselves are perceived when interacting with members of other groups. Vorauer and Quesnel also discuss the consequences of such concerns, and how they can differ for members of high- versus low-status groups. The information search model provides a number of useful directions for improving intergroup relations, including targeting the goals and mind-set that individuals hold when engaging in intergroup contact (such as approach and learning goals), and the salience of intergroup identity (e.g., making salient multicultural ideology). Vorauer and Quesnel further discuss how some interventions aimed at reducing prejudice and improving intergroup attitudes may, ironically, increase evaluative concerns and hinder their effectiveness.

In Chapter 24, Osborne, Davies, and Hutchinson (2017) discuss stereotypicality biases in the criminal justice system. The chapter provides a natural follow-up from the methodological focus on implicit prejudice provided by Yogeeswaran et al. in the previous part and discusses how such biases result in race-based injustices within the justice system. More generally, Osborne et al. provide a comprehensive review of research on how perceived stereotypicality (the extent to which one is believed to look like a prototypical member of one's group) may affect outcomes for people within the criminal justice system. This includes the likelihood of being shot by police, biases in eyewitness identification, and even an increased likelihood of being sentenced to death – a chilling effect referred to as "looking deathworthy" (Eberhardt, Davies, Purdie-Vaughns, & Johnson, 2006). Osborne et al. provide a comprehensive and systematic update of the accumulated studies that have consistently identified such biases, and they document the extent to which such biases can have a powerful effect on the outcomes experienced by disadvantaged and minority groups.

In Chapter 25, Paradies, Bastos, and Priest (2017) discuss the effects of prejudice and discrimination in another critical applied domain: that of health. The authors provide a comprehensive review of the accumulated body of research evidence consistently showing that perceived discrimination is linked with poorer health outcomes. The authors review research documenting this effect using different measures of perceived discrimination in different populations and across different types of health outcomes (such as mental health, physical health, and health-related behaviors). For instance, as the authors review, research in this area shows that following the 9/11 terrorist attacks in the United States, the birthrate of people of Arab descent in California decreased, and that the mechanism driving the effect was most likely a widespread and pervasive increase in discrimination and prejudice directed toward them (Lauderdale, 2006). This chapter spans the gap between the social-psychological study of prejudice and discrimination and research on epidemiology and public health. We hope that this chapter will scaffold further collaborative research between these two often disparate areas.

In Chapter 26, Bar-Tal and Avrahamzon (2017) discuss how societies adapt and develop a sociopsychological repertoire to help citizens cope with chronic stress in contexts of seemingly intractable and enduring conflict. Two such examples are the Palestinian-Israeli conflict and conflict in Northern Ireland. In this chapter, Bar-Tal and Avrahamzon focus specifically on how young children are socialized to function in contexts of intractable conflict and to develop what the authors refer to as the "sociopsychological infrastructure of conflict." This refers to the intergenerational transmission and maintenance of animosity and extremely strong negative stereotypes that delegitimize rival groups. The chapter provides an important window into the psychology of children living in contexts of intractable conflict and highlights the extremely early age at which children may begin to acquire the antecedents of delegitimization and animosity toward the rival group (as young as 2 years old). Disrupting this developmental process represents an important part of the solution for long-term peace building and conflict resolution.

In Chapter 27, Bilali and Staub (2017) discuss the use of interventions to reduce prejudice and violence using mass media in the Great Lakes region of Africa. Their chapter provides a case study outlining how psychological principles can be translated to help design evidence-based, tailored interventions, and how the effects of such interventions can be assessed. Kurt Lewin (1951) famously stated, "there is nothing so practical as a good theory." Bilali and Staub provide an excellent example of this adage in action in the context of a highly charged socio-political setting with a history of conflict. Their chapter offers concrete suggestions for how basic research on the psychological study of prejudice and intergroup relations can be translated into field experiments and from there into policy and intervention.

In Chapter 28, McFarland (2017) discusses his work on identification with all humanity. McFarland discusses how identification with all humanity represents the antithesis of prejudice, and he presents evidence for the gradual but steady increase in this broad meta-identity over the past few centuries. This includes the appearance of the concept of "crimes against humanity" and the Universal Declaration of Human Rights. The chapter presents a comprehensive review of recent findings showing that identification with all humanity predicts a range of promising outcomes in the quest for increased tolerance and conflict resolution, including international charity, knowledge of humanitarian concerns, and support for human rights. McFarland discusses a number of potential factors that may contribute to the development and socialization of identification with all humanity, including child-rearing practices, heritability, religious faith, and empathy. McFarland argues – and we agree – that the study of the development of identification with all humanity represents an important field of inquiry for research on the psychology of prejudice, and one with considerable potential for prejudice reduction in applied settings.

In the concluding chapter of the handbook, we turn to one of the key figures in the history of our discipline, Jane Elliott (2017). Jane Elliott is not a psychologist or researcher, but a teacher and activist. Elliott's work has been massively influential in informing members of the general public (and our students) about the experience of prejudice and has shaped much consequent public debate and research. In this chapter, she offers her perspective on a life spent campaigning and developing interventions to reduce discrimination.

In 1968, Jane Elliott was working as a grade-school teacher in the United States. It was directly after the death of Martin Luther King Jr. that Elliott entered her third-grade classroom, in her own words, "determined to teach my students about the ugliness of prejudice and the discrimination that results from it." Many of our students read secondary accounts of Elliott's Blue-eyed /Brown-eyed exercise in their undergraduate social psychology textbooks or watch footage from documentaries. Along with such summaries, they also read secondary analyses by social scientists discussing the psychological mechanisms through which Elliott's exercise operates to cause self-reflection intended to reduce discrimination. Here, Elliott offers her own account of the events leading up to the creation of the Brown-eyed/Blue-eyed exercise, her personal analysis of why the exercise is such a powerful intervention, and her reflections on how to reduce racism more generally. With her incisive wit, she challenges us as researchers, arguing that *prejudice is not the problem*. Instead, she suggests, we need to challenge systems (rather than individuals) and actions (rather than feelings). Comparisons can be drawn between the arguments that Elliott makes and those highlighted by other authors within this book.

Elliott's challenge to us is real, and difficult. She asks us to ensure that our work is not just for show – she calls on us to make a difference. On an empirical level, she also (indirectly) asks us to think about our methods and measures – are there ways that we can make sure that behavior is assessed (and not just attitudes), for example? Finally, she asks us to be brave. Again, she does not do this directly. Instead, through her stories, including the sometimes frightening reactions to her work, she demonstrates qualities much needed in those who work to combat inequality: persistence, dedication, and perhaps even chutzpah.

We are all indebted to Jane Elliott for her insightful work and fierce passion in developing and championing interventions aimed at reducing prejudice in schools and workplaces. Reading the textbook summaries of her Brown-eyed/Blue-eyed exercise inspired both of us to work in the area when we were undergraduates, and we hope that reading her personal account may do the same for the next generation. We dedicate this book to her.

References

Adorno, T., Frenkel-Brunswick, E., Levinson, D., & Sanford, R. (1950). *The authoritarian personality*. New York: Harper.

Allport, G. W. (1954). *The nature of prejudice*. Cambridge, MA: Addison-Wesley.

Bar-Tal, D., & Avrahamzon, T. (2017). Development of delegitimization and animosity in the context of intractable conflict. In C. Sibley & F. K. Barlow (Eds.), *Cambridge handbook of the psychology of prejudice*. Cambridge: Cambridge University Press.

Barlow, F. K., Sherlock, J., & Zietsch, B. P. (2017). Is prejudice heritable? Evidence from twin studies. In C. Sibley & F. K. Barlow (Eds.), *Cambridge handbook of the psychology of prejudice*. Cambridge: Cambridge University Press.

Bergh, R., & Akrami, N. (2017). Generalized prejudice: Old wisdom and new perspectives. In C. Sibley & F. K. Barlow (Eds.), *Cambridge handbook of the psychology of prejudice*. Cambridge: Cambridge University Press.

Bilali, R., & Staub, E. (2017). Interventions in real-world settings: Using media to overcome prejudice and promote intergroup reconciliation in Central Africa. In C. Sibley &

F. K. Barlow (Eds.), *Cambridge handbook of the psychology of prejudice*. Cambridge: Cambridge University Press.

Brewer, M. B. (2017). Intergroup discrimination: Ingroup love or outgroup hate? In C. Sibley & F. K. Barlow (Eds.), *Cambridge handbook of the psychology of prejudice*. Cambridge: Cambridge University Press.

Burns, M., Parker, L. R. M., & Monteith, M. J. (2017). Self-regulation strategies for combatting prejudice. In C. Sibley & F. K. Barlow (Eds.), *Cambridge handbook of the psychology of prejudice*. Cambridge: Cambridge University Press.

Connor, R. A., Glick, P., & Fiske, S. T. (2017). Ambivalent sexism in the twenty-first century. In C. Sibley & F. K. Barlow (Eds.), *Cambridge handbook of the psychology of prejudice*. Cambridge: Cambridge University Press.

Dobzhansky, T. (1973). Nothing in biology makes sense except in the light of evolution. *American Biology Teacher, 35*, 125–129.

Diedrichs, P. C., & Puhl, R. (2017). Weight bias: Prejudice and discrimination toward overweight and obese people. In C. Sibley & F. K. Barlow (Eds.), *Cambridge handbook of the psychology of prejudice*. Cambridge: Cambridge University Press.

Dixon, J., Durrheim, K., Stevenson, C., & Cakal, H. (2017). From prejudice reduction to collective action: Two psychological models of social change (and how to reconcile them). In C. Sibley & F. K. Barlow (Eds.), *Cambridge handbook of the psychology of prejudice*. Cambridge: Cambridge University Press.

Dixon, J. A., Durrheim, K., & Tredoux, C. (2007). Intergroup contact and attitudes toward the principle and practice of racial equality. *Psychological Science, 18*, 867–872.

Dixon, J., Tropp, L. R., Durrheim, K., & Tredoux, C. (2010). "Let them eat harmony": Prejudice-reduction strategies and attitudes of historically disadvantaged groups. *Current Directions in Psychological Science, 19*, 76–80.

Dovidio, J. F., Gaertner, S. L., & Pearson, A. R. (2017). Aversive racism and contemporary bias. In C. Sibley & F. K. Barlow (Eds.), *Cambridge handbook of the psychology of prejudice*. Cambridge: Cambridge University Press.

Dovidio, J. F., Glick, P., & Rudman, L. (2005). Introduction: Reflecting on *The nature of prejudice: Fifty years after Allport*. In J. F. Dovidio, P. Glick, & L. A. Rudman (Eds.), *On the nature of prejudice: Fifty years after Allport* (pp. 19–35). Malden, MA: Blackwell.

Duckitt, J. (2001). A dual-process cognitive-motivational theory of ideology and prejudice. In M. P. Zanna (Ed.), *Advances in experimental social psychology* (Vol. 33, pp. 41–113). New York: Academic Press.

Duckitt, J. (2010). *Historical overview*. In J. F. Dovidio, M. Hewstone, P. Glick & V. M. Esses (Eds.), *The SAGE handbook of prejudice, stereotyping and discrimination* (pp. 29–45). London: Sage.

Duckitt, J., & Sibley, C. G. (2017). The dual process motivational model of ideology and prejudice. In C. Sibley & F. K. Barlow (Eds.), *Cambridge handbook of the psychology of prejudice*. Cambridge: Cambridge University Press.

Eagly, A. H., & Diekman, A. B. (2005). What is the problem? Prejudice as an attitude-in-context. In J. F. Dovidio, P. Glick, & L. A. Rudman (Eds.), *On the nature of prejudice: Fifty years after Allport* (pp. 19–35). Malden, MA: Blackwell.

Eberhardt, J. L., Davies, P. G., Purdie-Vaughns, V. J., & Johnson, S. L. (2006). Looking deathworthy: Perceived stereotypicality of black defendants predicts capital-sentencing outcomes. *Psychological Science, 17*, 383–386.

Elliott, J. (2017). It's all about ignorance: Reflections from the Blue-eyed/Brown-eyed exercise. In C. Sibley & F. K. Barlow (Eds.), *Cambridge handbook of the psychology of prejudice*. Cambridge: Cambridge University Press.

Glick, P., & Fiske, S. T. (1996). The Ambivalent Sexism Inventory: Differentiating hostile and benevolent sexism. *Journal of Personality and Social Psychology, 70*, 491–512.

Greenwald, A. G. (2012). There is nothing so theoretical as a good method. *Perspectives on Psychological Science, 7*, 99–108.

Hammond, M. D., & Overall, N. C. (2017). Sexism in intimate contexts: How romantic relationships help explain the origins, functions, and consequences of sexist attitudes. In C. Sibley & F. K. Barlow (Eds.), *Cambridge handbook of the psychology of prejudice*. Cambridge: Cambridge University Press.

Jackman, M. R. (1994). *The velvet glove: Paternalism and conflict in gender, class, and race relations*. Berkley: University of California Press.

Lauderdale, D. S. (2006). Birth outcomes for Arabic-named women in California before and after September 11. *Demography, 43*, 185–201.

Lewin, K. (1951). *Field theory in social science: Selected theoretical papers* (D. Cartwright, Ed.). New York: Harper & Row.

Maitner, A. T., Smith, E. R., & Mackie, D. M. (2017). Intergroup emotions theory: Prejudice and differentiated emotional reactions toward outgroups. In C. Sibley & F. K. Barlow (Eds.), *Cambridge handbook of the psychology of prejudice*. Cambridge: Cambridge University Press.

McFarland, S. (2017). Identification with all humanity: The antithesis of prejudice, and more. In C. Sibley & F. K. Barlow (Eds.), *Cambridge handbook of the psychology of prejudice*. Cambridge: Cambridge University Press.

Ng, B. K. L., & Gervais, W. M. (2017). Religion and prejudice. In C. Sibley & F. K. Barlow (Eds.), *Cambridge handbook of the psychology of prejudice*. Cambridge: Cambridge University Press.

Osborne, D., Davies, P. G., & Hutchinson, S. (2017). Stereotypicality biases and the criminal justice system. In C. Sibley & F. K. Barlow (Eds.), *Cambridge handbook of the psychology of prejudice*. Cambridge: Cambridge University Press.

Paradies, Y., Bastos, J. L., & Priest, N. (2017). Prejudice, stigma, bias, discrimination, and health. In C. Sibley & F. K. Barlow (Eds.), *Cambridge handbook of the psychology of prejudice*. Cambridge: Cambridge University Press.

Poteat, V. P., & Birkett, M. (2017). Sexual prejudice: Advances in conceptual and empirical models. In C. Sibley & F. K. Barlow (Eds.), *Cambridge handbook of the psychology of prejudice*. Cambridge: Cambridge University Press.

Pratto, F., Sidanius, J., & Levin, S. (2006). Social dominance theory and the dynamics of intergroup relations: Taking stock and looking forward. *European Review of Social Psychology, 17*, 271–320.

Reynolds, K. J., Subasic, E., Batalha, L., & Jones, B. (2017). From prejudice to social change: a social identity perspective. In C. Sibley & F. K. Barlow (Eds.), *Cambridge handbook of the psychology of prejudice*. Cambridge: Cambridge University Press.

Sidanius, J., Cotterill, S., Sheehy-Skeffington, J., Kteily, N., & Carvacho, H. (2017). Social dominance theory: Explorations in the psychology of oppression. In C. Sibley & F. K. Barlow (Eds.), *Cambridge handbook of the psychology of prejudice*. Cambridge: Cambridge University Press.

Sidanius, J., & Pratto, F. (1999). *Social dominance: An intergroup theory of social hierarchy and oppression*. Cambridge: Cambridge University Press.

Sng, O., Williams, K. E. G., & Neuberg, S. L. (2017). Evolutionary approaches to stereotyping and prejudice. In C. Sibley & F. K. Barlow (Eds.), *Cambridge handbook of the psychology of prejudice*. Cambridge: Cambridge University Press.

Stephan, W. G., & Stephan, C. W. (2017). Intergroup threats. In C. Sibley & F. K. Barlow (Eds.), *Cambridge handbook of the psychology of prejudice*. Cambridge: Cambridge University Press.

Tropp, L. R., Mazziotta, A., & Wright, S. C. (2017). Recent developments in intergroup contact research: Affective processes, group status, and contact valence. In C. Sibley & F. K. Barlow (Eds.), *Cambridge handbook of the psychology of prejudice*. Cambridge: Cambridge University Press.

Vorauer, J. D., & Quesnel, M. (2017). Antecedents and consequences of evaluative concerns experienced during intergroup interaction: When and how does group status matter? In C. Sibley & F. K. Barlow (Eds.), *Cambridge handbook of the psychology of prejudice*. Cambridge: Cambridge University Press.

Ward, C., Szabo, A., & Stuart, J. (2017). Prejudice against immigrants in multicultural societies. In C. Sibley & F. K. Barlow (Eds.), *Cambridge handbook of the psychology of prejudice*. Cambridge: Cambridge University Press.

Wenzel, M., Waldzus, S., & Steffens, M. C. (2017). Ingroup projection as a challenge of diversity: Consensus about and complexity of superordinate categories. In C. Sibley & F. K. Barlow (Eds.), *Cambridge handbook of the psychology of prejudice*. Cambridge: Cambridge University Press.

Yogeeswaran, K., Devos, T., & Nash, K. (2017). Understanding the nature, measurement, and utility of implicit intergroup biases. In C. Sibley & F. K. Barlow (Eds.), *Cambridge handbook of the psychology of prejudice*. Cambridge: Cambridge University Press.

2 Evolutionary Approaches to Stereotyping and Prejudice

Oliver Sng, Keelah E. G. Williams, and Steven L. Neuberg

Males are stereotyped as more competitive than females, females as more caring than men, and African Americans as more physically aggressive and violent than European and Asian Americans. Heterosexuals are prejudiced against homosexuals, locals are prejudiced against immigrants, and religious people are prejudiced against atheists. As generalizations, these statements are supported by considerable bodies of empirical work, many of which are reviewed in the other chapters of this handbook.

Werner Heisenberg, the theoretical physicist, noted that "what we observe is not nature itself, but nature exposed to our method of questioning" (1958/1999, p. 58). The findings just described characterize the nature of one small subset of stereotypes and prejudices and emerge from methods of questioning derived from a variety of theoretical perspectives – perspectives focusing, for example, on ingroup/outgroup distinctions, social identity and self-enhancement processes, and a need to justify discriminatory behaviors against others. As we will see throughout this chapter, however, the nature of stereotypes and prejudices is often more nuanced and complex than what the questioning favored by such approaches allows us to discern. These nuances have important implications not only for our understanding of stereotyping and prejudice but also for the theoretical frameworks aiming to explain them.

Some of these nuances exist in the form of more textured conceptions of stereotyping and prejudice, missed by traditional methodological lenses focused at levels insufficiently fine to detect them. For example, when researchers use traditional measures to assess prejudices against groups as varied as gay men and Mexican Americans, respondents report feeling similarly prejudiced and negative toward the two groups. When researchers ask respondents about their specific emotional reactions to these groups, however, respondents report feeling quite differently toward the groups – feeling disgust toward gay men but fear of Mexican Americans (Cottrell & Neuberg, 2005). Other complexities have been missed because they occur beyond the scope of the investigative lenses derived from traditional frameworks. Consider, for example, that stereotypes of young African American men being dangerous are especially likely to come to mind for

The authors gratefully acknowledge financial support provided by National Science Foundation grant 1348983.

perceivers who are physically in a dark environment (Schaller, Park, & Mueller, 2003), or that a woman's current ovulatory stage influences her prejudices against outgroup men (McDonald, Donnellan, Cesario, & Navarrete, 2015). As conceptual variables, environmental darkness and fertility status lie well outside the theoretical architectures of traditional theories. That they nonetheless shape stereotype activation and prejudice has meaningful implications for our understanding of stereotyping and prejudice.

Although previously undetected via traditional perspectives, these nuances and many others have been uncovered with the theoretical lenses provided by evolutionary approaches. The aims of this chapter are to provide an overview of existing research inspired by evolutionary principles and to present hypotheses and findings related to stereotyping processes, stereotype content, prejudices, and discrimination. To anticipate, one can conceive of stereotyping, stereotypes, prejudices, and discrimination as functionally interlinked mental, affective, and behavioral tools designed by natural selection to enhance people's ability to identify and manage the threats and opportunities that arise amid the complex interdependencies of social living. We begin with a brief discussion of what an evolutionary approach is (and is not), and how it generates the affordance-management framework that conceptually captures the bulk of the presented research (see also Schaller & Neuberg, 2012; Neuberg & Schaller, 2016).

What Is an Evolutionary Approach?

What is an evolutionary approach to the study of prejudices and related phenomena? First, it is important to note that there is no singular evolutionary approach to prejudice, any more than there is a singular social psychological (or developmental or cognitive) approach to prejudice. Like social psychology, developmental psychology, and cognitive science, evolutionary psychology is a metatheory – a set of assumptions and principles that enable one to derive and test more specific theories, models, and hypotheses. What makes the evolutionary metatheory distinct is that it explicitly recognizes that the human brain has been shaped by biological selection pressures. This recognition is a simple one, but it enables the building of rich conceptual frameworks for understanding the different aspects of human thought, feelings, and behavior (e.g., Buss, 1995; Tooby & Cosmides, 1992).

Like any organ or biological system, the contemporary human brain is a product of natural selection (Darwin, 1871). The features of its anatomy, physiology, and neurochemistry (and accompanying mental processes and capacities) are therefore those that enhanced the reproductive fitness of our long-gone ancestors, relative to alternative features that existed at the time. For instance, individuals inclined to avoid predatory beasts were more likely than those without this inclination to survive such encounters, thereby increasing the likelihood they would successfully reproduce. To the extent that this avoidance inclination had a genetic component, and that the benefits of avoiding such animals existed for a long enough period of time, modern humans would come to be characterized by this avoidance adaptation and the cognitive and emotional inclinations causally linked to it.

An evolutionary approach thus (a) seriously considers the possibility that prejudices, stereotyping, stereotypes, and discrimination are in some aspects evolved adaptations, like the inclination to avoid dangerous animals, and (b) derives from this possibility various implications for understanding how these adaptations work, when they come into play, and for whom.

The usefulness of an evolutionary approach to prejudices and related phenomena is judged by the same criteria as any meta-approach: How well does it account for existing knowledge? How well does it predict novel findings? To what extent is it logically coherent? How well can it conceptually integrate phenomena? As judged by such criteria, the evolutionary approach has proven itself quite useful across psychology broadly (Buss, 2015), across the many realms of social psychology (e.g., Neuberg, Kenrick, & Schaller, 2010), across the subject matter of social cognition (Neuberg & Schaller, 2014), and, as we show here, within the more specific realms of prejudices, stereotypes, stereotyping, and discrimination (see also Kurzban & Leary, 2001; Neuberg & DeScioli, 2015; Neuberg & Schaller, 2016; Schaller & Neuberg, 2012).

Before proceeding, it is important to preempt several common misunderstandings about evolutionary approaches (for a more comprehensive discussion, see Kurzban, 2002; Neuberg et al., 2010). First, just because a behavior is an *adaptation* does not mean it is *adaptive* (i.e., beneficial for its possessor) in modern environments. The human preferences for fatty and sweet foods are adaptations for ancestral environments, in which calorically rich food was scarce, and thus inclinations to consume such food when it was available would have been biologically adaptive. Such scarcity no longer exists in much of the modern world, with the consequence that our evolved attraction to dietary fat and sugar often leads to overconsumption and serious medical problems. Adaptations need not be still adaptive.

The second misunderstanding is that because evolution is a natural process, because prejudices have evolutionary roots, and because "natural" is often conflated with "good," then prejudices and related phenomena must be good. Just because a process is natural, however, makes it neither good nor morally acceptable. The evolutionary perspective helps identify what *is* – and why it is – but makes no claim about whether it *ought* to be. Explaining is not justifying, and just because aspects of prejudices may be natural does not bestow on them moral value.

Third, and related to this point, it is often presumed that adaptations are conceived of as perfect solutions to problems. They are not. Rather, they are solutions that enhanced our ancestors' reproductive fitness *relative to* whatever alternative solutions were available to them at the time. An adaptation need not be "smart" in any absolute sense. That aspects of stereotyping and prejudice may be adaptations does not imply that they are perfect solutions to the problems they were designed by natural selection to solve.

Fourth, it is often presumed that evolved mechanisms are inflexible or inevitable. This is also incorrect. Just because we have an evolved preference for fats and sweets does not mean we are compelled to gorge ourselves on them. Just because we have an evolved inclination to fear young outgroup men does not mean we always seek to escape from, avoid, or attack them. Indeed, as we will see, functional *flexibility* is a fundamental implication of the evolutionary approach. Indeed, adaptations often depend critically on information from the environment, as when early developmental experiences, social learning, and culture play a strong role in determining which young men we identify as "outgroup."

Affordance Management

From an evolutionary perspective, the human mind has been shaped to address challenges to enhancing reproductive fitness – to perpetuate one's genes into future generations. Importantly, reproductive fitness is not just about successfully solving the challenge of mating, per se, but also about successfully solving a wide range of interconnected challenges (Kenrick, Griskevicius, Neuberg, & Schaller, 2010). One needs to survive in order to mate, which means acquiring nutrition and avoiding predation and disease. Moreover, individuals not only need to acquire a mate and successfully produce offspring but also to successfully parent to ensure that offspring themselves survive to reproduce. Furthermore, these challenges, such as protecting oneself from physical harm, acquiring resources, finding a mate, and caring for offspring, often entail addressing other challenges, such as gaining status, finding others to cooperate with on necessary tasks, and retaining one's mate.

Humans have long been highly interdependent social animals (Campbell, 1982; Richerson & Boyd, 1995), meaning that our ability to address fundamental challenges of reproductive fitness can be facilitated or hindered by the presence and actions of others. Although the social cooperation and coordination inherent to human sociality provides many opportunities and benefits to the individual, it also affords threats: for example, others may free-ride on one's efforts or take more than their fair share; they may commit violence or pass along infectious pathogens; they may espouse values and behave in ways that interfere with effective social coordination. An evolved psychology is therefore likely to be adapted to identify and address the particular types of social opportunities and threats afforded by others. We refer to the sets of evolved psychological mechanisms designed to address such threats and opportunities as *affordance-management systems* (Gibson, 1979; McArthur & Baron, 1983; Neuberg, Kenrick, & Schaller, 2010, 2011; Zebrowitz & Montepare, 2006). Stereotyping, prejudices, stereotypes, and discriminating behaviors are among the tools constituting these affordance-management systems.

Three themes run throughout much of the chapter. The first is that each of the different kinds of social opportunities and threats others pose often requires a qualitatively different response. Hence, multiple affordance-management systems are needed, each of which attends to and processes somewhat different information and generates somewhat different specific emotional and behavioral responses (Neuberg et al., 2011). That is, rather than reacting to a generalized threat with domain-general responses, people instead react to specific threats with domain-specific responses. One implication of this is that there are likely to exist qualitatively different prejudices and forms of discrimination to address the different threats others are perceived to pose. Rather than conceptualizing people's affective reactions to groups as prejudice (singular), it thus makes more sense to view them as prejudices (plural) – as different profiles of emotional responses (e.g., fear, disgust, anger) specific to the particular threats groups are believed to pose (Cottrell & Neuberg, 2005); we elaborate on this later.

The second theme relates to issues of accuracy and rationality in stereotyping and prejudice processes. Stereotyping processes, and the contents of stereotypes, have traditionally been viewed, and sometimes even defined, as inaccurate. In the same vein, prejudices and discriminatory behavior have also often been viewed as irrational. From an evolutionary affordance-management perspective, however, one would expect many stereotypes to possess meaningful kernels of truth. Even where they depart from accuracy, they might be expected to do so in highly predictable ways. Moreover, because cues to threat are imperfectly diagnostic, one would expect people to sometimes respond to objectively benign others with prejudices – but in ways that are "rational" in the sense that they are functionally tuned to shifts in perceived vulnerabilities. We elaborate on this later, too.

The third theme is that prejudices and discrimination are especially likely to be evoked when perceivers view themselves as interpersonally vulnerable. This felt vulnerability may be dispositional, as with some individuals who chronically view the world as a dangerous place. It may be situational, as when people find themselves in poorly lit, strange environments. It may be interpersonal, as when people encounter individuals from groups already stereotyped as threatening. It may be the result of all three, as when North Americans who are dispositionally fearful of attack and find themselves alone in a dark room are confronted with young African American men (Schaller et al., 2003). Prejudices and discriminating responses are functionally flexible, and their activation and engagement depend on interactions of vulnerability-relevant features of perceivers, their situations, and those being perceived.

Stereotyping: Why, and Which Categories?

Effective affordance management requires, first, that one identify the threats and opportunities potentially posed by others. The process of stereotyping can be viewed as serving that function.

To stereotype is to identify an individual as being a member of some group and then to infer that this individual possesses the characteristics typical of members of that group. The traditional understanding is that stereotyping serves to simplify the world for an information processor burdened by limited cognitive resources (Allport, 1954; Hamilton, 1981; Tajfel, 1969): By viewing a particular individual as being like typical members of some group, one need not engage in more effortful and lengthy attempts to understand him or her as a unique individual.

From an evolutionary perspective, however, conservation of mental resources and acts of simplifying, in and of themselves, cannot be the ultimate goal. Rather, we seek to understand others because they have affordance implications for us – they potentially pose threats and provide opportunities. Thus, the more fundamental goal of social perception needs to be a sufficiently accurate understanding – accurate enough that we can predict to some reasonable degree others' affordance-relevant actions. We want to know about others not only quickly and easily, but we want to know specific things about them – about whether, for example, they are inclined to cooperate with us, hurt us, love us, or feed us. The reason we so ubiquitously stereotype others is that, for our ancestors, (a) there were certain regularities between readily perceived features of others and their affordance-relevant behaviors, and (b) those individuals who used these regularities to make inferences about others – that is, who stereotyped in specific ways – would have, on average, interacted with others more effectively, enhancing their reproductive fitness relative to those who did not stereotype.

To say that stereotyping is an adaptation is not to say that it will necessarily lead to perfect inferences about others – about whether they are, for example, cooperative, trustworthy, or dangerous. As noted earlier, adaptations are not perfect solutions, but merely solutions that were better for our ancestors' reproductive fitness than whatever alternative solutions were available at the time. In fact, as we discuss later, several parts of the stereotyping process – the overgeneralization of cues that imply threat, the particular contents of certain stereotypes – do tend to be biased. They are biased, however, in ways that tend, on average, to reduce the likelihood that perceivers make the most costly of possible errors.

In addition, to say that stereotyping is an adaptation is not to say that social perceivers never move beyond stereotyping to more carefully attend to potentially individuating information about another. Indeed, the focus of an evolutionary approach on the need to obtain affordance-relevant information suggests specific circumstances under which people will be especially motivated to individuate others. As with other conceptual approaches, an evolutionary approach suggests that individuation becomes more likely when time to delve more deeply into another's inclinations is available, when there is reason to believe that one's stereotypes insufficiently capture a particular target's inclinations, and when nuanced inferences are especially important, such as when the perceiver's outcomes especially depend on the actions of the perceived (e.g., Fiske & Neuberg, 1990; Neuberg & Fiske, 1987; Pendry & Macrae, 1994). Evolutionary approaches also make more specific predictions about the use of stereotyping and individuating processes related to particular categories and stereotypes. For example, a perceiver currently concerned with physical safety may be especially likely to stereotype (and not spend the additional time and energy needed to individuate) young outgroup males, who – relative to outgroup females or older males – are believed to pose special risks of danger. In contrast, if there is less time pressure on making a social judgment, and judgments need to be made in especially complex domains of social life (e.g., managing social status) or in domains with significant long-term fitness implications (e.g., choosing a mate), one may be particularly likely to go beyond initial stereotyping in the hope of gaining a more nuanced understanding of the another. Just as stereotyping is likely an adaptation, so too is more thoughtful individuation (Neuberg, 1992). Social perceivers are functionally flexible, employing different strategies to gain understanding under different fitness-relevant circumstances.

From an evolutionary perspective, perceivers should categorize others in ways that, across human history, have enabled valid inferences about others' affordance-relevant capacities and inclinations. Of course, as revealed by work using the minimal group paradigm (e.g., Tajfel, Billig, Bundy, & Flament, 1971), people can generate a wide variety of seemingly arbitrary dimensions on which to categorize others. This does not mean, however, that the category dimensions used in "real-world" social perception tend to be arbitrary. Few of us categorize people by earlobe length or forearm thickness – and for good reason: Under most circumstances, such features provide little information about social opportunities and threats. Years of research reveal that people do categorize others, however, by age, sex, and race (for reviews, see Brewer, 1988; Fiske & Neuberg, 1990; Kinzler, Shutts, & Correll, 2010; Macrae & Quadflieg, 2010). Why are these features so important? And from an evolutionary perspective, what others might be similarly important? We briefly address each.

Age and Sex Stereotyping. Why are age and sex so often the basis of social categorization? Traditional work notes that physical cues to these dimensions are easily perceived, and that cultural norms and conventions teach that they are important. These are insufficient explanations, however. After all, other perceptually accessible features (e.g., shirt color) do not have the same impact on person perception. Moreover, cultural practices and norms regarding which features are important themselves need to be explained (i.e., *why* do cultures teach that age and sex are important features?). From an evolutionary perspective, age and sex are readily used as a basis for stereotyping because these features provide much information about the threats and opportunities others potentially pose.

Age and sex have long enabled diagnostic (albeit imperfect) inferences about others' potential abilities and capacities. Infants and young children are incompetent and require our care, young adults tend to be fertile and to possess physical capacities enabling strenuous physical work, and elderly people have acquired wisdom from experience. The differential biology of males and females provides valid cues regarding with whom we can successfully mate and have children, at whose body we can nurse, and by whose hand we would be most physically injured if assaulted.

In addition to enabling diagnostic inferences about others' potential abilities and capacities, age and sex enable diagnostic inferences about others' goals, strategies, and behavioral inclinations. To better understand this, consider life history theory – a biological framework that examines how organisms allocate energy and time to different tasks (e.g., growth, mating, parenting) across the life span (Charnov, 1993; Stearns, 1992). Given finite resources (e.g., time, energy), all organisms, including humans, face the problem of how to allocate resources to facilitate survival and reproduction (Hill & Kaplan, 1999; Kaplan & Gangestad, 2005). The optimal allocation strategy varies across three dimensions, two of which are age and sex. Age is important because devoting resources to mating is possible only after sexual maturity, whereas devoting resources to offspring care can only occur after reproduction. Sex is important because most female mammals are obliged to invest a greater minimal amount of biological resources in offspring, including gestation before birth and nursing after birth (Trivers, 1972). A secondary implication of this sex difference is that female mammals, including humans, tend to be choosier about their mates – they can create fewer offspring across their lifespan and thus the quality and survival of each one is of greater importance – and this leads to pressure on males to compete with one another to be chosen by females.

Because age and sex shape how people prioritize their goals and their behavioral strategies for achieving them, and because such behaviors carry affordance implications for social perceivers (e.g., in terms of mating possibilities, competition threats), social perceivers are likely to be attuned to others' age and sex and use these features to make inferences about others.

An evolutionary approach goes a step further. The affordance implications of age and sex depend on each other. Females, for instance, are fertile only within a particular age range, and although males tend to invest more energy into competing for mates than do females, this sex difference diminishes at older ages. It should thus be less useful for people to categorize others by age and sex independently than by specific age-sex intersectional subcategories (Neuberg & Sng, 2013). We elaborate on this latter point when discussing stereotype content.

Race Stereotyping. Throughout time, human social groups have included males and females across a wide range of ages. Moreover, age and sex can predict important information about social opportunities and threats. Hence, the social mind should be highly attuned to cues of age and sex, and these features should be used to anticipate others' behaviors.

In many ways, race is different. Human social groups have only very recently (in evolutionary time scales) included a diversity of races. Our human ancestors were unlikely to have encountered others of different races, meaning that there would have been no selection pressures for a psychology sensitive to race per se. Yet, people stereotype others by race. Why?

One possibility brings us back to life history theory. Along with age and sex, ecological circumstances are an important driver of organisms' behavioral strategies. Ecology is important because in unpredictable environments in which resources are scarce and mortality rates high, it is more adaptive to invest one's energy into reproducing early than into building one's body and accumulating skills and knowledge for future use. Put simply, delaying reproduction in an unpredictable and high-mortality environment could lead to death without having reproduced. This present-focused orientation has been termed a "fast" life history strategy and is associated with a suite of traits including earlier first sex, greater promiscuity, having more children, impulsivity, and antisocial behaviors including violence and criminality (e.g., Brumbach, Figueredo, & Ellis, 2009; Ellis, 2004; Figueredo et al., 2005; Figueredo et al., 2006; Griskevicius, Tybur, Delton, & Robertson, 2011). A "slow" life history strategy is composed of the opposite, more future-focused, traits and is more likely to emerge in ecologies characterized by sufficient resources, greater predictability, and lower mortality.

Behaviors comprising fast versus slow strategies potentially have important affordance implications for others. It is important for us to know, for example, whether a person we encounter is more or less likely to act impulsively, or whether a potential mate is interested in a short-term versus long-term relationship. Our ancestors who were able to discern the association between changing ecological circumstances (e.g., resulting from seasonality, droughts, natural disasters) and others' behaviors were likely to have better anticipated the social threats and opportunities others posed, consequently enhancing their reproductive fitness. We might thus expect modern humans to be sensitive to cues to others' home ecology and to stereotype others in terms of these ecologies (Neuberg & Sng, 2013; Williams, Sng, & Neuberg, 2016).

What does this have to do with race? In many places around the world, members of different races (or ethnicities, tribes, castes) are differentially distributed across ecologies. In the United States, African Americans are overrepresented in economically harsh and unpredictable environments, whereas European Americans are overrepresented in more economically sufficient and stable environments (Massey, 2004; Sampson, Raudenbush, & Earls, 1997). This correlation between race and ecology raises the possibility that perceivers may use race as a cue to the more fundamental ecology, thereby explaining the common use of race as a dimension for categorizing others.

A second possibility, independent of the first, is that race cues another feature people use to categorize others – coalitional membership. Ancestrally, people who looked very different from one another – for example, because they employed distinct bodily markings – often also belonged to different cooperative groups. Perhaps, then, people categorize others by race as a proxy for categorizing them by coalition. If so, when social perceivers are presented with direct information about an individual's coalitional membership, the individual's race should become less relevant as a basis for categorizing him or her. Indeed, when social perceivers receive information about both a target's coalitional membership and race, they become less likely to categorize that individual by race (Kurzban, Tooby, & Cosmides, 2001; Pietraszewski, Cosmides, & Tooby, 2014). Thus, because perceivers seem to be attuned to cues of coalitional group affiliations in general – a point we address later – race might be the basis for stereotyping because of its perceived association with distinct coalitional groups.

Disease-, coalitional-, and kin-based stereotyping. From an evolutionary perspective, other features are also likely to carry important affordance information. Given the threats that infectious diseases have long posed to individual survival and reproduction, people use cues associated with infectious disease (e.g., rashes, poxes, coughs) to categorize others as infectious. This is a significant challenge, however. The perceptible symptoms associated with infection vary greatly across pathogens and even across individuals infected with the same pathogen. Moreover, a huge number of different pathogens pose threats, and many evolve very rapidly. As a consequence, relying on any small set of specific cues to identify infectious others is likely to be ineffective over time. Instead, one might expect evolved psychologies to be sensitive to pathogens' more general tendency to leave atypical physical or behavioral marks on the infected individual and thus use a broad range of cues, including morphological and movement abnormalities, to implicitly categorize an individual as diseased (Schaller & Park, 2011). This is an important aspect of what is referred to as the *behavioral immune system* – an affordance-management system that influences behaviors with the goal of avoiding infection by pathogens. Indeed, social perceivers use many statistically abnormal features – including those linked to physical disability, obesity, and being elderly – to implicitly identify individuals as diseased (Duncan & Schaller, 2009; Park, Faulkner, & Schaller, 2003; Park, Schaller, & Crandall, 2007; Schaller & Neuberg, 2012).

Of course, having a movement disorder, being obese, and being heavily wrinkled are, at best, only weakly diagnostic of the presence of contagious pathogens. What this means is that many physically abnormal but pathogen-benign individuals will nonetheless be misidentified as posing a threat of infection. As with other threat-management systems, the behavioral immune system is biased toward avoiding the most costly of possible errors (Haselton & Nettle, 2006) – in this case, the cost of becoming infected with a dangerous pathogen (as opposed to the cost of avoiding a person even though they are not infected). As an illustration, consider the two types of errors a household smoke detector can make: It can falsely identify a dangerous fire when there is none (e.g., going off while bacon is smoking on the stovetop), with the cost of irritating the homeowner, or it can fail to detect an actual fire when there is one, with the potential cost of life to the homeowner. Because the latter error is much more costly than the former, smoke detectors are calibrated to avoid them, with the necessary consequence that the detector becomes more likely to make the opposite error – going off when there is no fire at all. Our psychological threat detectors are similarly calibrated to avoid the most costly errors – being infected, attacked, cheated – with the inevitable consequence that they, too, sometimes "go off" when the targets of our attention are actually benign

(Nesse, 2005; Neuberg et al., 2011). Consequently, morphologically abnormal but healthy individuals are nonetheless perceived to be potentially contagious (Schaller & Park, 2011), and non-threatening outgroup men are perceived to be dangerous (e.g., Becker, Neel, & Anderson, 2010; Maner et al., 2005; Schaller et al., 2003). Thus, although the process of stereotyping individuals as being members of threatening groups is error prone, these errors are not random. Rather, they follow a fairly straightforward "better safe than sorry" logic that, despite errors, on average enhances the fitness of the perceiver.

People also categorize others by their apparent coalitional affiliations, as mentioned earlier. Ancestral life was generally lived within small cooperative groups, although contact with other coalitions was not infrequent. Such inter-coalitional contact often posed a variety of threats, including violence. Indeed, aggressive intergroup conflict is believed to be a long-recurring feature of human social life, with evidence that it exists both within our primate relatives (Goodall, 1986; Wilson & Wrangham, 2003) and modern hunter-gatherers (Chagnon, 1988; Ferguson, 1984; Haas, 1990). Moreover, even within groups, competition for resources and mates leads to the formation of internal coalitions that have the potential to create intragroup violence. One would thus expect social perceivers to be sensitive to coalitional memberships and to stereotype others on that basis. One can view stereotyping by race, ethnicity, tribe, clan, religion, and other memberships – even arbitrary memberships as created via the minimal intergroup paradigm – as being examples of coalitional stereotyping.

From an evolutionary perspective, kinship should be another feature used to categorize and stereotype. Our ancestors who were able to discriminate between genetic relatives and non-relatives, and who used this ability to facilitate the survival and reproduction of related individuals, would have been more likely to pass their genes into future generations – with the consequence that kinship would be an important basis of contemporary stereotyping. An evolutionary approach certainly does not propose that individuals are born with knowledge of who their relatives are. Instead, an evolved relatedness-detection system would be attuned to cues that, in ancestral life, would have been reliably associated with kinship. Existing work has demonstrated that such cues include facial resemblance to the self, extended periods of co-residence, and attitudinal similarities (DeBruine, 2005; Lieberman, Tooby, & Cosmides, 2007; Park & Schaller, 2005).

In sum, we have seen that an evolutionary approach would anticipate that people stereotype others by age, sex, ecology, race, coalition, disease, and kinship. These features, among others, are used by social perceivers because they typically have – or at least had, for our ancestors – some diagnostic utility: They carry useful information about the threats and opportunities afforded by individuals with those features. Categorizing others as threatening, however, is potentially costly. Not only does it lead one to subsequently engage in energetically expensive behaviors to address the threat, but one may also be missing valuable opportunities while doing so. Stereotyping processes should thus be flexible – especially ready to engage certain categorizations and inferences when there is sufficient reason to believe that one is vulnerable to threat, but also more open to alternative categorizations when one feels more secure. Indeed, they are. For example, White perceivers led to be concerned about resource scarcity become more likely to categorize racially ambiguous faces as Black rather than White, and to view African Americans more stereotypically (Krosch & Amodio, 2014; Rodeheffer, Hill, & Lord, 2012). In a similar vein, White perceivers are especially likely to categorize an angry, racially ambiguous face as belonging to an outgroup when they feel dispositionally vulnerable to physical threat and believe themselves to be in a dangerous environment (Miller, Maner, & Becker, 2010). And perceivers are especially likely to categorize others by their physical attractiveness when in a highly invested romantic relationship and the target others are potentially same-sex competitors (Maner, Miller, Moss, Leo, & Plant, 2012). In all these cases, both the boundaries and the usage of social categories vary predictably by individual and situational characteristics. These characteristics are linked to felt vulnerabilities, in ways that one would expect if a function of categorization and stereotyping processes is to manage affordances (for broader reviews, see Neuberg, Becker, & Kenrick, 2013; Neuberg & Schaller, 2014).

Stereotype Content: Beliefs about Threats and Opportunities

The study of stereotype content has a considerable history (e.g., Devine & Elliot, 1995; Fiske, Cuddy, Glick, & Xu, 2002; Katz & Braly, 1933; Madon et al., 2001; Niemann, Jennings, Rozelle, Baxter, & Sullivan, 1994), and an evolutionary, affordance-management approach offers several insights.

First, the approach suggests that the most significant stereotypes about any group – the ones that are most likely to drive our prejudices and actions – will be those linked to important affordances. For example, because humans are concerned about self-protection, we should have prominent stereotypes about others' danger potential; because we are concerned about status, we should possess prominent stereotypes linked to groups' competitiveness; because we are concerned about mating, we should possess stereotypes linked to others' mate quality and availability. Moreover, because such fundamental concerns shift in prominence as a function of one's own life stage, sex, and current circumstances (Kenrick et al., 2010), the psychological prominence of such stereotypes may shift as well. For instance, implicit associations between faces of Black men and words related to dangerousness are stronger for perceivers who dispositionally feel vulnerable to physical violence and who are literally in the dark (Schaller et al., 2003). In a similar vein, associations between obesity and disease concepts are greater for perceivers who dispositionally feel vulnerable to infection and for those in whom infection threat had just been primed (Park, Schaller, & Crandall, 2007). Such findings illustrate not only a link between perceiver concerns and the presence of stereotypes relevant to those concerns but also that the psychological prominence of those affordance-relevant stereotypes changes with shifts in the prominence of those concerns.

Second, the affordance-management perspective suggests that the most prominent stereotypes will often exist at the intersections of important features – at the level of sub-categories. We can illustrate this by revisiting our discussion of sex and age categorization, as informed by life history theory. Recall that sex and age shape behavior in an interactive, rather than an independent, manner. If stereotypes exist to help perceivers anticipate the affordance-relevant behaviors of others, then one would also expect people's stereotypes to exist at the intersection of sex and age. That is, rather than having straightforward sex stereotypes – for example, that women are communal whereas men are agentic – people's stereotypes should be sensitive to sex-age intersections. They are. As one example, consider that males tend to invest more energy into mate competition than do females, but especially during prime mating ages. The sex difference in competitiveness is thus age dependent, and perceiver stereotypes ought to track this interactivity. Indeed, stereotypes of males as more competitive than females are especially pronounced for younger, as opposed to older, adult targets (Sng, Williams, & Neuberg, 2015).

Note that if one queries respondents only on their beliefs about males or females or only about young, middle-aged, or elderly people (as the traditional research has done), one never discovers age-sex sub-category nuances – or many others. Moreover, observing how humans (or other mammals) move through their natural worlds, it is not clear why independent stereotypes of "males" and "females" would ever spontaneously come to mind; after all, we never encounter males and females who are not also of a specific age. That people *can* report stereotypes at the level of "male" and "female" may only mean that they are able to transform their nuanced, complex stereotypes into a form that accommodates the constraints of our unnatural questions – constraints often imposed in tests of traditional theories.

A third insight adds another level of nuance. From an affordance-management approach, it is much less useful to know how an individual behaves in general than how that individual is likely to behave toward us *specifically* (or toward those we are invested in). One implication of this is that holding general stereotypes about others' traits – or cross-situational inclinations (e.g., "men are competitive") – will be less useful than holding stereotypes that reflect *toward whom* others are directing their behaviors (e.g., "men are competitive against other men"). For example, although males tend to invest more energy in mate competition than do females, females do invest in mate competition. Moreover, mate competition – for both women and men – tends to be directed toward reproductive-aged individuals of their *same sex*. One might therefore expect people's stereotypes of male and female competitiveness to track these patterns. Indeed, they do: Whereas people stereotype men to be more competitive than women *toward young men*, they actually stereotype women to be more competitive than men *toward young women* (Sng et al., 2015). Hence, stereotype content may in fact be "directed," carrying information about toward whom groups direct certain behaviors. This idea of directed stereotypes is novel and does not emerge from traditional theories.

Fourth, an evolutionary approach suggests there are social categories and stereotypes that have eluded the attention of traditional approaches to stereotyping and stereotype content. For example, the research discussed earlier reveals that people possess disease-linked stereotypes that they apply to people who are obese, disabled, and old (Schaller & Neuberg, 2012; Schaller & Park, 2011); such stereotypes do not derive readily from other theoretical frameworks. As a second example, following on our earlier discussion of the important role that ecology plays in shaping behavior, one would predict that people possess strong stereotypes based on the ecologies in which others live, and that these stereotypes would track the behavioral inclinations that these ecologies elicit. Ecologies in which resources are scarce and life is dangerously unpredictable elicit behaviors that are present focused, whereas ecologies in which resources are sufficient and life is predictable elicit behaviors that are future focused. Indeed, by tracking these actual ecology-behavior associations, people stereotype individuals from resource-poor and unpredictable neighborhoods as impulsive, aggressive, and less invested in education, compared to individuals from resource-sufficient and predictable neighborhoods. Such ecology stereotypes are readily applied to individuals within races, within levels of wealth, and in different cultures (Williams et al., 2016).

Fifth, implicit in this conceptualization is the idea that the most significant, affordance-relevant stereotypes will be, to some meaningful degree, accurate. This does not imply that such stereotypes describe well *all* individuals within any particular group, or even one member of a group perfectly well, but only that they will meaningfully describe, on average, the aggregate of individuals within any particular group. Some evidence suggests that this is indeed the case (e.g., Jussim, Cain, Crawford, Harber, & Cohen, 2009; Swim, 1994). Moreover, in line with the smoke detector principle (Nesse, 2005), inaccuracies in stereotype content are likely to be in the direction of exaggerating threat affordances. For example, given that the costs of being physically assaulted are typically greater than the costs of missing out on a possible friendly acquaintance, we might expect stereotypes held about young men from desperation ecologies to be biased in the direction of exaggerating their potential for physical aggressiveness.

In all, then, the evolutionary, affordance-management perspective has much to offer to enhance our understanding of the contents of people's stereotypes. Only recently, however, have researchers approached questions of stereotype content from such a perspective (Neuberg & Sng, 2013), and much work remains to be done.

Prejudices and Discrimination

Once one believes that an individual or group affords some potential opportunity or threat, effective affordance management requires one to act on that information in an attempt to either take advantage of the opportunity or remediate the threat. Prejudices and discrimination can be viewed as serving this function, with prejudices translating the perception of specific threats and opportunities into focused behaviors (discrimination) aimed at remediating the threat or exploiting the opportunity.

The evolutionary view of prejudice and discrimination differs somewhat from traditional conceptualizations, which generally define prejudice as a valenced evaluation or feeling toward a group or its members and discrimination as valenced actions directed at a group or its members (Allport, 1954; Fiske, 1998). From an evolutionary perspective, however, these conceptualizations as attitudes/evaluations and behaviors on general negative-positive continua are problematic. Because prejudices and discrimination serve the function of managing threats and opportunities, and because different threats and opportunities require different solutions, general "negative" or "positive" responses will typically be insufficient. For example, although anger and fear are similarly "negative" emotions, they engage quite different behaviors and serve quite different functions. It would not be particularly useful, for example, to charge with anger toward a gang of young men approaching with weapons or to run away with fear from a salesclerk who just cheated you out of change at the cash register. If social perception has evolved to be sensitive to specific challenges, one might expect prejudices and discrimination to be similarly sensitive.

Unlike affect, broadly construed, emotions carry such functional nuances, reflecting the specific affordances perceived to be in the environment and triggering relevant responses (Carver & Scheier, 1990; Cosmides & Tooby, 2000; Ekman, 1999; Nesse, 1990). Indeed, qualitatively distinct emotions are engaged by different threats and opportunities and facilitate qualitatively distinct behaviors (Frijda, 1986; Izard, 1991; Plutchik, 1980; Roseman, Wiest, & Swartz, 1994; Tomkins, 1963). For example, anger results from the appraisal that something has been illegitimately taken, and it facilitates approach to get that thing back; fear results from the appraisal that one is in physical danger, and it facilitates escape; and disgust results from the appraisal that one is at risk of physical or moral contaminants, and it facilitates avoidance of exposure and contact.

From an evolutionary perspective, then, one thinks of prejudice not as simple valenced (negative-positive) feelings about groups and their members but rather of prejudices (plural) as emotion-based feelings toward groups and their members. Some prejudices are primarily anger based; others primarily fear based; and others are grounded primarily in disgust, envy, and the like (Cottrell & Neuberg, 2005).

One important implication of this is that, to the extent that different groups are believed to pose qualitatively different threats, these groups should elicit qualitatively different prejudices and discriminatory actions. Indeed, they do (Cottrell & Neuberg, 2005; Cottrell, Richards, & Nichols, 2010). Moreover, such differentiated responses are observed even when traditional measures suggest that respondents' prejudices are similarly negative. For instance, whereas prejudices directed toward Mexican American men are largely characterized by fear, prejudices toward gay men are largely characterized by disgust. In cases such as these, traditional measures, focused as they are on general negativity, miss (and mask) important distinctions in how people feel about and act toward groups.

Recent research demonstrates that a threat-management approach to understanding prejudices can lend additional insights to the study of sexual prejudices. For example, simple ingroup-outgroup approaches would predict that heterosexuals would hold negative prejudices against non-heterosexuals, as a general outgroup, and this indeed appears to be the case when researchers employ traditional measures of prejudice. However, research that queries heterosexuals' reactions toward specific non-heterosexual subgroups – lesbians, gay men, bisexual women, bisexual men – suggests that conclusions drawn from traditional work are problematically simplified (Pirlott & Neuberg, 2014). Rather than revealing that heterosexuals hold straightforward, negative prejudices against non-heterosexuals, such studies show that sexual prejudices vary greatly depending on the sex of the heterosexual perceiver and the sex of the non-heterosexual target. Consider, for example, that college-aged heterosexual women are less prejudiced than heterosexual men against gay men – and, in fact, view gay men as favorably as they view straight men – or that straight men are less prejudiced against bisexual women than against bisexual men. Such findings are incompatible with the existence of a general negative sexual prejudice against non-heterosexuals, but consistent with the possibility that heterosexuals view (certain) non-heterosexuals of their own sex as posing threats of unwanted sexual interest.

Another new look at sexual prejudices builds on the finding that sexual prejudices have a prominent disgust component. Disgust evolved to help manage threats posed by infectious pathogens, so one might posit that sexually prejudiced individuals may be inclined to view homosexuality itself as a pathogen. Moreover, just as people strategically engage qualitatively distinct behavioral responses to the threat of pathogen infection depending on features that affect the likelihood of infection (e.g., network interconnectedness), early evidence suggests that sexually prejudiced individuals engage in qualitatively distinct antigay behaviors in response to these same types of factors (Filip-Crawford, 2015; Filip-Crawford & Neuberg, in press). Findings such as these are difficult to explain from existing, non-evolutionary approaches but readily emerge from an evolutionary affordance-management approach.

Just as identifying others as threatening imposes certain costs on a perceiver, so too does experiencing prejudices and engaging in behaviors to remediate those threats. Thus, just as stereotyping processes are functionally flexible – engaged particularly when vulnerability to the potential threat seems great – so too are prejudice and discriminatory processes. For example, as people become more concerned about contagious disease, they become more prejudiced against those exhibiting cues of physical abnormality or foreignness (e.g., Huang, Sedlovskaya, Ackerman, & Bargh, 2011; Park, Schaller, & Crandall, 2007; Young, Sacco, & Hugenberg, 2011). When growing economic competition is made salient, people become more prejudiced against groups stereotypically viewed as strong economic competitors (Butz & Yogeeswaran, 2011). When people's roles as caregivers are made salient, they express greater prejudices against potentially threatening outgroups (Gilead & Liberman, 2014). When people are concerned about threats to their groups' norms and values, they report greater prejudices against atheists (Cook, Cottrell, & Webster, 2015; Gervais, 2013; Varley, Filip-Crawford, Neuberg, & Nagoshi, 2015). And pregnant women in their first trimester – when the fetus is most vulnerable to infectious pathogens – hold more negative feelings toward foreigners (Navarrete, Fessler, & Eng, 2007).

Much empirical work in the traditional stereotyping and prejudice literatures has focused its lens on a particular gender-age combination – young outgroup men – and has demonstrated powerful stereotyping, prejudice, and discrimination effects. From the perspective of traditional stereotyping and prejudice theories, though, it is not a priori obvious why young men should elicit such pronounced reactions. A recent evolutionary approach, labeled the male warrior hypothesis, provides both a theoretical foundation and corresponding insights (McDonald, Navarette, & Van Vugt, 2012). As discussed earlier, young men, in particular, engage in greater intrasexual competition for mates. Because the formation of alliances and coalitions among males could enhance success in such competitions, one might expect evolution to have shaped a male coalitional psychology with specific functions, including aggression toward outgroup males. Indeed, explorations of chimpanzee behavior and human hunter-gatherer tribes suggest that, ancestrally, adult males were more likely than females to engage in coalitional violence (Chagnon, 1988; Ferguson, 1984; Goodall, 1986; Haas, 1990; Wilson & Wrangham, 2003). One would thus expect that, in contemporary times, men (more than women) would be more sensitive to threat from outgroup men (than outgroup women) and more aggressively prejudiced against outgroup members, especially outgroup men.

Consistent with these hypotheses, non-Black perceivers are especially likely to erroneously perceive anger in the facial expressions of Black men but not Black women (Maner et al., 2005), and it is more difficult to unlearn conditioned fear responses to outgroup men than to outgroup women (Navarrete et al., 2009). Men are especially willing to inflict punishments on same-sex outgroups, even when doing so incurs costs to their own group (Navarrete, McDonald, Molina, & Sidanius, 2010), and those men who are especially focused on coalitional issues are also especially prejudiced against outgroup men (McDonald et al., 2012). Moreover, in the United States, Black men have been targeted for greater discrimination than Black women in a variety of domains, including consumer markets and criminal sentencing (Ayres & Siegelman, 1995; Ayres & Waldfogel, 1994).

Like stereotyping and stereotypes, then, we find that prejudices and discrimination processes are strikingly nuanced. These nuances are not obviously predicted by traditional theories but are readily derived from evolutionary and affordance-management approaches.

Conclusions and Final Comments

The human brain has been shaped by biological selection processes to identify and manage a range of challenges to reproductive fitness, including threats and opportunities afforded by the presence and actions of others. From this perspective, one can conceive of stereotyping, stereotypes, prejudices, and discrimination as tools of affordance-management systems, designed to enhance people's ability to succeed amid the complex interdependencies of social living.

Evolutionary theory provides a powerful, integrated, and generative framework for understanding these processes and for addressing fundamental questions at the heart of the study of stereotyping and prejudice. *Why do we stereotype?* We stereotype because we need to quickly and easily predict, with some degree of accuracy, the opportunities and threats afforded by others. *Why do we stereotype on the basis of some features more than others?* We especially stereotype others by age, sex, ecology, coalition, disease, and kinship because for our ancestors these features had diagnostic utility, and by race because it is a cue (in the United States and elsewhere) for ecology and coalition; these features were useful for predicting the affordances of others. *Why do our stereotypes of different groups differ in the ways they do?* Stereotypes differ – and are not merely "negative" or "positive" – because different groups are perceived to present qualitatively different threats and opportunities, and stereotypes need to reflect these differences if they are to help social perceivers achieve their goals. *Why do we have prejudices, and what forms do they take?* We hold prejudices because as emotion-specific feelings, they translate the perception of specific threats and opportunities into focused behaviors that can remediate the threat or exploit the opportunity. This means that because different groups are perceived to pose qualitatively different threats and opportunities, people will also have qualitatively different prejudices toward them. *Under what circumstances are specific social categories, stereotypes, and prejudices engaged?* The use of specific social categories and the engagement of specific stereotypes and prejudices depend on the interaction of a perceiver's own vulnerabilities, his or her current situation, and the target being perceived. Thus, a social perceiver is especially likely to view a young man as dangerous and consequently fear him if the perceiver dispositionally believes the world to be dangerous, is in a potentially dangerous environment, and the young man is from a group already stereotyped as physically threatening. *To what extent, if any, are our stereotypes accurate and "rational"?* Because stereotypes and prejudices exist to help people manage the threats and opportunities inherent to social life, many stereotypes ought to possess meaningful kernels of truth yet slip into error in predictable ways – specifically, in ways that decrease the likelihood that perceivers hold the more costly (to them) of possible beliefs. And although certain prejudices may appear irrational in the sense that they are responses to imperfect assessments of threat, they are functionally calibrated to perceived vulnerability and do facilitate behaviors that are often actually useful for remediating such threats.

Useful theoretical approaches generate novel hypotheses and findings that lie outside the theoretical architectures of other approaches. By this standard, the evolutionary, affordance-management approach has done quite well. Some findings generated by this approach are novel via the depth and nuance they provide. Consider a few examples, as reviewed: People's prejudices are not merely negative or positive but instead comprise a wide range of specific emotions that are elicited by perceptions that others pose specific, functionally relevant threats. People's stereotypes often exist not at general levels (e.g., "male" or "female") but rather at more affordance-relevant intersections (e.g., "young men" or "middle-aged women"). Stereotypes are not beliefs about the general inclinations groups are perceived to possess (e.g., "young men are competitive") but rather beliefs about toward whom such inclinations are directed (e.g., "young men are competitive against young men"). Other findings generated by the affordance-management approach are novel via the theoretical breadth they provide – that is, by demonstrating certain prejudices or conceptualizing roles for certain variables, toward which the field had previously been blind. Consider these examples, as already reviewed: Heuristic cues to abnormality activate disease-based stereotypes and disgust-based prejudices to a large number of groups; pregnant women in their first trimester are particularly favorable toward their ingroups and particularly unfavorable toward their outgroups; environmental darkness enhances the activation of violence beliefs linked to certain groups but not others; it takes longer to unlearn experimentally conditioned anxious reactions to outgroup men than to outgroup women. By generating hypotheses and findings beyond the scope of traditional approaches, evolutionary approaches both deepen and broaden our understanding of prejudices and related phenomena.

Our overview has focused on the social perceiver – on the holder of stereotypes and prejudices, on the one stereotyping and discriminating. The evolutionary, affordance-management approach also has interesting implications, however, for the targets of these perceivers. After all, perceiver stereotypes and prejudices – and their discriminatory implications – constitute threats that targets themselves must manage. It is thus intriguing that when completing a survey makes salient to young Black men that they are viewed as dangerous, they consequently report that they would smile more at others to create a favorable first impression (Neel, Neufeld, & Neuberg, 2013). In a similar vein, obese individuals for whom stereotypes linked to disease were made salient became more likely to report wearing clean clothes (but not smiling) as a favored means of creating a favorable first impression. Recognizing that they are targeted by a functionally focused set of specific threat-based stereotypes, these targets aimed to better manage their social encounters by responding with a similarly functionally focused self-presentational strategy. The affordance-management perspective has important implications for both perceivers and targets, and the target side may be especially ripe for future research.

Early in the chapter we referred to Heisenberg's insight that "what we observe is not nature itself, but nature exposed to our method of questioning."

Methods of questioning, as derived from theory-based assumptions, can sometimes constrain discovery. If stereotypes are defined primarily as tools for simplifying our understanding of others, then we may attend little to their potential complexity and accuracy. If prejudice is viewed primarily as negative affect toward groups, then we may fail to see their potential emotional specificity – and thus miss the important nuances characterizing people's emotional and behavioral reactions to others. If we believe the function of prejudice is to enhance self-esteem or social identity, we fail to identify variables such as vulnerability to disease, environmental darkness, or a woman's reproductive status as being relevant for understanding prejudices. A complete toolbox for the stereotyping and prejudice researcher should contain multiple theoretical approaches. We argue that the evolutionary approach is an indispensable tool, both for generating novel predictions and discoveries and for illuminating what has been previously missed or misunderstood.

References

Allport, G. W. (1954). *The nature of prejudice*. Cambridge, MA: Addison-Wesley.

Ayres, I., & Siegeman, P. (1995). Race and gender discrimination in bargaining for a new car. *The American Economic Review, 85*, 304–321.

Ayres, I., & Waldfogel, J. (1994). A market test for race discrimination in bail setting. *Stanford Law Review, 46*, 987–1047.

Becker, D.V., Neel, R., & Anderson, U. (2010). Illusory conjunctions of angry facial expressions follow intergroup biases. *Psychological Science, 21*, 938–940.

Brewer, M. B. (1988). A dual process model of impression formation. In T. K. Srull & R. S. Wyer Jr. (Eds.), *Advances in social cognition* (Vol. *1*, pp. 1–36). Hillsdale, NJ: Lawrence Erlbaum Associates.

Brumbach, B. H., Figueredo, A. J., & Ellis, B. J. (2009). Effects of harsh and unpredictable environments in adolescence on development of life history strategies: A longitudinal test of an evolutionary model. *Human Nature, 20*, 25–51.

Buss, D. M. (1995). Evolutionary psychology: A new paradigm for social science. *Psychological Inquiry, 6*, 1–30.

Buss, D. M. (2016). *Handbook of evolutionary psychology* (2nd ed.). New York: John Wiley & Sons.

Butz, D. A., & Yogeeswaran, K. (2011). A new threat in the air: Macroeconomic threat increases prejudice against Asian Americans. *Journal of Experimental Social Psychology, 47*, 22–27.

Campbell, D. T. (1982). Legal and primary-group social controls. *Journal of Social and Biological Structures, 5*, 431–438.

Carver, C. S., & Scheier, M. F. (1990). Origins and functions of positive and negative affect: a control-process view. *Psychological Review, 97*(1), 19–35.

Chagnon, N. A. (1988). Life histories, blood revenge, and warfare in a tribal population. *Science, 239*, 985–992.

Charnov, E. L. (1993). *Life history invariants: Some explorations of symmetry in evolutionary ecology*. Oxford: Oxford University Press.

Cook, C. L., Cottrell, C. A., & Webster, G. D. (2015). No good without God: Antiatheist prejudice as a function of threats to morals and values. *Psychology of Religion and Spirituality, 7*, 217–226.

Cosmides, L., & Tooby, J. (2000). Evolutionary psychology and the emotions. In M. Lewis & J. M. Haviland-Jones (Eds.), *Handbook of emotions* (2nd ed., pp.91–115). New York: Guilford Press.

Cottrell, C. A., & Neuberg, S. L. (2005). Different emotional reactions to different groups: A sociofunctional threat-based approach to "prejudice." *Journal of Personality and Social Psychology, 88*, 770–789.

Cottrell, C. A., Richards, D. A. R., & Nichols, A. L. (2010). Predicting policy attitudes from general prejudice versus specific intergroup emotions. *Journal of Experimental Social Psychology, 46*, 247–254.

Darwin, C. (1871). *The descent of man, and selection in relation to sex*. London: John Murray.

DeBruine L. M. (2005). Trustworthy but not lust-worthy: Context-specific effects of facial resemblance. *Proceedings of the Royal Society of London, B, 272*, 919–922.

Devine, P. G., & Elliot, A. J. (1995). Are racial stereotypes really fading? The Princeton Trilogy revisited. *Personality and Social Psychology Bulletin, 21*, 1139–1150.

Duncan, L. A., & Schaller, M. (2009). Prejudicial attitudes toward older adults may be exaggerated when people feel vulnerable to infectious disease: Evidence and implications. *Analyses of Social Issues and Public Policy, 9*, 97–115.

Ellis, B. J. (2004). Timing of pubertal maturation in girls: An integrated life history approach. *Psychological Bulletin, 130*, 920–958.

Ekman, P. (1999). Facial expressions. In T. Dalgeish & M. J. Power (Eds.), *Handbook of cognition and emotion* (pp. 301–320). New York: Wiley.

Ferguson, R. B. (1984). *Warfare, culture, and environment*. Orlando, FL: Academic Press.

Figueredo, A. J., Vásquez, G., Brumbach, B. H., Schneider, S. M. R., Sefcek, J. A., Kirsner, B. R., & Jacobs, W. J. (2005). The K-Factor: Individual differences in life history strategy. *Personality and Individual Differences, 39*(8), 1349–1360.

Figueredo, A. J., Vásquez, G., Brumbach, B. H., Schneider, S. M. R., Sefcek, J. A., Tal, I. R., Hill, D., Wenner, C. J., & Jacobs, W. J. (2006). Consilience and life history theory: From genes to brain to reproductive strategy. *Developmental Review, 26*, 243–275.

Filip-Crawford, G. (2015). *Community interconnectedness and anti-gay behavior: A test of the Lay Disease-Spread Model of Homosexuality*. Unpublished Dissertation, Arizona State University.

Filip-Crawford, G., & Neuberg, S. L. (in press). Homosexuality and pro-gay ideology as pathogens? Implications of a disease-spread lay model for understanding anti-gay behaviors. *Personality and Social Psychology Review*. Advance online publication. 10.1177/1088868315601613

Fiske, S. T. (1998). Stereotyping, prejudice, and discrimination. In D. T. Gilbert, S. T. Fiske, & G. Lindzey (Eds.), *Handbook of social psychology* (4th ed., Vol. *2*, pp. 357–411). New York: McGraw-Hill.

Fiske, S. T., Cuddy, A. J., Glick, P., & Xu, J. (2002). A model of (often mixed) stereotype content: Competence and warmth respectively follow from perceived status and competition. *Journal of Personality and Social Psychology, 82*(6), 878–902.

Fiske, S. T., & Neuberg, S. L. (1990). A continuum of impression formation, from category-based to individuating processes: Influences of information and motivation on attention and interpretation. *Advances in Experimental Social Psychology, 23*, 1–74.

Frijda, N. H. (1986). *The emotions*. London: Cambridge University Press.

Gervais, W. M. (2013). In godlessness we distrust: Using social psychology to solve the puzzle of anti-atheist prejudice. *Social and Personality Psychology Compass, 7*(6), 366–377.

Gibson, J. J. (1979). *The ecological approach to visual perception*. Boston: Houghton, Mifflin.

Gilead, M., & Liberman, N. (2014). We take care of our own: Caregiving salience increases out-group bias in response to out-group threat. *Psychological Science, 25*(7), 1380–1387.

Goodall, J. (1986). *The chimpanzees of Gombe: Patterns of behavior*. Cambridge, MA: Belknap Press of Harvard University Press.

Griskevicius, V., Tybur, J. M., Delton, A. W., & Robertson, T. E. (2011). The influence of mortality and socioeconomic status on risk and delayed rewards: A life history theory approach. *Journal of Personality and Social Psychology, 100*(6), 1015–1026.

Haas, J. (1990). *The anthropology of war*. New York: Cambridge University Press.

Hamilton, D. L. (Ed.). (1981). *Cognitive processes in stereotyping and intergroup behavior*. Hillsdale, NJ: Lawrence Erlbaum Associates.

Haselton, M. G., & Nettle, D. (2006). The paranoid optimist: An integrative evolutionary model of cognitive biases. *Personality and Social Psychology Review, 10*, 47–66.

Heisenberg, W. (1999). *Physics and philosophy: The revolution in modern science*. (F. S. C. Northrop, Trans.). Amherst, NY: Prometheus Books (Original work published 1958).

Hill, K., & Kaplan, H. (1999). Life history traits in humans: Theory and empirical studies. *Annual Review of Anthropology, 28*, 397–430.

Huang, J. Y., Sedlovskaya, A., Ackerman, J. M., & Bargh, J. A. (2011). Immunizing against prejudice: Effects of disease protection on outgroup attitudes. *Psychological Science, 22*, 1550–1556.

Izard, C. E. (1991). *The psychology of emotions*. New York: Plenum Press.

Jussim, L., Cain, T. R., Crawford, J. T., Harber, K., & Cohen, F. (2009). The unbearable accuracy of stereotypes. In T. Nelson (Ed.), *The handbook of prejudice, stereotyping, and discrimination* (pp. 199–228). Mahwah, NJ: Lawrence Erlbaum Associates.

Kaplan, H. S., & Gangestad, S. W. (2005). Life history theory and evolutionary psychology. In D. M. Buss (Ed.), *The handbook of evolutionary psychology* (pp. 68–95). Hoboken, NJ: Wiley.

Katz, D., & Braly, K. (1933). Racial stereotypes of one hundred college students. *Journal of Abnormal and Social Psychology, 28*, 280–290.

Kenrick, D. T., Griskevicius, V., Neuberg, S. L., & Schaller, M. (2010). Renovating the pyramid of needs: Contemporary extensions built upon ancient foundations. *Perspectives on Psychological Science, 5*, 291–314.

Kinzler, K.D., Shutts, K., & Correll, J. (2010). Priorities in social categories. *European Journal of Social Psychology, 40*, 581–592.

Krosh, A. R., & Amodio, D. M. (2014). Economic scarcity alters the perception of race. *Proceedings of the National Academy of Sciences, 111*, 9079–9084.

Kurzban, R. (2002). Alas poor evolutionary psychology: Unfairly accused, unjustly condemned. *Human Nature Review, 2*, 99–109.

Kurzban, R., & Leary, M. R. (2001). Evolutionary origins of stigmatization: The functions of social exclusion. *Psychological Bulletin, 127*, 187–208.

Kurzban, R., Tooby, J., & Cosmides, L. (2001). Can race be erased? Coalitional computation and social categorization. *Proceedings of the National Academy of Sciences, 98*, 15387–15392.

Lieberman, D., Tooby, J., & Cosmides, L. (2007). The architecture of human kin detection. *Nature, 445*, 727–731.

Macrae, C. N., & Quadflieg, S. (2010). Perceiving people. In D. T. Gilbert, S. T. Fiske, & G. Lindzey (Eds.), *The handbook of social psychology* (5th ed., pp. 428–463). New York: McGraw-Hill.

Madon, S., Guyll, M., Aboufadel, K., Montiel, E., Smith, A., Palumbo, P., & Jussim, L. (2001). Ethnic and national stereotypes: The Princeton Trilogy revisited and revised. *Personality and Social Psychology Bulletin, 27*, 996–1010.

Maner, J. K., Kenrick, D. T., Becker, D. V., Robertson, T., Hofer, B., Delton, A. W., Neuberg, S. L., Butner, J., & Schaller, M. (2005). Functional projection: How fundamental social motives can bias interpersonal perception. *Journal of Personality and Social Psychology, 88*, 63–78.

Maner, J. K., Miller, S. L., Moss, J. H., Leo, J. L., & Plant, E. A. (2012). Motivated social categorization: Fundamental motives enhance people's sensitivity to basic social categories. *Journal of Personality and Social Psychology, 103*, 70–83.

Massey, D. S. (2004). Segregation and stratification: A biosocial perspective. *DuBois Review: Social Science Research on Race, 1*, 1–19.

McArthur, L. Z., & Baron, R. M. (1983). Toward an ecological theory of social perception. *Psychological Review, 90*, 215–238.

McDonald, M. M., Donnellan, M. B., Cesario, J., & Navarrete, C. D. (2015). Mate choice preferences in an intergroup context: Evidence for a sexual coercion threat-management system among women. *Evolution and Human Behavior, 36*, 438–445.

McDonald, M. M., Navarette, C. D., & Van Vugt, M. (2012). Evolution and the psychology of intergroup conflict: The male warrior hypothesis. *Philosophical Transactions of the Royal Society B, 367*, 670–679.

Miller, S. L., Maner, J. K., & Becker, D. V. (2010). Self-protective biases in group categorization: Threat cues shape the psychological boundary between "us" and "them." *Journal of Personality and Social Psychology, 99*, 62–77.

Navarrete, C. D., Fessler, D. M. T., & Eng, S. J. (2007). Elevated ethnocentrism in the first trimester of pregnancy. *Evolution and Human Behavior, 28*, 60–65.

Navarrete, C. D., McDonald, M. M., Molina, L. E., & Sidanius, J. (2010). Prejudice at the nexus of race and gender: An outgroup male target hypothesis. *Journal of Personality and Social Psychology, 98*, 933–945.

Navarrete, C. D., Olsson, A., Ho, A. K., Mendes, W. B., Thomsen, L., & Sidanius, J. (2009). Fear extinction to an out-group face: The role of target gender. *Psychological Science, 20*, 155–158.

Neel, R., Neufeld, S. L., & Neuberg, S. L. (2013). Would an obese person whistle Vivaldi? Targets of prejudice self-present to minimize the appearance of specific threats. *Psychological Science, 24*, 678–687.

Nesse, R. M. (1990). Evolutionary explanations of emotions. *Human Nature, 1*(3), 261–289.

Nesse, R. M. (2005). Natural selection and the regulation of defenses: A signal detection analysis of the smoke detector principle. *Evolution and Human Behavior, 26,* 88–105.

Neuberg, S. L. (1992). Evolution and individuation: The adaptiveness of non-stereotypical thought. *Psychological Inquiry, 3,* 178–180.

Neuberg, S. L., Becker, D. V., & Kenrick, D. T. (2013). Evolutionary social cognition. In D. E. Carlston (Ed.), *Oxford handbook of social cognition* (pp. 656–679). New York: Oxford University Press.

Neuberg. S. L., & Cottrell, C. A. (2006). Evolutionary bases of prejudices. In M. Schaller, J. A. Simpson, & D. T. Kenrick (Eds.), *Evolution and social psychology* (pp. 163–187). New York: Psychology Press.

Neuberg, S. L., & DeScioli, P. (2015). Prejudices: Managing threats to group life. In D. M. Buss (Ed.), *Handbook of evolutionary psychology* (2nd ed., Vol. *2,* 704–721). New York: Wiley.

Neuberg, S. L., & Fiske, S. T. (1987). Motivational influences on impression formation: Outcome dependency, accuracy-driven attention, and individuating processes. *Journal of Personality and Social Psychology, 53,* 431–444.

Neuberg, S. L., Kenrick, D. T., & Schaller, M. (2010). Evolutionary social psychology. In S. T. Fiske, D. Gilbert, & G. Lindzey (Eds.), *Handbook of social psychology* (pp. 761–796). New York: John Wiley & Sons.

Neuberg, S. L., Kenrick, D. T., & Schaller, M. (2011). Human threat management systems: Self-protection and disease avoidance. *Neuroscience and Biobehavioral Reviews, 35,* 1042–1051.

Neuberg, S. L., & Schaller, M. (2014). Evolutionary social cognition. In M. Mikulincer & P. R. Shaver (Eds.), *APA handbook of personality and social psychology: Vol. 1. Attitudes and social cognition,* pp. 3–45, E. Borgida & J. A. Bargh (Assoc. Eds.). Washington, DC: American Psychological Association.

Neuberg, S. L., & Schaller, M. (2016). An evolutionary threat-management approach to prejudices. *Current Opinion in Psychology, 7,* 1–5.

Neuberg, S. L., & Sng, O. (2013). A life history of social perception: Stereotyping at the intersections of age, sex, and ecology (and race). *Social Cognition, 31,* 696–711.

Niemann, Y. F., Jennings, L., Rozelle, R. M., Baxter, J. C., & Sullivan, E. (1994). Use of free responses and cluster analysis to determine stereotypes of eight groups. *Personality & Social Psychology Bulletin, 20*(4), 379–390.

Park, J. H., Faulkner, J., & Schaller, M. (2003). Evolved disease-avoidance processes and contemporary anti-social behavior: Prejudicial attitudes and avoidance of people with physical disabilities. *Journal of Nonverbal Behavior, 27,* 65–87.

Park, J.H., & Schaller, M. (2005). Does attitude similarity serve as a heuristic cue for kinship? Evidence of an implicit cognitive association. *Evolution and Human Behavior, 26,* 158–170.

Park, J. H., Schaller, M., & Crandall, C. S. (2007). Pathogen-avoidance mechanisms and the stigmatization of obese people. *Evolution and Human Behavior, 28,* 410–414.

Pendry, L. F., & Macrae, C. N. (1994). Stereotypes and mental life: The case of the motivated but thwarted tactician. *Journal of Experimental Social Psychology, 30,* 303–25.

Pietraszewski, D., Cosmides, L., & Tooby, J. (2014). The content of our cooperation, not the color of our skin: An alliance detection system regulates categorization by coalition and race, but not sex. *PLoS ONE*, *9*(2), e88534.

Pirlott, A. G., & Neuberg, S. L. (2014). Sexual prejudice: Avoiding unwanted sexual interest? *Social Psychological and Personality Science*, *5*, 92–101.

Plutchik, R. (1980). *Emotion: A psychoevolutionary synthesis*. New York: Harper & Row.

Richerson, P., & Boyd, R. (1995, January). *The evolution of human hypersociality*. Paper presented at the Ringberg Castle Symposium on Ideology, Warfare and Indoctrinability, Ringberg, Germany.

Rodeheffer, C. D., Hill, S. E., & Lord, C. G. (2012). Does this recession make me look Black? The effect of resource scarcity on the categorization of biracial faces. *Psychological Science*, *23*, 1476–1478.

Roseman, I. J., Wiest, C., & Swartz, T. S. (1994). Phenomenology, behaviors, and goals differentiate discrete emotions. *Journal of Personality and Social Psychology*, *67*, 206–221.

Sampson, R. J., Raudenbush, S. W., & Earls, F. (1997). Neighborhoods and violent crime: A multilevel study of collective efficacy. *Science*, *277*(5328), 918–923.

Schaller, M., & Neuberg, S. L. (2012). Danger, disease, and the nature of prejudice(s). In J. Olson & Zanna, M. P. (Eds.), *Advances in experimental social psychology* (Vol. *46*, pp. 1–55). Burlington, VT: Academic Press.

Schaller, M., & Park, J. H. (2011). The behavioral immune system (and why it matters). *Current Directions in Psychological Science*, *20*, 99–103.

Schaller, M., Park, J. H., & Mueller, A. (2003). Fear of the dark: Interactive effects of beliefs about danger and ambient darkness on ethnic stereotypes. *Personality and Social Psychology Bulletin*, *29*, 637–649.

Sng, O., Williams, K. E. G., & Neuberg, S. L. (2013, July) *Rethinking sex and age stereotypes: The need to manage threats and opportunities*. Paper presented at the 26th APS Annual Convention, San Francisco, CA.

Stearns, S. (1992). *The evolution of life*. Oxford: Oxford University Press.

Swim, J. K. (1994). Perceived versus meta-analytic effect sizes: An assessment of the accuracy of gender stereotypes. *Journal of Personality and Social Psychology*, *66*, 21–36.

Tajfel, H. (1969). Cognitive aspects of prejudice. *Journal of Biosocial Science*, *1*(S1), 173–191.

Tajfel, H., Billig, M. G., Bundy, R. P., & Flament, C. (1971). Social categorization and intergroup behaviour. *European Journal of Social Psychology*, *1*(2), 149–178.

Tooby, J., & Cosmides, L. (1992). The psychological foundations of culture. In J. H. Barkow, L. Cosmides, & J. Tooby (Eds.), *The adapted mind* (pp. 19–136). New York: Oxford University Press.

Tomkins, S. S. (1963). *Affect, imagery, consciousness: Vol. 2. The negative affects*. New York: Springer Verlag.

Trivers, R. L. (1972). Parental investment and sexual selection. In B. Campbell (Ed.), *Sexual selection and the descent of man* (pp. 136–179). Chicago: Aldine-Atherton.

Varley, A. H., Filip-Crawford, G., Neuberg, S. L., & Nagoshi, C. T. (2015). *Toward understanding anti-atheist prejudice: The roles of values-dissimilarity and belief in moralizing god(s)*. Unpublished manuscript, Arizona State University.

Williams, K. E. G., Sng, O., & Neuberg, S. L. (2016). Ecology-driven stereotypes override race stereotypes. *Proceedings of the National Academy of Sciences, 113*, 310–315.

Wilson, M. L., & Wrangham, R. W. (2003). Intergroup relations in chimpanzees. *Annual Review of Anthropology, 32*, 363–392.

Young, S. G., Sacco, D. F., & Hugenberg, K. (2011). Vulnerability to disease is associated with a domain-specific preference for symmetrical faces relative to symmetrical non-face stimuli. *European Journal of Social Psychology, 41*, 558–563.

Zebrowitz, L. A., & Montepare, J. (2006). The ecological approach to person perception: Evolutionary roots and contemporary offshoots. In M. Schaller, J. A. Simpson, & D. T. Kenrick (Eds.), *Evolution and social psychology* (pp. 81–113). New York: Psychology Press.

3 From Prejudice to Social Change: A Social Identity Perspective

Katherine J. Reynolds, Emina Subasic, Luisa Batalha, and Benjamin M. Jones

For more than 80 years, understanding the causes, consequences, and remedies for prejudice has been a central theme in social psychology. Prejudice, by definition, refers to the holding of negative attitudes toward others based exclusively on their membership of a given group (Brown, 1995, p. 6). Prejudice is a major area of academic enquiry because it is considered a necessary condition for discrimination, which affects the opportunities and well-being of its targets – the victims. Furthermore, when negative views about a particular group become widespread and shared, then intergroup conflict, violence, and civil unrest are more likely.

Much of social psychology, though, has focused on the concepts of prejudice and social change as largely distinct areas of inquiry underpinned by different levels of analysis. Many approaches to explaining prejudice are directed at individual-level factors such as personality and cognitive and motivation processes (which are potentially faulty and irrational). Other explanations of prejudice emphasize the role of system-level factors and argue that maintenance of the status quo and preservation of stable social hierarchies consequently result in the subjugation of particular minority groups. An alternative analysis is that prejudice and social change are both outcomes of ongoing and fluid intergroup relations whereby people's group memberships and relationships between groups play a central explanatory role. The overarching and fundamental questions of interest within this trajectory of work are how is the intergroup relationship perceived now and when and how does it change.

Drawing on the social identity perspective, which incorporates both social identity theory (Tajfel & Turner, 1979) and self-categorization theory (Turner, Hogg, Oakes, Reicher, & Wetherell, 1987), the aim of this chapter is to make a case for the interdependence of prejudice and social change. This more

This research was supported by an Australian Research Council (ARC) grant (LP120100446) and many of the ideas flow from an earlier ARC grant awarded to John C. Turner and Katherine Reynolds (2003–2007; DP0342645). We thank Corie Lin for her assistance with the preparation of the manuscript and the editors for their comments and suggestions.

integrated analysis relies on a new understanding of prejudice that rejects the premise that such attitudes and associated negative treatment are the product of flawed and faulty cognitive and motivational psychological processes (Oakes, Haslam, & Turner, 1994; Reynolds, Haslam, & Turner, 2012). Instead prejudice needs to be conceptualized, first and foremost, as an outcome of group processes and intergroup dynamics, whereby members of the majority and minority groups are positioned in a particular social relationship. Majority and minority do not refer to the simple numbers but to positions of power through cultural and economic dominance within a social system. The key point is that it is possible to connect (a) majority (dominant group) prejudice toward a minority, (b) minority groups' experiences of negative treatment (and their rejection of it), (c) increasing prejudice toward the majority group by the minority (and by the majority toward the minority), and (d) minority groups' (and their supporters') overt attempts at social change (e.g., protest, civil unrest, riots) and the majority group's attempts to maintain the status quo. Prejudice defined as negative attitudes related to people's group memberships can occur at various stages of this process. It can be viewed as a rational response to understandings of ingroup-outgroup relations and is expected to increase with attempts at social change and increased intergroup conflict.

Events in Ferguson (Missouri, spanning 2014–2015) highlight this sequence of events from prejudice to social change very clearly. During this time, news reports were filled with accusations of prejudice and discrimination by the Ferguson police department. Michael Brown, an 18-year-old African American male, was shot on August 9, 2014, by Darren Wilson, a 28-year-old Caucasian (White) police officer. Brown matched the description of a youth who had stolen cigars from a convenience store. An altercation broke out when Wilson confronted Brown and a friend, which eventually resulted in Wilson firing at least six shots at the unarmed Brown. Protests, riots, and looting followed the shooting, with a further outbreak in November 2014 when the decision was taken by a grand jury not to indict Wilson.

In response to ongoing unrest in Ferguson, the US Justice Department conducted an investigation into the Ferguson police department. Reporting in March 2015, it concluded there had been misconduct on behalf of the police officers involved. Specifically, this misconduct included the practice of using racial stereotypes and active discrimination against African American citizens. Quoting directly from the report: "Our investigation indicates that this disproportionate burden on African Americans cannot be explained by any difference in the rate at which people of different races violate the law. Rather, our investigation has revealed that these disparities occur, at least in part, because of unlawful bias against and stereotypes about African Americans" (Investigation into Ferguson Police Department, 2015, p. 5). The investigators also pointed out that "many officers appear to see some residents, especially those who live in Ferguson's predominantly African-American neighborhoods, less as constituents to be protected than as potential offenders and sources of revenue" (p. 2). The impact of these factors over time was a deterioration of trust and an undermining of "law enforcement legitimacy among African Americans in particular" (p. 2).

Events in Ferguson highlight the use of racial stereotypes and discriminatory practices within the police force, and the impact on targets of prejudice (including being harassed, treated unfairly, and possibly physically harmed). They also show connections between the minority group's experiences of prejudice and discrimination and civil unrest and protest. In this example, there is also political solidarity whereby majority group members join the fight for better conditions and treatment for the minority (Subasic, Reynolds, & Turner, 2008). There is a connection between the expression and experiences of prejudice and social change.

This case example showcases many of the points that are explored in detail in this chapter. The first part of the chapter is designed to highlight the split within the field between approaches that (a) address prejudice largely as a product of individual-level processes and/or an emphasis on system stability and (b) analyze the group and intergroup relations that account for both social stability and social change.

There is also a division depending on whether the focus is on the majority (perpetrator) or minority (victim). It is possible to classify much of the social psychology work along two main dimensions (see Figure 3.1). The first dimension is whether the targets of interest are members of the majority (dominant, advantaged) groups in society (i.e., perpetrators) or the members of minority (subordinate, disadvantaged) groups (i.e., victims of prejudice and discrimination). The second dimension is whether the relevant theories of prejudice are more oriented toward explaining system stability and the maintenance of the status quo or toward the conditions under which social change occurs. Through an exploration of the dominant approaches in each quadrant, it is possible to highlight current

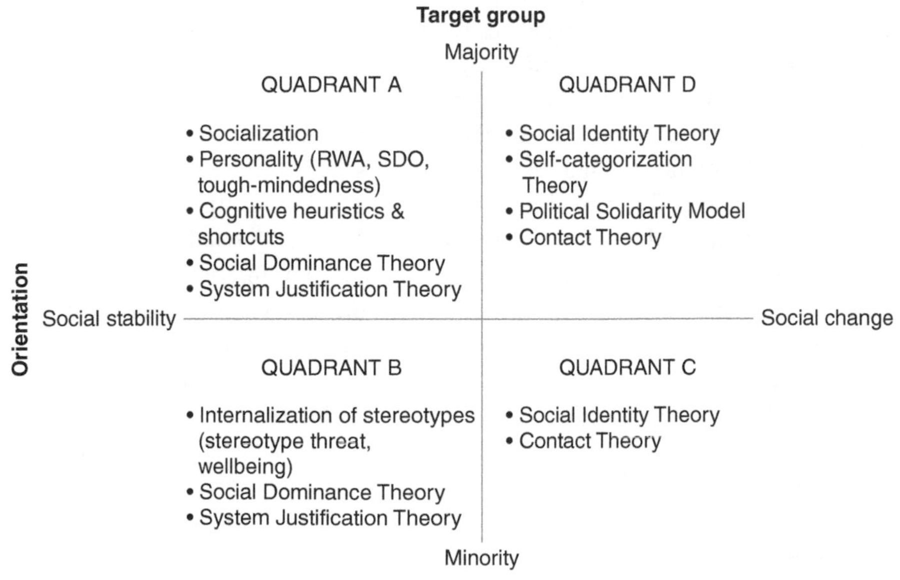

Figure 3.1 *Classification of social psychological theories of prejudice.*

explanations of prejudice within social psychology and the novel contribution of the social identity perspective becomes evident.

To begin with, each of the quadrants that are formed through the intersecting dimensions of minority or majority and the orientation to stability or change will be outlined in turn. We start with Quadrant A, where approaches largely target the majority and make a case for the inevitability of prejudice, and for system stability through the maintenance of the status quo. In Quadrant B, the target of interest is members of the minority group, the victims of prejudice and discrimination. Here there is evidence that stereotypes and negative treatment can be internalized, affecting the performance and well-being of its targets. In Quadrant C, the emphasis shifts away from social stability to social change. In particular, social identity theory has been used to explore how members of the minority group respond to their low-status, disadvantaged position in the social system (although many of the key points also can be applied to members of the majority group). The constructs of legitimacy, stability, and permeability that are central to social identity theory (Tajfel & Turner, 1979) are outlined. In the final quadrant, Quadrant D, attention is directed to the self-categorization theory analysis of subgroup and superordinate relations, and implications for explaining both system stability (justification) and system change (rejection; Reynolds, Jones, O'Brien, & Subasic, 2013; Turner et al., 1987; Turner & Reynolds, 2002).

Mapping the Social Psychology of Prejudice

Some historical context is useful to locate contemporary developments in prejudice research and their significance. There have been several important trends in theory and research on prejudice. Originally, prejudice was not deemed an important topic of inquiry, in that many prevailing attitudes that today we would label and study as "prejudice" were considered acceptable and normal. Psychological research (as part of the scientific racism movement) served to investigate ideas that certain groups were inferior as a result of biology, development, intellectual abilities, and character (e.g., Duckitt, 2001; Richards, 1997). Negative attitudes and treatment were not the subject of "prejudice." Such views were reasonable and founded on the basis of evidence of inferiority.

Only a few decades later, though, these notions of "victim" inferiority were rejected, and psychology embraced prejudice as a problem for the "perpetrator" (e.g., Duckitt, 1994, 2001; Richards, 1997). Since this time, the definition of prejudice has included both a description of the phenomenon as well as a psychological explanation for its occurrence (Turner, 2001). Not only is prejudice the holding of negative attitudes toward others based exclusively on their membership in a given group (e.g., Brown, 1995), it is also widely assumed that these attitudes are unreasonable and unfounded. Prejudiced attitudes are thus said to be held without warrant and involve judgments that are in contrast to the "facts" (Allport, 1954, p. 9). As Allport (1954) states, prejudice in general is "thinking ill of others without sufficient warrant" (p. 9), and ethnic prejudice in particular is "an antipathy based upon a faulty and inflexible generalization" (p. 9). Within this line of theorizing, the explanation for prejudice is already embedded in its definition – prejudice is a product of "flawed and faulty" psychology (Reynolds et al., 2012).

There is no doubt that many people find certain views about other groups and their treatment to be problematic and unjustified and are willing to take action to challenge such views. Prejudice can be challenged on moral, religious, and political grounds. It is possible to see why victims of prejudice, or those who want to see more just treatment for certain minority groups, would classify the perpetrators of such negativity as wrong, irrational, and biased. Calling the views of another group with whom you disagree faulty and irrational may be good politics. The critical issue is whether the lens of science supports the view that negative (and even positive) attitudes about groups are in fact the product of "faulty" psychological processes.

Ferguson, Branscombe, and Reynolds (2015; see also Reynolds & Turner 2001) ask whether it is possible that social and political objections to prejudice (especially among social scientists) may have been conflated with its definition. Ferguson and colleagues suggest that social scientists' objections to the negative treatment toward certain minority groups may reflect a redrawing of the boundaries of ingroup and outgroup relations such that those who are accused of being prejudiced have been recategorized as an outgroup, and the victims of such treatment recategorized as ingroup members. This potential overlap between the definition of prejudice and its cause is not widely discussed, but yet it has affected fundamentally the trajectory of theory and research on prejudice and stereotyping (Oakes et al., 1994; Reynolds et al., 2012). Much of the work on prejudice has focused on explaining "the secret's of man's [sic] irrational nature" (Allport, 1954, p. xv) and is represented in Quadrant A of Figure 3.1.

> **Quadrant A: Emphasis on majority processes and system stability**
> *Prejudice is an antipathy based on faulty and inflexible generalization. It may be felt or expressed. It may be directed toward a group or an individual of that group.* (Allport, 1954, p. 9)

Much of the existing social psychological theory and research on prejudice locates its causes largely within individual psychology, and as being the result of the functioning of ordinary motivational and cognitive processes. One clear example concerns the notion of prejudiced personality, which, it is argued, has its roots in biology, genes, and early socialization. The individual difference variables of interest include authoritarianism (RWA; e.g., Adorno, Frenkel-Brunswik, Levinson, & Sanford, 1950; Altemeyer, 1981), social dominance orientation (SDO; Sidanius & Pratto, 1999) and the Big Five personality factors (e.g., Ekehammer & Akrami, 2003). Although these measures differ in their emphasis, this work is united by the assumption that individual differences (e.g., high RWA, low openness) are relatively stable and are positively related to prejudice.

With respect to cognitive processes, the starting point is that prejudice is a product of cognitive error that originates from limitations in human information processes. People learn from their experience and from others around them (e.g., through peers, family, and the media) and form associations between membership of a particular group and negative attributes (that align with the existing dominant cultural and political beliefs). Given limitations in human information-processing capacity, these categorizations, heuristics and shortcuts (stereotypes, group generalizations) are used to form impressions of others and make sense of events (Fiske & Neuberg, 1990; Fiske & Taylor, 1991).

The simplification and generalization of social information through categorization are interpreted as adaptive. As a matter of cognitive necessity, then, humans categorize others and this leads to distorted and overgeneralized (but efficient) judgments. This analysis is often combined with the idea that people want to define themselves and, by extension, their group memberships positively (which draws on Tajfel and Turner's [1979] social identity theory, described in more detail in Quadrant C), which inevitably leads to one's own group memberships being treated more favorably than that of other groups (ingroup favoritism or bias; but see McGarty, 2001; Turner & Reynolds, 2001). The cognitive (cognitive economy and use of stereotypes, heuristics, and biases) and motivational explanations (desire for ingroup favoritism/ethnocentrism) combine into an analysis that explains how flawed and faulty group judgments are formed.

Social dominance theory (e.g., Sidanius & Pratto, 1999) and system justification theory (e.g., Jost & Banaji, 1994), although recognizing the role of intergroup relations in society (low- and high-status groups) and the impact of social processes, are placed in this quadrant because the root cause for negative stereotypes and prejudice are individual-level drives and needs. For social dominance theory, dominant-subordinate relations are an outcome of evolutionary processes. For system justification theory, there is a need to see the current social order as being fair and just. These individual-level factors serve to bias social relations toward the existing social order.

Aspects of these theories that relate more to group processes concern the analysis of the strategies that dominant groups use to maintain the status quo. In system justification theory (Jost & Banaji, 1994), it is explicitly recognized that high-status groups develop stereotypes, theories, and institutional structures that embed current arrangements. In social dominance theory, it is hierarchy-enhancing strategies and myths cultivated by the dominant group that emerge as important in maintaining the current dominant-subordinate relations. The main idea is that negative stereotypes can serve ideological functions and justify the treatment of certain groups in society (e.g., Jost & Banaji, 1994). In particular, they can justify the exploitation of some and the success of others in ways that make these differences seem legitimate, natural, and normal.

Although this is a brief summary of much work in social psychology on the topic of prejudice (other chapters in this volume address the ideas in more detail), for the purposes of this chapter it is useful to highlight the following points. First, it is clear that many of the major approaches in the field are located in this quadrant. A long list of individual-level factors is used to explain prejudice (i.e., stable personality, evolutionary drives, cognitive processes, motivational drives). The models, although acknowledging societal factors and socialization, do not fully engage with the interdependence between one's social position (e.g., status) and under-standings of group relations in shaping individual differences (e.g., RWA, neuroti-cism, openness) and the influence of individual differences on social and political attitudes.

Second, current explanations of prejudice concern its normality and inevitability, and in this way also deny the possibility of change. If prejudice is a product of fixed personality, how does it change? Turner (2006) draws the conclusion that there is a stability bias within social psychology, with much more energy directed at explaining current social arrangements rather than when and how they change. We argue that individual-level explanations of prejudice such as these often are fundamentally incompatible with other theories in social psychology on social change.

Quadrant B: The impact of prejudice and discrimination on individual members of the minority group

Suppose you heard over and over again that you were lazy, a simple child of nature, expected to steal and had inferior blood. Suppose [further] this view was forced on you by the majority of your fellow citizens. And suppose nothing you could do would change this opinion – because you happen to have black skin . . . One's reputation, whether false or true, cannot be hammered, hammered, hammered, into one's head without doing something to one's character. (Allport, 1954, pp. 138–139)

Research on the impact of prejudice and discrimination is included in Quadrant B of Figure 3.1. Allport (1954) dedicated a chapter of his book *The nature of prejudice* to the consequences of victimization. In his view, there are ego-defenses that vary from passive withdrawal (and well-hidden resentment), to strengthening ingroup ties, to action directed at the majority group. He recognized that one's character could be "persecution-produced" but that the precise impact would vary from individual to individual depending on a range of other life circumstances. Another ego defense strategy (which is rare in Allport's view) is to identify with the dominant group and come to experience self-hate with respect to being a member of the minority group (for similar arguments, see Jost & Banaji, 1994). An example provided by Allport was the unemployed during the Great Depression, where there was acceptance of shame and fault on the part of the individual members of this group. Allport argued this form of self-hate was related to the dominant ideology of individual responsibility and merit.

These same themes emerge within system justification theory where the internalization of societal stereotypes by minority group members can generate a "false consciousness" whereby people accept the stereotypes and their social disadvantage (Jost & Banaji, 1994). When members of disadvantaged groups internalize the systems' negative perceptions and treatment of them, they simultaneously accept that the position of higher-status groups is legitimate and thus the status quo is maintained. Evidence that low-status groups endorse beliefs where the majority outgroup is better than the ingroup (outgroup favoritism) and endorse system stereotypes are interpreted as support for system justification (e.g., Southern Italians rating Northern Italians more positively than their own group; Jost, Burgess, & Mosso, 2001).

Social stereotypes have the potential to become self-fulfilling and to affect behavior, especially when salient or contextually relevant. There is mounting evidence that even though members of the minority may be as competent and capable as members of the majority, when minority stereotypes are negative and salient, behavior becomes more aligned with that stereotype. Much of this work is conducted under the umbrella of *stereotype threat*, with implications for attitudes, memory, and behavior (e.g., Désert, Preaux, & Jund, 2009; Spencer, Logel, & Davies, 2015; Steele, Spencer, & Aronson, 2002).

Looking at the well-being consequences of victimization systematically, Schmitt, Branscombe, Postmes, and Garcia (2014) conducted a meta-analysis involving more than 300 studies and 140,000 participants. The aim was to assess the relationship between perceived discrimination and psychological well-being including self-esteem, depression, anxiety, psychological distress, and life satisfaction. The results indicated greater harm for disadvantaged groups ($r = -.24$) compared to advantaged groups ($r = -.10$). The internalization of negative social stereotypes thus affects well-being and performance, which can further contribute to ongoing disadvantage and low status.

Contexts in which certain group memberships and associated negative stereotypes are salient can be particularly damaging. Such evidence is leading to more concerted efforts to identify protective factors that can buffer the negative impact (Reynolds & Klik, 2016) and the conditions under which members of low-status minorities (perhaps with support from sympathetic majority group membership) will challenge the status quo and act to bring about social change. Coming together as a group and developing collective responses to discrimination are not only protective for well-being (e.g., Branscombe, Schmitt, & Harvey, 1999) but may be a catalyst for social change dynamics. These strategies involve group processes and draw heavily on core ideas within social identity theory. These are outlined in the next section on Quadrant C.

Quadrant C: Minority group membership and the conditions for social change

It is hardly surprising to say that the best way to predict whether a man [or woman] will harbour hostile attitudes towards a particular group and what will be the content of these attitudes is to find out how he [or she] understands the intergroup situation. (Tajfel, 1969, p. 81)

Quadrants C and D of Figure 3.1 incorporate research within the intergroup relations tradition, where the central idea is that prejudice is psychologically rational (but not necessarily any less objectionable and harmful) and is tied to contemporary group affiliations and intergroup relations (from the perceivers' vantage point). As Sherif (1967) pointed out, stereotypes and negative attitudes are "images shared . . . by large numbers of persons belonging to the same human groupings" (p. 234). Sherif did not accept that stereotypes and group-based perceptions were false or wrong because he believed such a view "evades the issue of stereotype formation by definition" (Sherif, 1967, p.23). Labeling such views as false means attention is not directed to their cause. Sherif's and Tajfel's (opening quote) ideas that negative stereotypes and prejudice are connected to human groupings and understandings of the intergroup situation have been developed and extended through social identity theory (Tajfel & Turner, 1979) and self-categorization theory (Turner et al., 1987).

A key construct in this approach is social identity, which captures people's self-definition and connections as group members. A continuum of identity was proposed that included both people's ability to think of themselves as individuals (personal identity: "I" and "me"), in contrast to other individuals, and as group members (social identity: "we" and "us") in contrast to other groups ("them"). The group is not an external classification based on sociological or other categories, but instead it has internal psychological meaning for members. At times, people can be oriented to each other and events through the lens of their psychological group memberships. So even if an individual sociologically is a member of the advantaged, high-status group, psychologically he or she may identify with members of the low-status group and act in solidarity with them (Subasic, et al., 2008). Equally, a member of a sociologically defined low-status group may identify with the high-status advantaged group.

Social identity theory and more recent developments in self-categorization theory are both distinctive because of their attention to the social change dynamics. Using the more specific language of social identity theory (Tajfel & Turner, 1979) it is argued that group members engage in social comparison and seek to positively differentiate their own group from other groups. These comparison processes involve categorization of self and others into groups (which is fundamental to all perception; Bruner, 1958), which increases awareness of a group's relative position – low or high status – in relation to some valued dimension. A critical question for social identity theory is how do the losers of these social comparisons achieve positive social identity and positive distinctiveness for their group. A number of strategies are identified and include social mobility, social creativity, and social competition, with the latter being the most likely to generate negative stereotypes, prejudice, and social antagonism. The perceived permeability, stability, and legitimacy of intergroup relations are central to explaining whether the minority group members act in ways that maintain the status quo (accepting or ignoring negative treatment) or act to bring about social change.

Put simply, people attempt social mobility (from a lower- to a higher-status group) when movement into a higher-status group is possible (the intergroup boundary is permeable) and there is an acceptance of, or acquiescence to, current intergroup relations (they are perceived as stable and/or legitimate). Social creativity is more likely when group boundaries are impermeable but there is a broad acceptance of the system. Here, group members seek to define "who they are" in the (larger) group in as positive a way as possible. In general, social creativity affords a form of positive group-based self-definition without broader changes to the position of different individuals or subgroups, and thereby it serves to maintain the status quo.

Finally, social competition depends on group boundaries being impermeable and insecure (unstable and/or illegitimate), leading low-status groups to act in ways to bring about social change. Social competition entails both a sense of illegitimacy and instability and a belief that change is possible (and necessary), often resulting in collective action aimed at challenging and overturning the existing status hierarchy. It also depends on the emergence of a sense of "us" in opposition to "them." Having group members who are committed and active is an important first step in attempts at social change (e.g., Kelly & Brienlinger, 1995) as it enables cooperation and coordinated action (e.g., protests, lobbying institutions, building alliances). Social competition, given its social change focus and direct threat to the status quo, heightens intergroup categorization (the ingroup-outgroup divide) and negative stereotypes, prejudice, and discrimination. Social competition is a strategy that emerges in response to social comparison, prejudice, and negative treatment and attempts to change the social position of the group (e.g., embed women's and gay rights) but is also a catalyst for further prejudice.

One of the other approaches in this quadrant (and quadrant D) is contact theory. Contact theory recognizes that positive interactions between people from different ethnic groups (minority and majority) can reduce fear and anxiety and/or increase empathy and/or group knowledge. As a result, negative attitudes toward outgroups decrease (Pettigrew & Tropp, 2008). Pettigrew and Tropp (2006) conducted a meta-analysis revealing a small but significant impact of contact on intergroup attitudes.

Using social identity terminology, contact may enhance individual mobility. Along these lines, there is evidence contact leads members of minority groups to be less likely to recognize inequality, and therefore less likely to engage in collective identification and collective action directed at social change (e.g., Dixon, Durrheim, & Tredoux, 2007; Wright & Baray, 2012). To be most effective, contact may need to be based on people's psychology and understandings as group members rather than on interpersonal interactions (e.g., Hewstone & Brown, 1986). The optimal conditions for contact such as institutional support, common goals, and equal status also suggest that group contact will be most beneficial when it occurs within a shared inclusive higher-order social identity (Reynolds, Batalha, Subasic, & Jones, 2015). In this way, positive contact needs to fit with the normative aspiration of the group for more tolerant group relations.

Based on these insights, the social identity perspective offers an explanation of the psychology of prejudice that is embedded in group psychology, ingroup and outgroup relations, and the dynamics of social change. In contrast to most of social psychology, where the group is portrayed as the cause of social and cognitive distortion and error (that underpins prejudice), within this alternative, group perception is normal and fundamental to what makes us human (e.g., the social brain hypothesis; Dunbar, 2009). According to Turner (2001), the group is "what makes possible social change, collective and political action to eliminate racism and prejudice, to aspire to new, more progressive social realities" (p. 1). The key message is that group psychology underpins the development of theories and beliefs about ourselves and society that can serve to accentuate and eliminate prejudice.

Quadrant D: Group membership and the conditions for social change

Human psychology does not make us prisoners of social structure. It makes us capable of collective action to change social structures and in turn re-fashion our identities, roles, personalities and beliefs. (Turner, 2006, p. 41)

The ideas stemming from social identity theory – that it is psychological group memberships and not sociological status that underpins system stability and social change – are developed further within self-categorization theory, which argues that people can define the self at different levels of inclusiveness. For example, one can define oneself as an individual in comparison to others, as a member of subgroups (ingroup and outgroup), and as a member of a more inclusive (superordinate) ingroup. These ideas have been directly applied to the area of prejudice and prejudice reduction through the common ingroup identity model (e.g., Gaertner, Dovidio, Anastasio, Bachman, & Rust, 1993). Common ingroup identification refers to the redefinition of group boundaries as to include "them" and, by so doing, becoming more inclusive (Gaertner et al., 1993) and can lead to favorable outgroup evaluations. It does so because the psychological distance between the self and the outgroup is reduced (Stone & Crisp, 2007). The importance of maintaining a salient subgroup identity at the same time as a higher-order identity (dual identity) is increasingly being recognized as a way of reducing intergroup discrimination but also fostering social change. Investigation of the relationship between social identity and prejudice has also acknowledged that people have many social identities and that this *identity complexity* is positively associated with tolerance for outgroups (Brewer & Pierce, 2005; Roccas & Brewer, 2002; Schmid, Al Ramiah, & Hewstone 2012; Schmid, Hewstone, Tausch, Cairns. & Hughes, 2009).

Exploring the dynamics between subgroup and superordinate levels further, it is possible to identify the conditions under which prejudice will be rejected and challenged (potentially leading to negative intergroup relations and increases in prejudice and social change). It is argued that system stability and justification are likely to emerge where there is superordinate identification on the part of both the minority and majority. System rejection and possible social change are likely to develop if an oppositional subgroup identity is defined in contrast to the hitherto superordinate group (Reynolds et al., 2013).

More specifically, when members of the group, regardless of their position within it (low or high status, minority or majority, leader or follower) are understood to be acting in line with the normative practices of the group (its culture), system stability is likely to be maintained. Under these conditions, group members will accept circumstances and "treatment" that an outside observer may consider disadvantageous or unfair (e.g., women resigning from paid work when married). It is when group members (individuals or subgroups) within the superordinate group come to perceive social arrangements as being illegitimate that cognitive alternatives to the status quo and motivations to bring such alternatives to the fore arise. Perceived illegitimacy emerges whenever an action violates some norm, value, rule, procedure, right, or obligation associated with a shared ingroup membership – a rule that "we are supposed to share." When this occurs, identification with the superordinate group and its authority figures is eroded, identification with a low-status minority is enhanced, and rejection of the system and associated collective action are likely.

The tension between superordinate ("we") and subgroup ("us" versus "them") social identities is central to the workings of (il)legitimacy and the dynamics of social change. Perceived legitimacy of a social authority that represents "us" at a higher level of self-definition, and identification with the group the social authority represents, are fundamentally linked. Where some system authority behaves legitimately, one is more likely to identify with and seek membership in the authority's group, at the expense of one's subordinate group. In such a situation, people will justify the higher-level self over the lower-level one. But when the actions of the system authority violate the shared higher-order ingroup identity, illegitimacy emerges. This, in turn, facilitates the superordinate group's recategorization as an outgroup, reduces identification with it, leads to increased identification with the contrasting subordinate ingroup, and makes it more likely that one will denigrate the system to justify and advance one's subordinate group's interests (e.g., Becker, Wright, Lubensky, & Zhou, 2013; Glasford & Calcagno 2012; Reynolds et al., 2013; Wiley, Srinivasan, Finke, Firnhaber, & Shilinksy, 2013; van Zomeren, Postmes, Spears, & Bettache, 2011). Under conditions where illegitimacy is coupled with instability, attempts at social change are likely to emerge coupled with a deterioration in intergroup relations and increases in prejudice.

These ideas are developed further within the political solidarity model of social change (Subasic et al., 2008). It is possible to conceptualize social change as a tripartite relationship among three (sociologically) defined groups: the authority (e.g., dominant leadership group), minority (e.g., disadvantaged group), and majority (e.g., other members of the system). Within this model, social stability or social change (where prejudice is actively rejected) involves the psychological connections between authority and majority, and majority and minority being maintained or redefined. Change is most likely when the majority shifts from identification with the authority to identification with the minority. The majority needs to come to identify at the subgroup level and support action that is in opposition to the hitherto authority (e.g., dominant group).

Here the example that opened the chapter can help illustrate this argument. Pointing to widespread intimidation and racial bias by the authority (Ferguson police) toward a minority (African Americans) is a way of eroding the legitimacy of the authority in the eyes of both the minority and majority. This then increases the likelihood that members of the majority will identify, and act in political solidarity, with the minority. An opposing dynamic is also possible where the dominant authority can seek to maintain influence and legitimacy (a concern also of social dominance theory and system justification theory) through acting in ways that maintain and strengthen its connection with the majority. For example, this might be achieved by arguing that most police in Ferguson are fair and just and are not prejudiced.

This analysis also has implications for the emergence of new forms of leadership (Subasic & Reynolds, 2011; Subasic, Reynolds, & Mohamed, 2015). Leadership is as much about being able to reflect and embody the group as it is about being able to create and shape "who we are" in ways that are meaningful to the group and advance particular "projects" (Haslam, Reicher, & Platow, 2013; Reicher, 2004; Subasic, Reynolds, 't Hart, Haslam, & Reicher, 2009). As the perceived illegitimacy of the authority's actions grows, new forms of influence and new leaders will be legitimized. Decreased identification with the system will lead to loss of influence by the established authorities and increased identification with those in opposition that best capture the momentum for change (Subasic et al., 2015; Turner, Reynolds, & Subasic, 2008). Those who are more extreme and radical will gain influence to the degree they harness the normative trajectory of the group ("us" versus "them"; Subasic et al., 2015). One clear outcome is that ingroup-outgroup divides will become sharper and negative intergroup attitudes stronger and more widespread. There is the potential for changes to the social structure that are more progressive and serve to eliminate prejudice (e.g., Turner, 2001).

Many of these ideas need to be refined and investigated through more detailed research. The analysis, though, is important in advancing understandings of both prejudice and social change. First, the old view of prejudice as flawed and faulty psychology driven by individual-level needs and motives is rejected. Prejudice is viewed, first and foremost, as a product of people's psychological group memberships, intergroup relations, and their understandings of such relations. Group psychology is not only the basis for prejudice; it also is the vehicle for eliminating it.

Second, system stability and social change (along with the potential to increase and eliminate prejudice) can be interpreted as outcomes of the same social identification processes, but precisely which will prevail depends on whether low-status individuals (and indeed those within the majority group) continue to identify with and see as legitimate the superordinate (system-level) group or whether they perceive the system as illegitimate and persecutory and come to identify more with their subordinate group.

Third, prejudice can be a cause and a consequence of social change. Negative treatment of minorities, under certain conditions, can be a catalyst for the emergence of an oppositional subgroup identity (rather than superordinate identity) and can lead to an increase in prejudice, discrimination, and social conflict. There is a link between prejudice and social change. What self-categorization theory and the related political solidarity model offer is an analysis that connects these two major areas of inquiry in social psychology, opening up new questions and directions for research.

Conclusions and Future Directions for Research

There is a core tension between the major theories that address prejudice and social change in social psychology. Theories focused on individual psychology (Quadrants A and B) start from a position that group perceptions (stereotypes, categorization, generalization) are faulty and flawed judgments. There is an emphasis on the inevitability of prejudice and the stability of the status quo (cognitive biases, dominant-subordinate hierarchies, ideologies, and stereotypes that serve to maintain the status quo). Turner (2006) makes this point clearly when he states: "The science prefers analyses that explain how and why social structures, intergroup and power relations, personalities and beliefs maintain and reproduce themselves, and indeed cannot be changed, rather than how and why society constantly generates forces for social change from within itself" (p. 46).

In contrast, social identity theory and self-categorization theory seek to address both social stability and social change. From this perspective, there is a pathway from prejudice to social change. This perspective starts from the position that our capacity to be group members as well as individuals is not negative but a plus for human beings. The analysis is distinctive in that it connects the victim experience of prejudice, experiences of negative treatment, and lack of opportunity in society to the dynamics of social change (e.g., Oakes et al., 1994; Reicher, 2012; Reynolds et al., 2012; Reynolds & Turner, 2001; Turner, 2001). Much can be gained by a shift from the inevitability of prejudice where group perception is understood to be the problem to a social change perspective.

Returning to the events in Ferguson outlined in the opening paragraphs, prejudice and discrimination by police can be understood as an outcome of certain understandings of the intergroup relationship between police and the African American community (that has developed over time in a broader context). The collective action by African Americans and their supporters (acting in political solidarity; Subasic et al., 2008) is one way to challenge it and bring about social change. The social identity perspective makes it clear that it is through group or collective psychology and coordinated action that prejudice both arises and can be challenged. There is some evidence that the efforts of African Americans in Ferguson and their supporters are having an impact. It is through acting collectively that there is hope that the future for Ferguson will be brighter.

References

Adorno, T. W., Frenkel-Brunswik, E., Levinson, D. J., & Sanford, R. N. (1950). *The authoritarian personality*. New York: Harper.

Allport, G. W. (1954). *The nature of prejudice*. Reading, MA: Addison-Wesley.

Altemeyer, B. (1981). *Right-wing authoritarians*. Winnipeg: University of Manitoba Press.

Becker, J. C., Wright, S. C., Lubensky, M. E., & Zhou, S. (2013). Friend or ally: Whether cross-group contact undermines collective action depends on what advantaged group members say (or don't say). *Personality and Social Psychology Bulletin, 39*, 442–455.

Branscombe, N. R., Schmitt, M. T., & Harvey, R. D. (1999). Perceiving pervasive discrimination among African Americans: Implications for group identification and well-being. *Journal of Personality and Social Psychology, 77*, 135–149. http://dx .doi.org/10.1037/0022-3514.77.1.135

Brewer, M. B., & Pierce, K. P. (2005). Social identity complexity and outgroup tolerance. *Personality and Social Psychology Bulletin, 31*, 428–437.

Brown, R. (1995). *Prejudice: Its social psychology*. London: Basil Blackwell.

Bruner, J. S. (1958). Social psychology and perception. In E. E. Maccoby, T. M. Newcomb, & E. L. Hartley (Eds.), *Readings in social psychology* (pp. 85–94). New York: Holt, Rinehart & Winston.

Désert, M., Préaux, M., & Jund, R. (2009). So young and already victims of stereotype threat: Socio-economic status and performance of 6 to 9 years old children on Raven's progressive matrices. *European Journal of Psychology of Education, 24*, 207–218. doi:10.1007/BF03173012

Dixon, J., Durrheim, K., & Tredoux, C. (2007). Intergroup contact and attitudes toward the principle and practice of racial equality. *Psychological Science, 18*, 867–872. doi: 10.1111/j.1467-9280.2007.01993.x

Duckitt, J. (1994). Conformity to social pressure and racial prejudice among White South Africans. *Genetic, Social, and General Psychology Monographs, 120*, 121–143.

Duckitt, J. (2001). A dual-process cognitive-motivational theory of ideology and prejudice. In M. P. Zanna (Ed.), *Advances in experimental social psychology*, Vol. 33 (pp. 41–113). San Diego, CA: Academic Press.

Dunbar, R. I. (2009). The social brain hypothesis and its implications for social evolution. *Annals of Human Biology, 36*, 562–572. doi: 10.1080/03014460902960289

Ekehammer, B., & Akrami, N. (2003). The relation between personality and prejudice: A variable and a person-centered approach. *European Journal of Personality, 17*, 449–464. doi: 10.1002/per.494

Ferguson, M. A., Branscombe, N. R., & Reynolds, K. J. (2011). The effect of intergroup comparison on willingness to perform sustainable behavior. *Journal of Environmental Psychology, 31*, 275–281. doi: 10.1016/j.jenvp.2011.04.001

Fiske, S. T., & Neuberg, S. L. (1990). A continuum of impression formation, from category-based to individuating processes: Influences of information and motivation on attention and interpretation. *Advances in Experimental Social Psychology, 23,* 1–74. doi: 10/1016/S.065-2601(08)60317-2

Fiske, S. T., & Taylor, S. E. (1991). *Social cognition,* 2nd ed. New York: McGraw-Hill.

Gaertner, S. L., Dovidio, J. F., Anastasio, P. A., Bachman, B. A., & Rust, M. C. (1993). The common ingroup identity model: Recategorization and the reduction of intergroup bias. *European Review of Social Psychology, 4,* 1–26. doi: 10.1080/14792779343000004

Glasford, D. E., & Calcagno, J. (2012). The conflict of harmony: Intergroup contact, commonality and political solidarity between minority groups. *Journal of Experimental Social Psychology, 48,* 323–328.

Haslam, S. A., Reicher, S. D., & Platow, M. J. (2013). *The new psychology of leadership: Identity, influence and power.* Sussex, UK: Psychology Press.

Hewstone, M., & Brown, R. (1986). Contact is not enough: An intergroup perspective on the "contact hypothesis." In M. Hewstone & R. Brown (Eds.), *Contact and conflict in intergroup encounters* (pp. 1–44). Oxford, UK: Blackwell.

Investigation into Ferguson Police Department. (2015). Retrieved from www.justice.gov /sites/default/files/opa/press-releases/attachments/2015/03/04/ferguson_police_ department_report.pdf

Jost, J. T., & Banaji, M. R. (1994). The role of stereotyping in system-justification and the production of false consciousness. *British Journal of Social Psychology, 33,* 1–27. doi: 10.1111/j.2044-8309.1994.tb01008.x

Jost, J. T., Burgess, D., & Mosso, C. O. (2001). Conflicts of legitimation among self, group, and system: the integrative potential of system justification theory. In J. T. Jost & B Major (Eds.), *The psychology of legitimacy.* Cambridge: Cambridge University Press.

Kelly, C., & Breinlinger, S. (1995). Identity and justice: Exploring women's participation in collective action. *Journal of Community and Applied Psychology, 5,* 41–57.

McGarty, C. (2001). Social identity theory does not maintain that identification produces bias, and self-categorization theory does not maintain that salience is identifica- tion: Two comments on Mummendey, Klink and Brown. *British Journal of Social Psychology, 40,* 173–176. doi: 10.1348/014466601164777

Oakes, P. J., Haslam, S. A., & Turner, J. C. (1994). *Stereotyping and social reality.* Oxford: Blackwell.

Pettigrew, T. F., & Tropp, L. R. (2006). A meta-analytic test of intergroup contact theory. *Journal of Personality and Social Psychology, 90,* 751–783. doi: 10.1037/0022-3514.90.5.751

Pettigrew, T. F., & Tropp, L. R. (2008). How does intergroup contact reduce prejudice? Meta-analytic tests of three mediators. *European Journal of Social Psychology, 38,* 922–934. doi: 10.1002/ejsp.504

Reicher, S. D. (2004). The context of social psychology: Domination, resistance and change. *Political Psychology, 25,* 40–62. doi: 10.1111/j.1467-9221.2004.00403.x

Reicher, S. D. (2012). From perception to mobilization: The shifting paradigm of prejudice. In J. Dixon & M. Levine (Eds.), *Beyond prejudice.* Oxford: Wiley-Blackwell.

Reynolds, K. J., Batalha, L., Subasic, E., & Jones, B. M. (2015). The social psychology of social (dis)harmony: Implications for political leaders and public policy. In J. P. Forgas, K. Fiedler & W. D. Crano (Eds.), *Social Psychology and Politics.* New York, NY: Psychology Press.

Reynolds, K. J., Haslam, S. A., & Turner, J. C. (2012). Social identity, prejudice and social change: Beyond the Allportian problematic. In J. Dixon & M Levin (Eds), *Beyond prejudice: Extending the social psychology of conflict, inequality and social change* (pp. 48–69). Cambridge: Cambridge University Press.

Reynolds, K. J., Jones, B. M., O'Brien, K., & Subasic, E. (2013). Theories of socio-political change and the dynamics of sub-group versus superordinate interests. *European Psychologist, 18,* 235–244. doi: 10.1027/1016-9040/a000159

Reynolds, K.J., & Klik, K.A. (2016). New developments in prejudice research: From its neural basis and impact on well-being to prejudice reduction. Current Opinion in Psychology, 11, 115–119.

Reynolds, K. J., & Turner, J. C. (2001). Prejudice as a group process: The role of social identity. In M. Augoustinos & K. Reynolds (Eds.), *Understanding prejudice, racism, and social conflict* (pp. 159–179). London: SAGE Publications Ltd.

Richards, G. (1997). *"Race," racism and psychology: Towards a reflexive history.* London: Routledge.

Roccas, S., & Brewer, M. B. (2002). Social identity complexity. *Personality and Social Psychology Review, 6,* 88–106.

Schmid, K., Al Ramiah, A., & Hewstone, M. (2012). Diversity and its consequences for outgroup, ingroup and neighbourhood trust: Indirect effects via intergroup contact and threat. *Unpublished manuscript.*

Schmid, K., Hewstone, M., Tausch, N., Cairns, E., & Hughes, J. (2009). Antecedents and consequences of social identity complexity: Intergroup contact, distinctiveness threat, and outgroup attitudes. *Personality and Social Psychology Bulletin, 35,* 1085–1098.

Schmitt, M. T., Branscombe, N. R., Postmes, T., & Garcia, A. (2014). The consequences of perceived discrimination for psychological well-being: A meta-analytic review. *Psychological Bulletin, 140,* 921–948. doi: 10.1037/a0035754

Sherif, M. (1967) *Group conflict and co-operation: Their social psychology.* London: Routledge and Kegan Paul.

Sidanius, J., & Pratto, F (1999). *Social dominance: An intergroup theory of social hierarchy and oppression.* Cambridge: Cambridge University Press.

Spencer, S. J., Logel, C., & Davies, P. G. (2015). Stereotype threat. *Annual Review of Psychology.* doi: 10.1146/annurev-psych-073115-103235

Steele, C. M., Spencer, S. J., & Aronson, J. (2002). Contending with group image: The psychology of stereotype and social identity threat. *Advances in Experimental Social Psychology, 34,* 379–440. doi:10.1016/S0065-2601(02)80009-0

Stone, C. H., & Crisp, R. J. (2007). Superordinate and subgroup identification as predictors of intergroup evaluation in common ingroup contexts. *Group Processes and Intergroup Relations, 10,* 493–513. doi: 10.1177/1368430207081537

Subasic, E., & Reynolds, K. J. (2011). Power consolidation in leadership change contexts: A social identity perspective. In P. 't Hart & J. Uhr (Eds.), *How power changes hands: Transition and succession in government.* Basingstoke: Palgrave Macmillan.

Subasic, E., Reynolds, K. J. & Mohamed, M. S. (2015). Changing identities to change society: Leadership as a contest for influence and collective mobilization. In K. J. Reynolds & N. Branscombe (Eds.), *Psychology of change: Life contexts, experiences, and identities.* New York: Psychology Press, pp. 246–263.

Subasic, E., Reynolds, K. J., 't Hart, P., Haslam, S. A., & Reicher, S. (2009). Leadership, social identity and the dynamics of influence in intergroup relations: A new understanding of social continuity and change. Successful grant submission to the Australian Research Council.

Subasic, E., Reynolds, K. J., & Turner, J. C. (2008). The political solidarity model of social change: Dynamics of self-categorization in intergroup power relations. *Personality and Social Psychology Review*, *12*, 330–352. doi:10.1177/1088868308323223

Tajfel, H. (1969). Cognitive aspects of prejudice. *Journal of Social Issues*, *25*, 79–97. doi: 10.1111/j.1540-4560.1969.tb00620.x

Tajfel, H., & Turner, J. C. (1979). An integrated theory of intergroup conflict. In W. G. Austin and S. Worchel (Eds.), *The social psychology of intergroup relations* (pp. 33–47). Monterey, CA: Brooks/Cole.

Turner, J. C. (2001, October 3). *The idea of prejudice in social psychology*. Freilich Foundation Eminent Lecture.

Turner, J. C. (2006). Tyranny, freedom and social structure: Escaping our theoretical prisons. *British Journal of Social Psychology*, *45*, 41–46. doi:10.1348/014466605X79840

Turner, J. C., Hogg, M. A., Oakes, P. J., Reicher, S. D., & Wetherell, M. S. (1987). *Rediscovering the social group: A self-categorization theory*. Oxford: Blackwell.

Turner, J. C., & Reynolds, K. J. (2001). The social identity perspective in intergroup relations: Theories, themes, and controversies. *Blackwell handbook of social psychology: Intergroup processes*, *4*, 133–152. doi:10.1002/9780470693421.ch7.

Turner, J. C., & Reynolds, K. J. (2002). From the inevitability of prejudice to the origins of social change: The emergence of perceived illegitimacy in intergroup relations. Grant submission Australian Research Council.

Turner, J. C., Reynolds, K. J., & Subasic, E. (2008). Identity confers power: The new view of leadership in social psychology. In P. 't Hart, & J. Uhr (Eds.), *Public leadership: Perspectives and practices* (pp. 57–72). Canberra: ANU E-press.

van Zomeren, M., Postmes, T., Spears, R., & Bettache, K. (2011). Can moral convictions motivate the advantaged to challenge social inequality? Extending the social identity model of collective action. *Group Processes & Intergroup Relations*, *14*, 735–753.

Wiley, S., Srinivasan, R., Finke, E., Firnhaber, J., & Shilinsky, A. (2013). Positive portrayals of feminist men increase men's solidarity with feminists and collective action intentions. *Psychology of Women Quarterly*, *37*, 61–71.

Wright, S. C., & Baray, G. (2012). Models of social change in social psychology: Collective action or prejudice reduction? Conflict or harmony? In J. Dixon & M. Levine (Eds.), *Beyond prejudice: Extending the social psychology of conflict, inequality and social change* (pp. 225–247). Cambridge: Cambridge University Press.

4 Ingroup Projection as a Challenge of Diversity: Consensus about and Complexity of Superordinate Categories

Michael Wenzel, Sven Waldzus, and Melanie C. Steffens

As is often done, we could begin such a chapter in a volume on intergroup conflict with a dire description of the state of human society and the continuing menace of social discrimination, prejudice, injustice, and ethnic violence. However, a children's book by the Austrian writer Edith Schreiber-Wicke (1990), whose title may be translated as "When the crows were still colorful," provides a fable that is more fun, yet insightful. It describes the story of the crows when they still came in all sorts of colors and patterns – orange with blue stripes, green with yellow spots, and so on – until one day a snowman asked the fateful (and probably spiteful) question of what a real, true crow looked like. Now the yellow-with-blue-spotted crows declared yellow with blue spots was the true color of crows, but the lilac crows argued the ur-crow was lilac colored, and all the other crows also claimed their colors were the real ones. There was arguing and quarreling; the crows began to fly with like-colored others only. The fighting ended only when one day a black rain turned all animals black. Afterward, only the crows stayed black and no longer had a reason to argue. The moral of the story? Obviously: ingroup projection is a challenge of diversity! And if we do not want to buy social harmony with dull sameness, we had better think of a more creative way to appreciate and enjoy differences.

Ingroup projection is the perception or claim that one's own group is more prototypical for a higher-order superordinate identity, hence more normative and positive, than a relevant comparison outgroup is, or more prototypical at least than the outgroup thinks the ingroup is. In the present chapter, we briefly outline the ingroup projection model (IPM; Mummendey & Wenzel, 1999; Wenzel, Mummendey, & Waldzus, 2007), discuss its key concepts and relevant recent findings, and essentially argue for two ways in which we need to construe our superordinate identities to reduce tension between diverse and divergent groups included in them: We need to advance consensus about the superordinate identity in question, and about the complexity of its representation.

Outline of the Ingroup Projection Model

Ingroup projection may be understood as a contemporary version and specification of an early concept in psychology and sociology: ethnocentrism (Gumplowicz, 1879; Sumner, 1906). Ethnocentrism describes a tendency of members to use their own group, its values and norms, as a judgmental reference standard for their social world, including other groups. Judging others by the standards of one's own group is likely to lead to a sense of superiority of one's group and the devaluation of others. However, whereas in ethnocentrism the imposition of one's own standards is somehow direct from one group to others (see Hegarty & Chryssochoou, 2005), in the concept of ingroup projection the process is mediated via the generalization of such standards to a higher-order identity in which *certain* other groups are included too; qua their inclusion in the higher-order, superordinate identity, these standards are seen as valid and applicable to those other groups. As a consequence, in contrast to ethnocentrism as an almost natural unfettered tendency, the process in ingroup projection is constrained by the social context and how individuals represent it.

The notion of ingroup projection is basically a corollary of self-categorization theory (Turner, Hogg, Oakes, Reicher, & Wetherell, 1987). This theory assumes that individuals use social categories to structure and give meaning to their social world, including their selves. They classify themselves as members of one category in contrast to others, more specifically, depending on the social context, as members of categories at various levels of inclusiveness: at an individual level (or even subindividual level, such as the real vs. ideal self), a group level (with groups obviously also differing in their breadth and inclusiveness), up to the human level (or even suprahuman level, such as living beings). These self-categorizations form the basis of an individual's contextually defined self-concept; self-categorization as a member of a group is the cognitive component of social identity (Tajfel & Turner, 1986).

The evaluative connotations of one's social identity derive from comparisons with relevant outgroups (although they may also form through intragroup interactions alone; Postmes, Spears, Lee, & Novak, 2005). Self-categorization theory assumes that comparisons between ingroup and outgroup imply that both are included in a superordinate, more inclusive category; only their shared inclusion makes two groups comparable (Turner et al., 1987). Their more abstract similarity at a superordinate level (e.g., humans have skin with pigmentation) allows their comparison at a group level (e.g., the ingroup's skin tone is lighter than the outgroup's). Moreover, the superordinate category may be represented in form of a contextually defined prototype (see Oakes, Haslam, & Turner, 1998), which constitutes the normative and positively valued position on the comparison dimension (e.g., the prototypical human skin tone is light olive). The groups are evaluated in terms of their relative closeness to that prototypical position, their relative prototypicality. The more prototypical a group is relative to a relevant comparison group, the more positively valued it is, and the higher in status and more deserving it is judged (see Wenzel, 2004).

When individuals self-categorize as members of an ingroup, they depersonalize and adopt their group's goal and values (Turner et al., 1987). Their commitment to their ingroup's goals and values means they are motivated and may experience ingroup pressures to advance their group's goals and its positive distinctiveness, status, power, or deservingness. This is where ingroup projection comes in, namely as the vehicle through which committed group members may seek to advance their group's standing by perceiving or portraying it as more prototypical for a salient and identity-relevant superordinate category, compared to a salient outgroup (Wenzel et al., 2007). On the flipside, to the degree that the ingroup claims to represent the prototype of the superordinate group (specifically, in terms that render the ingroup distinct from the outgroup), the comparison outgroup is perceived to be less prototypical, more deviant, less valued, and less deserving. Thus, ingroup projection should be related to ingroup favoritism (i.e., a relatively more positive evaluation and treatment of the ingroup). Conversely, to the extent that the outgroup is seen as deviating from the superordinate norm or questioning it, ingroup projection should be related to outgroup derogation and hostility. Hence, diversity (i.e., the presence of group differences) poses challenges when groups engage in projection and make their own the norm of the superordinate group.

Evidence across a Range of Intergroup Contexts

Fundamental Processes

There is good empirical evidence for these fundamental predictions of the IPM (for an earlier review, see Wenzel et al., 2007). For example, as processes of ingroup projection should generally apply to the perspectives of both groups in a salient intergroup context, this would lead to a perspective divergence between the groups about their relative prototypicality. Consistent with this, business administration students and psychology students disagreed about their relative prototypicality for students generally, with business administration students perceiving themselves as more prototypical than psychology students thought they were, and vice versa (Wenzel, Mummendey, Weber, & Waldzus, 2003). Similar patterns were found for chopper and sports bikers, primary and high school teachers, and East and West Germans (Waldzus, Mummendey, Wenzel, & Boettcher, 2004). Further evidence shows that members tend to engage in greater projection when they identify with both their ingroup (implying commitment to advance their group's goals) and the superordinate group (implying recurrence to it as a relevant normative referent), as the model predicts (Ullrich, Christ, & Schlüter, 2006; Wenzel et al., 2003; Waldzus, Mummendey, Wenzel, & Weber, 2003). Likewise, group members claim greater prototypicality specifically for ingroup attributes that are distinct from those of the outgroup in the given context. When Britons were the salient outgroup, German participants projected attributes on which Germans were stereotypically different from Britons; when Italians were the salient outgroup, Germans claimed greater prototypicality on attributes on which they were stereotypically different from Italians (Waldzus, Mummendey, & Wenzel, 2005). This is consistent with the idea that ingroup projection is most functional when distinctive and contextually group-defining features are considered prototypical.

Similarly, there is supportive evidence that perceived relative prototypicality is related to negative attitudes and behavioral intentions toward the outgroup (e.g., Waldzus et al., 2003, 2005; Wenzel et al., 2003), perceived legitimacy of higher ingroup status (Weber, Mummendey, & Waldzus, 2002), and perceptions of entitlement (Wenzel, 2001), including support for policies limiting the rights and opportunities of ethnic minorities (Huynh, Devos, & Altman, 2015). However, consistent with the model, relative ingroup prototypicality was related to negative outgroup attitudes only when the superordinate identity was positively valenced; when it was negatively valenced, the meaning of prototypicality reversed, with it being positively related to outgroup attitudes (Wenzel et al., 2003, Study 3). As a further theory-consistent qualification, the perceived relative prototypicality of the ingroup was only related to negative outgroup attitudes when the superordinate category was indeed inclusive of the outgroup. For example, Germans' perceived relative prototypicality for West Europeans (a category that does not include Poland) was not related to attitudes toward the Polish, but relative ingroup prototypicality for Europeans, which includes the Polish, was (Waldzus & Mummendey, 2004; see also Imhoff, Dotsch, Bianchi, Banse, & Wigboldus, 2011).

A meta-analysis reported by Wenzel et al. (2007) indicated a significant relationship of moderate size between relative prototypicality and intergroup attitudes. Two studies by Berthold, Mummendey, Kessler, Luecke, and Schubert (2012) found this relationship to be stronger for relative prototypicality measured in relation to the ideal, rather than actual, superordinate category, probably because the ideal implies a more prescriptive reference standard. Further, using cross-lagged regressions in a two-wave study on native Germans' attitudes toward immigrants, Kessler et al. (2010) found indications for causal effects of relative ingroup prototypicality on intergroup emotions and attitudes; however, they also found signs of the reverse causality, suggesting that ingroup projection may also serve as a justification of existing prejudices. This should not surprise: If, as assumed, motivational and normative pressures elicit ingroup projection based on one's identification with one's ingroup, then such motivations and norms may equally well stem from one's "anti-identification" with, and one's group's negative views toward, the outgroup. Later, we return to the question of the different social and epistemic functions of ingroup projection.

History, Humanity, and Holiness

Despite the identity-driven tendency to cast one's ingroup as the more prototypical group for a salient superordinate group, this is conditioned by the given social, historical, and ideological context. For example, in reunified Germany both East and West Germans rated West Germans as the more prototypical subgroup (even if they disagreed about the extent to which this was the case), which is not surprising as it was the East German system that collapsed whereas the West German one prevailed and integrated East Germany – going hand in hand with West Germans having economic and political dominance (Waldzus et al., 2004), as well as constituting the numerical majority. Similarly, while both Protestants and Catholics agreed on Northern Ireland being a relevant superordinate category, they both also perceived Protestants as having greater overlap with (prototypicality for) Northern Ireland (Noor, Brown, Taggart, Fernandez, & Coen, 2010). Protestants, while identifying more strongly with Northern Ireland than Catholics did, were less prepared to forgive the outgroup the more strongly they identified with the superordinate group. This is contrary to research showing a common superordinate categorization is beneficial for intergroup forgiveness (Wohl & Branscombe, 2005; see also Gaertner & Dovidio, 2000). Protestants might have considered their group as higher status and more deserving because of their greater prototypicality, and therefore they might have been less willing to make concessions to, and sympathize with, the outgroup *in particular* when they identified strongly with the superordinate group. Ingroup projection may thus be an important qualifier of the effects of common ingroup identity.

Indeed, even the most abstract of human social categories – humanity – widely considered the most sacrosanct, is not immune to these processes. Certainly, identification with humanity has regularly been found to be positively related with a number of prosocial outcomes such as the reduction of global inequality and the advancement of human rights (e.g., McFarland, Brown, & Webb, 2013; Reese, Proch, & Finn, 2015). However, the human category also seems to be a platform for ingroup projection processes, where distinct attributes of the ingroup in relation to a salient outgroup tend to be considered more typically human (Paladino & Vaes, 2009). Such a process mirrors the phenomenon of infra-humanization whereby an ingroup is perceived to be able to experience complex, uniquely human emotions more than a salient outgroup is (Leyens et al., 2000), which has been shown to underpin or express intergroup prejudices (e.g., Demoulin et al., 2004). Koval, Laham, Haslam, Bastian, and Wheelan (2012) found that such seeming projection held more specifically for negatively valenced attributes, suggesting that ingroup members may humanize their weaknesses to protect their group identity. Further evidence has supported the view that such ingroup projection processes may limit, or even pervert, the positive benefits commonly expected from a human identity. Reese, Berthold, and Steffens (2012) found that members of an economically developed country rated developed countries (the ingroup) as more prototypical for all humans than developing countries. There was furthermore evidence that ingroup prototypicality was positively related to perceived legitimacy of global inequality and, mediated by this, negatively related to behavioral intentions to advance the situation for developing countries and the idea of global equality. Reese, Berthold, and Steffens (2015) replicated these findings with regard to actual donation behavior: Claiming to be more human can make one less humane.

Finally, processes of ingroup projection do not stop at religion either (or, perhaps at religion least of all!). Lie and Verkuyten (2012) referred to Islam as a superordinate category and surveyed Turkish-Dutch Sunni Muslims and their feelings toward Alevi and Shiite Muslims. The authors found that Sunnis regarded their ingroup as more prototypical for Islam than Alevis and Shiites; perceived relative prototypicality was in turn negatively related to intergroup feelings toward these groups measured on a feeling thermometer.

There is thus good evidence for the basic principles of the ingroup projection model across a range of intergroup contexts, from the mundane to the politically charged, from the quintessentially human to the holy.

Advances in our Understanding of Ingroup Projection

The label "ingroup projection" should be understood as a metaphor. It is not meant as an expression of hidden drives and suppressed desires in a psychodynamic sense; and it does not privilege an understanding of the process as motivated and unconscious, rather than cognitive and heuristic, or strategic and deliberate; it may be all of these. Likewise, the process can be literally projective/inductive in that the representation of the higher-order group is infused by that of the lower-level ingroup, but it can also be introjective/deductive whereby the ingroup representation is assimilated to that of the superordinate category (e.g., classical infra-humanization whereby the ingroup is described in terms of quintessentially human emotions; Paladino & Vaes, 2009). Ingroup projection basically only describes the observation that people indicate their ingroup to be relatively more prototypical for a common superordinate category than other observers, such as members of a relevant outgroup, indicate it to be (Wenzel et al., 2007; see Figure 4.1).

Implicit Ingroup Projection

Recent research, however, has made some considerable advances in our understanding of the processes. First, ingroup projection can indeed be observed at a subliminal level and can occur spontaneously without cognitive control. Bianchi, Mummendey, Steffens, and Yzerbyt (2010) used a semantic priming technique and found that the superordinate group label presented as subliminal prime prior to lexical decisions (i.e., whether a presented letter string is a word or not a word) facilitated the recognition of typical ingroup attributes as words compared to typical outgroup attributes. The results suggest that ingroup traits were associated with the superordinate group more than outgroup traits.

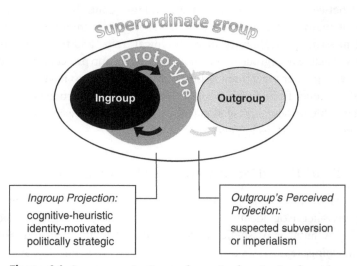

Figure 4.1 *Ingroup projection and perceived projection by outgroups.*

Another interesting technique by Imhoff et al. (2011) used the visual representation of the superordinate group as a measure of ingroup projection. A sample of Portuguese and German participants decided over hundreds of trials which one of two presented faces (randomly generated from one base image) was more European. The average of the faces chosen by each sample was then rated by two independent Portuguese and German samples. Both groups rated the average face resulting from the Portuguese sample as more typically Portuguese, and the face resulting from the German sample as more typically German. In other words, both Portuguese and Germans represented Europeans more in their own image.

Ingroup versus Social Projection

Ingroup projection has obvious similarities to the older concept of social projection, an individual's tendency to expect others to be similar to self (Allport, 1924; Krueger, 2007). While this tendency is likewise constrained by social categorization and applies in particular to others who are part of the same category as self (Clement & Krueger, 2002) – similar to ingroup projection applying to an inclusive, superordinate category – the reference point or anchor is the individual self rather than the ingroup (see also Otten & Wentura, 2001). Thus, the question is whether ingroup projection is indeed, as the theory presumes, a group-level phenomenon or whether it is a redundant concept, where the process is due to self-to-superordinate category projection. Bianchi, Machunsky, Steffens, and Mummendey (2009) investigated this question by having participants rate self, ingroup, outgroup, and superordinate group on a series of attributes (ingroup-typical, outgroup-typical, and irrelevant attributes). They calculated intraindividual partial correlations between ingroup and superordinate ratings (controlling for self), and between self and superordinate ratings (controlling for ingroup), as measures of ingroup and social projection, respectively. Ingroup projection was greater than social projection for ingroup-typical traits, and the former uniquely related to a measure of ingroup bias (Study 1); and ingroup projection but not social projection was greater when the ingroup was manipulated to have positive rather than negative value. These findings suggest that ingroup projection is distinct from, and not reducible to, social projection (for further evidence, see Imhoff & Dotsch, 2013; Machunsky & Meiser, 2009).

Cognitive-Heuristic and Identity-Motivated Ingroup Projection

Theoretically, we understand ingroup projection as a multifaceted process that can have cognitive-heuristic, identity-motivational, politically strategic, or ideological dimensions. A number of studies have contributed to the delineation of these different meanings (even if some of the researchers set out to privilege one meaning over others). Machunsky and Meiser (2009), for example, regard abstract, super-ordinate categories as rather ill-defined, yet individuals are often quite familiar with one particular part of them: their ingroup. Therefore, for questions of representation of a superordinate category, the ingroup constitutes a reasonable heuristic for inference. Illustrating their point, Machunsky and Meiser (2014a) argue and found that groups represented as prototypes (rather than exemplars) are easier, and hence more likely, to be used to infer the representation of a superordinate category, irrespective of whether or not the perceiver is implicated as a member. The authors argue that this cognitive mechanism alone may explain why ingroup projection occurs, as on positive attributes ingroups (and on negative attributes outgroups) tend to be represented in the form of prototypes. However, on top of representation effects, the authors also found a main effect of group membership (Study 3), suggesting that identity motives conjointly with cognitive mechanisms may account for ingroup projection.

Further empirical clues point to identity-motivational underpinnings of ingroup projection. As mentioned earlier, ingroup projection has been found to be posi-tively related to ingroup identification only when the evaluation of the super-ordinate category is positive (e.g., Wenzel et al., 2003), implying a motivation to maintain a positive social identity that ingroup projection may thus help satisfy (Tajfel & Turner, 1986). Moreover, highly prototypical groups often show stronger identification with superordinate categories and stronger correlations between subgroup and superordinate identification than subgroups that are less prototypical (Devos, Gavin, & Quintana, 2010). In line with an identity-serving function, ingroup projection was further enhanced when an outgroup posed a threat to the ingroup (Ullrich et al., 2006).

Indeed, whether ingroup projection is more of an identity-motivated or merely cognitive-heuristic process may depend on how much is at stake for the ingroup's identity. Consistent with this argument, Rosa and Waldzus (2012) observed in status-secure intergroup contexts, where the ingroup's higher status was stable, elevated levels of ingroup projection when participants responded under time pressure, cognitive load, or spontaneous responding instructions, thus presumably in a heuristic-processing mode. In contrast, when the ingroup's status was insecure, ingroup projection was more pronounced when there was no time pressure or when highly identified participants were instructed to respond thoughtfully (a systematic-processing mode; see Chaiken & Trope, 1999). Machunsky and Meiser (2014b) report equivalent results using manipulations of positive versus negative mood to induce heuristic and systematic processing, respectively. Hence, ingroup projection can be both a cognitive heuristic for efficient responding and a socially motivated, deliberate act of defending one's social identity.

Politically Strategic and Ideological Ingroup Projection

Not always, however, are group members, even those highly identified and committed, concerned with the positive portrayal of their group; sometimes the group's goals require a longer-term perspective than the immediate gratification through a positive identity. For example, members may present their group as poor to point to an inequity and demand redistribution (van Knippenberg & van Oers, 1984). Similarly, ingroup projection may not always be in the service of a positive evaluation of the ingroup but may rather be used strategically to promote other (longer-term) goals. Sindic and Reicher (2008) advanced this position in two studies set in the context of Scottish aspirations for independence from the British. They argued that Scots who support independence would seek to bolster their case by portraying the Scottish as *un*prototypical for Britain, thus emphasizing a lack of fit or belonging that supports the aim of secession. Indeed, the results showed that when the issue of independence was salient (and only then), support for independence was related to perceived relative prototypicality in a curvilinear way, with the latter declining at higher levels of support for independence. Further, when support for independence was relatively low, Scottish identification was positively related to relative prototypicality (ingroup projection); however, when support for independence was relatively strong, Scottish identification was negatively related to relative prototypicality. Strotmann (2007) found similar results for Catalan and Basque people in Spain, two regional groups with strong political aspirations for independence. This shows that ingroup projection is not only a function of group identification but rather depends on the group's goals and values. Ingroup projection (or the opposite: claimed unprototypicality) can be used strategically to advance the group's goals.

Moreover, perceptions of relative prototypicality can also be in the service of higher-order values and ideologies. For example, they could be used by both low- and high-status groups to justify existing social inequalities (Peker, 2009), for example, in line with the presumed palliative function of system justification (Jost, Gaucher, & Stern, 2015), or as an expression of commitment to values of the superordinate group that provides members with a positive social identity (Spears, Jetten, & Doosje, 2001). For example, in the context of salient economic status differences between African and European Americans in the United States, lower-status African Americans could describe European Americans as more prototypical than themselves on attributes such as entrepreneurship, justifying the status differences but, at the same time, elevating the attribute to a value of the superordinate group, Americans, that might distinguish it positively from other countries, also benefiting African Americans with a positive American identity (see Wenzel, 2002). On the other hand, ingroup projection could give expression to high-status group members' endorsement of an ideology that justifies group-based hierarchy and their own dominant position in it (Sibley, 2013). In sum, ingroup projection can be seen as having cognitive, motivational, strategic, and ideological underpinnings and functions.

Perceived Projection by Outgroups

The ingroup projection process implies that the outgroup is relatively unprototypical for a superordinate group that serves as a shared evaluative reference standard; to the extent that this is a positive standard, the outgroup is likely to be valued negatively, as deviant or inferior. More than that, the outgroup – just by being different, but probably in particular when seen as *choosing* to be different – may be regarded as challenging the representation of the superordinate group and what the ingroup perceives to be its defining values. Thus, outgroup members could be accused of engaging in *projection on their part*, trying to impose their values onto the representation of the superordinate category. Such an accusation could be made by dominant and dominated groups alike: A dominant majority may regard a minority's stubborn difference and unwillingness to assimilate as *subversion*, an attempt at undermining traditional values. Conversely, a low-power minority may regard a majority's dominance and insensitivity to difference as *cultural imperialism*, imposing its values on everyone else. From either perspective, perceived projection by outgroups could be an identity threat that triggers negative reactions (see Figure 4.1).

First, this reasoning can account for what may otherwise seem paradoxical effects of the endorsement of common identity, observed by Gómez and colleagues (Gómez, Dovidio, Huici, Gaertner, & Cuadrado, 2008; Gómez, Dovidio, Gaertner, Fernández, & Vázquez, 2013). Upon learning that ingroup members categorized ingroup (e.g., Spaniards) and outgroup (e.g., Eastern European immigrants) as being part of a common identity (e.g., Europeans), participants showed more positive orientations toward the outgroup; this is in line with the common ingroup identity model (Gaertner & Dovidio, 2000), which posits that a common, superordinate identity turns an outgroup into a higher-order ingroup to whom ingroup-favorable attitudes are extended. However, upon learning that the outgroup categorized both groups in the same way as part of a common identity, participants responded with *less* positive orientations. Thus, the outgroup's endorsement of a common identity did not have the same positive effect and indeed backfired. Gómez et al. (2013) showed that this backfiring effect was mediated by symbolic threat, measured as the perceived incompatibility of the groups' values. We can understand these results in terms of perceived projection by the outgroup: Outgroup members' statements of belonging to a shared superordinate category may be seen as a claim that their group (with its different values) is prototypical of, and equally fitting into, that group, an attempted subversion of values that the ingroup is likely to object to.

Indeed, measuring such perceptions directly, Von Oettingen (2012; Von Oettingen, Mummendey, & Steffens, 2015) found evidence that ingroups and outgroups not only objectively diverge in their relative prototypicality perceptions (as in Waldzus et al., 2004; Wenzel et al., 2003), but group members also tend to hold subjective perceptions of a divergence, *believing* that the outgroup thinks the ingroup is less relatively prototypical than they, the ingroup members, think it is. In the majority-minority contexts studied by Von Oettingen, it was in particular the prototypicality of the minority that was subject to such *meta-perceptive divergences*; for example, minority members tended to believe the majority considered the minority to be less prototypical than the minority members thought was the case. Moreover, there was evidence, above and beyond the effects of ingroup projection, that beliefs that the outgroup engaged in projection were predictive of negative intergroup attitudes (in particular among majority members, and minority members who maintained a separate subgroup identity). Indeed, suspected projection by an outgroup may elicit ingroup projection tendencies in response (see also Finley & Wenzel, 2003). Even when a contest over prototypicality is only in group members' minds, it is no less real in terms of the intergroup tensions it can cause.

Representations of the Superordinate Identity to Curb Ingroup Projection

It needs to be said that ingroup projection as such is not necessarily problematic. If members see their ingroup as highly prototypical, they may commit more strongly to the relevant superordinate category. Any project trying to promote a superordinate identity for the sake of large-scale cooperation, such as environmentalism mobilizing the global human community, might gain from such processes. However, if humanity, for example, is framed as an extension of Western, Christian, economically developed societies, groups that are minorities or just less powerful in the public discourse might believe they are not sufficiently represented. Under some circumstances, ingroup projection by dominating groups may condemn less-dominant subgroups to a stigma of deviance, which in turn undermines their access to resources and power that prototypical members of the superordinate category are entitled to. Thus, ingroup projection may at times be a means to legitimizing injustice and dysfunctional inequalities that prevent people from developing their full potential (Weber et al., 2002). Moreover, when groups disagree about their prototypicalities, whether or not an asymmetric status relation is involved, the seed is sown for misunderstandings and tension that all too easily escalate into outright conflict. In such circumstances, it would be desirable to curb ingroup projection.

As ingroup projection implicates the prototype of superordinate categories, the theorizing about remedies has focused above all on how such superordinate categories are represented cognitively and in discourse, and in particular how much scope there is in these representations for groups that are different from the mainstream. Broadly, one could think of two options (Mummendey & Wenzel, 1999; Wenzel et al., 2007): (a) superordinate categories that are only vaguely or minimally defined, thus otherwise undefinable, so that no subgroup can claim to represent the prototype better than others or (b) superordinate categories that are represented as complex so that different subcategories can be equally prototypical at the same time.

Vagueness, Complexity, Coherence, and Indispensability

As an example for the first option, vagueness, consider Bilewicz and Bilewicz's (2012) argument against the recently proposed concept of "omniculturalism" (Moghaddam, 2012), which suggests focusing on human commonalities before taking into account intercultural differences, as a tool to improve intercultural relations. Such omniculturalism, Bilewicz and Bilewicz argue, carries the risk that humanity is characterized by the distinctive features of one's own culture, which has historically served to justify Western colonial hegemony. Instead, they propose a more undefined notion of humanity, as "without a clear definition of what makes someone human, people would not deny humanity to outgroups" (Bilewicz & Bilewicz, 2012, p. 340).

Whether a representation of the superordinate category as undefined can reduce ingroup projection has been tested experimentally. In a study by Waldzus et al. (2003, Study 1) German participants rated Europeans on a number of attributes and then received false feedback about the results of a number of other surveys allegedly conducted with Germans rating Europeans on the same attributes. Half of the participants received rather consensual results showing rating profiles from the different surveys that were similar to the participant's own ratings (well-defined condition). The other half of the participants were shown heterogeneous rating profiles suggesting little consensus among Germans about what Europeans are like (undefined condition). As predicted, participants in the undefined condition showed less ingroup projection as indicated by reduced relative prototypicality of Germans vis-à-vis a relevant outgroup (Poles), which in turn led to more positive attitudes toward the outgroup.

However, the study by Waldzus et al. (2003) also points to limitations of undefined representations as a way to reduce ingroup projection: Participants who identified strongly with both Germans and Europeans showed relatively

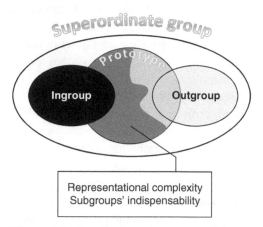

Figure 4.2 *Complex representations of the superordinate group.*

high scores of ingroup projection even in the undefined representation condition. It is possible that an undefined representation appears open to be defined for those with a strong motivation to do so.

The second option for curbing ingroup projection can be achieved by increasing the superordinate category's complexity (Figure 4.2). That way, superordinate categories are created that make prototypicality of outgroups not only possible but rather likely or even mandatory. Originally defined as a representation in which "the distribution of representative members on the prototypical dimension is ... multimodal" as compared to "unimodal" (Mummendey & Wenzel, 1999, p. 167), the more general aspect of complexity is that the superordinate category is represented as diverse, allowing different instantiations to be prototypical. It carries the notion of a group that would not be what it is without the recognition of intra-category differences between similarly representative yet distinct positions. A complex superordinate category implies accepting differences within this superordinate category as normative, which makes it unlikely that a subgroup that is different from the others will be stigmatized because of this difference. Indeed, a larger tradition of research studies how the appreciation of difference and diversity impacts intergroup relations, for instance, regarding effects of multiculturalist ideology (Park & Judd, 2005) or diversity beliefs in organizations (van Dick, van Knippenberg, Hägele, Guillaume, & Brodbeck, 2008).

Testing this experimentally, Waldzus et al. (2003, Study 2) asked German participants to describe either the diversity (complexity condition) or unity (control condition) of Europe. As predicted, whereas participants in the control condition indicated that Germans were more prototypical for Europe than the Polish out-group, in the complexity condition participants considered Germans and Polish as equally prototypical. Waldzus et al. (2005) replicated this finding with Italians and the British as outgroups.

The induction of complex superordinate category representations may come with a downside if it implies an over-inclusive and indistinct superordinate group with which members are less inclined to identify – in this case the benefits of a common identity might get lost. Peker, Crisp, and Hogg (2010) found evidence for reduced superordinate identification in response to a complexity operationalized as a greater number of descriptive attributes and subgroups. Instead, Peker et al. argue that to reduce ingroup projection without loss of identification, the superordinate category should show representational *coherence* – an organized and orderly representation that makes clear the contributions of ingroup and outgroups to the identity of the superordinate group. It should be noted though that the authors' operationalization of coherence, namely as symmetric alignment of the different subgroups' attributes in a table describing the superordinate category, was not without complexity (multiple dimensions, multiple subgroups, implied equal prototypicality). Still, the findings suggest that to be effective, complexity should not be chaos but rather a meaningful constellation.

An alternative way of thinking about positive implications of superordinate complexity is in terms of the subgroups' *indispensability* for the superordinate category. Verkuyten and colleagues (e.g., Verkuyten, Martinovic, & Smeekes, 2014) propose the concept of "indispensability" as an alternative to relative prototypicality. Prototypicality conventionally implies a graded category structure (see Turner et al., 1987) by which minorities would have little chance to be considered equally prototypical; but when thinking of a superordinate group as a combination of complementary subgroups (akin to a mosaic), even the smallest subgroup (mosaic piece) can be considered necessary and indispensable for the overall picture. Complexity can thus be thought of as complementarity of groups toward an overall identity. The ensuing perceived indispensability of outgroups has been found to be positively related to intergroup attitudes in Mauritius (Ng Tseung-Wong & Verkuyten, 2010), positive interethnic feelings in Malaysia (Verkuyten & Kahn, 2012), and support for immigrant rights in the Netherlands (Verkuyten et al., 2014).

Second-Order Conflict about Superordinate Representation

Two important implications have to be taken into account when inducing such complex superordinate categories. First, complex representations of superordinate categories do not necessarily *reduce* an ingroup's relative prototypicality. Rather, they lead to the perception of more *equal* prototypicality between subgroups. Depending on whether the ingroup started off from a high or low level of relative prototypicality, complexity might imply either a decrease or increase in relative ingroup prototypicality, respectively (Waldzus, 2010). For instance, where a minority group has shared in a consensual notion that it is less prototypical than a dominating majority (e.g., Waldzus et al., 2004), the idea of superordinate category complexity leads its members to perceive increased relative ingroup prototypicality (Alexandre, Waldzus, & Wenzel, 2016). Moreover, such a shift toward more equal prototypicality between subgroups does not necessarily mean that relations between subgroups become more harmonious. Rather, a complex framing of superordinate categories may represent a challenge to the status quo that could be seen as threatening by established higher-status groups, while it may facilitate cognitive alternatives to the status quo among minority groups (Tajfel & Turner, 1986) that foster dissatisfaction with its inferior position and tendencies to seek social change.

This idea leads to the second implication: Whether or not superordinate categories are seen as complex (or, more generally, represented in some form that implies the possibility for minority groups to be prototypical) might in itself become a battleground of dispute. Established dominating subgroups might reject such representations exactly because they put into question the legitimacy of their dominance. Indeed, Strotmann (2007) found that the induction of super-ordinate complexity (by triggering elaboration on the cultural richness and diversity in Spain) led Andalusians, a highly prototypical group in Spain, to identify less with this superordinate group, essentially withdrawing from a shared common ground. In contrast, powerless groups (often minorities) might frame superordinate categories as complex as part of their striving for social change (Saguy & Kteily, 2014). For instance, in Strotmann's (2007) research, groups that saw themselves as non-prototypical for Spain and that had strong social change ambitions (i.e., Catalans and Basques) perceived Spain to be more complex than highly prototypical subgroups did (i.e., Andalusians). Similarly, in an Irish context, Joyce, Stevenson, and Muldoon (2013) found in interviews that Irish Traveller participants proactively displayed and claimed what the authors called "hot" national identity (Reicher & Hopkins, 2001) to establish their Irishness, whereas Irish majority participants tended to disparage proactive displays of Irishness and seemed to endorse a "banal" (Billig, 1995) Irish identity that represents an assumed and unquestioned backdrop for their own unproblematic prototypicality. Thus, whereas minorities may seek to contest, majorities may seek to normalize a superordinate identity representation. More generally, the representation of superordinate categories as more or less open for minority subgroups' prototypicality depends on their functional role in actual intergroup relations.

Dominant Groups' Resistance to Complexity Interventions

The possibility that dominant groups regard the notion of superordinate identity complexity as a threat, questioning their greater prototypicality and status, is particularly problematic considering that interventions designed to break down prejudices and increase intergroup tolerance are typically aimed at dominant groups. It could be expected that members of dominant groups would generally not be very receptive to programs that seek to redefine superordinate identity as more complex, particularly if such interventions carry not only the abstract idea of diversity but also make salient its implementation in the concrete context (Yogeeswaran & Dasgupta, 2014).

Indeed, majority group members and participants who consider their ingroup prototypical of the superordinate group have been shown to report more uneasiness or threat after thinking about the diversity rather than unity of the superordinate group (Ehrke & Steffens, 2015; Steffens, Reese, Ehrke, & Jonas, 2015). In one study, US Americans were asked to think about the role of the United States in North America or in the world (Steffens et al., Experiment 3). As expected, US Americans thought they were highly prototypical of North Americans, but less so for the world population. They were then asked to think about either diversity or unity (either within North America or within the world). The results indicated more reported threat and less positive outgroup attitudes following diversity instructions in the North American context than in all other conditions. In other words, in a context in which members more (than less) strongly feel their subgroup represents the prototype, they may respond negatively to suggestions of superordinate diversity.

Similarly, there may be levels of diversity that are more (vs. less) taxing for subgroups that consider themselves prototypical, with diversity that includes particularly counter-prototypical groups likely to provoke more negative responses from a majority subgroup. Dieckmann, Steffens, and Methner (2015) investigated this in the context of metal music. The participants were death metal music fans who were a highly prototypical group among metal music fans. All of them were asked to think about the diversity of metal fans. However, half of them were presented with the examples of black metal fans and thrash metal fans, which are two other prototypical groups of metal fans; the other half were given examples of white metal fans and industrial metal fans, which are peripheral groups that are not regarded as "true" metal fans by some. After thinking about the diversity of metal fans and seeing peripheral rather than prototypical groups as examples, death metal fans disliked another peripheral group, nu metal fans, more. Further findings indicated that too much diversity appears to threaten the groupness of a superordinate group, and members of prototypical subgroups react to this threat by becoming more conservative and less inclusive and exhibiting negative attitudes toward peripheral groups.

The same can be true for "natural experiments" in diversity, such as increased diversity due to demographic shifts. In the US, for example, there are predictions that in coming decades non-Hispanic Whites will lose their numerical majority status and will represent less than 50% of the population. Danbold and Huo (2015, Study 1) found for White American participants such a perceived demographic shift to be related to prototypicality threat (i.e., the feeling that their status as prototypical Americans was threatened), particularly for those respondents who perceived prototypicality to be unevenly distributed (i.e., seeing Whites as more prototypical). Moreover, in an experimental Study 2, White American participants reacted to such information with prototypicality threat; mediated by this threat, they were less embracing of diversity in the

United States. In other words, increased diversity (whether naturally occurring or as an intervention strategy) can pose a threat to dominant groups and lead to the rejection of diversity (complexity) as an identity-defining property (see also Craig & Richeson, 2014; Outten, Schmitt, Miller, & Garcia, 2012). Hence, while complex superordinate identity might be an answer to the challenge of ingroup projection, it is not a simple one.

Consensus versus Complexity: Harmony and Social Change

As we are struggling with an answer, let us review what the question is (see Figure 4.3 for an overview of the model). Ingroup projection processes imply that members represent their own group as relatively more prototypical for a superordinate identity that also includes the outgroup, not necessarily more prototypical than the outgroup in absolute terms but relatively more prototypical than the outgroup grants (or is seen to grant) the ingroup to be. Indeed, because both sides of a given intergroup context can engage in ingroup projection, the groups are likely to show a perspective divergence in their perceptions of superordinate prototypicalities (Waldzus et al., 2004; Wenzel et al., 2003). A perceived divergence may be all the more likely as members may suspect outgroups of engaging in projection (Von Oettingen et al., 2015). The result would be disagreement, either tacit misunderstanding or explicit dissent (Kessler & Mummendey, 2009), which causes or reflects negative intergroup relations, discord, and discrimination. Based on this analysis, the question would be how to create greater consensus between the groups about their relative prototypicalities. With greater consensus, we may expect more intergroup harmony.

Toward this aim, one could think of approaches meant to overcome an ingroup-centric view and promote a better understanding of the outgroup's view. For example, Berthold, Leicht, Methner, and Gaum (2013) investigated the effects of

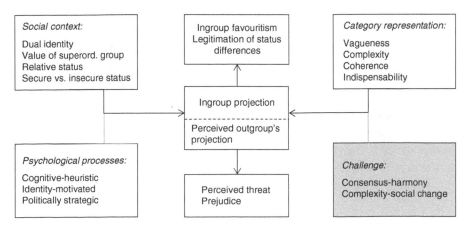

Figure 4.3 *Schematic map of the ingroup projection model.*

perspective taking and found that its positive effects on attitudes toward out-groups were mediated by reduced perceptions of relative ingroup prototypicality. Hence, perspective taking may be a means for reducing ingroup projection (as well as possibly perceived outgroup projection), thus reducing disagreement about prototypicality and increasing intergroup harmony. Likewise, superordinate identity complexity could be seen as an approach to facilitate intergroup consensus about the superordinate group's representation and the subgroups' prototypicalities (or indispensabilities), in that it portrays such perceptions as not being zero-sum. With one group's prototypicality not being at the cost of another group's prototypicality, each group's claims for prototypicality might be more agreeable to the other.

However, as we have seen, this is in fact not quite true, as members of dominant groups tend to resist such notions of complexity (e.g., Steffens et al., 2015). The reason is that more is at stake than mere agreement and harmony – namely, equality and respect (see Simon, Mommert, & Renger, 2015). Indeed, too much emphasis on consensus and the implied harmony may only enshrine social inequalities and foster a misguided contentment with the status quo (see Jost et al., 2015). A similar criticism has been raised against the contact hypothesis as an approach to improve intergroup relations, namely that its narrow focus on the reduction of prejudice and promotion of intergroup harmony helps cement the status quo and reduce motivations to seek social change toward greater equality between the groups (Dixon, Levine, Reicher, & Durrheim, 2012; Wright & Lubensky, 2009). If the goal is *social change* toward greater equality and justice, intergroup contact (and other approaches) would have to aim at greater complexity in the representation of superordinate identities, which affords included subgroups more equal prototypicality as a path to equal respect, status, and entitlements (Wenzel, 2013).

Complexity is therefore not necessarily a fluffy agreeable notion but can be rather inconvenient and hard work. However, it is also not an impossible one, as demonstrated in research by Ehrke, Berthold, and Steffens (2014), who found positive and lasting effects of diversity trainings on intergroup attitudes, mediated by the perceived complexity of a superordinate identity. Comparable findings were demonstrated in the context of a simulated United Nations conference to mitigate climate change, where diversity training increased the willingness to engage in collective action (Knab, 2015). Theoretical sophistication likewise helps, as demonstrated by Ehrke and Steffens (2015), who devised an approach that led autochthonous Germans to feel they themselves were not prototypical Germans in all respects; they were subsequently more receptive to a diversity manipulation and in response to it showed reduced ingroup bias.

Moreover, while a more complex superordinate identity representation implies social change that tends to be resisted by those who fear to lose their dominance, it might still be a more constructive path, for both winners and losers, compared to the alternative: seeking to overthrow dominance by converting others to one's group. For instance, Prislin and Filson (2009) found that minority members achieving social change (i.e., acceptance for their position) by advocating tolerance for diversity within a superordinate group showed greater levels of identification with the group compared to when they managed to convert majority members to their position. This was mediated by their perception that future differences would be regulated in a more conciliatory manner if the change came about through tolerance for different views rather than conversion of others to a new single view. Even majority members remained more strongly identified with the super-ordinate group after having lost their majority status, when the minority had advocated for greater tolerance of diversity. Hence, while complexity implies and requires social change, it might also help build common ground for it.

Above all, however, superordinate identity complexity is more likely to grow from a concerted approach, including consistent policy frameworks and institu-tions, as indicated in research by Sibley and Barlow (2009). These authors found that European Australian participants implicitly associated the superordinate cate-gory Australians more with their ingroup, European Australians, than with Indigenous Australians (mirroring US American=White findings by Devos & Banaji, 2005). In contrast, European New Zealanders associated the superordinate category New Zealanders equally strongly with Maori as with European New Zealanders. Importantly, the fact that this result was found on an implicit measure rules out the suspicion that answers were just driven by social desirability within an ideological climate demanding political correctness. While the quasi-experimental comparison with Australia defies clear conclusions, it is plausible that the histor-ical, institutional, and cultural acknowledgment of Maori in New Zealand (e.g., official bilingualism) fosters a more complex representation of New Zealanders – one that makes its subgroups more equally prototypical for their shared super-ordinate identity.

Coda

If it is mere consensus we want, then the fable of the crows, with which we started this chapter, would seem to provide the answer: a rain that turns all crows black – if there were such thing. In the human world, cultural homogenization would seem a close equivalent to black rain: All would be the same, and there would be nothing more to quarrel about. And, yet, as much as their sameness and blackness left the crows grumpy, the human world would be considerably bleaker, too. Colorful diversity is a more difficult project, requiring more creative responses as to what joins us all together, and probably a continuous re-creation of such responses too. One may wonder what would have happened if one crow, to the question what a real crow is like, had answered "colorful." Perhaps many more crows would have joined in, reaching consensus that no single crow coloring is the part that represents the whole; instead, the whole diversity of colors is needed to understand what crows are like.

References

Alexandre, J., Waldzus, S., & Wenzel, M. (2016). Complex inclusive categories of positive and negative valence and prototypicality claims in asymmetric intergroup relations. *British Journal of Social Psychology*. DOI: 10.1111/bjso.12148

Allport, F. H. (1924). *Social psychology*. Boston: Houghton Mifflin.

Berthold, A., Leicht, C., Methner, N., & Gaum, P. (2013). Seeing the world with the eyes of the outgroup: The impact of perspective taking on the prototypicality of the ingroup relative to the outgroup. *Journal of Experimental Social Psychology*, *49*, 1034–1041.

Berthold, A., Mummendey, A., Kessler, T., Luecke, B., & Schubert, T. (2012). When different means bad or merely worse. How minimal and maximal goals affect ingroup projection and outgroup attitudes. *European Journal of Social Psychology*, *42*, 682–690.

Bianchi, M., Machunsky, M., Steffens, M. C., & Mummendey, A. (2009). Like me or like us: Is ingroup projection just social projection? *Experimental Psychology*, *56*, 198–205.

Bianchi, M., Mummendey, A., Steffens, M. C., & Yzerbyt, V. Y. (2010). What do you mean by "European"? Evidence of spontaneous ingroup projection. *Personality and Social Psychology Bulletin*, *36*, 960–974.

Bilewicz, M., & Bilewicz, A. (2012). Who defines humanity? Psychological and cultural obstacles to omniculturalism. *Culture & Psychology*, *18*, 331–344.

Billig, M. (1995). *Banal nationalism*. London: Sage.

Chaiken, S., & Trope, Y. (Eds.). (1999). *Dual-process theories in social psychology*. New York: Guilford Press.

Clement, R. W., & Krueger, J. (2002). Social categorization moderates social projection. *Journal of Experimental Social Psychology*, 38, 219–231.

Craig, M. A., & Richeson, J. A. (2014). More diverse yet less tolerant? How the increasingly diverse racial landscape affects White Americans' racial attitudes. *Personality and Social Psychology Bulletin*, *40*, 750–761.

Danbold, F. & Huo, Y. J. (2015) No longer "All-American"? Whites' defensive reactions to their numerical decline. *Social Psychological and Personality Science*, *6*, 210–218.

Demoulin, S., Torres, R. R., Perez, A. R., Vaes, J., Paladino, M. P., Gaunt, R., . . . Leyens, J.-P. (2004). Emotional prejudice can lead to infra-humanisation. *European Review of Social Psychology*, *15*, 259–296.

Devos, T., & Banaji, M. R. (2005). American = White? *Journal of Personality and Social Psychology*, *88*, 447–466.

Devos, T., Gavin, K., & Quintana, F. J. (2010). Say "adios" to the American dream? The interplay between ethnic and national identity among Latino and Caucasian Americans. *Cultural Diversity and Ethnic Minority Psychology*, *16*, 37–49.

Dieckmann, J., Steffens, M. C., & Methner, N. (2015). *Back to the roots: When diversity evokes increased group-based conventionalism*. Manuscript submitted for publication.

Dixon, J., Levine, M., Reicher, S., & Durrheim, K. (2012). Beyond prejudice: Are negative evaluations the problem and is getting us to like one another more the solution? *Behavioral and Brain Sciences*, *35*, 411–425.

Ehrke, F., Berthold, A., & Steffens, M. C. (2014). How diversity training can change attitudes: Increasing perceived complexity of superordinate groups to improve intergroup relations. *Journal of Experimental Social Psychology*, *53*, 193–206.

Ehrke, F., & Steffens, M. C. (2015). *After all, are you that typical? Altering self-typicality to reduce backlash against perceived superordinate-group diversity*. Manuscript in preparation.

Ehrke, F., & Steffens, M. C. (2015). Diversity-Training: Theoretische Grundlagen und empirische Befunde (Diversity training: Theoretical foundations and empirical findings). In E. Hanappi-Egger & R. Bendl (Eds.), *Diversität, Diversifizierung und (Ent)Solidarisierung in der Organisationsforschung* (pp. 205–221). Wiesbaden: Springer VS.

Finley, S., & Wenzel, M. (2003, April). *Ingroup projection as a response to social identity threat*. Paper presented at the 32nd annual meeting of the Society of Australasian Social Psychologists, Sydney, Australia.

Gaertner, S. L., & Dovidio, J. F. (2000). *Reducing intergroup bias: The common ingroup identity model*. Philadelphia: Psychology Press.

Gómez, A., Dovidio, J. F., Gaertner, S. L., Fernandez, S., & Vazquez, A. (2013). Responses to endorsement of commonality by ingroup and outgroup members: The roles of group representation and threat. *Personality and Social Psychology Bulletin*, *39*, 419–431.

Gómez, A., Dovidio, J. F., Huici, C., Gaertner, S. L., & Cuadrado, I. (2008). The other side of we: When outgroup members express common identity. *Personality and Social Psychology Bulletin*, *34*, 1613–1626.

Gumplowicz, L. (1879). *Das Recht der Nationalität und Sprachen in Oesterreich-Ungarn [The right of nationality and languages in Austria-Hungary]*. Innsbruck, Austria: Wagner'sche Universitäts-Buchhandlung.

Hegarty, P., & Chryssochoou, X. (2005). Why "our" policies set the standard more than "theirs": Category norms and generalization between European Union countries. *Social Cognition*, *23*, 491–528.

Huynh, Q.-L., Devos, T., & Altman, H. R. (2015). Boundaries of American identity: Relations between ethnic group prototypicality and policy attitudes. *Political Psychology*, *36*, 449–468.

Imhoff, R., & Dotsch, R. (2013). Do we look like me or like us? Visual projection as self- or ingroup-projection. *Social Cognition*, *31*, 806–816.

Imhoff, R., Dotsch, R., Bianchi, M., Banse, R., & Wigboldus, D. H. (2011). Facing Europe: Visualizing spontaneous in-group projection. *Psychological Science*, *22*, 1583–1590.

Jost, J. T., Gaucher, D., & Stern, C. (2015). "The world isn't fair": A system justification perspective on social stratification and inequality. In M. Mikulincer, P. R. Shaver, J. F. Dovidio, & J. A. Simpson (Eds.), *APA handbook of personality and social psychology, Volume 2: Group processes* (pp. 317–340). Washington, DC: American Psychological Association.

Joyce, C., Stevenson, C., & Muldoon, O. (2013). Claiming and displaying national identity: Irish Travellers' and students' strategic use of "banal" and "hot" national identity in talk. *British Journal of Social Psychology*, *52*, 450–468.

Kessler, T., & Mummendey, A. (2009). Why do they not perceive us as we are? Ingroup projection as a source of intergroup misunderstanding. In S. Demoulin,

J.-P. Leyens, & J. F. Dovidio (Eds.), *Intergroup misunderstandings: Impact of divergent social realities* (pp. 135–152). New York: Psychology Press.

Kessler, T., Neumann, J., Mummendey, A., Berthold, A., Schubert, T., & Waldzus, S. (2010). How do we assign punishment? The impact of minimal and maximal standards on the evaluation of deviants. *Personality and Social Psychology Bulletin, 36*, 1213–1224.

Knab, N. (2015). *One world in diversity: Fostering international relations and collective action from a socio-psychological perspective.* Unpublished Masters thesis, University of Koblenz-Landau, Landau, Germany.

Koval, P., Laham, S. M., Haslam, N., Bastian, B., & Whelan, J. A. (2012). Our flaws are more human than yours: Ingroup bias in humanizing negative characteristics. *Personality and Social Psychology Bulletin, 38*, 283–295.

Krueger, J. I. (2007). From social projection to social behaviour. *European Review of Social Psychology, 18*, 1–35.

Leyens, J.-P., Paladino, P. M., Rodriguez-Torres, R., Vaes, J., Demoulin, S., Rodriguez-Perez, A., & Gaunt, R. (2000). The emotional side of prejudice: The attribution of secondary emotions to ingroups and outgroups. *Personality and Social Psychology Review, 4*, 186–197.

Lie, J. L. Y., & Verkuyten, M. (2012). Identity practices, ingroup projection, and the evaluation of subgroups: A study among Turkish-Dutch Sunnis. *The Journal of Social Psychology, 152*, 510–523.

Machunsky, M., & Meiser, T. (2009). Ingroup projection as a means to define the super-ordinate category efficiently: Response time evidence. *Social Cognition, 27*, 57–75.

Machunsky, M., & Meiser, T. (2014a). Cognitive components of ingroup projection: Prototype projection contributes to biased prototypicality judgments in group perception. *Social Psychology, 45*, 15–30.

Machunsky, M., & Meiser, T. (2014b). Us and them: Mood effects on ingroup projection. *European Journal of Social Psychology, 44*, 7–14.

McFarland, S., Brown, D., & Webb, M. (2013). Identification with all humanity as a moral concept and psychological construct. *Current Directions in Psychological Science, 22*, 194–198.

Moghaddam, F. M. (2012). The omnicultural imperative. *Culture & Psychology, 18*, 304–330.

Mummendey, A., & Wenzel, M. (1999). Social discrimination and tolerance in intergroup relations: Reactions to intergroup difference. *Personality and Social Psychology Review, 3*, 158–174.

Noor, M., Brown, R., Taggart, L., Fernandez, A., & Coen, S. (2010). Intergroup identity perceptions and their implications for intergroup forgiveness: The Common Ingroup Identity Model and its efficacy in the field. *The Irish Journal of Psychology, 31*, 151–170.

Oakes, P. J., Haslam, S. A., & Turner, J. C. (1998). The role of prototypicality in group influence and cohesion: Contextual variation in the graded structure of social categories. In S. Worchel, J. F. Morales, D. Paez, & J.-C. Deschamps (Eds.), *Social identity: International perspectives* (pp. 75–92). London: Sage.

Otten, S., & Wentura, D. (2001). Self-anchoring and in-group favoritism: An individual profiles analysis. *Journal of Experimental Social Psychology, 37*, 525–532.

Outten, H., Schmitt, M. T., Miller, D. A., & Garcia, A. L. (2012). Feeling threatened about the future: Whites' emotional reactions to anticipated ethnic demographic changes. *Personality and Social Psychology Bulletin, 38*, 14–25.

Paladino, M.-P., & Vaes, J. (2009). Ours is human: On the pervasiveness of infra-humanization in intergroup relations. *British Journal of Social Psychology, 48*, 237–251.

Park, B., & Judd, C. M. (2005). Rethinking the link between categorization and prejudice within the social cognition perspective. *Personality and Social Psychology Review, 9*, 108–130.

Peker, M. (2009). *Cognitive, motivational and ideological determinants of ingroup projection*. Unpublished Doctoral thesis, University of Kent, UK.

Peker, M., Crisp, R. J., & Hogg, M. A. (2010). Predictors of ingroup projection: The roles of superordinate category coherence and complexity. *Group Processes & Intergroup Relations, 13*, 525–542.

Postmes, T., Spears, R., Lee, A. T., & Novak, R. J. (2005). Individuality and social influence in groups: Inductive and deductive routes to group identity. *Journal of Personality and Social Psychology, 89*, 747–763.

Prislin, R., & Filson, J. (2009). Seeking conversion vs. advocating tolerance in pursuit of social change. *Journal of Personality and Social Psychology, 97*, 811–822.

Reese, G., Berthold, A., & Steffens, M. C. (2012). We are the world – and they are not: Prototypicality for the world community, legitimacy, and responses to global inequality. *Political Psychology, 33*, 683–700.

Reese, G., Berthold, A., & Steffens, M. C. (2015). *As high as it gets: Ingroup projection processes in the superordinate group humans*. Manuscript submitted for publication.

Reese, G., Proch, J., & Finn, C. (2015). Identification with all humanity: The role of self-definition and self-investment. *European Journal of Social Psychology*, advance online publication.

Reicher, S., & Hopkins, N. (2001). *Self and nation*. London: Sage.

Rosa, M., & Waldzus, S. (2012). Efficiency and defense motivated ingroup projection: Sources of prototypicality in intergroup relations. *Journal of Experimental Social Psychology, 48*, 669–681.

Saguy, T., & Kteily, N. (2014). Power, negotiations, and the anticipation of intergroup encounters. *European Review of Social Psychology, 25*, 107–141.

Schreiber-Wicke, E. (1990). *Als die Raben noch bunt waren [When the crows were still colorful]*. Stuttgart/Wien: Thienemann.

Sibley, C. G. (2013). Social dominance and representations of the national prototype: The exclusionary emphasis hypothesis of national character. *International Journal of Intercultural Relations, 37*, 212–224.

Sibley, C. G., & Barlow, F. K. (2009). Ubiquity of whiteness in majority group national imagination: Australian=White, but New Zealander does not. *Australian Journal of Psychology, 61*, 119–127.

Simon, B., Mommert, A., & Renger, D. (2015). Reaching across group boundaries: Respect from outgroup members facilitates recategorization as a common group. *British Journal of Social Psychology*, advance online publication.

Sindic, D., & Reicher, S. D. (2008). The instrumental use of group prototypicality judgments. *Journal of Experimental Social Psychology, 44*, 1425–1435.

Spears, R., Jetten, J., & Doosje, B. (2001). The (il)legitimacy of ingroup bias: From social reality to social resistance. In J. T. Jost & B. Major (Eds.), *The psychology of legitimacy: Emerging perspectives on ideology, justice, and intergroup relations* (pp. 332–362). New York: Cambridge University Press.

Steffens, M. C., Reese, G., Ehrke, F., & Jonas, K. J. (2015). *When does activating diversity alleviate, when does it increase intergroup bias? An ingroup projection perspective.* Manuscript submitted for publication.

Strotmann, B. (2007). *Regional and national identity in Spain – the role of relative prototypicality.* Unpublished Masters thesis, University of Marburg, Germany.

Sumner, W. G. (1906). *Folkways: A study of the sociological importance of usages, manners, customs, mores, and morals.* Boston: Ginn and Company.

Tajfel, H., & Turner, J. C. (1986). The social identity theory of intergroup behavior. In S. Worchel & G. Austin (Eds.), *Psychology of intergroup relations* (pp. 7–24). Chicago: Nelson-Hall.

Ng Tseung-Wong, C., & Verkuyten, M. (2010). Intergroup evaluations, group indispensability and prototypicality judgments: A study in Mauritius. *Group Processes & Intergroup Relations, 13,* 621–638.

Turner, J. C., Hogg, M. A., Oakes, P. J., Reicher, S. D., & Wetherell, M. S. (1987). *Rediscovering the social group: A self-categorization theory.* Oxford, UK: Basil Blackwell.

Ullrich, J., Christ, O., & Schlüter, E. (2006). Merging on Mayday: Subgroup and superordinate identification as joint moderators of threat effects in the context of European Union's expansion. *European Journal of Social Psychology, 36,* 857–876.

van Dick, R., van Knippenberg, D., Hägele, S., Guillaume, Y. R., & Brodbeck, F. C. (2008). Group diversity and group identification: The moderating role of diversity beliefs. *Human Relations, 61,* 1463–1492.

Van Knippenberg, A., & Van Oers, H. (1984). Social identity and equity concerns in intergroup perceptions. *British Journal of Social Psychology, 23,* 351–361.

Verkuyten, M., & Khan, A. (2012). Interethnic relations in Malaysia: Group identifications, indispensability and inclusive nationhood. *Asian Journal of Social Psychology, 15,* 132–139.

Verkuyten, M., Martinovic, B., & Smeekes, A. (2014). The multicultural jigsaw puzzle: Category indispensability and acceptance of immigrants' cultural rights. *Personality and Social Psychology Bulletin, 40,* 1480–1493.

Von Oettingen, M. (2012). *What they think matters! The role of (meta-)representations of the superordinate group among minority and majority members.* Unpublished Doctoral thesis, University of Jena, Germany.

Von Oettingen, M., Mummendey, A., & Steffens, M. C. (2015). *It depends on your perspective! The role of own and attributed superordinate group representations among majority and minority members.* Manuscript in preparation.

Waldzus, S. (2010). Complexity of superordinate self-categories and ingroup projection. In R. J. Crisp (Ed.), *The psychology of social and cultural diversity* (pp. 224–254). Chichester, UK: Wiley-Blackwell.

Waldzus, S., & Mummendey, A. (2004). Inclusion in a superordinate category, in-group prototypicality, and attitudes towards out-groups. *Journal of Experimental Social Psychology, 40,* 466–477.

Waldzus, S., Mummendey, A., & Wenzel, M. (2005). When "different" means "worse": In-group prototypicality in changing intergroup contexts. *Journal of Experimental Social Psychology, 41*, 76–83.

Waldzus, S., Mummendey, A., Wenzel, M., & Boettcher, F. (2004). Of bikers, teachers and Germans: Groups' diverging views about their prototypicality. *British Journal of Social Psychology, 43*, 385–400.

Waldzus, S., Mummendey, A., Wenzel, M., & Weber, U. (2003). Towards tolerance: Representations of superordinate categories and perceived in-group prototypicality. *Journal of Experimental Social Psychology, 39*, 31–47.

Weber, U., Mummendey, A., & Waldzus, S. (2002). Perceived legitimacy of intergroup status differences: Its prediction by relative ingroup prototypicality. *European Journal of Social Psychology, 32*, 449–470.

Wenzel, M. (2001). A social categorization approach to distributive justice: Social identity as the link between relevance of inputs and need for justice. *British Journal of Social Psychology, 40*, 315–335.

Wenzel, M. (2002). What is social about justice? Inclusive identity and group values as the basis of the justice motive. *Journal of Experimental Social Psychology, 38*, 205–218.

Wenzel, M. (2004). A social categorisation approach to distributive justice. *European Review of Social Psychology, 15*, 219–257.

Wenzel, M. (2013, April). *Intergroup contact: Perceived consensus about versus complexity of common identity.* Paper presented at the annual conference of the Society of Australasian Social Psychologists (SASP), Cairns, Australia.

Wenzel, M., Mummendey, A., & Waldzus, S. (2007). Superordinate identities and intergroup conflict: The ingroup projection model. *European Review of Social Psychology, 18*, 331–372.

Wenzel, M., Mummendey, A., Weber, U., & Waldzus, S. (2003). The ingroup as pars pro toto: Projection from the ingroup onto the inclusive category as a precursor to social discrimination. *Personality and Social Psychology Bulletin, 29*, 461–473.

Wohl, M. J. A., & Branscombe, N. R. (2005). Forgiveness and collective guilt assignment to historical perpetrator groups depend on level of social category inclusiveness. *Journal of Personality and Social Psychology, 88*(2), 288–303.

Wright, S. C., & Lubensky, M. E. (2009). The struggle for social equality: Collective action versus prejudice reduction. In S. Demoulin, J.-P. Leyens, & J. F. Dovidio (Eds.), *Intergroup misunderstandings: Impact of divergent social realities* (pp. 291–310). New York: Psychology Press.

Yogeeswaran, K. & Dasgupta, N. (2014). The devil is in the details: Abstract versus concrete construals of multiculturalism differentially impact intergroup relations. *Journal of Personality and Social Psychology, 106*, 772–789.

5 Intergroup Discrimination: Ingroup Love or Outgroup Hate?

Marilynn B. Brewer

Intergroup discrimination can be defined broadly as differential treatment of individuals based on social category membership. In many contexts, discrimination takes the form of ingroup bias, whereby members of one's own social categories are evaluated more positively or responded to more favorably than members of other social categories (outgroups). In much of the social psychological literature, discrimination is viewed as the behavioral component of prejudice.

In light of this conflation of prejudice and discrimination, it is interesting that ingroup bias is often referred to as ingroup *favoritism* (Tajfel, Billig, Bundy, & Flament, 1971), whereas prejudice is most often defined as outgroup *hostility* (see Dixon, Levine, Reicher, & Durrheim, 2012; Greenwald & Pettigrew, 2014). This chapter reviews theory and empirical research on the relationship between ingroup bias and outgroup hostility and argues that it is important to distinguish between these two loci of discrimination and to recognize that much intergroup discrimination takes the form of ingroup favoritism in the absence of outgroup antagonism.

Ingroup Bias and Ethnocentrism

Ethnocentrism was described by Sumner as a universal characteristic of human social groups whereby

> a differentiation arises between ourselves, the we-group, or in-group, and everybody else, or the others-group, out-groups. The insiders in a we-group are in a relation of peace, order, law, government, and industry, to each other ... Ethnocentrism is the technical name for this view of things in which one's own group is the center of everything, and all others are scaled and rated with reference to it ... Each group nourishes its own pride and vanity, boasts itself superior, exalts its own divinities, and looks with contempt on outsiders. (Sumner, 1906, pp. 12–13)

Over the past 50 years of empirical research on intergroup relations, this propensity to privilege ingroupers over outgroupers has been well established, confirming the power of *we-they* distinctions to produce differential evaluation, liking, and treatment of other persons depending on whether or not they are identified as members of the ingroup category.

Hundreds of studies in the laboratory and the field have documented ingroup favoritism in myriad forms (e.g., Brewer, 1979; Brewer & Campbell, 1976; Diehl, 1990; Mullen, Brown, & Smith, 1992). In addition to the allocation bias demonstrated in the minimal group experiments by Tajfel and his colleagues (Tajfel et al., 1971), preferential treatment and evaluation of ingroups relative to outgroups appear in evaluations of group products (e.g., Gerard & Hoyt, 1974), application of rules of fairness (Ancok & Chertkoff, 1983; Ng, 1984; Platow, McClintock, & Liebrand, 1990), attributions for positive and negative behavior (Hewstone, 1990; Weber, 1994), and willingness to trust and cooperate (Brewer & Kramer, 1986; Miller, Downs, & Prentice, 1998; Wit & Kerr, 2002; Yuki, Maddux, Brewer, & Takemura, 2005).

There is considerable evidence that such ingroup favoritism is considered normative in its own right (Blanz, Mummendey, & Otten, 1997; Jetten, Spears, & Manstead, 1996; Platow, O'Connell, Shave, & Hanning, 1995; Platow & Van Knippenberg, 2001) and that it is activated automatically when a group identity is salient (Otten & Moskowitz, 2000; Otten & Wentura, 1999). Automatic evaluative positivity toward minimal ingroups has been demonstrated to emerge in children at age five or six (Dunham & Emory, 2014) and has been postulated to have a genetic base (Lewis & Bates, 2010).

Decomposing Ingroup Bias

Despite the label implying a focus on ingroup attitudes ("ingroup bias," "ingroup favoritism"), the concept of "ingroup bias" is most often defined in social psychology textbooks and research literature as "positivity toward the ingroup *and* negativity toward outgroups." This implies a reciprocal relationship. This assumption of reciprocity was made explicit in Sumner's (1906) original treatment of ethnocentrism:

> The relation of comradeship and peace in the we-group and that of hostility and war towards others-groups are correlative to each other ... Loyalty to the group, sacrifice for it, hatred and contempt for outsiders, brotherhood within, warlikeness without – all grow together, common products of the same situation. (p. 12)

Empirically, however, ingroup bias is assessed as the difference between evaluations, affect, or treatment of ingroup members compared to outgroup members. Put more formally, net discrimination is, by definition, the difference in outcomes received by the ingroup (I) relative to those of the outgroup (O). But like any other difference score, variations in (I – O) can be parsed (theoretically) into components due to variation in favorability toward the ingroup and variation due to negativity toward the outgroup. Conceptually, we can represent this distinction by imagining an absolute standard of fairness or indifference, against which both

I and O could be evaluated. Differences between I and O could then take three forms, reflecting three types (or loci) of discrimination.

The first form (Type 1) reflects discrimination *for* the ingroup, wherein treatment of the ingroup is biased in a positive direction and treatment of the outgroup is indifferent. This form of discrimination is driven by differences between the extent to which the ingroup and outgroup activate positive evaluative processes. In this case, there may or may not be any explicit outgroup; just the generalized "others" is sufficient. Prejudice and discrimination arise from differential favorability/positivity toward those who share this ingroup identity, but without any corresponding negativity or hostility toward non-ingroup members. Discrimination results from withholding from others favors and benefits that are extended only to the ingroup.

The second type (Type 2) represents discrimination *against* the outgroup, wherein the outgroup is treated unfairly while treatment of the ingroup is indifferent (unbiased) with respect to the fairness standard. In other words, discrimination is driven by greater activation of negative evaluative processes for the outgroup than for the ingroup. Discrimination that is derived from outgroup antagonism (hate) is actively directed at harming or disadvantaging members of the outgroup, whether or not any personal or ingroup benefit is gained in the process.

Finally, a third form (Type 3) of discrimination involves differential treatment in favor of the ingroup *and* against the outgroup. This is the form associated with (actual or perceived) zero-sum situations, in which gains for the outgroup are seen as being achieved at the expense of the ingroup. It is the type of prejudice aroused when the outgroup is perceived as a threat, not only to the self but also to the integrity, interests, or identity of the ingroup as a whole. Discrimination derived from this form of prejudice is motivated more by ingroup protection (rather than enhancement) as well as antagonism toward the outgroup. In this case, activation of positive and negative evaluations is reciprocal.

Although the end result is the same in terms of relative standing of the ingroup and the outgroup, knowing the locus of the differential has significant implications for documenting and changing discriminatory behavior. For example, with Type 2 discrimination, the assumption is that if negative orientation toward the outgroup can be reduced, discrimination would be eliminated. But if discrimination is of Type 1, all of these efforts may be misplaced. Treating the outgroup more "fairly" does not necessarily eliminate positive biases that favor the ingroup. As Greenwald and Pettigrew put it, "unequal treatment can be produced as readily ... by helping members of an advantaged group as by harming members of a disadvantaged group" (2014, p. 670). Further, a great deal of social psychological research now suggests that it is Type 1 (ingroup favoring) discrimination that underlies much differential treatment of ingroup and outgroup members.

The Primacy of Ingroup Positivity

> Although we could not perceive our own ingroups excepting as they contrast to outgroups, still the ingroups are psychologically primary ... Hostility toward

outgroups helps strengthen our sense of belonging, but it is not required ...
The familiar is *preferred*. What is alien is regarded as somehow inferior, less
"good," but there is not necessarily hostility against it ... Thus, while a certain
amount of predilection is inevitable in all ingroup memberships, the reciprocal
attitude toward outgroups may range widely.

(Allport, 1954, p. 42; italics in original)

Allport's (1954) chapter on "Ingroup Formation" (from which this quotation is
taken) is one of the less-cited sections of his classic book *The Nature of Prejudice*,
but it warrants closer attention as a precursor to later research on ingroup bias and
intergroup discrimination. In this chapter, Allport postulated that ingroups are
"psychologically primary," in the sense that familiarity, attachment, and preference
for one's ingroups come prior to development of attitudes toward specific
outgroups.

Despite the widespread belief that ingroup positivity and outgroup derogation
are reciprocally related, empirical research demonstrates little consistent relation between the two. Indeed, results from both laboratory experiments and field
studies indicate that variations in ingroup positivity and social identification do
not systematically correlate with degree of bias or negativity toward outgroups
(Brewer, 1979, 1999; Hinkle & Brown, 1990; Struch & Schwartz, 1989). For
example, in a study of the reciprocal attitudes among 30 ethnic groups in
East Africa, Brewer and Campbell (1976) found that almost all of the groups
exhibited systematic differential positive evaluation of the ingroup over all
outgroups on dimensions such as trustworthiness, obedience, friendliness, and
honesty. However, the correlation between degree of positive ingroup regard and
social distance toward outgroups was essentially zero across the 30 groups.
The lack of correlation between intra-ethnic loyalty and interethnic hostility
was corroborated by analyses of coded data from an anthropological database of
186 societies (Cashdan, 2001).

The most direct experimental evidence for ingroup positivity as distinct from
outgroup negativity comes from a series of experiments by Gaertner and Dovidio,
who used various measures of cognitive processing to assess the locus of racial
prejudice in White college students (Gaertner & Dovidio, 1986; Gaertner &
McLaughlin, 1983). These methods were designed to measure independently
both negative and positive feelings about Blacks relative to Whites. One experiment, for instance, used a word association task to assess the relative speed of
recognition of associations between racial terms ("Black" and "White") and
various positive and negative words (e.g., smart, clean, or lazy, stupid).
Consistently in these and other reaction time experiments, the researchers have
found that the response to negative words is not affected by the pairing with
"Black" vs. "White," but responses to positive adjectives are significantly speeded
up when preceded by the word "White" compared to the response time following
"Black." Further, additional research indicates that Whites who consider
themselves low in prejudice make a conscious effort to suppress negative affective
reactions to Black stimuli, but show no suppression of differential positive affect

toward White stimuli. Apparently this more subtle ingroup positivity is not consciously recognized as a form of prejudice (see also Meertens & Pettigrew, 1997; Pettigrew & Meertens, 1995).

Experiments with the minimal intergroup situation also provide additional evidence that ingroup favoritism is prior to, and not necessarily associated with, outgroup negativity or hostility. Brewer (1979) reported that most minimal group studies that assessed ratings of the ingroup and outgroup separately found that categorization into groups leads to enhanced ingroup ratings in the absence of decreased outgroup ratings. Further, the positive ingroup biases exhibited in the allocation of positive resources in the minimal intergroup situation (Tajfel et al., 1971) are essentially eliminated when allocation decisions involve the distribution of negative outcomes or costs (e.g., Mummendey et al., 1992; Mummendey & Otten, 1998). These studies suggest that individuals are willing to differentially benefit the ingroup compared to outgroups but are reluctant to harm outgroups more directly.

Ingroup bias has been demonstrated in studies with young children, but the methodology employed in many of these studies does not discriminate whether bias is due to ingroup positivity or outgroup derogation. When methods that separate these two are used, evidence indicates that ingroup positivity is prior to and separate from development of outgroup derogation (Bennett, Lyons, Sani, & Barrett, 1998; Buttelmann & Bohm, 2014; Yee & Brown, 1992). In a review of developmental studies on intergroup attitudes, Cameron, Alvarez, Ruble, and Fuligni (2001) similarly concluded that young children tend to display a positivity bias toward their ingroup, without evidence of negativity toward outgroups.

Further evidence of the distinction between ingroup positivity and outgroup negativity was obtained in a set of experiments by Shah, Brazy, and Higgins (2004), who found that regulatory focus was differentially related to ingroup and outgroup attitudes. Specifically, individuals high in promotion focus (i.e., oriented toward achieving desired outcomes) demonstrated ingroup bias in positive emotions and approach behaviors. By contrast, individuals high in prevention focus (i.e., oriented toward avoiding undesirable outcomes) demonstrated negativity toward outgroups in emotions and avoidance behaviors.

Field research on intergroup relations provides further evidence for the independence of ingroup positivity and outgroup attitudes. In a study of Israeli attitudes toward ultraorthodox Jews, for instance, Struch and Schwartz (1989) found that positivity toward the ingroup was uncorrelated with negativity toward the outgroup, and that ingroup positivity and intergroup aggression had different predictors. Duckitt and Mphuthing (1998) conceptually replicated these findings in South Africa.

A large multicultural study factor analyzed measures of ethnocentrism and found good fit for a six-factor model with two second-order factors, distinguishing between intragroup (ingroup positivity, self-centeredness) and intergroup (outgroup hostility) manifestations of ethnocentrism (Bizumic, Duckitt,

Popadic, Dru, & Krauss, 2009). These findings resonate with research in political psychology that has established a conceptual distinction between patriotism (ingroup pride) and nationalism (ingroup superiority and intergroup hostility) (e.g., Bar-Tal, 1993; Kosterman & Feshbach, 1989; Roccas, Sagiv, Schwarz, Halvy, & Eidelson, 2008).

Overall then, experimental, developmental, and field research on ingroup bias and discrimination supports the contention that positivity toward ingroups and negativity toward outgroups are distinct forms of prejudice and have different antecedents and developmental trajectories. Research in both laboratory and field settings has come to acknowledge the important distinction between ingroup bias that reflects beneficence and positive sentiments toward the ingroup that are withheld from outgroups ("subtle" prejudice) and discrimination that reflects hostility, derogation, and intent to harm the outgroup ("blatant" prejudice) (Pettigrew & Meertens, 1995). This is not to say that ingroup-based discrimination is benign or inconsequential. Indeed (as is discussed later in this chapter), many forms of racism and sexism are probably attributable to discrimination based on ingroup preference rather than prejudice against outgroups (Brewer, 1996; Greenwald & Pettigrew, 2014). Nonetheless, the absence of positive regard and lack of trust for outgroups that is characteristic of most ingroup-outgroup differentiation can be conceptually and empirically distinguished from the presence of active hostility, distrust, and hate for outgroups that characterizes virulent prejudice.

Ingroup Bias: A Multilevel Phenomenon

The literature reviewed in the preceding section establishes that ingroup positivity and outgroup negativity are distinct concepts. The present section focuses more specifically on recent research that demonstrates the powerful effects of shared ingroup membership to cue cognitive, affective, and behavioral responses toward other persons. Social categorization of others as "us" (vs. "not us") influences responses across a range of levels of processing, from low-level attentional processes to high-level cognitive judgments and decision making.

Ingroup Influences on Perception and Attention

Face recognition bias and facial processing. A well-established finding in the social perception literature is the own-group face recognition bias – a significant difference in ability to correctly recognize previously seen faces of ingroup members compared to faces of outgroup members (see Young, Hugenberg, Bernstein, & Sacco, 2012, for review). Initially demonstrated with respect to recognition of racial/ethnic group members, one explanation of this memory bias is that perceivers have greater expertise in differentiating ingroup faces as a function of familiarity. Although this familiarity-expertise explanation has some support, it cannot account fully for the own-group recognition bias because the bias has been found even when familiarity is controlled for, and even when the ingroup-outgroup distinction is based on arbitrary categorization with no prior history of differential exposure to ingroup or outgroup category members (Bernstein, Young, & Hugenberg, 2007; Van Bavel & Cunningham, 2012; Van Bavel, Swencionis, O'Connor, & Cunningham, 2012). Further, own-race bias in face recognition can be eliminated when race is crosscut with another meaningful ingroup-outgroup categorization, such as shared university membership (Hehman, Mania, & Gaertner, 2010).

The finding that recognition bias occurs even for minimal groups suggests that the effect stems from differences in how faces are processed at the time of initial exposure. More specifically, it is hypothesized that cues to group membership attract more extensive processing of ingroup faces compared to faces that are not categorized as ingroup (Levin, 2000). This hypothesis is bolstered by findings that motivational factors influence the extent of own-group recognition bias (Pauker, Weisbuch, Ambady, Adams, & Sommers, 2009). Of particular interest is evidence that a perceiver's *need to belong* moderates the recognition bias. Specifically, individuals high in need to belong show a larger ingroup recognition bias effect; when need to belong is situationally activated (by a social exclusion experience), bias in recognition of own-team faces is enhanced (Van Bavel et al., 2012). Also consistent with the motivated attention hypothesis, an eye-tracking study by Kawakami and colleagues (Kawakami et al., 2014) demonstrated that participants attended more to the eyes of ingroup members than of outgroup members, that selective attention to eyes is affected by motivational factors, and that attention to eyes plays a role in the own-race recognition bias.

Neuroscience evidence. More direct evidence of differential processing of ingroup faces comes from social neuroscience research employing event-related brain potential (ERP) and brain-imaging methods. In ERP studies, increased amplitude in the N200 component of the brain waveform has been identified as an indicator that a stimulus is being processed as a face, with higher amplification associated with greater attention or depth of processing. An ERP study by Ito, Thompson, and Cacioppo (2004) revealed that the N200 component peaked higher in response to racial ingroup faces (compared to racial outgroups), and similar amplification differentials have been obtained for own-university faces (Hehman, Stanley, Gaertner, & Simons, 2011), and even for minimal ingroup categories (Ratner & Amodio, 2013). Since reduced N200 amplification is associated with later deficit in memory for previously shown faces (Ito et al., 2004), the ERP findings directly implicate motivated processing differences as an explanation for the own-group recognition memory bias.

In brain imaging research, fMRI activity in an area of the middle fusiform gyrus, known as the facial fusiform area (FFA), is also associated with processing of human faces and is correlated with memory performance. FFA activation has been found to be greater for ingroup race faces (Golby, Gabrieli, Chiao, & Eberhardt, 2001) and for own-team faces (Van Bavel, Packer, & Cunningham, 2011),

indicative of deeper processing and greater individuation of ingroup faces compared to faces not categorized as ingroup (Van Bavel, Packer, & Cunningham,
2008).

Van Bavel et al. (2011) specifically controlled for previous exposure by giving
participants an equal number of learning trials for ingroup team and outgroup team
members' faces before the fMRI phase of the study. In the scanner, participants
were presented with the previously learned ingroup and outgroup faces as well as
new, uncategorized faces not seen before. FFA activation was greater for ingroup
faces than for outgroup faces, which were found to be no different than the novel
control faces in terms of FFA activation. Although the implications of differential
activation of regions of the brain are yet to be fully explored, both ERP and fMRI
studies converge in suggesting that categorization of a person as ingroup or not
occurs very early in perceptual processing and influences subsequent attention and
extent of processing. Such differential processing appears to occur automatically
and outside of conscious awareness.

Ingroup Influences on Behavioral Orientations

One implication of the neurological evidence for ingroup bias is that ingroup
members are automatically responded to as more relevant or emotionally significant than non-ingroup members. Further behavioral research also indicates that
categorization of others as ingroupers elicits positive emotional responses such as
trust and empathy (Brewer, 1981; Sturmer, Snyder, Kropp, & Siem, 2006) and
associated approach behavioral orientations (Paladino & Castelli, 2008). These
spontaneous emotional states increase the propensity for engaging in prosocial
behavior, such as helping and cooperation.

Who deserves help? One line of research relevant to the assessment of intergroup discrimination is experiments on decisions about whether or not to help
another individual. Numerous field and lab experiments have demonstrated that
individuals are more likely to respond to a need for help from an ingroup member
than from outgroup members or individuals whose category membership is
unknown (Levine, Posser, Evans, & Reicher, 2005). Evidence that this differential
helping is motivated primarily by identification with the ingroup is provided by
results of experiments that examined the effects of physical pain on social identification and helping (Van Leeuwen, Ashton-James, & Hamaker, 2014). Compared
to a no-pain control condition, physical pain reduced helping of ingroup members
but had no effect on helping outgroupers, and the effect on ingroup helping was
mediated by reduction in group identification.

Differential responsiveness to ingroup or outgroup members is particularly
evident when the need for help is ambiguous or uncertain. For example, Gaertner
and Dovidio (1977) used the bystander intervention paradigm designed by Darley
and Latane (1968) to test effects of race on help giving as a function of how many
others were present during an apparent emergency. When the actual participant
believed she was alone with the victim (an experimenter confederate), there was no

difference in response to a Black or White confederate. Fully 88% of the subjects stood to help, and the speed of responding was equivalent for both ingroup and outgroup victims. However, when the subject believed that others were present – when responsibility to intervene was potentially diffused – a significant race-of-victim effect emerged. In this condition, 75% decided to help when the confederate was believed to be White, but only 37% stood to intervene when the confederate was believed to be Black. Further, subjects showed more physiological arousal (as indexed by change in heart rate) in response to the emergency involving a White victim, but less physiological response when the victim was Black and responsibility was diffused.

The results of this and other experiments by Gaertner and Dovidio demonstrate that Whites do not deliberately avoid helping Blacks – when help is clearly called for, Whites and Blacks are treated equivalently. However, when there is ambiguity in the situation – when the decision whether or not giving help is warranted is a judgment call – then the threshold for help giving is lower for ingroup members than for members of the outgroup.

Trust and cooperation. Uncertainty is also a factor when individuals must make a decision whether to trust another person or group of people when there is some risk that the other might exploit that trust to one's disadvantage. In experiments using various decision tasks in which participants must decide whether to put their trust in an anonymous stranger to benefit the trustor at some cost to themselves, knowing that the stranger shares a common group membership with the participant proves to be a strong determinant of the likelihood of choosing to trust (Foddy, Platow, & Yamagishi, 2009; Platow, Foddy, Yamagishi, Lim, & Chow, 2012; Yuki et al., 2005). Willingness to trust an ingroup member is greater than willingness to trust an outgrouper or a stranger whose category membership is unknown. What is critical for group-based trust is the *mutual* knowledge that oneself and the other share a common ingroup membership (Balliet, Wu, & De Dreu, 2014; Platow et al., 2012).

That knowledge of shared ingroup membership is sufficient to engender trust and cooperative behavior under conditions of risk and uncertainty has also been supported by results of numerous experiments in the social dilemmas literature. Social dilemmas are collective decision situations in which if individuals act in their own self-interest, the collective as a whole will be worse off. Cooperating in a social dilemma situation entails sacrificing immediate personal gain for the sake of collective welfare. Making salient a shared social identity has been demonstrated to increase cooperative behavior between strangers in dyadic exchanges such as prisoner's dilemma games (e.g., Dion, 1973; Miller et al., 1998) or investment games (e.g., Buchan, Croson, & Dawes, 2002; Tanis & Postmes, 2005), and in collective decision-making situations such as resource dilemmas (e.g., Balliet et al., 2014; Brewer & Kramer, 1986; Brewer & Schneider, 1990; Kramer & Goldman, 1995; Wit & Wilke, 1992) and public goods dilemmas (e.g., De Cremer & Van Vugt, 1999; Wit & Kerr, 2002).

Importantly, the effect of perceiving the collective as a shared ingroup is independent of the presence of outgroups (Gaertner, Iuzzini, Witt, & Orina, 2006). Even in intergroup situations, choosing to benefit the ingroup is not the same as choosing to disadvantage an outgroup. Halevy, Bornstein, and Sagiv (2008) designed an interesting modification of a two-group public goods dilemma in which individuals could decide whether to (a) keep all their monetary tokens to themselves, (b) donate to the ingroup (with benefits shared by all ingroup members), or (c) donate to the ingroup *and* inflict losses on the other group (at no cost to the ingroup). Overall, 63% of tokens were contributed to (b), but only 5% were contributed to choice (c). Clearly, almost all participants chose cooperation on behalf of an ingroup but avoided disadvantaging an outgroup.

In further experiments using a similar two-group public goods decision task, de Dreu (2010) found that individuals with a chronic prosocial value orientation report greater ingroup trust and make higher ingroup benefiting contributions compared to pro-self-oriented individuals, but they showed no difference in outgroup distrust or contributions to disadvantage the outgroup. Using the effects of administration of oxytocin to increase prosocial orientation, deDreu and colleagues (2010) found parallel effects on motivation to benefit ingroups but not to harm outgroups. Thirty minutes prior to the decision game, participants received an intranasal administration of oxytocin or a placebo. Across two experiments, compared to the placebo group, participants who had received a dose of oxytocin significantly increased their willingness to contribute resources to the ingroup (choice [b], but oxytocin had no effect on willingness to choose [c], which was relatively low in both conditions). Relatedly, oxytocin was also associated with increased reported trust of the ingroup but had no effect on outgroup trust, again demonstrating that enhanced positivity toward an ingroup does not entail negativity toward outgroups.

Ingroup Influences on Judgments of Justice and Fairness

Engaging social identities also influences perceptions of social justice and justice motives in general. Social psychological research provides evidence that group identification bounds the scope of people's concerns for distributive justice. For instance, Correia, Vala, and Aguiar (2007) found that learning about the suffering of an innocent victim in one's ingroup threatened participants' sense of a just world more than when the victim was a member of an outgroup. Wenzel (2000) found that only East and West Germans who strongly identified with the inclusive category "German" were likely to apply norms of equality to entitlements of all citizens (East and West) of the country. Similarly, Tyler and his colleagues have found that individuals who are highly identified with a group or organization are more likely to be concerned with procedural fairness (Huo, Smith, Tyler, & Lind, 1996; Tyler, Degoey, & Smith, 1996). And people appear to be *less* concerned about distributive or procedural justice for actions related to outgroups in intergroup contexts than they are in interpersonal contexts (Bruins, Platow, & Ng, 1995; Platow et al., 1995).

What is judged to be fair? Ingroup favoritism is particularly pernicious when it alters one's perception about the rules of fairness that should be applied when decisions about merit are being made. This is well illustrated by the results of an experiment by Ng (1984) using the minimal intergroup paradigm. After participants had been divided into arbitrary social categories, they had the opportunity to observe teams made up of one ingroup and one outgroup member performing a cooperative task. Across conditions, participants observed either a situation in which the ingroup member outperformed the outgroup member in contribution to the total product or one in which the outgroup member produced the greater contribution.

After viewing the performance outcomes, participants were asked to make a decision regarding the allocation of the team reward to the two team members. When the outgroup member outproduced the ingroup member, subjects were more likely to choose an equal allocation principle, a rule justified by the fact that it was a cooperative team task. However, when the ingroup member was the higher performer, they were likely to choose an equity principle whereby the ingrouper received more of the allocation, justified on the basis of relative merit. Further, the extent of over-allocation to the high producer was significantly greater when that contributor was an ingroup member than when the same performance differential was observed between two persons who were not categorized by an ingroup-outgroup distinction. Apparently, the threshold for application of the equity-merit principle is affected by whose merit is being judged.

Who deserves the benefit of the doubt? An effect known as the "intergroup attributional bias" refers to the finding that positive behaviors by fellow ingroup members are more likely to be attributed to dispositional causes (i.e., "he's a nice person") than are those same behaviors when performed by an outgroup member, and that negative actions by an ingroup member are more likely to be attributed to external reasons (e.g., "he was aggravated by the heat") (Hewstone, 1990). This attributional bias has been well established with respect to judgments made about ingroup behavior, but whether there is a parallel negative attributional bias for outgroups (i.e., negative behaviors over-attributed to dispositional causes) is less clear.

In one experimental test of the intergroup attribution bias with arbitrarily designated ingroup-outgroup categories, Weber (1994) found that attributions depended on strength of identification with the ingroup category. In this experiment, participants were assigned to arbitrary categories under conditions that promoted low or high identification with the ingroup. They then viewed a videotape in which an ingroup or an outgroup member either helped or refused to help an individual from the other group, and later they were asked to make ratings of the causes of that behavior as either internal (dispositional) or external (situationally caused).

When identification was low, attributions were unaffected by the group membership of the actor, and attributions for both positive and negative behaviors were approximately the same. Under high-identification conditions, however, there was a significant interaction between type of behavior and actor group membership in determining attributional ratings. In the case of helpful behavior, ratings were slightly more dispositional for the ingroup actor compared to the outgroup actor. But the major effect of group identity occurred on attributions for refusal to help. When exhibited by an ingroup member, this ambiguous negative behavior was seen as more clearly caused by the situation (i.e., as justified by the circumstances) than the same behavior from an outgroup member. Attributions for the outgrouper did not differ in the high- or low-identification conditions.

This finding is one illustration of a general "leniency bias" in favor of ingroups. Individuals attribute less blame (and recommend less severe punishment) for ingroup transgressions than for those of outgroups (Halabi, Statman, & Dovidio, 2015). As in the case of deciding whether or not to give help, biases in favor of the ingroup with respect to justifying negative behaviors are most likely to appear when the situation is ambiguous. When possible external justifications are present, ingroup members are less likely to be held accountable, or blamed, for negative behaviors or for failures to do something positive. The rule appears to be, when judgments are uncertain, give an ingroup member the benefit of the doubt. Coldly objective judgment seems to be reserved for members of outgroups.

Finding ways to justify undesirable actions by ingroup members extends even to transgressions that violate principles of morality or justice. Moral judgments appear to be flexible when shared ingroup membership is involved. In an illustrative experiment by Valdesolo and DeSteno (2007), participants observed another individual make a decision that benefited the decider to the disadvantage of another person and then were asked to rate how fair the decider had been. Fairness ratings were significantly higher when the decider was a member of the participant's (minimal) ingroup category than when the decider was an outgrouper. But fairness ratings for an outgroup category member were not significantly different from those made when the decider was uncategorized, again indicating that the bias is one of ingroup leniency rather than outgroup harshness. Even reprehensible behaviors such as torture are judged to be more morally justified when the perpetrator is one's ingroup nation rather than an outgroup (Tarrant, Branscombe, Warner, & Weston, 2012).

Invisible Discrimination

The influence of shared ingroup identity as a factor in decisions regarding justice and morality makes it clear that ingroup favoritism is not benign and can have serious social consequences. As said earlier, many forms of institutional racism and sexism are probably attributable to discrimination based on ingroup preference rather than prejudice against outgroups (Brewer, 1996; Greenwald & Pettigrew, 2014).

Although Allport (1954) acknowledged the prevalence of what he called "love-prejudice," he also stated that one reason we hear so little about this form of prejudice is that prejudices of this sort "create no social problem" (p. 25). In thinking that ingroup favoritism is benign unless accompanied by outgroup hate, Allport was certainly wrong. When not all social groups are equal in terms of size, status, or resources, ingroup bias on the part of more powerful or advantaged groups will create and perpetuate social inequity.

What is particularly pernicious about this is that discrimination based on ingroup favoritism is more difficult to detect than discrimination based on antagonism toward the less advantaged outgroups (Krieger, 1998). Acts of overt rejection, aggression, or vilification are visible to recipients, and the issue for assessing discrimination is to determine whether such acts were person based or category based. But how does one detect the *absence* of favoritism, leniency, or preferential attention? People have difficulty noticing things that do *not* happen in comparison to things that do. Thus, for instance, in the domain of work discrimination, "being fired or subjected to other forms of employment discipline are far more salient than not being assigned a particular account, not being introduced to important people, or not receiving encouragement, training, or other forms of mentoring" (Krieger, 1998, p. 1319).

In a review of job hiring discrimination research, Greenwald and Pettigrew (2014) conclude that difference in treatment of majority vs. minority group members is most often found in the presence vs. absence of helpful actions, rather than differential negative behaviors. When discrimination is based on ingroup positivity, outgroup members may be treated with relative objectivity (rather than contempt), and bias is only evident by comparison to warmer or more sympathetic treatment of ingroupers – a comparison that is often not available for observation. Discriminatory outcomes are often a product of what Freshman (2000) calls "ignore-ance" rather than rejection.

Even when the cumulative effects of ingroup favorability can be documented in the form of differential outcomes for members of advantaged and disadvantaged groups, such outcomes may not be attributed to discrimination. In legal contexts, ingroup favoritism is recognized as violating antidiscrimination law, but enforcement or sanctioning for this type of discrimination is mixed at best (Freshman, 2000; Krieger, 1998; but see Greenwald & Pettigrew, 2014, footnote 10, for evidence of recent change in direction in federal court opinions on this issue). Legal scholars have even argued explicitly that ingroup favoritism is not as bad as outgroup prejudice (see Freshman, 2000, pp. 354–355). Social psychological research indicates that laypersons also view ingroup favoritism as normative (Bruins et al., 1995; Platow et al., 1995) and that they reveal implicit preference for an ingroup member who discriminated in favor of fellow ingroup members over one who behaved in a fair, egalitarian way (Castelli, Tomelleri, & Zogmaister, 2008).

Legal scholar Linda Hamilton Krieger has argued that existing law may make it difficult to prove ingroup favoritism because this form of bias does not fit perceivers' "discrimination schema"; that is, it does not fit preexisting ideas about what discrimination looks like (Krieger, 1998, p. 1309). This speculation was well confirmed by results of a set of vignette experiments on discrimination judgments conducted by Pierce (2006). In these studies, participants were asked to put themselves in the role of an attorney being asked to assess whether there is evidence of discrimination in promotion practices of a particular company. As a reference point, participants were provided with normative information on the average rate of promotion in the relevant industry (e.g., 50%). They were then shown 10-year promotion statistics for the target company that revealed a 15% discrepancy in the rate of promotions received by members of one group (e.g., male employees) compared to another group (e.g., female employees). After reviewing the information, participants were asked to rate to what degree there appeared to be discrimination in the company.

The vignettes read by participants varied in how the discrepancy information was framed. In the *disadvantage frame* condition, the more favored group received promotions at the normative rate, whereas the less favored group was *denied* promotion at rate above the normative level. In the *advantage frame* condition, the less favored group was promoted at the normative rate, but the more favored group received promotions at a rate above the norm. Even though the ultimate disparity was the same in both frames, Pierce hypothesized that judged discrimination would be higher in the disadvantage frame than the advantage frame condition because the former would be a better fit to respondents' prototype of discrimination, namely, discrimination *against* a less advantaged group (rather than discrimination in favor of a more advantaged group). Across four experiments with different target social categories (gender, race, and university), this hypothesis was strongly supported. Participants consistently rated the disparity framed in terms of disadvantage as showing a greater degree of discrimination than the same disparity framed in terms of advantage (which was also rated as less unfair). This asymmetry in judged discrimination held even when the less favored group was the participants' own ingroup university! The finding that group-based advantage was less likely to be recognized as discrimination proved to be quite robust.

Overcoming Ingroup Favoritism

The difficulty of detecting ingroup favoritism and our reluctance to acknowledge it as a form of discrimination make this type of prejudice particularly challenging to deal with in pursuit of a more egalitarian, diverse society. Recognizing the presence of ingroup bias and its potential discriminatory effects is certainly a needed step, but mere awareness that we are inclined to respond more favorably and sympathetically to ingroup members may not be sufficient to correct for the effects of such favoritism. Ability to control effects of nonconscious bias requires not only awareness but also motivation and ability to make conscious corrections (Wilson & Brekke, 1994). Overriding negative prejudice through motivated control processes has proved to be possible (Gonsalkorale, Sherman, Allen, Klauer, & Amodio, 2011; Monteith, Ashburn-Nardo, Voils, & Czopp, 2002; Plant & Devine, 2009), but how do we correct for differential activation of attention, trust, and sympathy in dealings with ingroup members and their relative absence in responding to outgroupers?

Rather than suppressing ingroup positivity, a more fruitful approach to combatting discriminatory effects of ingroup bias may lie in changing perceptions of the ingroup. Whereas overcoming negative prejudice requires changing attitudes toward outgroups, combatting ill effects of positive prejudice requires changes in one's understanding of who is "us" – creating ingroups that are more inclusive, with less salient boundaries between us and not-us. Thus, a focus on ingroup inclusiveness may be an important direction for future work on reduction of intergroup discrimination.

Many of the strategies for reducing prejudicial attitudes against outgroups that have been studied in the social psychological literature can also be directed toward changing construal of relevant ingroups. Intergroup contact, for example, not only reduces negative affect toward outgroups but may also reduce salience of ingroup-outgroup distinctions through a process that Pettigrew (1997) referred to as "deprovincialization" (see also, Brewer, 2008). Redefining ingroup boundaries through recategorization or cross-categorization is effective in creating more inclusive ingroups (see Brewer & Gaertner, 2001). And taking advantage of our capacity for multiple social identities has the potential of reducing ingroup-outgroup distinctions and creating shared identity at a broad level of inclusiveness (Brewer, 2008, 2010).

At the limit, creating conditions that elicit identification with the global community has the potential for extending ingroup-based trust and sympathy to all humanity (McFarland, Webb, & Brown, 2012). In a cross-national study of global cooperation, Buchan et al. (2011) found that participation in globalized social, economic, and cultural networks increased the extent to which individuals identify with "the world as a whole," which in turn was associated with increased contributions to global (as opposed to local) shared resources. Like other superordinate category identities, global identity does not necessarily require sacrificing more local, distinct social identities but recognizing that the self and others can be categorized in terms of multiple shared identities, including common humanity (Albarello & Rubini, 2012). The capacity to activate common identity at times of consequential decision making makes it possible to harness the potential of ingroup love in the service of collective welfare in the broadest possible terms.

References

Albarello, F., & Rubini, M. (2012). Reducing dehumanisation outcomes towards Blacks: The role of multiple categorisation and of human identity. *European Journal of Social Psychology, 42*, 875–882.

Allport, G. (1954). *The nature of prejudice*. Reading, MA: Addison-Wesley.

Ancok, D., & Chertkoff, J. M. (1983). Effects of group membership, relative performance, and self-interest on the division of outcomes. *Journal of Personality and Social Psychology, 45*, 1256–1262.

Balliet, D., Wu, J., & De Dreu, C. (2014). Ingroup favoritism in cooperation: A meta-analysis. *Psychological Bulletin, 140*, 1556–1581.

Bar-Tal, D. (1993). Patriotism as fundamental beliefs of group members. *Politics and the Individual, 3*, 45–62.

Bennett, M., Lyons, E., Sani, F., & Barrett, M. (1998). Children's subjective identification with the group and in-group favouritism. *Developmental Psychology, 34*, 902–909.

Bernstein, M., Young, S., & Hugenberg, K. (2007). The cross-category effect: Mere social categorization is sufficient to elicit an own-group bias in face recognition. *Psychological Science, 15*, 706–712.

Bizumic, B., Duckitt, J., Popadic, D., Dru, V., & Krauss, S. (2009). A cross-cultural investigation into a reconceptualization of ethnocentrism. *European Journal of Social Psychology, 39*, 871–899.

Blanz, M., Mummendey, A., & Otten, S. (1997). Normative evaluations and frequency expectations regarding positive and negative outcome allocations between groups. *European Journal of Social Psychology, 27*, 165–176.

Brewer, M. B. (1979). In-group bias in the minimal intergroup situation: A cognitive motivational analysis. *Psychological Bulletin, 86*, 307–324.

Brewer, M. B. (1981). Ethnocentrism and its role in interpersonal trust. In M. Brewer and B. Collins (Eds.), *Scientific inquiry and the social sciences* (pp. 345–360). San Francisco: Jossey-Bass.

Brewer, M. B. (1996). In-group favoritism: The subtle side of intergroup discrimination. In D. Messick & A. Tenbrunsel (Eds.), *Codes of conduct: Behavioral research into business ethics* (pp. 160–170). New York: Russell Sage Foundation.

Brewer, M. B. (1999). The psychology of prejudice: In-group love or out-group hate? *Journal of Social Issues, 55*, 429–444.

Brewer, M. B. (2008). Deprovincialization: Social identity complexity and outgroup acceptance. In U. Wagner, L. Tropp, G. Finchilescu, & C. Tredoux (Eds.), *Improving intergroup relations. Building on the legacy of Thomas F. Pettigrew* (pp. 160–176). Oxford: Blackwell.

Brewer, M. B. (2010). Social identity complexity and acceptance of diversity. In R. Crisp (Ed.), *The psychology of social and cultural diversity* (pp. 11–33). Oxford: Wiley-Blackwell.

Brewer, M. B., & Campbell, D. T. (1976). *Ethnocentrism and intergroup attitudes: East African evidence*. Beverly Hills, CA: Sage.

Brewer, M. B., & Gaertner, S. L. (2001). Toward reduction of prejudice: Intergroup contact and social categorization. In R. Brown & S. Gaertner (Eds.), *Blackwell handbook of social psychology: Intergroup processes* (pp. 451–472). Oxford: Blackwell.

Brewer, M. B., & Kramer, R. M. (1986). Choice behavior in social dilemmas: Effects of social identity, group size, and decision framing. *Journal of Personality and Social Psychology, 50*, 543–549.

Brewer, M. B., & Schneider, S. (1990). Social identity and social dilemmas: A double-edged sword. In D. Abrams & M. Hogg (Eds.), *Social identity theory: Constructive and critical advances* (pp. 22–41). New York: Springer-Verlag.

Bruins, J., Platow, M., & Ng, S. H. (1995). Distributive and procedural justice in interpersonal and intergroup situations. *Social Justice Research*, *8*, 103–121.

Buchan, N., Brewer, M., Grimalda, G., Wilson, R., Fatas, E., & Foddy, M. (2011). Global social identity and global cooperation. *Psychological Science*, *22*, 821–828.

Buchan, N., Croson, R., & Dawes, R. M. (2002). Swift neighbors and persistent strangers: A cross-cultural investigation of trust and reciprocity in social exchange. *American Journal of Sociology*, *108*, 161–206.

Buttelmann, D., & Bohm, R. (2014). The ontogeny of the motivation that underlies in-group bias. *Psychological Science*, *25*, 921–927.

Cameron, J., Alvarez, J., Ruble, D., & Fuligni, A. (2001). Children's lay theories about ingroup and outgroups: Reconceptualizing research on prejudice. *Personality and Social Psychology Review*, *5*, 118–128.

Cashdan, E. (2001). Ethnocentrism and xenophobia: A cross-cultural study. *Current Anthropology*, *42*, 760–765.

Castelli, L., Tomelleri, S., & Zogmaister, C. (2008). Implicit ingroup metafavoritism: Subtle preference for ingroup members displaying ingroup bias. *Personality and Social Psychology Bulletin*, *34*, 807–818.

Correia, I., Vala, J., & Aguiar, P. (2007). Victim's innocence, social categorization, and the threat to the belief in a just world. *Journal of Experimental Social Psychology*, *43*, 31–38.

Darley, J. M., & Latane, B. (1968). Bystander intervention in emergencies: Diffusion of responsibility. *Journal of Personality and Social Psychology*, *8*, 377–383.

De Cremer, D., & Van Vugt, M. (1999). Social identification effects in social dilemmas: A transformation of motives. *European Journal of Social Psychology*, *29*, 871–893.

de Dreu, C. (2010). Social value orientation moderates ingroup love but not outgroup hate in competitive intergroup conflict. *Group Process and Intergroup Relations*, *13*, 701–713.

deDreu, C., Greer, L. L., Handgraaf, M. J., Shalvi, S., Van Kleef, G. A., Baas, M. . . . Feith, S. W. (2010). The neuropeptide oxytocin regulates parochial altruism in intergroup conflict among humans. *Science*, *328*, 1408–1411.

Diehl, M. (1990). The minimal group paradigm: Theoretical explanations and empirical findings. In W. Stroebe & M. Hewstone (Eds.), *European review of social psychology* (Vol. 1, pp. 263–292). Chicester, UK: John Wiley & Sons.

Dion, K. L. (1973). Cohesiveness as a determinant of ingroup-outgroup bias. *Journal of Personality and Social Psychology*, *28*, 163–171.

Dixon, J., Levine, M., Reicher, S., & Durrheim, K. (2012). Beyond prejudice: Are negative evaluations the problem and is getting us to like one another more the solution? *Behavioral and Brain Sciences*, *35*, 411–466.

Duckitt, J., & Mphuthing, T. (1998). Group identification and intergroup attitudes: A longitudinal analysis in South Africa. *Journal of Personality and Social Psychology*, *74*, 80–85.

Dunham, Y., & Emory, J. (2014). Of affect and ambiguity: The emergence of preference for arbitrary ingroups. *Journal of Social Issues*, *70*, 81–98.

Foddy, M., Platow, M., & Yamagishi, T. (2009). Group-based trust in strangers: The role of stereotypes and expectations. *Psychological Science*, *20*, 419–422.

Freshman, C. (2000). Whatever happened to anti-Semitism? How social science theories identify discrimination and promote coalitions between "different" minorities. *Cornell Law Review, 85*, 313–442.

Gaertner, L., Iuzzini, J., Witt, M., & Orina, M. (2006). Us without them: Evidence for an intragroup origin of positive in-group regard. *Journal of Personality and Social Psychology, 90*, 426–439.

Gaertner, S. L, & Dovidio, J. (1977). The subtlety of White racism, arousal, and helping behavior. *Journal of Personality and Social Psychology, 35*, 691–707.

Gaertner, S., & Dovidio, J. (1986). The aversive form of racism. In J. Dovidio & S. Gaertner (Eds.), *Prejudice, discrimination, and racism* (pp. 61–89). Orlando, FL: Academic Press.

Gaertner, S., & McLaughlin, J. (1983). Racial stereotypes: Associations and ascription of positive and negative characteristics. *Social Psychology Quarterly, 46*, 23–30.

Gerard, H. B., & Hoyt, M. (1974). Distinctiveness of social categorization and attitude toward in-group members. *Journal of Personality and Social Psychology, 29*, 836–842.

Golby, A., Gabrieli, J., Chiao, J., & Eberhardt, J. (2001). Differential responses in the fusiform region to same-race and other-race faces. *Nature Neuroscience, 4*, 845–850.

Gonsalkorale, K., Sherman, J. W., Allen, T. J., Klauer, K. C., & Amodio, D. M. (2011). Accounting for successful control of implicit racial bias: The roles of association activation, response monitoring, and overcoming bias. *Personality and Social Psychology Bulletin, 37*, 1534–1545.

Greenwald, A. G., & Pettigrew, T. F. (2014). With malice toward none and charity for some: Ingroup favoritism enables discrimination. *American Psychologist, 69*, 669–684.

Halabi, S., Statman, Y., & Dovidio, J. (2015). Attributions of responsibility and punishment for ingroup and outgroup members: The role of just world beliefs. *Group Processes and Intergroup Relations, 18*, 104–115.

Halevy, N., Bornstein, G., & Sagiv, L. (2008). "Ingroup love" and "outgroup hate" as motives for individual participation in intergroup conflict. *Psychological Science, 19*, 405–411.

Hehman, E., Mania, E., & Gaertner, S. (2010). Where the division lies: Common ingroup identity moderates the cross-race facial-recognition effect. *Journal of Experimental Social Psychology, 46*, 445–448.

Hehman, E., Stanley, E., Gaertner, S., & Simons, R. (2011). Multiple group membership influences face recognition: Recall and neurological evidence. *Journal of Experimental Social Psychology, 47*, 1262–1268.

Hewstone, M. (1990). The "ultimate attribution error"? A review of the literature on intergroup causal attribution. *European Journal of Social Psychology, 20*, 311–335.

Hinkle, S., & Brown, R. (1990). Intergroup comparisons and social identity: Some links and lacunae. In D. Abrams & M. Hogg (Eds.), *Social identity theory: Construction and critical advances* (pp. 48–70). London: Harvester Wheatsheaf.

Huo, Y., Smith, H., Tyler, T., & Lind, E. (1996). Superordinate identification, subgroup identification, and justice concerns. *Psychological Science, 7*, 40–45.

Ito, T., Thompson, E., & Cacioppo, J. (2004). Tracking the timecourse of social perception: The effects of racial cues on event-related brain potentials. *Personality and Social Psychology Bulletin, 30*, 1267–1280.

Jetten, J., Spears, R., & Manstead, A. R. (1996). Intergroup norms and intergroup discrimination: Distinctive self-categorization and social identity effects. *Journal of Personality and Social Psychology, 71,* 1222–1233.

Kawakami, K., Williams, A., Sidhu, D., Choma, B. L., Rodriguez-Bailón, R., Cañadas, E. . . . Hugenberg, K. (2014). An eye for the I: Preferential attention to the eyes of ingroup members. *Journal of Personality and Social Psychology, 107,* 1–20.

Kosterman, R., & Feshbach, S. (1989). Toward a measure of patriotic and nationalistic attitudes. *Political Psychology, 10,* 257–274.

Kramer, R. M., & Goldman, L. (1995). Helping the group or helping yourself? Social motives and group identity in resource dilemmas. In D. A. Schroeder (Ed.), *Social dilemmas: Perspectives on individuals and groups* (pp. 49–67). New York: Praeger.

Krieger, L. H. (1998). Civil rights Perestroika: Intergroup relations after affirmative action. *California Law Review, 86,* 1251–1333.

Levin, D. T. (2000). Race as a visual feature: Using visual search and perceptual discrimination tasks to understand face categories and the cross-race recognition deficit. *Journal of Experimental Psychology: General, 129,* 559–574.

Levine, M., Prosser, A., Evans, D., & Reicher, S. (2005). Identity and emergency intervention: How social group membership and inclusiveness of group boundaries shape helping behaviour. *Personality and Social Psychology Bulletin, 31,* 443–453.

Lewis, G. J., & Bates, T. C. (2010). Genetic evidence for multiple biological mechanisms underlying in-group favoritism. *Psychological Science, 21,* 1623–1628.

McFarland, S., Webb, M., & Brown, D. (2012). All humanity is my ingroup: A measure and studies of identification with all humanity. *Journal of Personality and Social Psychology, 103,* 830–853.

Meertens, R., & Pettigrew, T. F. (1997). Is subtle prejudice really prejudice? *Public Opinion Quarterly, 61,* 54–71.

Miller, D. T., Downs, J. S., & Prentice, D. A. (1998). Minimal conditions for the creation of a unit relationship: The social bond between birthdaymates. *European Journal of Social Psychology, 28,* 475–481.

Monteith, M., Ashburn-Nardo, L., Voils, C., & Czopp, A. (2002). Putting the brakes on prejudice: On the development and operation of cues for control. *Journal of Personality and Social Psychology, 83,* 1029–1050.

Mullen, B., Brown, R., & Smith, C. (1992). In-group bias as a function of salience, relevance, and status: An integration. *European Journal of Social Psychology, 22,* 103–122.

Mummendey, A., & Otten, S. (1998). Positive-negative asymmetry in social discrimination. *European Review of Social Psychology, 9,* 107–143.

Mummendey, A., Simon, B., Dietze, C., Grunert, M., Haeger, G., Kessler, S., . . . Schaferhoff, S. (1992). Categorization is not enough: Intergroup discrimination in negative outcome allocations. *Journal of Experimental Social Psychology, 28,* 125–144.

Ng, S. H. (1984). Equity and social categorization effects on intergroup allocation of rewards. *British Journal of Social Psychology, 23,* 165–172.

Otten, S., & Moskowitz, G. (2000). Evidence for implicit evaluative in-group bias: Affect-biased spontaneous trait inference in a minimal group paradigm. *Journal of Experimental Social Psychology, 36,* 77–89.

Otten, S., & Wentura, D. (1999). About the impact of automaticity in the minimal group paradigm: Evidence from affective priming tasks. *European Journal of Social Psychology, 29*, 1049–1071.

Paladino, M.-P., & Castelli, L. (2008). On the immediate consequences of intergroup categorization: Activation of approach and avoidance motor behavior toward ingroup and outgroup members. *Personality and Social Psychology Bulletin, 34*, 755–766.

Pauker, K., Weisbuch, M., Ambady, N., Adams, R., & Sommers, S. (2009). Not so Black and White: Memory for ambiguous group members. *Journal of Personality and Social Psychology, 96*, 795–810.

Pettigrew, T. F. (1997). Generalized intergroup contact effects on prejudice. *Personality and Social Psychology Bulletin, 23*, 172–185.

Pettigrew, T. F., & Meertens, R. (1995). Subtle and blatant prejudice in Western Europe. *European Journal of Social Psychology, 25*, 57–75.

Pierce, K. P. (2006). *Asymmetrical perceptions of group-based employment disparities: Differences in subjective evaluations of advantage-based and disadvantage-based discrimination.* Unpublished dissertation. Ohio State University.

Platow, M., Foddy, M., Yamagishi, T., Lim, L., & Chow, A. (2012). Two experimental tests of trust in in-group strangers: The moderating role of common knowledge of group membership. *European Journal of Social Psychology, 42*, 30–35.

Platow, M., McClintock, C., & Liebrand, W. (1990). Predicting intergroup fairness and in-group bias in the minimal group paradigm. *European Journal of Social Psychology, 20*, 221–239.

Platow, M., O'Connell, A., Shave, R., & Hanning, P. (1995). Social evaluations of fair and unfair allocations in interpersonal and intergroup situations. *British Journal of Social Psychology, 34*, 363–381.

Platow, M., & Van Knippenberg, D. (2001). A social identity analysis of leadership endorsement: The effects of leader ingroup prototypicality and distributive intergroup fairness. *Personality and Social Psychology Bulletin, 27*, 1508–1519.

Plant, E. A., & Devine, P. (2009). The active control of prejudice: Unpacking the intentions guiding control efforts. *Journal of Personality and Social Psychology, 96*, 640–652.

Ratner, K., & Amodio, D. (2013). Seeing "us vs them": Minimal group effects on neural encoding of faces. *Journal of Experimental Social Psychology, 49*, 298–301.

Roccas, S., Sagiv, L., Schwarz, S., Halvy, N., & Eidelson, R. (2008). Toward a unifying model of identification with groups: Integrating theoretical perspectives. *Personality and Social Psychology Review, 12*, 280–306.

Shaw, J., Brazy, P., & Higgins, E. T. (2004). Promoting us or preventing them: Regulatory focus and manifestations of intergroup bias. *Personality and Social Psychology Bulletin, 30*, 433–446.

Struch, N., & Schwartz, S. (1989). Intergroup aggression: Its predictors and distinctness from in-group bias. *Journal of Personality and Social Psychology, 56*, 364–373.

Sturmer, S., Snyder, M., Kropp, A., & Siem, B. (2006). Empathy-motivated helping: The moderating role of group membership. *Personality and Social Psychology Bulletin, 32*, 943–956.

Sumner, W. G. (1906). *Folkways.* New York: Ginn.

Tajfel, H., Billig, M., Bundy, R., & Flament, C. (1971). Social categorization and intergroup behaviour. *European Journal of Social Psychology, 1*, 149–178.

Tanis, M., & Postmes, T. (2005). A social identity approach to trust: Interpersonal perception, group membership and trusting behaviour. *European Journal of Social Psychology, 35*, 413–424.

Tarrant, M., Branscombe, N., Warner, R., & Weston, D. (2012). Social identity and perceptions of torture: It's moral when we do it. *Journal of Experimental Social Psychology, 48*, 513–518.

Tyler, T., Degoey, P., & Smith, H. (1996). Understanding why the justice of group procedures matters. *Journal of Personality and Social Psychology, 70*, 913–930.

Valdesolo, P., & DeSteno, D. (2007). Moral hypocrisy: Social groups and the flexibility of virtue. *Psychological Science, 18*, 689–690.

Van Bavel, J., & Cunningham, W. (2012). A social identity approach to person memory: Group membership, collective identification, and social role shape attention and memory. *Personality and Social Psychology Bulletin, 38*, 1566–1578.

Van Bavel, J., Packer, D., & Cunningham, W. (2008). The neural substrates of ingroup bias: A functional magnetic resonance imaging investigation. *Psychological Science, 19*, 1131–1139.

Van Bavel, J., Packer, D., & Cunningham, W. (2011). Modulation of the fusiform face area following minimal exposure to motivationally relevant faces: Evidence of ingroup enhancement (not outgroup disregard). *Journal of Cognitive Neuroscience, 23*, 3343–3354.

Van Bavel, J., Swencionis, J., O'Connor, R., & Cunningham, W. (2012). Motivated social memory: Belonging needs moderate the own-group bias in face recognition. *Journal of Experimental Social Psychology, 48*, 707–713.

Van Leeuwen, E., Ashton-James, C., & Hamaker, R. (2014). Pain reduces discrimination in helping. *European Journal of Social Psychology, 44*, 602–611.

Weber, J. G. (1994). The nature of ethnocentric attribution bias: In-group protection or enhancement? *Journal of Experimental Social Psychology, 30*, 482–504.

Wenzel, M. (2000). Justice and identity: The significance of inclusion for perceptions of entitlement and the justice motive. *Personality and Social Psychology Bulletin, 26*, 157–176.

Wilson, T., & Brekke, N. (1994). Mental contamination and mental correction: Unwanted influences on judgments and evaluations. *Psychological Bulletin, 116*, 117–142.

Wit, A. P., & Kerr, N. L. (2002). "Me versus just us versus us all": Categorization and cooperation in nested social dilemmas. *Journal of Personality and Social Psychology, 83*, 616–637.

Wit, A. P., & Wilke, H. (1992). The effect of social categorization on cooperation in three types of social dilemmas. *Journal of Economic Psychology, 13*, 135–151.

Yee, M., & Brown, R. (1992). Self-evaluations and intergroup attitudes in children aged three to nine. *Child Development, 63*, 619–629.

Young, S., Hugenberg, K., Bernstein, M., & Sacco, D. (2012). Perception and motivation in face recognition: A critical review of theories of the cross-race effect. *Personality and Social Psychology Review, 16*, 116–142.

Yuki, M., Maddux, W., Brewer, M. B., & Takemura, K. (2005). Cross-cultural differences in relationship- and group-based trust. *Personality and Social Psychology Bulletin, 31*, 48–62.

6 Intergroup Emotions Theory: Prejudice and Differentiated Emotional Reactions toward Outgroups

Angela T. Maitner, Eliot R. Smith, and Diane M. Mackie

> As a man I pity you, but as an official I must show you no mercy; as a politician I regard him as an ally, but as a moralist I loathe him.
>
> William James (1890/1983, p. 43)

Emotions, William James tells us, are embedded in identity. How I feel about you depends not only on who you are, but also on who *I* am. In an influential chapter merging theories of social identity and emotion felt toward other groups, Smith (1993) similarly argued that considering intergroup attitudes as a combination of appraisals, emotions, and action tendencies based in the perceiver's social identity could better explain shifting intergroup evaluations across contexts and could better predict differentiated intergroup outcomes than traditional models of prejudice.

In the more than 20 years since the publication of that work, intergroup emotions theory (Mackie, Devos, & Smith, 2000; Mackie, Maitner, & Smith, 2009; Mackie & Smith, 2002, 2015; Smith & Mackie, 2006, 2008; Smith, Seger, & Mackie, 2007) has grown and developed into a comprehensive theory of intergroup relations that provides a complementary perspective to traditional attitude models of prejudice. In this chapter, we rearticulate the central tenets of the theory and then focus on how social categorization and group identification – who *I* am – interact with context to influence individuals' appraisals, emotions, and behavioral intentions. We then focus on how three discrete emotional reactions elicit different and specific negative intergroup responses, before focusing on implications of intergroup emotions theory for improving intergroup relations. We finish with a discussion of current directions.

Intergroup Emotions Theory

Intergroup emotions theory (IET) suggests that when a particular social identity is activated, individuals will interpret events in terms of their implications for that ingroup, rather than for the individual personally. The more individuals identify with their currently activated social identity, the more extremely they will appraise group-relevant events. Group-based appraisals then elicit specific emotions and action tendencies. Because they are rooted in concerns for the group, we refer to such emotions as group based (see Niedenthal & Brauer, 2012). Intergroup relations are dynamic and ongoing, and thus individuals are expected to continuously reappraise changing situations, and their emotions to wax and wane, or amplify and change, along with changes in the intergroup context.

Research has been supportive of the proposed model (see Mackie & Smith, 2015, for a review). In a comprehensive demonstration of antecedent conditions and behavioral consequences of intergroup emotions, Gordijn, Yzerbyt, Wigboldus, and Dumont (2006) randomly assigned Colorado resident students at the University of Colorado to one of two conditions: to think of themselves as students or as Colorado residents. Participants were then asked to read a proposal to raise tuition for out-of-state students. Participants who were categorized as students appraised the proposal as *less* fair to the extent that they identified with being a student, as students were impacted negatively by the proposal (though these individuals themselves were not). Participants who were categorized as Colorado residents, on the other hand, appraised the proposal as *more* fair to the extent that they identified with their state, as the state would benefit from the tuition revenue (though these individuals themselves would not). The less fair participants appraised the proposal to be, the more anger they felt, and the stronger their desire to take action against the proposal. Thus, this study found that the way participants appraised the proposal was rooted in whether the outcome was beneficial or problematic for the activated identity, with appraisals amplified by group identification. Group-level appraisals influenced group-level emotions, which motivated support for intergroup action.

Antecedents of Group-Based Emotion

IET provides an important framework for predicting whether and how individuals will feel animosity toward other groups. According to the intergroup emotions model, the interplay of social categorization and social identification dictates whether and to what extent individuals will experience emotions toward other groups, and resultant appraisal processes explain what emotion individuals will feel. We consider each of these antecedents in turn.

Social categorization. In addition to being unique individuals, people can simultaneously be categorized as members of various groups ranging from committees, teams, and families, to national, ethnic, or religious groups. External circumstances or internal processes may lead an individual to self-categorize with a particular group at a particular time, with self-categorization shifting in response to anything from hearing one's national anthem, to noticing one's minority status, or thinking about one's personal beliefs.

Self-categorization theory (Turner, Hogg, Oakes, Reicher, & Wetherell, 1987) contends that when individuals are categorized as members of a group, they become depersonalized representatives of that group, taking on the goals and characteristics of a prototypical group member. We have shown that when people are categorized as members of a group, they consider information that is relevant to the group (but not necessarily to themselves) to take on personal relevance, indicating that their frame for perceiving the world is meaningfully changing (Maitner, Mackie, Claypool, & Crisp, 2010).

When individuals consider information to be relevant to them (as individuals or as group members), that information takes on emotional significance. A large body of work, of course, shows that when individuals are simply categorized into groups, they exhibit ingroup favoritism and, under the right circumstances, outgroup derogation (see Tajfel & Billig, 1974; Tajfel, Billig, Bundy, & Flament, 1971; Wenzel & Mummendey, 1996). Research on group-based emotion has more specifically shown that when individuals are categorized as members of a group, they experience emotion on behalf of those group memberships (Dumont, Yzerbyt, Wigboldus, & Gordijn, 2003; Gordijn, Wigboldus, & Yzerbyt, 2001; Gordijn et al., 2006; Mackie et al., 2000). In this work, participants learn about an event impacting a group with which they are or are not currently categorized. In general, participants experience more emotion when categorized as members of the affected group than when not so categorized.

Ray, Mackie, Rydell, and Smith (2008) showed that emotion directed toward specific outgroups waxes and wanes depending on salient levels of self-categorization. Participants tended to report more anger toward police when categorized as students, a group that has an antagonistic relationship with police, than when categorized as Americans, a group with a (historically) more positive relationship with police. In contrast, participants report relatively less anger toward Muslims when categorized as students (a group that generally values tolerance) than when categorized as Americans (a group that places a stronger value on security). Kuppens and Yzerbyt (2012) showed a similar effect, with female social science students reporting more anger, fear, and disgust toward Muslims when their identity as women had been made salient, relative to when their identity as social science students, young adults, or their personal identity had been made salient. They further showed that women's more negative emotional reactions were directed by different threat perceptions. Women felt more fear, for example, as a result of perceptions of threat to physical safety. They felt more anger as a result of increased perceptions of threats to safety and trust. In sum, the way participants both perceived and emotionally responded to a target outgroup was determined by social identity salience. Such work shows quite compellingly how animosity toward other groups is rooted in self-categorization.

Social identification. Individuals vary in the extent to which their identities are based in particular group memberships (Tajfel & Turner, 1986). So although all US citizens can be categorized as Americans, the extent to which that categorization impacts the individual varies. Tajfel (1981) defined social identity as "that part of an individual's self-concept which derives from his knowledge of membership in a social group (or groups) together with the value and emotional significance attached to that group membership" (p. 255). People who identify strongly with a particular group integrate group goals and motives prominently into their self-concept. High identifiers are then likely to make intergroup, rather than interpersonal, comparisons in ambiguous situations (Gurin, 1985), showing heightened attention to group, rather than individual, outcomes (Brewer & Gardner, 1996; Turner et al., 1987; see also Smith & Spears, 1996).

Research also shows that group identification impacts the extent to which individuals take group-level threats personally (e.g., McCoy & Major, 2003) and the extent to which individuals' behavior is affected by group-related threats (e.g., Schmader, 2002). Likewise, research suggests that identification moderates the extent to which individuals make appraisals and experience emotion on behalf of the group (e.g., Gordijn et al., 2006; McCoy & Major, 2003; Smith et al., 2007; Verkuyten, Drabbles, & van den Nieuwenhuijzen, 1999; Yzerbyt, Dumont, Wigboldus, & Gordijn, 2003). Similarly to Gordijn et al. (2006), Maitner (2007) showed that when individuals were categorized as Americans, those who identified more strongly felt more satisfied and less angry about a proposal that had positive consequences for Americans and negative consequences for students. At the same time, participants categorized as students who identified more strongly with that group felt more satisfied and less angry about a proposal that had positive consequences for students and negative consequences for Americans.

Identification also influences the extent to which individuals feel negative emotions toward outgroups. Mackie et al. (2000), for instance, showed that participants felt more anger toward a competitive outgroup, and reported a stronger desire to attack that outgroup the more they identified with their own group. Crisp, Heuston, Farr, and Turner (2007) showed that high identifiers felt angry but not sad when their team lost a match, whereas low identifiers felt sad but not angry. Research also shows that people feel more satisfied and less guilty when their groups aggress against other groups, to the extent that they identify with their own group (Doosje, Branscombe, Spears, & Manstead, 1998; Maitner, Mackie, & Smith, 2007). Thus identification plays an important role in dictating the *extent* to which individuals feel specific forms of animosity toward outgroup members, with high identifiers more likely to feel emotions such as anger toward the outgroup, and less likely to feel anger toward the ingroup or guilt on behalf of its actions.

Group-based appraisals. When individuals are categorized as members of a group, they tend to appraise and interpret the environment in line with group goals and outcomes, rather than individual goals and outcomes (e.g., Crocker, Voelkl, Testa, & Major, 1991; Dion & Earn, 1975; Gordijn et al., 2006; Hastorf & Cantril, 1954; Kuppens, Yzerbyt, Dandache, Fischer, and van der Schalk, 2013; Smith & Spears, 1996). Group-level appraisals assess the group's goals and resources in relation to the current social context. Thus, when an outgroup presents some sort of threat to the ingroup, individuals evaluate the threat against the ingroup's coping resources to determine their emotional reaction. Appraisals follow from shifting contexts and categorization, and they are then strengthened or biased by the importance of a social category to one's identity.

Specific patterns of group-based appraisals elicit specific patterns of group-based emotions. Perceiving a threatening group to be weak produces more outgroup-directed anger than perceiving the same group to be strong (Mackie et al., 2000) – when the outgroup is perceived as strong, it may instead elicit fear (Giner-Sorolla & Maitner, 2013). Perceiving harm to be unfair produces more anger than perceiving harm to be justified (Giner-Sorolla & Maitner, 2013; Gordijn et al., 2006; Halperin & Gross, 2011b; Livingstone, Spears, Manstead, & Bruder, 2009). Perceiving harm as ongoing produces more anger than perceiving that harm has been rectified (Maitner, Mackie, & Smith, 2006). Likewise, perceiving a group as competitive but weak or low in status elicits contempt, whereas perceiving a group as competitive and strong elicits envy (Cuddy, Fiske, & Glick, 2007). In other words, the specific assessment of group outcomes in a given context determines exactly *what form* emotional prejudices take on.

Group-Based Emotions and Behaviors

Thus far we have shown that categorization and identification, along with subsequent appraisal processes, elicit specific emotions directed toward specific outgroups. Although all group-based emotions are important to consider when investigating intergroup relations, three emotions – fear, anger, and contempt/disgust – have been studied extensively as important contributors to intergroup conflict.

Research has linked each of these emotions to specific target groups. Anger, for example, has been linked to Arabs (in a US sample; Dasgupta, DeSteno, Williams, & Hunsinger, 2009) and ethnic outgroups (at least for European men; Kuppens et al., 2012), whereas disgust has been linked to overweight people (Vartanian, Thomas, & Vanman, 2013) and gay men (Dasgupta et al., 2009; Inbar, Pizarro, & Bloom, 2012) in US samples. Correspondingly, Tapias, Glaser, Keltner, Vasquez, and Wickens (2007) showed that people who are dispositionally high in anger versus disgust are more prejudiced toward ethnic outgroups and gay men, respectively. In addition, incidental emotions strengthen prejudice and implicit bias toward groups that are the targets of corresponding emotions. That is, exposure to disgusting odors decreased warmth participants reported toward gay men but not other target outgroups (Inbar et al., 2012). Likewise, recalling a personal experience that had elicited disgust increased implicit bias against gay men, whereas incidental anger had no impact on bias toward that group. Recalling a personal experience that had elicited anger increased implicit bias against Arabs, but incidental disgust did not (Dasgupta et al., 2009). Thus, certain emotions may be linked to specific groups as a particular form of emotional prejudice; however, IET suggests that the way a particular group or its behavior is viewed in a particular context may also influence the emotions perceivers feel.

Outgroup-directed fear/anxiety. Anxiety results when individuals perceive that they have low or uncertain coping resources for confronting a motivationally relevant threat (Frijda, Kuipers, & ter Schure, 1989; Smith & Lazarus, 1993). Pioneering work on intergroup anxiety defined it as anxiety experienced when people anticipate or engage in intergroup contact (see Stephan, 2014). Building on this work, researchers have also investigated intergroup fear, which occurs in response to a broader range of group-relevant threats, including threats to group values, resources, or safety.

Studies have shown that intergroup fear uniquely motivates desires to move away from a fear-provoking, especially physically threatening, outgroup, seek information about the situation, take precautionary measures, negotiate with a threatening group, or help and support victims, but not to confront or attack the offending outgroup (Dijker, 1987; Dumont et al., 2003; Giner-Sorolla & Maitner, 2013; Kamans, Otten, & Gordijn, 2011; Lerner, Gonzalez, Small, & Fischhoff, 2003). For example, Americans' feelings of fear (but not anger) in response to the September 11, 2001, terrorist attacks predicted support for restrictions on civil liberties measured several months later (Skitka, Bauman, & Mullen, 2004), as well as support for deporting Arab Americans, Muslims, and first-generation immigrants (Skitka, Bauman, Aramovich, & Morgan, 2006). Fear clearly leads to a desire to avoid members of the offending group, although research shows that fear can lead to desires to confront or negotiate with an offending group when a conflict is intractable or ongoing (Giner-Sorolla & Maitner, 2013; Spanovik, Lickel, Denson, & Petrovic, 2010).

Research has also investigated collective angst, which is the specific concern for the future vitality of one's group (see Wohl & Branscombe, 2009). When ingroup members perceive threats to future longevity, they report desires to strengthen the ingroup (Wohl, Branscombe, & Reysen, 2010), show more forgiveness of past ingroup harm (Wohl & Branscombe, 2009), and show stronger opposition or exclusion of immigrants (Jetten & Wohl, 2012). However, collective angst is also associated with increased desires to compromise with enemy outgroups when doing so would help reduce particular threats (Halperin, Proat, & Wohl, 2013).

Outgroup-directed anger. Anger tends to result when individuals perceive that they have adequate coping resources for confronting a motivationally relevant threat (Frijda et al., 1989; Smith & Lazarus, 1993). Individuals experiencing anger report a strong desire to approach or confront the anger-inducing situation or outgroup (Frijda et al., 1989; Harmon-Jones, Sigelman, Bohlig, & Harmon-Jones, 2003). Indeed, outgroup-directed anger has proven to be a particularly potent predictor of the desire to take action against the offending group. Research has shown that outgroup-directed anger predicts ingroup bias, outgroup confrontation, active harm, radical responding, defense of ingroup positions to the outgroup, and support for ingroup members criticizing the outgroup (Kamans et al., 2011; Johnson & Glasford, 2014; Livingstone et al., 2009; Mackie et al., 2000; Smith et al., 2007; van Zomeren, Spears, Fischer, & Leach, 2004). Similarly, outgroup-directed anger predicts willingness to take action against harmful and unfair action perpetrated by one group against another (Gordijn et al., 2006; Maitner, 2007), with research investigating anger directed at terrorist actions or threats showing that anger leads to a desire to attack the offending group (Giner-Sorolla & Maitner, 2013), including support for aggressive military responses (Cheung-Blunden & Blunden, 2008; Sadler, Lineberger, Correll, & Park, 2005; Skitka et al., 2006). Outgroup-directed anger also increases the desire to support and affiliate with the ingroup (Smith et al., 2007), findings consistent with other research showing that this group emotion tends to increase ingroup identification (Kessler & Hollbach, 2005).

Compelling evidence for the role of anger leading to attack and confrontation behaviors also comes from research investigating the emotional consequences of engaging in behaviors incompatible with that action tendency (Maitner et al., 2006). We showed that when individuals felt anger about terrorist attacks shortly after September 11, anger was purged and satisfaction induced when the ingroup retaliated. We subsequently showed that outgroup-directed anger was purged only when the ingroup's response achieved a desired goal, which, in our work, meant securing an apology and retraction of insults. Satisfaction was induced any time the ingroup retaliated, whereas individuals got angry with ingroups that refused to confront anger-inducing outgroups. These findings provide evidence that group-based emotions functionally regulate intergroup behavior, shifting in response to changes in the intergroup context.

Outgroup-directed contempt/disgust. Contempt and disgust both result when people make downward comparisons within a domain that tends to be less personally important than a domain eliciting anger or fear (Frijda et al., 1989). Levin, Pratto, Matthews, Sidanius, and Kteily (2012) showed that intergroup disgust was predicted by value threats, with Lebanese participants reporting more disgust toward Americans the more they perceived Americans to hold values that were oppositional to those of Arabs. Both emotions motivate active and passive harm (Cuddy et al., 2007; Johnson & Glasford, 2014), and, in particular, elicit a tendency to avoid or exclude the provoking agent (Frijda et al., 1989; Mackie et al., 2000; Roseman, 1984; Roseman, Antoniou, & Jose, 1996).

Disgust is also uniquely related to a desire to forcefully expel or obliterate a stimulus (Plutchik, as cited in Roseman et al., 1996), and the combination of exclusion, active and passive harm, and desires to expel or obliterate may result in dehumanization of targets of these negative emotions. Harris and Fiske (2006), for instance, show that individuals processing information about members of groups toward which they feel contempt and disgust show no activation of the medial prefrontal cortex, a brain region implicated in social cognition. Individuals do, however, show activation in brain areas associated with disgust. In other words, it appears as though contempt and disgust result in a view of target groups as something less than human. Buckels and Trapnell (2013) likewise showed that incidental feelings of disgust promoted an implicit association between animals and arbitrary outgroups, again supporting the idea that feelings of disgust promote dehumanization of outgroups. Such strong emotion and accompanying dehumanization processes open the door to radical actions such as extermination and genocide (see Tausch et al., 2011). Intergroup hatred has been shown to elicit similarly extreme responses (Halperin, 2008).

Taken together, research has shown consistent support for the foundational claims of IET. First, findings show that intergroup emotions are embedded within identity and shift along with changes in self-categorization. Second, emotional tendencies may link to specific target groups, but emotions may also shift with shifting self-categorization or intergroup appraisals that reflect the dynamic social context. Finally, specific emotions predict differentiated action tendencies, allowing for a more differentiated prediction of intergroup hostilities.

Implications for Improving Intergroup Relations

Just as IET provides a framework for predicting and understanding how, when, and why individuals will feel dislike toward outgroups, it also provides a framework for understanding how, when, and why emotions felt toward other groups can be improved. Taking as a starting point the idea that emotional reactions are embedded in identity, the simplest implication is that shifting self-categorization also changes emotions (at least temporarily) toward outgroups. For example, when categorized as members of certain groups (e.g., Americans, women), Western individuals show comparatively high anti-Muslim reactions. However, Ray et al. (2008) and Kuppens and Yzerbyt (2012) showed that shifting self-categories from Americans to students or from women to individuals reduced negative emotions felt toward Muslims.

Prejudice reduction strategies that focus on recategorizing target outgroups may function in a similar way. The common ingroup identity model (see Dovidio & Gaertner, 1999; Gaertner, Mann, Murrell, & Dovidio, 1989), dual identity model (see Gaertner, Rust, Dovidio, Bachman, & Anastasio, 1994), and crossed categorization model (see Midgal, Hewstone, & Mullen, 1998) all take the same starting point. Specifically, they assume that if individuals can shift the dynamic between ingroup and target outgroup, reducing the threat perceived in the outgroup by bringing it into the ingroup or perceiving some overlapping shared category, animosity will be reduced. Elucidating the role of emotion in this process, Ray, Mackie, Smith, and Terman (2012) showed that cross-categorization reduced prejudice via discrete emotional responses. When individuals shared at least one group membership with a target person, they reported more positive emotions and intergroup attitudes.

Further, because IET adopts emotion models to understand intergroup relations, another implication is that emotion regulation strategies may be effective in helping improve intergroup relations. Halperin (2014) suggests that both indirect emotion regulation strategies, which attempt to change people's appraisals by providing specific and concrete messages to perceivers, and direct emotion regulation strategies, such as cognitive reappraisal, may be helpful in intractable conflicts. Indeed, research shows that if messages target specific appraisals, they can elicit emotions such as group-based guilt or decrease emotions such as intergroup anxiety, leading to positive intergroup consequences (see Čahajić-Clancy, Effron, Halperin, Liberman, & Ross, 2011; Halperin et al., 2012). Likewise, Halperin and Gross (2011a) showed that Israelis who engaged in cognitive reappraisal processes during the war in Gaza (in 2008) felt more hope and were more supportive of humanitarian aid for Palestinians. Perhaps more compellingly, Halperin, Porat, Tamir, and Gross (2013) trained Israeli participants in cognitive reappraisal one week before the Palestinian United Nations bid, then followed participants for five months after the event. They found that participants who received reappraisal training remained more supportive of conciliatory policies toward Palestinians five months later, because of reductions in intergroup anger. Thus it seems that reducing negative intergroup emotions has important implications for inter-group reconciliation.

A related area of work investigates intergroup apology and forgiveness, examining how apologies from one group toward another may reduce anger and desires for retaliation. Giner-Sorolla, Castano, Espinosa, and Brown (2007), for example, showed that apologies accompanied by offers of reparations (the director of a company offering to help clean up a chemical spill for which the company was responsible) were perceived as less insulting when targets expressed self-effacing shame ("he feels ashamed about the unfortunate incident," p. 521). In contrast, Wohl, Hornsey, and Bennett (2012) showed that when outgroups expressed secondary emotions such as shame and concern (relative to primary emotions such as anger and sadness) for wrong perpetrated against the ingroup, in this case, for the friendly fire death of soldiers, participants reported less forgiveness. Note, however, that such effects may be limited to individuals who dehumanize outgroup members. In a meta-analysis of intergroup forgiveness, van Tongeren, Burnette, O'Boyle, Worthington, and Forsyth (2014) showed that expressions of empathy and guilt increased intergroup forgiveness, whereas expressed negative emotions such as anger and fear reduced it. Thus emotional expressions in intergroup apologies clearly play an important role in eliciting intergroup forgiveness, likely through a dynamic reappraisal process, although results remain somewhat mixed in terms of which emotional expressions are most effective for eliciting reconciliation.

Exploring the role of *experienced* emotions in response to intergroup apology, Leonard, Mackie, and Smith (2011) showed that apologies reduced desires for retribution by reducing intergroup anger and increased forgiveness by increasing outgroup-directed respect. In the absence of intergroup apology, Tam et al. (2007) showed that felt anger reduced intergroup forgiveness. Taken together, this work suggests a critical role for intergroup emotions in the reconciliation process.

Current Trends and Future Directions

Recent work has begun pushing beyond the well-studied Western contexts to examine intergroup emotional processes in non-individualistic cultures, investigating implications for appraisals and behaviors. Other research has examined how group-based emotions are shared or communicated both within and between groups, and the implications of social sharing for intergroup attitudes.

Culture and intergroup emotion. Classic work from cultural psychology shows that in defining the self, people with independent self-construals tend to emphasize their unique characteristics, whereas people with interdependent self-construals tend to adopt goals and motives from important ingroups (see Markus & Kitayama, 1991). This simple definition suggests the untested hypothesis that people with interdependent senses of self would experience group-based emotions more strongly than people with independent senses of self.

More recent research has moved beyond this simple dichotomy. Leung and Cohen (2011), for example, suggest that cultures differ in the way individuals assess their self-worth. In dignity cultures such as the United States, self-worth is considered inalienable and therefore individuals are relatively impervious to personal feedback – positive or negative – from others. In honor and face cultures, on the other hand, self-worth is at least partially socially conferred. People in face cultures such as Japan earn their social worth by living up to the standards of their social roles, whereas people in honor cultures such as Turkey gain social worth from both internal and external sources. Because people from honor cultures have to both claim and defend their worth, they are often highly reactive to insults to their social image (see Rodriguez Mosquera, Manstead, & Fischer, 2002).

We argue that the nature of self-worth can influence how people perceive, interpret, and emotionally respond to events that have implications for individuals' social identities, with people aiming to defend and protect the social self most strongly when their identity is associated with honor norms. Recently, we have shown that within honor cultures, honor norms are conferred to some social identities (i.e., Arab) but not all (i.e., student; Maitner, Mackie, Pauketat, & Smith, 2015). Arab students read insults to either their Arab or student identity and reported emotional responses and behavioral intentions. When their honor-oriented (Arab) identity was insulted, participants reported more anger and shame than when their non-honor-oriented identity was insulted, or compared to members of a dignity culture (British students) who received the same insult. When their non-honor-oriented student identity was insulted, Arab participants reported no more anger or shame than members of a dignity culture (American students) who received the same insult. This work suggests that cultural processes may operate differently depending on which identity has been activated, with different cultural goals and values associated with different social identities. Activated cultural norms influenced the extremity to which participants reported self-protective emotional responses, but otherwise we found remarkable continuity of emotional processes across cultures.

Social sharing of intergroup emotions. Other contemporary work explores the relationship between emotional reactions experienced by group members and their group as a whole. Previous research has shown that negative ingroup actions may elicit negative emotions toward the ingroup (Maitner et al., 2007), and that negative emotions toward the ingroup decrease group identification whereas positive emotions felt toward the ingroup increase identification (Kessler & Hollbach, 2005). Because identification influences appraisals and emotions, this work suggests further that emotions are part of a dynamic feedback loop within the individual (Smith & Mackie, 2015). Other work has shown that when people learn about the emotional reactions of their fellow group members, their emotional reactions converge with those of their groups, especially when they are highly identified (Moons, Leonard, Mackie, & Smith, 2009; Smith et al., 2007). In this way, negative feelings toward outgroups may be shared (i.e., *inter*group emotions can converge at the *intra*group level).

More recent work has shown that a match between intergroup emotions felt by the individual and collective emotions felt by the group as a whole elicits self-categorization and support for collective action (Livingstone, Spears, Manstead, Bruder, & Shepherd, 2011). Consistently, but in the opposite direction, Goldenberg, Saguy, and Halperin (2014) showed that when individuals perceive that their group feels a different emotional reaction than they do themselves (such as when the group feels no anger in response to an offense), intergroup emotional reactions are exacerbated as individuals emotionally distance themselves from the collective (individuals report even more anger themselves). This is especially the case when the collective response is perceived as inappropriate. Rather than emotions always being shared within groups then, perceptions of the appropriateness of emotional reactions on the part of the group may increase or decrease individuals' own emotional reactions.

Communication of intergroup emotions. Other work has investigated the communication function of group-based emotion, both between ingroup and outgroup and to third-party observers. DeVos, van Zomeren, Gordijn, and Postmes (2013) showed that the communication of anger from victim to perpetrator group can elicit empathy, at least when maintaining a positive intergroup relationship is important to the perpetrating group. As a result, the communication of anger can actually reduce conflict between groups. Likewise, work investigating the experience of intergroup anger shows that feelings of intergroup anger can lead to an increased willingness for political compromise when anger is experienced in the absence of hatred in intractable conflicts (Halperin, Russell, Dweck, & Gross,

2011). Taken together this work suggests functionality in the experience and expression of anger for intergroup reconciliation.

Anger can also elicit empathy from third-party observers when communicated by powerful groups. Kamans, van Zomeren, Gordijn, and Postmes (2014) showed that third-party observers are more supportive of intergroup aggression when groups communicate emotional reactions that reflect their level of power within an intractable intergroup conflict. That is, observers were more likely to legitimize intergroup violence from lower-power groups that communicate that their aggressive behavior reflects both fear and their victim status. Observers also legitimized violence from higher-power groups that communicated anger, reflecting that they had been unfairly wronged, and therefore that their response was morally sound.

Taken together, new directions in the study of group-based emotion suggest first that intergroup emotions are elicited and function similarly across cultural contexts, although group goals and concerns may vary across cultures. Second, work on the social sharing of emotions shows that individuals may either adopt or distance themselves from collective emotions shared by the ingroup, depending on their levels of group identification and appraisals of the appropriateness of the group's emotional response. Finally, research suggests that the communication of even negative emotions between groups can have beneficial effects for intergroup relations, so long as it is experienced in the absence of hatred, or with some level of concern for improving intergroup relations.

Future developments. Future research may continue to explore these new directions, further developing the links among culture, social sharing, and communication of emotions both within and between groups. Significantly more research is needed to understand fully the extent to which emotional processes are universal or culturally specific. Certainly research on the interpersonal level suggests that emotions are differentially afforded in line with cultural values and practices (see Boiger, Güngör, Karasawa, & Mesquita, 2014). Emotions that are culturally afforded may be even more likely to be socially shared among group members, increasing identification and support for collective action in line with those afforded emotions, and reinforcing their frequent experience. Emotions that are not afforded within a particular cultural context, on the other hand, may be appraised as inappropriate and lead to social distancing.

Because different cultures experience and express emotions at different rates, the communication of emotions cross-culturally may be challenging. How, for example, is anger expressed by Turks, members of an honor culture for whom anger is afforded, perceived, and evaluated by face-oriented Japanese or dignity-oriented American targets? When such anger is expressed in response to an affront from either perceiver group, does it elicit sympathy and compromise as previous research suggests, or does it heighten conflict, as the situations and appraisals that are perceived as appropriate elicitors of anger responses vary across the three cultural groups? Such work could have important implications for global conflict and cooperation and may further elaborate challenges in intractable conflicts while pointing to potential solutions.

Conclusions

Over that past 20 years, an accumulating body of evidence suggests that knowing how individuals are categorized and what emotions they are feeling in particular contexts helps provide a more nuanced and differentiated set of predictions about intergroup relations, including understanding how negative evaluations change across contexts and are manifested in discriminatory behavior. Focusing on the role of emotion in intergroup relations has also led to the study of different forms of intervention and has motivated new bodies of work that investigate how processes are influenced by culture, as well as how the sharing and communication of emotion influences intra- and intergroup relations.

References

Boiger, M., Güngör, D., Karasawa, M., & Mesquita, B. (2014). Defending honour, keeping face: Interpersonal affordances of anger and shame in Turkey and Japan. *Cognition and Emotion*, *28*, 1255–1269. doi: 10.1080/02699931.2014.881324

Brewer, M. B., & Gardner, W. (1996). Who is this "we"? Levels of collective identity and self representations. *Journal of Personality and Social Psychology*, *71*, 83–93. doi: 10.1037/0022-3514.71.1.83

Buckels, E. E., & Trapnell, P. D. (2013). Disgust facilitates outgroup dehumanization. *Group Processes and Intergroup Relations*, *16*, 771–780. doi: 10.1177/1368430212471738

Čahajić-Clancy, S., Effron, D., Halperin, E., Liberman, V., & Ross, L. (2011). Affirmation, acknowledgment of ingroup responsibility, group-based guilt, and support for reparative measures. *Journal of Personality and Social Psychology*, *101*, 256–270. doi: 10.1037/a0023936

Cheung-Blunden, V., & Blunden, B. (2008). The emotional construal of war: Anger, fear and other negative emotions. *Peace and Conflict*, *14*, 123–149. doi:10.1080/10781910802017289

Crisp, R. J., Heuston, S., Farr, M. J., & Turner, R. (2007). Seeing red or feeling blue: Differentiated intergroup emotions and in-group identification in soccer fans. *Group Processes and Intergroup Relations*, *10*, 9–26. doi:10.1177/1368430207071337

Crocker, J., Voelkl, K., Testa, M., & Major, B. (1991). Social stigma: The affective consequences of attributional ambiguity. *Journal of Personality and Social Psychology*, *60*, 218–228. doi: 10.1037/0022-3514.60.2.218

Cuddy, A. J. C., Fiske, S. T., & Glick, P. (2007). The BIAS map: Behaviors from intergroup affect and stereotypes. *Journal of Personality and Social Psychology*, *92*, 631–648. doi: 10.1037/0022-3514.92.4.631

Dasgupta, N., DeSteno, D., Williams, L. A., & Hunsinger, M. (2009). Fanning the flames of prejudice: The influence of specific incidental emotions on implicit prejudice. *Emotion*, *9*, 585–591. doi: 10.1037/a0015961 deVos, B., van Zomeren, M., Gordijn, E. H., & Postmes, T. (2013). The communication of "pure" group-based anger reduces tendencies toward intergroup conflict because it increases out-group empathy. *Personality and Social Psychology Bulletin, 39,* 1043–1052. doi: 10.1177/0146167213489140

Dijker, A. J. (1987). Emotional reactions to ethnic minorities. *European Journal of Social Psychology, 17,* 305–325. doi: 10.1002/ejsp.2420170306

Dion, K. L., & Earn, B. M. (1975). The phenomenology of being a target of prejudice. *Journal of Personality and Social Psychology, 32,* 944–950. doi: 10.1037/0022-3514.32.5.944

Doosje, B., Branscombe, N. R., Spears, R., & Manstead, A. S. R. (1998). Guilty by association: When one's group has a negative history. *Journal of Personality and Social Psychology, 75,* 872–886. doi: 10.1037/0022-3514.75.4.872

Dovidio, J. F., & Gaertner, S. L. (1999). Reducing prejudice: Combating intergroup biases. *Current Directions in Psychological Science, 8,* 101–105. doi: 10.1111/1467-8721.00024

Dumont, M., Yzerbyt, V., Wigboldus, D., & Gordijn, E. H. (2003). Social categorization and fear reactions to the September 11th terrorist attacks. *Personality and Social Psychology Bulletin, 29,* 1509–1520. doi: 10.1177/0146167203256923

Frijda, N. H., Kuipers, P., & ter Schure, E. (1989). Relations among emotion, appraisal, and emotional action readiness. *Journal of Personality and Social Psychology, 57,* 212–228. doi: 10.1037/0022-3514.57.2.212

Gaertner, S. L., Mann, J., Murrell, A., & Dovidio, J. F. (1989). Reducing intergroup bias: The benefits of recategorization. *Journal of Personality and Social Psychology, 57,* 239–249. doi: 10.1037/0022-3514.57.2.239

Gaertner, S. L. Rust, M. C., Dovidio, J. R., Bachman, B. A., & Anastasio, P. A. (1994). The contact hypothesis: The role of a common ingroup identity on reducing intergroup bias. *Small Group Research, 25,* 224–249. doi: 10.1177/1046496494252005

Giner-Sorolla, R., Castano, E., Espinosa, P., & Brown, R. (2007). Shame expressions reduce the recipient's insult from outgroup reparations. *Journal of Experimental Social Psychology, 44,* 519–526. doi: 10.1016/j.jesp.2007.08.003

Giner-Sorolla, R., & Maitner, A. T. (2013) Angry at the unjust, scared of the powerful: Emotional responses to terrorist threat. *Personality and Social Psychology Bulletin, 39,* 1069–1082. doi: 10.1177/0146167213490803

Goldenberg, A., Saguy, T., & Halperin, E. (2014). How group-based emotions are shaped by collective emotions: Evidence for emotional transfer and emotional burden. *Journal of Personality and Social Psychology, 107,* 581–596. doi: 10.1037/a0037462

Gordijn, E. H., Wigboldus, D., & Yzerbyt, V. (2001). Emotional consequences of categorizing victims of negative outgroup behavior as ingroup or outgroup. *Group Processes and Intergroup Relations, 4,* 317–326. doi: 10.1177/1368430201004004002

Gordijn, E. H., Yzerbyt, V., Wigboldus, D., & Dumont, M. (2006). Emotional reactions to harmful intergroup behavior. *European Journal of Social Psychology, 36,* 15–30. doi: 10.1002/ejsp.296

Gurin, P. (1985). Women's gender consciousness. *Public Opinion Quarterly, 49,* 143–163. doi: 10.1086/268911

Halperin, E. (2008). Group-based hatred in intractable conflict in Israel. *The Journal of Conflict Resolution, 52*, 713–736. doi: 10.1177/0022002708314665

Halperin, E. (2014). Emotion, emotion regulation, and conflict resolution. *Emotion Review, 6*, 68–76. doi: 10.1177/1754073913491844

Halperin, E., Crisp, R. J., Husnu, S., Trzesniewski, K. H., Dweck, C., & Gross, J. J. (2012). Promoting intergroup contact by changing beliefs: Group malleability, intergroup anxiety, and contact motivation. *Emotion, 12*, 1192–1195. doi: 10.1037/a0028620

Halperin, E., & Gross, J. (2011a). Emotion regulation in violent conflict: Reappraisal, hope, and support for humanitarian aid to the opponent in wartime. *Cognition and Emotion, 25*, 1–9. doi: 10.1080/02699931.2010.536081

Halperin, E. & Gross, J. J. (2011b). Intergroup anger in intractable conflict: Long-term sentiments predict anger responses during the Gaza War. *Group Processes and Intergroup Relations, 14*, 477–488. doi: 10.1177/1368430210377459

Halperin, E., Porat, R., Tamir, M., & Gross, J. J. (2013). Can emotion regulation change political attitudes in intractable conflict? From the laboratory to the field. *Psychological Science, 24*, 106–111. doi: 10.1177/0956797612452572

Halperin, E., Proat, R., & Wohl, M. J. A. (2013). Extinction threat and reciprocal threat reduction: Collective angst predicts willingness to compromise in intractable intergroup conflicts. *Group Processes and Intergroup Relations, 16*, 797–813. doi: 10.1177/1368430213485994

Halperin, E., Russell, A. G., Dweck, C. S., & Gross, J. J. (2011). Anger, hatred, and the quest for peace: Anger can be constructive in the absence of hatred. *Journal of Conflict Resolution, 55*, 274–291. doi: 10.1177/0022002710383670

Harmon-Jones, E., Sigelman, J. D., Bohlig, A., & Harmon-Jones, C. (2003). Anger, coping, and frontal cortical activity: The effect of coping potential on anger-induced left frontal activity. *Cognition and Emotion, 17*, 1–24. doi: 10.1080/02699930302278

Harris, L. T., & Fiske, S. T. (2006). Dehumanizing the lowest of the low: Neuroimaging responses to extreme out-groups. *Psychological Science, 17*, 847–853. doi: 10.1111/j.1467-9280.2006.01793.x

Hastorf, A. H., & Cantril, H. (1954). They saw a game: a case study. *Journal of Abnormal & Social Psychology, 49*, 129–134. doi: 10.1037/h0057880

Inbar, Y., Pizarro, D. A., & Bloom, P. (2012). Disgusting smells cause decreased liking of gay men. *Emotion, 12*, 23–27. doi: 10.1037/a0023984

James, W. (1983). *Principles of psychology.* Cambridge, MA: Harvard University Press. Original work published 1890.

Jetten, J., & Wohl, M. J. A. (2012). The past as a determinant of the present: Historical continuity, collective angst, and opposition to immigration. *European Journal of Social Psychology, 42*, 442–450. doi: 10.1002/ejsp.865

Johnson, B. M., & Glasford, D. E. (2014). A threat-emotion profile approach to explaining active versus passive harm in intergroup relations. *Social Psychology, 45*, 399–407. doi: 10.1027/1864-9335/a000199

Kamans, E., Otten, S., & Gordijn, E. H. (2011). Power and threat in intergroup conflict. *Group Processes & Intergroup Relations, 14*, 293. doi:10.1177/1368430210372525

Kamans, E., van Zomeren, M., Gordijn, E. H., & Postmes, T. (2014). Communicating the right emotion makes violence seem less wrong: Power-congruent emotions lead outsiders to legitimize violence of powerless and powerful groups in intractable conflict. *Group Processes and Intergroup Relations, 17*, 286–305. doi: 10.1177/1368430213502562

Kessler, T., & Hollbach, S. (2005). Group-based emotion as determinants of ingroup identification. *Journal of Experimental Social Psychology, 41*, 677–685. doi: 10.1016/j.jesp.2005.01.001

Kuppens, T., & Yzerbyt, V. Y. (2012). Group-based emotions: The impact of social identity on appraisals, emotions, and behaviors. *Basic and Applied Social Psychology, 34*, 20–33. doi: 10.1080/01973533.2011.637474

Kuppens, T., Yzerbyt, V. Y., Dandache, S., Fischer, A. H., & van der Schalk, J. (2013). Social identity salience shapes group-based emotions through group-based appraisals. *Cognition and Emotion 27*, 1359–1377. doi: 10.1080/02699931.2013.785387

Kuppens, T., Pollet, T. V., Teixeira, C. P., Demoulin, S., Roberts, S. C., & Little, A. C. (2012). Emotions in context: Anger causes ethnic bias but not gender bias in men but not women. *European Journal of Social Psychology, 42*, 432–441. doi: 10.1002/ejsp.1848

Leonard, D. J., Mackie, D. M., & Smith, E. R. (2011). Emotional responses to intergroup apology mediate intergroup forgiveness and retribution. *Journal of Experimental Social Psychology, 47*, 1198–1206. doi:10.1016/j.jesp.2011.05.002

Lerner, J. S., Gonzalez, R. M., Small, D. A., & Fischhoff, B. (2003). Effects of fear and anger on perceived risks of terrorism: A national field experiment. *Psychological Science, 14*, 144–150. doi: 10.1111/1467-9280.01433

Leung, A. K.-Y., & Cohen, D. (2011). Within- and between-culture variation: Individual differences and the cultural logics of honor, face, and dignity cultures. *Journal of Personality and Social Psychology, 100*, 507–526. doi: 10.1037/a0022151

Levin, S., Pratto, F., Matthews, M., Sidanius, J., & Kteily, N. (2012). A dual process approach to understanding prejudice toward Americans in Lebanon: An extension to intergroup threat perceptions and emotions. *Group Processes and Intergroup Relations, 16*, 139–158. doi: 10.1177/1368430212443866

Livingstone, A. G., Spears, R., Manstead, A. S. R., & Bruder, M. (2009). Illegitimacy and identity threat in (inter)action: Predicting intergroup orientations among minority group members. *British Journal of Social Psychology, 48*, 755–775. doi: 10.1348/014466608X398591

Livingstone, A. G., Spears, R., Manstead, A. S. R., Bruder, M., & Shepherd, L. (2011). We feel, therefore we are: Emotion as a basis for self-categorization and social action. *Emotion, 11*, 754–767. doi: 10.1037/a0023223

Mackie, D. M., Devos, T., & Smith, E. R. (2000). Intergroup emotions: Explaining offensive action tendencies in an intergroup context. *Journal of Personality and Social Psychology, 79*, 602–616. doi: 10.1037/0022-3514.79.4.602

Mackie, D. M., Maitner, A. T., & Smith, E. R. (2009). Intergroup emotion theory. In T. D. Nelson (Ed.), *Handbook of prejudice, stereotyping, and discrimination* (pp. 285–307). New York: Psychology Press.

Mackie, D. M., & Smith, E. R. (2002). Intergroup emotions and the social self: Prejudice reconceptualized as differentiated reactions to outgroups. In J. P. Forgas &

K. D. Williams (Eds.), *The social self: Cognitive, interpersonal, and intergroup perspectives* (pp. 309–326). Philadelphia: Psychology Press.

Mackie, D. M., & Smith, E. R. (2015). Intergroup emotions. In M. Mikulincer & P. R. Shaver (Editors-in-chief), *APA handbook of personality and social psychology: Vol. 2. Group Processes*. Washington, DC: American Psychological Association.

Maitner, A. T. (2007). *Perceiving the world through group-colored glasses: Effects of self-categorization and group identification on attention and information processing*. Unpublished doctoral dissertation, University of California, Santa Barbara.

Maitner, A., Mackie, D. M., Claypool, H. M., & Crisp, R. J. (2010). Identity salience moderates processing of group-relevant information. *Journal of Experimental Social Psychology, 46*, 441–444. doi:10.1016/j.jesp.2009.11.010

Maitner, A. T., Mackie, D. M., Pauketat, J. V. T., & Smith, E. R. (2015). *The impact of culture and identity on emotional reactions to insults*. Unpublished manuscript.

Maitner, A. T., Mackie, D. M., & Smith, E. R. (2006). Evidence for the regulatory function of intergroup emotion: Implementing and impeding intergroup behavioral intentions. *Journal of Experimental Social Psychology, 42*, 720–728. doi:10.1016/j.jesp.2005.08.001

Maitner, A. T., Mackie, D. M., & Smith, E. R. (2007). Antecedents and consequences of satisfaction and guilt following in-group aggression. *Group Processes and Intergroup Relations, 10*, 223–237. doi:10.1177/1368430207075154

Markus, H. R., & Kitayama, S. (1991) Culture and the self: Implications for cognition, emotion, and motivation. *Psychological Review, 98*, 224–253. doi: 10.1037/0033-295X.98.2.224

McCoy, S. K., & Major, B. (2003). Group identification moderates emotional responses to perceived prejudice. *Personality and Social Psychology Bulletin, 29*, 1005–1017. doi: 10.1177/0146167203253466

Migdal, M. J., Hewstone, M., & Mullen, B. (1998). The effects of crossed categorization on intergroup evaluations: A meta-analysis. *British Journal of Social Psychology, 37*, 303–324. doi: 10.1111/j.2044-8309.1998.tb01174.x

Moons, W. G., Leonard, D. J., Mackie, D. M., & Smith, E. R. (2009). I feel our pain: Antecedents and consequences of emotional self-stereotyping. *Journal of Experimental Social Psychology, 45*, 760–769. doi:10.1016/j.jesp.2009.04.016

Niedenthal, P. M., & Brauer, M. (2012). Social functionality of human emotion. *Annual Review of Psychology, 63*, 259–285. doi: 10.1146/annurev.psych.121208.131605

Ray, D. G., Mackie, D. M., Rydell, R. J., & Smith, E. R. (2008). Changing categorization of self can change emotions about out-groups. *Journal of Experimental Social Psychology, 44*, 1210–1213. doi:10.1016/j.jesp.2008.03.014

Ray, D. G., Mackie, D. M., Smith, E. R., & Terman, A. W. (2012). Discrete emotions elucidate the effects of cross-categorization on prejudice. *Journal of Experimental Social Psychology, 48*, 55–69. doi: 10.1016/j.jesp.2011.07.011

Rodriguez Mosquera, P. M., Manstead, A. S. R., & Fischer, A. H. (2002). The role of honour concerns in emotional reactions to offences. *Cognition & Emotion, 16*, 143–163. doi: 10.1080/02699930143000167

Roseman, I. J. (1984). Cognitive determinants of emotion: A structural theory. *Review of Personality and Social Psychology, 5*, 11–36.

Roseman, I. J., Antoniou, A. A., & Jose, P. E. (1996). Appraisal determinants of emotions: Constructing a more accurate and comprehensive theory. *Cognition & Emotion, 10*, 241–277. doi: 10.1080/026999396380240

Sadler, M. S., Lineberger, M., Correll, J., & Park, B. (2005). Emotions, attributions, and policy endorsement in response to the September 11th terrorist attacks. *Basic and Applied Social Psychology, 27*, 249–258. doi:10.1207/s15324834basp2703_6

Schmader, T. (2002). Gender identification moderates stereotype threat effects on women's math performance. *Journal of Experimental Social Psychology, 38*, 194–201. doi: 10.1006/jesp.2001.1500

Skitka, L. J., Bauman, C. W., Aramovich, N. P., & Morgan, G. C. (2006). Confrontational and preventative policy responses to terrorism: Anger wants a fight and fear wants "them" to go away. *Basic and Applied Social Psychology, 28*, 375–384. doi:10.1207/s15324834basp2804_11

Skitka, L. J., Bauman, C. W., & Mullen, E. (2004). Political tolerance and coming to psychological closure following the September 11, 2001 terrorist attacks: An integrative approach. *Personality and Social Psychology Bulletin, 30*, 743–756. doi: 10.1177/0146167204263968

Smith, C. A., & Lazarus, R. S. (1993). Appraisal components, core relational themes, and the emotions. *Cognition and Emotion, 7*, 233–269. doi: 10.1080/02699939308409189

Smith, E. R. (1993). Social identity and social emotions: Toward new conceptualizations of prejudice. In D. M. Mackie & D. L. Hamilton (Eds.), *Affect, cognition, and stereotyping: Interactive processes in group perception* (pp. 297–315). San Diego: Academic Press.

Smith, E. R., & Mackie, D. M. (2006). It's about time: Intergroup emotions as time-dependent phenomena. In D. Capozza & R. Brown (Eds.), *Social identities: Motivational, emotional, and cultural influences*. New York: Psychology Press.

Smith, E. R., & Mackie, D. M. (2008). Intergroup emotions. In M. Lewis, J. Haviland-Jones, & L. Feldman Barrett (Eds.), *Handbook of emotions* (3rd ed., pp. 428–439). New York: Guilford Press.

Smith, E. R., & Mackie, D. M. (2015). Dynamics of group-based emotions: Insights from Intergroup Emotion Theory. *Emotion Review, 7*, 349–354. doi: 10.1177/1754073915590614

Smith, E. R., Seger, C. R., & Mackie, D. M. (2007). Can emotions be truly group-level? Evidence regarding four conceptual criteria. *Journal of Personality and Social Psychology, 93*, 431–446. doi: 10.1037/0022-3514.93.3.431

Smith, H. J., & Spears, R. (1996). Ability and outcome evaluations as a function of personal and collective (dis)advantage: A group escape from individual bias. *Personality and Social Psychology Bulletin, 22*, 690–704. doi: 10.1177/0146167296227004

Spanovic, M., Lickel, B., Denson, T. F., & Petrovic, N. (2010). Fear and anger as predictors of motivation for intergroup aggression: Evidence from Serbia and Republika Srpska. *Group Processes & Intergroup Relations, 13*, 725–739. doi:10.1177/1368430210374483

Stephan, W. G. (2014). Intergroup anxiety: Theory, research, and practice. *Personality and Social Psychology Review, 18*, 239–255. doi: 10.1177/1088868314530518

Tajfel, H. (1981). *Human groups and social categories*. Cambridge, UK: Cambridge University Press.

Tajfel, H., & Billig, M. (1974) Familiarity and categorization in intergroup behavior. *Journal of Experimental Social Psychology*, *10*, 159–170. doi: 10.1016/0022-1031(74)90064-X

Tajfel, H., Billig, M. G., Bundy, R. P., & Flament, C. (1971). Social categorization and intergroup behaviour. *European Journal of Social Psychology*, *1*, 149–178.

Tajfel, H., & Turner, J. C. (1986). The social identity theory of intergroup behavior. In W. Austin & S. Worchel (Eds.), *The social psychology of intergroup relations* (pp. 7–24). Chicago: Nelson Hall.

Tam, T., Hewstone, M., Cairns, E., Tausch, N., Maio, G., & Kenworthy, J. (2007). The impact of intergroup emotions on forgiveness in Northern Ireland. *Group Processes and Intergroup Relations*, *10*, 119–136. doi:10.1177/1368430207071345

Tapias, M. P., Glaser, J., Keltner, D., Vasquez, K., & Wickens, T. (2007). Emotion and prejudice: Specific emotions toward outgroups. *Group Processes and Intergroup Relations*, *10*, 27–39. doi: 10.1177/1368430207071338

Tausch, N., Becker, J. C., Spears, R., Christ, O., Saab, R., Singh, P., & Siddiqui, R. N. (2011). Explaining radical group behavior: Developing emotion and efficacy routes to normative and nonnormative collective action. *Journal of Personality and Social Psychology*, *101*, 129–148. doi:10.1037/a0022728

Turner, J. C., Hogg, M. A., Oakes, P. J., Reicher, S. D., & Wetherell, M. S. (1987). *Rediscovering the social group: A self-categorization theory*. Oxford, UK: Blackwell.

Van Tongeren, D. R., Burnette, J. L., O'Boyle, E., Worthington, E. L., Jr., & Forsyth, D. R. (2014). A meta-analysis of intergroup forgiveness. *The Journal of Positive Psychology*, *9*, 81–95. doi: 10.1080/17439760.2013.844268

van Zomeren, M., Spears, R., Fischer, A. H., & Leach, C. W. (2004). Put your money where your mouth is! Explaining collective action tendencies through group-based anger and group efficacy. *Journal of Personality and Social Psychology*, *87*, 649–664. doi: 10.1037/0022-3514.87.5.649

Vartanian, L. R., Thomas, M. A., & Vanman, E. J. (2013). Disgust, contempt, and anger and the stereotypes of obese people. *Eat Weight Discord*, *18*, 377–382. doi: 10.1007/s40519-013-0067-2

Verkuyten, M., Drabbles, M., & van den Nieuwenhuijzen, K. (1999). Self-categorization and emotional reactions to ethnic minorities. *European Journal of Social Psychology*, *29*, 605–619.

Wenzel, M., & Mummendey, A. (1996). Positive-negative asymmetry of social discrimination: A normative analysis of differential evaluations of in-group and out-group on positive and negative attributes. *British Journal of Social Psychology*, *35*, 493–507. doi: 10.1111/j.2044-8309.1996.tb01110.x

Wohl, M. J. A., & Branscombe, N. R. (2009). Group threat, collective angst, and ingroup forgiveness for the war in Iraq. *Political Psychology*, *30*, 193–217. doi: 10.1111/j.1467-9221.2008.00688.x

Wohl, M. J. A., Branscombe, N. R., & Reysen, S. (2010) Perceiving your group's future to be in jeopardy: Extinction threat induces collective angst and the desire to strengthen the ingroup. *Personality and Social Psychology Bulletin*, *36*, 898–910. doi: 10.1177/0146167210372505

Wohl, M. J. A., Hornsey, M. J., & Bennett, S. H. (2012). Why group apologies succeed and fail: Intergroup forgiveness and the role of primary and secondary emotions. *Journal of Personality and Social Psychology, 102*, 306–322. doi:10.1037/a0024838

Yzerbyt, V., Dumont, M., Wigboldus, D., & Gordijn, E. (2003). I feel for us: The impact of categorization and identification on emotions and action tendencies. *British Journal of Social Psychology, 42*, 533–549. doi: 10.1348/014466603322595266

7 Intergroup Threats

Walter G. Stephan and Cookie White Stephan

Intergroup Threats

We believe that intergroup threats play a significant role in causing the problems that plague intergroup relations. In this chapter, we lay out the reasoning and research on which this claim is based. We begin by addressing the causes of intergroup threats (see Figure 7.1). We argue that some types of people are more prone than others to perceive intergroup threats. Negative attitudes and related cognitions also play a role in causing intergroup threats. Likewise, prior intergroup relations and intergroup contact contribute to the perception of intergroup threats. In addition, the circumstances in which intergroup interactions occur can lead people to perceive that their group is under threat. Next, we argue that intergroup threats can lead to negative attitudes and expectations, activate cognitive biases, and reduce the effectiveness of cognitive processing. In addition, they often elicit negative emotions such as fear and anger. Perceived intergroup threats commonly lead to negative intentions and behaviors toward outgroups including aggression and discrimination. Intergroup threats can also generate retaliatory and other negative reactions from outgroups that further complicate intergroup relations. However, under some conditions intergroup threats can lead to positive outcomes such as amicable interactions and productive attempts to resolve conflicts. We end with a discussion of the implications of intergroup threats for intergroup interactions.

To encourage future research on intergroup threats, we speculate freely about their causes and consequences. We present examples of relevant research when they are available. Our presentation of these issues is shaped by our previous theoretical articles on intergroup threats, our disciplinary background (social psychology), and the fact that the overwhelming majority of the research on these topics has been conducted in Western countries.

Types of Intergroup Threats

Realistic and symbolic threats have been the focus of most of the extensive research on intergroup threats (Stephan, Ybarra, & Morrison, 2015). Realistic threats are those in which an outgroup is perceived to pose a threat of

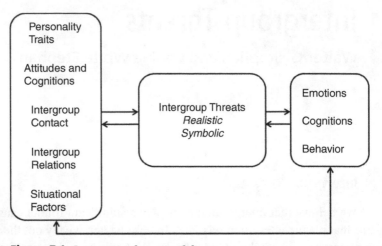

Figure 7.1 *Intergroup threat model.*

tangible harm to the ingroup. The potential types of tangible harm range from experiencing negative psychological outcomes such as frustration, embarrassment, feeling inept, being confused, or being perceived as prejudiced, to being concerned about being the target of physical harm, discrimination, economic loss, theft, destruction of personal property or being exposed to infectious diseases. In contrast, symbolic threats involve harm that is less tangible, such as threats to the integrity or validity of the ingroup's meaning systems – particularly its values, beliefs, norms, and morals.

Other distinctions among types of threat may also be important. For instance, threats may be targeted at an individual because of his or her membership in a social group or at the entire social group of which this person is a member. An experimental study of this distinction found that individual threats elicited more fear than anger, whereas threats to the ingroup as a whole elicited more anger than fear. Correspondingly, intergroup threats may be seen as originating from an individual member of an outgroup or from the outgroup as a whole. Reponses to threats originating from an individual member of another group may be quite different from responses to threats from the outgroup as a whole (e.g., retaliation is more likely to occur toward an individual than a group).

Antecedents of Intergroup Threats

Our review of the literature suggests that five categories of factors can predispose people to perceive intergroup threats: personality traits and related personal characteristics, attitudes and related cognitions, intergroup contact, intergroup relations, and situational factors.

Personality Traits and Related Characteristics

Two categories of personality traits may predispose people to perceive intergroup threats: those that lead individuals to be concerned that their own personal welfare is threatened by outgroups and those that lead people to be concerned that the welfare of their group is threatened by outgroups. Traits that are particularly likely to predispose people to feel individually threatened include insecurity, suspiciousness, mistrustfulness, fearfulness, rigidity, and beliefs that the world is dangerous. Individuals with these traits are concerned that other groups wish to harm them, which leads them to be vigilant regarding potential threats to the self from outgroups. There is little empirical research on these personality traits, although Matthews and Levin (2012) did find that viewing the world as dangerous was positively correlated with perceived threats from Muslims in a sample of American students.

Traits that lead people to be particularly worried that their ingroup as a whole is threatened include favoring well-ordered societies, supporting social inequality, adhering to strong belief systems (e.g., religious extremism), being ethnocentric, or being very conservative. People with these types of traits desire to maintain the current social order and are attuned to threats to that social order by outgroups. Research indicates that social dominance orientation (i.e., support for group-based inequalities) and right-wing authoritarianism (i.e., a preference for traditions and social order) are positively correlated with perceived threats against the ingroup (Matthews & Levin, 2012). In another study, higher levels of religiosity among Israeli Jews were positively correlated with perceived threats from Arabs (Butz et al., 2009). In addition, a study conducted in the United States found that political conservatism was positively correlated with perceived threats from terrorists (Crowson, 2009).

Social identity also plays a crucial role in causing people to perceive threats from outgroups. Highly ingroup-identified individuals consider the ingroup to be an important component of their self-definitions. As a result, they are more concerned about the welfare of the ingroup and the preservation of its values, beliefs, and practices than less ingroup-identified individuals. They also have more to lose than less ingroup-identified individuals if the ingroup is harmed or its values are undermined by outgroups. These concerns ultimately lead them to be more likely to attend to and perceive threats from outgroups than people who do not identify strongly with their ingroup. A number of studies have found that strength of identity with the ingroup is positively correlated with perceived intergroup threats. One study showed that perceived threats from Moroccans and Turks were positively correlated with national identity among students in the Netherlands (Verkuyten, 2009). A meta-analysis of studies of this relationship obtained results that were consistent with this finding (Riek, Mania, & Gaertner, 2006).

Attitudes and Related Cognitions

Although perceived intergroup threats can cause prejudice and negative stereotypes, it is also the case that prejudice and negative stereotypes can cause perceived intergroup threats (more on causality issues later). Prejudice and negative stereotypes can cause intergroup threats because they lead people to have negative expectations of outgroup members. People who are prejudiced may also be concerned that their negative views of the outgroup will be reciprocated. People who endorse ingroup social norms that proscribe outgroup contact often do so because they expect that harm will befall ingroup members who engage in outgroup contact.

In the research literature, prejudice has frequently been found to be correlated with perceived intergroup threats. For example, a study of samples of Blacks and Whites in the United States found that negative attitudes toward the other racial group were correlated with perceived threats from that group (Stephan, W. G., Boniecki, Ybarra, et al., 2002). Although the authors interpreted this finding to mean that threats lead to the negative attitudes, the reverse direction of causality is equally plausible – an issue we will return to later. A number of studies have found that negative stereotypes are also linked with perceived threats. For instance, in one study, negative stereotypes were positively correlated with perceived threats from immigrants in the Netherlands (Velasco Gonzalez, Verkuyten, Weesie, & Poppe, 2008). Other types of negative attitudes toward outgroups are also associated with perceiving intergroup threats. A study of 21 European countries found that opposition to immigration was positively correlated with perceived intergroup threats (Pereira, Vala, & Costa-Lopes, 2010). An experimental study employing participants from Germany demonstrated that negative beliefs about diversity can cause perceived threats (Kauff & Wagner, 2012). The German participants in this study read either an anti-diversity or a pro-diversity "newspaper" article that successfully created positive and negative beliefs about diversity. Participants in the anti-diversity condition subsequently reported higher levels of intergroup threats from immigrants than those in the pro-diversity condition.

Intergroup Contact

Low levels of intergroup contact can lead to perceptions of intergroup threats because low levels of contact are generally associated with a lack of knowledge of the outgroup (Pettigrew & Tropp, 2008). Ingroup members are unlikely to have accurate expectations for the behavior of outgroups and are likely to have a limited understanding of their motives, values, norms, and beliefs. This limited understanding is likely to lead to mistrust of outgroup members and uncertainty about how to interact with them. A lack of contact also means that people have had few opportunities to discover the values the two groups share in common.

Numerous studies indicate that amount of intergroup contact is negatively correlated with perceived threats across a wide range of group characteristics (ethnicity, nationality, religion, age, immigrants, sexual preferences). One of these studies examined perceived threats posed by Hindus and Muslims in India (Tausch, Hewstone, & Roy, 2009). The results indicated that the amount of contact with the other group was negatively correlated with these threats. Intergroup contact is also correlated with intergroup anxiety (a type of personal intergroup threat). Pettigrew and Tropp (2008) found that across 45 studies, the mean correlation between amount of contact and intergroup anxiety was −0.29.

Low levels of intergroup contact may also lead people to perceive the outgroup as dissimilar. In addition, a lack of contact implies that people have not had occasion to learn to empathize with outgroup members (Pettigrew & Tropp, 2008). Regarding the outgroup as dissimilar and being unable to empathize with them may lead to perceiving the outgroup as alien and therefore as threatening. An experimental study found that a fictitious immigrant group that was presented as having different values from German nationals was perceived as posing greater threats than an immigrant group with similar values (Rohmann, Florack, & Piontkowski, 2006, Study 2).

In terms of fostering perceived threats, negative contact with outgroups is likely to be even worse than a lack of contact. Negative contact generates experience-based negative expectations of outgroups that can form the basis for perceived threats. A study of American Whites indicated that negative contact with Blacks was positively correlated with perceived threats from Blacks (Aberson & Gaffney, 2008).

Intergroup Relations

Intergroup conflict, group power, relative status, and group size can have an impact on perceptions of intergroup threats. Intergroup conflict can generate perceptions of intergroup threats because people are likely to believe that the past is prelude to the present. The type of prior conflict (e.g., economic, political, religious, territorial), as well as its frequency, duration, and intensity, should influence the way that threats are perceived. In a study of Anglo-Canadians and Native Canadians, prior conflict with the other group was positively correlated with perceptions of intergroup threats in both groups (Corenblum & Stephan, W. G., 2001). Low-power groups would be expected to display greater perceived threats than high-power groups because high-power groups are in a position to exercise control over them. In line with this reasoning, in the Corenblum and W. G. Stephan (2001) study, the lower-power group perceived greater threats from the other group than did the higher-power group. However, high-power groups may feel threatened if they fear losing their power. Moreover, high-power groups are likely to respond vigorously to threats because they have so much to lose and they possess the means to do so.

The greater the status *differences* among groups in the same society, the more likely it is that both low- and high-status groups will feel threatened by the other group. Status differences lead to perceptions of threat by creating tensions in relations between low- and high-status groups. Perceived differences in status were found to be positively correlated with perceived intergroup threats in a study of Blacks and Whites in the United States (Stephan et al., 2002). In addition, the larger the outgroup is perceived to be, the more likely it is to be viewed as threatening. A study of outgroup size found that the percentage of foreigners in 17 European countries was positively correlated with perceived intergroup threats (McLaren, 2003).

Situational Factors

Situational factors have their effects on threats primarily during intergroup inter-actions. Situational factors may influence the degree to which people are concerned about negative psychological consequences (e.g., being embarrassed or frustrated, or feeling incompetent) as well as negative behavioral consequences (e.g., being discriminated against or physically harmed) for themselves and other members of their ingroup. Among the situational factors that are likely to activate these concerns are intergroup competition, a low ratio of ingroup to outgroup members in the interaction context, and status differences between groups in the situation. Other aspects of the situation that make intergroup interactions more difficult, such as language differences, a lack of clear social roles or structure, and a lack of familiarity with the situation, are also likely to lead people to feel threatened. Situational factors vary within and across contexts, with the result that situationally activated intergroup threats are often more fluid and transitory than other inter-group threats.

Research on situational factors has focused primarily on intergroup anxiety. For example, one study found that linguistic and cultural barriers to effective communication with foreign students (e.g., strong accents) were positively correlated with intergroup anxiety in an American sample (Spencer-Rodgers & McGovern, 2002). In another study, disrupting intergroup communications (interfering with people's ability to communicate during interethnic interactions) increased intergroup anxiety. In addition, it has been shown that unstructured (vs. structured) Black-White interactions in the United States increased intergroup anxiety compared to within-race interactions (Avery, Richeson, Hebl, & Ambady, 2009).

Consequences of Intergroup Threats

In our discussion of the consequences of intergroup threats, we explore three basic types of responses: emotional, cognitive, and behavioral. Understandably, people often react to intergroup threats with strong negative emotions because such threats can involve all that is meaningful to them, including their very existence. Their cognitions about the other group are likely to be equally negative. In addition, their cognitive processing may be muddled by the effects of their emotional reactions as well as the physiological arousal associated with these emotions. Together, negative emotions and cognitions can motivate people to engage in negative behaviors toward the outgroup, although under some conditions, intergroup threats can also cause positive behaviors.

Emotional Responses to Intergroup Threats

Feeling threatened by an outgroup leads to experiencing anxiety and fear, particularly if the individual believes he or she, or his or her group as a whole, cannot successfully counter the threats. Believing that a threat cannot be countered may also lead to feelings of intimidation, dread, helplessness, despair, vulnerability, humiliation, and even panic. If the outgroup threat implies that the ingroup will be less able to achieve desired goals, ingroup members may respond with frustration, hostility, resentment, or hatred. If people believe they can counter the threat, they are likely to feel anger or possibly rage toward the group that dares to threaten them. When the outgroup threats involve potential violations of the norms, values, or morals of the ingroup, ingroup members may respond with righteous indignation, outrage, contempt, disgust, scorn, or revulsion.

Research demonstrates that intergroup threats are positively correlated with reports of fear. For instance, in a Euro-American sample, Cottrell and Neuberg (2005) found that intergroup threats were positively correlated with fear toward an assortment of outgroups (African Americans, Asian Americans, Mexican Americans, Native Americans). Other studies have shown that intergroup threats are positively correlated with anger. In a study conducted in the United States, intergroup threats were correlated with anger toward people from the Muslim world (Matthews & Levin, 2012). Intergroup threats are also positively correlated with collective angst (Wohl, Branscombe, & Reysen, 2010), disgust (Matthews & Levin, 2012), contempt (Louis, Esses, & Lalonde, 2013), and *schadenfreude* (experiencing pleasure at the suffering of an outgroup; Leach, Spears, Branscombe, & Doosje, 2003). All of these negative emotional reactions to intergroup threats probably interfere with the capacity to experience emotional empathy toward outgroup members.

It is important to note that many of the emotional responses to intergroup threats are accompanied by physiological arousal, which has implications for cognitive processing and behavior. Several studies provide evidence that intergroup interaction can elicit physiological arousal, most likely because it is creates anxiety. In intergroup contexts, people experience increased blood pressure (Littleford, Wright, & Sayoc-Parial, 2005), higher cortisol levels (Gray, Mendes, & Denny-Brown, 2008), and greater left ventricular contractility and vasoconstriction (Blascovich, Mendes, Hunter, Lickel, & Kowai-Bell, 2001).

Attitudinal and Cognitive Responses to Intergroup Threats

When confronted with threats from other groups, people often respond with a cognitive appraisal of the type of threat, its magnitude, and the resources they have to cope with it (cf. Trawalter, Richeson, & Shelton, 2009). This appraisal is likely to be followed by a consideration of the options available to respond to the threat and an assessment of how quickly to take these actions. These appraisals, and the vigilance required to monitor threats, can place heavy demands on cognitive resources. Over time, these demands can deplete cognitive resources and lead to decrements in cognitive functioning, especially executive functioning (i.e., managing the deployment of cognitive resources). Cognitive depletion created by intergroup threats may also lead to a reliance on cognitive heuristics (e.g., representativeness, availability, similarity). In addition, cognitive depletion may eventually lower the quality of decision making, particularly with respect to how to respond to the threats.

Intergroup threats typically bias the content of cognitions about outgroups in a negative direction. Intergroup threats readily activate negative cognitions because these threats elicit negative emotions and because such threats raise concerns about negative consequences for the ingroup. Specifically, threats can arouse prejudice, stereotypes, and other negative beliefs about outgroups. Intergroup threats are also likely to lead to opposition to social policies favoring outgroups and support for policies and actions that have a negative impact on outgroups. An experimental study by Gonsalkorale, Carlisle, and von Hipple (2007) found that a manipulation of perceived intergroup threats led to increased stereotyping of Asians by White Australian students. Research also indicates that intergroup threats are often associated with negative attitudes toward outgroups. For instance, W. G. Stephan, Ybarra, and Bachman (1999) found that perceived intergroup threats were correlated with negative attitudes toward immigrants to the United States. In addition, a study conducted in China found that a threat to the Chinese economy by a British company increased implicit prejudice among Chinese students on the implicit association test (IAT; Yang, Shi, Luo, Shi, & Cai, 2014). Perceived intergroup threats have also been found to be negatively correlated with attitudes toward policies favoring compensatory treatment of minorities in South Africa (Durrheim et al., 2011). Other studies have found that perceived intergroup threats were positively correlated with exclusionary attitudes toward Palestinians in Israel (Ariely 2011) as well as opposition to the admission of Turkey to the European Union among citizens of Portugal (Pereira et al., 2010). In contrast to their effects on attitudes toward outgroups, intergroup threats are likely to strengthen both positive attitudes toward ingroups and ingroup identity. They may also strengthen core ingroup beliefs. Thus, extreme threats may breed extremism in response.

Intergroup threats may also amplify ingroup-outgroup cognitive biases such as attribution biases (e.g., the ultimate attribution error – making internal attributions for negative outgroup behaviors), memory biases (e.g., misanthropic memory, difficulty recalling stereotype-inconsistent information about outgroups), and a bias toward associating the outgroup with negative words and the ingroup with positive words (IAT; Banaji & Greenwald, 2013). A bias toward perceiving greater discrimination when being treated unfairly by outgroup vs. ingroup members (Dover, Major, Kunstman, & Sawyer, 2015) may also be magnified by intergroup threats. In addition, the bias toward perceiving outgroups as dissimilar to the ingroup, the outgroup homogeneity bias, a bias toward the overestimation of outgroup size, and the bias toward believing that outgroup stereotypes are difficult to disconfirm should be heightened by intergroup threats. Threats also appear to play a role in the "shooter bias," which is the bias toward "shooting" Black targets relative to White targets. In one study, Whites were more likely to believe that an unarmed person had a weapon if that person was a Black male rather than a Black female (or a White person of either sex; Plant, Gople, & Kustman, 2011). That is, the group that is stereotyped as most threatening was the most likely to be perceived as holding a weapon. A later study by Miller, Zielaskowski, and Plant (2012) found that for people who chronically perceive threats from outgroups, the shooter bias effect can even occur when the distinction between the ingroup and the outgroup is meaningless.

Moreover, intergroup threats may augment an inability to recognize outgroup faces and foster the dehumanization and infra-humanization of outgroups (Berti, Pevetti, & Battista, 2013; Hackel, Looser, & Bavel, 2014). The tendency to have more difficulty remembering atrocities committed by the ingroup than the same atrocities committed by an outgroup (Coman, Stone, Castano, & Hirst, 2014) may also be boosted by intergroup threats. Another cognitive bias that is likely to be amplified by intergroup threats is the tendency of ingroup members to exclude outgroups from their moral universe. The greater the threat (particularly symbolic threats), the more likely that outgroups will be considered to be morally inferior. In one study, perceived threats to Americans were negatively correlated with evaluations of the morality (as well as sociability and warmth) of a wide range of social groups (Kervyn, Fiske, & Yzerbyt, 2015). Excluding outgroups from the moral universe of the ingroup makes it easier to justify or condone actions toward the outgroup that would be considered immoral or illegal if directed at ingroup members (e.g., murder, torture, rape, assault, incarceration without due process, destruction of property, theft, starvation, denial of medical care). It has also been found that perceived intergroup threats were positively correlated with attitudes toward violence against Muslims in the Netherlands (Doosje, Loseman, & Bos, 2013). In Germany, perceived intergroup threats were found to be positively correlated with approval of torture during the interrogation of terrorists (Asbrock & Fritsche, 2013). A related study with a non-Muslim British sample found that the relationship between the perceived humanity of Muslims and proclivity to torture Muslims was mediated by perceived threats from Muslims (Viki, Osgood, & Phillips, 2013).

Behavioral Responses to Intergroup Threats

The behavioral responses to threat are enormously varied. They range from attacking the source of the threats through negotiations and appeasement to freezing from fear. At the individual level, responses to intergroup threats include aggression, harassment, discrimination, submission, begging for peace, and avoidance. In addition, intergroup threats can lead individuals to engage in a variety of negative nonverbal behaviors such as leaning away from outgroup members, frowning and scowling, averted gaze, physical distancing, speech disfluencies (e.g., false starts, fillers), and not touching outgroup members in circumstances where they would touch ingroup members (for a meta-analysis of the negative effects of interracial interactions on nonverbal behaviors, see Toosi, Babbitt, Ambady, & Sommers, 2012). At the group level, responses to intergroup threats include warfare, genocide, terrorism, sabotage, strikes, demonstrations, enacting laws to control outgroups, seeking compromise, capitulation, and flight. The negative emotions and cognitions elicited by intergroup threats, combined with any physiological arousal activated by intergroup threats, help fuel negative behavioral responses to intergroup threats.

The research literature provides evidence indicating that intergroup threats are associated with actual negative behaviors as well as negative intentions toward outgroups. For instance, intergroup anxiety was correlated with engaging in fewer effective intercultural communication behaviors in a US sample (e.g., resolving misunderstandings, capacity to interpret nonverbal behavior; Ulrey & Amason, 2001). Barlow and colleagues found that intergroup anxiety was correlated with avoiding Aboriginal Australians among both White and Asian Australians (Barlow, Louis, & Hewstone, 2009; Barlow, Louis, & Terry, 2010). A study done in Germany found that perceived intergroup threats were positively correlated with a willingness to use violence against foreigners (Wagner, Christ, & Pettigrew, 2008). Perceived intergroup threats have also been found to be positively correlated with discriminatory intentions toward immigrants in the Netherlands (Schleuter & Scheepers, 2010). Other studies have found that intergroup threats are related to reluctance to provide direct assistance to immigrants to Canada (Costello & Hodson, 2011) and offensive behavioral action tendencies toward the homeless in the Netherlands (Van Zomeren et al., 2007).

In addition to direct behavioral responses to intergroup threats, there may be indirect responses as well. For example, intergroup threats may activate negative performance-related stereotypes about the ingroup that lead ingroup members to be concerned that their task performance will confirm the negative stereotypes. These types of stereotype-based threats have been consistently found to cause decrements in performance on cognitive tasks (Aronson & McGlone, 2015).

Intergroup threats are also likely to affect group dynamics. For example, intergroup threats could promote groupthink (i.e., when desires to maintain group cohesion interfere with careful consideration of a wide range of options; Janis,

1982). Intergroup threats may also enhance group cohesion by bringing the group together to confront the threats. Threats may also lead people to engage in behaviors that strengthen ingroup identity; for example, a study of French Canadians found that perceived intergroup threats were positively correlated with sending their children to French Canadian schools – a type of boundary-maintenance behavior (Wohl, Branscombe, & Reysen, 2010, Study 2). The study by Matthews and Levin (2012), referred to earlier, found that perceived threats from Muslims led to stronger behavioral inclinations to preserve American values, such as prohibiting the teaching of Muslim values in schools or preventing children from reading books by Muslim authors. In addition, intergroup threats may cause the ingroup to be punitive toward members who deviate from ingroup norms, bolster the size of the ingroup, and lead to attempts to bind people to the ingroup. Alternatively, intergroup threats could cause disagreements among ingroup members as they confront the threats they face.

Although the behavioral responses to intergroup threats are primarily negative, intergroup threats can lead to positive behaviors under certain conditions. People who are motivated to appear non-prejudiced during intergroup interactions may consciously control their behavior to present themselves in a positive light (Vorauer, 2006, 2013). For example, a study by Mendes and Koslov (2013) found that when American White students were interacting with Blacks (during a get-acquainted conversation), they exhibited more positive nonverbal behaviors (smiling, laughing, nodding) than when interacting with Whites. In other cases, people may be legitimately interested in compromise and negotiation as an avenue to reduce intergroup threats and behave positively to achieve these goals.

The research on the consequences of intergroup threats supports our argument that intergroup threats have predominantly negative effects on intergroup relations. It would appear that many of the consequences occur with little or no conscious consideration. Given this pattern of negative behaviors and the relative lack of control that people seem to exercise over them, it is reasonable to ask if there is some deeper meaning that would help us understand why they occur. One answer to this question is that these negative responses serve an evolutionary function because they lead groups and their individual members to defend themselves against threats of harm from outgroups. Over the great expanse of human history, groups of people may have been more likely to survive if they were vigilant in their relationships with outgroups and sought to prepare themselves to actively ward off the threats posed by outgroups. Over time, some of these negative reactions may have become so automatic they have dropped out of conscious awareness. Negative responses would have been most adaptive when the outgroup actually was an "enemy" – in the sense that its members actually did pose threats to the ingroup. In modern societies, negative reactions to outgroup threats can create problems if the outgroup does not pose actual threats to the ingroup, especially if these negative responses have become nonconscious in nature.

A Note About Causality

The model we are proposing is basically a mediational model in which intergroup threats serve as mediators between their causes and consequences. In our model, the same variables sometimes show up as both causes and effects. For instance, negative attitudes toward outgroup members may cause ingroup members to perceive the outgroup as a threat to the ingroup (i.e., they fear that members of groups they dislike may want to harm them). But perceptions of intergroup threats can also heighten negative attitudes toward the outgroup. That is, causality is often reciprocal in our model.

The reciprocal causation model has important longitudinal implications. The cause and effect relationships in the model play out over time. For example, negative attitudes lead to the perception of threats, which leads to more negative attitudes, which leads to increased perceptions of threat, and so on. It is important to note that many of the studies we have cited examined intergroup threats as mediators between other sets of variables.

Numerous studies have shown that the effects of intergroup threats are moderated by other variables. This existing research on mediators and moderators is both complex and inconsistent. Nonetheless, it is important because finding consistent mediated and moderated relationships would be of enormous benefit in applied contexts.

Implications of Intergroup Threats for Intergroup Interactions

Intergroup interactions that occur when intergroup threats are present typically involve an iterative interplay of negative and positive emotions, cognitions, and behaviors. Each ingroup is an outgroup to the other group. The actions of members of one group impinge on the other group and elicit reactions from the other group that then impact the first group and so on throughout the interaction. In the final section of this chapter, we speculate on the implications of intergroup threats for intergroup interactions. In particular, we focus on the responses of outgroup members to the negative emotions, cognitions, and behaviors displayed by the ingroup (for a related discussion of the effects of being stigmatized on the stigmatized group, see Major, 2006).

When intergroup threats occur during intergroup interactions, they readily activate emotions that can interfere with productive and satisfying intergroup relationships. If members of an ingroup display negative emotions during intergroup interaction, they can trigger adverse responses from the outgroup. For instance, if intergroup threats activate fear in the ingroup, displaying this fear may lead outgroup members to take advantage of the ingroup by attempting to establish dominance or getting the ingroup to comply with their wishes. Ingroup displays of anger in response to intergroup threats could evoke aggression to counteract it, lead to avoidance or distancing, or cause submission and passivity among outgroup members. Outgroup members would also be expected to respond unfavorably to other negative emotional displays by the ingroup. For example, expressions of frustration or anxiety by the ingroup could elicit parallel emotional responses in outgroup members. Ingroup expressions of disgust, revulsion, loathing, disdain, or contempt are likely to lead to feelings of resentment in the outgroup, defensive assertions of self-worth, or a loss in self-worth (if the negative appraisals are accepted as valid by the outgroup). In addition, being a target of negative emotions is likely to reduce any empathy the outgroup might have for the ingroup.

Intergroup threats also have a detrimental effect on intergroup interactions because they distort ingroup members' perceptions and cognitions of the other group, as well as their capacity to think clearly and make sound decisions during intergroup interactions. For example, intergroup threats often lead to prejudice and negative stereotyping. These negative attitudes are likely to be communicated explicitly or implicitly to outgroup members who may reciprocate in kind. Being stereotyped or subjected to other negative evaluations may also lead to efforts by the outgroup to disprove them. The outgroup is also likely to respond to prejudice and stereotypes directed toward them with anger and resentment. In addition, outgroup members are likely to see ingroup members as biased against them.

People have a tendency to emphasize the homogeneity of outgroups, and they have difficulty differentiating outgroup members visually. Intergroup threats may amplify these tendencies, which would have the effect of making it more difficult for ingroup members to individualize outgroup members, thus interfering with effective intergroup interactions. Intergroup biases that lead to favoring the ingroup over the outgroup can result in the unfair distribution of resources. This ingroup favoritism bias would then be likely to cause perceptions of injustice on the part of outgroup members. Intergroup threats may also amplify the bias toward attributing positive behaviors by outgroup members to situational factors and negative behaviors by outgroup members to dispositional factors. If so, these erroneous attributions could lead to unfair negative evaluations of outgroup members with the result, again, that outgroup members feel they are being treated unjustly.

When intergroup threats cause ingroup members to treat outgroup members as less than human, it is likely to be experienced as humiliating and degrading and lead to resentment and hostility among members of the dehumanized group. In addition, to the extent that dehumanizing outgroups causes ingroup members to condone or engage in negative behaviors toward outgroup members, there is little doubt that the ingroup's acceptance of such behaviors will create ill will in the outgroup.

In multicultural/multiethnic workgroups, any depletion of cognitive resources brought about by intergroup threats will probably have a negative impact on the ability of ingroup members to process complex problems, formulate effective strategies, evaluate alternative options, generate creative solutions to problems, and make sound decisions more generally. The lowered quality of their contributions to multicultural/multiethnic workgroups is likely to harm relations between the groups.

When intergroup threats cause overt negative behaviors toward the outgroup (e.g., aggression, discrimination, avoidance), outgroup members may be offended, angered, or frustrated. Outgroup members may also respond with overt negative behaviors directed toward the ingroup. They may also be less cooperative, trusting, open, helpful, and empathic (Wlodarczyk, Basabe, & Bobowik, 2014) and more guarded and confrontational. Outgroup members also may reciprocate negative nonverbal behaviors directed at them. Correspondingly, if intergroup threats lead ingroup members to engage in positive behaviors, these behaviors, too, may be reciprocated, although in some cases they may be initially met with suspicion. When intergroup threats cause ingroup members to communicate poorly with outgroup members, it may engender misunderstandings and disagreements between the groups.

Although this chapter paints a rather gloomy picture of the impact of intergroup threats on intergroup interactions, these interactions need not be negative. If ingroup members wish to have productive interactions with the outgroup, they need to respond constructively to the negative reactions from the outgroup members, who may perceive that they are being threatened, even when few threats exist. Ingroup members can do this by being friendly, fair, open, helpful, concerned, and empathic toward the other group. In addition, ingroup members need to control the effects of feeling threatened on their own behavior toward the outgroup (e.g., by consciously attending to their own emotional, cognitive, and behavioral biases). People who are motivated to establish friendly relations with outgroups, work on common problems with them, monitor their own biases, and acquire new knowledge and new perspectives will find intergroup interactions immensely rewarding – even if they are bewildered and frustrated on occasion.

References

Aberson, C. L., & Gaffney, A. M. (2008). An integrated threat model of explicit and implicit attitudes. *European Journal of Social Psychology, 39*(5), 808–830.

Ariely, G. (2011). Spheres of citizenship: The role of distinct perceived threats in legitimizing allocation of political, welfare and cultural rights in Israel. *International Journal of Intercultural Relations, 35*(2), 213–225.

Aronson, J., & McGlone, M. S. (2015). Stereotype and social identity threat. In T. D. Nelson (Ed.) *Handbook of prejudice, stereotyping, and discrimination* (pp. 153–178). New York: Psychology Press.

Asbrock, F., & Fritsche, I. (2013). Authoritarian reactions to terrorist threat: Who is being threatened, the Me or the We? *International Journal of Psychology, 48*(1), 35–49.

Avery, D. R., Richeson, J. A., Hebl, M. R., & Ambady, N. (2009). It does not have to be uncomfortable: The role of behavioral scripts in Black–White interracial interactions. *Journal of Applied Psychology*, *94*(6), 1382–1393.

Banaji, M. R., & Greenwald, A. G. (2013). *Blindspot: Hidden biases of good people*. New York: Delacorte Press.

Barlow, F. K., Louis, W. R., & Hewstone, M. (2009). Rejected! Cognitions of rejection and intergroup anxiety as mediators of the impact of cross-group friendships on prejudice. *British Journal of Social Psychology*, *48*(3), 389–405.

Barlow, F. K., Louis, W. R., & Terry, D. J. (2010). Minority report: Social identity, cognitions of rejection and intergroup anxiety predicting prejudice from one racially marginalized group towards another. *European Journal of Social Psychology*, *40*(5), 805–818.

Berti, C., Pivetti, M., & Di Battista, S. (2013). The ontologization of Romani: An Italian study on the cross-categorization approach. *International Journal of Intercultural Relations*, *37*(4), 405–414.

Blascovich, J., Mendes, W. B., Hunter, S. B., Lickel, B., & Kowai–Bell, N. (2001). Perceiver threat in social interactions with stigmatized others. *Journal of Personality and Social Psychology*, *80*(2), 253–267.

Butz, D. Canetti, D., Halperin, E., Hobfoll, S. E., Shapira, O., & Hirsch-Hoefler, S. (2009). Authoritarianism, perceived threat and exclusionism on the eve of the Disengagement: Evidence from Gaza. *International Journal of Intercultural Relations*, *33*(6), 463–474.

Coman, A., Stone, C. B., Castano, E., & Hirst, W. (2014). Justifying atrocities: The effect of moral-disengagement strategies on socially shared retrieval-induced forgetting. *Psychological Science*, *25*(6), 1281–1285.

Corenblum, B., & Stephan, W. G. (2001). White fears and Native apprehensions: An integrated threat theory approach to intergroup attitudes. *Canadian Journal of Behavioral Science*, *33*(4), 251–268.

Costello, K., & Hodson, G. (2011). Social dominance-based threat reactions to immigrants in need of assistance. *European Journal of Social Psychology*, *41*(2), 220–231.

Cottrell, C. A., & Neuberg, S. L. (2005). Different emotional reactions to different groups: A sociofunctional threat-based approach to "prejudice." *Journal of Personality and Social Psychology*, *88*(5), 770–789.

Crowson, H. M. (2009). Predicting perceptions of symbolic and realistic threat from terrorists: The role of right-wing authoritarianism and social dominance orientation. *Individual Differences Research*, *7*(2) 113–118.

Doosje, B., Loseman, A., & Bos, K. (2013). Determinants of radicalization of Islamic youth in the Netherlands: Personal uncertainty, perceived injustice, and perceived group threat. *Journal of Social Issues*, *69*(3), 586–604.

Dover, T. L., Major, B., Kunstman, J. W., & Sawyer, P. J. (2015). Does unfairness feel different if it can be linked to group membership? Cognitive, affective, behavioral and physiological implications of discrimination and unfairness. *Journal of Experimental Social Psychology*, *56*, 96–103.

Durrheim, K., Dixon, J., Tredoux, C., Eaton, L., Quayle, M., & Clack, B. (2011). Predicting support for racial transformation policies: Intergroup threat, racial prejudice, sense of group entitlement and strength of identification. *European Journal of Social Psychology*, *41*(1), 23–41.

Gonsalkorale, K., Carlisle, K., & Von Hippel, W. (2007). Intergroup threat increases implicit stereotyping. *International Journal of Psychology and Psychological Therapy*, *7*(2), 189–200.

Gray, H. M., Mendes, W. B., & Denny-Brown, C. (2008). An in-group advantage in detecting intergroup anxiety. *Psychological Science*, *19*(12), 1233–1237.

Hackel, L. M., Looser, C. E., & Van Bavel, J. J. (2014). Group membership alters the threshold for mind perception: The role of social identity, collective identification, and intergroup threat. *Journal of Experimental Social Psychology*, *52*, 15–23.

Janis, I. L. (1982). *Groupthink*. Boston: Houghton Mifflin.

Kauff, M., & Wagner, U. (2012). Valuable therefore not threatening: The influence of diversity beliefs on discrimination against immigrants. *Social Psychological and Personality Science*, *3*(6), 714–721.

Kervyn, N., Fiske, S., & Yzerbyt, V. (2015). Forecasting the primary dimension of social perception: Symbolic and realistic threats together predict warmth in the stereotype content model. *Social Psychology*, *46*(1), 36–45.

Leach, C. W., Spears, R., Branscombe, N.R. & Doosje, B. (2003). Malicious pleasure: Schadenfreude at the suffering of another group. *Journal of Personality and Social Psychology*, *84*(5), 932.

Littleford, L. N., Wright, M. O. D., & Sayoc-Parial, M. (2005). White students' intergroup anxiety during same-race and interracial interactions: A multimethod approach. *Basic and Applied Social Psychology*, *27*, 85–94.

Louis, W. R., Esses, V. M., & Lalonde, R. N. (2013). National identification, perceived threat, and dehumanization as antecedents of negative attitudes toward immigrants in Australia and Canada. *Journal of Applied Social Psychology*, *43*(Suppl 2), 156–165.

Major, B. (2006). New perspectives on stigma and psychological well-being. In S. Levin & C. Van Laar (Eds.), *Stigma and group inequality: Social psychological perspectives* (pp. 193–210). Thousand Oaks, CA: Sage.

Matthews, M., & Levin, S. (2012). Testing a dual process model of prejudice: Assessment of group threat perceptions and emotions. *Motivation and Emotion*, *36*, 564–574.

McLaren, L. M. (2003). Anti-immigrant prejudice in Europe: Contact, threat perception, and preferences for the exclusion of migrants. *Social Forces*, *81*(3), 909–936.

Mendes, W. B., & Koslov, K. (2013). Brittle smiles: Positive biases toward stigmatized and outgroup targets. *Journal of Experimental Psychology: General*, *142*(3), 923.

Miller, S. L., Zielaskowski, K., & Plant, E. A. (2012). The basis of shooter biases: Beyond cultural stereotypes. *Personality and Social Psychology Bulletin*, *38*(10), 1358–1366.

Pereira, C., Vala, J., & Costa-Lopes, R. (2010). From prejudice to discrimination: The legitimizing role of perceived threat in discrimination against immigrants. *European Journal of Social Psychology*, *40*(7), 1231–1250.

Pettigrew, T. F., & Tropp, L. R. (2008). How does contact reduce prejudice? A meta-analytic test of three mediators. *European Journal of Social Psychology*, *38*(6), 922–934.

Plant, E. A., Goplen, J., & Kunstman, J. W. (2011). Selective responses to threat: The roles of race and gender in decisions to shoot. *Personality and Social Psychology Bulletin*, *37*(9), 1274–1281. doi: 0146167211408617

Riek, B. M., Mania, E. W., & Gaertner, S. L. (2006). Intergroup threat and outgroup attitudes: A meta-analytic review. *Personality and Social Psychology Review, 10*, 336–353.

Rohmann, A., Florack, A., & Piontkowski, U. (2006). The role of discordant acculturation attitudes in perceived threat: An analysis of host and immigrant attitudes in Germany. *International Journal of Intercultural Relations, 30*(6), 683–702.

Schlueter, E., & Scheepers, P. (2010). The relationship between outgroup size and anti-outgroup attitudes: A theoretical synthesis and empirical test of group threat and intergroup contact theory. *Social Science Research, 39*(2), 285–295.

Spencer-Rodgers, J., & McGovern, T. (2002). Attitudes toward the culturally different: The role of intercultural communication barriers, affective responses, consensual stereotypes, and perceived threat. *International Journal of Intercultural Relations, 26*(6), 609–631.

Stephan, W. G., Boniecki, K. A., Ybarra, O., Bettencourt, A., Ervin, K. S., Jackson, L. . . . Renfro, C. L. (2002). The role of threats in racial attitudes of Blacks and Whites. *Personality and Social Psychology Bulletin, 28*(9), 1242–1254.

Stephan, W. G., Ybarra, O., & Bachman, G. (1999). Prejudice toward immigrants. *Journal of Applied Social Psychology, 29*, 2221–2237.

Stephan, W. G., Ybarra, O., & Morrison, K. (2015). Intergroup threat theory. In T. D. Nelson (Ed.), *Handbook of prejudice, stereotyping, and discrimination* (pp. 255–278). New York: Psychology Press.

Tausch, N., Hewstone, M., & Roy, R. (2009). The relationships between contact, status and prejudice: An integrated threat theory analysis of Hindu-Muslim relations in India. *Journal of Community & Applied Social Psychology, 19*(2), 83–94.

Toosi, N. R., Babbitt, L. G., Ambady, N., & Sommers, S. R. (2012). Dyadic interracial interactions: A meta-analysis. *Psychological Bulletin, 138*(1), 1–27.

Trawalter, S., Richeson, J. A., & Shelton, J. N. (2009). Predicting behavior during interracial interactions: A stress and coping approach. *Personality and Social Psychology Review, 13*(3) 243–268.

Ulrey, K. L., & Amason, P. (2001). Intercultural communication between patients and health care providers: An exploration of intercultural communication effectiveness, cultural sensitivity, stress, and anxiety. *Health Communication, 13*(4), 449–463.

Van Zomeren, M., Fischer, A. H., & Spears, R. (2007). Testing the limits of tolerance: How intergroup anxiety amplifies negative and offensive responses to outgroup–initiated contact. *Personality and Social Psychology Bulletin, 33*(12), 1686–1699.

Velasco González, K., Verkuyten, M., Weesie, J., & Poppe, E. (2008). Prejudice towards Muslims in the Netherlands: Testing integrated threat theory. *British Journal of Social Psychology, 47*(4), 667–685.

Verkuyten, M. (2009). Support for multiculturalism and minority rights: The role of national identification and out-group threat. *Social Justice Research, 22*(1), 31–52.

Viki, G. T., Osgood, D., & Phillips, S. (2013). Dehumanization and self-reported proclivity to torture prisoners of war. *Journal of Experimental Social Psychology, 49*(3), 325–328.

Vorauer, J. D. (2006). An information search model of evaluative concerns in intergroup interaction. *Psychological Review, 113*(4), 862–886.

Vorauer, J. D. (2013). Getting past the self: Understanding and removing evaluative concerns as an obstacle to positive intergroup contact effects. In G. Hodson & M. Hewstone (Eds.), *Advances in intergroup contact* (pp. 23–48). New York: Psychology Press.

Wagner, U., Christ, O., & Pettigrew, T. F. (2008). Prejudice and group-related behavior in Germany. *Journal of Social Issues*, *64*(2), 403–416.

Wlodarczyk, A., Basabe, N., & Bobowik, M. (2014). The perception of realistic and symbolic threat and its influence on prejudice, ingroup favouritism and prosocial response: The native population in the face of immigration/Percepción de amenaza realista y simbólica, su influencia sobre el prejuicio, el favoritismo endogrupal y la respuesta prosocial: la población nativa ante la inmigración. *Revista de Psicología Social*, *29*(1), 60–89.

Wohl, M. J., Branscombe, N. R., & Reysen, S. (2010). Perceiving your group's future to be in jeopardy: Extinction threat induces collective angst and the desire to strengthen the ingroup. *Personality and Social Psychology Bulletin*, *36*(7), 898–910.

Yang, J., Shi, Y., Luo, Y. L., Shi, J., & Cai, H. (2014). The Brief Implicit Association Test is valid: Experimental evidence. *Social Cognition*, *32*(5), 449–465.

8 Social Dominance Theory: Explorations in the Psychology of Oppression

Jim Sidanius, Sarah Cotterill, Jennifer Sheehy-Skeffington, Nour Kteily, and Héctor Carvacho

Question: What is the difference between capitalism and communism?

Answer: Under capitalism you have the exploitation of man by man. Under communism it is just the reverse.

Russian saying

Despite impressive gains in the spread of quasi-democratic social practices and respect for human rights witnessed in the past hundred years (e.g., Pinker, 2011), intergroup discrimination, oppression, and violence continue to thrive within every modern social system. Whether one considers the marked discrimination against immigrants in the relatively egalitarian Sweden (Nordenstam & Ringström, 2013; Orange, 2013), the money-dominated elections of post-industrial states (Lessig, 2011), or the unambiguously oppressive dictatorships across the majority of the Arab world, systems of group-based social inequality and domination continue, despite our best efforts, to maintain their grip around the throats of democratic and egalitarian aspirations. While there are certainly vast differences in the degree of group-based social inequality across social systems, or across historical epochs within any given society, group-based social inequality appears to be a human universal present in all kinds of societies (see, e.g., Bowles, Smith, and Borgerhoff Mulder, 2010), even in hunter-gatherer communities (e.g., Ames, 2007; Arnold, 1993; Kennett, Winterhalder, Bartruff, & Erlandson, 2008).

Having made this basic observation of the near ubiquity of group-based social inequality, social dominance theory (SDT; Pratto, Sidanius, Stallworth, & Malle, 1994; Sidanius, 1993; Sidanius & Pratto, 1999) argues that many familiar types of group-based oppression (e.g., racism, sexism, nationalism, classism, religious intolerance, hostility toward the mentally ill) are essentially particular instantiations of a more general process through which dominant groups establish and maintain social, economic, and military supremacy over subordinate groups. Therefore, it is suggested that specific instantiations of oppression across social contexts cannot be comprehensively understood without serious consideration of the dynamic and multileveled forces producing and sustaining the phenomenon of group-based social hierarchy.

The Trimorphic Nature of Group-Based Social Hierarchy

SDT argues that there are essentially three related, yet qualitatively distinct types of group-based social hierarchy. The first type of hierarchical system is the "age system," in which those considered to be "adults" have more social, economic, and political power than those considered "juveniles." While the specific age separating one category in this system from another may vary between societies and within a given society over time, this dichotomy appears to be universal (James & James, 2008). The second form of group-based social hierarchy can be labeled "patriarchy" and is a system in which males have greater social, economic, and military power than females. While the degree of patriarchy can vary from relatively mild (e.g., Scandinavia) to relatively severe (e.g., Afghanistan), and the degree of patriarchy within a given society may vary over time, the presence of patriarchy itself appears be universal across human societies (Goldberg, 1994). Indeed, patriarchy may be a part of our evolutionary history: With the exception of bonobos (Pan *paniscus*), which can be described as a matriarchal species, patriarchy characterizes the other four great ape species (i.e., gorillas, orangutans, chimpanzees, and humans). Finally, we refer to the third and most antagonistic system of group-based social hierarchy as the "arbitrary-set" system. By arbitrary-set, we are referring to a hierarchically organized set of group distinctions that emerge as a function of historically and contextually evolved power and status differences between socially constructed groups, which therefore varies from culture to culture.

Mechanisms of Hierarchy Regulation: Hierarchy-Enhancing and Hierarchy-Attenuating Social Forces

Social dominance theorists posit that the exact degree of group-based social hierarchy in a given social system at any given time will be the point of equilibrium between two opposing sets of social forces: hierarchy-enhancing (HE) and hierarchy-attenuating (HA). This pair of forces operates at multiple levels, including individual-level dispositions toward (or against) hierarchy, attitudes and behaviors rooted in group membership, and systemic/institutional factors (Figure 8.1). Thus, HE social forces are composed of individual predispositions favoring hierarchy in society, the hierarchy-maintaining attitudes and behaviors of dominant (relative to subordinate) groups, and the joint operation of (system-level) hierarchy-enhancing social institutions (e.g., the police force), ideologies (e.g., the Protestant work ethic), and stereotypes that produce ever greater levels of group-based inequality. As the label implies, HA forces are those social forces that have exactly the opposite effect on group-based social

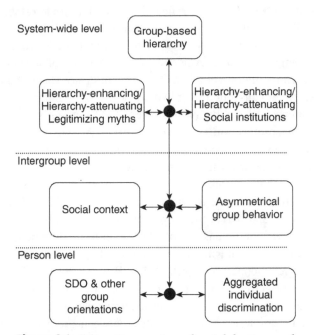

System-wide level

Intergroup level

Person level

Figure 8.1 *Schematic overview of social dominance theory (from Pratto, Sidanius, & Levin, 2006).*

inequality (see, e.g., Boehm, 1999). Examples of these forces are individual drives toward egalitarianism, welfare organizations and institutions such as the public defenders' office, and universalist ideologies such as the doctrine of global human rights.

SDT assumes that, generally speaking, dominant groups tend to support and enforce policies that entrench their advantages (i.e., HE policies), whereas subordinate group members tend to, but do not always, resist these policies. Indeed, the fact that members of dominant groups are more oriented toward preservation of the status quo than subordinates are toward challenging it is thought to be a factor contributing to the stability of hierarchical social systems. In this chapter, we not only review work illustrating the interactions between HE and HA social forces engaged in by dominant group members but also discuss advances in identifying and understanding the suboptimal behavioral and ideological orientations of subordinate group members.

Social Dominance Orientation

One of the several individual-level factors contributing to the creation and maintenance of group-based hierarchy is a construct known as social dominance orientation (SDO; Pratto et al., 1994; Sidanius & Pratto, 1999). Although SDO was initially conceptualized as the desire to have one's ingroup dominate socially relevant outgroups, it has been refined to reflect the general desire to establish and maintain hierarchically structured intergroup relations regardless of the position of one's own group(s) within this hierarchy (see Sidanius, Levin, Federico, & Pratto, 2001). Thus, for example, a Black American (e.g., member of a subordinate arbitrary-set group) with a high level of SDO would not desire Black Americans to dominate White Americans but rather would desire to maintain the extant hierarchical domination of Blacks by Whites, even at the ingroup's expense (for empirical support of this proposition, see Ho et al., 2012). A great deal of research has documented – using a variety of cross-sectional, longitudinal, and experimental methodologies – the various ways in which individual differences in SDO contribute to attitudes and behaviors that sustain hierarchy between groups in society (e.g., Guimond, Dambrun, Michinov, & Duarte, 2003; Ho et al., 2012; Kteily, Ho, & Sidanius, 2012; McFarland, 2010; Sibley & Liu, 2010). This research has also distinguished between two subdimensions of SDO, intergroup dominance (SDO-D) and intergroup anti-egalitarianism (SDO-E; Ho et al., 2012; see also Jost & Thompson, 2000; Kugler, Cooper, & Nosek, 2010). While SDO-D indexes one's desire to see some groups actively oppressed and is most strongly related to hostile attitudes such as old-fashioned racism, blatant dehumanization, and support for war, SDO-E taps into a preference for inequality between groups and is most strongly related to subtle forms of racism and hierarchy-enhancing social ideologies and careers (Ho et al., 2012; Kteily, Bruneau, Waytz, & Cotterill, 2015). Despite the prominence that the concept of SDO has had on the intergroup relations literature, social dominance theorists do not attempt to reduce the dynamics of intergroup discrimination or prejudice simply to individual differences in SDO. Rather, SDT is a multileveled theory that argues that group-based social hierarchy and its hydra-headed manifestations are the result of interactions among several processes operating at different levels of analysis (see Figure 8.1).

Contemporary Research Employing Social Dominance Theory

Since the last major review of social dominance theory (SDT) in 2006 (i.e., Pratto et al., 2006), researchers have continued to apply SDT to an understanding of attitudes and behaviors, including the maintenance of status boundaries, political party preference, labor union participation, support of harsh criminal sanctions, excessive use of police force, support for the death penalty and torture, and the dehumanization of low-status outgroups (see Table 8.1). Conceptual clarifications and extensions have also been proposed and tested, five of which we will review here: (a) the context-contingent effects of SDO, (b) the interface between empathy and SDO, (c) deepening our understanding of behavioral asymmetry, (d) introducing new thinking on ideology and the stability of intergroup differences, and (e) the development of the theory of gendered prejudice.

Table 8.1 *Social psychological domains in which social dominance theory has been applied (since 2005).*

Emotions
Hart, Hung, Glick, & Dinero, 2012
Hodson & Costello, 2007
Jeffries, Hornsey, Sutton, Douglas, & Bain, 2012
Kossowska, Bukowski, & Van Hiel, 2008
Laham, Tam, Lalljee, Hewstone, & Voci, 2009
Leone & Chirumbolo, 2008
Martin et al., 2014
Miller, Smith, & Mackie, 2004
Ratcliff, Bernstein, Cundiff, & Vescio, 2012
Van Hiel & Kossowska, 2006

Behavioral Intentions
Reese, Proch, & Cohrs, 2013

Collective Action
Henry, Sidanius, Levin, & Pratto, 2005
Levin, Henry, Pratto, & Sidanius, 2009

Competitiveness
Cozzolino & Snyder, 2008

Criminal Justice Attitudes and Outcomes
Dambrun, 2007
Gerber & Jackson, 2013
Green, Thomsen, Sidanius, Staerklé, & Potanina, 2009
Kemmelmeier, 2005
Kteily, Cotterill, Sidanius, Sheehy-Skeffington, & Bergh, 2014
Sidanius, Mitchell, Haley, & Navarrete, 2006
Perkins & Bourgeois, 2006

Cross-Cultural Comparisons
Fischer, Hanke, & Sibley, 2012
Lee, Pratto, & Johnson, 2011

Dehumanization
Costello & Hodson, 2011
Esses, Veenvliet, Hodson, & Mihic, 2008
Kteily et al., in press

Educational Attitudes and Performance
Cross, Cross, & Finch, 2010
Crowson & Brandes, 2010, 2014
Dambrun, Kamiejski, Haddad, & Duart, 2009
Sheehy-Skeffington & Sidanius, 2014a

Environmental Attitudes and Speciesism
Feygina, 2013
Jackson, Bitacola, Janes, & Esses, 2013
Milfont, Richter, Sibley, Wilson, & Fischer, 2013

Table 8.1 (*cont.*)

Health
Gilles et al., 2013
MacInnis, Busseri, Choma, & Hodson, 2013
Rosenthal & Levy, 2010
Sheehy-Skeffington & Sidanius, 2014b

The Invariance Hypothesis
Batalha, Reynolds, & Newbigin, 2011
Caricati, 2007
Dickens & Sergeant, 2008
Foels & Reid, 2010
Guimond, Chatard, Martinot, Crisp, & Redersdorff, 2006
Küpper & Zick, 2011
Lee et al., 2011
Levene & Dickens, 2008
Mata, Ghavami, & Wittig, 2010
McDonald, Navarrete, & Sidanius, 2011
Pula, McPherson, & Parks, 2012
Sidanius, Sinclair, & Pratto, 2006
Schmitt & Wirth, 2009
Snellman, Ekehammar, & Akrami, 2009
Wilson & White, 2010
Zakrisson, 2008

Intragroup Behavior
Islam & Zyohur, 2005
Roccato, 2008

Subdimensions of SDO
Hindriks, Verkuyten, & Coenders, 2014
Ho et al., 2012
Jost & Thompson, 2000
Kugler et al., 2010

Morality
Dhont & Hodson, 2014
Esses et al., 2008
Federico, Weber, Ergun, & Hunt, 2013
Ferreira, Fisher, Porto, Pilati, & Milfont, 2012
Kugler, Jost, & Noorbaloochi, 2014
Jackson & Gaertner, 2010
McFarland & Mathews, 2005
Milojev et al., 2014
Passini & Villano, 2013
Rios, Finkelstein, & Landa, 2014
Son Hing, Bobocel, Zanna, & McBride, 2007

Table 8.1 (*cont.*)

Nationalism, Patriotism, Support for War
Crowson, 2009
De Zavala, Cichocka, & Iskra-Golec, 2013
Livi, Leone, Falgares, & Lombardo, 2014

Organizational Behavior and the Workplace
Aiello, Pratto, & Pierro, 2013
Green & Auer, 2013
Haley & Sidanius, 2005
Martin et al., 2014
McKay & Avery, 2006
Nicol, 2009
Nicol, Rounding, & MacIntyre, 2011
Parkins, Fishbein, & Rithey, 2006
Pichler, Varma, & Bruce, 2010
Rosenblatt, 2012
Rosette, Carton, Bowes-Sperry, & Hewlin, 2013
Seelman & Walls, 2010
Shao, Resnick, & Hargis, 2011
Umphress, Simmons, Boswell, & Triana, 2007
Umphress, Smith-Crowe, Brief, Dietz, & Walkins, 2007

Personality and SDO
Bergh, Akrami, Sidanius, & Sibley, 2014
Leone, Desimoni, & Chriumbolo, 2014
Parkins, Ritchey, & Fishbein, 2006

Empathy
Bäckström & Björklund, 2007
Cheon et al., 2011
Chiao, Mathur, Harada, & Lipke, 2009
Sidanius et al., 2013

Political Attitudes and Legitimizing Ideologies
Bikman & Sunar, 2013
Bobbio, Canova, & Manganelli, 2010
Choma, Hanoch, Gummerum, & Hodson, 2013
Christopher, Zabel, Jones, & Marek, 2008
Costello & Hodson, 2009
Cotterill, Sidanius, Bhardwaj, & Kumar, 2014
Crawford, 2012
De Cremer, Cornelis, & Van Hiel, 2008
Esses & Hodson, 2006
Federico, Hunt, & Ergun, 2009
Green et al., 2010
Harding & Sibley, 2011
Hodson & Costello, 2007
Hodson & Esses, 2005
Jetten & Iyer, 2010

Table 8.1 (*cont.*)

Kteily, Sidanius, & Levin 2011
Kteily et al., 2012
Krauss, 2006
Levy, West, Ramirez, & Karafantis, 2006
Mosso, Briante, Aiello, & Russo, 2013
Oldmeadow & Fiske, 2007
Ramirez, Levy, Velilla, & Hughes, 2010
Sibley & Duckitt, 2010
Sibley & Wilson, 2007
Sibley, Wilson, & Robertson, 2007
Wilson & Sibley, 2013
Worthington, Navarro, Loewy, & Hart, 2008

Prejudice and Discrimination
Asbrock, Gutenbrunner, & Wagner, 2013
Asbrock, Sibley, & Duckitt, 2010
Bahns & Crandall, 2013
Bassett, 2010
Charles-Toussaint & Crowson, 2010
Cohrs & Stelzl, 2010
Costello & Hodson, 2009, 2014
Crowson & Brandes, 2010, 2014
Crowson & Gries, 2010
Crowson, Brandes, & Hurst, 2013
Danso, Sedlovskaya, & Suanda, 2007
Duckitt & Sibley, 2010
Duriez, 2011
Esses, Wagner, Wolf, Preseiser, & Wilbur, 2006
Feather & McKee, 2008
Gatto & Dambrun, 2012
Guimond et al., 2013
Guimond, De Oliveira, Kamiesjki, & Sidanius, 2010
Gutiérrez & Unzueta, 2013
Hodson, Rush, & MacInnis, 2010
Hodson, MacInnis, & Rush, 2010
Kteily et al., 2014
Kteily et al., 2012
Kteily et al., 2011
Leong, 2008
Levin et al., 2012
Levin, Pratto, Matthews, Sidanius, & Kteily, 2013
Malkin & Ben Ari, 2013
McFarland, 2010
Newman, Hartman, & Taber, 2014
Nickerson & Louis, 2008
O'Brien, Hunter, & Banks, 2007

Table 8.1 (*cont.*)

Onraet & Van Hiel, 2013
Pichler et al., 2010
Poteat & Mareish, 2012
Poteat & Spanierman, 2010
Schmid, Hewstone, Küpper, Zick, & Wagner, 2012
Sidanius, Haley, Molina, & Pratto, 2007
Sidanius & Pratto, 2012
Tausch & Hewstone, 2010
Thomsen et al., 2010
Thomsen, Green, & Sidanius, 2008
Umphress et al., 2008
Unzueta, Knowles, & Ho, 2012
Van Hiel & Kossowska, 2007
Vezzali & Giovannini, 2011
von Collani, Grumm, & Streicher, 2010

Social Perception
Alexander, Levin, & Henry, 2005
Ho, Sidanius, Levin, & Banaji, 2011
Ho, Sidanius, Cuddy, & Banaji, 2013
Kahn, Ho, Sidanius, & Pratto, 2009
Kteily et al., 2014
Levin et al., 2013
Newheiser, Tausch, Dovidio, & Hewstone, 2009
Simmons & Parks-Yancy, 2012
Snellmen Ekehammar, 2005
Yeagley, Morling, & Nelson, 2007
Thomsen et al., 2010

The Context-Contingent Effects of SDO

While it is well established that SDO is associated with generalized prejudice and hostility toward an array of groups (e.g., Altemeyer, 1998; McFarland & Adelson, 1996), more recent research has found that the association between SDO and outgroup hostility will be modified by the relative social status/power of the outgroup in question. For example, work by Henry et al. (2005) showed that while SDO was *positively* associated with support for aggression against Arabs (low status/power) among Americans (high status/power), and SDO was *negatively* associated with support for aggression against Americans among Arabs. In other words, those high in SDO are more likely to support violence by dominant groups against subordinate groups but less likely to support violence of subordinate groups against dominant groups.

In addition, violence directed at subordinate groups will be particularly severe when subordinates are perceived as violating group-status boundaries. For example, Thomsen et al. (2008) showed that while Right-Wing Authoritarianism Scale

(RWA) was somewhat positively associated with willingness to personally participate in government-sanctioned violence against foreign immigrants who did not assimilate to the values and norms of the host country, SDO was strongly associated with the willingness to personally participate in the government-sanctioned violence against immigrants who did assimilate to the values and norms of the host country (thus encroaching the high-status group's distinctiveness and boundaries). Relatedly, Kteily et al. (2014; also see Chapter 10, this volume) showed that the status of ambiguous targets (e.g., biracials) influences whether they are likely to be included in the ingroup, whereas high-SDO members of dominant groups were more likely to perceive low-status ambiguous targets in exclusionary terms (deeming them as more outgroup); this was not the case for high-status ambiguous targets (who were comparatively seen to be ingroup members). Research by Ho, Sidanius, Cuddy, and Banaji (2013) also showed that the related process of *hypodescent* (categorizing biracials in terms of their subordinate group membership) is influenced by a combination of high SDO and a sense of threat to the ingroup's standing. Thus, we can see that, as one would expect from a social dominance framework, high-SDO individuals will be most hostile toward members of subordinate groups attempting to breach the status/power boundary between subordinate and dominant groups.

SDO and Empathy

While SD theorists have long argued that SDO will tend to be negatively related to empathy (e.g., Bäckström & Björklund, 2007; Sidanius & Pratto, 1999), relatively new research has uncovered those brain regions that are implicated in this SDO/low-empathy connection. For example, Chiao and colleagues (Chiao et al., 2009) found that individuals' levels of SDO were strongly and negatively correlated with activity within those regions of the brain associated with the perception of pain in others. These brain regions included circuits in the mirror neuron system, the right inferior parietal lobe, and the left inferior frontal gyrus (see also Cheon et al., 2011).

In addition, in a set of cross-lagged analyses of panel (i.e., longitudinal) data using large samples in Belgium and New Zealand, recent work by Sidanius and colleagues (Sidanius et al., 2013) suggests a reciprocal relationship between SDO and empathy. That is, not only does the data suggest that one's level of empathy affects one's level of SDO, but individuals' levels of SDO also seem to influence empathy over time. Indeed, the effect of SDO on empathy appeared to be at least as strong as, if not stronger than, the reverse relationship.[1] This finding is in contrast to an important premise of the dual process model (see Chapter 10, this title, as well as Duckitt, 2001; Sibley & Duckitt, 2010), which argues that SDO – as an ideological variable – is driven by (rather than driving) personality factors such as empathy. If replicable, Sidanius et al.'s (2013) finding has important theoretical bearing on

1 However, for some limitations of cross-lag analysis, see Kenny, 1975.

our understanding of the status of SDO as either a personality variable or a sociopolitical ideology, or perhaps a mixture of both. Because we typically think of one's personality as driving one's sociopolitical ideologies (and not the reverse), it may be time to revisit the assumption among some theorists that SDO is exclusively a sociopolitical ideology.

Behavioral Asymmetry

One claim of SDT is that although group-based hierarchy is predominantly enforced and policed by high-power group members, low-power group members also play an important role in contributing to their own subordination. Sidanius and Pratto (1999, ch. 9) summarize how, on average, dominant social groups are much more successful than other groups in behaving in ways that enhance and maintain their dominant status, such as placing greater emphasis on educational achievement, saving money to acquire desirable commodities, and building social networks that help their friends and family have successful careers. On the other hand, members of subordinate social groups in a number of societies have a greater tendency to behave in group-debilitating ways, such as engaging in violence within and outside the home, school truancy, and unhealthy habits, including smoking and heavy alcohol consumption (e.g., Cauley, Donfield, LaPorte, & Warheftig, 1991; Steinberg, Dornbusch, & Brown, 1992; see Sidanius & Pratto, 1999, ch. 9, for a review). The argument is that these differences in the behaviors of dominant *vs.* subordinate groups might contribute to the entrenchment of hierarchy between groups in society.

This early observation has been buttressed by recent studies from across the social sciences. Public health researchers have highlighted the role of poor health-related decisions among members of subordinate groups in exacerbating inequalities in health outcomes along the socioeconomic spectrum (Lock, Pomerleau, Causer, & Altman, 2005), while political scientists observe that the poorest groups in society, though the ones with the greatest stake in debates concerning public spending, are the most quiescent and least politically engaged (Verba, Schlozman, & Brady, 1995; see also Cohen, Vigoda, & Samorly, 2001). Economists, meanwhile, highlight decisions made by those low in socioeconomic status that end up hampering their chances at social mobility, such as not opening a bank account (Bertrand, Mullainathan, & Shafir, 2006), not applying for available welfare support (Currie, 2004), engagement in rent-to-own contracts for expensive commodities (Zikmund-Fisher & Parker, 1999), and purchasing state lottery tickets at higher rates (despite these tickets offering the lowest rate of return of any legal gambling initiative; Clotfelter, Cook, Edell, & Moore, 1999; for a review, see Hall, 2012).

Rather than attribute such behavioral patterns to supposedly inherent inadequacies of members of subordinate groups, SDT points to ways in which these self-debilitating behaviors can be a product of the dynamics of oppression itself. The high incidence of violence among subordinate group members, for example, might be understood through extant theories regarding the tendency of people (a) to behave in ways that reinforce stereotypes imposed on them (Chen & Bargh, 1997; Snyder & Swann, 1978), (b) to take an oppositional stance to systems that oppress them (e.g., Ogbu, 2008), or (c) to channel anxiety about being at the bottom of increasingly unequal status hierarchies into aggressive interactions aimed at bolstering personal honor (Henry, 2009; Sidanius & Pratto, 1999, ch. 9). Research on stereotype threat allies with this approach, showing how mere reminders that one is in a group that has a bad reputation with respect to a trait being assessed, such as intelligence in the case of Black Americans, can trigger poorer performance on measures of that trait than when such reminders are absent (Steele & Aronson, 1995). Also supportive of the role of hierarchical dynamics in triggering hierarchy-supporting behaviors is evidence that perceived discrimination among low-status group members is strongly related to negative health behaviors (Pascoe & Smart, 2009).

Even more persuasive is evidence that experimentally induced experiences of low status or deprivation can elicit the same group-debilitating behaviors that were predicted by SDT (i.e., Sidanius & Pratto, 1999). In one line of studies concerning the psychological effects of poverty, behavioral economists induced a sense of resource scarcity in middle-income participants by asking them to play computerized games in which they had few versus plentiful resources (Shah, Mullainathan, & Shafir, 2012). Those who experienced scarcity ended up making decisions that hampered their game performance, such as borrowing resources from future rounds, and thus engaging in cycles of debt that mimic the damaging and self-reinforcing nature of financial debt among the poor (Shah et al., 2012). A follow-up set of studies shows how the cognitive constraints imposed by poverty can lead to the impression that the poor are less intelligent than the rich. Running experiments with shoppers in a New Jersey mall and sugar cane farmers in India, Mani, Mullainathan, Shafir, and Zhao (2013) demonstrated how the same person can appear to have less cognitive control and intelligence when he or she is preoccupied with financial strain, compared to when free of such financial worries. Experiments by Sheehy-Skeffington and Sidanius (2014a) demonstrate how such deficits in cognitive performance, and even downstream financial decisions, can be a product not only of absolute resource scarcity but also of relative scarcity, linking it back to the dynamics of oppression. In three studies, participants drawn from an American college, online, and low-income samples, who were randomly assigned to believe that they were near the bottom of the socioeconomic ladder, performed worse on three measures of executive functioning than did those led to believe they were near the top of the ladder. An additional study demonstrated that such impairments in executive functioning carried over into poor performance on a realistic financial task relying on such processes: identifying the best of three credit card loan offers (Sheehy-Skeffington & Sidanius, 2014a).

While the cognitive strain of poverty and low status may be one mechanism through which subordination elicits group-debilitating behavior, another important mechanism is the psychology of low social power. Recent research on this topic converges on the observation that being experimentally assigned to feel low in power triggers a prevention-focused, inhibition-oriented system of self-regulation (Keltner, Gruenfeld, & Anderson, 2003). This in turn impairs psychological responses supportive of one's own advancement, such as confidence (Anderson & Galinsky, 2006), awareness of rewards (Anderson & Berdahl, 2003), and engagement in goal-relevant actions (Berdahl & Martorana, 2006; Galinsky et al., 2003). Supportive of the claim that the psychology of powerlessness is a feature of intergroup disadvantage, Sheehy-Skeffington and Sidanius (2014b) showed that the experimentally induced perception that one is at the bottom of the socioeconomic hierarchy leads to a decrease in self-reported efficacy and control, which in turn increases the likelihood of making decisions that harm one's well-being.

In sum, the early claim that behavioral asymmetry of those at the top and bottom of the hierarchy is both a robust feature of, and contributor to, group-based social hierarchy has been bolstered by subsequent evidence originating across disciplines and national contexts. Even more intriguing is emerging evidence that the temporary experience of subordination itself can elicit behaviors that enhance such subordination through processes that would affect any of us were we to find ourselves in such situations.

Asymmetric Mobilization

SD theorists have also revisited ideas put forth in earlier work regarding ideological mechanisms that help sustain intergroup inequality. SDT proposes that in the same way that there are consequential differences in the behavioral repertoires of dominant and subordinate groups (Cauley et al., 1991; Skeffington & Sidanius, 2014a; Sidanius & Pratto, 1999; Steinberg et al., 1992), there are also differences in the patterns of ideological endorsement across the social status continuum (Levin et al., 1998; Mitchell & Sidanius, 1993; Sidanius, 1993; Sidanius, Pratto, & Rabinowitz, 1994). This is to say, in addition to adopting suboptimal behavioral patterns, subordinate groups are also less ideologically oriented in their groups' interest than are dominant groups (Sidanius & Pratto, 1999).

Cotterill et al. (2015) demonstrate that these patterns are more pervasive than work to date suggests, while also providing evidence for why they occur. The authors draw on ideas from the literature on the psychology of legitimacy (e.g., Jost & Major, 2001), which shows that high- and low-status groups alike are motivated to see the status quo as relatively fair and just (Jost & Banaji, 1994). An important observation from this literature is that for high-status groups, seeing the system as legitimate also means seeing the advantages enjoyed by one's group as legitimate (Jost, 2001; Jost & Burgess, 2002). On the other hand, for members of low-status groups, perceiving the system as legitimate is at odds with wanting the best for one's group (Jost, 2001; Jost & Burgess, 2002).

Furthering this reasoning, Cotterill et al. (in prep) predicted that the relatively pervasive tendency to perceive the status quo as legitimate might blunt group-serving behavior even among those low-status group members who care deeply about and identify strongly with the group. Empirically this should manifest in a relatively weak correlation between low-status ingroup identity (i.e., the degree to which a person thinks about himself as a member of a group to which he belongs) and group-serving beliefs (i.e., support for HA and rejection of HE beliefs). On the other hand, because seeing the system as legitimate is consistent with seeing high-status groups' advantage as legitimate, Cotterill et al. (in prep) did not expect legitimacy to hinder high-status groups from connecting their sense of identity with their interests. They predicted that there would be a relatively strong correlation between high-status identity and beliefs that serve the interests of high-status groups (i.e., support for HE and rejection of HA beliefs).[2]

In fact, Cotterill et al. (in prep) argued that the difference in the degree to which high- versus low-status groups mobilize identity in group-serving ways (termed asymmetric identity mobilization, or AIM) has implications for hierarchy maintenance. AIM suggests that highly identified members of subordinate groups, those individuals who extant literature suggests should be among the most likely to engage in collective action to improve the status of the group (Van Zomeren, Postmes, & Spears, 2008) are not necessarily endorsing ideological beliefs conducive to such action. Moreover, to the extent that high-status groups do connect their identity with their interests, we might expect hierarchy to become further entrenched.

The authors document evidence of AIM across five studies, using data from two countries, and in the context of real and artificial groups. First, using large-scale survey data from both higher- and lower-class students, the authors found that whereas there was a relatively strong connection between higher-class ingroup identity and support for HE, as well as rejection of HA ideologies, there was a significantly weaker connection between lower-class identity and support for HA and rejection of HE beliefs. Speaking to the generalizability of AIM, the same pattern was found using data from both Blacks and Whites in the United States and high versus low castes in India.

Furthermore, Cotterill et al. (in prep) found evidence of AIM in the context of an artificial groups paradigm. When group-based status differences were made to seem legitimate, there was a strong connection between high-status identity and

---

2 It is important to note that social dominance theorists have considered the relationship between identity and ideology before. Levin et al. (1998) found that a strong positive relationship between White ingroup identity and HE ideological beliefs, and a strong negative relationship between Black ingroup identity and HE beliefs (a phenomenon they termed ideological asymmetry, or IA, drawing on the classic SDT use of the term). This would suggest that Blacks mobilize identity in service of their respective group interests to the same extent as Whites. Cotterill et al. (in prep) point out, however, that these data were collected in the aftermath of the Rodney King beating, at a time when inequality was salient, and perceived system legitimacy was low for Black participants.

beliefs that serve the interests of the high-status group, and a significantly weaker connection between low-status identity and beliefs that serve the interests of the low-status group. This suggests that AIM is not simply a product of ongoing intergroup relations over the decades (e.g., the general history of violence and oppression seen in both the United States and India), but it seems to be a relatively basic aspect of group psychology.

Speaking to the question of why AIM occurs, the authors also found that decreasing perceived legitimacy in the context of artificial groups experimentally "turned off" AIM, significantly increasing the connection between subordinate ingroup identification and group-serving ideologies. In a final study, Cotterill et al. found the same moderation by legitimacy in the context of real groups. When lower-income participants believed that members of their class group were mistreated by a higher-class group, there was a significantly stronger connection between identification with these fellow group members, and support for policies that would help them (relative to when perceived treatment of their fellow group members was good).

The Theory of Gendered Prejudice (TGP)

One of the latest and most controversial extensions of SDT has been the further development of the theory of gendered prejudice (see McDonald et al., 2011). Built on the foundations of the Trivers's parental investment sexual selection theory (Trivers, 1972), and gender-related hypotheses derived from SDT (Sidanius & Pratto, 1999; Sidanius, Pratto, & Bobo, 1994; discussed later; see also Sidanius, Sinclair, & Pratto, 2006), the theory of gendered prejudice argues that there are important intergroup implications of the fact that over the course of evolutionary time, males and females have been faced with somewhat different reproductive challenges. Because of the considerably higher reproductive costs borne by females (i.e., in terms of placentation, gestation, birthing, lactation), and the fact that females are reproductively capable for a considerably shorter portion of their life cycles than are males, the two sexes will tend to pursue slightly different reproductive strategies. Specifically, females tend to be significantly choosier in their selection of a reproductive partner and will gravitate toward males in command of relatively high material and social resources and a willingness to devote these resources to the care and protection of the females' offspring. One of the primary ways in which males could accumulate these qualities attractive to females was to engage in extractive coalitional behavior together with other ingroup males to expropriate resources (e.g., hunting grounds, foraging territory, foodstuffs) from the males of out-groups. In addition, male access to reproductive assets could also be facilitated by constraining the reproductive choices of females (such as through mate guarding). This chronic predatory orientation toward outgroup males and the tendency to control the sexual choices of females are thought to have formed the basis of relatively high chronic levels of socially dominating attitudes and behaviors found among males (for evidence of the link between non-egalitarian attitudes and sexual behaviors, see Kelly, Dubbs, & Barlow, 2015).

According to the theory of gendered prejudice, this interplay between male and female reproductive strategies resulted in the following set of expectations: (a) On average, males will display higher levels of aggression and discrimination against arbitrary-set outgroups, and higher average SDO levels than females, everything else being equal (a thesis known as the invariance hypothesis); (b) males will not only tend to be the primary protagonists of arbitrary-set aggression but will also be the primary targets of this aggression (a thesis originally labeled the subordinate male target hypothesis and later developed into the outgroup male target hypothesis; see Navarrete, McDonald, Molina, & Sidanius, 2010); (c) the motives for outgroup discrimination will be somewhat different for ingroup males and females. Whereas outgroup discrimination will be proximally driven by some combination of outgroup aggression and social dominance orientation among males, among females outgroup discrimination will be proximally driven by fear, especially fear of sexual coercion at the hands of outgroup males (what is known as the differential motives hypothesis). In sum, the TGP essentially argues that outgroup discrimination and aggression are gendered phenomena and that the dueling reproductive strategies of males and females have sociopolitical implications for humans.

A good deal of research has found results consistent with TGP. In a large meta-analysis, Lee et al. (2011) employed 52,826 respondents (27,745 women), gleaned from 206 samples and 118 independent reports. The results showed robust male/female differences in SDO in line with the invariance hypothesis. Furthermore, the effect size of this gender difference in SDO was more than twice that of arbitrary-set differences in SDO.

Even more provocative is recent evidence consistent with the differential motives hypothesis. For example, Navarrete and colleagues (Navarrete, Fessler, Fleischman, & Geyer, 2009) found that racial bias against Black Americans tracked pregnancy risk across the menstrual cycle among young White women. The higher a woman's risk of conception, the higher the level of discrimination against Black Americans. Furthermore, additional interrogation of the data revealed that this correlation was conditioned by the degree to which the participants felt chronically vulnerable to sexual coercion. While there was a general tendency for anti-Black bias to increase as a function of conception risk, this relation was particularly pronounced among those women who felt chronically vulnerable to sexual coercion (Navarrete et al., 2009).

To assure themselves that these initial conception risk/prejudice results generalized across outgroups and were not simply restricted to Black targets, McDonald and colleagues (2011) performed an extension of the initial conception risk study by using male targets from minimal groups. Their results showed that for males perceived to be physically formidable, the greater a woman's conception risk, the greater the evaluative bias against males from minimal groups.

While the empirical evidence supporting TGP is encouraging thus far, much more work needs to be done to explore its limiting conditions and cultural generalizability.

Criticisms of Social Dominance Theory

Three major lines of criticism have been leveled against SDT. One concerns the causal status of SDO in driving sociopolitical attitudes and behaviors. A second line of criticism questions the validity of the invariance hypothesis concerning gender (see earlier). The third faults SDT for its alleged inability to account for social change. We discuss each of these criticisms in turn.

The Causal Status of SDO

In spite of the large set of phenomena with which SDO has been shown to correlate (see e.g., Table 8.1), the interpretation of these relationships has been the subject of some controversy. Critics have centered on two interrelated yet distinct issues – namely, SDO's role as a causal agent influencing downstream social attitudes and behaviors and its generality (Kreindler, 2005; Lehmiller & Schmitt, 2007; Schmitt, Branscombe, & Kappen, 2003; Turner & Reynolds, 2003; see also Reynolds & Turner, 2006).

With regards to this first issue, social dominance theorists have long treated SDO as both influenced by the social structure and context and influencing structure and context via its effects on intergroup attitudes and behaviors (i.e., as both a cause and an effect). However, some critics have argued that SDO is simply epiphenomenal, a "mere reflection" of existing attitudes toward particular social groups within a particular salient intergroup context (Turner & Reynolds, 2003). On this account, the relationship between SDO and a given variable – for example, racism – is explained by positing that participants complete the SDO scale holding a particular social group in mind. Thus, rather than SDO assessing support for hierarchy between groups in general (as the scale intends), participants might mentally substitute "groups" with "racial groups." If true, SDO would reflect nothing more than levels of participants' prior racism, and the SDO-racism relationship would be entirely epiphenomenal. Along similar lines, this perspective holds that the robust gender difference in SDO (Lee et al., 2011) can be accounted for by assuming that men and women complete the scale thinking about the implications of SDO for their respective gendered identities (Huang and Liu, 2005; Schmitt et al., 2003; see also Kreindler, 2005). This self-categorization perspective has received some empirical support. For example, Huang and Liu (2005) found that the gender difference in SDO was present when gender was salient in Taiwanese participants' minds, but not when membership in regional groups was primed. Similarly, in one study, Schmitt et al. (2003, Study 2) found that the SDO scores of participants specifically told to think about race were associated with their racism but not with their sexism.

Although we see this contextualist critique of SDO as informative, we do not agree that it undermines the generality of SDO or its status as a contributor to (rather than a mere reflection of) downstream social attitudes and behaviors. As suggested by Sibley and Liu (2010), we argue that although it is possible to prime specific contexts and thus influence the SDO scale to appear as a mere proxy for prior attitudes toward particular groups, it nevertheless typically (a) serves as a robust measure of support for intergroup hierarchy across social contexts and (b) predicts specific intergroup attitudes and behaviors. Several strands of research provide support for our assertions.

One line of research emphasizes SDO's generality (Kteily et al., 2012; Sibley & Liu, 2010). Thus, for example, Sibley and Liu (2010) modified items of the SDO scale to generate SDO scores that were specific to ethnic, gender, and age stratification. These items were measured in addition to the standard SDO scale, which was assessed with modified instructions to "think about groups in general." These authors found that support for hierarchy between groups in each of these specific contexts *uniquely* contributed to overall SDO scores, suggesting that SDO could not be accounted for by attitudes in any one of these contexts. Moreover, using hierarchical linear modeling, they determined that a large portion of the overall variance across the context-specific SDO measures was *between-person*, reflecting individual differences in support of inequalities across these contexts that were predicted by the general measure of SDO. Kteily et al. (2012) replicated and extended these ideas among an American community sample. Specifically, similar to Sibley and Liu (2010), these authors assessed the standard SDO scale, as well as a series of SDO items modified to focus on each of the race, age, and gender contexts. Using structural equation modeling, they showed that overall SDO scores (i.e., scores on the standard scale) were significantly and uniquely predicted by each of the scales assessing SDO levels with respect to race, age, and gender specifically. Consistent with Sibley and Liu (2010), this suggests that SDO cannot be thought to merely reflect attitudes in any one of these contexts alone. Kteily et al. (2012) further examined whether SDO's generality was dependent on providing, as Sibley and Liu (2010) had, instructions to "think about groups in general" prior to participants completing the SDO scale, by randomly assigning one group of participants (but not the other) to receive these instructions. In fact, this experimental manipulation had no effect: Across both conditions, SDO could not be reduced to any one of race-SDO, gender-SDO, or age-SDO. Beyond assessing these context-specific forms of SDO, these authors further observed that across experimental condition, SDO – measured on a single measurement occasion – was associated with a wide range of variables (from war support, to welfare opposition, to liking HE jobs and disliking HA jobs). Kteily and colleagues argued that it is highly unlikely that participants were thinking about all these groups simultaneously as they completed the SDO scale, making it difficult to conclude that these correlations could be explained by a contextualist account.

A related stream of research addressing the causal status of SDO has moved beyond cross-sectional studies and employed cross-lagged longitudinal designs. This research has provided strong support consistent with a causal role for SDO. For example, Thomsen et al. (2010) observed that whereas SDO significantly predicted White Americans' sense of ethnic victimization in 2000, controlling for levels of that variable in 1997, the reverse was not true. Consistent with the view of SDO as both a cause and effect, Sibley and Liu (2010) found some evidence of reciprocal cross-lagged paths between overall SDO and measures of context-specific inequality support over a 5-month period. Similarly, but over a 4-year period, Kteily et al. (2011) found that SDO and outgroup affect exerted significant cross-lagged effects on each other (see also Dhont, Van Hiel, & Hewstone, 2014; Sibley, Wilson, & Duckitt, 2007). However, when they assessed self-reported levels of friendship with racial outgroup members, they observed that SDO contributed to decreased outgroup friendships over time but not the reverse. Building on this recent research, evidence for SDO as a cause (as well as an effect) would benefit from experimental manipulations of SDO that documented increases in HE attitudes and behaviors across a range of social contexts.

In sum, SDO correlates with intergroup attitudes across a wide spectrum of social contexts, is uniquely associated with multiple context-specific inequality measures, and longitudinally predicts outgroup attitudes, (self-reported) behavior and even personality. Notwithstanding certain contextual influences on SDO, this pattern of results is highly inconsistent with a view of SDO as a mere epiphenomenon, shifting dramatically from one context to another. Rather, although SDO can be influenced to reflect context-specific attitudes, it seems to represent individuals' generalized orientation toward inequality between groups across social contexts, an orientation that has important social consequences.

The Invariance Hypothesis

As mentioned earlier, the invariance hypothesis states that males are expected to have higher SDO scores than females, all else being equal (see Sidanius & Pratto, 1999; Sidanius et al., 1994). More than 20 years of empirical research has shown this to be the most well-documented finding in the entire SDT literature[3] (see Lee et al., 2011). Thus, the controversy no longer concerns the facts of the case, but rather how this highly documented gender difference is to be interpreted. While cultural determinists and social role theorists (e.g., Eagly, 1987) prefer to interpret this gender difference as a result of socialization into social roles and context-specific power differences between men and women, SD theorists interpret this difference through the lens of evolutionary processes (see "Theory of Gendered Prejudice"). It is also possible, of course, that both perspectives are valid. SDO can

---

3 For competing evidence using much smaller samples, see Batalha et al., 2011. See also Küpper and Zick, 2011.

be partly socialized and evolutionary processes might predispose males toward higher SDO levels. The definitive adjudication between these two interpretations awaits future research.

Social Dominance Theory and Social Change

A final criticism of social dominance theory is the claim that it does not adequately account for social change (e.g., Huddy, 2004; Jost, 2011; Pratto, Stewart, & Bou Zeineddine, 2013; Turner & Reynolds, 2003). It is argued that by assuming the ubiquity of group-based hierarchy and the mechanisms that sustain it, SDT is not well equipped to account for changes to hierarchy. Indeed, the success of a growing field of research into collective action, much of which is based on social identity theory (see, e.g., Van Zomeren et al., 2008), might be seen as evidence that the latter theory is better equipped to account for incidents of group-based social protest and challenges to social hierarchy consistently observable in the global news media (Turner & Reynolds, 2003; see also Reicher, 2004). We break down this critique into two components, only one of which, we argue, is a valid criticism of SDT as originally formulated.

The first version of the social change-based critique of SDT is that it does not have coherent conceptual resources to deal with antiestablishment protest and other omnipresent social forces dedicated to challenging social hierarchy (Turner & Reynolds, 2003). We argue that this claim neglects SDT's explicit early theorizing of the presence, in every society, of forces that are not only hierarchy enhancing but also hierarchy attenuating. The latter includes egalitarian ideologies such as the United Nations Declaration of Human Rights, a broad range of counter-dominance discourses such as around the inegalitarian implications of capitalism, and social institutions that exert steady and continuous pressure toward more equal distribution of social value (Sidanius & Pratto, 1999; see also Boehm, 1999). It is precisely the dynamic nature of the clash between HE and HA forces, across levels of analysis, that uniquely equips SDT to account for complex societal processes and changes. Indeed, the original formulation of the theory acknowledged various types of social change that do occur, ranging from progressive legislative reforms (such as the American Civil Rights Acts of 1866, 1870, 1871, 1875, 1957, 1964, and 1965) that attenuated intergroup inequality, to separatist or anti-imperialist conflicts that destabilize, divide, or destroy societies (Sidanius & Pratto, 1999, pp. 35–36). Despite this, SD theorists point out that though the severity and specific nature of social hierarchy varies across time and social contexts, the fact of group-based social hierarchy itself seems to be a constant (see also Pratto et al., 2006). Thus, although the degree of domination and the specific groups dominating and being dominated might change, the phenomenon of group-based dominance seems remarkably stable. The 2012–2013 events in Egypt, where the Muslim Brotherhood supplanted an oppressive regime and then itself proceeded to quell opposition to its rule, provide a case in point. Thus, adequate theories of social change will need to explain not only the process by which oppressed groups supplant other oppressive groups but also the process by which hierarchy becomes re-entrenched. SDT provides the conceptual tools to explain both phenomena in turn. In other words, while the specific actors may change, the basic play remains the same.

A second version of this critique argues that whereas processes that radically alter societies are acknowledged in the theory, these processes are under-theorized and understudied within SDT (Pratto et al., 2013). Indeed, engaging in a dedicated examination of social change and of the assumptions of the theory regarding it may warrant more detailed development of some of the theory's nascent components. It is worth noting that the claim of SDT being logically incoherent, by assuming that which is to be proven – that is, the universality of group-based social hierarchy (Pratto et al., 2013) – misconstrues the basic assumptions and goals of SDT. The SDT project is not, in fact, trying to prove the universality or naturalness of group-based social hierarchy. Rather it starts with the observation that starting from the Holocene, human societies tend to be organized as group-based social hierarchies (see Bowles et al., 2010). Having made this observation, SDT then attempts to (a) engage in reverse engineering in trying to uncover the multileveled and interactive processes that are responsible for the production and maintenance of group-based hierarchy and (b) most importantly, explore how this form of social organization expresses itself in various forms of social oppression (e.g., racism, nationalism, and classism).

However, we agree that another area in need of more conceptual and empirical work is that of the balanced nature of HE and HA forces within societies and institutions, especially where such claims are grounded on assumed societal stability in a world in which many societies have in fact failed (Pratto et al., 2013). With this in mind, we are excited by ongoing conceptual innovations, such as on the multidimensional and fungible nature of power (Pratto, Lee, Tan, & Pitpitan, 2011), and the examination of meta-level, inter- and trans-societal dynamics (Pratto, Sidanius, Bou Zeineddine, Kteily, & Levin, 2014) which are extending and improving SDT's ability to speak to social instability and change.

Where Do We Go from Here? Some Remaining Questions

SD theorists have long argued that the production and maintenance of group-based hierarchy and its resultant systems of oppression are a function of processes operating at multiple levels of analysis. While some modest work has examined the processes responsible for the fit between individuals' sociopolitical attitudes (e.g., SDO levels, racism) and the hierarchical nature of social institutions in which individuals are embedded, the multilevel assumptions of SDT have yet to be comprehensively tested. There are a number of areas in which we need further evidence to clarify the specific multileveled interactive nature of the processes involved. In particular, we identify three aspects of a multilevel theory in which additional research is needed.

First, most of the research employing SDT as an organizing framework has used outcome variables at the individual level of analysis (for an exception see Mitchell & Sidanius, 1995). However, recent work has also begun to examine higher levels, looking at how between-nation differences in SDO are a function of such factors as nations' levels of democratization and gender empowerment (e.g., Fischer et al., 2012).

Second, we are in need of more research devoted to an examination of *cross-level* processes. We must begin to focus on the manner in which processes at one level of analysis both affect and are affected by processes at other levels of analysis (see, e.g., Hedström & Ylikoski, 2010; Staerklé, Sidanius, Green, & Molina, 2010). One rudimentary example of such cross-level processes is the person-institution work discussed by Haley and Sidanius (2005). These researchers began by reviewing evidence indicating that there is a matching or congruence between the hierarchy-relevant nature of social institutions and the hierarchy-relevant social attitudes and behavioral predispositions of personnel embedded within these institutions. For example, early work on SDT showed that Los Angeles police officers (i.e., hierarchy enhancers) had relatively high SDO scores, while attorneys in the public defender's office (i.e., hierarchy attenuators) had relatively low SDO scores (see Sidanius et al., 1994). Haley and Sidanius (2005) outlined five cross-level mechanisms that were argued to be responsible for this person-institution matching: (a) *self-selection*, or the tendency for individuals to select those social institutions that are congruent with their hierarchy-relevant social attitudes. For example, people with relatively high SDO scores will be positively attracted to careers in the internal security organizations (e.g., secret police), and negatively attracted to careers designed to help the stigmatized and the oppressed (e.g., civil rights organizations), (b) *institutional selection*, or the process by which social institutions will tend to select personnel with congruent hierarchy-relevant social attitudes and behavioral predispositions, (c) *institutional socialization*, or the tendency for the hierarchy-relevant social attitudes and behaviors of personnel to become increasingly congruent with continued exposure to hierarchy-relevant institutional culture. For example, evidence has shown that police trainees become increasingly hostile to Blacks as exposure to training within the police academy increases (see, e.g., Teahan, 1975; for a related example see Guimond, 2000). The fourth matching process is known as (d) *differential institutional reward*. This describes the tendency for personnel whose hierarchy-relevant social attitudes are congruent with the hierarchy-relevant institutional culture to be positively rewarded and personnel whose hierarchy-relevant social attitudes and behaviors are incongruent with the hierarchy-relevant culture of the institutions within which they are placed to be negatively rewarded. The fifth and last process thought to be responsible for the matching of individuals and social institutions, and to yet be empirically tested, is (e) *differential attrition*, or the tendency for incongruents to leave social roles or social institutions that do not fit with their ideological orientation.

Although Haley and Sidanius (2005) presented relatively strong evidence for the first four of these processes feeding into person-institutional matching, they had no data concerning the precise mediating mechanisms between person-institutional mismatch and personnel attrition. Perhaps even more important for SD theorizing, research has yet to explore the question as to whether or not the degree of group-based social hierarchy, at the system-wide level, is caused by or even associated with the degree of person-institutional congruence. These are exciting questions that can be answered with research techniques dedicated to exploring multiple levels of analysis.

Finally, a large lacuna in SDT research, linked to the social change critique, is a coherent and well-thought-out explanation accounting for the vast differences in the degree of group-based social hierarchy across cultures, nations, and time. One suspects that explanations for the substantial differences in the severity of group-based social hierarchy across societies are to be primarily found in the net effects of higher-level, exogenous factors such as chronic economic scarcity, vulnerability to invasion by outgroups, population density, disease load, and climactic conditions. While no efforts have yet been made to incorporate such contextual, macro-level factors into SDT, we suggest that such incorporation could prove to be extremely illuminating in understanding the dynamics and prospects for our socially hierarchical world.

References

Aiello, A., Pratto, F., & Pierro, A., (2013). Framing social dominance orientation and power in organizational context. *Basic and Applied Social Psychology, 35*, 487–495.

Alexander, M.G., Levin, S., & Henry, P. J. (2005). Image theory, social identity, and social dominance: Structural characteristics and individual motives underlying international images. *Political Psychology, 26*, 27–45.

Altemeyer, B. (1998). The other "authoritarian personality." *Advances in Social Psychology, 30*, 47–92.

Ames, K. (2007). Slavery, household production and demography on the southern Northwest Coast. In C. Cameron (Ed.), *Invisible citizens and their consequences* (pp. 138–158). Salt Lake City: University of Utah Press.

Anderson, C., & Berdahl, J. L. (2002). The experience of power: Examining the effects of power on approach and inhibition tendencies. *Journal of Personality and Social Psychology, 83*, 1362.

Anderson, C., & Galinsky, A. D. (2006). Power, optimism, and risk-taking. *European Journal of Social Psychology, 36*(4), 511–536.

Arnold, J. E. (1993). Labor and the rise of complex hunter-gathers. *Journal of Archaeological Science, 12*, 75–119.

Asbrock, F., Gutenbrunner, L., & Wagner, U. (2013). Unwilling, but not unaffected – Imagined contact effects for authoritarians and social dominators. *European Journal of Social Psychology, 43*, 404–412.

Asbrock, F., Sibley, C. G., & Duckitt, J. (2010). Right-wing authoritarianism and social dominance orientation and the dimensions of generalized prejudice: A longitudinal test. *European Journal of Personality, 24*, 324–340.

Bäckström, M., & Björklund, F. (2007). Structural modeling of generalized prejudice. *Journal of Individual Differences, 28*, 10–17.

Bahns, A. J., & Crandall, C. S. (2013). The opposite of backlash: High-SDO people show enhanced tolerance when gay people pose little threat. *European Journal of Social Psychology, 43*, 286–291.

Bassett, J. F. (2010).The effects of mortality salience and social dominance orientation on attitudes toward illegal immigrants. *Social Psychology, 41*, 52–55.

Batalha, L., Reynolds, K. J., & Newbigin, C. A. (2011). All else being equal: Are men always higher in social dominance orientation than women? *European Journal of Social Psychology, 41*, 796–806.

Berdahl, J. L., & Martorana, P. (2006). Effects of power on emotion and expression during a controversial group discussion. *European Journal of Social Psychology, 36*, 497–509.

Bergh, N. Akrami, N., Sidanius, J., & Sibley, C. G. (in press). Is group membership necessary for understanding generalized prejudice? A re-evaluation of why prejudices are interrelated. *Journal Personality and Social Psychology.*

Bertrand, M., Mullainathan, S., & Shafir, E. (2006). Behavioral economics and marketing in aid of decision making among the poor. *Journal of Public Policy and Marketing, 25*, 8–23.

Bikman, N., & Sunar, D. (2013). Difficult dialogs: Majority group members' willingness to talk about inequality with different minority groups. *International Journal of Intercultural Relations, 37*, 467–476.

Bobbio, A., Canova, L.,& Manganelli, A. M. (2010). Conservative ideology, economic conservatism, and causal attributions for poverty and wealth. DOI 10.1007/ s12144-010-9086-6

Boehm, C. (1999). *Hierarchy in the forest: The evolution of egalitarian behavior.* Cambridge, MA: Harvard University Press.

Bowles, S., Smith, E. A., & Borgerhoff Mulder, M. (2010). The emergence and persistence of inequality in premodern societies: Introduction to the special section. *Current Anthropology, 51*, 7–17.

Branscombe, N. R., Schmitt, M. T., & Harvey, R. D. (1999). Perceiving pervasive discrimination among Black Americans: Implications for group identification and well-being. *Journal of Personality and Social Psychology, 77*, 135–149.

Caricati, L. (2007). The relationship between social dominance orientation and gender: The mediating role of social values. *Sex Roles, 57*, 159–171.

Cauley, J. A., Donfield, S. M., LaPorte, R. E., & Warhaftig, N. E. (1991). Physical activity by socioeconomic status in two population based cohorts. *Medicine & Science in Sports & Exercise, 23*, 343–352.

Charles-Toussaint, G. C., & Crowson, M. H. (2010). Prejudice against international students: The role of threat perceptions and authoritarian dispositions in U.S. students. *The Journal of Psychology, 144*, 413–428.

Chen, M., & Bargh, J. A. (1997). Nonconscious behavioral confirmation processes: The self-fulfilling consequences of automatic stereotype activation. *Journal of Experimental Social Psychology, 33*(5), 541–560.

Cheon, B. K., Im, D.-M., Harada, T., Kim, Ji-S., Mathur, V. A., Scimeca . . . Chiao, J. Y. (2011). Cultural influences on neural basis of intergroup empathy. *NeuroImage*, *57*, 642–650.

Chiao, J. Y., Mathur, V. A., Harada, Y., & Lipke, T. (2009). Neural basis of preference for human social hierarchy versus egalitarianism. *Annals of the New York Academy of Sciences*, *1167*, 174–181.

Choma, B. L., Hanoch, Y., Gummerum, M., & Hodson, G. (2013). Relations between risk perceptions and socio-political ideology are domain- and ideology-dependent. *Personality and Individual Differences*, *54*, 29–34.

Christ, O., Sibley, C. G., & Wagner, U. (2012). Multilevel modeling in personality and social psychology. In K. Deaux & M. Snyder (Eds.), *The Oxford handbook of poersonality and social psychology* (pp. 239–260). Oxford: Oxford University Press.

Christopher, A. N., Zabel, K. L., Jones, J. R., & Marek, P. (2008). Protestant ethic ideology: Its multifaceted relationships with just world beliefs, social dominance orientation, and right-wing authoritarianism. *Personality and Individual Differences*, *45*, 473–477.

Clotfelter, C. T., Cook, P. J., Edell, J. A., & Moore, M. (1999). *State lotteries at the turn of the century: Report to the national gambling impact study commission.* Retrieved October 26, 2014, from http://govinfo.library.unt.edu/ngisc/reports/lotfinal.pdf.

Cohen, A., Vigoda, E., & Samorly, A. (2001). Analysis of the mediating effect of personal-psychological variables on the relationship between socioeconomic status and political participation: A structural equations framework. *Political Psychology*, *22*(4), 727–757.

Cohrs, J. C., & Stelzl, M. (2010). How ideological attitudes predict host society members' attitudes toward immigrants: Exploring cross-national differences. *Journal of Social Issues*, *66*, 673–694.

Costello, K. & Hodson, G. (2009). Exploring the roots of dehumanization: The role of animal–human similarity in promoting immigrant humanization. *Group Processes & Intergroup Relations*, *13*, 3–22.

Costello, K., & Hodson, G. (2011). Social dominance-based threat reactions to immigrants in need of assistance. *European Journal of Social Psychology*, *41*, 220–231.

Costello, K., & Hodson, G. (2014). Explaining dehumanization among children: The interspecies model of prejudice. *British Journal of Social Psychology*, *53*, 175–197.

Cotterill, S., Sidanius, J., Bhardwaj, A., & Kumar, V. (2014). Social dominance orientation and social attitudes in India: The mediation role of karma. *Journal of Social and Political Psychology*, *2*, 98–116.

Cotterill, S., Sidanius, J., Kteily, N., Ho, A., Bhardwaj, A., & Kumar, V. (2015). Ideological Undermobilization: The missing link between low-status ingroup identity and ideology. *Journal of Social and Political Psychology*, *2*, 98–116.

Cozzolino, P. J., & Snyder, M. (2008). Good times, bad times: How personal disadvantage moderates the relationship between social efforts to win. *Personality and Social Psychology Bulletin*, *34*, 1420–1433.

Crawford, J. T. (2012). The ideologically objectionable premise model: Predicting biased political judgments on the left and right. *Journal of Experimental Social Psychology*, *48*, 138–151.

Cross, J. R., Cross, T. L., & Finch, H. (2010). Maximizing student potential versus building community: An exploration of right-wing authoritarianism, social dominance orientation and preferred practice among supporters of gifted education. *Roeper Review, 32*, 235–248.

Crowson, M. H. (2009). Nationalism, internationalism, and perceived UN irrelevance: Mediators of relationships between authoritarianism and support for military aggression as part of the war on terror. *Journal of Applied Social Psychology, 39*, 1137–1162.

Crowson, M.H.,& Brandes, J. A. (2010). Predicting community opposition to inclusion in schools: The role of social dominance, contact, intergroup anxiety, and economic conservatism. *The Journal of Psychology, 144*, 121–144.

Crowson, M. H., & Brandes, J. A. (2014). Predicting pre-service teachers' opposition to inclusion of students with disabilities: A path analytic study. *Social Psychology of Education, 17*, 161–178.

Crowson, M. H., Brandes, J. A., & Hurst, R. J. (2013). Who opposes rights for persons with physical and intellectual disabilities? *Journal of Applied Social Psychology, 43*, E307–E318.

Crowson, M. H., & Gries, P. H. (2010). Do right-wing authoritarianism and social dominance orientation predict anti-China attitudes? *Psicología Política, 40*, 7–29.

Currie, J. (2004). *The take up of social benefits*. Working Paper No. 10488, National Bureau of Economic Research, Cambridge, MA.

Dambrun, M. (2007). Understanding the relationship between racial and support for the death penalty: The racist punitive bias hypothesis. *Social Justice Research, 20*, 228–249.

Danso, H. A., Sedlovskaya, A., Suanda, S. H. (2007). Perceptions of immigrants: Modifying the attitudes of individuals higher in social dominance orientation. *Personality and Social Psychology Bulletin, 33* doi: 10.1177/0146167207301015

Dambrun, M., Kamiejski, R., Haddadi, N., & Duarte, S. (2009). Why does social dominance orientation decrease with university exposure to the social sciences? The impact of institutional socialization and the mediating role of "geneticism." *European Journal of Social Psychology, 39*, 88–100.

De Cremer, D., Cornelis, I., & Van Hiel, A. (2008). To whom does voice in groups matter? Effects of voice on affect and procedural fairness judgments as a function of social dominance orientation. *Journal of Social Psychology, 148*, 61–76.

De Zavala, A. G., Cichocka, A., & Iskra-Golec, I. (2013). Collective narcissism moderates the effect of in-group image threat on intergroup hostility. *Journal of Personality and Social Psychology, 104*, 1019–1039.

Dhont, K., & Hodson, G. (2014). Why do right-wing adherents engage in more animal exploitation and meat consumption? *Personality and Individual Differences, 64*, 12–17.

Dhont, K., Van Hiel, A., & Hewstone, M. (2014). Changing the ideological roots of prejudice: Longitudinal effects of ethnic intergroup contact on social dominance orientation. *Group Processes & Intergroup Relations, 17*(1), 27–44.

Dickens, T. E., & Sergeant, M. J. T. (2008). Social dominance and sexual orientation. *Journal of Evolutionary Psychology, 6*, 57–71.

Duckitt, J. (2001). A dual-process cognitive-motivational theory of ideology and prejudice. *Advances in Experimental Social Psychology, 33*, 41–113.

Duckitt, J., & Sibley, C. G. (2010). Right-wing authoritarianism and social dominance orientation differentially moderate intergroup effects on prejudice. *European Journal of Personality, 24*, 583–601.

Duriez, B. (2011). Adolescent ethnic prejudice: Understanding the effects of parental extrinsic versus intrinsic goal promotion. *The Journal of Social Psychology, 151*, 441–454.

Eagly, A. (1987). *Sex differences in social behavior: A social role interpretation.* Hillsdale, NJ: Erlbaum.

Esses, V. M., & Hodson, G. (2006). The role of lay perceptions of ethnic prejudice in the maintenance and perpetuation of ethnic bias. *Journal of Social Issues, 62*, 453–468.

Esses, V. M., Veenvliet, S., Hodson, G., & Mihic, L. (2008). Justice, morality, and the dehumanization of refugees. *Social Justice Research, 21.* doi 10.1007/s11211-007-0058-4

Esses, V. M., Wagner, U., Wolf, C., Preiser, M., & Wilbur, C. J. (2006). Perceptions of national identity and attitudes toward immigrants and immigration in Canada and Germany. *International Journal of Intercultural Relations, 30*, 653–669.

Feather, N. T., & McKee, I. R. (2008). Values and prejudice: Predictors of attitudes towards Australian Aborigines. *Australian Journal of Psychology, 60*, 80–90.

Federico, C. M., Hunt, C. V., & Ergun, D., (2009). Hunr, and ideology: Translating "competitive jungles" and "dangerous worlds" into ideological reality. *Social Justice Research, 22*, 259–279.

Federico, C. M., Weber, C. R., Ergun, D., & Hunt, C. (2013). Mapping the connections between politics and morality: The multiple sociopolitical orientations involved in moral intuition. *Political Psychology, 34*, 589–610.

Ferreira, M. C., Fischer, R., Barreijros, P., Pilati, R., & Milfont, T. L. (2012). Unraveling the mystery of Brazilian Jeitinho: A cultural exploration of social norms. *Personality and Social Psychology Bulletin, 33*, 331–344.

Feygina, I. (2013). Social justice and the human–environment relationship: Common systemic, ideological, and psychological roots and processes. *Social Justice Research, 26*, 363–381.

Fischer, R., Hanke, K., & Sibley, C. G. (2012). Cultural and institutional determinants of social dominance orientation: A cross-cultural meta-analysis of 27 countries. *Personality and Social Psychology Bulletin, 33*, 437–467.

Foels, R., & Reid, L. D. (2010). Gender differences in social dominance orientation: The role of cognitive complexity. *Sex Roles, 62*, 684–692.

Galinsky, A. D., Gruenfeld, D. H., & Magee, J. C. (2003). From power to action. *Journal of Personality and Social Psychology, 85*, 453.

Gatto, J., & Dambrun, M. (2012). Authoritarianism, social dominance, and prejudice among junior police officers: The role of the normative context. *Social Psychology, 43*, 61–66.

Gerber, M. M., & Jackson, J. (2013). Retribution as revenge and retribution as just deserts. *Social Justice Research, 26*, 61–80.

Gilles, I., Bangerter, A., Clemence, A., Green, E. G. T., Krings, F., Mouton, A. . . . Wagner-Egger, P. (2013). Collective symbolic coping with disease threat and othering: A case of avian influenza. *British Journal of Social Psychology, 52*, 83–102.

Goldberg, S. (1994). *Why men rule: A theory of male dominance.* Chicago, IL: Open Court.

Green, E.G.T., & Auer, F. (2013). How social dominance orientation affects union participation: The role of union identification and perceived union instrumentality. *Journal of Community & Applied Social Psychology, 23*, 143–156.

Green, E. G. T., Krings, F., Staerklé, C., Bangerter, A., Wagner-Egger, P., & Bornand, T. (2010). Keeping the vermin out: Perceived disease threat and ideological orientations as predictors of exclusionary immigration attitudes. *Journal of Community & Applied Social Psychology, 20*, 299–316.

Green, E. G. T., Thomsen, L., Sidanius, J., Staerklé, C., & Potanina, P. (2009). Reactions to crime as a hierarchy regulating strategy: The moderating role of social dominance orientation. *Social Justice Research, 22*, 416–436.

Guimond, S. (2000). Group socialization and prejudice: The social transmission of intergroup attitudes and beliefs. *European Journal of Social Psychology, 30*, 335–354.

Guimond, S., Chatard, A., Martinot, D. M, Crisp, R., & Redersdorff, S. (2006). Social comparison, self-stereotyping, and gender differences in self-construals. *Journal of Personality and Social Psychology, 90*, 221–242.

Guimond, S., Crisp, R. J., De Oliveira, P., Kameijski, R., Keily, N., Kuepper, B. . . . Zick, A. (2013). Diversity policy, social dominance, and intergroup relations: Predicting prejudice in changing social and political contexts. *Journal of Personality and Social Psychology, 104*, 941–958.

Guimond, S., Dambrun, M., Michinov, N., & Duarte, S. (2003). Does social dominance generate prejudice? Integrating individual and contextual determinants of intergroup cognitions. *Journal of Personality and Social Psychology, 84*, 697–721.

Guimond, S., De Oliveira, P., Kamiesjki, R., & Sidanius, J. (2010). The trouble with assimilation: Social dominance and the emergence of hostility against immigrants. *Journal of Personality and Social Psychology, 34*, 642–650.

Gutiérrez, A. S., & Unzueta, M. M. (2013). Are admissions decisions based on family ties fairer than those that consider race? Social dominance orientation and attitudes toward legacy vs. affirmative action policies. *Journal of Experimental Social Psychology 49*, 554–558.

Harding, J. F., & Sibley, C. G. (2011). Social dominance and the disassociation between explicit and implicit representations of equality. *Journal of Community & Applied Social Psychology, 21*, 407–418.

Haley, H., & Sidanius, J. (2005). Person–organization congruence and the maintenance of group-based social hierarchy: A social dominance perspective. *Group Processes & Intergroup Relations, 8*(2), 187–203. doi: 10.1177/1368430205051067

Hall, C. C. (2012). Behavioral decision research, social class and implications for public policy. In H. R. Markus & S. T. Fiske (Eds.), *Facing social class: How societal rank influences interaction* (pp. 175–194). New York: Russell Sage Foundation.

Hart, J., Hung, J. A., Glick, P., & Dinero, R. E. (2012). He loves her, he loves her not: Attachment style as a personality antecedent to men's ambivalent sexism. *Personality and Social Psychology Bulletin, 38*, 1495–1505.

Hedström, P., & Ylikoski, P. (2010). Causal mechanisms in the social sciences. *Annual Review of Sociology, 36*(1), 49–67. doi: 10.1146/annurev.soc.012809.102632

Henry, P. J. (2009). Low-status compensation: A theory for understanding the role of status in cultures of honor. *Journal of Personality and Social Psychology, 97*(3), 451.

Henry, P. J., Sidanius, J., Levin, S., & Pratto, F. (2005). Social dominance orientation, authoritarianism, and support for intergroup violence between the Middle East and America. *Political Psychology*, *26*, 569–583.

Hindricks, P., Verkuyten, M., & Coenders, M. (2014). Dimensions of social dominance orientation: The roles of legitimizing myths and national identification. *European Journal of Personality*, *28*, 538–549. doi: 10.1002/per.1955

Ho, A. K., Sidanius, J., Cuddy, A., & Banaji, M. (2013). Status boundary enforcement and the categorization of Black-White biracials. *Journal of Experimental Social Psychology*, *49*, 940–943.

Ho, A. K., Sidanius, J., Levin, D., & Banaji, M. (2011). Evidence for hypodescent and racial hierarchy in the perception of biracial individuals. *Journal of Personality and Social Psychology*, *100*, 492–506.

Ho, A. K., Sidanius, J., Pratto, F., Levin, S., Thomsen, L., Kteily, N., & Sheehy-Skeffington, J. (2012). Social dominance orientation: Revisiting the structure and function of a variable predicting social and political attitudes. *Personality and Social Psychology Bulletin*, *38*, 583–606.

Hodson, G., & Costello, K. (2007). Interpersonal disgust, ideological orientations, and dehumanization as predictors of intergroup attitudes. *Psychological Science*, *18*, 691–698.

Hodson, G., & Esses, V. M. (2005). Lay perceptions of ethnic prejudice: Causes, solutions, and individual differences. *European Journal of Social Psychology*, *35*, 329–344.

Hodson, G., MacInnis, C. C., & Rush, J. (2010). Prejudice-relevant correlates of humor temperaments and humor styles. *Personality and Individual Differences*, *49*, 546–549.

Hodson, G., Rush, J., & MacInnis, C. C. (2010). A joke is just a joke (except when it isn't): Cavalier humor beliefs facilitate the expression of group dominance motives. *Journal of Personality and Social Psychology*, *99*, 660–682.

Huang, L., & Liu, J. (2005). Personality and social structural implications of the situational priming of social dominance orientation. *Personality and Individual Differences*, *38*(2), 267–276.

Huddy, L. (2004). Contrasting theoretical approaches to intergroup relations. *Political Psychology*, *25*, 947–967.

Islam, G., & Zyphur, M. J. (2005). Power, voice, and hierarchy: Exploring the antecedents of speaking up in groups. *Group Dynamics: Theory, Research, and Practice*, *9*, 93–103.

Jackson, L. E., & Gaertner, L. (2010). Mechanisms of moral disengagement and their differential use by right-wing authoritarianism and social dominance orientation in support of war. *Aggressive Behavior*, *36*, 238–250.

Jackson, L. M., Bitacola, L. M., Janes, L. M., & Esses, V. M. (2013). Intergroup ideology and environmental inequality. *Analyses of Social Issues and Public Policy*, *13*, 327–346.

James, A., & James, A. (2008). *Key concepts in childhood studies*. London: Sage Publications.

Jeffries, C. H., Horney, M. J., Sutton, R. M., Douglas, K. M., & Bain, P. G. (2012). The David and Goliath principle: Cultural, ideological, and attitudinal under-pinnings of the normative protection of low status groups from criticism. *Personality and Social Psychology Bulletin*, *20*, 1053–1065.

Jetten, J., & Iyer, A. (2010). Different meanings of the social dominance orientation concept: Predicting political attitudes over time. *British Journal of Social Psychology, 49*, 385–404.

Jost, J. T. (2011). System justification theory as compliment, complement, and corrective to theories of social identification and social dominance. In D. Dunning (Ed.), *Social motivation* (pp. 223–263). New York: Psychology Press.

Jost, J. T., & Banaji, M. R. (1994). The role of stereotyping in system-justification and the production of false consciousness. *British Journal of Social Psychology, 33*, 1–27.

Jost, J., Banaji, M., & Nosek, B. (2004). A decade of system justification theory: Accumulated evidence of conscious and unconscious bolstering of the status quo. *Political Psychology, 25*(6), 881–919.

Jost, J. T., & Burgess, D. (2000). Attitudinal ambivalence and the conflict between group and system justification motives in low status groups. *Personality and Social Psychology Bulletin, 26*, 293–305.

Jost, J. T., & Major, B. (2001). *The psychology of legitimacy: Emerging perspectives on ideology, justice, and intergroup relations.* Cambridge University Press.

Jost, J. T., & Thompson, E. P. (2000). Group-based dominance and opposition to equality as independent predictors of self-esteem, ethnocentrism, and social policy attitudes among African Americans and European Americans. *Journal of Experimental Social Psychology, 36*(3), 209–232. doi: 10.1006/jesp.1999.1403

Kahn, K., Ho, A. K., Sidanius, J., & Pratto, F. (2009). The space between us and them: Perceptions of status differences. *Group Processes & Intergroup Relations, 12*, 591–604.

Kelly, A. S., Dubbs, S. L., & Barlow, F. K. (2015). Social dominance orientation predicts heterosexual men's adverse reactions to romantic rejection. *Archives of Sexual Behavior, 44*, 903–919.

Keltner, D., Gruenfeld, D. H., & Anderson, C. (2003). Power, approach, and inhibition. *Psychological Review, 110*(2), 265.

Kemmelmeir, M. (2005). The effects of race and social dominance orientation in simulated juror decision making. *Journal of Applied Social Psychology, 35*, 1030–1045.

Kennett, D. J., Winterhalder, B., Bartruff, J., & Erlandson. J. (2008). An ecological model for the emergence of institutionalized social hierarchies in California's North Channel Islands. In Stephen Shennan (Ed.), *Evolutionary analysis of cultural behavior* (pp. 297–324). Berkeley: University of California Press.

Kenny, D. A. (1975). Cross-lagged panel correlation: A test for spuriousness. *Psychological Bulletin, 82*, 887–903.

Krauss, S. (2006). Does ideology transcend culture? A preliminary examination in Romania. *Journal of Personality, 74*. doi: 10.1111/j.1467-6494.2006.00408.x

Kreindler, S. (2005). A dual group processes model of individual differences in prejudice. *Personality and Social Psychology Review, 9*(2), 90–107.

Kteily, N., Bruneau, E., Waytz, A., & Cotterill, S. (2015). The "Ascent of Man": Theoretical and empirical evidence for blatant dehumanization. *Journal of Personality and Social Psychology.*

Kteily, N., Cotterill, S., & Sidanius, J., Sheehy-Skeffington, J., & Bergh, R. (2014). "Not one of us": Predictions and consequences of denying ingroup characteristics to ambiguous targets. *Personality and Social Psychology Bulletin, 40*, 1231–1247.

Kteily, N., Ho, A. K., & Sidanius, J. (2012). Hierarchy in the mind: The predictive power of social dominance orientation across social contexts and domains. *Journal of Experimental Social Psychology, 48*(2), 543–549.

Kteily, N. S., Sidanius, J., & Levin, S. (2011). Social dominance orientation: Cause or "mere effect"? Evidence for SDO as a causal predictor of prejudice and discrimination against ethnic and racial outgroups. *Journal of Experimental Social Psychology, 47*(1), 208–214.

Kugler, M. B., Cooper, J., & Nosek, B. A. (2010). Group-based dominance and opposition to equality correspond to different psychological motives. *Social Justice Research, 23*, 117–155.

Kugler, M., Jost, J. T., & Noorbaloochi, S. (2014). Another look at moral foundations theory: Do authoritarianism and social dominance explain liberal-conservative differences in "moral" intuitions. *Social Justice Research, 27*, 413–431.

Küpper, B., & Zick, A. (2011). Inverse gender gap in Germany: Social dominance orientation among men and women. *International Journal of Psychology, 46*, 33–45.

Laham, S. M., Tam, T., Lalljee, M., Hewstone, M., & Voci, A. (2010). Respect for persons in the intergroup context: Self–other overlap and intergroup emotions as mediators of the impact of respect on action tendencies. *Group Processes and Intergroup Relations, 13*, 301–317.

Lalonde, R. N., Giguere, B., Fontaine, M., & Smith, A. (2007). Social dominance orientation and ideological asymmetry in relation to interracial dating and transracial adoption in Canada. *Journal of Cross-Cultural Psychology, 38*, 559–572.

Lee, I., Pratto, F., & Johnson, B. T. (2011). Intergroup consensus/disagreement in support of group-based hierarchy: An examination of socio-structural and psycho-cultural factors. *Psychological Bulletin, 137*(6), 1029.

Lehmiller, J., & Schmitt, M. (2007). Group domination and inequality in context: Evidence for the unstable meanings of social dominance and authoritarianism. *European Journal of Social Psychology, 37*(4), 704–724.

Leone, L., & Chirumbolo, A. (2008). Conservatism as motivated avoidance of affect: Need for affect scales to predict conservatism measures. *Journal of Research in Personality, 42*, 755–762.

Leone, L., Desimoni, M., & Chirumbolo, A. (2014). Interest and expertise moderate the relationship between rightwing attitudes, ideological self-placement and voting. *European Journal of Personality, 28*(1), 2–13.

Lessig, L. (2011). *Republic, lost: How money corrupts Congress – and a plan to stop it.* New York: Hachette Book Group.

Levene, R., & Dickens, T. E. (2008). Sex-related invariance across cultures in an online role-playing game. *Journal of Evolutionary Psychology, 6*, 141–148.

Levin, S., Sidanius, J., Rabinowitz, J. L., & Federico, C. (1998). Ethnic identity, legitimizing ideologies and social status: A matter of ideological asymmetry. *Political Psychology, 19*, 373–404.

Leong, C-H. (2008). A multilevel research framework for the analyses of attitudes toward immigrants. *International Journal of Intercultural Relations, 32*, 115–129.

Levin, S., Henry, P.J., Pratto, F., & Sidanius, J. (2009). Social dominance and social identity in Lebanon: Implications for support of violence against the West. In Jeff Victoroff & Arie W. Kruglanski, (Eds.), *Psychology of terrorism: Classic and contemporary insights. Key readings in social psychology* (pp. 253–267). New York: Psychology Press.

Levin, S., Matthews, M., Guimond, S., Sidanius, J. Pratto., F., Nteily, N. ... Dover, T. (2012). Assimilation, multiculturalism, and colorblindness: Mediated and moderated relationships between social dominance orientation and prejudice. *Journal of Experimental Social Psychology 48*, 207–212.

Levin, S., Pratto, F., Matthews, M., Sidanius, J., & Kteily, N. (2013). A dual process approach to understanding prejudice toward Americans in Lebanon: An extension to intergroup threat perceptions and emotions. *Group Processes and Intergroup Relations, 16*, 139–158.

Levy, S. R., West, T. L., Ramirez, L., & Karanfantis, D. M. (2006). The Protestant work ethic: A lay theory with dual intergroup implications. *Group Processes & Intergroup Relations, 9*, 95–115.

Livi, S., Leone, L., Falgares, G., & Lombardo, F. (2014). Values, ideological attitudes and patriotism. *Personality and Individual Differences, 64*, 141–146.

Lock K., Pomerleau J., Causer L., Altmann, D. R., & McKee, M. (2005). The global burden of disease attributable to low consumption of fruit and vegetables: Implications for the global strategy on diet. *Bulletin of the World Health Organization, 85*, 100–108.

Malkin, G., & Ben Ari, R. (2013). Prejudice and "Vladimir's choice" among Israeli Arabs and Jews: Symmetrical vs. asymmetrical trends. *Group Processes & Intergroup Relations, 16*, 814–825.

Mani, A., Mullainathan, S., Shafir, E., & Zhao, J. (2013). Poverty impedes cognitive function. *Science, 341*(6149), 976–980.

Martin, D., Seppala, E., Heineberg, Y., Rossomando, T., Doty, J., Zimbardo, P. ... Zhou, Y. Y. (2014). Multiple facets of compassion: The impact of social dominance orientation and economic systems justification. *Journal of Business Ethics*. doi: 10.1007/s10551-014-2157-0

Mata, J., Ghavami, N. & Wittig, M. A. (2010). Understanding gender differences in early adolescents' sexual prejudice. *Journal of Early Adolescence, 30*, 50–75.

MacInnis, C. C., Busseria, M. A., Choma, B. L., & Hodson, G. (2013). The happy cyclist: Examining the association between generalized authoritarianism and subjective well-being. *Personality and Individual Differences, 55*, 780–793.

McDonald, M. M., Navarrete, C. D., & Sidanius, J. (2011). Developing a theory of gendered prejudice: An evolutionary and social dominance perspective. In R. Kramer, G. Leonardelli, & R. Livingston (Eds.), *Social cognition, social identity, and intergroup relations: A festschrift in honor of Marilynn Brewer* (pp. 189–220). New York: Psychology Press.

McFarland, S. (2010). Authoritarianism, social dominance, and other roots of generalized prejudice. *Political Psychology, 31*. doi: 10.1111/j.1467-9221.2010.00765.x

McFarland, S. G., & Adelson, S. (1996, July). *An omnibus study of personality, values, and prejudice.* Paper presented at the annual meeting of the International Society for Political Psychology, Vancouver, British Columbia.

McFarland, S., & Mathews, M. (2005). Who cares about human rights? *Political Psychology, 26*, 365–385.

McKay, P. F., & Avery, D. R. (2006). What has race got to do with it? Unraveling the role of racioethnicity in job seekers' reactions to site visits. *Personnel Psychology, 59*, 395–429.

Milfont, T. L., Richter, I., Sibley, C. G., Wilson, M. S., & Fischer, R. (2013). Environmental consequences of the desire to be dominate and be superior. *Personality and Social Psychology Bulletin*, *39*, 1127–1138.

Miller, D. A., Smith, E. R. & Mackie, D. M. (2004). Effects of intergroup contact and political predispositions on prejudice: Role of intergroup emotions. *Group and Intergroup Processes*, *7*, 221–237.

Milojev, P., Osborne, D., Greaves, L. M., Bulbulia, J., Wilson, M., Davies, C. L. … Sibley, C. G. (2014). Right-wing authoritarianism and social dominance orientation predict different moral signatures. *Social Justice Research*, *27*, 149–174.

Mitchell, M. & Sidanius, J. (1993). Group status and asymmetry in the relationship between ideology and death penalty support: A social dominance perspective. *National Journal of Sociology*, *7*, 67–93.

Mitchell, M., & Sidanius, J. (1995). Social hierarchy and executions in the United States: A social dominance perspective. The death penalty: A social dominance perspective. *Political Psychology*, *16*, 591–619.

Mosso, C., Briante, G., Aiello, A., & Russo, S. (2013). The role of legitimizing ideologies as predictors of ambivalent sexism in young people: Evidence from Italy and the USA. *Social Justice Research*, *26*, 1–17.

Navarrete, C. D., Fessler, D. M., Fleischman, D. S., & Geyer, J. (2009). Race bias tracks conception risk across the menstrual cycle. *Psychological Science*, *20*, 661–665.

Navarrete, C. D., McDonald, M. M., Molina, L. E., & Sidanius, J. (2010). Prejudice at the nexus of race and gender: An outgroup male target hypothesis. *Journal of Personality and Social Psychology*, *98*(6), 933.

Newheiser, A., Tausch, N., Dovidio, J. F., & Hewstone, M. (2009). Entitativity and prejudice: Examining their relationship and the moderating effect of attitude certainty. *Journal of Experimental Social Psychology*, *45*, 920–926.

Newman, B. J., Hartman, T. K., & Taber, C. S. (2014). Social dominance and the cultural politics of immigration. *Political Psychology*, *35*. doi: 10.1111/pops.12047

Nickerson, A. M., & Louis, W. R. (2008). Nationality versus humanity? Personality, identity, and norms in relation to attitudes toward asylum seekers. *Journal of Applied Social Psychology*, *38*, 796–817.

Nicol, A. A. M. (2009). Social dominance orientation, right-wing authoritarianism, and their relation with leadership styles. *Personality and Individual Differences*, *47*, 657–661.

Nicol, A. A. M., Roundint, K., & MacIntyre. (2011). The impact of social dominance orientation and right-wing authoritarianism on the relation between person–organization fit with commitment, satisfaction, and turnover intentions. *Personality and Individual Differences*, *51*, 893–898.

Nordenstam, S., & Ringström, A. (2013). Police database of Roma stirs outrage in Sweden. Reuters. www.reuters.com/article/2013/09/23/us-sweden-roma-idUSBRE 98M0EM20130923

O'Brien, K. S., Hunter, J. A., & Banks, M. (2007). Implicit anti-fat bias in physical educators: Physical attributes, ideology and socialization. *International Journal of Obesity*, *31*, 308–314.

Ogbu, J. U. (Ed.). (2008). *Minority status, oppositional culture, & schooling*. New York: Routledge.

Oldmeadow, J., & Fiske, S. T. (2007). System-justifying ideologies moderate status = competence stereotypes: Roles for belief in a just world and social dominance orientation. *European Journal of Social Psychology, 37*, 1135–1148.

Onraet, E., & Van Hiel, A. (2013). When threat to society becomes a threat to oneself: Implications for right-wing attitudes and ethnic prejudice. *International Journal of Psychology, 48*, 25–34. http://dx.doi.org/10.1080/00207594.2012.701747

Orange, R. (2013). Swedish riots spark surprise and anger. *The Guardian.* www.theguardian .com/world/2013/may/25/sweden-europe-news

Parkins, I. S., Fishbein, H. D., & Ritchey, P. N. (2006). The influence of personality on workplace bullying and discrimination. *Journal of Applied Social Psychology, 36*, 2554–2577.

Pascoe, E. A., & Smart, L. R. (2009). Perceived discrimination and health: A meta-analytic review. *Psychological Bulletin, 135*, 531–554.

Passini, S., & Villano, P. (2013). Judging moral issues in a multicultural society. *Swiss Journal of Psychology, 72*, 235–239.

Perkins, J. E., & Bourgeois, M. J. (2006). Perceptions of police use of deadly force. *Journal of Applied Social Psychology, 36*, 161–177.

Pichler, S., Varma, A., & Bruce, T. (2010). Heterosexism in employment decisions: The role of job misfit. *Journal of Applied Social Psychology, 40*, 2527–2555.

Ping Shao, C., Resnick, J., & Hargis, M. B. (2011). Helping and harming others in the workplace: The roles of personal values and abusive supervision. *Human Relations, 64*, 1051–1078.

Pinker, S. (2011). *The better angels of our nature: Why violence has declined.* New York: Viking Press.

Poteat, V. P., & Mereish, E. H. (2012). Ideology, prejudice, and attitudes toward sexual minority social policies and organizations. *Political Psychology, 33*. doi: 10.1111/ j.1467-9221.2012.00871.x

Poteat, V. P., & Spaniermen, L. B. (2010). Do the ideological beliefs of peers predict the prejudiced attitudes of other individuals in the group? *Group Processes and Intergroup Relations, 13*, 495–514.

Pratto, F., Lee, I., Tan, J., & Pitpitan, E. (2011). Power basis theory: A psycho-ecological approach to power. In D. Dunning (Ed.), *Social motivation* (pp. 191–222). New York: Psychology Press.

Pratto, F., Sidanius, J., Bou Zeineddine, F., Kteily, N., & Levin, S. (2014). When domestic politics and international relations intermesh: Subordinated publics' factional support within layered power structures. *Foreign Policy Analysis, 10*(2), 127–148.

Pratto, F., Sidanius, J., & Levin, S., (2006). Social dominance theory and the dynamics of intergroup relations: Taking stock and looking forward. *European Review of Social Psychology, 17*, 271–320.

Pratto, F., Sidanius, J., Stallworth, L. M., & Malle, B. F. (1994). Social dominance orienta- tion: A personality variable predicting social and political attitudes. *Journal of Personality and Social Psychology, 67*, 741–763.

Pratto, F., Stewart, A. L., & Bou Zeineddine, F. (2013). When inequality fails: Power, group dominance, and societal change. *Journal of Social and Political Psychology, 1*(1), 132–160. doi:10.5964/jspp.v1i1.97

Pula, K., McPherson, S., & Parks, C. D. (2012). Invariance of a two-factor model of social dominance orientation across gender. *Personality and Individual Differences, 52*, 385–389.

Ramirez, L., Levy, S. R., & Velilla, E., & Hughes, J. M. (2010). Considering the roles of culture and social status: The Protestant work ethic and egalitarianism. *Revista Latinoamericana de Psicología, 42*, 381–390.

Ratcliff, N. J., Bernstein, M. J., Cundiff, J. L., & Vescio, T. K. (2012). Seeing wrath from the top (through stratified lenses): Perceivers high in social dominance orientation show superior anger identification for high-status individuals. *Journal of Experimental Social Psychology, 48*, 1373–1376.

Reese, G., Proch, J., & Cohrs, J. C. (2014). Individual differences in responses to global inequality. *Analyses of Social Issues and Public Policy, 14*, 217–238.

Reicher, S. (2004). The context of social identity: Dominance, resistance, and change. *Political Psychology, 25*, 921–945.

Reynolds, K., & Turner, J. (2006). Individuality and the prejudiced personality. *European Review of Social Psychology, 17*, 233–270.

Rios, K., Finkelstein, S.R., & Landa, J. (2014). Is there a "fair" in fair-trade? Social dominance orientation influences perceptions of and preferences for fair-trade products. *Journal of Business Ethics*. doi: 10.1007/s10551-014-2221-9

Roccato, M. (2008). Right-wing authoritarianism, social dominance orientation, and attachment: An Italian study. *Swiss Journal of Psychology, 67*, 219–229.

Rosenblatt, V. (2012). Hierarchies, power inequalities, and organizational corruption. *Journal of Business Ethics, 111*, 237–251.

Rosenthal, L., & Levy, S. R. (2010). Understanding women's risk for HIV infection using social dominance theory and the four bases of gendered power. *Psychology of Women Quarterly, 34*, 21–35.

Rosette, A. S., Carton, A. M., Sperry, L. B., & Hewlin, P. F. (2013). Why do racial slurs remain prevalent in the workplace? Integrating theory on intergroup behavior. *Organization Science, 24*, 1402–1421.

Schmid, K., Hewstone, M., Küpper, B., Zick, A., & Wagner, U. (2012). Secondary transfer effects of intergroup contact: A cross-national comparison in Europe. *Social Psychology Quarterly, 75*, 28–51.

Schmitt, M. T., Branscombe, N., & Kappen, D. (2003). Attitudes toward group-based inequality: Social dominance or social identity? *British Journal of Social Psychology, 42*(2), 161–186.

Schmitt, M. T., & Wirth, J. H. (2009). Evidence that gender differences in social dominance orientation result from gendered self-stereotyping and group-interested responses to patriarchy. *Psychology of Women Quarterly, 33*, 429–436.

Seelman, K. L., & Walls, N. E. (2010). Person-organization incongruence as a predictor of right-wing authoritarianism, social dominance orientation, and heterosexism. *Journal of Social Work Education, 46*, 103–121.

Shah, A. K., Mullainathan, S., & Shafir, E. (2012). Some consequences of having too little. *Science, 338*, 682–685.

Sheehy-Skeffington, J., & Sidanius, J. (2014a). *Distracted looking up: Priming low socioeconomic status impairs executive functions*. Paper presented at the 17th General Meeting of the European Association of Social Psychology, Amsterdam, The Netherlands.

Sheehy-Skeffington, J., & Sidanius, J. (2014b). *Out of my hands: Low socioeconomic status diminishes perceptions of personal control and self-efficacy*. Manuscript under review.

Sibley, C. G. (2013). Social dominance and representations of the national prototype: The exclusionary emphasis hypothesis of national character. *International Journal of Intercultural Relations, 37*, 212–224.

Sibley, C. G., & Duckitt, J. (2010). The ideological legitimation of the status quo: Longitudinal tests of a social dominance model. *Political Psychology, 31*. doi: 10.1111/j.1467-9221.2009.00747.x

Sibley, C. G., & Liu, J. H. (2010). Social dominance orientation: Testing a global individual difference perspective. *Political Psychology, 31*(2), 175–207.

Sibley, C. G., & Wilson, M. (2007). Political attitudes and the ideology of equality: Differentiating support for liberal and conservative political parties in New Zealand. *New Zealand Journal of Psychology, 36*, 72–84.

Sibley, C. G., Wilson, M., & Duckitt, J. (2007). Antecedents of men's hostile and benevolent sexism: The dual roles of social dominance orientation and right-wing authoritarianism. *Personality and Social Psychology Bulletin, 33*(2), 160–172.

Sibley, C. G., Wilson, M. S., & Robertson, A. (2007). Differentiating the motivations and justifications underlying individual differences in Pakeha opposition to bicultural policy: Replication and extension of a predictive model. *New Zealand Journal of Psychology, 36*, 25–33.

Sidanius, J. (1993). The psychology of group conflict and the dynamics of oppression: A social dominance perspective. In S. Iyengar & W. McGuire (Eds.), *Explorations in Political Psychology* (pp. 183–219). Durham, NC: Duke University Press.

Sidanius, J., Haley, H., Molina, L., & Pratto, F. (2007). Vladimir's choice and the distribution of social resources: A group dominance perspective. *Group Processes and Intergroup Relations, 10*, 259–268.

Sidanius, J., Kteily, N., Sheehy-Skeffington, J., Ho, A., Sibley, C., & Duriez, B. (2013). "You're inferior and not worth our concern." *Journal of Personality, 81*, 313–323.

Sidanius, J., Levin, S., Federico, C., & Pratto, F. (2001). Legitimizing ideologies: The social dominance approach. In J. Jost & B. Major (Eds.), *The psychology of legitimacy: emerging perspectives on ideology, justice, and intergroup relations* (pp. 307–331). Cambridge University Press.

Sidanius, J., Liu, J., Shaw, J., & Pratto, F. (1994). Social dominance orientation, hierarchy-attenuators and hierarchy-enhancers: Social dominance theory and the criminal system. *Journal of Applied Social Psychology, 24*, 338–366.

Sidanius, J., Mitchell, M., Haley, H., & Navarrete, C. D. (2006). Support for harsh criminal sanctions and criminal justice beliefs: A social dominance perspective. *Social Justice Research, 19*, 433–449.

Sidanius, J., & Pratto, F. (1999). *Social dominance: An intergroup theory of social hierarchy and oppression*. New York: Cambridge University Press.

Sidanius, J., & Pratto, F. (2012). Social dominance theory. In P. A. M. Van Lange, A. W. Kruglanski, & E. T. Higgins (Eds.), *Handbook of theories of social psychology* (Vol. 2, pp. 418–438). London: Sage. doi:10.1348/014466603322127193

Sidanius, J., Pratto, F., & Bobo, L. (1994). Social dominance orientation and the political psychology of gender: A case of invariance? *Journal of Personality and Social Psychology, 67*, 998–101.

Sidanius, J., Pratto, F., & Mitchell, M. (1994). Ingroup identification, social dominance orientation, and differential intergroup social allocation. *Journal of Social Psychology*, *134*, 151–167.

Sidanius, J., Pratto, F., & Rabinowitz, J. (1994). Gender, ethnic status, and ideological asymmetry: A social dominance interpretation. *Journal of Cross-Cultural Psychology*, *25*, 194–216.

Sidanius, J., Sinclair, S., & Pratto, F. (2006). Social dominance orientation, gender and increasing college exposure. *Journal of Applied Social Psychology*, *36*, 1640–1653.

Sidanius, J., Van Laar, C., Levin, S., & Sinclair, S. (2003). Social hierarchy maintenance and assortment into social roles: A social dominance perspective. *Group Processes and Intergroup Relations*, *6*, 333–352.

Simmons, A. L., & Parks-Yancy, R. (2012). Were they joking? Depends on social dominance orientation. *Journal of Behavioral and Applied Management*, *13*(3), 213.

Snellman, A., & Ekehammar, B. (2005). Ethnic hierarchies, ethnic prejudice, and social dominance orientation. *Journal of Community & Applied Social Psychology*, *15*, 83–94.

Snellman, A., Ekehammar, B., & Akrami, N. (2009). The role of identification in social dominance orientation: Mediating or moderating the effect of sex? *Journal of Applied Social Psychology*, *39*, 999–1012.

Snyder, M., & Swann Jr., W. B. (1978). Behavioral confirmation in social interaction: From social perception to social reality. *Journal of Experimental Social Psychology*, *14* (2), 148–162.

Son Hing, L. S., Bobocel, D. R., Zanna, M. P., & McBridge, M. V. (2007). Authoritarian dynamics and unethical decision making: High social dominance orientation leaders and high right-wing authoritarianism followers. *Journal of Personality and Social Psychology*, *92*, 67–81.

Staerklé, C., Sidanius, J., Green, E., & Molina, L. (2010). Ethnic minority-majority asymmetry in national attitudes around the world: A multilevel analysis. *Political Psychology*, *31*, 491–519.

Steele, C. M., & Aronson, J. (1995). Stereotype threat and the intellectual test performance of African Americans. *Journal of Personality and Social Psychology*, *69*(5), 797.

Steinberg, L., Dornbusch, S., & Brown, B. B. (1992). Ethnic differences in adolescent achievement: An ecological perspective. *American Psychologist*, *47*(6), 723–729.

Tam, K-P., Leung, K-Y, & Chiu, C-Y. (2008). On being a mindful authoritarian: Is need for cognition always associated with less punitiveness? *Political Psychology*, *29*, 77–91.

Tausch, N., & Hewstone, M. (2010). Social dominance orientation attenuates stereotype change in the face of disconfirming information. *Social Psychology*, *41*,169–176.

Teahan, J. E. (1975). A longitudinal study of attitude shifts among Black and White police officers. *Journal of Social Issues*, *31*, 47–56.

Thomsen, L., Green, E. G., Ho, A. K., Levin, S., van Laar, C., Sinclair, S., & Sidanius, J. (2010). Wolves in sheep's clothing: SDO asymmetrically predicts perceived ethnic victimization among White and Latino students across three years. *Personality and Social Psychology Bulletin*, *36*(2), 225–238.

Thomsen, L., Green, E. G., & Sidanius, J. (2008). We will hunt them down: How social dominance orientation and right-wing authoritarianism fuel ethnic persecution of immigrants in fundamentally different ways. *Journal of Experimental Social Psychology, 44*, 1455–1464.

Trivers, R.L. (1972). Parental investment and sexual selection. In B. Campbell (Ed.), *Sexual selection and the descent of man* (pp.136–179). Chicago: Aldine-Atherton.

Turner, J., & Reynolds, K. (2003). Why social dominance theory has been falsified. *British Journal of Social Psychology, 42*(2), 199–206.

Umphress, E. E., Simmons, A. L., Boswell, W. R., & Triana, M. D. (2008). Managing discrimination in selection: The influence of directives from an authority and social dominance orientation. *Journal of Applied Psychology, 93*, 982–993.

Umphress, E. E., Smith-Crowe, K., Brief, A. P., Dietz, J., & Watkins, M. B. (2007). When birds of a feather flock together and when they do not: Status composition, social dominance orientation, and organizational attractiveness. *Journal of Applied Psychology, 92*, 396–409.

Unzueta, M. M, Knowles, E. D., & Ho, G. C. (2012). Diversity is what you want it to be: How social-dominance motives affect construals of diversity. *Psychological Science, 23*, 303–309.

Van Hiel, A., & Kossowska, M. (2006). Having few positive emotions, or too many negative feelings? Emotions as moderating variables of authoritarianism effects on racism. *Personality and Individual Differences, 40*, 919–930.

Van Hiel, A., & Kossowska, M. (2007). Contemporary attitudes and their ideological representation in Flanders (Belgium), Poland, and the Ukraine. *International Journal of Psychology, 42*, 16–26.

Van Vugt, M., De Cremer, D., & Janssen, D. P. (2007). Gender differences in cooperation and competition: The male-warrior hypothesis. *Psychological Science, 18*, 19–23.

Van Vugt, M., & Tybur, J. T. (in press). The evolutionary psychology of status. In D. Buss (Ed.), *Handbook of evolutionary psychology*. Hoboken, NJ: Wiley.

Van Zomeren, M., Postmes, T., & Spears, R. (2008). Toward an integrative social identity model of collective action: A quantitative research synthesis of three socio-psychological perspectives. *Psychological Bulletin, 134*(4), 504.

Verba, S., Schlozman, K. L., & Brady, H. E. (1995). *Voice and equality: Civic voluntarism in American politics* (Vol. *4*). Cambridge, MA: Harvard University Press.

Vezzali, L.,& Giovannini, D. (2011). Cross-group friendships, social dominance orientation and secondary transfer effect. *Testing, Psychometrics, Methodology in Applied Psychology, 18*, 181–194.

von Collani, G., Grumm, M., & Streicher, K. (2010). An investigation of the determinants of stigmatization and prejudice toward people living with HIV/AIDS. *Journal of Applied Social Psychology, 40*, 1747–1766.

Wilson, M. S. (2010). Assessing the "gender gap" in New Zealand politics: The mediating effects of social dominance orientation in student and general population. *New Zealand Journal of Psychology, 39*, 38–44.

Wilson, M. S., & Sibley, C. (2013). Social dominance orientation and right-wing authoritarianism: Additive and interactive effects on political conservatism. *Political Psychology, 34*, 277–284.

Wilson, M. S., & White, J. T. (2010). Assessing the "gender gap" in New Zealand politics: The mediating effects of social dominance orientation in student and general populations. *New Zealand Journal of Psychology, 39*, 38–44.

Worthington, R. L., Navarro, R. L., Loewy, M., & Hart, J. (2008). Color-blind racial attitudes, social dominance orientation, racial-ethnic group membership and college students' perceptions of campus climate. *Journal of Diversity in Higher Education, 1*, 8–19.

Yeagley, E., Morling, B., & Nelson, M. (2007). Nonverbal zero-acquaintance accuracy of self-esteem, social dominance orientation, and satisfaction with life. *Journal of Research in Personality, 41*(5), 1099–1106.

Zakrisson, I. (2008). Gender differences in social dominance orientation: Gender invariance may be situation invariance. *Sex Roles, 59*, 254–263.

Zikmund-Fisher, B. J., & Parker, A. M. (1999). Demand for rent-to-own contracts: A behavioral economic explanation. *Journal of Economic Behavior & Organization, 38*(2), 199–216.

9 The Dual Process Motivational Model of Ideology and Prejudice

John Duckitt and Chris G. Sibley

Early research on prejudice resulted in two important empirical observations. First, the kinds of social groups or categories that are targeted with prejudice vary markedly in different societies; and second, individuals within societies vary markedly in the degree to which they are generally prejudiced or generally tolerant. This suggested that we need two kinds of theories to explain prejudice. In the first case, societal or intergroup theories have focused on particular kinds of intergroup relations (e.g., intergroup competition, threat, or inequality) that would cause prejudice to be directed against specific groups and to be widely shared within a particular society. Thomas Pettigrew (1958) referred to this as the "specificity of prejudice." In the second case, individual difference theories have focused on certain stable characteristics of individuals (e.g., personality, values, motives, or ideological beliefs) that could cause them to be generally more or less prejudiced against all or most target groups. Early theorists referred to this as the "generality of prejudice" or "generalized prejudice" (e.g., Allport, 1954).

More recently, however, theories have emerged that can encompass both individual and intergroup factors within their explanatory frameworks. The dual process model (DPM) is one such approach. It was originally formulated to explain systematic individual differences in generalized prejudice, which it did in terms of two basic motivational orientations that dispose individuals to be generally prejudiced or tolerant. It also, however, proposed that these two motivational orientations would be largely activated by socially shared situational and intergroup factors (such as intergroup competition, threat, and inequality). In this way both individual and social or intergroup factors would operate together to generate prejudices. These prejudices are both specific (widely shared and directed against targets specific to a particular society) and generalized (with individuals in these societies varying systematically in the degree to which they were generally prejudiced or tolerant).

The DPM encompasses three closely intertwined explanatory contributions to the understanding of prejudice. First, it conceptualizes the two major social attitudinal predictors of individual differences in prejudice as expressions of two distinct motivational goal or value dimensions. Second, the DPM shows how these two motivationally based ideological dimensions are shaped by and emerge from different social and psychological bases. And third, the DPM provides an explanation of why these two motivationally based dimensions cause prejudice and describes how they operate in a complementary and interactive fashion with social and intergroup causes of prejudice. These explanatory contributions are successively described in the following three sections together with brief reviews of research testing their implications.

DPM 1: Two Motivationally Based Ideological Attitude Dimensions

In initially focusing on individual differences in prejudice, the DPM built most immediately on important findings by McFarland (1998; McFarland & Adelson, 1996) and Altemeyer (1998). These were that individuals' tendencies to be generally prejudiced or generally tolerant were powerfully (and relatively independently) predicted by two important individual difference dimensions, right-wing authoritarianism (RWA) and social dominance orientation (SDO; see Chapter 8, this title), with no other psychological factors adding notably to prediction.[1] The RWA scale was developed by Altemeyer (1981) to measure authoritarian attitudes, with items expressing beliefs in coercive social control, obedience, and respect for existing authorities, as well as conformity to traditional moral and religious norms. It refined and narrowed Adorno, Frenkel-Brunswick, Levinson, and Sanford's (1950) earlier "F" (fascist) scale. The SDO scale was developed by Pratto, Sidanius, Stallworth, and Malle (see also Chapter 8, this title) to measure "a general altitudinal orientation toward intergroup relations, reflecting whether one prefers such relations to be equal, versus hierarchical" (1994, p. 742). A great deal of research has subsequently confirmed the role of RWA and SDO as powerful predictors of prejudice (see meta-analyses by Proch, 2013; Sibley & Duckitt, 2008), and findings from longitudinal studies suggest that these effects are causal (e.g., Asbrock, Sibley, & Duckitt, 2010; Duriez, Vansteenkiste, Soenens, & De Witte, 2007; Kteily, Sidanius, & Levin, 2011; Sibley, Wilson, & Duckitt, 2007a).

RWA (and its predecessor, the F-scale) was originally seen as reflecting a personality dimension. However, research has shown that RWA is highly correlated with, and factors together with, attitudinal measures of social and cultural conservatism. On the other hand, SDO tends to be equivalently highly correlated with attitudinal measures of anti-egalitarianism and economic conservatism (for a review of evidence, see Duckitt & Sibley, 2009, pp. 99–100). These findings suggest that RWA and SDO are best viewed as direct measures of two broad social or ideological attitude dimensions. In addition, research has also shown that both

---

1 Some studies have reported significant additional effects (e.g., McFarland, 2010) but these effects have typically been weak and not consistently replicated.

RWA and SDO correlate powerfully with different kinds of social values or motivational goals, as for example assessed by the Schwartz Values Inventory or equivalent values measures (for a review of the evidence, see Duckitt & Sibley, 2010a, pp. 6–7). RWA is correlated with the higher-order value (or motivational goal) dimension of Conservation (values of Conformity, Tradition, Security) versus Openness (Self-direction, Stimulation, Hedonism), and SDO with the Self-enhancement (Power, Achievement) versus Self-transcendence (Universalism, Benevolence).

The DPM therefore explicitly conceptualized RWA and SDO as two broad motivationally (or value) based social attitude or ideological dimensions:

- RWA is defined as a threat-driven attitudinal expression of the values or motivational goals of collective security, control, stability, and order.
- SDO is defined as a competition-driven attitudinal expression of the values or motivational goals of power, dominance, and superiority.

This conceptualization then led on to explanations of how different sets of social and personality factors underlie the motivationally based dimensions of RWA and SDO, and of how and why RWA and SDO would operate to cause both generalized prejudice in individuals and socially shared patterns of prejudice directed against specific outgroups or minorities.

DPM 2: Social and Psychological Bases of Ideological Attitudes

The DPM was developed inductively by systematizing prior research findings into a coherent framework to explain how both psychological and situational factors influenced RWA (or social-cultural conservatism) and SDO (or anti-egalitarianism or economic conservatism). This model, which is summarized diagrammatically in Figure 9.1, proposes that the motivationally based values expressed in RWA and SDO are made chronically salient for individuals by both their personalities and their social worldview beliefs (formed by exposure to and socialization in particular social environments).

Thus, high RWA, which expresses the value or motivational goal of establishing and maintaining collective or societal security, order, stability, and cohesion (as opposed to individual freedom, autonomy, and self-expression) is made chronically salient for individuals by their socialized belief that the world they live in is dangerous, threatening, and unpredictable (as opposed to safe, secure, stable, and predictable). The causal personality traits would be those indicative of social conformity, which in the Big Five typology would be low Openness and high Conscientiousness. These traits result in a preference for order, structure, stability, and security. They therefore increase RWA directly, as well as indirectly through increasing dangerous world (DW) beliefs (since individuals higher in social

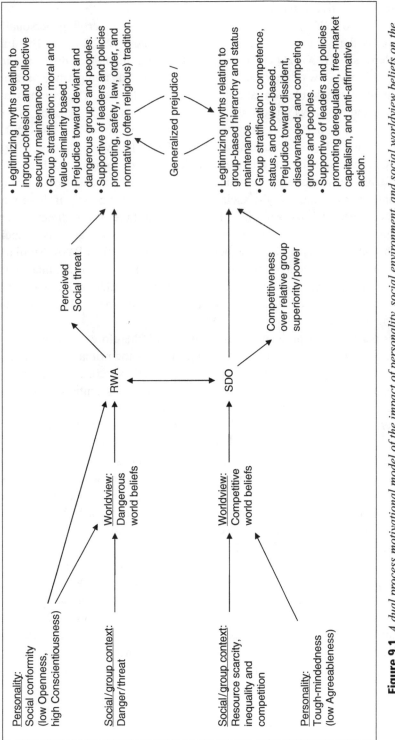

Figure 9.1 *A dual process motivational model of the impact of personality, social environment, and social worldview beliefs on the two ideological attitude dimensions of right-wing authoritarianism (RWA) and social dominance orientation (SDO) and corresponding prejudice-related outcomes.*

conformity should identify more strongly with the existing social order, and therefore be more sensitive to threats to it).

In the case of SDO, the model proposes that the underlying personality dimension is that of tough- versus tender-mindedness (i.e., low on Big Five Agreeableness or HEXACO Honesty-Humility), and this in turn disposes individuals to adopt a view of their social world as a ruthlessly competitive jungle in which the strong and able win, and the weak and unfit lose. This competitive-jungle worldview (CW) makes the value or motivational goals of power, dominance, and superiority over others chronically salient for individuals, which are then expressed attitudinally in high SDO. The two worldview beliefs, DW and CW, would tend to be relatively stable over time for individuals because of their origin in personality and socialization. However, they could change significantly with changes in the social environment, particularly if these were seen to be substantial and enduring. Thus, marked increases in threats to and disruption of societal order, cohesion, stability, and traditional values (social threat) should increase people's DW beliefs and therefore their RWA. Similarly, increases in the salience and importance of personal or group dominance and power over others, and of conflict and competition over relative dominance and power within society or between groups (competitive threat), should increase CW beliefs and therefore levels of SDO.[2]

The primary causal predictions from the DPM therefore are that the two ideological attitude dimensions of RWA and SDO, as the primary determinants of prejudice, emerge from two different sequential patterns. These involve particular trait dimensions (Big Five Openness and Conscientiousness versus Big Five Agreeableness and HEXACO Honesty-Humility respectively), and social environmental influences (social versus competitive threats respectively), which differentially influence individuals' social worldview beliefs (DW versus CW beliefs), and through them their ideological attitudes. This causal sequence can be seen as emerging developmentally, with the proposal being that basic behavioral dispositions or personality will start emerging in early childhood, and these (in conjunction with social environmental influences) will then influence the developmental socialization of schema-based worldview beliefs in later childhood and early adolescence. These will then (together with personality) influence the crystallization of values and ideological attitudes, which probably occur mainly in mid to later adolescence and early adulthood. While this causal pattern is directly predicted by the DPM, the model does not necessarily exclude possible reciprocal causal effects. For example, it seems quite possible that once values and ideological attitudes have crystallized, they help shape lifestyle, friendships, career choices, and romantic partners and then impact causally back on worldviews and personality dispositions. Self-justification and

2   DW and CW would be particularly high for those who would stand to lose from these threats – that is, for those in positions of traditional social authority in the case of DW, and those high in status, power, and dominance in the case of CW. Thus, although these social and competitive threats can often be differentiated, they would also overlap substantially, particularly in more traditional societies.

cognitive consistency would also produce reciprocal causal effects. Thus, whereas the model does not make any specific predictions about reciprocal causal effects, it does not exclude them.

This model of how personality, social situational factors, and social worldview might influence the ideological attitudes of RWA and SDO has generated a great deal of research over the past decade and a half using a variety of methodological approaches. Correlational studies have investigated cross-sectional relationships between personality or worldviews and ideological attitudes, while structural equation modeling (SEM) has been used to test all or most of the relationships proposed by the model simultaneously. Longitudinal studies have provided stronger tests of the causalities of these relationships, and experimental research has tested whether manipulating situational variables would have hypothesized effects on worldviews and through them on RWA and SDO. This research is reviewed in the following sections.

Correlational Studies

Much of the research on the relationship between the ideological attitudes of RWA and SDO and personality has used the Big Five personality trait dimensions. A meta-analytic review of this research in 2008 summarized the results of 71 studies using 22,068 participants (Sibley & Duckitt, 2008). The findings were fully consistent with the DPM, indicating that RWA was predicted primarily by low Openness (meta-analytic $r = -.36$)[3] and more weakly by higher Conscientiousness ($r = .15$), and that SDO was primarily predicted by low Agreeableness ($r = -.29$). This meta-analysis also confirmed that effects of these Big Five personality dimensions on prejudice would be largely mediated via RWA and SDO, as proposed by the DPM.

A more extensive recent meta-analysis including not only higher-order Big Five measures but also more specific, narrow-band personality trait measures (outside the Big Five framework) summarized the results of 1,115 studies over 60 years (Proch, 2013). The findings confirmed those from the earlier meta-analysis for both measures of the Big Five and the more specific traits measured outside the Big Five framework, since those predicting RWA were clearly classifiable as Openness and Conscientiousness subtraits, with the former much the stronger predictor. Those predicting SDO were clearly identifiable as Agreeableness subtraits.[4]

---

3 A qualification that can be noted here is that several studies have found that it is the cognition, curiosity, or intellect aspect of the higher-order Openness personality dimension rather than the experiential, culture, or aesthetics aspect that predicts RWA (Leone, Desimoni, & Chirumbolo, 2012; Onraet, Van Hiel, Roets, & Cornelis, 2011).

4 Proch (2013) did find two weak effects not predicted by the DPM, being a correlation of −.13 for Neuroticism with RWA, and −.12 for Openness with SDO. These would likely have been eliminated when controls for confounding variables were used, as indeed was the case for the similarly weak correlation between Openness and SDO in the Sibley and Duckitt (2008) meta-analysis.

Although these two meta-analyses used only self-report measures of personality, studies using interviewer, peer, and observer ratings of personality have obtained consistent findings (Block & Block, 2006; Cohrs, Kämfe-Hargrave, & Riemann, 2012; Lippa & Arad, 1999). A few studies have also investigated correlations between the HEXACO Big Six personality dimensions and found, again as expected by the DPM, that low Openness was the strongest predictor of RWA, and low Honesty-Humility of SDO (Lee, Ashton, Ogunfowora, Bourdage, & Shin, 2010; Leone et al., 2012; Sibley, Harding, Perry, Asbrock, & Duckitt, 2010).

Research on social worldviews and ideological attitudes was also recently reviewed and meta-analysed (Perry, Sibley, & Duckitt, 2013a). The findings over 46 studies and 12,939 participants found, again as expected by the DPM, that DW beliefs were substantially correlated with RWA (meta-analytic $r = .37$) and negligibly with SDO ($r = .08$), while CW beliefs were powerfully associated with SDO $(r = .53)$ and negligibly with RWA $(r = .11)$. Perry et al. (2013a) also refined the original worldview measures developed or adapted by Duckitt (2001) to eliminate item-content overlap between scales. They then replicated the meta-analytic effects in new research using the refined social worldview measures.[5] Perry and Sibley (2010) have also developed new frequency estimation indices that more directly assess the social schemas underlying dangerous and competitive worldview beliefs. This approach asks people to estimate the percentage of people in society that would engage in different dangerous/threatening or competitive/exploitative behaviors if they knew that they could get away with it. In two studies, these frequency estimation indices showed the expected pattern of covariation, with the DW schematic index predicting RWA and not SDO, and the CW schematic index predicting SDO and not RWA (see also Perry, Sibley, & Duckitt, 2013b).[6]

Numerous studies have shown that various individual-level indices or societal-level indicators of social threats predict RWA, or earlier measures of authoritarianism (for a recent brief overview, see Duckitt, 2013). Studies that have rated the degree of fear or concern people experience over social threat have also found significant positive correlations with RWA but not SDO (e.g., Choma, Hanoch, Hodson, & Gummerum, 2014; Shaffer & Duckitt, 2013; see also Duckitt & Fisher, 2003; Jugert & Duckitt, 2009; Napier, 2014). Other studies have used broad indices of various threats that did not differentiate between the kind of threats (social and competitive) that might differentially affect RWA and SDO and found, as would be predicted from the DPM, significant positive correlations with both RWA and SDO, though typically these would be more powerful for RWA (i.e., recent meta-analyses by Onraet, Van Hiel, Dhont, & Pattyn, 2013, and Onraet, Van Hiel, &

---

5 Perry et al.'s (2013a) new findings using the refined social worldview measures found a stronger correlation between DW and RWA than in the meta-analysis, which was similar in magnitude to that for CW and SDO.

6 A more recent study using an internet sample in Brazil did not replicate this, but this could have been due to a lack of differentiation between the two frequency estimation worldview measures which correlated at .80 in that sample (Cantal, Milfont, Wilson, & Gouveia, 2015).

Cornelis, 2013). These two meta-analyses also tested another important prediction from the DPM, which is that the kinds of threat that should influence these ideological attitudes would be external societal threats, rather than personal, psychological, or internal threats (e.g., anxiety, low self-esteem). The latter has been the prediction from earlier personality-based theories of authoritarianism or conservatism (e.g., Adorno et al., 1950; Allport, 1954; Jost, Glaser, Kruglanski, & Sulloway, 2003; Wilson, 1973). Both the two recent meta-analyses (for individual- and societal-level threat indices), however, showed that it was indeed external, societal-level threat, and not internal threat (when external threat was controlled) that predicted RWA and SDO (Onraet, Van Hiel, Dhont, & Pattyn, 2013; Onraet, Van Hiel, & Cornelis, 2013).

Overall, therefore, correlational studies have supported the differential relations proposed for personality and social worldview dimensions with ideological attitudes. These findings have clearly shown Big Five low Openness and high Conscientiousness, and DW beliefs, correlated with RWA. They have also clearly shown Big Five low Agreeableness (or HEXACO low Honesty-Humility) and CW beliefs correlated with SDO.[7] Moreover, research has also shown that it is external, societal-level threats that are correlated with ideological attitudes and not internal, psychological threats. While consistent with the DPM, these correlational effects have all pertained to hypothesized relationships tested separately from each other. More powerful tests of a complex model such as the DPM are possible using structural equation modeling, where all or most of the relationships proposed by the model can be tested simultaneously in the same sample, while controlling for measurement error. Such studies are reviewed in the next section.

Structural Equation Modeling (SEM)

A number of studies have used SEM to test the full DPM of how personality and social worldview beliefs might predict ideological attitudes (Duckitt, 2001; Duckitt, Wagner, du Plessis, & Birum, 2002; Leone e al., 2012; Sibley & Duckitt, 2009; Van Hiel, Cornelis, & Roets, 2007). These studies have used both student and community samples and have been conducted in four countries (Belgium, Italy, New Zealand, and the United States). Despite minor differences in some of the effects, they have overall obtained substantially consistent findings. The important consistent findings across all samples have been that the strongest predictors were low Openness (or Social Conformity) and DW

---

7 Research has also shown significant interaction between Big Five Openness and DW beliefs, or closely related social threat measures, in predicting RWA (Dallagio & Roccato, 2010) or Conservatism (see meta-analysis by Sibley, Osborne, & Duckitt, 2012). Specifically, the effects of Openness on RWA or Conservatism are stronger when DW beliefs are low (suggestive of a threat-constraint mechanism). Our analyses of preliminary data suggests the possibility that Big Five Agreeableness and CW beliefs may also interact significantly in predicting SDO, but with the effect stronger for persons higher in CW. Both effects seem intuitively plausible and not inconsistent with the DPM.

beliefs for RWA, and low Agreeableness (or low Honesty-Humility, or high Toughmindedness) and CW beliefs on SDO. Conscientiousness was a somewhat inconsistent and generally much weaker predictor of either RWA or DW beliefs. These SEM findings also indicated an interesting asymmetry in the way in which personality and worldview predicted ideological attitudes. The effects of low Agreeableness (or low Honesty-Humility, or high Toughmindedness) were invariably fully or largely mediated through CW beliefs, but those of low Openness (or Social Conformity) on RWA were mainly direct, and only weakly mediated through DW beliefs.[8]

Not all these SEM studies included measures of prejudice. However, those that did (Duckitt, 2001; Duckitt et al., 2002) and other SEM studies examining the effects of either the personality or social worldview constructs proposed by the model separately on both ideological attitudes and prejudice, clearly supported a further proposition from the DPM. This was that effects of personality and worldviews on prejudice would be entirely or largely mediated through RWA and SDO (Crowson, 2009; Ekehammar, Akrami, Gylje, & Zakrisson, 2004; Levin, Pratto, Matthews, Sidanius, & Kteily, 2012; Weber & Federico, 2007).

Longitudinal Research

The correlational findings reviewed in the previous two sections were impressively consistent with the effects predicted by the DPM, but they could not test the causalities proposed by the model. Longitudinal studies, while not able to conclusively test causal hypotheses, can provide stronger tests of such effects than correlational research. Accordingly, a number of longitudinal studies have investigated the tenets of the DPM. Of these, four published studies have investigated cross-lagged effects between the personality and social worldview variables specified as predictors by the DPM, and the ideological variables of RWA and SDO (Sibley & Duckitt, 2010, 2013; Sibley et al., 2007a; Sidanius et al., 2012).

Each of the causal effects predicted by the DPM were tested in between two and five independent samples in these four studies. Each of these predicted effects, except one that will be noted later, was statistically significant across all the studies and samples in which they were tested. Specifically, lower Openness was a significant cross-lagged predictor of RWA (but not SDO), lower Agreeableness (or a component such as empathy or compassion) of SDO (and not RWA), lower Openness of DW beliefs (and not CW beliefs), lower Agreeableness of CW beliefs (and not DW beliefs), higher DW beliefs of RWA (and not SDO), and higher CW beliefs of SDO (and not RWA).

---

8 There were additional statistically significant effects besides those noted here in the SEM studies, but these were generally weak and neither consistent across studies nor supported by the meta-analytic findings noted earlier. For example, the study by Van Hiel et al. (2007) found an effect of Neuroticism on lower RWA; Sibley and Duckitt (2009) found significant effects for Neuroticism on higher DW and higher CW, for Honesty-Humility on lower DW, and for Extraversion on higher CW and lower DW; Leone et al. (2012) found effects for Emotionality on higher DW and lower CW.

These findings thus supported the causal predictions from the DPM in how the two personality dimensions of Openness and Agreeableness, as well as worldview beliefs, might influence each other and the ideological attitudes of RWA and SDO. It was noted earlier that while the DPM model did not make any specific predictions about reciprocal or reversed causal effects, such effects would not be incompatible with the model and would be reasonably plausible, as long as they reversed effects between variables for which a causal linkage had been proposed. In several cases, significant reciprocal or reverse effects of this kind were found for variables expected to be causally linked. Thus, there was a significant reciprocal effect of higher RWA on DW (in one of the two samples studied), for higher SDO on CW (in both of two samples studied), for lower CW on Agreeableness (in the one sample studied), and for lower SDO on Agreeableness or components of Agreeableness (in all three of the samples studied). Of the total of 62 cross-lagged effects tested over the four studies and five samples, there were only two significant non-predicted effects (i.e., for variables not causally linked by the DPM). Both were weak and, given the number of analyses, might reflect Type 1 error.[9] Also, one effect that had originally been predicted by the DPM, that is, an effect of higher Big Five Conscientiousness on RWA, was not supported in either of the two samples in which it was tested.

To sum up, therefore, the causal predictions from the DPM were clearly supported by significant longitudinal cross-lagged effects. These were for Openness on DW and RWA, and for DW on RWA, as well as for Agreeableness (or components such as compassion or empathy) on CW and SDO, and for CW on SDO. The one effect originally predicted by the DPM that was not supported was for Conscientiousness (on both DW and RWA), which was nonsignificant in both the studies in which it was tested. This suggests that although Conscientiousness may be correlated with RWA, since this was supported by the two major meta-analyses reported (Proch, 2013; Sibley & Duckitt, 2008), its effects may not be causal. Alternatively, it is possible that any causal effects for Conscientiousness may have been too weak to be detected by the relatively low statistical power of the longitudinal studies in which it was tested. These cross-lagged longitudinal analyses also revealed significant reciprocal effects for variables that had been hypothesized by the DPM to be causally linked. These reciprocal effects were, however, not consistently significant except for a reciprocal effect of SDO on low Agreeableness (or components of it, such as empathy and compassion), which was consistent across three samples. This suggests that SDO may have a particularly notable tendency to have reciprocal causal effects on personality, such that when individuals explicitly adopt ideological attitudes expressive of competitive dominance and power (i.e., SDO), this may itself, and through associated lifestyle changes (e.g., friendship, partner, and career choices, and habitual interests and activities), facilitate

9 These were significant effects on SDO for higher Extraversion (Sibley & Duckitt, 2010) and lower Openness (Sibley & Duckitt, 2013).

emotional and behavioral tendencies to respond in a less kind, sympathetic, warm, and compassionate manner to others.

Finally, these conclusions have also been broadly supported by studies using different but reasonably comparable measures of personality and worldview beliefs to those specified by the DPM. For example, in respect of threat and ideological attitudes, Onraet, Dhont, and Van Hiel (2014) conducted a three-wave longitudinal study with a large nationally representative Dutch sample and found significant cross-lagged effects across both time periods for self-reported external threat (this included both DW beliefs and indicators of CW beliefs) on both RWA and SDO, with significant reciprocal effects also for RWA on threat. Mirisola, Roccato, Russo, Spagna, and Vieno (2014) also used a three-wave longitudinal design with a large and representative Italian sample and found increases in RWA in response to increases in perceived societal threat to safety and security.

Other longitudinal studies have also reported broadly consistent findings but have not used fully cross-lagged designs. Matthews, Levin, and Sidanius (2009) found significant longitudinal correlations between an economic threat item and SDO, and Rippl and Seipel (2012) found significant reciprocal longitudinal effects between ad hoc indices of threat and authoritarianism. Altemeyer (1996) found that becoming a parent (which should make social threats more salient) increased RWA, while Bonanno and Jost (2006) found increased conservatism in survivors of the 9/11 attacks in the United States, and Echebarria-Echabe and Fernandez-Guede (2006) found increases in RWA in Spanish samples following terrorist bomb attacks in Madrid. Analysis of archival data also indicates that higher societal threats were associated with elevated indicators of RWA in the United States over time (e.g., Doty, Peterson, & Winter, 1991; Sales, 1973).

In respect of personality and ideological attitudes, Block and Block (2006) found significant longitudinal effects for childhood behavioral ratings directly indicative of low Openness (i.e., indecisive, fearful, guilt prone) on sociopolitical conservatism at 23 years of age (see also, Fraley, Griffen, Belsky, & Roisman, 2012, who have reported similar long-term effects). And a pre-post-election over-time comparison in Taiwan by Liu, Huang, and McFedries (2008) found that supporters of the victorious party (previously in opposition) increased in RWA and SDO, effects that can plausibly be attributed to their party having gained governmental authority and political power dominance respectively.[10]

Experimental Research

Finally, correlational or longitudinal work is complemented by experimental work that definitively establishes causality. A number of experimental studies have

10 Interestingly, supporters of the losing party in this election, which had previously been in power, did not show reduced RWA and SDO. This was presumably because they did not see the shift in political and governmental power as stable and likely to endure, and this was indeed so, as their party did win the very next election.

shown that social situational factors influence RWA, SDO, or the social worldviews of DW and CW beliefs, as expected from the DPM.

Early correlational research had indicated that groups and individuals higher in power and status were higher in SDO (Sidanius & Pratto, 1999), and that the degree to which individuals identified with higher- or lower-status membership groups was associated with their having higher or lower SDO (e.g., Wilson & Liu, 2003). Experimental studies have shown that this effect does appear to be causal. For example, Guimond, Dambrun, Michinov, and Duarte (2003) found that assigning individuals to a high- versus low-power position (manager versus receptionist) increased levels of SDO, and other studies have shown that making membership of a high-power (as opposed to lower-power) and status group salient increased SDO (Huang & Liu, 2005; Schmitt, Branscombe, & Kappen, 2003). Further experimental research has supported these findings and qualified them by showing that it is when the social or group context involves competiveness from or toward other groups (i.e., competitive threats) that high-power positions, and identifying with high-power membership groups, increase SDO (De Oliveira, Guimond, & Dambrun, 2012; Morrison, Fast, & Ybarra, 2009; Morrision & Ybarra, 2008).

In the case of RWA, research has shown that experimental manipulations that increase or decrease social threat will have corresponding effects on RWA. For example, scenario-based experiments by Altemeyer (1988) found that participants reading about destabilizing political crises in their society increased in RWA. Experiments in which terrorist threats were made salient for participants similarly increased their levels of RWA (Asbrock & Fritsche, 2013; Fischer et al., 2010), while Fritsche, Cohrs, Kessler, and Bauer (2012) found that reminding participants of the destabilizing social threats posed by global warming also increased their levels of RWA. Moreover, experimental manipulations that induce feelings of physical safety were found to reduce social conservatism and resistance to change (i.e., indices equivalent to RWA), but not economic conservatism or acceptance of inequality (i.e., indices equivalent to SDO; Napier, 2014), and experimental manipulations to reduce threat eliminated the tendency for members of stigmatized (and therefore threatened) social groups to be higher on RWA (Henry, 2011).

Summing up, the experimental research reviewed here supports the propositions that competitively based group or personal dominance will increase SDO, and that social threats to societal stability, order, and cohesion will increase RWA. In addition, two experimental studies have tested more specific hypotheses derived from the DPM (Duckitt & Fisher, 2003; Jugert & Duckitt, 2009). Both these studies investigated whether social threat to societal stability and order would affect RWA and not SDO, and whether the effects would be mediated by DW beliefs, as predicted by the DPM. Social threat was manipulated by having participants read a hypothetical scenario depicting a dangerous and threatening future for their country, and the researchers found that this did indeed increase RWA and not

SDO, and that the threat-induced increase in RWA was fully mediated by higher DW beliefs.

Conclusions from Research on the Social and Psychological Bases of RWA, SDO

In concluding, it is clear that research evidence using a variety of approaches has supported the basic propositions of the DPM about the differential genesis and correlates of RWA and SDO as two distinct ideological attitude dimensions. Correlational studies and studies using SEM have shown that the Big Five personality dimensions of low Openness and high Conscientiousness and DW beliefs predict RWA, and that the Big Five personality dimension of low Agreeableness (or HEXACO Honesty-Humility) and CW beliefs predict SDO. A number of longitudinal studies have also supported the proposition that these effects of personality (though not for Conscientiousness) and social worldview on ideological attitudes are indeed causal. And finally, experimental evidence indicates that social situational variables have theoretically expected effects on RWA and SDO. Personal or group power and dominance, particularly if competitively based, increase SDO. On the other hand, threats to social order, security, and safety increase RWA. Moreover, several studies have shown that the effects of social threats to stability, collective security, and order are specific to RWA rather than SDO and that their effects on RWA were fully mediated through increased DW beliefs.

DPM 3: Effects of Ideological Attitudes on Prejudice

The DPM proposes that prejudiced attitudes emerge from two basic motivational goals and values, with one being threat-driven needs for group security and control, which are expressed in RWA, and the other being competition-driven needs for group dominance, superiority, and power, expressed in SDO. The proposition that a person high (as opposed to low) in RWA should be generally more reactive to social threat and more motivated to control social threat has ample research support. A number of experimental studies have shown that when participants were exposed to differing levels of social threat, those higher in RWA showed heightened reactivity to threat and more motivation to control the threat (Feldman, Lavine, Lodge, & Verhulst, 2010; Lavine et al., 1999; Lavine, Lodge, Polichak, & Taber, 2002). The DPM therefore proposes that this heightened reactivity to social threat, as well as the need to control threat, provides the motivational basis for prejudice against outgroups and minorities by persons higher in RWA. More specifically, it is proposed that persons high in RWA will be particularly negative to outgroups and minorities that seem to threaten collective or societal security, order, and stability and will favor policies, political parties, and beliefs (legitimizing myths) that emphasize the tough, punitive control of such potential threats.

The proposition that persons high (as opposed to low) in SDO would be generally more competitive over relative power and dominance, and more motivated to establish, maintain, and justify dominance and superiority over others, has also been well supported in research. For example, a series of experiments by Cozzolino and Snyder (2008) showed that when participants were placed in competitive situations in which their chances of victory were threatened, those high (as opposed to low) in SDO reacted to this competitive threat with increased greed, effort, and readiness to break rules to win at all costs. An experiment by De Cremer, Cornelis, and Van Hiel (2008) showed that having influence and power over group decisions ("voice") was more important to participants high (as opposed to low) in SDO, and research by Swami, Neofytou, Thirlwell, Taylor, and McCleary (2013) found that SDO (but not RWA) was a highly significant predictor of a drive for greater muscularity in men. Danso and Esses (2001) found that Whites who were high in SDO performed better on an ability test when tested by a Black (as opposed to a White) experimenter, presumably due to the presence of the Black experimenter cueing intergroup competitiveness for high SDO Whites, as well as motivation to maintain White dominance. Somewhat similarity, Eibach and Keegan (2006) found that White Americans who were high (as opposed to low) in SDO tended to frame advances by the Black minority toward greater equality as a competitive threat to their own status and privileges (i.e., their group dominance).

The DPM therefore proposes that this competiveness over relative power and dominance also provides the motivational basis for the prejudice against outgroups and minorities by persons higher in SDO. More specifically, persons high in SDO will be particularly negative and competitive toward lower-status or lower-power groups to justify and maintain their superiority over them. They will also be relatively negative toward outgroups that are seen as competing over or challenging relative group dominance or superiority. Persons high in SDO would also therefore favor policies, parties, or beliefs (legitimizing myths) that would promote and maintain group or personal dominance, superiority, and inequality. These processes are summarized diagrammatically in Figure 9.2.

The proposal that prejudiced attitudes are driven by the two motivational goals, expressed in RWA and SDO, generates three important testable hypotheses. First, it suggests that distinctive patterns of prejudice will be associated with RWA and SDO that may overlap but only partially. Thus, RWA and SDO may predict prejudice against the same outgroups and minorities but will also predict prejudice against different sets of outgroups and minorities. These differences in the patterns of prejudice associated with each will be directly related to, and explicable in terms of, their different motivational bases. Second, the DPM proposes that the two motives for prejudice will be expressed in the effects of RWA and SDO on prejudice being mediated by different kinds of motivationally biased perceptions of or feelings about the targeted outgroups or minorities. And third, the two basic

Intergroup Relations	Motivational Activation (Moderation)	Outgroup Perception (Mediation)
Social or intergroup threat from outgroup	Activates threat-driven collective security and social control motivation directed against the outgroup (stronger in high RWA persons, who therefore are more negative to threatening outgroups)	Outgroup therefore perceived as unjustifiably threatening group security, order, cohesion stability, and traditions, and therefore disliked and / or derogated
Salient intergroup categorization		
Intergroup dominance, inequality, and competitiveness over power-status	Activates competitively driven motivation to establish or maintain group dominance and superiority over the outgroup (stronger in high SDO persons, who therefore are more negative to subordinate or competitive groups)	Outgroup therefore perceived as competing over relative group dominance and status, and / or challenging the ingroup's legitimate social superiority and dominance, and therefore disliked and / or derogated

Figure 9.2 *A dual process motivational model of how intergroup or situational dynamics activate dual motivational goals expressed in the ideological attitudes of RWA and SDO to generate outgroup perceptions that result in outgroup prejudice.*

motives for prejudice in individuals will be activated by particular social or intergroup cues so that the effects of RWA and SDO on prejudice will be differentially moderated by those cues. These implications will be elaborated next and research bearing on each briefly reviewed.

Motivationally Based Differential Patterning of Prejudice

As noted, RWA and SDO index different motives for prejudice, and these motives may be elicited by the same outgroup or minorities. This would typically be the case for ethnic minorities that are low in both status and power (eliciting SDO-based prejudice), and socioculturally deviant from mainstream society and therefore threatening dominant norms, values, and traditions (eliciting RWA-based prejudice). Both RWA- and SDO-based prejudice may also be elicited to directly competing outgroups that activate both competition and threat-driven motives. However, these motives can also be differentially activated by outgroups or minorities, in which case RWA and SDO should predict prejudice differentially and in a manner consistent with their different motivational bases. This proposition has been supported by a number of studies investigating different kinds of prejudice or ethnocentrism.

One study that specifically set out to test this differential patterning of prejudice hypothesis found that RWA, and not SDO, predicted negative attitudes toward two specially selected groups that had been rated as likely to be seen as socially deviant and threatening traditional norms and values, but *not* likely to be seen as socially subordinate (rock stars and drug dealers; Duckitt, 2006). On the other hand, SDO, and not RWA, predicted negative attitudes to groups selected because they had been rated as socially subordinate and not socially threatening (people with a physical disability, housewives, and unemployment insurance beneficiaries).

Research has also shown that RWA and SDO predict different aspects of male sexism toward women. Sibley, Wilson, and Duckitt (2007b) showed that RWA was a better predictor of benevolently sexist (BS) attitudes toward women, which express support for traditional gender roles and resistance to social change. SDO, on the other hand, was the better predictor of hostile sexism (HS), which expresses competitive hostility to women and a desire to maintain dominance over them. Sibley et al. (2007b) also confirmed these differential effects in a further long-itudinal follow-up study showing significant cross-lagged effects of RWA on BS, and SDO on HS. Christopher and Wojda (2008) found the same differential effects with RWA predicting traditional role preference (a measure similar to BS), and SDO predicting employment scepticism (similar to HS), in the United States. More recently, Roets, Van Hiel, and Dhont (2012) found the same differential effects for RWA and SDO on men's BS and HS toward women in a Dutch community sample.[11]

There is also evidence that RWA and SDO predict different kinds of ethno-centrism. For example, Bizumic, Duckitt, Popadic, Dru, and Krauss (2009) identified two distinct dimensions of ethnocentrism with one termed "intergroup ethnocentrism" (with an emphasis on ingroup superiority over outgroups), which correlated primarily with SDO, and the other termed "intragroup ethnocentrism" (favoring the ingroup over individual group members), which correlated primarily with RWA. Stangor and Leary (2006) in their research also found that RWA was more strongly correlated with pro-ingroup than anti-outgroup attitudes, while SDO was more strongly correlated with anti-outgroup than pro-ingroup attitudes. Both these findings are clearly consistent with the conceptualization of RWA as expressing motivational goals of collective (or ingroup) security and cohesion, and SDO as expressing motivational goals of group dominance and superiority over others.

The DPM hypothesis that there should be fundamentally different patterns of prejudice for RWA and SDO has an important implication that is completely contrary to the widely held assumption of generalized prejudice. This assumption, deriving originally from Allport (1954) and Adorno et al. (1950), is that prejudices or negative intergroup attitudes will all correlate positively and form a single broad

---

11 Roets et al. (2012) also investigated men's and women's benevolent and hostile sexism *to men* and found, as expected, that women's RWA did predict BS to men. However, their SDO did not predict HS to men. As the researchers noted, the failure of SDO to predict women's HS to men would be expected because SDO should theoretically (according to both the DPM and social dominance theory) predict negative attitudes to subordinate groups (i.e., women) but not to dominant groups (i.e., in this case, men).

generalized prejudice dimension.[12] In contrast to this assumption of one broad dimension of generalized prejudice, the DPM expects there to be not just one but several generalized prejudice (or negative outgroup attitude) dimensions that will relate differently to RWA and SDO. This prediction was tested in research that factor analyzed negative attitudes to 24 social groups and found three distinct outgroup attitude dimensions (Duckitt & Sibley, 2007). As expected, one outgroup attitude dimension consisted of dangerous and threatening (and therefore potentially powerful) groups (e.g., terrorists, violent criminals) and was significantly independently associated only with RWA. A second outgroup attitude dimension consisted of low-status, disadvantaged groups (e.g., unattractive people, people with mental illness, obese people) and was significantly associated only with SDO. The third dimension consisted of dissident groups (e.g., prostitutes, feminists), most of which were deviant from traditional norms as well as some that challenged social inequality (e.g., protestors), which was primarily predicted by RWA, but also significantly by SDO.

A later study replicated these differential significant effects for RWA and SDO on the same three negative group attitude dimensions (Asbrock et al., 2010), and a longitudinal follow-up of the same participants six months later showed exactly the same cross-lagged effects significant (i.e., for RWA and SDO on the three group attitude dimensions). The reciprocal cross-lagged effects (of these three prejudice dimensions on RWA and SDO), on the other hand, were all nonsignificant, suggesting that causal impacts were from RWA and SDO to the prejudice dimensions and not vice versa. A more recent study was conducted in a different cultural setting (Brazil). Here, Cantal et al. (2015) obtained exactly the same pattern of significant differential effects for RWA and SDO on the same three negative group attitude dimensions.

The differential predictive power of SDO and RWA also holds in other domains. For example, a recent study by Milojev et al. (2014) showed that SDO and RWA predicted distinct individual differences in the combinations of moral foundations that people endorse. These combinations of moral foundations covered the five moral domains of Harm/Care, Fairness/Reciprocity, In-group/Loyalty, Authority/Respect, and Purity/Sanctity described by Haidt and Joseph (2004). SDO, on the one hand, tended to predict a specific profile of moral beliefs characterized by moderate/lukewarm support for multiple moral foundations. People high in RWA, on the other hand, tended to fit a profile of moral beliefs characterized by undifferentiated high support across moral foundations. Milojev et al. (2014) argued that difference in the links between SDO and RWA with distinct moral signatures occurred because SDO and RWA promote different moral justifications for prejudice and intergroup relations. RWA tended to predict conceptions of morality that emphasize binding foundations related to ingroup cohesion, whereas SDO

12 Allport, for example, expressed this as: "one of the facts of which we are most certain is that people who reject one outgroup will tend to reject other outgroups. If a person is anti-Jewish, he is likely to be anti-Catholic, anti-Negro, anti any out-group" (1954; p. 68).

tends to promote a view of morality that downplays the importance of social equality and fairness.

Overall, therefore, a good deal of research has shown that RWA and SDO have differential effects consistent with their different motivational bases on different forms and manifestations of prejudice, such as sexism and ethnocentrism. They have also been shown to predict negativity to different kinds of social groups specifically, as well as to different generalized group attitude dimensions as theoretically expected.[13]

Motivated Differential Mediation of Ideological Attitudes on Prejudice

An important prediction from the DPM is that because RWA and SDO express different motives or reasons for prejudice, their effects will be mediated by quite different perceptions of and feelings about the targeted groups. Specifically, the effects of RWA on outgroup negativity should be mediated by perceived social threat from the targeted groups, whereas the effects of SDO should be mediated by feelings of competitiveness over relative status and dominance toward the targeted groups.

These mediational effects have been supported in several empirical studies that investigated either RWA or SDO separately. Perceived threat has been found to mediate the effects of RWA on antigay prejudice in one study (Esses, Haddock, & Zanna, 1993), and on ethnic outgroups in another (Cohrs & Ibler, 2009). More recently, research by Kauff, Asbrock, Thörner, and Wagner (2013) found that perceived threat from multicultural policies mediated the effects of RWA on opposition to diversity and immigrants. In the case of SDO, two Canadian studies found that SDO was strongly correlated with anti-immigrant attitudes, and that this effect was mediated by the perception of economic competition from immigrants (Esses, Jackson, & Armstrong, 1998; Jackson & Esses, 2000).[14] More compelling evidence has come from studies that used measures of both RWA and SDO, together with indices of either one or both of perceived outgroup threat and outgroup competitiveness, to directly assess differential mediation. Research by Charles-Toussant and Crowson (2010) found that both RWA and SDO predicted US students' negative attitudes toward

---

13 Research has also shown differential effects for RWA and SDO consistent with theoretical expectation for a number of social outcomes other than prejudice. For example, RWA and SDO have been shown to differentially predict biased political judgments (Crawford, 2012), support for different kinds of right-wing political parties (Van Hiel & Mervielde, 2002), support for right-wing politicians who framed their messages in different ways (Crawford, Brady, Pilanski, & Erny, 2013), people's readiness to harm others (Asbrock, Nieuwoudt, Duckitt, & Sibley, 2011), different kinds of sentencing goals for offenders (Gerber & Jackson, 2013; McKee & Feather, 2008), social and economic policy attitudes (Perry & Sibley, 2013), evaluations of different media reports on different social policies (Crawford, Jussim, Cain, & Cohen, 2013), and readiness to eliminate a rival or competitor (McPherson & Parks, 2011).

14 RWA was included in these two studies but unusually did not correlate with anti-immigrant attitudes. Thus, mediation for RWA could not be assessed.

international students, with the effects for RWA being significantly mediated by perceived threat (both symbolic and real) from international students, whereas the effects for SDO were not.

Two other studies demonstrated differential mediation more comprehensively by using indices of both perceived threat and competition, and both RWA and SDO. This was the case for a study already noted in the previous section (Duckitt, 2006) that found that RWA predicted attitudes to groups preselected as socially threatening, and that SDO predicted attitudes to groups preselected to be low status or socially subordinate. This study also showed that the significant effects of RWA on outgroup attitudes were fully mediated by perceived outgroup threat. In contrast, the effects of SDO were not. Moreover, the significant effects for SDO on outgroup attitudes were mediated by perceived competitiveness, whereas the effects of RWA were not. More recently, Craig and Richeson (2014) found that support for strict immigration policies by US citizens was predicted by both RWA and SDO, with the effects for RWA (but not SDO) mediated by perceived cultural threat from immigrants, and the effects for SDO (but not RWA) mediated by perceived competition from immigrants.

Research examining the efficacy of intergroup contact on prejudice reduction for those high in SDO or RWA also supports the idea that RWA tends to express different motives or reasons for prejudice. In their formal integration of the DPM and intergroup contact theory, Asbrock, Christ, Duckitt, and Sibley (2012) argued that contact should be effective at reducing prejudice among those high in RWA, but less so, or not at all, for those high in SDO. The DPM states that RWA tends to predict prejudice on the basis of fear, perceptions of social threat, and differences in values or morals. Asbrock et al. (2012) reasoned that positive intergroup contact should be effective in reducing perceptions of social threat and hence prejudice for high RWAs. The same does not hold for SDO. People high in SDO tend to express prejudice as a way of legitimizing and maintaining social hierarchy – an end to a means, if you will.

Asbrock et al. (2012) theorized that expressions of prejudice based on the competition-driven motivation for dominance should thus be less amenable to reduction via intergroup contact, because they will be more likely to endorse prejudice strategically to help maintain hierarchy. Thus, while it should be possible for contact with outgroups to reduce perceptions of threat ("they are not really so different from us after all"), prejudice based on SDO should be harder to change, because intergroup contact should be less likely to reduce the perception that the outgroup is able to be exploited ("they are weak and ripe for exploitation").

Empirical research on the differential effects of contact on prejudice depending on SDO and RWA is somewhat mixed but generally supports a DPM perspective. With regard to RWA, Dhont and Van Hiel (2009) and Hodson, Harry, and Mitchell (2009) showed that positive intergroup contact was linked with less prejudice for those high in RWA. Results for SDO are less conclusive. Hodson (2008), for example, showed that intergroup contact reduced prejudice among higher-SDO

British convicts in a prison setting. This effect was replicated in an undergraduate sample collected by Dhont and Van Hiel (2009), but not in a broader community sample. Part of this ambiguity may have occurred because of the focus on SDO in isolation of RWA in some studies, which meant that the effect of RWA (which correlates with SDO) could not be statistically adjusted for. Finally, Asbrock et al. (2012) found good support for the predicted differential effects of SDO and RWA on contact in independent cross-sectional and longitudinal national probability samples. They showed that, as predicted by a DPM perspective, intergroup contact predicted reduced prejudice over time for those high in RWA. However, intergroup contact did not predict reduced prejudice over time for those high in SDO. Rather, the reverse occurred, with intergroup contact predicting reduced prejudice over time for those low in SDO (who were presumably more amenable to change in their attitudes following direct experience with the outgroup relative to those high in SDO).

Differential mediation of the effects of RWA and SDO consistent with the DPM has also been shown for other social outcomes relevant to prejudice, such as support for war. For example, McFarland (2005) found that both RWA and SDO predicted US students' support for the Iraq war, but that these effects were differentially mediated. The effect of RWA was mediated by perceived threat from Iraq, while the effect of SDO was mediated by a lack of concern for the human cost of the war (which would be consistent with the hard, tough-minded, competitive motivational orientation characteristic of SDO). Jackson and Gaertner (2010) obtained broadly similar findings: The significant effects of RWA and SDO on support for war were mediated by different moral disengagement mechanisms, with effects for RWA primarily mediated by moral justification (i.e., a morally justifiable defense of legitimate order and security), and those for SDO by dehumanizing-blaming victims (i.e., indicating a ruthlessly, competitive, tough-minded motivational orientation).

Summing up, therefore, a number of studies clearly support the hypothesis that the effects of RWA on outgroup negativity tend to be fully or substantially mediated by perceived threats and concerns about collective or societal security and order, whereas the effects of SDO are mediated by a tough-minded competiveness over relative dominance and superiority. Related to this, the available evidence suggests that intergroup contact may be more effective at reducing prejudice for those high in RWA than for those high in SDO, most likely because positive contact experiences are more effective at reducing perceived social threat than at reducing perceptions that the outgroup is in a weak or vulnerable position and could be potentially exploited or dominated (see Asbrock et al., 2012).

Motivationally Based Differential Contextual and Intergroup Activation of Prejudice

The DPM proposes that two basic and fundamentally human motivational goals underlie prejudice with one expressed in RWA (values of security, stability, order, control), and the other in SDO (values of power, dominance, superiority). These two motivational goals are not necessarily always important or salient for individuals, however, and only become salient when they are situationally activated by social threat or competition. They may then be motivationally directed against threatening or (potentially) competing outgroups. Thus, the DPM sees both individual motives and social and intergroup circumstances as necessarily involved in causing prejudice.

There are therefore two important predictions from the DPM. One is that the particular social and intergroup factors that activate the motivational goals underlying prejudice in individuals should also be important factors creating socially shared patterns of prejudice in societies and social groups generally. A second prediction is that in the case of individual attitudes, individuals' awareness of the intergroup relations of threat and competition in their societies or social group should interact with the strength of their personal motivational goals (for security and order, or power and dominance) to generate their personally held prejudiced attitudes against specific outgroups.

Thus, the DPM predicts first that the most important social and intergroup factors causing shared patterns of prejudice in societies should be intergroup relations of social threat (from an outgroup), and competition over relative dominance and superiority. The latter should be triggered either by intergroup social inequality (creating a need to justify existing dominance relations) or by direct intergroup competition over relative power, status, and dominance. The hypothesis that intergroup threat, competition, and inequality should be major social and intergroup causes of prejudice has been amply confirmed by a great deal of research (e.g., Bettencourt, Charlton, Dorr, & Hume, 2001; Riek, Mania, & Gaertner, 2006; Sidanius & Pratto, 1999). These factors have also been the focus of the most important intergroup and social-level theories of prejudice, such as realistic conflict theory (focusing on real intergroup threat or competition (e.g., Sherif, 1967), social identity theory (focusing on threats to group identity, intergroup competition, and inequality; Tajfel & Turner, 1979), terror management theory (intergroup threats to values and beliefs; Solomon, Greenberg, & Pyszczynski, 1991), and social dominance theory (focusing on intergroup inequality and dominance relations; see Chapter 8 in this book; Sidanius & Pratto, 1999).

The second prediction is that RWA and SDO should index differential reactivity to these social and intergroup factors and may thus moderate their effects (refer to Figure 9.2). Thus, persons high in RWA should be more reactive to intergroup threats than persons low in RWA, and therefore more prone to dislike threatening outgroups. Persons high in SDO should be more reactive to intergroup relations of competiveness or inequality in social status, power, and dominance relations than persons low in SDO, and therefore more prone to dislike groups or persons low in power and status, or those competing over relative power and status. More specifically, RWA should therefore predict outgroup prejudice more strongly when outgroups are socially threatening as opposed to nonthreatening, and SDO should predict outgroup prejudice more strongly when outgroups are competing over relative status or power (or are socially subordinate) as opposed to being noncompetitive (or not socially subordinate). These moderation hypotheses have been tested in both correlational research and research that has experimentally manipulated the salience or magnitude of outgroup threat or outgroup competition and relative status and power.

A number of such studies have looked at RWA or SDO separately. For example, research, some of which has been described earlier, has shown that experimentally manipulating factors to activate competitiveness over relative group dominance or superiority resulted in increased prejudice, aggression, cheating, or greed among persons high (as opposed to low) in SDO (Cozzolino & Snyder, 2008; Danso & Esses, 2001; De Cremer et al., 2008; Eibach & Keegan, 2006). In the case of RWA and threat, a large number of studies have shown that RWA (or closely similar measures of authoritarian attitudes) was more strongly predictive of prejudiced attitudes or similar outcome variables under socially threatening conditions (Cohrs & Ibler, 2009; Cohrs, Moschner, Maes, & Kielman, 2005; Feldman & Stenner, 1997; Kossowska et al., 2011; Rikert, 1998; Stenner, 2005). Recently, an impressive series of studies using both cross-national analyses and experimental research has shown that multicultural policies and situations increased prejudice toward immigrants and opposition to diversity, but only among persons high (but not low) in RWA. As expected, the significant effects were mediated by perceived threat (Kauff et al., 2013).

A number of studies have also used a variety of research strategies to directly test the DPM hypothesis that activating intergroup threat or competitiveness differentially moderates the effects of RWA and SDO on prejudice. For example, in a cross-national meta-analysis of 157 samples from 17 countries, Cohrs and Stelzl (2010) found that RWA was a particularly strong predictor of anti-immigrant attitudes in countries where immigrants were seen as increasing the crime rate (and would therefore be seen as socially threatening). On the other hand, SDO was the strongest predictor of anti-immigrant attitudes in countries with a higher relative unemployment rate for immigrants (where immigrants would be seen as competing for jobs). An experimental study by Dru (2007) directly supported the DPM differential moderation hypothesis by priming either (a) ingroup security and norm preservation or (b) group competitiveness. When ingroup security and preservation were made salient, RWA was a significant predictor of anti-immigrant attitudes whereas SDO was not. When group competitiveness was made salient, SDO significantly predicted anti-immigrant attitudes but RWA did not.

A number of other experimental studies have tested and supported the differential moderation hypothesis by manipulating descriptions of target groups to arouse concern over these groups either threatening collective security and order or presenting a competitive threat to relative group dominance and superiority. Duckitt and Sibley (2010b) investigated attitudes toward a bogus immigrant group ("Sandrians"), which was described as either socially deviant and unconventional (threatening ingroup norms and values; threat condition), or as disadvantaged and low in status and power (low-status condition), or as likely to compete for jobs and resources (competitive and socially threatening), or in neutral terms in a control condition (neither threatening nor competitive, and similar in status, skills, and culture to the host society). As predicted, neither RWA nor SDO predicted negativity to Sandrians in the control condition, only RWA predicted negativity in the outgroup threat condition, only SDO predicted negativity in the outgroup low-status condition, and both RWA and SDO predicted negativity in the outgroup threat and competition condition.

Craig and Richeson (2014) investigated attitudes toward ethnic minority immigrants by manipulating the national context (i.e., immigrants to participants' home country versus immigrants to foreign countries). Their findings were consistent with the DPM; RWA, but not SDO, predicted negativity to immigrants to their home country (since these threaten their ingroup's security and cohesion) but not toward those immigrating to foreign countries. SDO, on the other hand, predicted negativity for immigrants to both their own and foreign countries (expected since both domestic and foreign immigrants would be subordinate social groups, low in status and power).

A study by Thomson, Green, and Sidanius (2008) presented American and Swiss participants with a description of an immigrant who would not assimilate into their culture (threatening ingroup norms and cohesion) or an immigrant who was assimilating successfully (reducing inequality between immigrants and dominant majority). As hypothesized, RWA, and not SDO, predicted negativity toward the non-assimilating (socially threatening) immigrant, whereas SDO, and not RWA, predicted negativity toward the successfully assimilating (and therefore reducing ingroup dominance) immigrant. Cohrs and Asbrock (2009) depicted an immigrant group (Turks) as socially threatening to a sample of German students and, as expected, found that RWA and not SDO predicted significantly greater negativity to Turks. It should be noted that this experiment also had a second, "competitive," condition that did not find an expected effect for SDO on negativity to Turks. It seems likely, however, that this manipulation did not adequately manipulate intergroup competition from Turks.[15]

Finally, a recent series of experiments manipulated contextual variables (relevant to either ingroup security and cohesion or group dominance and inequality). They found differential moderation for the effects of RWA and SDO, as hypothesized by the DPM, on a range of political outcomes. For example, RWA (and not SDO) predicted intolerance for political groups when those groups were framed as threats to group norms and cohesion, and SDO (and not RWA) predicted intolerance for groups framed as threatening inequality and group dominance (Crawford & Pilanski, 2014). Crawford, Brady et al. (2013) found that RWA and SDO differentially predicted support for right-wing political candidates who framed

---

15 The manipulation for the "competitive" condition did not manipulate intergroup competition per se, but rather described Turks as being *personally* industrious, achievement orientated, and competitive. These are all traits that would generally be admired by persons high in SDO, and this positive (for high SDOs) depiction of Turks seems likely to have neutralized any effects that the manipulation may also have had on competitiveness.

their policy messages in terms of group cohesion or group status threats, respectively. In a further study, participants rated the amount of bias in articles supporting or opposing same-sex relationships (traditional values and norms manipulation) or affirmative action (equality and group dominance manipulation; Crawford, Jussim, et al., 2013). RWA predicted bias in the former condition, and SDO in the latter. And finally, Crawford (2012) found that RWA predicted more biased ratings on judgment issues concerning group conformity and traditional norms and values, whereas SDO predicted more biased ratings on judgment issues concerning group dominance and inequality.

Overall, therefore, the DPM hypothesis that social and contextual cues activating the motivational bases of RWA and SDO differentially moderate the effects of RWA and SDO on prejudice and other social outcomes has been supported in many studies, and particularly in studies that set out to test the hypothesis directly. Not surprisingly, given the difficulty of detecting interactions in psychological research (McClelland & Judd, 1993), a few studies have reported nonsignificant moderating effects for RWA or SDO with and what should theoretically be relevant contextual variables. However, this has tended to occur in research studies where detecting significant effects would be expected to be particularly difficult. For example, this has been the case where the target groups for prejudice have been real ethnic or social groups for whom there were already strong preexisting negative attitudes, as well as intergroup relations of threat and/or competitiveness, thus making it difficult for even powerful threat or competitiveness manipulations to significantly increase negativity to those groups (e.g., Esses et al., 1998; Meeus, Duriez, Vanbesselaere, Phalet, & Kuppens, 2009). Some cases studies have also reported no significant moderating effects for RWA or SDO when the presumed moderator was subjectively perceived threat or competiveness (for which mediating rather than moderating effects would be predicted by the DPM; e.g., Sidanius, Haley, Molina, & Pratto, 2007).

The issue of exactly how contextual variables might activate the motivational bases of RWA and SDO does raise interesting possibilities that have not yet been systematically investigated. For example, Cohrs and Ibler (2009) have suggested that because persons high in RWA see the social world as dangerous and threatening, they would be particularly likely to overreact to relatively weak or ambiguous outgroup threats, while persons low in RWA would tend to downplay relatively weak or ambiguous threats. This suggests that a dramatic escalation of outgroup threat or intergroup competition for such outgroups might have a stronger effect on persons low in RWA or SDO rather than high. This could happen, in the case of RWA, because highs might have already been negative to that outgroup (having overreacted to weak or ambiguous threats from it) creating a ceiling for any increase in threat, whereas lows might react more strongly to the dramatic disconfirmation of their prior minimization of threat.[16]

16 There is some support for this possibility from longitudinal research showing that persons initially low in RWA showed the greatest increases in RWA after exposure to social threat (Altemeyer, 1996; Mirisola et al., 2014)

Conclusions and Challenges

Most fundamentally, the DPM explains prejudice in terms of two basic and universally human motivational goals. These are competition-driven power, dominance, and superiority on the one hand, and threat-driven collective security and social control on the other. These motivational goals are activated by social and intergroup dynamics of threat, inequality, and competition, which generate group or societally shared patterns of prejudice. However, individuals, as a result of their personalities and socialization experiences (expressed in their social worldview beliefs), also differ in how important these motivational goals are for them. This is most directly expressed in their motivationally based social-ideological attitudes. These individual differences then determine the degree to which individuals react with outgroup prejudice to the intergroup relations of threat, competition, or inequality characterizing their particular group or society. In this way, the DPM integrates both social and intergroup factors, as well as individual differences, in explaining how prejudiced attitudes arise and are sustained for both individuals and in societies.

This chapter has outlined the core propositions of the DPM and reviewed research relevant to these propositions. This research has generally provided strong support for the model. However, important empirical issues remain that have not yet been adequately clarified. These issues, several of which were highlighted in this chapter, include the issue of exactly how intergroup dynamics and individual dispositions might interact to generate prejudice (see, e.g., Cohrs & Ibler, 2009), how genetic influences on prejudiced attitudes and their dual motivational and ideological determinants might be shaped and mediated through their underlying traits, worldviews, and values (see, e.g., Kandler, Bleidorn, & Riemann, 2012), and exactly how the effects of dispositional variables outside Big Five personality such as cognitive ability might be mediated through ideological attitudes (see, e.g., Hodson & Busseri, 2012).

In addition, the model faces various theoretical challenges. A crucial one is that of integrating values more explicitly into the model. The DPM has treated RWA and SDO as value-based social-attitudinal constructs and neglected the possibility that values may have independent predictive roles in their formation. Our preliminary analyses of new data have suggested that modeling values (security and control versus power and dominance) separately from RWA and SDO may reveal important effects. These analyses suggest that the effects of personality on ideological attitudes may be largely or fully mediated through values and worldviews, that the effects of social worldviews on ideological attitudes are mainly direct, and only partially mediated through values. They also show that the effects of values on prejudice seem to be largely or wholly mediated through ideological attitudes.[17]

---

17 Prior research by Duriez, Van Hiel, and Kossowska (2005) has also shown across multiple samples from different countries that the effect of values on prejudice was fully mediated by RWA and SDO. Their findings also indicated that the correlations between values and ideological attitudes were generally moderate and sometimes weak, which underlines the relative independence of these constructs and the need to model them separately.

If these effects are confirmed, it would support an important conclusion: Values of security-control and power-dominance do not themselves directly influence prejudice; it is only when these values are combined with particular worldviews that infuse them with threat or competitiveness that they become the kind of social-ideological attitudes that generate and sustain prejudiced attitudes.

In conclusion, therefore, the DPM attempts to provide an integrative framework for the explanation of prejudice and intergroup hostility in terms of two basic human motives (i.e., "fear" and "greed"; cf. Wildschut & Insko, 2007), their psychological underpinnings, and the social and intergroup circumstances that activate these motives in individuals and collectives. While the core propositions of the model have been supported by a great deal of research, the chapter has also highlighted a number of empirical and theoretical issues that need to be clarified.

References

Adorno, T., Frenkel-Brunswick, E., Levinson, D., & Sanford, R. (1950). *The authoritarian personality*. New York: Harper.

Allport, G. (1954). *The nature of prejudice*. Reading, MA: Addison-Wesley.

Altemeyer, B. (1981). *Right-wing authoritarianism*. Winnipeg, Manitoba, Canada: University of Manitoba Press.

Altemeyer, B. (1988). *Enemies of freedom: Understanding right-wing authoritarianism*. San Francisco: Jossey-Bass.

Altemeyer, B. (1996). *The authoritarian specter*. Cambridge, MA: Harvard University Press.

Altemeyer, B. (1998). The other "authoritarian personality." In M. Zanna (Ed.), *Advances in experimental social psychology* (Vol. *30*, pp. 47–92). San Diego: Academic.

Asbrock, F., Christ, O., Duckitt, J., & Sibley, C. G. (2012). Differential effects of intergroup contact for authoritarians and social dominators: A dual process model perspective. *Personality and Social Psychology Bulletin, 38*, 477–490.

Asbrock, F., & Fritsche, I. (2013). Authoritarian reactions to terrorist threat: Who is being threatened, the Me or the We. *International Journal of Psychology, 48*, 35–49.

Asbrock, F., Nieuwoudt, C., Duckitt, J., & Sibley, C. G. (2011). Societal stereotypes of warmth and competence and the permissiveness of intergroup behavior. *Analyses of Social Issues and Public Policy, 11*(1), 154–179.

Asbrock, F., Sibley, C. G., & Duckitt, J. (2010). Right wing authoritarianism, social dominance orientation and the dimensions of generalized prejudice: A longitudinal test. *European Journal of Personality, 24*, 324–340.

Bettencourt, B., Charlton, K., Dorr, N., & Hume, D. (2001). Status differences and in-group bias: A meta-analytic examination of the effects of status stability, status legitimacy, and group permeability. *Psychological Bulletin, 127*, 520–542.

Bizumic, B., Duckitt, J., Popadic, D., Dru, V., & Krauss, S. (2009). Psychological structure of ethnocentrism. *European Journal of Social Psychology, 39*, 871–899.

Block, J., & Block, J. H. (2006). Nursery school personality and political orientation two decades later. *Journal of Research in Personality, 40*, 734–749.

Bonanno, G., & Jost, J. (2006). Conservative shift among high-exposure survivors of the September 11th terrorist attacks. *Basic and Applied Social Psychology, 28*, 11–23.

Cantal, C., Milfont, T., Wilson, M., & Gouveia, V. (2015). Differential effects of right-wing authoritarianism and social dominance orientation on dimensions of generalized prejudice in Brazil. *European Journal of Personality, 29*, 17–27.

Charles-Toussant, G., & Crowson, H. M. (2010). Prejudice against international students: The role of threat perceptions and authoritarian dispositions in U.S. students. *Journal of Psychology, 144*, 413–428.

Choma, B., Hanoch, Y., Hodson, M., & Gummerum, G. (2014). Relations between risk perceptions and socio-political ideology are domain- and ideology-dependent. *Personality and Individual Differences, 54*, 29–34.

Christopher, A., & Wojda, M. (2008). Social dominance orientation, right-wing authoritarianism, sexism, and prejudice toward women in the workforce. *Psychology of Women Quarterly, 32*, 65–73.

Cohrs, J.C., & Asbrock, F. (2009). Right-wing authoritarianism and social dominance orientation and prejudice against threatening versus competitive outgroups. *European Journal of Social Psychology, 39*, 270–289.

Cohrs, J.C., & Ibler, S. (2009). Authoritarianism, threat, and prejudice: An analysis of mediation and moderation. *Basic and Applied Social Psychology, 31*, 81–94.

Cohrs, J. C., Moschner, B., Maes, J., & Kielmann, S. (2005). The motivational bases of right-wing authoritarianism and social dominance orientation: Relation to values and attitudes in the aftermath of September 11, 2001. *Personality and Social Psychology Bulletin, 31*, 1–10.

Cohrs, J. C., & Stelzl, M. (2010). How ideological attitudes predict host society members' attitudes toward immigrants: Exploring cross-national differences. *Journal of Social Issues, 66*, 673–694.

Cohrs, J. C., Kämfe-Hargrave, N., & Riemann, R. (2012). Individual differences in ideological attitudes and prejudice: Evidence from peer-report data. *Journal of Personality and Social Psychology, 103*, 343–361.

Cozzolino, P., & Snyder, M. (2008). Good times, bad times: How personal disadvantage moderates the relationship between social dominance and efforts to win. *Personality and Social Psychology Bulletin, 34*, 1420–1433.

Craig, M., & Richeson, J. (2014). Not in my backyard! Authoritarianism, social dominance orientation, and support for strict immigration policies at home and abroad. *Political Psychology, 35*, 417–429.

Crawford, J. (2012). The ideologically objectionable premise model: Predicting biased political judgments on the left and right. *Journal of Experimental Social Psychology, 48*, 138–151.

Crawford, J., Brady, J., Pilanski, J., & Erny, H. (2013). Differential effects of right-wing authoritarianism and social dominance orientation on political candidate support: The moderating role of message framing. *Journal of Social and Political Psychology, 1*, 5–28.

Crawford, J., Jussim, L., Cain, T., & Cohen, F. (2013). Right-wing authoritarianism and social dominance orientation differentially predict biased evaluations of media reports. *Journal of Applied Social Psychology, 43*, 163–174.

Crawford, J., & Pilanski, J. (2014). The differential effects of right-wing authoritarianism and social dominance orientation on political intolerance. *Political Psychology*, *35*, 557–575.

Crowson, H. M. (2009). Right-wing authoritarianism and social dominance orientation as mediators of worldview beliefs on attitudes related to the war on terror. *Social Psychology*, *40*, 93–103.

Dallagio, F., & Roccato, M. (2010). Right-wing authoritarianism, Big Five and perceived threat to safety. *European Journal of Personality*, *24*, 106–122.

Danso, H., & Esses, V. (2001). Black experimenters and the intellectual performance of White participants: The tables are turned. *Journal of Experimental Social Psychology*, *37*, 158–165.

De Cremer, D., Cornelis, I., & Van Hiel, A. (2008). To whom does voice in groups matter? Effects of voice on affect and procedural fairness judgments as function of social dominance orientation. *Journal of Social Psychology*, *148*, 61–76.

De Oliveira, P., Guimond, S., & Dambrun, M. (2012). Power and legitimizing ideologies in hierarchy-enhancing vs. hierarchy-attenuating environments. *Political Psychology*, *33*, 867–885.

Dhont, K., & Van Hiel, A. (2009). We must not be enemies: Interracial contact and the reduction of prejudice among authoritarians. *Personality and Individual Differences*, *46*, 172–177.

Doty, R., Peterson, B., & Winter, D. (1991). Threat and authoritarianism in the United States, 1978–1987. *Journal of Personality and Social Psychology*, *61*, 629–640.

Dru, V. (2007). Authoritarianism, social dominance orientation and prejudice: Effects of various self-categorization conditions. *Journal of Experimental Social Psychology*, *43*, 877–883.

Duckitt, J. (2001). A dual process cognitive-motivational theory of ideology and prejudice. In M. Zanna (Ed.), *Advances in experimental social psychology* (Vol. *33*, pp. 41–113). San Diego: Academic.

Duckitt, J. (2006). Differential effects of right wing authoritarianism and social dominance orientation on outgroup attitudes and their mediation by threat from competitiveness to outgroups. *Personality and Social Psychology Bulletin*, *32*, 684–696.

Duckitt, J. (2013). Introduction to the special section on authoritarianism in social context: The role of threat. *International Journal of Psychology*, *48*, 1–5.

Duckitt, J., & Fisher, K. (2003). The impact of social threat on worldview and ideological attitudes. *Political Psychology*, *24*, 199–222.

Duckitt, J., & Sibley, C. G. (2007). Right-wing authoritarianism, social dominance orientation and the dimensions of generalized prejudice. *European Journal of Personality*, *21*, 113–130.

Duckitt, J., & Sibley, C. G. (2009). A dual process motivational model of ideology, politics, and prejudice. *Psychological Inquiry*, *20*, 98–109.

Duckitt, J., & Sibley, C. G. (2010a). Personality, ideology, prejudice and politics: A dual process motivational model. *Journal of Personality*, *78*, 1861–1893.

Duckitt, J., & Sibley, C. G. (2010b). RWA and SDO differentially moderate intergroup effects on prejudice. *European Journal of Personality*, *24*, 583–601

Duckitt, J., Wagner, C., du Plessis, I., & Birum, I. (2002). The psychological bases of ideology and prejudice: Testing a dual process model. *Journal of Personality and Social Psychology*, *82*, 75–93.

Duriez, B., & Van Hiel, A., & Kossowska, M. (2005). Authoritarianism and social dominance in Western and Eastern Europe: The importance of the socio-political context and of political interest and involvement. *Political Psychology, 26,* 299–320.

Duriez, B., Vansteenkiste, M., Soenens, B., & De Witte, H. (2007). The social costs of extrinsic relative to intrinsic goal pursuits: Their relation with social dominance and racial and ethnic prejudice. *Journal of Personality, 75,* 757–782.

Echebarria-Echabe, A., & Fernandez-Guede, E. (2006). Effects of terrorism on attitudes and ideological orientation. *European Journal of Social Psychology, 36,* 259–265.

Eibach, R., & Keegan, T. (2006). Free at last: Social dominance, loss aversion, and White and Black Americans' differing assessment of racial progress. *Journal of Personality and Social Psychology, 90,* 453–467.

Ekehammar, B., Akrami, N., Gylje, M., & Zakrisson, I. (2004). What matters most to prejudice: Big Five personality, social dominance orientation, or right-wing authoritarianism? *European Journal of Personality, 18,* 463–482.

Esses, V., Haddock, G., & Zanna, M. (1993). Values, stereotypes, and emotions as determinants of intergroup attitudes. In D. Mackie & D. Hamilton (Eds.), *Affect, cognition, and stereotyping* (Vol. *17,* pp. 137–166). San Diego: Academic.

Esses, V., Jackson, L., & Armstrong, T. (1998). Intergroup competition and attitudes toward immigrants and immigration: An instrumental model of group conflict. *Journal of Social Issues, 54,* 699–724.

Feldman, S., & Stenner, K. (1997). Perceived threat and authoritarianism. *Political Psychology, 18,* 741–770.

Feldman, S., Lavine, H., Lodge, M., & Verhulst, B. (2010, July). *Seeing negative: Authoritarianism and automatic vigilance for threatening stimuli.* Paper presented at the 33rd annual meeting of the International Society for Political Psychology, San Francisco.

Fischer, P., Fischer, J., Frey, D., Such, M., Smyth, M., Tester, M., & Kasenmüeller, A. (2010). Causal evidence that terrorism salience increases authoritarian parenting practices. *Social Psychology, 41,* 246–254.

Fraley, R. C., Griffen, B., Belsky, J., & Roisman, D. (2012). Developmental antecedents of political ideology: A longitudinal investigation from birth to age 18 years. *Psychological Science, 23,* 1425–1431.

Fritsche, I., Cohrs, J. C., Kessler, T., & Bauer, J. (2012). Global warming is breeding social conflict: The subtle impact of climate change threat on authoritarian tendencies. *Journal of Environmental Psychology, 32,* 1–10.

Gerber, M., & Jackson, J. (2013). Retribution as revenge and retribution as just deserts. *Social Justice Research, 26,* 61–80.

Guimond, S., Dambrun, M., Michinov, N., & Duarte, S. (2003). Does social dominance generate prejudice: Integrating individual and contextual determinants of intergroup cognitions. *Journal of Personality and Social Psychology, 84,* 697–721.

Haidt, J., & Joseph, C. (2004). Intuitive ethics: How innately prepared intuitions generate culturally variable virtues. *Daedalus, 133*(4), 55–66.

Henry, P. J. (2011). The role of stigma in understanding ethnicity differences in authoritarianism. *Political Psychology, 32,* 419–438.

Hodson, G. (2008). Interracial prison contact: The pros for (socially dominant) cons. *British Journal of Social Psychology, 47,* 325–351.

Hodson, G., & Busseri, M. (2012). Bright minds and dark attitudes: Lower cognitive ability predicts greater prejudice through right-wing authoritarianism and low intergroup contact. *Psychological Science, 23*, 187–195.

Hodson, G., Harry, H., & Mitchell, A. (2009). Independent benefits of contact and friendship on attitudes toward homosexuals among authoritarians and highly identified heterosexuals. *European Journal of Social Psychology, 35*, 509–525.

Huang, L., & Liu, J. (2005). Personality and social structural implications of the situational priming of social dominance orientation. *Personality and Individual Differences, 38*, 267–276.

Jackson, L., & Esses, V. (2000). Effects of economic competition on people's willingness to help empower immigrants. *Group Processes and Intergroup Relations, 3*, 419–435.

Jackson, L., & Gaertner, L. (2010). Mechanisms of moral disengagement and their differential use by right-wing authoritarianism and social dominance orientation in support of war. *Aggressive Behavior, 36*, 238–250.

Jost, J., Glaser, J., Kruglanski, A., & Sulloway, F. (2003). Political conservatism as motivated social cognition. *Psychological Bulletin, 129*, 339–375.

Jugert, P., & Duckitt, J. (2009). A motivational model of authoritarianism: Testing personal and situational determinants. *Political Psychology, 30*, 693–719.

Kauff, M., Asbrock, F., Thörner, S., & Wagner, U. (2013). Side effects of multiculturalism – The interaction effect of a multicultural ideology and authoritarianism on prejudice and diversity beliefs. *Personality and Social Psychology Bulletin, 39*, 306–321.

Kandler, C., Bleidorn, W., & Riemann, R. (2012). Left or right? Sources of political orientation: The roles of genetic factors, cultural transmission, assortative mating, and personality. *Journal of Personality and Social Psychology, 102*, 633–645.

Kossowska, M., Trejtowicz, M., de Lemus, S., Bukowski, M., Van Hiel, A., & Goodwin, R. (2011). Relationships between right-wing authoritarianism, terrorism threat, and attitudes towards restriction of civil rights: A comparison among four European countries. *British Journal of Psychology, 102*, 245–259.

Kteily, N., Sidanius, J., & Levin, S. (2011). Social dominance orientation: Cause or mere effect? Evidence for SDO as a causal predictor of prejudice and discrimination against ethnic and racial outgroups. *Journal of Experimental Social Psychology, 47*, 208–214.

Lavine, H., Burgess, D. Snyder, M., Transue, J., Sullivan, J., Henry, B., & Wagner, S. (1999). Threat, authoritarianism, and voting: An investigation of personality and persuasion. *Personality and Social Psychology Bulletin, 25*, 337–347.

Lavine, H., Lodge, M., Polichak, J., & Taber, C. (2002). Explicating the black box through experimentation: Studies of authoritarianism and threat. *Political Analysis, 10*, 343–361.

Lee, K., Ashton, M., Ogunfowora, B., Bourdage, J., & Shin, K. (2010). The personality bases of socio-political attitudes: The role of honesty-humility and openness to experience. *Journal of Research in Personality, 44*, 115–119.

Leone, L., Desimoni, M., & Chirumbolo, A. (2012). HEXACO, social worldviews, and socio-political attitudes: A mediation analysis. *Personality and Individual Differences, 53*, 995–1001.

Levin, S., Pratto, F., Matthews, M., Sidanius, J., & Kteily, N. (2012). A dual process approach to understanding prejudice toward Americans in Lebanon: An extension to intergroup threat perceptions and emotions. *Group Processes and Intergroup Relations, 16,* 139–158.

Lippa, R., & Arad, S. (1999). Gender, personality, and prejudice: The display of authoritarianism and social dominance in interviews with college men and women. *Journal of Research in Personality, 33,* 463–493.

Liu, J., Huang, L., & McFedries, C. (2008). Cross-sectional and longitudinal differences in social dominance orientation and right wing authoritarianism as a function of political party preferences and social change. *Asian Journal of Social Psychology, 11,* 116–126.

Matthews, M., Levin, S., & Sidanius, J. (2009). A longitudinal test of the model of political conservatism as motivated social cognition. *Political Psychology, 30,* 921–936.

McClelland, G., & Judd, C. (1993). Statistical difficulties of detecting interactions and moderator effects. *Psychological Bulletin, 114,* 376–390.

McFarland, S. (1998, July). *Toward a typology of prejudiced persons.* Paper presented at annual meeting of the International Society of Political Psychology, Montreal, Canada.

McFarland, S. (2005). On the eve of war: Authoritarianism, social dominance, and American students' attitudes toward attacking Iraq. *Personality and Social Psychology Bulletin, 31,* 360–367.

McFarland, S. (2010). Authoritarianism, social dominance, and other roots of generalized prejudice. *Political Psychology, 31,* 453–477.

McFarland, S., & Adelson, S. (1996, July). *An omnibus study of personality, values, and prejudice.* Paper presented at the annual meeting of the International Society of Political Psychology, Vancouver, Canada.

McKee, I., & Feather, N. (2008). Revenge, retribution, and values: Social attitudes and punitive sentencing. *Social Justice Research, 21,* 138–163.

McPherson, S., & Parks, C. (2011). Intergroup and interindividual resource competition escalating into conflict: The elimination option. *Group Dynamics: Theory, Research, and Practice, 15,* 285–296.

Meeus, J., Duriez, B., Vanbesselaere, N., Phalet, K., & Kuppens, P. (2009). Examining dispositional and situational effects on outgroup attitudes. *European Journal of Personality, 23,* 307–328.

Milojev, P., Osborne, D., Greaves, L. M., Bulbulia, J., Wilson, M. S., Davies, C. L. ... Sibley, C. G. (2014). Right-wing authoritarianism and social dominance orientation predict different moral signatures. *Social Justice Research, 27,* 149–174.

Mirisola, A., Roccato, M., Russo, S., Spagna, G., & Vieno, A. (2014). Societal threat to safety, compensatory control, and right-wing authoritarianism. *Political Psychology, 35,* 795–812.

Morrision, K., Fast, N., & Ybarra, O. (2009). Group status, perceptions of threat, and support for social inequality. *Journal of Experimental Social Psychology, 45,* 204–210.

Morrision, K., & Ybarra, O. (2008). The effects of realistic threat and group identification on social dominance orientation. *Journal of Experimental Social Psychology, 44,* 156–163.

Napier, J. L. (2014, July). *Superheroes for change: Priming physical invulnerability facilitates progressive attitudes among conservatives.* Paper presented at the 36th Annual Meeting of the International Society for Political Psychology, Herzliya, Israel.

Onraet, E., Dhont, K., & Van Hiel, A. (2014). The relationships between internal and external threats and right-wing attitudes: A three-wave longitudinal study. *Personality and Social Psychology Bulletin, 40*, 712–725.

Onraet, E., Van Hiel, A., & Cornelis, I. (2013). Threat and right-wing attitudes: A cross-national approach. *Political Psychology, 35*, 791–803.

Onraet, E., Van Hiel, A., Dhont, K., & Pattyn, S. (2013). Internal and external threat in relationship with right-wing attitudes. *Journal of Personality, 81*, 233–248.

Onraet, E., Van Hiel, A., Roets, A., & Cornelis, I. (2011). The closed mind: "Experience" and "cognition" aspects of openness to experience and need for closure as psychological bases for right-wing attitudes. *European Journal of Personality, 25*, 184–197.

Perry, R., & Sibley, C. G. (2013). A dual-process motivational model of social and economic policy attitudes. *Analyses of Social Issues and Public Policy, 13*, 262–285.

Perry, R., & Sibley, C. G. (2010). Dangerous and competitive schemas: A new frequency estimation index of the dual process model's social worldviews component. *Personality and Individual Differences, 49*, 983–988.

Perry, R., Sibley, C. G., & Duckitt, J. (2013a). Dangerous and competitive worldviews: A meta-analysis of their associations with social dominance orientation and right-wing authoritarianism. *Journal of Research in Personality, 47*, 116–127.

Perry, R., Sibley, G. C., & Duckitt, J. (2013b). A comparison of broad-bandwidth and frequency-specific measures of competitive and dangerous worldviews. *Personality and Individual Differences, 54*, 284–288.

Pettigrew, T. (1958). Personality and socio-cultural factors in intergroup attitudes: A cross-national comparison. *Journal of Conflict Resolution, 2*, 29–42.

Pratto, F., Sidanius, J., Stallworth, L., & Malle, B. (1994). Social dominance orientation: A personality variable predicting social and political attitudes. *Journal of Personality and Social Psychology, 67*, 741–763.

Proch, J. (2013). *More than half a century of research on personality and prejudice: Where are we now and where do we go from here?* Unpublished PhD dissertation, Friedrich Schiller University, Jena, Germany.

Riek, B., Mania, E., & Gaertner, S. (2006). Intergroup threat and outgroup attitudes: A meta-analytic review. *Personality and Social Psychology Review, 10*, 336–353.

Rickert, E. (1998). Authoritarianism and economic threat: Implications for political behavior. *Political Psychology, 19*, 707–720.

Rippl, S., & Seipel, C. (2012). Threat appraisal and authoritarianism in context: Reactions to the European Union enlargement in border regions. *Journal of Applied Social Psychology, 11*, 2758–2775.

Roets, A., Van Hiel, A., & Dhont, K. (2012). Is sexism a gender issue? A motivated social cognition perspective on men's and women's sexist attitudes toward own and other gender. *European Journal of Personality, 26*, 350–359.

Sales, S. (1973). Threat as a factor in authoritarianism: an analysis of archival data. *Journal of Personality and Social Psychology, 28*, 44–57.

Schmitt, M., Branscombe, N., & Kappen, D. (2003). Attitudes toward group-based inequality: Social dominance or social identity? *British Journal of Social Psychology, 42*, 161–186.

Shaffer, B., & Duckitt, J. (2013). The dimensional structure of people's fears, threats, and concerns and their relationship with right-wing authoritarianism and social dominance orientation. *International Journal of Psychology, 48*, 6–17.

Sherif, M. (1967). *Group conflict and cooperation*. London: Routledge & Kegan Paul.

Sibley, C. G., & Duckitt, J. (2008). Personality and prejudice: A meta-analysis and theoretical review. *Personality and Social Psychology Review, 12*, 248–279.

Sibley, C. G., & Duckitt, J. (2009). Big-Five personality, social worldviews, and ideological attitudes: Further tests of a dual process cognitive-motivational model. *Journal of Social Psychology, 149*, 545–561.

Sibley, C. G., & Duckitt, J. (2010). The personality basis of ideology: A one-year longitudinal study. *Journal of Social Psychology, 150*, 540–559.

Sibley, C. G., & Duckitt, J. (2013). The dual process model of ideology and prejudice: A longitudinal test during a global recession. *Journal of Social Psychology, 153*, 448–466.

Sibley, C. G., Osborne, D., & Duckitt, J. (2012). Personality and political orientation: Meta-analysis and test of a threat-constraint model. *Journal of Research in Personality, 46*, 664–677.

Sibley, C. G., Harding, J., Perry, R., Asbrock, F., & Duckitt, J. (2010). Personality and prejudice: Extension to the HEXACO model of personality structure. *European Journal of Personality, 24*, 515–534.

Sibley, C. G., Wilson, M., & Duckitt, J. (2007a). Effects of dangerous and competitive worldviews on right wing authoritarianism and social dominance orientation over a five-month period. *Political Psychology, 28*, 357–371.

Sibley, C. G., Wilson, M., & Duckitt, J. (2007b). Antecedents of men's hostile and benevolent sexism: The dual roles of social dominance orientation and right-wing authoritarianism. *Personality and Social Psychology Bulletin, 33*, 160–172.

Sidanius, J., & Pratto, F. (1999). *Social dominance. An intergroup theory of social hierarchy and oppression*. Cambridge: Cambridge University Press.

Sidanius, J., Haley, H., Molina, L., & Pratto, F. (2007). Vladimir's choice and the distribution of social resources: A social dominance perspective. *Group Processes and Intergroup Relations, 10*, 257–265.

Sidanius, J., Kteily, N., Sheehy-Skeffington, J., Ho, A., Sibley, C. G., & Duriez, B. (2012). You're inferior and not worth our concern: The interface between empathy and social dominance orientation. *Journal of Personality, 81*, 313–323.

Solomon, S., Greenberg, J., & Pyszczynski, T. (1991). A terror management theory of social behavior: The psychological function of self-esteem and cultural worldviews. *Advances in Experimental Social Psychology, 24*, 93–159.

Stangor, C., & Leary, M. (2006). Intergroup beliefs: Investigations from the social side. In M. Zanna (Ed.), *Advances in experimental social psychology* (Vol. *38*, pp. 243–281). New York: Academic.

Stenner, K. (2005). *The authoritarian dynamic*. Cambridge: Cambridge University Press.

Swami, V., Neofytou, R., Thirlwell, H., Taylor, D., & McCleary, D. (2013). Social dominance orientation predicts drive for muscularity among British men. *Body Image, 10*, 653–656.

Tajfel, H., & Turner, J. (1979). An integrative theory of intergroup conflict. In W. Austin & S. Worchel (Eds.), *The social psychology of intergroup relations* (pp. 33–47). Monterey, CA: Brooks/Cole.

Thomsen, L., Green, E., & Sidanius, J. (2008). We will hunt them down: How social dominance orientation and right-wing authoritarianism fuel ethnic persecution of immigrants in fundamentally different ways. *Journal of Experimental Social Psychology, 44*, 1455–1464.

Van Hiel, A., Cornelis, I., & Roets, A. (2007). The intervening role of social worldviews in the relationship between the Five-Factor model of personality and social attitudes. *European Journal of Personality, 21*, 131–148.

Van Hiel, A., & Mervielde, I. (2002). Explaining conservative beliefs and political preferences: A comparison of social dominance orientation and authoritarianism. *Journal of Applied Social Psychology, 32*, 965–976.

Weber, C., & Federico, C. (2007). Interpersonal attachment and patterns of ideological belief. *Political Psychology, 28*, 389–416.

Wildschut, T., & Insko, C. (2007). Explanations of interindividual-intergroup discontinuity: A review of the evidence. *European Review of Social Psychology, 18*, 175–211.

Wilson, M., & Liu, J. (2003). Social dominance orientation and gender: The moderating role of gender identity. *British Journal of Social Psychology, 42*, 187–198.

Wilson, G. (1973). *The psychology of conservatism*. New York: Academic.

10 Is Prejudice Heritable? Evidence from Twin Studies

Fiona Kate Barlow, James M. Sherlock, and Brendan P. Zietsch

The idea of studying prejudice from a genetic standpoint may at first strike some as inappropriate. Genetic explanations of human emotion, thought, and behavior have often been used to justify prejudice, rather than explain it. Following the 1859 publication of Charles Darwin's theory of evolution in which he explained the change of traits over generations in both animal and plant species, Francis Galton aimed to apply evolutionary principles to human populations (Paul & Hasian, 1998). In 1883, Galton coined the term "eugenics" to describe the science of increasing the prevalence of desired traits within a population through selective breeding. While his ideas were initially challenged, they gained popularity in the early twentieth century, and multiple university departments began officially studying eugenics. Simultaneously, societies sprang up aiming to promote breeding in those of "high genetic quality" and supporting the forced sterilization of those of "low genetic quality" such as the mentally ill (Paul & Hasian, 1998).

By the 1930s, the most famous proponent of eugenics, Adolf Hitler, was rising to power. While some in England and America supported his aims and the principles of eugenics, many others were beginning to express concern about the use and validity of a eugenic approach. In the quote that follows, famed behavioral psychologist John Watson argued against a genetic understanding of human behavior. He posited that with enough resources, he would be able to make of a child what he chose, regardless of any "tendencies" that child might have:

> Give me a dozen healthy infants, well-formed, and my own specified world to bring them up in and I'll guarantee to take any one at random and train him to become any type of specialist I might select – doctor, lawyer, artist, merchant-chief and, yes, even beggar-man and thief, regardless of his talents, penchants, tendencies, abilities, vocations, and race of his ancestors. (Watson, 1930, p. 82)

Vitally, in the last sentence, Watson challenged racist assumptions of his time to state that he could achieve these goals irrespective of a child's race. Through their research, Watson and his contemporaries unequivocally demonstrated that there are large environmental impacts on the way that we behave. It is possible, however, that Watson's comments (and even research) were also political. At the time that he was working, anything other than a hard line on genetics could have been misused. Even today, so many years after Watson's writings, concerns about the potential misuse of genetic theorizing and data still remain. It is possible that such concerns account for the fact that there is comparatively little social-psychological work looking at the genetics of prejudice. What work there is, however, strongly suggests that we must examine the genetics of prejudice if we are to understand it. As this chapter reveals, a substantive proportion of variance in prejudice toward multiple groups, is in fact, heritable.

Nature vs. Nurture Debate

While social psychology has been slow to adopt genetic approaches when attempting to answer research questions, the same is not true of other areas within psychology. For example, in many ways developmental psychology is grounded in an ongoing debate about the extent to which nature (genetic factors) or nurture (environmental factors) makes us who we are. It is relatively uncontroversial to say that someone's eye color, hair color, or height are influenced, or even largely determined, by heritable factors. Something feels qualitatively different, however, about stating that "Tim's tendency to snap at his friends when he is tired" or "Yi's ability to have a good sense of humor when things get hard" is heritable in the same way that height is.

As humans, our huge frontal lobes give us the ability to reason, remember, and importantly build detailed narratives about who we are. To this end, who we are typically feels more than, and different from, the sum of our (genetic) parts. This perspective was perhaps most famously summarized by French philosopher René Descartes (1596–1650), who argued that the soul (or mind) and body were distinct and separable. To him, the body was material, following set laws of nature, whereas the soul (or mind) was not. Descartes, a devout Catholic, argued that the soul was instead determined by, or controlled by, God.

For many nonreligious people who hold this sentiment, parents and upbringing tend to take the place of "God." While we typically attribute our successes to stable, internal factors (Kelley, 1967), failures that we experience often feel like a direct consequence of insufficient parenting or traumatic early experiences. Developmental psychologists have heavily pursued this perspective, with particular responsibility falling on the mother. For example, Mary Ainsworth and colleagues (1978) argued that a child's temperament was a direct function of his or her mother's consistency. Lay explanations of parental responsibility for problems in children are also rife.

One instance can be found in our understanding of autism. Following the recognition of autism as a psychological disorder in 1943, scientists and parents attempted to understand the etiology of the disorder. Parents' difficulties interacting with their autistic children were speculated to be the cause, rather than the effect, of autism (Folstein & Rosen-Sheidley, 2001). Consequently, mothers of autistic children were dubbed "refrigerator mothers": cold, incapable, and responsible for their child's disorder. Similarly, parents of children with schizo-phrenia routinely blamed their behaviors (but not genes) for creating their child's mental illness (Peterson & Docherty, 2004). In other areas, one study found that Finnish people in an internet discussion primarily blamed the parents in the event that their child was overweight (Kokkonen, 2009). There was relative consensus among discussion participants that the parents of such children were "lousy," inadequately bonded to their children, and unable to practice appropriate child-rearing. A genetic contribution to children's weight was largely dismissed.

We see that anything that appears malleable (e.g., overweight, mental illness, attachment style) is easily and readily attributed to environmental rather than genetic factors. We also see that an absence of genetic understanding of human behavior can be used as a justification for judging others. In the case of tempera-ment, autism, schizophrenia, and weight, such judgments on parents are patently unfair. Each is highly heritable, with relatively little variance accounted for by shared, or home, environment (Freitag, 2007; Gejman, Sanders, & Duan, 2010; Saudino, 2005; Wardle, Carnell, Haworth, & Plomin, 2008).

But how do we know this? The answer lies in the twin study. After World War II, research on genetic influences on behavior commenced in earnest, following the development of statistical techniques outlined here. The field was termed "behavior genetics."

Quantitative Behavioral Genetics

Though grand in scope and scale, the attempt to discern the extent to which genes influence individual differences in a trait relies on a relatively simple premise. Key to the whole endeavor is the natural experiment provided by identical and nonidentical twins. Here, a quirk of biology has afforded researchers pairs of individuals who share 100% of their segregating genes (those inherited from their mother and father) and pairs who share only 50%. Whereas fraternal twins share only half of their parents' genetic material with each other, identical twins are for the most part genetic clones. Traits that are shared strongly between identical twins and weakly between nonidentical twins are presumably due to genes. Any similar-ity between twin pairs not attributable to genes must then be the product of the environment; so by quantifying genetic effects, researchers can determine to what degree differences between individuals are due to their genes and/or their environ-ment. The classical twin design, a mathematical model for estimating heritability, compares how a given trait covaries within identical twin pairs and nonidentical twin pairs to estimate the proportion of variation in a trait due to three separate factors: genetic influences (A and D), the shared environment (C), and any residual sources (E) (Neale & Cardon, 1992).

The broad-sense heritability (H^2) of a trait is the proportion of variance therein accounted for by all genetic factors. This estimate indicates the proportion of the

Box 10.1 Key terms in quantitative genetics

Alleles: alternative versions of a gene.

Phenotype: the observable characteristics of an organism.

Broad-sense heritability (H^2): the degree to which phenotypic variation reflects genetic variation (trait expression as a result of genes).

Narrow-sense heritability (h^2): the degree to which phenotypic variation reflects additive genetic variation.

Additive genetic variance (A): variance in a trait due to the sum of allelic effects within and across genes.

Nonadditive genetic variance (D): variance in a trait due to interactions between alleles such as dominance or epistasis.

Common environmental variance (C): variance due to any aspect of the environment shared by twins.

Residual variance (E): variance in a trait that causes twins to differ from each other.

difference between any two people due to their genetic inheritance. Genetic differences between people are the result of inheriting different alleles, which are alternative versions of genes, and their effects can be additive or interactive (see Box 10.1). Additive genitive effects (*A*) are the sum of allelic effects both within and across loci and are considered the narrow-sense heritability (h^2) of a trait. In contrast, nonadditive genetic variance (*D*) results from interactions between alleles, such as those involved in dominance (one allele at a locus is dominant and is expressed more than others) or epistasis (where the expression of an allele at one locus is dependent on alleles at one or more other loci). As illustrated in Figure 10.1, if additive genetic effects were the only source of variation in a trait, identical twins would be expected to correlate perfectly at 1.0, whereas nonidentical twins would only correlate at 0.5. If nonadditive genetic effects were the only source of variation in a trait, the resemblance between nonidentical twins would be much reduced relative to identical twins. In fact, nonidentical twins would be expected to correlate at .25 at most if dominance interactions were present. This would be further reduced if epistasis were occurring (for a detailed explanation of nonadditive genetic effects, see Posthuma et al., 2003). Identical twins, meanwhile, would still correlate perfectly as they would share the configuration of all of the genes underlying these interactions.

Twin studies can also estimate the effects of the shared environment on trait variation. The shared environment consists of any nongenetic source of variation in a trait that is shared between twins and, as a result, drives the pair to be more similar to each other. This may include aspects of the home such as socioeconomic status, parenting style, or the political affiliation of the household. Shared environmental effects will cause both identical and nonidentical twins to be more similar to each other, regardless of genetic relatedness. Thus, if the shared environment were the only source of variation in a trait, both identical and nonidentical twins would correlate at 1.0.

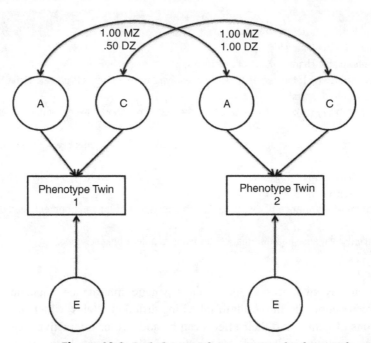

Figure 10.1 *Path diagram demonstrating the degree of resemblance between identical/monozygotic (MZ) and nonidentical/dizygotic (DZ) twins for additive genetic (A), shared environmental (C), and residual (E) influences. Phenotypic variance (equal for each twin pair) is influenced by latent factors A, C, and E. The variance associated with these factors is shared between twin pairs at varying magnitudes based on the zygosity of the twin pair and the characteristics of the factor itself. MZ twins share 100% of the variance caused by A, whereas DZ twins share half this influence. C is shared equally at 100% between identical and nonidentical twin pairs. By definition, E is the remaining unique variance in the phenotype not explained by A and C combined.*

Any variation that is not caused by genetic or shared environmental factors is estimated as residual variance. By definition, these influences cause twins to be different from each other; if residual sources of variance were the only factor influencing a trait, both identical and nonidentical twins would not correlate at all. Residual sources include any errors in measurement; chance biological effects (such as mutations or cancers); and of course the individual, idiosyncratic experiences of the twins. It is important to note that residual variance, and in particular measurement error, will constrain the upper limit of a trait's heritability. For example, even a trait that is 100% heritable (on the true values of the trait) will yield low estimates of heritability if the measure used is unreliable.

It is almost never the case that a single one of these factors can fully account for variation in a trait. Behavioral geneticists implement full-information maximum-likelihood modeling to generate variance component estimates (i.e., A, C/D, and E) that best fit the observed pattern of correlations between identical and nonidentical twins. These estimates are standardized to 1, so that each component represents the proportion of variation in a trait it accounts for as a percentage of total variance. By applying this model to multiple traits at once (i.e., a multivariate model), researchers are also able to generate estimates of the proportion of covariance between traits due to genetic and environmental effects. Further, the model can also provide estimates of a genetic correlation between traits. This indicates the degree of overlap in sources of genetic variation between two traits (i.e., shared genes).

Trait Heritability

Since the development of twin methodology, many thousands of studies have been run comparing the similarity in traits between monozygotic and dizygotic twins. A recent meta-analysis of the heritability of human traits allows for a comprehensive discussion of how (a) genetics, (b) shared environment, and (c) non-shared environment (and measurement error) contribute to physical and mental traits in general (Polderman et al., 2015). Polderman and colleagues (2015) looked at virtually all twin studies conducted between 1958 and 2012. In total, they examined results from 2,748 studies, investigating more than 7,000 traits, and composed of data offered from almost 15 million twin pair observations (note that some twins were used in multiple studies). Further, the sample was inherently cross-cultural: Twins came from 39 countries. The researchers found overwhelming evidence for the role of genes in both physical and psychological attributes. Tellingly, every single trait meta-analyzed was heritable to some degree. Overall, the reported heritability of traits in general was approximately 50%, with the majority of studies (approximately 70%) revealing no shared environmental effects on traits (note that idiosyncratic and individual experiences with parents will be captured under E, rather than C).

Social values and social interactions were among the least heritable traits. Approximately 30% of the variation in these types of traits was accounted for by genetic factors. Here, the shared environment did appear to have an impact, accounting for approximately 20% of the variance in social interactions and 30% of the variance in social values.[1] Prejudice, racism, and discrimination would all fall under this category but do not define it. Next we review studies that do explicitly investigate racism, sexism, and sexual prejudice. Further, we supplement these by reporting on the heritability of constructs that have been

---

1 This estimate should be interpreted with caution as couples tend to assortatively mate (i.e., are more alike than would be expected by chance) on social values (e.g., Eaves et al., 1999; Hatemi, Medland, Morley, Heath, & Martin, 2007; Martin et al., 1986; Zietsch, Verweij, Heath, & Martin, 2011), which can inflate estimates of shared environmental variance (see Verweij et al., 2008).

found to predict prejudice, political conservatism, right-wing authoritarianism and social dominance orientation, religiosity, and empathy (note that while each of these constructs predicts prejudice, we are in no way implying that they are necessarily associated with prejudice on the individual level or are the same as prejudice).

Genetics and Prejudice

One of the earliest studies to look at the heritability of social attitudes was conducted by Martin and colleagues (1986). In this work, data were collected from more than 4,000 twin pairs from Australia and the UK. Each twin had completed a modified version of the Wilson-Patterson Conservatism measure (Wilson & Patterson, 1968). In this measure, people are asked to indicate whether they agree, disagree, or are uncertain in response to a wide range of social issues aligned with conservative or liberal values. Issues included pajama parties (i.e., sleep-overs), casual living, nudist camps, chaperones, hippies, and cousin marriage. Of more relevance to the current chapter, issues also included those directed toward non-White people and women. Heritability estimates for these items, across both men and women, are reported in Table 10.1.

A study by Alford, Funk, and Hibbing (2005) also looked at the heritability of social attitudes as assessed by the Wilson-Patterson Conservatism measure. They examined data from more than 20,000 twins in the United States and their attitudes toward issues such as pacifism, foreign aid, immigration, women's liberation, gay rights, segregation, and busing (providing nonsegregated buses to transport children to nonsegregated schools). Estimates of the genetic and environmental influences on each of the issues relevant to the current chapter can be seen in Table 10.2.

Overall, conservatism (as measured by the 28-item version of the Wilson-Patterson measure of conservatism) was estimated to be 43% heritable, 22%

Table 10.1 *Variance component estimates for items on the Wilson-Patterson Conservatism scale (Wilson & Patterson, 1968) as reported in Martin et al. (1986).*

Attitude item	Heritability (A)	Shared Environment (C)	Residual Variance (E)
Working Mothers	.36	.09	.55
Coeducation	.07	.34	.59
Women Judges	.27	.14	.59
White Superiority	.40	.09	.51
Apartheid	.43	.05	.52
Mixed Marriage	.33	.12	.55

Table 10.2 *Variance component estimates for items on the Wilson-Patterson*
Conservatism scale (Wilson & Patterson, 1968), as report in Alford et al. (2005).

Attitude	Heritability	Shared Environment	Residual Variance (E)
Pacifism	.38	−.04	.66
Foreign Aid	.35	.06	.59
Immigration	.33	.12	.55
Women's Liberation	.33	.13	.54
Gay Rights	.28	.32	.40
Segregation	.27	.11	.62
Busing	.26	.16	.57

influenced by shared environment, and 35% due to residual sources (including error). Affect toward Democrats and Republicans was also moderately heritable (31%), with own party affiliation less so (14%; 41% accounted for by shared environment) (see also Eaves et al., 1999).

More recently, evidence for a genetic contribution to racial attitudes was found in the Minnesota Twins Political Survey (Orey & Park, 2012). The authors reported on data from 565 White twin sets. These twins were asked to rate how they felt toward Whites, Blacks, Hispanics, and Asians, from 0 = *very cool* to 1 = *very warm* (i.e., feelings thermometers). A measure of ethnocentrism was then calculated by subtracting how warm they felt toward non-Whites (averaged) from how warm they felt toward Whites. They found that 18% of the variance in ethnocentrism was accounted for by genetic factors, with 0% accounted for by shared environment and 82% accounted for by non-shared environment. It should be noticed that feelings thermometers yield inconsistent responses from individual respondents as well as between respondents (see Nelson, 2008; Wilcox, Sigelman, & Cook, 1989), and any error associated with this measure will constrain estimates of heritability.

Another study investigated prejudice against foreign nationals in Germany. Data were collected from 1,397 twins (Kandler, Lewis, Feldhaus, & Riemann, 2015). Their study used three measures of xenophobia (fear of foreignness). First, they measured direct prejudice toward non-European foreign nations (e.g., seeing foreign nationals as backstabbing, arrogant, and unfriendly). The second measure was discriminatory intent toward foreign nationals. This measure tapped into how much the participants thought that Swedes, Poles, Italians, and Turks living in Germany should be punished more and receive less social support than German nationals. Finally, they measured what they called narrow-sense xenophobia, with items tapping into whether people looked forward to and felt comfortable interacting with foreign nationals. Even after accounting for a range of control variables including spouses' social attitudes, prejudice toward non-European nationalities

(32%), discriminatory intent (31%), and narrow-sense xenophobia (43%) were all estimated to be substantially heritable. Conversely, the shared environment accounted for none of the variance overall of the attitudes investigated.

Another study using a subset of the twins used in Kandler et al. (2015) found that 38% of the variance in Germans' generalized prejudice was accounted for by genes, whereas 0% of the variance was caused by shared the environment (Lewis, Kandler, & Riemann, 2014). The authors also estimated the heritability of nationalism (the extent to which participants wanted to eject foreigners who did not love Germany from the country) and patriotism (the extent to which participants loved and were proud to be German) in this study. Nationalism was found to be due to both heritable (20%) and shared environmental (27%) factors, as was patriotism (29% and 9% respectively). Ingroup *love* (patriotism) and outgroup *hate* (prejudice) were found to be distinct heritable variables, with nationalism (a mix of ingroup love and outgroup hate) showing genetic correlations to each. Thus, we see genetic support for Marilynn Brewer's argument (Chapter 5, this title) about the distinct role of ingroup love when it comes to looking at how we come to preference one group over another.

A further set of studies investigated ingroup favoritism. In their first study, Lewis and Bates (2014) asked MZ and DZ twins how much they identified with their ethnic, racial, and religious ingroups, as well as the extent to which they preferred to spend time with members of their groups and placed importance on marrying within the group. They also asked twins to indicate the extent to which they were concerned about norm maintenance (which was referred to as "traditionalism"). This measure tapped into the extent that people approved of censorship and thought that moral and religious laws should be stricter. They found that 46% of the variance in ingroup favoritism and 20% of the variance in traditionalism were due to genetic factors. Conversely, only 7% and 19% of the variance in each were accounted for by shared environment, respectively. The genetic correlation between ingroup favoritism and traditionalism was estimated at $r = .59$, indicating a large degree overlap in the sources of genetic variation.

In a second study, Lewis and Bates (2014) conducted a conceptual replication of their first study. However, in this iteration they measured ingroup favoritism by looking at the difference between how warm participants felt toward their own group (White Americans) and other groups (Black, Hispanic, Muslim, and Asian Americans). To capture traditionalism, the authors measured right-wing authoritarianism (RWA), an ideological variable marked by submission to authorities and strong preference for established social order and norms (Adorno, Frenkel-Brunswik, Levinson, & Sanford, 1950; Altemeyer, 1988). In this study, 19% of the variance in ingroup favoritism was accounted for by genetic factors, and again, there was no influence of shared environment. RWA was 49% heritable, whereas 12% of the variation was due to shared environment and 39% to residual sources. Interestingly, the authors found that RWA and ingroup favoritism were statistically indistinguishable at the genetic level – they formed one latent factor (Lewis & Bates, 2014).

With regard to sexual minorities, Verweij et al. (2008) investigated the heritability of negative attitudes toward people who are not heterosexual. Sexually prejudiced responses toward statements such as "homosexuality is not immoral" or "[homosexuals are] dangerous as teachers" were summed across 10 items. Twin modeling revealed that 36% of variation in homophobic attitudes was due to additive genetic variance, in contrast to just 18% of variance accounted for by the shared environment.

In sum, then, the existing work on the heritability of attitudes toward people from different racial/ethnic groups, women, and non-heterosexuals demonstrates that genes have a marked and consistent influence on prejudice. Heritability estimates show that between 20% and 50% of the variation in various prejudicial attitudes is due to genetic effects.

Convergent evidence for the heritability of prejudice can also be found by examining the extent to which constructs robustly associated with prejudice are heritable. Of these, political orientation (as demonstrated in the studies using items from a measure of conservatism), RWA, and social dominance orientation (SDO: a preference for group-based hierarchies; Pratto, Sidanius, Stallworth, & Malle, 1994) stand out. Meta-analyses confirm that all three are robust predictors of prejudiced attitudes (Sibley & Duckitt, 2008). All three are also, as might be expected, heritable.

A recent German study found that 50% of the variance in RWA was accounted for by genetic factors, as opposed to just 7% (nonsignificant) in SDO (Kandler et al., 2015). Some authors have suggested that the heritability of RWA might be explained by an underlying "obedience to authority" factor that also explains religiosity and political conservatism (Ludeke, Johnson, & Bouchard, 2013). Further, in a study by Kandler, Bleidorn, and Riemann (2012), 872 twins (224 MZ pairs, 166 DZ pairs, and 92 unmatched pairs) reported on their personality and political attitudes. Political orientation was measured via eight items tapping in to two factors: (a) acceptance of inequality (e.g., intolerant and rejecting of minority groups) and (b) rejection of system change (e.g., conforming and patriotic). A right-wing orientation would be characterized by high acceptance of inequality and high rejection of system change. Personality was measured by the NEO-PI-R, measuring agreeableness, extroversion, conscientiousness, openness to experience, and neuroticism (Costa & McCrae, 2008).

Genetic factors explained political orientation more so than did shared environmental factors. Approximately 20% of the variance in acceptance of inequality was accounted for by additive genetic factors, and nearly 40% of the variance in rejection of system changes. Conversely, the shared environment was estimated to account for only 9% and 8% of the variance in the two political orientation factors, respectively. Substantive genetic correlations between personality and political orientation indicate that low levels of openness to experience and agreeableness genetically covary with acceptance of inequality. In contrast, high levels of extroversion and conscientiousness and low levels of openness to experience genetically covary with rejection of system change. It also appears that political orientations are maintained through assortative mating. Partners of twins were likely to share their spouse's political outlook, and thus their children are likely to share their parents' political leanings via genetic and shared environmental pathways.

It is unlikely that being conservative or liberal is directly genetically influenced – rather, the two ideologies represent underlying genetic factors that align with certain attitudes. A study drawing on Australian twin data found that approximately 24% of the variance in preference for a liberal versus a conservative government was heritable (Hatemi et al., 2007). However, participants were also asked what they thought their social class was, whether they attended church regularly, and how they felt about a range of social issues (e.g., gay rights, the monarchy, private school, and strict rules). The genetic variation in participants' voting behavior was almost entirely accounted for by a tendency to favor or oppose socialist principles. Other work has even shown that the extent to which people care about political issues at all (partisanship) is largely due to genetic factors, and not at all linked to shared environment (see also Hatemi, Alford, Hibbing, Martin, & Eaves, 2009; Settle, Dawes, & Fowler, 2009).

Further genetic evidence, independent of twin studies, comes from Benjamin et al. (2012), who used molecular-genetic-based statistical analysis of unrelated individuals to demonstrate the heritability of both social and economic attitudes. Unrelated individuals differ slightly in how genetically similar they are to one another, as a result of very distant relatedness. This variation in genetic related-ness can be compared with the variation in similarity on the trait, and an estimate can be derived for the trait's heritability as explained by the alleles included on the genotype chip (hundreds of thousands of single nucleotide polymorphisms across the genome). This methodology again indicates substantial heritability of social and economic attitudes. Further, the study sheds light on the genetic architecture of these attitudes, suggesting that genetic influences on political and economic preferences are the aggregate of many, many individually tiny allelic effects.

Religiosity, much like political conservatism, is also robustly linked to prejudice (Hall, Matz, & Wood, 2010). As is the case with political orientation, multiple studies show that religiosity is heritable. For example, a study of MZ and DZ twins raised apart (thus without shared environment) suggests that genes account for approximately 40% of the variance in both extrinsic and intrinsic religiosity (Bouchard, McGue, Lykken, & Tellegen, 1999). Complementing this study are numerous twin studies demonstrating the heritability of religiosity (e.g., Waller, Kojetin, Bouchard, Lykken, & Tellegen, 1990; Zietsch et al., 2011). Additionally, a small study of Polish twins found that religious fundamentalism was explained by a combination of genetic (38%) and shared environmental (46%) influences (Jakubowska & Oniszczenko, 2010). Where religiosity and traditional values are concerned, perceptions of immorality may contribute to prejudicial attitudes. In this regard, approximately half of the variation in moral disgust sensitivity (i.e., the extent to which moral transgressions illicit a disgust response) has been found to be heritable (Sherlock, Zietsch, Tybur, & Jern, 2016).

Finally, we turn our attention to empathy, altruism, and prosocial behavior (also as factors understood to be associated with prejudice; Dovidio et al., 2010). Here again, our genes come into play. A review paper examining the genetics of social behavior detailed research that looked at outcomes relevant to social behavior (Ebstein, Israel, Chew, Zhong, & Knafo, 2010). The authors reviewed work that convincingly demonstrated a heritable component of empathy, social responsiveness, empathetic concern, and aggression, even the extent to which people trust one another and behave in ultimatum and trust games. In terms of prosocial behavior, 50% of variance was accounted for by genetic factors in both boys and girls, with similar findings for social responsiveness (although here, shared environment appeared to play more of a role than it did in prosocial behavior).

Another twin study investigated the heritability of prosociality across a number of domains including civic duty, workplace commitment, and concern for the welfare of others (Lewis & Bates, 2011). The authors identified a common genetic factor underlying all domains that was thought to represent a prosociality mechanism. Approximately 65% and 44% of the variation in this underlying prosociality mechanism was due to genetic effects in females and males, respectively.

One study of South Korean twins tracked children's prosociality throughout development and concluded that genetic effects actually increased while shared environmental effects decreased with age (Hur & Rushton, 2007). The researchers concluded that 55% of variation in prosociality was due to genetic effects, while 45% was due to residual sources, leaving no influence on the shared environment. These estimates were also broadly congruent with estimates from Western samples (Rushton, 2004; Rushton, Fulker, Neale, Nias, & Eysenck, 1986).

In stark contrast to our capacity for love and empathy is the human tendency to aggress, which is all too frequently involved in, or a result of, prejudice. One meta-analysis looked at the heritability of antisocial behavior in the form of antisocial personality disorder and psychopathy (Ferguson, 2010). Additionally, the meta-analysis included studies that had investigated antisocial behavior itself, such as likelihood of aggression, violence, lying, and stealing. Generating estimates from 96,918 people over 38 studies, Ferguson (2010) convincingly demonstrated that the bulk of the variance in antisocial behavior was explained by genes (56%), with less explained by both the shared environment (11%) and residual influences (31%) combined.

Overall then, whether we look at prejudice toward racial groups, women, or non-heterosexuals, genes play a considerable role. Even when investigating factors associated with prejudice, we see that political conservatism, RWA, religiosity, empathy, prosocial behavior and altruism, and aggression all are heritable. This is perhaps no surprise, given that we opened with describing a meta-analysis showing that to date, all human traits measured appear to be heritable (Polderman et al., 2015). With this clear, it is now important to theorize about what this means for social psychology, and a psychological understanding of prejudice, where the goal is typically to change and improve intergroup relationships, rather than explain attitude stability. In short, the question becomes: What does this mean for the psychological study of prejudice?

Prejudice as Heritable and Malleable

Earlier in this chapter, we reviewed a study that looked at the heritability of attitudes toward, among other things, pajama parties (Martin et al., 1986). Attitudes toward pajama parties were included as a (presumably) reliable index of conservatism. Today, of course, pajama parties (or sleepovers) are uncontroversial. While attitudes toward them might be heritable, the extent to which this is meaningful is questionable. If we were to time travel as little as 500 or so years ago, we would likely have seen a highly heritable component to the belief that the earth was flat. Today, with the exception of a tiny minority of people, it is likely that acceptance of the earth as globular is at a ceiling. In short, while genetics may push us one way or the other on social attitudes, society (and social change) determines whether those attitudes are there to be supported. The heritability statistic that we have repeatedly referred to throughout this chapter relates only to within-population variance.

It is likely then (as argued by many others) that there are genetic factors that predispose us to the left or the right politically, for example. How this is expressed depends on the social situation, the media, the science available to us, and so on. While shared environmental effects within the home are relatively small in most cases, the twins who are measured in each study exist in a larger shared environment (whether it be state, country, or even world). This does not mean that understanding genes is unimportant, however.

Indeed, a psychological understanding of prejudice that ignores large genetic contributions is incomplete and objectively flawed. At the beginning of this chapter, we discussed the history of genetics, and eugenics and speculated that this history may have contributed to a motivated "blank slate" approach to human psychology (and social attitudes) in many psychologists. But wishing does not make it so. The research we have outlined shows overwhelmingly, and convincingly, that a blank slate understanding of prejudice is incorrect, and scientifically indefensible. The implications of this are manifold. For example, they suggest that some people (relative to others) will be more resistant to change. In line with this argument, Bourgeois (2002) found that in small group discussions (Study 2) consensus was less likely to be reached for highly, as opposed to weakly, heritable attitudes (see also Study 3).

It should be noted, however, that there is no single racist gene, or even racist genes, that have been identified. Many genes, each with a tiny effect, influence complex human traits (Chabris, Lee, Cesarini, Benjamin, & Laibson, 2015), and indeed molecular genetic studies have confirmed that this is the case for economic and social attitudes (Benjamin et al., 2012). Huge sample sizes (e.g., 100,000) are required to begin to find these genes, and that is one direction for future research in the area. In addition, genes can be switched on and off by environments. Further, effects identified as residual sources of variance are likely composed to some extent of the unique combination of someone with a particular set of genes encountering a particular social situation.

Perhaps most of all, this work calls for an increased emphasis on the interaction between an individual and his or her environment. Eventually, this will involve a rich understanding of the environments that regulate the activation of certain genes. In the short term, it might involve identifying the environments that interrupt the heritability of prejudice, or anti-prejudice interventions that work best for people who are genetically predisposed to be high in prejudice to begin with.

Conclusion

A frequent misconception regarding psychological traits is that they are either the result of nature or nurture. Sir Francis Galton (1874) describes the notion of nature and nurture as

> a convenient jingle of words, for it separates under two distinct heads the innumerable elements of which personality is composed. Nature is all that a man brings with himself into the world; nurture is every influence without that affects him after his birth. (p. 12)

However, rarely is it ever the case that one or the other is solely responsible for variation in a trait. More frequently, some complex interaction of the two is at play. In this chapter, we aimed to introduce prejudice researchers to research from behavioral genetics and called for investigation into the complex interactions that are likely at the heart of prejudice.

References

Adorno, T. W., Frenkel-Brunswik, E., Levinson, D. J., & Sanford, R. N. (1950). *The authoritarian personality.* New York: Harper & Brothers.

Ainsworth, M. D. S., Blehar, M. C., Waters, E., & Wall, S. (1978). *Patterns of attachment: A psychological study of the strange situation.* Hillsadale, NJ: Lawrence Erlbaum Associates.

Alford, J. R., Funk, C. L., & Hibbing, J. R. (2005). Are political orientations genetically transmitted? *American Political Science Review, 99*(02), 153–167.

Altemeyer, B. (1988). *Enemies of freedom: Understanding right-wing authoritarianism.* San Francisco: Jossey-Bass.

Benjamin, D. J., Cesarini, D., van der Loos, M. J. H. M., Dawes, C. T., Koellinger, P. D., Magnusson, P. K. E. ... Visscher, P. M. (2012). The genetic architecture of economic and political preferences. *Proceedings of the National Academy of Sciences of the United States of America, 109*(21), 8026–8031.

Bouchard, T., McGue, M., Lykken, D., & Tellegen, A. (1999). Intrinsic and extrinsic religiousness: Genetic and environmental influences and personality correlates. *Twin Research, 2*(02), 88–98.

Bourgeois, M. J. (2002). Heritability of attitudes constrains dynamic social impact. *Personality and Social Psychology Bulletin, 28*(8), 1063–1072.

Chabris, C. F., Lee, J. J., Cesarini, D., Benjamin, D. J., & Laibson, D. I. (2015). The fourth law of behavior genetics. *Current Directions in Psychological Science, 24*(4), 304–312.

Costa, P., & McCrae, R. (2008). The Revised NEO Personality Inventory (NEO-PI-R). In G. J. Boyle, G. Matthews, & D. H. Saklofske (Eds.), *The SAGE handbook of personality theory and assessment: Volume 2 – Personality measurement and testing* (pp. 179–199). London: SAGE Publications.

Darwin, C. (1859). *The origin of species by means of natural selection: or the preservation of favored races in the struggle for life*. London: John Murray.

Dovidio, J. F., Johnson, J. D., Gaertner, S. L., Pearson, A. R., Saguy, T., & Ashburn-Nardo, L. (2010). Empathy and intergroup relations. In M. Mikulincer & P. R. Shaver (Eds.), *Prosocial motives, emotions, and behavior: The better angels of our nature* (pp. 393–408). Washington, DC: American Psychological Association.

Eaves, L., Heath, A., Martin, N., Maes, H., Neale, M., Kendler, K. . . . Corey, L. (1999). Comparing the biological and cultural inheritance of personality and social attitudes in the Virginia 30,000 study of twins and their relatives. *Twin Research, 2*(02), 62–80.

Ebstein, R. P., Israel, S., Chew, S. H., Zhong, S., & Knafo, A. (2010). Genetics of human social behavior. *Neuron, 65*(6), 831–844.

Ferguson, C. J. (2010). Genetic contributions to antisocial personality and behavior: A meta-analytic review from an evolutionary perspective. *The Journal of Social Psychology, 150*(2), 160–180.

Folstein, S. E., & Rosen-Sheidley, B. (2001). Genetics of austim: Complex aetiology for a heterogeneous disorder. *Nature Reviews Genetics, 2*(12), 943–955.

Freitag, C. M. (2007). The genetics of autistic disorders and its clinical relevance: A review of the literature. *Molecular Psychiatry, 12*(1), 2–22.

Galton, F. (1874). *English men of science: Their nature and nurture*. London: Macmillan & Co.

Gejman, P. V., Sanders, A. R., & Duan, J. (2010). The role of genetics in the etiology of schizophrenia. *Psychiatric Clinics of North America, 33*(1), 35–66.

Hall, D. L., Matz, D. C., & Wood, W. (2010). Why don't we practice what we preach? A meta-analytic review of religious racism. *Personality and Social Psychology Review, 14*(1), 126–139.

Hatemi, P. K., Alford, J. R., Hibbing, J. R., Martin, N. G., & Eaves, L. J. (2009). Is there a "Party" in your genes? *Political Research Quarterly, 62*(3), 584–600.

Hatemi, P. K., Medland, S. E., Morley, K. I., Heath, A. C., & Martin, N. G. (2007). The genetics of voting: An Australian twin study. *Behavior Genetics, 37*(3), 435–448.

Hur, Y.-M., & Rushton, J. P. (2007). Genetic and environmental contributions to prosocial behavior in 2- to 9-year-old South Korean twins. *Biology Letters, 3*(6), 664–666.

Jakubowska, U., & Oniszczenko, W. (2010). The role of personality, cognitive, environmental and genetic factors as determinants of religious fundamentalism: A twin study in a Polish sample. *Studia Psychologica, 52*(3), 253.

Kandler, C., Bleidorn, W., & Riemann, R. (2012). Left or right? Sources of political orientation: The roles of genetic factors, cultural transmission, assortative mating, and personality. *Journal of Personality and Social Psychology, 102*(3), 633.

Kandler, C., Lewis, G. J., Feldhaus, L. H., & Riemann, R. (2015). The genetic and environmental roots of variance in negativity toward foreign nationals. *Behavior Genetics, 45*(2), 181–199.

Kelley, H. H. (1967). Attribution theory in social psychology. *Nebraska symposium on motivation*. Lincoln: University of Nebraska Press.

Kokkonen, R. (2009). The fat child – a sign of "bad" motherhood? An analysis of explanations for children's fatness on a Finnish website. *Journal of Community & Applied Social Psychology*, *19*(5), 336–347.

Lewis, G., & Bates, T. C. (2014). Common heritable effects underpin concerns over norm maintenance and in-group favoritism: Evidence from genetic analyses of right-wing authoritarianism and traditionalism. *Journal of Personality*, *82*(4), 297–309.

Lewis, G., Kandler, C., & Riemann, R. (2014). Distinct heritable influences underpin in-group love and out-group derogation. *Social Psychological and Personality Science*, *5*(4), 407–413.

Lewis, G. J., & Bates, T. C. (2011). A common heritable factor influences prosocial obligations across multiple domains. *Biology Letters*, *7*(4), 567–570.

Ludeke, S., Johnson, W., & Bouchard, T. J. (2013). "Obedience to traditional authority": A heritable factor underlying authoritarianism, conservatism and religiousness. *Personality and Individual Differences*, *55*(4), 375–380.

Martin, N. G., Eaves, L. J., Heath, A. C., Jardine, R., Feingold, L. M., & Eysenck, H. J. (1986). Transmission of social attitudes. *Proceedings of the National Academy of Sciences of the United States of America*, *83*(12), 4364–4368.

Neale, M. C., & Cardon, L. C. (1992). *Methodology for genetic studies of twins and families*. Boston: Kluwer Academic Publishers.

Nelson, S. C. (2008). Feeling thermometer. In P. J. Lavrakas (Ed.), *Encyclopedia of survey research methods* (p. 277). Thousand Oaks, CA: Sage Publications.

Orey, B. D. A., & Park, H. (2012). Nature, nurture, and ethnocentrism in the Minnesota Twin Study. *Twin Research and Human Genetics*, *15*(01), 71–73.

Paul, D. B., & Hasian, M. A. (1998). *Controlling human heredity: 1865 to the present*. London: Humanities Press International.

Peterson, E. C., & Docherty, N. M. (2004). Expressed emotion, attribution, and control in parents of schizophrenic patients. *Psychiatry*, *67*(2), 197–207.

Polderman, T. J. C., Benyamin, B., de Leeuw, C. A., Sullivan, P. F., van Bochoven, A., Visscher, P. M., & Posthuma, D. (2015). Meta-analysis of the heritability of human traits based on fifty years of twin studies. *Nature Genetics*, *47*(7), 702–709.

Posthuma, D., Beem, A. L., de Geus, E. J. C., van Baal, G. C. M., von Hjelmborg, J. B., Iachine, I., & Boomsma, D. I. (2003). Theory and practice in quantitative genetics. *Twin Research*, *6*(5), 361–376.

Pratto, F., Sidanius, J., Stallworth, L. M., & Malle, B. F. (1994). Social dominance orientation: A personality variable predicting social and political attitudes. *Journal of Personality and Social Psychology*, *67*(4), 741.

Rushton, J. P. (2004). Genetic and environmental contributions to pro-social attitudes: A twin study of social responsibility. *Proceedings of the Royal Society of London B: Biological Sciences*, *271*(1557), 2583–2585.

Rushton, J. P., Fulker, D. W., Neale, M. C., Nias, D. K. B., & Eysenck, H. J. (1986). Altruism and aggression: The heritability of individual differences. *Journal of Personality and Social Psychology*, *50*(6), 1192–1198.

Saudino, K. J. (2005). Behavioral genetics and child temperament. *Journal of Developmental and Behavioral Pediatrics*, *26*(3), 214–223.

Settle, J. E., Dawes, C. T., & Fowler, J. H. (2009). The heritability of partisan attachment. *Political Research Quarterly, 62*(3), 601–613.

Sherlock, J. M., Zietsch, B. P., Tybur, J. M., & Jern, P. (2016). The quantitative genetics of disgust sensitivity. *Emotion, 16*(1), 43–51.

Sibley, C. G., & Duckitt, J. (2008). Personality and prejudice: A meta-analysis and theoretical review. *Personality and Social Psychology Review, 12*(3), 248–279.

Verweij, K. J. H., Shekar, S. N., Zietsch, B. P., Eaves, L. J., Bailey, J. M., Boomsma, D. I., & Martin, N. G. (2008). Genetic and environmental influences on individual differences in attitudes toward homosexuality: An Australian twin study. *Behavior Genetics, 38*(3), 257–265.

Waller, N. G., Kojetin, B. A., Bouchard, T. J., Lykken, D. T., & Tellegen, A. (1990). Genetic and environmental influences on religious interests, attitudes, and values: A study of twins reared apart and together. *Psychological Science, 1*(2), 138–142.

Wardle, J., Carnell, S., Haworth, C. M. A., & Plomin, R. (2008). Evidence for a strong genetic influence on childhood adiposity despite the force of the obesogenic environment. *American Journal of Clinical Nutrition, 87*(2), 398–404.

Watson, J. B. (1930). *Behaviorism*. Chicago: University of Chicago Press.

Wilcox, C., Sigelman, L., & Cook, E. (1989). Some like it hot: Individual differences in responses to group feeling thermometers. *Public Opinion Quarterly, 53*, 246–257.

Wilson, G. D., & Patterson, J. R. (1968). A new measure of conservatism. *British Journal of Social and Clinical Psychology, 7*(4), 264–269.

Zietsch, B. P., Verweij, K. J. H., Heath, A. C., & Martin, N. G. (2011). Variation in human mate choice: Simultaneously investigating heritability, parental influence, sexual imprinting and assortative mating. *The American Naturalist, 177*(5), 605–616.

Prejudice in Specific Domains

PART II

Practice in Specific Domains

11 Understanding the Nature, Measurement, and Utility of Implicit Intergroup Biases

Kumar Yogeeswaran, Thierry Devos, and Kyle Nash

On July 17, 2014, plain-clothed officers from the New York Police Department (NYPD) approached Eric Garner, a 43-year-old African American man suspected of selling loose cigarettes. Garner argued he had not done anything wrong and wanted to be left alone. Officer Pantaleo attempted to handcuff Garner, who moved his arms asking not to be touched, after which Pantaleo put Garner in a chokehold from behind and pulled him to the ground. Other officers surrounded Garner, while Pantaleo pushed Garner's head down to the sidewalk. In a video of the incident, Garner is heard screaming, "I can't breathe" several times before losing consciousness. Seven minutes passed before an ambulance arrived, during which time, CPR was not performed. Garner was declared dead on arrival at the hospital.

Within a few months of this incident, other cases of police brutality toward young African American men came into the spotlight, including the fatal shootings of Michael Brown in Ferguson, Missouri; Tamir Rice in Cleveland, Ohio; Akai Gurley in Brooklyn, New York; and John Crawford near Dayton, Ohio. The common link between all these shootings was that they involved police officers and African American males between ages 12 and 43. Following the failure to indict officers involved in these cases, widespread demonstrations on the street called for justice (Gambino, Thrasher, & Epstein, 2014). Social movements including Twitter's "#BlackLivesMatter" and "#ICan'tBreathe" also called for action against police violence toward African Americans.

Despite public outcry over these cases, national surveys revealed a clear racial gap in perceptions of such incidents. Whereas 80% of African Americans believed that the shooting of Michael Brown raised racial issues that warranted discussion, only 37% of White Americans believed so. By contrast, 47% of White Americans believed race was getting more attention than it deserved (Anderson, 2014). To some individuals, race was irrelevant because there was no overt expression of racism. US Congressman Peter King, for example, argued that racial bias was irrelevant in Garner's death because racial epithets were not used by the police, and the officers would have treated Garner the same if he were a White male (Levine, 2014). Yet, federally collected data on police shootings reveal that young African

American men are 21 times more likely to be shot dead by police than their White counterparts (Gabrielson, Jones, & Sagara, 2014). King's comments reflect a view held by some that biases (whether in the form of stereotypes, prejudice, or discrimination) only exist if they are blatant, conscious, and deliberate. However, intergroup biases may also manifest themselves more implicitly in subtle, nonconscious, and automatic ways.

This chapter reviews the complex literature on the nature and meaning of implicit stereotyping and prejudice (collectively called "biases") – how they can be defined, their ubiquity, psychological processes underlying them, and contextual factors that increase or decrease their prevalence. We then describe how implicit biases can be measured using reaction-time and neurophysiological tools, before discussing how these tools can be used to understand social behavior. And finally, we conclude by offering avenues for future exploration.

Nature and Meaning of Implicit Biases

Intergroup research has established that prejudice and stereotyping often operate outside of conscious control or awareness. Even well-intentioned people who strongly endorse egalitarian values sometimes deviate from these principles as revealed by measures tapping affective or cognitive responses that are not consciously controllable. The initial enthusiasm for circumventing the limitations of self-report measures gave way to a wealth of theoretical and methodological advances (Gawronski & Payne, 2010). The aim of this section is to take stock of these advances and extract some key features of implicit biases.

Automatic and Nonconscious Processes

The conceptualization of implicit biases raises complex questions regarding the role of awareness, control, or intention (Moors & De Houwer, 2006). In some cases, the term "implicit" is used to describe responses that occur without conscious control (Payne, 2008). Here, the focus is on the inability to deliberately alter evaluations or thoughts. For example, it might be difficult for individuals to fake, tailor, or correct their automatic affective or cognitive responses to make them more consistent with the salient norms or values (Cvencek, Greenwald, Brown, Gray, & Snowden, 2010). If social desirability, impression management, or demand characteristics can affect self-reported attitudes and beliefs about social groups, these forces seem relatively inoperative in automatic responses.

The issue of non-consciousness has many layers (Gawronski, Hofmann, & Wilbur, 2006). It can refer to instances where individuals are unaware of the source of their prejudices and stereotypes (source awareness). This fits with the notion that implicit biases reflect past experiences that are inaccessible to introspection. Individuals might also be unaware of their preferences or the content of their thoughts (content awareness). Finally, individuals may not be aware of the impact that attitudes and beliefs have on other psychological processes (impact awareness). These distinctions nuance the idea that individuals are simply unaware of their implicit prejudices and stereotypes. In fact, recent evidence suggests that individuals can accurately assess their implicit attitudes toward one group compared to another (Hahn, Judd, Hirsh, & Blair, 2014).

Ubiquity of Implicit Biases

Implicit biases have been found to be relatively ubiquitous. Whether people are categorized by age, gender, race, ethnicity, nationality, sexual orientation, physical appearance, religion, socioeconomic status, or even trivial criteria, the resulting distinctions often elicit differential implicit attitudinal responses (i.e., a preference for one group over another) or implicit associations of traits or characteristics to specific groups (i.e., differentiation between groups on some descriptive dimension; Nosek et al., 2007). This is unsurprising given long-standing evidence for the role of categorical thinking in intergroup biases (Macrae & Bodenhausen, 2000; Tajfel, 1981). At that level, the novelty of implicit biases resides in the emphasis on processes that escape conscious control or awareness.

Implicit biases assessed via indirect measures tend to be stronger than explicit biases measured via self-report (Nosek et al., 2007). In some cases, striking dissociations between what individuals self-report and patterns obtained on indirect measures emerge. For example, ethnic minorities are implicitly perceived as being less American than Whites even when explicit knowledge or perceptions point in the opposite direction (Devos & Banaji, 2005; Devos & Ma, 2008). This points to a relative inability to override deeply held biases and align them with more conscious attitudes or beliefs. In other words, implicit biases reflect spontaneous affective or cognitive reactions to social groups regardless of whether perceivers endorse these reactions as valid or invalid, whereas explicit biases are based on propositions held as valid and relevant (Gawronski & Bodenhausen, 2006, 2014).

Variability and Context-Sensitivity of Implicit Biases

Implicit biases are not monolithic or unavoidable. In fact, they are extremely variable and context sensitive. For example, they vary as a function of individual or group differences. Stronger implicit biases are found among respondents who are not internally motivated to control prejudice (Devine, Plant, Amodio, Harmon-Jones, & Vance, 2002; Johns, Cullum, Smith, & Freng, 2008). Similarly, lower levels of implicit biases are found among individuals who interact with outgroup members on a regular basis (Dasgupta & Rivera, 2008; Tam, Hewstone, Harwood, Voci, & Kenworthy, 2006; Turner, Hewstone, & Voci, 2007). The tendency to implicitly favor ingroups over outgroups is stronger among individuals who belong to culturally valued or socially advantaged groups (Devos, Huynh, & Banaji, 2012).

Implicit biases also shift in response to a variety of contextual or situational interventions (Dasgupta, 2009; Gawronski & Sritharan, 2010). For example, reduction of implicit prejudice occurs as a result of extensive practice at overriding the dominant automatic prejudicial response (Devine, Forscher, Austin, & Cox, 2012; Kawakami, Dovidio, Moll, Hermsen, & Russin, 2000). Similarly, relatively limited exposure or generation of information contradicting preexisting associations may be sufficient to lower implicit biases (Blair, Ma, & Lenton, 2001; Dasgupta & Greenwald, 2001; Lenton, Bruder, & Sedikides, 2009; Rydell, Hamilton, & Devos, 2010). In the same vein, groups can be automatically evaluated differently as a function of the specific context in which they are encountered (Barden, Maddux, Petty, & Brewer, 2004; Wittenbrink, Judd, & Park, 2001).

Various mechanisms underlying contextual influences on implicit biases have been proposed (Gawronski & Bodenhausen, 2006; Gawronski & Sritharan, 2010; Lai, Hoffman, & Nosek, 2013). Some interventions operate through a form of retraining, meaning that individuals learn to link a concept with a social group in a way that differs or contradicts their preexisting associations. Shifting the context by temporarily considering situations or instances in which the preexisting associations might be undermined is a second possible mechanism. Finally, situational goals, motives, or behavioral strategies may alter the extent to which implicit biases are expressed. Often these differing mechanisms operate simultaneously, but they nonetheless need to be distinguished and some manipulations might play more potently on one of them. A recent comparison of the effectiveness of 17 interventions aimed at reducing implicit prejudice toward Blacks revealed that eight of them were effective – particularly ones that provided experience with counter-stereotypical exemplars, involved evaluative conditioning, or provided strategies to override biases. The other nine interventions were ineffective, particularly ones that required taking others' perspectives, considering egalitarian values, or inducing a positive emotion (Lai et al., 2014).

Processes Contributing to Implicit Biases

For a number of years, the case has been made that performance on implicit measures should not be thought of as process-pure assessments of automatic associations (Payne, 2008; Sherman, 2006). Instead, they should be conceptualized as tapping a mix of automatic and controlled processes. For instance, research documenting a racial bias in the propensity to shoot unarmed individuals has shown that this bias stems from an unintentional accessibility bias (e.g., "Blacks are more likely than Whites to carry guns") used to resolve ambiguities when control fails (Payne, Lambert, & Jacoby, 2002). Extending this conceptualization, the Quad model disentangles the contribution of four distinct processes on implicit tasks (Calanchini & Sherman, 2013; Conrey, Sherman, Gawronski, Hugenberg, & Groom, 2005). The processes are conceptualized as the activation of associations in memory (Activation), the ability to detect the correct responses (Detection), the ability to overcome automatic associations when they would produce an incorrect response (Overcoming Bias), and a guessing or response bias operating when other sources of responses are unavailable (Guessing).

This model has been used successfully to better understand how factors contributing to implicit biases are operating. For example, increased intergroup biases resulting from ego threat are associated only with increased activation of negative associations about outgroups (Allen & Sherman, 2011). Altering the impression of novel targets and exposing individuals to counter-stereotypic exemplars exclusively affects the automatic activation of underlying associations (Gonsalkorale, Allen, Sherman, & Klauer, 2010). Other strategies or interventions operate through two or more distinct processes. For example, counter-prejudicial training not only reduces the activation of associations, it also improves the detection of correct responses (Calanchini, Gonsalkorale, Sherman, & Klauer, 2013). The same approach can be used to grasp the role of group membership or individual differences in the magnitude of implicit biases (Gonsalkorale et al., 2010; Gonsalkorale, Sherman, Allen, Klauer, & Amodio, 2011).

Socio-Structural Factors Underlying Implicit Biases

At first blush, one may assume that implicit bias research focuses on intraindividual processes, failing to integrate the role of social dynamics. We contend, however, that this approach can shed light on the cultural and structural foundations of psychological processes and, conversely, the role that processes operating outside of conscious control and awareness play in manufacturing ideological systems and structural realities. The literature is replete with findings supporting this argument.

A common assumption is that implicit biases reflect repeated experiences within a given cultural context and develop through socialization processes (Devine, 1989; Greenwald & Banaji, 1995; Rudman, 2004). This assumption points to the role of a basic associative learning principle. For example, the associative-propositional evaluation (APE) model posits that implicit evaluations stem from associative links between mental concepts formed on the basis of spatiotemporal contiguities in the environment (Gawronski & Bodenhausen, 2006, 2014). Empirical evidence indeed shows that observed co-occurrences between objects and events create implicit associations (De Houwer, Thomas, & Baeyens, 2001). For example, when individuals are repeatedly exposed to names or images of cartoon creatures (e.g., "Metapod" or "Shelder") paired with positively vs. negatively valenced words (e.g., "exciting" vs. "awful") or images (a hot fudge sundae vs. a cockroach), their subsequent performance on a subliminal priming task reveals the formation of implicit attitudes about these cartoon creatures. Specifically, cartoon creatures initially paired with positive (rather than negative) stimuli facilitate the identification of positive adjectives but undermine the ability to quickly identify negative adjectives (Olson & Fazio, 2002).

Research stemming from a developmental perspective also highlights the social and cultural foundations of implicit biases. Children acquire implicit attitudes and beliefs that pervade the culture they are reared in fairly early on in life (Dunham, Baron, & Banaji, 2008; Olson & Dunham, 2010; Rutland, Cameron, Milne, & McGeorge, 2005). Relatedly, members of low-status, subordinate, or disadvantaged groups often display implicit attitudes and beliefs that perpetuate the ideological status quo (Devos, Gavin, & Quintana, 2010; Jost, Banaji, & Nosek, 2004; Newheiser, Dunham, Merrill, Hoosain, & Olson, 2014; Newheiser & Olson, 2012; Rudman, Feinberg, & Fairchild, 2002). Low-status groups such as the overweight and poor, for example, show an implicit preference for the dominant group (i.e., outgroup favoritism), even though doing so undermines their own status. These findings collectively suggest that implicit biases may be linked to socio-structural factors.

Research examining cross-national variations in implicit associations pro-vides yet another window into the societal foundations of implicit biases. For example, the extent to which science and math are implicitly associated with males more than females (implicit gender stereotypes) maps onto sex differ-ences in eighth-grade science and math achievement across 34 nations. Specifically, countries in which implicit gender stereotypes about science and math are stronger are also countries in which the gender gap in science and math performance is more pronounced (Nosek et al., 2009). Similarly, a study using 71 countries found a robust relation between the prevalence of obesity and the negativity toward overweight people (Marini et al., 2013). As the proportion of overweight people increased at the country level, so did negative implicit (but not explicit) attitudes toward overweight relative to thin people.

Although these findings are insufficient to establish causal pathways, they are consistent with the notion that implicit biases are embedded in social and cultural contexts. The merits of indirect measures, therefore, cannot be reduced to their capacity to assess attitudes and beliefs that do not fully enter consciousness or are not controllable. Theoretical and methodological advances in implicit social cognition provide a better understanding of the specific processes contributing to intergroup biases. These processes are highly dynamic and social in that they are bounded to a variety of contextual factors.

How Do We Measure Implicit Biases?

Social psychologists have developed several tools to capture implicit biases in the context of intergroup relations. Here we highlight two types of tools that do so – reaction-time measures and neurophysiological measures.

Reaction-Time (RT) Measures

RT measures have been used to capture a range of implicit biases including (a) implicit prejudices that assess the strength of association between social groups and positive vs. negative valence (e.g., good vs. bad words; Dovidio, Kawakami, & Gaertner, 2002; Fazio, Jackson, Dunton, & Williams, 1995; Greenwald, McGhee, & Schwartz, 1998); (b) implicit stereotypes that assess the strength of association between social groups and particular traits or beliefs (e.g., communal vs. agentic traits; math vs. humanities; Blair & Banaji, 1996; Nosek et al., 2007; Sekaquaptewa, Espinoza, Thompson, Vargas, & von Hippel, 2003); or (c) prototypicality within a superordinate group, which assesses the extent to which subgroups are perceived as belonging within a superordinate group (e.g., ethnic groups' fit within the nation; Devos & Banaji, 2005; Devos et al., 2010; Yogeeswaran, Dasgupta, & Gomez, 2012; Yogeeswaran, Dasgupta, Adelman, Eccleston, & Parker, 2011). In the section that follows, we focus on three of the most popular RT measures used in intergroup research.

Implicit Association Test (IAT). Perhaps the most popular of the RT tools, the IAT is a computer-based rapid response task that uses response latency as an indicator of the direction and strength of associations between two pairs of categories (e.g., two social groups and specific traits or valence; Greenwald et al., 1998). In the cross-national research on gender-science presented earlier (Nosek et al., 2009), participants would first be asked to complete practice trials where they simply categorize words associated with male vs. female or liberal arts vs. science using a left or right response key (Figure 11.1). After doing so, participants would be asked to categorize words associated with male or liberal arts using one response key, whereas the other response key would be used to indicate that a word associated with female or science appears on the screen (i.e., Male + Liberal Arts vs. Female + Science). However, in a subsequent block, they would respond with one key if the word on the screen is associated with female or liberal arts but use the other response key if it is associated with male or science (i.e., Female + Liberal Arts vs. Male + Science). If participants implicitly associate science more strongly with males than with females, they would have more ease categorizing stimuli in the latter configuration than the earlier (for details on calculation of IAT bias, see Greenwald, Nosek, & Banaji, 2003).

Priming. Originally developed by cognitive researchers, evaluative or affective priming represents another popular tool to measure implicit biases (Blair & Banaji, 1996; De Houwer, Teige-Mocigemba, Spruyt, & Moors, 2009; Dovidio, Kawakami, Johnson, Johnson, & Howard, 1997; Fazio et al., 1995). In an evaluative priming task examining attitudes toward White and African Americans, participants are told that their primary task is to categorize positive vs. negative words based on their valence (Figure 11.2). However, just prior to the word appearing on the screen, an image of a Black or White individual briefly flashes on the screen (De Houwer et al., 2009; Fazio & Olson, 2003). Prejudice researchers examine differences in RT or error rates in the categorization of positive and

Panel A. Single-categorization practice block (20 trials): left key = liberal arts; right key = science

Panel B. Single-categorization practice block (20 trials): left key = male; right key = female

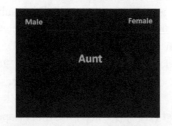

Panel C. Mixed-categorization blocks (20 trials in first block + 40 trials in second block): left key = male + liberal arts; right key = female + science

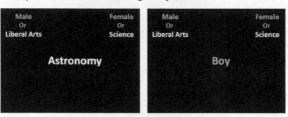

Panel D. Single-categorization practice block (20 trials): left key = female; right key = male

Panel E. Mixed-categorization blocks (20 trials in first block + 40 trials in second block): left key = female + liberal arts; right key = male + science

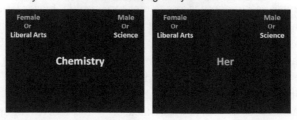

Figure 11.1 *Implicit Association Test procedure.*

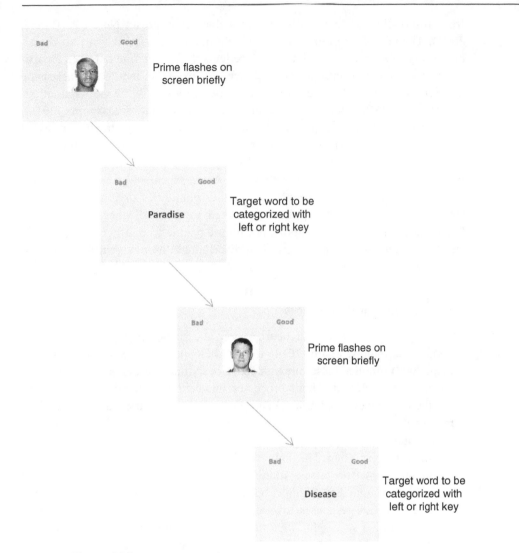

Figure 11.2 *Priming procedure.*

negative words following exposure to Black or White faces. If Black faces facilitate (quicker or more accurate) responses to negative words and impede (slower or more error prone) responses to positive words compared to priming of White faces, that indicates that participants have more unfavorable implicit attitudes toward Blacks relative to Whites (Fazio et al., 1995).

Go/No-Go Association Task (GNAT). Similar to the other measures, the GNAT (Nosek & Banaji, 2001) captures the direction and strength of associations between a target group and a specific trait or valence. However, the major difference between the GNAT from priming and the IAT is that the GNAT requires participants to respond only when the stimulus on screen is relevant (signal) but refrain from responding when the stimulus is a distracter (noise; Nosek & Banaji, 2001). The GNAT, therefore, provides a unique index of sensitivity or discriminability of signal from noise, which reflects the association between a particular group and a specific trait or valence. For example, in a GNAT assessing implicit associations between American nationality and White vs. Asian ethnicity (Devos & Ma, 2008; Yogeeswaran, Adelman, Parker, & Dasgupta, 2014), participants are first exposed to stimuli corresponding to the relevant categories (e.g., American symbols, foreign symbols, Asian faces, and White faces; Figure 11.3). Then in a critical block, participants are asked to respond by pressing the spacebar whenever they see Asian faces or American symbols, while ignoring images of people from other ethnicities or foreign symbols. However, in another block, they are asked to respond whenever they see White faces or American symbols, but ignore people from other ethnic groups and foreign symbols. The sensitivity or discriminability of signal from noise is indicative of associative strength (Nosek & Banaji, 2001).

Neurophysiological Measures

We hold, as many have, that neuroscience measures can tap implicit biases (Amodio, Bartholow, & Ito, 2014; Ito & Cacioppo, 2007; Stanley, Phelps, & Banaji, 2008). Implicit biases, though consciously inaccessible or uncontrollable, are nonetheless reflected in brain processes, and neurophysiological measures can index these neural events. Further, neurophysiological measures carry many of the same benefits as other implicit measures and can complement RT measures by offering unique capabilities. For example, while RT measures may be somewhat removed from the presumed mental processes, neuroscience measures can directly track ongoing mental processes. Additionally, certain processes may not have overt outcomes to examine. For example, response control may be critical in inhibiting automatic, negative responses toward outgroups (Amodio, 2014). However, if response control is successful, then there is no response to index. Neuroscience measures can probe the black box of such surreptitious behavior. Occasionally, implicit measures can interfere with subtle implicit processes as they unfold. Neuroscience measures can unobtrusively track these underlying processes. However, we do note that both controlled and automatic processes are reflected in neurophysiological measures. Moreover, one method is not generally better than others in measuring implicit processes (Ito & Caccioppo, 2007). The research question and experimental design determine which measure is most fitting. That said, two neuroscience methods stand at the fore.

Functional Magnetic Resonance Imaging (fMRI). This method is based on the hemodynamic response to brain activation, or blood-oxygenation-level dependent (BOLD) signal. To function, neural cells require oxygen carried by hemoglobin in the blood. Increased blood flow follows neural activity to replenish oxygen. Changes in oxygenation levels in the blood cause changes in the magnetic signal at these neural sites, which are detected by the MRI scanner.

Panel A. Practice blocks (10 trials): spacebar pressed when stimulus on screen fits with category label and ignored when stimulus does not correspond to category label

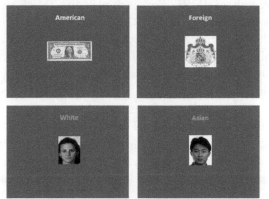

Panel B. Critical block (50 trials): spacebar pressed when White faces or American symbols appear on screen; no key pressed when any other stimuli appear on screen

Panel C. Critical block (50 trials): spacebar pressed when White faces or foreign symbols appear on screen; no key pressed when any other stimuli appear on screen

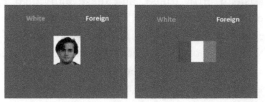

Panel D. Critical block (50 trials): spacebar pressed when Asian faces or foreign symbols appear on screen; no key pressed when any other stimuli appear on screen

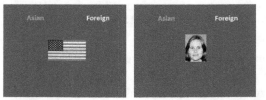

Panel E. Critical block (50 trials): spacebar pressed when Asian faces or American symbols appear on screen; no key pressed when any other stimuli appear on screen

Figure 11.3 *Go/No-Go Association Test procedure.*

The level of neural activity is thus inferred from the BOLD signal (Cacioppo et al., 2003). Spatial resolution, or determining the location of brain activation, is a particular strength of fMRI. For example, one fMRI study measured brain activation as participants viewed Black and White faces in the scanner (Richeson et al., 2003). In a separate session, the same participants completed an IAT assessing implicit attitudes toward Blacks vs. Whites before participants were asked to interact with a Black partner and subsequently perform the Stroop color-naming task that assessed cognitive control. Results revealed that viewing Black relative to White faces caused increased activity in several regions in the prefrontal cortex (PFC). Further, dorsolateral PFC activity to Black faces was associated with both implicit prejudice and Stroop interference after the interracial interaction. Together, these results suggested that viewing Black faces and interacting with a Black partner engage cognitive control-related processes.

Electroencephalography (EEG). EEG is based on recording and amplifying voltages on the scalp with electrodes positioned at particular locations on the head. The recorded voltages reflect the synchronous postsynaptic potentials of parallel pyramidal neurons, primarily in the cortex (Allison, Wood, & McCarthy, 1986). Derived from the continuously recorded EEG, event-related potentials (ERPs) reflect the brain's response to discrete stimuli or behaviors (Luck, 2014). ERPs are composed of positive and negative voltage deflections on the scalp measured for approximately one second (typically) in duration around the event of interest. An ERP is indexed for each trial of interest (e.g., all incongruent trials, all error trials), and these individual ERPs are then averaged to reduce measurement error. Different components with the averaged ERP and, presumably, different brain processes can then be quantified. For example, the N100 component is a negative voltage deflection that peaks at approximately 100 milliseconds after stimulus presentation (hence the name, N100). It is thought to reflect an automatic, perception-based process (Parasuraman, 1980). Research shows that the N100 is enhanced when viewing Black vs. White faces, which suggests that Black faces automatically capture attention to a greater degree than White faces (Ito & Urland, 2003). Temporal resolution, or determining when brain activation takes place, is a particular strength of EEG and ERPs.

EEG and fMRI have complementary strengths. Consider the two examples of prejudice research using fMRI and ERPs. In both studies, participants viewed Black and White faces as brain activity was assessed. In the fMRI study, several PFC regions were associated with viewing Black vs. White faces. Further, activation in the dorsolateral PFC predicted both IAT bias and depleted cognitive control (i.e., increased Stroop interference) after an intergroup interaction (Richeson et al., 2003). Thus, this fMRI study demonstrated brain activation to Black faces in a region linked to cognitive control and supported the idea that racial bias can prompt controlled responding in intergroup interactions. In the ERP study, the N100 component, which peaked only 122ms after stimulus presentation, was larger to Black faces compared to White faces (Ito & Urland, 2003). Thus, the ERP study demonstrated that Black faces elicit a rapid change in perceptual processing and supported the idea that Black faces elicit greater vigilance than White faces. Because of the complementary strengths of fMRI (spatial resolution) and EEG (temporal resolution), these studies together provide a more nuanced picture in which Black faces first elicit an automatic shift in attention followed by more sustained cognitive control, particularly in those who evidence implicit bias.

Relevance of Implicit Biases to Everyday Outcomes

As prejudice researchers, we are interested in more than just identifying the existence of implicit biases – we want to know if these implicit biases are epiphenomenal and remain confined to our mind or if they actually predict everyday outcomes. The section that follows unpacks the fairly young, but rich literature on this topic.

Utility of RT Measures for Intergroup Relations Research

For nearly two decades, research has explored the predictive effects of implicit biases, assessed via RT measures, on behavior and judgments. These findings show that implicit attitudes and stereotypes predict important outcomes.

Nonverbal behavior. Early work on implicit biases examined the relationship between implicit attitudes and stereotypes on nonverbal behavior such as eye contact, seating distance, body posture, smiling, friendliness, and comfort in the interaction (Amodio & Devine, 2006; Dovidio et al., 1997; Fazio et al., 1995; McConnell & Leibold, 2001). For example, implicit prejudice toward Black Americans (measured via priming) predicted unfriendly nonverbal behavior toward a Black interaction partner, whereas explicit prejudice predicted unfriendly verbal behavior toward a Black interaction partner (Dovidio et al., 2002). Similarly, implicit prejudice toward gay men predicted unfriendly nonverbal behavior toward a gay confederate; however, these implicit attitudes were unrelated to nonverbal behavior when perceivers consciously held egalitarian values or when they were high in behavioral control (Dasgupta & Rivera, 2006).

Job hiring. Implicit biases have also been shown to predict job hiring in several contexts (Agerström & Rooth, 2011; Kang, Dasgupta, Yogeeswaran, & Blasi, 2010; Rooth, 2010; Yogeeswaran & Dasgupta, 2010). For example, field experiments using real-life job recruiters revealed that both implicit attitudes and stereotypes about the professional competence of Arabs relative to Swedes predicted the probability that recruiters would call back a job candidate with an Arab/Muslim name. Explicit biases, by comparison, did not predict the probability of inviting job candidates with Arab/Muslim names (Rooth, 2010). Similarly, an implicit belief that the prototypical American is White rather than Asian predicted participants' willingness to hire White relative to Asian American candidates for a job in national security. However, this implicit belief had no impact on hiring decisions for an identical position in a private corporation (Yogeeswaran & Dasgupta, 2010).

Voting decisions. Implicit biases have also been used to predict people's willingness to vote for political candidates in elections (Devos & Ma, 2013; Greenwald, Smith, Sriram, Bar-Anan, & Nosek, 2009; Ma & Devos, 2014; Payne et al., 2010). Implicit attitudes toward Black vs. White Americans assessed a week before the 2008 US presidential election predicted voter preference for Barack Obama vs. John McCain, independent of explicit prejudice and political conservatism (Greenwald et al., 2009). Similarly, an implicit and explicit belief that the prototypical American is White independently predicted reduced willingness to vote for Obama and donate to his campaign (Devos & Ma, 2013). Collectively, these findings suggest that implicit biases predict voter decisions – sometimes over and above self-reported sentiments.

Medical decisions. Do implicit biases impact medical decisions made by highly trained professionals? In one study, physicians were found to have an implicit preference for Whites over Blacks and an implicit belief that Black patients are less cooperative than White patients, although no such self-reported sentiments were found. Importantly, these implicit biases predicted lower likelihood of recommending a life-saving treatment for Black relative to White patients reporting the same coronary symptoms (Green et al., 2007), suggesting that implicit biases predict decision making, even among highly trained professionals.

Economic decision making. Implicit biases have also been found to predict social trust and allocation of economic resources toward outgroups. For example, in a behavioral economic game capturing how much participants were willing to risk in an interaction with a stranger, participants' implicit attitudes predicted the overall disparity in the amount of money offered to an interaction partner who was Black vs. White (Stanley, Sokol-Hessner, Banaji, & Phelps, 2011). Participants showed greater trust in the group they implicitly favored, independent of their explicit feelings about the group. Similarly, negative implicit stereotypes about Jews, Blacks, and Asians predicted lower allocation of economic resources for student organizations run by these groups (Rudman & Ashmore, 2007). These findings collectively suggest that both implicit attitudes and stereotypes can predict economic decision making.

Meta-analytic findings. In 2009, a meta-analysis combining data from more than 30 studies examining the predictive validity of the IAT in particular on discriminatory behavior and judgments reported that the average predictive effect of implicit biases on discrimination was small to moderate ($r = .236$), while the average predictive effect for self-report measures was significantly smaller ($r = .117$; Greenwald, Poehlmann, Uhlmann, & Banaji, 2009). However, a subsequent meta-analysis using 27 of the 32 reports from Greenwald,

Poehlman, and colleagues' (2009) meta-analysis and an additional 18 reports published between 2007 and 2011 documented a weaker predictive effect of the IAT on discriminatory behavior and judgments (r = .148; Oswald, Mitchell, Blanton, Jaccard, & Tetlock, 2013). A closer examination of the two meta-analyses reveals that they used different criteria for inclusion of studies in their analyses. Whereas Greenwald, Poehlman, and colleagues (2009) included only findings that were guided by authors' expectations, Oswald and colleagues (2013) included any correlation between an IAT and discriminatory behavior even if there was no theoretical basis for a relationship between the two (Greenwald, Banaji, & Nosek, 2015). Regardless of the criteria used, it appears that implicit prejudices and stereotypes have at least a small predictive impact on intergroup behavior and judgments, sometimes over and above the use of self-report measures. These seemingly small effects, across time and the population, can cumulatively predict important consequences in real-world contexts (Greenwald et al., 2015).

Utility of Neuroscience Measures for Intergroup Relations Research

Whereas the utility of RT measures for intergroup research lies in their ability to predict behavior and judgments, neurophysiological measures can help intergroup researchers better understand mental processes underlying stereotyping and prejudice. A great deal of research has used fMRI and EEG to better probe the brain regions and potentials involved in implicit biases (Ito & Cacioppo, 2007; Phelps et al., 2000; Stanley et al., 2008).

Brain regions. Primary among brain regions involved in implicit biases may be the amygdala, a bilateral grouping of subcortical nuclei in the medial temporal lobes. The amygdala is associated with rapid responding to stimuli high in emotional intensity, such as threats and rewards (Ledoux, 2003). Thus, the amygdala has been a region of keen interest for researchers probing implicit biases. For example, one study examined the amygdala response to Black and White faces presented supraliminally and subliminally (Cunningham et al., 2004). Amygdala activation was higher to Black vs. White faces and was highest when Black faces were presented below conscious perception. Because the amygdala is strongly associated with threat sensitivity, these researchers suggested that amygdala activation reflected an automatic, negative evaluation of Black faces that was partially suppressed through cognitive control when Black faces were presented supraliminally. Although there is consensus that the amygdala response in prejudice is a response to motivationally important stimuli (Chekroud, Everett, Bridge, & Hewstone, 2014), patients with bilateral amygdala lesions also demonstrate levels of implicit biases against Blacks on an IAT on par with normative levels (Phelps Cannistraci, & Cunningham, 2003). The amygdala may thus be part of a broader neural network in implementing implicit biases.

Other structures that have been related to implicit biases include (among others) the insula and the medial prefrontal cortex (mPFC). The insula, located in the temporal cortex, is primarily associated with visceral and emotional states and is particularly linked to negative states such as disgust (Craig, 2009). Studies have also found that insula activation is associated with perception of outgroup members as opposed to ingroup members (Lieberman, Hariri, Jarcho, Eisenberger, & Bookheimer, 2005). These and other studies have been interpreted in line with the amygdala results as a kind of negative "gut" reaction to outgroups (Amodio, 2014).

The mPFC cortex is associated with social cognition, including self-other judgments (Mitchell, Macrae, & Banaji, 2006) and perspective taking (van Overwalle, 2009). In one study, participants showed reduced activation of the mPFC to group members stereotyped as being low in both warmth and competence as compared to individuals from non-stereotyped groups (Harris & Fiske, 2006). This reduced activation in the mPFC was believed to reflect dehumanization and an inability to perspective take with the stereotyped group (Harris & Fiske, 2006). This same region has also been implicated in biased behavior. For example, participants in one study viewed interactions of outgroup members who transgressed against ingroup members or ingroup members who transgressed against outgroup members while in an fMRI scanner (Baumgartner, Götte, Gügler, & Fehr, 2012). Participants were then given a chance to punish the transgressor, but at a personal (monetary) cost. Results demonstrated an ingroup bias, as evidenced by more leniency toward ingroup transgressors, was associated with increased activity in the mPFC. It appeared that perspective taking or humanization led to more favorable evaluations of the ingroup member despite the improper conduct; however, this same consideration was not extended to outgroup members.

Brain potentials. With millisecond precision, ERPs can shed light on the quick, automatic mental processes involved in implicit biases. For example, the P300 (or the late positive potential; LPP) is a positive-going waveform that begins roughly 250–300ms after an event, typically peaking within 300–500ms (Polich, 2007). A stimulus that is significantly different from a preceding set of stimuli (called an "oddball") elicits a larger P300 amplitude. Importantly for implicit bias research, the oddball P300 amplitude is higher when a negatively valenced target stimulus is presented within a set of positive stimuli or when a positively valenced target stimulus is presented within a set of negative stimuli (Ito & Cacioppo, 2000). Thus, P300 amplitudes can reflect the automatic evaluation of discrete stimuli, which should extend to the automatic evaluation of racial stimuli. Indeed, studies have shown that participants who score high on an explicit measure of prejudice demonstrate heightened P300 amplitude to White versus Black faces when presented with negative stimuli (Ito, Thompson, & Cacioppo, 2004). This suggests that overtly prejudiced participants find Black faces more negative than White faces.

The P300 has also been used to examine implicit categorization processes. For example, one study used this ERP component to measure the degree of differentiation between Blacks and the self (Phills, Kawakami, Tabi, Nadolny, & Inzlicht, 2011). After White participants completed repeated approach behaviors toward Black faces, they viewed a set of images of their own face, followed by a Black face or a White face. Results revealed that approach training decreased P300 amplitudes to Black faces that followed pictures of the self. The muted P300 amplitude thus reflected a reduced differentiation between the self and Blacks. Relatedly, another study showed that stereotype-discrepant information presented after both Black and White faces (e.g., educated and greedy for Black vs. musical and violent for White) elicited larger P300 peak amplitudes (Bartholow, Dickter, & Sestir, 2006).

Other ERP components associated with implicit biases include the N170, P200, and the N400. The N170 responds primarily to face stimuli and reflects a rapid and sophisticated integration of face perception processes (Eimer, 2000). For example, participants assigned to a novel ingroup demonstrated higher N170 amplitudes to faces from that ingroup compared to the newly formed outgroup, suggesting that people processed ingroup members more deeply (Ratner & Amodio, 2013). Similarly, following the presentation of Black faces, White faces, and images of cars, people with implicit biases showed higher N170 amplitudes to Black faces (Ofan, Rubin, & Amodio, 2011). Implicit biases against Blacks increased the salience of Black faces, perhaps as part of a threat detection process.

Relatedly, a more direct measure of threat detection may be the P200. Threatening images primarily enhance the P200. Notably, it is similarly enhanced when viewing Black compared to White faces (Ito & Urland, 2003). Consistent with this, P200 was higher to Blacks than Whites in a video game where participants were instructed to "shoot" or "not shoot" people with or without guns (Correll, Urland, & Ito, 2006). The degree to which the P200 was enhanced to Black relative to White targets predicted increased biases in the decision to shoot.

Finally, the N400 reflects semantic incongruity (Kutas & Federmeier, 2000). For example, a heightened N400 would be expected after the sentence "The apple tasted SPEEDY" compared to the sentence "The apple tasted SWEET." The N400 can thus be used to index racial stereotype accessibility. For example, Black and White faces followed by stereotype-incongruent words elicited larger N400 amplitudes compared to stereotype-congruent words (Hehman, Volpert, & Simons, 2013). Significantly, N400 amplitude to stereotype-incongruent words after Black faces was associated with higher levels of self-reported prejudice. Thus, the N400 reflected adherence to racial stereotypes.

Conclusions and Future Directions

The past few decades have shown a tremendous growth in the development of tools to capture implicit biases, exploration of processes underlying implicit biases, and research exploring their impact on everyday outcomes. In the section that follows, we outline some potential directions for future research.

Implicit Biases in Complex Intergroup Contexts

One avenue that is ripe for future research is exploring implicit biases in more complex intergroup contexts. Thus far, the focus has been on contexts defined based on a simple categorization (e.g., ethnicity, gender, or age), but many situations are characterized by more than one social identity and several categorical distinctions are relevant at once (e.g., ethnicity, immigration status, and gender). How do these differing social identities, with sometimes conflicting and at other times compounding stereotypes and prejudices, impact implicit biases? Studying these more complex configurations might be one of the next challenges for the field.

Implicit Biases from Multiple Perspectives

Whereas the bulk of research has focused on majority or dominant groups' implicit biases toward minorities and subordinate groups, future work should dedicate more attention to understanding implicit biases of minority or subordinate groups toward their own group and toward majority or dominant groups. Although some work suggests that minority and subordinate groups show implicit outgroup favoritism as a result of an internalization of implicit biases (Jost et al., 2004), these findings have been challenged by others (Olson, Crawford, & Devlin, 2009). A related direction for future work is to utilize an intergroup perspective and examine how majority groups' implicit biases impact minority group members, and how these in turn impact minority groups' attitudes and beliefs about their own group or the majority. Such an approach would help explain the dynamic ways in which implicit biases are enhanced or attenuated in intergroup contexts.

Structural and Contextual Factors Underlying Implicit Biases

The study of implicit biases might also benefit from integrating micro and macro levels of analyses. Although research on the malleability of implicit biases sheds light on the contextual and structural factors underlying implicit biases, we believe that more is to be done here. The focus should not be exclusively on dissecting psychological processes but also considering how these processes operate in specific sociocultural contexts. Linking micro and macro levels of analyses may provide a richer understanding of the structural and contextual foundations of implicit biases.

Broader Implications of Implicit Biases

Finally, the field may benefit from continuing to link implicit biases to outcomes of broader relevance to the public and other disciplines such as law, politics, business, health, criminal justice, and education. As evidenced in the cases of police brutality described at the beginning of this chapter, there is a clear divide in how the public sees such incidents, with a sizable portion of the population viewing race as irrelevant to such incidents because of the lack of overt expression of racial hatred. Researchers can do more to document and communicate the circumstances under which implicit biases translate into discriminatory outcomes. The policy implications of such research are also worth addressing more directly given the ubiquity of implicit biases. As implicit biases are highly context sensitive, research might not tell us about ways to eradicate prejudices and stereotypes given that fluctuations in implicit biases tend to be short-lived. However, such research can provide a window into the kind of contexts that will perpetuate these biases and those that are more likely to foster inclusion and acceptance.

Concluding Remark

Research on implicit biases has shown tremendous growth in the past two decades and will continue to be a central theme of social psychological research in the years to come. In this chapter, we provided a selective overview of the large and complex literature on implicit biases including what they are, how they can be assessed, and their benefits to the field of intergroup relations. Our goal was not to capture all the exciting work in the field but rather to focus on the big picture, encouraging readers to see the forest instead of the trees.

References

Agerström, J., & Rooth, D. (2011). The role of automatic obesity stereotypes in real hiring discrimination. *Journal of Applied Psychology, 96*(4), 790–805. doi:10.1037/a0021594

Allen, T., & Sherman, J. (2011). Ego threat and intergroup bias: A test of motivated-activation versus self-regulatory accounts. *Psychological Science, 22*(3), 331–333.

Allison, T., Wood, C., & McCarthy, G. (1986). The central nervous system. In M.G.H. Coles, E. Donchin, & S.W. Porges (Eds). *Psychophysiology: Systems, processes, and applications* (pp. 5–25). New York: Guilford Press.

Amodio, D. (2014). The neuroscience of prejudice and stereotyping. *Nature Reviews Neuroscience, 15*, 670–682.

Amodio, D., Bartholow, B., & Ito, T. (2014). Tracking the dynamics of the social brain: ERP approaches for social cognitive and affective neuroscience. *Social Cognitive and Affective Neuroscience, 9*(3), 385–393.

Amodio, D. M., & Devine, P. G. (2006). Stereotyping and evaluation in implicit race bias: Evidence for independent constructs and unique effects on behavior. *Journal of Personality and Social Psychology, 91*(4), 652–661. doi:10.1037/0022-3514.91.4.652

Anderson, M. (2014). Vast majority of Blacks view the criminal justice system as unfair. Pew Research Center. Retrieved from www.pewresearch.org/fact-tank/2014/08/12/vast-majority-of-blacks-view-the-criminal-justice-system-as-unfair/

Barden, J., Maddux, W., Petty, R., & Brewer, M. (2004). Contextual moderation of racial bias: The impact of social roles on controlled and automatically activated attitudes. *Journal of Personality and Social Psychology, 87*(1), 5–22.

Bartholow, B., Dickter, C., & Sestir, M. (2006). Stereotype activation and control of race bias: Cognitive control of inhibition and its impairment by alcohol. *Journal of Personality and Social Psychology, 90*(2), 272.

Baumgartner, T., Götte, L., Gügler, R., & Fehr, E. (2012). The mentalizing network orchestrates the impact of parochial altruism on social norm enforcement. *Human Brain Mapping, 33*(6), 1452–1469.

Blair, I., & Banaji, M. (1996). Automatic and controlled processes in stereotype priming. *Journal of Personality and Social Psychology, 70*(6), 1142–1163.

Blair, I., Ma, J., & Lenton, A. (2001). Imagining stereotypes away: The moderation of implicit stereotypes through mental imagery. *Journal of Personality and Social Psychology, 81*(5), 828–841.

Cacioppo, J., Berntson, G., Lorig, T., Norris, C., Rickett, E., & Nusbaum, H. (2003) Just because you're imaging the brain doesn't mean you can stop using your head: A primer and set of first principles. *Journal of Personality and Social Psychology, 85*, 650–661.

Calanchini, J., Gonsalkorale, K., Sherman, J., & Klauer, K. (2013). Counter-prejudicial training reduces activation of biased associations and enhances response monitoring. *European Journal of Social Psychology, 43*(5), 321–325.

Calanchini, J., & Sherman, J. (2013). Implicit attitudes reflect associative, non-associative, and non-attitudinal processes. *Social and Personality Psychology Compass, 7*(9), 654–667.

Chekroud, A., Everett, J., Bridge, H., & Hewstone, M. (2014). A review of neuroimaging studies of race-related prejudice: Does amygdala response reflect threat? *Frontiers in Human Neuroscience, 8*, 179.

Conrey, F., Sherman, J., Gawronski, B., Hugenberg, K., & Groom, C. (2005). Separating multiple processes in implicit social cognition: The Quad model of implicit task performance. *Journal of Personality and Social Psychology, 89*(4), 469–487.

Correll, J., Urland, G. R., & Ito, T. A. (2006). Event-related potentials and the decision to shoot: The role of threat perception and cognitive control. *Journal of Experimental Social Psychology, 42*(1), 120–128.

Craig, A. (2009). How do you feel – now? The anterior insula and human awareness. *Nature Reviews Neuroscience, 10*, 59–70.

Cunningham, W., Johnson, M., Raye, C., Gatenby, J., Gore, J., & Banaji, M. (2004). Separable neural components in the processing of Black and White faces. *Psychological Science, 15*(12), 806–813.

Cvencek, D., Greenwald, A., Brown, A., Gray, N., & Snowden, R. (2010). Faking of the Implicit Association Test is statistically detectable and partly correctable. *Basic and Applied Social Psychology, 32*(4), 302–314.

Dasgupta, N. (2009). Mechanisms underlying the malleability of implicit prejudice and stereotypes: The role of automaticity and cognitive control. In T. D. Nelson (Ed.),

Handbook of prejudice, stereotyping, and discrimination (pp. 267–284). New York: Psychology Press.

Dasgupta, N., & Greenwald, A. (2001). On the malleability of automatic attitudes: Combating automatic prejudice with images of admired and disliked individuals. *Journal of Personality and Social Psychology, 81*(5), 800–814.

Dasgupta, N., & Rivera, L. (2006). From automatic antigay prejudice to behavior: The moderating role of conscious beliefs about gender and behavioral control. *Journal of Personality and Social Psychology, 91*(2), 268–280.

Dasgupta, N., & Rivera, L. (2008). When social context matters: The influence of long-term contact and short-term exposure to admired outgroup members on implicit attitudes and behavioral intentions. *Social Cognition, 26*(1), 112–123.

De Houwer, J., Teige-Mocigemba, S., Spruyt, A., & Moors, A. (2009). Implicit measures: A normative analysis and review. *Psychological Bulletin, 135*(3), 347–368.

De Houwer, J., Thomas, S., & Baeyens, F. (2001). Association learning of likes and dislikes: A review of 25 years of research on human evaluative conditioning. *Psychological Bulletin, 127*(6), 853–869.

Devine, P. (1989). Stereotypes and prejudice: Their automatic and controlled components. *Journal of Personality and Social Psychology, 56*(1), 5–18.

Devine, P., Forscher, P., Austin, A., & Cox, W. (2012). Long-term reduction in implicit race bias: A prejudice habit-breaking intervention. *Journal of Experimental Social Psychology, 48*(6), 1267–1278.

Devine, P., Plant, E., Amodio, D., Harmon-Jones, E., & Vance, S. (2002). The regulation of explicit and implicit race bias: The role of motivations to respond without prejudice. *Journal of Personality and Social Psychology, 82*(5), 835–848.

Devos, T., & Banaji, M. (2005). American = White? *Journal of Personality and Social Psychology, 88*(3), 447–466.

Devos, T., Gavin, K., & Quintana, F. (2010). Say "adios" to the American dream? The interplay between ethnic and national identity among Latino and Caucasian Americans. *Cultural Diversity and Ethnic Minority Psychology, 16*(1), 37–49.

Devos, T., Huynh, Q.-L., & Banaji, M. R. (2012). Implicit self and identity. In M. R. Leary & J. P. Tangney (Eds.), *Handbook of self and identity* (2nd ed., pp. 155–179). New York: Guilford Press.

Devos, T., & Ma, D. S. (2008). Is Kate Winslet more American than Lucy Liu? The impact of construal processes on the implicit ascription of a national identity. *British Journal of Social Psychology, 47*(2), 191–215.

Devos, T., & Ma, D. (2013). How "American" is Barack Obama? The role of national identity in a historic bid for the White House. *Journal of Applied Social Psychology, 43*(1), 214–226.

Dovidio, J., Kawakami, K., & Gaertner, S. (2002). Implicit and explicit prejudice and interracial interaction. *Journal of Personality and Social Psychology, 82*(1), 62–68.

Dovidio, J., Kawakami, K., Johnson, C., Johnson, B., & Howard, A. (1997). On the nature of prejudice: Automatic and controlled processes. *Journal of Experimental Social Psychology, 33*(5), 510–540.

Dunham, Y., Baron, A., & Banaji, M. (2008). The development of implicit intergroup cognition. *Trends in Cognitive Sciences, 12*(7), 248–253.

Eimer, M. (2000). The face-specific N170 component reflects late stages in the structural encoding of faces. *Neuroreport, 11*(10), 2319–2324.

Fazio, R., Jackson, J., Dunton, B., & Williams, C. (1995). Variability in automatic activation as an unobtrusive measure of racial attitudes: A bona fide pipeline? *Journal of Personality and Social Psychology, 69*(6), 1013–1027.

Fazio, R., & Olson, M. (2003). Implicit measures in social cognition research: Their meaning and uses. *Annual Review of Psychology, 54*, 297–327.

Gambino, L., Thrasher, S., & Epstein, K. (2014). Thousands march to protest police brutality in major US cities. *The Guardian*. Retrieved from www.theguardian.com/us-news/2014/dec/13/marchers-protest-police-brutality-new-york-washington-boston

Gabrielson, R., Jones, R. G., & Sagara, E. (2014). Deadly force, in Black and White. *ProPublica*. Retrieved from www.propublica.org/article/deadly-force-in-black-and-white?utm_source=et&utm_medium=email&utm_campaign=dailynewsletter

Gawronski, B., & Bodenhausen, G. (2006). Associative and propositional processes in evaluation: An integrative review of implicit and explicit attitude change. *Psychological Bulletin, 132*(5), 692–731.

Gawronski, B., & Bodenhausen, G. (2014). Implicit and explicit evaluation: A brief review of the associative–propositional evaluation model. *Social and Personality Psychology Compass, 8*(8), 448–462.

Gawronski, B., Hofmann, W., & Wilbur, C. (2006). Are "implicit" attitudes unconscious? *Consciousness and Cognition: An International Journal, 15*(3), 485–499.

Gawronski, B., & Payne, B. K. (2010). *Handbook of implicit social cognition: Measurement, theory, and applications*. New York: Guilford Press.

Gawronski, B., & Sritharan, R. (2010). Formation, change, and contextualization of mental associations: Determinants and principles of variations in implicit measures. In B. Gawronski & B. K. Payne (Eds.), *Handbook of implicit social cognition: Measurement, theory, and applications* (pp. 216–240). New York: Guilford Press.

Gonsalkorale, K., Allen, T., Sherman, J., & Klauer, K. (2010). Mechanisms of group membership and exemplar exposure effects on implicit attitudes. *Social Psychology, 41*(3), 158–168.

Gonsalkorale, K., Sherman, J., Allen, T., Klauer, K., & Amodio, D. (2011). Accounting for successful control of implicit racial bias: The roles of association activation, response monitoring, and overcoming bias. *Personality and Social Psychology Bulletin, 37*(11), 1534–1545.

Green, A. R., Carney, D. R., Pallin, D. J., Ngo, L. H., Raymond, K. L., Iezzoni, L. I., & Banaji, M. R. (2007). Implicit bias among physicians and its prediction of thrombolysis decisions for Black and White patients. *Journal of General Internal Medicine, 22*(9), 1231–1238.

Greenwald, A., & Banaji, M. (1995). Implicit social cognition: Attitudes, self-esteem, and stereotypes. *Psychological Review, 102*(1), 4–27.

Greenwald, A., Banaji, M., & Nosek, B. (2015). Statistically small effects of the Implicit Association Test can have societally large effects. *Journal of Personality and Social Psychology, 108*(4), 553–561.

Greenwald, A., McGhee, D., & Schwartz, J. (1998). Measuring individual differences in implicit cognition: The Implicit Association Test. *Journal of Personality and Social Psychology, 74*(6), 1464–1480.

Greenwald, A., Nosek, B., & Banaji, M. (2003). Understanding and using the Implicit Association Test: I. An improved scoring algorithm. *Journal of Personality and Social Psychology*, *85*(2), 197–216.

Greenwald, A., Poehlman, T., Uhlmann, E., & Banaji, M. (2009). Understanding and using the Implicit Association Test: III. Meta-analysis of predictive validity. *Journal of Personality and Social Psychology*, *97*(1), 17–41.

Greenwald, A., Smith, C., Sriram, N., Bar-Anan, Y., & Nosek, B. (2009). Implicit race attitudes predicted vote in the 2008 U.S. Presidential election. *Analyses of Social Issues and Public Policy (ASAP)*, *9*(1), 241–253.

Hahn, A., Judd, C., Hirsh, H., & Blair, I. (2014). Awareness of implicit attitudes. *Journal of Experimental Psychology: General*, *143*(3), 1369–1392.

Harris, L., & Fiske, S. (2006). Dehumanizing the lowest of the low neuroimaging responses to extreme out-groups. *Psychological Science*, *17*(10), 847–853.

Hehman, E., Volpert, H. I., & Simons, R. F. (2013). The N400 as an index of racial stereotype accessibility. *Social Cognitive and Affective Neuroscience*, *9*(4), 544–552.

Ito, T., & Cacioppo, J. (2000). Electrophysiological evidence of implicit and explicit categorization processes. *Journal of Experimental Social Psychology*, *36*(6), 660–676.

Ito, T., & Cacioppo, J. (2007). Attitudes as mental and neural states of readiness: Using physiological measures to study implicit attitudes. In B. Wittenbrink & N. Schwarz (Eds.), *Implicit measures of attitudes* (pp. 125–158). New York: Guilford Press.

Ito, T., Thompson, E., & Cacioppo, J. (2004). Tracking the time-course of social perception: The effects of racial cues on event-related brain potentials. *Personality and Social Psychology Bulletin*, *30*(10), 1267–1280.

Ito, T., & Urland, G. (2003). Race and gender on the brain: Electrocortical measures of attention to the race and gender of multiply categorizable individuals. *Journal of Personality and Social Psychology*, *85*(4), 616–626.

Johns, M., Cullum, J., Smith, T., & Freng, S. (2008). Internal motivation to respond without prejudice and automatic egalitarian goal activation. *Journal of Experimental Social Psychology*, *44*(6), 1514–1519.

Jost, J., Banaji, M., & Nosek, B. (2004). A decade of system justification theory: Accumulated evidence of conscious and unconscious bolstering of the status quo. *Political Psychology*, *25*(6), 881–920.

Kang, J., Dasgupta, N., Yogeeswaran, K., & Blasi, G. (2010). Are ideal litigators White? Measuring the myth of colorblindness. *Journal of Empirical Legal Studies*, *7*(4), 886–915.

Kawakami, K., Dovidio, J., Moll, J., Hermsen, S., & Russin, A. (2000). Just say no (to stereotyping): Effects of training in the negation of stereotypic associations on stereotype activation. *Journal of Personality and Social Psychology*, *78*(5), 871–888.

Kutas, M., & Federmeier, K. (2000). Electrophysiology reveals semantic memory use in language comprehension. *Trends in Cognitive Sciences*, *4*(12), 463–470.

Lai, C., Hoffman, K., & Nosek, B. (2013). Reducing implicit prejudice. *Social and Personality Psychology Compass*, *7*(5), 315–330.

Lai, C., Marini, M., Lehr, S., Cerruti, C., Shin, J.-E. L., Joy-Gaba, J. . . . Nosek, B. (2014). Reducing implicit racial preferences: I. A comparative investigation of 17 interventions. *Journal of Experimental Psychology: General*, *143*(4), 1765–1785.

LeDoux, J. (2003). The emotional brain, fear, and the amygdala. *Cellular and Molecular Neurobiology, 23*(4–5), 727–738.

Lenton, A., Bruder, M., & Sedikides, C. (2009). A meta-analysis on the malleability of automatic gender stereotypes. *Psychology of Women Quarterly, 33*(2), 183–196.

Levine, S. (2014). Peter King says Eric Garner would not have died from chokehold were he not obese. *Huffington Post*. Retrieved from www.huffingtonpost.com/2014/12/03/peter-king-eric-garner_n_6265748.html

Lieberman, M., Hariri, A., Jarcho, J., Eisenberger, N., & Bookheimer, S. (2005). An fMRI investigation of race-related amygdala activity in African-American and Caucasian-American individuals. *Nature Neuroscience, 8*(6), 720–722.

Luck, S. (2014). *An introduction to the event-related potential technique*. Cambridge, MA: MIT Press.

Ma, D., & Devos, T. (2014). Every heart beats true, for the red, white, and blue: National identity predicts voter support. *Analyses of Social Issues and Public Policy, 14*, 22–45.

Macrae, C., & Bodenhausen, G. (2000). Social cognition: Thinking categorically about others. *Annual Review of Psychology, 51*, 93–120.

Marini, M., Sriram, N., Schnabel, K., Maliszewski, N., Devos, T., Ekehammar, B. ... Nosek, B. (2013). Overweight people have low levels of implicit weight bias, but overweight nations have high levels of implicit weight bias. *PLoS ONE, 8*, e83543.

McConnell, A., & Leibold, J. (2001). Relations among the Implicit Association Test, discriminatory behavior, and explicit measures of racial attitudes. *Journal of Experimental Social Psychology, 37*(5), 435–442.

Mitchell, J., Macrae, C. N., & Banaji, M. (2006). Dissociable medial prefrontal contributions to judgments of similar and dissimilar others. *Neuron, 50*(4), 655–663.

Moors, A., & De Houwer, J. (2006). Automaticity: A theoretical and conceptual analysis. *Psychological Bulletin, 132*(2), 297–326.

Newheiser, A., Dunham, Y., Merrill, A., Hoosain, L., & Olson, K. (2014). Preference for high status predicts implicit outgroup bias among children from low-status groups. *Developmental Psychology, 50*(4), 1081–1090.

Newheiser, A., & Olson, K. (2012). White and Black American children's implicit intergroup bias. *Journal of Experimental Social Psychology, 48*(1), 264–270.

Nosek, B., & Banaji, M. (2001). The Go/No-go Association Task. *Social Cognition, 19*(6), 625–666.

Nosek, B., Smyth, F., Hansen, J., Devos, T., Lindner, N., Ranganath, K. ... Banaji, M. (2007). Pervasiveness and correlates of implicit attitudes and stereotypes. *European Review of Social Psychology, 18*(1), 36–88.

Nosek, B., Smyth, F., Sriram, N., Lindner, N., Devos, T., Ayala, A. ... Greenwald, A. (2009). National differences in gender-science stereotypes predict national sex differences in science and math achievement. *Proceedings of the National Academy of Sciences of the United States of America, 106*(26), 10593–10597.

Ofan, R., Rubin, N., & Amodio, D. (2011). Seeing race: N170 responses to race and their relation to automatic racial attitudes and controlled processing. *Journal of Cognitive Neuroscience, 23*(10), 3153–3161.

Olson, M., Crawford, M., & Devlin, W. (2009). Evidence for the underestimation of implicit ingroup favoritism among low-status groups. *Journal of Experimental Social Psychology, 45*, 1111–1116.

Olson, K., & Dunham, Y. (2010). The development of implicit social cognition. In B. Gawronski & B. K. Payne (Eds.), *Handbook of implicit social cognition: Measurement, theory, and applications* (pp. 241–254). New York: Guilford Press.

Olson, M., & Fazio, R. (2002). Implicit acquisition and manifestation of classically conditioned attitudes. *Social Cognition, 20*(2), 89–104.

Oswald, F., Mitchell, G., Blanton, H., Jaccard, J., & Tetlock, P. (2013). Predicting ethnic and racial discrimination: A meta-analysis of IAT criterion studies. *Journal of Personality and Social Psychology, 105*(2), 171–192.

Parasuraman, R. (1980). Effects of information processing demands on slow negative shift latencies and N100 amplitude in selective and divided attention. *Biological Psychology, 11*(3), 217–233.

Payne, B. K. (2008). What mistakes disclose: A process dissociation approach to automatic and controlled processes in social psychology. *Social and Personality Psychology Compass, 2*(2), 1073–1092.

Payne, B. K., Krosnick, J., Pasek, J., Lelkes, Y., Akhtar, O., & Tompson, T. (2010). Implicit and explicit prejudice in the 2008 presidential election. *Journal of Experimental Social Psychology, 46*, 367–374.

Payne, B. K., Lambert, A., & Jacoby, L. (2002). Best laid plans: Effects of goals on accessibility bias and cognitive control in race-based misperceptions of weapons. *Journal of Experimental Social Psychology, 38*(4), 384–396.

Phelps, E., Cannistraci, C., & Cunningham, W. (2003). Intact performance on an indirect measure of race bias following amygdala damage. *Neuropsychologia, 41*(2), 203–208.

Phelps, E., O'Connor, K., Cunningham, W., Funayama, E., Gatenby, J., Gore, J., & Banaji, M. (2000). Performance on indirect measures of race evaluation predicts amygdala activation. *Journal of Cognitive Neuroscience, 12*(5), 729–738.

Phills, C., Kawakami, K., Tabi, E., Nadolny, D., & Inzlicht, M. (2011). Mind the gap: Increasing associations between the self and Blacks with approach behaviors. *Journal of Personality and Social Psychology, 100*(2), 197–210.

Polich, J. (2007). Updating P300: An integrative theory of P3a and P3b. *Clinical Neurophysiology, 118*(10), 2128–2148.

Ratner, K., & Amodio, D. (2013). Seeing "us vs. them": Minimal group effects on the neural encoding of faces. *Journal of Experimental Social Psychology, 49*(2), 298–301.

Rooth, D. (2010). Automatic associations and discrimination in hiring: Real-world evidence. *Labour Economics, 17*, 523–534.

Richeson, J., Baird, A., Gordon, H., Heatherton, T., Wyland, C., Trawalter, S., & Shelton, J. (2003). An fMRI investigation of the impact of interracial contact on executive function. *Nature Neuroscience, 6*(12), 1323–1328.

Rudman, L. (2004). Sources of implicit attitudes. *Current Directions in Psychological Science, 13*(2), 79–82.

Rudman, L., & Ashmore, R. (2007). Discrimination and the Implicit Association Test. *Group Processes & Intergroup Relations, 10*(3), 359–372. doi:10.1177/1368430207078696

Rudman, L., Feinberg, J., & Fairchild, K. (2002). Minority members' implicit attitudes: Automatic ingroup bias as a function of group status. *Social Cognition, 20*(4), 294–320.

Rutland, A., Cameron, L., Milne, A., & McGeorge, P. (2005). Social norms and self-presentation: Children's implicit and explicit intergroup attitudes. *Child Development, 76*(2), 451–466.

Rydell, R., Hamilton, D. L., & Devos, T. (2010). Now they are American, now they are not: Valence as a determinant of the inclusion of African Americans in the American identity. *Social Cognition, 28*(2), 161–179.

Sekaquaptewa, D., Espinoza, P., Thompson, M., Vargas, P., & von Hippel, W. (2003). Stereotypic explanatory bias: Implicit stereotyping as a predictor of discrimination. *Journal of Experimental Social Psychology, 39*(1), 75–82.

Sherman, J. (2006). On building a better process model: It's not only how many, but which ones and by which means? *Psychological Inquiry, 17*(3), 173–184.

Stanley, D., Sokol-Hessner, P., Banaji, M., & Phelps, E. (2011). Implicit race attitudes predict trustworthiness judgments and economic trust decisions. *Proceedings of the National Academy of Sciences of the United States of America, 108*(19), 7710–7775.

Stanley, D., Phelps, E., & Banaji, M. (2008). The neural basis of implicit attitudes. *Current Directions in Psychological Science, 17*(2), 164–170.

Tajfel, H. (1981). *Human groups and social categories: Studies in social psychology.* Cambridge: Cambridge University Press.

Tam, T., Hewstone, M., Harwood, J., Voci, A., & Kenworthy, J. (2006). Intergroup contact and grandparent-grandchild communication: The effects of self-disclosure on implicit and explicit biases against older people. *Group Processes & Intergroup Relations, 9*(3), 413–429.

Turner, R., Hewstone, M., & Voci, A. (2007). Reducing explicit and implicit outgroup prejudice via direct and extended contact: The mediating role of self-disclosure and intergroup anxiety. *Journal of Personality and Social Psychology, 93*(3), 369–388.

Van Overwalle, F. (2009). Social cognition and the brain: A meta-analysis. *Human Brain Mapping, 30*(3), 829–858.

Wittenbrink, B., Judd, C., & Park, B. (2001). Spontaneous prejudice in context: Variability in automatically activated attitudes. *Journal of Personality and Social Psychology, 81*(5), 815–827.

Yogeeswaran, K., Adelman, L., Parker, M., & Dasgupta, N. (2014). In the eyes of the beholder: National identification predicts differential reactions to ethnic identity expressions. *Cultural Diversity & Ethnic Minority Psychology, 20*(3), 362–369.

Yogeeswaran, K., & Dasgupta, N. (2010). Will the "real" American please stand up? The effect of implicit national prototypes on discriminatory behavior and judgments. *Personality and Social Psychology Bulletin, 36*(10), 1332–1345.

Yogeeswaran, K., Dasgupta, N., Adelman, L., Eccleston, A., & Parker, M. T. (2011). To be or not to be (ethnic): Public vs. private expressions of ethnic identification differentially impact national inclusion of White and non-White groups. *Journal of Experimental Social Psychology, 47*(5), 908–914.

Yogeeswaran, K., Dasgupta, N., & Gomez, C. (2012). A new American dilemma? The effect of ethnic identification and public service on the national inclusion of ethnic minorities. *European Journal of Social Psychology, 42*(6), 691–705.

12 Aversive Racism and Contemporary Bias

John F. Dovidio, Samuel L. Gaertner, and Adam R. Pearson

In the United States, the 1960s and early 1970s were characterized by significant societal changes. The Civil Rights Movement and social, political, and moral forces stimulated these changes to address racism by White Americans toward Black Americans and achieve the nation's historical egalitarian ideals. With the Civil Rights legislation and other federal mandates, it was no longer simply immoral to discriminate against Blacks; it was now also illegal. Surveys and national polls revealed significant reductions in overt expressions of prejudice among Whites toward Blacks (Dovidio & Gartner, 2004). This unprecedented change in race relations in the United States changed the nature of racial attitudes, from blatant to subtle, and consequently the study of prejudice in psychology (Dovidio, 2001). In other countries, similar normative changes have reduced blatant expressions of prejudice while more subtle, yet equally pernicious, forms of bias persist (see Pettigrew & Meertens, 1995).

This chapter reviews the development of theory about contemporary forms of racism – focusing primarily on aversive racism – tracing the evolution of this perspective, describing key empirical evidence, and identifying productive avenues for future research. We begin by reviewing relations among different theories of subtle contemporary racism and discussing work on implicit prejudice and its relationship to aversive racism. We then consider the implications of aversive racism for interventions to reduce bias and identify promising new directions for research on contemporary racism, in general, and aversive racism, in particular.

Overview of Theories of Subtle Racism

The changing social norms and values shaped by the civil rights era posed unique challenges to the study of prejudice. Although overt expressions of prejudice and negative stereotyping have substantially declined, in part because of new normative pressures toward egalitarianism, privately held beliefs continue to reflect negative racial attitudes and beliefs. One effect of these new norms was that people appeared to more deliberately manage how others perceived their racial attitudes. For example, when expressing attitudes under conditions in which they were led to believe their true attitudes could be detected (e.g., bogus pipeline; Roese & Jamieson, 1993), Whites displayed significantly more negative attitudes toward Blacks than when they reported their attitudes under more normal conditions. This effect occurred, in part, because people normally consciously manage self-reports of prejudice and interracial behaviors to appear nonbiased.

Changes in law and societal norms toward the affirmation of egalitarian values in the 1960s also prompted another important change – a shift in the nature of racial prejudice in the United States. Many Whites not only altered their public attitudes to appear less prejudiced but also developed a private self-concept of being non-prejudiced. They genuinely embraced these egalitarian norms and internalized them. These changes to the expression and self-control of racial attitudes, along with methodological advances in capturing subtle and unintended manifestations of bias, spawned a new era of research on race relations, beginning in the 1970s. We briefly describe four historically influential approaches to understanding subtle racism dating from this period: symbolic, modern, ambivalent, and aversive forms of racism.

Symbolic Racism

Symbolic racism theory (Sears & Henry, 2005) developed in response to a practical problem: the failure of traditional self-report measures to predict people's responses to racially targeted policies and Black political candidates. Sears, Henry, and Kosterman (2000) observed, "Few Whites now support the core notions of old-fashioned racism ... Our own view is that the acceptance of formal equality is genuine but that racial animus has not gone away; it has just changed its principal manifestations" (p. 77). Symbolic racism involves four basic belief components that reflect the confluence of politically conservative, individualistic values and early acquired negative racial affect that typically emerge in adolescence before many other sociopolitical beliefs. These include (a) discrimination against Blacks is "a thing of the past,"(b) Blacks' failure to progress is attributable to their unwillingness to work hard enough, (c) Blacks make excessive demands, and (d) Blacks have gotten more than they deserve. The components are typically measured using self-reported responses (see Henry & Sears, 2002).

Symbolic racism predicts people's political attitudes and behavior better than do measures of old-fashioned racism, realistic threats, and perceived intergroup competition, non-racial ideologies (e.g., individualism, egalitarianism), and political affiliation and ideology (Sears & Henry, 2005). Specifically, symbolic racism uniquely predicts White Americans' attitudes toward a range of racially relevant policies, including busing for school integration and affirmative action, as well as less explicitly race-targeted policies that disproportionately affect blacks, such as policies relating to crime and welfare. Symbolic racism also predicts opposition to

Black political candidates, as well as support for ethnocentric White candidates, such as former Ku Klux Klan leader David Duke (Tesler & Sears, 2010).

Modern Racism

Modern racism theory was derived from symbolic racism theory; however, the two positions diverge on the hypothesized origins of bias. Whereas symbolic racism proposes that Whites' negative attitudes are primarily rooted in concerns that Blacks threaten Whites' worldviews by violating principles of individualism, modern racism theory hypothesizes that various forms of negative affect (e.g., fear, disgust), which may be acquired through early socialization and modeling, persist into adulthood. Both theories, though, assume that negative racial attitudes are expressed indirectly and symbolically, in terms of more abstract social and political issues (e.g., opposition to school integration, ostensibly to support neighborhood schools; see McConahay, 1986).

Modern racism is assessed using the Modern Racism Scale, a self-report measure similar to that used to assess symbolic racism. The scale was originally designed to be an indirect measure of racism that is less susceptible to social desirability concerns (McConahay, 1986). Like symbolic racism, modern racism predicts voting against political candidates who are Black or sympathetic toward Blacks, and voting against policies designed to assist Blacks such as affirmative action and school integration programs. It also predicts these political attitudes better than do measures of political conservatism, identification as a Democrat or Republican, education, and most importantly, personal interests in the outcomes of a vote (Henry, 2009).

The modern and symbolic racism approaches have been challenged on similar conceptual grounds. Because the scales are not direct measures of stereotypes or prejudice against Blacks, critics have argued that both modern racism and symbolic racism scales tap non-racial principles underlying conservatism (such as opposition to excessive government intervention) rather than racial attitudes, per se, and there is evidence that a subset of high modern racism scorers are, indeed, principled conservatives rather than racists (Son Hing, Chung-Yan, Hamilton, & Zanna, 2008). Other critiques of the Modern Racism Scale have contended that this measure should no longer be classified as an indirect measure but, rather, as a blatant measure of racism. Indeed, responses on the Modern Racism Scale appear to be more susceptible to social desirability influences and self-presentational concerns than in the past (Calanchini & Sherman, 2013). As McConahay (1986) noted 30 years ago, "It is expected that new items will have to be generated for the Modern Racism Scale as new issues emerge in American race relations and some of the current items become more reactive while the ambivalence lingers" (p. 123). Nevertheless, items from the Modern Racism Scale still predict responses to political issues (e.g., evaluations of Obama versus McCain during the 2008 presidential campaign, support for government policies benefiting Blacks) in ways over and above measures of blatant prejudice toward Blacks (Ditonto, Lau, & Sears, 2013).

Ambivalent Racism

Another important psychological insight into contemporary forms of prejudice and discrimination involved the recognition of the ambivalence that many Whites hold toward Blacks. Pioneering work by Katz (1981) proposed the existence of Whites' ambivalent attitudes toward Blacks. Katz (1981; see also Katz, Wackenhut, & Hass, 1986) noted that attitudes toward Blacks often involve sympathy and a desire to be fair and egalitarian, as well as negative affective reactions (Dovidio & Gaertner, 2004; Gaertner & Dovidio, 1986; Katz, 1981). These inconsistent and opposing elements create psychological tension that amplifies responses to the associated groups and their members (Katz, 1981). Response amplification involves responding more intensely, positively or negatively, to members of stigmatized groups than non-stigmatized groups as a consequence of the psychological tension involved in some forms of bias (e.g., toward Blacks and people with disabilities). For instance, when participants were induced to be overly harsh in their evaluation of a Black person (compared to giving mild negative feedback or a harsh evaluation of a White person), they compensated by subsequently helping the Black person more (including more than the harshly evaluated White person (Katz, Glass, Lucido, & Farber, 1979). However, when White participants responded overly negatively to a confederate (administering noxious vs. non-offensive noise) and were not given the opportunity to compensate for their harsh action by helping the confederate in a subsequent task, they denigrated the Black confederate uniquely strongly (Katz, Glass, & Cohen, 1973). These and other findings by Katz and his colleagues (see Katz et al., 1986) provide general support for the concept of ambivalence-amplification.

Aversive Racism

Whereas modern and symbolic racism characterize the attitudes of political conservatives, aversive racism characterizes the biases of those who are politically and socially liberal (Nail, Harton, & Decker, 2003) and believe that they are not prejudiced, but whose unconscious negative feelings and beliefs nevertheless get expressed in subtle, indirect, and often rationalizable ways. In 1970, Kovel distinguished between dominative and aversive racism. Dominative racism is the "old-fashioned," blatant form. According to Kovel, the dominative racist is the "type who acts out bigoted beliefs – he [sic] represents the open flame of racial hatred" (p. 54). Building on Kovel's (1970) distinction, over the past 45 years we have explored the existence and operation of aversive racism among White Americans. Aversive racism is hypothesized to be qualitatively different from blatant, old-fashioned, racism. Aversive racists sympathize with victims of past injustice, support principles of racial equality, and genuinely regard themselves as non-prejudiced, but at the same time they possess conflict-ing, often nonconscious, negative feelings and beliefs about Blacks that are rooted in basic psychological processes (e.g., social categorization) that promote racial bias (Dovidio & Gaertner, 2004; Gaertner & Dovidio, 1986; Pearson, Dovidio, & Gaertner, 2009). In addition, the negative feelings that aversive racists have toward Blacks do not reflect open hostility or hatred. Instead, aversive racists' reactions typically involve discomfort, anxiety, or fear. That is, while they find Blacks aversive, they find any suggestion that they might be prejudiced aversive as well. In addition, in some instances aversive racism can reflect the expression of more positive feelings toward Blacks than toward Whites (Gaertner et al., 1997; Greenwald & Pettigrew, 2014). The experience of differential positivity rather than negativity toward racial ingroup and out-group members similarly can obscure self-recognition of prejudicial attitudes.

Like symbolic and modern racism, aversive racism is hypothesized to operate in subtle and indirect ways. However, unlike symbolic and modern racism approaches that utilize self-report scales to measure these concepts and have largely focused on their relationship to political behavior, work on aversive racism has examined a broad array of responses to Blacks and Whites. Because the basic premises of aversive racism are not tied to specific scale items and the US political context, the principles of aversive racism are applic-able to behaviors of dominant groups toward minorities in other nations that also have strong societal egalitarian values, such as Canada (Son Hing et al., 2008), England (Hodson, Hooper, Dovidio, & Gaertner, 2005), the Netherlands (Kleinpenning & Hagendoorn, 1993), Portugal (de França & Monteiro, 2013), and Spain (Wojcieszak, 2015).

The aversive racism framework also helps identify when discrimination against Blacks and other minority groups will occur. Because aversive racists consciously endorse egalitarian values and truly believe that they are non-prejudiced, they will not act inappropriately when discrimination would be obvious to others and themselves. Specifically, when they are presented with a situation in which the normatively appropriate response is clear, aversive racists will not discriminate against Blacks. In these contexts, aversive racists will be especially motivated to avoid feelings, beliefs, and behaviors that could be associated with racist intent. However, discrimination will occur in situations in which normative structure is weak, when the guidelines for appropriate behavior are vague, when the basis for social judgment is ambiguous, or when one can justify or rationalize a negative response on the basis of some factor other than race. Under these circumstances, aversive racists may engage in behaviors that ultimately harm Blacks but in ways that allow aversive racists to maintain their self-image as non-prejudiced.

Support for the aversive racism framework has been obtained across a broad range of paradigms and participant populations. Early tests of the aversive racism framework focused on prosocial behavior for both theoretical and practical rea-sons. Theoretically, because aversive racists are hypothesized to be particularly effective at censoring negative behavior toward Blacks, the biases associated with aversive racism may often manifest as differential prosocial responses toward Whites and Blacks in need. Indeed, it was research on the differential behavior of Whites toward Black and White motorists who were stranded on a highway that represented the first empirical work on aversive racism (Gaertner, 1973). The results of a meta-analysis of 31 experiments on Whites' interracial helping behavior conducted over the past 40 years evidence a stable pattern of discrimination reflective of aversive racism that has not subsided over time (Saucier, Miller, & Doucet, 2005). Based on these findings, the authors concluded that racism and discrimination against Blacks "can and will exist as long as individuals harbor negativity toward Blacks at the implicit level" (p. 14).

Aversive racism is also influential in selection decisions in employment and college admission, interpersonal judgments, and policy and legal decisions (see Dovidio & Gaertner, 2004; Knight, Guiliano, & Sanchez-Ross, 2001; Sommers & Ellsworth, 2000). For example, Dovidio and Gaertner (2000) examined White college students' support for hiring Black and White applicants for a selective campus position within the same college in the years 1989 and 1999. When the candidates' credentials clearly qualified or disqualified them for the position, there was no discrimination against the Black candidate (i.e., the highly qualified Black candidate was just as likely to be hired as the highly qualified White candidate). However, when candidates' qualifications for the position were less obvious and the appropriate decision was more ambiguous (moderate qualifications), White participants recommended a Black candidate significantly less often than a White candidate with exactly the same credentials. Whereas overt expressions of prejudice (measured by items on a self-report scale) declined over this 10-year period, the pattern of subtle discrimination in selection decisions remained essentially unchanged.

Additional research offers further insight into processes that underlie these effects. When ambiguous or mixed credentials are involved, people systematically weigh credentials differently based on their unconscious biases. For example, when providing input to college admission decisions for candidates with mixed credentials (e.g., strong high school grades but modest standardized scores, or vice versa), White college students emphasized the credential that White candidates were stronger in relative to Black candidates as being the more valid predictor of success in college. This differential weighting of the credentials, in turn, justified students' stronger recommendations of White than Black candidates for admission (Hodson, Dovidio, & Gaertner, 2002; see also Brief, Dietz, Cohen, Pugh, and Vaslow, 2000, for employment bias against Blacks; Rooth, 2007, for hiring biases against Muslims).

Recent developmental research is also supportive of the hypothesized role of egalitarian norms in the dynamics of aversive racism. Developmentally, older children are more aware of egalitarian norms than are younger children, and thus they may be more likely to show patterns consistent with aversive racism, whereas younger children may display more blatant intergroup bias. For instance, de França and Monteiro (2013, Study 1) found that younger White Portuguese children (ages 5–7) generally favored other White children over Black children in the distribution of rewards (candy) regardless of how they performed on a task. Older children (ages 8–10) rewarded relatively poorly performing Black children less than White children but, consistent with the aversive racism perspective, did not discriminate against Black relative to White children when they performed equally well. In another study (de França & Monteiro, 2013, Study 1), increasing the salience of egalitarian norms through the presence of an adult reduced bias in helping a White relative to a Black child for the older children but not for younger children.

Further support for this developmental time-course was obtained by McGillicuddy-De Lisi, Daly, and Neal (2006), who found evidence of aversive racism in the way that 10-year-olds distributed resources to Black and White story characters. Whereas younger children (7- to 8-year-olds) distributed money equivalently, regardless of race, age, performance, or need, older children (9- to 10-year-olds) showed evidence of differential allocation by race, consistent with aversive racism. Older children allocated less money to needy Black than to needy White children but allocated more money to Black than to White children who performed unusually successfully on the designated task. Furthermore, whereas the younger children justified their allocations based on principles of equality for both Black and White targets, the older children made different justifications for their allocations for White and Black targets, appealing to principles of equality for the former and equity (i.e., deservingness) for the latter. Together, these findings implicate a window of middle-to-late childhood for the emergence of cognitive and behavioral strategies that allow aversive racists to establish and maintain a non-prejudiced self-concept while engaging in subtle discriminatory practices.

More generally, the studies cited show that, in contrast to the dramatic decline in overt expressions of prejudice, subtle forms of discrimination persist and, despite their subtlety, can be as consequential and pernicious as more overt forms. In addition to the outcomes detailed earlier in the context of hiring and helping behavior, even minor discriminatory patterns can have substantial effects over time. For instance, computer simulations of corporate hiring decisions demonstrate that even a slight systematic bias (a 1% bias against women in performance assessments) compounds to produce a substantial underrepresentation of women in top-level management positions (Martell, Lane, & Emrich, 1996), which approximates the actual gender disparity in top-level management positions today (35% women vs. 65% men).

Early work on aversive racism had limited means to assess people's hypothesized unconscious attitudes and beliefs. Major developments in assessing implicit biases over the past several decades, however, have offered a solution to this problem (see Chapter 11 by Yogeeswaran, Devos, and Nash for a full discussion of measures of implicit bias). Whereas self-report methods today are often used to assess explicit attitudes, implicit attitudes can be assessed through a wide range of methodologies, including response latency tasks, memory tasks, and physiological measures (e.g., heart rate and galvanic skin response), as well as indirect self-report measures (e.g., biases in behavioral and trait attributions). In the next section, we discuss research on implicit attitudes and its relevance to aversive racism.

Aversive Racism and Implicit Bias

Among the most common techniques for assessing implicit, automatically activated (and potentially unconscious) attitudes are response latency techniques (Fazio & Olson, 2003; Gaertner & McLaughlin, 1983). As Yogeeswaran et al. review (Chapter 11, this title), response-time techniques have been commonly used to test the strength of association between social groups and positive or negative valence (implicit attitudes) and particular traits or beliefs (implicit stereotypes), as well as the extent to which subgroups (e.g., Blacks) are perceived as belonging within a superordinate group (e.g., Americans).

One of the most popular response-time techniques is the Implicit Association Test (IAT; see Greenwald, Poehlman, Uhlmann, & Banaji, 2009). The IAT relies on the basic assumption that people are faster categorizing groups of stimuli that are similar in valence than groups of stimuli that are dissimilar in valence. For instance, research using the Race-IAT has shown that people who associate negativity with Blacks are quicker to respond when images of Blacks and unpleasant words share a response key than when images of Blacks and pleasant words share a response key (Greenwald et al., 2009). Importantly, responses on these types of measures are difficult to control and are often unintended. Implicit attitudes are acquired early in life (Rudman, Phelan, & Heppen, 2007) from repeated exposure to positive or negative information about a group, or a lack of exposure, either through socialization or direct experience, and can be resistant to change in response to new information (Gregg, Seibt, & Banaji, 2006; Smith & DeCoster, 2000; see also Yogeeswaran et al.'s chapter in this title).

Consistent with the aversive racism framework, in a large sample of more than 14,000 US Whites, whereas most (59.4%) appeared non-prejudiced on a self-report (explicit) measure, a large majority (71.5%) nevertheless showed evidence of implicit bias on the Race-IAT that was largely dissociated from their explicit (self-reported) views (Greenwald & Krieger, 2006). Moreover, the percentage of respondents who display pro-White implicit race bias varies relatively little by age, sex, political ideology, and educational attainment (Greenwald & Krieger, 2006). For instance, more liberal individuals display less explicit prejudice on self-report measures but show pro-White implicit racial bias at levels equal to those of conservatives. Also, whereas younger children exhibit racial bias both explicitly and implicitly, as they grow older and more responsive to egalitarian norms, explicit bias tends to decline but implicit bias remains high (Baron & Banaji, 2006; Dunham, Baron, & Banaji, 2008).

Initially, research on implicit attitudes focused on developing and refining measurement techniques, distinguishing implicit from explicit measures, and clarifying the origins and meaning of implicit measures of attitudes. More recent work has examined the predictive validity of implicit measures. A meta-analysis by Greenwald et al. (2009; cf. Oswald, Mitchell, Blanton, Jaccard, & Tetlock, 2013) of 122 research reports found that both implicit measures of attitudes such as the IAT and explicit measures predicted a range of behaviors to attitude objects (explicit attitudes average $r = .36$ and implicit attitudes average $r = .27$). However, the predictive validity of explicit measures for socially sensitive issues was much weaker. Across a range of racial issues in particular (e.g., willingness to hire a Black job applicant [Ziegert & Hanges, 2005], subjective and neural threat responses to Blacks [Phelps et al., 2000], affective and nonverbal expressions toward Blacks [McConnell & Leibold, 2001]), implicit attitudes (average $r = .24$) were a better predictor overall than explicit attitudes (average $r = .12$).

Notably, different theoretical perspectives suggest that a key factor in the relative validity of implicit and explicit measures for predicting behavior is the context in which the behavior occurs and the type of behavior being examined (Dovidio et al., 2001; Dovidio, Kawakami, Smoak, & Dovidio, 2009). For example, Fazio's (1990) MODE model indicates that whereas implicit measures will better predict spontaneous behaviors, explicit measures will better predict deliberative behaviors, including those in situations in which social desirability factors are salient (Fazio & Olson, 2003). Accordingly, the relative influence of explicit and implicit attitudes depends on the type of response that is made. Whereas explicit attitudes shape more deliberative responses in which the costs and benefits of various courses of action are weighed, implicit attitudes influence behaviors that are less controllable and responses that people do not view as indicative of their attitude.

Consistent with this distinction, and paralleling the findings in racial contexts in the United States, in a Canadian sample, Son Hing et al. (2008) found that when assessing candidates with more moderate qualifications, evaluators recommended White candidates more strongly for a position than Asian candidates with identical credentials. However, when evaluating candidates with exceptionally strong qualifications, no such selection bias emerged. Moreover, the researchers found that implicit bias against Asians (as measured by an IAT), but not explicit prejudice, predicted weaker support for hiring Asian candidates who had moderate qualifications. However, when the Asian candidate had distinctively strong qualifications, neither implicit nor explicit prejudice predicted the hiring decision.

Divergent effects of implicit and explicit racial attitudes can also fuel divergent perspectives and experiences of Blacks and Whites in interracial interactions. Dovidio, Kawakami, and Gaertner (2002) demonstrated that whereas Whites' explicit (self-reported) racial attitudes predicted their relatively controllable verbal expressions in their interactions with Blacks, Whites' implicit attitudes, which were generally negative, predicted their nonverbal behaviors. Moreover, Black interaction partners weighed the nonverbal behavior more heavily than the verbal behavior in their impressions of the White partner and the interaction. Thus, Whites and Blacks had divergent perspectives in their interactions, and Blacks' awareness of conflicting positive verbal and negative nonverbal behavior undermined how trustworthy they saw the White interaction partner.

Stigmatization and discrimination can have profound effects on the health of members of disadvantaged groups (see Paradies, Bastos, and Priest, Chapter 25, this title). Implicit biases of physicians can have a substantial impact on the quality of health care that Blacks receive and ultimately affect their health and well-being. For example, White physicians generally see themselves as non-prejudiced and color blind but also harbor negative implicit racial biases toward Blacks (Sabin, Rivara, & Greenwald, 2008). Physicians' implicit biases predict medical recommendations, such as lower quality of coronary care for Black patients (Green et al., 2007), in ways independent of explicit racial bias. The effects of implicit bias may be particularly influential for medical issues that may evoke stereotypical beliefs about Blacks (e.g., illegal drug use). For instance, physicians higher in implicit bias are substantially less willing to prescribe narcotics to ease the pain of Black patients than White patients (Sabin & Greenwald, 2012). Also, consistent with research on the influence of implicit racial bias in social interactions (Dovidio et al., 2002), doctors higher in implicit bias speak faster to and have shorter visits with Black patients (Cooper et al., 2012), and they display less warmth in their medical interactions (Penner et al., 2010). Overall, physicians higher in implicit bias are less patient centered in their care of Black patients (Blair et al., 2013; Cooper et al., 2012).

Moreover, as suggested by the aversive racism framework, the combination of explicit and implicit attitudes is also an important determinant of physician-patient relations. Penner et al. (2010) found that although Black patients generally perceived doctors higher in implicit racial bias less favorably, this effect was particularly pronounced when doctors were low in explicit prejudice but high in implicit bias – the aversive racist profile. Specifically, Black patients who interacted with aversive racist physicians were less satisfied with the interaction and felt less close to their physicians than Black patients who interacted with other physicians, including physicians who were high on both implicit and explicit bias. These effects may be due, in part, to a lack of awareness of personal bias among implicitly biased physicians. As in Dovidio et al.'s (2002) study, the perceptions of doctors themselves were based primarily on their explicit racial attitudes: Doctors higher in explicit bias reported that they involved Black patients less in the medical decision-making process during the visit.

Taken together, current research reveals that implicit biases contribute in significant ways to racism. They shape disparate treatment of minorities in ways independent of explicit (self-reported) personal biases.

Implications for Interventions

Prejudice-reduction techniques have traditionally been concerned with changing conscious attitudes (explicit attitudes) and obvious expressions of bias, and they have commonly utilized educational programs aimed at combatting such views and behaviors (Stephan & Stephan, 2001). However, antibias education programs often prove to be ineffective in producing intended outcomes in organizations (e.g., Kalev, Dobbin, & Kelly, 2006) and educational settings (Yeager & Walton, 2011), as well as among the general public (see Paluck & Green, 2009). Contemporary forms of racism, such as aversive racism, can be more difficult to combat than more blatant forms because they are expressed subtly and indirectly. Members of high-status groups are less attuned to cues of subtle discrimination than to blatant bias (Salvatore & Shelton, 2007), and groups victimized by bias often fail to recognize the role that subtle discrimination plays in their disadvantage. Aversive racists already recognize prejudice as harmful, but they do not recognize that *they* are prejudiced. Other techniques are thus required. In this section, we consider different types of interventions for reducing subtle bias.

Reducing Implicit Bias

To the extent that most Whites in the United States endorse egalitarian values, one obvious strategy to combat contemporary bias is to tailor interventions to minimize or eliminate implicit bias. Indeed, new techniques have been developed to modify implicit biases and their expression (Lai et al., 2014). These techniques include approaches that encourage people to think of members of other groups more in terms of their individual qualities than as primarily members of their racial or ethnic groups. Examples of these techniques include training in perspective taking and empathic responding or increasing exposure to counter-stereotypic members and actions of the negatively stereotyped group. However, implicit attitudes are "habits of mind" (Devine, 1989) that may be deeply entrenched, and thus difficult, if not impossible, to unlearn completely. As a consequence, although the various techniques identified by Lai et al. (2014) may temporarily inhibit the activation of implicit biases in a given context, the effects may not be durable. To the extent that media, social models, and other societal influences reinforce stereotypes and justify group hierarchies (Jost et al., 2012; Sidanius & Pratto, 1999), implicit biases can become reactivated beyond the lab.

In addition, interventions to address implicit bias by suppressing negative attitudes and stereotypes can have paradoxical effects. Because conscious efforts to suppress implicit biases are cognitively taxing, implicit biases may be especially pronounced and influential (i.e., producing a "rebound effect"; Monteith, Sherman, & Devine, 1998) when those cognitive resources are depleted and the ability to control one's behavior consciously is diminished (Trawalter & Richeson, 2006).

Implicit cognition plays a particularly important role in shaping behavior when cognitive control is impaired, for example, by fatigue or tasks that strain cognitive resources. Attempts to suppress implicit bias can also affect impressions of others. Because suppression can make implicit biases hyperaccessible due to rebound, these thoughts can influence the attributions of Black partners in social interactions, leading to more negative impressions of them in ways that can justify negative reactions to them (Pearson, Dovidio, Phills, & Onyeador, 2014). Also, emphasizing the automatic nature of implicit bias can lead people to believe that their biases are fixed rather than malleable, which may reduce motivations to present bias (Neel & Shapiro, 2012).

Although bias control has traditionally been conceptualized in terms of conscious efforts to inhibit negative attitudes and stereotypes that become activated in one's mind, studies suggest that biases may also be combatted at the implicit level through non-conscious processes that inhibit their activation in the first place (Calanchini, Gonsalkorale, Sherman, & Klauer, 2013). For instance, individuals with chronic explicit race-related egalitarian goals spontaneously activate egalitarian thoughts when primed with Black (vs. White) faces, whereas individuals who do not report such goals do not (Moskowitz, Salomon, & Taylor, 2000). In addition, individuals with chronic egalitarian goals do not exhibit the automatic activation of racial stereotypes that Whites typically demonstrate when exposed to Blacks (Park, Glaser, & Knowles, 2008). Activating egalitarian goals even temporarily, for example, by having people describe a personal incident in which they failed to be egalitarian toward Blacks, can subsequently inhibit non-conscious racial stereotyping (see Moskowitz & Ignarri, 2009, for a review).

In general, whereas conscious efforts to avoid stereotyping may often fail or even exacerbate bias because individuals lack insight into the processes that promote and regulate it, implicit egalitarian goals may succeed by co-opting the very psychological mechanisms that sustain it, replacing stereotypic associations with egalitarian or atypical associations when perceiving or interacting with members of other racial and ethnic groups. However, developing implicit egalitarian goals may often require extended practice to establish (Devine, Forscher, Austin, & Cox, 2012).

Correcting for Unconscious Bias

Rather than attempting to alter implicit biases, another approach involves intervening to inhibit the unfair consequences of this bias through conscious control. Many Whites believe that unfair bias against Blacks is no longer prevalent and that anti-White bias is a bigger societal problem than anti-Black bias (Norton & Sommers, 2011). In addition, aversive racists who do acknowledge that prejudice exists and is harmful do not recognize that they are prejudiced.

A foundational step in combatting the influence of subtle bias in admissions decisions is thus educating those making decisions about the existence of implicit prejudice and subtle bias and their personal susceptibility to these influences. The decision process therefore needs to be structured in ways that facilitate the detection of bias. For instance, because people can rationalize preferences in complex decisions in many ways, they can readily justify decisions about a given individual. However, bias that is subtle in a particular case becomes much more apparent when its cumulative effects are considered. Thus, one particularly effective way for addressing subtle bias is to assess the outcomes of a set of decisions in terms of whether the desired diversity among candidates has been achieved (Crosby, Clayton, Alksnis, & Hemker, 1986). In addition, reminding individuals of their personal accountability for detecting and correcting for unconscious bias promotes fairer, less biased decision making in employment contexts (Nadler, Lowery, Grebinoski, & Jones, 2014). Because implicit biases affect decision making subtly and unintentionally, good intentions are not sufficient to eliminate this bias. Instead, the emphasis of diversity efforts needs to recognize diversity early in the decision-making process and in assessing the outcomes.

One implication of this approach is that it is important that people acknowledge race and its potential effects on their behavior, rather than attempting to be color blind and dismiss the influence of race on their perceptions, cognitions, feelings, and actions. Whites are typically motivated to avoid seeing themselves as racially biased and often adopt a color-blind strategy when engaging in interracial interactions, particularly when they anticipate racial tension (Apfelbaum, Norton, & Sommers, 2012). However, efforts to be color blind can sometimes produce rebound effects, causing biases to become activated even more strongly. Indeed, Uhlmann and Cohen (2005) found that participants who were more confident in the objectivity of their judgments were also more likely to discriminate against equally qualified female candidates for a stereotypically male job (chief of police), inflating criteria that favored male over female candidates. Ironically, the act of affirming a non-prejudiced self-image can, in some cases, further increase the likelihood that even ostensibly non-prejudiced individuals will discriminate (see also Effron, Cameron, & Monin, 2009; Monin & Miller, 2001).

Whites' attempts to be color blind can also alienate minority group members, who generally seek acknowledgment of their racial identity and further contribute to interracial distrust. Apfelbaum, Sommers, and Norton (2008) found that although avoidance of race was seen as a favorable strategy by Whites for promoting more positive interracial interactions, in practice failure to acknowledge race actually predicted decrements in Whites' nonverbal friendliness and resulted in greater perceptions of racial prejudice by Black interaction partners. By contrast, a multicultural perspective, which involves the appreciation of differences and common connections, represents a promotion focus (Scheepers, Saguy, Dovidio, & Gaertner, 2014) that encourages mutual understanding and cooperation. When members of different groups adopt a multicultural orientation in their interaction, they generally show greater responsiveness to one another's goals, attitudes, and needs, and the interaction is more productive and mutually satisfying (Vorauer, Gagnon, & Sasaki, 2009).

Harnessing Egalitarian Motives

It may also be possible to capitalize on aversive racists' good intentions and induce self-motivated efforts to reduce the impact of unconscious biases by making them aware of these biases. Son Hing, Li, and Zanna (2002) examined responses of people identified as non-prejudiced (low in both explicit and implicit prejudice) and aversive racists (low in explicit prejudice but high in implicit prejudice) to self-awareness of one's own hypocrisy. In a study conducted in Canada with Asians as the target minority group, participants were assigned to either a hypocrisy condition, in which they reflected on situations in which they had reacted negatively or unfairly toward an Asian person, or to a control condition, in which they were not asked to write about such situations. The researchers predicted that making people aware of violations of their egalitarian principles would arouse guilt among aversive racists (who harbor negative feelings toward Asians) and thus produce compensatory behavior when recommending funding for Asian student groups among aversive racists but not among non-prejudiced participants. The results supported the predictions. Aversive racists in the hypocrisy condition experienced uniquely high levels of guilt and displayed the most generous funding recommendations for the Asian Students' Association. The funding recommendations of truly low-prejudiced participants, however, were not affected by the hypocrisy manipulation. Son Hing et al. (2002) concluded that making people aware of their biases is particularly effective at reducing bias among people who explicitly endorse egalitarian principles while also possessing implicit biases – the factors that characterize aversive racists.

Work by Monteith and colleagues (see Monteith, Arthur, & Flynn, 2010, for a review) further indicates that when low-prejudiced people recognize discrepancies between their behavior (i.e., what they *would* do) and their personal standards (i.e., what they *should* do) toward minorities, they feel guilt and compunction, which subsequently produces motivations to respond without prejudice in the future. With practice, these individuals learn to reduce prejudicial responses and respond in ways that are consistent with their non-prejudiced personal standards. When extended over time, this process of self-regulation can produce sustained changes in even automatic negative responses.

Dovidio, Kawakami, and Gaertner (2000) found that greater discrepancies between what one would do and should do produced higher levels of guilt among Whites in an initial experimental session, and this relationship occurred primarily for low-prejudiced participants. These findings indicate the potential recruitment of self-regulatory processes for low-prejudiced but not high-prejudiced participants. When participants returned three weeks later, there was generally greater alignment (i.e., smaller discrepancy) between what one would and should do – an indication that both high-prejudiced and low-prejudiced participants showed a decrease in overt expressions of bias. However, both groups differed in terms of the extent to which they internalized these changes. Low-prejudiced Whites who had larger initial discrepancies showed greater reductions in implicit stereotyping; in contrast, for high-prejudiced Whites the relationship was weaker and nonsignificant.

Nevertheless, feedback suggesting successful self-regulation in some cases may backfire. Mann and Kawakami (2012) explored the effect of goal feedback on outgroup discrimination and ingroup favoritism, as well as implicit racial attitudes. In a series of studies, participants showed greater racial bias after receiving feedback that they were progressing on egalitarian goals compared to feedback that they were failing on egalitarian goals or a no-feedback condition. Specifically, participants who were told that they were progressively becoming more egalitarian subsequently sat farther away from Blacks and closer to Whites and demonstrated greater implicit racial prejudice. Thus, feedback that signals reduced need to monitor and regulate one's responses may undermine Whites' egalitarian motives. Nevertheless, Whites who are both aware of their biases and remain concerned about displaying biases show a high level of motivation to engage in activities (e.g., training) to eliminate their racial bias over time (Perry, Murphy, & Dovidio, 2015).

Taken together, these findings demonstrate that the good intentions of aversive racists can be harnessed to promote self-initiated change in both conscious and unconscious biases with sufficient awareness, effort, and practice.

Redirecting the Forces of Ingroup Bias

According to the aversive racism framework, the negative attitudes and feelings that develop toward members of other groups are rooted in basic socio-cognitive processes. One such process is the categorization of people into ingroups and outgroups (see Dovidio & Gaertner, 2010, for a review). Because categorization is a basic process fundamental to intergroup bias, this process has been targeted in efforts to combat the negative effects of aversive racism.

The common ingroup identity model (Gaertner & Dovidio, 2000, 2012) is one such intervention approach that harnesses social categorization as a means to reduce intergroup bias and has received strong empirical support in interventions with both child and adult populations. Specifically, if members of different groups are induced to think of themselves as a single superordinate ingroup rather than as two separate groups, attitudes toward former outgroup members will become more positive by reaping the benefits of ingroup status. Enhancing the salience of a common ingroup identity has been shown to inhibit the activation of both implicit (Van Bavel & Cunningham, 2009) and explicit (Gaertner & Dovidio, 2000) biases. Thus, by changing the basis of categorization from race to an alternative, inclusive dimension, one can alter who "we" are and who "they" are, undermining a potent contributing force to contemporary racism. The formation of a common identity, however, need not require groups to forsake their subgroup identities. It is possible for members to conceive of themselves as holding a "dual identity" in which other identities and a superordinate identity are salient simultaneously (Crisp, Stone, & Hall, 2006; Gaertner & Dovidio, 2009).

This intervention was used in a primary care setting with Black patients being seen by non-Black physicians (Penner et al., 2013). Compared to a standard-of-care control condition, Black patients who were induced to feel a common identity and team goal (successful resolution of their medical problem) had more successful interactions. Black patients in the common identity condition, compared to a control condition, reported more trust of their physician four weeks later. This greater trust led to greater subsequent adherence to the physician's treatment recommendations.

Future Directions

The past decade has seen substantial progress in understanding manifestations and expressions of subtle bias, and particularly in the development of techniques for assessing implicit forms of bias, incorporating perspectives from affective and cognitive neuroscience and psychophysiological research. Next, we consider three domains that have received comparatively less attention and represent particularly promising areas for future research: (a) conditions under which implicit biases may be expressed blatantly, (b) the relationship between contemporary bias and intimate relations, and (c) extensions of the dynamics of aversive racism to other groups.

From Subtle to Overt Bias: The Inversion Problem

Research described in this chapter suggests that "everyday" prejudice, bias within the latitude of normal expression, provides a foundation that, under appropriate conditions, can be manifested in actions that systematically disadvantage members of other groups. This unfair treatment can sometimes escalate to intentional physical harm. Indeed, history is replete with examples, from Rwanda, the former Yugoslavia, and the Holocaust during World War II, demonstrating how neighbors who had been living in apparent harmony can suddenly become violent enemies. Modern-day examples also abound, such as the recent rise in blatant homophobia in Russia and Africa and Islamophobia in the United States and Europe. Moreover, events such as the terrorist attack of 9/11 can create strong negative associations with a group (Muslims) that was not strongly stigmatized previously (Esses, Dovidio, & Hodson, 2002).

How and when do aversive biases become overt? Because aggression and intergroup violence are usually normatively sanctioned, aversive racists may be particularly inhibited in engaging in interracial aggression in most contexts. Nevertheless, given their underlying negative feelings and beliefs, aversive racists may also be especially susceptible to disinhibiting influences that can lead to overt hostility and aggression. As Stephan and Stephan (2001) propose, interracial anxiety can amplify Whites' affective reactions and consequently produce more extreme behavioral responses to Blacks than to Whites. Thus, the more diffuse emotions of anxiety and discomfort that are experienced by aversive racists and typically lead to avoidance can readily be transformed into more intense negative emotions that motivate open aggression and hostility toward Blacks (see Dovidio, Pearson, Gaertner, & Hodson, 2008). Mullen (1986), for instance, found that interracial violence by Whites against Blacks often occurs within a social context that permits or encourages aggression. His analysis of newspaper reports of Blacks being lynched by White mobs revealed that violence against Blacks was more likely when Whites were part of a larger group and experienced greater anonymity and deindividuation (see also Leader, Mullen, & Abrams, 2007). Thus, factors that normally disinhibit aggressive behavior, such as provocation and anonymity, may be especially potent within intergroup contexts for promoting interracial aggression toward Blacks.

Laws and legal processes may also facilitate progression to more overt forms of discrimination. Research on aversive racism has shown that disparate treatment is most likely to occur in combination with other factors that provide non-racial justifications for negative treatment, and that disparate treatment often represents ingroup favoritism (pro-White responses) rather than outgroup antipathy (anti-Black responses; Gaertner et al., 1997; Greenwald & Pettigrew, 2014). However, when the normative context supports it, these dynamics can lead to direct physical harm. In the context of the government-sanctioned death penalty, Blacks who are perceived more stereotypically are more likely to receive the death penalty in capital cases (Eberhardt, Davies, Purdie-Vaughns, & Johnson, 2006); in addition, greater implicit dehumanization of Blacks predicts greater violence by police officers toward black children suspected of crimes (Goff, Jackson, Di Leone, Culotta, & DoTomasso, 2014). Unconscious biases can influence how evidence is perceived and weighed, affecting assessments of guilt, and once a defendant is judged guilty, they can affect the severity of recommended punishment in ways that reinforce stereotypes of Blacks as criminals and fuel dehumanization and distrust.

Contemporary Bias and Intimate Relationships

Close relationships represent an important new context for studying aversive racism, given the uniquely intimate nature of these exchanges and the well-documented power of cross-group friendships and romantic relationships to combat bias (Davies, Wright, Aron, & Comeau, 2013; Page-Gould, Mendoza-Denton, & Tropp, 2008). One in three Americans (35%) indicates that a member of his or her immediate family or a close relative is currently married to someone of a different race (Wang, 2012). Processes that help form and maintain social bonds in interpersonal relationships may, therefore, also be essential for developing cross-group friendships and intimate relationships that can promote positive intergroup attitudes as well as egalitarian norms in social networks through extended contact processes (see Davies et al., 2013).

"Big data" approaches, analyzing survey responses and behaviors of more than 30 million online daters – nearly one-third of the US population under age 40 – offer a unique window into actual dating habits of a large and growing segment of the American public (see Rudder, 2014a; and Curington, Ken-Hou, & Lundquist, 2015). Cross-sectional analyses of online daters' self-reported preferences show increasing openness to interracial dating and interracial marriage. However, online daters' behaviors (e.g., private attractiveness ratings, who communicates with and dates whom) show evidence of substantial and in some cases intensified racial bias, with White men and women rating Blacks as less attractive, and dating Blacks less often, than those of other racial and ethnic groups (Rudder, 2014b; and Curington et al., 2015, for similar findings showing strong preferences for White versus non-White among multiethnic online datees).

These effects are mirrored in national marriage statistics. In 2010, 17% of US Blacks and 26% of US Hispanics married outside of their race, whereas only 9% of Whites entered interracial marriages (Wang, 2012). Among Blacks and Hispanics, newlyweds who married Whites tended to have higher educational attainment than did those who married within their own racial or ethnic group.

Aversive Racism beyond Black-White Relations

Aversive and other contemporary forms of racism are hypothesized to result from the conflict between persistent negative feelings or beliefs and social norms inhibiting bias against Blacks. However, norms concerning egalitarian treatment vary substantially across groups (Crandall, Eshleman, & O'Brien, 2002), as do legal restrictions. In the United States, as of 2015, federal laws prohibit employment discrimination on the basis of age, race, ethnicity, disability, and religion, but not on the basis of weight, economic status, gender identity, or sexual orientation. At the state level, 52% of the US lesbian, gay, bisexual, and transgender (LGBT) population currently live in states that do not prohibit employment discrimination based on sexual orientation or gender identity (see www.lgbtmap.org). Thus, whereas subtle bias may characterize responses to groups with legal protections, blatant biases may be commonly expressed toward groups, such as obese or poor people, who are not protected and perceived to be responsible for their disadvantage. Nevertheless, changing public opinion and legal decisions, such as the 2015 US Supreme Court decision to support federal and state recognition of same-sex marriage, can signal new egalitarians norms for LGBT individuals. As a consequence, bias that was previously largely blatant toward gay men and lesbians may now more commonly be expressed in more subtle and rationalizable forms – an aversive form of bias.

Beyond the extension to different groups and types of intergroup relations, future research on aversive racism might productively consider responses to groups with multiple or intersectional identities. Traditionally, race in the United States was socially defined in strict binary terms. "One drop of Black blood" defined a person as Black rather than White, and multiracial individuals were treated as Blacks (*hypodescent*; Ho, Sidanius, Levin, & Banaji, 2011). In part stimulated by the prominence of President Barack Obama, the category 'multiracial' has become more widely recognized and applied, one that may in some ways be more appealing than either White or Black. Nevertheless, notions of hypodescent persist in contemporary society in ways that can impact everyday relationships and broader societal intergroup relations. Curington et al. (2015), for instance, examined messages sent between heterosexual men and women between 2003 and 2010 on a large US dating site and found that multiracial men and women are increasingly preferred above all other groups, including Whites. Nevertheless, persistent pro-White and anti-Black biases in dating preferences were found, with online daters generally preferring White multiethnic individuals to non-Whites.

Considering differentiated responses to people with intersectional identities can help provide a more nuanced and comprehensive understanding of contemporary bias. For example, because Black men are viewed as more prototypical of the category Black than are Black women, they may be the primary target under conditions that elicit subtle bias, while Black women's "intersectional invisibility" may insulate them from this bias (Purdie-Vaughns & Eibach, 2008). However, when egalitarian norms are salient, Black women may benefit less from compensatory actions or policies than Black men. Thus, when multiple or intersectional identities are involved, subtle bias may be even more complex than research on this topic has previously considered.

Additional research might identify processes that generalize across different stigmatized groups that may contribute to the "spread" of contemporary forms of bias within and between social networks. For instance, people are more tolerant of discrimination against minorities after overhearing racist jokes (Ford & Ferguson, 2004) and exposure to cues as subtle as an antiracism T-shirt can influence unconscious bias (Lun, Sinclair, Glenn, & Whitchurch, 2007).

Research on prejudice has typically not examined social influence beyond dyadic interactions in the laboratory; however, emerging research on social networks may offer some clues. In a large field experiment in US high schools, Paluck (2011) trained student leaders (Peer Trainers) to confront expressions of prejudice in five randomly assigned high schools across a period of five months and compared their responses to those of students awaiting training in five control schools. Whereas the treatment Peer Trainers' egalitarian attitudes (assessed through self-report) spread only to close friends five months post-training, their anti-prejudice behavior (signing a gay rights petition) spread to both friends and acquaintances, including to individuals outside of the Peer Trainers' school network. These findings suggest that conformity of non-prejudiced behavior may precede the internalization of egalitarian attitudes among more peripherally connected individuals. A comprehensive understanding of both structural (e.g., relationship networks) as well as psychological factors can, thus, help guide the development of interventions that may more effectively combat contemporary forms of bias and its transmission.

Conclusion

In virtually all societies, across time and cultures, groups are organized hierarchically, with some groups consistently enjoying greater privilege and resources than others. Racism operates to maintain the power and status of dominant groups over other groups. However, as a function of social, political, and historical forces, racism is manifested in different ways. In the later 1930s through the 1950s, stimulated politically by the Nazis' rise to power in Germany, historically by the Holocaust, and intellectually by the classic work on the authoritarian personality (Adorno, Frenkel-Brunswik, Levinson, & Sanford, 1950), racial biases were seen as not simply disruptions in rational processes but also as dangerous aberrations from normal thinking. Stimulated further by the civil rights movement in the 1960s, traditional blatant expressions of prejudice rapidly declined in the United States, but subtle and indirect forms – symbolic, modern, ambivalent, and aversive – emerged.

Aversive racism, the main focus of this chapter, represents a distinct form of contemporary bias that characterizes the racial attitudes of well-intentioned, typically politically liberal people, who genuinely endorse egalitarian values and believe that they are not prejudiced. The recent directions in aversive racism research, which we have identified in this chapter, help broaden the theoretical perspective both practically and conceptually. Practically, the dynamics of aversive racism are not restricted to White Americans' responses to Black Americans but to other traditionally disadvantaged groups, and this phenomenon occurs cross-nationally. It also affects formal and consequential interactions and outcomes related to legal processes, employment, and health care. Theoretically, the study of aversive racism contributes to understanding structural factors (e.g., color-blind policies), intergroup relations (e.g., group mistrust and conflict), interpersonal interaction (e.g., nonverbal communication), and intrapersonal emotional (e.g., emotion regulation) and cognitive (implicit cognition) processes.

The particular challenge of studying contemporary forms of bias, such as aversive racism, is not simply in identifying the basic psychological processes that underlie bias, which may be common across societies and groups, but also the unique social and political factors that may systematically alter the ways that contemporary biases manifest. These forces may increase the subtlety of the expression of bias or, in some cases, alter the normative context in ways that justify open discrimination. Furthermore, understanding and communicating information about contemporary bias can alter the nature of racism and shape the emergence of new forms of bias. As Gergen (1973) observed more than four decades ago, "The dissemination of psychological knowledge modifies the patterns of behavior on which the knowledge is based" (p. 309). Thus, making people aware of how their behavior can reflect subtle prejudice or discrimination may, at least for some individuals, motivate them to express negative racial attitudes in even more indirect and less obvious ways, to insulate them from the recognition by others or themselves of their racial bias. Nevertheless, understanding the dynamics of contemporary bias is ultimately necessary to address bias at its psychological roots and thereby contribute to more equitable and sustainable societies that benefit all groups.

References

Adorno, T. W., Frenkel-Brunswik, E., Levinson, D. J., & Sanford, R. N. (1950). *The authoritarian personality*. New York: Harper.

Apfelbaum, E. P., Norton, M. I., & Sommers, S. R. (2012). Racial color blindness: Emergence, practice, and implications. *Current Directions in Psychological Science, 21*, 205–209.

Apfelbaum, E. P., Sommers, S. R., & Norton, M. I. (2008). Seeing race and seeming racist? Evaluating strategic colorblindness in social interaction. *Journal of Personality and Social Psychology, 95*, 918–932.

Baron, A. S., & Banaji, M. R. (2006). The development of implicit attitudes: Evidence of race evaluations from ages 6, 10 & adulthood. *Psychological Science, 17*, 53–58.

Blair, I. V., Steiner, J. F., Fairclough, D. L., Hanratty, R., Price, D. W., Hirsh, H. K. ... Havranek, E. P. (2013). Clinicians' implicit ethnic/racial bias and perceptions of care among Black and Latino patients. *Annals of Family Medicine, 11*, 43–52.

Brief, A. P., Dietz, J., Cohen, R. R., Pugh, S. D., & Vaslow, J. B. (2000). Just doing business: Modern racism and obedience to authority as explanations for employment discrimination. *Organizational Behavior and Human Decision Processes, 81*, 72–97.

Calanchini, J., Gonsalkorale, K., Sherman, J. W., & Klauer, K. C. (2013). Counter-prejudicial training reduces activation of biased associations and enhances response monitoring. *European Journal of Social Psychology, 43*, 321–325.

Calanchini, J., & Sherman, J. W. (2013). Implicit processes reflect associative, non-associative, and non-attitudinal processes. *Social and Personality Psychology Compass, 7*, 654–667.

Cooper, L. A., Roter, D. L., Carson, K. A., Beach, M. C., Sabin, J. A., Greenwald, A. G., & Inui, T. S. (2012). The associations of clinicians' implicit attitudes about race with medical visit communication and patient ratings of interpersonal care. *American Journal of Public Health, 102*, 979–987.

Crandall, C. S., Eshleman, A., & O'Brien, L. (2002). Social norms and the expression and suppression of prejudice: The struggle for internalization. *Journal of Personality and Social Psychology, 82*, 359–378.

Crisp, R. J., Stone, C. H., & Hall, N. R. (2006). Recategorization and subgroup identification: Predicting and preventing threats from common ingroups. *Personality and Social Psychology Bulletin, 32*, 230–243.

Crosby, F., Clayton, S., Alksnis, O., & Hemker, K. (1986). Cognitive biases in the perception of discrimination: The importance of format. *Sex Roles, 14*, 637–646.

Curington, C. V., Ken-Hou, L., & Lundquist, J. H. (2015). Positioning multiraciality in cyberspace: Treatment of multiracial daters in an online dating website. *American Sociological Review, 80*, 764–788.

de França, D. X., & Monteiro, M. B. (2013). Social norms and the expression of prejudice: The development of aversive racism in children. *European Journal of Social Psychology, 43*, 263–271.

Davies, K., Wright, S. C., Aron, A., & Comeau, J. (2013). Intergroup contact through friendship: Intimacy and norms. In G. Hodson & M. Hewstone (Eds.), *Advances in intergroup contact* (pp. 200–230). New York: Psychology Press.

Devine, P. G. (1989). Stereotypes and prejudice: The automatic and controlled components. *Journal of Personality and Social Psychology, 56*, 5–18.

Devine, P. G., Forscher, P. S., Austin, A. J., & Cox, W. T. (2012). Long-term reduction in implicit bias: A prejudice habit-breaking intervention. *Journal of Experimental Social Psychology, 48*, 1267–1278.

Ditonto, T. M., Lau, R. R., & Sears, D. (2013). AMPing racial attitudes: Comparing the power of explicit and implicit racism measures in 2008. *Political Psychology, 34*, 487–510.

Dovidio, J. F. (2001). On the nature of contemporary prejudice: The third wave. *Journal of Social Issues, 57*, 829–849.

Dovidio, J. F., & Gaertner, S. L. (2000). Aversive racism and selection decisions: 1989 and 1999. *Psychological Science, 11*, 319–323.

Dovidio, J. F., & Gaertner, S. L. (2004). Aversive racism. In M. P. Zanna (Ed.), *Advances in experimental social psychology* (Vol. *36*, pp. 1–51). San Diego, CA: Academic Press.

Dovidio, J. F., & Gaertner, S. L. (2010). Intergroup bias. In S. T. Fiske, D. Gilbert, & G. Lindzey (Eds.), *Handbook of social psychology* (Vol. *2*, 5th ed., pp. 1084–1121). New York: Wiley.

Dovidio, J. F., Kawakami, K., & Gaertner, S. L. (2000). Reducing contemporary prejudice: Combating explicit and implicit bias at the individual and intergroup level. In S. Oskamp (Ed.), *Reducing prejudice and discrimination* (pp. 137–163). Hillsdale, NJ: Erlbaum.

Dovidio, J. F., Kawakami, K., & Gaertner, S. L. (2002). Implicit and explicit prejudice and interracial interaction. *Journal of Personality and Social Psychology, 82*, 62–68.

Dovidio, J. F., Kawakami, K., Smoak, N., & Gaertner, S. L. (2009). The nature of contemporary racial prejudice: Insights from implicit and explicit measures of attitudes. In R. E. Petty, R. H. Fazio, & P. Brinol (Eds.), *Attitudes: Insights from the new implicit measures* (pp. 165–192). New York: Psychology Press.

Dovidio, J. F., Pearson, A. R., Gaertner, S. L., & Hodson, G. (2008). On the nature of contemporary prejudice: From subtle bias to severe consequences. In V. M. Esses

& R. A. Vernon (Eds.), *Explaining the breakdown of ethnic relations: Why neighbors kill* (pp. 41-60). Malden, MA: Blackwell.

Dunham, Y., Baron, A. S., & Banaji, M. R. (2008). The development of implicit intergroup cognition. *Trends in Cognitive Sciences, 12,* 248–253.

Eberhardt, J. L., Davies, P. G., Purdie-Vaughns, V., & Johnson, S. L. (2006). Looking deathworthy: Perceived stereotypicality of Black defendants predicts capital-sentencing outcomes. *Psychological Science, 17,* 383–386.

Effron, D. A., Cameron, J. S., & Monin, B. (2009). Endorsing Obama licenses favoring Whites. *Journal of Experimental Social Psychology, 45,* 590–593.

Esses, V. M., Dovidio, J. F., & Hodson, G. (2002). Public attitudes toward immigration in the United States and Canada in response to the September 2001 "Attack on America." *Analysis of Social Issues and Public Policy, 2,* 69–85.

Fazio, R. H. (1990). Multiple processes by which attitudes guide behavior: The MODE Model as an integrative framework. In M. P. Zanna (Ed.), *Advances in experimental social psychology* (Vol. *23*, pp. 75–109). Orlando, FL: Academic Press.

Fazio, R. H., & Olson, M. A. (2003). Implicit measures in social cognition: Their meaning and use. *Annual Review of Psychology, 54,* 297–327.

Ford, T. E., & Ferguson, M. A. (2004). Social consequences of disparagement humor: A prejudice norm theory. *Personality and Social Psychology Review, 8,* 79–94.

Gaertner, S. L. (1973). Helping behavior and racial discrimination among liberals and conservatives. *Journal of Personality and Social Psychology, 25,* 335–341.

Gaertner, S. L., & Dovidio, J. F. (1986). The aversive form of racism. In J. F. Dovidio & S. L. Gaertner (Eds.), *Prejudice, discrimination, and racism* (pp. 61–89). Orlando, FL: Academic Press.

Gaertner, S. L., & Dovidio, J. F. (2000). *Reducing intergroup bias: The Common Ingroup Identity Model.* Philadelphia, PA: The Psychology Press.

Gaertner, S. L., & Dovidio, J. F. (2009). A Common Ingroup Identity: A categorization-based approach for reducing intergroup bias. In T. Nelson (Ed.), *Handbook of prejudice* (pp. 489–506). Philadelphia, PA: Taylor & Francis.

Gaertner, S. L., & Dovidio, J. F. (2012). Reducing intergroup bias: The Common Ingroup Identity Model. In P. A. M. Van Lange, A. W. Kruglanski, & E. T. Higgins (Eds.), *Handbook of theories of social psychology* (Vol. *2*, pp. 439–457). Thousand Oaks, CA: Sage.

Gaertner, S. L., Dovidio, J. F., Banker, B., Rust, M. C., Nier, J. & Ward, C. M. (1997). Does pro-whiteness necessarily mean anti-blackness? In M. Fine, L. Powell, L. Weis, & M. Wong (Eds.), *Off White* (pp. 167–178). New York: Routledge.

Gaertner, S. L., & McLaughlin, J. (1983). Racial stereotypes: Associations and ascriptions of positive and negative characteristics. *Social Psychology Quarterly, 46,* 23–30.

Gergen, K. J. (1973). Social psychology as history. *Journal of Personality and Social Psychology, 26,* 309–320.

Goff, P. A., Jackson, M. C., Di Leone, B. A. L., Culotta, C. M., & DoTomasso, N. A. (2014). The essence of innocence: Consequences of dehumanizing Black children. *Journal of Personality and Social Psychology, 106,* 526–545.

Green, A. R., Carney, D. R., Pallin, D. J., Ngo, L. H., Raymond, K. L., Iezzoni, L. I., & Banaji, M. R. (2007). Implicit bias among physicians and its predictions of thrombolysis decisions for Black and White patients. *Journal of General Internal Medicine, 22,* 1231–1238.

Greenwald, A. G., & Krieger, L. H. (2006). Implicit bias: Scientific foundations. *California Law Review, 94*, 945–967.

Greenwald, A. G., & Pettigrew, T. F. (2014). With malice toward none: Ingroup favoritism enables discrimination. *American Psychologist, 69*, 669–684.

Greenwald, A. G., Poehlman, T. A., Uhlmann, E. L., & Banaji, M. R. (2009). Understanding and using the Implicit Association Test: III. Meta-analysis of predictive validity. *Journal of Personality and Social Psychology, 97*, 17–41.

Gregg, A. P., Seibt, B., & Banaji, M. R. (2006). Easier done than undone: Asymmetry in the malleability of implicit preferences. *Journal of Personality and Social Psychology, 90*, 1–20.

Henry, P. J. (2009). Modern racism. In J. M. Levine & M. A. Hogg (Eds.), *Encyclopedia of group processes and intergroup relations* (pp. 575–577). Thousand Oaks, CA: Sage.

Henry, P. J., & Sears, D. O. (2002). The Symbolic Racism 2000 Scale. *Political Psychology, 23*, 253–283.

Hodson, G., Dovidio, J. F., & Gaertner, S. L. (2002). Processes in racial discrimination: Differential weighting of conflicting information. *Personality and Social Psychology Bulletin, 28*, 460–471.

Hodson, G, Hooper, H., Dovidio, J. F., & Gaertner, S. L. (2005). Aversive racism in Britain: Legal decisions and the use of inadmissible evidence. *European Journal of Social Psychology, 35*, 437–448.

Ho, A., Sidanius, J., Levin, D. T., & Banaji, M. R. (2011). Evidence for hypodescent and racial hierarchy in the categorization and perception of biracial individuals. *Journal of Personality and Social Psychology, 100*, 492–506.

Jost, J. T., Liviatan, I., van der Toorn, J., Ledgerwood, A., Mandisodza, A., & Nosek, B. A. (2012). System justification: A motivational process with implications for social conflict. In E. Kals & J. Maes (Eds.), *Justice and conflicts: Theoretical and empirical contributions* (pp. 315–327). New York: Springer.

Kalev, A., Dobbin, F., & Kelly, E. (2006). Best practices or best guesses? Assessing the efficacy of corporate affirmative action and diversity policies. *American Sociological Review, 71*, 589–617.

Katz, I. (1981). *Stigma: A social psychological analysis*. Hillsdale, NJ: Erlbaum.

Katz, I., Glass, D. C., & Cohen, S. (1973). Ambivalence, guilt, and scapegoating of minority group victims. *Journal of Experimental Social Psychology, 9*, 423–436.

Katz, I., Glass, D. C., Lucido, D., & Farber, J. (1979). Harm-doing and victim's racial or orthopedic stigma as determinants of helping behavior. *Journal of Personality, 47*, 340–364.

Katz, I., Wackenhut, J., & Hass, R. G. (1986). Racial ambivalence, value duality, and behavior. In J. F. Dovidio & S. L. Gaertner (Eds.), *Prejudice, discrimination, and racism* (pp. 35–59). Orlando, FL: Academic Press.

Kleinpenning, G., & Hagendoorn, L. (1993). Forms of racism and the cumulative dimension. *Social Psychology Quarterly, 56*, 21–36.

Knight, J. L., Guiliano, T. A., & Sanchez-Ross, M. G. (2001). Famous or infamous? The influence of celebrity status and race on perceptions of responsibility for rape. *Basic and Applied Social Psychology, 23*, 183–190.

Kovel, J. (1970). *White racism: A psychohistory*. New York: Pantheon.

Lai, C. K., Marini, M., Lehr, S. A., Cerruti, C., Shin, J.-E., Joy-Gaba, J. A. . . . Nosek, B. A. (2014). Reducing implicit racial preferences: I. A comparative investigation of 17 interventions. *Journal of Experimental Psychology: General, 143*, 1765–1785.

Leader, T., Mullen, B., & Abrams, D. (2007). Without mercy: The immediate impact of group size on lynch mob atrocity. *Personality and Social Psychology Bulletin, 33*, 1340–1352.

Lun, J., Sinclair, S., Glenn, C., & Whitchurch, E. (2007). (Why) do I think what you think? Epistemic social tuning and implicit prejudice. *Journal of Personality and Social Psychology, 93*, 957–972.

Mann, N. H., & Kawakami, K. (2012). The long, steep path to equality: Progressing on egalitarian goals. *Journal of Experimental Psychology: General, 141*, 187–197.

Martell, R. F., Lane, D. M., & Emrich, C. E. (1996). Male-female differences: A computer simulation. *American Psychologist, 51*, 157–158.

McConahay, J. B. (1986). Modern racism, ambivalence, and the Modern Racism Scale. In J. F. Dovidio & S. L. Gaertner (Eds.), *Prejudice, discrimination, and racism* (pp. 99–125). Orlando, FL: Academic Press.

McConnell, A. R., & Leibold, J. M. (2001). Relations among the Implicit Association Test, discriminatory behavior, and explicit measures of racial attitudes. *Journal of Experimental Social Psychology, 37*, 435–442.

McGillicuddy-De Lisi, A. V., Daly, M., & Neal, A. (2006). Children's distributive justice judgments: Aversive racism in Euro-American children? *Child Development, 77*, 1063–1080.

Monin, B., & Miller, D. T. (2001). Moral credentials and the expression of prejudice. *Journal of Personality and Social Psychology, 81*, 33–43.

Monteith, M. J., Arthur, S. A., & Flynn, S. M. (2010). Self-regulation and bias. In J. F. Dovidio, M. Hewstone, P. Glick, & V. M. Esses (Eds.). *SAGE handbook of prejudice, stereotyping, and discrimination* (pp. 493–507). London: Sage.

Monteith, M. J., Sherman, J. W., & Devine, P. G. (1998). Suppression as a stereotype control strategy. *Personality and Social Psychology Review, 2*, 63–82.

Moskowitz, G. B., & Ignarri, C. (2009). Implicit volition and stereotype control. *European Review of Social Psychology, 20*, 97–145.

Moskowitz, G. B., Salomon, A. R., & Taylor, C. M. (2000). Preconsciously controlling stereotyping: Implicitly activated egalitarian goals prevent the activation of stereotypes. *Social Cognition, 18*, 151–177.

Mullen, B. (1986). Atrocity as a function of lynch mob composition: A self-attention perspective. *Personality and Social Psychology Bulletin, 12*, 187–197.

Nadler, J. T., Lowery, M. R., Grebinski, J., & Jones, R. G. (2014). Aversive discrimination in employment interviews: Reducing effects of sexual orientation bias with accountability. *Psychology of Sexual Orientation and Gender Diversity, 1*, 480–488.

Nail, P. R., Harton, H. C., & Decker, B. P. (2003). Political orientation and modern versus aversive racism: Tests of Dovidio and Gaertner's (1998) integrated model. *Journal of Personality and Social Psychology, 84*, 754–770.

Neel, R., & Shapiro, J. R. (2012). Is race bias malleable? Whites' lay theories of racial bias predict divergent strategies for interracial interactions. *Journal of Personality and Social Psychology, 103*, 101–120.

Norton, M. I., & Sommers, S. R. (2011). Whites see racism as a zero-sum game that they are now losing. *Perspectives on Psychological Science, 6*, 215–218

Oswald, F. L., Mitchell, G., Blanton, H., Jaccard, J., & Tetlock, P. E. (2013). Predicting ethnic and racial discrimination: A meta-analysis of IAT criterion studies. *Journal of Personality and Social Psychology, 105*, 171–192.

Page-Gould, E., Mendoza-Denton, R., & Tropp, L. R. (2008). With a little help from my cross-group friend: Reducing anxiety in intergroup contexts through cross-group friendship. *Journal of Personality and Social Psychology, 95*, 1080–1094.

Paluck, E. L., & Green, D. P. (2009). Prejudice reduction: What works? A critical look at evidence from the field and the laboratory. *Annual Review of Psychology, 60*, 339–367.

Paluck, E. L. (2011). Peer pressure against prejudice: A high school field experiment examining social network change. *Journal of Experimental Social Psychology, 47*, 350–358.

Park, S. H., Glaser, J., & Knowles, E. D. (2008). Implicit motivation to control prejudice moderates the effect of cognitive depletion on unintended discrimination. *Social Cognition, 26*, 401–419.

Pearson, A. R., Dovidio, J. F., & Gaertner, S. L. (2009). The nature of contemporary prejudice: Insights from aversive racism. *Social and Personality Psychology Compass, 3*, 314–338.

Pearson, A. R., Dovidio, J. F., Phills, C. E., & Onyeador, I. N. (2014). Attitude-goal correspondence and interracial interaction: Implications for executive function and impression formation. *Journal of Experimental Social Psychology, 49*, 907–914.

Penner, L. A., Dovidio, J. F., West, T. W., Gaertner, S. L., Albrecht, T. L., Dailey, R. K., & Markova, T. (2010). Aversive racism and medical interactions with Black patients: A field study. *Journal of Experimental Social Psychology, 46*, 436–440.

Penner, L. A., Gaertner, S. L., Dovidio, J. F., Hagiwara, N., Porcerelli, J., Markova, T., & Albrecht, T. L. (2013). A social psychological approach to improving the outcomes of racially discordant medical interactions. *Journal of General Internal Medicine, 28*, 1143–1149.

Perry, S. P., Murphy, M. C., & Dovidio, J. F. (2015). Modern prejudice: Subtle, but unconscious? The role of bias awareness in Whites' perceptions of personal and others' biases. *Journal of Experimental Social Psychology, 61*, 64–78.

Pettigrew, T. F., & Meertens, R. W. (1995). Subtle and blatant prejudice in Western Europe. *European Journal of Social Psychology, 25*, 57–75.

Phelps, E. A., O'Conner, K. J., Cunningham, W. A., Funayama, E. S., Gatenby, J. C., Gore, J. C., & Banaji, M. R. (2000). Performance on indirect measures of race evaluation predicts amygdala activation. *Journal of Cognitive Neuroscience, 12*, 1–10.

Purdie-Vaughns, V., & Eibach, R. P. (2008). Intersectional invisibility: The distinctive advantages and disadvantages of multiple subordinate-group identities. *Sex Roles, 59*, 377–391.

Roese, N. J., & Jamieson, D. W. (1993). Twenty years of bogus pipeline research: A critical review and meta-analysis. *Psychological Bulletin, 114*, 363–375.

Rooth, D. (2007). Automatic associations and discrimination in hiring: Real world evidence. *Labour Economics, 17*, 523–534.

Rudder, C. (2014a). *Dataclysm: Who we are (when we think no one's looking).* New York: Crown Publishers.

Rudder, C. (2014b). *Race and attraction, 2009–2014.* Retrieved from http://oktrends .okcupid.com/

Rudman, L. A., Phelan, J. E., & Heppen, J. B. (2007). Developmental sources of implicit attitudes. *Personality and Social Psychology Bulletin, 33*, 1700–1713.

Sabin, J. A., & Greenwald, A. G. (2012). The influence of implicit bias on treatment recommendations for 4 common pediatric conditions: Pain, urinary tract infection, attention deficit hyperactivity disorder, and asthma. *American Journal of Public Health, 102*, 988–995.

Sabin, J. A., Rivara, F. P., & Greenwald, A. G. (2008). Physician implicit attitudes and stereotypes about race and quality of medical care. *Medical Care, 46*, 678–685.

Salvatore, J., & Shelton, J. N. (2007). Cognitive costs of exposure to racial prejudice. *Psychological Science, 18*, 810–815.

Saucier, D. A., Miller, C. T., & Doucet, N. (2005). Differences in helping Whites and Blacks: A meta-analysis. *Personality and Social Psychology Review, 9*, 2–16.

Scheepers, D., Saguy, T., Dovidio, J. F., & Gaertner, S. L. (2014). A shared dual identity promotes cardiovascular challenge response during interethnic interaction. *Group Processes & Intergroup Relations, 17*, 324–341.

Sears, D. O., & Henry, P. J. (2005). Over thirty years later: A contemporary look at symbolic racism. In M. P. Zanna (Ed.), *Advances in experimental social psychology* (Vol. 37, pp. 95–150). San Diego, CA: Academic Press.

Sears, D. O., Henry, P. J., & Kosterman, R. (2000). Egalitarian values and the origins of contemporary American racism. In D.O. Sears, J. Sidanius, & L. Bobo (Eds.), *Racialized politics: The debate about racism in America* (pp. 75–117). Chicago: University of Chicago Press.

Sidanius, J., & Pratto, F. (1999). *Social dominance: An intergroup theory of social hierarchy and oppression.* New York: Cambridge University Press.

Smith, E. R., & DeCoster, J. (2000). Dual-process models in social and cognitive psychology: Conceptual integration and links to underlying memory systems. *Personality and Social Psychology Review, 4*, 108–131.

Sommers, S. R., & Ellsworth, P. C. (2000). Race in the courtroom: Perceptions of guilt and dispositional attributions. *Personality and Social Psychology Bulletin, 26*, 1367–1379.

Son Hing, L. S., Chung-Yan, G., Hamilton, L., & Zanna, M. (2008). A two-dimensional model that employs explicit and implicit attitudes to characterize prejudice. *Journal of Personality and Social Psychology, 94*, 971–987.

Son Hing, L. S., Li, W., & Zanna, M. P. (2002). Inducing hypocrisy to reduce prejudicial responses among aversive racists. *Journal of Experimental Social Psychology, 38*, 71–78.

Stephan, W. G., & Stephan, C. W. (2001). *Improving intergroup relations.* Thousand Oaks, CA: Sage.

Tesler, M., & Sears, D. O. (2010). *Obama's race: The 2008 election and the dream of a post-racial America.* Chicago: University of Chicago Press.

Trawalter, S., & Richeson, J. A. (2006). Regulatory focus and executive function after interracial interactions. *Journal of Experimental Social Psychology, 42,* 406–412.

Uhlmann, E. L., & Cohen, G. L. (2005). Constructed criteria: Redefining merit to justify discrimination. *Psychological Science, 16,* 474–480.

Van Bavel, J. J., & Cunnigham, W. A. (2009). Self-categorization with a novel mixed-race group moderates automatic social and racial biases. *Personality and Social Psychology Bulletin, 35,* 321–335.

Vorauer, J. D., Gagnon, A., & Sasaki, S. J. (2009). Salient intergroup ideology and intergroup interaction. *Psychological Science, 20,* 838–845.

Wang, W. (2012). *The rise of intermarriage: Rates, characteristics vary by race and gender.* Retrieved from www.pewsocialtrends.org/2012/02/16/the-rise-of-intermarriage /2/#chapter-1-overview

Wojcieszak, M. (2015). Aversive racism in Spain – Testing the theory. *International Journal of Public Opinion Research, 27,* 22–45.

Yeager, D. S. & Walton, G. M. (2011). Social-psychological interventions in education: They're not magic. *Review of Educational Research, 81,* 267–301.

Ziegert, J. C., & Hanges, P. J. (2005). Employment discrimination: The role of implicit attitudes, motivation, and a climate for racial bias. *Journal of Applied Psychology, 90,* 554–562.

13 Ambivalent Sexism in the Twenty-First Century

Rachel A. Connor, Peter Glick, and Susan T. Fiske

Gender-based inequality is pervasive. Historically and cross-culturally, men have held more resources, power, and status than women. Despite general trends toward gender equality, male dominance remains a global reality. As of 2014, the global gender gap in economic participation and opportunity, which includes gender gaps in income, labor force participation, and professional advancement, stood at 60% (Hausmann, Tyson, Bekhouche, & Zahidi, 2014). If progress toward gender equality continues at the same pace, it will take until 2095 to completely close this gap. Yet in contrast to characterizations of intergroup relations as hostile and competitive, gender relations are predominantly cooperative – individual men and women consistently engage in and sustain close relationships with members of the other sex, whether friends, parents, siblings, or significant others. Herein lies the gender relationship paradox. How is the tension between male hegemony and male-female intimacy reconciled?

Ambivalent sexism theory (Glick & Fiske, 1996) recognizes that sexism entails a mixture of antipathy and subjective benevolence:

- *Hostile sexism* corresponds to classic definitions of prejudice as antipathy (Allport, 1954) and reflects the hostile derogation of women who pose a threat to the gender hierarchy (e.g., feminists).
- *Benevolent sexism* is "a set of interrelated attitudes toward women that are sexist in terms of viewing women stereotypically and in restricted roles but that are subjectively positive in feeling (for the perceiver)" (Glick & Fiske, 1996, p. 491). Benevolent sexism bestows affection on women who embrace limited but traditional gender roles (e.g., housewives). Hence, although benevolent sexism may appear positive, it presumes and reinforces women's subordinate status.

Ambivalent sexism theory argues that hostile and benevolent sexism are, in fact, not conflicting but complementary ideologies that present a resolution to the gender relationship paradox. By offering male protection and provision to women in exchange for their compliance, benevolent sexism recruits women as unwitting participants in their own subjugation, thereby obviating overt coercion. Hostile sexism serves to safeguard the status quo by punishing those who deviate from traditional gender roles.

This chapter discusses ambivalent sexism as a coordinated system of control that serves male dominance and limits women's power across personal, economic, and political domains. First, we review ambivalent sexism theory, focusing on ambivalent sexism's system-justifying functions. The second section addresses how ambivalent sexism polices women's bodies through the threat of rape, sexual harassment, and violence, as well as oppressive beauty ideals. The third section covers the economic and political domain, discussing how ambivalent sexism perpetuates gender discrimination at work. Fourth, we outline ways of reducing sexism, highlighting the particular challenges in identifying and confronting bias created by subtle sexism. Last, we offer recommendations for future research.

Ambivalent Sexism Theory

Ambivalent sexism theory (Glick & Fiske, 1996) holds that sexism is composed of two distinct yet complementary ideologies. Hostile sexism (HS) involves overtly misogynistic and competitive attitudes toward women, whereas benevolent sexism (BS) consists of subjectively favorable but patronizing attitudes toward women. Hostile sexism views gender relations in combative terms: Women are seen as seeking to usurp men's power in various ways, via their sexuality, by claiming discrimination, or through feminist activism. Benevolent sexism romanticizes heterosexual relationships and regards women as the perfect complement to men, but it also depicts women as weak and in need of male protection, thus emphasizing women's lower status. Glick and Fiske (1996) developed the Ambivalent Sexism Inventory (ASI) to measure hostile and benevolent sexism. This self-report measure, which has demonstrated reliability and validity in multinational studies (Glick et al., 2000; Glick et al., 2004), consists of 22 items that assess HS (e.g., "Women seek to gain power by getting control over men") and BS (e.g., "Women should be cherished and protected by men"). See Table 13.1 for a copy of the ASI.

Sources of Sexist Ambivalence

Ambivalent sexism emerges from the confluence of patriarchy, gender role differentiation, and female-male interdependence (Glick & Fiske, 1996). Each of these elements is associated with a set of hostile and benevolent attitudes toward women that legitimize male dominance. Social role theory posits that physical strength differences between men and women, in tandem with certain societal and ecological conditions, historically determined the distribution of men and women into social roles (Eagly & Wood, 2012). These factors led to men performing roles that granted them greater decision-making power, authority, and access to resources, setting the stage for patriarchy. However, whereas other long-standing relationships of inequality (such as race and class) involve limited contact between groups, in gender relations, the biology of sex and reproduction necessitates close, sustained contact between men and women. In other intergroup relations, avoiding or

Table 13.1 *The Ambivalent Sexism Inventory (ASI).*

Relationships Between Men and Women

Below is a series of statements concerning men and women and their relationships in contemporary society. Please indicate the degree to which you agree or disagree with each statement using the following scale:

0	1	2	3	4	5
Disagree Strongly	Disagree Somewhat	Disagree Slightly	Agree Slightly	Agree Somewhat	Agree Strongly

B(I)   1. No matter how accomplished he is, a man is not truly complete as a person unless he has the love of a woman.

H   2. Many women are actually seeking special favors, such as hiring policies that favor them over men, under the guise of asking for "equality."

B(P)* 3. In a disaster, women ought not necessarily to be rescued before men.

H   4. Most women interpret innocent remarks or acts as being sexist.

H   5. Women are too easily offended.

B(I)* 6. People are often truly happy in life without being romantically involved with a member of the other sex.

H*   7. Feminists are not seeking for women to have more power than men.

B(G)   8. Many women have a quality of purity that few men possess.

B(P)   9. Women should be cherished and protected by men.

H   10. Most women fail to appreciate fully all that men do for them.

H   11. Women seek to gain power by getting control over men.

B(I)   12. Every man ought to have a woman whom he adores.

B(I)* 13. Men are complete without women.

H   14. Women exaggerate problems they have at work.

H   15. Once a woman gets a man to commit to her, she usually tries to put him on a tight leash.

H   16. When women lose to men in a fair competition, they typically complain about being discriminated against.

B(P) 17. A good woman should be set on a pedestal by her man.

H*   18. There are actually very few women who get a kick out of teasing men by seeming sexually available and then refusing male advances.

B(G) 19. Women, compared to men, tend to have a superior moral sensibility.

B(P) 20. Men should be willing to sacrifice their own well being in order to provide financially for the women in their lives.

H*   21. Feminists are making entirely reasonable demands of men.

B(G) 22. Women, as compared to men, tend to have a more refined sense of culture and good taste.

© 1995 by Peter Glick and Susan T. Fiske. Use of this scale requires permission of one of the authors. *Source:* Adapted with permission from Glick and Fiske (1996). *Note:* H = Hostile Sexism, B = Benevolent Sexism, (P) = Protective Paternalism, (G) = Complementary Gender Differentiation, (I) = Heterosexual Intimacy, * = reverse-scored item.

excluding the subordinate group often serves the dominant group's interests. The intimate, dyadic nature of male-female relationships demands a different approach. Purely exclusionary or hostile tactics are unlikely to work because men want to maintain amicable relationships with women.

Using direct force carries risks for dominant groups, but overt force is particularly risky when the lives of dominant and subordinate group members are intertwined (Jackman, 1994). Overt force protects the dominant group's privileged position but offers no incentives for the subordinate group to participate in the unequal system. As a result, subordinate group members may show limited cooperation, or worse, active resistance. When groups are highly interdependent, a subtler form of control, ostensibly benevolent paternalism, is more effective at system maintenance because it masks inequalities and elicits desired behavior from subordinates (Glick & Fiske, 1996; Jackman, 1994). Both dominants and subordinates may view the dominant group's higher status as warranted because the dominants "know what's best" and allegedly have benevolent intentions toward the subordinate group. Contrary to true benevolence, however, the dominant group's main concern is to maintain its superior status and resources while mollifying the subordinates on whom they depend. Jackman (1994) characterized this strategy as the iron fist, which lies within the velvet glove. For ambivalent sexists, when the velvet glove of benevolent sexism fails to keep women in their place, the iron fist of hostile sexism emerges. Put another way, BS represents the "carrot" dangled in front of women to motivate them to accept inequality, while HS represents the "stick" that beats them when they do not.

Hostile and benevolent sexism each include subcomponents related to paternalism (the notion that men should rule), gender differentiation (distinguishing the genders through roles and stereotypes), and heterosexual intimacy (sexuality and intimate relationships). The paternalistic component goes directly to the heart of supporting men's power and status. Hostile sexism's *dominative paternalism* defends men's greater power. In contemporary societies in which women have experienced gains in status, this entails viewing women as trying to take men's power and gain unfair advantages over men. Benevolent sexism's *protective paternalism* component justifies limiting women's access to resources and masculine roles as necessary to protect and to serve their best interests.

The gender differentiation subcomponents of hostile and benevolent sexism solve a second challenge: demarcating gender boundaries, which is necessary for preserving status distinctions. Spatial separation as a mode of differentiation features prominently in class and race relations (Jackman, 1994). In contrast, because gender relations involve intimate contact, group boundaries must be enforced primarily through distinct roles – expectations that define socially acceptable behavior for men and women. Hostile sexism's *competitive gender differentiation* justifies male dominance by depicting only men as having the necessary characteristics for high-status positions. Its benevolent counterpart, *complementary gender differentiation*, ascribes positive, albeit low-status traits (e.g., morality) to women and emphasizes the complementarity of men's and women's stereotypical attributes.

Finally, the heterosexuality component attempts to maintain men's advantaged position in the gender hierarchy while accommodating their dependence on women for heterosexual sex and relationships. Hostile sexism's *heterosexual hostility* attempts to control and restrict women's sexuality, expressing the fear that women can use sex to manipulate men. Benevolent sexism's *heterosexual intimacy* component idealizes women as romantic partners and views heterosexual romantic relationships as necessary to "complete" a man.

Functions of Ambivalent Sexism

Despite their overall subordination, women are not completely powerless or subject to men's will. Rather, intergroup attitudes are negotiated, with each group influencing the other. However, by virtue of their social position, men, as the dominant group, have greater power to define intergroup stereotypes and attitudes. Notably, maintaining gender inequality does not require that individual men consciously intend to control or dominate women. Gender inequality becomes routinized through the widespread diffusion and acceptance of sexist ideology, which serves to explain and justify inequalities (Johnson, Dowd, & Ridgeway, 2006).

Benevolent sexism is crucial in persuading women to accept the unequal arrangement. Women resist HS (Barreto & Ellemers, 2005; Glick et al., 2000; Glick et al., 2004) but tend to view BS as relatively harmless (Becker & Swim, 2011; Bosson, Pinel, & Vandello, 2010) or even romantic (Rudman & Heppen, 2003). Compared to HS, BS seems like an attractive offer; it promises to provide women with male protection and preferential treatment in return for their cooperation (Fischer, 2006; Glick et al., 2000; Hammond, Sibley, & Overall, 2013). But the positive veneer of benevolent sexism hides its insidious nature: BS increases women's satisfaction with the gender status quo, thus undermining women's resistance to gender inequality (Becker & Wright, 2011; Connelly & Heesacker, 2012; Hammond & Sibley, 2011; Kay & Jost, 2003). Further, as its ideological complement, BS renders HS more palatable (Napier, Thorisdottir, & Jost, 2010), and women's endorsement of BS predicts greater willingness to endorse HS over time (Sibley, Overall, & Duckitt, 2007).

Indicating their ideological complementarity, HS and BS consistently exhibit strong, positive correlations at the national level (Fiske & North, 2014; Glick et al., 2000; Glick et al., 2004). That is, comparing across nations, in those countries where citizens score high on BS, they also score high on HS. The cross-national correlation approaches .90, an almost perfect relationship. In addition, both components of ambivalent sexism positively predict indicators of gender inequality that assess gender gaps in longevity, standards of living, and access to power and education (Brandt, 2011; Glick et al., 2000; Glick et al., 2004). Together, the interrelated components of ambivalent sexism serve to bolster male dominance by dictating a set of gender-specific rules that circumscribe women's personal, economic, and political power. To this end, hostile and benevolent sexism serve specific functions: BS rewards women who accept their submissive role (e.g., traditional women), and HS punishes women who deviate from their prescribed roles (e.g., career women, feminists; Glick, Diebold, Bailey-Werner, & Zhu, 1997).

Supporting ambivalent sexism theory, HS predicts negative and BS predicts positive attitudes toward and stereotypes of women. Glick et al. (2000) asked participants in 12 countries to list traits they associate with women and to rate each trait in terms of its negativity and positivity. HS predicted negative trait ratings, and BS predicted positive trait ratings, after controlling for shared variance between HS and BS. Further, consistent with their roles in maintaining inequality, HS and BS are positively related to other system-justifying ideologies. HS correlates with competitive intergroup ideology (social dominance orientation; Christopher & Mull, 2006; Sibley, Wilson, & Duckitt, 2007) and modern racism (Glick & Fiske, 1996). In contrast, BS is associated with right-wing authoritarianism, which predicts prejudice toward groups perceived as socially threatening (Christopher & Mull, 2006; Sibley et al., 2007).

Policing Women's Bodies

Efforts to control women's bodies range from overt interpersonal tactics, such as violence and sexual assault, to subtle, societally sanctioned methods of control, such as sexual objectification. This section focuses on how, in the interest of maintaining the gender status quo, ambivalent sexism justifies physical and sexual aggression toward "bad" women (e.g., temptresses, hostile competitors), while extending protection to "good" women (e.g., chaste, traditional women).

Interpersonal Physical and Sexual Violence

Relationship partners pose a major threat to women's safety. Women are more likely than men to be assaulted or murdered by a relationship partner (Browne & Williams, 1993; Lauritsen & Heimer, 2008). Violence toward women committed by male intimates occurs with disturbing frequency, both within the United States and across the world. A 2010 summary report of the National Intimate Partner and Sexual Violence Survey estimated that more than 40% of American women have experienced physical or sexual violence at the hands of their intimate partners (Black et al., 2011). According to a report by the World Health Organization (2013), 30% of women worldwide who have been in a relationship have experienced physical and/or sexual violence by their intimate partner, and as many as 38% of women who are murdered are victims of intimate partners.

Serious intimate partner violence often stems from motives to control a relationship partner. Intimate terrorism, a form of relationship violence that is primarily perpetrated by males, involves using psychologically, sexually, and physically abusive behavior to manipulate a romantic partner (Johnson, 2006).

While men also suffer from physical violence committed by their partners, they do not experience sexual violence or severe physical violence (e.g., hit with a fist or hard object, kicked, choked, beaten, burned, or have a knife or a gun used on them) to the same extent women do (Black et al., 2011). In addition, intimate partner violence by a woman is often defensive, a response to a male partner's violence, rather than motivated by the desire to control the male partner (Johnson, 2006).

Perhaps counterintuitively, close contact between groups licenses the dominant group's use of violence against subordinates (Jackman, 1994), as is reflected in the attitude that spousal violence is a private matter. When violence is committed by a relationship partner rather than a stranger, women are less likely to recognize the gendered nature of violence and more likely to tolerate the abuse.

Hostile Sexism Not surprisingly, men's hostile sexism predicts aggression toward women. Men high in hostility toward women report more frequently engaging in verbal aggression toward relationship partners, and sexual aggression toward women (Forbes, Adams-Curtis, & White, 2004). Men high (versus low) in HS hold more positive attitudes toward wife beating and are more likely to blame women as having somehow elicited the abuse they receive (Glick, Sakallı-Uğurlu, Ferreira, & de Souza, 2002; Sakallı, 2001). Qualitative work involving interviews with male domestic violence perpetrators demonstrates the role HS plays in legitimizing aggression toward female partners. Male perpetrators espoused beliefs that, as the superior sex, men have the right to use violence to put women "in their place" (Wood, 2004). When they did not receive the respect and deference they expected from their partners, they felt justified in responding with violence. Empirical research supports that men who are most invested in protecting male dominance are more likely to sexually harass following a threat to male status (Dall'Ara & Maass, 1999; Maass, Cadinu, Guarnieri, & Grasselli, 2003).

Several studies find that HS predicts the endorsement of rape myths (e.g., Glick & Fiske, 1996), which are "attitudes and beliefs that are generally false but widely and persistently held, and that serve to deny and justify male sexual aggression against women" (Lonsway & Fitzgerald, 1994, p. 134). A common rape myth is that women sexually manipulate men and then falsely "cry rape" (Lonsway & Fitzgerald, 1994). By depicting male-female relations as a power struggle in which women are eager to use their sexuality to overthrow men's authority, HS facilitates the minimization and tolerance of sexual aggression toward women (e.g., Russell & Trigg, 2004). Emphasizing HS's function in bolstering male dominance, individuals who endorse hostile-power relation beliefs (e.g., that women want to take power away from men) minimize the seriousness of a rape incident and blame the victim, but only when the alleged perpetrator is a high-status male. In contrast, hostile beliefs do not predict minimization of the incident or victim blame when the perpetrator is a high-status female (Yamawaki, Darby, & Queiroz, 2007). Hostile sexism also underpins the myth that women who dress provocatively, walk alone late at night, or initiate sexual activity are "asking for it" (e.g., Sakallı-Uğurlu, Salman, & Turgut, 2010). Men's HS predicts rape proclivity (e.g., would they coerce a woman into sex) in an acquaintance rape scenario, mediated by perceptions that the victim actually wants to have sex, despite her refusal (Abrams, Viki, Masser, & Bohner 2003; Masser, Viki, & Power, 2006).

Within intimate relationships, men's HS creates greater antagonism, leading to more negative behaviors that might precipitate aggression. Hammond and Overall (2013) conducted longitudinal studies of committed heterosexual couples. They found that men's HS scores predicted more negative interpretations of their female partners' behavior than the female partners' reports would support. Consistent with the hostile sexist view that women seek to manipulate and control men, high HS men were more likely to characterize their partners' behavior as manipulative, leading to increased antagonism and poorer relationship quality, which are risk factors for violence in intimate relationships (for a more detailed account of the repercussions of men's HS in intimate relationships, see Hammond & Overall, Chapter 14, this title).

In sum, hostile sexist beliefs legitimize aggression toward women on the grounds that women provoke male aggression when they violate gender norms. In light of the literature just reviewed, it is not surprising that many women find BS preferable to HS (e.g., Fischer, 2006; Glick et al., 2000); however, BS also contributes to justifying violence toward women.

Benevolent Sexism   Whereas HS uses violence as a means of coercion and control, BS takes a different tack: offering provisory protection from male aggression as long as women conform to gender stereotypes. In accordance with its function in upholding gender roles, BS fosters negativity toward women who do not adhere to gender-role prescriptions regarding female sexuality (Sakallı-Uğurlu & Glick, 2003). BS predicts victim blaming and excusing the perpetrator in cases of acquaintance rape (Yamawaki, 2007). In a study examining perceptions of rape perpetrators, participants read hypothetical scenarios describing an acquaintance or a stranger rape (Viki, Abrams, & Masser, 2004). When the female victim was raped by an acquaintance, participants high in BS (versus low) ascribed less responsibility to the perpetrator and recommended more lenient jail sentences. In contrast, participants' BS did not predict perpetrator blame or recommended sentence length in the stranger rape condition. In acquaintance rape, the ambiguity surrounding the consensuality of sex allows for perceptions that a victim's behavior encouraged the rape (Abrams et al., 2003). Consistent with beliefs that women are the gatekeepers of sexuality, research shows that BS predicts victim blame when a victim violates gender stereotypes and is a "bad" rape victim (e.g., does not physically resist the attacker), two factors that have been previously confounded in research (Masser, Lee, & Kimmie, 2010). Thus, the benefits of BS are conferred on women who adhere to role prescriptions regarding female sexuality (e.g., "chaste" women) but withheld from women who engage in promiscuous behavior (Sibley & Wilson, 2004).

Ironically, the threat of male violence leads women to seek protection, which, due to men's greater status and control of resources, only men are positioned to provide. This "protection racket" leads women to endorse BS; in societies where men are high in HS, women show stronger endorsement of BS (Glick et al., 2000; Glick et al., 2004). Experimental research demonstrates that women who are told that men are generally high in HS show greater endorsement of BS, compared to a control group (Fischer, 2006). Thus, research supports that women endorse BS out of self-protective motives, in response to perceived danger from men. For instance, BS is associated with rape-myth acceptance for women but not men, perhaps reflecting beliefs that women are protected from rape if they behave in line with expectations (Forbes et al., 2004). Furthermore, the perceived threat of violence from an intimate partner may lead women to accept BS and its attendant role prescriptions (Expósito, Herrera, Moya, & Glick, 2010). In encouraging women to devote their energies to intimate relationships rather than to cultivating personal success, however, BS only increases their dependence within relationships (see Hammond & Overall, Chapter 14, this title).

A particularly troubling consequence is that BS disarms women, making them more vulnerable to violence. In a series of studies, Durán, Moya, and Megías (2011, 2014) showed that (a) women respond less negatively to a hypothetical sexual assault committed by a male relationship partner when they believe he is a benevolent sexist; (b) this effect may be explained by interpretations of a man's sexual aggression as evidence of his attraction to his partner; and (c) people high in BS are less likely to consider a hypothetical sexual assault as rape, mediated by beliefs that sex is a marital right for men and a marital duty for women. Women view BS as attractive in a male partner, without realizing that BS and HS coexist in individuals, and in fact, univalent sexists are rarer than ambivalent sexists (Kilianski & Rudman, 1998; Sibley & Becker, 2012). Paralleling the classic cycle of abuse, women may find that the honeymoon period ends and the abuse begins when they do not conform to an ambivalent sexist partner's expectations. Without sufficient social or economic resources, women are less able to leave relationships. Thus, women may become trapped in the "entangling net of conditional love," striving to meet their partner's expectations to preclude hostile abuse (Jackman, 1994, p. 78).

Objectification

Objectification theory (Fredrickson & Roberts, 1997) focuses on the negative consequences (e.g., body dissatisfaction) women experience because of a cultural context promoting a sexually evaluative focus on women's appearance. Merging objectification theory and system justification theory (Jost, Banaji, & Nosek, 2004),

Calogero (2013) argues that sexual objectification is part of a larger system of social control that maintains gender inequality, undermining women externally, by treating them as objects, and internally, via self-objectification. In other words, men's objectification of women is not just about sexual interest, but also about keeping women in a subordinate role. From this perspective, it is not surprising to find relations between ambivalently sexist ideology and objectification. As in other areas, HS and BS seem to complement each other: HS reinforces men's objectification of women and BS reinforces women's self-objectification.

Hostile Sexism   Research provides evidence for HS's role in the implicit dehumanization of women through sexual objectification. An fMRI study found that (a) men high in HS are quicker to pair sexualized women (e.g., a woman pictured in a bikini) with first-person verbs (push, pull) and clothed women with third-person verbs (pushes, pulls), indicating reduced perceptions of sexualized women's agency; and (b) males high in HS show decreased activation in brain areas involved with mentalizing (attributing mental states to others) and increased activation in brain areas involved with object manipulation when viewing photographs of sexualized women (Cikara, Eberhardt, & Fiske, 2011). Suggesting that HS is part of a broader pattern of female dehumanization, individuals high in HS are less likely to attribute positive, secondary (i.e., uniquely human) emotions to women (Viki & Abrams, 2003). However, highlighting the need for further research in this area, more recent research suggests HS may specifically predict dehumanization of sexualized female targets, as the implicit dehumanization of women as a group is unrelated to men's endorsement of hostile sexism (Rudman & Mescher, 2012).

Benevolent Sexism   Women's recurrent experiences of being reduced to their bodies and/or body parts can lead them to self-objectify, to "treat themselves as objects to be looked at and evaluated" (Fredrickson & Roberts, 1997, p. 177). Self-objectification leads women to persistently police their bodily appearance and strive to meet feminine beauty standards, while de-emphasizing success in other areas. Calogero (2013) views self-objectification as a type of internalized social control, related to BS, that encourages women to adopt gender-congruent roles and behaviors. In support of this assertion, exposure to benevolent and complementary sexism (a combination of HS and BS) increases women's (but not men's) state self-objectification, self-surveillance, and body shame (Calogero & Jost, 2011). Moreover, merely observing another woman being treated in a benevolent sexist way increases women's preoccupation with appearance and body shame (Shepherd et al., 2011).

Some studies (e.g., Oswald, Franzoi, & Frost, 2012), however, suggest that BS is associated with greater body esteem only to the extent that women feel successful in increasing their attractiveness to men. Franzoi (2001) found that women high (more so than women low) in BS reported using more cosmetics to prepare for a date, a strategy to increase their attractiveness, and also reported higher body esteem. Body surveillance may temporarily boost self-esteem for some women, insofar as it makes them feel more attractive (Breines, Crocker, & Garcia, 2008). Thus, like BS, self-objectification appears to offer benefits for some women; but in encouraging women's adherence to prescriptive roles, it ultimately legitimizes gender inequality. Further, this research suggests that in activating gender stereo-types (and rewards associated with conformity to stereotypes), BS facilitates women's self-objectification.

Control of Economic and Political Resources

Although gender gaps in health and educational attainment are approach-ing convergence, gender gaps in political decision-making power, wages, and high-status professions persist (Hausmann et al., 2014). Women have increasingly moved into mid-level management roles but remain underrepresented in the high-est-paying and most powerful positions (Eagly & Carli, 2007). In the United States, women make up only 5% of CEOs in Fortune 500 companies, 17% of Fortune 500 board members, and 19% of congressional representatives (Parker, Horowitz, Wang, Brown, & Patten, 2015). In Iceland, the current world leader in women's political empowerment, the gender gap in political leadership is around 34% (Hausmann et al., 2014). Both HS and BS promote barriers to closing these gaps.

According to Eagly and Carli (2007), modern forms of sexism and discrimi-nation no longer resemble a "glass ceiling"; rather, they represent a series of complicated hurdles to women's advancement. In particular, ambivalent sexism poses a paradox for working women; BS attributes to women low-status char-acteristics that are not valued in male-typed positions (i.e., communality, warmth), and HS punishes women who display high-status characteristics valued in the workplace (i.e., agency, competence). As a result, women often must choose between being liked or respected, and they risk being undervalued as workers either way.

Hostile Sexism

As a result of gender stereotypes that associate agency and competence with men (Prentice & Carranza, 2002), women must worker harder to demonstrate these qualities to secure high-status positions. However, by behaving agentically, women violate proscriptive gender stereotypes that prohibit them from display-ing the high-status, self-promoting behaviors typically associated with men (e.g., dominance; Rudman, Moss-Racusin, Glick, & Phelan, 2012). As a result, agentic women encounter penalties that non-agentic women do not. Although they are judged as similarly competent to agentic men, agentic women are seen as less likable (e.g., Heilman, Wallen, Fuchs, & Tamkins, 2004). This well-documented phenomenon is known as backlash (Rudman et al., 2012). In one example of backlash research, Phelan, Moss-Racusin, and Rudman (2008) had participants view and evaluate videotaped interviews of male and female applicants for a leadership position. The applicants either presented themselves as communal (e.g., emphasizing interpersonal skills) or agentic (e.g., emphasizing leadership ability). Participants rated the female agentic applicant as less socially skilled and less hirable than the agentic male applicant. Moreover, participants justified the agentic female's lower hirability by devaluing her competence and assigning greater weight to her low social skills. Multiple studies show that agentic women face hiring discrimination (Rudman, 1998; Rudman & Glick, 1999), social disapproval (Heilman et al., 2004), and disadvantage in salary negotiations (Bowles, Babcock, & Lai, 2007). HS fuels backlash against women who violate gender roles, predicting negative attitudes toward women in leadership positions (Masser & Abrams, 2004; Sakallı-Uğurlu & Beydogan, 2002), greater preference for male over female authorities (Rudman & Kilianski, 2000), and a lower likelihood of voting for a non-stereotypical female political candidate (Gervais & Hillard, 2011).

Hostile sexist beliefs that successful women are dominant and power hungry justify backlash (Rudman & Fairchild, 2004; Rudman & Glick, 2001). Characterizing agentic women as "overly dominant" allows perceivers to justify hostile discrimination toward women who violate gendered expectancies (Rudman et al., 2012). Female political candidates who are perceived as violating gender roles by seeking power suffer at the polls, whereas male candidates do not; this voting bias is partially explained by moral outrage resulting from perceptions that female candidates who express power-seeking goals are less caring and supportive (Okimoto & Brescoll, 2010). Furthermore, HS predicts endorsement of attitudes that justify discrimination against women in promotions. People high in HS are more likely to agree that women have an unfair advantage over men in promotions, report more resentment of perceived female advantage, and blame women for the promotion gender gap (Feather & Boeckmann, 2007). In addition, men high in HS report less guilt regarding gender inequality in the workplace. As a result, HS predicts gender discrimination in hiring and promotion (e.g., Masser & Abrams, 2004). Consistent with this research, Connor and Fiske (2016) find that HS legitimizes gender income inequality by encouraging system-justifying explanations for disparities in men's and women's economic outcomes. Specifically, politically conservative participants exposed to HS, compared to those not exposed to HS, exhibit greater acceptance of gender income inequality; this effect is explained by their greater endorsement of attributions for the gender income gap that blame women for their economic disadvantage.

Benevolent Sexism

Whereas HS promotes overtly hostile backlash toward women, BS fosters more subtle, paternalistic forms of discrimination toward women in the workplace.

By ascribing female-stereotypical characteristics to women, BS preserves beliefs in women's lower competence, thereby justifying discrimination against them and supporting male privilege (Glick & Fiske, 1996). The perceived incongruity between the characteristics women are believed to possess and the characteristics required for success in male-typed roles leads to discrimination, due to women's perceived "lack of fit" (Eagly & Karau, 2002; Heilman, 2001).

Research illustrates at least two ways in which BS subtly undermines women in the workplace. First, BS leads to patronizing treatment that seems positive but ultimately puts women at a disadvantage. For instance, male managers give female, relative to male, subordinates more symbolic rewards, such as praise, but this comes at the cost of allocating fewer valued resources, such as promotions (Biernat, Tocci, & Williams, 2012; Vescio, Gervais, Snyder, & Hoover, 2005). This "praise over pay" effect may be tied to benevolent sexist beliefs that women value procedurally fair treatment in the workplace over monetary rewards (Belliveau, 2012).

In addition, patronizing treatment reduces women's chances for advancement by restricting their access to on-the-job development opportunities, such as challenging assignments and critical feedback that develop new skills and opportunities for promotion. Male managers high in BS give women less challenging work assignments (King et al., 2012). One explanation for the excessive praise women sometimes receive is a leniency bias (see Harber, 1998) stemming from lower expectations for women and a desire not to hurt their presumed fragile feelings. Compared to female managers, male managers, in both the energy and health care industries, reported receiving more negative feedback from supervisors, but also more challenging developmental work experiences, which are important for gaining job skills and improving performance (King et al., 2012). In comparison to hostile discrimination, paternalistic treatment of women by male managers is more likely to go unnoticed and may even be rewarded (Becker, Glick, Ilic, & Bohner, 2011).

Patronizing behavior can include over-helping or offers to help that presume the target's incompetence at a task (Nadler, 2002). Patronizing help poses a difficult dilemma for women: Accepting patronizing help hurts women's perceived competence, but rejecting it hurts their perceived warmth. In contrast, men face no penalty for rejecting help (Becker et al., 2011).

Perhaps most insidiously, BS leads women to behave in ways that confirm gender stereotypes, even when they do not personally endorse BS. Exposure to BS (e.g., by merely proofreading BS items from the Ambivalent Sexism Inventory) leads women to ascribe less importance to competence and academic achievement (Barreto, Ellemers, Piebinga, & Moya, 2010), reduces women's willingness to challenge gender discrimination (Becker & Wright, 2011), and increases women's acceptance of the social system as a whole (Jost & Kay, 2005). In line with work on stereotype threat, BS also diminishes women's cognitive performance in a workplace setting by increasing women's self-doubt (Dardenne, Dumont, & Bollier, 2007). Women exposed to BS show increased activity in neural regions associated with suppressing intrusive thoughts, report more frequently experiencing intrusive thoughts of their incompetence, and recall a greater number of past situations in which they felt incompetent (Dardenne et al., 2007; Dardenne et al., 2013; Dumont, Sarlet, & Dardenne, 2010).

In part, BS undermines women's economic chances by fostering reliance on men to provide, leading them to value pleasing their male relationship partners more than succeeding at work (see Hammond & Overall, Chapter 14, this title). For example, women who endorse BS are more likely to accept a male partner's paternalistic restrictions prohibiting them from accepting an internship opportunity (Moya, Glick, Expósito, de Lemus, & Hart, 2007), value their male partner's career success over their own (Chen, Fiske, & Lee, 2009), and show decreased interest in leadership and high-paying, high-status occupations (Rudman & Heppen, 2003). In conclusion, by fostering subtle discrimination toward women and leading women to define themselves and behave in gender-stereotypic ways, BS subtly undermines women in the workplace.

Reducing Sexism

Ambivalent sexism theory highlights the need for prejudice-reduction interventions specific to sexism. As a result of the unique features of gender relations, sexism researchers cannot simply co-opt strategies designed to reduce other forms of prejudice. Increased intergroup contact, for example, will have little effect in reducing sexism; in fact, close contact between men and women reinforces gender status divisions (Jackman, 1994; Ridgeway & Correll, 2004). Other challenges in reducing sexism include women's reliance on men for status and resources, which increases the costs of confronting sexism, and BS's positive stereotypes of women, which make sexism more appealing, more difficult to recognize, and more difficult to confront. The following sections discuss ways to reduce and confront sexism, as well as the particular challenges associated with even recognizing, let alone confronting, BS.

Decreasing Endorsement

Two recent studies present promising interventions to reduce sexism. The Workshop Activity for Gender Equity Simulation in the Academy (WAGES–Academic; Cundiff, Zawadzki, Danube, & Shields, 2014), allows participants to experience the accumulative effects of subtle sexism in the workplace. WAGES uses experiential learning to minimize reactance against sex discrimination claims and increase feelings of self-efficacy in confronting sexism, which create barriers to sexism-reduction interventions. A second intervention (developed by de Lemus, Navarro, Velásquez, Ryan, & Megías, 2014) aims to reduce sexism and increase awareness of gender inequality by targeting the bases of gendered power. Participation in these programs increases perceptions of subtle sexism as harmful, reduces endorsement of sexism, and increases willingness to act for gender equality (Cundiff et al., 2014; de Lemus et al., 2014; Zawadzki, Shields Danube, & Swim, 2013).

Confronting Sexism

Confronting sexist incidents is another strategy for reducing sexism that can potentially increase perpetrators' awareness of their sexist behavior, reduce the likelihood they will behave in a similar way in the future, and even establish situational norms that discourage sexist behavior from others (Czopp, Monteith, & Mark, 2006). In addition to reducing bias, confrontation has positive personal outcomes for targets of sexism. Women who confront sexism feel more satisfied, competent, self-confident, and empowered (Gervais, Hillard, & Vescio, 2010; Hyers, 2007).

Despite women's desire to confront sexism, they often avoid doing so because of fears about violating prescriptive gender roles (e.g., of feminine modesty and niceness) and backlash for behaving assertively (Hyers, 2007; Shelton & Stewart, 2004), a fear that may be well founded (e.g., Kaiser & Miller, 2001). When deciding whether to confront sexism, women weigh the costs and benefits of doing so (Good, Moss-Racusin, & Sanchez, 2012). The costs and benefits vary, based on how people confront (i.e., the message they use) and who confronts (i.e., the source of confrontation), influencing a confrontation's likelihood of succeeding.

Hostile confrontations (e.g., labeling an offender as sexist) may backfire, resulting in less accepting reactions to the confrontation, as well as more negative evaluations of and greater hostility toward the confronter (Becker & Barreto, 2014; Czopp et al., 2006). Moreover, women who aggressively confront sexism may inadvertently confirm an offender's hostile sexist beliefs about women. In contrast, assertive, but nonaggressive confrontations may still evoke negative reactions, but they are seen as less threatening and produce more accepting responses (Becker & Barreto, 2014; Czopp et al., 2006).

The confronter's group membership also influences how offenders respond to confrontation. When men confront sexism, offenders experience greater self-directed negative affect, view the confronter more positively, and perceive the confrontation as more legitimate (Czopp & Monteith, 2003; Drury & Kaiser, 2014). Perceptions of men as acting against group interest seem to enhance their credibility as confronters (Drury & Kaiser, 2014). Male allies can also empower women to confront sexism. Female targets of sexism are more likely to take action against sexism by filing a complaint when a male suggests they have been targets of sexism (Cihangir, Barreto, & Ellemers, 2014). Given their greater structural power, men are often better positioned than women to confront sexism, particularly when offenders also hold power (Ashburn-Nardo, Blanchar,

Petersson, Morris, & Goodwin, 2014). However, as Drury and Kaiser (2014) note, it is important that men engage as equal partners in the fight against sexism rather than act as paternalistic protectors of women.

Challenges Associated with Confronting BS

BS is particularly challenging to confront because, unlike HS, people do not readily recognize BS as sexism and view it as relatively harmless (Barreto & Ellemers, 2005; Bosson et al., 2010). Of course, if targets fail to recognize sexism, they will not confront it, thereby unwittingly reinforcing sexist behavior (Ashburn-Nardo et al., 2014). Further, BS serves system-justifying functions for both men and women; it alleviates the dissonance associated with women's lower-status position and increases life satisfaction for women as well as men (Connelly & Heesacker, 2012; Hammond & Sibley, 2011; Jost & Kay, 2005). Finally, because paternalistic behavior comes couched as benevolent helping or protection, confronting benevolently sexist acts may be viewed as especially impolite, aggressive, and ungrateful (e.g., Becker et al., 2011).

Given these challenges, how can BS effectively be confronted and reduced? Research suggests the most effective way to reduce endorsement of BS is to highlight its harmful consequences. Simply attending to daily sexist experiences reduces women's endorsement of BS; however, it does not affect men's BS endorsement, unless they are made more aware of the harm BS causes (which also further reduces women's BS endorsement; Becker & Swim, 2011, 2012). Moreover, individuals exposed to information about BS's harm evaluate a benevolently sexist man more negatively and view him as more sexist (Becker & Swim, 2012). As a result of its apparent positivity, BS may often be well intentioned, as suggested by research showing that an internal motivation to behave in a non-prejudiced manner actually increases paternalistic discrimination (Fehr & Sassenburg, 2009). Once alerted to the negative consequences of BS, however, individuals high in internal motivation to behave in non-prejudiced ways show decreased paternalistic discrimination.

Few studies have directly addressed ways of confronting BS. Extant work shows that even women who politely reject BS face backlash (e.g., Becker et al., 2011). In masculine domains, however, the benefits of confronting patronizing behavior may outweigh the costs, at least when behavior is explicitly patronizing. When women confront (compared to when they do not), they are seen as more competent, thus more qualified for a male-typed job (Becker et al., 2011); but because women who confront lose perceived warmth, they may still face penalties for confronting (e.g., Rudman, 1998). Future research is needed to determine how reactions to confronting BS differ when patronizing behavior is more subtle, as this is likely to increase the costs of confronting. For example, because BS involves (subjectively) positive treatment of women, people confronted about subtle paternalistic behavior may be more likely to respond with patronizing amusement or hostility (Czopp & Monteith, 2003).

Future Directions

The research reviewed in this chapter shows that ambivalent sexism reinforces gender-status divisions and inequality across multiple domains. Interpersonally, ambivalent sexism resembles a "protection racket" that leads women to seek male protection from male-instituted violence. Ambivalent sexism also reinforces women's subordinate position by facilitating the sexual objectification of women, which leads women to adopt restrictive self-views and stereotype-congruent behaviors. In the public domain (e.g., work and politics), hostile and benevolent sexism create barriers to women's advancement in political and professional positions, often forcing women to choose between being respected or liked. Although many effects have been well researched, gaps in the literature remain, suggesting avenues for future research.

First, research on reducing sexism is sparse, but increasing. The positive effects from recent educational interventions (e.g., workshops and demonstrations) give cause for optimism for their use as a prevention strategy. Implementing and testing these strategies within organizations represent important directions for further research. The focus on prevention is particularly important, given the well-demonstrated costs of confronting sexist behavior as it happens – especially benevolently sexist acts. We hope that future research will find effective strategies individuals can use to confront daily acts of sexism that avoid or minimize the social penalties confronters typically face. The biggest challenge will be to devise interventions and methods of confronting benevolently sexist acts.

Second, notably less effort has been dedicated to examining ambivalent sexism toward men as compared to women. Glick and Fiske (1999) also devised measures of hostility toward men (HM) and benevolence toward men (BM). HM attributes socially undesirable, but high-status traits to men (e.g., aggressiveness, arrogance), thereby legitimating male dominance. In contrast, BM valorizes men's traditional role as women's protectors and providers, while reinforcing the need for women to provide domestic care of men in close relationships (e.g., "women ought to take care of their men at home, because men would fall apart if they had to fend for themselves"; Glick & Fiske, 1999). Hostile and benevolent sexism toward men and women are correlated, arise from the same structural factors, and similarly predict national-level indicators of gender inequality (Glick et al., 2004). Underscoring the importance of examining ambivalent sexism toward men and women, HM (in contrast to HS, BS, or BM) uniquely contributes to perceived stability of male dominance (Glick & Whitehead, 2010). HM suggests that even though male dominance may not be legitimate, it is likely to be inevitable because men mainly care about asserting dominance, untampered with concern for others.

Although research sheds light on the psychological processes underlying women's endorsement of sexism, it is also vital to understand why sexism, particularly BS, appeals to individual men. Beyond system-justifying motives, many men may endorse BS because compared to HS, it is a "nice" way to be manly. Benevolent sexism toward women and men provides scripts for behavior in heterosexual relationships; without BS, men (and women) may have difficulty navigating heterosexual romance (see Overall, Sibley, & Tan, 2011, for possible benefits of men's BS to heterosexual relationship quality). Research studying relationship partners' levels of ambivalent sexism provides insight into how BS guides men's and women's behavior in intimate relationships. The following chapter by Hammond and Overall focuses specifically on research exploring the relational aspect of ambivalent sexism theory. To the extent men derive a positive self-image from their role as protector and provider, female partners' rejection of BS not only poses a threat to their social identities but also to their personal identities. The reality is that achieving gender equality requires that men change too, and researchers must be willing to help men "remake masculinities" in ways that support gender equality (Connell, 2005).

A fourth understudied area relates to intersectionality. Paternalistic protection is reserved for women who adhere to traditionally feminine roles; to the extent women are seen as violating gender roles, they are deemed unworthy of protection. Future researchers might explore how intersecting identities shape the experience of benevolent sexism. For example, are certain women (i.e., those who embody "ideal" femininity: White, middle class or rich, beautiful, young, heterosexual, mothers) more likely to receive the benefits of BS? There is evidence that this selective chivalry occurs in the courtroom. To cite a grim example, although defendants who murder women are more likely to be sentenced to death than those who kill men, defendants who kill White women are more than twice as likely to receive a death sentence than those who kill Black women (Holcomb, Williams, & Demuth, 2004). Other research suggests that the current measure of BS does not adequately capture sexist beliefs among African Americans and Latino/a Americans (Hayes & Swim, 2013). Thus, researchers should attend to how women with intersectional identities experience sexism, as well as how HS and BS interact with and reinforce other forms of prejudice.

Conclusion

Nearly two decades of research, conducted across various nations, broadly support ambivalent sexism theory's contention that BS and HS represent complementary ideologies, the carrot and the stick, that reinforce gender inequality across both private (e.g., close relationships) and public (e.g., the workplace) domains. The research also amply demonstrates BS's negative effects, even though it seems subjectively favorable and fosters discrimination with a smile, couched as help, provision, or protection. Further, BS has been shown to be especially effective in undermining women's resistance to inequality. Gaps in the research remain, however, particularly regarding how intersecting identities shape sexism. Moving ahead in the twenty-first century, we encourage future researchers to address the gaps identified here to further understanding of the mechanisms by which ambivalent sexism perpetuates inequality and how it can be combatted.

References

Abrams, D., Viki, G. T., Masser, B., & Bohner, G. (2003). Perceptions of stranger and acquaintance rape: The role of benevolent and hostile sexism in victim blame and rape proclivity. *Journal of Personality and Social Psychology, 84*, 111–125.

Allport, G. W. (1954). *The nature of prejudice*. Reading, MA: Addison-Wesley.

Ashburn-Nardo, L., Blanchar, J. C., Petersson, J., Morris, K. A., & Goodwin, S. A. (2014). Do you say something when it's your boss? The role of perpetrator power in prejudice confrontation. *Journal of Social Issues, 70*(4), 615–636.

Barreto, M., & Ellemers, N. (2005). The burden of benevolent sexism: How it contributes to the maintenance of gender inequalities. *European Journal of Social Psychology, 35*(5), 633–642.

Barreto, M., Ellemers, N., Piebinga, L., & Moya, M. (2010). How nice of us and how dumb of me: The effect of exposure to benevolent sexism on women's task and relational self-descriptions. *Sex Roles, 62*(7–8), 532–544.

Becker, J. C., Glick, P., Ilic, M., & Bohner, G. (2011). Damned if she does, damned if she doesn't: Consequences of accepting versus confronting patronizing help for the female target and male actor. *European Journal of Social Psychology, 41*(6), 761–773.

Becker, J. C., & Swim, J, K. (2011). Seeing the unseen attention to daily encounters with sexism as way to reduce sexist beliefs. *Psychology of Women Quarterly, 35*(2), 227–242.

Becker, J. C., & Swim, J. K. (2012). Reducing endorsement of benevolent and modern sexist beliefs: Differential effects of addressing harm versus pervasiveness of benevolent sexism. *Social Psychology, 43*(3), 127–137.

Becker, J. C., & Wright, S. C. (2011). Yet another dark side of chivalry: Benevolent sexism undermines and hostile sexism motivates collective action for social change. *Journal of Personality and Social Psychology, 101*, 62–77.

Becker, J. C., & Barreto, M. (2014). Ways to go: Men's and women's support for aggressive and nonaggressive confrontation of sexism as a function of gender identification. *Journal of Social Issues, 70*(4), 668–686.

Belliveau, M. A. (2012). Engendering inequity? How social accounts create vs. merely explain unfavorable pay outcomes for women. *Organization Science, 23*(4), 1154–1174.

Black, M. C., Basile, K. C., Breiding, M. J., Smith, S. G., Walters, M. L., Merrick, M. T. . . . Stevens, M. R. (2011). *The National Intimate Partner and Sexual Violence Survey (NISVS)*. Atlanta, GA: NCIPC, CDC.

Biernat, M., Tocci, M. J., & Williams, J. C. (2012). The language of performance evaluations: Gender-based shifts in content and consistency of judgment. *Social Psychological and Personality Science, 3*(2), 186–192.

Bosson, J. K., Pinel, E. C., & Vandello, J. A. (2010). The emotional impact of ambivalent sexism: Forecasts versus real experiences. *Sex Roles*, *62*(7–8), 520–531.

Bowles, H. R., Babcock, L., & Lai, L. (2007). Social incentives for gender differences in the propensity to initiate negotiations: Sometimes it does hurt to ask. *Organizational Behavior and Human Decision Processes*, *103*(1), 84–103.

Brandt, M. J. (2011). Sexism and gender inequality across 57 societies. *Psychological Science*, *22*(11), 1413–1418.

Breines, J. G., Crocker, J., & Garcia, J. A. (2008). Self-objectification and well-being in women's daily lives. *Personality and Social Psychology Bulletin*, *34*(5), 583–598.

Browne A., Williams K. R. (1993). Gender, intimacy, and lethal violence: Trends from 1976 through 1987. *Gender & Society*, *7*(1), 78–98.

Calogero, R. M. (2013). On objects and actions: Situating self-objectification in a system justification context. In S. J. Gervais (Ed.), *Objectification and (de) humanization* (pp. 97–126). New York: Springer.

Calogero, R. M., & Jost, J. T. (2011). Self-subjugation among women: Exposure to sexist ideology, self-objectification, and the protective function of the need to avoid closure. *Journal of Personality and Social Psychology*, *100*, 211–228.

Chen, Z., Fiske, S. T., & Lee, T. L. (2009). Ambivalent sexism and power-related gender-role ideology in marriage. *Sex Roles*, *60*(11–12), 765–778.

Christopher, A. N., & Mull, M. S. (2006). Conservative ideology and ambivalent sexism. *Psychology of Women Quarterly*, *30*(2), 223–230.

Cihangir, S., Barreto, M., & Ellemers, N. (2014). Men as allies against sexism. SAGE Open. doi: 10.1177/2158244014539168

Cikara, M., Eberhardt, J. L., & Fiske, S. T. (2011). From agents to objects: Sexist attitudes and neural responses to sexualized targets. *Journal of Cognitive Neuroscience*, *23*(3), 540–551.

Connell, R. W. (2005). Change among the gatekeepers: Men, masculinities, and gender equality in the global arena. *Signs*, *40*(1), 1801–1825.

Connelly, K., & Heesacker, M. (2012). Why is benevolent sexism appealing? *Psychology of Women Quarterly*, *36*(4), 432–443.

Connor, R. A., & Fiske, S. T. (2016). Not minding the gender income gap: Hostile sexism, conservatism, and attributed choice in a moral framework. Manuscript submitted for publication.

Cundiff, J. L., Zawadzki, M. J., Danube, . L., & Shields, S. A. (2014). Using experiential learning to increase the recognition of everyday sexism as harmful: The WAGES intervention. *Journal of Social Issues*, *70*(4), 703–721.

Czopp, A. M., & Monteith, M. J. (2003). Confronting prejudice (literally): Reactions to confrontations of racial and gender bias. *Personality and Social Psychology Bulletin*, *29*(4), 532–544.

Czopp, A. M., Monteith, M. J., & Mark, A. Y. (2006). Standing up for a change: Reducing bias through interpersonal confrontation. *Journal of Personality and Social Psychology*, *90*, 784–803.

Dall'Ara, E., & Maass, A. (1999). Studying sexual harassment in the laboratory: Are egalitarian women at higher risk? *Sex Roles*, *41*, 681–704.

Dardenne, B., Dumont, M., & Bollier, T. (2007). Insidious dangers of benevolent sexism: Consequences for women's performance. *Journal of Personality and Social Psychology*, *93*(5), 764–779.

Dardenne, B., Dumont, M., Sarlet, M., Phillips, C., Balteau, E,. Degueldre, C. . . . Collette, F. (2013). Benevolent sexism alters executive brain responses. *Neuroreport*, *24*(10), 572–577.

de Lemus, S., Navarro, L., Velásquez, M. J., Ryan, E., & Megías, J. L. (2014). From sex to gender: A university intervention to reduce sexism in Argentina, Spain, and El Salvador. *Journal of Social Issues*, *70*(4), 741–762.

Drury, B. J., & Kaiser, C. R. (2014). Allies against sexism: The role of men in confronting sexism. *Journal of Social Issues*, *70*(4), 637–652.

Dumont, M., Sarlet, M., & Dardenne, B. (2010). Be too kind to a woman, she'll feel incompetent: Benevolent sexism shifts self-construal and autobiographical memories toward incompetence. *Sex Roles*, *62*(7–8), 545–553.

Durán, M., Moya, M., & Megías, J. L. (2011). It's his right, it's her duty: Benevolent sexism and the justification of traditional sexual roles. *Journal of Sex Research*, *48*(5), 470–478.

Durán, M., Moya, M., & Megías, J. L. (2014). Benevolent sexist ideology attributed to an abusive partner decreases women's active coping responses to acts of sexual violence. *Journal of Interpersonal Violence*, *29*(8), 1380–1401.

Eagly, A. H., & Carli, L, L. (2007). *Through the labyrinth*. Boston: Harvard Business Press.

Eagly, A. H., & Karau, S. J. (2002). Role congruity theory of prejudice toward female leaders. *Psychological Review*, *109*(3), 573–598.

Eagly, A, H., & Wood, W. (2012). Social role theory. In P. Van Lange, A. W. Kruglanski & E. T. Higgins (Eds.), *Handbook of theories of social psychology* (pp. 458–476). London: Sage.

Expósito, F., Herrera, M. C., Moya, M., & Glick, P. (2010). Don't rock the boat: Women's benevolent sexism predicts fears of marital violence. *Psychology of Women Quarterly*, *34*(1), 36–42.

Feather, N. T., & Boeckmann, R. J. (2007). Beliefs about gender discrimination in the workplace in the context of affirmative action: Effects of gender and ambivalent attitudes in an Australian sample. *Sex Roles*, *57*(1–2), 31–42.

Fehr, J., & Sassenberg, K. (2009). Intended and unintended consequences of internal motivation to behave nonprejudiced: The case of benevolent discrimination. *European Journal of Social Psychology*, *39*(6), 1093–1108.

Fischer, A. R. (2006). Women's benevolent sexism as reaction to hostility. *Psychology of Women Quarterly*, *30*(4), 410–416.

Fiske, S. T., & North, M. S. (2015). Measures of stereotyping and prejudice: Barometers of bias. In G. Boyle & D. Saklofske (Eds.), *Measures of personality & social psychological constructs* (pp. 684-718). Cambridge, MA: Elsevier/Academic Press.

Forbes, G. B., Adams-Curtis, L. E., & White, K. B. (2004). First- and second-generation measures of sexism, rape myths and related beliefs, and hostility toward women. Their interrelationships and association with college students' experiences with dating aggression and sexual coercion. *Violence against Women*, *10*(3), 236–261.

Franzoi, S. L. (2001). Is female body esteem shaped by benevolent sexism? *Sex Roles*, *44*(3–4), 177–188.

Fredrickson, B. L., & Roberts, T. A. (1997). Objectification theory. *Psychology of Women Quarterly*, *21*(2), 173–206.

Gervais, S. J., & Hillard, A. L. (2011). A role congruity perspective on prejudice toward Hillary Clinton and Sarah Palin. *Analyses of Social Issues and Public Policy*, *11*(1), 221–240.

Gervais, S. J., Hillard, A. L., & Vescio, T. K. (2010). Confronting sexism: The role of relationship orientation and gender. *Sex Roles*, *63*(7–8), 463–474.

Glick, P., Diebold, J., Bailey-Werner, B., & Zhu, L. (1997). The two faces of Adam: Ambivalent sexism and polarized attitudes toward women. *Personality and Social Psychology Bulletin*, *23*, 1323–1334.

Glick, P., & Fiske, S. T. (1996). The Ambivalent Sexism Inventory: Differentiating hostile and benevolent sexism. *Journal of Personality and Social Psychology*, *70*(3), 491–512.

Glick, P., & Fiske, S. T. (1999). The ambivalence toward men inventory. *Psychology of Women Quarterly*, *23*(3), 519–536.

Glick, P., Fiske, S. T., Mladinic, A., Saiz, J. L., Abrams, D., Masser, B. ... & López, W. L. (2000). Beyond prejudice as simple antipathy: Hostile and benevolent sexism across cultures. *Journal of Personality and Social Psychology*, *79*(5), 763–775.

Glick, P., Lameiras, M., Fiske, S. T., Eckes, T., Masser, B., Volpato, C. ... & Wells, R. (2004). Bad but bold: Ambivalent attitudes toward men predict gender inequality in 16 nations. *Journal of Personality and Social Psychology*, *86*(5), 713–728.

Glick, P., Sakallı-Uğurlu, N., Ferreira, M. C., & de Souza, M. A. (2002). Ambivalent sexism and attitudes toward wife abuse in Turkey and Brazil. *Psychology of Women Quarterly*, *26*(4), 292–297.

Glick, P., & Whitehead, J. (2010). Hostility toward men and the perceived stability of male dominance. *Social Psychology*, *41*(3), 177–185.

Good, J. J., Moss-Racusin, C. A., & Sanchez, D. T. (2012). When do we confront? Perceptions of costs and benefits predict confronting discrimination on behalf of the self and others. *Psychology of Women Quarterly*, *36*, 210–226.

Hammond, M. D., & Overall, N. C. (2013). Men's hostile sexism and biased perceptions of intimate partners: Fostering dissatisfaction and negative behavior in close relationships. *Personality and Social Psychology Bulletin*, *39*(12), 1585–1599.

Hammond, M. D., & Sibley, C. G. (2011). Why are benevolent sexists happier? *Sex Roles*, *65*(5–6), 332–343.

Hammond, M. D, Sibley, C. G, & Overall, N. C. (2013). The allure of sexism: Psychological entitlement fosters women's endorsement of benevolent sexism over time. *Social Psychological and Personality Science*, *5*(4), 422–429.

Harber, K. D. (1998). Feedback to minorities: Evidence of a positive bias. *Journal of Personality and Social Psychology*, *74*(3), 622–628.

Hausmann, R., Tyson, L. D., Bekhouche, Y., & Zahidi, S. (2014). *The global gender gap report*. Geneva, Switzerland: World Economic Forum.

Hayes, E. R., & Swim, J. K. (2013). African, Asian, Latina/o, and European Americans' responses to popular measures of sexist beliefs: Some cautionary notes. *Psychology of Women Quarterly*, *37*(2), 155–166.

Heilman, M. E. (2001). Description and prescription: How gender stereotypes prevent women's ascent up the organizational ladder. *Journal of Social Issues*, *57*(4), 657–674.

Heilman, M. E., Wallen, A. S., Fuchs, D., & Tamkins, M. M. (2004). Penalties for success: Reactions to women who succeed at male gender-typed tasks. *Journal of Applied Psychology, 89*(3), 416–427.

Holcomb, J. E., Williams, M. R., & Demuth, S. (2004). White female victims and death penalty disparity research. *Justice Quarterly, 21*(4), 877–902.

Hyers, L. L. (2007). Resisting prejudice every day: Exploring women's assertive responses to anti-Black racism, anti-Semitism, heterosexism, and sexism. *Sex Roles, 56*(1–2), 1–12.

Jackman, M. R. (1994). *The velvet glove.* Berkeley: University of California Press.

Johnson, C., Dowd, T. J., & Ridgeway, C. L. (2006). Legitimacy as a social process. *Annual Review of Sociology, 32*, 53–78.

Johnson, M. P. (2006). Conflict and control: Gender symmetry and asymmetry in domestic violence. *Violence against Women, 12*(11), 1003–1018.

Jost, J. T., Banaji, M. R., & Nosek, B. A. (2004). A decade of system justification theory: Accumulated evidence of conscious and unconscious bolstering of the status quo. *Political Psychology, 25*(6), 881–919.

Jost, J. T., & Kay, A. C. (2005). Exposure to benevolent sexism and complementary gender stereotypes: Consequences for specific and diffuse forms of system justification. *Journal of Personality and Social Psychology, 88*(3), 498–509.

Kaiser, C. R., & Miller, C. T. (2001). Stop complaining! The social costs of making attributions to discrimination. *Personality and Social Psychology Bulletin, 27*(2), 254–263.

Kay, A. C., & Jost, J. T. (2003). Complementary justice: Effects of "poor but happy" and "poor but honest" stereotype exemplars on system justification and implicit activation of the justice motive. *Journal of Personality and Social Psychology, 85*(5), 823–837.

Kilianski, S. E., & Rudman, L. A. (1998). Wanting it both ways: Do women approve of benevolent sexism? *Sex Roles, 39*(5–6), 333–352.

King, E. B., Botsford, W., Hebl, M. R., Kazama, S., Dawson, J. F., & Perkins, A. (2012). Benevolent sexism at work: Gender differences in the distribution of challenging developmental experiences. *Journal of Management, 38*(6), 1835–1866.

Lauritsen, J. L., & Heimer, K. (2008). The gender gap in violent victimization, 1973–2004 *Journal of Quantitative Criminology, 24*(2), 125–147.

Lonsway, K. A., & Fitzgerald, L. F. (1994). Rape myths in review. *Psychology of Women Quarterly, 18*, 133–164.

Maass, A., Cadinu, M., Guarnieri, G., & Grasselli, A. (2003). Sexual harassment under social identity threat: The computer harassment paradigm. *Journal of Personality and Social Psychology, 85*(5), 853–870.

Masser, B., & Abrams, D. (2004). Reinforcing the glass ceiling: The consequences of hostile sexism for female managerial candidates. *Sex Roles, 51*(9–10), 609–615.

Masser, B., Lee, K., & McKimmie, B. M. (2010). Bad woman, bad victim? Disentangling the effects of victim stereotypicality, gender stereotypicality and benevolent sexism on acquaintance rape victim blame. *Sex Roles, 62*(7–8), 494–504.

Masser, B., Viki, G. T., & Power, C. (2006). Hostile sexism and rape proclivity amongst men. *Sex Roles, 54*(7–8), 565–574.

Moya, M., Glick, P., Expósito, F., de Lemus, S., & Hart, J. (2007). It's for your own good: Benevolent sexism and women's reactions to protectively justified restrictions. *Personality and Social Psychology Bulletin, 33*(10), 1421–1434.

Nadler, A. (2002). Inter–group helping relations as power relations: Maintaining or challenging social dominance between groups through helping. *Journal of Social Issues, 58*(3), 487–502.

Napier, J. L., Thorisdottir, H., & Jost, J. T. (2010). The joy of sexism? A multinational investigation of hostile and benevolent justifications for gender inequality and their relation to subjective well-being. *Sex Roles, 62*(7–8), 405–419.

Okimoto, T. G., & Brescoll, V. L. (2010). The price of power: Power seeking and backlash against female politicians. *Personality and Social Psychology Bulletin, 36*(7), 923–936.

Oswald, D. L., Franzoi, S. L., & Frost, K. A. (2012). Experiencing sexism and young women's body esteem. *Journal of Social and Clinical Psychology, 31*(10), 1112–1137.

Overall, N. C., Sibley, C. G., & Tan, R. (2011). The costs and benefits of sexism: Resistance to influence during relationship conflict. *Journal of Personality and Social Psychology, 101*(2), 271–290.

Parker, K., Horowitz, J. M., Wang, W., Brown, A., & Patten, E. (2015). *Women and leadership*. Washington, DC: Pew Research Center.

Phelan, J. E., Moss-Racusin, C. A., & Rudman, L. A. (2008). Competent yet out in the cold: Shifting criteria for hiring reflect backlash toward agentic women. *Psychology of Women Quarterly, 32*(4), 406–413.

Prentice, D. A., & Carranza, E. (2002). What women and men should be, shouldn't be, are allowed to be, and don't have to be: The contents of prescriptive gender stereotypes. *Psychology of Women Quarterly, 26*(4), 269–281.

Ridgeway, C. L., & Correll, S. J. (2004). Unpacking the gender system: A theoretical perspective on gender beliefs and social relations. *Gender & Society, 18*(4), 510–531.

Rudman, L. A. (1998). Self-promotion as a risk factor for women: The costs and benefits of counterstereotypical impression management. *Journal of Personality and Social Psychology, 74*(3), 629–645.

Rudman, L. A., & Fairchild, K. (2004). Reactions to counterstereotypic behavior: The role of backlash in cultural stereotype maintenance. *Journal of Personality and Social Psychology, 87*(2), 157–176.

Rudman, L. A., & Glick, P. (1999). Feminized management and backlash toward agentic women: The hidden costs to women of a kinder, gentler image of middle managers. *Journal of Personality and Social Psychology, 77*(5), 1004–1010.

Rudman, L. A., & Glick, P. (2001). Prescriptive gender stereotypes and backlash toward agentic women. *Journal of Social Issues, 57*(4), 743–762.

Rudman, L. A., & Heppen, J. B. (2003). Implicit romantic fantasies and women's interest in personal power: A glass slipper effect? *Personality and Social Psychology Bulletin, 29*(11), 1357–1370.

Rudman, L. A., & Mescher, K. (2012). Of animals and objects: Men's implicit dehumanization of women and likelihood of sexual aggression. *Personality and Social Psychology Bulletin, 38*(6), 734–746.

Rudman, L. A., & Kilianski, S. E. (2000). Implicit and explicit attitudes toward female authority. *Personality and Social Psychology Bulletin, 26*(11), 1315–1328.

Rudman, L. A., Moss-Racusin, C. A., Glick, P., & Phelan, J. E. (2012). Reactions to vanguards: Advances in backlash theory. In P. G. Devine & E. A. Plant (Eds.), *Advances in experimental social psychology* (Vol. *45*, pp.167–227). San Diego, CA: Academic Press.

Russell, B. L., & Trigg, K. Y. (2004). Tolerance of sexual harassment: An examination of gender differences, ambivalent sexism, social dominance, and gender roles. *Sex Roles, 50*(7–8), 565–573.

Sakallı, N. (2001). Beliefs about wife beating among Turkish college students: The effects of patriarchy, sexism, and sex differences. *Sex Roles, 44*(9–10), 599–610.

Sakallı-Uğurlu, N., & Beydogan, B. (2002). Turkish college students' attitudes toward women managers: The effects of patriarchy, sexism, and gender differences. *Journal of Psychology, 136*(6), 647–656.

Sakallı-Uğurlu, N., & Glick, P. (2003). Ambivalent sexism and attitudes toward women who engage in premarital sex in Turkey. *Journal of Sex Research, 40*(3), 296–302.

Sakallı-Uğurlu, N., Salman, S., & Turgut, S. (2010). Predictors of Turkish women's and men's attitudes toward sexual harassment: Ambivalent sexism, and ambivalence toward men. *Sex Roles, 63*(11–12), 871–881.

Shepherd, M., Erchull, M. J., Rosner, A., Taubenberger, L., Queen, E.F., & McKee, J. (2011). "I'll get that for you": The relationship between benevolent sexism and body self-perceptions. *Sex Roles, 64*(1–2), 1–8.

Shelton, J. N., & Stewart, R. E. (2004). Confronting perpetrators of prejudice: The inhibitory effects of social costs. *Psychology of Women Quarterly, 28*(3), 215–223.

Sibley, C. G., & Becker, J. C. (2012). On the nature of sexist ambivalence: Profiling ambivalent and univalent sexists. *European Journal of Social Psychology, 42*(5), 589–601.

Sibley, C. G., Overall, N. C., & Duckitt, J. (2007). When women become more hostilely sexist toward their gender: The system-justifying effect of benevolent sexism. *Sex Roles, 57*(9–10), 743–754.

Sibley, C. G., & Wilson, M. S. (2004). Differentiating hostile and benevolent sexist attitudes toward positive and negative sexual female subtypes. *Sex Roles, 51*(11–12), 687–696.

Sibley, C. G., Wilson, M. S., & Duckitt, J. (2007). Antecedents of men's hostile and benevolent sexism: The dual roles of social dominance orientation and right-wing authoritarianism. *Personality and Social Psychology Bulletin, 33*(2), 160–172.

Vescio, T. K., Gervais, S. J., Snyder, M., & Hoover, A. (2005). Power and the creation of patronizing environments: The stereotype-based behaviors of the powerful and their effects on female performance in masculine domains. *Journal of Personality and Social Psychology, 88*(4), 658–672.

Viki, G. T., & Abrams, D. (2003). Infra-humanization: Ambivalent sexism and the attribution of primary and secondary emotions to women. *Journal of Experimental Social Psychology, 39*(5), 492–499.

Viki, G. T., Abrams, D., & Masser, B. M. (2004). Evaluating stranger and acquaintance rape: The role of benevolent sexism in perpetrator blame and recommended sentence length. *Law and Human Behavior, 28*(3), 295–303.

Wood, J. T. (2004). Monsters and victims: Male felons' accounts of intimate partner violence. *Journal of Social and Personal Relationships*, *21*(5), 555–576.

World Health Organization. (2013). *Global and regional estimates of violence against women*. Geneva, Switzerland: WHO.

Yamawaki, N. (2007). Rape perception and the function of ambivalent sexism and gender-role traditionality. *Journal of Interpersonal Violence*, *22*(4), 406–423.

Yamawaki, N., Darby, R., & Queiroz, A. (2007). The moderating role of ambivalent sexism: The influence of power status on perception of rape victim and rapist. *Journal of Social Psychology*, *147*(1), 41–56.

Zawadzki, M. J., Shields, S. A., Danube, C. L., & Swim, J. K. (2013). Reducing the endorsement of sexism using experiential learning: The workshop activity for gender equity simulation (WAGES). *Psychology of Women Quarterly*, *38*(1), 75–92.

14 Sexism in Intimate Contexts: How Romantic Relationships Help Explain the Origins, Functions, and Consequences of Sexist Attitudes

Matthew D. Hammond and Nickola C. Overall

How can we characterize and understand the relationship between men and women? One answer to this question involves group membership, including the relative social roles men and women "ought to" occupy and thus the extent to which men versus women hold status and power in society. Another involves intimate heterosexual relationships, such as how men and women "ought to" care for each other in their close, personal relationships. These answers highlight the complexities of the relationship between men and women, which can be considered as both intergroup and competitive and interpersonal and cooperative.

As outlined by ambivalent sexism theory (Glick & Fiske, 1996, 2001) these conflicting concerns of power and intimacy produce two related forms of sexist attitudes toward women (see Connor, Glick, & Fiske, Chapter 13, this title). *Hostile sexism* encompasses competitive attitudes that cast women as incompetent, overly emotional, and attempting to unfairly undermine men's power. These attitudes reinforce men's advantaged societal status by threatening and denigrating women who could challenge men's power. However, protecting societal-level advantages in this manner comes at the expense of men attaining security and satisfaction within intimate heterosexual relationships. *Benevolent sexism* arises to offset these costs and facilitate men's relationship needs. Benevolent sexism characterizes the relationship between men and women as mutually beneficial and based on complementary traits and social roles: Men are "completed" by cherishing and protecting female partners who, in turn, adopt the role of warm, supportive caregivers.

In their chapter, Connor et al. examined how ambivalent attitudes restrict women's political, economic, and personal power. On the basis of that foundational chapter, here we take a more fine-grained look at the central role that dynamics within romantic relationships play in the emergence, functions, and consequences of hostile and benevolent sexism toward women. Tables 14.1 and 14.2 summarize

Table 14.1 *Summary of key points demonstrating that intimate relationships are central to understanding the emergence, function, and consequences of men's sexist attitudes toward women.*

Chapter Section	Key Points Derived from Ambivalent Sexism Theory and Associated Research
Men's Hostile Sexism and Intimate Relationships	• Hostile sexism stems from competition between men and women and expresses aggressive attitudes toward women who are perceived to be a threat to men's power. • Mutual interdependence in close relationships means that hostile sexism is an ineffective way to (a) influence women and (b) fulfill men's relationship needs and goals, which depend on women's cooperation. • Fears that women will exploit men's dependence trigger aggressive responses toward intimate partners by men who strongly endorse hostile sexism. • Negative perceptions and aggressive behavior associated with men's hostile sexism elicit resistance from female partners and undermine relationship satisfaction and stability. • Thus, men cannot both protect their power in intimate relationships and attain their relationship needs and goals, which is a key reason why benevolent forms of sexism exist.
Men's Benevolent Sexism and Intimate Relationships	• Benevolent sexism stems from the need for intimacy between men and women and expresses subjectively positive evaluations and care toward women who fulfill these needs. • Benevolent sexism offers a romantic, idealized version of heterosexual intimacy where men cherish, protect, and provide for women who adopt supportive, caregiving roles. • This positive depiction of intimate relationships disguises the ways in which benevolent sexism perpetuates men's power while facilitating the fulfillment of men's relationships needs. • Men who endorse benevolent sexism are appealing to women as relationship partners and also behave in ways that facilitate the fulfillment of men's intimacy and relatedness needs. • Men's benevolent sexism also functions to maintain and promote men's power by (a) shaping relationship interactions in ways that undermine women's competence and (b) withdrawing praise and protection from women who do not conform to benevolently sexist ideals.

the principles derived from ambivalent sexism theory and associated research that we review in this chapter. We begin by examining men's endorsement of hostile and benevolent sexism (Table 14.1). We first outline the difficulties that men's hostile sexism creates in romantic relationships and consider how these deficits necessitate benevolent sexism. We then consider the ways men's benevolent

Table 14.2 *Summary of key points demonstrating that intimate relationships are central to understanding the emergence, function, and consequences of women's sexist attitudes toward women.*

Chapter Section	Key Points Derived from Ambivalent Sexism Theory and Associated Research
Women's Benevolent Sexism and Intimate Relationships	• Benevolent sexism is appealing to women; women adopt and endorse benevolent sexism because it promises protection, provision, and reverence to women. • The benefits that benevolent sexism promises to women are primarily delivered by intimate partners, which means that women's endorsement of benevolent sexism is shaped and maintained by perceiving that their partner endorses benevolent sexism. • Women's endorsement of benevolent sexism plays a key role in maintaining gender inequality through fostering women's investment in traditional, relationship-focused roles. • Women's endorsement of benevolent sexism also has relationship costs, including women becoming more vulnerable if the promises of benevolent sexism are unfulfilled. • Thus, even though the content of benevolent sexism idealizes intimate relationships, it ultimately functions to provide men advantages at the cost of women's independence and well-being.
Women's Hostile Sexism and Intimate Relationships	• Women's endorsement of benevolent sexism also fosters stronger hostile attitudes toward women, but we know little about the origins or functions of women's hostile sexism. • Women may strongly endorse hostile sexism in contexts of competition with other women, such as when depending on an intimate partner means that women in nontraditional roles are threatening to their own relationship position and well-being, or when women compete with other women in dating domains. • Women's hostile sexism has puzzling effects in romantic relationships, such as lower desires for warm, romantic partners and greater satisfaction even when faced with relationship problems. • Women's hostile sexism may foster relationship dependence by enabling favorable downward comparisons to other women which enhance self- and relationship worth.

sexism functions within intimate relationships to facilitate men's intimacy needs while maintaining and promoting their power. In the second half of the chapter, we turn to women's endorsement of benevolent and hostile sexism (Table 14.2). We review evidence showing that the relationship structure promised by benevolent sexism is appealing to women but has harmful personal and relationship consequences for them. We then offer a more speculative account of the role and impact of women's endorsement of hostile sexism. At the end of the chapter, we consider other ways in which relationship processes can inform our understanding of sexist attitudes toward women and outline important future research directions.

Men's Hostile Sexism and Intimate Relationships

It is not surprising that men's hostile attitudes toward women create difficulties in intimate heterosexual relationships. A key reason for these difficulties is that hostile sexism clashes with the mutual interdependence that exists in heterosexual relationships; men and women depend on each other for the fulfillment of key needs (e.g., intimacy, support, reproduction). Indeed, the more that people care for and commit to their relationship partners, the more their future goals and happiness depend on the partner's continued love and investment (Kelley & Thibaut, 1978; Rusbult & Buunk, 1993). Even in unequal societies, such interdependence gives women power in relationships (at least more power than they have outside the home). Thus, unlike at the societal level where men typically have more social power, men are as dependent as women in intimate relationships for the fulfillment of relationship needs and desires.

Mutual interdependence and the resulting dyadic power women hold in intimate relationships are critical to understanding the emergence, function, and consequences of sexist attitudes. First, the ability for women to influence and resist influence in intimate contexts challenges the power that men who endorse hostile sexism strive to attain. Second, the potential for women to hold power over men elicits aggressive responses from men who endorse hostile sexism. Such responses not only damage relationships but also undermine men's ability to achieve their relationship goals. It is precisely these relationship costs that make benevolent sexism a crucial counterpart to hostile sexism, working within intimate contexts to maintain men's power. Following, we examine each of these premises by reviewing research investigating how the content and effects of sexist attitudes shape and are shaped by intimate relationships (see upper section of Table 14.1).

Aggressive and threatening attitudes directed at women who could challenge men's power are at the heart of hostile sexism. Hostile sexism portrays the relationship between men and women as a competition over power, describing women as threatening men's power "by getting control over men" and using the "guise of equality" to get ahead of men (Ambivalent Sexism Inventory; Glick & Fiske, 1996). Accordingly, hostile sexism tends to target women who challenge men's societal dominance. For example, men who endorse hostile sexism evaluate feminists and career women more negatively but do not view homemakers more negatively (Glick, Diebold, Bailey-Werner, & Zhu, 1997). Although hostile sexism may often be directed toward women who challenge men's societal-level power, these power concerns also manifest at the interpersonal level as warnings that women will exploit men's relational dependence to subvert men's power. For example, hostile sexism expresses fears that women will seek to humiliate or manipulate men in relationships by "seeming sexually available and then refusing male advances" or putting men "on a tight leash" (Ambivalent Sexism Inventory; Glick & Fiske, 1996).

Indeed, a growing body of research demonstrates that rather than the power concerns associated with hostile sexism being restricted to maintaining dominance outside the home, the inevitable dependence experienced within relationships is threatening and triggers men's attempts to sustain power and control. Hostile sexism encompasses beliefs that men are shamed if they lose dominance in their relationship (Chen, Fiske, & Lee, 2009), and men who endorse hostile sexism express greater fears of intimacy (Yakushko, 2005). Stronger endorsement of hostile sexism is also associated with more punitive attitudes toward partners who are seen to be challenging men's authority (e.g., partners who "do not behave well should be treated severely"; Chen et al., 2009, p. 771) and a greater acceptance of violent behavior and verbal aggression toward intimate partners (Forbes, Adams-Curtis, & White, 2004; Forbes, Jobe, White, Bloesch, & Adams-Curtis, 2005; Yamawaki, Ostenson, & Brown, 2009; also see Connor, Glick, & Fiske, Chapter 13, this title).

Evidence also suggests that such aggressive relationship responses are due to power-relevant concerns and associated negative perceptions of female partner's intentions. Men who endorse hostile sexism experience heightened dissatisfaction when their relationships are marked by conflict and disagreement, which is precisely when challenges to power are at the fore (Hammond & Overall, 2013a). In addition, when couples are trying to influence each other during conflict discussions, men who strongly endorse hostile sexism are less open to their partner's perspective and exhibit greater aggressive communication (Overall, Sibley, & Tan, 2011). Moreover, biased by fears that women seek to exploit men's dependence, men who more strongly endorse hostile sexism see common relationship behaviors, such as criticism and affection, more negatively (i.e., more critical and less affectionate) than they actually are (Hammond & Overall, 2013a; also see Herrera, Expósito, & Moya, 2012). These negatively biased perceptions, in turn, result in men who strongly endorse hostile sexism, feeling more manipulated by their partners, experiencing less satisfaction in their relationship, and behaving more aggressively toward their partners (Hammond & Overall, 2013a).

Not surprisingly, the negative relationship perceptions and aggressive behavior associated with men's hostile sexism is damaging to relationships (see Fletcher, Simpson, Campbell, & Overall, 2013). Highlighting the importance of dyadic interdependence, however, the destructive relationship effects of men's hostile sexism rest on how men's concerns over being manipulated or controlled prompt destructive and defensive attempts to protect power, which are resisted by female partners. For example, the aggressive communication exhibited by men who endorse hostile sexism elicits greater defensiveness and hostility from their female partners, and in turn men who endorse hostile sexism are less able to obtain the changes they want in their relationship (Overall et al., 2011). Thus, ideologies that punish women who challenge men's power are inevitably undermined by the interdependencies that exist between men and women within intimate relationships. Hostile sexism is not an effective form of control in relationships because the resistance that is evoked in female partners means that men cannot both protect their power and attain their relationship needs and goals. Moreover, the destructive consequences of efforts to protect power undermine the satisfaction of both partners and place relationships at risk of dissolution.

Men's Benevolent Sexism and Intimate Relationships

The reactance and damage hostile sexism creates in intimate relationships are precisely why benevolent sexism exists. Rather than fight against women's dyadic power, benevolent sexism acknowledges heterosexual men's reliance on women for the fulfillment of their relational needs, such as emotional closeness, sexual intimacy, and reproduction (Glick & Fiske, 1996). Benevolent sexism presents an idealized version of heterosexual relationships by expressing that men are only "complete" when they have the love of a woman and that men's role is to cherish, protect, and provide for the women in their lives. Benevolent sexism also positively differentiates women from men, such as revering women's sensitivity, empathy, and communal orientation. Of importance, however, the reverence of women's interpersonal qualities and relationship-based roles expressed by benevolent sexism continues to position women as lower in status than men, which creates relationship interactions that undermine women's competence. Moreover, benevolent sexism also reduces the degree to which women's dyadic power can challenge men's societal power by only offering reverence, provision, and protection to women who conform to benevolently sexist prescriptions and therefore support and accept men holding advantaged control over societal power. Thus, as we describe later (and summarized in the lower section of Table 14.1), the subjectively positive depictions of men and women in intimate relationships disguises the ways in which benevolent sexism maintains gender inequality from within intimate contexts.

The content of benevolent sexism expresses a romanticized and idealized version of heterosexual intimacy in which men are gallant protectors of women. Benevolent sexism overlaps with prescriptions of chivalry in dating contexts, such as men paying on a first date (Viki, Abrams, & Hutchinson, 2003), being protective toward intimate partners (Sarlet, Dumont, Delacollette, & Dardenne, 2012), and romantic ideals that couples are destined to be together and should be able to read each other's minds (Hammond & Overall, 2013b; Hart, Hung, Glick, & Dinero, 2012). Indeed, the promise to "love and cherish" in traditional wedding vows is similar to the prescription that "women should be cherished and protected by men." Critically, however, benevolent prescriptions involve specific relationship roles in which men bear the responsibility to provide for women who, in return, should be supportive caregivers. By suffusing romantic ideals about men's and women's relationship roles, benevolent sexism puts up a subjectively positive façade that is harder to detect as sexist than hostile sexism (Barreto & Ellemers, 2005; Riemer, Chaudoir, & Earnshaw, 2014), behind which benevolent sexism provides two central advantages for men: (a) facilitating the attainment of men's relationship needs and goals while (b) supporting men's power by withdrawing protection from women who do not adopt traditional gender norms.

The romantic tone of benevolent sexism is successful in promoting men's access to satisfying relationships. Men who are described as endorsing benevolently sexist attitudes are considered relatively attractive partners by women (Bohner, Ahlborn, & Steiner, 2010; Kilianski & Rudman, 1998). Moreover, men's agreement with benevolent sexism is associated with a range of positive relationship outcomes, from more friendly interactions when meeting new women (Goh & Hall, 2015) to greater relationship satisfaction in long-term, committed relationships (Hammond & Overall, 2013b; Sibley & Becker, 2012). Consistent with the idealized portrayal of relationships, one reason men who endorse benevolent sexism are more satisfied is that men's benevolent sexism promotes more rose-colored views of intimate partners. For example, Hammond and Overall (2013a) found that men who more strongly endorsed benevolent sexism interpreted their female partners' daily behaviors as relatively less critical and more caring than they actually were. A second reason that men are more fulfilled in relationship contexts, however, is that men's benevolent sexism leads to more positive, caring behavior that is successful at influencing interdependent partners. Men who endorse benevolent sexism are more open to their partner and express lower hostility during conflict discussions, which facilitates greater happiness and cooperation in their partners (Overall et al., 2011).

However, the subjectively positive responses enacted by men who endorse benevolent sexism are nonetheless infused by a representation that women should be cared for because they need help and are less capable than men. Even though such benevolently sexist expressions carry a caring or romantic flavor, they undermine and restrict women's competence and thus promote men's high-status position. Outside of relationship contexts, for example, offers of help coated in expressions of benevolent sexism, such as men saying "don't worry, male co-workers will cooperate and help you to get used to the job," interfere with women's task performance and reduce women's feelings of competence (Dardenne, Dumont, & Bollier, 2007, p. 767; also see Barreto, Ellemers, Piebinga, & Moya, 2010; Salomon, Burgess, & Bosson, 2015). Behavioral expressions of benevolent sexism from romantic partners also function this way and may have a greater impact given the ongoing nature of couples' interactions. For example, men who endorse benevolent sexism are more likely to take over their female partners' goal pursuits by providing plans and solutions while ignoring their partners' own abilities to strive and achieve their goals (Hammond & Overall, 2015; also see Shnabel, Bar-Anan, Kende, Bareket, & Lazar, 2016). This type of support leads partners to feel less goal-related competence (Hammond & Overall, 2015), revealing that men's "protect and provide" behaviors that are prompted by benevolent sexism impinge on women's efficacy and thus will likely undermine women's ability to achieve independent success.

As outlined in the prior chapter (Connor, Glick, & Fiske, Chapter 13), another way that benevolent sexism works to maintain women's lower status and social power is by offering reverence and protection to women conditional on women's conformity to traditional gender norms. In particular, the care and protection promised by benevolent sexism for women who embody loyal, warm relationship roles accompanies harsh, punitive evaluations of women who do not. Although men who endorse benevolent sexism are generally intolerant of violence toward women (e.g., Obeid, Chang, & Ginges, 2010; Sakalli, 2001), men who endorse benevolent sexism attribute relatively more blame to the victims of rape when those victims are portrayed as being unfaithful to partners (Abrams, Viki, Masser, & Bohner, 2003; Viki & Abrams, 2002). Similarly, in scenarios in which husbands rape their wives, participants attributed relatively more blame to the wives when husbands were described as endorsing benevolent sexism (Durán, Moya, Megías, & Viki, 2010). One impetus for why benevolent sexism, rather than hostile sexism, is linked with negative evaluations of women who do not conform to traditional relationship ideals is men's investment in building and maintaining relationships, such as placing women "on a pedestal" and being "willing to sacrifice their own well-being" for partners (Ambivalent Sexism Inventory; Glick & Fiske, 1996). All of these efforts to protect and care for women appear to provide men who endorse benevolent sexism the pretext for harsh retaliation when women do not meet their expected ideals.

In sum, benevolent sexism arises to offset the pitfalls of men's hostile sexism within interdependent heterosexual relationships (see Table 14.1). Men's endorsement of benevolent sexism involves an idealization of romantic relationships involving men who adopt a gallant provider role being completed by women who adopt the complementary role of managing the relationship and domestic domains. The romantic prescriptions associated with benevolent sexism mean that men are considered to be relatively appealing relationship partners and approach relationship interactions with openness and positivity. However, the caring expressions of benevolent sexism are (a) weighted by paternalistic offers of help that restrict women's personal competencies and (b) replaced by harsh treatment when women do not meet benevolently sexist standards of loyalty and interpersonal warmth. Both of these relationship-level pathways ultimately reinforce the societal-level stereotypes that women are interpersonally warm but incompetent, therefore perpetuating men's advantaged high-status position. Thus, key ways that benevolent sexism functions to maintain gender inequality occur within intimate relationships. In addition, as we discuss next, these functions are particularly powerful because the relationship promises that perpetuate men's societal power also persuade women to endorse benevolent sexism.

Women's Benevolent Sexism and Intimate Relationships

A principal reason benevolent sexism is so effective at sustaining gender inequalities is because its romantic appeal entices women to accept and invest in men's advantaged access to societal power. As we summarized in the upper section of Table 14.2, the promise that men will prioritize intimate relationships and be devoted and caring providers is central to persuading women to support men's careers and societal advantages. Importantly, women's revered and protected position is offered within intimate relationships by their male partners, which means that women adopt benevolent sexism when their intimate partners endorse benevolent sexism. Women's internalization of benevolent sexism is particularly important in sustaining gender inequality because it encourages women to invest in their relationships rather than their careers or independent success, which fosters dependence on their partner's career successes and status. Moreover, because benevolent sexism encourages women to invest in their relationship at the expense of their own achievements outside the home, when their relationships fall short of benevolent ideals (as they realistically will), women who endorse benevolent sexism experience heightened dissatisfaction. Thus, women's endorsement of benevolent sexism not only restricts their aspirations, it also makes women particularly dependent on their relationships and more vulnerable when relationships do not go well. In the following sections, we lay out the theoretical and empirical underpinning of these claims (also see Table 14.2).

How Relationships Foster and Sustain Women's Benevolent Sexism. The appeal for women's adoption and endorsement of benevolent sexism rests on its romantic promises that women will be protected, revered, and provided for by their male intimate partners. These promises are particularly appealing to women because of their disadvantaged access to career success and legal power and the existence of aggression toward women to sustain their low-power position (Glick & Fiske, 1996; Jackman, 1994). For example, women's endorsement of benevolent attitudes is highest in countries with the greatest gender inequality and most prevalent levels of violence toward women (Brandt, 2011; Glick et al., 2000). In addition, priming women with threatening information that men hold aggressive attitudes toward women increases women's agreement with benevolent sexism (Fischer, 2006). These findings suggest that women are motivated to adopt benevolent sexism in the face of aggression toward women because of the prescriptions that "men should protect women." Of course, the promise of protection has been described as a protection racket because benevolent sexism legitimizes violence toward women when they are not deemed to be chaste, loyal partners (as we described earlier) and provides a justification for hostile sexism by defining the behaviors and traits that are "acceptable" for women (Glick & Fiske, 2001; also see Connor, Glick, & Fiske, Chapter 13, this title). Thus, women's endorsement of benevolent sexism works to uphold the existing acceptance of men's aggression toward nontraditional women.

Benevolent sexism is not just appealing because of the protection it offers but also because of the prescriptions that men should care for, cherish, and revere women. Thus, even in highly egalitarian countries in which security against violence is provided by legal protection and normative intolerance of aggression toward women, benevolent sexism continues to be attractive to women. First, even in relatively egalitarian countries women face greater discrimination than men and less opportunity for career achievements (United Nations Development Programme, 2014). The promise of a strong, caring provider should be appealing to women when the reality of career paths makes it easier for men than women to succeed. Second, the qualities of warmth and trustworthiness prescribed by benevolent sexism reflect the most important and desirable qualities that people report in a romantic partner (Buss, 1988; Fletcher, Simpson, Thomas, & Giles, 1999), meaning that the promise of an adoring and dedicated partner is an important enticement for women because it is a heightened version of qualities that are attractive to almost everyone.

A growing body of research confirms that the personal benefits promised by benevolent sexism encourage women's endorsement of benevolent sexism. Women agree more with benevolently sexist attitudes that are personally phrased (e.g., "I should be set on a pedestal by my man") compared to when those same attitudes express benefits to women in general (e.g., "career women should be set on a pedestal"; Becker, 2010). Similarly, women (but not men) who believe that they are more deserving of praise and material gains (i.e., high in psychological entitlement) demonstrate greater endorsement of benevolent sexism both concurrently and increasingly over time (Hammond, Sibley, & Overall, 2014; also see Grubbs, Exline, & Twenge, 2014). These studies suggest that the appeal of benevolent sexism to women is the benefits it prescribes, including attaining financial support, praise, and (dyadic) power. Given that psychological entitlement is higher in Western countries (Twenge & Campbell, 2010) and women need less protection when societal norms renounce overtly sexist attitudes, this motivation for endorsing benevolent sexism may be critical in sustaining benevolent sexism in relatively egalitarian contexts.

Regardless of which aspect of benevolent sexism has the most appeal, the promised protection, provision, and reverence are primarily delivered within intimate relationship by male partners. This fact has an important implication – intimate relationships should be a primary domain in which women should be allured into agreeing with benevolent sexism (Jackman, 1994; Ridgeway & Smith-Lovin, 1999). In particular, benevolent sexism should be particularly enticing if women perceive that their male partner endorses benevolent sexism and will therefore provide the protection, provision, and reverence benevolent sexism offers women. In a series of recent studies, Hammond, Overall, and Cross (2016) suggest that women's internalization of benevolent sexism depends on their perceptions of their partner's benevolent sexism. Women endorsed benevolent sexism more strongly, and maintained this stronger endorsement over time, when they perceived that their male partner endorsed benevolent sexism. In contrast, women's endorsement of benevolent sexism decreased over time when they perceived that their partner did not endorse it. Experimental manipulations also supported this pattern; when women were presented with information suggesting their partner likely endorsed benevolent sexism more (versus less) than they thought, women reported subsequently stronger (versus weaker) endorsement of it. In contrast, men's agreement with benevolent sexism was not shaped by existing or manipulated perceptions of their partner's sexist attitudes across studies.

In sum, women's adoption and sustained endorsement of benevolent sexism occurs when women perceive that the care and reverence promised by benevolent sexism is accessible and likely to be provided by their intimate partners. Thus, it is the perceived availability of relationship benefits that contributes to women's internalization of sexist attitudes that, as we discuss next, ultimately serve to reinforce existing gender inequality.

The Costs of Women's Benevolent Sexism. As summarized by Connor et al. (Chapter 13, this title), women's endorsement of benevolent sexism functions to perpetuate men's societal advantages by encouraging women to invest in traditional, relationship-focused roles at the expense of pursuing independent success. Women who endorse benevolent sexism hold stronger beliefs that they should be empathetic, sensitive, and warm in their relationships and forgo their own careers to support their partner's careers (e.g., Chen et al., 2009; Lee, Fiske, Glick, & Chen, 2010). Accordingly, cross-national and meta-analytical research has shown that women who endorse benevolent sexism more strongly prefer partners who are older and who have relatively higher levels of material resources (Eastwick et al., 2006; Sibley & Overall, 2011). Women who endorse benevolent sexism also hold lower ambitions for independent success, such as lower educational and career goals (e.g., Fernández, Castro, Otero, Foltz, & Lorenzo, 2006; Sinclair, Huntsinger, Skorinko, & Hardin, 2005). The resulting dependence on their partner's career achievement and associated provision is further exacerbated by women who endorse benevolent sexism being more accepting when their partners make unjustified career decisions for them (Moya, Glick, Expósito, de Lemus, & Hart, 2007) and believing their own career success is threatening to male partners (Expósito, Herrera, Moya, & Glick, 2010).

Given these personal costs to women are an important way in which benevolent sexism sustains gender inequality, it is not surprising that the literature has primarily focused on how women's investment in relationship roles arising from benevolent sexism undermine their direct access and attainment of social resources and power. However, because benevolent sexism encourages women to put their stake in their relationship, women are more vulnerable when relationships do not go well. The realities of romantic relationships mean that couples will inevitably face disagreement or conflict. These events will likely be particularly jarring for women who expect, and are invested in, a cherished relationship role. For example, women who more strongly endorse benevolent sexism exhibit greater hostility and resistance in conflict interactions when their partners do not endorse benevolent sexism, presumably because their partners are not treating them in the way they expect (Overall et al., 2011). Women who endorse benevolent sexism accept that men have advantaged power outside the home on the premise that their investment into a relationship caretaker and homemaker role will be respected and revered. When partners do not live up to their end of the bargain, or their relationship is not the idyllic picture benevolent sexism promises, women should be much less satisfied.

Indeed, a bulk of work has shown that when relationships and partners do not match ideal standards, people evaluate their relationships more negatively (Fletcher et al., 1999), and the resulting dissatisfaction is magnified for those who possess more romanticized relationship beliefs (Knee, Patrick, & Lonsbary, 2003). More idealistic and unrealistic relationship expectations are also associated with more negative and extreme reactions to relationship problems, conflict, and hurtful partner behavior (McNulty & Karney, 2004). The prescriptions and expectations encompassed by benevolent sexism operate in the same fashion – the relationship satisfaction of women who endorse benevolent sexism is more sensitive to whether the promises of benevolent sexism are fulfilled in their relationships. Hammond and Overall (2013b) found that women who more strongly endorsed benevolent sexism were relatively more dissatisfied and hurt when facing relationship problems and daily conflicts or disagreement with their partner (also see Casad, Salazar, & Macina, 2015; Hammond & Overall, 2014).

One reason women who endorse benevolent sexism are more vulnerable to relationship difficulties is that benevolently sexist prescriptions require women to forgo personal competencies to instead focus on the relationship domain, meaning that it becomes all the more important that the relationship is successful. Moreover, when women have invested more time, effort, and resources into their relationship, and therefore the more there is to lose if the relationship dissolves, women who endorse benevolent sexism should become even more sensitive to the extent to which their concession of power to men (outside of the relationship domain) is being met by fulfillment of the promises of benevolent sexism. Accordingly, in the studies reported by Hammond and Overall (2013b), the drops in satisfaction occurring when women who endorsed benevolent sexism faced problems or conflict were magnified further in longer-term relationships.[1] In particular, the more women who endorsed benevolent sexism had invested in their relationship, the sharper their declines in relationship satisfaction when they faced relationship conflict in their daily lives. Thus, the promise of a protected, cherished, and

---

[1] Even when the relationship meets the benevolently sexist ideal, women are likely vulnerable in other ways. For example, women who have an accident that causes physical disability may no longer meet the standards of warmth and support required for the protection and provision offered by benevolent sexism (see Fine & Asch, 1981).

revered relationship position that incentivizes women's adoption of a relationship-focused role rather than pursuit of independent success also leaves women's relationship well-being more susceptible to problems and disagreement and does so the more and the longer that they invest in their relationships.

It may seem strange that benevolent sexism jeopardizes women's relationship satisfaction when (a) it is the promise of relationship benefits that entices women's agreement of these attitudes, and (b) a primary function of benevolent attitudes is to promote men's fulfillment of relational and intimacy needs, which depends on women's investment and satisfaction. However, the way in which benevolent sexism encourages intimate interdependence and legitimizes men's adoption of the provider role is by reducing women's independent opportunities and fostering reliance on the relationship. Thus, benevolent sexism is sexist because it prioritizes men's advantages over women's well-being. The epitome of this imbalance is illustrated by weighing the benefits and costs of benevolent sexism for both men and women: Men benefit from enacting the role of chival-rous provider as a function of their own benevolent sexism and associated caring behaviors. In contrast, women benefit from benevolent sexism as a function of their male partner's endorsement of its reverent attitudes and to the extent their own role embodies a warm (but not competent) ideal that is complementary to men's competent role. Thus, women remain dependent on their male partners for the benefits of benevolent sexism, and they only receive these when their male partners are willing to provide them.

Women's Hostile Sexism and Intimate Relationships

As with men's sexist attitudes, benevolent sexism and hostile sexism operate in tandem. Thus, a further way that benevolent sexism functions to maintain gender inequality is by undermining women's resistance to hostile sexism (see the lower section of Table 14.2). Women who endorse benevolent sexism are more likely to express stronger endorsement of hostile sexism over time (Sibley, Overall, & Duckitt, 2007; Sibley & Perry, 2010), suggesting that as women invest in a traditional, dependent relationship role, they are more willing to accept derogatory attitudes toward other nontraditional women. Women who invest in relationship-focused roles and traits may seem to have little impetus to hold derogatory attitudes toward women outside of relationship domains, such as career women and feminists (Becker, 2010; Glick et al., 1997). However, consider the romantic promises of benevolent sexism that describe how men and women have unique compatibility within the limits of an intimate relationship, reframing male and female intimate partners as a team. As women become invested in their male partner's opportunities to gain power, status, and resources, other women who do not adopt traditional roles represent a potential threat to their own well-being, thereby opening the door for hostile sexism. The role of relationship investment and dependence fostering women's hostile attitudes to other women is an important area of future investigation.

Other important interpersonal contexts in which women's hostile sexism may manifest most strongly are dating relationships and the early stages of relationship formation. Indeed, one study examining the development of sexist attitudes across adolescence indicates that women (but not men) who have had more relationship experience are likely to endorse hostile sexism more strongly (de Lumus, Moya, & Glick, 2010). Although we can only speculate about the underlying reasons, it is likely that women's competition with other women is an important source of hostile attitudes (as it is for men's hostile sexism; Sibley, Wilson, & Duckitt, 2007). For example, hostile sexism may be particularly appealing to women who are seeking intimate partners because hostile sexism (a) is congruous with antagonism toward female competitors and (b) helps protect self-esteem by offering a rationale for experiencing rejection as losing out to "manipulative" women. Similarly, women's exposure to, or experiences of, violence in dating contexts may prompt endorsement of hostile sexism as a way to rationalize aggressive acts and separate the self from women who "ought to" be targets of men's aggression (see Glick et al., 2000).

Understanding the origins of women's hostile sexism will also help resolve puzzling effects found in romantic relationships. For example, when women endorse hostile sexism more strongly, they report greater satisfaction in their relationship, and these higher levels of relationship satisfaction are sustained even in relationships that report high levels of problems (Hammond & Overall, 2013b). Moreover, Lee et al. (2010) found that American women who more strongly endorse hostile sexism also express relatively *lower* desire for a partner who is warm and romantic – qualities that are generally considered the most important in a partner (e.g., Fletcher et al., 1999). Why would holding hostile views of women in nontraditional roles influence women's evaluations about their own relationships and desired partners? One answer may be that women who endorse hostile sexism report more positive evaluations of their own relationships and are less selective when finding partners because they make downward comparisons to women who are not in committed relationships (e.g., Frye & Karney, 2002). Again, therefore, hostile sexism may provide a way of protecting or bolstering feelings of self- and relationship worth by enabling favorable comparisons to single women who must manipulate men or are unable to provide for themselves. As we discuss next, examining these possibilities in future investigations has important implications for understanding how sexist attitudes emerge, function, and can be reduced.

Future Research into the Interpersonal Origins and Consequences of Sexism

The bulk of this chapter has focused on existing evidence for the ways in which intimate relationships contribute to the emergence, function, and consequences of sexist attitudes toward women. The research on women's hostile sexism is sparse, however, and we raised a number of possibilities of relationship-related dynamics that would be fruitful areas of investigation. In this section, we briefly consider other ways in which relationships play a role in fostering and modifying the endorsement of sexist attitudes. For example, we discussed earlier the ways in which relationships are central to women's adoption of sexist attitudes. Intimacy-related motives may also foster men's endorsement of benevolent sexism and hostile sexism, alongside the cultural, economic, and societal factors discussed by Connor et al. (Chapter 13, this title). We have also focused on intimate romantic relationships, but familial and platonic relationships should also shape the origins and consequences of sexism. We consider these two issues, outlining important directions for future research.

The Interpersonal Origins of Men's Ambivalent Sexism. Prior research has established that individual differences in the drive to preserve the hierarchical power structure of group relations foster men's hostile sexism, whereas the drive for protecting the ingroup from harm and preserving existing traditional norms fosters men's benevolent sexism (Duckitt, 2001; Sibley, Wilson, & Duckitt, 2007). The societal-level concerns over competition and cooperation that predict greater sexism echo the ambivalent interpersonal concerns linked with sexism that we have highlighted in this chapter – men's fear over losing power when depending on women (hostile sexism) and idealization of women's capacity to complete men with their love in an intimate relationship (benevolent sexism). Thus, in addition to individual differences, the balance between competition and cooperation in men's interpersonal relationships is also likely to influence men's agreement with sexist attitudes.

Indeed, men's dependence on women for intimacy, support, and reproduction is proposed to generate benevolent sexism (Glick & Fiske, 1996; Glick & Hilt, 2000). Just as benevolent sexism appeals to women because of the promise of care and provision, benevolent sexism is also attractive to men because its chivalrous behavioral scripts and characterizations of men as gallant providers promise men a way to successfully negotiate romantic goals, such as finding a partner (Glick & Fiske, 2001; Viki et al., 2003). Some research does support that intimacy needs are indeed one motivator of men's endorsement of benevolent sexism. Men higher in attachment anxiety, who possess strong desires for intimacy and closeness, tend to endorse benevolent sexism more strongly (Hart et al., 2012), and men's endorsement of benevolent sexism is highest in adolescence and early adulthood – particularly among male teenagers who have greater relationship experience (de Lumus et al., 2010; also see Garaigordobil & Aliri, 2013; Glick & Fiske, 1996). These correlational findings suggest an important relational motivator of men's sexism: Experiencing doubts about being able to attain women's love may motivate men to endorse benevolent sexism as they look to adopt a romantically attractive identity.

In addition, if relationship desires and experiences are one pathway to benevolent sexism, they should also modify men's hostile sexism given that the same dependence and idealization of women at the heart of benevolent sexism also fosters fears about women's potential power over men (Glick & Fiske, 1996). For example, one possible interpersonal origin of hostile sexism is that it promises protection against the risks of being emotionally dependent on another person (see Murray, Holmes, & Collins, 2006). Indeed, men who are higher in attachment anxiety and harbor intense fears of being rejected and abandoned by close others express greater hostile sexism independent of concerns about men and women competing for power in society (Hart et al., 2012). Hostile sexism may offer protection against the (perceived) loss of identity and control when depending on others by perpetuating traditional masculine norms of independence, self-reliance, and dominance (e.g., Bem, 1974), and by blaming women for being emotionally unpredictable and subversive to justify dependency-related insecurities. Thus, future research may investigate how hostile sexism functions to suppress men's relational worries and protect men's identity and self-control. Of course, in this chapter we have already discussed the aggressive and destructive behaviors linked with men's hostile sexism (see also Hammond & Overall, 2013b; Overall et al., 2011). So, if endorsing hostile sexism does protect men's sense of self against the threat of relationship dependence, it does so at the expense of relationship well-being.

Sexism in Non-Romantic Interpersonal Contexts. This chapter focused on romantic heterosexual relationships in understanding the manifestation and consequences of sexist attitudes because it is within this domain in which the interdependence between men and women is greatest, and thus the strongest emotional and cognitive ambivalence exists between the need for intimacy versus the threat of abandonment (Glick & Fiske, 1996; Jackman, 1994; Ridgeway & Smith-Lovin, 1999). Nonetheless, men and women are interdependent in other interpersonal relationships, including familial bonds and close friendship circles. Consistent with our focus on romantic relationships as a primary source of individuals' adoption of sexist attitudes, parent-child associations of gender attitudes tend to be relatively weak (Tenenbaum & Leaper, 2002). Nonetheless, even though children may not adopt the same attitudes held by their parents, parent-child interactions are still likely to establish normative beliefs concerning gender and intimate relationships. Moreover, if ambivalent sexism partly arises from individuals' experiences of conflicting motives between group status and romantic relationships, then a critical period for sexist attitudes should be individuals' development from adolescence into adulthood (see Glick & Hilt, 2000). Accordingly, examining how parent-adolescent relationship dynamics contribute to the emergence, functions, and consequences of sexist attitudes is an important area for future research.

Sexist attitudes are also likely to emerge and be sustained in less intimate social networks, including school and workplace groups, neighborhoods, and religious communities. For example, non-intimate interactions play a determining role in the legitimization of sexist expressions. For example, telling sexist jokes in social circles propagates ideas that sexism is more normative and acceptable (Ford, Wentzel, & Lorion, 2001). In turn, men who more strongly endorse sexist attitudes find sexist humor more amusing and less offensive, presumably leading to repetition and propagation of those sexist ideas (Greenwood & Isbell, 2002; Thomas & Esses, 2004). Conversely, men's interpersonal interactions likely play a powerful role in confronting sexism, such as responding to a sexist remark by speaking up and challenging the speaker. Men's confrontation of sexist remarks elicits relatively more guilt in offenders, suggesting that because men are not perceived to be personally invested or emotionally responding to sexist expressions, men may be more effective at curtailing future sexist remarks (Cihanger, Barreto, & Ellemers, 2014; Czopp & Monteith, 2003; Drury & Kaiser, 2014). Future research that investigates how sexist expressions emerge and are perpetuated within social circles will provide important information about how interpersonal expressions of sexism can shape and reinforce the normative sexist attitudes that function to maintain societal-level gender inequality.

Conclusion

We have covered numerous ways in which romantic relationships between men and women shape the ways in which sexist attitudes toward women are adopted and endorsed, and in turn, function to maintain men's societal advantages. Our main points derived from ambivalent sexism theory, and the research that we have reviewed, are summarized in Tables 14.1 and 14.2. Sexist attitudes toward women are unique among prejudices because they arise from simultaneous drives for competition and cooperation: Men hold more status and power relative to women in society, yet men and women are interdependent within intimate, heterosexual relationships. Investigating dynamics within romantic relationships demonstrates the ambivalence that is central to these attitudes. Hostile sexism encompasses derogation and aggression toward nontraditional women in society, but it is actually detrimental to men's personal lives, fostering dissatisfaction, conflict, and resistance in female partners. Benevolent sexism is a necessary complement to hostile sexism by fostering satisfying and subjectively caring relationship behaviors to provide men access to intimacy and influence within relationship domains. Of importance, however, benevolent sexism produces relationship behaviors and beliefs that operate from within relationships to maintain men's power and status at a societal level.

Benevolent sexism redirects the focus of gender relations from societal comparisons of men's and women's relative advantages to an idyllic view of men and women as intimate partners: Women who invest fully in a traditional, supportive relationship role are provided and cared for by men. Thus, benevolent sexism appeals to both men and women because it suffuses romantic ideas of "true love," offering women a position on a pedestal and offering men a partner to revere and adore. These gendered relationship roles restrict women to a position in which their access to resources, valued qualities, and relationship satisfaction are all more dependent on their male partner fulfilling the role of protector and provider. This system is so powerful because, for any given couple, a complementary union in which one partner is a devoted protector and provider and the other partner is adored and cherished has many benefits and has the potential to be a foundation for a stable, satisfying relationship. But, hostile sexism and benevolent sexism do not work solely in one relationship. Sexist attitudes function from within relationships to ensure that *all* men are characterized as competent, responsible providers for women, who should *all* be warm, supportive caregivers. Thus, through prompting patterns of praise and threat toward women in interpersonal interactions, benevolent sexism and hostile sexism ultimately reinforce men's advantages over women that exist across societies.

References

Abrams, D., Viki, G. T., Masser, B., & Bohner, G. (2003). Perception of a stranger and acquaintance rape: The role of benevolent and hostile sexism in victim blame and rape proclivity. *Journal of Personality and Social Psychology, 84*, 111–125. doi: 10.1177/1077801206291663

Barreto, M., & Ellemers, N. (2005). The burden of benevolent sexism: How it contributes to the maintenance of gender inequalities. *European Journal of Social Psychology, 35*, 633–642. doi: 10.1002/ejsp.270

Barreto, M., Ellemers, N., Piebinga, L., & Moya, M. (2010). How nice of us and how dumb of me: The effect of exposure to benevolent sexism on women's task and relational self-descriptions. *Sex Roles, 62*, 532–544. doi: 10.1007/s11199-009-9699-0

Baumeister, R. F., & Leary, M. R. (1995). The need to belong: Desire for interpersonal attachments as a fundamental human motivation. *Psychological Bulletin, 117*, 497–529. doi: 10.1037/0033-2909.117.3.497

Becker, J. C. (2010). Why do women endorse hostile and benevolent sexism? The role of salient female subtypes and personalization of sexist contents. *Sex Roles, 62*, 453–467. doi: 10.1007/s11199-009-9707-4

Bem, S. L. (1974). The measurement of psychological androgyny. *Journal of Consulting and Clinical Psychology, 42*, 155–162. doi: 10.1037/h0036215

Bohner, G., Ahlborn, K., & Steiner, R. (2010). How sexy are sexist men? Women's perception of male response profiles in the ambivalent sexism inventory. *Sex Roles, 62*, 568–582. doi: 10.1007/s11199-009-9665-x

Brandt, M. J. (2011). Sexism and gender inequality across 57 societies. *Psychological Science, 22*, 1413–1418. doi: 10.1177/0956797611420445

Buss, D. M. (1988). The evolution of human intrasexual competition: Tactics of mate attraction. *Journal of Personality and Social Psychology, 54*, 616–628. doi: 10.1037/0022-3514.54.4.616

Casad, B. J., Salazar, M. M., & Macina, V. (2015). The real versus the ideal: Predicting relationship satisfaction and well-being from endorsement of marriage myths and benevolent sexism. *Psychology of Women Quarterly, 39*, 119–129. doi: 0361684314528304

Chen, Z., Fiske, S. T., & Lee, T. L. (2009). Ambivalent sexism and power-related gender-role ideology in marriage. *Sex Roles, 60*, 765–778. doi: 10.1007/s11199-009-9585-9

Cihangir, S., Barreto, M., & Ellemers, N. (2014). Men as allies against sexism. *SAGE Open, 4*, doi: 2158244014539168.

Czopp, A. M., & Monteith, M. J. (2003). Confronting prejudice (literally): Reactions to confrontations of racial and gender bias. *Personality and Social Psychology Bulletin, 29*, 532–544. doi: 10.1177/0146167202250923

Dardenne, B., Dumont, M., & Bollier, T. (2007). Insidious dangers of benevolent sexism: Consequences for women's performance. *Journal of Personality and Social Psychology, 93*, 764–779. doi: 10.1037/0022-3514.93.5.764

de Lemus, S., Moya, M., & Glick, P. (2010). When contact correlates with prejudice: Adolescents' romantic relationship experience predicts greater benevolent sexism in boys and hostile sexism in girls. *Sex Roles, 63*, 214–225. doi: 10.1007/s11199-010-9786-2

Drury, B. J., & Kaiser, C. R. (2014). Allies against sexism: The role of men in confronting sexism. *Journal of Social Issues, 70*, 637–652. doi: 10.1111/josi.12083

Duckitt, J. (2001). A dual process cognitive-motivational theory of ideology and prejudice. In M. P. Zanna (Ed.), *Advances in experimental social psychology* (Vol. *33*, pp. 41–113). San Diego, CA: Academic Press. 41–114. doi: 10.1016/s0065-2601(01)80004-6

Durán, M., Moya, M., Megías, J. L., & Viki, G. T. (2010). Social perception of rape victims in dating and married relationships: The role of perpetrator's benevolent sexism. *Sex Roles, 62*, 505–519. doi: 10.1007/s11199-009-9676-7

Eastwick, P. W., Eagly, A., Glick, P., Johannesen-Schmidt, M. C., Fiske, S. T., Blum, A. M. B. . . . Volpato, C. (2006). Is traditional gender ideology associated with sex-typed mate preferences? A test in nine nations. *Sex Roles, 54*, 603–614. doi: 10.1007/s11199-006-9027-x

Expósito, F., Herrera, M. C., Moya, M., & Glick, P. (2010). Don't rock the boat: Women's benevolent sexism predicts fears of marital violence. *Psychology of Women Quarterly, 34*, 36–42. doi: 10.1111/j.1471-6402.2009.01539.x

Fernández, M., Castro, Y., Otero, M., Foltz, M., & Lorenzo, M. (2006). Sexism, vocational goals, and motivation as predictors of men's and women's career choice. *Sex Roles, 55*, 267–272. doi: 10.1007/s11199-006-9079-y

Fine, M., & Asch, A. (1981). Disabled women: Sexism without the pedestal. *Journal of Sociology and Social Welfare, 8*, 233–248.

Fischer, A. R. (2006). Women's benevolent sexism as reaction to hostility. *Psychology of Women Quarterly, 30*, 410–416. doi: 10.1111/j.1471-6402.2006.00316.x

Fletcher, G. J. O., Simpson, J. A., Campbell, L., & Overall, N. C. (2013). *The science of intimate relationships*. Cambridge: Wiley-Blackwell.

Fletcher, G. J., Simpson, J. A., Thomas, G., & Giles, L. (1999). Ideals in intimate relationships. *Journal of Personality and Social Psychology, 76*, 72–89. doi: 10.1037/0022-3514.76.1.72

Forbes, G. B., Adams-Curtis, L. E., & White, K. B. (2004). First-and second-generation measures of sexism, rape myths, and related beliefs, and hostility toward women: Their interrelationships and association with college students' experiences with dating aggression and sexual coercion. *Violence Against Women, 10*, 236–261. doi: 10.1177/1077801203256002

Forbes, G. B., Jobe, R. L., White, K. B., Bloesch, E., & Adams-Curtis, L. E. (2005). Perceptions of dating violence following a sexual or nonsexual betrayal of trust: Effects of gender, sexism, acceptance of rape myths, and vengeance motivation. *Sex Roles*, *52*, 165–173. doi: 10.1007/s11199-005-1292-6

Ford, T. E., Wentzel, E. R., & Lorion, J. (2001). Effects of exposure to sexist humor on perceptions of normative tolerance of sexism. *European Journal of Social Psychology*, *31*, 677–691. doi: 10.1002/ejsp.56

Frye, N. E., & Karney, B. R. (2002). Being better or getting better? Social and temporal comparisons as coping mechanisms in close relationships. *Personality and Social Psychology Bulletin*, *28*, 1287–1299. doi: 10.1177/01461672022812013

Garaigordobil, M., & Aliri, J. (2013). Ambivalent Sexism Inventory: Standardization and normative data in a sample of the basque country. *Behavioral Psychology-Psicologia Conductual*, *21*, 173–186.

Glick, P., Diebold, J., Bailey-Werner, B., & Zhu, L. (1997). The two faces of Adam: Ambivalent sexism and polarized attitudes toward women. *Personality and Social Psychology Bulletin*, *23*, 1323–1334. doi: 10.1177/01461672972312009

Glick, P., & Fiske, S. T. (1996). The Ambivalent Sexism Inventory: Differentiating hostile and benevolent sexism. *Journal of Personality and Social Psychology*, *70*, 491–512. doi: 10.1037//0022-3514.70.3.491

Glick, P., & Fiske, S. T. (2001). An ambivalent alliance: Hostile and benevolent sexism as complementary justifications for gender inequality. *American Psychologist*, *56*, 109–118. doi: 10.1037/0003-066X.56.2.109

Glick, P., Fiske, S. T., Mladinic, A., Saiz, J., Abrams, D., Masser, B. . . . López, W. L. (2000). Beyond prejudice as simple antipathy: Hostile and benevolent sexism across cultures. *Journal of Personality and Social Psychology*, *79*, 763–775. doi: 10.1037//0022-3514.79.5.763

Glick, P., & Hilt, L. (2000). Combative children to ambivalent adults: The development of gender prejudice. In T. Eckes & M. Trautner (Eds.), *Developmental social psychology of gender* (pp. 243–272). Mahwah, NJ: Erlbaum.

Goh, J. X. & Hall, J. A. (2015). Nonverbal and verbal expressions of men's sexism in mixed-gender interactions. *Sex Roles*, *72*, 252–261. doi: 10.1007/s11199-015-0451-7

Greenwood, D., & Isbell, L. M. (2002). Ambivalent sexism and the dumb blonde: Men's and women's reactions to sexist jokes. *Psychology of Women Quarterly*, *26*, 341–350. doi: 10.1111/1471-6402.t01-2-00073

Grubbs, J. B., Exline, J. J., & Twenge, J. M. (2014). Psychological entitlement and ambivalent sexism: Understanding the role of entitlement in predicting two forms of sexism. *Sex Roles*, *70*, 209–220. doi: 10.1007/s11199-014-0360-1

Hammond, M. D., & Overall, N. C. (2013a). Men's hostile sexism and biased perceptions of intimate partners: Fostering dissatisfaction and negative behavior in close relationships. *Personality and Social Psychology Bulletin*, *39*, 1585–1599. doi: 10.1177/0146167213499026

Hammond, M. D., & Overall, N. C. (2013b). When relationships do not live up to benevolent ideals: Women's benevolent sexism and sensitivity to relationship problems. *European Journal of Social Psychology*, *43*, 212–223. doi: 10.1002/ejsp.1939

Hammond, M. D., & Overall, N.C. (2014). Endorsing benevolent sexism magnifies willingness to dissolve relationships when facing partner-ideal discrepancies. *Personal Relationships*, *21*, 272–287. doi: 10.1111/pere.12031

Hammond, M. D., Sibley, C. G., & Overall, N. C. (2014). The allure of sexism: Psychological entitlement fosters women's endorsement of benevolent sexism over time. *Social Psychological and Personality Science, 5*, 421–428. doi: 10.1177/1948550613506124

Hammond, M. D., & Overall, N. C. (2015). Benevolent sexism and support of romantic partner's goals: Undermining women's competence while fulfilling men's intimacy needs. *Personality and Social Psychology Bulletin, 41*, 1180–1194. doi: 10.1177/0146167215593492

Hammond, M. D., Overall, N. C., & Cross, E. J. (2016). Internalizing sexism in close relationships: The perceived sexism of partners maintains women's endorsement of benevolent sexism. *Journal of Personality and Social Psychology, 110*, 214–238. doi: 10.1037/pspi0000043

Hart, J., Hung, J. A., Glick, P., & Dinero, R. E. (2012). He loves her, he loves her not: Attachment style as a personality antecedent to men's ambivalent sexism. *Personality and Social Psychology Bulletin, 38*, 1495–1505. doi: 10.1177/0146167212454177

Herrera, M. C., Expósito, F., & Moya, M. (2012). Negative reactions of men to the loss of power in gender relations: Lilith vs. Eve. *The European Journal of Psychology Applied to Legal Context, 4*, 17–42. doi: 10.1037/e506052012-248

Jackman, M. R. (1994). *The velvet glove: Paternalism and conflict in gender, class, and race relations*. Berkeley: University of California Press.

Kelley, H. H., & Thibaut, J. W. (1978). *Interpersonal relations: A theory of interdependence*. New York: Wiley.

Kilianski, S. E., & Rudman, L. A. (1998). Wanting it both ways: Do women approve of benevolent sexism? *Sex Roles, 39*, 333–352. doi: 10.1023/A:1018814924402

Knee, C. R., Patrick, H., & Lonsbary, C. (2003). Implicit theories of relationships: Orientations toward evaluation and cultivation. *Personality and Social Psychology Review, 7*, 41–55. doi: 10.1207/S15327957PSPR0701_3

Lee, T. L., Fiske, S. T., Glick, P., & Chen, Z. (2010). Ambivalent sexism in close relationships: (Hostile) power and (benevolent) romance shape relationship ideals. *Sex Roles, 62*, 583–602. doi: 10.1007/s11199-010-9770-x

McNulty, J. K., & Karney, B. R. (2004). Positive expectations in the early years of marriage: Should couples expect the best or brace for the worst? *Journal of Personality and Social Psychology, 86*, 729–743. doi: 10.1037/0022-3514.86.5.729

Moya, M., Glick, P., Expósito, F., de Lemus, S., & Hart, J. (2007). It's for your own good: Benevolent sexism and women's reactions to protectively justified restrictions. *Personality and Social Psychology Bulletin, 33*, 1421–1434. doi: 10.1177/0146167207304790

Murray, S. L., Holmes, J. G., & Collins, N. L. (2006). Optimizing assurance: The risk regulation system in relationships. *Psychological Bulletin, 132*, 641–666. doi: 10.1037/0033-2909.132.5.641

Obeid, N., Chang, D. F., & Ginges, J. (2010). Beliefs about wife beating: An exploratory study with Lebanese students. *Violence Against Women, 16*, 691–712. doi: 10.1177/1077801210370465

Overall, N. C., Sibley, C. G., & Tan, R. (2011). The costs and benefits of sexism: Resistance to influence during relationship conflict. *Journal of Personality and Social Psychology, 101*, 271–290. doi: 10.1037/a0022727

Ridgeway, C. L., & Smith-Lovin, L. (1999). The gender system and interaction. *Annual Review of Sociology, 25*, 191–216. doi: 10.1146/annurev.soc.25.1.191

Riemer, A., Chaudoir, S., & Earnshaw, V. (2014). What looks like sexism and why? The effect of comment type and perpetrator type on women's perceptions of sexism. *The Journal of General Psychology, 141*, 263–279. doi: 10.1080/00221309.2014.907769

Rusbult, C. E., & Buunk, B. P. (1993). Commitment processes in close relationships: An interdependence analysis. *Journal of Social and Personal Relationships, 10*, 175–204. doi: 10.1177/026540759301000202

Sakalli, N. (2001). Beliefs about wife beating among Turkish college students: The effects of patriarchy, sexism, and sex differences. *Sex Roles, 44*, 599–610. doi: 10.1080/00223980209604825

Salomon, K., Burgess, K. D., & Bosson, J. K. (2015). Flash fire and slow burn: Women's cardiovascular reactivity and recovery following hostile and benevolent sexism. *Journal of Experimental Psychology: General, 144*, 469–479. doi: 10.1037/xge0000061

Sarlet, M., Dumont, M., Delacollette, N., & Dardenne, B. (2012). Prescription of protective paternalism for men in romantic and work contexts. *Psychology of Women Quarterly, 36*, 444–457. doi: 10.1177/0361684312454842

Shnabel, N., Bar-Anan, Y., Kende, A., Bareket, O., & Lazar, Y. (2016). Help to perpetuate traditional gender roles: Benevolent sexism increases engagement in dependency-oriented cross-gender helping. *Journal of Personality and Social Psychology, 110*, 55–75. doi: 10.1037/pspi0000037

Sibley, C. G., & Becker, J. C. (2012). On the nature of sexist ambivalence: Profiling ambivalent and univalent sexists. *European Journal of Social Psychology, 42*, 589–601. doi: 10.1002/ejsp.1870

Sibley, C. G., & Overall, N. C. (2011). A dual-process motivational model of ambivalent sexism and gender differences in romantic partner preferences. *Psychology of Women Quarterly, 35*, 303–317. doi: 10.1177/0361684311401838

Sibley, C. G., Overall, N. C., & Duckitt, J. (2007). When women become more hostilely sexist toward their gender: The system justifying effect of benevolent sexism. *Sex Roles, 57*, 743–754. doi: 10.1007/s11199-007-9306-1

Sibley, C. G., & Perry, R. (2010). An opposing process model of benevolent sexism. *Sex Roles, 62*, 438–452. doi: 10.1007/s11199-009-9705-6

Sibley, C. G., Wilson, M. S., & Duckitt, J. (2007). Antecedents of men's hostile and benevolent sexism: The dual roles of social dominance orientation and right-wing authoritarianism. *Personality and Social Psychology Bulletin, 33*, 160–172. doi: 10.1177/0146167206294745

Sinclair, S., Huntsinger, J., Skorinko, J., & Hardin, C. D. (2005). Social tuning of the self: Consequences for the self-evaluations of stereotype targets. *Journal of Personality and Social Psychology, 89*, 160–175. doi: 10.1037/0022-3514.89.2.160

Tenenbaum, H. R., & Leaper, C. (2002). Are parents' gender schemas related to their children's gender-related cognitions? A meta-analysis. *Developmental Psychology, 38*, 615–630. doi: 10.1037//0012-1649.38.4.615

Thomas, C. A., & Esses, V. M. (2004). Individual differences in reactions to sexist humor. *Group Processes & Intergroup Relations, 7*, 89–100. doi: 10.1177/1368430204039975

Twenge, J. M., & Campbell, W. K. (2010). *The narcissism epidemic: Living in the age of entitlement*. New York: Simon & Schuster.

United Nations Development Programme. (2014). *Human development report 2014*. Retrieved from hdr.undp.org/en/2014-report/download

Viki, G. T., & Abrams, D. (2002). But she was unfaithful: Benevolent sexism and reactions to rape victims who violate traditional gender role expectations. *Sex Roles, 47*, 289–293. doi: 10.1023/A:1021342912248

Viki, G. T., Abrams, D., & Hutchison, P. (2003). The "true" romantic: Benevolent sexism and paternalistic chivalry. *Sex Roles, 49*, 533–537. doi: 10.1023/A:1025888824749

Yakushko, O. (2005). Ambivalent sexism and relationship patterns among women and men in Ukraine. *Sex Roles, 52*, 589–596. doi: 10.1007/s11199-005-3727-5

Yamawaki, N., Ostenson, J., & Brown, R. C. (2009). The functions of gender role traditionality, ambivalent sexism, injury, and frequency of assault on domestic violence perception: A study between Japanese and American college students. *Violence Against Women, 15*, 1126–1142. doi: 10.1177/1077801209340758

15 Religion and Prejudice

Ben K. L. Ng and Will M. Gervais

From a religious point of view, if God had thought homosexuality is a sin, he would not have created gay people.

Howard Dean, Former Governor of Vermont

If a man has sexual relations with a man as one does with a woman, both of them have done what is detestable. They are to be put to death; their blood will be on their own heads.

Leviticus 20:13, New International Version

A woman helps feed and clothe poor children in the slums of India: How likely is it that her religion motivated her to do so? A man votes against marriage equality for gay men and lesbians: How likely is it that his religion motivated him to do so? As Allport (1954) noted more than half a century ago, religion has a paradoxical relationship with prejudice. In his words, "[religion] makes and unmakes prejudice." In the more than six decades since Allport made this observation, social psychologists have tried to pin down the precise relationship between religion and prejudice.

Early work in this area attempted to fractionate religion into distinct components that respectively predicted more and less prejudice. In this view, some "core" element of religion may predict tolerance, while other aspects of religion (or nonreligious constructs that tend to nonetheless correlate with religiosity) might engender outgroup enmity. This tradition has a long history, indeed, as William James (1902) noted:

> The plain fact is that men's minds are built, as has been often said, in water-tight compartments. Religious after a fashion, they yet have many other things in them beside their religion, and unholy entanglements and associations inevitably obtain. The basenesses so commonly charged to religion's account are thus, almost all of them, not chargeable at all to religion proper, but rather to religion's wicked practical partner, the spirit of corporate dominion. And the bigotries are most of them in their turn chargeable to religion's wicked intellectual partner, the spirit of dogmatic dominion, the passion for laying down the law in the form of an absolutely closed-in theoretic system.

This search for "religion proper" and the unfortunate "wicked practical partners" of religiosity dominated research on religion and prejudice for decades. Scores of studies from the 1960s to the 1990s conceptualized various measures of religiosity such as extrinsic/intrinsic religious orientation (Allport, 1966; Allport & Ross,

1967), quest (Batson, 1976; Batson & Ventis, 1982), and fundamentalism (McFarland, 1989) in hopes of disentangling this paradox. These religious measures were often examined in conjunction with prejudice measures related to outgroups such as gay men and lesbians, African Americans, and atheists. In recent years, researchers have expanded the scope of their inquiry beyond a search for different facets of religiosity and their relationships to prejudice to instead consider the evolutionary, cultural, and cognitive motivations for the association between religion and prejudice (e.g., Blogowska & Saroglou, 2011; Brandt & Reyna, 2014; Mavor, Louis, & Laythe, 2011; Preston, Ritter, & Hernandez, 2010; Rothschild, Abdollahi, & Pyszczynski, 2009).

A concurrent line of inquiry deals with the evolutionary, cognitive, and cultural underpinnings of religion itself (e.g., Atran & Norenzayan, 2004; Barrett, 2000; Boyer, 2001; Gervais, 2013a; Henrich, 2009; Norenzayan & Gervais, 2013; Norenzayan et al., 2016; Norenzayan & Shariff, 2008). Researchers in this area deal with questions such as: "Why do we have religion?" "How do we come to believe in a supernatural agent we can neither see nor feel?" "What is the role of cultural evolution in the spread and survival of some religions but not others?" and "What makes people nonbelievers?" Independent of prejudice research, this body of research deals with the roots and transmission of religious concepts and beliefs. Recent years have seen dramatic advances in tackling these questions, with evidence backed by findings from development psychology, anthropology, and cognitive neuroscience. Nonetheless, many fundamental questions are still subject to contentious debate.

The central argument of this chapter can be stated directly: We propose that an understanding of religion's role in prejudice is facilitated when viewed in the context of both the evolution of religion and the evolution of prejudice. Thus, understanding the origins of religion can contribute to the study of religion and prejudice by highlighting the potential adaptive functions of prejudice against outgroups and individuals. This chapter is not an attempt to supplant early findings in the religion and prejudice literature. Rather, it is an attempt to catalyze more integrative research programs on religion and prejudice, based on more nuanced understandings of the origins of religion and prejudice, respectively.

As an overview, this chapter begins by outlining recent work on the potential evolutionary origins of religion. Next, we summarize recent work outlining the evolutionary underpinnings of prejudice. Finally, we weave these two strands together and highlight three distinct forms of prejudice that can be – we argue – better understood in light of the evolution of both religion and prejudice: (a) anti-Muslim prejudice, (b) antigay prejudice, and (c) anti-atheist prejudice.

The Evolution of Religion

Over the past two decades, two slightly different theoretical camps have emerged, attempting to account for the evolution of religion. They are commonly known as the adaptationist and the by-product accounts of religion. The apparent schism between the two perspectives may largely result from each trying to describe different patterns regarding religion worldwide. Adaptationist perspectives attempt to explain the near-ubiquity of religion in the face of its apparent costliness, while by-product accounts tend to focus instead on the common cognitive structure of religious and supernatural concepts worldwide. As a result, adaptationist accounts suggest that some religious beliefs and behaviors may be evolutionary adaptations for cooperative group living (Johnson & Bering, 2006; Johnson & Krüger, 2004; Sosis & Alcorta, 2003), while by-product accounts propose that religious concepts arise spontaneously from the workings of, and spread culturally because of, psychological processes that evolved for other purposes (Barrett, 2000, 2004; Boyer, 2001). We briefly review both accounts and then attempt to reconcile them.

Generally speaking, adaptationist frameworks tend to view religion as an adaptation for navigating the recurrent challenges of group cooperation. This is an evolutionary challenge because successful group living requires costly investments from group members. Free riders, however, can reap the benefits of cooperation without having to contribute personal resources to the group, inevitably jeopardizing the functioning of the group (Sober & Wilson, 1999). Several aspects of religion, including both religious beliefs and religious practices, may help overcome the problem of free riding. For example, belief in a monitoring and potentially punishing supernatural agent can facilitate cooperation and reduce the temptation to cheat if believers perceive it to be a credible threat (Bering & Johnson, 2005; Johnson, 2005; Johnson & Krüger, 2004). In contrast, other approaches emphasize the role of practice, rather than belief. Some researchers have argued that religious ritual serves as a costly signal of loyalty to a group (Irons, 2001; Sosis, 2006). Costly commitments promote intragroup cooperation by communicating trustworthiness to others while preventing free riders from exploiting cooperative benefits without first signaling their commitment to the group. Both supernatural punishment and costly signaling approaches may operate in concert, and both speak to the cultural recurrence of beliefs and practices across successful religious groups.

The by-product account makes the claim that supernatural beliefs began as a cultural by-product of a suite of psychological processes evolved to serve other functions (Boyer, 2001, 2003). In this account, supernatural belief emerges as a recurrent by-product of other social-cognitive faculties such as theory of mind – also termed mind perception or mentalizing – and teleological reasoning. Theory of mind is defined as the ability to detect and correctly infer the minds of others (Baron-Cohen, 1995; Frith & Frith, 2003). It supplies the cognitive foundation for our belief in mind-body dualism (Bloom, 2007). Our intuitive sense of mind-body dualism allows us to conceptualize a physical body without a mind, and more importantly a mind without a body. Plausibly, the ability to represent disembodied minds is central to widespread belief in supernatural agents who possess humanlike goals, beliefs, and desires (Barrett & Keil, 1996; Guthrie,

1993). Similarly, teleological reasoning – reasoning based on the assumption that there is a purpose to the world – seems to be a cognitive default. Developmental studies have shown that children at a relatively young age display a proclivity toward imbuing the natural world with purpose (e.g., Kelemen, 1999a, 1999b, 2004). Moreover, teleological appeals tend to persist into adulthood (Kelemen & Rosset, 2009) and become accepted even by scientists when their cognitive resources are limited (Kelemen, Rottman, & Seston, 2013). To the extent that people view objects in the world as existing for a purpose or function, they may infer the presence of a supernatural designer who imbues the world with that purpose. Thus, both mentalizing and teleological reasoning may provide some intuitive support for notions of supernatural agency.

Intuitive support for supernatural beliefs may be further elaborated through cultural evolution, leading to the transmission and, subsequently, sustenance of religious faith over time (Gervais, Willard, Norenzayan, & Henrich, 2011; Norenzayan & Gervais, 2013). Transmission of faith via cultural learning can take several forms. Some types of mental representations are especially memorable, emotionally evocative, and potentially actionable, leading to a class of *content-biased* social-learning strategies (Robert & Richerson, 1985; Sperber & Sperber, 1996). For example, people find minimally counterintuitive concepts – such as supernatural agents – especially memorable, potentially giving minimally counterintuitive concepts an advantage in cultural transmission (e.g., Barrett & Nyhof, 2001). On the other hand, some *context-biased* learning strategies focus more on the sources, rather than contents, of cultural information. Within context learning biases, several strategies have been formulated. One strategy encourages cultural learners to attend to cultural models based on skills, success, and prestige – prestige bias (Henrich & Gil-White, 2001). Credibility-enhancing displays (CREDs) build on learners' motivation to avoid being deceived by cultural models. If models engage in behaviors that would be costly if contrary beliefs were privately held, learners are more likely to trust and embrace those beliefs (Henrich, 2009). Other strategies include (but are not limited to) conformist bias, success-based bias, and familiarity-based learning (Rendell et al., 2011). While intuitive support for supernatural beliefs is important, it is insufficient to explain the maintenance of religious belief. Cultural evolution contributes by providing the mechanism (i.e., content and context bias) through which supernatural beliefs can be passed on, both spatially (person to person) and temporally (generation to generation).

While adaptationist and by-product accounts are often cast as competing hypotheses, they can be easily and productively combined (Norenzayan et al., 2016). The capacity to mentally represent supernatural agents likely emerges as a by-product of ordinary social cognition (e.g., Gervais, 2013b) and subsequent cultural learning can stabilize belief in specific supernatural agents in different groups. At the same time, other aspects of religions – belief in moralizing gods, credibility-enhancing displays, and costly signals – can then act as potential cooperative adaptations at the level of cultural evolution (see, e.g., Norenzayan et al., 2016).

Evolution of Prejudice(s)

Classic social-psychological approaches view prejudice as essentially unidimensional (e.g., Allport, 1954; Brewer & Brown, 1998). We like people who are like us, and we dislike dissimilar others. We experience ingroup love and outgroup hate. In recent years, however, some evolutionary models of prejudice have instead proposed that different prejudices derive from psychological mechanisms that evolved during our evolutionary past to solve a suite of adaptive problems (Krebs & Denton, 1997; Kurzban & Leary, 2001; Neuberg, Smith, & Asher, 2000; Schaller, Park, & Faulkner, 2003). From an evolutionary perspective, it thus makes more sense to speak of *prejudices*, with each prejudice characterizing a specific reaction to a specific individual or group of people (Neuberg, Kenrick, & Schaller, 2010), rather than *prejudice* as a unitary phenomenon encompassing broad negative reactions to diverse groups.

One of the first systematic evolutionary accounts of prejudice (Kurzban & Leary, 2001) proposed that our ancestral environment was fraught with distinct adaptive challenges such as competition for resources and mates and parasitic avoidance. Specific psychological mechanisms evolved during our evolutionary history that may have helped our ancestors manage these threats by influencing their reactions to groups and individuals that were perceived as threats in each domain. Prejudice can thus be thought of as our specific reactions to groups and individuals perceived as posing specific adaptive threats. Hence, contemporary prejudices may persist because they conferred adaptive advantages to our ancestors by specifying how different individuals and groups should be confronted, instead of employing a one-size-fits-all strategy. Different social groups and individuals present unique threats to survival, thus requiring distinct reactions, based specifically on the threats they are perceived to pose (Cottrell & Neuberg, 2005; Kurzban & Leary, 2001). For example, prejudice toward gays can be typified by a disgust reaction because gays are viewed as health hazards (Cottrell & Neuberg, 2005). Disgust in turn activates our disease-avoidance system, which facilitates behaviors such as social avoidance and opposition to gay rights (Cottrell, Richards, & Nichols, 2010). African Americans, however, are considered a threat to physical safety, prompting our self-protective system by inducing fear (Cottrell & Neuberg, 2005). Combined, these insights highlight another important aspect of evolutionary approaches to prejudice. Instead of viewing prejudice as existing solely at the level of groups (e.g., why Whites and Blacks might not get along), this approach also views inferences made about individuals as perhaps equally important. So, for example, different racial groups might be viewed as contestants in an intergroup conflict, engendering prejudice at the group level. On the other hand, people may heuristically view morphological irregularities in others as signs of disease and thus avoid those individuals not because of any group-level inferences, but solely because of individual-level inferences. To foreshadow, in terms of religion and prejudice, we view both intergroup conflict and individual inference processes as important for the relationship between religion and different types of prejudices, with some characterized by intergroup conflict and others arising solely at the level of individual inferences.

At the intergroup level, one potent route to prejudice stems from our evolved coalitional psychology (Kurzban & Leary, 2001). Our coalitional psychology functions as a cognitive system designed to promote intragroup cooperation while distancing ourselves from outgroup members (Tooby & Cosmides, 1988). Therefore, our coalitional psychology triggers not just within-group cooperation (Wilson & Sober, 1994) but also often drives between-group competition and prejudice (Alexander, 1979; Sidanius & Pratto, 2001). Research in intergroup processes comports with this view, as ingroup identification often leads to discrimination, competition, and sometimes even violence toward outgroup members (Insko, Pinkley, Harring, & Holton, 1987; Sheriff, 1966; Tajfel, Billig, Bundy, & Flament, 1971). At the same time, we also emphasize that while intergroup competition often drives prejudice, it does not follow that all prejudices stem from intergroup competition. Many prejudices are plausibly driven solely by inferences made about the threats individuals may pose, and subsequent reactions to them.

Integrating the Evolutions of Religion and Prejudice

In this section, we attempt to combine evolutionary accounts of both religion and prejudice into an integrated (albeit admittedly speculative) model of religion and prejudice. First, we outline how threats to fundamental elements of religion might lead to prejudice. Next, using three test cases, we explicitly spell out the perceived threats exemplified by each prejudice target and describe their underlying psychology and relation to religion.

Religion and Prejudice

Constructing a taxonomy of the core dimensions of religion is a challenging task. Despite the challenge, numerous attempts have been made (Allport & Ross, 1967; Batson, Schoenrade, & Ventis, 1993; Hood, Hill, & Williamson, 2005; Pargament, 2001; Voas, 2007). Saroglou's (2011) more recent attempt at synthesizing the previous taxonomies led to his "Big Four" religious dimensions: (a) *believing* in transcendent entities (e.g., personal gods); (b) *bonding*, or a deep emotional experience with others, usually via rituals; (c) *behaving* according to religious moral norms; and (d) *belonging* to a community or tradition.

While the four dimensions are not definite claims about what religion is, they can certainly help illustrate how different aspects of religion can be related to the evolutions of both religion and prejudice. For example, our capacity for mentally representing supernatural agents may have contributed to the dimension of belief because believing requires first and foremost the ability to mentalize. Similarly, the dimensions of bonding and belonging may be linked to religious rituals, thought to foster commitment to the group. Behaving on the other hand could have been influenced by the belief in a god who monitors and punishes norm violators. Furthermore, because the dimensions are proposed to be the core of religion, any real or perceived external threat to any dimension by any outgroup or individual could potentially lead to prejudice as a way of handling the perceived threat.

Beliefs/Believing

Believing is characterized by the motivation to hold a set of religious ideas. This dimension is exemplified by an intrinsic orientation. People with an intrinsic orientation see religion as an end in itself (Allport & Ross, 1967). Studies on intrinsic orientation often suggest a negative association with prejudice (Allport & Ross, 1967; Donahue, 1985; McFarland, 1989). Because an intrinsic orientation is primarily about transcendence, spiritual connection with god, and meaning, we speculate that people high in intrinsic orientation may be less likely to track coalitions, alliances, and enemies, all else equal. For instance, self-reported spirituality is positively associated with the value of universalism (Saroglou & Galand, 2004) and greater willingness to help an unknown target (Saroglou, Pichon, Trompette, Verschueren, & Dernelle, 2005). Insofar as god beliefs suppress activation of coalitional psychology, the capacity to track cues of coalition will be reduced, subsequently diminishing prejudices driven primarily by coalitional psychology. However, prejudices driven largely by non-coalitional factors may be unrelated or even positively related to belief.

Behaving/Practices

Morality is a subject many (especially contemporary), albeit not all, religions are concerned with. Therefore, central to morality-concerned religions is how one ought to behave in accord with the moral norms of one's group. According to Haidt and Graham (2007), morality can be divided into five broad foundations: harm, fairness, authority, loyalty, and purity. The first two foundations can be categorized as "individualizing" foundations, because they are about individual rights and protection. The next three foundations are bundled into "binding" foundations because they function to bind people into social groups such as families and religions. While all five foundations are important to religion, the binding foundations are especially so because group solidarity is important for stabilizing religion (Graham & Haidt, 2010). When binding foundations are violated, our coalitional tracking system will be activated as a way of responding to a potential impediment to group functioning and cooperation. Because different groups have different norms, religious norms allow the identification and sorting of people into their respective groups.

Religious fundamentalism potentially serves as a useful, albeit indirect, measure of motivation to adhere to religious norms. Fundamentalism reflects an unwavering belief in a set of religious teachings (Altemeyer & Hunsberger, 1992). People who score high on religious fundamentalism may thus be highly motivated to defend their religious beliefs, and at the same time discriminate against those who violate their beliefs. Right-wing authoritarianism, while not necessarily a religious measure, has a close association with fundamentalism and is often related to obedience to authority, adherence to social conventions, and need for social order (Altemeyer & Hunsberger, 2005). The attitudinal expressions of conventionalism and need for social order of right-wing authoritarians are especially relevant here because they highlight the motivation to conform, as well as the expectation that others should conform, to social and religious norms for group order and cohesion to be maintained.

To assess the determinants and role of right-wing authoritarianism on prejudice, a dual process model has been proposed to account for two distinct ideological attitudes (social dominance orientation being the other dimension) that differentially contribute to prejudice (Duckitt & Sibley, 2010; Duckitt, Wagner, Du Plessis, & Birum, 2002). This approach sees right-wing authoritarianism as an ideological attitude derived from an underlying personality trait labeled as social conformity (Duckitt, 2001). Empirical findings based on the dual process model suggest that there is a direct as well as an indirect effect of social conformity on right-wing authoritarianism, mediated by a belief in a dangerous world. Because the trait of social conformity implies an importance placed on both personal and social order, right-wing authoritarians are thus likely to be sensitive to groups that are a threat to such an order. In line with our argument that threat to a core dimension of religion can lead to prejudice, right-wing authoritarians' sensitivity to threats to the existing social order may lead them to feel threatened and subsequently be prejudiced against two types of outgroups deemed as disruptors of order: (a) dangerous groups that threaten both personal and social safety (e.g., drug dealers and violent criminals) and (b) social deviants who violate traditional ingroup norms and values (e.g., protestors and atheists; Duckitt & Sibley, 2007).

The dual process model proposes that the underlying mechanism associated with prejudice is different for right-wing authoritarianism and social dominance. For right-wing authoritarianism, the route to prejudice is thought to be via perceived threat from outgroups, whereas for social dominance orientation, the proposed mechanism is group competitiveness. The corollary is that each ideological belief should thus differentially predict prejudice toward different outgroups. Specifically for right-wing authoritarianism, the model hypothesized and found empirical support showing that right-wing authoritarianism but not social dominance orientation predicted prejudice against socially deviant groups that are thought to undermine socially established norms and values (Duckitt, 2006). Importantly, the relationship between right-wing authoritarianism and prejudice was mediated by perceived social threat and not group competitiveness (Duckitt, 2006), lending support to the dual process model as well as our argument that perceived threat leads to prejudice as a form of threat management.

Consequently, fundamentalism and right-wing authoritarianism are associated with the need to uphold both religious truths and values promoting obedience to religious authorities. Because morals and norms are often derived from scriptures and authorities, religious fundamentalists and right-wing authoritarians are likely to not only abide strictly by those norms but also to expect others to adhere to them. When other groups and individuals deviate from these norms, however, they are violating what is perceived as sacred to both religious fundamentalists and right-wing authoritarians. Consequently, norm violators tend to be discriminated against. Gays are a good example of perceived norm violators, especially in relation to purity violations (Inbar, Pizarro, & Bloom, 2009). Studies on antigay prejudice have found that religious fundamentalism and right-wing authoritarianism are often reliable predictors of negative attitudes toward gays (Brandt & Reyna, 2010; Hunsberger, 1996; Laythe, Finkel, Bringle, & Kirkpatrick, 2002). In essence, groups with different moral norms from the ingroup likely trigger coalitional psychology, motivating the need to differentiate between allies and enemies, promoting prejudice.

Belonging/Affiliation

Belonging is marked by identification not with religion per se, but with a religious group or community. Extrinsic religiosity is one measure embracing this aspect of religion because people high in extrinsic religiosity view religion as a means to an end. They are motivated by the status, security, and social networking benefits religion affords them (Allport & Ross, 1967; Batson & Ventis, 1982). Because extrinsically religious people value religion mostly for social needs, people who are biased toward this orientation are motivated to accommodate people who can provide those needs, while shunning others who fail to make the cut. Indeed, extrinsic religiosity is positively correlated with prejudice toward religious out-groups (Allport & Ross, 1967; Herek, 1987; Hoge & Carroll, 1973).

Both fundamentalism and right-wing authoritarianism may represent aspects of belonging, suggesting that belonging is associated with our coalitional tendencies. Extrinsic orientation, fundamentalism, and right-wing authoritarianism can be considered measures of coalitional inclination. Take right-wing authoritarianism as an example. In the previous section, we elaborated on how right-wing authoritarians are motivated to establish and maintain social order, based in part on the underlying personality trait of social conformity. Therefore, right-wing authoritarians should be attentive to groups that disrupt the social order they strive to keep. When disruptions are detected, coalitional psychology should likewise be triggered

playing a relatively more positive implicit attitude toward
Muslims (Rowatt et al., 2005). Perception of Muslims as
of norms and values is a threat to one's ingroup that requires
ment. In other words, differing religious norms can be seen as

norms of the ingroup are not threatened, two possible routes
One can respond either by avoiding any interaction or by
ess. Matthews and Levin (2012) set out to test both hypoth-
hat perception of threat to ingroup values was positively
eelings of disgust (avoidance) and anger (approach) toward
sentangle the relationship, value threat was experimentally
be either high or low. Disgust and anger were evaluated as
tors. Results provide initial evidence that perceiving Muslims
r threat to one's values increases feelings of disgust but not anger.
avoidance of all things Muslim. However, other studies support
ting out against Muslims. For example, negative attitudes toward
associated with more support for several aspects of the war on
s & Gross, 2013). One possible explanation for the contradictory
hat while Matthews and Levin's study focused on value difference,
Gross had participants rate Muslims on several traits such as "violent"
and "trustworthy." This may have primed participants to increase their support for the war on terror as an act of retaliation against the perceived violent
nature Muslims.

If group identification augments group differences, then church attendance
can be an additional marker of affiliation that will predict anti-Muslim prejudice. Attendance at church has the ability to increase commitment to coalitional identities (Atran, 2003). When coalitional commitment is enhanced,
group differences should be intensified, creating room for prejudice to
develop. This can be contrasted with prayer frequency. Because prayers
should not trigger coalitional cues, church attendance but not prayers should
predict anti-Muslim prejudice. Ginges et al. (2009) pitted attendance with
prayers and found that attendance at religious services but not prayers predicted support for suicide attacks, an extreme form of prejudice, to benefit the
ingroup. While this study can only speak to the broader interreligion conflict
perspective, the general mechanism can be applied to explain more specific
(i.e., anti-Muslim) prejudices, supporting the view that perceived differences
in group practices may result in aggressive behaviors toward, rather than
avoidance of, Muslims. This leads to more avenues of research regarding
circumstances under which avoidance or approach might be triggered as
a dominant response to threats. In sum, anti-Muslim prejudice may originate
from our evolved coalitional psychology that alerts us to discrepancies in
group practices, while differing religious norms and practices serves as a clear
line of group demarcation.

to identify those who are associated with the disruptions as uncooperative outgroup
members.

When primed with affiliation-based religious terms, people show an increase in
prosocial intentions, but only to ingroup members (Preston & Ritter, 2013).
Furthermore, support for suicide attacks, an extreme form of parochial altruism
(Choi & Bowles, 2007), is correlated with attendance at religious services instead
of prayers to gods (Ginges, Hansen, & Norenzayan, 2009). Attendance at religious
services – a form of collective ritual – is thought to enhance coalitional commitment by boosting positive benefits related to intragroup cooperation. Additionally,
rituals typically signal ingroup commitment that may be associated with increased
intergroup conflict (Ginges, Atran, Medin, & Shikaki, 2007). Prayers to gods,
however, do not seem to reinforce coalitional psychology and may in fact diminish
it. This is perhaps due to prayers' emphasis on a relationship with god, rather than
promoting ingroup identification. To the extent that practices such as religious
services bolster our sense of belonging to a group, coalitional psychology will be
activated, perhaps promoting prejudice against other groups.

Integrated Framework

In the previous section, we described the plausible links between some core
dimensions of religion and prejudice. To date, however, most of the accumulated
evidence examining religion and prejudice use only general measures without
considering specific reactions to different groups and individuals as evolutionary
models advocate (Cottrell & Neuberg, 2005; Neuberg & Cottrell, 2008; Schaller &
Neuberg, 2008).

To overcome this deficit, our integrated model seeks to specify the distinct threats
different groups and individuals are perceived to pose, and then make speculative
predictions about how religion might exacerbate or attenuate the respective responses
triggered by those perceived threats. Two sources of threats are pertinent to our
model: norm violation and group affiliation. Violations to moral norms – group
loyalty, authority, and purity (Graham & Haidt, 2010) – should elicit distinct threats.
For example, violation of purity norms might result in the spread of diseases and
pathogens, which is a threat to one's health. On the other hand, disobedience to
authority and disloyalty to the group might signal reluctance to comply with group
norms, which can be seen as a threat to cooperation. Similarly, a lack of affiliation
with a religious community or affiliation with an irreligious community or communities with different religious narratives and beliefs will plausibly evoke different
threats. Once identified, threats can be dealt with via (a) suppression, (b) norm
enforcement, or (c) avoidance (Phelan, Link, & Dovidio, 2008).

Three Test Cases for Our Integrated Framework

We apply our integrated model to three types of prejudice in the religion and
prejudice literature as preliminary test cases.

I   Anti-Muslim Prejudice   Muslims currently face rampant discrimination in the United States. We use anti-Muslim prejudice as a test case to more broadly illustrate how prejudice can arise between religious groups. In this sense, anti-Muslim prejudice – and enmity between religious groups more broadly – likely emerges as an intergroup phenomenon, highly influenced by evolved coalitional psychology. Anti-Muslim prejudice may be based on perceived differences in religious practices, customs, and values. For example, Muslims are prohibited from eating pork, while no such restrictions are imposed on Christians. Muslims also pray at specific times five times a day, while Christians usually attend church services once a week. When such practices differ, intergroup differences likely become more salient, activating coalitional psychology. Once triggered, detection of alliances is based on identifying members with the same religious traditions, while those with a contrasting set of practices are classified as an outgroup. Perceived dissimilarities in group norms and values thus become sources of threat. Two plausible routes to managing the threat are available. One can either socially avoid coming into contact with Muslims (only living in a neighborhood without Muslims) for fear of being tainted with impurities associated with Islam or actively try to impose the ingroup's norms by acting out against Muslims (e.g., aggression). In sum, religion may heighten coalitional concerns, driving intergroup conflict between religious groups. In a majority Christian country such as the United States, this may increase anti-Muslim prejudice.

II   Antigay Prejudice   While anti-Muslim prejudice likely emerges from intergroup processes, we view antigay prejudice as plausibly being more driven by individual-level inferences. Specifically, antigay prejudice may stem from both the perceived violation of purity norms and the heuristic pathogen threats associated with homosexuality (e.g., Cottrell & Neuberg, 2005). Some facets of religion may exacerbate the heuristic purity and pathogen-based inferences that drive antigay prejudice. Because purity norms are integral to religion, especially in religious rituals, violation of purity norms is an especially salient threat to many religious groups and individuals. When purity threat is present, disgust is often activated as a way of avoiding interaction with gays. Thus, in sum, religion may heighten sensitivity to purity cues and, in turn, lead to negative inferences about, and avoidance of, gay men and lesbians.

III   Anti-Atheist Prejudice   Trust is central to social life, but an individual's trustworthiness must be only indirectly inferred (Simpson, 2007). Religious believers may come to use religious belief as a cue to who can be trusted. After all, many people view religion as a necessary component of morality (Pew, 2007). Without belief in a god, atheists might be viewed as moral wildcards who are capable of engaging in various immoral actions (Gervais,

2014). Thus, for religious believe[r] cooperative threats and therefore Shariff, & Norenzayan, 2011). As wit may derive more from inferences rega ness, rather than any perceived inte atheists. Religious belief is likely a ke Believers are more likely to view relig As a result, they will be more morally su of individual atheists.

In the next three sections, we treat each te potential areas to be explored in the future.

Anti-Muslim Prejudice

Since the 9/11 terrorist attack on the toward Muslims have occupied a central stage i saw an initial decline in prejudice toward Musli Muslims rose from 2005 to 2010 (Pew, 2010). A s respondents admitted to at least feeling a little pr highest compared to other religious groups (Gallup, here on anti-Muslim prejudice, our aim is to illust intergroup conflict between religious groups. Our fra Muslim prejudice results from perceived differences traditions, which in turn trigger evolved coalitional p system then demarcates alliances and enemies accordin practices the religion of the ingroup, in this case a maje A Gallup poll (Gallup, 2009b) supports this prediction, w disagreeing that Christianity and Islam are the sam a Christian, Muslims become an especially salient outgroup that the practice of Islam is at odds with Christianity.

Using both explicit and implicit measures examining attitu psychological studies have documented a positive associa aspects of religiosity (e.g., fundamentalism) and anti-Muslim Pargament, Mahoney, & Trevino, 2008; Rowatt, Franklin, & Co Slik & Konig, 2006). Using explicit measures of negative Muslims, Rowatt and colleagues (2005) found a positive correla mentalism and right-wing authoritarianism. Likewise, a higher Muslims as desecrators of Christian values and teachings led to l explicit anti-Muslim attitudes (Raiya et al., 2008). Measures usin Association Test (IAT) demonstrated similar results. Participants s higher end of the Christian orthodoxy scale (highly correlated with ism) were quicker to pair Christians names with positive words and M

Antigay Prejudice

In 2013, the UN Human Rights Office created a series of ads succinctly portraying antigay prejudice (Radcliffe, 2013). The ads showed that when people Google search "gays should" using the Google auto-complete function, they are most likely to be completed by words "be killed" and "die." Type in the words "gays shouldn't" and the computer churns out "be allowed to marry" or "be allowed to adopt." In 2011, an FBI hate crime report showed that 21% of hate crimes were motivated by a sexual orientation bias (FBI, 2011). While the causes of suicide and suicide attempts among gay youths are multifaceted, a poll by the Public Religion Research Institute (PRRI, 2010) saw two-thirds of respondents perceiving a connection between negative messages from religious institutions and suicide rates among gay and lesbian youths. Although explicit acceptance of gay men and lesbians seems to be on the rise, subtle prejudice still persists, with potentially grave consequences.

Past research on antigay prejudice is replete with findings of a positive relationship between measures of religiosity and prejudice against gays (Finlay & Walther, 2003; Herek & Capitanio, 1996; Laythe et al., 2002; Rowatt et al., 2006). For instance, religious attendance and membership in a conservative religious denomination is associated with antigay prejudice (Finlay & Walther, 2003; Fisher, Derison, Polley, Cadman, & Johnston, 1994). A meta-analysis of religion and prejudice against gays and lesbians found measures such as fundamentalism, church attendance, and endorsement of orthodoxy to have a small but reliably positive relationship with negative attitudes toward homosexuals (Whitley, 2009). However, a small set of studies measuring extrinsic orientation and quest found either null results or a negative relation with antigay prejudice (Bassett et al., 2000; Batson et al., 1993).

A majority of these studies, however, face a number of inferential complications because of the correlational nature of the study designs. Even when primes using religious concepts are used to test the effect of religion on prejudice (Johnson, Rowatt, & LaBouff, 2012), information linking cognitive representations of those primes to antigay prejudice is absent. When mediators are tested (Johnson, Labouff, Rowatt, Patock-Peckham, & Carlisle, 2012; Shen, Yelderman, Haggard, & Rowatt, 2013), they tend to be measures (e.g., fundamentalism and right-wing authoritarianism) that have religious elements in them (Altemeyer, 1988; Altemeyer & Hunsberger, 1992). The general consensus though is that gays are considered a value-violating outgroup. The precise nature of the violated value and the resulting reaction, though, remain unclear.

Our framework posits that rather than being a strictly intergroup phenomenon, antigay prejudice may stem more from individual-level inferences. Individual gays are viewed both as a threat to a crucial moral domain in religion – purity – and as potential pathogen threats (e.g., Cottrell & Neuberg, 2005), subsequently activating feelings of disgust as a means of avoiding interaction. Purity concern is part and parcel of religion, especially pertaining to religious rituals (Shweder, Much, Mahapatra, & Park, 1997). For example, baptism, which is common for Christians, Sikhs, and Mandaeanists, is a water purification ritual that is symbolic of body cleansing. In Islam, "wudu" or washing parts of the body before worship is a common practice as well (Katz, 2005). Religious scriptures are similarly filled with verses intimately related to purity (Psalm 51:10; 1 Corinthians 6:9–10; Quran 4:43, 9:108; Vishnu Purana 4:24; Bhagavad-Gita 5:11). Additionally, food prohibitions in many religions such as Muslim halal laws, vegetarianism in Buddhism, and kosher laws in Judaism are intimately tied to the cleansing of one's body and state of mind, further suggesting the importance of purity.

To the extent that contemporary religions strongly prohibit same-sex marriage and the notion of sex between people of the same biological sex, gays are violating purity-based moral values. Gay marriage is a direct violation of the sanctification of marriage, while sex between same-sex partners is often perceived as contributing to the spread of sexual diseases and illnesses, posing a health threat to the religious community. Purity-related violations are costly if diseases spread into the community. To minimize threats to the self and the group, our human threat management system evolved two distinct and domain-specific systems, one for self-protection and one for disease avoidance (Neuberg, Kenrick, & Schaller, 2011). The disease avoidance system can be observed in humans by our emotional disgust and rejection of food potentially contaminated by parasites (Rozin, Millman, & Nemeroff, 1986). An adaptationist viewpoint of the disease avoidance system, however, goes beyond pathogen disgust. Humans are also prone to be disgusted sexually (Fessler & Navarrete, 2004; Lieberman, Tooby, & Cosmides, 2007) and morally (Haidt, McCauley, & Rozin, 1994). Purity violations and disgust are intimately related to the disease avoidance system. Therefore, a gay individual's violation of the purity domain activates disease avoidance systems, which in turn produces feelings of disgust and behavioral avoidance.

Many of the relevant findings, however, are not situated directly in a religious context. Only a handful of studies indirectly examined religious perception of purity threat and disgust toward gays. For example, conservatives – a political group that tends to be highly religious – are more disgust sensitive, especially toward issues pertaining to purity such as gay marriage (Inbar et al., 2009). Disgust is also strongly associated with a socially conservative value system that subsumes measures of religious fundamentalism and right-wing authoritarianism (Terrizzi, Shook, & Ventis, 2010).

Furthermore, given that disgust can exist in different forms according to distinct adaptive problems (Tybur, Lieberman, & Griskevicius, 2009), evidence is lacking on how the different forms of disgust are related to antigay prejudice as a function of religiosity. Speculatively, perhaps nonreligious people might be more concerned about physical disgust, presumably as a result of the perceived connection between gay sex and disease. However, moral disgust might be the dominant response instead for religious individuals because gay marriage is to identify those who are associated with the disruptions as uncooperative outgroup members.

When primed with affiliation-based religious terms, people show an increase in prosocial intentions, but only to ingroup members (Preston & Ritter, 2013). Furthermore, support for suicide attacks, an extreme form of parochial altruism (Choi & Bowles, 2007), is correlated with attendance at religious services instead of prayers to gods (Ginges, Hansen, & Norenzayan, 2009). Attendance at religious services – a form of collective ritual – is thought to enhance coalitional commitment by boosting positive benefits related to intragroup cooperation. Additionally, rituals typically signal ingroup commitment that may be associated with increased intergroup conflict (Ginges, Atran, Medin, & Shikaki, 2007). Prayers to gods, however, do not seem to reinforce coalitional psychology and may in fact diminish it. This is perhaps due to prayers' emphasis on a relationship with god, rather than promoting ingroup identification. To the extent that practices such as religious services bolster our sense of belonging to a group, coalitional psychology will be activated, perhaps promoting prejudice against other groups.

Integrated Framework

In the previous section, we described the plausible links between some core dimensions of religion and prejudice. To date, however, most of the accumulated evidence examining religion and prejudice use only general measures without considering specific reactions to different groups and individuals as evolutionary models advocate (Cottrell & Neuberg, 2005; Neuberg & Cottrell, 2008; Schaller & Neuberg, 2008).

To overcome this deficit, our integrated model seeks to specify the distinct threats different groups and individuals are perceived to pose, and then make speculative predictions about how religion might exacerbate or attenuate the respective responses triggered by those perceived threats. Two sources of threats are pertinent to our model: norm violation and group affiliation. Violations to moral norms – group loyalty, authority, and purity (Graham & Haidt, 2010) – should elicit distinct threats. For example, violation of purity norms might result in the spread of diseases and pathogens, which is a threat to one's health. On the other hand, disobedience to authority and disloyalty to the group might signal reluctance to comply with group norms, which can be seen as a threat to cooperation. Similarly, a lack of affiliation with a religious community or affiliation with an irreligious community or communities with different religious narratives and beliefs will plausibly evoke different threats. Once identified, threats can be dealt with via (a) suppression, (b) norm enforcement, or (c) avoidance (Phelan, Link, & Dovidio, 2008).

Three Test Cases for Our Integrated Framework

We apply our integrated model to three types of prejudice in the religion and prejudice literature as preliminary test cases.

I Anti-Muslim Prejudice   Muslims currently face rampant discrimination in the United States. We use anti-Muslim prejudice as a test case to more broadly illustrate how prejudice can arise between religious groups. In this sense, anti-Muslim prejudice – and enmity between religious groups more broadly – likely emerges as an intergroup phenomenon, highly influenced by evolved coalitional psychology. Anti-Muslim prejudice may be based on perceived differences in religious practices, customs, and values. For example, Muslims are prohibited from eating pork, while no such restrictions are imposed on Christians. Muslims also pray at specific times five times a day, while Christians usually attend church services once a week. When such practices differ, intergroup differences likely become more salient, activating coalitional psychology. Once triggered, detection of alliances is based on identifying members with the same religious traditions, while those with a contrasting set of practices are classified as an outgroup. Perceived dissimilarities in group norms and values thus become sources of threat. Two plausible routes to managing the threat are available. One can either socially avoid coming into contact with Muslims (only living in a neighborhood without Muslims) for fear of being tainted with impurities associated with Islam or actively try to impose the ingroup's norms by acting out against Muslims (e.g., aggression). In sum, religion may heighten coalitional concerns, driving intergroup conflict between religious groups. In a majority Christian country such as the United States, this may increase anti-Muslim prejudice.

II Antigay Prejudice   While anti-Muslim prejudice likely emerges from intergroup processes, we view antigay prejudice as plausibly being more driven by individual-level inferences. Specifically, antigay prejudice may stem from both the perceived violation of purity norms and the heuristic pathogen threats associated with homosexuality (e.g., Cottrell & Neuberg, 2005). Some facets of religion may exacerbate the heuristic purity and pathogen-based inferences that drive antigay prejudice. Because purity norms are integral to religion, especially in religious rituals, violation of purity norms is an especially salient threat to many religious groups and individuals. When purity threat is present, disgust is often activated as a way of avoiding interaction with gays. Thus, in sum, religion may heighten sensitivity to purity cues and, in turn, lead to negative inferences about, and avoidance of, gay men and lesbians.

III Anti-Atheist Prejudice   Trust is central to social life, but an individual's trustworthiness must be only indirectly inferred (Simpson, 2007). Religious believers may come to use religious belief as a cue to who can be trusted. After all, many people view religion as a necessary component of morality (Pew, 2007). Without belief in a god, atheists might be viewed as moral wildcards who are capable of engaging in various immoral actions (Gervais,

2014). Thus, for religious believers, individual atheists may be viewed as cooperative threats and therefore viewed with distrust (e.g., Gervais, Shariff, & Norenzayan, 2011). As with antigay prejudice, anti-atheist prejudice may derive more from inferences regarding an individual atheists' trustworthiness, rather than any perceived intergroup conflict between believers and atheists. Religious belief is likely a key contributor to anti-atheist prejudice. Believers are more likely to view religion as a key contributor to morality. As a result, they will be more morally suspicious of atheists, leading to distrust of individual atheists.

In the next three sections, we treat each test case more thoroughly and highlight potential areas to be explored in the future.

Anti-Muslim Prejudice

Since the 9/11 terrorist attack on the World Trade Center, attitudes toward Muslims have occupied a central stage in America. Although post-9/11 saw an initial decline in prejudice toward Muslims, negative attitudes toward Muslims rose from 2005 to 2010 (Pew, 2010). A similar poll found that 43% of respondents admitted to at least feeling a little prejudice toward Muslims, the highest compared to other religious groups (Gallup, 2009a). Although we focus here on anti-Muslim prejudice, our aim is to illustrate broader patterns about intergroup conflict between religious groups. Our framework predicts that anti-Muslim prejudice results from perceived differences in religious practices and traditions, which in turn trigger evolved coalitional psychology. Our coalition system then demarcates alliances and enemies according to whether or not one practices the religion of the ingroup, in this case a majority Christian ingroup. A Gallup poll (Gallup, 2009b) supports this prediction, with 68% of respondents disagreeing that Christianity and Islam are the same. Consequently, to a Christian, Muslims become an especially salient outgroup because of the belief that the practice of Islam is at odds with Christianity.

Using both explicit and implicit measures examining attitudes toward Muslims, psychological studies have documented a positive association between some aspects of religiosity (e.g., fundamentalism) and anti-Muslim prejudice (Raiya, Pargament, Mahoney, & Trevino, 2008; Rowatt, Franklin, & Cotton, 2005; van der Slik & Konig, 2006). Using explicit measures of negative attitudes toward Muslims, Rowatt and colleagues (2005) found a positive correlation with fundamentalism and right-wing authoritarianism. Likewise, a higher endorsement of Muslims as desecrators of Christian values and teachings led to higher levels of explicit anti-Muslim attitudes (Raiya et al., 2008). Measures using the Implicit Association Test (IAT) demonstrated similar results. Participants scoring on the higher end of the Christian orthodoxy scale (highly correlated with fundamentalism) were quicker to pair Christians names with positive words and Muslim names with negative words, displaying a relatively more positive implicit attitude toward fellow Christians than Muslims (Rowatt et al., 2005). Perception of Muslims as pursuing a different set of norms and values is a threat to one's ingroup that requires attention and management. In other words, differing religious norms can be seen as coalitional cues.

To ensure that the norms of the ingroup are not threatened, two possible routes can be undertaken. One can respond either by avoiding any interaction or by attempting to aggress. Matthews and Levin (2012) set out to test both hypotheses and found that perception of threat to ingroup values was positively associated with feelings of disgust (avoidance) and anger (approach) toward Muslims. To disentangle the relationship, value threat was experimentally manipulated to be either high or low. Disgust and anger were evaluated as potential mediators. Results provide initial evidence that perceiving Muslims to hold a greater threat to one's values increases feelings of disgust but not anger. This led to the avoidance of all things Muslim. However, other studies support the idea of acting out against Muslims. For example, negative attitudes toward Muslims are associated with more support for several aspects of the war on terror (Sides & Gross, 2013). One possible explanation for the contradictory findings is that while Matthews and Levin's study focused on value difference, Sides and Gross had participants rate Muslims on several traits such as "violent" and "untrustworthy." This may have primed participants to increase their support for the war on terror as an act of retaliation against the perceived violent nature of Muslims.

If group identification augments group differences, then church attendance can be an additional marker of affiliation that will predict anti-Muslim prejudice. Attendance at church has the ability to increase commitment to coalitional identities (Atran, 2003). When coalitional commitment is enhanced, group differences should be intensified, creating room for prejudice to develop. This can be contrasted with prayer frequency. Because prayers should not trigger coalitional cues, church attendance but not prayers should predict anti-Muslim prejudice. Ginges et al. (2009) pitted attendance with prayers and found that attendance at religious services but not prayers predicted support for suicide attacks, an extreme form of prejudice, to benefit the ingroup. While this study can only speak to the broader interreligion conflict perspective, the general mechanism can be applied to explain more specific (i.e., anti-Muslim) prejudices, supporting the view that perceived differences in group practices may result in aggressive behaviors toward, rather than avoidance of, Muslims. This leads to more avenues of research regarding circumstances under which avoidance or approach might be triggered as a dominant response to threats. In sum, anti-Muslim prejudice may originate from our evolved coalitional psychology that alerts us to discrepancies in group practices, while differing religious norms and practices serves as a clear line of group demarcation.

a violation of sacred values. If so, the nonreligious should be more inclined to avoid interaction with gays, but the religious will seek ways to preserve their sacred values. One way is via antigay legislation; another is to engage in aggressive behaviors. It is also possible that if the physical aspect is made salient, the primary response is avoidance regardless of religiosity, but active engagement becomes the prepotent response when the focus is on the moral dimension. In sum, while our model posits that antigay prejudice may be a result of disgust toward purity violations, it is more likely to be an individual-level, rather than group-level, reaction.

Anti-Atheist Prejudice

Even though anti-atheist prejudice is less prominent in the media than either Islamophobia or antigay prejudice, it is nevertheless a common occurrence. A case in point is a social experiment that a group of shoe retailers decided to carry out (AtheistBerlin, 2012). On November 21, 2012, they sent 89 people two packages, each containing a pair of shoes. One package was sealed with a packing tape branded with the word "atheist" on it and the other with a neutral tape. The packages were sent all over the United States (49 states) from Berlin via USPS. Because all packages were sent at the same time, they should have arrived at roughly the same time. That was not the case. In fact, the atheist-branded packages took on average three days longer to arrive and they were 10 times more likely to disappear than packages with neutral tapings. While definitive conclusions cannot be made, discrimination from USPS employees based on religion (or lack thereof) is a possibility.

Contemporary opinion polls tell a similar story. In one poll, only 45% of respondents were willing to vote for a qualified atheist presidential candidate. This was the lowest percentage out of several other minority candidates and also the only one who was unable to receive a majority vote (Jones, 2007). And in 2014, a Pew poll found that 53% of Americans would not vote for an atheist as a presidential candidate, with 22% who would not vote for a marijuana user and 35% for someone who had an extramarital affair (Pew, 2014). In a sociological survey, Americans rated atheists as the group least likely to agree with their vision of American (40%), a full 13% more than for Muslims (Edgell, Gerteis, & Hartmann, 2006). Atheists were also the least favored in this survey as a potential marriage partner, with 48% of the respondents opposing having an atheist in the family. The prevalence of atheists (Zuckerman, 2007) coupled with the many instances of discrimination call for a need to understand not just the traditional between-religious conflicts but also conflicts arising from the religious-nonreligious divide.

Our theoretical framework suggests that anti-atheist prejudice arises primarily in the domain of trust. People often use religion as a cue to who can be trusted (Tan &

Vogel, 2008), perhaps because they view belief in a morally concerned god as a useful deterrent to antisocial behavior. Therefore, to the extent that atheists do not believe in god, they are likely to be distrusted on the basis of their perceived tendency to be morally unregulated. As with antigay prejudice, we hypothesize that anti-atheist prejudice primarily emerges at the individual, rather than intergroup, level.

To examine distrust as the motivation for anti-atheist prejudice, a series of studies using the conjunction fallacy paradigm (Tversky & Kahneman, 1983) were conducted by Gervais and colleagues (2011). In the classic conjunction fallacy task, a description of Linda as an outspoken and politically active single woman was given to participants. They were then asked to decide which was more probable: (A) Linda is a bank teller or (B) Linda is a bank teller and a feminist. A conjunction fallacy is committed when one chooses option B. This is because participants intuitively judged the description as more representative of a feminist even though statistically speaking, option A is the correct answer. When the target's description fits a particular group membership, people tend to commit the fallacy. Gervais and colleagues took advantage of this by having descriptions fitting of someone who is untrustworthy and measuring the tendency for participants to commit the fallacy using a variety of groups, including atheists. In their second study, participants read a description of an untrustworthy and selfish target as follows:

> Richard is 31 years old. On his way to work one day, he accidentally backed his car into a parked van. Because pedestrians were watching, he got out of his car. He pretended to write down his insurance information. He then tucked the blank note into the van's window before getting back into his car and driving away. Later the day, Richard found a wallet on the sidewalk. Nobody was looking, so he took all of the money out of the wallet. He then threw the wallet in a trash can.

Participants next had to decide which option was more probable of Richard, that he was (A) a teacher or (B) a teacher and "XXXXX." "XXXXX" was manipulated to be a Christian, a Muslim, a rapist, or an atheist. If "XXXXX" is a rapist for example, and if participants chose B, it means that they think Richard is a teacher who is also a rapist. Committing the fallacy by choosing B when Richard was presented as an atheist is thus an indirect measure of people's intuitive association between an atheist and the trait of untrustworthiness. Participants were significantly more likely to pick option B in the atheist condition compared to the other conditions (except the rapist condition) with consistently large effects. Two additional studies varying the descriptions and the groups for comparisons showed similar results, suggesting that anti-atheist prejudice is by and large driven by distrust toward nonbelievers and not disgust or general unpleasantness. An additional follow-up study demonstrated the context specificity of distrust in a job selection survey. Participants were given information about two job candidates and they had to decide which candidate was suitable for a waitressing job – a low-trust position – and which was better as a daycare worker – a high-trust position. The candidates were similar in all attributes (e.g., gender, educational background) except religiosity. One was presented as a religious person while the other was an atheist. When the candidate was religious, participants preferred that candidate to be a daycare worker compared to the atheist candidate and vice versa for the waitressing job. These studies are consistent with the possibility that distrust is central to anti-atheist prejudice.

Further support for our integrated framework comes from research on the psychological interchangeability between gods and secular authorities, underpinned by the ability of both to provide people with a sense of psychological control (Kay, Gaucher, Napier, Callan, & Laurin, 2008; Kay, Shepherd, Blatz, Chua, & Galinsky, 2010). By extension, both gods and the government may also serve the role of encouraging prosociality while staving off the temptation to behave immorally. While disbelief may indicate distrust, as described previously, insofar as other forms of effective surveillance are in place (e.g., secular authority) to ensure that antisocial behaviors do not go undetected, the role of a moralizing god can potentially be replaced, diminishing the need to remain distrustful of atheists. Indeed, when primed with concepts associated with secular authorities, participants reported reduced distrust of atheists (Gervais & Norenzayan, 2012), but not reduced prejudice against other groups. Two cross-national analyses provide additional support, finding that believers residing in countries with a strong secular rule of law are less politically intolerant of atheists, a measure that has an extensive overlap with assessing atheist distrust (Norenzayan & Gervais, 2015).

Our integrated framework when applied to anti-atheist prejudice provides a more complete picture than many other accounts. Instead of merely presenting evidence of anti-atheist prejudice as a general negative attitude, our framework specifically posits that distrust is a core feature of anti-atheist prejudice. By understanding what drives anti-atheist prejudice, future studies can more effectively find ways to reduce anti-atheist prejudice by focusing on distrust instead of more general negative attitudes. For example, might an atheist who displays a willingness to commit to cooperation by incurring costs to the self during the previous iteration of a trust game be seen as more trustworthy and less likely to defect in the future? Is distrust a general phenomenon regardless of whether one is a hard-line atheist who thinks religion is toxic (e.g., Hitchens, 2008), an atheist who finds value in some aspects of religion (e.g., De Botton, 2012), or a person who has no religious affiliation but does not consider himself/herself to be an atheist? With the current rise of the religiously unaffiliated in America (Pew, 2015), it is fruitful to explore if the religious do in fact distinguish and subsequently vary the level of distrust according to the type of atheist one is perceived to be. To conclude, anti-atheist prejudice is primarily driven by distrust because atheists, by virtue of their lack of belief in a god, are perceived as being incapable of regulating their moral behaviors.

Concluding Remarks

In this chapter, we sought to expand on research in religion and prejudice by integrating recent evolutionary accounts of both. To do so, we reviewed both adaptationist and by-product accounts of religion and then attempted to reconcile them. In sum, the capacity to represent supernatural agents may arise as a by-product of ordinary nonreligious cognition, but different religious representations can have adaptive functions for promoting ingroup cooperation. Next, we discussed the benefits of adopting an evolutionary approach to understanding stereotyping and prejudice. The core insight from this approach is that different forms of prejudice can be viewed as specific reactions to deal with recurrent adaptive challenges. Thus, rather than thinking of "prejudice" as a unitary construct, it urges researchers to consider "prejudices" as functionally distinct complexes of reactions to individuals and groups heuristically viewed as posing specific functional threats. Next, we argued that threats to different core dimensions of religion (i.e., believing, behaving, and belonging) can induce different threat perceptions and consequently unique prejudices to manage each threat. Therefore, by incorporating evolutionary approaches to both religion and prejudices, our integrated model makes precise predictions about religion and prejudice based on the unique characteristics different religious groups and individuals possess.

We highlighted the utility of our framework by considering three test cases: anti-Muslim prejudice, antigay prejudice, and anti-atheist prejudice. Instead of merely suggesting an association between some form of religious measures and prejudice against Muslims, gays, and atheists, we were able to make more explicit predictions. For example, our model posits that prejudice against gays can be characterized by disgust, but anti-atheist prejudice is distinctly associated with distrust. Differentiating between prejudices not only stimulates more fruitful research and offers a more nuanced perspective in religion and prejudice, it also highlights the need for customized interventions aimed at reducing prejudice (e.g., Kurzban, Tooby, & Cosmides, 2001). When the specific underlying causes of different prejudices are recognized, specific steps can be taken to address those causes. While some interventions – such as intergroup contact – may reduce prejudices broadly, others – such as reminders of secular authority (Gervais & Norenzayan, 2012) – might more surgically target only a single prejudice.

The previous half century has seen massive gains in understanding the evolution of religion and prejudice, respectively. At the same time, there is a wealth of available evidence on the relationship between certain religious constructs (e.g., intrinsic vs. extrinsic religiosity) and various prejudices. We propose a model that may help organize existing research on religion and prejudice. Further, as our model is currently both descriptive and speculative, it suggests more avenues for researchers to generate and test specific hypotheses about the relationship between religion and different prejudices, hopefully leading to effective interventions for reducing given prejudices. Our integrated model should thus be seen as a profitable albeit unfinished product in the pursuit of organizing and building on the literature on religion and prejudice.

References

Alexander, R. D. (1979). *Darwinism and human affairs*. Seattle: University of Washington Press.

Allport, G. W. (1954). *The nature of prejudice*. Reading, MA: Addison-Wesley.

Allport, G. W. (1966). The religious context of prejudice. *Journal for the Scientific Study of Religion*, 447–457.

Allport, G. W., & Ross, J. M. (1967). Personal religious orientation and prejudice. *Journal of Personality and Social Psychology, 5*(4), 432.

Altemeyer, B. (1988). *Enemies of freedom: Understanding right-wing authoritarianism*. San Francisco: Jossey-Bass.

Altemeyer, B., & Hunsberger, B. (1992). Authoritarianism, religious fundamentalism, quest, and prejudice. *The International Journal for the Psychology of Religion, 2*(2), 113–133.

Altemeyer, B., & Hunsberger, B. (2005). Fundamentalism and authoritarianism. In R. F. Paloutzian & C. L. Park (Eds.), *Handbook of the psychology of religion and spirituality* (pp. 378–393). New York: Guilford Press.

AtheistBerlin. (2012). USPS Discrimination Against Atheism? from www.atheistberlin .com/atheist/?study

Atran, S. (2003). Genesis of suicide terrorism. *Science, 299*(5612), 1534–1539.

Atran, S., & Norenzayan, A. (2004). Religion's evolutionary landscape: Counterintuition, commitment, compassion, communion. *Behavioral and Brain Sciences, 27*(06), 713–730.

Baron-Cohen, S. (1995). *Mindblindness: An essay on autism and theory of mind*. Cambridge, MA: MIT Press.

Barrett, J. L. (2000). Exploring the natural foundations of religion. *Trends in Cognitive Sciences, 4*(1), 29–34.

Barrett, J. L. (2004). *Why would anyone believe in God?*: Walnut Creek, CA: AltaMira Press.

Barrett, J. L., & Keil, F. C. (1996). Conceptualizing a nonnatural entity: Anthropomorphism in God concepts. *Cognitive Psychology, 31*(3), 219–247.

Barrett, J. L., & Nyhof, M. A. (2001). Spreading non-natural concepts: The role of intuitive conceptual structures in memory and transmission of cultural materials. *Journal of Cognition and Culture, 1*(1), 69–100.

Bassett, R. L., Hodak, E., Allen, J., Bartos, D., Grastorf, J., Sittig, L., & Strong, J. (2000). Homonegative Christians: Loving the sinner but hating the sin. *Journal of Psychology and Christianity, 19*(3), 258–269.

Batson, C. D. (1976). Religion as prosocial: Agent or double agent? *Journal for the Scientific Study of Religion*, 29–45.

Batson, C. D., Schoenrade, P., & Ventis, W. L. (1993). *Religion and the individual: A social-psychological perspective*. New York: Oxford University Press.

Batson, C. D., & Ventis, W. L. (1982). *The religious experience: A social-psychological perspective*. New York: Oxford University Press.

Bering, J. M., & Johnson, D. D. (2005). "O Lord . . . You perceive my thoughts from afar": Recursiveness and the evolution of supernatural agency. *Journal of Cognition and Culture, 5*(1), 118–142.

Blogowska, J., & Saroglou, V. (2011). Religious fundamentalism and limited prosociality as a function of the target. *Journal for the Scientific Study of Religion, 50*(1), 44–60.

Bloom, P. (2007). Religion is natural. *Developmental Science, 10*(1), 147–151.

Boyer, P. (2001). *Religion explained: The evolutionary origins of religious thought*. New York: Basic Books.

Boyer, P. (2003). Religious thought and behaviour as by-products of brain function. *Trends in Cognitive Sciences, 7*(3), 119–124.

Brandt, M. J., & Reyna, C. (2010). The role of prejudice and the need for closure in religious fundamentalism. *Personality and Social Psychology Bulletin, 36*, 715–725.

Brandt, M. J., & Reyna, C. (2014). To love or hate thy neighbor: The role of authoritarianism and traditionalism in explaining the link between fundamentalism and racial prejudice. *Political Psychology, 35*(2), 207–223.

Brewer, M. B., & Brown, R. J. (1998). *Intergroup relations*. In D. T. Gilbert, S. T. Fiske, & G. Lindzey (Eds.), *Handbook of social psychology* (4th ed., pp. 554–594). Boston: McGraw-Hill.

Choi, J.-K., & Bowles, S. (2007). The coevolution of parochial altruism and war. *Science, 318*(5850), 636–640.

Cottrell, C. A., & Neuberg, S. L. (2005). Different emotional reactions to different groups: A sociofunctional threat-based approach to "prejudice." *Journal of Personality and Social Psychology, 88*(5), 770.

Cottrell, C. A., Richards, D. A., & Nichols, A. L. (2010). Predicting policy attitudes from general prejudice versus specific intergroup emotions. *Journal of Experimental Social Psychology, 46*(2), 247–254.

De Botton, A. (2012). *Religion for atheists: A non-believer's guide to the uses of religion*. London: Penguin.

Donahue, M. J. (1985). Intrinsic and extrinsic religiousness: The empirical research. *Journal for the Scientific Study of Religion*, 418–423.

Duckitt, J. (2001). A dual-process cognitive-motivational theory of ideology and prejudice. *Advances in Experimental Social Psychology, 33*, 41–113.

Duckitt, J., Wagner, C., Du Plessis, I., & Birum, I. (2002). The psychological bases of ideology and prejudice: Testing a dual process model. *Journal of Personality and Social Psychology, 83*(1), 75.

Duckitt, J. (2006). Differential effects of right wing authoritarianism and social dominance orientation on outgroup attitudes and their mediation by threat from and competitiveness to outgroups. *Personality and Social Psychology Bulletin, 32*(5), 684–696.

Duckitt, J., & Sibley, C. G. (2007). Right wing authoritarianism, social dominance orientation and the dimensions of generalized prejudice. *European Journal of Personality, 21*(2), 113–130.

Duckitt, J., & Sibley, C. G. (2010). Personality, ideology, prejudice, and politics: A dual-process motivational model. *Journal of Personality, 78*(6), 1861–1894.

Edgell, P., Gerteis, J., & Hartmann, D. (2006). Atheists as "other": Moral boundaries and cultural membership in American society. *American Sociological Review, 71*(2), 211–234.

FBI. (2011). FBI Releases 2011 Hate Crime Statistics [Press release]. Retrieved from www .fbi.gov/news/pressrel/press-releases/fbi-releases-2011-hate-crime-statistics

Fessler, D. M., & Navarrete, C. D. (2004). Third-party attitudes toward sibling incest: Evidence for Westermarck's hypotheses. *Evolution and Human Behavior, 25*(5), 277–294.

Finlay, B., & Walther, C. S. (2003). The relation of religious affiliation, service attendance, and other factors to homophobic attitudes among university students. *Review of Religious Research*, 370–393.

Fisher, R. D., Derison, D., Polley, C. F., Cadman, J., & Johnston, D. (1994). Religiousness, religious orientation, and attitudes towards gays and lesbians. *Journal of Applied Social Psychology, 24*(7), 614–630.

Frith, U., & Frith, C. D. (2003). Development and neurophysiology of mentalizing. *Philosophical Transactions of the Royal Society B-Biological Sciences, 358*(1431), 459–473. doi: 10.1098/rstb.2002.1218

Gallup. (2009a). In U.S., religious prejudice stronger against Muslims. Retrieved from www .gallup.com/poll/125312/religious-prejudice-stronger-against-muslims.aspx

Gallup. (2009b). Religious perceptions in America with an in-depth analysis of U.S. attitudes toward Muslims and Islam. Retrieved from www.clubmadrid.org /img/secciones/SSP_MWF_WorldReligion_Report_en-US_final.pdf

Gervais, W. M. (2013a). Religious cognition. In V. Saroglou (Ed.), *Religion, personality, and social behavior* (pp. 71–95). New York: Psychology Press.

Gervais, W. M. (2013b). Perceiving minds and gods: How mind perception enables, constrains, and is triggered by belief in gods. *Perspectives on Psychological Science, 8*(4), 380–394.

Gervais, W. M. (2014). Everything is permitted? People intuitively judge immorality as representative of atheists. *PloS One, 9*(4), e92302.

Gervais, W. M., & Norenzayan, A. (2012). Reminders of secular authority reduce believers' distrust of atheists. *Psychological Science, 23*, 483–491.

Gervais, W. M., Shariff, A. F., & Norenzayan, A. (2011). Do you believe in atheists? Distrust is central to anti-atheist prejudice. *Journal of Personality and Social Psychology, 101*(6), 1189.

Gervais, W. M., Willard, A. K., Norenzayan, A., & Henrich, J. (2011). The cultural transmission of faith: Why innate intuitions are necessary, but insufficient, to explain religious belief. *Religion, 41*(3), 389–410.

Ginges, J., Atran, S., Medin, D., & Shikaki, K. (2007). Sacred bounds on rational resolution of violent political conflict. *Proceedings of the National Academy of Sciences, 104*(18), 7357–7360.

Ginges, J., Hansen, I., & Norenzayan, A. (2009). Religion and support for suicide attacks. *Psychological Science, 20*(2), 224–230.

Graham, J., & Haidt, J. (2010). Beyond beliefs: Religions bind individuals into moral communities. *Personality and Social Psychology Review, 14*(1), 140–150. doi: 10.1177/1088868309353415

Guthrie, S. (1993). *Faces in the clouds*. New York: Oxford University Press.

Haidt, J., & Graham, J. (2007). When morality opposes justice: Conservatives have moral intuitions that liberals may not recognize. *Social Justice Research, 20*(1), 98–116.

Haidt, J., McCauley, C., & Rozin, P. (1994). Individual differences in sensitivity to disgust: A scale sampling seven domains of disgust elicitors. *Personality and Individual Differences*, *16*(5), 701–713.

Henrich, J. (2009). The evolution of costly displays, cooperation and religion: Credibility enhancing displays and their implications for cultural evolution. *Evolution and Human Behavior*, *30*(4), 244–260.

Henrich, J., & Gil-White, F. J. (2001). The evolution of prestige: Freely conferred deference as a mechanism for enhancing the benefits of cultural transmission. *Evolution and Human Behavior*, *22*(3), 165–196.

Herek, G. M. (1987). Religious orientation and prejudice: A comparison of racial and sexual attitudes. *Personality and Social Psychology Bulletin*, *13*(1), 34–44.

Herek, G. M., & Capitanio, J. P. (1996). "Some of my best friends": Intergroup contact, concealable stigma, and heterosexuals' attitudes toward gay men and lesbians. *Personality and Social Psychology Bulletin*, *22*, 412–424.

Hitchens, C. (2008). *God is not great: How religion poisons everything*. New York: Twelve.

Hoge, R., & Carroll, J. W. (1973). Religiosity and prejudice in northern and southern churches. *Journal for the Scientific Study of Religion*, 181–197.

Hood, R. W., Hill, P. C., & Williamson, W. P. (2005). *The psychology of religious fundamentalism*. New York: Guilford Press.

Hunsberger, B. (1996). Religious fundamentalism, right-wing authoritarianism, and hostility toward homosexuals in non-Christian religious groups. *The International Journal for the Psychology of Religion*, *6*(1), 39–49.

Inbar, Y., Pizarro, D. A., & Bloom, P. (2009). Conservatives are more easily disgusted than liberals. *Cognition and Emotion*, *23*(4), 714–725.

Insko, C. A., Pinkley, R. L., Harring, K., & Holton, B. (1987). Minimal conditions for real groups: Mere categorization or competitive between category behavior. *Representative Research in Social Psychology*, *17*, 5–36.

Irons, W. (2001). Religion as a hard-to-fake sign of commitment. *Evolution and the capacity for commitment*, 292–309.

James, W. (1902). *The varieties of religious experience*. New York: Random House.

Johnson, D. D. (2005). God's punishment and public goods. *Human Nature*, *16*(4), 410–446.

Johnson, D. D., & Bering, J. M. (2006). Hand of God, mind of man: Punishment and cognition in the evolution of cooperation. *Evolutionary Psychology*, *4*(1), 219–233.

Johnson, D. D., & Krüger, O. (2004). The good of wrath: Supernatural punishment and the evolution of cooperation. *Political Theology*, *5*(2), 159–176.

Johnson, M. K., Labouff, J. P., Rowatt, W. C., Patock-Peckham, J. A., & Carlisle, R. D. (2012). Facets of right-wing authoritarianism mediate the relationship between religious fundamentalism and attitudes toward Arabs and African Americans. *Journal for the Scientific Study of Religion*, *51*(1), 128–142.

Johnson, M. K., Rowatt, W. C., & LaBouff, J. P. (2012). Religiosity and prejudice revisited: In-group favoritism, out-group derogation, or both? *Psychology of Religion and Spirituality*, *4*(2), 154–168. doi: DOI 10.1037/a0025107

Jones, J. M. (2007). Some Americans reluctant to vote for Mormon, 72-year-old presidential candidates; Strong support for black, women, Catholic candidates. Retrieved from www.gallup.com/poll/26611/some-americans-reluctant-vote-mormon-72year old-presidential-candidates.aspx

Katz, M. H. (2005). The study of Islamic ritual and the meaning of wuḍū'. *Der Islam, 82*(1), 106–145.

Kay, A. C., Gaucher, D., Napier, J. L., Callan, M. J., & Laurin, K. (2008). God and the government: Testing a compensatory control mechanism for the support of external systems. *Journal of Personality and Social Psychology, 95*(1), 18.

Kay, A. C., Shepherd, S., Blatz, C. W., Chua, S. N., & Galinsky, A. D. (2010). For God (or) country: The hydraulic relation between government instability and belief in religious sources of control. *Journal of Personality and Social Psychology, 99*(5), 725.

Kelemen, D. (1999a). Function, goals and intention: Children's teleological reasoning about objects. *Trends in Cognitive Sciences, 3*(12), 461–468.

Kelemen, D. (1999b). Why are rocks pointy? Children's preference for teleological explanations of the natural world. *Developmental Psychology, 35*(6), 1440.

Kelemen, D. (2004). Are children "intuitive theists"? Reasoning about purpose and design in nature. *Psychological Science, 15*(5), 295–301.

Kelemen, D., & Rosset, E. (2009). The human function compunction: Teleological explanation in adults. *Cognition, 111*(1), 138–143.

Kelemen, D., Rottman, J., & Seston, R. (2013). Professional physical scientists display tenacious teleological tendencies: Purpose-based reasoning as a cognitive default. *Journal of Experimental Psychology: General, 142*(4), 1074.

Krebs, D. L., & Denton, K. (1997). Social illusions and self-deception: The evolution of biases in person perception. *Evolutionary Social Psychology,* 21–48.

Kurzban, R., & Leary, M. R. (2001). Evolutionary origins of stigmatization: The functions of social exclusion. *Psychological Bulletin, 127*(2), 187.

Kurzban, R., Tooby, J., & Cosmides, L. (2001). Can race be erased? Coalitional computation and social categorization. *Proceedings of the National Academy of Sciences, 98*(26), 15387–15392.

Laythe, B., Finkel, D. G., Bringle, R. G., & Kirkpatrick, L. A. (2002). Religious fundamentalism as a predictor of prejudice: A two-component model. *Journal for the Scientific Study of Religion, 41*(4), 623–635.

Lieberman, D., Tooby, J., & Cosmides, L. (2007). The architecture of human kin detection. *Nature, 445*(7129), 727–731.

Matthews, M., & Levin, S. (2012). Testing a dual process model of prejudice: Assessment of group threat perceptions and emotions. *Motivation and Emotion, 36*(4), 564–574.

Mavor, K. I., Louis, W. R., & Laythe, B. (2011). Religion, prejudice, and authoritarianism: Is RWA a boon or bane to the psychology of religion? *Journal for the Scientific Study of Religion, 50*(1), 22–43.

McFarland, S. G. (1989). Religious orientations and the targets of discrimination. *Journal for the Scientific Study of Religion,* 324–336.

Neuberg, S. L., & Cottrell, C. A. (2008). Managing the threats and opportunities afforded by human sociality. *Group Dynamics: Theory, Research, and Practice, 12*(1), 63.

Neuberg, S. L., Kenrick, D. T., & Schaller, M. (2010). Evolutionary social psychology. In S. T. Fiske, D. T. Gilbert, & G. Lindzey (Eds.), *Handbook of social psychology* (5th ed., Vol. 2, pp. 761–796). New York: Wiley.

Neuberg, S. L., Kenrick, D. T., & Schaller, M. (2011). Human threat management systems: Self-protection and disease avoidance. *Neuroscience & Biobehavioral Reviews, 35*(4), 1042–1051.

Neuberg, S. L., Smith, D. M., & Asher, T. (2000). Why people stigmatize: Toward a biocultural framework. In T. Heatherton, R. Kleck, M. Hebl & J. Hull (Eds.), *The social psychology of stigma* (pp. 31–61). New York: Guilford Press.

Norenzayan, A., & Gervais, W. M. (2012). The cultural evolution of religion. *Creating consilience: Integrating the sciences and the humanities*, 243–265.

Norenzayan, A., & Gervais, W. M. (2013). The origins of religious disbelief. *Trends in Cognitive Sciences*, *17*(1), 20–25.

Norenzayan, A., & Gervais, W. M. (2015). Secular rule of law erodes believers' political intolerance of atheists. *Religion, Brain & Behavior*, *5*(1), 3–14.

Norenzayan, A., Shariff, A., Gervais, W., Willard, A., Slingerland, E., & Henrich, J. (2016). The cultural evolution of prosocial religions. *Behavioral and Brain Sciences*, *39*.

Norenzayan, A., & Shariff, A. F. (2008). The origin and evolution of religious prosociality. *Science*, *322*(5898), 58–62.

Pargament, K. I. (2001). *The psychology of religion and coping: Theory, research, practice.* New York: Guilford Press.

Pew. (2007). Chapter 3. Views of religion and morality. Retrieved from www.pewglobal.org /2007/10/04/chapter-3-views-of-religion-and-morality/

Pew. (2010). Public remains conflicted over Islam. Retrieved from www.pewforum.org /files/2010/08/Islam-mosque-full-report.pdf

Pew. (2014). For 2016 hopefuls, Washington experience could do more harm than good. Retrieved from www.people-press.org/2014/05/19/for-2016-hopefuls-washington-experience-could-do-more-harm-than-good/

Pew. (2015). America's changing religious landscape. Retrieved from www.pewforum.org /2015/05/12/americas-changing-religious-landscape/

Phelan, J. C., Link, B. G., & Dovidio, J. F. (2008). Stigma and prejudice: One animal or two? *Social Science & Medicine*, *67*(3), 358–367.

Preston, J. L., & Ritter, R. S. (2013). Different effects of religion and God on prosociality with the ingroup and outgroup. *Personality and Social Psychology Bulletin*, *39*, 1471–1483.

Preston, J. L., Ritter, R. S., & Ivan Hernandez, J. (2010). Principles of religious prosociality: A review and reformulation. *Social and Personality Psychology Compass*, *4*(8), 574–590.

PRRI. (2010). Survey | Less than 1-in-5 give America's places of worship high marks on handling issue of homosexuality. Retrieved from http://publicreligion.org /research/2010/10/less-than-1-in-5-give-americas-places-of-worship-high-marks -on-handling-issue-of-homosexuality/#.VVuo7PlViko

Radcliffe, C. (2013). UN campaign reveals shocking, depressing gay Google auto-complete function. Retrieved from www.huffingtonpost.com/charles-radcliffe/google-auto-complete-gays_b_4153399.html

Raiya, H. A., Pargament, K. I., Mahoney, A., & Trevino, K. (2008). When Muslims are perceived as a religious threat: Examining the connection between desecration, religious coping, and anti-Muslim attitudes. *Basic and Applied Social Psychology*, *30*(4), 311–325.

Rendell, L., Fogarty, L., Hoppitt, W. J. E., Morgan, T. J. H., Webster, M. M., & Laland, K. N. (2011). Cognitive culture: Theoretical and empirical insights into social learning strategies. *Trends in Cognitive Science*, *15*(2), 68–76.

Robert, B., & Richerson, P. J. (1985). *Culture and the evolutionary process*. Chicago: University of Chicago Press.

Rothschild, Z. K., Abdollahi, A., & Pyszczynski, T. (2009). Does peace have a prayer? The effect of mortality salience, compassionate values, and religious fundamentalism on hostility toward out-groups. *Journal of Experimental Social Psychology*, *45*(4), 816–827.

Rowatt, W. C., Franklin, L. M., & Cotton, M. (2005). Patterns and personality correlates of implicit and explicit attitudes toward Christians and Muslims. *Journal for the Scientific Study of Religion*, *44*(1), 29–43.

Rowatt, W. C., Tsang, J. A., Kelly, J., LaMartina, B., McCullers, M., & McKinley, A. (2006). Associations between religious personality dimensions and implicit homosexual prejudice. *Journal for the Scientific Study of Religion*, *45*(3), 397–406.

Rozin, P., Millman, L., & Nemeroff, C. (1986). Operation of the laws of sympathetic magic in disgust and other domains. *Journal of Personality and Social Psychology*, *50*(4), 703.

Saroglou, V. (2011). Believing, bonding, behaving, and belonging: The Big Four religious dimensions and cultural variation. *Journal of Cross-Cultural Psychology*, *42*(8), 1320–1340.

Saroglou, V., & Galand, P. (2004). Identities, values, and religion: A study among Muslim, other immigrant, and native Belgian young adults after the 9/11 attacks. *Identity*, *4*(2), 97–132.

Saroglou, V., Pichon, I., Trompette, L., Verschueren, M., & Dernelle, R. (2005). Prosocial behavior and religion: New evidence based on projective measures and peer ratings. *Journal for the Scientific Study of Religion*, *44*(3), 323–348.

Schaller, M., & Neuberg, S. L. (2008). Intergroup prejudices and intergroup conflicts. In C. Crawford & D. L. Krebs (Eds.), *Foundations of evolutionary psychology: Ideas, issues, and applications* (pp. 399–412). Mahwah, NJ: Erlbaum.

Schaller, M., Park, J., & Faulkner, J. (2003). Prehistoric dangers and contemporary prejudices. *European Review of Social Psychology*, *14*(1), 105–137.

Shen, M. J., Yelderman, L. A., Haggard, M. C., & Rowatt, W. C. (2013). Disentangling the belief in God and cognitive rigidity/flexibility components of religiosity to predict racial and value-violating prejudice: A Post-Critical Belief Scale analysis. *Personality and Individual Differences*, *54*(3), 389–395.

Sheriff, M. (1966). *Group conflict and cooperation*: London: Routledge and Kegan Paul.

Shweder, R., Much, N., Mahapatra, M., & Park, L. (1997). The "Big Three" of morality (autonomy, community, divinity) and the "Big Three" explanations of suffering. In A. Brandt & P. Rozin (Eds.), *Morality and health* (pp. 119–169). New York: Routledge.

Sidanius, J., & Pratto, F. (2001). *Social dominance: An intergroup theory of social hierarchy and oppression*. New York: Cambridge University Press.

Sides, J., & Gross, K. (2013). Stereotypes of Muslims and support for the war on terror. *The Journal of Politics*, *75*(03), 583–598.

Simpson, J. A. (2007). Psychological foundations of trust. *Current Directions in Psychological Science*, *16*(5), 264–268. doi: 10.1111/j.1467-8721.2007.00517.x

Sober, E., & Wilson, D. S. (1999). *Unto others: The evolution and psychology of unselfish behavior*. Cambridge, MA: Harvard University Press.

Sosis, R. (2006). Religious behaviors, badges, and bans: Signaling theory and the evolution of religion, in P. McNamara (Ed.), *Where God and science meet: How brain and evolutionary studies alter our understanding of religion*, *1*, 61–86, Bridgeport, CT: Praeger Publishing.

Sosis, R., & Alcorta, C. (2003). Signaling, solidarity, and the sacred: The evolution of religious behavior. *Evolutionary Anthropology: Issues, News, and Reviews*, *12*(6), 264–274.

Sperber, D., & Sperber, D. (1996). *Explaining culture*. Oxford: Blackwell Publishers.

Tajfel, H., Billig, M. G., Bundy, R. P., & Flament, C. (1971). Social categorization and intergroup behaviour. *European Journal of Social Psychology*, *1*(2), 149–178.

Tan, J. H., & Vogel, C. (2008). Religion and trust: An experimental study. *Journal of Economic Psychology*, *29*(6), 832–848.

Terrizzi, J. A., Shook, N. J., & Ventis, W. L. (2010). Disgust: A predictor of social conservatism and prejudicial attitudes toward homosexuals. *Personality and Individual Differences*, *49*(6), 587–592.

Tooby, J., & Cosmides, L. (1988). The evolution of war and its cognitive foundations. *Institute for Evolutionary Studies Technical Report*, *88*(1), 1–15.

Tversky, A., & Kahneman, D. (1983). Extensional versus intuitive reasoning: The conjunction fallacy in probability judgment. *Psychological Review*, *90*(4), 293–315. doi: 10.1037/0033-295x.90.4.293

Tybur, J. M., Lieberman, D., & Griskevicius, V. (2009). Microbes, mating, and morality: Individual differences in three functional domains of disgust. *Journal of Personality and Social Psychology*, *97*(1), 103–122. doi: 10.1037/a0015474

van der Slik, F. W., & Konig, R. P. (2006). RESEARCH: Orthodox, humanitarian, and science-inspired belief in relation to prejudice against Jews, Muslims, and ethnic minorities: The content of one's belief does matter. *The International Journal for the Psychology of Religion*, *16*(2), 113–126.

Voas, D. (2007). Surveys of behaviour, beliefs and affiliation: Micro-quantitative. In J. Beckford & N. Demerath III (Eds.), *The SAGE handbook of the sociology of religion* (pp. 144–166). London: Sage.

Whitley Jr., B. E. (2009). Religiosity and attitudes toward lesbians and gay men: A meta-analysis. *International Journal for the Psychology of Religion*, *19*(1), 21–38.

Wilson, D. S., & Sober, E. (1994). Reintroducing group selection to the human behavioral sciences. *Behavioral and Brain Sciences*, *17*(04), 585–608.

Zuckerman, P. (2007). Atheism: Contemporary numbers and patterns. In M. Martin (Ed.), *The Cambridge companion to atheism* (pp. 47–66). Cambridge: Cambridge University Press.

16 Sexual Prejudice: Advances in Conceptual and Empirical Models

V. Paul Poteat and Michelle Birkett

Considerable advances have occurred in the study of prejudice against sexual minorities (e.g., lesbian, gay, bisexual, or transgender individuals) across multiple fields of psychology in recent years. With this growing attention, scholars have proposed more refined and nuanced conceptualizations of sexual prejudice, documented varied ways in which it is expressed, identified multiple underlying predictors, and pointed to emerging issues that require concerted interdisciplinary approaches to address. There is also a substantial literature base documenting discrimination against sexual minorities and its many physical, mental, and behavioral health consequences (Katz-Wise & Hyde, 2012; Meyer, 2003). For the purpose of this chapter, however, we focus on the construct of sexual prejudice itself and seek to provide an understanding of individual factors and social processes that contribute to its development and perpetuation.

Operationalizing Sexual Prejudice

Scholars have proposed and used varying terminology for the continually evolving concept of sexual prejudice as it is now understood; of these terms, "homophobia" (largely attributed to Weinberg, 1972) has been the most enduring and widely used in research and popular culture. Herek (2004) provided a rich review and critique of these terms, with an emphasis on homophobia, and considered the historical and societal context in which this term first originated and was later revised. In his critique, Herek noted important limitations to the term "homophobia," including (a) it rarely refers to an intense, irrational fear of sexual minorities; (b) it is framed through the lens of psychopathology but is not meant as a diagnosis; (c) it has inadequately reflected the role of broader social norms and processes in shaping individuals' attitudes; (d) more recently its operationalization has become diffuse as a consequence of being applied to a rather large range of ideas; and (e) it is often considered synonymous with prejudice toward gay men specifically rather than sexual minorities more expansively. Consequently, although many researchers use the term "homophobia" to capture a range of interrelated concepts (e.g., individuals' negative attitudes toward non-heterosexuals, discriminatory social policies or institutions), it has steadily been replaced by terms such as "sexual stigma," "heterosexism," and "sexual prejudice," which we describe next.

Sexual stigma may be defined as the collective belief among members of society that non-heterosexual identities, feelings, or behaviors are wrong and inferior to heterosexual identities, feelings, or behaviors (Herek, 2004). As denoted by its name, sexual stigma incorporates facets of the social-psychological concept of stigma (Crocker, Major, & Steele, 1998; Goffman, 1963; Major & O'Brien, 2005). As a stigmatized group, non-heterosexual individuals are thus wholly defined and treated on the basis of this singular aspect of their identity, occupy a subordinate position in the hierarchy of society, and face marginalization and discrimination.

Heterosexism refers to the ways in which social institutions and systems perpetuate the normativity of heterosexuality, sexual stigma, and the marginalization of non-heterosexuality (Herek, 2004). For instance, heterosexism is exemplified in laws that define marriage as between only one man and one woman or that prohibit adoption by same-sex couples, language that assumes heterosexuality or denotes non-heterosexuality as subordinate, as well as ideological norms and positions espoused by certain institutions (e.g., political or religious institutions) that endorse or condone stigma against non-heterosexuality.

Finally, *sexual prejudice* can be defined as negative attitudes toward individuals based on their non-heterosexual group membership, such as lesbian, gay, or bisexual individuals and their communities (Herek, 2004). Thus, sexual prejudice – as an attitude – represents a general tendency for an individual to make a negative evaluation of another person, in this case based on that person's sexual minority group membership (Eagly & Chaiken, 1993; Herek, 2004). This contemporary shift in how sexual prejudice has been defined, as well as sexual stigma and heterosexism, is particularly relevant for social psychologists. Essentially, it moves the conceptualization from a clinically based framework to a framework founded on core social psychology theories and issues such as those on intergroup relations and conflict, social stigma, and broader research on prejudice.

Identifying a Comprehensive Set of Factors Contributing to Sexual Prejudice

Studies have identified a range of factors linked to sexual prejudice that offer a more comprehensive explanation for why some individuals are more likely than others to hold stronger sexual prejudice attitudes. As noted in the prior section, although a range of terms has been used across these studies, their focus has still coalesced around the study of negative attitudes toward sexual minorities (primarily lesbians and gay men). In this section, we review some of the most prominent and widely studied factors associated with sexual prejudice. There are several ways to organize these factors as they relate to one another. Broadly, some represent individual psychological constructs, whereas others reflect a set of interpersonal and social constructs. We first review individual factors associated with sexual prejudice and then extend this focus to interpersonal and social factors.

Individual Factors Associated with Sexual Prejudice

Individual attributes and several major belief systems have been connected to sexual prejudice. In the interest of space, we focus on patterns that have been identified based on gender, gender ideology, social dominance orientation, right-wing authoritarianism, and identity centrality. Still, we note that multiple other individual factors have been connected to sexual prejudice, including empathy and perspective taking, religious ideologies, and political ideologies (Johnson, Brems, & Alford-Keating, 1997; Pearte, Renk, & Negy, 2013; Whitley, 2009). While outside the scope of this chapter, these too warrant continued attention.

Gender differences and gender ideology. At a basic level, gender differences in sexual prejudice are robust across many studies, with men reporting higher levels than women (Herek, 2000; Hollekim, Slaatten, & Anderssen, 2012; Kite & Whitley, 1996; Monto & Supinski, 2014). At the same time, there is variation in this pattern when considering prejudice toward specific sexual minority populations. For instance, some findings indicate that these gender differences apply to prejudice toward gay men, but that gender differences are less sizable or are nonsignificant for prejudice toward lesbian women (Kite & Whitley, 1996; Whitley & Ægisdóttir, 2000). In other studies, heterosexual men report greater prejudice toward gay men than they do toward lesbian women, whereas heterosexual women do not make this distinction in their attitudes (Herek, 1988; LaMar & Kite, 1998; Mata, Ghavami, & Wittig, 2010). Still other studies have shown gender differences between heterosexual men and women on their attitudes toward bisexual men but not on their attitudes toward bisexual women (Mulick & Wright, 2011), possibly because heterosexual men hold less negative attitudes toward bisexual women than bisexual men, thus attenuating these gender differences. Indeed, similar to patterns found when looking at prejudice toward gay men and lesbian women, heterosexual men report greater prejudice toward bisexual men than they do toward bisexual women, whereas heterosexual women do not make this distinction (Yost & Thomas, 2012). These findings underscore the need for research to consider sexual prejudice toward specific populations of sexual minorities and by specific dominant groups. Doing so would allow researchers to identify whether a unique set of factors contributes to these specific forms of sexual prejudice and explain why these different patterns emerge based on gender.

Masculine ideology beliefs offer a potential explanation for the distinct gender-based patterns for sexual prejudice toward gay and bisexual men and toward lesbian and bisexual women. Although multiple forms of masculinity have been described, the prevailing form of masculine ideology in society remains one that includes explicit sexual prejudice, particularly toward gay men (Epstein, 2001; Kimmel, 1997; Mahalik et al., 2003; Pascoe, 2007; Pleck, Sonenstein, & Ku, 1994). Men are socialized from childhood through adulthood to adhere to this belief system, and many report feeling pressured to prove both their masculinity and heterosexuality to their peers (Pascoe, 2007; Phoenix, Frosh, & Pattman, 2003). Indeed, there are significant associations between traditional masculine ideology beliefs and sexual prejudice (Mahalik et al., 2003; Parrott, Adams, & Zeichner, 2002; Pleck et al., 1994; Stotzer & Shih, 2012). This socialization of masculine roles and beliefs among men that includes a denigration of gay men (or non-heterosexual men more broadly) could partly explain why heterosexual men report stronger prejudice toward gay and bisexual men than do heterosexual women, as well as why this pattern may be weaker for prejudice toward lesbian or bisexual women. Similarly, in a sexist society female same-sex and opposite-sex relationships are sexualized and objectified by heterosexual men and women's agency is devalued (Fredrickson & Roberts, 1997; Hill & Fischer, 2008); because of their marginalized position based on gender, non-heterosexual women's violation of heterosexist norms may be viewed as less threatening among heterosexual men.

Dominance and authoritarianism. Social dominance orientation (SDO) and right-wing authoritarianism (RWA) are two prominent ideologies that have been examined extensively in the social psychology research on prejudice (Sibley & Duckitt, 2008). First, SDO is based within social dominance theory, which stipulates that hierarchies exist in societies wherein some groups are in positions with greater power and access to resources than others (Pratto, Sidanius, Stallworth, & Malle, 1994). SDO represents one's level of support and preference for group-based hierarchies, and these anti-egalitarian beliefs are used to justify the existence and acceptability of hierarchies in which some groups are dominant over others (Pratto et al., 1994). Second, RWA is based in the authoritarianism literature (Adorno, Frenkel-Brunswik, Levinson, & Sanford, 1950; Altmeyer, 1988) and reflects adherence to traditional social conventions, submission to those deemed legitimate authority figures, and support for the punishment of those who break such conventions (Altemeyer, 1988). Both SDO and RWA are strong predictors of prejudice, often acting in a parallel and additive manner (Duckitt & Sibley, 2007; Duckitt, Wagner, du Plessis, & Birum, 2002; Levin, Pratto, Matthews, Sidanius, & Kteily, 2013; Sibley, Robertson, & Wilson, 2006). For a recent review of the effects of SDO and RWA on prejudice, see Duckitt and Sibley's chapter on the dual process model (Chapter 9, this title).

Specific to sexual prejudice, SDO and RWA are both significantly associated with this form of prejudice when they are considered independent of each other

(Duckitt & Sibley, 2007; Haddock, Zanna, & Esses, 1993; Mata et al., 2010; Poteat, Espelage, & Green, 2007; Poteat & Spanierman, 2010; Whitley, 1999). When their joint contribution is considered, however, studies suggest that RWA is more strongly associated with sexual prejudice than SDO. For example, when controlling for the effect of RWA, the unique effect of SDO in predicting sexual prejudice often is reduced to nonsignificance (Duckitt & Sibley, 2007; Poteat & Spanierman, 2010; Webster, Burns, Pickering, & Saucier, 2014). RWA may be a particularly strong predictor of sexual prejudice because sexual minorities are often viewed as challenging and threatening historical, cultural, and religious norms; traditional values; and conventions (Haddock et al., 1993; Miceli, 2005). Although SDO contributes less to the prediction of sexual prejudice relative to RWA, it remains relevant and offers an explanation for why some individuals endorse stronger levels of sexual prejudice. Just as masculine ideology beliefs provide a partial explanation for gender differences on sexual prejudice, so too does SDO. Mata and colleagues (2010) found that SDO partially mediated the differences between adolescent boys and girls on their levels of sexual prejudice. As found in the SDO literature, individuals in dominant groups (e.g., heterosexual men) often report higher levels of SDO than those in subordinate and marginalized groups (Guimond, Dambrun, Michinov, & Duarte, 2003; Pratto et al., 1994). Thus, countering sexual prejudice among some individuals likely will require addressing both their dominant and authoritarian beliefs.

The fact that sexual prejudice is associated with both RWA and SDO could also capture the somewhat contradictory claims made by those who hold negative attitudes toward sexual minorities: namely, that sexual minorities are simultaneously considered to be a serious threat (a point that would elicit negativity from high-RWA individuals) while they are also stereotyped as weak and subordinate (a point that would elicit negativity from high-SDO individuals). Notwithstanding the robustness of these findings and the strength of the associations between SDO, RWA, and sexual prejudice, there is still a need for future research to consider whether SDO and RWA vary in the strength with which they are associated with prejudice toward specific sexual minority populations. It might be, for example, that SDO is particularly important in predicting antigay prejudice, as gay men are often stereotyped as ineffectual. Conversely, lesbian women do not face this same stereotype, and prejudice toward them may be less conceptually related to hierarchy maintenance. Potentially, this more specific focus could offer clearer explanations for how these ideological beliefs are associated with sexual prejudice and suggest mechanisms by which they come to predict prejudice toward certain sexual minority populations.

Identity importance and centrality. The importance and centrality that heterosexual individuals place on their sexual orientation identity (i.e., being "straight") in relation to their overall sense of identity is associated with their level of sexual prejudice and antigay behavior (Poteat, DiGiovanni, & Scheer, 2013). Similarly, men who report a stronger desire that their gender identity and expression not be interpreted in a way that would misidentify them as non-heterosexual also report stronger levels of sexual prejudice (Falomir-Pichastor & Mugny, 2009). These associations can be framed within social identity theory (Tajfel & Turner, 1986). As noted in this theory, individuals engage in behaviors to differentiate themselves from outgroup members to create positive ingroup distinctiveness, and to decrease any threat of being misclassified as a member of an outgroup (Tajfel & Turner, 1986). For individuals who hold strongly negative attitudes toward sexual minorities, their sexual orientation social identity may be particularly salient and thus be a primary category that they use to classify others as either an accepted ingroup member or a highly derogated outgroup member. Further, because people high in sexual prejudice ascribe such negative attitudes toward individuals in the non-heterosexual social category, they may be especially averse to others misidentifying them as a member of that group. Individuals who identify more strongly with their ingroup are more likely to engage in differentiating behaviors (Jetten, Spears, & Manstead, 1997). Antigay behavior may be one overt form of differentiating behavior among individuals who hold strong sexual prejudice attitudes. Consequently, individuals may engage in antigay behavior as a way to emphasize their heterosexual group membership to others and to preemptively abate any anticipated threat from others to classify them as a sexual minority.

Several issues need greater attention in this area of research. Although the association between sexual orientation identity importance and sexual prejudice has been identified, more research is needed to test the causal order and longitudinal associations between these factors. As noted in developmental intergroup theory (Bigler & Liben, 2006), establishing the psychological relevance and salience of a social category can lead to the formation of stereotypes and prejudice based on the use of that category. This process would suggest that raising the salience of sexual orientation identity among heterosexual individuals could lead them to form stereotypes and negative attitudes toward sexual minorities. In turn, holding strong negative attitudes toward sexual minorities could reinforce and maintain the ongoing salience of this social identity among these heterosexual individuals because, for them, the negativity of being misclassified as a sexual minority would be particularly elevated.

Another unique issue to be addressed as part of this area of research is the visibility of sexual orientation identity. Relative to other social identities, sexual orientation identity may not be as readily visible or as accurately assumed by others (Stern, West, Jost, & Rule, 2013). It is possible that such uncertainty could affect how individuals interact and potentially magnify associations between identity salience and prejudice or between identity salience and differentiating behavior compared to these associations for other social categories. Because sexual orientation may be more of a hidden identity, there may be uncertainty or hypervigilance around identifying ingroup and outgroup members and signifying one's own group identity. For instance, heterosexual men might make deliberate statements about their heterosexuality when they engage in actions that might lead others to question their sexual orientation (Bosson, Prewitt-Freilino, & Taylor, 2005; Pascoe, 2007).

Interpersonal and Social Factors Associated with Sexual Prejudice

Despite growing attention to sexual prejudice, the predominant focus has been on individual psychological factors underlying these attitudes. Much less attention has been given to the broader social context in which these attitudes are socialized and expressed or to how the broader social context exerts effects on sexual minorities (Birkett & Espelage, 2015; Mustanski, Birkett, Greene, Hatzenbuehler, & Newcomb, 2014; Poteat, 2007). Nevertheless, the sizable literature base on prejudice in general has underscored the effects of social factors and interpersonal experiences in shaping individuals' prejudiced attitudes. In this section, we focus on two factors: the effects of intergroup contact and friendships with sexual minorities and the effects of peer socialization and group norms.

Intergroup contact and friendships. There is much support for Allport's (1954) intergroup contact hypothesis that under optimal conditions, contact with outgroup members can reduce prejudice and discrimination (refer to Chapter 6, this title). The benefits of intergroup contact are especially high within the context of peer friendships (Pettigrew & Tropp, 2006). Congruent with this larger literature base, direct contact and friendships with sexual minorities are associated with lower sexual prejudice (Herek, 2002; Herek & Capitanio, 1996; Hodson, Harry, & Mitchell, 2009; Smith, Axelton, & Saucier, 2009). Heterosexual individuals who have more sexual minority friends report lower sexual prejudice than those without these friendships (Herek & Capitanio, 1996; Hodson et al., 2009; Vonofakou, Hewstone, & Voci, 2007). These studies have also considered various mechanisms by which intergroup contact and friendships with sexual minorities predict lower sexual prejudice, including lower intergroup anxiety and greater attitude strength (Mereish & Poteat, 2015; Vonofakou et al., 2007). These findings thus indicate that intergroup anxiety may be a strong driver of sexual prejudice and that such anxiety is amenable to change through contact.

More research is needed to examine mechanisms by which direct contact and friendships with sexual minorities could reduce sexual prejudice. In addition to giving continued attention to the factors of intergroup anxiety and attitude strength, studies might focus on other factors known to be strongly associated with sexual prejudice in particular, such as SDO, RWA, or masculine ideology beliefs. Do intergroup friendships modify these beliefs and, in turn, sexual prejudice attitudes? Do sexual minority friendships tend to have stronger effects on some beliefs more than others? Also, studies should consider attributes of the relationships that heterosexuals have with sexual minority peers (e.g., length of the friendship, level of closeness) as well as attributes of sexual minority peers themselves that magnify or attenuate the effects of such friendships on sexual prejudice. For example, bidirectionality is likely at play. That is, just as contact reduces sexual prejudice in heterosexuals, it is likely that sexual prejudice also drives contact. For example, it is unlikely that someone high in sexual prejudice will seek out sexual minority friends. Interestingly, it is those who are presumably most resistant to contact with sexual minorities who would benefit from it the most. Understanding how sexual minority friendships are developed and encouraged should therefore also be a focus of future research. Broadly, these factors could give a clearer indication of optimal conditions under which sexual prejudice is reduced. Finally, as we later note, certain group norms and inter-personal dynamics should be considered in terms of how they shape individuals' sexual prejudice.

In addition to direct contact, the extended contact hypothesis suggests that an individual's knowledge that another ingroup member has outgroup friendships can decrease prejudice (Wright, Aron, McLaughlin-Volpe, & Ropp, 1997). These extended friendships predict lower prejudice over and above direct friendships (Turner, Hewstone, & Voci, 2007). Such types of extended friendships with sexual minorities are related to lower sexual prejudice (Hodson et al., 2009; Mereish & Poteat, 2015). Additional research is needed to examine the connection between extended friendships with sexual minorities and sexual prejudice. Direct contact or friendships with sexual minorities may not always be possible, especially in contexts where sexual minorities may face elevated risks for self-disclosing their sexual orientation. Future research should identify specific mechanisms by which knowledge of another heterosexual peer's friendships with sexual minorities leads heterosexual individuals to evaluate or change their own sexual prejudice attitudes or the conditions under which this process is most likely to occur. For example, are heterosexuals with sexual minority friends more likely to challenge the sexual prejudice of their peers who do not have sexual minority friends? At an even broader level of extended contact, future research might consider the effects of increased visibility of sexual minority characters, actors, and public figures on television and in other forms of social media.

Peer socialization and group norms. As noted earlier, intergroup contact through peer friendships can have a powerful effect on reducing prejudice. More broadly than having sexual minority friends, peers in general exert a significant influence on one another across developmental periods from childhood to adult-hood (Arnett, 2008; Prinstein & Dodge, 2008). Peers come to have an even larger role in socializing attitudes and behaviors during adolescence as individuals come to spend more time with peers (Brechwald & Prinstein, 2011). Social network theories (McPherson, Smith-Lovin, & Cook, 2001) provide a framework for examining and understanding these peer-related patterns. In general, individuals tend to affiliate with peers who express similar attitudes and behaviors, and this selection effect results in basic peer homophily (McPherson et al., 2001). Beyond this selection effect, peers can influence one another over time through ongoing socialization processes (e.g., establishing and enforcing group norms) that can result in even greater peer similarity and influence members' attitudes and beha-viors (Brechwald & Prinstein, 2011). Emerging findings, primarily among adoles-cents, are beginning to show how these processes apply to sexual prejudice and discriminatory behavior.

There is initial evidence for peer similarity on sexual prejudice, supportive of the basic homophily principle of social network theories (Birkett & Espelage, 2015;

Poteat, 2007). These studies collected friendship nominations among adolescents within schools, in which social network analysis was used to identify cohesive friendship groups. Based on these identified group memberships, adolescents within the same peer group report similar levels of sexual prejudice and engage in similar rates of discriminatory behavior (Birkett & Espelage, 2015; Poteat, 2007). There is also evidence of ongoing peer socialization of these attitudes and behaviors: The sexual prejudice of adolescents' peers predicts their own ensuing levels of sexual prejudice and discriminatory behavior (Birkett & Espelage, 2015; Poteat, 2007).

Although peer similarity and socialization have been identified in relation to sexual prejudice, some issues remain to be addressed. For instance, it is likely that most individuals do not deliberately select their friends based specifically on their level of sexual prejudice. Rather, individuals may select friends based on broader and more overarching worldviews, morals or values, or ideological beliefs that, in turn, could result in a level of shared prejudice or anti-prejudice attitudes. This process should be tested directly in future research. Similarly, certain factors could magnify or attenuate the level of similarity among peers in their sexual prejudice. For instance, some individuals may indeed select peers who share closely similar prejudice or anti-prejudice attitudes if this is an important quality to them. Also, some individuals give greater preference to shared behaviors and interests over shared attitudes and beliefs, something that has been connected in the general literature to low and high levels of self-monitoring (Gangestad & Snyder, 2000). Self-monitoring could also account for why some individuals are more similar to their peers than others on levels of prejudice and should be examined.

Other beliefs and behaviors of adolescents' friends that collectively reflect peer group norms account for individuals' sexual prejudice over and above effects attributable to the individual. In this case, we revisit the relevance of SDO and RWA, discussed earlier for their contributions as individual ideological beliefs. In addition to individual-level SDO, social dominance theory stipulates that individuals in hierarchy-enhancing environments will report higher levels of prejudice than individuals in hierarchy-attenuating environments (Pratto et al., 1994). Hierarchy-enhancing environments are those that reinforce and condone social inequality, whereas hierarchy-attenuating environments are those that reject social inequality and promote egalitarianism. For instance, individuals' own levels of prejudice and SDO have been examined in relation to their membership in hierarchy-enhancing and hierarchy-attenuating careers (Pratto, Stallworth, Sidanius, & Siers, 1997; Sidanius, van Laar, Levin, & Sinclair, 2003).

We have extended this examination to look at how sexual prejudice might be present in peer groups that are more hierarchy-enhancing or hierarchy-attenuating in nature (Poteat et al., 2007). We found that adolescents who were members of peer groups that collectively reported higher levels of dominance than other groups (i.e., were more hierarchy-enhancing) also reported higher levels of sexual prejudice, even when controlling for each individual's level of SDO. In effect, an individual who was a member of a hierarchy-enhancing peer group reported even stronger sexual prejudice than another individual who espoused equivalent levels of SDO but who was a member of a peer group that was less hierarchy-enhancing. Consequently, individuals who reported the strongest levels of sexual prejudice were those who held strong SDO beliefs and whose peers also held strong SDO beliefs. The same kind of peer group contextual effect has been found for RWA: Individuals who are members of highly authoritarian peer groups report even stronger levels of sexual prejudice, over and above levels that would be anticipated based on their own level of RWA (Poteat & Spanierman, 2010). In fact, similar to patterns that have been identified at the individual level (Duckitt & Sibley, 2007), collective RWA group norms are stronger predictors of an individual's sexual prejudice than collective SDO group norms (Poteat & Spanierman, 2010).

Finally, studies have noted the negative effects of prejudice on individuals' intergroup interactions (e.g., Dovidio, Kawakami, & Gaertner, 2002), but there has been much less attention to whether prejudice affects interactions among close friends. Recent findings have shown that levels of sexual prejudice within peer groups do affect the interpersonal dynamics and quality of interactions among peers in the group (e.g., Poteat, Mereish, & Birkett, 2015). We found that adolescents who reported stronger sexual prejudice reported poorer interpersonal interactions with peers they had nominated as friends. We also documented contextual effects tied to collective levels of prejudice at the group level. In effect, adolescents who reported the most negative interactions with their friends were those who personally reported high levels of sexual prejudice and whose friends also reported high levels of sexual prejudice. This effect was evident even when accounting for the overall aggressive nature of the group, as well as sexual orientation, age, gender, and group size and sexual orientation composition. Moreover, adolescents in groups with stronger initial group-level sexual prejudice reported progressively worse interactions with their peers seven months later.

Of interest, group-level sexual prejudice only predicted ensuing negative interactions, not positive interactions. Because relationship qualities are multi-dimensional (Furman, 1996), some relationships have many negative qualities even when exhibiting positive qualities. If the effects of holding prejudice attitudes were unilaterally negative, this would likely risk a breakdown of peer groups. Because some relational needs (e.g., emotional support) continue to be met in groups espousing high levels of prejudice, prejudice may endure despite some of the more caustic interactions that it exacerbates. Several processes could explain why sexual prejudice predicts increasingly poorer peer relationships. As sexual prejudice is associated with dominance, ongoing attempts to establish and maintain dominance within these groups could lead to increasingly negative interactions and homophobic exchanges among these peers. Similarly, these peers may engage in certain antagonistic behavior to "prove" their heterosexuality. Ultimately, these findings suggest why prejudice can be difficult to change: Prejudice attitudes and associated behaviors serve a relational function (Connolly, 2000; Guerin, 2003; Pascoe, 2007) despite their other negative effects. Continued attention to how peers contribute to the perpetuation of prejudice as well as attention to how prejudice itself affects the interactions that occur within peer groups is critical.

The Development of Sexual Prejudice: The Need for More Dynamic Models

Up to this point, we have considered a range of individual and social factors that account for variability across individuals in their sexual prejudice attitudes. However, with the exception of our discussion on peer socialization and intergroup contact, there has been a general assumption of relative stability in these attitudes as held by any one individual. Granted, one defining feature of an attitude is that it is relatively enduring (Eagly & Chaiken, 1993); yet, when considering individuals' sexual prejudice over an expansive period of time, it is quite possible that their attitudes exhibit some degree of change. Individual changes in sexual prejudice could occur as a result of direct and formalized interventions (e.g., through a school's use of an anti-bullying program that addresses bias-based harassment or guest speakers in college courses) or from naturally occurring processes or circumstances (e.g., continual development of one's own worldviews or a friend's disclosure of his or her sexual minority identity). Nevertheless, longitudinal studies, or even cross-sectional cohort comparisons, on potential developmental changes in sexual prejudice are few in number. Moreover, the lack of research is pronounced for periods prior to adulthood. The absence of research during these periods is especially concerning because stereotyping and prejudice could be more malleable to change in earlier developmental periods compared to adulthood given the many simultaneous advances in other aspects of development (e.g., cognitive development) that could contribute to variability and change in prejudice (Bigler & Liben, 2006).

To our knowledge, no studies have considered stereotypes or attitudes toward sexual minorities prior to early adolescence. During these later developmental periods, however, cross-sectional cohort comparisons do suggest a general trend of decreasing sexual prejudice from early to late adolescence and from late adolescence into adulthood (Hoover & Fishbein, 1999; Horn, 2006). Although this overall trend provides a foundational pattern, several limitations come from cross-sectional comparisons. It is difficult to differentiate the extent to which cohort differences represent actual changes in attitudes within individuals from the effects that could be due to unique characteristics of each cohort. More importantly, these findings convey only a singular pattern of change when it is quite likely that there is substantial variability across individuals in whether or how their sexual prejudice attitudes change during any developmental period. Further, beyond the identification of different trends, research is needed to identify factors that account for patterns of change in sexual prejudice.

A few studies have begun to use longitudinal data from individuals to identify patterns of change in sexual prejudice, and to identify factors that account for different patterns of change. For example, using data from four time points to consider changes in sexual prejudice among adolescents from ages 12 to 18, Poteat and Anderson (2012) identified several patterns of change. Boys reported initially higher levels of sexual prejudice toward gay men and lesbian women than did girls; moreover, while sexual prejudice toward gay men decreased among girls from early to late adolescence, boys showed no significant decrease in their sexual prejudice toward gay men. In contrast, boys and girls reported significant and comparable decreases in prejudice toward lesbians from early to late adolescence. Finally, fluctuations in individuals' SDO over this period corresponded significantly with fluctuations in their sexual prejudice toward gay men and lesbians.

With data from older age groups, a study by Hooghe and Meeusen (2012) also considered patterns of change in sexual prejudice using two time points of data from individuals when they were age 18 and then when they were age 21. Congruent with the findings of Poteat and Anderson (2012), these authors also found that men reported initially higher levels of sexual prejudice than women (the study considered sexual prejudice in general and not toward specific sexual minority populations). Also, sexual prejudice among women decreased more than it did among men between the first and second time points. The authors also found that having more sexual minority friends at age 18 predicted decreased sexual prejudice at age 21, though more so for men than for women. Finally, they found that higher levels of SDO and conservative gender role beliefs at age 18 predicted increased levels of sexual prejudice at age 21.

These emerging findings point to the need for continued longitudinal research on developmental changes in sexual prejudice, and they highlight several key issues that require greater attention. As we have noted in other sections of this chapter, research needs to consider attitudes held toward specific sexual minority populations. This need was highlighted by the findings of Poteat and Anderson (2012) showing distinct patterns of change for boys in their attitudes toward gay men and attitudes toward lesbians. Not only may individuals hold distinctly different degrees of prejudice toward specific sexual minority populations (Whitley & Ægisdóttir, 2000; Yost & Thomas, 2012) but also changes in their attitudes toward one group may not automatically imply equivalent changes in their attitudes toward other sexual minority groups. Building on the findings of both of these studies, future research should also identify other individual and social factors that could capture variability across individuals in whether and how their attitudes toward sexual minorities change over time. Also, expanded beyond the focus on sexual prejudice, research should consider whether trajectories of change in sexual prejudice align with or are distinct from trajectories of change in other forms of prejudice. Such studies should consider factors that could account for any similarities or differences in these patterns. For instance, several models have been proposed that suggest certain ways in which individuals cluster various minority groups together, as well as different stereotype dimensions along which certain minority groups are categorized and associated with one another (Asbrock, Sibley, & Duckitt, 2010; Duckitt & Sibley, 2007; Fiske, Cuddy, Glick, & Xu, 2002). It would be informative to determine if trajectories of change in prejudice attitudes are similar for attitudes held toward those groups that tend to fall within the same cluster or along similar stereotype dimensions.

The Intersection of Sexual Orientation with Multiple Stigmatized Identities

An overarching issue that must be better addressed in future research on sexual prejudice relates to points of intersectionality across social identities (e.g., in reference to how sexual orientation intersects with other social identities such as race, gender identity or expression, social class, or disability, among others). How is sexual prejudice expressed similarly or differently toward individuals based on their other privileged or stigmatized identities? How do individuals in dominant groups view sexual minority individuals with multiple marginalized identities, some of which may be more visible than others (e.g., sexual minorities of color, sexual minorities with disabilities, or sexual minorities living in poverty)? Attention to these issues could highlight complex cognitive processes that produce variability in sexual prejudice toward specific populations of sexual minorities. Given that individuals come to be wholly defined and treated based on their stigmatized identity, how does this process occur when some individuals have multiple stigmatized identities (e.g., do some identities take precedent, are individuals with other stigmatized identities assumed to be heterosexual)? Are multiple forms of prejudice activated for individuals in dominant groups when they encounter sexual minorities from these backgrounds? The fact that some studies suggest that individuals with multiple stigmatized identities experience even greater health concerns (Mustanski, Garofalo, & Emerson, 2010; Russell, Everett, Rosario, & Birkett, 2014) further underscores the need to consider these issues in future research.

A focus on intersectionality of stigmatized identities highlights the particular need for research on anti-transgender prejudice and how this form of prejudice differs from sexual prejudice. Transgender individuals are sometimes included in research examining the effects of sexual prejudice on LGB individuals, given their often shared experiences within the broader sexual minority community. At the same time, this approach has several shortcomings. First, sexual orientation and gender identity are two distinct aspects of a person's identity; thus, transgender individuals may identify as either heterosexual or as a sexual minority. The nuanced experiences of transgender individuals are lost when research examines the LGBT community as a homogenous whole. Second, transgender individuals often face prejudice from cisgender heterosexual individuals as well as from cisgender sexual minorities (Weiss, 2003), and further attention to anti-trans prejudice within the LGB community is warranted. Third, there is great diversity within the transgender community itself, as individuals differ in gender identification, fluidity, decisions or abilities to utilize medical treatments (such as hormones or surgery), and identity development trajectories.

Some work has begun to assess anti-transgender prejudice separate from sexual prejudice. For example, Hill and Willoughby (2005) and Nagoshi and colleagues (2008) have both developed assessments of anti-transgender prejudice. The latter assessment was based on Bornstein's (1998) tool for assessing a person's discomfort with gender nonconforming people, and research with this measure has shown it to be highly correlated with stronger sexual prejudice, right-wing authoritarianism, religious fundamentalism, and hostile sexism (Nagoshi et al., 2008). As transgender people gain increased visibility, a deeper understanding of the components of anti-transgender prejudice and its association with other factors is necessary.

Finally, research is needed on cisgender and heterosexual privilege. This is in line with the broader movement of research on social issues to become more systemic. By shifting the discourse away from a solitary focus on disadvantages faced by sexual and gender minorities, and by examining advantages conferred to heterosexual and cisgender individuals, a more complete analysis of dominant power structures will be possible. This holistic perspective is better suited to demonstrate how the privileges afforded to individuals based on dominant group membership (e.g., according to race, gender, sexual orientation, religion) contribute to and maintain oppressive systems (e.g., Case, Iuzzini, & Hopkins, 2012; Israel, 2012) and is less likely to further perpetuate oppression by decentralizing dominant group members as the norm against which sexual and gender minorities are compared (Israel, 2012; Serano, 2007).

Beyond Prejudice: Extending the Focus to Affirming Attitudes

In an even broader sense than individual developmental changes in sexual prejudice, there have been gradual societal and cultural shifts in how sexual minorities have come to be seen, along with a growing awareness of the often blatant discrimination they face (Baunach, 2012; Brewer, 2014). Perhaps as a reflection of this shift, contemporary research in the area of sexual prejudice has increasingly emphasized the need for studies to expand and incorporate attention to actively affirming attitudes and behaviors toward sexual minorities. Expressing low levels of sexual prejudice is not synonymous with holding explicitly affirming attitudes toward sexual minorities (Fingerhut, 2011; Pittinsky, Rosenthal, & Montoya, 2011). Thus, direct attention to heterosexual allies (i.e., individuals who express affirming attitudes and engage in advocacy to counter discrimination and to promote the equality of sexual minorities; Russell, 2011) is a critical and much-needed complementary focus to the continued attention to sexual prejudice and discrimination. In addition to the factors we have noted earlier in this chapter, a unique set of factors could also lead some heterosexual individuals to adopt explicitly affirming attitudes and to engage in behaviors that directly challenge established discriminatory norms against sexual minorities (Duhigg, Rostosky, Gray, & Wimsatt, 2010; Montgomery & Stewart, 2012; Russell, 2011). This represents a burgeoning and promising area for future research, and one that would offer a much more comprehensive understanding of attitudes toward sexual minorities – one that expressly includes negative and positive attitudes.

Conclusion

As the study of sexual prejudice continues to advance, emerging findings in this area have highlighted new avenues of research. In this chapter, our aim was to provide an overview of how the conceptualization of sexual prejudice itself has evolved as well an overview of the many factors that contribute to and perpetuate these attitudes; it is by no means exhaustive in its coverage of the topic. Nevertheless, our hope is that by providing this foundational knowledge and by identifying several key areas that warrant closer attention, this chapter will add to the literature in a way that promotes the next generation of studies on sexual prejudice as well as empirically informed efforts to not only reduce sexual prejudice but also to cultivate affirming attitudes and societal norms for sexual minorities.

References

Adorno, T., Frenkel-Brunswik, E., Levinson, D., & Sanford, N. (1950). *The authoritarian personality.* New York: Harper.

Allport, G. W. (1954). *The nature of prejudice.* Cambridge, MA: Addison-Wesley.

Altemeyer, B. (1988). *Enemies of freedom: Understanding right-wing authoritarianism.* San Francisco, CA: Jossey-Bass.

Arnett, J. J. (2008). Socialization in emerging adulthood: From the family to the wider world, from socialization to self-socialization. In J. E. Grusec & P. D. Hastings (Eds.), *Handbook of socialization: Theory and research* (pp. 208–231). New York: Guilford Press.

Asbrock, F., Sibley, C. G., & Duckitt, J. (2010). Right-wing authoritarianism and social dominance orientation and the dimensions of generalized prejudice: A longitudinal test. *European Journal of Personality, 24*, 324–340.

Baunach, D. M. (2012). Changing same-sex marriage attitudes in America from 1988 through 2010. *Public Opinion Quarterly, 76*, 364–378.

Bigler, R. S., & Liben, L. S. (2006). A developmental intergroup theory of social stereotypes and prejudice. In R. Kail (Ed.), *Advances in child development and behavior* (Vol. *34*, pp. 39–89). New York: Academic Press.

Birkett, M., & Espelage, D. L. (2015). Homophobic name-calling, peer groups, and masculinity: The socialization of homophobic behavior in adolescents. *Social Development, 24*, 184–205.

Bornstein, K. (1998). *My gender workbook*. New York: Routledge.

Bosson, J. K., Prewitt-Freilino, J. L., & Taylor, J. N. (2005). Role rigidity: A problem of identity misclassification? *Journal of Personality and Social Psychology, 89*, 552–565.

Brechwald, W. A., & Prinstein, M. J. (2011). Beyond homophily: A decade of advances in understanding peer influence processes. *Journal of Research on Adolescence, 21*, 166–179.

Brewer, P. R. (2014). Public opinion about gay rights and gay marriage. *International Journal of Public Opinion Research, 26*, 279–282.

Case, K. A., Iuzzini, J., & Hopkins, M. (2012). Systems of privilege: Intersections, awareness, and applications. *Journal of Social Issues, 68*, 1–10.

Connolly, P. (2000). Racism and young girls' peer-group relations: The experiences of South Asian girls. *Sociology, 34*, 499–519.

Crocker, J., Major, B., & Steele, C. (1998). Social stigma. In D. Gilbert, S. T. Fiske, & G. Lindzey (Eds.), *Handbook of social psychology* (4th ed., Vol. *2*, pp. 504–553). Boston: McGraw-Hill.

Dovidio, J. F., Kawakami, K., & Gaertner, S. E. (2002). Implicit and explicit prejudice and interracial interactions. *Journal of Personality and Social Psychology, 82*, 62–68.

Duckitt, J., & Sibley, C. G. (2007). Right wing authoritarianism, social dominance orientation and the dimensions of generalized prejudice. *European Journal of Personality, 21*, 113–130.

Duckitt, J., Wagner, C., du Plessis, I., & Birum, I. (2002). The psychological bases of ideology and prejudice: Testing a dual process model. *Journal of Personality and Social Psychology, 83*, 75–93.

Duhigg, J. M., Rostosky, S. S., Gray, B. E., & Wimsatt, M. K. (2010). Development of heterosexuals into sexual-minority allies: A qualitative exploration. *Sexuality Research and Social Policy, 7*, 2–14.

Eagly, A. H., & Chaiken, S. (1993). *The psychology of attitudes*. Orlando, FL: Harcourt Brace Jovanovich.

Epstein, D. (2001). Disciplining and punishing masculinities: An introduction. *Men and Masculinities, 4*, 115–117.

Falomir-Pichastor, J. M., & Mugny, G. (2009). "I'm not gay … I'm a real man!": Heterosexual men's gender self-esteem and sexual prejudice. *Personality and Social Psychology Bulletin, 35*, 1233–1243.

Fingerhut, A. W. (2011). Straight allies: What predicts heterosexuals' alliance with the LGBT community? *Journal of Applied Social Psychology, 41*, 2230–2248.

Fiske, S. T., Cuddy, A. J. C., Glick, P., & Xu, J. (2002). A model of (often mixed) stereotype content: Competence and warmth respectively follow from perceived status and competition. *Journal of Personality and Social Psychology, 82*, 878–902.

Fredrickson, B. L., & Roberts, T. (1997). Objectification theory: Toward understanding women's lived experiences and mental health risks. *Psychology of Women Quarterly, 21*, 173–206.

Furman, W. (1996). The measurement of friendship perceptions: Conceptual and methodological issues. In W. M. Bukowski, A. F. Newcomb, & W. W. Hartup (Eds.), *The company they keep: Friendships in childhood and adolescence* (pp. 41–65). Cambridge: Cambridge University Press.

Gangestad, S. W., & Snyder, M. (2000). Self-monitoring: Appraisal and reappraisal. *Psychological Bulletin, 126*, 530–555.

Goffman, E. (1963). *Stigma: Notes on the management of spoiled identity.* Englewood Cliffs, NJ: Prentice Hall.

Guerin, B. (2003). Combating prejudice and racism: New interventions from a functional analysis of racist language. *Journal of Community and Applied Social Psychology, 13*, 29–45.

Guimond, S., Dambrun, M., Michinov, N., & Duarte, S. (2003). Does social dominance generate prejudice? Integrating individual and contextual determinants of intergroup cognitions. *Journal of Personality and Social Psychology, 84*, 697–721.

Haddock, G., Zanna, M. P., & Esses, V. M. (1993). Assessing the structure of prejudicial attitudes: The case of attitudes toward homosexuals. *Journal of Personality and Social Psychology, 65*, 1105–1118.

Herek, G. M. (1988). Heterosexuals' attitudes toward lesbians and gay men: Correlates and gender differences. *Journal of Sex Research, 25*, 451–477.

Herek, G. M. (2000). The psychology of sexual prejudice. *Current Directions in Psychological Science, 9*, 19–22.

Herek, G. M. (2002). Gender gaps in public opinion about lesbians and gay men. *Public Opinion Quarterly, 66*, 40–66.

Herek, G. M. (2004). Beyond "homophobia": Thinking about sexual prejudice and stigma in the twenty-first century. *Sexuality Research and Social Policy, 1*, 6–24.

Herek, G. M., & Capitanio, J. P. (1996). "Some of my best friends": Intergroup contact, concealable stigma, and heterosexuals' attitudes toward gay men and lesbians. *Personality and Social Psychology Bulletin, 22*, 412–424.

Hill, M. S., & Fischer, A. R. (2008). Examining objectification theory: Lesbian and heterosexual women's experiences with sexual- and self-objectification. *The Counseling Psychologist, 36*, 745–776.

Hill, D. B., & Willoughby, B. L. B. (2005). The development and validation of the genderism and transphobia scale. *Sex Roles, 53*, 531–544.

Hodson, G., Harry, H., & Mitchell, A. (2009). Independent benefits of contact and friendship on attitudes toward homosexuals among authoritarians and highly identified heterosexuals. *European Journal of Social Psychology, 39*, 509–525.

Hollekim, R., Slaatten, H., & Anderssen, N. (2012). A nationwide study of Norwegian beliefs about same-sex marriage and lesbian and gay parenthood. *Sexuality Research and Social Policy, 9*, 15–30.

Hooghe, M., & Meeusen, C. (2012). Homophobia and the transition to adulthood: A three-year panel study among Belgian late adolescents and young adults, 2008–2011. *Journal of Youth and Adolescence, 41*, 1197–1207.

Hoover, R., & Fishbein, H. D. (1999). The development of prejudice and sex role stereotyping in White adolescents and White young adults. *Journal of Applied Developmental Psychology, 20*, 431–448.

Horn, S. S. (2006). Heterosexual adolescents' attitudes and beliefs about homosexuality and gay and lesbian peers. *Cognitive Development, 21*, 420–440.

Israel, T. (2012). 2011 Society of Counseling Psychology presidential address: Exploring privilege in counseling psychology: Shifting the lens. *The Counseling Psychologist, 40*, 158–180.

Jetten, J., Spears, R., & Manstead, A. S. R. (1997). Strength of identification and intergroup differentiation: The influence of group norms. *European Journal of Social Psychology, 27*, 603–609.

Johnson, M. E., Brems, C., & Alford-Keating, P. (1997). Personality correlates of homophobia. *Journal of Homosexuality, 34*, 57–69.

Katz-Wise, S. L., & Hyde, J. S. (2012). Victimization experiences of lesbian, gay, and bisexual individuals: A meta-analysis. *Journal of Sex Research, 49*, 142–167.

Kimmel, M. S. (1997). Masculinity as homophobia: Fear, shame, and silence in the construction of gender identity. In M. M. Gergen & S. N. Davis (Eds.), *Toward a new psychology of gender* (pp. 223–242). Florence, KY: Taylor & Frances.

Kite, M. E., & Whitley, B. E. (1996). Sex differences in attitudes toward homosexual persons, behaviors, and civil rights: A meta-analysis. *Personality and Social Psychology Bulletin, 22*, 336–353.

LaMar, L., & Kite, M. (1998). Sex differences in attitudes toward gay men and lesbians: A multidimensional perspective. *Journal of Sex Research, 35*, 189–196.

Levin, S., Pratto, F., Matthews, M., Sidanius, J., & Kteily, N. (2013). A dual process approach to understanding prejudice toward Americans in Lebanon: An extension to intergroup threat perceptions and emotions. *Group Processes and Intergroup Relations, 16*, 139–158.

Mahalik, J. R., Locke, B. D., Ludlow, L. H., Diemer, M. A., Scott, R. P. J., Gottfried, M., & Freitas, G. (2003). Development of the Conformity to Masculine Norms Inventory. *Psychology of Men and Masculinity, 4*, 3–25.

Major, B., & O'Brien, L. T. (2005). The social psychology of stigma. *Annual Review of Psychology, 56*, 393–421.

Mata, J., Ghavami, N., & Wittig, M. A. (2010). Understanding gender differences in early adolescents' sexual prejudice. *Journal of Early Adolescence, 30*, 50–75.

Mereish, E. H., & Poteat, V. P. (2015). Effects of heterosexuals' direct and extended friendships with sexual minorities on their attitudes and behaviors: Intergroup anxiety and attitude strength as mediators and moderators. *Journal of Applied Social Psychology, 45*, 147–157.

Meyer, I. H. (2003). Prejudice, social stress, and mental health in lesbian, gay, and bisexual populations: Conceptual issues and research evidence. *Psychological Bulletin, 129*, 674–697.

Miceli, M. S. (2005). Morality politics vs. identity politics: Framing processes and competition among Christian right and gay social movement organizations. *Sociological Forum, 20*, 589–612.

McPherson, M., Smith-Lovin, L., & Cook, J. M. (2001). Birds of a feather: Homophily in social networks. *Annual Review of Sociology, 27*, 415–444.

Montgomery, S. A., & Stewart, A. J. (2012). Privileged allies in lesbian and gay rights activism: Gender, generation, and resistance to heteronormativity. *Journal of Social Issues, 68*, 162–177.

Monto, M. A., & Supinski, J. (2014). Discomfort with homosexuality: A new measure captures differences in attitudes toward gay men and lesbians. *Journal of Homosexuality, 61*, 899–916.

Mulick, P. S., & Wright, L. W. (2011). The Biphobia Scale a decade later: Reflections and additions. *Journal of Bisexuality, 11*, 453–457.

Mustanski, B., Birkett, M., Greene, G. J., Hatzenbuehler, M. L., & Newcomb, M. E. (2014). Envisioning an America without sexual orientation inequities in adolescent health. *American Journal of Public Health, 104*, 218–225.

Mustanski, B. S., Garofalo, R., & Emerson, E. M. (2010). Mental health disorders, psychological distress, and suicidality in a diverse sample of lesbian, gay, bisexual, and transgender youths. *American Journal of Public Health, 100*, 2426–2432.

Nagoshi, J. L., Adams, K. A., Terrell, H. K., Hill, E. D., Brzuzy, S., & Nagoshi, C. T. (2008). Gender differences in correlates of homophobia and transphobia. *Sex Roles, 59*, 521–531.

Parrott, D. J., Adams, H. E., & Zeichner, A. (2002). Homophobia: Personality and attitude correlates. *Personality and Individual Differences, 32*, 1269–1278.

Pascoe, C. J. (2007). *Dude, you're a fag: Masculinity and sexuality in high school.* Los Angeles: University of California Press.

Pearte, C., Renk, K., & Negy, C. (2013). Explaining variation in relations among intrinsic religiosity, political conservatism, and homonegativity, as a function of authoritarianism's three components: An expansion on recent literature. *Sexuality Research and Social Policy, 10*, 97–109.

Pettigrew, T. F., & Tropp, L. R. (2006). A meta-analytic test of intergroup contact theory. *Journal of Personality and Social Psychology, 90*, 751–783.

Phoenix, A., Frosh, S., & Pattman, R. (2003). Producing contradictory masculine subject positions: Narratives of threat, homophobia, and bullying in 11–14 year old boys. *Journal of Social Issues, 59*, 179–195.

Pittinsky, T. L., Rosenthal, S. A., & Montoya, R. M. (2011). Measuring positive attitudes toward outgroups: Development and validation of the Allophilia Scale. In L. R. Tropp & R. K. Mallett (Eds.), *Moving beyond prejudice reduction: Pathways to positive intergroup relations* (pp. 41–60). Washington, DC: American Psychological Association.

Pleck, J. H., Sonenstein, F. L., & Ku, L. C. (1994). Attitudes toward male roles among adolescent males: A discriminant validity analysis. *Sex Roles, 30*, 481–501.

Poteat, V. P. (2007). Peer group socialization of homophobic attitudes and behavior during adolescence. *Child Development, 78*, 1830–1842.

Poteat, V. P., & Anderson, C. J. (2012). Developmental changes in sexual prejudice from early to late adolescence: The effects of gender, race, and ideology on different patterns of change. *Developmental Psychology, 48*, 1403–1415.

Poteat, V. P., DiGiovanni, C. D., & Scheer, J. R. (2013). Predicting homophobic behavior among heterosexual youth: Domain general and sexual orientation-specific factors at the individual and contextual level. *Journal of Youth and Adolescence, 42*, 351–362.

Poteat, V. P., Espelage, D. L., & Green, H. D. (2007). The socialization of dominance: Peer group contextual effects on homophobic and dominance attitudes. *Journal of Personality and Social Psychology, 92*, 1040–1050.

Poteat, V. P., Mereish, E. H., & Birkett, M. (2015). The negative effects of prejudice on interpersonal relationships within adolescent peer groups. *Developmental Psychology, 51*, 544–553.

Poteat, V. P., & Spanierman, L. B. (2010). Do the ideological beliefs of peers predict the prejudiced attitudes of other individuals in the group? *Group Processes and Intergroup Relations, 13*, 495–514.

Pratto, F., Sidanius, J., Stallworth, L M., & Malle, B. F. (1994). Social dominance orientation: A personality variable predicting social and political attitudes. *Journal of Personality and Social Psychology, 67*, 741–763.

Pratto, F., Stallworth, L. M., Sidanius, J., & Siers, B. (1997). The gender gap in occupational role attainment: A social dominance approach. *Journal of Personality and Social Psychology, 72*, 37–53.

Prinstein, M. J., & Dodge, K. A. (2008). *Understanding peer influence in children and adolescents*. New York: Guilford Press.

Russell, G. M. (2011). Motives of heterosexual allies in collective action for equality. *Journal of Social Issues, 67*, 376–393.

Russell, S. T., Everett, B. G., Rosario, M., & Birkett, M. (2014). Indicators of victimization and sexual orientation among adolescents: Analyses from youth risk behavior surveys. *American Journal of Public Health, 104*, 255–261.

Serano, J. (2007). *Whipping girl: A transsexual woman on sexism and the scapegoating of femininity*. Emeryville, CA: Seal Press.

Sibley, C. G., & Duckitt, J. (2008). Personality and prejudice: A meta-analysis and theoretical review. *Personality and Social Psychology Review, 12*, 248–279.

Sibley, C. G., Robertson, A., & Wilson, M. S. (2006). Social dominance orientation and right-wing authoritarianism: Additive and interactive effects. *Political Psychology, 27*, 755–768.

Sidanius, J., van Laar, C., Levin, S., & Sinclair, S. (2003). Social hierarchy maintenance and assortment into social roles: A social dominance perspective. *Group Processes and Intergroup Relations, 6*, 333–352.

Smith, S. J., Axelton, A. M., & Saucier, D. A. (2009). The effects of contact on sexual prejudice: A meta-analysis. *Sex Roles, 61*, 178–191.

Stern, C., West, T. V., Jost, J. T., & Rule, N. O. (2013). The politics of gaydar: Ideological differences in the use of gendered cues in categorizing sexual orientation. *Journal of Personality and Social Psychology, 104*, 520–541.

Stotzer, R. L., & Shih, M. (2012). The relationship between masculinity and sexual prejudice in factors associated with violence against gay men. *Psychology of Men and Masculinity, 13*, 136–142.

Tajfel, H., & Turner, J. C. (1986). The social identity theory of intergroup conflict. In S. Worchel & W. G. Austin (Eds.), *Psychology of intergroup relations* (pp. 7–24). Chicago: Nelson-Hall.

Turner, R. N., Hewstone, M., & Voci, A. (2007). Reducing explicit and implicit outgroup prejudice via direct and extended contact: The mediating role of self-disclosure and intergroup anxiety. *Journal of Personality and Social Psychology, 93*, 369–388.

Vonofakou, C., Hewstone, M., & Voci, A. (2007). Contact with outgroup friends as a predictor of meta-attitudinal strength and accessibility of attitudes towards gay men. *Journal of Personality and Social Psychology, 92*, 804–820.

Webster, R. J., Burns, M. D., Pickering, M., & Saucier, D. A. (2014). The suppression and justification of prejudice as a function of political orientation. *European Journal of Personality, 28*, 44–59.

Weinberg, G. (1972). *Society and the healthy homosexual.* New York: St. Martin's.

Weiss, J. T. (2003). GL vs. BT: The archaeology of biphobia and transphobia within the U.S. gay and lesbian community. *Journal of Bisexuality, 3*, 25–55.

Whitley, B. E. (1999). Right-wing authoritarianism, social dominance orientation, and prejudice. *Journal of Personality and Social Psychology, 77*, 126–134.

Whitley, B. E. (2009). Religiosity and attitudes toward lesbians and gay men: A meta-analysis. *International Journal for the Psychology of Religion, 19*, 21–38.

Whitley, B. E., & Ægisdóttir, S. (2000). The gender belief system, authoritarianism, social dominance orientation, and heterosexuals' attitudes toward lesbians and gay men. *Sex Roles, 42*, 947–967.

Wright, S. C., Aron, A., McLaughlin-Volpe, T., & Ropp, S. A. (1997). The extended contact effect: Knowledge of cross-group friendships and prejudice. *Journal of Personality and Social Psychology, 73*, 73–90.

Yost, M. R., & Thomas, G. D. (2012). Gender and binegativity: Men's and women's attitudes toward male and female bisexuals. *Archives of Sexual Behavior, 41*, 691–702.

17 Weight Bias: Prejudice and Discrimination toward Overweight and Obese People

Phillippa C. Diedrichs and Rebecca Puhl

Why did they call me names? I was a nice little girl. Is there a name for this?

Why am I supposed to hate myself until I reach my "ideal" weight? Is there a name for this?

Why do I rarely see anyone who looks like me in women's magazines, on TV, or in the movies? Is there a name for this?

Why can't large people go to the theatre or ride on a plane in comfort? Is there a name for this?

Why was a job withheld from me because *"we can't have you out in front"*? Is there a name for this?

Yes, there is a name for this – the name is discrimination.

(Johnson, 2001, p. 101)

Definition and Prevalence of Weight Bias

Weight bias refers to stigmatization, bullying, prejudice, and discrimination against overweight and obese individuals based on their body weight and appearance (Puhl & Brownell, 2003). It can manifest in prejudiced implicit and explicit attitudes, including the attribution of negative stereotypes (e.g., unattractive, lazy, unclean, gluttonous, unintelligent, unhealthy) toward overweight and obese people. It also includes discriminatory actions toward an individual based on their weight and appearance, such as suboptimal health care and employment inequities. As this chapter shows, extensive evidence demonstrates that overweight and obese individuals are at significantly greater risk for institutional and interpersonal prejudice and discrimination because of their higher weight (Carr & Friedman, 2005). Although a substantial amount of research, policy, advocacy, and social action has been dedicated to understanding the causes of, and methods for preventing, other forms of discrimination (e.g., race and sexuality), policy and social action addressing weight bias has thus far been limited (Brownell, 2005). It has been suggested that weight bias is the last socially acceptable form of discrimination (Puhl & Brownell, 2001). This neglect is concerning given research demonstrating that experiencing weight bias can impair psychological and physical health, hinder economic and employment opportunities, and impede academic performance and education.

In the United States, weight discrimination is one of the most common forms of discrimination reported by women and men (Puhl, Andreyeva, & Brownell, 2008). Unlike other forms of discrimination that have remained stable in recent decades, reports of weight discrimination were found to increase by 66%, from 7% in 1995–1996 to 12% in 2004–2006 (Andreyeva, Puhl, & Brownell, 2008). This increase was present even after controlling for increasing rates of obesity. Compared to men, women have heightened vulnerability to weight bias, even at lower levels of overweight. While men appear to be at risk of discrimination at a body mass index (BMI) of 35 or higher (i.e., equivalent to Class II or III "severe" obesity), women experience a significant increase in risk of weight discrimination at a lower BMI of 27 (i.e., equivalent to the overweight category, and just two points above the "normal weight" range) (Puhl et al., 2008).

Although most prevalence data on weight bias comes from the United States, a recent multinational study of 2,866 adults in Canada, the United States, Iceland, and Australia found that levels of explicit weight bias were consistent across countries (Puhl, Latner, O'Brien, Luedicke, Danielsdottir et al., 2015). The same data indicated that adults reported body weight to be the most common reason that children are bullied in their country, and weight-based bullying was viewed to be significantly more common than bullying related to race/ethnicity, sexual orientation, and religion (Puhl, Latner, O'Brien, Luedicke, Forhan et al., 2015). A smaller anthropological study of 680 adults in 10 countries (American Samoa, Puerto Rico, Tanzania, Mexico, Paraguay, the United Kingdom, Argentina, the United States, New Zealand, and Iceland) also reported that weight bias was present in all countries studied. The authors concluded that there appears to be a "shared model of obesity that transcends populations including traditionally fat-positive societies," and that there is a "profound global diffusion of negative ideas about obesity" (Brewis, Wutich, Fallette-Cowden, & Rodriguez-Soto, 2011, p. 269). In sum, the available data suggest that weight bias is a global issue. Given that an estimated 2.1 billion people are overweight or obese globally (Ng et al., 2014), it is also an issue with significant scope for impact.

Sources of Weight Bias

A substantial and growing body of research indicates that weight bias is prevalent among children, adolescents, adults, employers, health professionals, and mass media (Hebl, Ruggs, Singeltary, & Beal, 2008). The field of research, while consistent in demonstrating negative attitudes toward overweight and obese people, is limited by a tendency to rely on measures of prejudiced attitudes, rather than overt discriminatory behaviors. Although recent research suggests that self-report measures of weight-based prejudice predict discriminatory behaviors (O'Brien, Latner, Ebneter, & Hunter, 2013), some of the attitudinal measures used in this field have not been rigorously evaluated in terms of their psychometric properties, nor have they been used consistently across studies (Puhl & Latner, 2012). This makes the evaluation and comparison of findings across studies difficult. Nevertheless, the consistency of findings across 50 years of research suggests that children, adolescents, and adults are frequent targets and sources of weight bias, and that weight bias is prevalent across the lifespan and multiple settings.

Children. Many studies have shown that children hold prejudiced attitudes and engage in bullying and harassment toward overweight and obese peers. Weight bias was first documented among children in the 1960s and has since been observed in preschool children as young as age 3 (Cramer & Steinwert, 1998). One of the earliest studies asked more than 600 children ages 10–11 to rate the likeability of children of various body weights depicted in series of drawings (Richardson, Goodman, Hastorf, & Dornbusch, 1961). Overweight children were overwhelmingly rated as least likeable, and this finding has since been replicated consistently in other studies (e.g., Bacardi-Gascon, Leon-Reyes, & Jimenez-Cruz, 2007). One replication study indicated that weight bias among children has worsened from 1961 to 2001 (Latner & Stunkard, 2003). Further, other research (e.g., Rich et al., 2008) has found that children as young as age 4 are more likely to assign negative attributes (e.g., lazy, dirty, mean, ugly, stupid) to overweight children and are less likely to choose them as friends, in comparison to lower-weight children. Merely being in the proximity of an overweight child can also result in weight bias, regardless of whether or not the children being targeted are overweight themselves (Penny & Haddock, 2007). This research as a whole suggests that weight bias begins at an early age.

Adolescents. Studies investigating appearance- and weight-related teasing indicate that adolescents frequently engage in weight-biased attitudes and behaviors. In a study of 3,500 children from 47 schools across Europe, physical appearance was identified as the most common reason for making fun of other children (British Council, 2008). A Canadian study of more than 5,000 adolescents, ages 11–16, found that adolescents were more likely to verbally and physically victimize overweight and obese adolescents compared to peers who were of average weight (Janssen, Craig, Boyce, & Pickett, 2004). A recent study with 4,364 Dutch adolescents found that adolescents with a higher BMI were more like be the target and source of bullying (Jansen et al., 2014). Within the United States, multiple studies surveying youth, parents, and teachers indicate that weight-based bullying is viewed to be the most frequent form of bullying that youth experience at school (Puhl, Luedicke, & DePierre, 2013), and that the prevalence of weight-based teasing is similar across race and ethnic groups (van den Berg, Neumark-Sztainer, Eisenberg, & Haines, 2008). For example, in 2011, the US National Education Association issued a nationwide survey of more than 5,000 educators and showed that teachers viewed weight-based bullying to be more problematic than bullying because of a student's gender, sexual orientation, or disability (Bradshaw, Waasdorp, & O'Breman, 2013). Even among ethnic minority adolescents who experience race-based harassment, weight-based bullying has been reported by these youth as the most frequent form of peer harassment experienced by girls and the second most common among boys (Bucchianeri, Eisenberg, & Neumark-Sztainer, 2013). For a comprehensive review of studies examining weight-based bullying in North American and Australian samples, see Tang-Peronard and Heitmann (2008). Collectively, this body of research provides evidence that adolescents exhibit weight bias.

Adults. Adults frequently demonstrate negative attitudes toward, and prejudice against, overweight and obese individuals across a range of settings. A study of more than 4,000 men and women from North America found that adults have more negative implicit and explicit attitudes toward overweight individuals compared to lower-weight individuals (Schwartz, Vartanian, Nosek, & Brownell, 2006). Similar results have been found among adults in Canada, Iceland, and Australia (Puhl, Latner, O'Brien, Luedicke, Danielsdottir et al., 2015). Adults frequently stereotype overweight and obese individuals as being less attractive, successful, motivated, intelligent, happy, healthy, and popular than lower-weight individuals (Schwartz et al., 2006). Studies suggest that men, White individuals, and younger adults are more likely to display weight bias (Puhl, Latner, O'Brien, Luedicke, Danielsdottir et al., 2015). Furthermore, while research indicates that overweight and obese people are less likely to express weight bias than people of lower body weights, some overweight and obese adults also report holding negative attitudes and prejudice toward other overweight and obese people, demonstrating an ingroup bias (Alperin, Hornsey, Hayward, Diedrichs, & Barlow, 2014).

Weight bias expressed by adults has been documented in many settings, including education (Latner & Schwartz, 2005), employment (Rudolph, Wells, Weller, & Batles, 2009), professional management (Fikkan & Rothblum, 2005), and even health care (Sabin, Marini, Nosek, & Brownell, 2012). Within health care, studies have consistently demonstrated weight bias by health care providers across a range of specialities, including doctors (Bocquier et al., 2005), nurses (Brown & Thompson, 2007), dietitians (Oberrieder, Walker, Monroe, & Adeyanju, 1995), psychologists (Davis-Coelho, Waltz, & Davis-Coelho, 2000), physiotherapists (Setchell, Watson, Jones, Gard, & Briffa, 2014), and preservice medical and maternity care students (Mulherin, Miller, Barlow, Diedrichs, & Thompson, 2013). Provider attitudes include views that obese patients are lazy, lacking self-control and willpower, personally to blame for their weight, non-compliant with treatment, and deserve to be targets of derogatory humor (Glauser, Roepke, Stevenin, Dubois, & Ahn, 2015; Phelan et al., 2014; Wear, Aultman, Varley, & Zarconi, 2006). A study of 2,284 physicians found that weight bias is as pervasive among medical doctors as it is among the general public (Sabin et al., 2012). Of concern, evidence has increasingly indicated that weight biases by health professionals can reduce the quality of care they provide to their patients, such as spending less time in appointments (Hebl, Xu, & Mason, 2003), providing less education about health (Bertakis, 2005), expressing less desire to help their patients, and reporting that treating obesity is "more annoying" and a greater waste of their time compared to providing care to their lower-weight patients (Hebl et al., 2003).

Media. Weight bias is frequently communicated and reinforced in media through the idealization and overrepresentation of lower-weight bodies, and through the consistent negative and stereotyped depiction of overweight and obese individuals (Ata & Thompson, 2010). Within television shows and movies, characters who appear to be overweight or obese are often ridiculed, depicted as engaging in stereotypical behaviors (e.g., eating or bingeing), and are less likely to have positive social interactions (Greenberg, Eastin, Hofschire, Lachlan, & Brownell, 2003; Himes & Thompson, 2007). For example, researchers analyzed verbal comments in North American prime-time television comedies in the late 1990s–early 2000s and found that higher-weight characters received significantly more negative appearance-related comments (followed by more canned audience laughter) than their lower-weight counterparts (Fouts & Vaughan, 2002). This suggests to viewers that it is both undesirable to have a higher body weight and socially acceptable to overtly ridicule overweight and obese individuals.

Reality weight-loss television shows have also been critiqued for perpetuating anti-fat attitudes and stereotyping. *The Biggest Loser* is a well-known reality weight-loss TV program aired in 30 countries that features obese contestants engaging in a competition to lose weight. Several experimental studies have demonstrated that exposure to this program increases negative attitudes toward obese persons, reinforces beliefs that obesity is simply an issue of personal responsibility, and worsens exercise-related attitudes (Berry, McLeod, Pankratow, & Walker, 2013; Dornoff et al., 2012; Yoo, 2012). Furthermore, an Australian qualitative study found that obese adults report that they believe *The Biggest Loser* is derogatory and treats people with obesity like "a side show at some kind of circus" (Thomas, Hyde, & Komesaroff, 2007, p. 211).

Multiple studies document weight bias in news media. Content analysis indicates that 72% of the images accompanying US news stories about obesity are stigmatizing, with overweight and obese people significantly more likely than lower-weight individuals to be featured in images with their heads obscured, wearing fewer clothes, and in situations where they are eating or drinking (Heuer, McClure, & Puhl, 2011). Indeed, in online news reports, 65% of overweight or obese adults and 77% of overweight or obese children are portrayed in a negative and stereotyped manner (Puhl, Peterson, DePierre, & Luedicke, 2013). This is particularly concerning as news media strongly shape public perceptions and, in some cases, public policy (Kim & Wills, 2007). Furthermore, viewing news media images of overweight or obese people portrayed in a negative manner has been shown experimentally to result in more negative attitudes toward obese people among consumers (McClure, Puhl, & Heuer, 2011).

Weight bias is also perpetuated in newer forms of media. An extraction of social media posts on *Twitter*, *Facebook*, *YouTube*, and blogs over two months in early 2012 found 2.2 million posts including the words, "fat," "overweight," or "obese/obesity" (Wen-ying, Prestin, & Kunath, 2014). The most common discourse surrounding these words was derogatory and demonstrated stigma toward overweight individuals. Another content analysis of *YouTube* videos containing examples of fat stigmatization found that adults, adolescents, and children were all targets of weight bias, and that these videos were viewed at a high rate, receiving on average 2.4 million views (Hussin, Frazier, & Thompson, 2011). Indeed, *YouTube* videos featuring overweight people receive significantly more views if they feature weight-based teasing and ridicule (Yoo & Kim, 2012).

Weight bias presented in youth-targeted media is of particular concern. Multiple studies conducting comprehensive content analyses of children's television shows, films, cartoons, and books indicate that overweight characters are depicted as being aggressive, antisocial, evil, cruel, unattractive, unfriendly, disliked by others, less intelligent, and eating food while thinner characters are more often portrayed as sociable, kind, successful, popular, and attractive (Herbozo, Tantleff-Dunn, Gokee-Larose, & Thompson, 2004; Klein & Shiffman, 2006; Robinson, Callister, & Jankoski, 2008; Throop et al., 2014). Research additionally shows that increased media exposure is associated with holding more negative attitudes toward overweight individuals among children (e.g., Latner, Rosewall, & Simmonds, 2007). In summary, evidence shows that weight bias is extensively communicated to children, adolescents, and adults in mass media. The widespread prevalence of weight bias is particularly concerning in light of its negative consequences.

Consequences of Weight Bias

Numerous studies have documented negative consequences of weight bias for overweight and obese individuals across a number of key living areas, including health, employment, and education. Although there are limitations of this existing evidence, such as reliance on retrospective accounts of weight bias, use of experimental manipulations in artificially controlled settings (rather than real life observed or experienced acts of discrimination), and a lack of research outside of North America, the consistency of findings regarding the negative consequences of weight bias across more than four decades of research is compelling.

Health. Overweight and obese individuals often experience poor psychological and physical health as a consequence of experiencing weight bias (Puhl & Suh, 2015). Negative outcomes include increased risk of depression, anxiety, low self-esteem, substance abuse, and suicidality. For example, perceived weight discrimination was associated with substantial psychiatric morbidity and comorbidity in a sample of 22,231 overweight and obese individuals (Hatzenbuehler, Keyes, & Hasin, 2009). There is also correlational and prospective evidence that after controlling for actual body weight, school level, and socioeconomic status, adolescent boys and girls who are bullied and harassed about their weight are more likely to experience depression, body dissatisfaction, low self-esteem, and suicidal ideation than those who are not teased (Shroff & Thompson, 2004; Thompson, Herbozo, Himes, & Yamamiya, 2005). Furthermore, other studies with Australian,

Swedish, and North American adolescent samples have found that experiencing weight-related teasing mediates the relationship between body mass index (BMI) and body dissatisfaction (Eisenberg, Neumark-Sztainer, & Story, 2003; Gleason, Alexander, & Somers, 2000). This suggests that experiencing weight bias can have a direct effect on body dissatisfaction, and in some cases can explain the relationship between BMI and body dissatisfaction. Many of these negative psychological consequences occur even after controlling for factors such as BMI, obesity onset, and gender, suggesting that negative psychological consequences emerge from stigmatizing experiences rather than from body weight per se.

Ironically, although concerns around higher weight and ill health are sometimes used to justify weight bias and body shaming, physical health is also compromised as a result of being the target of weight bias (Puhl & Brownell, 2003). Specifically, experiencing weight bias is associated with an increased risk of engaging in disordered eating behaviors, resistance to physical activity, increased weight gain, and physiological stress. Studies have found that overweight adolescents who experience weight-related teasing are more likely to engage in binge eating and unhealthy weight control behaviors than overweight and obese adolescents who do not experience weight-based teasing (e.g., Wertheim, Koerner, & Paxton, 2001). Longitudinal research has also found that after controlling for actual weight, experiencing weight bias in the form of weight-related teasing directly predicts the onset of dietary restrictions and bulimic tendencies (Haines, Neumark-Sztainer, Eisenberg, & Hannan, 2006). Furthermore, more recent longitudinal studies (in both the United States and the UK) have demonstrated that experiences of weight discrimination (but not other forms of discrimination) increase the risk of becoming and remaining obese over time (Jackson, Beeken, & Wardle, 2014; Sutin & Terracciano, 2013). Increasing research has also documented physiological reactivity in response to exposure to weight bias, including increased cortisol reactivity, blood pressure, and other measures of physiological stress (Major, Eliezer, & Rieck, 2012). Thus, evidence to date suggests that a range of adverse health consequences can occur as a result of weight bias.

Health Care. Research investigating health care services provides further evidence for the negative health consequences of experiencing weight bias. Specifically, research suggests that overweight and obese women may avoid seeking health care for fear of being targets for weight bias from health professionals (Amy, Aalborg, Lyons, & Keranen, 2006). A North American study found that overweight and obese women were more reluctant to have pelvic examinations than lower-weight women (Adams, Smith, Wilbur, & Grady, 1993). The reluctance of these women to seek health care may be well founded, as the same study showed that 17% of the 1,300 physicians surveyed were hesitant to carry out pelvic examinations for obese women. Further, there is evidence that derogatory comments made by medical staff are more common during pelvic examinations of overweight patients than lower-weight patients (Adams et al., 1993).

Overweight and obese women are also more likely than average-weight women to perceive specific weight-related barriers to seeking and receiving appropriate health care. These include previous negative attitudes and disrespectful treatment from doctors; small patient gowns, exam tables, and equipment; and past experiences of unsolicited weight-loss advice, even when weight was unrelated to the presenting medical condition (Wear et al., 2006). Furthermore, exposure to stigmatizing news stories in the media about obesity is associated with reduced support for medical policies that may improve overweight and obese women's health care and treatment (Brochu, Pearl, Puhl, & Brownell, 2014). Collectively, these results suggest weight bias results in suboptimal health care for overweight and obese people, and that being a target of weight bias within health care settings may lead some overweight and obese women to delay seeking medical care.

Income and Employment. Evidence indicates that overweight and obese people may be penalized in earnings, opportunities, and disciplinary action in employment. An analysis of the salaries reported in longitudinal studies of adults in Germany and the United States revealed that after controlling for age, education, marital status, and a range of other related factors, overweight and obese adults earned significantly less than average-weight adults (Judge & Cable, 2010). Specifically, overweight German women and men on average earned USD $1,843 and $146 less per year, respectively, than their average-weight counterparts. Interestingly, underweight men also earned significantly less than average-weight men, perhaps reflecting the current dominant cultural ideals for male attractiveness, which emphasize a lean and muscular body type, as opposed to small or heavier builds (Diedrichs & Lee, 2010). In the United States, overweight women and men earned $1,276.64 and $146.04 less annually than their average- and below-weight counterparts (Judge & Cable, 2010). Speaking to the ultrathin dominant standards for female beauty prevalent in Western societies, women who were average weight earned a staggering $389,300 less than below-average-weight women over a 25-year career. Others studies provide further evidence of income penalties for overweight and obese individuals (e.g., Johar & Katayama, 2012).

Studies have experimentally examined the potential for weight bias in employment settings. A meta-analysis of these studies found that overweight individuals are consistently discriminated against in work settings and hiring practices (Rudolph et al., 2009). One study randomly assigned participants to view identical resumes with small photos of either women in the "normal" weight BMI category or women in the obese category. Obese women were rated as significantly poorer on the job selection criteria and perceived leadership potential, their proposed starting salaries were lower, and they were less likely to be selected for the job (O'Brien et al., 2013). Similar experimental studies show that obese people are less likely to be given promotions (Rothblum, Brand, Millers, & Oetjen, 1990), more likely to be assigned to least desirable "back of the shop" sales territories (Bellizzi & Hasty, 1998), receive more disciplinary action (Bellizzi & Hasty, 2001), and receive poorer customer service (King, Shapiro, Hebl, Singeltary, & Turner, 2006). Evidently, weight bias is pervasive in employment settings.

Education. The most common place where children experience weight bias is at school (Latner & Schwartz, 2005). Schoolteachers and staff have been identified as sources of weight bias and potential targets for interventions to reduce weight bias (Puhl, Latner, O'Brien, Luedicke, Forhan et al., 2015). Not surprisingly, weight bias appears to negatively affect grades at school. Evidence shows that obese students receive significantly lower academic grades in school and university than "normal"-weight students, despite scoring just as well on intelligence and achievement tests, suggesting that lower grades are not due to their "inability to master scholastic material" (MacCann & Robers, 2013). Student reports confirm that their experiences of weight-based bullying at school have harmed their grades and led them to avoid going to school to escape harassment (Puhl & Luedicke, 2012). There is also some evidence to suggest that despite comparable grades and academic performance, overweight and obese adolescents are less likely to be accepted to high-ranking universities and are less to receive financial support from their parents while at university, even after controlling for income, ethnicity, and family size (Canning & Mayer, 1966; Crandall, 1991).

Children's internalized weight bias is also likely to impact their academic performance. Studies in Finland, China, and the United States indicate that irrespective of their actual body weight, adolescent girls who perceive themselves to be overweight and/or report dissatisfaction with their weight achieve poorer academic grades (Florin, Shults, & Stettler, 2011; Mikkilä, Lahti-Koski, Pietinen, Virtanen, & Rimpela, 2003; Xie et al., 2006). Furthermore, another study indicated that 31% of adolescents sampled in the UK say that they avoid classroom debate and absent themselves from school on days they lack confidence in their appearance (Lovegrove & Rumsey, 2005).

Theoretical Explanations for Weight Bias

A number of theories have been proposed to explain why overweight and obese individuals are stigmatized. These range from theories that explain individual-level psychological mechanisms for weight bias (e.g., attribution theory, social consensus theory) as well as sociocultural theory, which situates weight bias within feminist and social justice frameworks. This section briefly reviews one of the most well-supported individual-level theories for weight bias, attribution theory, in addition to providing a short overview of sociocultural theory for weight bias (see Puhl & Brownell, 2003, for a more detailed analysis of individual-level theories; see Saguy, 2012, for a more detailed analysis of critical sociocultural theory).

Attribution Theory. Attribution theory argues that people try to make sense of their social world through causal explanations or attributions about events and behaviors that are primarily external or internal (Heider, 1958). External attributions ascribe outcomes to factors beyond individual control, and internal attributions to those within individual control. Studies show that internal attributions are often used to justify the social and economic disadvantage of stigmatized groups (Doosje & Branscombe, 2002).

Body weight is determined by a complex interaction of modifiable and non-modifiable biological, behavioral, social, and environmental factors (e.g., genetics, hormones, dietary intake, physical activity levels, socioeconomic status; Swinburn et al., 2011). Research has consistently found that people who hold an ideology that endorses individual responsibility are more likely to stigmatize overweight and obese individuals (e.g., Pearl & Lebowitz, 2014; Puhl & Brownell, 2003). Specifically, people who make internal attributions about the causes of weight and believe that weight is within an individual's control (i.e., individuals can change their weight through will power, exercise, and dietary choices) are more likely to hold negative attitudes toward overweight and obese people (Crandall, 1994). This finding is robust in studies of individualist cultures (e.g., United States, Australia, Poland, Iceland, and Canada; Puhl, Latner, O'Brien, Luedicke, Danielsdottir et al., 2015); however, it is less clear in collectivist cultures (e.g., India, Turkey, and Venezuela; Crandall et al., 2008). While attribution theory is well supported by correlational and experimental studies as being a useful explanation of weight bias, and there is merit in challenging weight controllability beliefs in interventions that aim to reduce weight bias, some scholars have suggested that it lends itself to reinforcing weight bias because external attributions of weight may stigmatize fat bodies as being "diseased" (Saguy & Riley, 2005). Accordingly, critical theorists have situated weight bias as a social and cultural problem rooted in gender, race, and social class injustices.

Sociocultural Theory. Critical, feminist, and fat acceptance scholars have posited that weight bias reflects the intersection of social justice issues surrounding gender, race, and class inequalities (Saguy & Almeling, 2008). Indeed, the gendered nature of weight bias, whereby women are more likely to experience and be disadvantaged by weight-based discrimination, provides support for this (Fikkan & Rothblum, 2012). Feminist scholars (e.g., Bordo, 1993; Orbach, 2010) have argued that the dominant social hatred of fat bodies is an expression of the historical pressure women have faced to conform to narrowly defined cultural beauty ideals, which in recent centuries have emphasized thin and slender female bodies as indicators of attractiveness and success. Further, the fact that ethnic minority and lower-income groups are more likely to be overweight or obese (likely due to disparities in access to health care, fresh unprocessed food, and environments that are conducive to safe and pleasurable physical activity) has led others to argue that weight bias stems from social and environmental injustices (Saguy, 2012). Furthermore, it has been argued that framing obesity and weight bias purely in terms of risky health behaviors runs the risk of legitimizing social inequalities and health disparities (Saguy & Riley, 2005). Thus, recognizing weight bias as an issue reflecting both social injustice and public health may be important in efforts to better understand and combat this problem. It is likely that multi-level strategies including individual through to macro-level intervention will be necessary to reduce weight bias.

Interventions to Address Weight Bias

Taken together, the research summarized in this chapter suggests that interventions to reduce weight bias are urgently needed, given its widespread prevalence and negative consequences. Intervention efforts to address weight bias are multi-level, ranging from individual psychosocial interventions through to media, public health, and policy approaches.

Psychosocial Interventions. In line with attribution theory, evidence shows that interventions that aim to educate adults about the multiple determinants of weight (i.e., biological, behavioral, social, and environmental factors) and challenge weight controllability beliefs can result in a reduction in negative attitudes toward overweight and obese individuals. For example, in separate studies, Crandall (1994) and Puhl, Schwartz, and Brownell (2005) found that reading a brief article that emphasized the importance of uncontrollable factors in weight determination (e.g., genetics and physiology) was associated with more positive attitudes toward overweight and obese individuals than reading an article about the physiology of stress or an article that highlighted controllable factors associated with weight (e.g., diet and exercise). Further, Diedrichs and Barlow (2011) observed reductions in weight bias, relative to controls, that were maintained at 3-week follow-up among Australian preservice health students after a brief 2-hour education intervention outlining the multiple determinants of weight. Other studies, however, have found limited or no support for challenging controllability beliefs to reduce weight bias (e.g., Teachman, Gapinski, Brownell, Rawlins, & Jeyaram, 2003). Therefore, it has been suggested that further research examine additional bias-reduction strategies, as it is unlikely that challenging weight controllability beliefs will be sufficient on its own as a method to reduce weight bias (O'Brien, Puhl, Latner, Mir, & Hunter, 2010)

Among children, the results of interventions that aim to change weight controllability beliefs to reduce weight bias are mixed (e.g., Anesbury & Tiggemann, 2000; Bell & Morgan, 2000). However, evidence suggests that children's picture books that promote positive body image (e.g., *Shapesville* by Mills and Osborne, 2003) can significantly reduce weight bias among 5- to 9-year-old girls (Dohnt & Tiggemann, 2008). Furthermore, school-based eating disorder prevention programs that focus on promoting positive body image, intuitive eating, and media literacy have shown some success in reducing weight bias among children and adolescents in controlled trials (e.g., Kater, Rohwer, & Londre, 2002).

Media and Public Health Interventions. Encouragingly, research and advocacy efforts, particularly from the fields of body image and eating disorders prevention, have dedicated concerted effort to increasing body size diversity and the positive portrayal of people with higher weights in advertising and media imagery. For example, the findings of experimental body image research, which consistently documents that exposure to larger "plus-size" models is associated with positive body image and consumer reactions, have underpinned advocacy efforts to address the overrepresentation of idealized images of thin and hyper-muscular models in advertising and media (e.g., Diedrichs & Lee, 2010, 2011). Specifically, politicians have used this research to lobby for the regulation of advertising in an effort to promote greater body size diversity (British All Party Parliamentary Group on Body Image, 2012). In a positive step, the Australian government has developed a voluntary media code of conduct to improve body image, which, among other recommendations, encourages brands and media out-lets to showcase people of diverse body sizes in their advertising and media images (Paxton, 2015). The uptake and effectiveness of this code and other advocacy efforts, however, are yet to be formally evaluated.

The US-based Rudd Center for Food Policy and Obesity has produced a number of resources that aim to reduce weight bias in the media. Specifically, it has published media guidelines that aim to reduce weight-biased reporting and por-trayal of overweight and obese individuals (Rudd Center for Food Policy and Obesity, 2015). In addition, the center has a free online repository of images featuring unbiased portrayals of people with larger bodies available for use by media outlets, educators, and health professionals. An experimental study evalu-ated the impact of these images and found that exposure to images in the gallery was associated with less weight-biased attitudes compared to the stereotyped portrayals of larger bodies usually displayed in the media (Pearl, Puhl, & Brownell, 2012).

There have also been calls for a reorientation of public health campaigns from a focus on weight and obesity to a "weight-inclusive approach" (e.g., Tylka et al., 2014). A weight-inclusive approach focuses on encouraging all individuals, irrespective of their body weight, to eat nutritious food in response to internal hunger cues and to engage in physical activity that is sustainable and pleasurable. Indeed, surveys and experimental research have indicated that nationally represen-tative samples of the US public respond more positively to public health messages that promote health behaviors without a focus on weight or obesity (Puhl, Luedicke, & Peterson, 2013; Puhl, Peterson, & Luedicke, 2013). Alternatively, public health messages perceived as being weight biased are seen as being less likely to motivate health behavior change.

Social Policy and Legislation. Social policy refers to policies designed to support the well-being of society and may include legislation, regulations, guide-lines, public comment and persuasion, and the government allocation of taxpayer funds to particular initiatives (Paxton, 2015). In the context of weight bias, social policy initiatives could include school-based anti-bullying strategies, legislation to protect people from weight-based discrimination, and media regulations to reduce the overrepresentation of idealized lower-weight bodies. There is broad public support for these types of social policy approaches to reduce weight bias, evidenced in representative samples of the US public; convenience samples of adults from Australia, Iceland, and Canada; and parents and educators (Puhl & Heuer, 2011;

Puhl, Latner, O'Brien, Luedicke, Forhan et al., 2015; Puhl, Neumark-Sztainer, Austin, Luedicke, & King, 2014).

Despite social support, few social policy and legislative approaches have been implemented to address weight bias. Perhaps most concerning is that unlike other forms of discrimination, it remains legal to discriminate on the basis of weight. Exceptions to this include limited options for legal recourse through disability antidiscrimination laws for very high-weight individuals in the United States (Pomeranz & Puhl, 2013), and an antidiscrimination workplace law that was enacted in France in 2001 that included provisions about physical appearance (e.g., height, weight, attractiveness; Viprey, 2002). Nevertheless, it is evident that if weight bias is to be addressed on a broad scale, social policy and legislative strategies require ongoing and urgent attention.

Future Directions for Research, Intervention, and Advocacy

This chapter has outlined the definition, prevalence, sources, consequences, theories, and intervention approaches for weight bias. Weight bias is pervasive and associated with numerous negative consequences for children and adults. Although some progress has been made in individual-level and media interventions to address weight bias, social policy and legislative remedies are lacking, and few, if any, interventions have been disseminated on a broad scale. To rapidly and strategically advance research, intervention, and advocacy efforts dedicated to reducing weight bias, we make the following recommendations. First, to improve the quality of evidence, researchers need to pay careful attention to the validity and consistency of scales and tools used to assess weight bias, and to increase the use of behavioral measures of bias and discrimination. Second, it is imperative to expand the breadth of research in this field to include representative, multi-country, and ethnically diverse samples. Third, although the evidence for the prevalence and consequences of weight bias is reasonably well established, effective interventions to address this problem are acutely needed and require urgent attention in research and advocacy efforts. Given the success of research, social action, and advocacy efforts in other areas of prejudice (e.g., race, age, disability, gender), researchers and advocates can learn from prejudice reduction research in these fields (e.g., Alperin et al., 2014) and work together in more coordinated, systematic ways to help reduce weight bias and its devastating consequences for those affected.

References

Adams, C. H., Smith, N. J., Wilbur, D. C., & Grady, K. E. (1993). The relationship of obesity to the frequency of pelvic examinations: Do physician and patient attitudes make a difference? *Women and Health, 20,* 45–57.

Alperin, A., Hornsey, M. J., Hayward, L. E., Diedrichs, P. C., & Barlow, F. K. (2014). Applying the contact hypothesis to anti-fat attitudes: Contact with overweight people is related to how we interact with our bodies and those of others. *Social Science and Medicine, 123,* 37–44.

Amy, N. K., Aalborg, A., Lyons, P., & Keranen, L. (2006). Barriers to routine gynecological cancer screening for White and African-American obese women. *International Journal of Obesity, 30,* 147–155.

Andreyeva, T., Puhl, R. M., & Brownell, K. D. (2008). Changes in perceived weight discrimination among Americans, 1995–1996 through 2004–2006. *International Journal of Obesity, 16,* 1129–1134.

Anesbury, T., & Tiggemann, M. (2000). An attempt to reduce negative stereotyping of obesity in children by changing controllability beliefs. *Health Education Research, 15,* 145–152.

Ata, R. N., & Thompson, J. K. (2010). Weight bias in the media: A review of recent research. *Obesity Facts, 3,* 41–46.

Bacardi-Gascon, M., Leon-Reyes, M. J., & Jimenez-Cruz, A. (2007). Stigmatization of overweight Mexican children. *Child Psychiatry & Human Development, 38,* 99–105.

Bell, S. K., & Morgan, S. B. (2000). Children's attitudes and behavioral intentions toward a peer presented as obese: Does a medical explanation for obesity make a difference? *Journal of Pediatric Psychology, 25,* 137–145.

Bellizzi, J. A., & Hasty, R. W. (1998). Territory assignment decisions and supervising unethical selling behavior: The effects of obesity and gender as moderated by job-related factors. *Journal of Personal Selling and Sales Management, 18,* 35–49.

Bellizzi, J. A., & Hasty, R. W. (2001). The effects of a stated organizational policy on inconsistent disciplinary action based on salesperson gender and weight. *Journal of Personal Selling and Sales Management, 21,* 189–198.

Berry, T. R., McLeod, N. C., Pankratow, M., & Walker, J. (2013). Effects of *Biggest Loser* exercise depictions on exercise-related attitudes. *American Journal of Health Behavior, 37,* 96–103.

Bertakis, K. D., & Azari, R. (2005). The impact of obesity on primary care visits. *Obesity Research, 13,* 1615–1622.

Bocquier, A., Verger, P., Basdevant, A., Andreotti, G., Baretge, J., Villani, P., & Paraponaris, A. (2005). Overweight and obesity: Knowledge, attitudes and practices of general practitioners in France. *Obesity Research, 13,* 787–795.

Bordo, S. (1993). *Unbearable weight: Feminism, Western culture, and the body.* Berkeley: University of California Press.

Bradshaw, C. P., Waasdorp, T. E., & O'Breman, L. M. (2013). Teachers' and education support professionals' perspectives on bullying and prevention: Findings from a National Education Association study. *School Psychology Review, 42,* 280–297.

Brewis, A. A., Wutich, A., Fallette-Cowden, A., & Rodriguez-Soto, I. (2011). Body norms and fat stigma in global perspective. *Current Anthroplogy, 52*(2), 269–276.

British All-Party Parliamentary Group on Body Image. (2012). Reflection on Body Image Report. www.berealcampaign.co.uk/assets/filemanager/documents/appg_body_image_final.pdf

British Council. (2008). Inclusion and diversity in education (INDIE) research findings.

Brochu, P. M., Pearl, R. M., Puhl, R. M., & Brownell, K. D. (2014). Do media portrayals of obesity influence support for weight-related medical policy? *Health Psychology*, *33*, 197–200.

Brown, I., & Thompson, J. (2007). Primary care nurses' attitudes, beliefs and own body size in relation to obesity management. *Journal of Advanced Nursing*, *60*, 535–543.

Brownell, K. D. (2005). The social, scientific, and human context of prejudice and discrimination based on weight. In K. D. Brownell, R. M. Puhl, M. B. Schwartz, & L. Rudd (Eds.), *Weight bias: Nature, consequences and remedies* (pp. 1–11). New York: Guilford Press.

Bucchianeri, M. M., Eisenberg, M. E., & Neumark-Sztainer, D. (2013). Weightism, racism, classism, and sexism: Shared forms of harassment in adolescents. *Journal of Adolescent Health*, *53*, 47–53.

Canning, H., & Mayer, J. (1966). Obesity – its possible effect on college acceptance. *New England Journal of Medicine*, *275*, 1172–1174.

Carr, D., & Friedman, M. A. (2005). Is obesity stigmatizing? Body weight, perceived discrimination, and psychological well-being in the United States. *Journal of Health and Social Behavior*, *46*(3), 244–259.

Cramer, P., & Steinwert, T. (1998). Thin is good, fat is bad: How early does it begin? *Journal of Applied Developmental Psychology*, *19*, 429–451. doi: 10.1016/s0193-3973(99)80049-5

Crandall, C. S. (1991). Do parents discriminate against their heavyweight daughters? *Personality and Social Psychology Bulletin*, *21*, 724–735.

Crandall, C. S. (1994). Prejudice against fat people: Ideology and self-interest. *Journal of Personality and Social Psychology*, *66*, 882–894.

Crandall, C. S., D'Anello, S., Sakalli, N., Lazarus, E., Wieczorkowska Nejtardt, G., & Feather, N. T. (2008). An attribution-value model of prejudice: Anti-fat attitudes in six nations. *Personality and Social Psychology Bulletin*, *27*, 30–37.

Davis-Coelho, K., Waltz, J., & Davis-Coelho, B. (2000). Awareness and prevention of bias against fat clients in psychotherapy. *Professional Psychology: Research and Practice*, *31*, 682–684.

Diedrichs, P. C., & Barlow, F. K. (2011). How to lose weight bias fast! Evaluating a brief anti-weight bias intervention. *British Journal of Health Psychology*, *16*, 846–861.

Diedrichs, P. C., & Lee, C. (2010). GI Joe or average Joe? The impact of average-size and muscular fashion models on men's and women's body image and advertisement effectiveness. *Body Image*, *7*, 218–226.

Diedrichs, P. C., & Lee, C. (2011). Waif goodbye! Average-size female models promote positive body image and appeal to consumers. *Psychology & Health*, *26*, 1273–1291.

Dohnt, H. K., & Tiggemann, M. (2008). Promoting positive body image in young girls: An evaluation of "Shapesville." *European Eating Disorders Review*, *16*, 222–233.

Doosje, B., & Branscombe, N. R. (2002). Attributions for the negative historical actions of a group. *European Journal of Social Psychology*, *33*(2), 235–248.

Dornoff, S. E., Hinman, N. G., Koball, A. M., Storfer-Isser, A., Carhart, V. L., Baik, K. D., & Carels, R. A. (2012). The effects of reality television on weight bias: An examination of the *Biggest Loser*. *Obesity*, *29*, 993–998.

Eisenberg, M., Neumark-Sztainer, D., & Story, M. (2003). Associations of weight-based teasing and emotional well-being among adolescents. *Archives of Pediatric and Adolescent Medicine*, *157*, 733–738.

Fikkan, J. L., & Rothblum, E. D. (2005). Weight bias in employment. In K. D. Brownell, R. M. Puhl, M. B. Schwartz, & L. Rudd (Eds.), *Weight bias: Nature, consequences and remedies* (pp. 15–28). New York: Guilford Press.

Fikkan, J. L., & Rothblum, E. D. (2012). Is fat a feminist issue? Exploring the gendered nature of weight bias. *Sex Roles, 66*, 575–592.

Florin, T. A., Shults, J., & Stettler, N. (2011). Perception of overweight is associated with poor academic performance in US adolescents. *Journal of School Health, 81*, 663–670.

Fouts, G., & Vaughan, K. (2002). Television situation comedies: Male weight, negative references, and audience reactions. *Sex Roles, 46*, 439–442.

Glauser, T. A., Roepke, N., Stevenin, B., Dubois, A. M., & Ahn, S. M. (2015). Physician knowledge about and perceptions of obesity management. *Obesity Research and Clinical Practice, 9*, 573–583.

Gleason, J. H., Alexander, A. M., & Somers, C. L. (2000). Later adolescents' reactions to three types of childhood teasing: Relations with self-esteem and body image. *Social Behavior and Personality, 28*, 471–480.

Greenberg, B. S., Eastin, M., Hofschire, L., Lachlan, K., & Brownell, K. D. (2003). Portrayals of overweight and obese individuals on commercial television. *American Journal of Public Health, 93*, 1342–1348.

Haines, J., Neumark-Sztainer, D., Eisenberg, M., & Hannan, P. J. (2006). Weight teasing and disordered eating behaviors in adolescents: Longitudinal findings from Project EAT (Eating Among Teens). *Pediatrics, 117*, 209–215.

Happer, C., & Philo, G. (2013). The role of the media in construction of public belief and social change. *Journal of Social and Political Psychology, 1*. doi: 10.5964/jspp.v1i1.96

Hatzenbuehler, M. L., Keyes, K. M., & Hasin, D. S. (2009). Associations between perceived weight discrimination and the prevalence of psychiatric disorders in the general populations. *Obesity, 17*, 2033–2039.

Hebl, M. R., Ruggs, E. N., Singeltary, L., & Beal, D. J. (2008). Perceptions of obesity across the lifespan. *Obesity*, S46–S52.

Hebl, M. R., Xu, J., & Mason, M. F. (2003). Weighing the care: Patients' perceptions of physician care as a function of gender and weight. *International Journal of Obesity, 27*, 269–275.

Heider, F. (1958). *The psychology of interpersonal relationships*. New York: Wiley.

Herbozo, S., Tantleff-Dunn, S., Gokee-Larose, J., & Thompson, J. K. (2004). Beauty and thinness messages in children's media: A content analysis. *Eating Disorders, 12*, 21–34.

Heuer, C., McClure, K. J., & Puhl, R. M. (2011). Obesity stigma in online news: A visual content analysis. *Journal of Health Communication, 16*, 976–987.

Himes, S. M., & Thompson, J. K. (2007). Fat stigmatization in television shows and movies: A content analysis. *Obesity, 15*, 712–718.

Hussin, M., Frazier, S., & Thompson, J. K. (2011). Fat stigmatization on YouTube: A content analysis. *Body Image, 8*, 90–92.

Jackson, S. E., Beeken, R. J., & Wardle, J. (2014). Perceived weight discrimination and changes in weight, waist circumference, and weight status. *Obesity, 22*, 2485–2488.

Jansen, P. W., Verlinden, M., Dommisse-van Berkel, A., Mieloo, C. L., Raat, H., Hofman, A. . . . Tiemeier, H. (2014). Teacher and peer reports of overweight and bullying among young primary school children. *Pediatrics, 134*, 473–480

Janssen, I., Craig, W. M., Boyce, W. F., & Pickett, W. (2004). Associations between overweight and obesity with bullying behaviors in school-aged children. *Pediatrics*, *113*, 1187–1194.

Johar, M., & Katayama, H. (2012). Quantile regression analysis of body mass and wages. *Health Economics*, *21*, 597–611.

Johnson, C. (2001). *Self esteem comes in all sizes*. Carlsbad, CA: Gurze Books.

Judge, T. A., & Cable, D. M. (2010). When it comes to pay, do the thin win? The effect of weight on pay for men and women. *Journal of Applied Psychology*, *96*, 95–112.

Katcr, K. J., Rohwer, J., & Londre, K. (2002). Evaluation of an upper elementary school program to prevent body image, eating, and weight concerns. *Journal of School Health*, *72*, 199–204.

Kim, S. H., & Wills, L. A. (2007). Talking about obesity: News framing of who is responsible for causing and fixing the problem. *Journal of Health Communication*, *12*, 359–376.

King, E. B., Shapiro, J. R., Hebl, M. R., Singeltary, L., & Turner, S. (2006). The stigma of obesity in customer service: A mechanism for remediation and bottom-line consequences of interpersonal discrimination. *Journal of Applied Psychology*, *91*, 579–593.

Klein, H., & Shiffman, K. S. (2006). Messages about physical attractiveness in animated cartoons. *Body Image*, *3*, 353–363.

Latner, J. D., Rosewall, J. K., & Simmonds, M. B. (2007). Childhood obesity stigma: Association with television, videogame, and magazine exposure. *Body Image*, *4*, 147–155.

Latner, J. D., & Schwartz, M. B. (2005). Weight bias in a child's world. In K. D. Brownell, R. M. Puhl, M. B. Schwartz, & L. Rudd (Eds.), *Weight bias: Nature, consequences, and remedies* (pp. 54–67). New York: Guilford Press.

Latner, J. D., & Stunkard, A. J. (2003). Getting worse: The stigmatization of obese children. *Obesity Research*, *11*, 452–456.

Lovegrove, E., & Rumsey, N. (2005). Ignoring it doesn't make it stop: Adolescents, appearance, and bullying. *The Cleft Palate-Craniofacial Journal*, *42*, 33–44.

MacCann, C., & Robers, R. D. (2013). Just as smart but not as successful: Obese students obtain lower school grades but equivalent test scores to nonobese students. *International Journal of Obesity*, *37*, 40–46.

Major, B., Eliezer, D., & Rieck, H. (2012). The psychological weight of weight stigma. *Social Psychology and Personality Science*, *3*, 651–658.

McClure, K. J., Puhl, R. M., & Heuer, C. (2011). Obesity in the news: Do photographic images of obese people influence antifat attitudes? *Journal of Health Communication*, *16*, 359–371.

Mikkilä, V., Lahti-Koski, M., Pietinen, P., Virtanen, S. M., & Rimpela, M. (2003). Associates of obesity and weight dissatisfaction among Finnish adolescents. *Public Health Nutrition*, *6*, 49–56.

Mills, A., & Osbourne, B. (2003). *Shapesville*. Carlsbad, CA: Gurze Books.

Mulherin, K., Miller, Y. D., Barlow, F. K., Diedrichs, P. C., & Thompson, R. (2013). Weight stigma in maternity care: Women's experiences and care providers' attitudes. *BMC Pregnancy and Childbirth*, *13*(19).

Ng, M., Fleming, T., Robinson, M., Blake, T., Graetz, N., Margano, C. ... Gakidou, E. (2014). Global, regional, and national prevalence of overweight and obesity in children and adults during 1980–2013: A systematic analysis for the Global Burden of Disease Study 2013. *The Lancet, 384*(9945), 766–781.

O'Brien, K., Latner, J. D., Ebneter, D., & Hunter, J. A. (2013). Obesity discrimination: The role of physical appearance, personal ideology, and anti-fat prejudice. *International Journal of Obesity, 37*, 455–460.

O'Brien, K., Puhl, R. M., Latner, J. D., Mir, A. S., & Hunter, J. A. (2010). Reducing anti-fat prejudice in preservice health students: A randomized trial. *International Journal of Obesity, 18*, 2138–2144.

Oberrieder, H. R., Walker, R., Monroe, D., & Adeyanju, M. (1995). Attitudes of dietetics students and registered dieticians toward obesity. *American Journal of the Dietetic Association, 95*, 916–914.

Orbach, S. (2010). *Bodies*. London: Profile Books.

Paxton, S. J. (2015). Social policy and prevention of body image and eating disorders. In M. Levine & L. Smolak (Eds.), *The Wiley-Blackwell handbook of eating disorders* (pp. 655–668). New York: John Wiley & Sons.

Pearl, R. M., & Lebowitz, M.S. (2014). Beyond personal responsibility: Effects of causal attributions for overweight and obesity on weight-related beliefs, stigma, and policy support. *Psychology & Health, 29*, 1176–1191.

Pearl, R. M., Puhl, R. M., & Brownell, K. D. (2012). Positive media portrayals of obese persons: Impact on attitudes and image preferences. *Health Psychology, 31*, 821–829.

Penny, H., & Haddock, G. (2007). Anti-fat prejudice among children: The "mere proximity" effect in 5–10 year olds. *Journal of Experimental Social Psychology, 43*, 678–683.

Phelan, S. M., Dovidio, J. F., Puhl, R. M., Burgess, D. J., Nelson, D. B., & Yeazel, M. W. (2014). Implicit and explicit weight bias in a national sample of 4,732 medical students: The medical student CHANGES study. *Obesity, 22*, 1201–1208.

Pomeranz, J. L., & Puhl, R. M. (2013). New developments in the law for obesity discrimination and protection. *Obesity, 21*, 469–471.

Puhl, R. M., Andreyeva, T., & Brownell, K. D. (2008). Perceptions of weight discrimination: Prevalence and comparison to race and gender discrimination in America. *International Journal of Obesity, 32*, 992–1000.

Puhl, R. M., & Brownell, K. D. (2001). Bias, discrimination and obesity. *Obesity Research, 9*, 788–805.

Puhl, R. M., & Brownell, K. D. (2003). Psychosocial origins of obesity stigma: Toward changing a powerful and pervasive bias. *Obesity Reviews, 4*, 213–227.

Puhl, R. M., & Heuer, C. (2011). Public opinion about laws to prohibit weight discrimination in the United States. *Obesity, 19*, 74–82.

Puhl, R. M., & Latner, J. D. (2012). Weight bias: New science on a significant social problem. *Obesity, 16*, S1-S2.

Puhl, R. M., Latner, J. D., O'Brien, K., Luedicke, J., Danielsdottir, S., & Forhan, M. (2015). A multinational examination of weight bias: Predictors of anti-fat attitudes across four countries. *International Journal of Obesity, 39*, 1166–1173.

Puhl, R. M., Latner, J. D., O'Brien, K., Luedicke, J., Forhan, M., & Danielsdottir, S. (2015). Cross-national perspectives about weight-based bullying in youth: nature, extent and remedies. *Pediatric Obesity, 11*, 241–250.

Puhl, R. M., & Luedicke, J. (2012). Weight-based victimization among adolescents in the school setting: Emotional reactions and coping behaviors. *Journal of Youth and Adolescence, 41*, 27–40.

Puhl, R. M., Luedicke, J., & DePierre, J. A. (2013). Parental concerns about weight-based victimization in youth. *Childhood Obesity, 9*, 540–548.

Puhl, R. M., Luedicke, J., & Peterson, L. (2013). Public reactions to obesity-related health campaigns: A randomized controlled trial. *The American Journal of Preventive Medicine, 45*, 36–48.

Puhl, R. M., Neumark-Sztainer, D., Austin, S. B., Luedicke, J., & King, K. M. (2014). Setting policy priorities to address eating disorders and weight stigma: Views from the field of eating disorders and the US general public. *BMC Public Health, 14*, 524.

Puhl, R. M., Peterson, J. L., DePierre, J. A., & Luedicke, J. (2013). Headless, hungry, and unhealthy: A video content analysis of obese persons portrayed in online news. *Journal of Health Communication, 18*, 686–702.

Puhl, R. M., Peterson, J. L., & Luedicke, J. (2013). Fighting obesity or obese persons? Public perceptions of obesity-related health messages. *International Journal of Obesity, 37*, 774–782.

Puhl, R. M., Schwartz, M. B., & Brownell, K. D. (2005). Impact of perceived consensus on stereotypes about obese people: A new approach for reducing bias. *Health Psychology. Special Section on Dissemination, 24*, 517–525.

Puhl, R. M., & Suh, Y. (2015). Health consequences of weight stigma: Implications for obesity prevention and treatment. *Current Obesity Reports, 4*, 182–190.

Rich, S. S., Essery, E. V., Sanborn, C. F., DiMarco, N. M., Morales, L. K., & LeClere, S. M. (2008). Predictors of body size stigmatisation in Hispanic preschool children. *Obesity, 16*, S11–S17.

Richardson, S. A., Goodman, N., Hastorf, A. H., & Dornbusch, S. M. (1961). Cultural uniformity in reaction to physical disabilities. *American Sociological Review, 26*, 467–480.

Robinson, T., Callister, M., & Jankoski, T. (2008). Portrayal of body weight on children's television sitcoms: A content analysis. *Body Image, 5*, 141–151.

Rothblum, E. D., Brand, P. A., Millers, C. T., & Oetjen, H. A. (1990). The relationship between obesity, employment discrimination, and employment related victimization. *Journal of Vocational Behavior, 37*, 251–266.

Rudd Center for Food Policy and Obesity. (2015). Guidelines for media portrayals of individuals affected by obesity. Retrieved from www.uconnruddcenter.org/files/Pdfs/MediaGuidelines_PortrayalObese(1).pdf

Rudolph, C. W., Wells, C. L., Weller, M. D., & Batles, B. B. (2009). A meta-analysis of empirical studies of weight-based bias in the workplace. *Journal of Vocational Behavior, 74*, 1–10.

Sabin, J. A., Marini, M., Nosek, B. A., & Brownell, K. D. (2012). Implicit and explicit anti-fat bias among a large sample of medical doctors by BMI, race/ethnicity and gender. *PloS One, 7*, e48448.

Saguy, A. C. (2012). Why fat is a feminist issue. *Sex Roles, 66*, 600–607.

Saguy, A. C., & Almeling, R. (2008). Fat in the fire? Science, the news media, and the "obesity epidemic." *Sociological Forum, 23*, 53–83.

Saguy, A. C., & Riley, K. W. (2005). Weight both sides: Morality, mortality, and framing contests over obesity. *Journal of Health Politics, Policy and Law, 30*, 869–923.

Schwartz, M. B., Vartanian, L. R., Nosek, B. A., & Brownell, K. D. (2006). The influence of one's own body weight on implicit and explicit anti-fat bias. *Obesity, 14*, 440–447.

Setchell, J., Watson, B., Jones, L., Gard, M., & Briffa, K. (2014). Physiotherapists demonstrate weight stigma: A cross-sectional survey of Australian physiotherapists. *Journal of Physiotherapy, 60*, 157–162.

Shroff, H., & Thompson, J. K. (2004). Body image and eating disturbance in India: Media and interpersonal influences. *International Journal of Eating Disorders, 35*, 198–203.

Sutin, A. R., & Terracciano, A. (2013). Perceived weight discrimination and obesity. *PloS One, 8*, e70048.

Swinburn, B. A., Sacks, G., Hall, K. D., McPherson, K., Finegood, D. T., Moodie, M. L., & Gortmaker, S. L. (2011). The global obesity pandemic: Shaped by global drivers and local environments. *Lancet, 378*, 804–814.

Tang-Peronard, J. L., & Heitmann, B. L. (2008). Stigmatization of obese children and adolescents, the importance of gender. *Obesity Reviews, 9*, 522–534.

Teachman, B. A., Gapinski, K. D., Brownell, K. D., Rawlins, M., & Jeyaram, S. (2003). Demonstrations of implicit anti-fat bias: The impact of providing causal information and evoking empathy. *Health Psychology, 22*, 68–78.

Thomas, S., Hyde, J., & Komesaroff, P. (2007). "Cheapening the struggle": Obese people's attitudes toward *The Biggest Loser*. *Obesity Management, 3*, 210–215.

Thompson, J. K., Herbozo, S., Himes, S., & Yamamiya, Y. (2005). Effects of weight-related teasing adults. In K. D. Brownell, R. M. Puhl, M. B. Schwartz, & L. Rudd (Eds.), *Weight bias: Nature, consequence, and remedies.* (pp. 137–149). New York: Guilford Press.

Throop, E. M., Skinner, A. C., Perrin, A. J., Steiner, M. J., Odulana, A., & Perrin, E. M. (2014). Pass the popcorn: "Obeseogenic" behaviors and stigma in children's movies. *Obesity, 22*, 1694–1700.

Tylka, T. L., Annunziato, R. A., Burgard, D., Danielsdottir, S., Shuman, E., Davis, C., & Calogero, R. M. (2014). The weight-inclusive versus weight-normative approach to health: Evaluating the evidence for prioritizing well-being over weight loss. *Journal of Obesity.* doi: http://dx.doi.org/10.1155/2014/983495

van den Berg, P., Neumark-Sztainer, D., Eisenberg, M. E., & Haines, J. (2008). Racial/ethnic differences in weight-related teasing in adolescents. *Obesity, 16*(S2), S3-S10. doi: 10.1038/oby.2008.445

Viprey, M. (2002). New anti-discrmination law adopted. Retrieved from www.eurofound.europa.eu/observatories/eurwork/articles/law-and-regulation/new-anti-discrimination-law-adopted

Wear, D., Aultman, J. M., Varley, J. D., & Zarconi, J. (2006). Making fun of patients: Medical students' perceptions and use of derogatory and cynical humor in clinical settings. *Academic Medicine, 81*, 454–462.

Wen-ying, S. C., Prestin, A., & Kunath, S. (2014). Obesity in social media: A mixed methods analysis. *Translational Behavioral Medicine, 4*, 314–323.

Wertheim, E. H., Koerner, J., & Paxton, S. J. (2001). Longitudinal predictors of restrictive eating and bulimic tendencies in three different age groups of adolescent girls *Journal of Youth and Adolescence, 30*, 69–81.

Xie, B., Chou, C. P., Spruijt-Metz, D., Reynolds, K., Clark, F., Palmer, P. H. ... Johnson, C. A. (2006). Weight perception, academic performance, and psychological factors in Chinese adolescents. *American Journal of Health Behavior, 30,* 115–124.

Yoo, J. H. (2012). No clear winner. Effects of *The Biggest Loser* on the stigmatization of obese persons. *Health Communication, 28,* 294–303.

Yoo, J. H., & Kim, K. (2012). Obesity in the new media: A content analysis of obesity videos on YouTube. *Health Communication, 27,* 294–303.

18 Prejudice Against Immigrants in Multicultural Societies

Colleen Ward, Agnes Szabo, and Jaimee Stuart

Migration is one of the most ancient traditions of humankind. From the beginning of human history, people have been moving places and crossing cultural and societal borders to search for new opportunities and a better life or to flee from war and natural disasters. Although migration is not a modern phenomenon, because of recent technological advancements in communication and transportation, moving across countries has become easier than ever before. This has resulted in a marked worldwide increase in the migrant stock over the past 50 years. In 2013, more than 230 million people were living as international immigrants, and it is projected that the migrant population will reach 400 million by 2050 (Martin, 2013).

Globally, four major migration pathways can be identified. The largest exchange (36%) occurs between regions of the Global South, that is, people from less affluent countries moving to other undeveloped regions. The second largest flow (35%) goes from the Global South to the Global North, that is, people from undeveloped regions migrating to the developed world. It is worth noting that the South to North migration continues to rise and is soon expected to become the primary trend. International relocation within the Global North is also considerable (23%), whereas North to South migration contributes only a small proportion (6%) to the global trends. Although there are no notable gender differences in migration trends, age appears to be a significant factor. Of all immigrants, 15% are younger than age 20, and approximately 74% belong to the working-age population. In sum, the majority of international immigrants (59%) currently reside in the developed world, where, according to recent statistics, migration has become the primary source of population growth, highlighting its growing significance in terms of economic prosperity and sustainable social development (UN, 2013).

At the same time, it is important to recognize that migration is not just an economic matter; it also has important implications for individuals and societies. As a result of globalization, demographic expansion, and increasing diversity within and across nations, plural societies are facing a wide range of social issues stemming from a multicultural reality, in which firsthand intercultural contact is an indispensable part of everyday experiences. Navigating these multiethnic contemporary societies has become increasingly complex and challenging, fostering public resistance to immigration and negative intergroup attitudes. Consequently, safeguarding social cohesion, ensuring inclusion, and enhancing positive inter-group relations have been recognized as key political objectives in the Western world.

A number of initiatives have been put in place by governments of major immigrant-receiving countries aiming to improve social cohesion by taking a stand against prejudice, combatting discrimination and racism, and fostering cross-cultural understanding. Such programs include the Living in Harmony Initiative in Australia, Multiculturalism Policy in Canada, and the EQUAL Development Partnerships in the European Union. Although social policy seems to be making headway in promoting social cohesion, xenophobia has been on the rise since the late 1980s. In recent years, anti-immigrant attitudes have been expressed more openly and have been one of the major foci of political and public debates (Hooghe, Trappers, Meuleman, & Reeskens, 2008; Semyonov, Raijman, & Gorodzeisky, 2006; Zick, Wagner, van Dick, & Petzel, 2001). Large comparative data sets, such as the latest wave of the European Social Survey and the International Social Survey Program, also confirm that negative sentiments and anti-immigrant attitudes are increasingly widespread and accepted among host country nationals across the globe.

In this chapter, we present a brief overview of intergroup theory and research on attitudes toward immigrants. We also consider contributions from acculturation psychology, examining the relations between immigrants and members of the receiving society in an interactive context as a function of how immigrants are expected to adapt and "fit into" the country of settlement and how immigrants themselves wish to manage issues of cultural maintenance and participation. We then synthesize these two strands of research in a discussion of multiculturalism. Finally, we propose ways in which relations between immigrants and members of the receiving society can be enhanced and enriched.

Explaining Prejudice Against Immigrants with Intergroup Theories

A number of frameworks have been developed under the general umbrella of intergroup theory as a response to a growing need to understand individual behavior and attitudes in multiethnic and multicultural group settings. Many of these theories emphasize the role of perceived threat and competition in the development of negative attitudes toward immigrants. The integrated threat theory (ITT; Stephan & Stephan, 2000; see also Stephan & Stephan, Chapter 7, this title) identifies the conditions that prevent or hinder the development of positive inter-group relations and differentiates four basic motives of perceived threat. Realistic threat arises when the outgroup is perceived to pose a risk to the health and well-being or the economic and political status of the ingroup. Symbolic threat is fueled by perceived differences in cultural practices, norms, values, and beliefs. Negative stereotypes, that is, generalized beliefs about the undesirable characteristics of the outgroup, lead to the anticipation of unpleasant interactions and negative outcomes. Finally, the theory posits that when people from different groups come into contact, they might experience intergroup anxiety, which involves feelings of uneasiness, fear of being devalued and threat to one's self-concept.

Integrated threat theory has been intensively tested in multiethnic settings and proved to be a useful framework to investigate host nationals' attitudes toward immigrants (Leong, 2008; Stephan, Renfro, Esses, Stephan, & Martin, 2005; Stephan, Ybarra, & Bachman, 1999; Stephan, Ybarra, Martinez, Schwarzwald, & Tur-Kaspa, 1998; Ward & Masgoret, 2008). For example, a study by Stephan et al. (1998) in Spain and Israel demonstrated that a combination of the four types of threat into a latent factor was associated with higher levels of prejudice against immigrants. When looking at the components individually, interpersonal factors, such as intergroup anxiety and negative stereotyping, showed the strongest relationship with negative attitudes toward immigrants. Although this study was correlational in nature, the findings have been confirmed in a series of experiments with university students in the United States (Stephan et al., 2005). More specifically, when participants read articles that either described immigrants as posing both symbolic and realistic threat or included negative stereotypes about the target group, they reported higher levels of prejudice against immigrants. Similarly, when the researchers manipulated the level of intergroup anxiety, those in the high-anxiety group reported less favorable attitudes toward the target immigrant group.

Similar to integrated threat theory, the unified instrumental model of group conflict (UIMGC; Esses, Jackson, & Armstrong, 1998; Esses, Jackson, & Bennett-AbuAyyash, 2010) places a strong emphasis on threat in the escalation of intergroup conflict. According to the UIMGC, resource stress in the presence of relevant and distinctive outgroups gives rise to intergroup competition. It is suggested that competition for resources can be motivated by scarcity, unequal access, and desire for an unequal distribution of these resources. The last factor is an individual difference variable, which is generally operationalized in terms of social dominance orientation (SDO; Sidanius & Pratto, 1999; see also Sidanius, Cotterill, Sheehy-Skeffington, Kteily & Carvacho, Chapter 8, this title). Furthermore, the theory proposes that perceived group competition is supported by both cognitive and affective psychological mechanisms. The cognitive component involves zero-sum/fixed beliefs regarding competitive situations, in which a gain for one group entails a corresponding loss for the other group. These beliefs, however, are accompanied by a range of negative emotions, such as anxiety and fear induced by the competitors and the high-stake situation. In general, people are motivated to utilize competition-reducing strategies. Discrimination and negative stereotyping are applied to reduce the competitiveness of the relevant outgroup. Another way to reduce intergroup competition is by increasing the competitive advantage of the ingroup. Finally, groups might apply avoidant strategies to eliminate the source of competition.

Esses et al. (1998) have argued that skilled immigrants are a potential group for the study of the unified instrumental model of group conflict, as they can successfully compete for resources and are often perceived as competitors by host nationals. With respect to attitudes toward immigrants, the theory has been supported by research in North America, New Zealand, and Europe (Esses, Dovidio, Jackson, & Armstrong, 2001; Jackson & Esses, 2000; Masgoret, 2004; Meuleman, Davidov, & Billiet, 2009). Comparing 17 European countries, Meuleman et al. (2009) found that a large influx of immigrants within a short period of time and high levels of unemployment were the best predictors of anti-immigrant attitudes. In countries where unemployment is persistently high, immigration is often perceived as an economic threat by increasing competition for resources. In another comparative study using data from the International Social Survey Program, Mayda (2006) showed that the average level of education in the working-age population affected attitudes toward immigrants. In particular, in countries that attracted skilled and highly educated immigrants, the working-age population had more negative attitudes toward immigration. This is in line with Meuleman et al.'s (2009) finding indicating that the characteristics of the labor market and competition for resources are influential factors in the evolution of negative intergroup attitudes.

In a series of experiments, Esses and colleagues (Esses et al., 1998, 2001; Jackson & Esses, 2000) examined the role of perceived competition in the job market, zero-sum beliefs, and individual differences in the prediction of negative attitudes toward a fictional group of immigrants (Sardinians) and immigrants in general. Participants in the high-competition condition reported less favorable attitudes toward immigrants and less support for Sardinian immigration, perceived Sardinians less positively, and were less willing to support immigrant empowerment. In addition, individual differences in right-wing authoritarianism (RWA) and social dominance orientation predicted more negative outcomes in terms of intergroup attitudes and support for immigration. Furthermore, the research demonstrated that the relationship between social dominance orientation and attitudes toward immigrants was mediated by zero-sum beliefs. Specifically, those high in social dominance orientation were more likely to believe that acceptance of immigrants posed risks of unfavorable outcomes for the Canadian ingroup. The researchers argued that negative stereotyping, opposition to immigration, and lack of support for immigrant settlement programs demonstrate the utilization of competition-reducing strategies.

As evidenced by the program of research by Esses and colleagues (Esses et al., 1998, 2001; Jackson & Esses, 2000), individual difference variables, such as acceptance of and desire for hierarchy or authoritarian views, also play an important role in the prediction of intergroup attitudes. In connection with prejudice and discrimination, the two most widely researched intra-psychological constructs are right-wing authoritarianism and social dominance orientation. Those characterized by high levels of right-wing authoritarianism adhere to social conventions (conventionalism), display hostile emotions and endorse aggression (authoritarian aggression), and are willing to legitimize and submit to authorities (authoritarian submission; Altemeyer, 1998). Social dominance theory (SDT) posits that individual differences can be observed in the extent to which people desire their ingroup to dominate and be superior (Pratto, Sidanius, Stallworth, & Malle, 1994; Sidanius & Pratto, 1999). Previous research has consistently shown that both right-wing authoritarianism and social dominance orientation are associated with negative attitudes toward a wide range of outgroups, including ethnic minorities and immigrants (Akrami, Ekehammar, & Araya, 2000; Altemeyer, 1998; Guimond, 2000; Guimond, Dambrun, Michinov, & Duarte, 2003; Pratto et al., 1994).

Drawing on the self-identity research tradition, social identity theory (SIT; Tajfel, 1978; Tajfel & Turner, 1986) provides another prolific approach to the study of individual differences in intergroup relations and discrimination. Tajfel and Turner (1986) proposed that social identity is created through identification with groups within which an individual is embedded. The theory posits that people are motivated to maintain high levels of self-esteem and a positive social identity by making favorable comparisons between the ingroup and relevant outgroups. Verkuyten (2010) argues that SIT is a particularly relevant framework for the study of intergroup processes and attitudes toward immigrants, since status positions and group identification become salient in multicultural environments. Indeed, previous research conducted in major immigrant-receiving countries (e.g., Canada, Great Britain, and Germany) shows that ingroup favoritism assessed in the form of nationalism, as opposed to patriotism or international identity, leads to outgroup derogation and negative attitudes toward immigrants (Esses, Dovidio, Semenya, & Jackson, 2005; Mummendey, Klink, & Brown, 2001). Similarly, a study by Martinovic and Verkuyten (2013) in the Netherlands suggested that high national identifiers reject immigrants because of their autochthonous beliefs, that is, rights and ownership attributed to the primo-occupants of a territory. Furthermore, their findings indicated that this relationship was stronger for those who perceived the immigrant outgroups as threatening the status and power of the Dutch ingroup.

While studies converge to link threat to prejudice and discrimination, empirical evidence suggests that positive intergroup contact can diminish these negative effects. The contact hypothesis (Allport, 1954), one of the most influential and widely researched frameworks for the study of intergroup relations, postulates that interactions between members of different social groups can promote positive attitudes and reduce intergroup bias. If personal contact occurs between individuals of equal status who share common goals, are willing to cooperate, and enjoy the support of authorities in their encounter, prejudice and conflict can be markedly reduced (Pettigrew, 1997). A meta-analysis of more than 500 studies by Pettigrew and Tropp (2006) provided supporting evidence for the contact hypothesis indicating that intergroup contact is typically associated with decreased levels of prejudice. Furthermore, their analyses suggested that the positive effects of contact on intergroup attitudes were stronger under the optimal conditions.

Specifically in the context of immigration and interethnic relations, both cross-sectional and longitudinal studies have indicated that intercultural contact can effectively reduce intergroup anxiety and improve host nationals' attitudes toward immigrants (Binder et al., 2009; Brown & Hewstone, 2005; Van Oudenhoven, Groenewoud, & Hewstone, 1996; Voci & Hewstone, 2003). For example, Stephan, Diaz-Loving, and Duran (2000) examined intergroup attitudes of Mexicans and Americans. Their findings suggested that although threat predicted negative attitudes, in both groups the quality and amount of intercultural contact were related to decreased levels of perceived threat. In addition, quality of contact exerted a direct positive effect on intergroup attitudes. These findings show that having frequent and positive interactions with members of outgroups has the capacity to foster positive relations by reducing perceived threat.

Ward and Masgoret (2006) tested the contact hypothesis, integrated threat theory, unified instrumental model of group conflict, and social dominance theory in an integrative model with members of the general public in New Zealand. They found that perceived intergroup threat, measured in the forms of zero-sum beliefs and realistic and symbolic threat, was associated with less positive attitudes toward immigrants. However, perceptions of threat were influenced by individual difference variables. Specifically, those who reported lower levels of social dominance orientation and more positive attitudes toward diversity experienced decreased levels of intergroup threat. In addition, intercultural contact had a positive indirect effect on perceived threat through intergroup anxiety. Frequency of contact with immigrants was linked to reduced intergroup anxiety, which in turn led to lower levels of perceived threat and then more positive attitudes toward immigrants. This research highlights that contact does not necessarily have a direct impact on intergroup attitudes; however, it can facilitate positive intercultural relations by reducing the negative feelings of fear and anxiety experienced in a multicultural group setting.

The contact hypothesis stimulated a large body of research and theorizing on the conditions that facilitate positive intergroup relations and reduce prejudice, discrimination, and stereotyping. One of the theoretical approaches that emphasizes the role of inclusion is the common ingroup identity model (CIIM) by Gaertner, Dovidio, and Bachman (1996). According to the CIIM, stereotypes and discrimination can be attenuated through categorization of group membership. More specifically, Gaertner and colleagues argue that by shifting the cognitive representation of groups to a superior category, while maintaining subgroup identities, an inclusive social identity can be created, thus generating ingroup favoritism and more positive attitudes toward former outgroup members. A study with high school students demonstrated the positive effects of a superordinate identity in a multiethnic setting (Gaertner, Rust, Dovidio, Bachman, & Anastasio, 1994). Findings indicated that perceiving the student body as one inclusive group and at the same time acknowledging the presence of different subgroups were associated with lower intergroup bias and more positive intergroup affect. Similarly, an investigation in Belgium by Billiet, Maddens, and Beerten (2003) highlighted the impact of a superordinate national identity in the prediction of positive attitudes toward foreigners. On the other hand, a study with Canadian and German participants suggested that the positive effect of an inclusive identity might vary as a function of the social context (Esses, Wagner, Wolf, Preiser, & Wilbur, 2006). Specifically, perceptions of national identity as being inclusive of immigrants were related to more positive intergroup attitudes in Canada but exerted harmful effects in Germany. These findings provide insight into potential cross-cultural differences in the effectiveness of strategies and programs designed to facilitate positive intergroup relations.

Understanding and Explaining Prejudice Toward Immigrants: Contributions from Acculturation Psychology

Although intergroup and acculturation theory and research have evolved as distinct fields, they can be seen as reflecting reciprocal sets of phenomena associated with intercultural contact (Berry, 2006; Ward & Leong, 2006). Accordingly, benefits can be gained by synthesizing the two approaches. Acculturation theory posits that intercultural contact prompts consideration of two key issues: (a) the extent to which heritage culture will be maintained and (b) the extent to which contact with other groups and participation in the wider society are sought (Berry, 1980, 1997). Cultural maintenance coupled with participation represents integration. Separation and assimilation are characterized solely by cultural maintenance or participation, respectively, and when neither maintenance nor participation is achieved, marginalization results. These four acculturation strategies are differentially associated not only with the psychological and sociocultural adaptation of immigrants, but also with intercultural relations between immigrants and members of receiving societies (Berry & Sam, 2016).

Early research by Berry and colleagues in Canada showed that integrationist views were in opposition to separation, assimilation, and marginalization and were associated with lower levels of ethnocentrism and more positive outgroup perceptions (Berry & Kalin, 1995; Berry, Kalin, & Taylor, 1977). More recent research in Europe has likewise concluded that the preference for integration is linked to more positive intergroup relations for immigrants and members of the receiving society (Zagefka & Brown, 2002). Conversely, the endorsement of assimilation by majority group members is associated with greater ingroup bias, as well as more prejudiced and less tolerant attitudes against immigrants (Kosic, Mannetti, & Sam, 2005; Piontkowski, Florack, Hoelker, & Obdrzalek, 2000), particularly for those who have strong national identities (Gieling, Thijs, & Verkuyten, 2014).

It is often the case, however, that the acculturation preferences of new immigrants do not match the acculturation expectations of members of the receiving society. There is strong international evidence that immigrants consistently prefer integration

(Berry, Phinney, Sam, & Vedder, 2006; Ward & Leong, 2006), but the preferences of members of the host community are more variable. Canadians and New Zealanders favor integration (Berry & Kalin, 1995; Berry et al., 1977; Ward, 2009; Ward & Masgoret, 2008). Evidence is mixed for Germans, with studies reporting both preferences for assimilation (Zick et al., 2001) and integration (Rohmann, Florack, & Piontkowski, 2006), while the Dutch and Italians favor assimilation and integration compared to separation and marginalization (Kosic et al., 2005; Van Oudenhoven, Prins, & Buunk, 1998). The variability in these patterns is likely due not only to different assessment methods (e.g., use of vignettes, survey items) but also the target immigrant group. Indeed, Montreuil and Bourhis (2001) reported that although integration is strongly preferred overall in Canada, in Quebec the acceptance of assimilation, separation, and exclusion is greater for "devalued" immigrant groups (e.g., Haitian) compared to "valued" ones (e.g., French).

The significance of the match-mismatch of acculturation preferences and expectations is highlighted in the interactive acculturation model (IAM; Bourhis, Moïse, Perreault, & Senécal, 1997) that links state policies to the dynamic interplay of immigrant and receiving community approaches to acculturation. The model proposes that state immigration policies are intertwined with state ideologies, ranging on a continuum from pluralist to ethnist, and that these policies and ideologies impact the acculturation preferences of immigrants and members of the receiving community. Moreover, it is argued that convergence and divergence of acculturation attitudes and behaviors affect intergroup relations. For example, agreement on integration or assimilation is proposed to lead to consensual outcomes and positive intergroup relations. In contrast, immigrant preference for integration in an assimilationist environment is associated with problematic outcomes characterized by partial disagreement and leading to a degree of negative stereotyping and discrimination. The negative outcomes are more pronounced in conflictual circumstances, such as immigrants preferring integration when segregation is imposed.

The complexity of the interactive acculturation model as well as the variable probability that each match or mismatch actually occurs in contemporary democracies have prevented a systematic test of all conditions and combinations; however, the underlying principles have been tested in research that has examined concordance and discordance of immigrant-host views. Discordance between the acculturation attitudes of the majority and the attitudes they attribute to immigrants is associated with more threatening and less enriching relations (Piontkowski, Rohmann, & Florack, 2002). Furthermore, discordance on the cultural maintenance issue and the contact-participation issue independently contributes to the prediction of realistic threat, symbolic threat, and intergroup anxiety for both majority group members and immigrants, above and beyond the effects of negative intergroup contact (Rohmann et al., 2006). For immigrants more specifically, discordance is also associated with greater perceived discrimination (Jasinskaja-Lahti, Liebkind, Horenczyk, & Schmitz, 2003).

Both the interactive acculturation model (Bourhis et al., 1997) and the concordance model (CM; Piontkowski et al., 2002) accentuate the dynamic nature of the relationship between immigrants and members of the wider society. It is also important to recognize, however, that there is often a gap between what immigrants prefer and what they achieve, in other words between ideal and real acculturation strategies or between attitudes and behaviors (Navas, Rojas, Garcia, & Pumares, 2007; Ward & Kus, 2012). New immigrants may not initially have the language proficiency or culture-specific skills to interact effectively with members of the receiving community, and these must be learned over time (Ward, Bochner, & Furnham, 2001). There is some evidence that first-generation immigrants move from separation to integration during the course of their residence in the settlement country (Ho, 1995) and that integration is more common in the second generation because of an increasingly strong orientation to the national culture (Phinney, Berry, Vedder, & Liebkind, 2006).

Moving to Multiculturalism: Merging Acculturation and Intergroup Research

The relationship between the acculturation orientations preferred by immigrants and those imposed by the larger society can be seen in Berry's (2001, 2003) depiction of intercultural strategies. More specifically, the left side of Figure 18.1 illustrates options for immigrants in response to the question: "How shall *we* deal with these issues?" while the right side of the figure depicts the views of members of the larger society in response to the question: "How should *they* deal with these issues?" Depending on the perspective of immigrants versus members of the

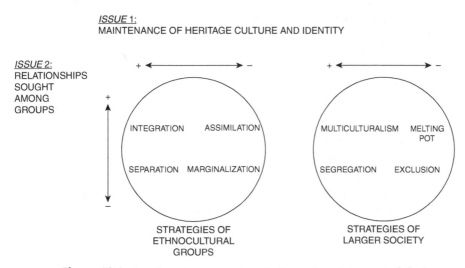

Figure 18.1 *Acculturation strategies of ethno-cultural groups and the larger society (Berry, 2003).*

receiving society, acculturation may unfold as integration and multiculturalism, assimilation and melting pot, separation and segregation, or marginalization and exclusion. Of particular relevance here is the identification of multiculturalism as an intercultural strategy, where immigrant groups maintain their heritage cultures and participate equitably in the wider society. Indeed, Berry has argued that diversity without equal participation will lead to separation or segregation; equal participation without diversity will result in assimilation or the pursuit of the melting pot; in the absence of diversity and equity, marginalization and exclusion will likely occur; but when both diversity and equity are present, integration and multiculturalism are found. Multiculturalism as an intercultural strategy can be examined in terms of ideology – beliefs that cultural diversity is valuable for society and should be accommodated in ways that facilitate equitable participation (Berry et al., 1977) and in terms of policies and practices that support this ideology. Most psychological research has concentrated on the former, which is discussed in the next section.

Multicultural Ideology

There is strong evidence that a multicultural ideology is associated with less ethnocentrism, more tolerance, greater recognition but less expression of bias, and more positive attitudes toward immigrants, immigration, and liberal immigration policies (Apfelbaum, Norton, & Sommers, 2012; Berry, 2006; Richeson & Nussbaum, 2004; Ryan, Casas, & Thompson, 2010; Ward & Masgoret, 2006, 2008; Wolsko, Park, & Judd, 2006; Zagefka, Brown, Broquard, & Martin, 2007). It is also associated with a lower level of perceived social distance between immigrants and majority group members (Hindriks, Verkuyten, & Coenders, 2014). Furthermore, support for multiculturalism has been shown to lead to greater contact between members of the receiving community and immigrants and to more positive intergroup behaviors (Hui, Chen, Leung, & Berry, 2015). Wolsko et al. (2006) concluded that endorsement of multiculturalism leads to perceptions of greater differences across ethnic groups but more positive perceptions of ethnic outgroups; conversely, support for assimilation is related to perceptions of greater homogeneity among ethnic outgroups and more negative perceptions of ethnic outgroups. Assimilationists have also been shown to hold strong ingroup biases and anticipate relationships with immigrants to be more negative (Piontkowski et al., 2000). This is not to suggest that multiculturalism is the panacea for all intergroup struggles. Research has also suggested that its effectiveness in enhancing intergroup relations can be moderated by personal factors such as general level of prejudice (Vorauer & Sasaki, 2011) and situational factors, including the level of perceived threat and conflict (Correll, Park, & Smith, 2008; Sasaki & Vorauer, 2013).

Although multicultural ideologies have been linked to more positive intergroup perceptions and relations for both immigrants and members of the host community, multicultural attitudes are more strongly endorsed by minority groups, as reported in Schalk-Soekar's (2007) review of data from 21 countries. Perceived threat is a major contributor to these group differences (Verkuyten, 2009b). Research by Tip and colleagues found that Britons' perceptions of Pakistanis' preferences for cultural maintenance negatively affected their support for multiculturalism and that this relationship was mediated by identity threat (Tip et al., 2012). Indeed, Berry et al. (1977) argued that the development of a secure cultural identity is a cornerstone for multiculturalism, noting that confidence in one's identity underpins the broader acceptance of diversity and that when confidence is achieved, mutual intergroup acceptance increases. Certainly research has found associations between positive attitudes toward multiculturalism and self-esteem (Verkuyten, 2009a) and life satisfaction (Breugelmans & van de Vijver, 2004) in majority group members. In Berry's own research, confidence has been operationalized as feelings of security in cultural and economic domains, that is, the inverse of feeling threatened.

A second factor that contributes to the rejection of a multicultural ideology by majority group members is the notion of exclusion. In the United States, Whites implicitly and explicitly associate multiculturalism with exclusion, and this lessens their support for multicultural policies and practices (Plaut, Garnett, Buffardi, & Sanchez-Burks, 2011). There are, however, strategies that can be implemented to enhance a sense of inclusiveness, including priming Whites to identify as "European American," leading them to feel a sense of belonging to an ethnic group, and increasing their support for multiculturalism. It is worth noting at this point that in Berry's (1997) theory and research on immigration and multiculturalism, aligned to Canada's multicultural policy, all groups are viewed as cultural groups, and although the terms "dominant" and "nondominant" are used to describe their power differentials, the equation of "mainstream" culture with that of the dominant group is avoided. These distinctions are rarely made in other cultural contexts; indeed, some might question whether Berry's optimistic views based on multiculturalism in Canada are equally valid and relevant in most of the world's culturally plural nations. Multiculturalism and its implications for relations between immigrants and members of the receiving society are explored in a sociopolitical context in the next section.

Multicultural Societies

At the national level, multiculturalism is generally understood in terms of the ethnic, cultural, religious, and linguistic diversity that is commonplace in most countries. In recent times, the increase in immigration-driven cultural heterogeneity has been a contentious issue in North America, Europe, and Australasia where diversity has been linked to a range of negative social outcomes, including greater anti-immigrant sentiments, perceived threat, and hostile ethnic attitudes in the wider society (Bloemraad & Wright, 2014; Putnam, 2007; Schneider, 2008). These outcomes, however, are not inevitable (Kesler & Bloemraad, 2010), and multidisciplinary research converges to conclude that the impact of diversity on intercultural relations is shaped by broader demographic, social, and political factors. Among the most important of these is multicultural policy, which varies significantly across countries.

Comparative research shows that policies exert positive influences on at least some aspects of intergroup relations as immigrants experience more belongingness in terms of citizenship acquisition, have higher levels of trust, and report lower levels of discrimination in countries with more multicultural policies (Koopmans, Statham, Giugni, & Passy, 2005; Wright & Bloemraad, 2012). In addition to, and often aligned with, public policies are widespread consensual beliefs and evaluations about diversity, equity, and acculturation options. At the national level, normative cultural ideologies set the stage for intercultural interactions and relations between immigrants and members of the receiving society, and as is the case at the individual level of psychological research, country-level studies indicate that inclusive ideologies are negatively related to threat (Scheepers, Gijsberts, & Coenders, 2002). All in all, understanding and interpreting the correlates and consequences of multiculturalism at the societal level requires an in-depth analysis of these three dimensions. This is particularly important in practical terms as the popular rhetoric about the success and failure of multiculturalism is situated at the country level; however, for our purposes, it is the link between national- and individual-level factors relating to prejudice toward immigrants that is of greatest interest.

Breugelmans and van de Vijver (2004) were among the first to explore this in their research on multicultural attitudes and behaviors. They examined the effects of perceived norms for multiculturalism as a threat and perceived norms for support of multiculturalism in Dutch society as predictors of majority group members' multicultural attitudes and behaviors. As hypothesized, they found that threat norms exerted a significant negative effect and support norms exerted a positive effect on multicultural attitudes (e.g., valuing diversity, endorsing integration) and self-reported behaviors (e.g., contact with nonnative groups). A similar line of research is in development by Stuart and Ward (2015) with the construction and validation of their Subjective Multiculturalism Scale. Paralleling the key components of multiculturalism, the three-factor measure requires respondents to act as cultural informants about diversity (e.g., it is likely that you will interact with people from many different cultures on a given day), equity (e.g., few ethnic minorities are in leadership positions), and ideology (e.g., most people think multiculturalism is a bad thing) in their country. Using national-level data from the International Social Survey Program (ISSP; see www.gesis.org/issp/modules/issp-modules-by-topic/national-identity/2003/) on attitudes to diversity and Breugelmans and van de Vijver's (2004) measure of multicultural attitudes, the researchers found that perceptions of multicultural ideology in New Zealand and the United States were significantly and positively related both to national attitudes to diversity and to one's own multicultural attitudes. Although perceptions of diversity were unrelated to one's own attitudes, in both New Zealand and the

United States perceived equity norms were associated with more negative attitudes toward multiculturalism, suggesting the possibility that equity may be perceived as threatening. Although this line of research is in its early stages, it does point to the wider sociopolitical climate as affecting multicultural attitudes.

This issue of sociopolitical context was also taken up in comparative research by Guimond et al. (2013) in their study of diversity policies, ideologies, and prejudice in Canada, Germany, the United States, and the United Kingdom. With reference to international databases on diversity policies, the Multicultural Policy Index (MPI, see www.queensu.ca/mcp/index.html) and the Migrant Integration Policy Index (MIPEX, see www.mipex.eu), the countries were ranked as high (Canada), medium (United States and United Kingdom) or low (Germany) in terms of pro-diversity policies. Students in the four countries reported on perceived norms for multiculturalism as well as their own personal attitudes. As predicted, there were significant differences in perceived norms with Canada viewed as having the strongest norms for multiculturalism, Germany the lowest, and the United States and the United Kingdom falling in between. Then, examining patterns of anti-Muslim prejudice, the researchers found the lowest level of prejudice in Canadians, the highest in Germans, and intermediate levels in Americans and Britons, with the former more closely resembling Canadians and the latter more similar to Germans.

In addition to the comparative analyses, Guimond et al. (2013) proposed a model whereby national-level policies generate normative cultural ideologies, including ideologies about multiculturalism and assimilation, and that these normative ideologies affect individual ideologies and, in turn, intergroup attitudes and behaviors, including prejudice and discrimination. Accordingly, the researchers tested an integrative causal model with pathways from national diversity policies to three mediating variables – normative cultural ideologies, personal cultural ideologies, and intra-personal factors regarded as general social psychological determinants of intergroup attitudes and behaviors (in this case Social Dominance Orientation). Each of these three factors was proposed to have direct paths to intergroup attitudes and behaviors; in addition, the effects of perceived normative ideologies and intrapersonal factors were proposed to be partially mediated by personal cultural ideologies. The data generated a good fit to the model with significant paths as predicted, with the exception of the link between country and SDO.

Guimond, de la Sablonnière, and Nugier (2014) extended their discussion of sociopolitical context in studies of intergroup relations, pointing out that most research, particularly experimental research, has been conducted in a single country at a single point in time and posing the question as to whether context might moderate experimental results on multiculturalism. This is an issue long recognized by cross-cultural psychologists and examined in the International Comparative Study of Ethno-cultural Youth (Berry et al., 2006). Although this 13-nation project was focused on the psychological and sociocultural adaptation of immigrant youth, it did capture some aspects of intergroup relations, including intercultural contact and perceived discrimination. Overall, the project showed that sociopolitical context relates in systematic ways to psychological processes and outcomes.

One important domain was that of cultural identity. In recent settler societies such as Australia and New Zealand, ethnic identities were positively and significantly correlated, reflecting integration, and opening up the possibility that a superordinate national common ingroup could enhance intercultural relations (Phinney et al., 2006). The reverse was true in former colonial countries such as Germany, France, and the Netherlands, calling into question the effectiveness of such an approach to enhancing intercultural relations in these contexts. Another important analysis considered cultural diversity and diversity policies across the 13 countries in relation to the experiences of immigrant youth (Vedder, van de Vijver, & Liebkind, 2006). This analysis was subsequently extended in part to include national attitudes toward immigrants (Ward & Stuart, 2013). The analyses revealed that in more culturally diverse countries, immigrant youth perceived more discrimination, engaged in more ethnic behaviors (specifically more ingroup contact and less contact with national peers), and reported lower levels of life satisfaction. At the same time, more diversity policies predicted stronger endorsement of integration, stronger ethnic and national orientations, and better sociocultural adaptation (fewer behavioral problems and better school adjustment). Finally, research showed that negative attitudes toward immigrants at the national level predicted lower levels of life satisfaction in immigrant youth (Ward & Stuart, 2013).

To date, psychological studies of intergroup relations based on cross-cultural and multinational studies are rare. What little evidence is available points to the importance of the sociopolitical context, including the extent of cultural diversity, diversity policies, and diversity ideologies, for acculturation and intercultural relations (Berry et al., 2006; Guimond et al., 2013, 2014; Ward & Stuart, 2013). We believe that synthesizing theory and research from acculturation and social psychology in comparative studies, though difficult, provides a more meaningful and comprehensive approach to understanding and explaining prejudice against immigrants. To those ends, Guimond et al.'s (2013) integrative conceptual framework for culture-general and culture-specific determinants of intergroup attitudes and behaviors provides a good start. However, we would suggest that country-level factors should not be limited to diversity policies but also include national attitudes about diversity and associated cultural ideologies as well as diversity indices. We also argue that distinctions should be made between country-level and individual-level factors in comparative research in multi-level designs and analyses. More specifically, it is important to recognize that what Guimond et al. (2013, 2014) refer to as cultural norms of integration are more appropriately described as perceived cultural norms, as in psychological research, including studies by Guimond and colleagues, individuals act as cultural informants about their national norms. Our adaptation of Guimond et al.'s (2013, 2014) model is presented in Figure 18.2 as a means of guiding future research on prejudice against immigrants.

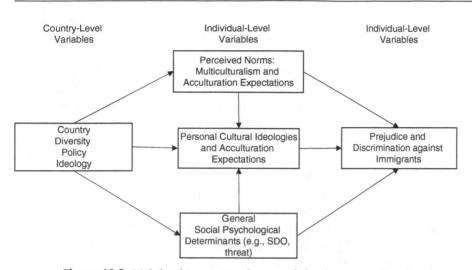

Figure 18.2 *Multilevel integrative framework for the cross-cultural study of prejudice and discrimination against immigrants (adapted from Guimond et al., 2014).*

Conclusion

Migration and cultural diversity are now key features of contemporary societies, and it is clear from the research discussed in this chapter that acculturation and intergroup relations can no longer be studied in isolation. Rather, these areas of research should be viewed as complementary to each other, and our theorizing concerning prejudice against immigrants in multicultural societies needs to expand to accommodate both of these research streams. This is particularly timely as models of immigrant adaptation are increasingly becoming models of mutual adaptation that take into account the reactions of majority groups to cultural diversity and the reciprocal transformations of identity, attitudes, and behaviors that occur within the majority culture as a result of intercultural contact (Bourhis et al., 1997; Piontkowski et al., 2002).

It is well established that cultural diversity affords both risks and benefits. Under the right circumstances, all groups can flourish in a multicultural society; yet as outlined in this chapter, diverse environments can also generate intergroup hostility and precipitate negative psychological and social consequences. An important implication of both acculturation and intergroup research on prejudice toward immigrants is that it is not the cultural diversity itself that seems to be the major problem. Rather, it is the management of cultural diversity and the presence or absence of supportive multicultural policies and ideologies that drives the development and maintenance of social cohesion. This is not surprising as multicultural policy tends to be predicated on ideologies of acceptance of diversity, which, in turn, encourage the maintenance of traditional ethnic cultures along with fair and equitable participation of all cultural groups in the wider society. However, while governments, institutions, and organizations can enact multicultural policies and prohibit blatant prejudice or discrimination, they cannot regulate the attitudes and perceptions of host society members, which ultimately enact the everyday instances of unfair treatment toward immigrants and ethnic minorities.

Kymlicka (2012) notes that during the 1970s to 1990s, multiculturalism was seen as a remedy for negative intercultural relations arising from increasing cultural diversity. However, there has since been a retreat from multiculturalism and its purported failure to both help the intended beneficiaries (minorities themselves) and to increase social capital, cohesion, and trust in the wider society. However, it is suggested that the "failure" of multiculturalism is not the fault of policies of acceptance and equity for members of diverse cultural groups, but rather it is the failure to situate multiculturalism in historic and national contexts. Kymlicka (2012) suggests that as a result of the backlash against multiculturalism, the discourse has shifted to civic integration and superordinate national identity or "post-multiculturalism." This view, however, tends to place the onus on minorities to fit in and adapt to the norms, values, and practices of the wider society; it ignores wider contextual factors, particularly how members of a culturally plural society perceive their environment and experience "everyday multiculturalism," and it does little to explicate the differences in outcomes for those who live in culturally diverse contexts and have little intercultural contact versus those in the same environments who have extensive intercultural contact.

Recent research has suggested that for multiculturalism to succeed, ethnic minorities need to be included into the representation of national identity, and a shift must occur from an exclusive to an inclusive definition of the national prototype where members of the majority group also consider themselves to be a subgroup of the national culture (Reynolds, Batalha, Subasic, & Jones, 2015). Research on the common ingroup identity model (as outlined earlier in this chapter) has shown that creating a superordinate identity has positive consequences for intergroup attitudes, but this approach can also distract attention from inequity and reduce collective action by minority group members (Dovidio, Gaertner, & Saguy, 2009). The negative effects of a common ingroup identity on social action can be attenuated by the recognition and endorsement of distinct subgroup identities within a superordinate identity, or a "dual identity," which has been likened to "integration" within acculturation frameworks (Dovidio et al., 2009; Glasford & Dovidio, 2011).

The research on social capital also offers promising avenues to capitalize on the benefits of multiculturalism. Specifically, research finds that environments (from the neighborhood level to the national level) that have higher levels of diversity also experience substantially more problems with the creation of various kinds of social capital, cooperation, and trust (Stolle, Soroka, & Johnston, 2008). Yet, it is recognized that intercultural contact among individuals from dissimilar groups within these settings fosters a superordinate identity and is more beneficial for civic values and attitudes than social interactions among homogeneous individuals (Putnam, 2007). Illuminating these contradictory positions, Stolle and colleagues (2008) found that even though diversity had negative effects on trust at both the national and neighborhood levels, individuals who live in diverse environments and regularly talk with their neighbors are not negatively affected by diversity at all. Indeed, contextual diversity interacts with individual behaviors, and the strength and nature of social ties in these environments are critical to the resulting social outcomes, as illustrated in the following quote:

> In short . . . while diversity itself (without contact) may push interpersonal trust downwards, interaction and actual experiences with members of other social or racial groups can have counteracting positive effects. It is diversity without contact that is most problematic (Stolle et al., 2008, p. 61).

Notably, the effects of positive intergroup contact have been found to go beyond the individual and extend to the broader social network. Christ and colleagues (2014) found that across seven studies, individuals' outgroup attitudes are more favorable when living in contexts where people have more positive intergroup contact. They suggest that social levels of positive intergroup contact reduce prejudice for everyone, even individuals who have had no direct contact themselves, provided that other ingroup members engage in positive intergroup contact. Following on from this research, Hewstone and colleagues (Hewstone, 2015; Schmid, Al Ramiah, & Hewstone, 2014) have tested and found support for a model where all indirect effects from diversity to trust via contact and threat were positive, such that diversity was associated with increased contact, which, in turn, was associated with less threat, and therefore indirectly increased trust. The studies demonstrate that contact at the contextual level (schools, neighborhoods, and workplaces) can have positive spillover effects for society at large under the right conditions (Christ et. al, 2014).

In conclusion, it is important to clarify that the empirical research data indicate that exposure to cultural diversity does not increase negative intergroup relations in a deterministic way. Rather, the interplay between acculturative and intergroup processes is dynamic and multi-leveled. Our adaptation of Guimond et al.'s (2013, 2014) model attempts to engage with these issues and provide a meaningful way to bridge the gaps between these disparate literatures. Furthermore, it is suggested that future research concerning the implications of migration on prejudice within multicultural societies should look to both general models of adaptation (the factors that reduce prejudice across national contexts) as well as culture-specific models of adaptation (the factors that reduce prejudice in a specific social context, potentially with a specific group). Therefore, we also encourage this model to be contextualized so that we can move beyond the notions of an ideal form of multiculturalism and begin to understand how all groups fare within the multitude of distinct, culturally diverse nations that now exist on the global stage.

References

Akrami, N., Ekehammar, B., & Araya, T. (2000). Classical and modern racial prejudice: A study of attitudes toward immigrants in Sweden. *European Journal of Social Psychology, 30*(4), 521–532. doi: 10.1002/1099-0992(200007/08)30:4<521:: Aid-Ejsp5>3.0.Co;2-N

Allport, G. W. (1954). *The nature of prejudice.* Cambridge, MA: Addison-Wesley.

Altemeyer, B. (1998). The other authoritarian personality. In M. Zanna (Ed.), *Advances in experimental social psychology* (Vol. *30*, pp. 47–92). San Diego, CA: Academic Press.

Apfelbaum, E. P., Norton, M. I., & Sommers, S. R. (2012). Racial color blindness: Emergence, practice, and implications. *Current Directions in Psychological Science, 21*(3), 205–209. doi: 10.1177/0963721411434980

Berry, J. W. (1980). Acculturation as varieties of adaptation. In A. M. Padilla (Ed.), *Acculturation: Theory, models and some new findings* (pp. 9–25). Boulder, CO: Westview.

Berry, J. W. (1997). Immigration, acculturation, and adaptation. *Applied Psychology: An International Review 46*(1), 5–34. doi: 10.1111/j.1464-0597.1997.tb01087.x

Berry, J. W. (2001). A psychology of immigration. *Journal of Social Issues, 57*(3), 615–631. doi: 10.1111/0022-4537.00231

Berry, J. W. (2003). Conceptual approaches to acculturation. In K. Chung, P. Balls Organista, & G. Marin (Eds.), *Acculturation: Advances in theory, measurement, and applied research* (pp. 17–37). Washington, DC: American Psychological Association.

Berry, J. W. (2006). Mutual attitudes among immigrants and ethnocultural groups in Canada. *International Journal of Intercultural Relations, 30*(6), 719–734. doi: 10.1016/j.ijintrel.2006.06.004

Berry, J. W., & Kalin, R. (1995). Multicultural and ethnic attitudes in Canada: An overview of the 1991 national survey. *Canadian Journal of Behavioral Science, 27*(3), 301–320. doi: 10.1037/0008-400x.27.3.301

Berry, J. W., Kalin, R., & Taylor, D. M. (1977). *Multiculturalism and ethnic attitudes in Canada.* Ottawa: Minister of State for Multiculturalism.

Berry, J. W., Phinney, J., Sam, D. L., & Vedder, P. (2006). *Immigrant youth in cultural transition: Acculturation, identity, and adaptation across national contexts.* Mahwah, NJ: Erlbaum.

Berry, J. W., & Sam, D. L. (2016). Theoretical perspectives. In J. W. Berry & D. L. Sam (Eds.), *Cambridge handbook of acculturation psychology* (2nd ed., pp. 11–29). Cambridge: Cambridge University Press.

Billiet, J., Maddens, B., & Beerten, R. (2003). National identity and attitude toward foreigners in a multinational state: A replication. *Political Psychology, 24*(2), 241–257. doi: 10.1111/0162-895x.00327

Binder, J., Zagefka, H., Brown, R., Funke, F., Kessler, T., Mummendey, A. . . . Leyens, J. P. (2009). Does contact reduce prejudice or does prejudice reduce contact? A longitudinal test of the contact hypothesis among majority and minority groups in three European countries. *Journal of Personality and Social Psychology, 96*(4), 843–856. doi: 10.1037/A0013470

Bloemraad, I., & Wright, M. (2014). "Utter failure" or unity out of diversity? Debating and evaluating policies of multiculturalism. *International Migration Review, 48*, 292–334. doi: 10.1111/Imre.12135

Bourhis, R. Y., Moïse, L. C., Perreault, S., & Senècal, S. (1997). Towards an interactive acculturation model: A social psychological approach. *International Journal of Psychology, 32*(6), 369–386. doi: 10.1080/002075997400629

Breugelmans, S. M., & van de Vijver, F. J. R. (2004). Antecedents and components of majority attitudes toward multiculturalism in the Netherlands. *Applied Psychology: An International Review, 53*(3), 400–422. doi: 10.1111/j.1464-0597.2004.00177.x

Brown, R., & Hewstone, M. (2005). An integrative theory of intergroup contact. In M. Zanna (Ed.), *Advances in experimental social psychology* (Vol. *37*, pp. 255–343). San Diego, CA: Academic Press.

Christ, O., Schmid, K., Lolliot, S., Swart, H., Stolle, D., Tausch, N. . . . Hewstone, M. (2014). Contextual effect of positive intergroup contact on outgroup prejudice. *Proceedings of the National Academy of Sciences of the United States of America, 111*(11), 3996–4000. doi: 10.1073/pnas.1320901111

Correll, J., Park, B., & Smith, J. A. (2008). Colorblind and multicultural prejudice reduction strategies in high-conflict situations. *Group Processes & Intergroup Relations, 11*(4), 471–491. doi: 10.1177/1368430208095401

Dovidio, J. F., Gaertner, S. L., & Saguy, T. (2009). Commonality and the complexity of "we": Social attitudes and social change. *Personality and Social Psychology Review, 13*(1), 3–20. doi: 10.1177/1088868308326751

Esses, V. M., Dovidio, J. F., Jackson, L. M., & Armstrong, T. L. (2001). The immigration dilemma: The role of perceived group competition, ethnic prejudice, and national identity. *Journal of Social Issues, 57*(3), 389–412. doi: 10.1111/0022-4537.00220

Esses, V. M., Dovidio, J. F., Semenya, A. H., & Jackson, L. M. (2005). Attitudes toward immigrants and immigration: The role of national and international identity. In D. Abrams, M. A. Hogg, & J. M. Marques (Eds.), *The social psychology of inclusion and exclusion* (pp. 317–337). New York: Psychology Press.

Esses, V. M., Jackson, L. M., & Armstrong, T. L. (1998). Intergroup competition and attitudes toward immigrants and immigration: An instrumental model of group conflict. *Journal of Social Issues, 54*(4), 699–724. doi: 10.1111/0022-4537.911998091

Esses, V. M., Jackson, L. M., & Bennett-AbuAyyash, C. (2010). Intergroup competition. In J. F. Dovidio, M. Hewstone, P. Glick, & V. M. Esses (Eds.), *Handbook of prejudice, stereotyping, and discrimination* (pp. 225–240). London: Sage.

Esses, V. M., Wagner, U., Wolf, C., Preiser, M., & Wilbur, C. J. (2006). Perceptions of national identity and attitudes toward immigrants and immigration in Canada and Germany. *International Journal of Intercultural Relations, 30*(6), 653–669. doi: 10.1016/j.ijintrel.2006.07.002

Gaertner, S. L., Dovidio, J. F., & Bachman, B. A. (1996). Revisiting the contact hypothesis: The induction of a common ingroup identity. *International Journal of Intercultural Relations, 20*(3–4), 271–290. doi: 10.1016/0147-1767(96)00019-3

Gaertner, S. L., Rust, M. C., Dovidio, J. F., Bachman, B. A., & Anastasio, P. A. (1994). The contact hypothesis: The role of a common ingroup identity on reducing intergroup bias. *Small Group Research, 25*(2), 224–249. doi: 10.1177/1046496494252005

Gieling, M., Thijs, J., & Verkuyten, M. (2014). Dutch adolescents' tolerance of Muslim immigrants: The role of assimilation ideology, intergroup contact, and national identification. *Journal of Applied Social Psychology, 44*(3), 155–165. doi: 10.1111/Jasp.12220

Glasford, D. E., & Dovidio, J. F. (2011). E pluribus unum: Dual identity and minority group members' motivation to engage in contact, as well as social change. *Journal of Experimental Social Psychology, 47*(5), 1021–1024. doi: 10.1016/j. jesp.2011.03.021

Guimond, S. (2000). Group socialization and prejudice: The social transmission of intergroup attitudes and beliefs. *European Journal of Social Psychology, 30*(3), 335–354. doi: 10.1002/(SICI)1099-0992(200005/06)30:33.0.CO;2-V

Guimond, S., Crisp, R. J., De Oliveira, P., Kamiejski, R., Kteily, N., Kuepper, B. ... Zick, A. (2013). Diversity policy, social dominance, and intergroup relations: Predicting prejudice in changing social and political contexts. *Journal of Personality and Social Psychology, 104*(6), 941–958. doi: 10.1037/A0032069

Guimond, S., Dambrun, M., Michinov, N., & Duarte, S. (2003). Does social dominance generate prejudice? Integrating individual and contextual determinants of intergroup cognitions. *Journal of Personality and Social Psychology, 84*(4), 697–721. doi: 10.1037/0022-3514.84.4.697

Guimond, S., de la Sablonnière, R., & Nugier, A. (2014). Living in a multicultural world: Intergroup ideologies and the societal context of intergroup relations. *European Review of Social Psychology, 25*(1), 142–188. doi: 10.1080/10463283.2014.957578

Hewstone, M. (2015). Consequences of diversity for social cohesion and prejudice: The missing dimension of intergroup contact. *Journal of Social Issues, 71*(2), 417–438. doi: 10.1111/Josi.12120

Hindriks, P., Verkuyten, M., & Coenders, M. (2014). Interminority attitudes: The roles of ethnic and national identification, contact, and multiculturalism. *Social Psychology Quarterly, 77*(1), 54–74. doi: 10.1177/0190272513511469

Ho, E. S. (1995). *The challenge of culture change: The cross-cultural adaptation of Hong Kong Chinese adolescent immigrants in New Zealand.* Unpublished doctoral thesis. Hamilton: University of Waikato.

Hooghe, M., Trappers, A., Meuleman, B., & Reeskens, T. (2008). Migration to European countries: A structural explanation of patterns, 1980–2004. *International Migration Review, 42*(2), 476–504. doi: 10.1111/j.1747-7379.2008.00132.x

Hui, B. P. H., Chen, S. X., Leung, C. M., & Berry, J. W. (2015). Facilitating adaptation and intercultural contact: The role of integration and multicultural ideology in dominant and non-dominant groups. *International Journal of Intercultural Relations, 45*, 70–84. doi: 10.1016/j.ijintrel.2015.01.002

Jackson, L. M., & Esses, V. M. (2000). Effects of perceived economic competition on people's willingness to help empower immigrants. *Group Processes & Intergroup Relations, 3*, 419–435. doi: 10.1177/1368430200003004006

Jasinskaja-Lahti, I., Liebkind, K., Horenczyk, G., & Schmitz, P. (2003). The interactive nature of acculturation: Perceived discrimination, acculturation attitudes and stress among young ethnic repatriates in Finland, Israel and Germany. *International Journal of Intercultural Relations, 27*(1), 79–97. doi: Pii S0147-1767(02)00061-5

Kesler, C., & Bloemraad, I. (2010). Does immigration erode social capital? The conditional effects of immigration-generated diversity on trust, membership, and participation across 19 countries, 1981–2000. *Canadian Journal of Political Science, 43*(2), 319–347. doi: 10.1017/S0008423910000077

Koopmans, R., Statham, P., Giugni, M., & Passy, F. (2005). *Contested citizenship: Immigration and cultural diversity in Europe.* Minneapolis: University of Minnesota Press.

Kosic, A., Mannetti, L., & Sam, D. L. (2005). The role of majority attitudes towards outgroup in the perception of the acculturation strategies of immigrants. *International Journal of Intercultural Relations, 29*(3), 273–288. doi: 10.1016/j.ijintrel.2005.06.004

Kymlicka, W. (2012). *Multiculturalism: Success, failure, and the future.* Report for the Migration Policy Institute. Retrieved from www.migrationpolicy.org/research/TCM-multiculturalism-success-failure

Leong, C. H. (2008). A multilevel research framework for the analyses of attitudes toward immigrants. *International Journal of Intercultural Relations, 32*(2), 115–129. doi: 10.1016/j.ijintrel.2007.10.002

Martin, P. (2013). The global challenge of managing migration. Report by the Population Reference Bureau. *Population Bulletin, 68*, 2–18.

Martinovic, B., & Verkuyten, M. (2013). "We were here first, so we determine the rules of the game": Autochthony and prejudice towards outgroups. *European Journal of Social Psychology, 43*(7), 637–647. doi: 10.1002/Ejsp.1980

Masgoret, A. M. (2004, August). *Examining the bases of intergroup competition and its role in determining immigration attitudes in New Zealand.* Paper presented at the XXVI International Conference of Psychology, Beijing, China.

Mayda, A. M. (2006). Who is against immigration? A cross-country investigation of individual attitudes toward immigrants. *Review of Economics and Statistics, 88*(3), 510–530. doi: 10.1162/rest.88.3.510

Meuleman, B., Davidov, E., & Billiet, J. (2009). Changing attitudes toward immigration in Europe, 2002–2007: A dynamic group conflict theory approach. *Social Science Research, 38*(2), 352–365. doi: 10.1016/j.ssresearch.2008.09.006

Montreuil, A., & Bourhis, R. Y. (2001). Majority acculturation orientations toward "valued" and "devalued" immigrants. *Journal of Cross-Cultural Psychology, 32*(6), 698–719. doi: 10.1177/0022022101032006004

Mummendey, A., Klink, A., & Brown, R. (2001). Nationalism and patriotism: National identification and outgroup rejection. *British Journal of Social Psychology, 40*, 159–172. doi: 10.1348/014466601164740

Navas, M., Rojas, A. J., Garcia, M., & Pumares, P. (2007). Acculturation strategies and attitudes according to the relative acculturation extended model (RAEM): The perspectives of natives versus immigrants. *International Journal of Intercultural Relations, 31*(1), 67–86. doi: 10.1016/j.ijintrel.2006.08.002

Pettigrew, T. F. (1997). Generalized intergroup contact effects on prejudice. *Personality and Social Psychology Bulletin, 23*(2), 173–185. doi: 10.1177/0146167297232006

Pettigrew, T. F., & Tropp, L. R. (2006). A meta-analytic test of intergroup contact theory. *Journal of Personality and Social Psychology, 90*(5), 751–783. doi: 10.1037/0022-3514.90.5.751

Phinney, J., Berry, J. W., Vedder, P., & Liebkind, K. (2006). The acculturation experience: Attitudes, identities and behaviors of immigrant youth. In J. W. Berry, J. Phinney, D. L. Sam, & P. Vedder (Eds.), *Immigrant youth in cultural transition: Acculturation, identity and adaptation across national contexts* (pp. 71–116). Mahwah, NJ: Lawrence Erlbaum.

Piontkowski, U., Florack, A., Hoelker, P., & Obdrzalek, P. (2000). Predicting acculturation attitudes of dominant and non-dominant groups. *International Journal of Intercultural Relations, 24*(1), 1–26. doi: 10.1016/S0147-1767(99)00020-6

Piontkowski, U., Rohmann, A., & Florack, A. (2002). Concordance of acculturation attitudes and perceived threat. *Group Processes and Intergroup Relations, 5*, 221–232. doi: 10.1177/1368430202005003003

Plaut, V. C., Garnett, F. G., Buffardi, L. E., & Sanchez-Burks, J. (2011). "What about me?" Perceptions of exclusion and Whites' reactions to multiculturalism. *Journal of Personality and Social Psychology, 101*(2), 337–353. doi: 10.1037/A0022832

Pratto, F., Sidanius, J., Stallworth, L. M., & Malle, B. F. (1994). Social dominance orientation: A personality variable predicting social and political attitudes. *Journal of Personality and Social Psychology, 67*(4), 741–763. doi: 10.1037/0022-3514.67.4.741

Putnam, R. D. (2007). E pluribus unum: Diversity and community in the twenty-first century The 2006 Johan Skytte Prize Lecture. *Scandinavian Political Studies, 30*(2), 137–174. doi: 10.1111/j.1467-9477.2007.00176.x

Reynolds, K. J., Batalha, L., Subasic, M., & Jones, B. M. (2015). The social psychology of social (dis)harmony: Implications for political leaders and public policy. In J. P. Forgas, K. Fiedler, & W. D. Crano (Eds.), *Social psychology and politics* (pp. 337–356). New York: Psychology Press.

Richeson, J. A., & Nussbaum, R. J. (2004). The impact of multiculturalism versus color-blindness on racial bias. *Journal of Experimental Social Psychology, 40*(3), 417–423. doi: 10.1016/j.jesp.2003.09.002

Rohmann, A., Florack, A., & Piontkowski, U. (2006). The role of discordant acculturation attitudes in perceived threat: An analysis of host and immigrant attitudes in Germany. *International Journal of Intercultural Relations, 30*(6), 683–702. doi: 10.1016/j.ijintrel.2006.06.006

Ryan, C. S., Casas, J. F., & Thompson, B. K. (2010). Interethnic ideology, intergroup perceptions, and cultural orientation. *Journal of Social Issues, 66*(1), 29–44. doi: 10.1111/j.1540-4560.2009.01631.x

Sasaki, S. J., & Vorauer, J. D. (2013). Ignoring versus exploring differences between groups: Effects of salient color-blindness and multiculturalism on intergroup attitudes and behavior. *Social and Personality Psychology Compass, 7*, 246–259. doi: 10.1111/spc3.12021

Schalk-Soekar, S. (2007). *Multiculturalism: A stable concept with many ideological and political aspects.* Unpublished doctoral dissertation. Tilburg, the Netherlands: Tilburg University.

Scheepers, P., Gijsberts, M., & Coenders, M. (2002). Ethnic exclusionism in European countries: Public opposition to civil rights for legal migrants as a response to perceived ethnic threat. *European Sociological Review, 18*(1), 17–34. doi: 10.1093/Esr/18.1.17

Schmid, K., Al Ramiah, A., & Hewstone, M. (2014). Neighborhood ethnic diversity and trust: The role of intergroup contact and perceived threat. *Psychological Science*, *25*(3), 665–674. doi: 10.1177/0956797613508956

Schneider, S. L. (2008). Anti-immigrant attitudes in Europe: Outgroup size and perceived ethnic threat. *European Sociological Review*, *24*(1), 53–67. doi: 10.1093/Esr/Jcm034

Semyonov, M., Raijman, R., & Gorodzeisky, A. (2006). The rise of anti-foreigner sentiment in European societies, 1988–2000. *American Sociological Review*, *71*(3), 426–449.

Sidanius, J., & Pratto, F. (1999). *Social dominance: An intergroup theory of social hierarchy and oppression*. Cambridge: Cambridge University Press.

Stephan, W. G., Diaz-Loving, R., & Duran, A. (2000). Integrated threat theory and inter-cultural attitudes – Mexico and the United States. *Journal of Cross-Cultural Psychology*, *31*(2), 240–249. doi: 10.1177/0022022100031002006

Stephan, W. G., Renfro, C. L., Esses, V. M., Stephan, C. W., & Martin, T. (2005). The effects of feeling threatened on attitudes toward immigrants. *International Journal of Intercultural Relations*, *29*(1), 1–19. doi: 10.1016/j.ijintrel.2005.04.011

Stephan, W. G., & Stephan, C. W. (2000). An integrated threat theory of prejudice. In S. Oskamp (Ed.), *Claremont symposium on applied psychology* (pp. 23–46). Hillsdale, NJ: Erlbaum.

Stephan, W. G., Ybarra, O., & Bachman, G. (1999). Prejudice toward immigrants. *Journal of Applied Social Psychology*, *29*(11), 2221–2237. doi: 10.1111/j.1559-1816.1999.tb00107.x

Stephan, W. G., Ybarra, O., Martinez, C. M., Schwarzwald, J., & Tur-Kaspa, M. (1998). Prejudice toward immigrants to Spain and Israel: An integrated threat theory analysis. *Journal of Cross-Cultural Psychology*, *29*(4), 559–576. doi: 10.1177/0022022198294004

Stolle, D., Soroka, S., & Johnston, R. (2008). When does diversity erode trust? Neighborhood diversity, interpersonal trust and the mediating effect of social interactions. *Political Studies*, *56*(1), 57–75. doi: 10.1111/j.1467-9248.2007.00717.x

Stuart, J., & Ward, C. (2015, June). *The construction and validation of the Subjective Multiculturalism Scale*. Paper presented at the IX Biennial Conference of the International Academy for Intercultural Research, Bergen, Norway.

Tajfel, H. (1978). *Differentiation between social groups: Studies in the social psychology of intergroup relations*. New York: Academic Press.

Tajfel, H., & Turner, J. C. (1986). The social identity theory of intergroup behavior. In S. Worchel & W. Austin (Eds.), *Psychology of intergroup relations* (pp. 7–24). Chicago: Nelson-Hall.

Tip, L. K., Zagefka, H., Gonzalez, R., Brown, R., Cinnirella, M., & Na, X. (2012). Is support for multiculturalism threatened by … threat itself? *International Journal of Intercultural Relations*, *36*(1), 22–30. doi: 10.1016/j.ijintrel.2010.09.011

United Nations. (2013). *International migration report 2013*. New York: Author.

Van Oudenhoven, J. P., Groenewoud, J. T., & Hewstone, M. (1996). Cooperation, ethnic salience and generalization of interethnic attitudes. *European Journal of Social Psychology*, *26*(4), 649–661. doi: 10.1002/(Sici)1099-0992(199607)26:4<649::Aid-Ejsp780>3.0.Co;2-T

Van Oudenhoven, J. P., Prins, K. S., & Buunk, P. B. (1998). Attitudes of minority and majority members towards adaptation of immigrants. *European Journal of Social*

Psychology, 28(6), 995–1013. doi: 10.1002/(Sici)1099– 0992(1998110) 28:6<995::Aid-Ejsp908>3.0.Co;2–8

Vedder, P., van de Vijver, F. J. R., & Liebkind, K. (2006). Predicting immigrant youths' adaptation across countries and ethno-cultural groups. In J. W. Berry, J. Phinney, D. L. Sam, & P. Vedder (Eds.), *Immigrant youth in cultural transition: Acculturation, identity and adaptation across national contexts* (pp. 143–166). Mahwah, NJ: Lawrence Erlbaum.

Verkuyten, M. (2009a). Self-esteem and multiculturalism: An examination among ethnic minority and majority groups in the Netherlands. *Journal of Research in Personality, 43*(3), 419–427. doi: 10.1016/j.jrp.2009.01.013

Verkuyten, M. (2009b). Support for multiculturalism and minority rights: The role of national identification and outgroup threat. *Social Justice Research, 22*(1), 31–52. doi: 10.1007/s11211-008-0087-7

Verkuyten, M. (2010). Multicultural recognition and ethnic minority rights: A social identity perspective. *European Review of Social Psychology, 17*, 148–184. doi: 10.1080/ 10463280600937418

Voci, A., & Hewstone, M. (2003). Intergroup contact and prejudice toward immigrants in Italy: The mediational role of anxiety and the moderational role of group salience. *Group Processes & Intergroup Relations, 6*(1), 37–54. doi: 10.1177/ 1368430203006001011

Vorauer, J. D., & Sasaki, S. J. (2011). In the worst rather than the best of times: Effects of salient intergroup ideology in threatening intergroup interactions. *Journal of Personality and Social Psychology, 101*(2), 307–320. doi: 10.1037/A0023152

Ward, C. (2009). Acculturation and social cohesion: Emerging issues for Asian immigrants in New Zealand. In C. H. Leong & J. W. Berry (Eds.), *Intercultural relations in Asia: Migration and work effectiveness* (pp. 3–22). Singapore: World Scientific.

Ward, C., Bochner, S., & Furnham, A. (2001). *The psychology of culture shock*. London: Routledge.

Ward, C., & Kus, L. (2012). Back to and beyond Berry's basics: The conceptualization, operationalization and classification of acculturation. *International Journal of Intercultural Relations, 36*(4), 472–485. doi: 10.1016/j.ijintrel.2012.02.002

Ward, C., & Leong, C. H. (2006). Intercultural relations in plural societies: Theory, research and application. In D. L. Sam & J. W. Berry (Eds.), *Cambridge handbook of acculturation psychology* (pp. 484–503). Cambridge: Cambridge University Press.

Ward, C., & Masgoret, A. M. (2006). An integrative model of attitudes toward immigrants. *International Journal of Intercultural Relations, 30*(6), 671–682. doi: 10.1016/j. ijintrel.2006.06.002

Ward, C., & Masgoret, A. M. (2008). Attitudes toward immigrants, immigration, and multiculturalism in New Zealand: A social psychological analysis. *International Migration Review, 42*(1), 227–248. doi: 10.1111/j.1747-7379.2007.00119.x

Ward, C., & Stuart, J. (2013, June). *Population, policy and psychology: The impact of multiculturalism on the psychological well-being of immigrant youth*. Paper presented at the North American Regional Conference of the International Association for Cross-cultural Psychology, Los Angeles, CA.

Wolsko, C., Park, B., & Judd, C. (2006). Considering the Tower of Babel: Correlates of assimilation and multiculturalism among ethnic minority and majority groups in the United States. *Social Justice Research, 19,* 277–306. doi: 10.1007/s11211-006-0014-8

Wright, M., & Bloemraad, I. (2012). Is there a trade-off between multiculturalism and socio-political integration? Policy regimes and immigrant incorporation in comparative perspective. *Perspectives on Politics, 10*(1), 77–95. doi: 10.1017/S1537592711004919

Zagefka, H., & Brown, R. (2002). The relationship between acculturation strategies, relative fit and intergroup relations: Immigrant-majority relations in Germany. *European Journal of Social Psychology, 32*(2), 171–188. doi: 10.1002/Ejsp.73

Zagefka, H., Brown, R., Broquard, M., & Martin, S. L. (2007). Predictors and consequences of negative attitudes toward immigrants in Belgium and Turkey: The role of acculturation preferences and economic competition. *British Journal of Social Psychology, 46,* 153–169. doi: 10.1348/014466606x111185

Zick, A., Wagner, U., van Dick, R., & Petzel, T. (2001). Acculturation and prejudice in Germany: Majority and minority perspectives. *Journal of Social Issues, 57*(3), 541–557. doi: 10.1111/0022–4537.00228

19 Generalized Prejudice: Old Wisdom and New Perspectives

Robin Bergh and Nazar Akrami

Some individuals seem to carry prejudice with them, from context to context, from attitudes toward one group to attitudes toward other, seemingly unrelated, groups. This reveals itself in correlations between different kinds of prejudice, for example, against Jews and old people. This observation also represents one of the oldest lessons in the prejudice literature (Allport, 1954; Hartley, 1946). What is perhaps more startling is just how much of the variance is shared between different prejudices. More than half of the individual variability in devaluing attitudes toward immigrants; women; gays; and old, overweight, or disabled people can be traced to the same underlying factor (generalized prejudice; see Bergh, Akrami, & Ekehammar, 2012; Ekehammar & Akrami, 2003). Such a big chunk of variance would seem difficult to overlook in the pursuit of a comprehensive understanding of prejudice.

In this chapter we initially cover some basic empirical findings and discuss how descriptions of generalized prejudice factor(s) have developed over time. What they all have in common is the idea that devaluing and/or negative attitudes are generalized across group domains (e.g., against various ethnic, age, and religious groups). However, as we elaborate, there are also important themes that differentiate certain views. Second, we discuss some proposed contradictions to generalized prejudice research, as connected to a declining popularity of the concept since Allport's time. We note how many of these seeming contradictions can be resolved by statistical reappraisals. In the final section, we discuss a new perspective on what generalized prejudice represents. A central question here is whether generalized prejudice is associated more with a comprehensive concern for societal "order" rather than reflecting an "us versus them" mentality.

The Empirical "Fact"

Generalized prejudice is primarily reflected in the correlation between measures of devaluation of different groups. Hartley (1946) was one of the pioneers in examining this issue. His participants provided social distance ratings for 39 social groups (mainly ethnic ones), but also three fictitious groups (e.g., Pireneans). He found many substantial correlations between the various group evaluations, including the fictitious ones.[1] Some eight years on, and many studies later, Allport (1954) proclaimed that the generalization of prejudice was "one of the facts of which we are most certain" (p. 68). As provocative as that may sound, and as much as scholars have since departed from his views, there is strong evidence for the basic idea that prejudice reproduces across targets.

The finding of correlated prejudices has been replicated across a broad range of cultural contexts, such as Brazil (Cantal, Milfont, Wilson, & Gouveia, 2015), Germany (Zick et al., 2008), New Zealand (Duckitt & Sibley, 2007), Romania (Krauss, 2002), Scandinavia (Bäckström & Björklund, 2007), the Soviet Union (McFarland, Ageyev, & Abalakina, 1993), and the United States (Bierly, 1985). The most commonly examined targets have been various ethnic and religious minorities, women, and gays (see references from Table 19.1). However, prejudice toward people who have a disability or are old, overweight, or unemployed also fit into the same attitudinal pattern (e.g., Bergh et al., 2012; Duckitt & Sibley, 2007). The use of balanced and well-validated measures has also safe-guarded against dismissing the correlations in terms of response biases such as acquaintance (e.g., Bäckström & Björklund, 2007; Ekehammar & Akrami, 2003). More important, it has also been demonstrated that generalized prejudice is consistent in self- and peer ratings, thus providing strong support for conceptual communalities (Cohrs, Kämpfe-Hargrave, & Riemann, 2012). A few studies have also found a generalized prejudice factor using implicit prejudice measures (e.g., McFarland & Mattern, 2001). However, unlike a generalized prejudice factor based on explicit measures, the implicit counterpart seems largely unrelated to personality and ideological beliefs (Bergh et al., 2012; Cunningham, Nezlek, & Banaji, 2004).

Explanations of prejudice in terms of personality differences have historically gone hand-in-hand with the generalization of these attitudes across targets, and there is a good reason for that. Generalized prejudice suggests that regardless of whether the situation happens to make salient gender, ethnicity, or religion, it tends to be the same individuals who express more prejudice. Indeed, (explicit) generalized prejudice seems to follow regular and fundamental principles of personality psychology – namely, that these individual differences are coherent across contexts and stable over time (see Asbrock, Sibley, & Duckitt, 2010; Zick et al., 2008). In line with these observations, it has been repeatedly shown that individual differences in generalized prejudice are predicted by core personality characteristics (e.g., Ekehammar & Akrami, 2003; Sibley & Duckitt, 2008).

---

1 Fink (1971) found fewer significant correlations than Hartley (1946) when changing the response format, but his study also had poorer statistical power. Methodological artifacts was an issue in the early work on generalized prejudice, but as described in the main text, many of these have been dealt with in more recent work.

The Anti-Outgroup Perspective

Statistically speaking, generalized prejudice can be modeled as a latent factor manifesting itself in evaluations of a range of groups. As with any latent factor though, it remains for researchers to describe its meaning. Allport (1954) was one of the first to do so. He proposed that some people are simply "anti any outgroup" (p. 68). Adorno, Frenkel-Brunswik, Levinson, and Sanford (1950) used a different label (ethnocentrism[2]), but they shared the view that the factor centered on a generic derogation of outgroups.

Although descriptions of generalized prejudice vary, there is one theme that they nonetheless share. The common theme is that the targets are discussed as *outgroups*. To attest to this point, Table 19.1 summarizes all definitions of generalized prejudice (to our knowledge) since the year 2000.[3] Indeed, many scholars have adopted Allport's (1954) view that the outgroup notion is both a *sufficient* and *necessary* condition for generalized prejudice (i.e. whenever a number of outgroup evaluations are considered, a generalized prejudice factor should be expected). However, as described under the next heading, a few scholars have questioned if it is sufficient, and they have suggested narrower definitions.

From Any Outgroup to Some Outgroups

Questioning the simplicity of the anti any outgroup argument, Duckitt (2001) argued that systematic individual differences in prejudice tend to be underpinned by either fear (associated with authoritarianism) or a struggle for power (associated with social dominance; see Duckitt & Sibley, Chapter 9, this title). In the first case, Duckitt (2001) proposed that "outgroups will be disliked because they are seen as threatening and dangerous to social or group cohesion, security, order, values, and stability" (p. 85) and in the latter case, he proposed that "outgroups will be derogated because they are seen as inferior, weak, inadequate, and failures" (p. 85). Consequently, Duckitt (2001, 2006) implied that prejudice should generalize across outgroups, but only insofar that they are dangerous or derogated. He also proposed that the different motives for prejudice should be reflected in distinct factors of group negativity. Indeed, low warmth toward groups such as

---

2 Papers on correlated forms of prejudice and latent prejudice factors often treat generalized prejudice and ethnocentrism as synonymous concepts (e.g., Kinder & Kam, 2009; McFarland, 2010), but many that focus primarily on ethnocentrism tend to treat the concept as more multi-faceted (e.g., Bizumic, Duckitt, Popadic, Dru, & Krauss, 2009). This chapter is about generalized prejudice, and the term "ethnocentrism" is relevant here only insofar that it is used to describe the data underpinning the notion of generalized prejudice (i.e., interrelated prejudices; see, e.g., Cunningham et al., 2004). Finally, group-based enmity (Zick et al., 2008) is another term for describing the same phenomenon.

3 We focus on definitions that discuss the generalization of prejudice across quite distinct domains. We do not include papers discussing generalizability (solely) across, for example, ethnic groups (i.e., more domain-specific prejudice).

Table 19.1 *Descriptions of generalized prejudice (or ethnocentrism in studies primarily focusing on correlated prejudices, i.e., generalized prejudice).*

1. "It seems reasonable to assume that prejudice toward one group indicates an increased tendency to harbor prejudice toward other groups. Such a position is consistent with Allport's (1954) view that 'people who reject one out-group will tend to reject other out-groups. If a person is anti-Jewish, he is likely to be anti-Catholic, anti-Negro, anti- any out-group' (p. 68). This point also has been made more recently by Ray and Lovejoy (1986), who hold that 'to be ethnocentric . . . implies that one will dislike all out-groups. To dislike just one out-group would be incoherent' (p. 563)" (Agnew, Thompson, & Gaines, 2000, p. 405).

2. "Allport (1954/1979) argued that prejudice towards multiple different outgroups are often so highly correlated as to constitute a 'generality of prejudice'. . . . Two individual differences constructs [RWA & SDO] have been shown to be strong and complementary predictors of generalized prejudice in the decades following Allport's observation. Recent research also supports Allport's conceptualization . . . These studies typically show high correlations between attitude measures referring to different outgroups, indicating that persons reporting favourable attitudes towards some outgroups tend to be generally more favourable towards other outgroups, while persons who are hostile or prejudiced towards certain outgroups tend to be generally less favourable towards others" (Asbrock, Sibley, & Duckitt, 2010, pp. 324–325).

3. "Prejudices toward a variety of target groups are found to be highly correlated indicating a generalized tendency (e.g., Akrami, Ekehammar, & Bergh, 2011). Importantly, the observation of such a generalized tendency across targets laid the very foundation for the personality approach to prejudice (see Adorno, Frenkel-Brunswik, Levinson, & Sanford, 1950; Allport, 1954). The guiding idea here is quite simple: If individuals displaying prejudice toward one out-group also do it toward other out-groups (including nonexisting ones, see Hartley, 1946) then it makes sense to start looking for an explanation within the individual" (Bergh, Akrami, & Ekehammar, 2012, p. 614).

4. "A prejudiced person might develop a general outgroup attitude when confronted with several ethnic outgroups. Starting from this perspective, the present study considers attitudes among adolescent majority members encountering several non-Western immigrant groups. [new paragraph] The theory of an authoritarian personality suggests that people with negative outgroup attitudes should also maintain a general outgroup attitude. Even other individualistic explanations of prejudice (e.g. Allport, 1954/1979) may suggest that individuals can develop a generally prejudiced personality and thus also a general and negative attitude toward several outgroups" (Bratt, 2005, pp. 447–448).

5. "We are particularly interested in understanding individual differences in generalized prejudice (GP), i.e., the tendency to dislike outgroup members no matter which particular group they belong to" (Bäckström & Björklund, 2007, p. 10).

6. "The historical roots of this finding that prejudices are generalized across outgroups can be traced back to the seminal work of Adorno and colleagues (1950), who used the term ethnocentrism popularized by Sumner (1906; see Bizumic, 2014) to define this disposition for individuals to generalize their prejudices. However, this definition is theoretically distinct from the original meaning of ethnocentrism as the tendency to view one's own ingroup as the center of everything and to devalue outgroups because of an overvaluation of the ingroup (Sumner, 1906). For this reason, Allport (1954) used the term generalized attitude to refer to the disposition to hold many prejudices. [new paragraph] This generalized prejudice idea suggests that individuals' negative attitudes towards distinct outgroups will all tend to be positively correlated and factor together as a single prejudice dimension" (Cantal, Milfont, Wilson, & Gouveia, 2015, p. 17).

Table 19.1 (*cont.*)

7. "An individual differences account of prejudice builds on the observation that people prejudiced against one outgroup typically tend to be prejudiced against other outgroups as well (e.g. Allport, 1954). In several studies prejudices against a range of outgroups were so highly correlated that they could reasonably be treated as indicators of a generalized prejudice factor" (Cohrs & Asbrock, 2009, p. 270).

8. "Consistent with notions that prejudice typically generalizes across different target groups (e.g., Akrami, Ekehammar, & Bergh, 2011; Altemeyer, 1998; Ekehammar, Akrami, Gylje, & Zakrisson, 2004; McFarland, 2010; Zick et al., 2008), we focus on generalized prejudice rather than prejudices toward specific groups ... because we measured prejudice in relation to gay men and lesbians, people with disabilities, and foreigners ... only data from participants who indicated that they were of German nationality, did not live with a disability, and had a heterosexual orientation were kept for the analyses" (Cohrs, Kämpfe-Hargrave, & Riemann, 2012, pp. 344, 347).

9. "Whereas prejudice may be seen as negative evaluation of and hostility toward a social group, ethnocentrism includes the tendency to form and maintain negative evaluations and hostility toward multiple groups that are not one's own. Evidence for an ethnocentric disposition comes from consistently high correlations between prejudices toward various outgroups ... [Generalized prejudice studies] have been taken to suggest that individuals high in ethnocentrism will derogate any outgroup regardless of contact and in the absence of group competition" (Cunningham, Nezlek, & Banaji, 2004, p. 1333).

10. "More than half a century ago, Gordon W. Allport noted that 'one of the facts of which we are most certain is that people who reject one out-group will tend to reject other outgroups. If a person is anti-Jewish, he is likely to be anti-Catholic, anti-Negro, anti any out-group' (Allport 1954: 68). In other words, prejudice is understood as a unitary phenomenon by this research group. We build upon these approaches and consider enmity toward different minority groups as being closely related to each other and deriving from a generalized attitude toward out-groups" (Davidov, Thörner, Schmidt, Gosen, & Wolf, 2011, p. 483).

11. "Prejudice tends to be generalized over targets. Persons who are less favorable to one out-group or minority tend to be less favorable to other out-groups or minorities. This has been documented empirically by strong positive correlations between attitudes to different out-groups" (Duckitt, 2001, p. 41).

12. "This means that persons reporting favourable attitudes to some outgroups tend to be generally more favourable toward other outgroups, while persons who are hostile or prejudiced to certain outgroups tend to be generally less favourable to others. These findings suggest that there should be just one broad dimension of generalized prejudice directed across all or most outgroups. They also suggest that some relatively stable characteristic of individuals makes them prone to be prejudiced against socially rejected outgroups and minorities in general (Adorno et al., Allport). The current study examines the degree to which ... there are consistencies between negative attitudes toward a range of different groups held by the individual" (Duckitt & Sibley, 2007, pp. 113–114).

13. "Attitudes to various out-groups seem to be highly correlated among people irrespective of their social background. Thus, this generalized prejudice (cf. Allport, 1954) can be seen as deriving from one or more basic personality traits" (Ekehammar & Akrami, 2003, p. 450).

14. "Generalized prejudice is a tendency to respond with prejudice toward any outgroup (Allport, 1954; Duckitt, 1992)" (Ekehammar, Akrami, Gylje, & Zakrisson, 2004, p. 464).

Table 19.1 (*cont.*)

15. "As observed by Allport (1954): 'One of the facts of which we are most certain is that people who reject one out-group will tend to reject other out-groups. If a person is anti-Jewish, he is likely to be anti-Catholic, anti-Negro, anti any out-group' (p. 68). [new paragraph] Such patterns of generalized prejudice have been observed in multiple studies, across multiple types of outgroups, in multiple cultures" (Hodson & Dhont, 2015, p. 4).

16. "By ethnocentrism we refer to a deep-seated psychological predisposition that partitions the world into ingroups and outgroups – into "us" and "them" . . . Ethnocentrism divides the world into two opposing camps. From an ethnocentric point of view, groups are either 'friend' or they are 'foe,' eliciting loyalty and favoritism on the one hand or suspicion and disdain on the other. Ethnocentrism is commonly expressed through stereotypes . . . After being asked to judge whites on this score [hardworking vs. lazy and intelligent vs. unintelligent], respondents are asked to make the same judgment, this time about blacks, Asian Americans, and Hispanic Americans" (Kam & Kinder, 2012, pp. 326–328).

17. "Insofar as ethnocentrism entails hostility directed not at a single out-group but at many out-groups, these applications of realistic group conflict theory, however successful they may be in explaining particular instances of conflict, simply do not speak to ethnocentrism as we conceive it. From the perspective of group conflict theory, generalized prejudice is possible only in the presence of multiple and simultaneous intergroup conflicts. But we are interested in ethnocentrism in precisely this sense. Ethnocentrism is generalized prejudice. If our question is why some people are ethnocentric while others are not, why some but not others are predisposed to take many kinds of difference as warrant for condescension or contempt, then group conflict theory cannot take us very far. More promising, as we are about to see, is the theory of authoritarianism . . . These results . . . offer clear support for the conception of ethnocentrism as generalized prejudice" (Kinder & Kam, 2009, pp. 11, 139).

18. "Generalized prejudice, which Adorno et al. (1950) labeled 'ethnocentrism,' is a prejudice against all outgroups, whether they are ethnic, sexual, or even fictional" (Krauss, 2002, p. 1257).

19. "The tendency for prejudices against different outgroups to be correlated has been found in many times and places (e.g., Adorno, Frenkel-Brunswik, Levinson, & Sanford, 1950; Allport and Kramer, 1946; Altemeyer, 1996; Bierly, 1985; Hartley, 1946; McFarland, Ageyev, & Abalakina, 1993). When balanced-scale measures are used, the typical correlation between two prejudices is about .50 (Duckett, 1992). That figure sustains Allport's assertion, while leaving plenty of room for different prejudices to be influenced by prejudice-specific causes (Whitley, 1999) and for social norms and ethnic conflicts to intensify some prejudices but not others (Prothro, 1952; Pettigrew, 1959). [new paragraph] But why, as the correlation suggests, are some people more disposed toward prejudice against outgroups than are others? That is the question explored here. This disposition was first labeled 'ethnocentrism' (Adorno et al., 1950), adopting a term introduced by Sumner (1906). But because the disposition includes many non-ethnic prejudices – sexism, religious hostilities, antihomosexuality, etc. – Allport (1954) referred to prejudice as a 'generalized attitude.' Because the correlations extend even to fictitious groups such as 'Danireans' and 'Wallonians' (Hartley, 1946), a generalized tendency to respond with prejudice toward many outgroups is apparent. Following Allport, the term 'generalized prejudice' is used here. [new paragraph] Because the correlation among prejudices suggested a source 'deep within the structure of the person' (Adorno et al., 1950, p. 223), the construct of the authoritarian personality was developed as an effort to understand 'the kinds of psychological dispositions – fears, anxieties, values, impulses' (Sanford, 1956, p. 267) that undergird ethnocentrism (or here, generalized prejudice)" (McFarland, 2001, p. 1).

Table 19.1 (*cont.*)

20. "A generalized tendency to respond with prejudice toward many outgroups is evident. Adorno et al. (1950) adopted Sumner's (1906) term 'ethnocentrism' to describe this disposition to hold many prejudices. Because the disposition includes many nonethnic prejudices – sexism, antihomosexuality, etc., along with extreme ingroup patriotism (called 'pseudopatriotism' by Adorno et al., p. 107) – Allport (1954) referred to it as a 'generalized attitude.' Following Allport, the term 'generalized prejudice' is used here" (McFarland, 2010, pp. 453–454).

21. "Prejudices against outgroups are highly correlated and reflect a general disposition to reject outgroups that the Adorno group called ethnocentrism . . . Are prejudices against outgroups highly correlated among Russians as they are among Western populations? The Soviet Union had different outgroups than does the West, but a similar pattern was expected. Communists are an outgroup victim of prejudice among Western authoritarians, and prejudice against communists is highly correlated with other racial, ethnic, and sexual prejudices (see McFarland, 1989a). In the Soviet Union, capitalists, dissidents, and champions of democracy were appropriate outgroups, and negative attitudes toward these groups were expected to be correlated with the common prejudices based on race, sex and age" (McFarland, Ageyev, & Abalakina, 1993, pp. 201–202).

22. "Different forms of prejudice, targeting different out-groups (e.g. homosexuals, immigrants, Muslims), are typically correlated (Adorno, Frenkel-Brunswick, Levinson, & Stanford, 1950; Allport, 1954). Scholars have considered this 'generality of prejudice' as a strong indication that individual differences in prejudice vary as a function of stable personality attributes" (Meeusen & Dhont, 2015, p. 585)

23. "Prejudice targeting different outgroups [is] strongly correlated (e.g. Akrami et al., 2011; Allport, 1954; Bierly, 1985). The idea is that if one holds negative attitudes toward some outgroups, e.g. immigrants, one will also dislike other outgroups, like homosexuals, religious minorities or disabled people, a phenomenon referred to as 'generalized prejudice' or a 'general devaluation of outgroups' " (Meeusen & Kern, 2016, p. 1).

24. "The predisposition of individuals to respond with prejudice to any out-group is denoted as generalized prejudice (GP) following Allport's (1954) terminology. GP is conceptualized as a personality trait that is based on empirical findings showing that, for example, racism, sexism, anti-Semitism, or negative attitudes toward homosexuals were highly correlated among people, so they could be reduced to form one GP factor (e.g., Bierly, 1985; Ekehammar et al., 2004)" (Roth & von Collani, 2007, p. 141).

25. "The predisposition of individuals to respond with prejudice to any kind of out-group is denoted as generalized prejudice following Allport's (1954) terminology" (von Collani & Grumm, 2009, p. 111).

26. "The GFE syndrome encompasses prejudices toward different groups that are, within a stable structure, substantially interrelated over a period of time even though the level of approval can vary across time, cultures, and individuals. They are proposed to be interrelated because they all mirror a generalized devaluation of out-groups, that is, GFE" (Zick et al., 2008, p. 364).

Note. Table adapted from Bergh, Akrami, Sidanius, & Sibley (in press).

violent criminals, drug dealers, and terrorists (primarily dangerous) can be teased apart from low warmth toward, for example, disabled, unattractive, and unemployed people (primarily derogated; Duckitt & Sibley, 2007; see also Asbrock et al., 2010; Cantal et al., 2015).

Despite of the influence of Duckitt's dual process model (see Duckitt and Sibley, Chapter 9, this title), the proposed derogation dimension has received more attention than the dangerous one. The focus on derogation also represents a shift from Allport's (1954) original writing. Derogation typically implies a bias in which one group is devalued compared to another one, and it does not necessitate absolute antipathy as Allport described prejudice. Indeed, many scholars have argued that prejudice should not be equated with antipathy (e.g., Glick & Fiske, 2001; Jackman, 1994). In line with such perspectives, Zick and associates (2008) suggested that targets of generalized prejudice are outgroups that are seen as "*unequal in value* by 'reasons,' for example, of economic uselessness, lower levels of civilization, or abnormal sexual practices" (p. 364, emphasis added). Like Allport, they stressed an ingroup-outgroup dynamic, but they also proposed that status and power differentials further restrain the boundaries of generalized prejudice. As such, Zick et al. (2008) examined devaluation of, for example, Jews, Muslims, foreigners, gays, and homeless people. Indeed, this represents a rather "typical" set of target groups in contemporary studies on generalized prejudice (see also Akrami, Ekehammar, & Bergh, 2011; Bäckström & Björklund, 2007; Cohrs et al., 2012; McFarland, 2010).

Positioning an Old Concept in a Modernized Literature

Many contemporary perspectives on prejudice have been proposed as alternatives to approaching prejudice as a generalized attitude, and the personality underpinnings thereof (e.g., Cottrell & Neuberg, 2005; Mackie & Smith, 2004). In some cases, it is also argued that the alternatives disprove the latter perspective (e.g., Reynolds & Turner, 2006). Here we address some of these viewpoints, and we argue that there is little reason, statistically or conceptually, to portray them as mutually exclusive to the generalized prejudice notion.

Prejudice Is Both Contextual and Context Independent

To argue that prejudice is entirely target-unspecific and context-independent is clearly simplistic and easily disproven by observation. However, replace "entirely" with "in part" and it makes perfect psychometric sense. Any two psychological measures that overlap have a common part that is independent of the specifics of its components. In this case, the measures would be for specific prejudices anchored in particular group contexts. Expanding this to three or more measures, three variance components need to be considered: (a) strictly common variance (shared by all measures), (b) strictly specific variance (no overlap with other measures), and

(c) variance shared by a subset of measures. The last variance component has been referred to as "dirty variance" because it dilutes the distinction between common and specific variance in classic psychometrics (Little, Cunningham, Shahar, & Widaman, 2002). However, borrowing from hierarchical personality models (e.g., McCrae & Costa, 2008), we refer to this as facet variance because it is the variance giving rise to multiple sub-factors, positioned between the individual measures and higher-order factors. Figure 19.1 illustrates such a hierarchical structure of prejudice, based on these variance components.

It should be noted that studies on generalized prejudice have traditionally focused on the common variance, and as such it is also less dependent on the context. In contrast, perspectives that stress how different groups are associated with different emotional, cognitive, and behavioral reactions (e.g., Cottrell & Neuberg, 2005; Eagly & Diekman, 2005; Fiske, Cuddy, & Glick, 2007; Mackie & Smith, 2004) capitalize on nonrandom specific and facet variance in different measures. Indeed, Figure 19.1 further illustrates how many popular perspectives on prejudice can be positioned at different levels in this hierarchical structure.

A few papers approach prejudice this way, and by paying more careful attention to different components of variance, they reveal how these are linked different explanations (Akrami et al., 2011; Meeusen & Kern, 2016; Zick et al., 2008). Importantly, such perspectives resolve the presumed contradiction between the generalized prejudice notion and different contextual perspectives.

Prejudice Displays Both Multidimensionality and Unity

A unidimensional view on prejudice has not only been criticized by social psychologists, it has also been challenged from within the personality and ideology approach (Duckitt, 2001, 2006). Indeed, if different prejudices fall along divergent dimensions, then it could be seen as a challenge to the very notion of generalized prejudice. Still, there are two counterarguments to such an inference. First, group negativity (as reflected in warmth ratings) is unequivocally multifaceted, for instance, toward housewives versus drug dealers (Asbrock et al., 2010; Duckitt & Sibley, 2007; Cantal et al., 2015). However, it is an open question if this holds true with other conceptualizations of prejudice and different types of measures.

Second, for many targets of prejudice, the two theoretical dimensions (fear and derogation) are intertwined, and there are also non-negligible correlations between the extracted factors (e.g., Asbrock et al., 2010). This opens up the possibility of hierarchical factor models, whereby a higher-order factor accounts for the communalities between different sub-factors. In such models, it is easy to reconcile the idea of generalized prejudice as capturing common variance of all targets (a higher-order factor) with Duckitt's reasoning about sub-factors (as reflected in facet variance; see Figure 19.1).

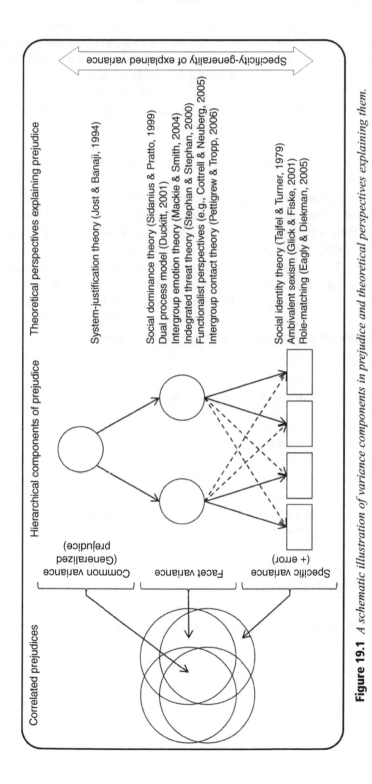

Figure 19.1 *A schematic illustration of variance components in prejudice and theoretical perspectives explaining them.*

Prejudice Is a Matter of Both Personality and Social Identity

The observation of generalized prejudice gave rise to the notion of "prejudiced personalities" (e.g., Adorno et al., 1950), and that idea has been the target of many objections from social identity theorists (e.g., Brown, 2010; Reynolds & Turner, 2006). Social identity theorists argue for fluidity in prejudice and self-definitions; personality psychologists argue for relative stability, both in (generalized) prejudice and self-definitions. Personality scholars have claimed that traits predict prejudice; social identity scholars claim that traits are irrelevant (see Reynolds & Turner, 2006). The list of disagreements could go on, and this schism has been described as one of the most severe in the personality and social psychology literature (Hodson, 2009).

Statistically speaking, the data from personality and social identity research rarely speak against each other; they speak *past* each other. They do so because they tend to be orthogonal. Mean levels of prejudice are often fairly changeable, but individual differences are often fairly stable (Akrami, Ekehammar, Bergh, Dahlstrand, & Malmsten, 2009). Furthermore, group membership predicts specific variance in prejudice, whereas basic personality variables predict the common variance (i.e., generalized prejudice; Akrami et al., 2011). Considering such basic statistical principles, there is little reason to argue that social identity research contradicts a personality approach, or the other way around.

A New Perspective on the Nature of Generalized Prejudice

Arguably the generalized prejudice concept has strengths that are difficult to negate in a comprehensive view on prejudice. However, in this last section we address a potential reservation that has gone unnoticed, and it is one that targets the generalized prejudice literature as a whole. More specifically, we return to the idea that generalized prejudice should involve (some) outgroups (see Table 19.1). Rather than asking if an ingroup-outgroup dynamic is insufficient for understanding generalized prejudice (e.g., Duckitt, 2001; Zick et al., 2008), we pose the question if it is even necessary. Finally, from the perspective that the ingroup-outgroup distinction may well be unnecessary, we review what the necessary conditions might be instead.

Removing Axioms from Definitions of (Generalized) Prejudice

To address if it is necessary for targets of generalized prejudice to be outgroups, we need to first consider how prejudice is defined in itself. Indeed, prejudice is commonly approached as an intergroup attitude (i.e., between "us" and "them") of negative valence (e.g., Dovidio & Gaertner, 2010; Stephan & Stephan, 2000). From such a perspective, it is an oxymoron to question if generalized prejudice by necessity involves outgroups. However, to limit prejudice to between-group attitudes is to imply, for instance, that sexist prejudice toward women is only possible by men. To incorporate sexism as a kind of prejudice, it is necessary to define the concept in a broader sense – one that can be construed on other criteria than group membership.

In a broader sense, prejudice could be defined as group *devaluation*. First of all, this definition circumvents the issue if prejudice has to be negative. Ageism, sexism, and racism all have benevolent and ambivalent aspects (Fiske et al., 2007; Jackman, 1994), and as such they are incompatible with defining prejudice as antipathy (see also Glick & Fiske, 2001). However, they all fit within a devaluation perspective, such that sexism is devaluation (overall) of women compared to men, and so on. A second feature of this definition is that devaluation can indeed be based on many other criteria than the ingroup-outgroup distinction. For example, from this viewpoint prejudice can manifest itself along dimensions of status and power, such that a low-power group is devalued compared to a high-power one. Importantly, this bias could be independent of group membership (see Jost & Banaji, 1994).

As seen through this lens, generalized prejudice represents a generic form of group devaluation. It can incorporate, for example, sexism, ageism, paternalistic racism, and other attitudes that have benevolent aspects. Still, groups targeted by more hostility or negativity, such as Muslims and gays, are certainly devalued as well (Herek, 2000; Kteily, Bruneau, Waytz, & Cotterill, 2015), and as such they should also be indicative of generalized prejudice. Indeed, this perspective accounts for the breadth of targets that empirically fit into a generalized prejudice factor (see Table 19.1 references; see also Brown, 2010). In contrast, Allport's (1954) assumption of outgroup antipathy would seem limited in this regard. Thus, rather than invoking his axiomatic assumptions, we could ask an empirical question: How important is group membership for understanding the observation that group devaluations are generalized across targets?

From Some Outgroups to No Ingroup-Outgroup Dynamic?

Consider the finding that sexism (toward women) is strongly indicative of generalized prejudice, and this holds true also when women are included as participants. This has been shown in nationally representative samples (Zick et al., 2008) and even in cases where female participants represent a clear numerical majority (Akrami et al., 2011). Unless the results for sexism were entirely underpinned by male participants, this would suggest that generalized prejudice could involve ingroups. This in turn implies a challenge to the view that generalized prejudice necessarily involves an ingroup-outgroup dynamic (see Table 19.1).

To demonstrate that some individuals are biased toward most any (or some) outgroups, it would be natural to (a) show that devaluing or negative sentiments are correlated for different outgroups and to (b) show that these correlations are not due to some other explanation. This is what generalized prejudice research has typically aimed to do. However, the correlations in the literature do not merely involve outgroup ratings. Practically all studies include prejudices that are known to represent ingroup definitions for many participants (e.g., sexism for women), or lack demographic information about group membership (e.g., failing to assess sexual orientation when assessing sexual prejudice), or use targets with unclear ingroup-outgroup boundaries (e.g., poor people). Finally, while most targets may represent outgroups for most participants, the more fundamental problem is that there exist alternative ways of explaining the observed correlations.

As noted earlier, groups can be devalued along other dimensions than group membership. However, studies on generalized prejudice systematically confound two important dimensions that are theoretically distinct – group membership and group status (see Mullen, Brown, & Smith, 1992). They also disregard power differentials across groups. Specifically, studies assessing generalized prejudice are almost exclusively based on evaluations of marginalized or stigmatized groups. The exception is the inclusion of fictitious groups (e.g., Hartley, 1946). However, there is a confound to consider in this case as prejudiced participants may think of unfamiliar ethnic groups as less powerful or "unimportant" (as compared to, for example, a US ingroup). To further illustrate the problem, consider the finding that prejudiced White heterosexuals devalue both Blacks and gays. From that finding alone, it is impossible to know whether this reflects a bias based on group membership (as Allport argued) or a bias based on stigma/status. Also, without disentangling such influences (group membership and group status), the data also call for caution regarding conclusions about interaction effects (as implied by perspectives stressing a bounded outgroup derogation; see Duckitt, 2001; Zick et al., 2008).

Because of the inferential problems outlined earlier, the role of group membership remains an open question in the existing studies on generalized prejudice. However, there some are indications that group membership may be more peripheral than typically assumed. Authoritarianism and social dominance are strong predictors of prejudice toward marginalized groups (e.g., Duckitt & Sibley, Chapter 9, this title; McFarland, 2010), but in minimal groups, where the impact of status and power differences has been nullified, their predictive power is substantially weaker (see, e.g., Amiot & Bourhis, 2005; Reynolds et al., 2007; Sidanius, Pratto, & Mitchell, 1994). Also, recent experiments indicate that minimal group biases, as well as absolute ingroup positivity and outgroup negativity, are null-correlated with conventional generalized prejudice factors (Bergh, Akrami, Sidanius, & Sibley, in press). As such, generalized prejudice seems orthogonal to both ingroup love and outgroup hate (cf. Brewer, 1999). Moreover, in these studies, group identification explained minimal group biases but not generalized prejudice. Instead, a number of personality covariates revealed an opposite pattern – they explained generalized prejudice but not minimal group biases. Additional studies showed a similar pattern for real target groups – basic personality traits predicted biases based on status and power, but not biases or negativity based on group membership in isolation (Bergh et al., 2015). Also, in line with the finding that generally prejudiced individuals score higher on sexism (e.g., Akrami et al., 2011), these studies showed that this is indeed true for both men and women. Likewise, individuals with a high level of generalized prejudice were more biased toward overweight people, even when they were overweight themselves. These findings also fit with Crandall's (1994) observation that anti-overweight prejudice is unrelated or only very weakly associated with one's own weight, but that it is strongly related to racism.

What the studies in the previous paragraph have in common is that they all challenge the notion that generalized prejudice is first and foremost an "us versus them" phenomenon. Just as much research has shown that the anti-outgroup criteria are insufficient for explaining how prejudice generalizes across different groups (see, e.g., Asbrock et al., 2010; Duckitt & Sibley, 2007; Zick et al., 2008), this research suggests that the anti-outgroup criteria might be peripheral altogether. This question has clear theoretical and practical implications. If seemingly xenophobic individuals do not care that much about "us" and "them," but rather about maintaining status and power differences between groups, then researchers and policy makers should be advised to construe prejudice interventions accordingly. Most prejudice interventions focus on intergroup contact and/or altered group categorizations (e.g., Paluck & Green, 2009), but if a large component of the variance between individuals in prejudice does not center on ingroup biases, then these interventions might, to some extent, be treating an epiphenomenon (where the more "real" problem is inequality; see Dixon, Levine, Reicher, & Durrheim, 2012; Glick & Fiske, 2001).

Generalized Prejudice as a General Threat Sensitivity

There is a risk of ending up in a theoretical void when questioning an ingroup-outgroup dynamic in generalized prejudice – if it is not about xenophobia, lacking contact, and so on, then where does it come from? Answers to that question are available when insights from the threat literature on prejudice (see Stephan and Stephan, Chapter 7, this title) and Duckitt's dual-process model are combined with system justification theory (Jost & Banaji, 1994). The threat literature suggests that prejudice emerges as a response to perceived threats that outgroups pose to one's ingroup, in either a symbolic (e.g., moral values) or a realistic sense (e.g., economic costs). Similarly, Duckitt's dual-process model (see Duckitt & Sibley, Chapter 9, this title) suggests that authoritarianism and a dangerous worldview stem from close-mindedness and symbolic group threats (and security threats), whereas social dominance and competitive worldviews stem from tough-mindedness and realistic group threats.

Most research here has focused on the differences, rather than the similarities, between these mentalities (Duckitt & Sibley, 2010). Also, when authoritarianism and dominance predict prejudice toward the same targets, the suggestion is that these groups are broadly dissident and associated with double threats (norm-violating/dangerous and resource-demanding/competitive; see Duckitt & Sibley, 2007, 2010). However, from such a perspective the overlap between different perceived threats seems almost coincidental – it is not in itself explained. Furthermore, prejudices correlate even when they do not have double threat attributes. For example, prejudice against gays is substantially correlated with prejudice against people with disabilities (e.g., Bäckström & Björklund, 2007; Cohrs et al., 2012), even though these groups seem rather orthogonal in what threats they might pose (symbolic in the first case, realistic [economic] in the latter). Another example of generalizations across threat domains is found in the stigma literature. For example, Kurzban and Leary (2001) argued that fear of parasitic infections could lead to "aesthetic" stigmas (e.g., against unattractive people), whereas a fear of exploitation could explain stigmatization of the poor and unemployed. Nonetheless, the attitudes in these cases show a substantial overlap (see, e.g., Duckitt & Sibley, 2007). Equally important, various threats evidently trigger prejudice, but to whom are these threats directed? Do they represent threats to an ingroup (as traditionally studied)? Or are threats at different levels (individual, group, and society) equally relevant? People high on authoritarianism, who see the world as dangerous, are not just sensitive to perceived outgroup threats; they are argued to be equally (if not more) sensitive to threats from within their group (Duckitt, 1989; see also Marques, Yzerbyt, & Leyens, 1988). Similarly, dominant individuals, who see the world as inherently competitive, also reveal their orientation toward power in interpersonal settings (Son Hing, Bobocel, Zanna, & McBride, 2007). These findings make little sense when prejudice is only explained in "us versus them" terms. However, if we consider the possibility that the primary concern of authoritarian and dominant individuals may not be a particular ingroup-outgroup relation, but a community or society at large (see Ho et al., 2012), they make all the more sense. Drawing on such concerns for the societal stability, as described in system-justification theory (Jost & Banaji. 1994), a different view of generalized prejudice emerges: Generally prejudiced individuals lash out against most any threat to the social/societal "order" (e.g., hierarchy).

The notion that prejudiced individuals are concerned about societal order, and react to threats to it, is described in detail in the writing on both authoritarianism and social dominance (e.g., Duckitt, 2001; Sidanius & Pratto, 1999). Again, however, these constructs are theorized to invoke such concerns in fundamentally different ways (see earlier discussion). Still, is there any evidence of communalities (as implied by the perspective on generalized prejudice presented)? Some data suggest so. For example, there is evidence of spillover effects, such that realistic threats (e.g., economic conditions) affect targets of prejudice that are mainly associated with the symbolic dimension (see Andersen & Fetner, 2008). Also, at the zero-order level, where the shared variance of authoritarianism and dominance has not been partialed out, there is evidence of both variables predicting prejudice toward symbolically and realistically threatening groups (e.g., Cantal et al., 2015; Ekehammar et al., 2004). So while regression analysis reveals the unique effects and the existence of facet variability (see Figure 19.1), the correlations speaks of a broader pattern of communalities that cut across different threat mentalities and different prejudices. Indeed, generalized prejudice can involve both ingroup and outgroup targets (see previous section), and it spans across groups that could challenge the societal order in a symbolic (e.g., gays and Muslims; Zick et al., 2008) and realistic sense (e.g., poor people; Cunningham et al., 2004).

If generalized prejudice were underpinned by system-justification motives, then societal threats would not only affect specific prejudices; they would also have a direct effect on levels of generalized prejudice. Indeed, Zick and associates (2008) found that generalized prejudice was directly influenced by the thought of Germans not standing their ground economically compared to immigrants. That effect was even stronger than the direct effect on anti-immigrant prejudice. More broadly, a number of studies have shown that prejudice can increase and decrease in a uniform fashion across group domains, thus suggesting that higher-order communalities have meaning (e.g., Vasiljevic & Crisp, 2013; Vezzali & Giovannini 2012). In sum, the core tenets of this integrative perspective, stressing communalities in prejudice toward groups perceived as realistical and symbolic threats to the societal order (rather than threatening an ingroup) are summarized in Figure 19.2. The figure also illustrates how targets falling outside the scope of generalized prejudice are those that are low on both dimensions, and these would tend to be majority groups and those having more power or status.

The perspective on generalized prejudice discussed here also provides further implications for the relation between personality and social identity research. If prejudice is group devaluation (cf. Glick & Fiske, 2001), it follows that ingroup biases represent a subcategory thereof: It is prejudice specifically based on group membership. As for this particular subcategory, personality might be largely irrelevant (e.g., Reynolds & Turner, 2006). However, if ingroup biases represent one subcategory of prejudiced attitudes, then there is also room for personality to explain biases occurring along other demarcation lines. Indeed, the perspective discussed here holds that generalized prejudice captures biases based on power and status differentials, or what might be called "system-justifying biases" (as contrasted with ingroup biases; see Jost & Banaji, 1994). For such biases, there are indeed good reasons to argue for personality correlates (Pratto, Sidanius, & Levin, 2006; see also Sidanius, Cotterill, Sheehy-Skeffington, Kteily, & Carvacho, Chapter 8, this title).

Summary and Conclusions

Different prejudices share a common core – generalized prejudice – and this observation has guided decades of research. The definition of generalized prejudice has developed from incorporating most any outgroup to a narrower

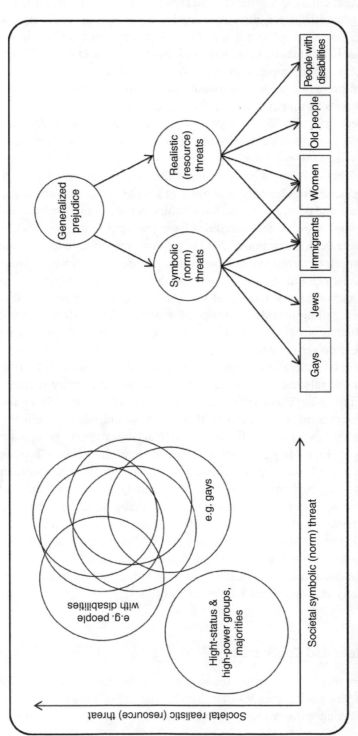

Figure 19.2 *A schematic illustration of devaluation of groups perceived as symbolically or realistically threatening a societal "order." Alternative conceptualizations of the facets are possible (such as security/norms and competition/derogation), but the emphasis here is on the overarching communalities.*

inclusion of outgroups that are disadvantaged or seen as threatening in various ways. The literature also includes a number of reservations against the generalized prejudice notion, but these can be clearly resolved by statistical reappraisals. Thus, summarizing recent findings we described a hierarchical view on prejudice – including a higher-order factor (generalized prejudice), facet-level variance, and specific variance – where different explanations are valid at different levels. For example, personality variables display robust relations with the higher-order factor (and facets), whereas the lowest level is better accounted for by predictors such as group membership and more specific stereotypes and emotional reactions. Finally, we reviewed findings challenging an "us versus them" perspective of generalized prejudice. Generalized prejudice can encompass ingroups, at least when they are in a disadvantaged position, and such findings seem to revolve around a generic tendency to lash out against most any group (ingroup or outgroup) threatening the societal order. Taken together, the reviewed research indicates that Allport's (1954) view on generalized prejudice may not have been entirely accurate, despite still being widely endorsed (see Table 19.1). Even so, the relevance of generalized prejudice is not negated. It has been an important piece in the prejudice puzzle, and it calls for further attention.

References

Adorno, T., Frenkel-Brunswik, E., Levinson, D. J., & Sanford, R. (1950). *The authoritarian personality*. New York: Harper.

Agnew, C. R., Thompson, V. D., & Gaines, S. O. (2000). Incorporating proximal and distal influences on prejudice: Testing a general model across outgroups. *Personality and Social Psychology Bulletin, 26*, 403–418.

Akrami, N., Ekehammar, B., & Bergh, R. (2011). Generalized prejudice: Common and specific components. *Psychological Science, 22*, 57–59.

Akrami, N., Ekehammar, B., Bergh, R., Dahlstrand, E., & Malmsten, S. (2009). Prejudice: The person in the situation. *Journal of Research in Personality, 43*, 890–897.

Allport, G. W. (1954). *The nature of prejudice*. Cambridge, MA: Addison-Wesley.

Allport, G. W., & Kramer, B. M. (1946). Some roots of prejudice. *Journal of Psychology, 22*, 9–39.

Altemeyer, B. (1996). *The authoritarian specter*. Cambridge, MA: Harvard University Press.

Altemeyer, B. (1998). The other "authoritarian personality." In M. P. Zanna (Ed.), *Advances in experimental social psychology* (Vol. *30*, pp. 47–92). San Diego, CA: Academic Press.

Amiot, C. E., & Bourhis, R. Y. (2005). Ideological beliefs as determinants of discrimination in positive and negative outcome distributions. *European Journal of Social Psychology, 35*, 581–598.

Andersen, R., & Fetner, T. (2008). Economic inequality and intolerance: Attitudes toward homosexuality in 35 democracies. *American Journal of Political Science, 52*, 942–958.

Asbrock, F., Sibley, C. G., & Duckitt, J. (2010). Right-wing authoritarianism and social dominance orientation and the dimensions of generalized prejudice: A longitudinal test. *European Journal Personality, 340*, 324–340.

Bäckström, M., & Björklund, F. (2007). Structural modeling of generalized prejudice. *Journal of Individual Differences, 28*, 10–17.

Bergh, R., Akrami, N., & Ekehammar, B. (2012). The personality underpinnings of explicit and implicit generalized prejudice. *Social Psychological and Personality Science, 3*, 614–621.

Bergh, R., Akrami, N., Sidanius, J., & Sibley, C. (in press). Is group membership necessary for understanding generalized prejudice? A re-evaluation of why prejudices are interrelated. *Journal of Personality and Social Psychology.*

Bierly, M. M. (1985). Prejudice toward contemporary outgroups as a generalized attitude. *Journal of Applied Social Psychology, 15*, 189–199.

Bizumic, B. (2014). Who coined the concept of ethnocentrism? A brief report. *Journal of Social and Political Psychology, 2*, 3–10.

Bizumic, B., Duckitt, J., Popadic, D., Dru, V., & Krauss, S. (2009). A cross-cultural investigation into a reconceptualization of ethnocentrism. *European Journal of Social Psychology, 39*, 871–899.

Bratt, C. (2005). The structure of attitudes toward non-Western immigrant groups: Second-order factor analysis of attitudes among Norwegian adolescents. *Group Processes and Intergroup Relations, 8*, 447–469.

Brewer, M. B. (1999). The psychology of prejudice: Ingroup love and outgroup hate? *Journal of Social Issues, 55*, 429–444.

Brown, R. (2010). *Prejudice. Its social psychology* (2nd ed.). Oxford: Wiley-Blackwell.

Cantal, C., Milfont, T. L., Wilson, M. S., & Gouveia, V. V. (2015). differential effects of right-wing authoritarianism and social dominance orientation on dimensions of generalized prejudice in Brazil. *European Journal of Personality, 27*, 17–27.

Cohrs, J. C., & Asbrock, F. (2009). Right-wing authoritarianism, social dominance orientation and prejudice against threatening and competitive ethnic groups. *European Journal of Social Psychology, 39*, 270–289.

Cohrs, J. C., Kämpfe-Hargrave, N., & Riemann, R. (2012). Individual differences in ideological attitudes and prejudice: Evidence from peer-report data. *Journal of Personality and Social Psychology, 103*, 343–361.

Cottrell, C. A, & Neuberg, S. L. (2005). Different emotional reactions to different groups: A sociofunctional threat-based approach to "prejudice." *Journal of Personality and Social Psychology, 88*, 770–789.

Crandall, C. S. (1994). Prejudice against fat people: Ideology and self-interest. *Journal of Personality and Social Psychology, 66*, 882–894.

Cunningham, W. A., Nezlek, J. B., & Banaji, M. R. (2004). Implicit and explicit ethnocentrism: Revisiting the ideologies of prejudice. *Personality and Social Psychology Bulletin, 30*, 1332–1346.

Davidov, E., Thörner, S., Schmidt, P., Gosen, S., & Wolf, C. (2011). Level and change of group-focused enmity in Germany: Unconditional and conditional latent growth curve models with four panel waves. *Advances in Statistical Analysis, 95*, 481–500.

Dixon, J., Levine, M., Reicher, S., & Durrheim, K. (2012). Beyond prejudice: Are negative evaluations the problem and is getting us to like one another more the solution? *Behavioral and Brain Sciences*, *35*, 411–466.

Dovidio, J. F., & Gaertner, S. L. (2010). Intergroup bias. In S. T. Fiske, D. T. Gilbert, & G. Lindzey (Eds.), *Handbook of social psychology* (pp. 1084–1121). Hoboken, NJ: Wiley.

Duckitt, J. (1989). Authoritarianism and group identification: A new view of an old construct. *Political Psychology*, *10*, 63–84.

Duckitt, J. (1992). *The social psychology of prejudice*. New York: Praeger.

Duckitt, J. (2001). A dual-process cognitive-motivational theory of ideology and prejudice. In M. P. Zanna (Ed.), *Advances in experimental social psychology* (Vol. *33*. pp. 41–113). San Diego, CA: Academic Press.

Duckitt, J. (2006). Differential effects of right wing authoritarianism and social dominance orientation on outgroup attitudes and their mediation by threat from and competitive-ness to outgroups. *Personality and Social Psychology Bulletin*, *32*, 684–696.

Duckitt, J., & Sibley, C. G. (2007). Right-wing authoritarianism, social dominance orientation and the dimensions of generalized prejudice. *European Journal of Personality*, *130*, 113–130.

Duckitt, J., & Sibley, C.G. (2010). Personality, ideology, prejudice and politics: A dual process motivational model. *Journal of Personality*, *78*, 1861–1893.

Eagly, A. H., & Diekman, A. B. (2005). What is the problem? Prejudice as an attitude-in-context. In J. F. Dovidio, P. Glick, & L. Rudman (Eds.), *On the nature of prejudice: Fifty years after Allport* (pp. 19–35). Malden, MA: Blackwell.

Ekehammar, B., & Akrami, N. (2003). The relation between personality and prejudice: A variable- and a person-centred approach. *European Journal of Personality*, *17*, 449–464.

Ekehammar, B., Akrami, N., Gylje, M., & Zakrisson, I., B. (2004). What matters most to prejudice: Big Five personality, social dominance orientation, or right-wing authoritarianism? *European Journal of Personality*, *18*, 463–482.

Fink, H. C. (1971). Fictitious groups and the generality of prejudice: An artifact of scales without neutral categories. *Psychological Reports*, *29*, 359–365.

Fiske, S. T., Cuddy, A. J. C., & Glick, P. (2007). Universal dimensions of social cognition: Warmth and competence. *Trends in Cognitive Sciences*, *11*, 77–83.

Glick, P., & Fiske, S. T. (2001). An ambivalent alliance. Hostile and benevolent sexism as complementary justifications for gender inequality. *American Psychologist*, *56*, 109–118.

Hartley, E. L. (1946). *Problems in prejudice*. New York: Kings Crown.

Herek, G. M. (2000). The psychology of sexual prejudice. *Current Directions in Psychological Science*, *9*, 19–22.

Ho, A. K., Sidanius, J., Pratto, F., Levin, S., Thomsen, L., Kteily, N., & Sheehy-Skeffington, J. (2012). Social dominance orientation: Revisiting the structure and function of a variable predicting social and political attitudes. *Personality and Social Psychology Bulletin*, *38*, 583–606.

Hodson, G. (2009). The puzzling person–situation schism in prejudice research. *Journal of Research in Personality*, *43*, 247–248.

Hodson, G., & Dhont, K. (2015). The person-based nature of prejudice: Individual difference predictors of intergroup negativity. *European Review of Social Psychology, 26*, 1–42.

Jackman, M. R. (1994). *The velvet glove: Paternalism and conflict in gender, class, and race relations*. Berkeley: University of California Press.

Jost, J. T., & Banaji, M. R. (1994). The role of stereotyping in system-justification and the production of false consciousness. *British Journal of Social Psychology, 33*, 1–27.

Kam, C. D., & Kinder, D. R. (2012). Ethnocentrism as a short-term force in the 2008 American presidential election. *American Journal of Political Science, 56*, 326–340.

Kinder, D. R., & Kam, C. D. (2009). *Us against them*. Chicago: University of Chicago Press.

Krauss, S. W. (2002). Romanian authoritarianism 10 years after communism. *Personality and Social Psychology Bulletin, 28*, 1255–1264.

Kteily, N., Bruneau, E., Waytz, A., & Cotterill, S. (2015). The ascent of man: Theoretical and empirical evidence for blatant dehumanization. *Journal of Personality and Social Psychology, 109*, 901–931.

Kurzban, R., & Leary, M. R. (2001). Evolutionary origins of stigmatization: The functions of social exclusion. *Psychological Bulletin, 127*, 187–208.

Little, T. D., Cunningham, W. A., Shahar, G., & Widaman, K. F. (2002). To parcel or not to parcel: Exploring the question and weighing the merits. *Structural Equation Modeling, 9*, 151–173.

Mackie, D. M., & Smith, E. R. (2004). *From prejudice to intergroup emotions: Differentiated reactions to social groups*. New York: Psychology Press.

Marques, J. M., Yzerbyt, V. Y., & Leyens, J. P. (1988). The "black sheep effect": Extremity of judgments towards ingroup members as a function of group identification. *European Journal of Social Psychology, 18*, 1–16.

McCrae, R. R., & Costa Jr., P. T. (2008). The five-factor theory of personality. In O. P. John, R. W. Robins, & L. A. Pervin (Eds.), *Handbook of personality: Theory and research* (3rd ed., pp. 159–180). New York: Guilford.

McFarland, S. G. (1989). Religious orientations and targets of discrimination. *Journal for the Scientific Study of Religion, 28*, 324–336.

McFarland, S. G. (2001). *Prejudiced people: Individual differences in explicit prejudice*. Unpublished manuscript.

McFarland, S. (2010). Authoritarianism, social dominance, and other roots of generalized prejudice. *Political Psychology, 31*, 453–477.

McFarland, S. G., Ageyev, V., & Abalakina, M. (1993). The authoritarian personality in the United States and the former Soviet Union: Comparative studies. In W. F. Stone, G. Lederer, & R. Christie (Eds.), *Strengths and weaknesses: The authoritarian personality today* (pp. 199–228). New York: Springer.

McFarland, S. G. & Mattern, K. (2001). *Generalized Explicit and Implicit Prejudice*. Unpublished manuscript.

Meeusen, C., & Dhont, K. (2015). Parent-child similarity in common and specific components of prejudice: The role of ideological attitudes and political discussion. *European Journal Personality, 29*, 585–598.

Meeusen, C., & Kern, A. (2016). The relation between societal factors and different forms of prejudice: A cross-national approach on target-specific and generalized prejudice. *Social Science Research, 55*, 1–15.

Mullen, B., Brown, R., & Smith, C. (1992). Ingroup bias as a function of salience, relevance, and status: An integration. *European Journal of Social Psychology*, *22*, 103–122.

Paluck, E. L., & Green, D. P. (2009). Prejudice reduction: What works? A review and assessment of research and practice. *Annual Review of Psychology*, *60*, 339–367.

Pettigrew, T. F. (1959). Regional differences in anti-Negro prejudice. *Journal of Abnormal and Social Psychology*, *59*, 28–36.

Pratto, F., Sidanius, J., & Levin, S. (2006). Social dominance theory and the dynamics of intergroup relations: Taking stock and looking forward. *European Review of Social Psychology*, *17*, 271–320.

Prothro, E. T. (1952). Ethnocentrism and anti-Negro attitudes in the deep south. *Journal of Abnormal and Social Psychology*, *47*, 105–108.

Reynolds, K. J., & Turner, J. C. (2006). Individuality and the prejudiced personality. *European Review of Social Psychology*, *17*, 233–270.

Reynolds, K. J., Turner, J. C., Haslam, S. A., Ryan, M. K., Bizumic, B., & Subasic, E. (2007). Does personality explain in-group identification and discrimination? Evidence from the minimal group paradigm. *British Journal of Social Psychology*, *46*, 517–539.

Roth, M., & von Collani, G. (2007). A head-to-head comparison of Big-Five types and traits in the prediction of social attitudes: Further evidence for a five-cluster typology. *Journal of Individual Differences*, *28*, 138–149.

Sanford, N. (1956). The approach of the authoritarian personality. In J. L. McCary (Ed.), *Psychology of personality: Six modern approaches* (pp. 261–282). New York: Grove Press.

Sibley, C. G., & Duckitt, J. (2008). Personality and prejudice: A meta-analysis and theoretical review. *Personality and Social Psychology Review*, *12*, 248–279.

Sidanius, J., & Pratto, F. (1999). *Social dominance: An intergroup theory of social hierarchy and oppression*. New York: Cambridge University Press.

Sidanius, J., Pratto, F., & Mitchell, M. (1994). In-group identification, social dominance orientation, and differential intergroup social allocation. *Journal of Social Psychology*, *134*, 151–167.

Son Hing, L. S., Bobocel, D. R., Zanna, M. P., & McBride, M. V. (2007). Authoritarian dynamics and unethical decision making: High social dominance orientation leaders and high right-wing authoritarianism leaders. *Journal of Personality and Social Psychology*, *92*, 67–81.

Stephan, W. G., & Stephan, C. W. (2000). An integrated threat theory of prejudice. In S. Oskamp (Ed.), *Reducing prejudice and discrimination* (pp. 23–45). Mahwah, NJ: Erlbaum.

Sumner, W. G. (1906). *Folkways*. New York: Ginn.

Vasiljevic, M., & Crisp, R. J. (2013). Tolerance by surprise: Evidence for a generalized reduction in prejudice and increased egalitarianism through novel category combination. *PLoS ONE*, *8*, e57106.

Vezzali, L., & Giovannini, D. (2012). Secondary transfer effect of intergroup contact: The role of intergroup attitudes, intergroup anxiety and perspective taking. *Journal of Community & Applied Social Psychology*, *22*, 125–144.

von Collani, G., & Grumm, M. (2009). On the dimensional structure of personality, ideological beliefs, social attitudes, and personal values. *Journal of Individual Differences, 30*, 107–119.

Whitley, B. E. (1999). Right-wing authoritarianism, social dominance orientation, and prejudice. *Journal of Personality and Social Psychology, 77*, 126–134.

Zick, A, Wolf, C., Küpper, B., Davidov, E., Schmidt, P., & Heitmeyer, W. (2008). The syndrome of group focused enmity: The interrelation of prejudices tested with multiple cross sectional and panel data. *Journal of Social Issues, 64*, 363–383.

PART III

Prejudice Reduction and Analysis in Applied Contexts

20 Recent Developments in Intergroup Contact Research: Affective Processes, Group Status, and Contact Valence

Linda R. Tropp, Agostino Mazziotta, and Stephen C. Wright

What are the consequences of bringing people from diverse groups together? Does it enhance trust and goodwill, or does it lead to mistrust and hostility? More than 60 years ago, social scientists offered initial evidence and theoretical perspectives regarding how contact between members of different groups can reduce intergroup hostility and promote positive intergroup attitudes (see Allport, 1954; Williams, 1947). Since then, Allport's (1954) formulation of intergroup contact theory has become one of the most enduring models in the history of social psychology (Brewer & Brown, 1998), as well as one of psychology's best strategies to improve intergroup relations (Pettigrew & Tropp, 2011).

This chapter provides an overview of recent theorizing and research on intergroup contact with a focus on three key developments in the literature. First, we highlight the special role of affective processes and friendship in improving intergroup attitudes while considering both direct and indirect forms of intergroup contact. We then review the differential effects and implications of contact among members of minority and majority groups and describe how contact effects reach far beyond shifts in intergroup attitudes. Finally, we discuss the effects of both positive and negative intergroup contact on attitudes and relations between groups.

Effects of Direct Contact

Research reveals the crucial roles that affective processes play in contact effects, both in terms of the kinds of contact that are most likely to improve intergroup attitudes and the kinds of positive outcomes we can expect from such contact (see Pettigrew & Tropp, 2011). With survey data from seven European samples, seminal work by Pettigrew (1997) showed that intergroup contact in the form of cross-group friendships was consistently and negatively associated with a range of prejudice measures, particularly those assessing feelings of sympathy and admiration toward the outgroup. In line with Pettigrew's (1997) findings, other studies indicate that cross-group friendships relate more strongly to reduced prejudice than more distant forms of contact (Herek & Capitanio, 1996), particularly when affective dimensions of prejudice such as feelings and emotions toward outgroup members are involved (Tropp & Pettigrew, 2005a).

Cross-group friendships. Empirical interest in the special role of cross-group friendships has expanded and corroborated these early findings through longitudinal, meta-analytic, and experimental research. Longitudinal surveys in several countries have shown that greater cross-group friendships predict more positive intergroup attitudes over time (Binder et al., 2009; Levin, van Laar, & Sidanius, 2003; Swart, Hewstone, Christ, & Voci, 2011). Meta-analytic research by Davies, Tropp, Aron, Pettigrew, and Wright (2011) lends further support, demonstrating that cross-group friendships predict more positive intergroup attitudes irrespective of how friendship is measured – whether assessed as numbers or percentages of cross-group friends or as reported closeness to or time spent with cross-group friends. Experimental studies also show that both developing new cross-group friendships (Page-Gould, Mendoza-Denton, & Tropp, 2008; Wright, Brody, & Aron, 2005) and reflecting on existing cross-group friendships (Page-Gould, Mendoza-Denton, Alegre, & Siy, 2010) can improve intergroup attitudes.

Contact quantity and quality. Paralleling this emphasis on cross-group friendships, other work has usefully distinguished between the quantity and quality of intergroup contact. Building on Allport's (1954) formulation of optimal conditions for contact, contact quality has often been operationalized in terms of the participant's subjective sense of these conditions – for example, feeling that the contact is cooperative and supported and that members of both groups are regarded as equals (Dixon, Tropp, et al., 2010, Islam & Hewstone, 1993). Others have stressed the importance of affective closeness and intimacy as markers of high-quality intergroup contact; indeed, some propose that the potential for members of different groups to become friends should be regarded as its own optimal condition for contact (Cook, 1962; Pettigrew, 1998), or that the optimal contact can be construed as conditions that facilitate the development of cross-group friendships (Wright et al., 2005; Wright, 2009). Although the broad conclusion is that contact between members of different groups generally improves intergroup attitudes (Pettigrew & Tropp, 2011), it is now well established that not all types of contact are equal. Contact quantity alone is limited in its impact on intergroup attitudes, whereas contact quality – especially when defined as close relationships across group boundaries – is much more influential (Tropp & Pettigrew, 2005a).

Mediators of contact effects. Substantial research also highlights the importance of affect in the processes through which contact improves intergroup attitudes. Affective pathways such as reducing intergroup anxiety (Barlow, Louis, & Hewstone, 2009; Islam & Hewstone, 1993, Paolini, Hewstone, Cairns, & Voci, 2004) and promoting intergroup empathy toward the outgroup (Finlay & Stephan,

2000) have emerged as key mediators of the contact-prejudice relationship. Meta-analytic work confirms these findings (Pettigrew & Tropp, 2008), while also showing that these pathways function largely independently of each other. Similarly, longitudinal studies indicate that over time, high-quality contact such as cross-group friendships predicts lower intergroup anxiety (Levin et al., 2003) as well as greater intergroup empathy (Swart et al., 2011).

Effects of Indirect Contact

The growing focus on affective processes is also consistent with theorizing by Wright, Aron, and colleagues (Aron et al., 2004; Wright, Aron, & Tropp, 2002; Wright et al., 2005), who suggest that close cross-group contact can shift our broader understandings of intergroup relationships and can impact intergroup attitudes even in the absence of direct contact. In recent years, many scholars have highlighted the importance of indirect forms of contact (see Dovidio, Eller, & Hewstone, 2011; Vezzali, Hewstone, Capozza, Giovanni, & Wölfer, 2014; Wright & Aron, 2010, for reviews), as these offer strategies through which a relatively small number of direct cross-group friendships can have a wider impact on intergroup relations. Prominent among these perspectives is the extended contact effect introduced by Wright, Aron, McLaughlin-Volpe, and Ropp (1997), which holds that the mere "knowledge that an ingroup member has a close relationship with an outgroup member can lead to more positive intergroup attitudes" (p. 73). Across two survey studies, these authors showed that independent of their own direct cross-group contact, White, Latino(a), and Black Americans who knew of greater numbers of cross-ethnic friendships reported more positive intergroup attitudes than those who knew of fewer cross-ethnic friendships. Subsequent survey studies have shown similar effects across a wide range of groups and contexts, including Catholics and Protestants in Northern Ireland (Tam, Hewstone, Kenworthy, & Cairns, 2009); South Asians and Whites in the United Kingdom (Turner, Hewstone, & Voci, 2007); Spaniards and immigrants in Spain (Gómez, Tropp, & Fernandez, 2011); Germans in relation to "foreigners" in Germany (Christ et al., 2010); and heterosexuals in relation to gay men (Mereish & Poteat, 2015).

These correlational findings have been complemented by controlled experiments offering causal evidence of the effects of extended contact on intergroup attitudes (see Lemmer & Wagner, 2015, for review). Laboratory research by Wright and colleagues (1997) used variants of minimal group procedures (Tajfel, Billig, Bundy, & Flament, 1971) in which participants watched two confederates – ostensibly one ingroup member and one outgroup member – work together on a puzzle and act as though they were close friends, strangers, or disliked acquaintances. Compared to those who watched pairs of strangers or disliked acquaintances, those who watched a cross-group friendship pair reported more positive evaluations of the outgroup.

Experimental studies in applied contexts have revealed similar patterns of effects. For example, Cameron, Rutland, and Brown (2007) found that British schoolchildren who listened to stories depicting cross-group friendships between British and refugee children offered more positive evaluations of refugees than children who heard the same stories depicting friendships between two British children. Similar effects have been found for children's attitudes toward children with disabilities (Cameron & Rutland, 2006), Finnish adolescents' attitudes toward "foreigners" (Liebkind & McAlister, 1999), and Italian adolescents' attitudes toward immigrants (Vezzali, Stathi, & Giovannini, 2012).

Mediators of extended contact effects. A number of processes have been proposed to account for these effects of extended contact. Observing others engaged in intergroup contact can reduce anxieties associated with cross-group interactions (West & Turner, 2014). There is also evidence that extended contact works by creating a meaningful connection between oneself and the outgroup, referred to as the "inclusion of the outgroup in the self" (Turner, Hewstone, Voci, & Vonofakou, 2008; Wright, Aron, & Brody, 2008), whereby the positive feelings typically reserved for the self (and ingroup) are extended to the outgroup and its members. Extended contact can also change our perceptions of both ingroup norms – how we believe members of our group relate to the outgroup – and outgroup norms – how we believe outgroup members relate to the ingroup (Gómez et al., 2011; Turner et al., 2008). In a powerful field experiment in Rwanda, Paluck (2009) showed that exposure to a radio soap opera that included positive contact between Hutus and Tutsis changed respondents' beliefs about norms for relations between the groups, and led to more positive intergroup behavior. Related work by Mazziotta, Mummendey, and Wright (2011) highlights the value of presenting ingroup role models who demonstrate that and how cross-group contact can be successful; observing positive cross-group interactions not only encouraged more positive intergroup attitudes but also enhanced participants' beliefs about their ability to navigate cross-group interactions successfully. Thus, changing perceptions of norms may be a particularly valuable means through which extended and other indirect forms of contact can influence the broader relations between groups.

Relationships between direct and indirect contact. A recent meta-analysis (Lemmer & Wagner, 2015) suggests that both indirect and contact interventions are effective in improving intergroup attitudes, and studies typically show modest positive correlations between the two forms of contact (Mazziotta, Rohmann, Wright, De Tezanos-Pinto, & Lutterbach, 2015; Mereish & Poteat, 2015). Extended contact may be especially predictive of intergroup attitudes in contexts where opportunities for direct contact are limited, whereas direct contact plays a stronger role when it is possible (Christ et al., 2010). Importantly, indirect forms of contact may help to prepare people for direct contact with members of other groups. For example, longitudinal survey research with undergraduates in the United States has shown that positive extended contact prior to college significantly predicts students' formation of cross-group friendships during college (Schofield,

Hausmann, Ye, & Woods, 2010). Experimental research also indicates that extended contact can lead to more positive nonverbal behavior during a subsequent cross-group interaction, which in turn leads one's partner to perceive the interaction as more positive (West & Turner, 2014). In sum, indirect contact involving knowledge of and exposure to positive and successful cross-group interactions can supplement or set the stage for direct contact as a means of improving intergroup attitudes.

Contact Effects Among Minority and Majority Groups

Beyond extending the scope of intergroup contact to include both direct and indirect forms, new generations of research have identified important differences in the nature and experience of intergroup contact among members of different groups depending on their status. Group status plays a defining role in relations between groups (Bobo, 1999), as the attitudes of majority group members are often linked to their privileged status, while the attitudes of minorities are often based in the anticipation of prejudice and discrimination from the majority group (see Monteith & Spicer, 2000).[1] Meta-analytic and longitudinal studies also show that the effects of contact are typically weaker among members of minority groups than among members of the majority group (Binder et al., 2009; Tropp & Pettigrew, 2005b). Moreover, research has uncovered differences in minority and majority group members' experiences during intergroup contact, along with differences in the perceptions and expectations they bring to contact situations (see Devine & Vasquez, 1998; Shelton, Richeson, & Vorauer, 2006; Tropp, 2006).

Different anxieties in intergroup relationships. Members of both minority and majority groups may be concerned about how they will be perceived by outgroup members (Sigelman & Tuch, 1997; Vorauer, 2006), and they arc both likely to feel anxious about engaging in cross-group interactions (Plant & Devine, 2003; Stephan & Stephan, 1985; Tropp, 2003). Nonetheless, given their divergent views of intergroup relationships, their anxieties are often based in different concerns: Members of majority groups are especially likely to experience anxiety about being perceived as prejudiced, whereas members of minority groups are more likely to be anxious about becoming the target of prejudice (Devine & Vasquez, 1998).

Different motivations and goals in intergroup relationships. Correspondingly, members of minority and majority groups may have different motivations and goals as they approach contact with each other. Members of majority groups tend to seek acceptance and assurance of their moral integrity, while members of minority groups seek respect and empowerment (Bergsieker,

1 Here, we use the terms "minority" and "majority" to refer to groups of different status in a broader social hierarchy, where "minority" is meant to refer to groups that have been socially devalued, subordinate, and/or historically disadvantaged, while "majority" is meant to refer to groups that have been socially valued, dominant, and/or historically advantaged.

Shelton, & Richeson, 2010; Shnabel, Nadler, Ullrich, Dovidio, & Carmi, 2009); to the extent that their respective needs are satisfied, members of these groups demonstrate greater willingness to engage with the other group and greater optimism for their future relations (Shnabel et al., 2009). Relatedly, willingness to engage in contact may be predicted by different psychological factors for members of these groups: Majority group members' interest often stems from their own beliefs and valuing of diversity, whereas minority group members' interest often stems from their perceptions of the majority group's beliefs and values around diversity, social integration, and interest in contact (Tropp & Bianchi, 2006; Zagefka, González, & Brown, 2011).

Different preferences for representations of intergroup relationships. In line with their distinct motivations and concerns, members of minority and majority groups also tend to differ in their preferred representations of intergroup relationships. Majority group members prefer representations that minimize the salience of group differences and emphasize common ties across groups (see Saguy, Tausch, Dovidio, Pratto, & Singh, 2010; Wolsko, Park, Judd, & Wittenbrink, 2000), while members of minority groups tend to prefer representations that highlight the distinctiveness of their group identity when ties are established across group boundaries (see Hehman et al., 2011; Ryan, Hunt, Weible, Peterson, & Casas, 2007). These trends suggest that members of minority groups value positive acknowledgment of their group identities (Eggins, Haslam, & Reynolds, 2002; Hornsey & Hogg, 2000), such that they may feel more positively inclined toward cross-group interactions when group identities are explicitly recognized (Tropp & Bianchi, 2007).

Extended contact among minority and majority groups. Research also points to distinct processes in extended contact for members of minority and majority groups. Although these groups tend not to differ in their mean levels of extended contact (Gómez et al., 2011) or in overall effects of extended contact on intergroup attitudes (Turner et al., 2007; Wright et al., 1997), some work indicates that perceived outgroup norms play a greater role in extended contact for minority groups than for majority groups (Gómez et al., 2011). Taken together with other work cited previously (Tropp & Bianchi, 2006; Zagefka et al., 2011), these findings suggest that members of minority groups may attend carefully to cues from the majority group, and they may become less willing to engage in contact to the extent that they anticipate disregard or rejection (see Tropp, 2006).

Contact Effects Beyond Shifting Intergroup Attitudes

Granted, intergroup contact research has traditionally been focused on the perspectives of majority groups toward the goal of shifting intergroup attitudes toward the reduction of intergroup prejudice (Allport, 1954). Yet research has highlighted the importance of thinking more broadly about the potential outcomes and implications of intergroup contact (see Dixon & Levine, 2012; Tropp & Mallett, 2011). Along with improving intergroup attitudes, emerging research shows how contact can impact a variety of other outcomes relevant to relations between groups.

Potential beneficial effects of contact. Through positive contact experiences, group members' views of and approaches to relations between groups can shift in many beneficial ways. Contact can enhance trust between groups (Tam et al., 2009; Tropp, 2008), and feelings of inclusion within the broader social context in which contact occurs (Mendoza-Denton & Page-Gould, 2008). Positive contact in the past can also facilitate more positive contact experiences in the future (Page-Gould et al., 2010; Paolini et al., 2014), a greater willingness to help outgroup members in need (Oliner & Oliner, 1988), and a tendency to have a more diverse social networks later in life (Ellison & Powers, 1994). Moreover, close cross-group relationships are associated with more positive beliefs about outgroup members' intentions (Powers & Ellison, 1995; Tropp, Hawi, O'Brien, et al., under review), as well as a stronger desire to improve relations between groups (Sigelman & Welch, 1993). Indeed, even in contexts of violent intergroup conflict (see Wagner & Hewstone, 2012), positive contact experiences can enhance a willingness to forgive, and a desire for intergroup reconciliation (Čehajić, Brown, & Castano, 2008; Hewstone, Cairns, Voci, Hamberger, & Niens, 2006; Tam et al., 2009; Tropp et al., under review).

Positive contact experiences can also enhance support for policies designed to reduce intergroup inequality among members of high-status majority groups. Experimental research shows that Whites who developed a friendship with a Black or Latino(a) partner showed less support for state ballot initiatives that would ban affirmative action, end bilingual education, and tighten controls on immigration, compared to those who developed a friendship with a White partner (Wright et al., 2005). Large-scale survey research also shows that White South Africans who reported positive contact with Black South Africans were less likely to indicate opposition to compensatory policies (e.g., scholarships) and preferential policies (e.g., affirmative action) that would promote the advancement of Black South Africans (Dixon, Durrheim et al., 2010). Similarly, positive contact with Palestinians predicts greater willingness to compromise and make reparations among Jewish Israelis (Maoz & Ellis, 2008), and positive contact with immigrants predicts greater support for pro-immigration policies among citizens of the United States and many Western European countries (Fetzer, 2000; Pettigrew, Wagner, & Christ, 2007). Thus, although improving intergroup attitudes has been a primary focus in contact research, the positive impacts of contact can extend far beyond improved intergroup attitudes.

Potential detrimental effects of contact. Despite the clear benefits of positive contact, researchers have importantly begun to question the exclusive focus on these benefits, while raising concerns about contact's "darker side" (Dixon, Levine, Reicher, & Durrheim, 2012; Wright, 2001). In our enthusiastic pursuit of the harmony afforded by positive contact, we may have underemphasized its relationship to other important routes to achieving social equality, such as collective action and resistance by members of low-status minority groups. Although the goals of promoting intergroup harmony and fighting for social equality are not necessarily in conflict, the underlying psychological processes supporting these two routes to these goals may be: Contact focuses on creating harmony between groups, while collective action has at its core conflict between groups (Wright & Baray, 2012; Wright & Lubensky, 2009).

A growing body of research shows that while positive contact can improve intergroup attitudes, it can at the same time reduce the likelihood that members of low-status minority group members will seek to protect the interests of their groups and engage in activities to challenge intergroup inequality. Wright and Lubensky (2009) found that among Black and Latino(a) Americans, positive contact with Whites was associated with more positive attitudes toward Whites, but also with less support for collective action to advance equality; they also showed that this effect was mediated in part by reduced identification with their low-status group and a stronger belief that individual personal advancement was possible. Similar findings have been observed among Arab Israelis in relation to Jewish Israelis (Saguy, Tausch, Dovidio, & Pratto, 2009), among Māori New Zealanders in relation to European New Zealanders (Barlow, Sibley, & Hornsey, 2012), and among Muslims in relation to Hindus in India (Saguy et al., 2010). Parallel results have been found in South Africa where among Black South Africans, positive contact with Whites predicts more positive intergroup attitudes and trust, yet lower perceptions of racial discrimination (see Dixon, Tropp et al., 2010), and less support for social policies that could advance racial equality (Dixon, Durrheim, & Tredoux, 2007).

Additional studies provide stronger evidence of causal direction. Using longitudinal survey data from Black and Latino(a) Americans, Tropp, Hawi, Van Laar, and Levin (2012) observed that greater friendships with Whites predicted significantly lower perceptions of discrimination over time and lower subsequent support for ethnic activism. Experimentally, Becker, Wright, Lubensky, and Zhou (2013) showed that members of the LGBT community who were primed to recall positive contact with a heterosexual friend or family member known to be unsupportive of same-sex marriage indicated lower intentions to engage in ongoing protests supporting same-sex marriage, compared to participants in a "no prime" control condition. In addition to obscuring perceptions of discrimination and undermining intentions to engage in collective action, it has also been proposed that positive contact can blur intergroup boundaries, leading group members to focus more on commonalities between groups and deflect attention away from inequalities (Wright & Lubensky, 2009; see also Dovidio, Saguy, Gaertner, & Thomas, 2012); consistent with this view, members of low-status groups who have contact with high-status groups where commonalities are emphasized may develop overly optimistic expectations of fair treatment by members of high-status groups (Saguy et al., 2009).

In summary, there is growing evidence that positive contact, in addition to creating more positive attitudes, can encourage members of high-status majority groups to support policies that can benefit low-status minority groups. However, positive contact between these groups can also have the unintended consequences of reducing minority group members' perceptions of discrimination, identification with their own low-status group, recognition of structural inequality, and intentions to challenge the status quo and take action to promote minority group interests. Yet these undesirable effects need not always occur. For example, the experimental research by Becker et al. (2013) also reveals that when members of a low-status minority group have contact with a member of the high-status majority group, and that high-status group partner clearly indicates that he or she supports greater equality and sees existing inequalities as illegitimate, the undermining effect of positive contact on collective action can be erased. Greater research attention is therefore needed to specify conditions under which positive contact between minority and majority groups need not interfere with, or may even enhance, commitment to collective efforts to dismantle status inequalities.

Effects of Positive and Negative Contact

In addition to specifying potentially beneficial and detrimental effects of positive contact, recent years have witnessed growing interest in studying the effects of both positive and negative contact experiences (Barlow, Paolini et al., 2012; Graf, Paolini, & Rubin, 2014; Paolini et al., 2014; Paolini, Harwood, & Rubin, 2010; Pettigrew, 2008; Techakesari et al., 2015). Across a range of intergroup contexts, this work shows that people typically experience more positive intergroup encounters than negative ones. At the same time, the research suggests that negative contact is more strongly associated with negative intergroup attitudes than positive contact is with positive intergroup attitudes (Barlow, Paolini et al., 2012). This asymmetry is especially likely to occur when cognitive dimensions of intergroup attitudes, such as stereotypes or beliefs about the outgroup, are measured (Aberson, 2015; Mazziotta, Rohmann, Wright, & De Tezanos-Pinto, 2014); this is likely because negative contact heightens the salience of social categories and is consistent with the negative expectations people have for relations with outgroup members (Paolini et al., 2010). However, Graf and colleagues (2014) provide evidence that while negative contact may have a stronger influence on intergroup attitudes, positive contact may outweigh its influence by occurring more frequently.

Effects of positive and negative contact among minority and majority groups. Although most investigations of positive and negative contact effects have concentrated on members of majority groups, Stephan and colleagues' (2002) large-scale survey importantly investigated the effects of negative contact among both Black and White Americans; their findings showed that Blacks reported having experienced more negative contact with Whites than Whites reported having experienced with Blacks. Similarly, in a secondary analysis of US national survey data, Tropp (2007) found that Black Americans reported significantly greater perceptions of racial discrimination than Whites, and greater perceptions of racial discrimination inhibited the effects of contact on positive attitudes toward Whites. Experimental and diary studies further show that exposure to prejudice and discrimination can undermine racial and ethnic minorities' willingness to engage in contact with members of the White majority (Shelton & Richeson, 2006; Tropp, 2003). These initial findings point to the need for greater efforts to integrate the emerging research on positive and negative contact effects with earlier findings on minority-majority differences in perceptions of and experiences with intergroup contact.

Effects of positive and negative contact in contexts of intergroup conflict. The relative effects of positive and negative contact may be further influenced by the degree to which the larger intergroup relationship is marked by past or ongoing conflict (see Wagner & Hewstone, 2012). However, studies conducted in conflict zones report encouraging effects of intergroup contact, even in the face of violent intergroup conflict. Indeed, even after taking into account suffering, loss, and exposure to violence resulting from intergroup conflict, studies between religious groups in Northern Ireland and racial groups in South Africa show that positive contact can predict greater intergroup trust, more positive beliefs about outgroup members' intentions, and greater willingness to work toward intergroup reconciliation (Al Ramiah & Hewstone, 2013; Hewstone et al., 2006; Tropp et al., under review). Studies in Northern Ireland and Cyprus show that extensive positive intergroup contact in the past can buffer the effects of a negative contact experience in the present (Paolini et al., 2014). Moreover, meta-analytic research indicates that positive contact interventions can improve intergroup attitudes, even when used after periods of intergroup violence (Lemmer & Wagner, 2015). Although more work is needed to understand how the temporal sequencing of positive and negative contact contributes to their effects, existing work suggests that positive contact can contribute to many positive intergroup outcomes in conflict settings, whether it occurs before or after periods of negative contact.

Effects of positive and negative extended contact. To date, little work has investigated the effects of positive and negative extended contact. However, Mazziotta and colleagues (2015) show that, like direct contact, positive extended contact was reported more often than negative extended contact, and that both positive and negative forms of extended contact uniquely predicted Germans' attitudes toward Turks (Study 1) and Muslims (Study 2). Similarly, research by LaBianca, Brass, and Gray (1998) suggests that having friends who report negative relations with outgroup members predicts stronger perceptions of intergroup conflict, whereas having friends who report positive relations with outgroup members predicts weaker perceptions of intergroup conflict. These initial findings provide important reminders that relations between groups are embedded in broader social and historical contexts where both positive and negative intergroup encounters may be experienced directly or indirectly, and where both can impact group members' intergroup attitudes and behaviors.

Concluding Remarks

Despite its long history, empirical and theoretical advances in the intergroup contact literature remain as vibrant as ever and have contributed to a true renaissance in our understanding of contact effects, leading us to many new insights and important research directions. In this chapter, we have focused on three key recent developments in intergroup contact research – namely, the roles of affective processes, group status, and the valence of contact experiences. Consensus is growing that while intergroup contact can influence a variety of intergroup outcomes, it is the affective elements of these contact experiences – such as intergroup closeness and anxiety – that are most influential. Emerging bodies of research also show that while positive contact can promote positive intergroup attitudes, trust, and a range of other beneficial intergroup outcomes, it may inadvertently undermine some efforts to promote social change. As our field continues to advance, we call for greater synthesis and integration across these new developments – for example, identifying the similarities and differences in how affective processes drive the effects of direct and indirect forms of positive and negative contact; studying the implications of affective processes for shifting intergroup attitudes as well as for challenging social inequalities; and enhancing our understanding of how both positive and negative contact, in their direct and indirect forms, affect intergroup attitudes and motivations for social change among members of both minority and majority groups. Adding layers of conceptual complexity – through emphasizing both direct and indirect forms of contact, the experiences of both minority and majority groups, and the nature of both positive and negative contact experiences – presents a real challenge for contemporary researchers, but it appears that many are rising to the challenge. Inspired by these new developments, future generations of research promise to offer more comprehensive and far-reaching insights regarding how people's experiences with members of other groups can shift not only their own attitudes and intentions toward other groups but also their contributions to shaping and influencing social policies and institutions that will guide broader societal relations between groups.

References

Aberson, C. L. (2015). Positive intergroup contact, negative intergroup contact, and threat as predictors of cognitive and affective dimensions of prejudice. *Group Processes and Intergroup Relations*, *18*, 743–760.

Allport, G. W. (1954). *The nature of prejudice*. Reading, MA: Addison-Wesley.

Al Ramiah, A., & Hewstone, M. (2013). Intergroup contact as a tool for reducing, resolving, and preventing intergroup conflict: Evidence, limitations, and potential. *American Psychologist*, *68*, 527–542.

Aron, A., McLaughlin-Volpe, T., Mashek, D., Lewandowski, G., Wright, S. C., & Aron, E. N. (2004). Including others in the self. *European Review of Social Psychology*, *15*, 101–132.

Barlow, F. K., Louis, W. R., & Hewstone, M. (2009). Rejected! Cognitions of rejection and intergroup anxiety as mediators of the impact of cross-group friendships on prejudice. *British Journal of Social Psychology*, *48*, 389–405.

Barlow, F. K., Paolini, S., Pedersen, A., Hornsey, M. J., Radke, H. R. M., Harwood, J. . . . Sibley, C. G. (2012). The contact caveat: Negative contact predicts increased prejudice more than positive contact predicts reduced prejudice. *Personality and Social Psychology Bulletin*, *38*, 1629–1643.

Barlow, F. K., Sibley, C. G., & Hornsey, M. J. (2012). Rejection as a call to arms: Inter-racial hostility and support for political action as outcomes of race-based rejection in majority and minority groups. *British Journal of Social Psychology*, *51*, 167–177.

Becker, J. C., Wright, S. C., Lubensky, M. E., & Zhou, S. (2013). Friend or ally: Whether cross-group contact undermines collective action depends what advantaged group members say (or don't say). *Personality and Social Psychology Bulletin*, *39*, 442–455.

Bergsieker, H. B., Shelton, J. N., & Richeson, J. A. (2010). To be liked versus respected: Divergent goals in interracial interactions. *Journal of Personality and Social Psychology*, *99*, 248–264.

Binder, J., Zagefka, H., Brown, R., Funke, F., Kessler, T., Mummendey, A., . . . Leyens, J.-P. (2009). Does contact reduce prejudice or does prejudice reduce contact? A longitudinal test of the contact hypothesis amongst majority and minority groups in three European countries. *Journal of Personality and Social Psychology*, *96*, 843–856.

Bobo, L. D. (1999). Prejudice as group position: Microfoundations of a sociological approach to racism and race relations. *Journal of Social Issues*, *55*, 445–72.

Brewer, M. B., & Brown, R. (1998). Intergroup relations. In D. T. Gilbert, S. T. Fiske, & G. Lindzey (Eds.), *The handbook of social psychology* (Vol. *2*, pp. 554–594). New York: McGraw-Hill.

Cameron, L., & Rutland, A. (2006). Extended contact through story reading in school: Reducing children's prejudice toward the disabled. *Journal of Social Issues*, *62*, 469–488.

Cameron, L., Rutland, A., & Brown, R. (2007). Promoting children's positive intergroup attitudes towards stigmatized groups: Extended contact and multiple classification skills training. *International Journal of Behavioral Development*, *31*, 454–466.

Čehajić, S., Brown, R. & Castano, E. (2008). Forgive and forget? Antecedents and consequences of intergroup forgiveness in Bosnia and Herzegovina. *Political Psychology*, *29*, 351–367.

Christ, O., Hewstone, M., Tausch, N., Wagner, U., Voci, A., Hughes, J., & Cairns, E. (2010). Direct contact as a moderator of extended contact effects: Cross-sectional and longitudinal impact on outgroup attitudes, behavioral intentions, and attitude certainty. *Personality and Social Psychology Bulletin*, *36*, 1662–1674.

Cook, S. W. (1962). The systematic analysis of socially significant events: A strategy for social research. *Journal of Social Issues, 18,* 66–84.

Davies, K., Tropp, L. R., Aron, A., Pettigrew, T. F., & Wright, S. C. (2011). Cross-group friendships and intergroup attitudes: A meta-analytic review. *Personality and Social Psychology Review, 15,* 332–351.

Devine, P. G., & Vasquez, K. A. (1998). The rocky road to positive intergroup relations. In J. L. Eberhardt & S. T. Fiske (Eds.), *Confronting racism: The problem and the response* (pp. 234–262). Thousand Oaks, CA: Sage.

Dixon, J., Durrheim, K., Tredoux. C., Tropp, L., Clack, B., Eaton, L., & Quayle, M. (2010). Challenging the stubborn core of opposition to equality: Racial contact and policy attitudes. *Political Psychology, 31,* 831–855.

Dixon, J., Durrheim, K., & Tredoux, C. (2007). Intergroup contact and attitudes toward the principle and practice of racial equality. *Psychological Science, 18,* 867–872.

Dixon, J., & Levine, M. (2012). *Beyond prejudice: Extending the social psychology of conflict, inequality and social change.* New York: Cambridge University Press.

Dixon, J., Levine, M., Reicher, S., & Durrheim, K. (2012). Beyond prejudice: Are negative evaluations the problem and is getting us to like one another more the solution? *Behavioral and Brain Sciences, 35,* 411–425.

Dixon, J., Tropp, L. R., Durrheim, K., & Tredoux, C. (2010). "Let them eat harmony": Prejudice-reduction strategies and attitudes of historically disadvantaged groups. *Current Directions in Psychological Science, 19,* 76–80.

Dovidio, J. F., Eller, A., & Hewstone, M. (2011). Improving intergroup relations through direct, extended, and other forms of indirect contact. *Group Processes and Intergroup Relations, 14,* 147–160.

Dovidio, J. F., Saguy, T., Gaertner, S. L., & Thomas, E. L. (2012). From attitudes to (in) action: The darker side of "we." In J. Dixon & M. Levine (Eds.), *Beyond prejudice: Extending the social psychology of conflict, inequality and social change* (pp. 248–268). New York: Cambridge University Press.

Eggins, R. A., Haslam, S. A., & Reynolds, K. J. (2002). Social identity and negotiation: Subgroup representation and superordinate consensus. *Personality and Social Psychology Bulletin, 28,* 887–899.

Ellison, C. G., & Powers, D. A. (1994). The contact hypothesis and racial attitudes among Black Americans. *Social Science Quarterly, 75,* 385–400.

Fetzer, J. S. (2000). *Public attitudes toward immigration in the United States, France, and Germany.* New York: Cambridge University Press.

Finlay, K., & Stephan, W. G. (2000). Reducing prejudice: The effects of empathy on intergroup attitudes. *Journal of Applied Social Psychology, 30,* 1720–1737.

Gómez, A., Tropp, L. R., & Fernandez, S. (2011). When extended contact opens the door to future contact: Testing the effects of extended contact on attitudes and intergroup expectancies in majority and minority groups. *Group Processes and Intergroup Relations, 14,* 161–173.

Graf, S., Paolini, S., & Rubin, M. (2014). Negative intergroup contact is more influential, but positive intergroup contact is more common: Assessing contact prominence and contact prevalence in five Central European countries. *European Journal of Social Psychology, 44,* 536–547.

Hehman, E., Gaertner, S. L., Dovidio, J. F., Mania, E. W., Guerra, R., Wilson, D. C., & Friel, B. M. (2011). Group status drives minority and majority integration preferences. *Psychological Science, 23*, 46–52.

Herek, G. M., & Capitanio, J. P. (1996). "Some of my best friends": Intergroup contact, concealable stigma, and heterosexuals' attitudes toward gay men and lesbians. *Personality and Social Psychology Bulletin, 22*, 412–424.

Hewstone, M., Cairns, E., Voci, A., Hamberger, J., & Niens, U. (2006). Intergroup contact, forgiveness, and experience of "the troubles" in Northern Ireland. *Journal of Social Issues, 62*, 99–120.

Hornsey, M. J., & Hogg, M. A. (2000). Assimilation and diversity: An integrative model of subgroup relations. *Personality and Social Psychology Review, 4*, 143–156.

Islam, M. R., & Hewstone, M. (1993). Dimensions of contact as predictors of intergroup anxiety, perceived out-group variability, and out-group attitude: An integrative model. *Personality and Social Psychology Bulletin, 19*, 700–710.

LaBianca, G., Brass, D. J., & Gray, B. (1998). Social networks and perceptions of intergroup conflict: The role of negative relationships and third parties. *Academy of Management Journal, 41*, 55–67.

Lemmer, G., & Wagner, U. (2015). Can we really reduce ethnic prejudice outside the lab? A meta-analysis of direct and indirect contact interventions. *European Journal of Social Psychology, 45*, 152–168.

Levin, S., van Laar, C., & Sidanius, J. (2003). The effects of ingroup and outgroup friendship on ethnic attitudes in college: A longitudinal study. *Group Processes and Intergroup Relations, 6*, 76–92.

Liebkind, K., & McAlister, A. L. (1999). Extended contact through peer modelling to promote tolerance in Finland. *European Journal of Social Psychology, 29*, 765–780.

Maoz, I., & Ellis, D. (2008). Intergroup communication as a predictor of Jewish-Israeli agreement with integrative solutions to the Israeli-Palestinian conflict: The mediating effects of outgroup trust and guilt. *Journal of Communication, 58*, 490–507.

Mazziotta, A., Mummendey, A., & Wright, S. C. (2011). Vicarious intergroup contact effects: Applying social-cognitive theory to intergroup contact research. *Group Processes and Intergroup Relations, 14*, 255–274.

Mazziotta, A., Rohmann, A., Wright, S. C., & De Tezanos-Pinto, P. (2014, June). *The effects of positive and negative day-to-day contact experiences.* Paper presented at the 10th Biennial Conference of the Society of the Psychological Study of Social Issues, Portland.

Mazziotta, A., Rohmann, A., Wright, S. C., De Tezanos-Pinto, P., & Lutterbach, S. (2015). (How) Does positive and negative extended cross-group contact predict direct cross-group contact and intergroup attitudes? *European Journal of Social Psychology, 45*, 653–667.

Mendoza-Denton, R., & Page-Gould, E. (2008). Can cross-group friendships influence minority students' well-being at historically white universities? *Psychological Science, 19*, 933–939.

Mereish, E., & Poteat, V. P. (2015). Effects of heterosexuals' direct and extended friendships with sexual minorities on their attitudes and behaviors: Intergroup anxiety and attitude strength as mediators and moderators. *Journal of Applied Social Psychology, 45*, 147–157.

Monteith, M. J., & Spicer, C. V. (2000). Contents and correlates of Whites' and Blacks' racial attitudes. *Journal of Experimental Social Psychology, 36*, 125–154.

Oliner, S. P., & Oliner, P. M. (1988). *The altruistic personality: Rescuers of Jews in Nazi Europe*. New York: Free Press.

Page-Gould, E., Mendoza-Denton, R., & Tropp, L. R. (2008). With a little help from my cross-group friend: Reducing anxiety in intergroup contexts through cross-group friendship. *Journal of Personality and Social Psychology, 95*, 1080–1094.

Page-Gould, E., Mendoza-Denton, R., Alegre, J. M., & Siy, J. O. (2010). Understanding the impact of cross-group friendship on interactions with novel outgroup members. *Journal of Personality and Social Psychology, 98*, 775–793.

Paluck, E. L. (2009). Reducing intergroup prejudice and conflict using the media: A field experiment in Rwanda. *Journal of Personality and Social Psychology, 96*, 574–587.

Paolini, S., Harwood, J., & Rubin, M. (2010). Negative intergroup contact makes group memberships salient: Explaining why intergroup conflict endures. *Personality and Social Psychology Bulletin, 36*, 1723–1738.

Paolini, S., Harwood, J., Rubin, M., Husnu, S., Joyce, N., & Hewstone, M. (2014). Positive and extensive intergroup contact in the past buffers against the disproportionate impact of negative contact in the present. *European Journal of Social Psychology, 44*, 548–562.

Paolini, S., Hewstone, M., Cairns, E., & Voci, A. (2004). Effects of direct and indirect cross-group friendships on judgments of Catholics and Protestants in Northern Ireland: The mediating role of an anxiety-reduction mechanism. *Personality and Social Psychology Bulletin, 30*, 770–786.

Pettigrew, T. F. (1997). Generalized intergroup contact effects on prejudice. *Personality and Social Psychology Bulletin, 23*, 173–185.

Pettigrew, T. F. (1998). Intergroup contact theory. *Annual Review of Psychology, 49*, 65–85.

Pettigrew, T. F. (2008). Future directions for intergroup contact theory and research. *International Journal of Intercultural Relations, 32*, 187–199.

Pettigrew, T. F., & Tropp, L. R. (2008). How does intergroup contact reduce prejudice? Meta-analytic tests of three mediators. *European Journal of Social Psychology, 38*, 922–934.

Pettigrew, T. F., & Tropp, L. R. (2011). *When groups meet: The dynamics of intergroup contact*. New York: Psychology Press.

Pettigrew, T. F., Wagner, U., & Christ, O. (2007). The predictors of anti-immigration attitudes. Comparing German results with those of Canada and the United States. *Du Bois Review, 4*, 19–39.

Plant, E. A., & Devine, P. G. (2003). The antecedents and implications of interracial anxiety. *Personality and Social Psychology Bulletin, 29*, 790–801.

Powers, D. A., & Ellison, C. G. (1995). Interracial contact and black racial attitudes: The contact hypothesis and selectivity bias. *Social Forces, 74*, 205–226.

Ryan, C. S., Hunt, J. S., Weible, J. A., Peterson, C. R., & Casas, J. F. (2007). Multicultural and colorblind ideology, stereotypes, and ethnocentrism among Black and White Americans. *Group Processes and Intergroup Relations, 10*, 617–637.

Saguy, T., Tausch, N., Dovidio, J. F., & Pratto, F. (2009). The irony of harmony: Intergroup contact can produce false expectations for equality. *Psychological Science, 20*, 114–121.

Saguy, T., Tausch, N., Dovidio, J. F., Pratto, F., & Singh, P. (2010). Tension and harmony in intergroup relations. In R. P. Shaver & M. Mikulincer (Eds.), *Understanding and reducing aggression, violence, and their consequences* (pp. 333–348). Washington, DC: American Psychological Association.

Schofield, J. W., Hausmann, L. R. M., Ye, F., & Woods, R. L. (2010). Intergroup friendships on campus: Predicting close and casual friendships between White and African American first-year college students. *Group Processes and Intergroup Relations*, *13*, 585–602.

Shelton, J. N., & Richeson, J. A. (2006). Ethnic minorities' racial attitudes and contact experiences with white people. *Cultural Diversity and Ethnic Minority Psychology*, *12*, 149–164.

Shelton, J. N., Richeson, J. A., & Vorauer, J. D. (2006). Threatened identities and interethnic interactions. *European Review of Social Psychology*, *17*, 321–358.

Shnabel, N., Nadler, A., Ullrich, J., Dovidio, J. F., & Carmi, D. (2009). Promoting reconciliation through the satisfaction of the emotional needs of victimized and perpetrating group members: The needs-based model of reconciliation. *Personality and Social Psychology Bulletin*, *35*, 1021–1030.

Sigelman, L., & Tuch, S. A. (1997). Metastereotypes: Blacks' perceptions of Whites' stereotypes of Blacks. *Public Opinion Quarterly*, *61*, 87–101.

Stephan, W. G., Boniecki, K. A., Ybarra, O., Bettencourt, A., Ervin, K. S., Jackson, L. A. . . . Renfro, C. L. (2002). The role of threats in the racial attitudes of Blacks and Whites. *Personality and Social Psychology Bulletin*, *28*, 1242–1254.

Stephan, W. G., & Stephan, C. W. (1985). Intergroup anxiety. *Journal of Social Issues*, *41*, 157–175.

Swart, H., Hewstone, M., Christ, O., & Voci, A. (2011). Affective mediators of intergroup contact: A three-wave longitudinal study in South Africa. *Journal of Personality and Social Psychology*, *101*, 1221–1238.

Tajfel, H., Billig, M. G., Bundy, R. P., & Flament, C. (1971). Social categorization and intergroup behaviour. *European Journal of Social Psychology*, *1*, 149–178.

Tam, T., Hewstone, M., Kenworthy, J., & Cairns, E. (2009). Intergroup trust in Northern Ireland. *Personality and Social Psychology Bulletin*, *35*, 45–59.

Techakesari, P., Barlow, F. K., Hornsey, M. J., Sung, B., Thai, M., & Chak, J. L. Y. (2015). An investigation of positive and negative contact as predictors of intergroup attitudes in the United States, Hong Kong, and Thailand. *Journal of Cross-Cultural Psychology*, *46*, 454–468.

Tropp, L. R. (2003). The psychological impact of prejudice: Implications for intergroup contact. *Group Processes and Intergroup Relations*, *6*, 131–149.

Tropp, L. R. (2006). Stigma and intergroup contact among members of minority and majority status groups. In S. Levin & C. van Laar (Eds.), *Stigma and group inequality: Social psychological perspectives* (pp. 171–191). Mahwah, NJ: Erlbaum.

Tropp, L. R. (2007). Perceived discrimination and interracial contact: Predicting interracial closeness among Black and White Americans. *Social Psychology Quarterly*, *70*, 70–81.

Tropp L. R. (2008). The role of trust in intergroup contact: Its significance and implications for improving relations between groups. In U. Wagner, L. R. Tropp, G. Finchilescu, & C. Tredoux (Eds.), *Improving intergroup relations: Building on the legacy of Thomas F. Pettigrew* (pp. 91–106). Malden, MA: Blackwell.

Tropp, L. R., & Bianchi, R. A. (2006). Valuing diversity and interest in intergroup contact. *Journal of Social Issues, 62*, 533–551.

Tropp, L. R., & Bianchi, R. A. (2007). Interpreting references to group membership in context: Feelings about intergroup contact depending on who says what to whom. *European Journal of Social Psychology, 37*, 153–170.

Tropp, L. R., Hawi, D. R., Van Laar, C., & Levin, S. (2012). Cross-ethnic friendships, perceived discrimination, and their effects on ethnic activism over time: A longitudinal investigation of three ethnic minority groups. *British Journal of Social Psychology, 51*, 257–272.

Tropp, L. R., Hawi, D., O'Brien, T. C., Gheorghiu, M., Zetes, A., & Butz, D. (under review). *Intergroup contact and the potential for post-conflict reconciliation: Studies in South Africa and Northern Ireland.*

Tropp, L. R., & Mallett, R. K. (2011). *Moving beyond prejudice reduction: Pathways to positive intergroup relations.* Washington, DC: American Psychological Association.

Tropp, L. R., & Pettigrew, T. F. (2005a). Differential relationships between intergroup contact and affective and cognitive indicators of prejudice. *Personality and Social Psychology Bulletin, 31*, 1145–1158.

Tropp, L. R., & Pettigrew, T. F. (2005b). Relationships between intergroup contact and prejudice among minority and majority status groups. *Psychological Science, 16*, 951–957.

Turner, R. N., Hewstone, M., & Voci, A. (2007). Reducing explicit and implicit outgroup prejudice via direct and extended contact: The mediating role of self-disclosure and intergroup anxiety. *Journal of Personality and Social Psychology, 93*, 369–388.

Turner, R. N., Hewstone, M., Voci, A., & Vonofakou, C. (2008). A test of the extended intergroup contact hypothesis: The mediating role of intergroup anxiety, perceived ingroup and outgroup norms, and inclusion of the outgroup in the self. *Journal of Personality and Social Psychology, 95*, 843–860.

Vezzali, L., Hewstone, M., Capozza, D., Giovannini, D., & Wölfer, R. (2014). Improving intergroup relations with extended and vicarious forms of indirect contact. *European Review of Social Psychology, 25*, 314–389.

Vezzali, L., Stathi, S., & Giovannini, D. (2012). Indirect contact through book reading: Improving adolescents' attitudes and behavioral intentions toward immigrants. *Psychology in the Schools, 49*, 148–162.

Vorauer, J. D. (2006). An information search model of evaluative concerns in intergroup interaction. *Psychological Review, 113*, 862–886.

Wagner, U., & Hewstone, M. (2012). Intergroup contact. In L. R. Tropp (Ed.), *The Oxford handbook of intergroup conflict* (pp. 193–209). New York: Oxford University.

West, K., & Turner, R. N. (2014). Using extended contact to improve physiological responses and behavior toward people with schizophrenia. *Journal of Experimental Social Psychology, 50*, 57–64.

Williams, R. M. Jr. (1947). *The reduction of intergroup tensions.* New York: Social Science Research Council.

Wolsko, C., Park, B., Judd, C. M., & Wittenbrink, B. (2000). Framing interethnic ideology: Effects of multicultural and color-blind perspectives on judgments of groups and individuals. *Journal of Personality and Social Psychology, 78*, 635–654.

Wright, S. C. (2001). Strategic collective action: Social psychology and social change. In R. Brown & S. Gaertner (Eds.), *Blackwell handbook of social psychology: Intergroup processes* (pp. 409–430). Malden, MA: Blackwell.

Wright, S. C. (2009). Cross-group contact effects. In S. Otten, T. Kessler, & K. Sassenberg (Eds.), *Intergroup relations: The role of emotion and motivation* (pp. 262–283). New York: Psychology Press.

Wright, S. C., & Aron, A. (2010). The extended contact effect. In J. Levine & M. A. Hogg (Eds.), *The encyclopedia of group processes and intergroup relations* (pp. 265–267). Thousand Oaks, CA: Sage.

Wright, S. C., Aron, A., McLaughlin-Volpe, T., & Ropp, S. A. (1997). The extended contact effect: Knowledge of cross-group friendships and prejudice. *Journal of Personality and Social Psychology, 73*, 73–90.

Wright, S. C., Aron, A., & Brody, S. M. (2008). Extended contact and including others in the self: Building on the Allport/Pettigrew legacy. In U. Wagner, L. R. Tropp, G. Finchilescu, & C. Tredoux (Eds.), *Improving intergroup relations: Building on the legacy of Thomas F. Pettigrew* (pp. 143–159). Malden, MA: Blackwell.

Wright, S. C., Aron, A., & Tropp, L. R. (2002). Including others (and their groups) in the self: Self-expansion theory and intergroup relations. In J. P. Forgas & K. Williams (Eds.), *The social self: Cognitive, interpersonal and intergroup perspectives* (pp. 343–363). Philadelphia: Psychology Press.

Wright, S. C. & Baray, G. (2012). Models of social change in social psychology: Collective action or prejudice reduction, conflict or harmony. In J. Dixon & M. Levine (Eds.), *Beyond prejudice: Extending the social psychology of intergroup conflict, inequality and social change* (pp. 225–247). Cambridge: Cambridge University Press.

Wright, S. C., Brody, S. M., & Aron, A. (2005). Intergroup contact: Still our best hope for improving intergroup relations. In C. S. Crandall & M. Schaller (Eds.), *The social psychology of prejudice: Historical perspectives* (pp. 115–142). Lawrence, KS: Lewinian Press.

Wright, S. C., & Lubensky, M. (2009). The struggle for social equality: Collective action vs. prejudice reduction. In S. Demoulin, J.-P. Leyens, & J. F. Dovidio (Eds.), *Intergroup misunderstandings: Impact of divergent social realities* (pp. 291–310). New York: Psychology Press.

Zagefka, H., González, R., & Brown, R. (2011). How minority members' perceptions of majority members' acculturation preferences shape minority members' own acculturation preferences: Evidence from Chile. *British Journal of Social Psychology, 50*, 216–233.

21 From Prejudice Reduction to Collective Action: Two Psychological Models of Social Change (and How to Reconcile Them)

John Dixon, Kevin Durrheim, Clifford Stevenson, and Huseyin Cakal

Even when the social order appears intractable, social change is constantly unfolding all around us, finding expression in the accumulation of small acts of resistance as much as in dramatic moments of revolution. Psychologists should take interest in the dynamics of social change, whether mundane or dramatic, for at least two reasons. First, the explanation of when and why change occurs – or fails to occur – requires analysis of ordinary people's thoughts, feelings, and behaviors. To understand fully the conditions under which people act in ways that support or challenge the status quo, we simply cannot afford to overlook the role of psychological factors. Second and related, processes of social change invite us to (re)appraise the moral and political implications of psychological knowledge. How do we reduce discrimination against others? When do we recognize and challenge social inequality and when do we accept or even endorse it? How can we create more inclusive forms of identity and community? Such questions elide the traditional division between scholarship and advocacy. They require us to demonstrate how psychological knowledge helps create a more just and tolerant society. Perhaps less comfortably, they require us to recognize how our discipline may be complicit in maintaining social inequalities.

In this chapter, we discuss two psychological models of social change, namely prejudice reduction and collective action. Both models focus on the problem of improving relations between groups to reduce social inequality and discrimination. However, they propose different psychological pathways to the achievement of this goal and prioritize different core questions. As we shall see, the prejudice reduction model primarily addresses the question "How can we get individuals to like one another more?" whereas the collective action model primarily addresses the question "How can we get individuals to mobilize together to challenge inequality?"

The first section of the chapter elaborates the fundamental principles and underlying assumptions of these models. The second section explores the relationship between the two models of change, focusing on the allegation that prejudice reduction exerts counterproductive effects on collective action. The chapter's conclusion advocates a *contextualist* perspective on social change. We hold that any evaluation of the efficacy of psychological models of change must remain sensitive to the "stubborn particulars" (Cherry, 1995) of local conditions and the affordances and obstacles embedded there.

Prejudice Reduction

How could it be that in a culture of law, order and reason there could have survived the irrational remnants of ancient racial and religious hatreds? How to explain the willingness of great masses of people to tolerate the mass extermination of their fellow citizens.

(Adorno, Frenkel-Brunswik, Levinson, & Sanford, 1950, p. v)

Taken from the preface to the *Authoritarian Personality*, Adorno et al.'s famous quotation captures some basic features of the modern concept of prejudice. Initially, this concept highlighted a general distinction between rational thinking and thinking corrupted by irrational biases. However, in the early years of the last century, "prejudice" came to refer more narrowly to the expression of unreasonable dislike toward members of other social groups. In the years following the Second World War, commentators such as Allport and Kramer (1946), Saenger (1953), and Allport (1954) gathered compelling evidence of the scale, nature, and consequences of the problem of prejudice, focusing particularly on the damage done by racism and anti-Semitism in American society. They also presented an unfavorable picture of the mental life of bigots, flagging the rigid and "stenciled" quality of their thinking; their ego fragility and intolerance of ambiguity; and, above all, the irrational nature of their antipathy for members of minority groups.

This early work often adopted an individual differences approach to explaining prejudice. It espoused a "rotten apple" perspective (cf. Henriques et al., 1984), tracing the causes of prejudice to the dynamics of "maladjusted" personality development. As the field developed, alternative causal models gained currency, and the core image of the nature of the prejudiced person shifted. In the so-called second phase of prejudice research (cf. Dovidio, 2001), prejudice was viewed as the unfortunate by-product of ordinary cognitive processes such as categorization, attribution, and stereotyping. The core image of the authoritarian bigot gave way to the image of the "cognitive miser," engaging in efficient yet fallible forms of information processing. Researchers also recognized increasingly that individual prejudice might reflect group-level norms, identity dynamics, and instrumental goals rather than personal irrationality (Sherif et al., 1961; Tajfel & Turner, 1986). In its most recent phase, prejudice research has been dominated by so-called dual process models, as exemplified, for example, by research that distinguishes between conscious and implicit attitudes toward others (see Durrheim, Quayle, & Dixon, 2016). The figure of the aversive racist – whose surface support for racial tolerance and equality is offset by unconscious antipathies – shows how this latest wave of prejudice research is complicating standard images of the "old-fashioned" or "redneck" bigot (Dovidio & Gaertner, 2004).

One of the most enduring contributions of prejudice research arises from its implications for promoting social change. From the outset, prejudice researchers sought not only to understand but also to transform relations of social inequality and discrimination. As Lippitt and Radke (1946, p. 167) insisted in an early commentary: "The need for an understanding of the dynamics of prejudice has no equivalent importance in the social sciences. In no other aspects of interpersonal and intergroup relations is there a more urgent need for social scientists to *get out and do something* [our emphasis]." In the ensuing decades, many social scientists answered this rallying cry: They got out and did something. Numerous interventions to reduce prejudice were devised, tested, and applied across a wide range of social and cultural settings and types of intergroup relations (see Paluck & Green, 2009, for a comprehensive overview). Examples include interventions to promote intergroup contact, common identification, empathic awareness, and cooperative learning.

It is important to acknowledge, of course, that different theoretical conceptions of the nature of prejudice have inspired different solutions to the problem. If one's starting assumption is that the "cognitive processes of prejudiced people are in general different from the cognitive processes of tolerant people" (Allport, 1954, p. 170), for example, then this points toward a rather different approach to prejudice reduction than if one assumes that prejudice reflects intergroup competition for scarce resources (see also Long, 1951). Similarly, if one treats prejudice as a largely conscious, controlled, and deliberative response, then this has different implications for practical intervention than if one treats it as an implicit, uncontrolled, and automatic response (e.g., Olsen & Fazio, 2006).

Nevertheless, we want to identify some general principles that underlie the entire project of prejudice reduction, laying the foundations for the model of social change it promotes. These principles inform researchers' conception of (a) the primary agents of change, (b) the primary psychological mechanisms through which change occurs, and (c) the behavioral changes that ultimately shape broader patterns of social inequality.

Agents of change. The prejudice reduction model focuses overwhelmingly on changing the hearts and minds of members of historically advantaged groups, whose bigotry is viewed as the main cause of social problems such as racism, xenophobia, and homophobia. Whereas in the early years of the last century, the victims of social inequality and discrimination were often viewed as bringing misfortune on themselves (e.g., as a result of intellectual deficiencies), the rise of prejudice research heralded an important and progressive ideological shift (Samelson, 1978). The prejudices of the historically advantaged increasingly became viewed as the main problem that required solution. Prejudice reduction became viewed as the answer to that problem.

Underlying psychological processes. The prejudice reduction model of social change posits a series of internal cognitive and affective shifts in the mind of the bigot. The cognitive shifts enable the prejudiced person to formulate a more accurate view of social reality and relations or at least to moderate the tendency to perceive others as mere exemplars of social groups. Stereotype reduction is the best example this process of "de-biasing," which typically involves the rational correction of faulty beliefs about others (see Oakes, Haslam, & Turner (1994) for a critique of this approach). Early in the history of prejudice research, however, psychologists realized that stereotype reduction was by no means an automatic consequence of exposure to counter-stereotypic information. They found that even in the face of seemingly contradictory evidence, cognitive processes such as subtyping and confirmation bias often preserve stereotypes. They are preserved, too, by individuals' emotional investments in maintaining the differences between "us" and "them." To echo Allport's (1954) observation: "Defeated intellectually," prejudice all too often "lingers emotionally" (p. 328).

Proponents of the prejudice reduction model have thus also targeted the transformation of our reactions to others on an emotional level. Whereas the extent to which prejudice necessarily involves holding false beliefs about others is much debated, the assumption that it involves disliking them is widely shared. As such, the challenge of getting people to like one another more – or at least to hate one another less – lies at the heart of many prejudice reduction interventions. As well as tackling generalized negativity, such interventions have targeted the reduction of specific negative feelings such as anxiety and threat as well as the promotion of specific positive feelings such as empathy and forgiveness (e.g., see Pettigrew & Tropp, 2008).

Behavioral outcomes and their social and political implications. The aim of prejudice reduction interventions is not merely to get dominant group bigots to have more positive thoughts and feelings about members of other groups. If this were the case, then such interventions would have remained an interesting, but ultimately inconsequential, distraction to the project of combatting social inequality. Rather, the promise on which the voluminous prejudice literature rests is more provocative and far reaching. It posits the existence of an intimate relationship between prejudice reduction, transformations in individual behavior, and the reduction of social inequality on a broader scale.

Proponents of this model do not always make the underlying mechanisms of change transparent. Indeed, the pathway from psychological to behavioral to social change is often presumed rather than explicitly evidenced or evaluated. Nevertheless, it is possible to piece together the assumptions involved, for they underwrite the promise of psychological work on prejudice. In changing the thoughts and feelings that the advantaged harbor toward the disadvantaged, prejudice reduction is also believed to decrease the likelihood that they will actively discriminate against them in situations that matter, for example, job interviews, jury deliberations, policing, educational assessments, mortgage-lending decisions, and so on. In turn, this process is assumed to gradually erode inequality at a collective and institutional level. Closely related, by decreasing the likelihood that the historically advantaged will act in ways that defend their privileges, prejudice reduction also undermines the so-called stubborn core of resistance to social change at a societal scale (Dixon et al., 2010a). It weakens, for instance, resistance to policies such as affirmative action, educational quotas, and increased taxation of the rich. In these ways, the psychological rehabilitation of dominant group bigots is believed to mediate individual and collective behaviors that promote social change in a broader sense.

Critics have long harbored doubts about the efficacy of this model of change. They have warned of the limits of an individualistic account of the origins of systemic inequality and thus of interventions to promote change through the improvement of personal thoughts and feelings about others (Henriques et al., 1984). They have questioned, too, the extent to which we should put our faith in a model of change that relies on persuading members of advantaged groups to accept the fundamental injustice of the privileges they enjoy and then to embrace policies that progressively undermine those privileges (Reicher, 2007). Historical evidence, they have suggested, does not give much cause for optimism about the success of this strategy. All too often, power is not so much passively ceded by the advantaged as actively seized by the disadvantaged (Dixon, Levine, Reicher, & Durrheim, 2012), which brings us to our second model of social change.

Collective Action

As Owen thought of his child's future, there sprang up within him a feeling of hatred and fury against his fellow workmen. They were the enemy – those ragged-trousered philanthropists, who not only quietly submitted like so many cattle to their miserable slavery for the benefit of others, but defended it and opposed and ridiculed any suggestion of reform. They were the real oppressors – the men who spoke of themselves as "the likes of us" who, having lived in poverty all their lives, considered that what had been good enough for them was good enough for their children.

(Tressell, 1914, pp. 39–40)

As its name suggests, the collective action model of social change explains the conditions under which members of a group act together to improve their status, reduce inequality, or achieve some related group goal. Although the roots of this model of social change lie outside of psychology – notably in Marxist and socialist thought and in related sociological and historical work on mass movements – psychological motivations are central to understanding when and why collective action occurs, a theme powerfully captured in Robert Tressell's (1914) socialist novel *The Ragged-Trousered Philanthropists*. In this novel, Tressell details a young activist's passionate, and often frustrating, struggle to rouse his fellow workers to challenge class inequalities in Edwardian England. By presenting a series of extended conversations between this activist, Frank Owen, and a group of working-class laborers, Tressell explores the challenges of motivating the histori-cally disadvantaged to abandon their "philanthropic" acceptance of inequality and act together to challenge it. At its most basic level, the psychology of collective action can similarly be characterized as an attempt to understand how "ragged-trousered philanthropists" become political activists.

We should immediately add that this problem has generated far less attention than the problem of prejudice reduction within our discipline. Whereas prejudice reduction has inspired many thousands of studies and attracted millions of dollars of funding, collective action has been embraced with noticeably less enthusiasm. Indeed, it could be argued that psychologists have often treated any kind of rebellious intergroup behavior as inherently dangerous, a perspective captured in a long tradition of research on crowd psychology (Reicher, 2002). Witness the scathing indictment of mass behavior presented by Gustave Le Bon, whose work laid the foundations for modern research on deindividuation accounts of collective behavior (e.g., Zimbardo, 1969). Submerged within the mass, Le Bon (1896, pp. 55–56) observed in a notorious passage, individuals tend to display "impul-siveness, irritability, incapacity to reason, the absence of judgment and of critical spirit, the exaggeration of the sentiments and others besides – which are almost always observed in beings belonging to inferior forms of evolution – in women, savages and children, for instance."

Notwithstanding this general ideological bias against collective behavior and mass protest in particular (see also Reicher & Stott, 2011, for a more recent case study), psychologists have also provided concepts, theories, and evidence that have enabled the development of the collective action model of social change. Stouffer and colleagues' (1949) classic work on relative deprivation sheds light on a range of seemingly paradoxical findings, laying the foundations for a rich body of research on the social psychology of intergroup justice (see Walker & Pettigrew, 1984). This work showed that objective structural conditions of poverty, mistreat-ment, and disadvantage are not in themselves sufficient to explain why people perceive the social inequality as unfair. Psychological factors such as the nature of social comparisons made and the degree to which the status quo is perceived as legitimate play a crucial role. Their work helped explain why, for example, those living in the worst material circumstances in a society are often not the most dissatisfied with their lot in life.

Tajfel and Turner's (1986) social identity theory similarly advanced the field by underlining the importance of group identification as a driving force of collective action and clarifying the ideological conditions under which subordinate groups are likely to band together to challenge the social order. When group boundaries are perceived as sharply defined and impermeable, group identities salient, and the social order unstable and illegitimate, they argued, then collective action to challenge the status quo becomes more likely. Building on this general theoretical framework, several distinct but related strands of work on collective action have flourished over the past few decades. The (elaborated) social identity model of crowd behavior developed by Reicher and colleagues (Drury & Reicher, 2009; Reicher, 1982; see also Stott & Drury, 2000) and the dual pathway model of collective action theory developed by Van Zomeren and colleagues (Van Zommeren, Postmes, & Spears, 2008; Van Zomeren, Spears, Fischer, & Leach, 2004) exemplify two exciting developments in the field. Klandermans and colleagues' work on the psychology of protests and the role of politicized collective identities exemplifies another (Klandermans, 1997, 2002; Simon & Klandermans, 2001).

Our concern in this chapter is not with the details of specific theories of collective action. Rather, as in our discussion of prejudice reduction, we want to outline some general principles that inform this model of social change. These principles again specify (a) the main agents of change, (b) the main psychological mechanisms through which change occurs, and (c) the individual and collective behaviors that are presumed to alter wider patterns of social inequality.

Agents of change. Although its proponents do not deny that members of historically advantaged groups may participate in mass protest, the collective action model has generally focused on the role of the disadvantaged in promoting social change. There are at least two good reasons for this focus. First, the disadvantaged typically have less access to institutional sources of power and must therefore rely to a far greater degree on the power of mass resistance to effect change. Second, given that many social struggles are designed to undermine systems of hierarchy and privilege, the disadvantaged typically have most to gain from collective action.

Underlying psychological processes. As anticipated earlier, the collective action model of social change focuses on psychological processes that encourage individuals to recognize injustice and become motivated to do something about it. A number of key processes are consistently identified in the literature, uniting otherwise distinct theoretical traditions (see also Simon & Klandermans, 2001; Van Zommeren et al., 2008). First, a strong sense of social identity is generally agreed to be critical. When individuals perceive themselves as belonging to a common social category and feel an emotional attachment to that category, then collective action is more likely to occur. Conversely, the experience of engagement in collective action may itself lead to stronger identification with the group or even a redefinition of participants' self-definitions (cf. Drury & Reicher, 2000). Second and related, collective action is often impelled by perceptions of injustice about the treatment of a common ingroup. Of particular significance here are perceptions that arise through intergroup comparisons in which the relative social statuses of "us" and "them" are directly contrasted, fomenting what Runciman (1966) called a sense of "fraternalistic deprivation." Third, this typically leads to negative emotions such as anger, frustration, and outrage, which are arguably the most immediate predictors of participation in collective action. Fourth, such action also becomes more likely when the social order is perceived as unstable and when group members develop a sense of collective efficacy and empowerment. Again, the act of participating in mass protest can in itself be an empowering and transformative experience.

As Drury and Reicher (2009) note, when participation is "understood as instantiating one's collective identity against one's oppressors, then empowerment can develop into a virtuous cycle of broader, deeper, and more advanced resistance" (p. 722).

Behavioral outcomes and their social and political implications. Collective action can take many forms and find expression in different kinds of behaviors. The anti-apartheid struggle, for instance, was marked by mass strikes that sought to cripple the apartheid economy, marches protesting particular apartheid laws, and violent clashes with the South African police in the townships. In an especially imaginative expression of collective resistance during the 1980s, black protesters drew attention to the injustice (not to mention ridiculousness) of beach segregation by staging a campaign of occupations under the banner "All God's beaches for all God's people." In this case, mass protests took the form of picnicking on Whites-only beaches and taking rebellious dips in Whites-only seas (Durrheim & Dixon, 2001).

Research on collective action has attempted to catalog its various forms and to map its social, psychological, and political implications. Psychological work, for example, has distinguished between normative and nonnormative, violent and nonviolent, and incidental and sustained collective action (e.g., see Tausch et al., 2011). It has shown how the psychological pathways that lead to different forms of collective action may vary, even if many of the core processes are similar. Our key point here, however, is not to open up these complexities. We want to make a simpler observation. Collective action is not about getting (psychologically reformed) individuals to treat other individuals better in the hope that this may indirectly change the status quo. Rather, it is about getting members of disadvantaged communities to act together to challenge the status quo directly, that is, to become a group not only of but also for itself.

Whether or not this process is ultimately effective, of course, is a moot point, and one that its champions sometimes gloss over. Mass protests can result in violent repressions that intensify inequality and leave the disadvantaged in a deteriorating rather than improving situation. The availability of personal and collective resources, effective communication and coordination structures, the capacity to form allegiances with third parties, the political/military power and unity of opposition forces can all play a vital role in determining the success of any social struggle. Moreover, mass protest may also lead to unanticipated consequences in which, for example, the overthrow of one repressive regime creates the conditions under which another can form.

Similarly, the idea that members of disadvantaged groups who view the social order as legitimate or believe that social mobility is possible can necessarily be characterized as holding a distorted view of social reality has attracted criticism. For one thing, it disregards the fact that the disadvantaged may have sound reasons for embracing the status quo under certain conditions. For instance, an unequal social system may present short-term material benefits and opportunities that a disadvantaged community may be quite right to recognize, especially if the viable alternatives are not present. For one thing, it begs the questions of who is in a position to define objectively the nature and causes of social inequality or judge the validity of others' political beliefs. Debates surrounding the Marxist concept of ideological "false consciousness" and of the entire "dominant ideology" thesis (Abercrombie & Turner, 1978) highlight some of the complexities involved here. They also offer an intriguing, if as yet relatively unexplored, counterpoint to psychological work that emphasizes the tendency of subordinate group members to accept their own subordination.

Relationship Between the Two Models of Change

It is intuitive to presuppose that our two models of social change, prejudice reduction and collective action, inform complementary interventions to promote social change. On the one hand, prejudice reduction works by tackling the cognitive and emotional biases of members of dominant groups and, in so doing, reducing their tendency to discriminate against members of subordinate groups. On the other hand, collective action works by mobilizing the disadvantaged to challenge social inequality from the bottom up. In this way, these models of change could be seen as mutually sustaining movements within a common process of creating social justice.

In a provocative series of book chapters, however, Steve Wright and his colleagues have complicated this simple story (e.g., see Wright, 2001; Wright & Baray, 2012; Wright & Lubensky, 2009), opening up a new tradition of research on the so-called ironic (Dixon et al., 2010b) or sedative (Cakal, Hewstone, Schwar, & Heath, 2011) effects of prejudice reduction on collective action. They argue that the surface complementarity of these models belies deeper social psychological – and indeed political – tensions that may ultimately prove irreconcilable.

Prejudice reduction increases positive intergroup emotions and beliefs, while decreasing negative reactions to members of other groups. Prejudice reduction lessens the salience of intergroup boundaries and their associated social identities and thus weakens processes of intergroup comparison and differentiation. Above all, prejudice reduction fosters harmonious relations between hitherto divided and unequal communities. It does so both by correcting negative beliefs about the disadvantaged and by extending the emotional good will of the advantaged toward those who are less fortunate than themselves. Like a pebble thrown into a pond, its effects are assumed to ripple outward gently to transform intergroup relations at an institutional and collective level.

By contrast, as Table 21.1 highlights, collective action sets in motion an opposing set of social and psychological processes. Rather than diminishing intergroup comparisons and decreasing the salience of group identities, collective action typically requires the disadvantaged to identify strongly as a social group and to make intergroup comparisons that highlight social inequalities. Collective action

Table 21.1 *Two models of social change*

Model of Change	Main Agents of Change	Interventions	Psychological Processes	Behavioral Outcomes
Prejudice reduction model	Members of historically advantaged groups	Intergroup contact; cooperative interdependence; reeducation; empathy arousal	Stereotype reduction; more positive affect; decreased salience of group boundaries and identities	Reduction of individual acts of discrimination; reduction of intergroup conflict
Collective action model	Members of historically disadvantaged groups	Empowerment; consciousness raising; coalition building	Sense of injustice; collective anger; collective efficacy; increased salience of group boundaries and identities	Collective action to change the status quo

works by fostering rather than reducing ostensibly negative emotions, especially a sense of anger at the status quo, which provides the psychological impetus to act collectively. Above all, collective action works not by fostering harmony, but by enabling confrontation with existing relations of power and status: a process that typically brings the historically disadvantaged into direct conflict with representatives (or functionaries) of the historically advantaged.

These tensions between a model of change based on promoting intergroup harmony and a model of change based on promoting intergroup conflict play out not only at a psychological but also at a sociopolitical level. A growing body of research has suggested that prejudice reduction interventions may well be effective at improving the thoughts and feelings that the disadvantaged espouse toward the advantaged. However, they also reduce their tendency to acknowledge, reject, or challenge social inequality and this may have profound consequences for whether or not social change occurs (Dixon et al., 2012).

Consider, for example, emerging work on the consequences of intergroup contact (see Tropp, Mazziotta, & Wright, Chapter 20, this title) – one of the most extensively researched interventions to reduce prejudice. By increasing intergroup empathy, decreasing intergroup anxiety, and providing richer information about others, contact has been shown to improve intergroup attitudes, reduce negative stereotypes, and increase positive responses such as forgiveness and trust (see Pettigrew & Tropp, 2011, for a comprehensive review). For this reason, the contact hypothesis (Allport, 1954) has "long been considered one of psychology's most effective strategies for improving intergroup relations" (Dovidio, Gaertner, & Kawamaki, 2003, p. 5).

Mounting evidence suggests, however, that positive experiences of contact with the advantaged can have paradoxical effects on the political attitudes and collective action orientations of the disadvantaged (see Dixon et al., 2010c, for a review).

This evidence has been gathered from research conducted in the United States (Glasford & Calcagno, 2011; Tropp, Hawi, van Laar, & Levin 2012; Taush, Saguy, & Bryson, in press), South Africa (Cakal, 2011; Dixon et al., 2007, 2010b), Israel (Saguy, Tausch, Dovidio, & Pratto, 2009; Saugy & Chernyak-Hai, 2012), India (Tausch, Saguy, & Singh, 2009), and New Zealand (Sengupta & Sibley, 2013). It has used an array of research designs, types of intergroup relations, and political indicators relevant to collective action; and it has produced a broadly convergent set of findings (see also Tropp et al., Chapter 20, this title).

These findings indicate that positive intergroup contact reduces subordinate group members'

- Support for policies designed to redress inequality (e.g., Sengupta & Sibley, 2013)
- Readiness to perceive the members of the ingroup as suffering from collective discrimination (e.g., Dixon et al., 2010b)
- Feelings of anger at unjust treatment (e.g., Tausch et al., in press)
- Political solidarity with members of similarly disadvantaged groups (e.g., Glasford & Calcagno, 2011)
- Most important, willingness to participate in collective action to change social inequality (e.g., Becker et al., 2013; Cakal et al., 2011; Tropp et al., 2012; Saguy et al., 2009)

At the same time, such contact increases subordinate group members'

- Willingness to perceive the existing status hierarchy as legitimate (e.g., Saguy et al., 2009)
- Belief in the possibility of social mobility (e.g., Tausch et al., 2015)
- Readiness to perceive that members of the dominant groups will treat members of subordinate groups fairly (e.g., Saguy & Chernyak-Hai, 2012)

Explaining the pathway from positive contact to collective action, researchers such as Cakal et al. (2011), Tausch et al. (2015), Tropp et al. (2012), and Wright & Lubensky (2009) present evidence that positive interactions with the advantaged tend to reduce disadvantaged group members' perceptions of injustice, identification with the ingroup, sense that group boundaries are "closed" and that social mobility is difficult, and anger at injustice. These psychological shifts in turn reduce their willingness to support, or participate in, collective action (see also Tropp et al., Chapter 20, this title).

Of course, this process varies depending on the nature of contact experiences. Contact in which intergroup relations of power and status are explicitly flagged (Becker et al., 2013) or where encounters are negatively experienced by subordinate group members (cf. Barlow et al., 2012) may prove to be exceptions. However, given that contact interventions generally seek to promote harmonious exchanges – and that dominant group members are often motivated to keep issues of power and status off the table during intergroup encounters (Saguy & Dovidio, 2013) – the paradoxical effects of contact on minority political attitudes arguably illustrate deep-lying tensions between models of social change based on prejudice reduction and models based on collective action (see Dixon et al., 2012, for further discussion).

Echoing this idea, researchers working in other fields of inquiry have warned that exploitative intergroup relations are often characterized not by overt antipathy, but by mixed or even ostensibly positive emotions and behaviors. Jackman's (1994) sociological work has shown how many long-standing systems of intergroup inequality (e.g., gender relations in patriarchal societies) are swathed in the "coercive embrace" of paternalistic affection, which has a "shimmering allure" for members of both advantaged and disadvantaged groups alike. Similarly, emerging psychological research on benevolent sexism (Glick & Fiske, 2001), common identification (Dovidio, Gaertner, & Saguy, 2009), positive dehumanization (Haslam & Loughnan, 2012), and even intergroup helping (Durrheim, Jacobs, & Dixon, 2014; Nadler, 2002) demonstrates how negative evaluations need not underpin the problem of social inequality.

A fiortori, getting people to like one another more is not necessarily the solution (Dixon et al., 2012). Indeed, in some circumstances at least, prejudice reduction and other interventions to promote social harmony may actually make social change more difficult to achieve. As Wright and Baray (2012) emphasize:

> Although it is clear efforts to reduce rampant antipathy, overt expressions of hostility, and active denigration of other groups would need to be part of a scheme to improve many intergroup relations, it also appears reasonable to consider the limitations of a focus on prejudice reduction, and recognize that it may actually directly conflict with another important means by which positive social change occurs – collective action. Failure to recognize these limitations will very likely lead us into the trap that many members of the advantage group seem to fall into – assuming that because interpersonal interactions across groups are convivial and warm that intergroup inequalities are either gone or are acceptable. (p. 242)

Conclusion: Toward a Contextualist Resolution

William McGuire (1983) once advocated what he called a contextualist approach to social psychology (later elaborated into his perspectivist approach). Two of the guiding principles of his approach are particularly apposite to our discussion of models of social change in this chapter. First, any social psychological theory will benefit from empirical confrontation across as wide a range of contexts and everyday settings as possible. Crucially, this enables not only its falsification but also, equally important, the specification of its boundary conditions. The second principle is a corollary of the first. Social psychologists should actively seek out conditions where their theoretical models and associated hypotheses do not seem to apply; that is, where predicted effects and relationships are weaker, nonexistent, or even reversed. Increasingly, we have come to view the tensions between collective action and prejudice reduction models of social change in such contextualist terms. The resolution of these tensions will not, in our view, involve a generic denouement. Rather, it will involve careful, qualified, and contextually attuned work that appraises the social, political, and psychological opportunities – and obstacles – to social change within and across a range of social contexts. In the spirit of McGuire, we end the chapter by considering two contexts in which the efficacy of collective action and prejudice reduction interventions to promote social change might well vary.

The first context is post-apartheid South Africa, a society where the first and second authors of this chapter have conducted research for more than 20 years. Most of this research has explored the relationship between intergroup contact and attitudes toward the transformation of structures of racial inequality in the post-apartheid era. In a series of national surveys, for example, we found that Black South Africans who reported having positive contact with White South Africans tended to have more favorable intergroup attitudes (as measured on dimensions such as trust and warmth). At the same time, such contact was associated with lower levels of support for government policies designed to address inequality, such as land restitution and affirmative action (Dixon et al., 2007).

In a follow-up study, we found that positive contact with Whites was also associated with decreased acknowledgment of racial discrimination among Black South Africans (Dixon et al., 2010b). Intriguingly, we found that these effects were partly mediated by (positive) intergroup attitudes. When the disadvantaged hold positive feelings toward members of a historically advantaged group, our analysis suggested, then it becomes more difficult for them to treat the advantaged as beneficiaries of inequality. Consequently, they may be less motivated to act in ways that challenge the status quo. This may help explain why paternalistic relationships – marked by ostensibly affectionate and helpful intergroup exchanges – can play an insidious role in maintaining existing power relations in post-apartheid society (see Durrheim, Jacobs, & Dixon, 2014, for a case study).

Based on these and similar findings, we have come to question the limits of the prejudice reduction model that has dominated psychological research on social change for most of the past century. Indeed, we have contributed to emerging debates about the limits of what Wetherell and Potter (1992) once called the "prejudice problematic" (e.g., Dixon et al., 2012). We have argued that the entire project of "getting us to like one another more" is sometimes a distraction from the main struggle to achieve social inequality. Worse, by diminishing the extent to which the historically disadvantaged recognize and resist broader forms of injustice, this project may sometimes contribute to the very problem that it is trying resolve.

It is important, however, to flag the boundary conditions within which this critique of the prejudice reduction model of social change applies. Our work has focused almost exclusively on relations within a society marked by long-standing, continuing, institutionalized patterns of racial discrimination: a society where absolute and relative levels of poverty make it one of the most unequal countries on Earth. In this society, Black citizens continue to struggle for access to basic health care, education, employment, and housing; their life expectancy, health, wealth, and opportunities for social mobility are grossly diminished as a result. In this society, too, the project of creating racial harmony through prejudice reduction is, in our view, of limited relevance to the promotion of social equality, at least at the present historical juncture. Indeed, it is worth noting that many of the significant political advances achieved in South Africa over the past 25 years, including the dismantling of apartheid, have largely been the result of sustained collective action – often in the face of violent repression – by the disadvantaged and their allies. They have had little or nothing to do with the improvement of the racial attitudes and stereotypes of White South Africans.

To say this is not to claim that prejudice reduction is intrinsically flawed, however, or to deny it has value in certain circumstances. To the contrary, in circumstances where social equality has been broadly achieved, prejudice reduction can be effective in combatting some of the other legacies that affect social life in post-conflict societies. The program of work conducted by Miles Hewstone, the late Ed Cairns, and their colleagues in Northern Ireland evidences some of the potential benefits of prejudice reduction in a society where significant advances have been made in terms of the achievement of social justice, but where problems of intergroup conflict linger (e.g., Hewstone et al., 2006).

Although Northern Ireland has a long history of (sectarian) discrimination and inequality, in the years following the end of "The Troubles," much has been done to address its legacy. Major advances have been made, for example, in terms of key issues of political representation and the reform of institutions of policing and criminal justice. Moreover, although poverty and disadvantage certainly exist in Northern Ireland, they are neither as severe as the South African situation nor, crucially, are they structured so overwhelmingly along intergroup lines. Many of Northern Ireland's current problems relate to issues of fear and distrust between Protestant and Catholic communities, persistently high levels of segregation, conflict over the expression of cultural differences, and of course the ever present threat of sectarian violence. This threat creates numerous problems at the level of everyday life.

Bairner and Shirlow (2003) demonstrated, for instance, how use of public facilities designed to benefit the whole community (e.g., leisure centers) may be curtailed by fears about where they are located. Protestants are often reluctant to use facilities located in or near Catholic areas, while Catholics are similarly reluctant to use facilities located in or near Protestant areas.

In this kind of context, as Hewstone and colleagues' work demonstrates powerfully, prejudice reduction interventions such as promoting intergroup contact are of potentially vital importance (e.g., Hewstone et al., 2006; Hughes et al., 2008). They have the capacity to increase empathy and forgiveness across intergroup divisions, reduce the dehumanization of others, dampen intergroup threat and anxiety, and thus improve how individuals treat one another in everyday settings. Ultimately, as is happening in Northern Ireland, they may inform government initiatives to promote good relations and to create urban environments where citizens feel safe, trusting of one another, and able to mingle freely.

Our broader point is that the formulation "prejudice reduction versus collective action" is potentially as limiting as the presumption that the two models of change are simply compatible. The deeper challenge will be to explore how the relationship between these two models of change plays out within particular social contexts and to specify the conditions under which interventions based on these models are effective, ineffective, or even counterproductive in creating a more just society.

References

Abercrombie, N., & Turner, B. S. (1978). The dominant ideology thesis. *British Journal of Sociology, 29*, 149–170.

Adorno, T. W., Frenkel-Brunswik, E., Levinson, D. J., & Sanford, R. N. (1950). *The authoritarian personality.* New York: Harper.

Allport, G. W., & Kramer, B. M. (1946). Some roots of prejudice. *Journal of Psychology, 22*, 9–39.

Allport, G. W. (1954). *The nature of prejudice.* Garden City, NY: Doubleday.

Bairner, A., & Shirlow, P. (2003). When leisure turns to fear: Fear, mobility and ethno-sectarianism in Belfast. *Leisure Studies, 22*, 203–221.

Barlow, F. K., Paolini, S., Pedersen, A., Hornsey, M. J., Radke, H. R. M., Harwood, J., & Sibley, C. G. (2013). The contact caveat: Negative contact predicts increased prejudice more than positive contact predicts reduced prejudice. *Personality and Social Psychology Bulletin, 38*, 1629–1643.

Becker, J. C., Wright, S. C., Lubensky, M. E., & Zhou, S. (2013). Friend or ally: Whether cross-group contact undermines collective action depends on what advantaged group members say (or don't say). *Personality and Social Psychology Bulletin, 39*, 442–455.

Cakal, H., Hewstone, M., Schwar, G., & Heath, A. (2011). An investigation of the social identity model of collective action and the "sedative" effect of intergroup contact amongst Black and White students in South Africa. *British Journal of Social Psychology, 50*, 606–627.

Cherry, F. (1995). *The stubborn particulars of social psychology: Essays on the research process.* London: Routledge.

Dixon, J., Durrheim, K., & Tredoux, C. (2007). Intergroup contact and attitudes toward the principle and practice of racial equality. *Psychological Science, 18*, 867–872.

Dixon, J., Durrheim, K., Tredoux, C., Tropp, L. R., Clack, B., & Eaton, E. (2010b). A paradox of integration? Interracial contact, prejudice reduction and Black South Africans' perceptions of racial discrimination. *Journal of Social Issues, 66*, 401–416.

Dixon, J., Durrheim, K., Tredoux, C. G., Tropp, L. R., Clack, B., Eaton, L., & Quayle, M. (2010a). Challenging the stubborn core of opposition to equality: Racial contact and policy attitudes. *Political Psychology, 31*, 831–856.

Dixon, J., Levine, M., Reicher, S., & Durrheim, K. (2012). Beyond prejudice: Are negative evaluations the problem and is getting us to like one another more the solution? *Behavioral and Brain Sciences*, *35*, 411–425.

Dixon, J., Tropp, L. R., Durrheim, K., & Tredoux, C. G. (2010c). "Let them eat harmony": Prejudice reduction and the political attitudes of historically disadvantaged groups. *Current Directions in Psychological Science*, *19*, 76–80.

Dovidio, J. F. (2001). On the nature of contemporary prejudice: The third wave. *Journal of Social Issues*, *57*, 829–849.

Dovidio, J. F., & Gaertner, S. L. (2004). Aversive racism. In M. P. Zanna (Ed.), *Advances in experimental social psychology* (Vol. *36*, pp. 1–52). San Diego, CA: Academic Press.

Dovidio, J. F., Gaertner, S. L., & Kawakami, K. (2003). Intergroup contact: The past, present, and the future. *Group Processes & Intergroup Relations*, *6*, 5–21.

Dovidio, J. F., Gaertner, S. L., & Saguy, T. (2009). Commonality and the complexity of "we": Social attitudes and social change. *Personality and Social Psychology Review*, *13*, 3–20.

Drury, J. & Reicher, S. (2000). Collective action and psychological change: The emergence of new social identities. *British Journal of Social Psychology*, *39*, 579–604.

Drury, J., & Reicher, S. (2009). Collective psychological empowerment as a model of social change: Researching crowds and power. *Journal of Social Issues*, *65*, 707–725.

Durrheim, K., & Dixon, J. A. (2001). The role of place and metaphor in racial exclusion: South Africa's beaches as sites of shifting racialization. *Ethnic and Racial Studies*, *24*, 433–450.

Durrheim, K., Jacobs, N. & Dixon, J. (2014). Explaining the paradoxical effects of intergroup contact: Paternalistic relations and systems justification in domestic labour in South Africa. *International Journal of Intercultural Relations*, *41*, 150–164.

Durrheim, K., Quayle, M., & Dixon, J. (2016). Prejudice as identity performance: The struggle for the nature of prejudice. *Political Psychology*, *37*, 17–35.

Durrheim, K., Quayle, M. & Dixon, J. (forthcoming). Prejudice as identity performance: The struggle for the nature of prejudice. *Political Psychology*.

Glasford, D. E., & Calcagno, J. (2011). The conflict of harmony: Intergroup contact, commonalty and political solidarity between disadvantaged groups. *Journal of Experimental Social Psychology*, *48*, 323–328.

Glick, P., & Fiske, S. T. (2001). An ambivalent alliance: Hostile and benevolent sexism as complementary justifications for gender inequality. *American Psychologist*, *56*, 109–118.

Haslam, N., & Loughnan, S. (2012). Dehumanization and prejudice. In J. Dixon & M. Levine (Eds.), *Beyond prejudice: Extending the social psychology of intergroup conflict, inequality and social change*. Cambridge: Cambridge University Press.

Henriques, J., Hollway, W., Urwin, C., Venn, C., & Walkerdine, V. (1984). *Changing the subject*. London: Methuen.

Hewstone, M., Cairns, E., Voci, A., Hamberger, J., & Niens, U. (2006). Intergroup contact, forgiveness, and experience of "The Troubles" in Northern Ireland. *Journal of Social Issues*, *62*, 99–120.

Hughes, J., Campbell, A., Hewstone, M., & Cairns, E. (2008). What's there to fear? A comparative study of responses to the outgroup in mixed and segregated areas of Belfast. *Peace and Change*, *33*, 522–548.

Jackman, M. R. (1994). *The velvet glove: Paternalism and conflict in gender, class, and race relations*. Berkeley: University of California Press.

Klandermans, B. (1997). *The social psychology of protest*. Oxford: Blackwell.

Klandermans, B. (2002). How group identification helps to overcome the dilemma of collective action. *American Behavioral Scientist, 45*, 887–900.

Le Bon, G. (1895, trans. 1947). *The crowd: A study of the popular mind*. London: Ernest Benn.

Lippitt, R., & Radke, M. J. (1946). New trends in the investigation of prejudice. *Annals of the American Academy of Political and Social Science, 244*, 167–76.

Long, H. H. (1951). Race prejudice and social change. *American Journal of Sociology, 57*, 15–19.

McGuire, W. (1983). A contexutalist theory of knowledge: Its implications for innovation and reform in psychological research. In L. Berkowitz (Ed.), *Advances in experimental social psychology* (Vol. *16*, pp. 1–47). Thousand Oaks, CA: Academic Press.

Nadler, A. (2002). Inter-group helping relations as power relations: Helping relations as affirming or challenging inter-group hierarchy. *Journal of Social Issues, 58*, 487–503.

Oakes, P. J., Haslam, S. A., & Turner, J. C. (1994). *Stereotyping and social reality*. Oxford: Blackwell.

Olson, M. A., & Fazio, R. H. (2006). Reducing automatically-activated racial prejudice through implicit evaluative conditioning. *Personality and Social Psychology Bulletin, 32*, 421–433.

Paluck, E. L. & Green, D. P. (2009). Prejudice reduction: What works? A review and assessment of research and practice. *Annual Review of Psychology, 60*, 339–367.

Pettigrew, T. F., & Tropp, L. R. (2008). How does intergroup contact reduce prejudice? Meta-analytic tests of three mediators. *European Journal of Social Psychology, 38*, 922–934.

Pettigrew, T. F., & Tropp, L. R. (2011). *When groups meet: The dynamics of intergroup contact*. Philadelphia: Psychology Press.

Reicher, S. D. (1982). The determination of collective behavior. In H. Tajfel (Ed.), *Social identity and intergroup relations* (pp. 41–83). Cambridge: Cambridge University Press.

Reicher, S. (2002). The psychology of crowd dynamics. In M. A. Hogg & R. S. Tindale (Eds.), *Blackwell handbook of social psychology: Group processes* (pp. 182–208). Oxford: Blackwell.

Reicher, S. (2007). Rethinking the paradigm of prejudice. *South African Journal of Psychology, 37*, 820–834.

Reicher, S., & Stott, C. (2011). *Mad mobs and Englishmen: Myths and realities of the 2011 riots*. London: Robinson.

Runciman, W. G. (1966). *Relative deprivation and social justice: A study of attitudes to social inequality in twentieth-century England*. Berkeley: University of California Press.

Saenger, G. (1953). *The social psychology of prejudice*. New York: Harper.

Saguy, T., & Chernyak-Hai, L. (2012). Intergroup contact can undermine disadvantaged group members' attributions to discrimination. *Journal of Experimental Social Psychology, 48*, 714–720.

Saguy, T., & Dovidio, J. (2013). Insecure status relations shape preferences for the content of intergroup contact. *Personality and Social Psychology Bulletin, 39*, 130–142.

Saguy, T., Tausch, N., Dovidio, J., & Pratto, F. (2009). The irony of harmony: Intergroup contact can produce false expectations for equality. *Psychological Science, 20,* 14–121.

Samelson, F. (1978). From "race psychology" to "studies in prejudice": Some observations on the thematic reversal in social psychology. *Journal of the History of the Behavioral Science, 14,* 265–278.

Sengupta, N. K., & Sibley, C. G. (2013). Perpetuating one's own disadvantage: Intergroup contact enables the ideological legitimation of inequality. *Personality and Social Psychology Bulletin, 39,* 1391–1403.

Sherif, M., Harvey, O. J., White, B. J., Hood, W. R., & Sherif, C. (1961). *Intergroup conflict and cooperation: The Robber's Cave Experiment.* Norman: University of Oklahoma Press.

Simon, B., & Klandermans, B. (2001). Politicized collective identity: A social psychological analysis. *American Psychologist, 56,* 319–331.

Stott, C. J., & Drury, J. (2000) Crowds, context & identity: Dynamic categorization processes in the "poll tax riot." *Human Relations, 53,* 247–273.

Stouffer, S. A., Suchman, E. A., DeVinney, L. C., Starr, S. A., & Williams, R. M. (1949). *The American soldier: Adjustment to army life* (Vol. *1*). Princeton, NJ: Princeton University Press.

Tajfel, H., & Turner, J. C. (1986). The social identity theory of inter-group behavior. In S. Worchel & L. W. Austin (Eds.), *Psychology of intergroup relations* (pp. 7–24). Chicago: Nelson-Hall.

Tausch, N., Becker, J. C., Spears, R., Christ, O., Saab, R., Singh, P., & Siddiqui, R. N. (2011). Explaining radical group behavior: Developing emotion and efficacy routes to normative and non-normative collective action. *Journal of Personality and Social Psychology, 101,* 129-148.

Tausch, N., Saguay, T., & Bryson, J. (2015). How does intergroup contact undermine collective action among disadvantaged groups? The roles of group-based anger and individual mobility orientation. *Journal of Social Issues, 71,* 536-553.

Tausch, N., Saguy, T., & Singh, P. (2009). *Contact between Muslims and Hindus: Benefits and limitations.* Unpublished Manuscript.

Tressell, R. (1914/2005). *The ragged-trousered philanthropists.* Oxford: Oxford Classics.

Tropp, L. R., Hawi, D., van Laar, C., & Levin, S. (2012). Perceived discrimination, cross ethnic friendships and their effects on ethnic activism over time: A longitudinal investigation of three ethnic minority groups. *British Journal of Social Psychology, 51,* 257–272.

Van Zomeren, M., Spears, R., Fischer, A., & Leach, C. W. (2004). Put your money where your mouth is! Explaining collective action tendencies through group-based anger and group efficacy. *Journal of Personality and Social Psychology, 87,* 649–664.

Van Zommeren, M., Postmes, T., & Spears, R. (2008). Toward an integrative social identity model of collective action: A quantitative research synthesis of three socio-psychological perspectives. *Psychological Bulletin, 134,* 504–535.

Walker, I., & Pettigrew, T. F. (1984). Relative deprivation theory: An overview and conceptual critique. *British Journal of Social Psychology, 23,* 301–310.

Wetherell, M., & Potter, J. (1992). *Mapping the language of racism: Discourse and the legitimation of exploitation*. Hertfordshire: Harvester Wheatsheaf.

Wright, S. C. (2001). Strategic collective action: Social psychology and social change. In R. Brown & S. L. Gaertner (Eds.), *Intergroup processes: Blackwell handbook of social psychology* (Vol. *4*, pp. 409–430). Oxford: Blackwell.

Wright, S. C., & Baray, G. (2012). Models of social change in social psychology: Collective action or prejudice reduction, conflict or harmony. In J. Dixon & M. Levine (Eds.), *Beyond prejudice: Extending the social psychology of intergroup conflict, inequality and social change*. Cambridge: Cambridge University Press.

Wright, S. C., & Lubensky, M. (2009). The struggle for social equality: Collective action vs. prejudice reduction. In S. Demoulin, J. P. Leyens, & J.F. Dovidio (Eds.), *Intergroup misunderstandings: Impact of divergent social realities* (pp. 291–310). New York: Psychology Press.

Zimbardo, P. G. (1969). The human choice: Individuation, reason, and order vs. deindividuation, impulse and chaos. In W. J. Arnold & D. Levine (Eds.), *Nebraska symposium on motivation* (Vol. *17*, pp. 237–307). Lincoln: University of Nebraska Press.

22 Self-Regulation Strategies for Combatting Prejudice

Mason D. Burns, Laura Ruth M. Parker,
and Margo J. Monteith

In September 2013, police shot and killed Jonathan Ferrell as they responded to a call about a possible breaking and entering in a Charlotte, North Carolina, neighborhood (King & Stapleton, 2013). Jonathan had been in a serious car accident and sought help after escaping the car through the back window. When he approached a nearby home, the homeowner called 911 and reported that Jonathan was trying to break in. When the police arrived, Jonathan ran toward them, likely disoriented and seeking assistance for his injuries. As he approached, he was shot and killed by an officer on the scene. Why were the homeowner and police officers so quick to assume that Jonathan was dangerous? Would the evening have ended differently if Jonathan were not a young, Black man? Perhaps. The evaluations and judgments of the officers and homeowner were potentially swayed by the subtle but powerful influence of racial biases.

Despite the decline in overtly hostile and blatant forms of racial prejudice since the civil rights movement in the United States, subtle forms of bias remain widespread with pervasive consequences. Data from Project Implicit, an online demonstration website assessing people's implicit biases, shows that on average people visiting the website demonstrate significant anti-Black bias on a race implicit association task (Nosek, Banaji, & Greenwald, 2002). People also show implicit biases related to other racial groups and based on gender, religion, and age (Axt, Ebersole, & Nosek, 2014; Nosek et al., 2002). These widely held implicit biases can become activated automatically, without a person's awareness or intention, and can meaningfully influence people's evaluations and judgments. For example, as implicit racial bias increased, White doctors were less likely to treat Black patients presenting with symptoms of a heart attack with a potentially life-saving treatment to reduce blood clots (Green et al., 2007). In addition, once activated, these subtle biases can influence the people's responses regardless of their levels of explicit, consciously endorsed prejudice. Even people who sincerely endorse egalitarian beliefs and believe themselves to be non-prejudiced may possess and be swayed by subtle biases (e.g., Devine, 1989).

If these biases are widely held and influence people's thoughts, feelings, and actions, how can people combat them? Their biases may conflict with social norms and/or their internal standards. If people remain unaware that their thoughts, feelings, and behaviors are inconsistent with personal and societal standards, the bias will live on, unchallenged and unchecked. Alternatively, people may become aware of the conflict between their biased response and societal and personal egalitarian standards. In this case, awareness of the inconsistency may prompt people to attempt to self-regulate their biased responses. In this way, self-regulation has the potential to limit the influence of and ultimately reduce discriminatory outcomes.

Self-regulation involves goal setting and applying effort to achieve goals, often through the exertion of self-control (Mischel, 1996). Whether the goal is to study more or eat less, to achieve goals, individuals must regulate related thoughts and behaviors. The regulation of both implicit and explicit stereotyping and prejudice is no different. Like all forms of self-regulation, the ability to regulate stereotyping and prejudice requires the detection of discrepancies between goals and actions, the initiation of behaviors to reach a goal, assessing progress toward that goal, and adjusting behaviors accordingly (e.g., Carver & Scheier, 1990). While different self-regulatory strategies may involve some unique processes, all highlight the importance of effort, ability, and motivation.

In this chapter, we first discuss the role of motivation in the self-regulation of bias. Then, we discuss a variety of strategies for self-regulating outgroup bias and their consequences. We review strategies that involve suppressing or blocking stereotypes from the mind and the potential consequences of these strategies. We also discuss motivational and learning processes that facilitate vigilance against biases, inhibition of biases, and ultimately replacement of biases with non-prejudiced responses. Self-regulation can also involve establishing simple *if-then* statements that can be effective in reducing biased expressions. Following discussion of these self-regulation strategies, we address the consequences of people's use of self-regulation during interracial interactions, including possible costs to regulators but also advantages for the quality of interactions. Finally, we consider how interpersonal confrontations of biases may spark the self-regulation of prejudice in others.

The literature concerning the self-regulation of bias, like the broader literature on stereotyping and prejudice, is marked by an overrepresentation of research concerning Whites' bias in relation to Blacks in the United States. This is due to a variety of factors, including the pervasiveness of this type of bias both historically and contemporarily in the United States. Readers will find that empirical research summarized in this chapter likewise frequently focuses on the regulation of anti-Black bias, although certainly not exclusively. Perhaps more important, we wish to highlight that the theories and strategies relevant to self-regulation that we discuss should apply to intergroup biases broadly as long as the conditions for regulation (e.g., sufficient motivation) have been met.

Motivation to Self-Regulate

Regardless of the specific self-regulation strategy, the ability to success-fully regulate bias depends in large part on motivation to do so. However, the motivation to control prejudice is not a unitary construct that people either have or do not have. Instead, this motivation can come from external and internal sources and vary according to their strength (Plant & Devine, 1998). When motivation to regulate prejudice is primarily external, social norms, fear of disapproval from others, or other pressures from external sources drive self-regulation. However, when motivation to regulate is primarily internal, personal egalitarian beliefs and internal standards drive self-regulation. Low-prejudice individuals are often highly internally motivated to regulate prejudice because egalitarianism is personally important to them (e.g., Devine, 1989). Some people are simultaneously motivated by both external and internal sources.

Drawing from self-determination theory (e.g., Ryan & Deci, 2000), Legault and colleagues conceptualized motivation to regulate bias on a continuum from non-self-determined to self-determined (Legault, Green-Demers, Grant, & Chung, 2007). Taking a developmental approach, this view of motivation posits that individuals start with no motivation to regulate or respond without bias. This lack of motivation, labeled "amotivation," will develop into external regulation as individuals begin to feel external pressures to be egalitarian (e.g., social norms). For people with external regulation, the motivation to reduce prejudiced behaviors stems from self-presentational concerns in specific situations. Over time, individuals may begin to develop affective reactions to self-regulatory failures. Anxiety, guilt, and fear motivate these people to engage in "introjected regulation." When individuals start to value egalitarianism as an important societal norm, but before it becomes incorporated into their self-concept, they engage in "identified regulation." With the integration of egalitarian values into the self-concept, people will engage in more self-determined prejudice regulatory efforts, or "integrated regulation." Finally, when regulating bias is purely internally driven, inherently satisfying, and a core component of their self-concept, people are deemed "intrinsically motivated" to respond without bias.

Motivation to respond without prejudice affects when people will engage in self-regulation, and the effectiveness of their efforts. Because they are attuned primarily to external norms and social pressure, people with less self-determined, more external forms of motivation are more likely to engage in self-regulation only in situations where external forces are relatively strong and salient. On the other hand, people with more self-determined and internal forms of motivation are likely to engage in self-regulation more consistently, and even in the absence of external pressure, because they are driven by their personal, deeply held beliefs and standards to avoid bias (e.g., Plant & Devine, 1998). Furthermore, people with more self-determined, internal motivations to respond without prejudice may be more effective at regulating bias and its negative consequences. Self-determined motivations to regulate prejudice help individuals buffer the negative impact of intergroup threat, whereas non-self-determined motivations exacerbate the effects of intergroup threat (Legault & Green-Demers, 2012). In addition, when motivation to respond without prejudice was experimentally manipulated, individuals who read brochures emphasizing their personal autonomy in regulating prejudice reported greater self-determined motivations and lower levels of both implicit and explicit prejudice relative to individuals who read a brochure emphasizing society's expectations against prejudice (Legault et al., 2007). Devine, Plant, and Amodio (2002) likewise showed that self-reported motivations vary with the ability to control implicit as well as explicit bias.

In sum, when people have sufficient motivation, they will engage in efforts to respond without bias. Next, we examine a variety of strategies that people may use to regulate bias.

Strategies for Regulating Outgroup Bias

Stereotype Suppression

When faced with the prospect of having biased thoughts or engaging in biased actions, people may attempt to avoid bias by suppressing any stereotypic thoughts that come to mind. Unfortunately, stereotype suppression often backfires because of an ironic monitoring process in the mind (Macrae, Bodenhausen, Milne, & Jetten, 1994; Wegner, 1994). According to Wegner's (1994) model of mental control, efforts to actively avoid certain (e.g., prejudiced) thoughts require active monitoring of ongoing thought processes to detect and then suppress the unwanted content. This monitoring process subsequently primes individuals with the unwanted thoughts, unfortunately increasing their accessibility. To illustrate, Macrae and colleagues (1994) instructed participants to suppress stereotypic thoughts when writing about a day in the life of a skinhead. On a subsequent writing task, participants who had initially suppressed stereotypic thoughts provided more stereotypic comments about skinheads than participants who did not initially suppress stereotypes (Study 1). Similar effects have been obtained with behavioral measures of stereotyping (Study 2) and stereotype accessibility measures (Study 3). This ironic stereotype rebound also emerges when people self-instigate suppression rather than being explicitly instructed to suppress (Macrae, Bodenhausen, & Milne, 1998).

Despite potential pitfalls, stereotype suppression can be effective if people possess internal motivation or sufficient cognitive resources (Monteith, Sherman, & Devine, 1998). People who are internally motivated to avoid stereotyping and/or low in prejudice are less likely to experience stereotype rebound, presumably because they have practice with suppression and accessible non-biased replacements (Monteith, Spicer, & Tooman, 1998). Stereotype rebound may also be avoided among people who are less practiced at suppression if they possess sufficient cognitive resources to continue monitoring their thoughts following suppression (Gailliot, Plant, Butz, & Baumeister, 2007; Monteith, Spicer et al., 1998; Wyer, Sherman, & Stroessner, 2000).

Color Blindness

Whereas stereotype suppression involves the active avoidance of stereotypes, color blindness involves ignoring group-based differences (Goff, Jackson, Nichols, & DiLeone, 2013; Rattan & Ambady, 2013). For example, someone may claim "I don't see color; I just see people." Color blindness may appear to be an easy and straightforward way to avoid prejudice. Unfortunately, it has limited benefits and many negative consequences. Correll, Park, and Smith (2008) found that strategic color blindness reduced explicit prejudice, but only short term. Following a 20-minute delay, adopting a color-blind ideology resulted in a rebound of explicit bias. In addition, participants who adopted a color-blind ideology did not show any differences in implicit bias. Other research similarly suggests that although color blindness may result in less stereotyping (e.g., Wolsko, Park, Judd, & Wittenbrink, 2000), avoiding racial categorization may actually increase prejudice (Richeson & Nussbaum, 2004), ethnocentrism (Ryan, Hunt, Weible, Peterson, & Casas, 2007), failure to recognize discrimination (Apfelbaum, Pauker, Sommers, & Ambady, 2010), and failure to support programs aimed at discrimination amelioration (Mazzocco, Cooper, & Flint, 2012). Troublingly, strategically ignoring race can impede interracial interactions and cooperative tasks. For example, participants who adopted strategic color blindness in an interracial interaction were perceived as less friendly by Black interaction partners (Apfelbaum, Sommers, & Norton, 2008). Finally, color blindness can impair performance on cooperative tasks where the discussion of race can be useful or beneficial (Norton, Sommers, Apfelbaum, Pura, & Ariely, 2006).

In sum, although stereotype suppression and color blindness may be useful forms of prejudice regulation in some cases, these strategies are limited forms of regulation. By requiring individuals to suppress intrusive thoughts of stereotypes or race, these strategies often lead to the ironic increase of these unwanted thoughts. By focusing on preventing thoughts from entering one's mind, these strategies do not provide individuals with the tools to set long-term egalitarian goals and may fail to produce lasting change.

The Self-Regulation Model of Prejudice

The self-regulation of prejudice model (SRP; Monteith, 1993) provides an alternative self-regulatory strategy whereby individuals actively monitor their environment in order to detect and replace biased thoughts rather than simply

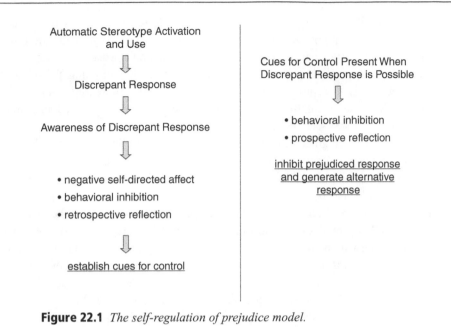

Figure 22.1 *The self-regulation of prejudice model.*

ignoring or attempting to suppress them. As shown in Figure 22.1, the SRP begins with the well-documented finding that the automatic activation and application of stereotypes are very common, even among individuals who are egalitarian minded (e.g., Banaji, Hardin, & Rothman, 1993; Bargh, Chen, & Burrows, 1996; Devine, 1989; Greenwald & Banaji, 1995). For people who value egalitarianism and wish to control prejudice because of their personal standards, reliance on stereotypes constitutes self-relevant discrepancies. Similarly, externally motivated people can experience discrepancies when their biased responses conflict with standards imposed by others (Monteith, Devine, & Zuwerink, 1993; Monteith, Mark, & Ashburn-Nardo, 2010). When individuals become aware of their discrepant responses, the SRP model outlines a series of consequences that facilitate future self-regulatory efforts.

According to the SRP, once a biased response is recognized as discrepant with one's standards, individuals experience increased negative affect. This negative affect is directed toward the self (e.g., guilt and disappointment with the self) if one's biased response conflicts with internalized personal standards and is a more generalized discomfort if the biased response violates external standards (see Higgins, 1987). In keeping with motivation and learning theories (Gray, 1982; Gray & McNaughton, 1996), awareness of a discrepant response results in the activation of the behavioral inhibition system (BIS) and in the momentary disruption of ongoing responding. When the BIS is activated, individuals pay more attention to the features of the situation related to the discrepancy, called "retrospective reflection." Taken together, these consequences of a discrepant response result in the formation of associations between the discrepancy, stimuli present, and the negative affect experienced – referred to as "cues for control." When these cues are present in future situations, they will trigger activation of the BIS. BIS activation causes behavioral inhibition and "prospective reflection," prompting a person to pay more attention to his or her ongoing thoughts and behaviors. This disruption of ongoing responding and increased attention will allow individuals to inhibit prejudiced responses before they occur and generate alternate responses.

To illustrate, imagine Andy, a White man, is walking through a crowded mall. Like many people, Andy thinks of himself as a tolerant, fair, and egalitarian person. As Andy is walking, he happens to see a Black man holding a purse. The thought, "I bet he stole that purse" automatically enters Andy's mind. Just then, he sees a woman emerge from a store, take the purse, and put it over her shoulder. Suddenly, Andy realizes that he stereotyped the Black man as a criminal. Andy might wonder why he had this negative thought. Why did he assume this man was a thief when he was just standing there? Would Andy have responded the same way if the man were White? He feels guilty, and the natural activity of the BIS causes him to momentarily pause and note stimuli in this situation (e.g., his location, what he was doing, the race of the other person). On encountering these cues in the future when a similarly biased response may occur, Andy's BIS will likely become activated, and he will be able to inhibit biased thoughts while maintaining an egalitarian mind-set.

Empirical Support for the Self-Regulation Model of Prejudice

We turn now to an examination of empirical support for each aspect of the SRP model. Central to the SRP is the idea that individuals are capable of detecting discrepancies between their biased responses and their more egalitarian standards for responding. To understand people's ability to detect discrepancies, researchers have used the Should-Would Discrepancy Questionnaire (e.g., Devine, Monteith, Zuwerink, & Elliot, 1991; Monteith et al., 1993; Monteith & Voils, 1998; Monteith & Mark, 2005). The Should-Would Discrepancy Questionnaire asks participants to rate the extent to which they *should* act in a biased way and the extent to which they *would* act in a biased way across numerous situations. For instance, participants rate the extent they *should* feel uncomfortable sitting next to a Black person on a bus and the extent to which they *would* feel uncomfortable doing so. Research using this task consistently demonstrates that many participants report that their *shoulds* are more prejudiced than their *woulds*, thus revealing discrepancies.

Importantly, people attend to and are aware of discrepancies in their everyday lives. Monteith et al., (2010) asked White participants to recall and describe past instances in which they thought about, felt about, or behaved toward Blacks in ways that they recognized were discrepant from either their personal standards or social standards. Following this interview, participants completed the Should-Would Discrepancy Questionnaire. Most participants reported discrepancy experiences (e.g., feeling afraid of Black men on the subway). In addition, the number of reported discrepancy experiences was positively related to the magnitude of scores on the questionnaire. Monteith and Voils (1998) examined whether responses on the questionnaire predict actual behaviors in situations where one might respond in a prejudiced way. White participants who had completed the questionnaire during a separate mass testing procedure were brought to the lab for a study on humor. Participants evaluated many jokes, some of which played on negative stereotypes of Blacks, while experiencing either high or low cognitive load. Low-prejudice participants who had reported larger discrepancies between their *shoulds* and *woulds* were more likely to positively evaluate racist jokes if they were under high rather than low cognitive load. However, low-prejudice participants with smaller discrepancies evaluated these same racially biased jokes unfavorably even when they were distracted. In other words, participants' self-reported ability to regulate biased responses corresponded to their actual ability to control biased responding to the racial jokes.

Such discrepancy-related findings suggest that individuals are often aware of their outgroup biases that conflict with their standards for responding. Does awareness of discrepancies give rise to affective reactions, as the SRP suggests? Prior research has consistently shown that individuals low in prejudice who experience larger discrepancies when completing the Should-Would Questionnaire subsequently report elevated levels of negative self-directed affect, relative to participants with smaller discrepancies. Importantly, this type of affect is critical for consistently motivating subsequent efforts to control prejudice (e.g., Monteith, 1993). Conversely, high-prejudice individuals who experience larger discrepancies when completing the Should-Would Questionnaire subsequently report greater general discomfort, but not greater negative self-directed affect, than their counterparts with smaller discrepancies (e.g., Devine et al., 1991; Monteith et al., 1993). Although discomfort can motivate self-regulation in some situations, it is less likely to do so as consistently as negative self-directed affect.

The discrepancy-affect link has been demonstrated in other ways as well. Fehr and Sassenberg (2010) had participants complete an Implicit Association Test (IAT) and receive feedback suggesting they held negative attitudes toward Arabs. To the extent that this IAT feedback was discrepant from the individual's self-standards, participants reported greater guilt and dissatisfaction with themselves (see also Monteith, Voils, & Ashburn-Nardo, 2001). Discrepancy-related affect has also been induced experimentally by leading participants to believe that they have made biased responses (e.g., Monteith, 1993; Monteith, Ashburn-Nardo, Voils, & Czopp, 2002). For instance, Amodio, Devine, and Harmon-Jones (2007) provided participants with fixed feedback concerning their neurological reactions in response to viewing images of White, Black, and Asian faces. Participants low in prejudice were led to believe that EEG recordings indicated negative reactions to Black faces relative to White and

Asian faces. Following this fixed feedback, participants reported greater guilt relative to baseline levels measured previously.

In addition to prompting feelings of guilt, the SRP model posits that awareness of discrepant responses prompts behavioral inhibition, or the disruption of ongoing responses. Monteith et al. (2002) gave low-prejudice, White participants fixed physiological feedback suggesting they were reacting negatively to images of Blacks. This feedback caused participants to pause briefly, taking milliseconds longer than a comparison condition to advance to the next screen. Such momentary pauses theoretically facilitate retrospective reflection, or attending closely to features of the environment associated with the discrepancy. Furthermore, this behavioral inhibition serves an important purpose, directing attention to the discrepancy and related information. When the low-prejudice participants in Monteith et al.'s (2002) investigation were asked to list their thoughts about the experiment at the end of the study, participants who believed they had negative reactions to photos of Blacks were significantly more likely to list thoughts associated with their negative feedback, their reactions to the feedback, and race-related topics than participants who believed they had negative reactions to neutral pictures (see also Monteith, 1993).

Awareness of discrepant responses leads to feelings of guilt and to behavioral inhibition; however, these outcomes alone are not enough to facilitate effective self-regulation. If Andy from our earlier example simply notices and reflects on how he behaved in a prejudiced way, he is no less likely to be biased in the future. Rather, to change his future behavior he must form associations between the discrepancy, negative affect, and features of the environment to encode cues for control. When he recognizes these relevant cues in the future, he will be able to inhibit or replace biased responses and prevent another discrepancy from occurring.

To examine the development and operation of these cues for control, Monteith (1993, Study 2) gave low-prejudice participants feedback that they were prone to subtly biased homophobic reactions. In an ostensibly separate study, these participants evaluated 12 jokes, two of which were based on stereotypes about gays. Believing that this second task was unrelated to their feedback, the participants recognized the cues they had established previously (e.g., a task dealing with stereotypes of homosexuals) and inhibited their prejudiced responses. Specifically, participants who received discrepant feedback took longer to evaluate these jokes and evaluated the jokes less favorably than participants in a control condition. In other research, low-prejudiced participants completed a race-based IAT and received bogus feedback that they were biased against Blacks (Monteith et al., 2002). In a second supposedly unrelated task, participants were presented with a series of single words and were asked to indicate whether they liked or disliked each word. Embedded among fillers were traditionally Black names that had also been used earlier in the IAT. To the extent that participants experienced guilt following IAT feedback, they took longer to evaluate the Black names (prospective reflection) and evaluated them more favorably.

The process of generating alternatives to prejudiced responses can involve replacement with non-biased responses, as in the earlier examples, or other processes. For instance, people may gather more information and individuate outgroup members (e.g., Fiske & Neuberg, 1990; Fiske, Lin, & Neuberg, 1999) or initiate positive intergroup contact (e.g., Esses & Dovidio, 2002) as a means to generating non-biased responses.

Before concluding this section, we wish to underscore that self-regulating prejudice through the steps outlined by the SRP model applies well to low-prejudice individuals who personally value egalitarianism. However, the SRP model can also apply to high-prejudice individuals who are externally motivated to control their prejudice. For instance, when White participants were led through a guided interview concerning the development of cues for control, one high-prejudice participant reported the following:

> My roommate's Black and sometimes when we're watching shows they kinda like make the Blacks look trashy, you know like on Jerry Springer . . . I was laughing at it but he wasn't really and it kind of automatically made me feel like I had done something wrong so I felt bad . . . I didn't want him to think, "Well he looks like some kind of racist."

When asked about future concern and intent to regulate, the same participant responded as follows:

> If something on TV comes up that's like shady you know it's like I think about it . . . you know I think about it to make sure that it doesn't happen again in case he actually was mad about it. I wouldn't laugh out loud if I thought maybe it would be offensive to someone else. I'm just a little more careful now. (Monteith et al., 2010)

Through external pressures such as those reported by this one participant, the SRP can help explain how individuals high in prejudice establish cues for control – albeit for external reasons.

Implementation Intentions

For people to successfully self-regulate, they must be able to recognize cues that lead to prejudice responses. On acknowledging these situational features, people can take steps to prevent themselves from falling into similar prejudiced patterns of behavior in the future. By establishing implementation intentions (Fujita, 2011; Gollwitzer, 1999; Gollwitzer & Sheeran, 2006) people form specific *if-then* plans of action to follow when they encounter a specific cue for control. In the case of regulating prejudice, an individual might form the *if-then* plan: "If I see a Black person at the mall, then I will think this person is shopping." When such implementation intentions are formed, the cues activating these statements (i.e., seeing a Black person at the mall) become more salient and the intended *then* response (i.e., assuming the person is shopping) occurs more quickly, reflexively (Gollwitzer & Brandstätter, 1997), and with less effort (Bayer, Achtziger, Gollwitzer, & Moskowitz, 2009).

As a means of regulating bias, implementation intentions can be useful by defining desired outcomes. For example, Stewart and Payne (2008) instructed participants to form the implementation intention to think "good" when they saw a Black person during a race-IAT or to think "safe" when engaging in the weapon-identification task (a task assessing implicit associations between weapons versus neutral objects with Whites and Blacks; Payne, 2001). Forming this simple implementation intention significantly reduced automatic stereotype bias on both tasks. Similarly, Mendoza, Gollwitzer, and Amodio (2010) investigated how implementation intentions affect responding on the Shooter Bias Task (Correll, Park, Judd, & Wittenbrink, 2002). The Shooter Bias Task is a computerized program whereby participants are instructed to "shoot" when an image of an armed person appears and "not shoot" when an image of an unarmed person appears. Previous research demonstrates a consistent bias whereby people incorrectly shoot unarmed Black targets more frequently than unarmed White targets (Correll et al., 2002). Participants given the implementation intention to ignore the race of the target or to focus on whether the person was armed or not made fewer errors than those without such implementation intentions (Mendoza et al., 2010).

As a result of the specificity of *if-then* statements, forming specific implementation intentions may not have generalized bias reduction effects. That is, although forming the implementation intention "If I see a Black person at the mall, I will think this person is shopping" may help in the context of a mall or shopping centers, this implementation intention may be ineffective across more diverse situations. Additionally, broader implementation intentions such as "If I see a Black person, then I will ignore this person's race" may result in ironic negative consequences (Apfelbaum et al., 2008; Apfelbaum et al., 2010; Vorauer, Gagnon, & Sasaki, 2009). Nonetheless, implementation intentions can be used effectively in conjunction with other regulatory strategies. For instance, once a cue for control has been identified, pairing this cue with an implementation intention to think carefully before responding can help slow down automatic responding and encourage people to take in more information before engaging in a behavior (Mendoza et al., 2010).

Self-Regulation, Executive Function, and Intergroup Contact

All of the self-regulation strategies discussed in this chapter require effort. Monitoring one's thoughts and behaviors, paying attention to cues in the environment, and inhibiting prejudiced responses can be taxing. Because implicit and explicit bias can affect how both Whites and Blacks experiences interracial interactions (Dovidio, Kawakami, & Gaertner, 2002), effective regulation is needed. However, cognitive depletion resulting from effortful regulation may reduce the quality of the interracial interaction. Consistent with this possibility, many of the problems Whites experience in interracial interactions stem from their desire to appear non-prejudiced, their desire to avoid offending interaction partners, and their uncertainty about the best way to achieve these positive outcomes (Apfelbaum et al., 2008; Plant, 2004; Richeson & Shelton, 2007).

Richeson and Shelton (2003) examined some of the difficulties associated with regulation during interracial interactions by measuring Whites' implicit racial attitudes (via the IAT) prior to an interaction with a White or a Black experimenter. Interestingly, Whites higher in implicit bias demonstrated more positive nonverbal behaviors toward their Black interaction partner relative to Whites lower in bias. Following the interaction, participants completed a measure of cognitive depletion. Because interracial interactions require a great deal of self-regulation among individuals higher in implicit racial bias, these participants experienced greater cognitive impairment after interacting with a Black, but not White, experimenter.

Increased regulatory efforts have also been induced experimentally through manipulating concern with appearing prejudiced. In one line of research, White participants complete a race IAT before being randomly assigned to a prejudice concern condition or a control condition (Richeson & Trawalter, 2005). Participants in the prejudice concern condition received IAT feedback telling them that "most people are more prejudiced than they think they are." Participants then interacted with either a White or Black interaction partner and completed a measure of cognitive depletion. Participants induced to be more concerned about prejudice prior to the interaction experienced greater self-regulatory demands and suffered greater cognitive depletion if they interacted with a Black partner than if they interacted with a White partner.

Though interracial interactions can be cognitively depleting, research points to a number of strategies to help reduce depletion associated with self-regulation. For instance, individuals who adopt an approach or promotion mind-set are less depleted following self-regulation relative to individuals who adopt avoidance or prevention mind-sets (Oertig et al., 2013; Trawalter & Richeson, 2006). In addition, research from the broader self-regulation literature suggests that positive affect (Tice, Baumeister, Shmeuli, & Muraven, 2007), regulatory practice (Gailliot et al., 2007), and the use of implementation intentions can reduce depletion following self-regulation (Webb & Sheeran, 2003).

Inroads to Self-Regulation: Interpersonal Confrontations

Even if individuals are motivated and able to self-regulate their biases, they may not always notice their own biased responses. By pointing out biases, interpersonal confrontations may encourage bias regulation. Czopp, Monteith, and Mark (2006) examined the self-regulatory consequences of interpersonal confrontations of prejudice. At the beginning of the study, participants generated inferences about individuals based on a single photograph and a small amount of information about the person. For example, participants saw a picture of a White man and the description "This person works with numbers." Participants then freely generated a description of this person such as "accountant" or "math teacher." Embedded within 20 photograph-description pairs were critical trials with a photograph of a Black man paired with descriptions likely to yield a stereotypic response (e.g., "This person can be found behind bars" might elicit the response "criminal" rather than a non-stereotypic alternative such as "bartender"). Then some participants were confronted about their stereotype-consistent responses. Following the confrontation, participants reported greater guilt and self-disappointment and provided significantly fewer stereotypic responses on a later stereotype inference task than non-confronted participants (Czopp et al., 2006).

Confrontations are more or less effective at reducing bias depending on the type of bias confronted and characteristics of the confronter. For instance, confrontations of racism are often effective in reducing subsequent racially biased responses. However, people may view confrontations of sexism as illegitimate or unnecessary because social norms against sexism are weaker than those against racism (Fiske & Stevens, 1993) and gender stereotypes are often perceived as positive (Czopp & Monteith, 2003). Indeed, research directly comparing confrontations of racism and sexism find that confrontations of gender bias result in less guilt, less corrective behaviors, less concern, and greater amusement relative to confrontations of racism (Czopp & Monteith, 2003; Gulker, Mark, & Monteith, 2013).

Characteristics of the confronter similarly influence the efficacy of a confrontation. For instance, while nontargets (e.g., males who confront sexism toward women) may have difficulty recognizing bias or may not feel comfortable confronting racism or sexism, these confrontations may be more effective than confrontations by target group members (Czopp & Monteith, 2003; Drury & Kaiser, 2014; Gulker et al., 2013; Rasinski & Czopp, 2010; Saunders & Senn, 2009). Because confronting sexism/racism has no apparent benefit for men/Whites, nontarget confrontations are perceived as less self-interested and more persuasive (Drury & Kaiser, 2014; Gervais & Hillard, 2014; Gulker et al., 2013).

Finally, beyond bringing to light one's own biases, confrontations also help encourage self-regulation by creating egalitarian norms and expectations of others. These norms may then help motivate individuals with egalitarian self-concepts to live up to these standards and regulate negative thoughts and behaviors in the future (e.g., Blanchard, Crandall, Brigham, & Vaughn, 1994; Blanchard, Lilly, & Vaughn, 1991; Monteith, Deneen, & Tooman, 1996).

Conclusion

As we have seen in this chapter, the accumulated evidence of people's ability to successfully regulate stereotypes and prejudice demonstrates that bias can be tamed. Although several strategies may help people regulate their bias, some strategies are more effective than others at promoting long-term reduction of bias across a variety of situations. Furthermore, people's internal and external motivations to respond without prejudice play a role in the effectiveness of their efforts to respond without bias. Self-regulation strategies can have important consequences for people's lives, as demonstrated by the reviewed literature on self-regulation and interracial interactions.

Although we believe self-regulation is an effective and useful means for reducing prejudice, it is no silver bullet. To successfully combat bias, people must first be aware of the need for self-regulation of bias. For this reason, interpersonal confrontations of prejudice are an effective way to jump-start the self-regulatory process in others. Confrontations not only increase people's awareness of their own biased responses but also decrease the likelihood that they will make the same biased response in the future. Beyond awareness of the need for self-regulation, people need to know how to implement effective strategies to achieve control, and they need to be sufficiently motivated to practice self-regulatory strategies with consistency and persistence. These factors stand between the capability for and the realization of successful self-regulation.

To the extent that subtle bias contributes to ongoing inequality and discrimination, self-regulation strategies provide useful tools for combatting both subtle bias and its pernicious consequences. Once again, the tragic death of Jonathan Ferrell has raised concerns in the eyes of the public that subtle biases may contribute to harsher and more punitive treatment of young Black men at the hands of police officers. Sadly, this is not the only event of police shootings involving Blacks where racial biases have been implicated. The deaths of Trayvon Martin, Michael Brown, Sandra Bland, and other young Black Americans have all led to greater media coverage of and public attention toward persisting racial prejudice and inequality in the United States. For example, in his piece published in the wake of Michael Brown's death, "The Science of Why Cops Shoot Young Black Men," Chris Mooney (2014) explored the role implicit bias may play in the shooting deaths of Black men and women at the hands of the police. Although retroactively determining whether race actually did play a role in these types of situations is not possible, we do know from the vast literature that intergroup biases, often subtle in nature and unintended, continue to support unequal playing fields and disparate outcomes. Efforts to raise awareness of and teach strategies for effective self-regulation are sorely needed because of the persistence of subtle bias and the potential of self-regulation to stop bias in its tracks.

References

Amodio, D. M., Devine, P. G., & Harmon-Jones, E. (2007). A dynamic model of guilt: Implications for motivation and self-regulation in the context of prejudice. *Psychological Science, 18*, 524–530.

Apfelbaum, E. P., Pauker, K., Sommers, S. R., & Ambady, N. (2010). In blind pursuit of racial equality? *Psychological Science, 21*, 157–1592.

Apfelbaum, E. P., Sommers, S. R., & Norton, M. I. (2008). Seeing race and seeming racist? Evaluating strategic colorblindness in social interaction. *Journal of Personality and Social Psychology, 95*, 918–932.

Axt, J. R., Ebersole, C. R., & Nosek, B. A. (2014). The rules of implicit evaluation by race, religion, and age. *Psychological Science, 25*, 1804–1815.

Banaji, M. R., Hardin, C., & Rothman, A. J. (1993). Implicit stereotyping in person judgment. *Journal of Personality and Social Psychology, 65*, 272–281.

Bargh, J. A., Chen, M., & Burrows, L. (1996). Automaticity of social behavior: Direct effects of trait construct and stereotype activation on action. *Journal of Personality and Social Psychology, 71*, 230–244.

Bayer, U. C., Achtziger, A., Gollwitzer, P. M., & Moskowitz, G. (2009). Responding to subliminal cues: Do if-then plans facilitate action preparation and initiation without conscious intent? *Social Cognition, 27*, 183–201.

Blanchard, F. A., Crandall, C. S., Brigham, J. C., & Vaughn, L. A. (1994). Condemning and condoning racism: A social context approach to interracial settings. *Journal of Applied Psychology, 79*, 993–997.

Blanchard, E. A., Lilly, T., & Vaughn, L. A. (1991). Reducing the expression of racial prejudice. *Psychological Science, 2*, 101–105.

Carver, C. S., & Scheier, M. F. (1990). Origins and functions of positive and negative affect: A control-process view. *Psychological Review, 97*, 19–35.

Correll, J., Park, B., Judd, C. M., & Wittenbrink, B. (2002). The police officer's dilemma: Using ethnicity to disambiguate potentially threatening individuals. *Journal of Personality and Social Psychology, 83* 1314–1329.

Correll, J., Park, B., & Smith, J. A. (2008). Colorblind and multicultural prejudice reduction strategies in high-conflict situations. *Group Processes & Intergroup Relations, 11*, 471–491.

Czopp, A. M., & Monteith, M. J. (2003). Confronting prejudice (literally): Reactions to confrontations of racial and gender bias. *Personality and Social Psychology Bulletin, 29*, 532–544.

Czopp, A. M., Monteith, M. J., & Mark, A. Y. (2006). Standing up for a change: Reducing bias through interpersonal confrontation. *Journal of Personality and Social Psychology, 90*, 784–803.

Devine, P. G. (1989). Stereotypes and prejudice: Their automatic and controlled components. *Journal of Personality and Social Psychology, 56*, 5–18.

Devine, P. G., Monteith, M. J., Zuwerink, J. R., & Elliot, A. J. (1991). Prejudice with and without compunction, *Journal of Personality and Social Psychology, 60*, 817–830.

Devine, P. G., Plant, E. A., & Amodio, D. M. (2002). The regulation of explicit and implicit race bias: The role of motivations to respond without prejudice. *Journal of Personality and Social Psychology, 85*, 835–848.

Dovidio, J. F., Kawakami, K., & Gaertner, S. L. (2002). Implicit and explicit prejudice and interracial interactions. *Journal of Personality and Social Psychology, 82*, 62–68.

Drury, B. J., & Kaiser, C. R. (2014). Allies against sexism: The role of confronting sexism. *Journal of Social Issues, 70*, 637–652.

Esses, V. M., & Dovidio, J. F. (2002). The role of emotions in determining willingness to engage in intergroup contact. *Personality and Social Psychology Bulletin, 28*, 1202–1214.

Fehr, J., & Sassenberg, K. (2010). Willing and able: How internal motivation and failure help to overcome prejudice. *Group Processes and Intergroup Relations*, *13*, 167–181.

Fiske, S. T., Lin, M., & Neuberg, S. (1999). The continuum model. In S. Chaiken & Y. Trope (Eds.), *Dual-process theories in social psychology* (pp. 231–254). New York: Guilford Press.

Fiske, S. T., & Neuberg, S. L. (1990). A continuum of impression formation, from category-based to individuating processes: Influences of information and motivation on attention and interpretation. *Advances in Experimental Social Psychology*, *23*, 1–74.

Fiske, S. T., & Stevens, L. E. (1993). What's so special about sex? Gender stereotyping and discrimination. In S. Oskamp & M. Costanzo (Eds.), Gender issues in contemporary society (Claremont Symposium on Applied Social Psychology) (Vol. *6*, pp. 173–195). Thousand Oaks, CA: Sage Publications.

Fujita, K. (2011). On conceptualizing self-control as more than the effortful inhibition of impulses. *Personality and Social Psychology Review*, *15*, 352–366.

Gailliot, M. T., Plant, E. A., Butz, D. A., & Baumeister, R. F. (2007). Increasing self-regulatory strength can reduce the depleting effect of suppressing stereotypes. *Personality and Social Psychological Bulletin*, *33*, 281–294.

Gervais, S. J., & Hillard, A. L. (2014). Confronting sexism as persuasion. Effects of a confrontation's recipient, source, message, and context. *Journal of Social Issues*, *70*, 653–667.

Goff, P. A., Jackson, M. C., Nichols, A. H., & DiLeone, B. A. L. (2013). Anything but race: Avoiding racial discourse to avoid hurting you or me. *Psychology*, *4*, 335–339.

Gollwitzer, P. M. (1999). Implementation intentions: Strong effects of simple plans. *American Psychologist*, *54*, 493–503.

Gollwitzer, P. M., & Brandstätter, V. (1997). Implementation intentions and effective goal pursuit. *Journal of Personality and Social Psychology*, *73*, 186–199.

Gollwitzer, P. M., & Sheeran, P. (2006). Implementation intentions and goal achievement: A meta-analysis of effects and processes. In M. P. Zanna (Ed.), *Advances in experimental social psychology* (pp. 60–119). San Diego, CA: Academic Press.

Gray, J. A. (1982). *The neuropsychology of anxiety: An enquiry into the functions of the septo-hippocampal system*. New York: Oxford University Press.

Gray, J. A., & McNaughton, N. (1996). The neuropsychology of anxiety: Reprise. In D. A. Hope (Ed.), *Nebraska Symposium on Motivation, 1995: Perspectives on anxiety, panic, and fear. Current theory and research in motivation* (Vol. *43*, pp. 61–134). Lincoln: University of Nebraska Press.

Green, A. R., Carney, D. R., Palling, D. J., Ngo, L. H., Raymond, K. L., Iezzoni, L. I., & Banaji, M. R. (2007). Implicit bias among physicians and its prediction of thrombolyosis decision for Black and White patients. *Journal of General Internal Medicine*, *22*, 1231–1238.

Greenwald, A. B., & Banaji, M. R. (1995). Implicit social cognition: Attitudes, self-esteem, and stereotypes, *Psychological Review*, *102*, 4–27.

Gulker, J. E., Mark, A. Y., & Monteith, M. J. (2013). Confronting prejudice: The who, what, and why of confrontation effectiveness. *Social Influence*, *8*, 280–293.

Higgins, E. T. (1987). Self-discrepancy theory: A theory relating self and affect. *Psychological Review*, *94*, 319–340.

King, J., & Stapleton, A. (2013, September 9). Charlotte police kill ex-FAMU player who may have been running to them for help, *CNN*. Retrieved from http://edition.cnn .com/2013/09/15/justice/north-carolina-police-shooting/

Legault, L., & Green-Demers, I. (2012). The protective role of self-determined prejudice regulation in the relationship between intergroup threat and prejudice. *Motivation and Emotion, 36*, 143–158.

Legault, L., Green-Demers, I., Grant, P., & Chung, J. (2007). On the self-regulation of implicit and explicit prejudice: A self-determination theory perspective. *Personality and Social Psychology Bulletin, 33*, 732–749.

Macrae, C. N., Bodenhausen, G. V., & Milne, A. B. (1998). Saying no to unwanted thoughts: Self-focus and the regulation of mental life. *Journal of Personality and Social Psychology, 74*, 578–589.

Macrae, C. N., Bodenhausen, G. V., Milne, A. B., & Jetten, J. (1994). Out of mind but back in sight: Stereotypes on the rebound. *Journal of Personality and Social Psychology, 67*, 808–817.

Mazzocco, P. J., Cooper, L. W., & Flint, M. (2012). Different shades of racial color-blindness: The role of prejudice. *Group Processes & Intergroup Relations, 15*, 167–178.

Mendoza, S. A., Gollwitzer, P. M., & Amodio, D. M. (2010). Reducing the expression of implicit stereotypes: Reflexive control through implementation intentions. *Personality and Social Psychology Bulletin, 46*, 512–523.

Mischel, W. (1996). From good intentions to willpower. In P. M. Gollwitzer & J. A. Bargh (Eds.), *The psychology of action: Linking cognition and motivation to behavior* (pp. 197–218). New York, NY: Guilford Press.

Monteith, M. J. (1993). Self-regulation of prejudiced responses: Implications for progress in prejudice reduction efforts. *Journal of Personality and Social Psychology, 65*, 469–485.

Monteith, M. J., Ashburn-Nardo, L., Voils, C. I., & Czopp, A. M. (2002). Putting the brakes on prejudice: On the development and operation of cues for control. *Journal of Personality and Social Psychology, 83*, 1029–1050.

Monteith, M. J., Deneen, N. E., & Tooman, G. D. (1996). The effect of social norm activation on the expression of opinions concerning gay men and Blacks. *Basic and Applied Social Psychology, 18*, 267–287.

Monteith, M. J., Devine, P. G., & Zuwerink, J. R. (1993). Self-directed versus other-directed affect as a consequence of prejudice-related discrepancies. *Journal of Personality and Social Psychology, 64*, 198–210.

Monteith, M. J., & Mark, A. Y. (2005). Changing one's prejudice ways: Awareness, affect, and self-regulation. *European Review of Social Psychology, 16*, 113–154.

Monteith, M. J., Mark, A.Y., & Ashburn-Nardo, L. (2010). The self-regulation of prejudice: Toward understanding its lived character. *Group Processes and Intergroup Relations, 13*, 183–200.

Monteith, M. J., Sherman, J., & Devine, P. G. (1998). Suppression as a stereotype control strategy. *Personality and Social Psychology Review, 2*, 63–82.

Monteith, M. J., Spicer, C. V., & Tooman, G. (1998). Consequences of stereotype suppression: Stereotypes on and not on the rebound. *Journal of Experimental Social Psychology, 34*, 355–377.

Monteith, M. J., & Voils, C. I. (1998). Proneness to prejudiced responses: Toward understanding the authenticity of self-reported discrepancies. *Journal of Personality and Social Psychology, 75*, 901–916.

Monteith, M. J., Voils, C. I., & Ashburn-Nardo L. (2001). Taking a look underground: Detecting, interpreting, and reacting to implicit racial biases. *Social Cognition, 19*, 365–417.

Mooney, C. (2014, December). The science of why cops shoot young Black men: And how to reform our bigoted brains. *Mother Jones.* Retrieved from www.motherjones .com/politics/2014/11/science-of-racism-prejudice

Norton, M. I., Sommers, S. R., Apfelbaum, E. P., Pura, N., & Ariely, D. (2006). Color blindness and interracial interactions: Playing the political correctness game. *Psychological Science, 17*, 949–953.

Nosek, B. A., Banaji, M. R., & Greenwald, A. G. (2002). Harvesting implicit group attitudes and beliefs from a demonstration website. *Group Dynamics and Intergroup Relations, 6*, 101–115.

Oertig, D., Schüler, J., Schnelle, J., Brandstätter, V., Roskes, M., & Elliot, A. J. (2013). Avoidance goal pursuit depletes self-regulatory resources. *Journal of Personality, 81*, 365–375.

Payne, B. K. (2001). Prejudice and perception: The role of automatic and controlled processes in misperceiving a weapon. *Journal of Personality and Social Psychology, 81*, 181–192.

Plant, E. A. (2004). Responses to interracial interactions over time. *Personality and Social Psychology Bulletin, 30*, 1458–1471.

Plant, E. A., & Devine, P. G. (1998). Internal and external motivation to respond without prejudice. *Journal of Personality and Social Psychology, 75*, 811–832.

Rasinski, H. M., & Czopp, A. M. (2010). The effect of target status on witnesses' reactions to confrontations of bias. *Basic and Applied Social Psychology, 32*, 8–16.

Rattan, A., & Ambady, N. (2013). Diversity ideologies and intergroup relations: An examination of colorblindness and multiculturalism. *European Journal of Social Psychology, 43*, 12–21.

Richeson, J. A., & Nussbaum, R. J. (2004). The impact of multiculturalism versus color-blindness on racial bias. *Journal of Experimental Social Psychology, 40*, 417–423.

Richeson, J. A., & Shelton, J. N. (2007). Negotiating interracial interactions: Costs, consequences, and possibilities. *Current Directions in Psychological Science, 16*, 316–320.

Richeson, J. A., & Shelton, J. N. (2003). When prejudice does not pay: Effects of interracial contact on executive function. *Psychological Science, 14*, 287–290.

Richeson, J. A., & Trawalter, S. (2005). Why do interracial interactions impair executive function? A resource depletion account. *Journal of Personality and Social Psychology, 88*, 934–947.

Ryan, E. L., & Deci, R. M. (2000). The "what" and "why" of goal pursuits: Human needs and self-determination of behavior. *Psychological Inquiry, 11*, 227–268.

Ryan, C. S., Hunt, J. S., Weible, J. A., Peterson, C. R., & Casas, J. F. (2007). Multicultural and colorblind ideology, stereotypes, and ethnocentrism among Black and White Americans. *Group Processes & Intergroup Relations, 10*, 617–637.

Saunders, K. A., & Senn, C. Y. (2009). Should I confront him? Men's reactions to hypothetical confrontations of peer sexual harassment. *Sex Roles*, *61*, 399–415.

Stewart, B. D., & Payne, B. K. (2008). Bringing automatic stereotyping under control: Implementation intentions as efficient means of thought control. *Personality and Social Psychology Bulletin*, *34*, 1332–1345.

Tice, D. M., Baumeister, R. F., Shmueli, D., & Muraven, M. (2007). Restoring the self: Positive affect helps improve self-regulation following ego depletion. *Journal of Experimental Social Psychology*, *43*, 379–384.

Trawalter, S., & Richeson, J. A. (2006). Regulatory focus and executive function after interracial interactions. *Journal of Experimental Social Psychology*, *42*, 406–412.

Vorauer, J. D., Gagnon, A., & Sasaki, S. J. (2009). Salient intergroup ideology and intergroup interaction. *Psychological Science*, *20*, 838–845.

Webb, T. L., & Sheeran, P. (2003). Can implementation intentions help to overcome ego-depletion? *Journal of Experimental Social Psychology*, *39*, 279–286.

Wegner, D. M. (1994). Ironic processes of mental control. *Psychological Review*, *101*, 34–52.

Wolsko, C., Park, B., Judd, C. M., & Wittenbrink, B. (2000). Framing interethnic ideology: Effects of multicultural and color-blind perspectives on judgments of groups and individuals. *Journal of Personality and Social Psychology*, *78*, 635–354.

Wyer, N. A., Sherman, J. W., & Stroessner, S. J. (2000). The roles of motivation and ability in controlling the consequences of stereotype suppression. *Personality and Social Psychology Bulletin*, *26*, 13–25.

23 Antecedents and Consequences of Evaluative Concerns Experienced During Intergroup Interaction: When and How Does Group Status Matter?

Jacquie D. Vorauer and Matthew Quesnel

Individuals often evidence substantial egocentrism by virtue of being preoccupied with themselves and how they appear to others during social interaction. For example, people overestimate the extent to which others' behavior is caused by and directed toward them personally (Zuckerman et al., 1983), perceive that others pay more attention to them than is actually the case (Gilovich, Medvec, & Savitsky, 2000), and even exaggerate others' focus on their failures and mishaps (Savitsky, Epley, & Gilovich, 2001). Such egocentric biases may sometimes seem counterintuitive, as when they lead individuals to reach overly pessimistic conclusions about how they are viewed. However, the biases are readily understandable through the lens of contemporary theories emphasizing how individuals' fundamental motivation to maintain a sense of belonging and acceptance leads them to continuously monitor their social standing with others (e.g., Leary & Downs, 1995).

Critical from an intergroup relations perspective is that individuals do not leave this motivation for social acceptance – or the egocentric biases that it fosters – behind when they enter intergroup interaction situations. Although myriad forces are of course operative in these settings, individuals' basic human desire to understand and manage their social standing with others remains very much in play.

What does this mean for intergroup relations? The information search model (Vorauer, 2006) drew on existing research and theory to make a range of predictions regarding antecedents and consequences of evaluative concerns during intergroup interaction. A key premise of the model was that these concerns could have a variety of negative implications for intergroup relations. Although at the time clear evidence supported of some of the model's propositions, other propositions were largely speculative. In the decade or so since then, research has been conducted that speaks to many of these originally untested, or sparsely tested, ideas, and more data from members of minority or lower-status groups are available now than was initially the case.

Accordingly, we review the new research and assess the extent to which the findings support versus contradict key propositions of the model. Because of space limitations, we focus on group memberships defined by ethnic background and broad themes, especially with respect to consequences. We place particular emphasis on the evidence for similarities versus differences across members of higher- and lower-status groups. We conclude by considering implications for intervention and identifying what we see as important next steps for research in this area.

Antecedents of Evaluative Concerns

What factors prompt individuals to be preoccupied with evaluative concerns in intergroup contexts? In the theoretical framework provided by the information search model, uncertainty about and importance attached to others' evaluations are both critical.

Uncertainty

According to the model, uncertainty is elevated in intergroup relative to intragroup exchanges, a function of perceived group differences, experience, and ambiguity and elevated for majority as compared to minority group members.

Is Uncertainty Elevated in Intergroup Exchanges and a Function of Perceived Group Differences, Experience, and Ambiguity? The model drew on extant research to argue that uncertainty generally tends to be higher in intergroup than intragroup interaction, and evidence consistent with this idea has continued to accumulate. For example, Avery, Richeson, Hebl, and Ambady (2009) found that under baseline conditions White individuals appeared to be more anxious in exchanges with Black than White interaction partners. Gray, Mendes, and Denny-Brown (2008) found that both White and Black individuals appeared more anxious in intergroup than intragroup interaction, although these effects were only detected by same-ethnicity observers.

The proposition that uncertainty is elevated in intergroup contexts was based in part on an assumption that uncertainty is reduced by experience, which is typically more limited in the intergroup case. And indeed, considerable evidence exists for a link between real, indirect, or imagined intergroup contact experience and reductions in self-reported intergroup anxiety (see Stephan, 2014, for a review).

Notably, however, the measures that have been used in this area have overwhelmingly tended to center on anxiety rather than uncertainty per se. Despite being related constructs, anxiety and uncertainty are distinct in that anxiety more clearly involves negative affect and for that reason should be more directly related to prejudice (see, e.g., Logan, Steel, & Hunt, 2015). Moreover, although anxiety measures have varied in terms of whether they include items tapping uncertainty, even when such items are included they focus on a broad state rather than on uncertainty about evaluation in particular.

To rectify this situation, Sakamoto (2013) conducted a series of studies focusing specifically on evaluative uncertainty, individuals' uncertainty about how they are viewed. In her most directly relevant experiment (Study 1), university students with a majority or minority ethnic background (i.e., White/European or Asian) engaged in an ostensible intergroup or intragroup interaction and then completed measures of evaluative uncertainty. A response latency measure indexed how long it took participants to indicate whether their ostensible partner in the study thought that they possessed a series of traits, with longer response times taken as reflective of greater uncertainty. An "uncertainty as a gap" measure asked participants how much they wanted to know and how much they thought they knew about their partner's impression of them and uncertainty was assessed in terms of the gap between the "want" and "know" ratings. In a confidence measure, participants estimated their partner's feelings toward them and then indicated their confidence in these judgments. Results from the response latency and confidence measures both indicated greater uncertainty in the context of intergroup as compared to intragroup exchanges, and this effect was not moderated by whether participants were majority or minority group members. There was no effect of exchange type on the uncertainty as a gap measure.

In sum, although most of the studies here have examined anxiety rather than uncertainty per se, taken as a whole the available evidence continues to be broadly consistent with the proposition that evaluative uncertainty is elevated in intergroup as compared to intragroup contexts and that intergroup contact experience reduces uncertainty. Both of these effects appear to occur for members of higher- and lower-status groups, although research examining the effects of intergroup contact on prejudice suggests stronger contact effects for majority than minority group members (e.g., Barlow, Hornsey, Thai, Sengupta, & Sibley, 2013; Tropp & Pettigrew, 2005). Whether this is also the case with respect to evaluative uncertainty is currently unclear, especially as some research suggests that the effect of intergroup friendships on feeling understood in intergroup contexts is stronger for minority as compared to majority group members (Shelton, Douglass, Garcia, Yip, & Trail, 2014; see also Mendoza-Denton & Page-Gould, 2008). Other research focusing on cross-group friendship has found that experimentally prompting such experiences reduces cortisol reactivity over time in members of higher- and lower-status groups (White and Latino/a Americans) who are high in race-based rejection sensitivity and more generally reduces anxious mood regardless of rejection sensitivity or group membership (Page-Gould, Mendoza-Denton, & Tropp, 2008; see also Davies, Tropp, Aron, Pettigrew, & Wright, 2011, for further evidence along these lines). Our review did not locate any studies specifically examining links from perceived group differences or ambiguity to uncertainty.

Is Uncertainty Elevated for Majority Group Members? If uncertainty is a negative function of experience, it follows that majority group members should experience more evaluative uncertainty than minority group members in intergroup contexts by virtue of having had less intergroup contact. In line with this proposition, several studies indicate that minority group members are less anxious than majority group members in unscripted intergroup exchanges (Avery et al., 2009) and when intergroup exchanges involve discussing race (Trawalter & Richeson, 2008), although the role of experience per se in accounting for these effects is unclear.

In the previously mentioned research by Sakamoto (2013) directly probing evaluative uncertainty, results on the "uncertainty as a gap" measure indicated that majority group members were more uncertain than minority group members, but there were no effects of group membership on the other measures. Overall, then, evidence for greater uncertainty experienced by majority as compared to minority group members in intergroup contexts is limited.

Importance

According to the model, pragmatic importance attached to outgroup members' evaluations is elevated for members of lower-status groups as compared to members of higher-status groups because of asymmetries in control over valued resources in society: For predicting and controlling their own outcomes, it is valuable for individuals to know powerful others' evaluations of them regardless of whether those evaluations are taken to heart. Self-evaluative importance centers on different domains for members of lower- versus higher-status groups as a function of perceived legitimacy of the group status difference. Specifically, when members of higher-status groups perceive their own group to be enjoying unfair advantage (low perceived legitimacy), they are predicted to view members of lower-status groups as "morality experts" who are the best judges of who is accountable or forgiven for group-based transgressions. When members of lower-status groups accept the social system as fair and legitimate (high perceived legitimacy), they are predicted to view members of higher-status groups as "competence experts" by virtue of their having the skills and characteristics necessary for success and achievement in society (Table 23.1). Evaluative concerns with a concomitant focus on morality versus competence are predicted to result.

Is Pragmatic Importance Elevated for Members of Lower-Status Groups?

Research by Lammers, Gordijn, and Otten (2008) provides indirect support for the basic idea that members of lower-status groups should attach heightened pragmatic importance to a higher-status group's perspective by virtue of its greater control of resources. These researchers found that individuals belonging to a lower-power group were more likely than those belonging to a higher-power

Table 23.1 *Predictions made by information search model (Vorauer, 2006) regarding pragmatic and self-evaluative importance attached to outgroup's perspective.*

		Lower-Status Group	Higher-Status Group
Type of Importance	Pragmatic	High	Low
	Self-Evaluative	• HIGH when perceived legitimacy of group status difference is HIGH • Focus: COMPETENCE	• HIGH when perceived legitimacy of group status difference is LOW • Focus: MORALITY

group to activate meta-stereotypes regarding the outgroup's evaluation of the ingroup and generally documented a connection between belonging to a lower-power group and trying to take outgroup members' perspective.

Does Self-Evaluative Importance Center on Different Domains for Members of Lower- versus Higher-Status Groups as a Function of Perceived Legitimacy?   Vorauer and Sakamoto (2008) directly tested the model's predictions regarding self-evaluative importance. In an initial study involving White and First Nations Canadians, participants completed a measure of the perceived legitimacy of the group status difference and then imagined an exchange with a member of one of these groups and indicated how much they cared about the other person's impression of them. Consistent with the model, results indicated that First Nations Canadians tended to assign greater importance to an outgroup as compared to an ingroup member's opinion with increasing perceived legitimacy, whereas White Canadians showed the opposite pattern. A second study replicated this pattern of effects with White and Chinese Canadians participating in an ostensibly real intergroup or intragroup exchange and dependent measures centering on evaluative concerns.

A third study again involved ostensible exchanges between White and Chinese Canadians but was modified to manipulate rather than measure perceived legitimacy of the group status difference and to include measures of perceived expertise in morality- and achievement-related domains as well as importance. The basic interactive effect of relative group status and legitimacy on importance accorded to outgroup relative to ingroup members' opinions was once again evident, more clearly establishing the causal influence of perceived legitimacy. Moreover, in line with predictions, Chinese Canadians perceived a White Canadian as a better judge of their competence than a Chinese Canadian only when legitimacy was high, and White Canadians perceived a Chinese Canadian as a better judge of their moral goodness than a White Canadian only when legitimacy was low. Also as predicted by the model, these effects on perceived expertise accounted for the effects that were evident on importance.

In a fourth and final study, the interactive effects of group status and perceived legitimacy on egocentric biases that have been linked to evaluative concerns were probed in face-to-face exchanges between White and Chinese Canadians. Results revealed that for Chinese Canadians, higher perceived legitimacy was related to exaggerating the cues reflecting negative competence evaluations that were evident in the White Canadian partner's behavior (self-as-targeting), whereas for White Canadians, lower perceived legitimacy was related to exaggerating the cues reflecting positive moral qualities conveyed by their own behavior (signal amplification). In addition, at higher levels of perceived legitimacy Chinese Canadians exaggerated their transparency with respect to competence-relevant traits, whereas at lower levels of perceived legitimacy White Canadians exaggerated their transparency with respect to morality-relevant traits.

Although Vorauer and Sakamoto's (2008) findings generally provided good support for the model's propositions regarding expertise and self-evaluative importance, there were some exceptions. First, although in Study 4 White and Chinese Canadians each evidenced egocentric bias in the particular domain that was predicted to be important to them as a function of perceived legitimacy, for Chinese Canadians the egocentrism involved exaggerating negative evaluative cues in an interaction partner's behavior, whereas for White Canadians the egocentrism involved exaggerating positive cues in their own behavior. This pattern could conceivably reflect the connection of lower power to negative affect and attention to other people's actions or Chinese Canadians' higher levels of collectivism. Regardless, the pattern suggests that the way evaluative concerns manifest in egocentric bias may vary according to group status.

Second, the results of Study 3 indicated that for White Canadians, lower perceived legitimacy was associated with perceptions of Chinese Canadians having relatively greater competence as well as moral expertise. The lack of specificity here might reflect the centrality of morality-relevant judgments to interpersonal evaluations and could indicate that the model's predictions regarding domain specificity do not hold for members of higher-status groups. However, the predicted specificity was evident for members of higher- and lower-status groups in the measures of egocentric bias in Study 4 and is also consistent with the findings of subsequent research.

Specifically, although perceived legitimacy has not typically been incorporated as a moderator variable, evidence continues to accumulate that members of higher-status groups (usually White individuals) are generally concerned with avoiding the appearance of prejudice (e.g., Crosby & Monin, 2007; Goff, Steele, & Davies, 2008; Harber, Stafford, & Kennedy, 2010; Mendes & Koslov, 2013) and that members of lower-status groups are generally concerned about potential negative evaluations of their performance in a variety of achievement domains (e.g., Taylor & Walton, 2011; Woodcock, Hernandez, Estrada, & Schultz, 2012).

In this research literature, the experiences and perceptions of members of higher- versus lower-status groups are typically examined separately, with distinct research paradigms. However, some recent work has taken a more integrative approach. For example, Shnabel, Ullrich, Nadler, Dovidio, and Aydin (2013) found that members of higher-status groups responded more positively to feedback that an outgroup member viewed them as warm, whereas members of lower-status groups responded more positively to feedback that an outgroup member viewed them as competent.

Consider also a series of studies by Bergsieker, Shelton, and Richeson (2010) probing divergent self-presentational goals pursued by White versus Black and Latino Americans during interracial interaction. Consistent with the idea that in intergroup interaction, members of higher-status groups are preoccupied with assessments of their morality whereas members of lower-status groups are preoccupied with assessments of their competence, in two initial studies involving imagined intergroup interaction Black and Latino individuals attached more importance than White individuals to being respected as opposed to liked and to appearing competent as opposed to moral; White individuals showed the opposite pattern. The differential importance attached to morality versus competence judgments by ethnic minority versus White participants was replicated in the context of real dyadic relations and face-to-face interaction and was not evident in same-race exchanges. These researchers also documented behavioral consequences of White versus ethnic minority individuals' divergent impression management goals, demonstrating that in intergroup exchanges White individuals' goals to be liked and appear moral lead them to display ingratiation behavior and that Black individuals' goals to be respected and appear competent lead them to display self-promotion behavior. Mendes and Koslov's (2013) research indicating that White individuals interacting with a Black partner exhibit more smiling and laughing relative to both their Black partners and White individuals engaged in same-race exchanges corroborate these findings.

Although Bergsieker et al.'s (2010) data focus on individuals' goals for how they want to appear to outgroup members rather than the perceived expertise of outgroup members, they are clearly consistent with the information search model's propositions regarding distinct domains of evaluative concern for members of higher- versus lower-status groups. One finding obtained by Bergsieker et al. (2010) was inconsistent with the model, however. One of their studies included 17 pairs composed of one White and one Asian individual, and for these pairs no divergent goal pattern was evident. The researchers argue that the content of group stereotypes rather than status differences per se may be critical for producing divergent goals, with the exception occurring here because Asian individuals are not stereotyped as incompetent and White individuals may be less concerned about being viewed as immoral in the context of this relationship.

It is not clear how to reconcile these findings with those obtained by Vorauer and Sakamoto (2008) with White and Chinese Canadians. Conceivably, however, Bergsieker et al.'s (2010) participants may not have perceived the overall societal group status difference between White and Asian Americans to be relevant to the groups in the actual study context, namely, students at an elite university. Determining the impact of general versus local perceived group status differences is important theoretically and also for enhancing our ability to predict the focus and intensity of individuals' intergroup evaluative concerns across different contexts.

As well, neither Shnabel et al. (2013) nor Bergsieker et al. (2010) examined the moderating role of perceived legitimacy. In two studies involving experimentally manipulated group status and status legitimacy, Siem, Von Oettingen, Mummendey, and Nadler (2013) found that members of higher-status groups had stronger social acceptance than empowerment needs particularly when legitimacy was low. This finding is broadly consistent with the information search model's predictions, although there is some slippage between the constructs of evaluative concerns and these researchers' assessment of acceptance and empowerment needs: Only the acceptance items focused on outgroup members' impressions, whereas the empowerment items focused instead on direct behavioral control. This slippage might help account for why the effects for members of lower-status groups run counter to the information search model's predictions. Specifically, Siem et al. (2013) found that for members of lower status groups, the tendency to have stronger empowerment than social acceptance needs was greater when legitimacy was low (rather than high as predicted by the model). A close look at the means suggests that this pattern was driven in part by a tendency for members of lower-status groups to report greater acceptance needs (the construct most relevant to evaluative concern) when legitimacy was high. However, this post hoc analysis is clearly speculative.

Uncertainty × Importance = Evaluative Concern

According to the information search model, individuals' evaluative concerns during intergroup interaction are a joint function of their uncertainty regarding and the importance they attach to an outgroup member's view of them. To date, this proposition has not been tested. Indeed, uncertainty and importance have been examined separately rather than together.

That said, some indirect evidence exists for links from both importance and uncertainty to evaluative concerns. The differential implications of perceived legitimacy for the importance that members of lower- versus higher-status groups attached to outgroup members' views of them in Vorauer and Sakamoto's (2008) Study 1 were directly echoed in the results for evaluative concern in Study 2 and in the egocentric biases reflective of evaluative concern that individuals exhibited during intergroup interaction in the final study.

As well, although uncertainty has not often been measured, several studies have included interventions that appear to constitute rather direct manipulations of uncertainty along with measures relevant to evaluative concerns. Avery et al. (2009) found that giving White individuals a clear interaction role to follow reduced the anxiety that they displayed nonverbally during an interaction with a Black (but not a White) partner. Richeson and Trawalter (2005) found that giving White individuals a script to follow reduced the depletion they evidenced on a Stroop color-naming task following an exchange with a Black (but not a White) confederate (an initial study linked such depletion to concern with appearing prejudiced).

Summary

The evidence currently available is consistent with the idea that evaluative uncertainty is elevated in intergroup relative to intragroup exchanges for members of both lower- and higher-status groups. The path from intergroup contact to reduced evaluative uncertainty is also supported, although there is reason to believe that the connection might be stronger for majority than minority group members for contact per se (i.e., as opposed to cross-group friendship). The evidence is equivocal as to whether majority group members generally experience higher evaluative uncertainty than minority group members. Links from perceived group differences and ambiguity of intergroup interaction to uncertainty have not been empirically established.

The predictions with respect to importance have generally been quite clearly supported. Specifically, some evidence suggests that pragmatic importance is elevated for members of lower- relative to higher-status groups. More substantial evidence indicates that for members of higher-status groups, self-evaluative importance attached to outgroup members' point of view centers on moral domains whereas for members of lower-status groups it centers on achievement domains. Some results indicate that perceived legitimacy of the group status difference is positively related to self-evaluative importance for members of lower-status groups and negatively related for members of higher-status groups, although the evidence here is not entirely consistent. Questions also remain as to the applicability of these effects across all lower-status–higher-status intergroup relations. The proposition that uncertainty and importance interact to predict evaluative concerns has not been tested, but there is indirect evidence that both uncertainty and importance feed evaluative concerns.

Consequences of Evaluative Concerns

What are the consequences of being preoccupied with evaluation in intergroup contexts? The information search model articulated a series of information search activities and attendant uncertainty reduction outcomes triggered by evaluative concerns that can have negative downstream implications for intergroup relations. Specifically, evaluative concerns can render intergroup exchanges taxing and frustrating for everyone involved by virtue of triggering inhibited and disrupted behavior that is difficult to read. The stage is then set for miscommunications, defensive reactions, and ultimately more negative attitudes.

By and large, although many gaps remain and predictors are often prejudice, rejection concerns, or anxiety rather than evaluative concerns per se, research in this area suggests that evaluative concerns have similar negative implications for lower- and higher-status group members' own experience of intergroup exchanges and for their interaction partner's experience as well.

Own Experience

In research by Sasaki and Vorauer (2010, Study 2) examining executive resource depletion, one member of an intragroup or intergroup interacting dyad was instructed to adopt an impression formation or evaluative concern mind-set prior to a 15-minute "get-acquainted" discussion. Those individuals who were prompted to adopt an evaluative concern mind-set exhibited greater executive resource depletion than those who adopted an impression formation mind-set, as assessed by scores on a Stroop task completed after the discussion. This effect was equally evident across intragroup and intergroup pairs and regardless of whether a member of a lower- (Asian Canadian) or higher-status group (White Canadian) was given the mind-set instructions.

Parallel effects have been documented with respect to stress responses such as cortisol reactivity. Trawalter, Adam, Chase-Lansdale, and Richeson (2012) found that White individuals' concerns with appearing prejudiced were positively associated with anxious behavior and cortisol reactivity during intergroup but not intragroup contact. Page-Gould et al. (2008) found that both White and Latino/a individuals' race-based rejection sensitivity was associated with increased cortisol reactivity during an initial intergroup encounter. The increased cortisol reactivity and cognitive depletion associated with evaluative concerns in intergroup interactions could have negative consequences for individuals' inhibition of stereotypes (Amodio, 2009).

Interaction Partner's Experience

In a daily diary study of roommate pairs, Shelton, West, and Trail (2010) found that for both White and ethnic minority individuals, concerns about appearing prejudiced were associated with anxious behaviors and being less liked by their roommate; this pattern was only evident in interracial roommate pairs. Along similar lines, West, Shelton, and Trail (2009) found that for both White and ethnic minority individuals, greater anxiety experienced during interactions with their roommate increased their roommate's anxiety and decreased their roommate's interest in future contact with them, again a pattern that was only evident in interracial roommate pairs. In Sasaki and Vorauer's (2010) research, individuals who adopted an evaluative concern rather than an impression formation mind-set led their interaction partner to experience greater executive resource depletion, an effect that was equally evident across intragroup and intergroup pairs and regardless of whether a member of a lower- or higher-status group was given the mind-set instructions.

Evidence from research on evaluative concerns in academic settings suggests that individuals' desire to avoid appearing prejudiced can lead to negative outcomes for members of lower-status groups in situations where honest and critical feedback is important. For example, Crosby and Monin (2007) found that concerns with avoiding prejudice led individuals to provide less useful and cautionary advice when in the role of advisor to a Black as compared with a White student looking to take on a challenging course schedule. Other studies have found similar outcomes for constructive feedback on written essays (e.g., Croft & Schmader, 2012), suggesting that members of higher-status groups concerned with avoiding appearing prejudiced may exhibit a positivity bias, overcompensating and failing to provide constructive feedback that could help enhance lower-status group members' future performance.

Other research focusing on avoidant reactions has found that for White Americans, higher external motivation to avoid prejudice is associated with looking toward but then away from Black faces, that is, showing a "vigilance-avoidance" pattern of attention indicative of anxiety and perceived threat (Richeson & Trawalter, 2008). MacInnis and Hodson (2012) found that White Canadians who were led to believe that a Black Canadian participant perceived them as biased (referred to as a personal meta-stereotype) chose to avoid interaction with the person.

Although behavior was not examined, Son and Shelton (2011) found that for Asian Americans, concerns about being stereotyped as a result of their ethnicity were related to feeling anxious and concerned about appearing competent (intelligent) during intergroup contact and a desire to avoid intergroup contact. Méndez, Gómez, and Tropp (2007) found that Spanish individuals who perceived that immigrants viewed their group negatively had less desire for contact with immigrants. In research by Kamans, Gordijn, Oldenhuis, and Otten (2009), Dutch Moroccan teenagers who had negative attitudes toward the Dutch and perceived that they were viewed through the lens of a negative meta-stereotype reported aggressive and destructive behavioral intentions toward society as a whole. Barlow, Louis, and Terry (2010) found that both Asian and European Australians who perceived Aboriginal Australians as likely to reject them reported a desire to avoid intergroup contact. Barlow, Sibley, and Hornsey (2012) found that perceiving race-based rejection predicted hostile feelings toward outgroups for both majority (White New Zealanders) and minority (Māori New Zealanders) groups. However, there were differences here as well, with intergroup anxiety serving as a mediator only for majority group members and increased ethnic identification and support for political action being associated with perceived rejection only for minority group members.

Work outside of the intergroup domain further points to potentially distinct reactions by members of lower- versus higher-status groups to perceived rejection. Çelik, Lammers, van Beest, Bekker, and Vonk (2013) found that being rejected for incompetence prompts feelings of sadness, whereas being rejected for lack of warmth prompts feelings of anger. To the extent that lower- and higher-status group members' distinct areas of evaluative concern leave them overly ready to perceive rejection as being competence- versus liking-based respectively, these individuals may then exhibit distinct affective reactions in negative or conflictual intergroup exchanges that suggest rejection. Indeed, Vorauer and Kumhyr's (2001) finding that Aboriginal Canadians paired with a higher-prejudice White Canadian partner experienced negative self-directed affect rather than negative other-directed affect is consistent with this possibility. Further, when taken together with the distinct areas of evaluative concern experienced by members of lower- versus higher-status groups, recent work by Holoien and Fiske (2013) demonstrating that when individuals seek to appear competent they downplay their warmth and vice versa suggests that when they are concerned with evaluation, members of lower-status groups might downplay their warmth in intergroup exchanges.

There is also perhaps some indication that members of lower- versus higher-status groups differ in their propensity to exhibit egocentric projection when experiencing evaluative concerns. In their first study, Holoien, Bergsieker, Shelton, and Alegre (2015) found that the more that White individuals were concerned with their cross-race roommate seeing them as kind and open minded, the more egocentric projection that they showed in their estimates of how much they understood their roommate, whereas no such relation occurred for minority (Black or Asian) individuals. Moreover, individuals' overestimation of their understanding of their roommate was associated with lower reports of relationship quality by the roommate. It is possible that if a measure more clearly related to concerns about being respected had been included, a similar connection to egocentric projection would have been evident for minority individuals as well. Nonetheless, it has to be acknowledged that to date most of the evidence for egocentric bias prompted by evaluative concerns has come from studies of members of higher-status groups.

Summary

Although operationalizations of evaluative concerns vary, research to date suggests that across members of lower- and higher-status groups such concerns have similar negative implications for individuals' own experience of intergroup exchanges and for their responses to outgroup interaction partners. That said, research from outside the intergroup domain indicates that the differential focus of these groups' concerns on competence and achievement versus morality and likability may lead to systematic divergences in affective reactions and self-presentation behaviors that have implications for their interaction partners' experiences. More research is needed on the connection of evaluative concerns to avoidant behavior and egocentric bias for members of lower-status groups.

Implications for Intervention

We now consider how research testing the information search model's propositions can inform efforts to improve intergroup relations.

Intergroup Contact

Substantial evidence indicates that intergroup contact generally renders intergroup attitudes more favorable (e.g., Pettigrew & Tropp, 2006). At the same time, in many cases evaluative concerns can pose an obstacle to positive intergroup contact effects, leading individuals to avoid intergroup exchanges and rendering the exchanges that do occur awkward and strained (see Vorauer, 2013, for a review). Moreover, the egocentric inferences prompted by evaluative concerns can reduce individuals' readiness to generalize from positive exchanges with individual outgroup members to the outgroup as a whole. For example, Vorauer (2008) found that White Canadians who were concerned with being unprejudiced drew inferences about the worthiness of their ingroup rather than about outgroup members (First Nations or Chinese Canadians) from the tenor of an intergroup exchange.

Clearly, then, any factor that serves to reduce evaluative concerns has the potential to enhance positive intergroup contact effects. By virtue of reducing uncertainty, intergroup contact experience may itself serve to reduce evaluative concerns in subsequent intergroup exchanges, such that initial experiences set the stage for improved experiences in the future and the benefits of intergroup contact are enhanced over time. In view of the aforementioned obstacles, however, factors that more directly divert individuals away from a focus on outgroup members' evaluations of them may play an important role in accelerating this process.

As suggested by Sasaki and Vorauer's (2010) research in which the mind-set that individuals adopted during intergroup contact was experimentally manipulated, instantiating an alternative mind-set centering on learning about the other person holds a great deal of promise in this regard for members of both lower- and higher-status groups. Further along these lines, Goff et al. (2008) demonstrated that instantiating a learning goal led White individuals to sit closer to Black interaction partners, and Migacheva and Tropp (2013) found that learning orientation was positively associated with comfort and interest in intergroup interaction for both White and Black Americans (see Murphy, Richeson, & Molden, 2011, for a review). In this research, learning orientation was directly invoked or measured, but as reviewed later similar types of mind-sets instantiated indirectly via salient intergroup ideology might be similarly beneficial in terms of diverting individuals away from an egocentric preoccupation with their own evaluation.

Salient Intergroup Ideology

In two studies involving ostensible and face-to-face interaction between White and Aboriginal Canadians, Vorauer, Gagnon, and Sasaki (2009) found that salient multicultural ideology prompted a focus on learning about the other person that fostered more positive behavior by members of both groups. Priming antiracism did not have any consistent effects. Salient color-blind ideology fostered a prevention orientation in White Canadians that led them to express negative affect toward their Aboriginal Canadian interaction partner. This result is consistent with research by Holoien and Shelton (2012) demonstrating that White Americans primed with color blindness as opposed to multiculturalism behave in a more prejudiced manner during intergroup exchanges and leave their ethnic minority interaction partners more depleted. Notably, although Vorauer, Gagnon, and Sasaki (2009) found effects of salient color blindness on White Canadians' behavior, they did not find that this ideology affected Aboriginal Canadians' behavior. Color blindness did seem to enhance Aboriginal Canadians' sense of identity security, but only in the ostensible interaction paradigm in which they were not confronted with a White Canadian who had also been primed with color blindness.

Color-blind ideology encourages a focus on fundamental human qualities that everyone shares and on not attending to (or even seeing) color. Whereas the first component centering on shared qualities would seem to have the potential to minimize evaluative concerns, the latter component suggesting self-monitoring and suppression of inappropriate responses instead seems apt to exacerbate them (see, e.g., Plant, Devine, & Peruche, 2010). Consistent with this idea, related approaches that emphasize similarities and common bonds without an explicit mandate to ignore group membership seem to be more reliably beneficial. For example, West, Pearson, Dovidio, Shelton, and Trail (2009) found that perceptions of common ingroup identity were beneficial in sustaining friendship between cross-race roommate dyads. This effect was evident for both White and minority individuals and partially mediated by reduced anxiety.

Focusing on individual-level perceived similarity, West, Magee, Gordon, and Gullett (2014) found that being induced to perceive similarity on self-revealing attributes peripheral to intergroup interaction has a variety of positive effects for both White and ethnic minority individuals, such as reducing anxiety, enhancing the accuracy of their perceptions of their outgroup interaction partner's relationship intentions, and improving task performance. Notably, as these authors suggest, because individuals induced to perceive similarity also believed that their partners were made aware of the similarity, reduction in individuals' concern about what their outgroup partner thought of them might have contributed to the effects that were evident for the perceived similarity manipulation.

Although no direct evidence indicates that salient multiculturalism reduces evaluative concerns, Vorauer, Gagnon, and Sasaki's (2009) finding that this ideology enhances focus on learning about an outgroup interaction partner is highly suggestive, as is research indicating that salient multiculturalism heightens reactivity to outgroup members' qualities and behavior (Vorauer & Sasaki, 2011). In light of the link between evaluative concerns and disruption of the connection between attitudes and behavior, research indicating that salient multiculturalism heightens the extent to which individuals' behavior toward outgroup members is attitude consistent (Vorauer & Sasaki, 2010) also points to a link between salient multiculturalism and reduced evaluative concerns. Indeed, as Murphy et al. (2011) suggest, reduced evaluative concerns may generally contribute to the positive effects that have been documented for approach, promotion, and learning goals in intergroup contact situations (see also Neel & Shapiro, 2012).

Empathy

Empathy is another approach to enhancing individuals' focus on and attention to others that may on the surface seem much more direct, and hence more promising, than salient multiculturalism. Research suggests, however, that although in the abstract empathy can readily foster self-other merging and concomitant positive feelings, when enacted in the context of an intergroup exchange where there is the potential for evaluation, it can backfire and be harmful rather than beneficial (see Vorauer, 2013, for a review). Stepping inside an outgroup member's shoes in the midst of interaction can lead individuals to focus on what that outgroup member thinks of them and, accordingly, to activate meta-stereotypes about how the outgroup views the ingroup (Vorauer & Sasaki, 2009) and to evidence the disrupted behavior pattern characteristic of evaluative concerns (Vorauer, Martens, & Sasaki, 2009). Specifically, drawing together the results of these several studies examining empathy in the context of intergroup exchanges, empathizing with an outgroup interaction partner leads individuals to focus on how they are evaluated by the outgroup member in reference to a meta-stereotype. Lower-prejudice individuals perceive that they will be viewed as especially open minded and tolerant (i.e., as different from "most White people") and become complacent, ultimately behaving less positively. In contrast, higher-prejudice individuals perceive that they will be viewed in terms of the meta-stereotype. They respond to this imagined criticism by engaging in draining self-regulation that results in more positive behavior, at least in the short term, but that may also prompt future avoidance of intergroup contact. They also defensively derogate the outgroup member.

Recent research has demonstrated that it is only imagine-other perspective taking, and not imagine-self perspective taking, that prompts meta-stereotype activation and interferes with drawing positive inferences about the outgroup from a favorable contact experience (Vorauer & Sasaki, 2014). The two forms of perspective taking are distinct in that imagine-self perspective taking involves individuals imagining how they themselves would feel if they were in the target's place, whereas imagine-other perspective taking involves imagining how the target feels and his or her own distinct individual viewpoint. Thus imagine-other perspective taking more directly leads individuals to a position in which they can think about the target's particular impressions of them. Notably, although imagine-self perspective taking was not harmful, it was not associated with any clear benefits either.

Taken as a whole, this research suggesting that empathy and perspective taking can increase evaluative concerns points away from encouraging this approach in actual interaction situations. However, it must be noted that all of the studies on this issue have focused on members of higher-status groups, with members of lower-status groups serving only as targets.

Summary

Although intergroup contact generally has favorable implications for intergroup attitudes and can serve to reduce uncertainty and anxiety, evaluative concerns experienced in these situations can pose an obstacle to positive intergroup contact effects. A variety of strategies designed to improve intergroup relations may serve to reduce, or ironically enhance, these concerns in intergroup interaction situations, with concomitant implications for how the exchanges unfold. Specifically, research suggests that for members of higher-status groups, encouraging empathy or perspective taking in intergroup interaction situations can backfire by virtue of enhancing evaluative concerns. In contrast, rendering multiculturalism salient may reduce such concerns by directing individuals' attention out toward their outgroup interaction partner. Encouraging approach, promotion, and learning goals may be similarly beneficial by virtue of reducing individuals' preoccupation with saying or doing the wrong thing (Murphy et al., 2011).

However, members of lower-status groups have almost always served only as targets in this research, such that the effects of the mind-sets and ideologies on their behavior are unclear. One exception is the research by Vorauer, Gagnon, and Sasaki (2009) in which various intergroup ideologies were primed in members of both lower- and higher-status groups. Multicultural ideology was similarly beneficial across both groups, whereas color blindness had negative implications for higher- but not lower-status group members' behavior. Conceivably, ideologies that directly focus on avoiding prejudice have different implications according to whether an individual's group is typically considered to be the target or perpetrator of prejudice. The implications of empathy and perspective taking for evaluative concerns seem apt to be similar across members of lower- and higher-status groups, although lower-status group members' behavioral reactions might center more on promoting their own competence than on conveying warmth. Future research with members of lower-status groups is needed before clear conclusions can be drawn on either count.

Conclusion and Future Directions

One key theme to emerge from research on evaluative concerns in intergroup interaction is that such concerns can have a variety of negative effects on individuals' affect, cognition, and behavior in such contexts irrespective of individuals' intergroup attitudes. Indeed, together with individuals' fundamental aversion to the possibility of negative evaluation, norms in contemporary Western society may over time lead such concerns to become an increasingly important predictor of negative treatment of outgroup members and contact avoidance relative to prejudiced attitudes per se (see also Finchilescu, 2010).

Research indicates that although the focus of their concerns differs, there are many parallels across members of lower- and higher-status groups in terms of how a preoccupation with evaluation can detract from the positivity of intergroup interaction experiences and behavior. However, with respect to interventions, we currently have much better insight into the approaches that exacerbate versus reduce higher-status group members' evaluative concerns than we do for members of lower-status groups. Moreover, the range of outcomes considered needs to be expanded.

Specifically, we see three gaps to be filled in research probing the implications of evaluative concerns for the efficacy of interventions to improve intergroup relations. The first is the aforementioned shortage of studies directly examining the perspective of members of lower-status groups, that is, including these individuals in studies in a role other than target.

Second, we need to identify means of implementing strategies such as empathy that minimize the activation of evaluative concerns and thus pave the way for the more beneficial potential effects of the strategies to unfold. For example, empathy may lead to more reliably positive other-focused responses when individuals have meaningful individuating information about the target of their efforts to which they can direct their attention. Antiracism messages might be more effective if they also emphasize the malleability of racial bias, which tends to foster a learning orientation (Neel & Shapiro, 2012), or if reframed in a positive manner to focus on human rights.

Third, a review of the types of dependent measures that have typically been included in studies in this area reveals a clear emphasis on positive feelings and behaviors, outcomes that are more highly valued by members of higher- than lower-status groups: Whereas members of higher-status groups place a premium on ensuring smooth and pleasant intergroup exchanges and on being liked (Bergsieker et al., 2010), members of lower-status groups are relatively more focused on enhancing their power and control (Saguy, Dovidio, & Pratto, 2008). The question thus arises as to how evaluative concerns affect outcomes of importance to members of lower-status groups such as feeling respected, exerting power, and having a voice – outcomes that may prove more important to social change and reconciliation processes than positive intergroup evaluations

(Dixon, Tropp, Durrheim, & Tredoux, 2010; Shnabel, Nadler, Ullrich, Dovidio, & Carmi, 2009).

Although evaluative concerns involve attending to others' behavior in a manner typically associated with lower power, the situation is potentially complicated by the content of the meta-stereotypes that are activated. Specifically, for members of higher-status groups concerns with evaluation are in fact directly tied to the high-power position of their group (especially if that elevated position is seen as illegitimate), such that the net effect on power-relevant affect, cognition, and behavior is unclear. In contrast, for members of lower-status groups there is a "double whammy" of sorts given that these individuals' evaluative concerns are tied to the lower-power position of their group, such that their concerns may be accompanied by activation of meta-stereotypes about ineffectiveness and incompetence. Coupled with the value that members of lower-status groups attach to power-relevant outcomes, evaluative concerns may be particularly detrimental to them in this respect. The information search model did not directly address power-relevant outcomes. However, learning more about how various intergroup interventions affect power-relevant outcomes and the role played by evaluative concerns in accounting for these effects are pressing goals for future research.

References

Amodio, D. M. (2009). Intergroup anxiety effects on the control of racial stereotypes: A psychoneuroendocrine analysis. *Journal of Experimental Social Psychology*, *45*(1), 60–67.

Avery, D. R., Richeson, J. A., Hebl, M. R., & Ambady, N. (2009). It does not have to be uncomfortable: The role of behavioral scripts in Black–White interracial interactions. *Journal of Applied Psychology*, *94*(6), 1382.

Barlow, F. K., Hornsey, M. J., Thai, M., Sengupta, N. K., & Sibley, C. G. (2013). The wallpaper effect: The contact hypothesis fails for minority group members who live in areas with a high proportion of majority group members. *PloS One, 8* (12), e82228.

Barlow, F. K., Louis, W. R., & Terry, D. J. (2010). Minority report: Social identity, cognitions of rejection and intergroup anxiety predicting prejudice from one racially marginalized group towards another. *European Journal of Social Psychology*, *40*(5), 805–818. Retrieved from http://search.proquest.com/doc view/754051612?accountid=14569

Barlow, F. K., Sibley, C. G., & Hornsey, M. J. (2012). Rejection as a call to arms: Inter-racial hostility and support for political action as outcomes of race-based rejection in majority and minority groups. *British Journal of Social Psychology*, *51*(1), 167–177. doi: http://dx.doi.org/10.1111/j.2044-8309.2011.02040.x

Bergsieker, H. B., Shelton, J. N., & Richeson, J. A. (2010). To be liked versus respected: Divergent goals in interracial interactions. *Journal of Personality and Social Psychology*, *99*(2), 248–264. doi: http://dx.doi.org/10.1037/a0018474

Çelik, P., Lammers, J., van Beest, I., Bekker, M. H. J., & Vonk, R. (2013). Not all rejections are alike; competence and warmth as a fundamental distinction in social rejection. *Journal of Experimental Social Psychology, 49*(4), 635–642. doi: http://dx.doi .org/10.1016/j.jesp.2013.02.010

Croft, A., & Schmader, T. (2012). The feedback withholding bias: Minority students do not receive critical feedback from evaluators concerned about appearing racist. *Journal of Experimental Social Psychology, 48*(5), 1139–1144.

Crosby, J. R., & Monin, B. (2007). Failure to warn: How student race affects warnings of potential academic difficulty. *Journal of Experimental Social Psychology, 43*(4), 663–670. doi: http://dx.doi.org/10.1016/j.jesp.2006.06.007

Davies, K., Tropp, L. R., Aron, A., Pettigrew, T. F., & Wright, S. C. (2011). Cross-group friendships and intergroup attitudes: A meta-analytic review. *Personality and Social Psychology Review, 15*(4), 332–351. doi: http://dx.doi.org/10.1177/ 1088868311411103

Dixon, J., Tropp, L. R., Durrheim, K., & Tredoux, C. (2010). "Let them eat harmony": Prejudice-reduction strategies and attitudes of historically disadvantaged groups. *Current Directions in Psychological Science, 19*(2), 76–80. doi: http://dx.doi.org/ 10.1177/0963721410363366

Finchilescu, G. (2010). Intergroup anxiety in interracial interaction: The role of prejudice and metastereotypes. *Journal of Social Issues, 66*, 334–351. doi: 10.1111/j.1540-4560.2010.01648.x

Gilovich, T., Medvec, V. H., & Savitsky, K. (2000). The spotlight effect in social judgment: an egocentric bias in estimates of the salience of one's own actions and appearance. *Journal of personality and social psychology, 78*(2), 211.

Goff, P. A., Steele, C. M., & Davies, P. G. (2008). The space between us: Stereotype threat and distance in interracial contexts. *Journal of Personality and Social Psychology, 94*(1), 91–107. doi: http://dx.doi.org.uml.idm.oclc.org/10.1037/0022-3514.94.1.91

Gray, H. M., Mendes, W. B., & Denny-Brown, C. (2008). An in-group advantage in detecting intergroup anxiety. *Psychological Science, 19*(12), 1233–1237. doi: http://dx.doi.org/10.1111/j.1467-9280.2008.02230.x

Harber, K. D., Stafford, R., & Kennedy, K. A. (2010). The positive feedback bias as a response to self-image threat. *British Journal of Social Psychology, 49*(1), 207–218. doi: http://dx.doi.org/10.1348/014466609X473956

Holoien, D. S., Bergsieker, H. B., Shelton, J. N., & Alegre, J. M. (2015). Do you really understand? achieving accuracy in interracial relationships. *Journal of Personality and Social Psychology, 108*(1), 76–92. doi: http://dx.doi.org/10.1037/pspi0000003

Holoien, D. S., & Fiske, S. T. (2013). Downplaying positive impressions: Compensation between warmth and competence in impression management. *Journal of Experimental Social Psychology, 49*(1), 33–41. doi: http://dx.doi.org/10.1016/j.je sp.2012.09.001

Holoien, D. S., & Shelton, J. N. (2012). You deplete me: The cognitive costs of color-blindness on ethnic minorities. *Journal of Experimental Social Psychology, 48*(2), 562–565. doi: http://dx.doi.org/10.1016/j.jesp.2011.09.010

Kamans, E., Gordijn, E. H., Oldenhuis, H., & Otten, S. (2009). What I think you see is what you get: Influence of prejudice on assimilation to negative meta-stereotypes among Dutch Moroccan teenagers. *European Journal of Social Psychology, 39*(5), 842–851. doi: http://dx.doi.org/10.1002/ejsp.593

Leary, M. R., & Downs, D. L. (1995). Interpersonal functions of the self-esteem motive: The self-esteem system as a sociometer. In M. R. Leary & J. P. Tangney (Eds.), *Efficacy, agency, and self-esteem* (pp. 123–144). New York: Plenum Press.

Logan, S., Steel, Z., & Hunt, C. (2015). Investigating the effect of anxiety, uncertainty and ethnocentrism on willingness to interact in an intercultural communication. *Journal of Cross-Cultural Psychology, 46*(1), 39–52. doi: http://dx.doi.org/ 10.1177/0022022114555762

MacInnis, C., & Hodson, G. (2012). "Where the rubber hits the road" en route to inter-group harmony: Examining contact intentions and contact behaviour under meta-stereotype threat. *British Journal of Social Psychology, 51*(2), 363–373. doi: http://dx.doi.org/10.1111/j.2044-8309.2010.02014.x

Mendes, W. B., & Koslov, K. (2013). Brittle smiles: Positive biases toward stigmatized and outgroup targets. *Journal of Experimental Psychology: General, 142*(3), 923–933. doi: http://dx.doi.org/10.1037/a0029663

Méndez, E., Gómez, Á., & Tropp, L. R. (2007). When metaperceptions are affected by intergroup processes. *International Journal of Psychology & Psychological Therapy, 7*(2), 237–250. Retrieved from http://search.proquest.com/docview/ 621845460?accountid=14569

Mendoza-Denton, R., & Page-Gould, E. (2008). Can cross-group friendships influence minority students' well-being at historically white universities? *Psychological Science, 19*(9), 933–939. doi: http://dx.doi.org/10.1111/j.1467-9280.2008.02179.x

Migacheva, K., & Tropp, L. R. (2013). Learning orientation as a predictor of positive intergroup contact. *Group Processes & Intergroup Relations, 16*(4), 426–444. Retrieved from http://search.proquest.com/docview/1449308269?accountid=14569

Murphy, M. C., Richeson, J. A., & Molden, D. C. (2011). Leveraging motivational mindsets to foster positive interracial interactions. *Social and Personality Psychology Compass, 5*(2), 118–131. doi: http://dx.doi.org/10.1111/j.1751-9004.2010.00338.x

Neel, R., & Shapiro, J. R. (2012). Is racial bias malleable? Whites' lay theories of racial bias predict divergent strategies for interracial interactions. *Journal of Personality and Social Psychology, 103*, 101–120. Retrieved from http://dx.doi.org/10.1037/ a0028237

Page-Gould, E., Mendoza-Denton, R., & Tropp, L. R. (2008). With a little help from my cross-group friend: Reducing anxiety in intergroup contexts through cross-group friendship. *Journal of Personality and Social Psychology, 95*(5), 1080–1094. doi: http://dx.doi.org/10.1037/0022-3514.95.5.1080

Pettigrew, T. F., & Tropp, L. R. (2006). A meta-analytic test of intergroup contact theory. *Journal of Personality and Social Psychology, 90*(5), 751–783. doi: http://dx.doi .org/10.1037/0022-3514.90.5.751

Plant, E. A., Devine, P. G., & Peruche, M. B. (2010). Routes to positive interracial interactions: Approaching egalitarianism or avoiding prejudice. *Personality and Social Psychology Bulletin, 36*(9), 1135–1147. doi: http://dx.doi.org/10.1177/ 0146167210378018

Richeson, J. A., & Trawalter, S. (2005). Why do interracial interactions impair executive function? A resource depletion account. *Journal of Personality and Social Psychology, 88*(6), 934–947. doi: http://dx.doi.org/10.1037/0022-3514.88.6.934

Richeson, J. A., & Trawalter, S. (2008). The threat of appearing prejudiced and race-based attentional biases. *Psychological Science*, *19*(2), 98–102. doi: http://dx.doi.org/10.1111/j.1467-9280.2008.02052.x

Saguy, T., Dovidio, J. F., & Pratto, F. (2008). Beyond contact: Intergroup contact in the context of power relations. *Personality and Social Psychology Bulletin*, *34*, 432–445.

Sakamoto, Y. (2013). *Does she hate me? or does she like me? Evaluative uncertainty during intergroup contact* (Order No. AAINR78916). Available from PsycINFO. (1449320007; 2013-99200-277). Retrieved from http://search.proquest.com/docview/1449320007?accountid=14569

Sasaki, S. J., & Vorauer, J. D. (2010). Contagious resource depletion and anxiety? Spreading effects of evaluative concern and impression formation in dyadic social interaction. *Journal of Experimental Social Psychology*, *46*(6), 1011–1016. doi: http://dx.doi.org/10.1016/j.jesp.2010.07.003

Savitsky, K., Epley, N., & Gilovich, T. (2001). Do others judge us as harshly as we think? Overestimating the impact of our failures, shortcomings, and mishaps. *Journal of Personality and Social Psychology*, *81*(1), 44.

Shnabel, N., Nadler, A., Ullrich, J., Dovidio, J. F., & Carmi, D. (2009). Promoting reconciliation through the satisfaction of the emotional needs of victimized and perpetrating group members: The needs-based model of reconciliation. *Personality and Social Psychology Bulletin*, *35*(8), 1021–1030.

Shnabel, N., Ullrich, J., Nadler, A., Dovidio, J. F., & Aydin, A. L. (2013). Warm or competent? Improving intergroup relations by addressing threatened identities of advantaged and disadvantaged groups. *European Journal of Social Psychology*, *43*(6), 482–492. Retrieved from http://search.proquest.com/docview/1519507478?accountid=14569

Shelton, N., Douglass, S., Garcia, R. L., Yip, T., & Trail, T. E. (2014). Feeling (mis) understood and intergroup friendships in interracial interactions. *Personality and Social Psychology Bulletin*, *40*(9), 1193–1204. doi: http://dx.doi.org/10.1177/0146167214538459

Shelton, J. N., West, T. V., & Trail, T. E. (2010). Concerns about appearing prejudiced: Implications for anxiety during daily interracial interactions. *Group Processes & Intergroup Relations*, *13*(3), 329–344. doi: http://dx.doi.org/10.1177/1368430209344869

Siem, B., Von Oettingen, M., Mummendey, A., & Nadler, A. (2013). When status differences are illegitimate, groups' needs diverge: Testing the needs-based model of reconciliation in contexts of status inequality. *European Journal of Social Psychology*, *43*(2), 137–148. doi: http://dx.doi.org/10.1002/ejsp.1929

Son, D., & Shelton, J. N. (2011). Stigma consciousness among Asian Americans: Impact of positive stereotypes in interracial roommate relationships. *Asian American Journal of Psychology*, *2*(1), 51–60. doi: http://dx.doi.org/10.1037/a0022651

Stephan, W. G. (2014). Intergroup anxiety: Theory, research, and practice. *Personality and Social Psychology Review*, *18*(3), 239–255. doi: http://dx.doi.org/10.1177/1088868314530518

Taylor, V. J., & Walton, G. M. (2011). Stereotype threat undermines academic learning. *Personality and Social Psychology Bulletin*, *37*(8), 1055–1067. doi: http://dx.doi.org/10.1177/0146167211406506

Trawalter, S., Adam, E. K., Chase-Lansdale, P., & Richeson, J. A. (2012). Concerns about appearing prejudiced get under the skin: Stress responses to interracial contact in the moment and across time. *Journal of Experimental Social Psychology, 48*(3), 682–693. doi: http://dx.doi.org/10.1016/j.jesp.2011.12.003

Trawalter, S., & Richeson, J. A. (2008). Let's talk about race, baby! When Whites' and Blacks' interracial contact experiences diverge. *Journal of Experimental Social Psychology, 44*(4), 1214–1217. doi: http://dx.doi.org/10.1016/j.jesp.2008.03.013

Tropp, L. R., & Pettigrew, T. F. (2005). Relationships between intergroup contact and prejudice among minority and majority status groups. *Psychological Science, 16* (12), 951–957. doi: http://dx.doi.org/10.1111/j.1467-9280.2005.01643.x

Vorauer, J. D. (2006). An information search model of evaluative concerns in intergroup interaction. *Psychological Review, 113*(4), 862.

Vorauer, J. (2008). Unprejudiced and self-focused: When intergroup contact is experienced as being about the ingroup rather than the outgroup. *Journal of Experimental Social Psychology, 44*(3), 912–919. doi: http://dx.doi.org/10.1016/j.jesp.2007.10.002

Vorauer, J. D. (2013). Getting past the self: Understanding and removing evaluative concerns as an obstacle to positive intergroup contact effects. In M. R. Leary & J. P. Tangney (Eds.), *Advances in intergroup contact* (pp. 23–48). New York: Psychology Press.

Vorauer, J. D., Gagnon, A., & Sasaki, S. J. (2009). Salient intergroup ideology and intergroup interaction. *Psychological Science, 20*(7), 838–845. doi: http://dx.doi.org/10.1111/j.1467-9280.2009.02369.x

Vorauer, J., & Kumhyr, S. M. (2001). Is this about you or me? Self- versus other-directed judgments and feelings in response to intergroup interaction. *Personality and Social Psychology Bulletin, 27*(6), 706–719. doi: http://dx.doi.org/10.1177/0146167201276006

Vorauer, J. D., Martens, V., & Sasaki, S. J. (2009). When trying to understand detracts from trying to behave: Effects of perspective taking in intergroup interaction. *Journal of Personality and Social Psychology, 96*(4), 811–827. doi: http://dx.doi.org/10.1037/a0013411

Vorauer, J. D., & Sakamoto, Y. (2008). Who cares what the outgroup thinks? Testing an information search model of the importance individuals accord to an outgroup member's view of them during intergroup interaction. *Journal of Personality and Social Psychology, 95*(6), 1467.

Vorauer, J. D., & Sasaki, S. J. (2009). Helpful only in the abstract? Ironic effects of empathy in intergroup interaction. *Psychological Science, 20*(2), 191–197. doi: http://dx.doi.org/10.1111/j.1467-9280.2009.02265.x

Vorauer, J. D., & Sasaki, S. J. (2010). In need of liberation or constraint? How intergroup attitudes moderate the behavioral implications of intergroup ideologies. *Journal of Experimental Social Psychology, 46*(1), 133–138. doi: http://dx.doi.org/10.1016/j.jesp.2009.08.013

Vorauer, J. D., & Sasaki, S. J. (2011). In the worst rather than the best of times: Effects of salient intergroup ideology in threatening intergroup interactions. *Journal of Personality and Social Psychology, 101*(2), 307–320. doi: http://dx.doi.org/10.1037/a0023152

Vorauer, J. D., & Sasaki, S. J. (2014). Distinct effects of imagine-other versus imagine-self perspective taking on prejudice reduction. *Social Cognition, 32*(2), 130–147. doi: http://dx.doi.org/10.1521/soco.2014.32.2.130

West, T. V., Magee, J. C., Gordon, S. H., & Gullett, L. (2014). A little similarity goes a long way: The effects of peripheral but self-revealing similarities on improving and sustaining interracial relationships. *Journal of Personality and Social Psychology, 107*(1), 81–100. doi: http://dx.doi.org/10.1037/a0036556

West, T. V., Pearson, A. R., Dovidio, J. F., Shelton, J. N., & Trail, T. E. (2009). Superordinate identity and intergroup roommate friendship development. *Journal of Experimental Social Psychology, 45*(6), 1266–1272. doi: http://dx.doi.org/10.1016/j.jesp.2009.08.002

West, T. V., Shelton, J. N., & Trail, T. E. (2009). Relational anxiety in interracial interactions. *Psychological Science, 20*(3), 289–292. doi: http://dx.doi.org/10.1111/j.1467-9280.2009.02289.x

Woodcock, A., Hernandez, P. R., Estrada, M., & Schultz, P. W. (2012). The consequences of chronic stereotype threat: Domain disidentification and abandonment. *Journal of Personality and Social Psychology, 103*(4), 635–646. doi: http://dx.doi.org/10.1037/a0029120

Zuckerman, M., Kernis, M. H., Guarnera, S. M., Murphy, J. F., & Rappoport, L. (1983). The egocentric bias: Seeing oneself as cause and target of others' behavior. *Journal of Personality, 51*(4), 621–630. Retrieved from http://uml.idm.oclc.org/login?url=http://search.proquest.com.uml.idm.oclc.org/docview/616922194?accountid=14569

24 Stereotypicality Biases and the Criminal Justice System

Danny Osborne, Paul G. Davies, and Shirley Hutchinson

Michael Brown, age 18. Tony Robinson, age 19. Amadou Diallo, age 22. Oscar Grant III, age 22. Freddie Gray, age 25. Akai Gurley, age 28. Jerame Reid, age 36. Eric Garner, age 43. Tamir Rice, age 12. These are just some of the names of innocent Black men (and, in the case of Tamir Rice, boys) who fell prey to the use of deadly force by police officers over the past few years in the United States. Although these victims vary considerably in terms of their age, their place of residence, and the circumstances surrounding their death, a common thread unites them; they all poignantly bring to light race-based injustices within the criminal justice system.

Unfortunately, racial disparities in the courts have long been noted (Alexander, 2010; Snowball & Weatherburn, 2007; Sudbury, 2013). For example, research from the United States shows that Blacks are nearly seven times more likely than Whites to serve time in prison by the time they reach their early 30s (Pettit & Western, 2004). Though some argue that these disparities are based on different rates of offending and other legitimate factors (see Klein, Petersilia, & Turner, 1990), studies show that after controlling for various legally relevant factors, race-based differences in criminal justice outcomes still exist (see Austin & Allen, 2000; Bales & Piquero, 2012; Mitchell & MacKenzie, 2004). In short, racial disparities can be found throughout the criminal justice system.

To a certain extent, race-based injustices such as the ones noted above may be (partly) explained – though certainly not excused – by the implicit associations that exist between race and crime (see Eberhardt, Goff, Purdie, & Davies, 2004). Specifically, Yogeeswaran, Devos, and Nash (Chapter 11, this title) note that implicit biases originate from socialization processes and operate outside of aware-ness. As such, crime-related stereotypes about Blacks may lead police officers and others within the criminal justice system to *unintentionally* misinterpret ambiguous information in a stereotype-consistent manner (see Levinson & Young, 2010). When involving life-or-death decisions, these basic cognitive biases may give rise to the unnecessary use of deadly force. In other words, basic psychological processes that underlie stereotyping and implicit biases may (partially) account for the noted racial disparities found in the courts (for a detailed review of the literature on implicit biases, see Yogeeswaran et al. (Chapter 11, this title).

The aim of the current chapter is to examine the practical implications of these (and other) biases by providing an overview of contemporary research on race and the judicial system. Because excellent treatments of this field exist (e.g., Alexander, 2010; Flexon, 2012; Gross & Mauro, 1989; Mitchell & MacKenzie, 2004; Sudbury, 2013), we build on this literature by focusing on the effects that *within*-race differences in one's appearance have on criminal justice outcomes. This research has, however, predominately developed in North America. As such, our review is – by necessity – confined to disparities between Blacks and Whites within the US courts. Disparities in the treatment of minorities by the judicial system have, however, been noted across the globe (see Snowball & Weatherburn, 2007; Sudbury, 2013). Nevertheless, to provide continuity to our review, we focus on race-based disparities in the United States.

We start by providing a review of the literature on racial biases within the criminal justice system. We then introduce the concept of perceived stereotypicality and provide a historical overview of the impact that stereotypicality biases have had on the treatment of Blacks in the United States. Next, we outline the existing literature on the effects of perceived stereotypicality on criminal justice outcomes, followed by a review of recent studies on the relationship between eyewitness identifications and perceived stereotypicality. We conclude with suggestions for future research.

Race and Crime

The list of names that opened this chapter provides a poignant reminder of the gravity of race-based disparities in criminal justice outcomes. Indeed, minorities are treated harsher than majority group members at every stage of the criminal justice system (e.g., see Flexon, 2012; Mustard, 2001; Spohn, 2000; Sweeney & Haney, 1992). Such treatment disparities call into question the fairness of our courts and constitute a serious threat to the legitimacy of the judicial system. Although our primary aim is to examine within-race disparities in criminal justice outcomes, a review of between-race biases is needed to provide context to the current chapter.

One approach toward assessing biases in the courts is to simulate the experience of jurors in a controlled laboratory setting. Specifically, in jury simulation studies, mock jurors (i.e., participants) are presented with information about a supposed crime and are then usually asked to evaluate the defendant on a variety of dimensions such as his or her guilt, likelihood of recidivism, and other attributes relevant to the given case, as well as to provide sentencing recommendations. Before making these judgments, the suspect's race, details of the crime (e.g., the victim's race, type of crime), and/or procedures in the courtroom (e.g., juror instructions, strength of the evidence against the defendant) are often manipulated. The aim of these studies is to determine whether the race of a defendant *could* affect how actual jurors assess a case.

Though limited in terms of external validity, jury simulation studies identify potential sources of bias in the courts. All else being equal, mock jurors indicate that Black defendants appear more culpable (Johnson, Whitestone, Jackson, & Gatto, 1995; Sommers & Ellsworth, 2000) and violent (Sommers & Ellsworth, 2000) than White defendants. Mock jurors are also more likely to convict (Sommers & Ellsworth, 2001) and later recommend harsher sentences for Black (vs. White) defendants (Jones & Kaplan, 2003; Sweeney & Haney, 1992). Indeed, Mitchell, Haw, Pfeifer, and Meissner's (2005) meta-analysis covering more than 30 years of jury simulation studies found that perceptions of guilt were higher and sentence recommendations were harsher for Black defendants than they were for White defendants. These studies show that there is a clear potential for racial biases to affect the decision-making process of jurors in the real world.

Unfortunately, research on actual courtroom proceedings identifies similar race-based disparities in criminal justice outcomes. To begin, Blacks are overrepresented in the prisons relative to their presence in the general population (see Alexander, 2010; Bales & Piquero, 2012; Pettit & Western, 2004). Although different rates of offending may partly explain this imbalance in the prison population, racial biases (Austin & Allen, 2000; Bridges & Steen, 1998; Spohn, 2000) and overly punitive responses to "stereotypically Black" crimes (e.g., the "war on drugs"; see Alexander, 2010; Austin & Allen, 2000) are implicated in the current overrepresentation of Blacks in jail. Moreover, after controlling for various mitigating and extenuating factors, Blacks and other racial minorities who are convicted of a criminal offense receive longer prison sentences than their White counterparts (Mustard, 2001; Spohn, 2000).

The literature documenting racial disparities in the use of the death penalty provides particularly unsettling evidence of racial biases in the criminal justice system. Specifically, Black defendants are more likely than White defendants to be sentenced to death after being convicted of a capital offense (Flexon, 2012; Gross & Mauro, 1984, 1989). Moreover, racial disparities in death sentences are particularly pronounced when the victims are White (e.g., see Baldus, Woodworth, Zuckerman, & Weiner, 1997–1998; Flexon, 2012; Gross & Mauro, 1989). For example, Pierce and Radelet (2010–2011) found that 30% of Black defendants who were convicted of killing a White victim in East Baton Rouge Parish, Louisiana, received a capital sentence, whereas only 12% of White defendants convicted of similar crimes were sentenced to death. Others confirm that defendants are more than three times more likely to receive a death sentence if convicted of killing a White, relative to a Black, victim (e.g., Radelet & Pierce, 2010). Racial disparities within the criminal justice system are literally a matter of life and death.

The disproportionate use of the death penalty against Blacks is further complicated by the literature on wrongful convictions. Specifically, Blacks are more likely than Whites to be wrongfully convicted of a crime (see Gross, 2008; Gross, Jacoby, Matheson, Montgomery, & Patil, 2005; Smith & Hattery, 2011). Indeed, as of this writing, the Innocence Project (2015) notes that 325 convictions have been overturned by DNA evidence since 1989. Whereas Whites constitute less than 30% of these cases, more than 62% of wrongful convictions were of Black defendants.

Coupled with the previously mentioned race-based differences in capital sentencing, racial disparities in wrongful convictions are a particularly serious miscarriage of justice.

A number of steps have been taken to purge the courts of racial biases. Indeed, mandatory minimums and other sentencing guidelines have been introduced to eliminate race-based disparities from the courts. Whereas some evidence suggests that these procedures have been effective at eliminating between-race differences in sentencing outcomes (see Blair, Judd, & Chapleau, 2004; Pizzi, Blair, & Judd, 2005), the offenses and associated sentences that fall under the jurisdiction of many mandatory minimums disproportionately affect minorities[1] (Alexander, 2010; Tonry, 1995). Moreover, racial biases are more likely to occur during the decision to incarcerate than when administering sentences (Abrams, Bertrand, & Mullainathan, 2012; Spohn, 2000). Finally, despite the use of these safeguards, race-based disparities in criminal justice outcomes are still present in the post-reform period (Flexon, 2012; Gross & Mauro, 1984, 1989).

Perceived Stereotypicality

Although race has been the major focus of research on disparities in criminal justice outcomes, an emerging literature has begun to examine the effect that within-race differences in appearance have on people's treatment by the courts. Specifically, research on "perceived stereotypicality,"[2] which we define as *the degree to which a person looks like a typical member of his or her racial/ ethnic group*, demonstrates that within-race variations in people's perceived appearance affect how others treat minorities. Accordingly, people whose appearance is perceived to be highly stereotypic of their group (i.e., high on perceived stereotypicality) are seen as more representative of their group than those whose appearance is perceived to deviate from their group's prototype (i.e., low on

---

1 This is perhaps best illustrated in the disparity between mandatory minimums for trafficking crack (versus powder) cocaine. Specifically, a controversial US federal sentencing guideline passed in 1986 mandated that drug convictions for trafficking five grams of crack cocaine (i.e., a stereotypically Black crime; see Skorinko & Spellman, 2013) carry a mandatory minimum five-year prison sentence. The same mandatory minimum penalty for trafficking powder cocaine, however, would only be imposed for suspects who are caught with 500 grams or more of powder cocaine. In practice, Alexander (2010) notes that the policy disproportionately disadvantaged Blacks (for a review of the controversial 100:1 policy, see Spade, 1996).

2 Many terms have been used to capture biases based on variations in perceived appearance such as Afrocentric bias (e.g., Blair et al., 2004), racial phenotypicality bias (e.g., Maddox, 2004), skin tone bias (e.g., Maddox & Gray, 2002), and perceived stereotypicality bias (e.g., Eberhardt, Davies, Purdie-Vaughns, & Johnson, 2006), to name a few. Nevertheless, for consistency purposes, we use the term "perceived stereotypicality" when reviewing these separate traditions. Though we recognize that there are subtle differences between these various constructs, we prefer the term "perceived stereotypicality" because it (a) acknowledges the subjective aspect of determining whether one appears representative of his or her racial group and (b) ties the construct to the stereotyping literature (arguably) better than the other terms.

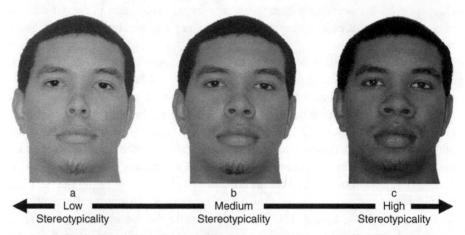

Figure 24.1 *Example of variations in perceived stereotypicality. The given target's appearance has been digitally altered to appear low (a), medium (b), or high (c) in perceived stereotypicality.*

perceived stereotypicality; Blair, Judd, Sadler, & Jenkins, 2002; Livingston & Brewer, 2002).

Because most research on perceived stereotypicality has focused on variability within the Black community, our chapter examines people's perceptions of – and responses to – the appearance of Blacks. To illustrate, variations in the perceived stereotypicality of Blacks are shown in Figure 24.1. Whereas the person in Figure 24.1a has a light skin tone, a narrow nose, and thin lips, the person in Figure 24.1c has a dark skin tone, a broad nose, and thick lips; the person in Figure 24.1b falls between these two end points. Accordingly, the persons in Figures 24.1a, 24.1b, and 24.1c would be described as being low, medium, and high on perceived stereotypicality, respectively. Before demonstrating the impact that variation in perceived stereotypicality has on criminal justice outcomes, a brief history of stereotypicality biases is needed. We now turn to this literature.

History of Stereotypicality Biases

Despite only just recently receiving attention from psychologists (see Maddox, 2004), stereotypicality biases have long existed. Indeed, evidence of stereotypicality biases in the United States dates back to (at least) the days of slavery. Specifically, Blacks who were perceived to be less phenotypically stereotypic were sold on the slave market at higher prices than Blacks who were seen as more phenotypically stereotypic (Drake & Cayton, 1962; Kotlikoff, 1979; Myrdal, 1944). Likewise, house servants were more likely than field hands to be low on perceived stereotypicality (Kotlikoff, 1979; Russell, Wilson, & Hall, 1993). These findings suggest that Blacks who were low on perceived stereotypicality were valued more – and (arguably) treated better – than Blacks who were high on perceived stereotypicality during the long period of slavery in the United States.

Unfortunately, stereotypicality biases continue to affect the lives of Blacks in the United States. Indeed, experiences with both interpersonal and institutional forms of discrimination vary by level of perceived stereotypicality (see Klonoff & Landrine, 2000; Uzogara, Lee, Abdou, & Jackson, 2014). Hebl, Williams, Sundermann, Kell, and Davies (2012) found that Blacks who were high on perceived stereotypicality had fewer cross-race friends (Studies 1 and 3) and were less likely to have their friend requests accepted on Facebook by non-Black Facebook users (Study 2) than their counterparts who were low on perceived stereotypicality. Relatedly, Blacks who are high on perceived stereotypicality (a) are rated as less attractive (Hill, 2002), (b) are seen as less likeable (Hagiwara, Kashy, & Cesario, 2012), and (c) report experiencing more discrimination (Hersch, 2006; Klonoff & Landrine, 2000) than Blacks who are low on perceived stereotypicality.

Stereotypicality biases are also found within the employment sector. Specifically, Blacks who are high on perceived stereotypicality are less likely to be recommended for a position (Goldsmith, Hamilton, & Darity, 2006) – and subsequently hired (Goldsmith et al., 2006; Wade, Romano, & Blue, 2004) – than their counterparts who are low on perceived stereotypicality. Once hired, perceived stereotypicality is negatively associated with Blacks' income (Hersch, 2006; Hochschild & Weaver, 2007). Critically, the negative relationship between perceived stereotypicality and socioeconomic status remains even after accounting for people's family background (Hill, 2000; Monk, 2014). In short, levels of perceived stereotypicality have broad implications for the lives of Blacks.

Stereotypicality biases also exist within the Black community (see Russell et al., 1993). Dating back to Clark and Clark's (1950) seminal research, studies have shown that many Blacks demonstrate a preference for light skin tone (Hall, 1992; Hill, 2002). Indeed, financially successful Blacks are more likely than their less successful counterparts to marry partners who are low on perceived stereotypicality (Hunter, 2002). Monk (2014) also found that Blacks' level of perceived stereotypicality was negatively correlated with their spouses' educational attainment. Uzogara and colleagues (2014) note, however, that those who are either high or low on perceived stereotypicality are more likely than their counterparts who are seen as moderately stereotypic to be treated unfairly on the basis of their skin tone within the Black community. These studies highlight the multifaceted ways in which stereotypicality biases continue to affect the Black community.

Stereotypicality Biases and the Criminal Justice System

Since the early 2000s, scholars have examined stereotypicality biases within the justice system (see Blair, Judd, & Chapleau, 2004; Eberhardt et al.,

2006; Kahn & Davies, 2011; Pizzi et al., 2005). These studies show that variations in perceived stereotypicality affect how suspects are treated (a) starting from when the perceiver assesses whether or not a crime is being committed (Kahn & Davies, 2011), (b) moving to an assessment of a suspect's guilt (Eberhardt et al., 2004), and (c) concluding with the sentencing of the alleged perpetrator (Blair et al., 2004; Eberhardt et al., 2006; Gyimah-Brempong & Price, 2006). Thus, despite only recently capturing legal scholars' attention, stereotypicality biases are deeply entrenched within the criminal justice system.

In terms of initial perceptions, Blacks who are high on perceived stereotypicality are more likely to be negatively stereotyped than their counterparts who are low on perceived stereotypicality (see Blair et al., 2002; Livingston & Brewer, 2002; Maddox & Gray, 2002). Accordingly, the former group is more likely than the latter group to be seen as criminal (Eberhardt et al., 2004; Kleider, Cavrak, & Knuycky, 2012) – an association that has dire implications within the context of ambiguous situations. Indeed, research implementing the "shoot, don't shoot" videogame paradigm in which participants must quickly decide whether or not a suspect is carrying a weapon (see Correll, Park, Judd, & Wittenbrink, 2002) shows that Blacks who are high on perceived stereotypicality are more likely than Blacks who are low on perceived stereotypicality to be mistakenly seen as carrying a gun and subsequently shot (Kahn & Davies, 2011).

Moving from the initial context of a crime to the courtroom, research shows that perceived stereotypicality also influences assessments of a defendant's guilt. Levinson and Young (2010) conducted a jury simulation study in which mock jurors were shown a photo of a defendant who was either low or high on perceived stereotypicality during the presentation of evidence from a supposed trial. Participants were then asked to indicate the extent to which the evidence implicated the defendant, as well as whether or not they believed the defendant was guilty. Consistent with the stereotypicality biases reported earlier, results indicated that participants believed the evidence was more indicative of guilt – and were subsequently more likely to believe the defendant was guilty – after seeing a defendant who was high (vs. low) on perceived stereotypicality.

Finally, research within actual criminal proceedings reveals similar stereotypicality biases. Specifically, a suspect's level of perceived stereotypicality is positively associated with sentence length (see Gyimah-Brempong & Price, 2006; Viglione, Hannon, & DeFina, 2011). Viglione and colleagues (2011) analyzed data on actual prison sentences administered to more than 12,000 Black women and found that the sentences for defendants who were high on perceived stereotypicality were 12% longer than those for Black women who were low on perceived stereotypicality. Likewise, Blair et al. (2004) assessed the sentences administered to a random sample of male convicts and found that convicts' level of perceived stereotypicality was positively associated with their sentence length. Moreover, these results held after controlling for extenuating factors including the seriousness of the crime, severity of concurrent offenses, and number of prior offenses. Thus, perceived stereotypicality was an independent predictor of actual sentence length.

Eberhardt and colleagues (2006) provide perhaps the most poignant demonstration of the impact that stereotypicality biases have on the severity of prison sentences. These authors located more than 600 actual courtroom cases involving death-eligible offenses and had a group of naïve participants rate the perceived stereotypicality of a subset of Black suspects who were convicted of murdering White victims. After controlling for factors known to affect sentence severity, Eberhardt and colleagues (2006) found that Black defendants who were high on perceived stereotypicality were more than twice as likely as Black defendants who were low on perceived stereotypicality to receive the death penalty. Thus, stereotypicality biases have dire consequences for Blacks who encounter the judicial system.

Eyewitness (Mis)Identifications

Wrongful convictions are another type of criminal justice outcome that could reveal disparities based on perceived stereotypicality. As previously mentioned, Blacks are vastly overrepresented in the cases of DNA-based exonerations identified since 1989 (Gross, 2008; Gross et al., 2005; Innocence Project, 2015). Notably, mistaken eyewitness identifications are present in more than 70% of all these wrongful convictions (see Gross, 2008; Gross et al., 2005; Innocence Project, 2015). Although many have (at least implicitly) assumed that those who are mistakenly identified are randomly chosen from a lineup, research has begun to examine the possibility that eyewitnesses unintentionally make systematic errors when they mistakenly identify a suspect (see Osborne & Davies, 2014). Specifically, eyewitnesses' expectations about a suspect's appearance may systematically alter their memory of a perpetrator's level of perceived stereotypicality.

Though research has yet to assess the possibility that stereotypicality biases contribute to actual cases of mistaken identification, experimental evidence provides indirect support for this thesis. Indeed, research shows that variations in perceived stereotypicality influence the cross-race effect – a robust phenomenon in which people are less accurate at remembering other-race (vs. own-race) faces (Brigham, Bennett, Meissner, & Mitchell, 2007; Meissner & Brigham, 2001; Wells & Olson, 2001). Knuycky, Kleider, and Cavrak (2014) demonstrated that mock witnesses presented with a target-absent lineup (i.e., a lineup that does not include the real perpetrator) were more than twice as likely to mistakenly identify a suspect who was high (vs. low) on perceived stereotypicality. Moreover, although some evidence suggests that the cross-race effect can be eliminated by conceiving other-race faces as part of the ingroup (see Cassidy, Quinn, & Humphreys, 2011; Hehman, Mania, & Gaertner, 2010), reductions in the cross-race effect are limited to faces that are low on perceived stereotypicality (see Pauker et al., 2009). In short,

Whites experience considerable difficulty attempting to recall faces that are high on perceived stereotypicality.

In addition to being less accurate at remembering faces that are high (vs. low) on perceived stereotypicality, people may systematically misremember others' level of perceived stereotypicality. Indeed, pairing a racially ambiguous face with the label "Black" leads people to perceive the given face as higher on perceived stereotypicality than if the same face had been labeled "White" (Study 2; Levin & Banaji, 2006). Similarly, faces paired with hairstyles that are stereotypically Black are seen as being higher in perceived stereotypicality than are the same faces paired with stereotypically Latino hairstyles (MacLin & Malpass, 2001). On the other hand, priming people with counter-stereotypes leads them to recall Blacks as having a lighter skin tone than had they been primed with stereotypic words (Ben-Zeev, Dennehy, Goodrich, Kolarik, & Geisler, 2014). Importantly, contextual cues such as these fundamentally change how racially ambiguous faces are processed at the early stages of facial perception (Willadsen-Jensen & Ito, 2014). In other words, the context in which a person is seen can alter people's memory of the person's level of perceived stereotypicality.

To explain how environmental cues such as these could produce systematic errors in eyewitness identification, Osborne and Davies (2014) developed the contextual model of eyewitness identification (CMEI). As shown in Figure 24.2, the model assumes that the type of crime committed activates racial stereotypes about the perpetrator. Specifically, stereotypically White crimes (e.g., hate crimes or serial killing; see Osborne & Davies, 2013; Skorinko & Spellman, 2013) should activate stereotypes about White perpetrators, whereas stereotypically Black crimes (e.g., gang activity and drive-by shootings; see Osborne & Davies, 2013; Skorinko & Spellman, 2013) should activate stereotypes about Black perpetrators. In turn, activation of these stereotypes is expected to alter eyewitnesses'

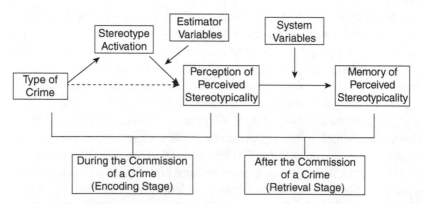

Figure 24.2 *Contextual model of eyewitness identification in which the crime type affects eyewitness identification via stereotype activation. Estimator and system variables moderate this relationship at separate stages of the identification process. Figure adapted from Osborne and Davies (2014).*

perception – and subsequent memory – of the perpetrator's level of perceived stereotypicality in a stereotype-consistent manner (i.e., higher or lower in perceived stereotypicality). As a result of this biased memory trace, eyewitnesses may make systematic errors during the identification process.

To assess this possibility, Osborne and Davies (2013) randomly assigned participants to watch a slideshow containing photos of an ostensible suspect to a crime. Before watching the slideshow, participants were told the suspect was accused of either a stereotypically Black crime or a stereotypically White crime. After receiving this information, participants watched the slideshow, completed a 10-minute distractor task, and were subsequently asked to identify the suspect from a morph that gradually changed the suspect's appearance from low to high perceived stereotypicality. Consistent with the CMEI, participants who believed they were watching a person accused of a stereotypically Black crime later remembered the suspect as being higher in perceived stereotypicality than did participants who believed they were watching a person accused of a stereotypically White crime.

Subsequent research has replicated and extended these findings. Specifically, the memory biases reported earlier are limited to cases involving Black suspects and White victims (Davies, Hutchinson, Osborne, & Eberhardt, 2016; Hutchinson, Davies, & Osborne, 2014). Moreover, Osborne, Davies, and Hutchinson (in preparation) have shown that participants *only* misremember a suspect's level of perceived stereotypicality if they are told beforehand of the type of crime the suspect is accused of committing. This suggests that encoding (rather than retrieval) errors cause these memory biases, coinciding with other research showing that stereotypicality biases fundamentally alter the perception of a person's face (Willadsen-Jensen & Ito, 2014). Thus, rather than being objectively perceived, a suspect's level of perceived stereotypicality can be influenced by a variety of factors surrounding the commission of a crime.

Limitations and Directions for Future Research

Although the extant literature has done an excellent job documenting the existence of stereotypicality biases within the criminal justice system, a number of limitations to this research should be noted. For one, studies examining stereotypicality biases often confound multiple physical features when assessing perceived stereotypicality (see Hagiwara et al., 2012). Specifically, the perceived stereotypicality of Blacks is typically operationalized in terms of variations in both (a) skin tone and (b) Afrocentric features (i.e., nose width and lip thickness). As such, the extent to which any one of these facial features uniquely contributes to the stereotypicality biases identified in the research presented in the current chapter is unknown.

In light of this limitation, research suggests that the effects of these distinct physical features on criminal justice outcomes may be additive (rather than inter-active). Hagiwara and colleagues (2012) showed that both skin tone and Afrocentric features had main effects on people's (implicit and explicit) negativity toward Blacks. Specifically, White participants reported more negative responses toward Blacks who had (a) a dark skin tone and (b) a high proportion of Afrocentric features than they did toward Blacks who had (a) a light skin tone and (b) a low percentage of Afrocentric features, respectively. Skin tone and Afrocentric features did not, however, interact to predict participants' affective responses toward Blacks. Although these results imply that skin tone and Afrocentric features independently contribute to stereotypicality biases within the judicial system, additional work is needed to examine the generalizability of these findings to the courtroom.

Perhaps more problematic than the operationalization of perceived stereotypi-cality is the near-exclusive focus on stereotypicality biases within the United States. Specifically, as noted at the outset of this chapter, the majority of research on perceived stereotypicality has been pursued in North America. Although these studies advance our understanding of the pernicious effects that perceived stereotypicality have on Blacks' treatment within the criminal justice system, the dominate focus on US-based race relations has overshadowed the develop-ment of a more inclusive understanding of stereotypicality biases that extends beyond the experience of Blacks. Indeed, a major challenge facing the literature on perceived stereotypicality is to demonstrate its relevance outside of the United States.

Although we are unaware of research examining stereotypicality biases in courtrooms outside of the United States, a few studies have assessed the effects of perceived stereotypicality among other minority groups in nonlegal settings. Specifically, Sidanius, Peña, and Sawyer (2001) have shown that skin tone is inversely associated with perceived social status among Latinos from the Dominican Republic. Likewise, Uhlmann, Dasgupta, Elgueta, Greenwald, and Swanson (2002) showed that both American Latinos (Study 1) and Chileans (Study 2) have an implicit bias favoring light (vs. dark) skin. Finally, Houkamau and Sibley (2015) demonstrated that self-ratings of perceived stereotypicality negatively correlate with homeownership among Māori in New Zealand. Together, these studies indicate that stereotypicality biases extend beyond members of the Black community. Nevertheless, future research is needed to see if these biases also pervade the criminal justice system in their respective countries.

Future research should also further examine the effects of perceived stereotypi-cality on eyewitness memory. Indeed, the literature reviewed here suggests that stereotypicality biases may systematically influence whom eyewitnesses mistakenly identify from a police lineup (Davies et al., 2016; Hutchinson et al., 2014; Osborne & Davies, 2013). Although we explicitly developed the CMEI to address this possibility (see Osborne & Davies, 2014), a number of propositions within the model remain untested (e.g., the effects of estimator and system variables on encoding and retrieval errors, respectively). Moreover, the extent to which crime types systematically affect eyewitnesses' memory of a perpetrator's level of perceived stereotypicality in the real world is unknown. As such, we look forward to future research that examines these possibilities.

A final suggestion for the literature on perceived stereotypicality is to identify ways of eliminating stereotypicality biases from the criminal justice system. Though this is admittedly an ambitious goal, research demonstrates that it is possible to prevent between-race biases from affecting sentencing decisions (e.g., Blair et al., 2004; Pizzi et al., 2005). Indeed, as noted by Yogeeswaran and colleagues (Chapter 11, this title), the context-specific nature of implicit stereotyping implies that it is possible to refrain from acting on automatically activated biases. That said, stereotypicality biases appear to be harder to control than traditional between-group stereotypes (Blair, Judd, & Fallman, 2004; Hagiwara et al., 2012; Livingston & Brewer, 2002). As such, a difficult road lies ahead for those who aim to eliminate stereotypicality biases from the courtroom. The gravity of these biases should, however, motivate the continued pursuit of both between- and within-group racial equality in the criminal justice system.

Conclusion

Although stereotypicality biases have existed for centuries, psychologists have only just begun to systematically examine their presence in the criminal justice system. Critically, we now know that these biases are (at least) as insidious as the between-race biases that have been identified in the past. Indeed, stereotypicality biases influence how minorities are treated at all stages of the criminal justice system. Moreover, stereotypicality biases even occur in the context of eyewitness identifications. By understanding and bringing these biases to light, we aim to mitigate their influence on the perversions of justice we have become too accustomed to seeing in contemporary society. Only then can we truly argue that the scales of justice are balanced toward equality.

References

Abrams, D., Bertrand, M., & Mullainathan, S. (2012). Do judges vary in their treatment of race? *Journal of Legal Studies*, *41*(2), 347–383. doi: 10.1086/666006

Alexander, M. (2010). *The new Jim Crow: Mass incarceration in the age of colorblindness*. New York: The New Press.

Austin, R. L., & Allen, M. D. (2000). Racial disparity in arrest rates as an explanation of racial disparity in commitment to Pennsylvania's prisons. *Journal of Research in Crime and Delinquency*, *37*(2), 200–220. doi: 10.1177/0022427800037002003

Baldus, D. C., Woodworth, G., Zuckerman, D., & Weiner, N. A. (1997–1998). Racial discrimination and the death penalty in the post-Furman era: An empirical and legal overview with recent findings from Philadelphia. *Cornell Law Review, 83*, 1638–1770.

Bales, W. D., & Piquero, A. R. (2012). Racial/ethnic differentials in sentencing to incarceration. *Justice Quarterly, 29*(5), 742–773. doi: 10.1080/07418825.2012.659674

Ben-Zeev, A., Dennehy, T. C., Goodrich, R. I., Kolarik, B. S., & Geisler, M. W. (2014). When an "educated" Black man becomes lighter in the mind's eye: Evidence for a skin tone memory bias. *SAGE Open, 4*(1), 1–9. doi: 10.1177/2158244013516770

Blair, I. V., Judd, C. M., & Chapleau, K. M. (2004). The influence of Afrocentric facial features in criminal sentencing. *Psychological Science, 15*(10), 674–679. doi: 10.1111/j.0956-7976.2004.00739.x

Blair, I. V., Judd, C. M., & Fallman, J. L. (2004). The automaticity of race and Afrocentric facial features in social judgments. *Journal of Personality and Social Psychology, 87*(6), 763–778. doi: 10.1037/0022-3514.87.6.763

Blair, I. V., Judd, C. M., Sadler, M. S., & Jenkins, C. (2002). The role of Afrocentric features in person perception: Judging by features and categories. *Journal of Personality and Social Psychology, 83*(1), 5–25. doi: 10.1037/0022-3514.83.1.5

Bridges, G. S., & Steen, S. (1998). Racial disparities in official assessments of juvenile offenders: Attributional stereotypes as mediating mechanisms. *American Sociological Review, 63*(4), 554–570. doi: 10.2307/2657267

Brigham, J. C., Bennett, L. B., Meissner, C. A., & Mitchell, T. L. (2007). The influence of race on eyewitness memory. In R. C. L. Lindsay, D. F. Ross, J. D. Read, & M. P. Toglia (Eds.), *The handbook of eyewitness psychology: Volume II: Memory for people* (Vol. *II*, pp. 257–281). Mahwah, NJ: Lawrence Erlbaum Associates.

Cassidy, K. D., Quinn, K. A., & Humphreys, G. W. (2011). The influence of ingroup/outgroup categorization on same- and other-race face processing: The moderating role of inter-versus intra-racial context. *Journal of Experimental Social Psychology, 47*(4), 811–817. doi: 10.1016/j.jesp.2011.02.017

Clark, K. B., & Clark, M. P. (1950). Emotional factors in racial identification and preference in Negro children. *Journal of Negro Education, 19*(3), 341–350. doi: 10.2307/2966491

Correll, J., Park, B., Judd, C. M., & Wittenbrink, B. (2002). The police officer's dilemma: Using ethnicity to disambiguate potentially threatening individuals. *Journal of Personality and Social Psychology, 83*(6), 1314–1329. doi: 10.1037/0022-3514.83.6.1314

Davies, P. G., Hutchinson, S., Osborne, D., & Eberhardt, J. L. (2016). Victim's race and sex leads to eyewitness misidentification of perpetrator's phenotypic stereotypicality. *Social Psychological and Personality Science, 7*(6), 491–499. doi: 10.1177/1948550616644655

Drake, S. C., & Cayton, H. (1962). The measure of a man. In S. C. Drake & H. Cayton (Eds.), *Black metropolis: A study of Negro life in a northern city* (Vol. 2, pp. 495–525). New York: Harper.

Eberhardt, J. L., Davies, P. G., Purdie-Vaughns, V. J., & Johnson, S. L. (2006). Looking deathworthy: Perceived stereotypicality of black defendants predicts capital-sentencing outcomes. *Psychological Science, 17*(5), 383–386. doi: 10.1111/j.1467-9280.2006.01716.x

Eberhardt, J. L., Goff, P. A., Purdie, V. J., & Davies, P. G. (2004). Seeing black: Race, crime, and visual processing. *Journal of Personality and Social Psychology, 87*(6), 876–893. doi: 10.1037/0022-3514.87.6.876

Flexon, J. L. (2012). *Racial disparities in capital sentencing: Prejudice and discrimination in the jury room*. El Paso, TX: LFB Scholarly Publishing LLC.

Goldsmith, A. H., Hamilton, D., & Darity, W. (2006). Shades of discrimination: Skin tone and wages. *The American Economic Review, 96*(2), 242–245. doi: 10.1257/000282806777212152

Gross, S. R. (2008). Convicting the innocent. *Annual Review of Law and Social Science, 4*(1), 173–192. doi: 10.1146/annurev.lawsocsci.4.110707.172300

Gross, S. R., Jacoby, K., Matheson, D. J., Montgomery, N., & Patil, S. (2005). Exonerations in the United States 1989 through 2003. *Journal of Criminal Law and Criminology, 95*(2), 523–560.

Gross, S. R., & Mauro, R. (1984). Patterns of death: An analysis of racial disparities in capital sentencing and homicide victimization. *Stanford Law Review, 37*(1), 27–153. doi: 10.2307/1228652

Gross, S. R., & Mauro, R. (1989). *Death and discrimination: Racial disparities in capital sentencing*. Boston, MA: Northeastern University Press.

Gyimah-Brempong, K., & Price, G. N. (2006). Crime and punishment: And skin hue too? *American Economic Review, 96*(2), 246–250. doi: 10.1257/000282806777212530

Hagiwara, N., Kashy, D. A., & Cesario, J. (2012). The independent effects of skin tone and facial features on Whites' affective reactions to Blacks. *Journal of Experimental Social Psychology, 48*(4), 892–898. doi: 10.1016/j.jesp.2012.02.001

Hall, R. E. (1992). Bias among African-Americans regarding skin color: Implications for social work practice. *Research on Social Work Practice, 2*(4), 479–486. doi: 10.1177/104973159200200404

Hebl, M. R., Williams, M. J., Sundermann, J. M., Kell, H. J., & Davies, P. G. (2012). Selectively friending: Racial stereotypicality and social rejection. *Journal of Experimental Social Psychology, 48*(6), 1329–1335. doi: 10.1016/j.jesp.2012.05.019

Hehman, E., Mania, E. W., & Gaertner, S. L. (2010). Where the division lies: Common ingroup identity moderates the cross-race facial-recognition effect. *Journal of Experimental Social Psychology, 46*(2), 445–448. doi: 10.1016/j.jesp.2009.11.008

Hersch, J. (2006). Skin-tone effects among African Americans: Perceptions and reality. *The American Economic Review, 96*(2), 251–255. doi: 10.2307/30034652

Hill, M. E. (2000). Color differences in the socioeconomic status of African American men: Results of a longitudinal study. *Social Forces, 78*(4), 1437–1460. doi: 10.2307/3006180

Hill, M. E. (2002). Skin color and the perception of attractiveness among African Americans: Does gender make a difference? *Social Psychology Quarterly, 65*(1), 77–91. doi: 10.2307/3090169

Hochschild, J. L., & Weaver, V. (2007). The skin color paradox and the American racial order. *Social Forces, 86*(2), 643–670. doi: 10.1353/sof.2008.0005

Houkamau, C. A., & Sibley, C. G. (2015). Looking Māori predicts decreased rates of home ownership: Institutional racism in housing based on perceived appearance. *PLoS One, 10*(3), e0118540. doi: 10.1371/journal.pone.0118540

Hunter, M. L. (2002). "If you're light you're alright": Light skin color as social capital for women of color. *Gender and Society*, *16*(2), 175–193. doi: 10.1177/0891243202016002003

Hutchinson, S., Davies, P. G., & Osborne, D. (2014). The influence of stereotypes on eyewitness recall of perceived stereotypicality. In C. Pracana (Ed.), *Psychology applications & developments* (pp. 337–344). Lisbon, Portugal: Science Press.

Innocence Project. (2015). *DNA exonerations nationwide*. Retrieved from www.innocenceproject.org

Johnson, J. D., Whitestone, E., Jackson, L. A., & Gatto, L. (1995). Justice is still not colorblind: Differential racial effects of exposure to inadmissible evidence. *Personality and Social Psychology Bulletin*, *21*(9), 893–898. doi: 10.1177/0146167295219003

Jones, C. S., & Kaplan, M. F. (2003). The effects of racially stereotypical crimes on juror decision-making and information-processing strategies. *Basic and Applied Social Psychology*, *25*(1), 1–13. doi: 10.1207/S15324834BASP2501_1

Kahn, K. B., & Davies, P. G. (2011). Differentially dangerous? Phenotypic racial stereotypicality increases implicit bias among ingroup and outgroup members. *Group Processes & Intergroup Relations*, *14*(4), 569–580. doi: 10.1177/1368430210374609

Kleider, H. M., Cavrak, S. E., & Knuycky, L. R. (2012). Looking like a criminal: Stereotypical black facial features promote face source memory error. *Memory & Cognition*, *40*(8), 1200–1213. doi: 10.3758/s13421-012-0229-x

Klein, S., Petersilia, J., & Turner, S. (1990). Race and imprisonment decisions in California. *Science*, *247*(4944), 812–816. doi: 10.1126/science.2305254

Klonoff, E. A., & Landrine, H. (2000). Is skin color a marker for racial discrimination? Explaining the skin color–hypertension relationship. *Journal of Behavioral Medicine*, *23*(4), 329–338.

Knuycky, L. R., Kleider, H. M., & Cavrak, S. E. (2014). Line-up misidentifications: When being "prototypically Black" is perceived as criminal. *Applied Cognitive Psychology*, *28*(1), 39–46. doi: 10.1002/acp.2954

Kotlikoff, L. J. (1979). The structure of slave prices in New Orleans, 1804 to 1862. *Economic Inquiry*, *17*(4), 496–518. doi: 10.1111/j.1465-7295.1979.tb00544.x

Levin, D. T., & Banaji, M. R. (2006). Distortions in the perceived lightness of faces: The role of race categories. *Journal of Experimental Psychology: General*, *135*(4), 501–512. doi: 10.1037/0096-3445.135.4.501

Levinson, J. D., & Young, D. (2010). Different shades of bias: Skin tone, implicit racial bias, and judgments of ambiguous evidence. *West Virginia Law Review*, *112*(2), 307–350.

Livingston, R. W., & Brewer, M. B. (2002). What are we really priming? Cue-based versus category-based processing of facial stimuli. *Journal of Personality and Social Psychology*, *82*(1), 5–18. doi: 10.1037/0022-3514.82.1.5

MacLin, O. H., & Malpass, R. S. (2001). Racial categorization of faces: The ambiguous race face effect. *Psychology, Public Policy, and Law*, *7*(1), 98–118. doi: 10.1037//1076-8971.7.1.98

Maddox, K. B. (2004). Perspectives on racial phenotypicality bias. *Personality and Social Psychology Review*, *8*(4), 383–401. doi: 10.1207/s15327957pspr0804_4

Maddox, K. B., & Gray, S. A. (2002). Cognitive representations of Black Americans: Reexploring the role of skin tone. *Personality and Social Psychology Bulletin*, *28*(2), 250–259. doi: 10.1177/0146167202282010

Meissner, C. A., & Brigham, J. C. (2001). Thirty years of investigating the own-race bias in memory for faces: A meta-analytic review. *Psychology, Public Policy, and Law*, *7* (1), 3–35. doi: 10.1037/1076-8971.7.1.3

Mitchell, O., & MacKenzie, D. L. (2004). *The relationship between race, ethnicity, and sentencing outcomes: A meta-analysis of sentencing research.* Washington, DC: U.S. Department of Justice, National Institute of Justice.

Mitchell, T. L., Haw, R. M., Pfeifer, J. E., & Meissner, C. A. (2005). Racial bias in mock juror decision-making: A meta-analytic review of defendant treatment. *Law and Human Behavior*, *29*(6), 621–637. doi: 10.1007/s10979-005-8122-9

Monk, E. P. (2014). Skin tone stratification among Black Americans, 2001–2003. *Social Forces*, *92*(4), 1313–1337. doi: 10.1093/sf/sou007

Mustard, D. B. (2001). Racial, ethnic, and gender disparities in sentencing: Evidence from the U.S. federal courts. *Journal of Law and Economics*, *44*(1), 285–314. doi: 10.1086/320276

Myrdal, G. (1944). *An American dilemma.* New York: Harper & Row.

Osborne, D., & Davies, P. G. (2013). Eyewitness identifications are affected by stereotypes about a suspect's level of perceived stereotypicality. *Group Processes & Intergroup Relations*, *16*(4), 488–504. doi: 10.1177/1368430212454927

Osborne, D., & Davies, P. G. (2014). Crime type, perceived stereotypicality, and memory biases: A contextual model of eyewitness identification. *Applied Cognitive Psychology*, *28*(3), 392–402. doi: 10.1002/acp.3009

Osborne, D., Davies, P. G., & Hutchinson, S. (in preparation). Expectations of appearance: Encoding errors underlie stereotype-consistent memory biases of a suspect's perceived stereotypicality.

Pauker, K., Weisbuch, M., Ambady, N., Sommers, S. R., Adams Jr., R. B., & Ivcevic, Z. (2009). Not so black and white: Memory for ambiguous group members. *Journal of Personality and Social Psychology*, *96*(4), 795–810. doi: 10.1037/a0013265

Pettit, B., & Western, B. (2004). Mass imprisonment and the life course: Race and class inequality in U.S. incarceration. *American Sociological Review*, *69*(2), 151–169. doi: 10.1177/000312240406900201

Pierce, G. L., & Radelet, M. L. (2010–2011). Death sentencing in East Baton Rouge Parish, 1990–2008. *Louisiana Law Review*, *71*, 647–674.

Pizzi, W. T., Blair, I. V., & Judd, C. M. (2005). Discrimination in sentencing on the basis of Afrocentric features. *Michigan Journal of Race and Law*, *10*(2), 327–353.

Radelet, M. L., & Pierce, G. L. (2010). Race and death sentencing in North Carolina, 1980–2007. *North Carolina Law Review*, *89*, 2119–2160.

Russell, K., Wilson, M., & Hall, R. (1993). *The color complex: The politics of skin color among African Americans.* New York: Harcourt Brace Jovanovich.

Sidanius, J., Peña, Y., & Sawyer, M. (2001). Inclusionary discrimination: Pigmentocracy and patriotism in the Dominican Republic. *Political Psychology*, *22*(4), 827–851. doi: 10.1111/0162-895X.00264

Skorinko, J. L., & Spellman, B. A. (2013). Stereotypic crimes: How group-crime associations affect memory and (sometimes) verdicts and sentencing. *Victims &*

Offenders: An International Journal of Evidence-based Research, Policy, and Practice, 8(3), 278–397. doi: 10.1080/15564886.2012.755140

Smith, E., & Hattery, A. J. (2011). Race, wrongful conviction & exoneration. *Journal of African American Studies, 15*(1), 74–94. doi: 10.1007/s12111-010-9130-5

Snowball, L., & Weatherburn, D. (2007). Does racial bias in sentencing contribute to Indigenous overrepresentation in prison? *Australian & New Zealand Journal of Criminology, 40*(3), 272–290. doi: 10.1375/acri.40.3.272

Sommers, S. R., & Ellsworth, P. C. (2000). Race in the courtroom: Perceptions of guilt and dispositional attributions. *Personality and Social Psychology Bulletin, 26*(11), 1367–1379. doi: 10.1177/0146167200263005

Sommers, S. R., & Ellsworth, P. C. (2001). White juror bias: An investigation of prejudice against Black defendants in the American courtroom. *Psychology, Public Policy, and Law, 7*(1), 201–229. doi: 10.1037/1076-8971.7.1.201

Spade Jr., W. (1996). Beyond the 100:1 ratio: Toward a rational cocaine sentencing policy. *Arizona Law Review, 38*, 1233–1290.

Spohn, C. (2000). Thirty years of sentencing reform: The quest for a racially neutral sentencing process. *Criminal Justice, 3*, 427–501.

Sudbury, J. (Ed.). (2013). *Global lockdown: Race, gender, and the prison-industrial complex*. New York: Routledge.

Sweeney, L. T., & Haney, C. (1992). The influence of race on sentencing: A meta analytic review of experimental studies. *Behavioral Sciences & the Law, 10*(2), 179–195. doi: 10.1002/bsl.2370100204

Tonry, M. (1995). *Malign neglect: Race, crime, and punishment in America*. New York: Oxford University Press.

Uhlmann, E., Dasgupta, N., Elgueta, A., Greenwald, A. G., & Swanson, J. (2002). Subgroup prejudice based on skin color among Hispanics in the United States and Latin America. *Social Cognition, 20*(3), 198–225. doi: 10.1521/soco.20.3.198.21104

Uzogara, E. E., Lee, H., Abdou, C. M., & Jackson, J. S. (2014). A comparison of skin tone discrimination among African American men: 1995 and 2003. *Psychology of Men & Masculinity, 15*(2), 201–212. doi: 10.1037/a0033479

Viglione, J., Hannon, L., & DeFina, R. (2011). The impact of light skin on prison time for Black female offenders. *Social Science Journal, 48*(1), 250–258. doi: 10.1016/j.soscij.2010.08.003

Wade, T. J., Romano, M. J., & Blue, L. (2004). The effect of African American skin color on hiring preferences. *Journal of Applied Social Psychology, 34*(12), 2550–2558. doi: 10.1111/j.1559-1816.2004.tb01991.x

Wells, G. L., & Olson, E. A. (2001). The other-race effect in eyewitness identification: What do we do about it? *Psychology, Public Policy, and Law, 7*(1), 230–246. doi: 10.1037/1076-8971.7.1.230

Willadsen-Jensen, E., & Ito, T. A. (2014). The effect of context on responses to racially ambiguous faces: Changes in perception and evaluation. *Social Cognitive and Affective Neuroscience, 10*(7): 885–892. doi: 10.1093/scan/nsu134

25 Prejudice, Stigma, Bias, Discrimination, and Health

Yin Paradies, João Luiz Bastos, and Naomi Priest

Operationalizing Prejudice, Stigma, Bias, and Discrimination in Health Research

Prejudice, stigma, bias, and discrimination are all expressions of oppression, "a concept that describes a relationship between groups or categories of people in which a dominant group benefits from the systematic abuse, exploitation, and injustice directed toward a subordinate group" (Johnson, 2000, p. 293). While a myriad of typologies exist concerning definitions and manifestations of prejudice, stigma, bias, and discrimination, in the public health literature, oppression is frequently conceptualized across three distinct, but interrelated, levels (Jones, 2000; Paradies, 2006):

- internalized (or intrapersonal) prejudiced attitudes or beliefs, frequently based on notions of supposedly innate superiority/inferiority, which may be subscribed to either by members of dominant social groups or by subordinate ones;
- interpersonal discriminatory interactions between people, with varying degrees of frequency and intensity, including manifestations from racially motivated assault to verbal abuse, ostracism, and exclusion; and
- systemic or structural, which includes bias in societal institutions, laws, policies, and social practices. Of note, this level may be thought of as the one that sets the context and increases or decreases the likelihood of the first two types of oppression outlined here.

In the mid-twentieth century, the psychological concept of prejudice (Allport, 1954) and the sociological phenomenon of stigma (Goffman, 1963) gave rise to two lines of inquiry, which have only recently begun to converge in relation to their use within health research (Phelan, Link, & Dovidio, 2008), with ongoing calls to better understand the relationship between these concepts (Hatzenbuehler & Link, 2014; Hatzenbuehler, Phelan, & Link, 2013; Stuber, Meyer, & Link, 2008). For example, a stigma framework has often been referenced when studying specific illnesses or morbidities, such as mental illness and HIV/AIDS, while prejudice and discrimination have been foregrounded in studies of racism and health. In addition, the concept of bias is commonly utilized within health care contexts as a way of describing unconscious forms of discrimination, often labeled implicit bias (Paradies, Truong, & Priest, 2014; Shavers et al., 2012; Van Ryn et al., 2011). Within public health, researchers have tended to define and measure discrimination as the behavioral manifestations of prejudice, stigma, and bias, thus considering discrimination a real-world manifestation of oppression with potential adverse health consequences.

Although it may seem self-evident that discrimination, prejudice, stigma, and bias are unhealthy for both individuals and societies, quantitative health research on oppression only began in earnest with a review by Krieger (1999). As well as reviewing 20 studies on discrimination and health, Krieger considered frameworks, methods, and approaches used in this field of study. Critically, in doing so, Krieger clearly states that the unfair treatment inherent in discrimination is morally reprehensible whether or not it is detrimental to health and well-being (Krieger, 1999). In concordance with this view, rather than serving primarily as further opprobrium against discrimination, health research on this topic aims to further our understanding of, and capacity to counteract, oppression as a determinant of population health disparities. As discussed in more detail later, such research has demonstrated that discrimination has varied impacts on health-related behaviors and mental and physical health, as well as social outcomes that influence health status. Studies have also investigated a range of factors that mediate and/or moderate the relationship between discrimination and health.

To date, relevant literature has largely focused on the detrimental impacts of experiences of discrimination that are self-reported by members of target minority groups, especially African Americans, women, GLBTIQ[1] communities, and indigenous peoples. This has included elucidation of how self-reported experiences of oppression underlie specific population patterns of health inequities (i.e., unfair and avoidable health differentials between social groups), and the nature of any etiological relation between discrimination and multiple health outcomes, including mental illnesses, deleterious health behaviors, and poor physical outcomes (Krieger, 2014). For instance, racial or ethnic health differentials have been attributed, at least in part, to the fact that individuals from specific social groupings, such as Black or indigenous people, are more likely to be exposed to acute and/or chronic forms of oppression, which in turn, put them at a heightened risk of ill health.

Importantly, the health consequences of systemic and structural forms of oppression have remained largely under-examined to date (although see, e.g., Feagin & Bennefield, 2014; Gee, 2002; Gee & Ford, 2011; Lukachko, Hatzenbuehler, & Keyes, 2014; Mendez, Hogan, & Culhane, 2011). Similarly, the association between internalized oppression and health has also received limited attention (although see Bryant, 2011; Chae, Nuru-Jeter, & Adler, 2012;

---

1 Gay, lesbian, bisexual, transgender, intersex, queer, and questioning.

Carr, Szymanski, Taha, West & Kaslow, 2014; Chae, Lincoln, Adler, & Dyme et al., 2010; Cort, Gwebu, Tull, Cox, & Modize, 2013; Krieger et al., 2011; Krieger et al., 2013; Tull, Cort, Gwebu, & Gwebu, 2007; Tull, Sheu, Butler, & Cornelious, 2005).

Some public heath scholars (Bastos, 2012; Parker, 2012) argue that such emphasis on individual-level discrimination, despite the previously mentioned multi-level conceptualization of oppression, is due to a widespread influence of *functionalism* on social psychology and social epidemiology in the past few decades (Berard, 2008). Following this paradigm, oppression is rarely seen as a social process beyond personal interactions, thus reflecting structural systems of power and domination that maintain silence or avoid disrupting dominant systems. For example, Phelan et al. (2008) conceptualize stigma and prejudice as structural features of modern societies that have specific purposes: (a) exploitation and domination, (b) enforcement of social norms, and (c) disease avoidance. In other words, each of these would be to keep people down, keep people in, and keep people away, respectively. According to these scholars, these specific functions of oppression should be emphasized in both public health and related areas of inquiry.

In addition to a focus on discrimination as an individual-level phenomenon, an implicit notion that perpetrators of prejudice are themselves "unhealthy" was evident during the 1950s and 1960s, when prejudice in social psychology was characterized as "faulty cognition" (Reicher, 2007, p. 820) or implicated in personality disorders (Adorno, Frenkel-Brunswick, Levinson, & Sanford, 1950; Bell, 1980; Sibley, Harding, Perry, Asbrock, & Duckitt, 2010). Interestingly, explicit examination of health impacts for perpetrators of discrimination has emerged recently in public health research (see the Conclusion for details).

As well as predominantly focusing on interpersonal discrimination, existing studies across disciplines have largely conceptualized prejudice (Meyer, 2003a) and discrimination (Brondolo, Brady, Libby, & Pencille, 2011) as a psychosocial stressor (Bastos, Celeste, Faerstein, & Barros, 2010), with consequent mental, physical, and behavioral impacts. Health outcomes most commonly studied have included depression, anxiety, and stress. In addition, despite a range of attributes that form the basis of discrimination in society, scholarship has predominantly focused on racism with much fewer studies examining sexism, heterosexism, weight bias, mental illness stigma, disability, or HIV status, whether in combination or in isolation (Krieger, 2014). For example, 66% of the studies included in a systematic review of discrimination and health focused on racism (Pascoe & Richman, 2009), while this figure was 64% in a more recent study by Schmitt, Branscombe, Postmes, and Garcia (2014). As the second most commonly studied form of discrimination, sexism was the focus of 14% (Pascoe & Richman, 2009) and 7% (Schmitt et al., 2014) of studies examined in these two reviews.

Measuring Oppression in Health Research

According to Blank, Dabady, and Citro (2004), there are four main methodological approaches to assess discrimination, bias, prejudice, or stigma, whether from an internalized, interpersonal, or systemic perspective:

- laboratory experiments, which expose, for example, White and Black participants (often randomly allocated) to various scenarios in controlled conditions;
- field experiments, also known as audit or paired-testing studies, which, for example, could involve ascertaining differential treatment between matched pairs of Blacks and Whites randomly allocated to seek housing (in person, over the phone, or via correspondence);
- statistical analysis of observational data and natural experiments, which investigate the association between a variable – often regarded as a marker of oppression (e.g., race, sex, or social class) – and a specific outcome. The residual association between the variables, after taking into account other relevant observed characteristics, is attributed to oppression; and
- indicators of discrimination from survey and administrative records, which rely on self-reports of, say, racial attitudes and perceived experiences of discrimination.

Computer-assisted reaction-time measures and neurophysiological methods have also emerged recently as a new method to assess implicit attitudes (Yogeeswaran, Devos, & Nash, Chapter 11, this title). Each of these methodological approaches has its own purposes, strengths, and limitations and can be used conjointly to address specific types of research questions (Blank et al., 2004). In health research, although field experiments have been utilized (Paradies et al., 2014; Planas, García, Bustelo, Carcamo, & Martinez, 2015), statistical analysis of observational data and, even more so, indicators of discrimination from survey records predominate. This is, in part, due to the emphasis on an individual-level perspective as discussed earlier.

The most common approach, use of indicators of discrimination, typically involves the administration of measures (i.e., psychometric scales) of self-reported experiences of discrimination to survey participants, for example, the Schedule of Sexist Events (Landrine & Klonoff, 1996). With these approaches, the association between self-reported discriminatory experiences and health outcomes or patterns of health inequalities may be tested in the context of multivariable models, including confounding adjustment and examination of effect modification. This approach often focuses on specific stigmatized population groups and, in contrast to research using observational data discussed earlier, explicit comparison between these groups and the non-stigmatized are rarely undertaken (Lewis, Cogburn, & Williams, 2015).

The development of self-reported discrimination scales has been characterized by two key assessment procedures: one-stage and two-stage measurement. One-stage approaches involve explicit terminology related to a specific driver of discriminatory experiences as the reasons for unfair, differential, or negative treatment, for example, Schedule of Racist Events (Landrine & Klonoff, 1996). In contrast, the two-stage approach involves an initial question about unfair or discriminatory experiences with a nested item then asking the respondent to attribute this experience to one or more of their ascribed or acquired social characteristics (e.g., gender, sexuality, socioeconomic position). Two key scales that use this two-stage approach are mentioned later. Typically, the extent of discrimination reported is higher in the one- vs. two-stage approach, with debate in the literature over whether such enhanced reporting is more accurate or overestimated (Lewis et al., 2015). More generally, the literature suggests that censure from others (Kaiser, Dyrenforth, & Hagiwara, 2006; Kaiser & Major, 2006), attributional ambiguity (Kaiser & Miller, 2001), and just-world beliefs (Barreto & Ellemers, 2015) result in under- rather than over-reporting of discrimination (Krieger et al., 2010; Krieger et al., 2011).

A three-stage approach instrument was also developed, in which the interviewee is first asked whether he/she experienced differential treatment; then what was/ were the perceived reason/s for such treatment/s; and, finally, if he/she felt discriminated against in the circumstance/s to which he/she referred (Bastos, Faerstein, Celeste, & Barros, 2012). This instrument was devised to disentangle harmful differential treatment effects from their interpretation as discriminatory events; however, no systematic research on the purportedly distinctive effects of these phenomena has yet been conducted.

In general, it may be argued that all survey instruments already developed, following any of the three aforementioned approaches, are still in their initial stages of psychometric assessment and refinement, such that further research is needed to better and comprehensively assess oppression from an individual perspective (Atkins, 2014; Bastos et al., 2010; Yoo & Pituc, 2013). Within this nascent state of the field, the two-stage Everyday Discrimination Scale (Williams, Yu, Jackson, & Anderson, 1997) and the Experiences of Discrimination scale (Krieger, Smith, Naishadham, Hartman, & Barbeau, 2005) are notable in their extent of psychometric testing to date (Chana, Trana, & Nguyen, 2012; Cunningham et al., 2011; Kim, Sellbom, & Ford, 2014; Lewis, Yang, Jacobs, & Fitchett, 2012; Peek, Nunez-Smith, Drum, & Lewis, 2011; Reeve et al., 2011; Stucky et al., 2011). However, some potential major challenges to be faced in this line of inquiry are whether:

- it would be appropriate to devise a *universal* oppression scale, which could be cross-culturally adaptable to multiple contexts, as well as various population groups, such that results across studies are directly comparable;
- experiencing and perpetrating discrimination (e.g., attitudes or behaviors) should be simultaneously assessed in the same survey; and
- the method of data collection (e.g., face-to-face interviews, self-administered questionnaires, and computer-assisted techniques) differentially impacts the reporting of oppression, affecting its validity and reliability (Bastos et al., 2010).

The previously mentioned approaches should ideally be complemented by further consideration of subtle discrimination, including positive stereotypes (Czopp, Kay, & Cheryan, 2015). Although shown to be just as damaging to health as overt forms of discrimination (Jones et al., 2016), subtle discrimination has received relatively little attention to date (cf. Sibley, 2011) as has measurement of ecologic or group-level investigations of oppression. Such studies could incorporate measures of residential segregation, minority representation in government, mortgage redlining (Gee, 2002), and area-level racial climate (Chae et al., 2015) as markers of systemic oppression. Specific measures for various periods in the life course are also required to accommodate developmental and socio-cognitive capacities of respondents, particularly children and adolescents.

Pathways Between Oppression and Ill Health

As noted earlier, in practice, the impact of oppression has predominately been measured through its expression as unfair or negative differential treatment (i.e., discrimination). Such treatment can impact on health in a number of ways, including but not limited to:

- reduced access to social outcomes such as employment, housing, and education and/or increased exposure to risk factors (e.g., pollution);
- maladaptive cognitive, emotional, and behavioral responses including diminished participation in healthy behaviors and/or increased engagement in unhealthy behaviors;
- allostatic load and concomitant patho-psychological processes; and
- physical injury as a result of identity-motivated assault.

Building on conceptual diagrams and existing scholarship (Harrell et al., 2011; Paradies, 2006; Pascoe & Richman, 2009; Williams, 1997), Figure 25.1 broadly details these multiple pathways linking discrimination to ill health. Although the mechanisms proposed to explain the observed associations between discriminatory experiences and health outcomes are multiple and varied (Gee, Walsemann, & Brondolo, 2012; Harrell et al., 2011; Paradies, 2006; Williams & Mohammed, 2013), it is important to note that not all of these pathways have been thoroughly examined in empirical studies as yet (Priest et al., 2013) and, clearly, discrimination is not the only determinant of the mechanisms and health end-points shown. Moreover, pathways through which discrimination affects multiple health outcomes may change over time, and across distinct sociocultural contexts, depending on various manifestations, perpetrators, and targets.

There is now overwhelming evidence that one's living and working conditions as well as social and economic opportunities, education, income, wealth, and status are the primary determinants of health across human populations (Braveman,

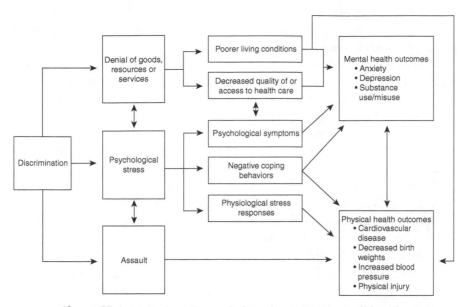

Figure 25.1 *Multiple pathways linking discrimination to ill health. Adapted from Paradies et al. (2013).*

Egerter, & Williams, 2011). As touched on earlier, it is also clear that various forms of discrimination impact directly on these social resources and, hence, on health and well-being across the life course, including mental, emotion, and physical injury resulting from identity-motivated assault (Herek, 2009; Shannon, Rospenda, Richman, & Minich, 2009).

Key aspects of the social determinants of health model are health-related thoughts, emotions, and behaviors. In relation to discrimination, there is now emerging evidence of phenomena such as hypervigilance (Clark, Benkert, & Flack, 2006; Hicken, Lee, Ailshire, Burgard, & Williams, 2013), anticipatory/ attributional anxiety (Mendes, McCoy, Major, & Blascovich, 2008; Sawyer, Major, Casad, Townsend, & Mendes, 2012), and rumination (Borders & Hennebry, 2015; Borders & Liang, 2011) as responses to discrimination that are, at least in some contexts, maladaptive, with a range of detrimental health effects. In addition, other research indicates that passive (rather than active) coping (Pearson et al., 2014; Schmader, Croft, Whitehead, & Stone, 2013; Szymanski & Henrichs-Beck, 2014) as a response to discrimination may be associated with ill health.

There is now also nascent evidence of the relationship between discrimination and reduced engagement in healthy behaviors including sleep (Slopen et al., 2016) and physical activity (Edwards & Cunningham, 2013; Shelton et al., 2009; Womack et al., 2014), while other studies have shown that discrimination can lead to more unhealthy behaviors such as alcohol consumption (Goto, Couto, & Bastos, 2013; Gilbert & Zemore, 2016) and smoking (Lewis et al., 2015). These behavioral changes may occur through either conscious or semiconscious forms of stress coping or more indirectly and unconsciously via reduced self-regulation (Smart Richman & Lattanner, 2014).

Whether or not discrimination is consciously perceived by its targets, a series of negative emotional responses and physiological arousal may ensue. Studies indicate that the hypothalamic-pituitary-adrenal (HPA) axis may be activated with consequent release of cortisol (i.e., a steroid hormone released in response to stress or other physiologic factors). This is important given that flat cortisol slopes are frequently associated with outcomes such as poor mental health, higher breast cancer mortality, and cardiovascular disease (Zeiders, Hoyt, & Adam, 2014). However, empirical studies on the association between discrimination and the HPA axis activity are still inconsistent, suggesting that the direction of effect (increased or decreased HPA axis stimulation in response to discrimination) depends on a range of factors, which are not fully understood at present (Berger & Sarnyai, 2015). The stressful response to discrimination may also activate the sympathetic-adrenalmedullary axis, which often leads to changes in the cardiovascular system, including increased heart rate and blood pressure (Williams & Mohammed, 2013). Nevertheless, research on the association between discrimination and cardiovascular outcomes, specifically heart rate variability (HRV), is scarce. Existing studies suggest a direct relation between perceived discrimination and low HRV, which is known to be a prognostic factor for myocardial infarction and diabetic neuropathy (Berger & Sarnyai, 2015).

Another potential pathway from discrimination to negative health outcomes has been referred to as "allostatic load," a maladaptive process by which the human body adapts to changing demands over time, which leads to increased secretion of glucocorticoids and pro-inflammatory cytokines (Juster, McEwen, & Lupien, 2010). These are known to affect specific areas of the brain and contribute to metabolic changes, which are potential risk factors for chronic diseases (Harrell et al., 2011), with emerging evidence from longitudinal studies of the intersection between discrimination, allostatic load, and health outcomes (cf. Brody et al., 2014).

The Impact of Oppression on Health

A comprehensive review by Pascoe and Richman (2009), combined with a meta-analysis, examined 192 studies on the association between perceived discrimination and mental and physical health. In all, 134 of these studies were included in the meta-analysis, which showed that discrimination had a significant negative effect on both mental and a somewhat weaker but still significant negative association with physical health (Pascoe & Richman, 2009).

A more recent meta-analysis by Schmitt et al. (2014) examined the relationship between discrimination and mental health and well-being (negative and positive) in 328 independent effect sizes (N = 144,246), including associations adjusted for different covariates. Correlational data measuring both perceived discrimination and psychological well-being (e.g., self-esteem, depression, anxiety, psychological distress, life satisfaction) were reviewed. Using a random-effects model, the mean weighted effect size was significantly negative, indicating harm ($r = -.23$). Effect sizes were larger for disadvantaged groups ($r = -.24$) compared to advantaged groups ($r = -.10$), larger for children compared to adults, larger for perceptions of personal discrimination compared to group discrimination, and weaker for racism and sexism compared to other types of oppression. The negative relationship was significant across different operationalizations of well-being but was somewhat weaker for positive outcomes (e.g., self-esteem, positive affect) than for negative outcomes (e.g., depression, anxiety, negative affect). Importantly, the effect size was significantly negative even in longitudinal studies that controlled for prior levels of well-being ($r = -.15$).

Although findings from these meta-analyses are compelling, the majority of these correlational data still come from cross-sectional investigations whose participants were selected according to convenience sampling schemes (Goto et al., 2013). Most studies did not explicitly state the theoretical framework guiding the statistical analysis, and have an overemphasis on adolescents and adults from specific ethnic or racial categories, living in the United States. Therefore, the potential generalizability of the current findings as well as the causal nature of the reported associations remain a matter of concern.

Discrimination has also been associated with physiological indicators such as hypertension (Dolezsar, McGrath, Herzig, & Miller, 2014); obesity, coronary artery calcification, inflammation, allostatic load, cortisol levels, c-reactive protein, e-selectin, oxidative stress, and telomere length (Lewis, Cogburn, & Williams, 2015); as well as behaviors including eating habits, smoking, and substance use (Smart Richman & Hatzenbuehler, 2014).

Nonetheless, the association between individual-level oppression and physical health outcomes has not been as consistent as the relationship with mental health. Blood pressure is a representative case in this regard. Even though pioneering studies on the health effects of discrimination took blood pressure and related cardiovascular outcomes as their dependent variables, no consistent pattern of correlation has been demonstrated in the literature. Out of 50 association tests assessed in a previous literature review (Couto, Goto, & Bastos, 2012), 20 were not indicative of either a direct or an inverse relationship between interpersonal discrimination and blood pressure or hypertension.

The relation between oppression and health behaviors has been intensively investigated in the United States, particularly among non-Hispanic Blacks. The studies on this topic have progressed from consistently showing an association between, for example, self-reports of discrimination and substance use/abuse to assessing the causal mechanisms (especially potential cognitive mediators) linking oppression and health behaviors. It is also notable that the statistical associations have been investigated in the context of prospective cohort studies.

For instance, Whitbeck, Hoyt, McMorris, Chen, and Stubben (2001) revealed that discriminatory experiences predicted depression, anger, and delinquent behaviors in a Native American sample. In addition, they showed that anger and delinquent behaviors mediated the effects of discrimination on early substance abuse. Furthermore, Gibbons et al. (2010), prospectively studying a sample of African American youth, showed that the simultaneous inclusion of hostility, anger, depression, and anxiety in the same statistical model confirmed these previous results by Whitbeck et al. (2001) – the indirect path from discrimination to substance use/abuse through anger was statistically significant. This led the authors to conclude that the central construct mediating the association between discrimination and substance use was anger/hostility, and not depression or anxiety. Recent findings from a Brazilian study carried out with undergraduate students also support the idea that discrimination is linked to health outcomes and health behaviors via distinct interlinking pathways: While discrimination may affect self-rated health through anxiety, depression, physical activity, and fruit/vegetable consumption, these associations with discrimination were mediated by discomfort with discriminatory experiences (Bastos, Celeste, Silva, Priest, & Paradies, 2015).

Quasi-experimental studies have also revealed the influence of oppressive social environments. Groundbreaking work by Lauderdale (2006) hypothesized that the terrorists attacks of September 11, 2001, in the United States would lead to an increase in discrimination against people of Arab descent, including its potential deleterious effects on birth outcomes. Based on data from the California birth information system, Lauderdale was able to demonstrate that there was an increase in preterm birth and low birth weight among Arab women in the six months following the attacks, which was not mirrored in any other ethnic or racial group. Prior to September 11, pregnant Arab women had rates of preterm birth and low birth weight similar to those observed among the non-Hispanic White population. A similar study in Michigan, however, with the same design and target population did not result in any significant findings (El-Sayed, Hadley, & Galea, 2008).

Another example of the health effects of oppressive environments comes from 16 states in the United States that banned same-sex marriage in 2004. Longitudinal data collected before and after the bans revealed that non-heterosexual adults in states that banned same-sex marriage experienced a third more mood and alcohol-use disorders, and 2.5 times more generalized anxiety disorders (Hatzenbuehler, McLaughlin, Keyes, & Hasin, 2010), while both heterosexual and non-heterosexual respondents in states without bans experienced no significant changes in such health outcomes. Other studies have demonstrated that the ill-health effects of such systemic discrimination are independent of interpersonal discrimination (Smart Richman & Hatzenbuehler, 2014).

A Dynamic Life-Course Perspective on Oppression

There is a growing global scientific consensus that the origins of adult disease and health inequalities are often found among early life experiences and exposures with early life adversity, such as poverty, abuse, domestic violence, and traumatic stress, shown to influence health later in life, including physical and mental health and cardiovascular, metabolic, and immune function (Shonkoff, Boyce, & McEwen, 2009). Children and youth are thus considered particularly vulnerable to discrimination's harmful effects, as with other forms of early life adversity. Much of the research on discrimination among children and youth has focused on racial discrimination, with emerging evidence documenting the importance of discrimination due to sexual orientation and weight (Garnett et al., 2014; Meyer, 2003b; Puhl & Latner, 2007). Deleterious health effects of subjective experiences of racial discrimination have been documented across countries and racial ethnic groups for this age group (Priest et al., 2013). This includes both direct experiences, where children and youth themselves are targets of discrimination, as well as vicarious experiences, that is, hearing about or seeing another person's experience of discrimination (Harrell, 2000; Mansouri & Jenkins, 2010) or the impact of carers or close family members experiencing discrimination that children and youth may or may not witness (Bécares, Nazroo, & Kelly, 2015; Kelly, Bécares, & Nazroo, 2013; Priest, Paradies, Stevens, & Bailie, 2012). Direct childhood experiences of racial discrimination have been associated with poorer mental health and well-being and increased behavior problems in elementary-school-aged children, and with poorer mental health and increased delinquent behavior and tobacco, alcohol, and substance use in adolescence (Priest et al., 2013). Evidence of the effects of racial discrimination on child physical health outcomes is less consistent, likely a result of few studies in this area to date, as well as delayed onset between exposure to discrimination and outcomes such as obesity, cardiovascular, and other chronic diseases, with future work required using more sensitive biomarkers (Priest et al., 2013).

Experiences of racial discrimination have been found to be associated with flatter (unhealthier) diurnal cortisol slopes for racial/ethnic minority youth (Zeiders, Hoyt, & Adam, 2014). Vicarious discrimination, in the form of carer experiences, has been associated with physical health outcomes such as preterm birth and low birth weight among African Americans in the United States (Mustillo et al., 2004), increased common illnesses in Australian indigenous children under age 7 (Priest et al., 2012), more visits to the doctor for illnesses among 14-month-old Latino children in the United States (Halim, Yoshikawa, & Amodio, 2013), and with poor mental health outcomes in African American preschoolers (Caughy, O'Campo, & Muntaner, 2004), ethnic minority 5-year-olds in the UK (Kelly et al., 2013), as well as African American and racial/ethnic minority adolescents in the United

States (Ford, Hurd, Jagers, & Sellers, 2013; Gibbons, Gerrard, Cleveland, Wills, & Brody, 2004; Tran, 2014).

Rather than an episodic phenomenon, oppression is more likely to manifest across a wide range of life domains, individual lifetimes, and generations. Endeavors to investigate discrimination comprehensively should therefore aim to assess exposure to bias over the life course, with evidence particularly under-developed for early childhood and preadolescent periods and for trajectories of exposure and effects throughout childhood and into adulthood (Priest et al., 2013). How the timing of first and early experiences of discrimination and the accumulation of such incidents over the life course affect the onset and course of illness, both uniquely and in combination with other stress, resilience, and resistance factors, is as yet unknown. A life-course lens for a comprehensive empirical assessment of how racism can influence health has been outlined by Gee et al. (2012). They highlight the importance of attending to sensitive periods, the interdependence in exposures among persons, latency periods, stress proliferation processes, historical period, and birth cohort. However, research and analytic models that capture the complexity of these social determinants of health, their clustering and accumulation, and the biological pathways through which they operate to influence health across the life span are currently scant (Adler, Bush, & Pantell, 2012).

Intersectionality and Health

Research remains limited regarding how multiple aspects of oppression relate to one another and can combine, additively and interactively, with other environmental risks and resources to affect health. Investigating health effects of multiple levels of oppression in relation to a single social identity remains important. However, recognition is growing of the need for theoretical and empirical research in this field to move beyond analyzing single categories to consider simultaneous interactions between different dimensions of social identity (e.g., race/ethnicity, gender, class) and the impact on health of systems and processes of oppression and domination (e.g., racism, classism, sexism) that operate at the micro and macro levels (Hankivsky, 2012). These intersectional approaches question the isolation and prioritization of a single social position and highlight the potential of varied interrelationships of social identities and interacting social processes in the production of inequities (Browne & Misra, 2003; Crenshaw, 1989; Hankivsky, 2012).

Within discrimination and health research, the health impacts of discrimination have been found to be invariant by the personal characteristic for which discrimination was attributed to by the target (Williams et al., 2012), while a meta-analysis provided broader support for this finding in relation to mental health (Schmitt et al., 2014). However, there was evidence that health impacts were worse for groups subject to forms of discrimination that are still somewhat societally acceptable (e.g., those who are overweight) compared to much more socially unacceptable forms of discrimination (e.g., racial). Deleterious health impacts of multiple forms of discrimination across multiple social identities (e.g., race, sex) as proposed in the double jeopardy hypothesis have also been documented (Grollman, 2012, 2014). There is thus an ongoing need to not only move beyond racial discrimination as the most commonly studied form of oppression in this field (Smart Richman and Hatzenbuehler, 2014) but also to consider how multiple forms of oppression are interrelated, and how they combine interactively, not just additively, to influence health (Bauer, 2014).

As an example of such emerging research, a study by Carr et al. (2014) found that while only racism had an direct association with depression among 144 African American women in the US southeast, both racism and sexual objectification had an indirect effect mediated through internalization (attributing responsibility to oneself) while gendered racism had no significant association with this health outcome. Another study in Brazil showed that not only were self-reports of age, race, and class discrimination correlated, being discriminated against based simultaneously on these three factors was associated with the highest frequency of common mental disorders, which could not be explained by the effect of each type of discrimination in isolation (Bastos, Barros, Celeste, Paradies, & Faerstein, 2014). Among Latina/o adults, additive and interactive effects of multiple forms of oppression on mental health have recently been shown, across two forms of external oppression (racist discrimination and heterosexist discrimination) and internalized oppression (racism and heterosexism; Velez, Moradi, & DeBlaere, 2014). Other researchers have begun to ask if experiences of diverse forms of oppression are unrelated (i.e., independent), inversely related (i.e., where increased reporting of racism results in reduced reporting of sexism), positively associated, or even qualitatively different when experienced in combination (i.e., effect moderation or interaction in a statistical sense), with extant empirical work demonstrating positive correlations between various self-reported experiences of discrimination (Harnois, 2014).

Greater attention is required within quantitative health research to the explicit theorization (Veenstra, 2013) and application of intersectionality to improve understanding of patterns of inequalities within intersectional groups and the likely individual- and group-level causes of these, including interactions between dimensions of oppression and privilege across levels (Bauer, 2014). It is argued that doing so is consistent with ecosocial theory (Krieger, 2012) and other cross-disciplinary biopsychosocial approaches that reflect the complexity of how social, behavioural, and environmental factors become biologically embodied (Bauer, 2014).

Conclusion

Many of the challenges outlined throughout this chapter may be fruitfully addressed by the adoption of a broader sociocultural perspective on how oppression operates in the social realm and on the social functions it exerts. Such a perspective is key to conceptualizing oppression beyond cognitive/emotional processes in which individual ideological orientations, stigmas, prejudices, and other factors play important roles. This will add important dimensions to the existing research largely focused on individual-level oppression and its antecedents and health consequences, as well as having the potential to broaden existing concerns with specific single types of oppression (e.g., racism, sexism, ageism), while encompassing a greater diversity of target populations and nation contexts. We would like to end with a brief sketch of promising new directions in the field of oppression and health:

- the interacting health impacts of both perpetrating and being the target of racism (and other forms of oppression; Gong and Xu, 2014; Hamburger, Basile, & Vivolo, 2011; Zadro & Gonsalkorale, 2014), especially given emerging evidence that holding racist attitudes can be associated with ill health (Kwate & Goodman, 2014; Samson, 2015) along with calls to study the link between such attitudes and experiences of racism within specific localities (Habtegiorgis, Paradies, & Dunn, 2014);
- computer-assisted techniques to assess internalized oppression such as the Implicit Association Test (IAT) in terms of pro-White bias (i.e., internalized racism; Chae et al., 2014) for African Americans as well as implicit association between self and being a victim of discrimination (Krieger et al., 2013), including their relationship with various health outcomes and interplay with survey-based approaches as well as approaches that may be superior to the IAT (Orey, Craemer, & Price, 2013); and
- the specific contribution that discrimination makes to health disparities, which has been examined in only a handful of studies to date (Ikram et al., 2015; Lewis, Cogburn, & Williams, 2015).

We hope the body of work brought together in this chapter will help researchers carry out studies capable of enhancing our knowledge of the issue and ultimately foster fair and equitable social environments conducive to health and well-being.

References

Adler, N., N. R. Bush, & M. S. Pantell. (2012). Rigor, vigor, and the study of health disparities. *Proceedings of the National Academy of Sciences 109* (Supplement 2), 17154–17159.

Adorno, T., Frenkel-Brunswick, E., Levinson, D., & Sanford, R. N. (1950). *The authoritarian personality.* New York: Harper & Brothers.

Allport, G. (1954). *The nature of prejudice.* Reading, MA: Addison-Wesley.

Atkins, R. (2014). Instruments measuring perceived racism/racial discrimination: Review and critique of factor analytic techniques. *Int J Health Serv 44* (4):711–34.

Barreto, M., & Ellemers, N. (2015). Detecting and experiencing prejudice: New answers to old questions. *Advances in Experimental Social Psychology, 52*, 139–219.

Bastos, F. I. (2012). Forum: Stigma, discrimination and health: Policies and research challenges. Postscript. *Cad Saude Publica, 28*(1), 190–193.

Bastos, J. L., Barros, A. J., Celeste, R. K., Paradies, Y., & Faerstein, E. (2014). Age, class and race discrimination: Their interactions and associations with mental health among Brazilian university students. *Cad Saude Publica, 30* (1), 175–186.

Bastos, J. L., Celeste, R. K., Faerstein, E., & Barros, A. J. (2010). Racial discrimination and health: A systematic review of scales with a focus on their psychometric properties. *Soc Sci Med, 70* (7), 1091–1099.

Bastos, J. L., Celeste, R. K., Silva, D. A., Priest, N., & Paradies, Y. C. (2015). Assessing mediators between discrimination, health behaviors and physical health outcomes: A representative cross-sectional study. *Soc Psychiatry Psychiatr Epidemiol.*

Bastos, J. L., Faerstein, E., Celeste, R. K., & Barros, A. J. (2012). Explicit discrimination and health: Development and psychometric properties of an assessment instrument. *Rev Saude Publica, 46*(2), 269–278.

Bauer, G. R. (2014). Incorporating intersectionality theory into population health research methodology: Challenges and the potential to advance health equity. *Social Science & Medicine, 110*, 10–17.

Bécares, L., Nazroo, J., & Kelly, Y. (2015). A longitudinal examination of maternal, family, and area-level experiences of racism on children's socioemotional development: Patterns and possible explanations. *Social Science & Medicine, 142*, 128–135.

Bell, C. (1980). Racism: A symptom of the narcissistic personality. *Journal of the American Medical Society, 72*(7), 661–665.

Berard, T. J. (2008). The Neglected Social Psychology of Institutional Racism. Sociology Compass, 2.

Berger, M., & Sarnyai, Z. (2015). "More than skin deep": Stress neurobiology and mental health consequences of racial discrimination. *Stress, 18*(1), 1–10.

Blank, R. M., Dabady, M., & Citro, C. F. (2004). *Measuring racial discrimination: Panel on methods for assessing discrimination.* Washington, DC: National Academies Press.

Borders, A., & Hennebry, K. A. (2015). Angry rumination moderates the association between perceived ethnic discrimination and risky behaviors. *Personality and Individual Differences, 79*(0), 81–86.

Borders, A., & Liang, C. T. H. (2011). Rumination partially mediates the associations between perceived ethnic discrimination, emotional distress, and aggression. *Cultural Diversity & Ethnic Minority Psychology, 17*(2), 125–133.

Braveman, P., Egerter, S., & Williams, D. R. (2011). The social determinants of health: Coming of age. *Annual Review of Public Health, 32*, 381–398.

Brody, G. H., Lei, M. K., Chae, D. H., Yu, T., Kogan, S. M., & Beach, S. R. H. (2014). Perceived discrimination among African American adolescents and allostatic load: A longitudinal analysis with buffering effects. *Child Development, 85*(3), 989–1002.

Brondolo, E., Brady, N., Libby, D., & Pencille, M. (2011). Racism as a psychosocial stressor. In A. Baum & R. Contrada, (Eds.), *Handbook of stress science* (pp. 167–184). New York: Springer.

Browne, I., & Misra, J. (2003). The intersection of gender and race in labor markets. *Annual Review of Sociology, 29*, 487–513.

Bryant, W. W. (2011). Internalized racism's association with African American male's propensity for violence. *Journal of Black Studies, 42*(4), 690–707.

Carr, E. R., Szymanski, D.M., Taha, F., West, L.M., & Kaslow, N. J. (2014). Understanding the link between multiple oppressions and depression among African American women: The role of internalization. *Psychology of Women Quarterly, 38*(2), 233–245.

Caughy, M. O., O'Campo, P. J., & Muntaner, C. (2004). Experiences of racism among African American parents and the mental health of their preschool-aged children. *Am J Public Health, 94*(12), 2118–2124.

Chae, D.H., Clouston, S., Hatzenbuehler, M. L., Kramer, M. R., Cooper, H. L. F., Wilson, S.M. ... Link, B. G. (2015). Association between an internet-based measure of area racism and black mortality. *PLoS One, 10*(4).

Chae, D. H., Nuru-Jeter, A. M., & Adler, N. E. (2012). Implicit racial bias as a moderator of the association between racial discrimination and hypertension: A study of midlife African American men. *Psychosomatic Medicine, 74*(9), 961–964.

Chae, D. H., Nuru-Jeter, A. M., Adler, N. E., Brody, G. H., Lin, J., Blackburn, E. H., & Epel, E. S. (2014). Discrimination, racial bias, and telomere length in African-American men. *American Journal of Preventive Medicine* (2), 103.

Chae, D. H., Lincoln, K. D., Adler, N. E., & Leonard Dyme, S. (2010). Do experiences of racial discrimination predict cardiovascular disease among African American men? The moderating role of internalized negative racial group attitudes. *Social Science and Medicine, 71*(6), 1182–1188.

Chana, K. T., Trana, T. V., & Nguyen, T. N. (2012). Cross-cultural equivalence of a measure of perceived discrimination between Chinese-Americans and Vietnamese-Americans. *Journal of Ethnic and Cultural Diversity in Social Work, 21*(1), 20–36.

Clark, R., Benkert, R. A., & Flack, J. M. (2006). Large arterial elasticity varies as a function of gender and racism-related vigilance in Black youth. *Journal of Adolescence Health, 39*, 562–569.

Cort, M. A., Gwebu, E. T., Tull, E. S., Cox, N. A., & Modise, T. (2013). The differential gender effect of internalized racism on abdominal obesity in KwaZulu-Natal, South Africa. *The Social Science Journal, 50*(4), 557–564.

Couto, P. F., Goto, J. B., & Bastos, J. L. (2012). Blood pressure and interpersonal discrimination: Systematic review of epidemiologic studies. *Arq Bras Cardiol, 99*(4), 956–963.

Crenshaw, K. (1989). *Demarginalizing the intersection of race and sex: A Black feminist critique of antidiscrimination doctrine, feminist theory and antiracist politics.* University of Chicago Legal Forum, pp. 139–167.

Cunningham, T. J., Berkman, L. F., Gortmaker, S. L., Kiefe, C. I., Jacobs, D. R., Seeman, T. E., & Kawachi, I. (2011). Assessment of differential item functioning in the experiences of discrimination index: The Coronary Artery Risk Development in Young Adults (CARDIA) study. *American Journal of Epidemiology, 174*, 1266–1274.

Czopp, A. M., Kay, A. C., & Cheryan, S. (2015). Positive stereotypes are pervasive and powerful. *Perspect Psychol Sci, 10*(4), 451–463.

Dolezsar, C. M., McGrath, J. J., Herzig, A. J. M., & Miller, S. B. (2014). Perceived racial discrimination and hypertension: A comprehensive systematic review. *Health Psychology, 33*(1), 20–34.

Edwards, M. B., & Cunningham, G. (2013). Examining the associations of perceived community racism with self-reported physical activity levels and health among older racial minority adults. *Journal of Physical Activity and Health, 10,* 932–939.

El-Sayed, A., Hadley, C., & Galea, S. (2008). Birth outcomes among Arab Americans in Michigan before and after the terrorist attacks of September 11. *Ethnicity & Disease, 18*(3), 348–356.

Feagin, J., & Bennefield, Z. (2014). Systemic racism and U.S. health care. *Social Science & Medicine, 103,* 7–14.

Ford, K. R., Hurd, M., Jagers, R. J., & Sellers, R. M. (2013). Caregiver experiences of discrimination and African American adolescents' psychological health over time. *Child Development, 84*(2), 485–499.

Garnett, B., Raveche, K., Masyn, E., Austin, S. B., Miller, M., Williams, D. R., & Viswanath, K. (2014). The intersectionality of discrimination attributes and bullying among youth: An applied latent class analysis. *Journal of Youth and Adolescence, 43*(8), 1225–1239.

Gee, G. C. (2002). A multilevel analysis of the relationship between institutional and individual racial discrimination and health status. *Am J Public Health, 92*(4), 615–623.

Gee, G. C., & Ford, C. L. (2011). Structural racism and health inequities, old issues, new directions. *Du Bois Review, 8*(1), 115–132.

Gee, G. C., Walsemann, K. M., & Brondolo, E. (2012). A life course perspective on how racism may be related to health inequities. *Am J Public Health, 102*(5), 967–974.

Gibbons, F. X., Etcheverry, P. E., Stock, M. L., Gerrard, M., Weng, C. Y., Kiviniemi, M., & O'Hara, R. E. (2010). Exploring the link between racial discrimination and substance use: What mediates? What buffers? *J Pers Soc Psychol, 99*(5), 785–801.

Gibbons, F. X., Gerrard, M., Cleveland, M. J., Wills, T. A., & Brody, G. (2004). Perceived discrimination and substance use in African American parents and their children: A panel study. *J Pers.Soc Psychol, 86*(4), 517–529.

Gilbert, P. A., & Zemore, S. E. (2016). Discrimination and drinking: A systematic review of the evidence. *Social Science & Medicine, 161,* 178–194.

Goffman, E. 1963. *Stigma: Notes on the management of spoiled identity.* Englewood Cliffs, NJ: Prentice Hall.

Gong, F., & Xu, J. (2014). Mental illness and discrimination. In W.C. Cockerham, R. Dingwall, & S. Quah, (Eds.), *The Wiley Blackwell encyclopedia of health, illness, behavior, and society* (pp. 1572–1577). Chicester: Wiley-Blackwell.

Goto, J. B., Couto, P. F., & Bastos, J. L. (2013). Systematic review of epidemiological studies on interpersonal discrimination and mental health. *Cad Saude Publica, 29*(3), 445–459.

Grollman, E. A. (2012). Multiple forms of perceived discrimination and health among adolescents and young adults. *Journal of Health and Social Behavior, 53*(2), 199–214.

Grollman, E. A. (2014). Multiple disadvantaged statuses and health: The role of multiple forms of discrimination. *Journal of Health and Social Behavior, 55*(1), 3–19.

Habtegiorgis, A., Paradies, Y., & Dunn, K. (2014). Are racist attitudes related to experiences of racial discrimination? Within sample testing utilizing nationally representative survey data. *Social Science Research, 47*, 178–191.

Halim, M. L., Yoshikawa, H., & Amodio, D. M. (2013). Cross-generational effects of discrimination among immigrant mothers: Perceived discrimination predicts child's healthcare visits for illness. *Health Psychology, 32*(2), 203–211.

Hamburger, M. E., Basile, K. C., & Vivolo, A. M. (2011). *Measuring bullying victimization, perpetration, and bystander experiences: a compendium of assessment tools.* Atlanta, GA: Centers for Disease Control and Prevention, National Center for Injury Prevention and Control.

Hankivsky, O. (2012)3. Women's health, men's health, and gender and health: Implications of intersectionality. *Social Science and Medicine, 74*, 1712–1720.

Harnois, C. E. (2014). Are perceptions of discrimination unidimensional, oppositional, or intersectional? Examining the relationship among perceived racial-, ethnic-, gender-, and age-based discrimination. *Sociological Perspective, 57*(4), 470–480.

Harrell, C. J. P., Burford, T. I., Cage, B. N., McNair Nelson, T., Shearon, S., Thompson, A., & Green, S. (2011). Multiple pathways linking racism to health outcomes. *Du Bois Review, 8*(1), 143–157.

Harrell, S. P. 2000. A multidimensional conceptualization of racism-related stress: Implications for the well-being of people of color. *American Journal of Orthopsychiatry, 70*(1), 42–57.

Hatzenbuehler, M. L., & Link, B. G. (2014). Introduction to the special issue on structural stigma and health. *Social Science & Medicine, 103*, 1–6.

Hatzenbuehler, M. L., McLaughlin, K. A. Keyes, K. M. and Hasin. D. S. 2010. The impact of institutional discrimination on psychiatric disorders in lesbian, gay, and bisexual populations: A prospective study. *Am J Public Health, 100*(3), 452–459.

Hatzenbuehler, M. L., Phelan, J. C., & Link, B. G. (2013). Stigma as a fundamental cause of population health inequalities. *American Journal of Public Health, 103*(5), e1–e9.

Herek, G. M. (2009). Hate crimes and stigma-related experiences among sexual minority adults in the United States: Prevalence estimates from a national probability sample. *J Interpers Violence, 24*(1), 54–74.

Hicken, M. T., Lee, H., Ailshire, J., Burgard, S. A., & Williams, D. R. (2013). "Every shut eye, ain't sleep": The role of racism-related vigilance in racial/ethnic disparities in sleep difficulty. *Race and Social Problems, 5*(2), 100–112.

Ikram, U.Z., Snijder, M. B., Fassaert, T. J., Schene, A. H., Kunst, A. E., & Stronks, K. (2015). The contribution of perceived ethnic discrimination to the prevalence of depression. *Eur J Public Health, 25*(2), 243–248.

Johnson, A. G. (2000). Oppression. In A. G. Johnson (Ed.), *The Blackwell dictionary of sociology: A user's guide to sociological language.* Oxford: Blackwell Publishers.

Jones, C. P. (2000). Levels of racism: A theoretic framework and a gardener's tale. *Am J Public Health, 90*(8), 1212–1215.

Jones, K. P., Peddie, C. I., Gilrane, V. L., King, E. B., & Gray, A.L. (2016). Not so subtle: A meta-analytic investigation of the correlates of subtle and overt discrimination. *Journal of Management, 42*(6), 1588–1613.

Juster, R. J., McEwen, B. S., & Lupien, S. J. (2010). Allostatic load biomarkers of chronic stress and impact on health and cognition. *Neuroscience and Biobehavioral Reviews, 35*(1), 2–16.

Kaiser, C. R., Dyrenforth, P. S., & Hagiwara, N. (2006). Why are attributions to discrimination interpersonally costly? A test of system- and group-justifying motivations. *Personality & Social Psychology Bulletin, 332*(11), 1523–1536.

Kaiser, C. R., & Major, B. (2006). A social psychological perspective on perceiving and reporting discrimination. *Law & Social Inquiry, 31*(4), 801–830.

Kaiser, C. R., & Miller, C. T. (2001). Stop complaining! The social costs of making attributions to discrimination. *Personality & Social Psychology Bulletin, 27*(2), 254–263.

Kelly, Y., Bécares, L., & Nazroo, J. (2013). Associations between maternal experiences of racism and early child health and development: Findings from the UK Millennium Cohort Study. *Journal of Epidemiology and Community Health, 67*(1), 35–44.

Kim, G., Sellbom, M., & Ford, K. L. (2014). Race/ethnicity and measurement equivalence of the Everyday Discrimination Scale. *Psychological Assessment, 26*(3), 892–900.

Krieger, N. (1999). Embodying inequality: A review of concepts, measures, and methods for studying health consequences of discrimination. *Int J Health Serv, 29*(2), 295–352.

Krieger, N. (2012). Methods for the scientific study of discrimination and health: An ecosocial approach. *American Journal of Public Health Online*, e1–e10.

Krieger, N. (2014). Discrimination and health inequities. In L. F. Berkman, I. Kawachi & M. M. Glymour (Eds.), *Social epidemiology* (pp. 63–125). New York: Oxford.

Krieger, N., Carney, D., Lancaster, K., Waterman, P. D., Kosholeva, A., & Banaji, M. (2010). Combining explicit and implicit measures of racial discrimination in health research. *American Journal of Public Health, 100*(8), 1485–1492.

Krieger, N., Smith, K., Naishadham, D., Hartman, C., & Barbeau, E. M. (2005). Experiences of discrimination: Validity and reliability of a self-report measure for population health research on racism and health. *Soc Sci Med, 61*(7), 1576–1596.

Krieger, N., Waterman, P. D., Kosheleva, A., Chen, J. T, Smith, D. R., Carney, G. G. . . . Freeman, E. R. (2013). Racial discrimination & cardiovascular disease risk: My body, my story study of 1005 US-born Black and White community health center participants (US). *PLoS One, 8*(10), e77174.

Krieger, N., Waterman, P. D., Kosholeva, A., Chen, J. T., Carney, D.R., and et al. (2011). Exposing racial discrimination: Implicit & explicit measures – the my body, my story study of 1005 US-born Black & White community health center members. *PLoS One, 6*(11), e27636.

Kwate, N. O. A., & Goodman, M. S. (2014). An empirical analysis of White privilege, social position and health. *Social Science & Medicine, 116*(0), 150–160.

Landrine, H., & Klonoff, E. A. (1996). The schedule of racist events: A measure of racial discrimination and a study of its negative physical and mental health consequences. *Journal of Black Psychology, 22*(2), 144–168.

Lauderdale, D. S. (2006). Birth outcomes for Arabic-named women in California before and after September 11. *Demography, 43*(1), 185–201.

Lewis, T. T., Cogburn, C. D., & Williams, D. R. (2015). Self-reported experiences of discrimination and health: Scientific advances, ongoing controversies, and emerging issues. *Annual Review of Clinical Psychology, 11*(28), 407–440.

Lewis, T. T., Yang, F. M., Jacobs, E. A., & Fitchett, G. (2012). Racial/ethnic differences in responses to the Everyday Discrimination Scale: A differential item functioning analysis. *American Journal of Epidemiology, 175*(5), 391–401.

Lukachko, A., Hatzenbuehler, M. L., & Keyes, K. M. (2014). Structural racism and myocardial infarction in the United States. *Social Science & Medicine*, *103*(0), 42–50.

Mansouri, F., & Jenkins, L. (2010). Schools as sites of race relations and intercultural tension. *Australian Journal of Teacher Education*, *35*(7), 93–108.

Mendes, W. B., McCoy, S., Major, B., & Blascovich, J. (2008). How attributional ambiguity shapes physiological and emotional responses to social rejection and acceptance. *Journal of Personality and Social Psychology*, *94*(2), 278–291.

Mendez, D. D., Hogan, V. K., & Culhane, J. 2011. Institutional racism and pregnancy health: Using home mortgage disclosure act data to develop an index for mortgage discrimination at the community level. *Public Health Reports*, *126*(Suppl. 3), 102–114.

Meyer, I. H. (2003a). Prejudice as stress: Conceptual and measurement problems. *Am J Public Health*, *93*(2), 262–265.

Meyer, I. H. (2003b). Prejudice, social stress, and mental health in lesbian, gay, and bisexual populations: Conceptual issues and research evidence." *Psychological Bulletin*, *129*(5), 674–697.

Mustillo, S., Krieger, N., Gunderson, E. P., Sidney, S., McCreath, H., & Kiefe, C. I. (2004). Self-reported experiences of racial discrimination and Black-White differences in preterm and low-birthweight deliveries: The CARDIA study. *American Journal of Public Health*, *94*(12), 2125–2131.

Orey, B. D. A., Craemer, T., & Price, M. (2013). Implicit racial attitude measures in Black samples: IAT, subliminal priming, and implicit black identification. *PS: Political Science & Politics*, *46*(3), 550.

Paradies, Y. (2006). Defining, conceptualizing and characterizing racism in health research. *Critical Public Health*, *16*(2), 143–157.

Paradies, Y., Priest, N., Ben, J., Truong, M., Gupta, A., Pieterse, A. … Gee, G. (2013). Racism as a determinant of health: A protocol for conducting a systematic review and meta-analysis. *Systematic Reviews*, *2*(85).

Paradies, Y., Truong, M., & Priest, N. (2014). A systematic review of the extent and measurement of healthcare provider racism. *Journal of General Internal Medicine*, *29*(2), 364–387.

Parker, R. (2012). Stigma, prejudice and discrimination in global public health. *Cad Saude Publica*, *28*(1), 164–169.

Pascoe, E. A., & Richman, L. S. (2009). Perceived discrimination and health: A meta-analytic review. *Psychological Bulletin*, *135*(4), 531–554.

Pearson, M. R., Derlega, V. J., Henson, J. M., Holmes, K. Y., Ferrer, R. A., & Harrison, S. B. (2014) Role of neuroticism and coping strategies in psychological reactions to a racist incident among African American university students. *J Black Psychol*, *40* (1), 81–111.

Peek, M. E., Nunez-Smith, M., Drum, M., & Lewis, T. T. (2011). Adapting the everyday discrimination scale to medical settings: Reliability and validity testing in a sample of African American patients. *Ethnicity and Disease*, *21*(4), 502–509.

Phelan, J. C., Link, B. G., & Dovidio, J. F. (2008). Stigma and prejudice: One animal or two? *Soc Sci Med*, *67*(3), 358–367.

Planas, M., García, P. J., Bustelo, M., Carcamo, C. P., & Martinez. S. (2015). Effects of ethnic attributes on the quality of family planning services in Lima, Peru: A randomized crossover trial. *PLoS One*, *10*(2), e0115274.

Priest, N., Paradies, Y., Stevens, M., & Bailie, R. (2012). Exploring relationships between racism, housing and child illness in remote Aboriginal communities. *Journal of Epidemiology and Community Health, 66*(5), 440–447.

Priest, N., Paradies, Y., Trenerry, B., Truong, M., Karlsen, S., & Kelly, Y. (2013). A systematic review of studies examining the relationship between reported racism and health and wellbeing for children and young people. *Social Science and Medicine, 95*, 115–127.

Puhl, R., & Latner, J. (2007). Stigma, obesity, and the health of the nation's children. *Psychological Bulletin, 133*(4), 557–580.

Reeve, B. B., Willis, G., Shariff-Marco, S. and et.al. (2011). Comparing cognitive interviewing and psychometric methods to evaluate a racial ethnic discrimination scale. *Field Methods, 23*(4), 397–419.

Reicher, S. (2007). Rethinking the paradigm of prejudice. *South African Journal of Psychology, 37*(4), 820–834.

Samson, F. L. (2015). Racial resentment and smoking. *Social Science & Medicine, 126*(0), 164–168.

Sawyer, P. J., Major, B., Casad, B. J., Townsend, S. S. M., & Mendes, W. B. (2012). Discrimination and the stress response: Psychological and physiological consequences of anticipating prejudice in interethnic interactions. *American Journal of Public Health, 102*(5), 1020–1026.

Schmader, T., Croft, A., Whitehead, J., & Stone, J. (2013). A peek inside the targets' toolbox: How stigmatized targets deflect discrimination by invoking a common identity. *Basic and Applied Social Psychology, 35*(1), 141–149.

Schmitt, M. T., Branscombe, N. R., Postmes, T., & Garcia, A. (2014). The consequences of perceived discrimination for psychological well-being: A meta-analytic review. *Psychological Bulletin, 140*(4), 921–948.

Shannon, C. A., Rospenda, K. M., Richman, J. A., & Minich, L. M. (2009). Race, racial discrimination, and the risk of work-related illness, injury, or assault: Findings from a national study. *J Occup Environ Med, 5*(4), 441–448.

Shavers, V. L., Fagan, P. Jones, D. and Et al. (2012). The state of research on racial/ethnic discrimination in the receipt of health care. *American Journal of Public Health, 102*(5), 953–966.

Shelton, R. C., Puleo, E., Bennett, G. G., McNeill, L. H., Goldman, R. E., & Emmons, K. M. (2009). Racial discrimination and physical activity among low-income-housing residents. *Amer J Preventive Medicine, 37*(6), 541–545.

Shonkoff, J. P., Boyce, W., & McEwen, B. (2009). Neuroscience, molecular biology, and the childhood roots of health disparities: Building a new framework for health promotion and disease prevention. *JAMA, 301*, 2252–2259.

Sibley, C. G. (2011). The BIAS-Treatment Scale (BIAS-TS): A measure of the subjective experience of active and passive harm and facilitation. *J Pers Assess, 93*(3), 300–315.

Sibley, C. G., Harding, J. F., Perry, R., Asbrock, F., & Duckitt, J. (2010). Personality and prejudice: Extension to the HEXACO personality model. *European Journal of Personality, 24*, 515–534.

Slopen, N., et al. (2016). Discrimination and sleep: a systematic review. Sleep Medicine *18*: 88–95.

Smart Richman, L., & Hatzenbuehler, M. L. (2014). A multilevel analysis of stigma and health: Implications for research and policy. *Policy Insights from the Behavioral and Brain Sciences*, *1*, 213–221.

Smart Richman, L., & Lattanner, M. R. (2014). Self-regulatory processes underlying structural stigma and health. *Social Science & Medicine*, *103*, 94–100.

Stuber, J., Meyer, I., Link, B. (2008). Stigma, prejudice, discrimination and health. *Soc.Sci. Med.*, *67*(3), 351–357.

Stucky, B. D., and et.al. (2011). An item factor analysis and item response theory-based revision of the Everyday Discrimination Scale. *Cultural Diversity and Ethnic Minority Psychology*, *17*(2), 175–185.

Szymanski, D. M., & Henrichs-Beck, C. (2014). Exploring sexual minority women's experiences of external and internalized heterosexism and sexism and their links to coping and distress. *Sex Roles*, *70*(1–2), 28–42.

Tran, A. T. (2014). Family contexts: Parental experiences of discrimination and child mental health. *American Journal of Community Psychology*, *53*(1–2), 37–46.

Tull, E. S., Cort, M. A., Gwebu, E. T., & Gwebu, K. (2007). Internalized racism is associated with elevated fasting glucose in a sample of adult women but not men in Zimbabwe. *Ethn.Dis.*, *17*(4), 731–735.

Tull, E. S., Sheu, Y. T., Butler, C., & Cornelious, K. (2005). Relationships between perceived stress, coping behavior and cortisol secretion in women with high and low levels of internalized racism. *Journal of the National Medical Association*, *97*(2), 206–212.

Van Ryn, M., Burgess, D. J., Dovidio, J., Phelan, S. M., Saha, S., Malat, J. . . . Perry, S. P. (2011). The impact of racism on clinician cognition, behavior and clinical decision making. *Du Bois Review*, *8*(1), 199–218.

Veenstra, G. (2013). The gendered nature of discriminatory experiences by race, class, and sexuality: A comparison of intersectionality theory and the subordinate male target hypothesis. *Sex Roles*, *68*, 646–659.

Velez, B. L., Moradi, B., & DeBlaere, D. (2014). Multiple oppressions and the mental health of sexual minority Latina/o individuals. *The Counseling Psychologist*.

Whitbeck, L. B., Hoyt, D. R., McMorris, B. J., Chen, X., & Stubben, J. D. (2001). Perceived discrimination and early substance abuse among American Indian children. *J Health Soc Behav*, *42*(4), 405–424.

Williams, D. R. (1997). Race and health: Basic questions, emerging directions. *Ann Epidemiol*, *7*(5), 322–333.

Williams, D. R., & Mohammed, S. A. (2013). Racism and health I: Pathways and scientific evidence. *Am Behav Sci*, *57*(8).

Williams, D. R., Yu, Y., Jackson, J. S., & Anderson, N. B. (1997). Racial differences in physical and mental health: Socioeconomic status, stress, and discrimination. *Journal of Health Psychology*, *2*(3), 335–351.

Williams, D. R., Rahwa Haile, S. A., Mohammed, A. H., Sonnega, J. Jackson, J. S., & Stein, D. J. (2012). Perceived discrimination and psychological well-being in the USA and South Africa. *Ethnicity & Health*, *17*(1–2), 111–133.

Womack, V.Y., Ning, H., Lewis, C. E., Loucks, E. B., Puterman, E., Reis, J. . . . Carnethon, M. R. (2014). Relationship between perceived discrimination and sedentary behavior in adults. *Amer J Health Behav*, *38*(5), 641–649.

Yoo, H. C., & Pituc, S. T. (2013). Assessments of perceived racial stereotypes, discrimination, and racism. In *APA handbooks in psychology* (pp. 605–451). Washington, DC: American Psychological Association.

Zadro, L., & Gonsalkorale, K. (2014). Sources of ostracism: The nature and consequences of excluding and ignoring others. *Current Directions in Psychological Science*, *23*(2), 93–97.

Zeiders, K. H., Hoyt, L. T., & Adam, E. K. (2014). Associations between self-reported discrimination and diurnal cortisol rhythms among young adults: The moderating role of racial-ethnic minority status. *Psychoneuroendocrinology*, *50*, 280–288.

26 Development of Delegitimization and Animosity in the Context of Intractable Conflict

Daniel Bar-Tal and Talia Avrahamzon

Understanding acquisition and development of stereotypes and prejudice by young children in the context of intractable conflicts is a special challenge for social, developmental, and political psychologists, because these concepts play a major role in the dynamics of the hostile intergroup relations between the rivals (i.e., the parties involved in intractable conflicts). In this type of conflict, societies, as a result of the severe conditions of life, develop and later maintain sociopsychological repertoires, of which extremely negative stereotypes and strong prejudice are an inseparable part. The very negative stereotypes are denoted in *delegitimization*, defined as follows:

> Categorization of a group, or groups, into extremely negative social categories that exclude it, or them, from the sphere of human groups that act within the limits of acceptable norms and/or values, since these groups are viewed as violating basic human norms or values and therefore deserve maltreatment. (Bar-Tal & Hammack, 2012, p. 30)

Prejudice refers to the attitude that people hold toward another group (e.g., Leyens, Yzerbyt, & Schadron, 1994; Stroebe & Insko, 1989). However, in the context of intractable conflict, the negative attitude experienced by rival society members is strong. Therefore, we refer to such prejudice as *animosity*, which conjures emotions of hatred and anger, to stress its particular nature (see Jung et al., 2002). Though delegitimization and animosity are learned similarly as are all stereotypes and attitudes, they are special reflections of the context of intractable conflicts. They are acquired by children as a direct result of their exposure to violence, and other experiences as well, and are imparted to them implicitly and explicitly by agents of socialization. These agents include the family, as well as those at institutionalized levels, through educational systems, media, or political organizations. This chapter elucidates the unique process of the early acquisition of delegitimization (very negative stereotyping) and animosity (very strong prejudice) by children who grow up in societies that are involved in intractable conflict with all its implications. First, the chapter elaborates on the nature of the intractable conflicts, as the unique context in which children develop and acquire their intergroup repertoire of stereotypes and prejudice.

Sociopsychological Dynamics of Intractable Conflicts

Intractable conflicts are defined as violent confrontations between political, cultural, or ethnic groups, and between states as well as within different groups within one state (often ethnic groups). Examples include the Palestinian-Israeli conflict and conflicts in Sri Lanka, Northern Ireland, the Balkans, and Cyprus. Building on Kriesberg's (1998) model, Bar-Tal presented seven characteristics of intractable conflict: (a) *total*, fought over goals that are viewed as existential for the survival of the group; (b) *violent*, including wars, terror, military encounters that lead to losses, suffering, and destruction; (c) perceived as irresolvable and zero sum in nature; (d) central because it preoccupies the involved societies; (e) demands extensive investment of resources; and (f) lasts at least 25 years (see Bar-Tal, 1998, 2013). The context of intractable conflict consists of severe and harsh conditions, including chronic stress, feelings of insecurity, a sense of deprivation, fear, hardship, bereavement, and continuous threats. To adapt, involved societies develop a sociopsychological repertoire, which fulfills the needs of the society members who are coping with the stress. This repertoire also withstands the rival by enabling society members' mobilization to participate in the conflict, including the sacrifice of their lives. The repertoire consists of societal beliefs[1], as well as attitudes and shared emotions, which eventually crystalize into collective memory,[2] ethos of conflict,[3] and collective emotional orientation[4] – together called the *sociopsychological infrastructure of conflict*. In this infrastructure, the systematic institutionalization of delegitimization and animosity of the rival plays a central role not only in the collective memory and ethos of conflict but also in the collective emotional orientation.

The cognitive part of the infrastructure is based on eight themes of societal beliefs: (a) *societal beliefs about the justness of one's own goals* outline the contested goals, indicate their crucial importance, and provide their explanations and rationales; (b) *societal beliefs about security* stress the importance of personal safety and national survival and outline the conditions for their achievement; (c) *societal beliefs of positive collective self-image* concern the ethnocentric tendency to attribute positive traits, values, and behavior to one's own society; (d) *societal beliefs of victimization* concern the self-presentation of the ingroup as the victim of the conflict; (e) *societal beliefs of patriotism* generate attachment to the country and

---

1 Societal beliefs are defined as shared cognitions by the society members that address themes and issues that the society members are particularly occupied with, and which contribute to their sense of uniqueness (Bar-Tal, 2000).
2 Collective memory of conflict describes the outbreak of the conflict and its course, providing a coherent and meaningful picture of what has happened from the societal perspective (Bar-Tal, 2007, 2013; Devine-Wright, 2003; Papadakis, Perstianis, & Welz, 2006; Tint, 2010).
3 Ethos of conflict is defined as the configuration of central societal shared beliefs that provide a particular dominant orientation to a society and give meaning under the conditions of intractable conflict (Bar-Tal, 2013).
4 Collective emotional orientation refers to societal characterization of an emotion that is reflected on individual and collective levels in a sociopsychological repertoire, as well as in tangible and intangible societal symbols such as cultural products or ceremonies (Bar-Tal, 2001, 2013).

society by propagating loyalty, love, care, and sacrifice; (f) *societal beliefs of unity* refer to the importance of ignoring internal conflicts and disagreements during intractable conflicts to unite the society's forces in the face of an external threat; (g) *societal beliefs of peace* refer to peace as the ultimate desire of the society; and (h), the focus of this chapter, *societal beliefs of delegitimizing the opponent* concern beliefs that deny the adversary's humanity. These themes reflect contents of ethos of conflict and of collective memory.[5]

The negative stereotyping toward the rival group in the form of delegitimization develops because the rival not only threatens the lives of the society members but also inflicts heavy harm by killing and wounding fellow patriots, destroys property, and frequently performs diverse atrocities. It is closely related to the strong prejudice in the form of animosity, various emotions (such as hatred and fear), and also has behavioral implications. Delegitimization[6] and animosity under the conditions of intractable conflict provide an excellent explanation of why the rival performs violence, allows maltreatment and harm of the rival as retribution and prevention, and facilitates overall mobilization of the society members to participate in the violence.

In the described conditions of intractable conflict, it is obvious that children, from a very young age, are exposed directly and indirectly to experiences and information that contribute to their acquisition of delegitimization of and animosity toward the rival. This chapter focuses on these processes. But first we will say few words about the acquisition of prejudice.

Acquisition of Prejudice

The acquisition and development of prejudice toward racial and ethnic groups were a focus in many disciplines for much of the twentieth century, with a particular focus from the 1980s on ethnic-racial socialization (Priest, Walton, White, Kowal, & Paradies, 2014). Ethnic-racial socialization is the process that involves both explicit and implicit messages about the "meaning and significance of race and ethnicity; racial and ethnic group membership and identity; racial and

---

5 The detection of the eight themes is based on extensive systematic studies in the Israeli Jewish society involved in intractable conflict (see Bar-Tal, 2007; Oren 2009). In addition these themes were found to be dominant in other societies engaged in intractable conflict such as among Serbs, Kosovars, Albanians, Croats, and Bosnians (MacDonald, 2002), among Hutus in Rwanda (Slocum-Bradley, 2008), and among Greek and Turkish Cypriots (Hadjipavlou, 2007; Papadakis, 2008).

6 People engage in delegitimization in at least six ways: *dehumanization*, categorizing a group as nonhuman (e.g., snakes, savages, monsters); *outcasting*, categorization of the rival into groups that are considered as violators of pivotal social norms (e.g., murderers, psychopaths, terrorists); *trait characterization*, attributing traits that are considered extremely negative and unacceptable in a given society (e.g., idiots or parasites); use of *political labels*, labels with names of political groups that are absolutely rejected by the values of the delegitimizing group (e.g., Nazis or communists); *group comparison*, when the delegitimized group is labeled by the name of a group that traditionally serves as an example of negativity in the delegitimizing group (e.g., vandals); and *enemy*, a group that threatens to do harm and therefore arouses feelings of hostility (Bar-Tal & Hamack, 2012).

ethnic stratification; and intergroup and intragroup interactions" (Priest et al., 2014, p. 2).

A recent systematic review of 30 years of ethnic-racial socialization research (Priest et al., 2014) found much of the research during the past two decades has focused on the following four themes: cultural socialization, preparation for bias, promotion of mistrust, and egalitarianism (see Boykin & Toms, 1985; Hughes et al., 2006, for the development of these constructs). A noted gap in this field of research is the limited focus on ethnic-racial socialization of young children younger than age 6 (only 18 of the 92 studies in the review focused on or included children younger than age 6). This is noteworthy given evidence that children develop awareness of racial and ethnic difference and even prejudice earlier than age 6 (Bar-Tal & Teichman, 2005). The review also identified an overwhelming majority of studies undertaken in the United States (where 86 of the 92 studies in the review were from the United States), primarily centered on racial relations between Black and White Americans.

Our point of departure is a well-established premise stating that context plays a crucial role in the acquisition of stereotypes and prejudice in all its forms (e.g., Divine, 1989; Hirschfeld, 1996; Raabe & Beelman, 2011; Sherif, Harvey, White, Hood, & Sherif, 1961). This premise is embedded in the understanding that children's repertoires must be understood and considered in the societal and cultural context in which they live. This view is well conceptualized and supported by seminal theoretical and empirical contributions in developmental psychology (see, e.g., Bronfenbrenner, 1979; Cole, 1992; Goodnow, 1990; Scribner, 1990; Vygotsky, 1978; and Barrett, 2007, specifically for children's national enculturation). The specific focus of our interest is intractable conflict, in which children from an early age undergo ethnic-racial socialization. In its wider form, this can be called *political socialization* and can be defined as follows: processes through which individuals in a society shape their beliefs, attitudes, motivations, values, and patterns of behaviors that relate to the realm of the political world with all its aspects and issues (e.g., Dawson, Prewitt, & Dawson, 1977; Niemi & Sobieszek, 1977).

Applying the terms "ethnic-racial socialization" and "political socialization" enables the exploration of prejudice acquisition and associated behavior from an ecological perspective (see Broffenbrenner, 1979), whereby children are both exposed to and shaped by socialization delivered implicitly and explicitly from parents and other significant adults, peers, education (curricula and pedagogy), societal institutions, the media, and the political mechanisms.

The Context of Intractable Conflict

Of special importance for understanding the effects of the context of intractable conflict on the ethnic-racial socialization and political socialization of children is the evolution of a culture of conflict that is hegemonic in many of the intractable conflicts during their climax. A culture of conflict develops when societies saliently integrate into their culture tangible and intangible symbols, created to communicate a particular meaning about the prolonged and continuous experiences of living in the context of sustained and violent conflict (Bar-Tal, 2013; Geertz, 1973; Ross, 1998). Symbols of a conflict (e.g., glorified heroes from the past and present, commemorating ceremonies for the fallen soldiers, sacred goals of the conflict, or delegitimized presentation of the rival) become hegemonic elements in the culture of societies involved in intractable conflict: They provide the dominant meaning about the present reality, about the past, and about future goals and serve as guides for individual action. Ann Swidler's (1986, p. 273) discussion of culture as "a 'tool kit' of rituals, symbols, stories, and world views" that people use to construct "strategies of action" is an important addition and can serve as a foundation for the present discussion.

It is possible to suggest that solidification of a culture of conflict includes the following six features: (a) An inherent part of the socialization indicates that the elements of the culture of conflict, including the societal beliefs of the narratives, myths, and symbols are transferred to the society members through a socialization process in its widest meaning, from childhood to old age. Channels of communication and formal and informal institutions impart and disseminate messages that reflect the culture of conflict with its major themes. (b) Extensive sharing suggests that the societal beliefs of the sociopsychological infrastructure and the accompanying emotions are widely shared by society members. (c) Wide application means that the repertoire of the culture of conflict is not only held by society members but is also put into active use by them in their daily conversations, being chronically accessible. In addition, it appears to be dominant in public discourse via societal channels of mass communication. Finally, it is also expressed in institutional ceremonies, commemorations, memorials, and so on. (d) Expression in cultural products indicates that the leading themes of sociopsychological infrastructure are expressed also through cultural products such as literary books, TV programs, films, theater plays, visual arts, monuments, and so on. (e) Appearance in educational materials shows that the contents of the sociopsychological infrastructure appear in the textbooks used in schools and even in higher education as central themes of socialization. (f) Symbols of the culture of conflict become routinized into everyday life experiences. In other words, society members experience various symbols of the conflict in their daily lives (see Bar-Tal, Abutbul, & Raviv, 2014).

Thus, as the culture of conflict develops, the processes of institutionalization, socialization, and dissemination transmit, propagate, and maintain the societal beliefs of collective memory and ethos of conflict, as well as group-based emotions among society members. This repertoire becomes easily accessible, solidified, and dominant. The development of the culture of conflict is unavoidable because of the intensive psychological experiences that society members go through during intractable conflict. These powerful experiences leave their mark on every aspect of societal life, including on how children acquire their beliefs and attitudes about the rival. We now extensively elaborate on this process.

Acquisition Processes of Delegitimization and Animosity

We propose four premises to highlight how delegitimization and animosity in children in intractable conflicts are developed and sustained, at both individual and societal levels. First, in the context of intractable conflict, acquisition of delegitimization and animosity occurs earlier than previously thought and may even appear among children as young as age 2. A study by Bar-Tal and Teichman (2005) even showed that children age 1.5–2.0 express a negative connation to the word "Arab" before they acquire this word and learn this concept. Second, societal agents of political socialization participate in the sociopolitical development of young children, who impart delegitimization and animosity toward the rival. Third, as a result of the socialization processes and direct exposure to various aspects of conflict-related events, children form delegitimization and animosity as part of the systematic and coherent system of beliefs, attitudes, and emotions pertaining to conflict. That is, delegitimization and animosity are inseparable parts of the sociopsychological infrastructure embossed in the culture of conflict that societies develop in the context of intractable conflict. Finally, we propose that the delegitimization and animosity toward the rival, as part of the repertoire absorbed by children at an early age, may have a latent influence on the solidification of their later sociopsychological systems of beliefs and attitudes as adults. These premises in turn highlight serious consequences of political socialization, as well as ethnic-racial socialization processes, of young children in societies involved in intractable conflict. Of special importance are the last two premises because they shed focal light on the place of the delegitimization and animosity in the holistic analysis of the sociopsychological dynamics of intractable conflicts.

Early Acquisition of Delegitimization and Animosity

The conception of groups and their accompanying distinctions between ingroup favoritism and outgroup prejudice emerges at a young age, especially when children have an inherent need to make distinctions between the ingroup and the outgroup (see Bennett, Lyons, Sani, & Barrett, 1998; Doyle & Aboud, 1995; Kowalski, 2003; Rubin, Bukowski, & Parker, 2006). This categorization contributes to the development of one's social identity, which is

> That part of an individual's self-concept which derives from his [or her] knowledge of his [or her] membership of a social group (or groups) together with the value and emotional significance attached to that membership. (Tajfel, 1978, p. 63)

Unsurprisingly, children typically (although not always) display a more positive attitude toward the ingroup than the outgroup (e.g., Barrett, 2007; Bigler, Brown, & Markell, 2001; Nesdale & Flesser, 2001; Teichman, 2001).

The categorizing of race develops as young as age 3, when children develop racial awareness and are capable of ascribing difference (see Aboud, 1988; Dunham, Chen, & Banaji, 2013). With regard to ethnic groups, children are receptive to developing and redeveloping prejudiced attitudes from as young as ages 3 to 6 (Aboud, 1988; Aboud & Doyle, 1996; Connolly, 2012; Katz & Kofkin, 1997). Social-cognitive theorists (see Aboud, 1988) would argue that during these early years, the preschool child has an egocentric social perspective and preference to his or her own group. It is not until ages 8 to 10 that cognitive maturation occurs, and evidence starts to reveal a reduction in outgroup bias or ingroup favoritism (see Hailey & Olson, 2013; Raabe & Beelman, 2011, for further discussion on the development of racial attitudes). Noting the developmental trajectory of the acquisition of prejudice in non-conflict contexts, we can question whether the development, attainment of prejudice, categorizing of ingroups and outgroups, and the accompanying ethnic-racial socialization are different for children in intractable conflicts.

In intractable conflicts, the psychosocial repertoire stabilizes ingroup and polarizes outgroup beliefs, emotions, and attitudes. Unsurprisingly, in intractable conflicts, children's preference for the ingroup is even stronger than for children not in intractable conflicts, and it appears earlier because the societal goal is to increase the identification of society members with their own group, at the micro and macro levels (Bar-Tal, 1996; Bar-Tal & Teichman, 2005; Brown, 2000; Oppenheimer, 2006). In a special edition of the *European Journal of Developmental Psychology*, Oppenheimer and Barrett (2011) set out to investigate children's national identifications and attitudes to national ingroups and outgroups as determinants of the understanding of the enemy and the presence of enemy images (Barrett, 2007; Oppenheimer, 2006,). Using the National Identification Scale as well as ingroup/outgroup attitudes scale, the study included 12 national groups involving Bosnian and Serbian children (Bosnia), Greek Cypriot and Turkish Cypriot children (Cyprus), Catholic and Protestant children (Northern Ireland), Basque and Spanish children (the Basque Country), Jewish and Arab children (Israel), and Dutch and English children (The Netherlands and England). Oppenheimer found that a child's affect toward its national ingroup is often correlated with the strength of national identification, and that the ingroup was judged more favorably than the outgroup.

In contrast to ingroup favoritism, children's view of the rival outgroup is a strong indication of the strength of prejudice acquisition in intractable conflicts. Oppenheimer (2011) found that groups currently engaged with conflict had higher negative attitudes toward the outgroup compared to groups not currently experiencing conflict. Interestingly, those states that had conflict in the past still revealed traditional enemy outgroups that were viewed less positively than neutral outgroups (Barrett, 2007; Oppenheimer, 2011). Oppenheimer (2011) concluded, "the perception of the ingroup and its evaluation is dependent on the sociohistorical setting and on the position of the national group in a particular setting" (p. 15*)*. As Mertan (2011) suggests, such findings are in support of Tajfel's social identity theory, whereby intergroup relations affect children's intergroup attitudes. In intractable conflicts, this can be attributed to the greater awareness of threat, salience of the differences between groups, and the intensification of national identity.

The earlier acquisition of prejudice for children in intractable conflicts is subject to their earlier ethnic-racial and political socialization. According to Bar-Tal, Diamond, and Nasie (in press), political socialization is an inseparable part of children's daily lives in intractable conflicts. It is possible to say that life in the context of intractable conflict imprints the life of the society members from the day an individual is born and becomes an active absorber of experiences and information. Infants may hear sirens, shootings, bombardment, and/or detect emotional distress of their family members (Meijer, 1985). As an infant or toddler grows, these experiences become more concrete, identifiable, understandable, and meaningful. That is, as the trajectories of development advance, children have a wider scope of experiences -qualitatively and quantitatively- and then form coherent and comprehensive worldviews of the conflict.

In this context, a three-level analysis to political socialization should be used. First, as *observations*, children are exposed implicitly and explicitly to the conflict, including narratives of the enemy and the ingroup. This can occur through seeing or hearing symbols, images, or experiences associated with the conflict (Bar-Tal et al., 2014), including checkpoints, soldiers, monuments, sirens, and family distress (Bar-Tal et al., in press). Most pertinent to animosity acquisition, children are exposed to ingroup and outgroup categorization, including societal beliefs of delegitimization of the rival, a positive collective self-image, and beliefs of collective self-victimhood.

Second, as *instructions*, children are engaged in direct discussions and debates regarding the conflict with a range of socialization agents, including peers, family members, and teachers. Third, *as direct experiences of violence*, the most pervasive level is firsthand experience of the conflict, through loss or injury to themselves or someone they know, as well as through the destruction of known property, detention, or becoming a refugee (see Cairns, 1996, and Slone, 2009, for examples of children's exposure to violence).

Thus it is not surprising that for children raised in conflict, the increased preference toward the ingroup and negativity toward the outgroup occur at an earlier age than it does for children not raised in conflict (Bar-Tal, 1996, 2007; Oppenheimer, 2011; Teichman & Bar-Tal, 2008). Bar-Tal and Teichman (2005) found, based on their research with Jewish Israelis, that children as young as ages 2 and 3 develop intergroup attitudes (Teichman & Bar-Tal, 2008). Moreover, a study found children who were not yet age 2, before acquiring the word "Arab" and its concept, associate this word with negative connotation (Bar-Tal & Teichman, 2005). Connolly (2002) supports this observation in Northern Ireland, where children as young as age 3 were internalizing cultural preferences and symbols, such as preferences toward specific flags.

Other examples are Bar-Tal and Teichman's studies in Israel during the 1990s (see also Nasie, Diamond, & Bar-Tal, in press). They revealed that children age 3 to 6 described Arabs not only with negative stereotypes and attributes but also with violent behavior. The children also expressed extreme emotions of hate toward Arabs (for further Israeli examples, see Bar-Tal, 1996; Bar-Tal, Spivak, & Castel-Bazelet, 2003; Israeli-Diner, 1993; Ovadia, 1993). Of special note is the finding showing that Israeli Jewish children acknowledge the violent role their group plays in the conflict, yet they saw this as positive based on the justness of Israeli goals, a positive self-view, and especially delegitimization of the rival that requires self-defense.

Importantly, children ages 8 to 9 involved in violent conflict do not show an attenuation of ingroup love and outgroup hate compared to children in non-violent contexts. Conversely, children age 10 reported a renewed elevation in prejudice toward the outgroup or rival (Teichman & Bar-Tal, 2008; for further information see Augustinos & Rosewarne, 2001; Bar-Tal & Teichman, 2005; Black-Gutman & Hickson, 1996; Raabe & Beelmann, 2011; Rutland, 1999; Teichman, 2001; Vaughan, 1987). In Oppenheimer's review (Oppenheimer, 2011) this occurred for children in societies recently and previously experiencing conflict including Spain (Raizabal & Oritz, 2011), Cyprus (Mertan, 2011), Bosnia (Oppenheimer & Midzik, 2011), and Northern Ireland (Gallagher & Cairns, 2011).

In sum, early exposure to conflict (including violence), political socialization, and ethnic-racial socialization (specifically ingroup and outgroup categorization) provide children in intractable conflict with different experiences to those of children who do not live in the context of intractable conflicts (for Israel-Palestinian examples, see Slone, 2009, Landau et al., 2010; for South Africa, see Straker, Mendelsohn, Moosa, & Tudin, 1996; for Sierre Leone, see Mcintyre & Thusi, 2003; for Northern Ireland, see Muldoon and Trew, 2000; for Lebanon, see Macksoud & Aber, 1996; and for Sarajevo, see Husain et al., 1998). It is this early exposure to conflict, combined with the psychological repertoire of societal beliefs, attitudes, and emotions, and the collective memories, that feed the delegitimization and animosity.

Societal Agents of Ethnic-Racial and Political Socialization

The second premise this chapter presents is that societal agents of ethnic-racial and political socialization participate in the sociopolitical development of young children. These agents impart delegitimization and animosity toward the rival. Socialization agents present content that instills the societal beliefs of the sociopsychological repertoire of the conflict, including delegitimization of the rival, in order to emphasize justness of the conflict, a positive self-collective image, and a self-collective sense of victimhood. Unlike the universal nature of the sociopsychological repertoire within different intractable conflicts, the agents and contents differ between intractable conflicts, depending on whether the ingroup has a state or formal political autonomous infrastructure (Bar-Tal, 2013). When a society has a state, it also has all the channels of communication, and institutions such as the educational system, to impart the societal beliefs of culture of conflict (e.g., Israeli Jews or Turks). But when a society does not have a state, it needs to use informal agents of socialization and informal channels such as a family (e.g., Palestinians or Kurds).

It is noted that there is limited empirical evidence to determine which agent is most influential in affecting the development of young children's attitudes and beliefs (Deng, 2012), especially macro socialization agents (Priest et al., 2014). Although there are many socialization agents at play including parents, peers, education system (pedagogy, curricula, and the institution), literature, and the media, this chapter focuses on parents (as the primary socialization agent), as well as education and media (both are major agents of institutionalizing and disseminating delegitimization and animosity).

Parents. Parents play a critical role in both the ethnic-racial and political socialization of their children. Parents do so explicitly (through instructions of attitudes and behavior, modeling, supporting decisions, and disciplining) and implicitly (by controlling agents, content, and environmental exposure to the world; see Bar-Tal et al., in press; Maccoby, 1992, Milner, 1983). Priest et al.'s (2014) review highlighted that many of the studies they focused on looked at the delivery of ethnic-racial socialization from parents, who were overwhelmingly considered to be the key influential factor of ethnic-racial socialization (86 of 92 studies indicated this to be the case, although consistent measures were not used across the studies).

In the context of the Israeli-Palestinian conflict, one of the main sources of information regarding the rival for young children is parents and other members of the family (Bar-Tal, Teichman, & Zohar, 1994, ages 5–6.5; Ben-Dov, 2000, ages 3–4; Ben Shabat, 2010, ages 6–7; Edres, 2006, ages 5–6). Parents were identified by 81% of children as a key source of information about the outgroup (Arabs). A number of studies explored the exchanges between parents and their children (see Bar-Tal et al., in press; Myers-Walls, Myers-Bowman, & Pelo, 1993; Shamai, 2001). Other studies have identified that children as young as age 3 were able to have discussions with their parents and specifically making reference to the conflict (O'Malley, Blankemeyer, Walker, & Dellmann-Jenkins, 2007).

Educational system. The educational system – both kindergartens and schools – in the context of intractable conflict contributes to political and ethnic-racial socialization in two ways: first, by transmitting societal beliefs and the dominant narratives through a range of education methods including pedagogical practices, curricula, textbooks, and ceremonies; and second, by offering one-sided narratives of the collective memory and discouraging critical thinking. The educational system differs from families as it is often controlled by the government, for whom a primary goal is to explicitly impart to the next generation a society's ideology and ethos, values, goals, myths, and narratives (Apple, 1979; Beckerman & Zembylas, 2012; Bordieu, 1973; Podeh, 2002). Furthermore, in the school setting, the collective experiences, such as collective grief, collective mourning, or collective pride, are central to developing a group identity (Beckerman & Zembylas, 2012).

In studies undertaken in Israel, Bar-Tal et al. (2003) found that 64% of 5- to 6.5-year-old children reported that they acquired information about the conflict from their kindergarten teachers; Ben Shabat (2010) found that 50% of the 6- to 7-year-old children in her study reported that they acquired information about the conflict from their school or kindergarten; and Ovadia (1993) found that about 30% of the 3- to 6-year-old children in his study reported that their main source about the conflict was their kindergarten. Bar-Tal and Ozer (2009) and Furman (1999) both determined that teachers in kindergartens emphasize themes within the repertoire such as national security, justification of the army and war, justness of their own goals, and self-perceived righteousness (see Nasie, Diamond, & Bar-Tal, 2015).

Textbooks are also powerful disseminating tools of conflict-related content (e.g., Adwan, Bar-Tal, & Wexler, 2016; Bar-Tal, 1998; Papadakis, 2008; Perera, 1991) for two reasons. First, as education tends to be compulsory, all children are accessing the same messages via textbooks. Second, textbooks carry weight as being authoritative and objective sources of knowledge. Bar-Tal's earlier studies (1998 and Bar-Tal & Zoltak, 1989) highlighted that as early as in the first grade, Israeli textbooks had introduced the reality of the conflict, and at the second grade they already made reference to most of the eight conflict-related societal beliefs.

Schools are also used as a platform for the school community to perform rituals, memorials, and ceremonies that reflect the themes of the ethos of conflict and collective memory, with direct reference to the negative nature of the rival (Bar-Tal & Ozer, 2009; Eldan, 2006). Similarly, in their studies of Israel and Cyprus, Beckerman and Zembylas (2012) go further and note the persuasive role national mourning plays within the school, again as a strategy to maintain the hegemony of the conflict.

Television. Television has an influencing role in imparting societal beliefs, attitudes, and patterns of behaviors. Numerous studies highlight television as a main source of information regarding conflict (Barret, 2007; Blankemeyer, Walker, & Svitak, 2009; Cairns, 1987; Cairns, Hunter, & Herring, 1980; Covell, 1996; Lemish & Götz, 2007). As with other socialization agents, if there is limited or no objective or balanced information, children become more susceptible to the biased information being presented on television programs (Barrett & Short, 1992).

Studies in Israel indicate that television is a major source of information on the conflict for children. In Israel, Warshel (2007) reported that 88% of the Jewish Israeli children ages 6 to 10 reported television as a source of information about the conflict, followed by parents and teachers. Probably few television programs regarding the conflict are aimed at children, and thus it has been suggested that the programs the children were referring to were news programs. Access to news would seem to heighten children's views of the conflict, as well as leading to the gathering and interpreting of information on Arabs, possibly without awareness or guidance from adults (Nasie et al., 2015).

In sum, delegitimization and animosity enable children and adults alike to view the rival as the enemy: immoral, evil, and faceless (Keen, 1986), and requiring annihilation (Alexander, Brewer, & Herrmann, 1999; Bar-Tal & Hammack, 2012). This view, coupled with mistrust and hatred (Bar-Tal & Hamack, 2012), creates a negative intergroup repertoire. The overt delegitimization of the rival constantly appears in public discourse as well as in cultural products – for example, as presented in films or literature (Bar-Tal & Teichman, 2005; Bekerman & Maoz, 2005; Durante, Volpato, & Fiske, 2010) – and becomes a fundamental part of the culture of conflict that maintains intractable conflicts (Bar-Tal, 2013).

Formation of Repertoire by Children: The Power of Delegitimization

The third premise presented in this chapter suggests that as a result of the socialization processes within a culture of conflict and direct exposure to various aspects of conflict-related events, children form delegitimization and animosity as part of a systematic and coherent system of beliefs, attitudes, and emotions pertaining to conflict. That is, as already noted, delegitimization and animosity do not stand alone in the realm of the sociopsychological repertoire but are an inseparable part of the sociopsychological infrastructure that societies develop in the context of intractable conflict.

It is well documented that children (and adults) make sense of the conflict by forming a perceived holistic and meaningful view of the conflict, their own group, and of the rival (e.g., Bar-Tal, 1996; MacMullin & Odeh, 1999; Masalha, 2003; Miljević-Ridjički &Lugomer-Armano, 1994; Povrzanovic, 1997). In fact, in societies engaged in intractable conflict, children adopt an ethos of conflict with its themes of justness of own goals, security, positive collective self-image, one's own victimization, patriotism, unity and peace and negative stereotyping, and in many cases, delegitimization of the rival. Also, as discussed, through a range of socialization agents, children acquire narratives of ethos of conflict and collective memory with the same themes, as well as emotions related to the conflict, including fear and hatred toward to the rival. The most comprehensive study to explore children's deconstruction and understanding of this meaningful view, or psycho-social repertoire, was undertaken in Israel by Ben Shabat (2010). Sixty Jewish children ages 6 to 7 were interviewed about the themes of ethos of conflict. The results showed that they grasped almost fully its themes, and that it had become part of their repertoire.

In a study undertaken in Croatia, Miljević-Ridjički and Lugomer-Armano (1994) found that children as young as age 3 were able to articulate knowledge and emotions regarding the war, as well as concepts associated with supporting the ingroup as well as delegitimizing the other. The children also expressed other societal beliefs during the interviews, including justness of their own ingroup goals (self-defense, safety, and freedom), self-victimization ("the [others] want to take our homeland" and for conflict "we are only defending ourselves, ours [people] are fighting to save our lives"), and used attributes "good" and "brave" to describe the ingroup and its actions. The children also expressed fear, mainly about who became refugees. According to Connolly's (2002) research and further research with Connolly, Kelly, and Smith (2009) in Northern Ireland, young children identified a preference for national symbols such as flags, colors, and marches, even prior to an understanding of what the symbols actually represented (for other studies, see Myers-Bowman, Waler, & Myers-Walls, 2005, in Yugoslavia; Raviv, Bar-Tal, Koren-Silvershatz, & Raviv, 1999, in Israel).

This premise indicates that delegitimization and animosity in cases of intractable conflict cannot be seen as an isolated sociopsychological reaction, but must be viewed as part of a system of societal beliefs that form a holistic, systematic, meaningful, and comprehensive outlook on perceived reality. This system serves functions of describing reality, explaining the causes that led to this reality, and justifying the violent behavior of the ingroup (Bar-Tal & Hammack, 2012). In this system, societal beliefs of delegitimization may be seen as key beliefs that have a crucial impact on the way that reality is perceived and the group behaves.

This systemic view has a number of implications. First, it provides a cohesive outlook that combines a number of themes of societal beliefs that complement the specific perspectives provided by delegitimization and animosity. In the context of intractable conflict, it was found that the themes of ethos of conflict and collective memory form a holistic stance (Bar-Tal, Sharvit, Halperin, & Zafran, 2012; Gopher, 2006). Second, delegitimization and animosity, as part of the system, receive support from other societal beliefs with which they are in an interrelationship. These include societal beliefs of justness of own goals, self-collective victimhood, self-collective positive view, patriotism, and unity. Some serve as causes and other as effects, while some even perform both roles in the system as delegitimization. When a group believes that its own goals are just, it delegitimizes the rival that does not accept this justness. By carrying on violence, the rival is viewed as a delegitimized group, and the own group is perceived as being a victim and also as being moral (Bar-Tal, 2003). Subsequently, this system of beliefs becomes a sociopsychological barrier to resolving the conflict peacefully. Third, the system of beliefs is difficult to change. It becomes resistant to persuasion because of its supportive interrelated structure, which can be considered as a type of conflict ideology (Bar-Tal et al., 2012; Tetlock, 1989). Ideology is considered to be a closed system of systematically formulated beliefs that guide reality perception and behavior (van Dijk,

1998). Hence, it reduces openness to information and its processing. Eagly and Chaikin (1993, 1998) similarly proposed that embeddedness of beliefs and attitudes in an interrelated system creates resistance to change because their coherent structure creates dependency and support among the beliefs and attitudes in this system (e.g., Rokeach, 1964). Changing one belief and/or attitude requires a change of other beliefs and attitudes as well. Accordingly, it may be assumed that the mode of thinking of those who hold an ideology is characterized (relative to those who do not hold it) by an inclination to adhere to that which is familiar; to be selective in searching for information; and to think in a biased, simplistic, and stereotypical way (Feldman, 2003; Jost, Glaser, Kruglanski, & Sulloway, 2003).

Effects of Early Socialization

The final premise suggests that delegitimization and animosity, as part of the system of societal beliefs and attitudes of the culture of conflict absorbed by children at an early age, may have influence on their later sociopsychological repertoire as adults. As stated previously, children by the age of 2 or 3 begin to learn content related to the conflict, and by ages 5 to 7 possess most of the repertoire of the ethos of conflict, including delegitimization and animosity toward the outgroup. This process is unavoidable in a society involved in intractable conflict. In fact, the acquisition and use of this repertoire is an important indicator for membership in, and identification with, a society. By adulthood, members hold in their repertoire the beliefs, attitudes, values, and emotions regarding the conflict, even if they do not express them.

It is acknowledged that although longitudinal evidence is limited, extensive evidence still reveals the continuity between childhood experiences and the formation of an adult's beliefs and attitudes (Bandura, 1986; Hess & Torney, 2005; Kagan & Moss, 1962). In fact, social psychologists have established that early socialization, with the acquisition of negative stereotypes and prejudice, has a lasting impact on the lives of society members in their adulthood. It thus plays a major role in the dynamics of intergroup relations (Augoustinos & Rosewarne, 2001; Devine, 1989; Dovidio, Kawamaki, & Beach, 2001; Sears & Levy, 2003).

Most society members solidify their societal beliefs in adulthood in line with the imparted beliefs by agents such as parents, the education system, and the media. These beliefs are acquired in early age and eventually form a crystalized system of beliefs that corresponds to the themes of the ethos of conflict and collective memory. In this case, early learnings are well reflected in adulthood. We recognize that some society members eventually form peace-oriented views regarding the conflict that include positive stereotypes of the rival. This process may take place because of parents' socialization, of peace socialization of other agents, as well as specific experiences that affected their view of the conflict (see Nasie, Bar-Tal, & Schnaidman, 2014). Nevertheless, there is substantial evidence that the early-acquired delegitimization and animosity of the rival also have an effect on peace-oriented individuals, in spite of their new repertoire that negates the early learning.

This premise is supported by stereotyping research; Devine (1989) found that the early acquisition of negative stereotypes has an imprinting effect on the individual and continues to exist into adulthood, even among those who acquire alternative beliefs (Devine, 1989; Dovidio et al., 2001; Sears & Levy, 2003). Further, *implicit* intergroup attitudes appear to be relatively stable between childhood and adulthood (Dunham, Baron, & Banaji, 2006, 2007). Regarding implicit attitudes, a recent study by Dunham et al. (2013) found that implicit ingroup preference is a tendency that emerges very early in life, appearing as soon as intergroup categories are acquired at around ages 3 to 4. This tendency is also found among adolescents, and then among adults. As with other elements of ethnic-racial socialization, stereotypes (and in intractable conflict, extending that to delegitimization of the rival) are presented by a range of socialization agents and are well learned and highly accessible, even prior to the development of the cognitive ability to challenge their validity (Dovidio, Evans, & Tyler, 1986; Higgins, King, & Mavin, 1982). From this work on implicit stereotyping, we see that the presence of a member of a target group leads to automatic activation of relevant stereotypes.

It is possible to acquire new beliefs about the outgroup; however, given that the stereotypes have been presented since early childhood, the process of challenging the beliefs related to the stereotypes requires conscious cognitive resources and motivation (Devine, 1989; Devine, Plant, Amodio, Harmon-Jones, & Vance, 2002; Fiske, 1989). When this does not occur, a return to the early learned stereotype occurs, even unconsciously. If the effects of the stereotypes acquired in childhood impact adult reactions in relatively normal contexts, then we can claim that they can definitely be found in the powerful context of intractable conflict. In support of this premise, pioneering Israeli studies by Sharvit (2007, 2014) demonstrated that even when people develop and act on the basis of alternative beliefs and attitudes that are in contrast with the conflict-supporting sociopsychological repertoire, the ethos of conflict learned at an early age continues to be stored as implicit beliefs and attitudes. These in turn automatically influence information-processing functioning in times of stress. Thus this experiment clearly demonstrated that the societal beliefs of the ethos of conflict exist in the psychological repertoires of most members of Israeli Jewish society who have undergone socialization processes in the reality of intractable conflict, even among those who have rejected the ethos beliefs and adopted alternative dovish beliefs as a result of later learning. We can then suggest that society members living in the context of intractable conflict cannot escape from the early learning, and the later influence, of themes of the ethos of conflict that include delegitimization and animosity. This influence can be either direct and conscious or indirect and automatic.

Implications and Conclusions

This chapter presented specific research about the acquisition of delegitimization and animosity by young children who live under the conditions of intractable conflict. This repertoire is imparted to children implicitly and explicitly (from birth) through parents, peers, education systems (even in the early childhood education systems through the celebration of festivals and historical events), the media, and in the broader political milieu. Bar Tal and Hammack (2012) argue that this very explicit, normative, and institutionalized expression of delegitimization and animosity guides behaviors and serves as a glass through which to interpret information and experiences. In fact, they noted that "violence and narratives become intertwined and institutionalized in conflict settings in such a way that they reproduce the status quo of a conflict" (p. 38). The way in which children explicitly and implicitly participate in ethnic-racial and political socialization in intractable conflicts enables them to play a role in society, at the micro and macro levels. It also contributes to the cycle of the conflict as the children take their acquired negative stereotypes (delegitimization) and strong prejudice (animosity) into adulthood. They become part of the conflict supporting ideology that serves as a pillar of the culture of conflict that characterizes societies engaged in intractable conflict. As long as there is no sign of possible peace, this repertoire is functional for meeting the challenges that the intractable conflict poses to the society, both on individual and collective levels. But when a light appears at the end of the tunnel, and signs of a possible peace-making process become realistic, the same repertoire becomes a barrier to the process of peace building that includes negotiation (Bar-Tal & Halperin, 2011). Beliefs of delegitimization and attitudes of animosity feed mistrust, hatred, and hostility that prevent any meaningful embarking on the peace road. Changing the view of the rival is one of the first necessary conditions if societies involved in intractable conflict really wish to begin negotiations to settle their conflict peacefully.

The full recognition of the rival as a partner with whom it is possible to negotiate a peaceful settlement of the conflict is based on belief contents that legitimize, equalize, differentiate, and personalize the rival (see Bar-Tal & Teichman, 2005). *Legitimization* allows viewing the opponent as belonging to an acceptable category of groups behaving within the boundaries of international norms, with whom it is possible and even desired to terminate the conflict and construct positive relations. *Equalization* turns the rival into an equal partner with whom it is possible to establish new relations. *Differentiation* leads to heterogenization of the rival group. It enables a new perception of the rival group that has hitherto been viewed as a homogeneous and monolithic hostile entity. *Personalization* allows people to view the rival group not as a depersonalized entity but as a group made up of individuals with ordinary human characteristics, concerns, needs, and goals.

Bar-Tal and Hammock (2012) suggest five approaches for specifically reducing delegitimization and ultimately conflict resolution, peace building, and reconciliation: (a) *Pragmatic conflict resolution:* the peaceful cessation of violence is an essential condition for reducing delegitimization practices. Northern Ireland presents a prime case study for this way. (b) *Recognition and political protections:* this focuses on the formal recognition of the rival, such as in the Oslo Peace Accords, which explicitly noted the mutual legitimization of both groups to exist. (c) *Structural symmetry:* this requires both sides to commit to a new relationship by restructuring social, economic, and political spaces, where the ultimate purpose is to equalize the power structures. For example, when there is an economic difference between rival groups, attention must be given to closing the gap. Again, Northern Ireland provides a good example of this goal (Byrne, Staandish, Arnold, Fissuh, & Irvin, 2009). (d) *Deinstitutionalization of delegitimization:* this focuses on the need for systemic changes in the delivery of messages and imagery regarding the outgroup. Specifically, in Northern Ireland a national media initiative for children was implemented with the aim of reducing stereotyping and delegitimization (see Connolly, Fitzpatrick, Gallagher, & Harris, 2006). In addition, the breakdown in institutionalizing stereotypes will enable the deconstructing of monolithic identities, which Bar-On (2005) argues is essential in achieving any form of reconciliation. Finally, (e) *rescripting master narratives:* the need for both sides to acknowledge the other's narratives and their own not as the absolute truth (see Bekerman & Zembylas, 2012, on teaching contested narratives).

Knowing about the early acquisition and effects of the delegitimization and animosity in intractable conflicts, it is unsurprising that any attempt to resolve intractable conflict needs to not only address the practical consideration of the conflict but also the sociopsychological repertoire at all levels of socialization and its agents. The child, the adult, and the society as a whole need to adopt a new repertoire via the expression of new narratives that break down stereotypes and prejudice. Through a new narrative, institutional and societal changes in attitudes, perceptions, and praxis will be engendered (Trimiklinotis, 2013), providing a foundation for the lasting peace. Yet, it must be recognized and accepted that to change the societal system of beliefs and attitudes that feed the continuation of the conflict, the societies that yearn for peace need to carry their change into the institutions that very young children attend. It is there where the construction of delegitimization and animosity begins.

References

Aboud, F. (1988). *Children and prejudice*. New York: Blackwell.

Aboud, F. E., & Doyle, A. B. (1996). Parental and peer influences on children's racial attitudes. *International Journal of Intercultural Relations, 20*(3/4), 371–383.

Adwan, S., Bar-Tal, D., & Wexler, B. (2016). Portrayal of the other in Palestinian and Israel schoolbooks: A comparative study. *Political Psychology, 37*, 201–217.

Alexander, M. G., Brewer, M. B., & Herrmann, R. K. (1999). Images and affect: A functional analysis of out-groups stereotypes. *Journal of Personality and Social Psychology, 77*, 78–93.

Apple, M. W. (1979). *Ideology and curriculum*. London: Routledge & Kegan Paul.

Augoustinos, M., & Rosewarne, D. L. (2001). Stereotype knowledge and prejudice in children. *British Journal of Developmental Psychology, 19*, 143–156.

Bandura, A. (1986). *Social foundations of thoughts and action: A social cognitive theory*. Englewood Cliffs, NJ: Prentice Hall.

Bar-On, D. (2005). Empirical criteria for reconciliation in practice. *Intervention, 3*(3), 180–191.

Bar-Tal, D. (1996). Development of social categories and stereotypes in early childhood: The case of "The Arab" concept formation, stereotype, and attitudes by Jewish children in Israel. *International Journal of Intercultural Relations, 20*, 341–370.

Bar-Tal, D. (1998). Societal beliefs in times of intractable conflict: The Israeli case. *International Journal of Conflict Management, 9*, 22–50.

Bar-Tal, D. (2000). *Shared beliefs in a society: Social psychological analysis*. Thousand Oaks, CA: Sage.

Bar-Tal, D. (2001). Why does fear override hope in societies engulfed by intractable conflict, as it does in the Israeli society? *Political Psychology, 22*, 601–627.

Bar-Tal, D. (2003). Collective memory of physical violence: Its contribution to the culture of violence. In E. Cairns & M. D. Roe (Eds.), *The role of memory in ethnic conflict* (pp. 77–93). Houndmills: Palgrave Macmillan.

Bar-Tal, D. (2007). *Living with the conflict: Sociopsychological analysis of the Israeli-Jewish society*. Jerusalem: Carmel (in Hebrew).

Bar-Tal, D. (2013). *Intractable conflicts: Sociopsychological foundations and dynamics*. Cambridge: Cambridge University Press.

Bar-Tal, D., Abutbul, G., & Raviv, A. (2014). The culture of conflict and its routinization. In C. Kinnvall, T. Capelos, H. Dekker, & P. Nesbitt-Larking (Eds.), *Handbook of global political psychology* (pp. 407–427). London: Palgrave.

Bar-Tal, D., Diamond, A., & Nasie, M. (in press). The political socialization of young children in intractable conflicts. *International Journal of Behavioral Development*.

Bar-Tal, D., & Halperin, E. (2011). Sociopsychological barriers to conflict resolution. In D. Bar-Tal (Ed.), *Intergroup conflicts and their resolution: A social psychological perspective*. New York: Psychology Press.

Bar-Tal, D., & Hammack, P. L. (2012). Conflict, delegitimization, and violence. In L. R. Tropp (Ed.), *The Oxford handbook of intergroup conflict* (pp. 29–52). New York: Oxford University Press.

Bar-Tal, D., & Ozer, I. (2009). *How ethos of conflict is transmitted during Holocaust Day, Memorial Day, and Independence Day by teachers of kindergartens in mixed city*. Unpublished manuscript (in Hebrew).

Bar-Tal, D., Sharvit, K., Halperin, E., & Zafran, A. (2012). Ethos of conflict: The concept and its measurement. *Peace and Conflict: Journal of Peace Psychology, 18*, 40–61.

Bar-Tal, D., Spivak, K., & Castel-Bazelet, I. (2003). *Collective memory of children in kindergarten (age 5–6) as a function of religiosity*. Unpublished manuscript (in Hebrew).

Bar-Tal, D., & Teichman, Y. (2005). *Stereotypes and prejudice in conflict: Representations of Arabs in Israeli Jewish Society*. Cambridge: Cambridge University Press.

Bar-Tal, D., Teichman, Y., & Zohar, O. (1994). *Young children's stereotype of "an Arab" as reported in an interview and represented in drawings*. Unpublished manuscript.

Bar-Tal, D., & Zoltak, S. (1989). Images of an Arab and Jewish-Arab relations in school readers. *Megamot, 32*, 301–317 (in Hebrew).

Barrett, M. (2007). *Children's knowledge, beliefs and feelings about nations and national groups*. Hove, UK: Psychology Press.

Barrett, M., & Short, J. (1992). Images of European people in a group of 5–10 year old English school children. *British Journal of Developmental Psychology 10*(4), 339–365.

Bekerman, Z., & Maoz, I. (2005). Troubles with identity: Obstacles to coexistence education in conflict ridden societies. *Identity: An International Journal of Theory and Research, 5*, 341–357.

Ben-Dov, I. (2000). *Development of category, stereotype and prejudice toward Arabs among Jewish children of pre-school age (3–6)*. PhD dissertation, Tel Aviv University.

Ben Shabat, C. (2010). *Collective memory and ethos of conflict acquisition during childhood: Comparing children attending state-secular and state-religious schools in Israel*. Master thesis submitted to School of Education, Tel Aviv University (in Hebrew).

Bennett, M., Lyons, E., Sani, F., & Barrett, M. (1998). Children's subjective identification with the group and in-group favoritism. *Developmental Psychology 34*, (5), 902–909.

Bekerman, Z., & Zembylas, M. (2012). *Teaching contested narratives*. Cambridge: Cambridge University Press.

Bigler, R., Brown, C., & Markell, M. (2001). When groups are not created equal: Effects of group status on the formation of intergroup attitudes in children. *Child Development, 72*(4), 1151–1162.

Black-Gutman, D., & Hickson, F. (1996). The relationship between racial attitudes and social-cognitive development in children: An Australian study. *Developmental Psychology, 32*(3), 448–456.

Blankemeyer, M., Walker, K., & Svitak, E. (2009). The 2003 war in Iraq: An ecological analysis of American and Northern Irish children's perceptions. *Childhood, 16*, 229–247.

Bourdieu, P. (1973). Cultural reproduction and social reproduction. In R. Brown (Ed.), *Knowledge, education and cultural change* (pp. 71–112). London: Tavistock.

Boykin, A. W., & Toms, F. D. (1985). Black child socialization. In H. P. McAdoo & J. L. McAdoo (Eds.), *Black children: Social, educational and parental environments* (pp. 159–173). Los Angeles: Sage.

Bronfenbrenner, U. (1979). *The ecology of human development: Experiments by nature and design*. Boston: Harvard University Press.

Brown, R. (2000). Social identity theory: Past achievements, current problems and future challenges. *European Journals of Social Psychology, 30*, 745–778.

Byrne, S., Standish, K., Arnold, J., Fissuh, E., & Irvin, C. (2009). Economic aid: The end of phase II and the impact on sustainable peacebuilding in Northern Ireland. *Journal of Intervention and State Building, 3*, 345–363.

Cairns, E. (1987). *Caught in crossfire: Children and the Northern Ireland conflict*. Syracuse: Syracuse University Press.

Cairns, E. (1996). *Children in political violence*. Oxford, UK: Blackwell.

Cairns, E. D., Hunter, D., & Herring, L. (1980). Young children's awareness of violence in Northern Ireland: The influence of Northern Irish television in Scotland and Northern Ireland. *British Journal of Social and Clinical Psychology, 19*, 3–6.

Cole, M. (1992). Culture and cognitive development: From cross-cultural comparisons to model systems of cultural mediation. In A. F. Healy, S. M. Kosslyn, & R. M. Shiffrin (Eds.), *Essays in honor of William K. Estes* (pp. 279–305). Hillsdale, NJ: Erlbaum.

Connolly, P. (2002). Researching young children's perspectives on "the Troubles" in Northern Ireland. *Child Care in Practice, 8*(1), 58–64.

Connolly, P. (2012). *Too young to notice? Young children's attitudes toward, and awareness of, ethnic divisions*, Public Lecture, 28 November, Faculty of Human Sciences, Macquarie University, Australia.

Connolly, P., Fitzpatrick, S., Gallagher, T., & Harris, P. (2006). Addressing diversity and inclusion in the early years in conflict-affected societies: A case study of the Media Initiative for Children – Northern Ireland. *International Journal for Early Years Education, 14*(3), 263–278.

Connolly, P., Kelly, B., & Smith, A. (2009). Ethnic habitus and young children: A case study of Northern Ireland. *European Early Childhood Education Research Journal, 17*, 217–232.

Covell, K. (1996). National and gender differences in adolescents' war attitudes. *International Journal of Behavioral Development, 19*, 871–883.

Dawson, R., Prewitt, P., & Dawson, K. (1977). *Political socialization*. Boston: Little Brown.

Deng, L. Y. F. (2012). "Parenting about peace": Exploring Taiwanese parents' and children's perceptions in a shared political and sociocultural context. *Family Relations: Interdisciplinary Journal of Applied Family Studies, 61*, 115–128.

Devine, P. G. (1989). Stereotypes and prejudice: Their automatic and controlled components. *Journal of Personality and Social Psychology, 56*, 5–18.

Devine, P. G., Plant, E. A., Amodio, D. M., Harmon-Jones, E., & Vance, S. L. (2002). The regulation of explicit and implicit race bias: The role of motivations to respond without prejudice. *Journal of Personality and Social Psychology, 82*, 835–848.

Devine-Wright, P. (2003). A theoretical overview of memory and conflict. In E. Cairns & M. D. Roe (Eds.), *The role of memory in ethnic conflict* (pp. 9–33). New York: Palgrave Macmillan.

Dovidio, J. F., Evans, N. E., & Tyler, R. B. (1986). Racial stereotypes: The content of their cognitive representations. *Journal of Experimental Social Psychology, 22*, 22–37.

Dovidio, J. F., Kawakami, K., & Beach, K. R. (2001). Implicit and explicit attitudes: Examination of the relationship between measures of intergroup bias. In R. Brown & S. L. Gaertner (Eds.), *Blackwell handbook of social psychology: Intergroup processes* (pp. 175–197). Malden, MA: Blackwell.

Doyle, A. B., & Aboud, F. E. (1995). A longitudinal study of White children's racial prejudice as a social-cognitive development. *Merrill Palmer Quarterly, 41*(2), 209–228.

Dunham, Y., Baron, A. S., & Banaji, M. R. (2006). From American city to Japanese village: A cross-cultural investigation of implicit race attitudes. *Child Development, 77,* 1268–1281.

Dunham, Y., Baron, A. S., & Banaji, M. R. (2007). Children and social groups: A developmental analysis of implicit consistency in Hispanic Americans. *Self and Identity, 6,* 238–255.

Dunham, Y., Chen, E. E., & Banaji, M. R. (2013). Two signatures of implicit intergroup attitudes: Developmental invariance and early enculturation. *Psychological Science, 24*(6), 860–868.

Durante, F., Volpato, C. & Fiske, S. T. (2010). Using the stereotype content model to examine group depictions in fascism: An archival approach. *European Journal of Social Psychology, 40,* 465–483.

Eagly, A. H., & Chaiken, S. (1993). *The psychology of attitudes.* Fort Worth, TX: Harcourt Brace Jovanovich.

Eagly, A.H., & Chaiken, S. (1998). Attitude structure and function. In D. T. Gilbert, S. T. Fiske, & G. Lindzey (Eds.), *The handbook of social psychology* (Vol. *1,* pp. 269–322). New York: MacGraw-Hill.

Edres, S. (2006). *The images of Arabs and Jews held by Arab children as a function of age and town.* Unpublished master's thesis, Tel Aviv University (in Hebrew).

Eldan, M. (2006). *Imparting collective memory by secular and religious kindergarten teachers.* Unpublished master's thesis, Tel Aviv University (in Hebrew).

Feldman, S. (2003). Enforcing social conformity: A theory of authoritarianism. *Political Psychology, 24,* 41–74.

Fiske, S. T. (1989). Examining the role of intent: Toward understanding its role in stereotyping and prejudice. In J. S. Uleman & J. A. Bargh (Eds.), *Unintended thought* (pp. 253–283). New York: Guilford Press.

Furman, M. (1999). Army and war: Collective narratives of early childhood in contemporary Israel. In E. Lomsky-Feder & E. Ben-Ari (Eds.), *The military and militarism in Israeli society* (pp. 141–168). Albany: State University of New York Press.

Gallagher, E., & Cairns, E. (2011). National identity and in-group/out-group attitudes: Catholic and Protestant children in Northern Ireland, *European Journal of Developmental Psychology, 8*(1), 58–73.

Geertz, C. (1973). *The interpretation of cultures.* New York: Basic Books.

Goodnow, J. J. (1990). The socialization of cognition: What's involved? In J. W. Stigler, R. A. Shweder, & G. Herdt (Eds.), *Cultural psychology* (pp. 259–286). Cambridge: Cambridge University Press.

Gopher, U. (2006). *Antecedents to the ethos of conflict in Israeli-Jewish society.* Master's thesis, Tel Aviv University (in Hebrew).

Hadjipavlou, M. (2007). The Cyprus conflict: Root causes and implications for peacebuilding. *Journal of Peace Research, 44*(3), 349–365.

Hailey, S. E., & Olson, K. R. (2013). A social psychologist's guide to the development of racial attitudes. *Social and Personality Psychology Compass, 7,* 457–469.

Hess, R. D., & Torney, J. V. (2005). *The development of political attitudes in children.* New Brunswick, NJ: Aldine Transaction.

Higgins, E. T., King, G. A., & Mavin, G. H. (1982). Individual construct accessibility and subjective impressions and recall. *Journal of Personality and Social Psychology, 43,* 35–47.

Hirschfeld, L. A. (1996). *Race in the making. Cognition, culture, and the child's construction of human kinds.* Cambridge, MA: MIT Press.

Hughes, D., Rodriguez, J., Smith, E. P., Johnson, D. J., Stevenson, H. C., & Spicer, P. (2006). Parents' ethnic-racial socialization practices: A review of research and directions for future study. *Developmental Psychology, 42*(5), 747–770.

Husain, S. A., Nair, J., Holcomb, W., Reid, J. C., Vargas, V., & Nair, S. S. (1998). Stress reactions of children and adolescents in war and siege conditions. *American Journal of Psychiatry, 155,* 1718–1719.

Israeli-Diner, G. (1993). *Stereotypes of Arabs among nursery-school children.* Unpublished master's thesis, Tel Aviv University (in Hebrew).

Jost, J. T., Glaser, J., Kruglanski, A. W., & Sulloway, F. (2003). Exceptions that prove the rule: Using a theory of motivated social cognition to account for ideological incongruities and political anomalies. *Psychological Bulletin, 129,* 383–393.

Jung, K., Ang, H. S., Leong, M. S., Tan, J. S., Pornpitakpan, C., & Kau, K. A. (2002). A typology of animosity and its cross-national validation. *Journal of Cross-Cultural Psychology, 33,* 525–539.

Kagan, J., & Moss, H. A. (1962). *Birth to maturity.* New York: Wiley

Katz, P. A., & Kofkin, J. A. (1997). Race, gender and young children. In S. Luthar, J. Burack, D. Cicchetti, & J. Weisz (Eds.), *Developmental perspectives on risk and pathology* (pp. 51–74). New York: Cambridge University Press.

Keen, S. (1986). *Faces of the enemy: Reflections of the hostile imagination.* San Fransisco: Harper and Row.

Kriesberg, L. (1998). Intractable conflicts. In E. Weiner (Ed.), *The handbook of interethnic coexistence* (pp. 332–342). New York: Continuum.

Kowalski, K. (2003). The emergence of ethnic and racial attitudes in preschool-aged children. *Journal of Social Psychology, 143*(6), 677–690.

Landau, S. F., Gvirsman, S. D., Huesmann, L. R., Dubow, E. F., Boxer, P., Ginges, J., & Shikaki, K. (2010). The effects of exposure to violence on aggressive behavior: The case of Arab and Jewish children in Israel. In K. Österman (Ed.), *Indirect and direct aggression* (pp. 321–343). Berlin: Peter Lang.

Lemish D., & Götz, M. (Eds.). (2007). *Children and media in times of conflict and war.* Cresskill, NJ: Hampton.

Leyens, J. P., Yzerbyt, V., & Schadron, G. (1994). *Stereotypes and social cognition.* London: Sage.

Maccoby, E. E., (1992). The role of parents in the socialization of children: An historical overview. *Developmental Psychology, 28,* 1006–1017.

MacDonald, D. B. (2002). *Balkan holocausts? Serbian and Croatian victim-centered propaganda and the war in Yugoslavia.* Manchester: Manchester University Press.

Macksoud, M., & Aber, L. (1996). The war experiences and psychosocial development of children in Lebanon. *Child Development, 67,* 70–88.

Masalha, S. (2003). Children and violent conflict: A look at the inner world of Palestinian children via their dreams. Palestine-Israel. *Journal of Politics, Economics & Culture, 10,* 62–70

MacMullin, C., & Odeh, J. (1999). What is worrying children in the Gaza Strip? *Child Psychiatry and Human Development, 30,* 55–70.

McIntyre, A., & Thusi, T. (2003). Children and youth in Sierra Leone's peace-building process. *African Security Review, 12*(2), 73–80.

Meijer, A. (1985). Child psychiatric sequelae of maternal war stress. *Acta Psychiatrica Scandinavia, 72*, 505–511.

Mertan, B. (2011). Children's perception of national identity and in-group/out-group attitudes: Turkish-Cypriot school children. *European Journal of Developmental Psychology, 8*(1), 74–86.

Miljević-Ridjički, R., & Lugomer-Armano, G. (1994). Children's comprehension of war. *Child Abuse Review, 3*, 134–144.

Milner, D. (1983). *Children and race: Ten years on.* East Grinstead, Sussex: West Lock Educational Co. Ltd.

Muldoon, O. T., & Trew, K. (2000). Children's experience and adjustment to conflict related events in Northern Ireland. *Peace Psychology: Journal of Peace and Conflict, 6* (2), 157–176

Myers-Bowman, K. S., Walker, K., & Myers-Walls, J. A. (2005). "Differences between war and peace are big": Children from Yugoslavia and the United States describe peace and war. *Peace and Conflict: Journal of Peace Psychology, 11*, 177–198.

Myers-Walls, J. A., Myers-Bowman, K. S., & Pelo, A. (1993). Parents as educators about war and peace. *Family Relations, 42*, 66–73.

Nasie, M., Diamond, A. H., & Bar-Tal, D. (in press). Young children in intractable conflicts: The Israeli case. *Personality and Social Psychology Review.*

Nasie, M., Bar-Tal, D., & Shnaidman, O. (2014). Activists in Israeli radical peace organizations: Their personal stories about joining and taking part in these organizations. *Peace and Conflict: Journal of Peace Psychology, 20*, 313–329.

Nesdale, D., & Flesser. D. (2001). Social identity and the development of children's group attitudes. *Child Development, 72*(2), 506–517.

Niemi, R., & Sobieszek, B. (1977). Political socialization. *Annual Review of Sociology, 3*, 209–233.

O'Malley, C. J., Blankemeyer, M., Walker, K., & Dellmann-Jenkins, M. (2007). Children's reported communication with their parents about war. *Journal of Family Issues, 28*, 1639–1662.

Oppenheimer, L. (2006). The development of enemy images: A theoretical contribution. *Peace and Conflict: Journal of Peace Psychology, 12*(3), 269–292.

Oppenheimer, L. (2011). Comparative analyses: Are there discernable patterns in the development of and relationships among national identification and in-group/out-group attitudes? *European Journal of Developmental Psychology, 8*(1), 116–132.

Oppenheimer, L., & Barrett, M. (2011). National identity and in-group/out-group attitudes in children: The role of sociohistorical settings. An introduction to the special issue. *European Journal of Developmental Psychology, 8*(1), 1–4.

Oppenheimer, L., & Midzic, E. (2011). National identification and in-group/out-group attitudes with Bosniak and Serbian children in Bosnia. *European Journal of Developmental Psychology, 8*(1), 43–57.

Oren, N. (2005). *The impact of major events in the Arab-Israeli conflict on the ethos of conflict of the Israeli Jewish society (1967–2000).* Doctoral dissertation, Tel-Aviv University.

Oren, N. (2009). *The Israeli ethos of conflict 1967–2005.* Working Paper #27. Fairfax, VA: Institute for Conflict Analysis and Resolution, George Mason University. Retrieved from http://icar.gmu.edu/wp_27oren.pdf

Ovadia, G. (1993). *Stereotypes toward Arabs of kindergarten-age children.* Unpublished master's thesis, Tel Aviv University (in Hebrew).

Papadakis, Y. (2008). *History education in divided Cyprus: A comparison of Greek Cypriot and Turkish Cypriot school books on the "history of Cyprus."* PRIO report 2/2008. Oslo: International Peace Research Institute.

Papadakis, Y., Perstianis, N., & Welz, G. (Eds.). (2006). *Divided Cyprus: Modernity, history, and an island in conflict.* Bloomington: Indiana University Press.

Perera, S. (1991). *Teaching and learning hatred: The role of education and socialization in Sri Lankan ethnic conflict.* PhD dissertation, University of California, Santa Barbara.

Povrzanovic, M. (1997). Children, war and nation: Croatia 1991–4. *Childhood: A Global Journal of Child Research, 4,* 81–102.

Podeh, E. (2002). *The Arab-Israeli conflict in Israeli history textbooks, 1948–2000.* Westport, CT: Bergin & Garvey.

Priest, N., Walton, J., White, F., Kowal, E., & Paradies, Y. (2014). Understanding the complexities of ethnic-racial socialization processes for both minority and majority groups: A 30-year systematic review. *International Journal of Intercultural Relations, 43,* 139–155.

Raabe, T., & Beelmann, A. (2011). Development of ethnic, racial, and national prejudice in childhood and adolescence: A multinational meta-analysis of age difference. *Child Development, 82*(6), 1715–1737.

Raviv, A., Bar-Tal, D., Koren-Silveshatz, L., & Raviv, A. (1999). Beliefs about war, conflict and peace in Israel as a function of developmental, cultural and situational factors. In A. Raviv, L. Oppenheimer, & D. Bar-Tal (Eds.), *How children understand war and peace* (pp. 161–189). San Francisco: Jossey Bass.

Reizábal, L., & Ortiz, G. (2011). National identity and ingroup/out-group attitudes with Basque and Basque-Spanish children growing up in the Basque Country. *European Journal of Developmental Psychology, 8*(1), 98–115.

Rokeach, M. (1964). *The three Christs of Ypsilanti.* New York: New York Review of Books.

Ross, M. H. (1998). The cultural dynamics of ethnic conflict. In D. Jacquin, A. Oros, & M. Verweij (Eds.), *Culture in world politics* (pp. 156–186). Houndmills: Macmillan.

Rutland, A. (1999). The development of national prejudice, in-group favoritism and self-stereotypes in British children. *British Journal of Social Psychology, 38*(1), 55–70.

Scribner, S. (1990). A sociocultural approach to the study of mind. In G. Greenberg & E. Tobach (Eds.), *Theories of the evolution of knowing. The T. C. Schneirla Conference Series* (Vol. 4, pp. 107–120). Hillsdale, NJ: Erlbaum.

Sears, D. O., & Levy, S. (2003). Childhood and adult political development. In D. O. Sears, L. Huddy, & R. Jervis (Eds.), *Oxford handbook of political psychology* (pp. 60–109). New York: Oxford University Press.

Shamai, M. (2001). Parents' perceptions of their children in a context of shared political uncertainty. *Child and Family Social Work, 6,* 249–260.

Sharvit, K. (2007). *Activation of the ethos of conflict while coping with stress resulting from intractable conflict.* PhD dissertation, Tel Aviv University.

Sharvit, K. (2014). How conflict begets conflict: Activation of the ethos of conflict in times of distress in a society involved in an intractable conflict. *Journal of Experimental Social Psychology, 55,* 252–261.

Sherif, M., Harvey, O. J., White, B. J., Hood, W. R. & Sherif, C. W. (1961). *Intergroup cooperation and competition: The Robbers Cave experiment*, Norman, OK: University Book Exchange.

Slocum-Bradley, N. (Ed.). (2008). *Promoting conflict or peace through identity*, London: Ashgate.

Slone, M. (2009). Growing up in Israel: Lessons on understanding the effects of political violence on children. In B.K. Barber (Ed.), *Adolescents and war: How youth deal with political violence* (pp. 81–104). New York: Oxford University Press.

Straker, G., Mendelsohn, M., Moosa, F., & Tudin, P. (1996). Violent political contexts and the emotional concerns of township youth. *Child Development, 67*, 46–54.

Stroebe, W., & Insko, C. A. (1989). Stereotype, prejudice, and discrimination: Changing conceptions in theory and research. In D. Bar-Tal, C. F. Graumann, A. W. Kruglanski, & W. Stroebe (Eds.), *Stereotyping and prejudice* (pp. 3–34). New York: Springer-Verlag.

Swidler, A. (1986). Culture in action: Symbols and strategies. *American Sociological Review, 51*(2), 273–286.

Tajfel, H. (1978). Social categorization. Social identity, and social comparison. In H. Tajfel (Ed.), *Differentiation between social groups* (pp. 61–76). London: Academic Press.

Teichman, Y. (2001). The development of Israeli children's images of Jews and Arabs and their expression in human figure drawings. *Developmental Psychology, 37*, 749–761.

Teichman, Y., & Bar-Tal, D. (2008). Acquisition and development of shared psychological intergroup repertoire in a context of an intractable conflict. In S. M. Quintana & C. McKown (Eds.), *Handbook of race, racism, and the developing child* (pp. 452–482). Hoboken: John Wiley & Sons, Inc.

Tetlock, P. E. (1989). Structure and function in political belief systems. In A. R. Pratkanis, S. J. Breckler, & A. G. Greenwald (Eds.), *Attitude structure and function* (pp. 129–152). Hillsdale, NJ: Erlbaum.

Tint, B. (2010). History, memory and intractable conflict. *Conflict Resolution Quarterly, 27*(3), 239–256.

Trimikliniotis, N. (2013). Sociology of reconciliation: Learning from comparing violent conflicts and reconciliation processes. *Current Sociology, 61*, 244.

Van Dijk, T. A. (1998). *Ideology: A multidisciplinary approach*. London: Sage.

Vygotsky, L. S. (1978). *Mind in society: The development of higher psychological processes*. Cambridge, MA: Harvard University Press.

Warshel, Y. (2007). "As though there is peace": Opinions of Jewish-Israeli children about watching Rechov Sumsum/Shara'a Simsim amidst armed political conflict. In D. Lemish & M. Götz (Eds.), *Children and media in times of conflict and war* (pp. 309–332). Cresskill, NJ: Hampton.

27 Interventions in Real-World Settings: Using Media to Overcome Prejudice and Promote Intergroup Reconciliation in Central Africa

Rezarta Bilali and Ervin Staub

Prejudice is one of the most studied topics in social psychology, and much of this work has an explicit applied focus on prejudice reduction. Yet, we have a long road ahead in designing and rigorously assessing the effectiveness of evidence-based prejudice reduction interventions in real-world settings. In a review of prejudice reduction literature, Paluck and Green (2009) showed that less than half the studies in this area assessed the *causal* impact of prejudice reduction interventions, and of these, most were conducted in laboratory settings. Of the field experimental studies (11% of all studies reviewed), the vast majority were conducted in schools. Moreover, the research in this area relies heavily on student populations in Western countries (Henry, 2008). Consequently, we know little about prejudice reduction in conflict-affected countries, and in contexts of ongoing violence or its aftermath.

In the past decade, however, important theoretical and empirical developments in social psychology have started to address the nature of intergroup relations in conflict-affected countries, broadening the scope of interventions from prejudice reduction to more generally improving intergroup relations and promoting reconciliation. Premises of influential social psychological theories, such as social identity theory (see Chapter 3) or contact hypothesis (see Chapter 6), have been tested and extended to a number of ongoing and post-conflict settings including Bosnia, Cyprus, Israel, Lebanon, Northern Ireland, Rwanda, and so on (e.g., Čehajić, Brown, & Castano, 2008; Kanazayire, Licata, Melotte, Dusingizemungu, & Azzi, 2014). In addition, new concepts and approaches have been developed to capture psychological and social processes unique to contexts of violent conflict (e.g., Chapter 26 in this title; Bar-Tal, 2007; Kelman, 1990; Staub, 1989, 2011). Exciting and productive research programs have emerged on intergroup reconciliation (e.g., Shnabel & Nadler, 2008; Staub, 2011), victimhood (e.g., Noor, Brown, Gonzalez, Manzi, & Lewis, 2012; Vollhardt, 2012; Vollhardt & Bilali, 2015), intergroup forgiveness (e.g., Tam et al., 2007), and intergroup apologies (e.g., Blatz, Schumann, & Ross, 2009). These new developments have practical implications, as the principles and findings can guide interventions to promote reconciliation and reduce prejudice in conflict settings (e.g., Hameiri, Bar-Tal, & Halperin, 2014).

In this chapter, we aim to contribute to this growing literature in two important ways. First, despite the important strides made, our knowledge of psychological interventions in conflict and post-conflict settings is limited and at an early stage of development. We overview a research program on an intervention (a mass media campaign) that uses psychological principles and knowledge to prevent violence, reduce prejudice, and promote intergroup reconciliation in one of the world's most violent regions, the Great Lakes Region of Africa. From this, we draw implications about our understanding of prejudice reduction and reconciliation and highlight avenues for future research. Our second goal is to emphasize the ways in which research, theory, and practice can inform one another, and discuss the benefits and challenges of conducting field research in these settings. Although we, the psychologists working in this area, are driven by a motivation to contribute to practice and policy, typically we are not trained in designing and implementing interventions. Therefore, we highlight important considerations that scholars and practitioners need to consider as we move from basic research to recommendations for policy and intervention. To achieve this goal, we describe the design and implementation of the mass media intervention using psychological principles from its conception to its implementation at scale. We will discuss the translation of psychological principles to specific contexts, the steps and challenges of implementing such interventions in new and difficult settings, and research assessing this intervention's efficacy.

Contexts of Conflict in the Great Lakes Region of Africa: Rwanda, Burundi, and the DRC

Conflicts in the Great Lakes Region (Rwanda, Burundi, and DRC) are interconnected because of cultural and historical ties, arbitrarily drawn borders, and massive exodus of populations during and after violent incidents (Lemarchand, 2009). Rwanda and Burundi have similar ethnic compositions (about 85% of the population is Hutu, 14% Tutsi, and 1% Twa), whereas numerous ethnic clans, including Hutus and Tutsis, populate the eastern provinces of DRC. The conflicts in the DRC revolve around matters of territory and land ownership, tribes and ethnicity, and power and wealth, among multiple parties.

Before the colonial time, Tutsis were dominant in Rwanda and Burundi; under Belgian oversight, the Tutsis' power and privilege were enhanced and Hutus were oppressed – conditions that created intergroup animosity. In Rwanda, Hutus took over power from Tutsis in a violent uprising in 1959–1962, whereas in Burundi the Tutsi minority remained in power till early 1990s. The violence targeting Tutsis during the power switch in Rwanda resulted in a large migration of Tutsis to the neighboring countries. Over the years there were occasional mass killings of Tutsis, with further exodus. Not allowed reentry to Rwanda and not granted citizenship rights in the host countries, these exiles formed armed groups to attack Rwanda. The latest and strongest of these groups, the Rwandan Patriotic Front (RPF), invaded Rwanda in 1990, triggering the three-year civil war that preceded the 1994 genocide. The 1959 uprising against Tutsis in Rwanda resolved Tutsis in Burundi to maintain power at any cost, leading to further repression and exclusion of Hutus from important institutions. A failed Hutu rebellion in 1972 in Burundi was followed by systematic violence of genocidal proportions carried out by the Tutsi gendarmerie, resulting in hundreds of thousands of Hutus killed and a massive Hutu exodus to the neighboring countries (Lemarchand, 2009). The stories of the 1972 massacres influenced the historical memories of the Hutus in the region (Lemarchand, 2009, p. 139). In 1993, Burundi held its first democratic and free elections, resulting in the victory of Melchior Ndadaye, who became the first democratically elected president and the first Hutu president. However, Ndadaye was assassinated a few months after the elections, resulting in a brutal civil war in which Hutu groups carried out revenge attacks on Tutsis amounting to genocidal acts (International Commission of Inquiry for Burundi, 2002), followed by violent attacks by the Tutsi military on Hutus.

Not long after the turmoil in Burundi, in 1994, following a peace agreement, about 800,000 Tutsis and a large number of moderate Hutus were murdered in a period of 100 days in Rwanda. The RPF resumed fighting and managed to stop the genocide. About a million and a half Hutus left Rwanda after the RPF took power, many settling in camps along the border in Zaire, now the Democratic Republic of the Congo (DRC). Among them were the genocide perpetrators, who in incursions into Rwanda were killing more Tutsis (Reyntjens, 2009). The new Rwandan army, now under Tutsi rule, twice invaded the Congo. In addition to fighting the genocidaires, they killed a large number of Hutus, possibly between 200,000 and 300,000 (Prunier, 2009). Many of the ethnic Tutsis from eastern Congo were also involved in the mass violence against the Hutu refugee camps in the DRC. Rwanda's military presence and actions in eastern Congo have led to great resentment and animosity among the Congolese population toward Rwandophone (i.e., people of Rwandan origin) populations. Although the war in the DRC officially ended in 2002, the violence continues in the eastern provinces through rebel groups, large-scale rape, displacement of civilians, and other human rights abuses (Human Rights Watch, 2012).

Programs, Policies, and Interventions to Overcome Mass Violence

This overview sheds light on the cyclical nature of conflicts and the complexity of intergroup relations in the Great Lakes Region of Africa. At the psychological level, such extreme violence has a significant impact on all segments of the population: survivors, perpetrators, and bystanders. It shatters victims' assumptions about the world and their relationships with others (e.g., McCann & Pearlman, 1990; Pearlman & Saakvitne, 1995) and makes them feel threatened and vulnerable (Staub, 1989, 2003, 2011; Staub & Pearlman, 2001, 2006). As in the Great Lakes Region, the roles of victims and perpetrators often shift, as all groups may have endured victimization or perpetrated harm at different points in time. At a psychological level, the groups involved experience the world as dangerous, and outgroups are seen as untrustworthy (Staub, 1998, 2011). This might result in an increased sensitivity to new threats and a tendency to protect the ingroup by all means, including preemptive violence (Staub, 1998). Perpetrators, in order to justify their actions, as well as protect themselves from the emotional consequences of their actions (such as empathic distress, guilt, and shame), devalue and dehumanize the victims and blame them for bringing the violence on themselves (Staub, 2011).

These processes pose formidable challenges to efforts to reduce prejudice, promote reconciliation, and stop cycles of violence in these settings. Governments endorse different policies to address the consequences of violence and promote unity and social cohesion in its aftermath. Burundi's and Rwanda's approaches to addressing the past and building peace in the aftermath of violence are both substantial (albeit different), whereas in eastern DRC such top-down approaches are nonexistent. Specifically, the ethnic groups in Burundi agreed on a political power-sharing solution in which Hutus and Tutsis hold respectively 60% and 40% of the posts in the government and national assembly (Lemarchand, 2009). However, Burundi has failed to directly address its violent past, postponing the agreed-upon creation of a truth commission to establish the truth and responsibilities for the violence of the past decades (Vandeginste, 2014). Some studies suggest that civilians in Burundi are more likely to prefer "forgiving and forgetting" over punishment and seeking the truth about the past, likely because of the political and societal risks of such processes (e.g., potential for renewed violence and hostility, Samii, 2013; Uvin, 2009).

By contrast, in the aftermath of genocide in Rwanda, the Tutsi-dominated government has instituted extensive policies and programs to address the past, including a transitional justice system (i.e., the Gacaca courts, which are in part the Rwandan version of a truth and reconciliation commission set to uncover the truth about the genocide and in part trying the perpetrators of violence against Tutsis), as well as a range of policies under the "unity and reconciliation" campaign. These include policies that prohibit identification based on ethnicity, and reeducation programs to teach a portion of the Rwandan population the sanctioned history of Rwanda. These policies and some problematic implementations of Gacaca trials have received critiques by scholars (e.g., Clark, 2010; Hodgkin, 2006). These critiques highlight their potentially harmful implications for society (for a discussion of these policies from a psychological perspective, see Bilali, 2014; Moss, 2014; Staub, 2014). While there is little empirical research to shed light on the effects of these policies and programs on intergroup attitudes, preliminary work provides some support for both the policies and critiques of the policies. For example, in two studies, Rime, Kanyangara and colleagues (Kanyangara, Rime, Philippot, & Yzerbyt, 2007; Rime, Kanyangara, Yzerbyt, & Paez, 2011) found mixed effects (both positive and negative) of participation in the Gacaca trials. Participation in Gacaca increased posttraumatic stress (PTSD; see also Brounéus, 2010) but reduced shame among survivors. It also reduced PTSD but increased shame and guilt among prisoners. However, both survivors and perpetrators experienced more negative primary emotions (e.g., fear, sadness) after participation. The findings also showed ambivalence with regard to intergroup outcomes. On one hand, participation in Gacaca was related to more positive outgroup stereotypes and lower perceived outgroup homogeneity. On the other hand, survivors who participated in Gacaca exhibited more revenge feelings, less inclination to forgive, and less willingness for intergroup contact. These mixed effects may have been due in part to the emotional consequences of reliving traumatic events, and in part to the complexity of the Gacaca process, which attempted to establish the truth, while also trying perpetrators, in front of primarily Hutu communities, with witnesses (and most likely survivors) exposed to negative reactions by the relatives of perpetrators (Broneus, 2010). Some of the negative reactions by Hutus may have been enhanced as a result of the one-sided nature of the justice process, with violence against Hutus not acknowledged or addressed (Staub, 2014). In addition to government programs and policies, a large number of nongovernmental actors (civil society and international organizations) have made efforts intervening in these contexts, each promoting its own theories of change. Few of these efforts are theory-or evidence-based, and even fewer are rigorously studied. Such efforts provide excellent opportunities for scholars to set up collaborations with practitioners and test theoretical premises in the field. In the rest of the chapter, we describe the development and evaluation of an approach – a public education campaign – using psychological theory for intervening in these settings.

Development of a Mass Media Campaign to Prevent Violence and Promote Reconciliation in the Aftermath of Mass Violence

In the summer of 1999, psychologists Ervin Staub (coauthor of this chapter) and Laurie Pearlman were invited to Rwanda to initiate interventions to promote healing and reconciliation in the aftermath of the genocide. They first conducted a two-week workshop with 35 Rwandese staff of local and international NGOs that focused on promoting healing and rebuilding communities after the genocide. The workshop was structured in a way that would provide participants with information about theory and research to help with understanding the roots of mass violence (Staub, 1989, 2003), the effects of trauma after mass violence, and avenues to healing (McCann & Pearlman, 1990; Pearlman & Saakvitne, 1995). Different examples of mass violence and genocide in the world were used to exemplify basic principles, and participants themselves applied these principles to the genocide in Rwanda. Participants engaged in extensive discussion and small-group activities that aimed toward integrating this knowledge with participants' own experiences during and after the genocide. In informal evaluations at the end of the workshops, participants reported that the experience had a powerful impact on them. It helped them make meaning out of their personal and their group's experiences with violence, empowered them by providing tools to engage with traumatic experiences in a supportive manner, and gave them hope that new violence could be prevented.

Staub, Pearlman, Gubin, and Hagengimana (2005) set out to experimentally test the effectiveness of this approach by assessing its impact on trauma and orientation toward the other group. Staub and Pearlman trained facilitators on this approach, who then facilitated community discussions (including both Tutsis and Hutus). The outcomes in the community groups led by facilitators trained by Staub and Pearlman were compared to outcomes in community groups led by facilitators who did not undergo training, as well as to members of groups that received no intervention. The assessment was done at three points in time: before the start of the intervention, at the end of the intervention, and two months after the intervention. Two months after the intervention, compared to both control groups, the intervention groups reported significantly less trauma symptoms, more positive orientation by members of each group toward the other, more "conditional forgiveness" (i.e., willingness to forgive under certain conditions, for example, if the perpetrators make amends), a more complex understanding of the roots of violence, and more readiness to reconcile (for detailed descriptions, see Staub et al., 2005).

Staub and Pearlman then used this approach in workshops with varied groups in Rwanda, including leaders and journalists. With leaders, they used the knowledge about the origins and the impact of genocide on populations to discuss national policies and practices. With journalists, they discussed ways in which media reporting might either increase or reduce the likelihood of renewed violence (Staub, 2011; Staub & Pearlman, 2006).

Based on the findings of this research and on participants' feedback on various training workshops, as well as their theoretical work, Staub (2011) concluded that examining and understanding the societal, cultural, and psychological influences that lead to extreme violence might help humanize both victims and perpetrators, by showing that such violence is the outcome of a human process. Understanding the roots of violence and learning about similar ways that others have suffered seem to help survivors see their common humanity with others, mitigate negative attitudes toward themselves, and help them see perpetrators (as well as passive bystanders) as human beings in spite of their horrible actions (Staub et al., 2005). In line with this idea, in a survey conducted in Burundi, Rwanda, and the DRC, Vollhardt and Bilali (2015) found that perceiving commonalities between the ingroup's and other group's suffering was related to more positive intergroup attitudes across national contexts. Staub (2006) also argued that viewing mass violence as a result of a multitude of factors that in combination increase the likelihood of violence should reduce perpetrators' defensiveness (by reducing portrayals of perpetrators as innately evil), thus making it more likely for them to acknowledge their responsibility. Similarly, it has been suggested that understanding psychological trauma, including both the symptoms of posttraumatic stress disorder (American Psychiatric Association, 1994) and the profound effects of traumatic experiences on the self, can contribute to healing (Allen, 2001; Rosenbloom & Williams, 1999).

To scale up the efforts in preventing renewed violence and promoting intergroup reconciliation, Staub and Pearlman's approach (i.e., increasing the understanding of the roots and evolution of violence and its effects on victims, witnesses, and perpetrators, as well as increasing understanding of the effects of trauma and avenues to healing) was adapted to a large-scale public education campaign via media that we describe in the next section.

Media Education Campaign via Radio

The media campaign that we describe was initiated in collaboration with Radio La Benevolencija's Humanitarian Tools Foundation. Radio La Benevolencija has broadcast fictional radio dramas in Rwanda since 2004 (*Musekeweya* or *New Dawn*), in Burundi since 2006 (*Murikira Ukuri* or *Shedding Light on the Truth*), and in the DRC since 2006 (*Kumbuka Kesho* or *Remember Tomorrow*). These dramas are designed to prevent violence and promote positive intergroup relations. The main programs consist of weekly soap operas with embedded educational content to communicate the role of various macro- and micro-level factors that increase the likelihood that individuals engage in or support violence (e.g., the role of difficult life conditions, cultural-societal characteristics, encouragement of blind obedience in society, historical devaluation of some groups) and might contribute to the evolution of mass violence and genocide (see Staub, 1989, 1998, 2011; Staub & Pearlman, 2006).

In Rwanda this educational content has been embedded in a fictional story of conflict between villages (see www.labenevolencija.org/; also Staub, 2011). The conflict begins when there is a drought. One of the villages that was granted by the authorities a piece of rich land that lies between the two villages has enough food, while people in the other village go hungry. This latter village, led by a negative leader who is in part motivated by personal issues, attacks the other village to steal its food. This is followed by a long history of conflict, and eventually reconciliation.

The radio campaign aims toward cognitive change (insight, awareness, and learning) as well as behavioral change (modeling and social learning and invoking learning by doing). The information embedded in the radio drama through events and the words and actions of the characters aims to educate the population about the roots and evolution of violence. It also aims to educate people about the complex trauma that violence creates and encourages active bystandership (i.e., taking action in the face of evil), which has the potential to prevent escalation and stop violence (Staub, 2006; Staub & Pearlman, 2006; Staub et al., 2005). Similarly, building on the workshops and training sessions led by Staub and Pearlman, the media campaign rests on the idea that understanding the roots of group-based violence, as well as the avenues to prevention and reconciliation, will inoculate people to the influences that promote violence. In addition, the media campaign draws from Bandura's (1986) social cognitive theory by using role models to portray desirable behaviors, such as encouraging people to take action to prevent violence or to resist calls to violence. This approach is also in line with Freire's (1973) critical consciousness approach to social change, which emphasizes the role of critical reflection (i.e., understanding and analyzing the role of social conditions underlying oppression) and critical action (i.e., acting to change these conditions) to promote positive social change.

Communication messages to guide the creation of educational content. Theories and research about the origins of genocide, the traumatic impact of violence, healing, and reconciliation were summarized in brief "communication messages." First, 12 messages were used, which were afterward expanded to 35 messages to give a more detailed sense of origins, trauma, healing, and reconciliation. The step-by-step nature of the evolution of both the negative and positive processes was also summarized in a narrative "continuum."

Three examples of the messages include (a) national, ethnic, or religious groups, or ideological groups that arise in difficult times, and their leaders tend to scapegoat other groups and create destructive ideologies; (b) passivity by witnesses/bystanders affirms the perpetrators and facilitates the evolution of harm doing; and (c) establishing the complex truth about past group relations and about conflict and violence and developing a shared view of history are important for reconciliation. As part of addressing this last communication message, we indicated that there are divergent views of history and showed the challenge in discussing them. The following is a relevant segment from *Muwekeweya*, the radio drama in Rwanda:

THE TEACHER: (Moderately) Mugenga, without defending yourselves, don't you know that it is you the people of Bumanzi who are the culprits for the disaster? (The conflict with the other village and the attack by the other village on them.)

MUGENGA: (Angry) How should we be held responsible when the land was officially given to us!

THE TEACHER: Even though you didn't take it by force, you should have shared it with the people in Muhumuro with whom you shared it before! I say it impartially as I hail from neither Muhumuro nor Bumanzi.

MUGENGA: (Indignant) You don't deserve being listened to! Fabiya, I won't talk to you anymore! Our children are in trouble if you teach them such things!

THE TEACHER: Look! Why do people call a spade a spade and you get angry and start insulting them! Does being at loggerheads with someone give you the right to insult them? (From Staub, 2011, p. 450)

The Design, Implementation, and Adaptation of Mass Media Intervention

Although the general approach in developing these interventions is the same across national sites, the implementation is country specific. The prototype intervention was first designed in Rwanda and then adapted to Burundi and the Eastern DRC. Specifically, six implementation features (Durlak & Dupre, 2008; see also Dane & Schneider, 1998) – adaptation, fidelity, quality, dosage, participant responsiveness, program reach – are considered in each country (Table 27.1).

Table 27.1 *Features of the implementation of the intervention.*

Features of Implementation Strategy	Definition (from Durlak & Dupre, 2008)	Design and Implementation of the Radio Drama Interventions
Fidelity	Does the intervention correspond to the originally intended program?	• Same training manual and educational content across sites • Periodic training of scriptwriters on educational content and education entertainment strategy • Same procedures to produce programs across sites • Regular monitoring of the implementation
Dosage	How much of the intended program has been delivered?	• One episode (4–5 scenes) of 30 minutes broadcast on a weekly basis, repeated twice a week • Each episode includes 1–2 educational messages, embedded in the story, repeated several times in different episodes • Broadcast for several years
Quality	Are the program components conducted correctly and delivered clearly?	• All scripts reviewed by an academic expert who assesses educational content • Regular feedback through listener groups and focus group discussions
Participant responsiveness	Does the program stimulate and hold the interest and attention of participants?	• Feedback from listeners (through letters, SMS, phone calls) • Periodic surveys assessing listeners' interest, perceptions of goals, identification with characters, etc.
Adaptation	How is the program modified during the implementation?	• Prior to intervention: adaptation of the educational material and story to the cultural, historical, and sociopolitical context • During the intervention: ongoing adaptations consider changes in the sociopolitical context over the course of the program
Program reach	Who is the target audience? How representative is it?	• Periodic audience surveys to assess the popularity and the reach of the program

First, to ensure proper *adaptation* of the educational principles to specific cultural and political contexts, baseline research is conducted to assess the audience's relevant knowledge, attitudes, and behaviors in each country. The findings of this work are used to shape the specific goals and design of the intervention. Then, representatives of civil society groups, government agencies, and the local staff meet to assess the relevance of the educational messages in their context. These local partners and staff adapt the educational content to the local context and design the fictional setting of the conflict, in line with the nature of intercommunity relations in each country. For instance, in Burundi, the radio drama *Murikira Ukuri* portrays the conflict between two fictional ethnic groups that differ in education level and income opportunities, wealth, and representation in governance. This makes the story accessible to Burundians, who can relate to the complex power relations and grievances of the fictional groups. In Rwanda, the main story line of the soap opera *Musekeweya* portrays the evolution and cycles of violence between two villages. The violence starts in response to unjust distribution of resources by authorities (who gave ownership of a fertile valley to one of the villages), and worsens as a drought results in shortage of food, especially in the poorer village. In the DRC, the story includes conflict among multiple clans, and a variety of other social problems pertinent to the DRC context, including corruption, child labor, child soldiers, and poverty. Despite the similarities between fiction and reality, the stories are designed in a way that makes it difficult for listeners to identify their ethnic group with one of the fictional groups to reduce the possibility that listeners take sides and use preexisting schemas and beliefs about their conflict to understand the fictional story.

Fidelity of an intervention refers to whether it corresponds to the originally intended program (i.e., whether the educational messages are communicated accurately). Closely monitoring the implementation of the intervention ensures its fidelity. Local scriptwriters and producers undergo periodic training on the educational content, and a psychologist with relevant expertise reviews the scripts prior to their broadcast and provides feedback on the implementation of the messages. In ongoing formative research, listener groups offer feedback on different aspects of the program (e.g., whether the messages are understood, whether the show is interesting). These measures are important in ensuring the *quality* of the intervention over time.

It is not enough, however, that an intervention is of high quality and has fidelity. Whether the intervention reaches the intended populations (*program reach*) and *participants' responsiveness* to the intervention are also important. Periodic representative surveys assess the reach and popularity of the mass media intervention. In addition, listeners have the opportunity to send their feedback through SMS and letters to the producers. In yearly workshops, civil society representatives and the local staff reevaluate the scope of the intervention and design the storyline for the following year by taking into consideration feedback from listeners, the results of evaluation studies, and the changes in the sociopolitical context.

Dosage refers to the amount of intended program that needs to be delivered to observe effects. Determining dosage is probably the most difficult task in social interventions, as we lack studies to inform such decisions, and dosage should likely vary depending on the needs in a particular context. Moreover, dosage can mean different things. For instance, in the context of the mass media intervention, it refers to the frequency and length of each broadcast, as well as the frequency of educational messages and the length of time during which they are repeated. The radio dramas are broadcast twice a week, for 30 minutes each, by now over many years. Based on evaluation research and listener feedback, we have learned that programs might be more effective if they focus on a fewer number of messages that are conveyed with higher frequency for a longer period of time. These recommendations have been implemented in the design of the radio dramas.

Does Mass Media Intervention Reduce Prejudice and Promote Reconciliation?

A series of studies have examined the impact of the soap opera intervention on intergroup relations in Rwanda, Burundi, and the DRC. We have summarized the results of four studies (Bilali & Vollhardt, 2013, 2015; Bilali, Vollhardt, & Rarick, 2016; Paluck, 2009; for the Rwanda evaluation, see also Staub & Pearlman, 2009, and Staub, 2011) that have assessed the impact of the intervention in Table 27.2 (in Table 27.2, a "+" sign refers to effects in the predicted direction, whereas a "−" sign refers to the effects contrary to the goals of the program) and further discuss these findings in the following section.

In addition, two studies in the DRC have tested specific mechanisms of change, specifically the role of discussions (Paluck, 2010) and the impact of role modeling of collective action (Bilali, Vollhardt, & Rarick, 2017). In the following sections, we aim to integrate the results of these studies, discuss the mechanisms of change, and consider explanations for the differential effects of the intervention across sites. We draw hypotheses for future research and raise important questions regarding the design and implementation of social psychological interventions in different settings.

The Impact of the Prototype Radio Soap Opera in Rwanda

During its first year of the show, Paluck (2009) carried out a one-year randomized impact study in which she randomly assigned 14 communities across Rwanda to either an experimental or a control group. Forty individuals in each community were randomly selected to listen to either the reconciliation soap opera or a soap opera focusing on health. During the course of one year, the groups listened on a regular basis to the assigned radio soap opera. At the end of the year, the study revealed

Table 27.2 *Summary of research findings assessing the impact of reconciliation radio dramas in Rwanda, Burundi, and the DRC.*

	Rwanda	Burundi	DRC
Outgroup orientation: social distance, trust, active bystandership			
Advise children to marry within ingroup (r) [1,3,4]	+	+	+
There is mistrust in my community (r) [1]	ns	N/A	N/A
It is naïve to trust the outgroup (r) [1,2,3]	++	+	N/A
If an outgroup member is treated unfairly, I try to stop it [2]	N/A	+	N/A
Conformity			
If I disagree with something someone is doing or saying, I keep quiet (r) [1,3]	+	ns	N/A
People should defer to leaders without questioning them (r) [3,4]	N/A	ns	-
Ingroup superiority			
My group is superior (r) [3,4]	N/A	+	ns
My group is more moral relative to other groups (r) [3,4]	N/A	+	ns
Responsibility attributions			
The other group is responsible for problems in the country (r) [3]	N/A	+	N/A
My group has no responsibility for problems in the country [3]	N/A	+	N/A
Tolerance			
A good leader makes sure my group gets ahead (r) [4]	N/A	N/A	-
Discussing with other groups makes things worse (r) [4]	N/A	N/A	-
It causes too much confusion/to allow expression of different views (r) [1,2,3,4]	+	+	ns
Beliefs about victimhood and the past of the conflict			
Competitive victimhood (r) [2,3,4]	+	+	+
Inclusive victimhood [2,3,4]	+	ns	+
The history I have learned from my family is the only true history (r) [2,3]	+	+	N/A
I try to understand other group's perspective of history [2,3]	+	ns	N/A
Beliefs about evolution of violence			
Violence is more likely if we obey leaders blindly [3]	N/A	ns	N/A
If I stand by while others commit evil acts, I am also responsible [1,3]	ns	ns	N/A
When we do not intervene when someone is treated in an unfair way, we allow violence to evolve [3]	N/A	-	N/A
Violence comes out suddenly (r) [1]	ns	N/A	N/A
Mass violence grows out of small acts [1]	ns	N/A	N/A
When people marry from different groups, this contributes to peace [1]	ns	N/A	N/A
Empathy for other people [1]	+	N/A	N/A
Cooperative behavior [1]	+	N/A	N/A

Notes: The table summarizes the results of four studies conducted in Rwanda, Burundi, and the DRC. The upper scripts refer to specific studies: [1] Paluck (2009), [2] Bilali and Vollhardt (2013), [3] Bilali, Vollhardt, and Rarick (2016), [4] Bilali and Vollhardt (2015). "+" refers to effects in the predicted direction, "−" refers to effects contrary to the goals of the program, "ns" refers to null results, "r" refers to reversed coded items; "N/A" means that the item was not asked in that context.

that the intervention increased outgroup trust and reduced social distance toward outgroups. In addition, reconciliation drama listeners were more likely to engage in cooperative behavior in real group settings and in role-plays that addressed community problems. They were more likely to report engaging in, rather than just advocating, reconciliation activities (such as approaching someone who harmed them or whom they harmed; Paluck, 2009; Paluck & Green, 2009). Listeners of the reconciliation soap opera were also more likely to show empathy for genocide survivors, political prisoners, and poor people.

One of the challenges of the soap opera's popularity in Rwanda – about 90% of the population listen to the broadcast of the radio drama – is that, without a comparison group not exposed to the drama, it is hard to assess the long-term impact of the program. In light of this, Bilali and Vollhardt (2013) employed an innovative approach to evaluation by drawing on the psychological literature on priming, which refers to activating in a subtle way a representation or association in memory. They used audio priming (specifically, they made the soap opera salient by exposing participants to the voice of one of its main characters) to assess whether *Musekeweya* influenced people's willingness to engage with different versions of history, their victimhood beliefs, and outgroup trust. Participants completed an audio-delivered questionnaire in which the items were recorded either in the voice of one of the characters of the radio drama or in the voice of an unknown actor. Listeners who were primed with *Musekeweya* through the voice of its character exhibited more historical perspective taking (i.e., were less likely to report that their group's version of history is the only true history, and more likely to report that they try to understand other groups' perspective of history), reported higher outgroup trust, and less competitive and more inclusive victimhood (i.e., seeing others as having suffered similarly to themselves).

Do the Positive Effects of the Radio Drama Generalize to Contexts of Burundi and the DRC?

Five years after the start of the broadcast in Burundi, we replicated and extended the findings in Rwanda to the context in Burundi (Bilali et al., 2016). We used a statistical technique (propensity score matching) to match listeners and non-listeners in a series of demographic characteristics, regional background, and experiences with violence. We subsequently assessed the differences between matched listeners and non-listeners in a series of outcomes. As shown in Table 27.2, the results replicated Paluck's findings in Rwanda with regard to the soap opera's positive influence on outgroup trust and social distance. In addition, soap opera listeners were more likely than non-listeners to acknowledge the ingroup's responsibility for violence, and they were less likely to blame the outgroup. This seems an important finding, in that not only perpetrators but also members of groups that have perpetrated violence usually resist acknowledging their group's responsibility (Staub, 2011). They were also less likely to perceive the ingroup as superior to the outgroup. However, unlike in Rwanda, the radio drama in Burundi did not influence dissent and obedience to leaders. The effects of the drama on active bystandership were mixed such that listeners reported speaking out more if they witness bullying of an outgroup member (i.e., higher active bystandership); however, they also were less likely to report that the passivity of bystanders contributes to violence.

In the South and North Kivu provinces of the DRC, Bilali and Vollhardt (2015) used the same methodology as in Rwanda (i.e., audio priming) to assess the radio drama's associations with a variety of intergroup attitudes. The results also revealed mixed effects of the radio drama in the DRC. In line with the goals of the intervention, priming of the radio drama was related to higher inclusive and less exclusive (competitive) victimhood, as well as to more tolerance of intergroup marriages. Contrary to the goals of the intervention, however, participants exposed to the character's voice were more likely than those in the control group to agree that people should obey leaders without asking questions (i.e., more obedience), that a good leader should promote the ethnic ingroup's success, and that discussions between members of different ethnic or political groups make things worse.

Understanding the Heterogeneity of Media Intervention Effects Across National Sites

There are several potential explanations for the heterogeneity of effects of the media intervention in different national contexts. It is possible that the observed differences across settings might be due to the adaptation and implementation features of the intervention. For instance, the implementation of the intervention in DRC might be of lower quality or the story might be less entertaining. This in turn might lead to listeners' lower identification with the characters, and subsequently to a lower impact of the show. To examine this possibility, Bilali and Vollhardt (2015, Study 2) conducted focus group discussions to examine how listeners perceived and engaged with the media intervention. The results of focus group discussions did not support this explanation. Listeners in the DRC identified with the show and its characters, found the show to be realistic, and understood its main goal and message related to peaceful coexistence. Listeners also seemed to endorse the behaviors modeled in the drama.

Alternatively, the same intervention might have a differential impact depending on the features of the context (e.g., differences in the sociopolitical contexts and historical conflict, existing dominant narratives), which might moderate the intervention's effects. Next, we discuss two such potential moderators: the role of dominant social norms and narratives and the characteristics of the conflict (i.e., the degree of ongoing violence and insecurity).

Existing narratives and social norms. Drawing on the differences in the impact of the radio drama in Rwanda and Burundi, Bilali et al. (2016) hypothesized that the impact of an intervention might depend on the degree to which the ideas put forth by the intervention counteract or resonate with existing societal and institutional norms. While the radio drama was associated with higher reports of dissent and lower reports of obedience toward leaders in Rwanda, it failed to affect these outcomes in Burundi. Narratives that emphasize the role of obedience in perpetuating the genocide are common in post-genocide Rwanda. One possibility is that the radio drama might be effective in amplifying these resonant beliefs and narratives in Rwanda but might not be as effective in a context where these narratives are less familiar (Bilali et al., 2016).

It is also possible that interventions might be more likely to produce social change when the societal conditions are facilitative of these changes. Consistent with this idea, in Rwanda, Paluck and Green (2009) found heterogeneity of experimental effects of the radio drama intervention in two communities: a community of Tutsi survivors of genocide and a Hutu community in a region that was a seat of Hutu extremism prior to the genocide. In the Hutu community where there was heightened government surveillance, the radio drama did not influence dissent, presumably because dissent was not a safe behavioral option for this community. In a Tutsi genocide survivor community, participants were more likely to publicly admit that there is mistrust in their community as a result of the intervention. This is likely because this community felt lower censorship (relative to the Hutu community) from the government with regard to free expression of opinions (Paluck & Green, 2009). Staub (2014) has noted that the contextual constraints (e.g., limitations on freedom of speech and political activity in Rwanda) might limit expressions of the effects of the intervention that stress values and behaviors that counter these societal norms (e.g., moderate authority, pluralism). However, it is also possible that such changes might be latent and might emerge when political conditions change, as proposed by Vallacher, Coleman, Nowak, and Bui-Wrzonsinska's (2010) dynamical systems theory (Staub, 2011, 2014).

Contexts of ongoing violence versus aftermath of violence. As suggested earlier, the inconsistent and mixed impact of the radio drama in the DRC as compared to the generally positive impact in Rwanda and Burundi raises questions about whether the characteristics of the conflicts in these countries might account for the differences. Different from Rwanda and Burundi, the violence in the DRC is ongoing, resulting in insecurity and fear among the population. People living in conditions of ongoing violence and insecurity are faced with different challenges and needs than people in post-conflict settings where violence has diminished (see Stevens, Eagle, Kaminer, & Higson-Smith, 2013). For these reasons, Bilali and Vollhardt (2015) argued that the effectiveness of radio drama interventions (and more generally of peace-building interventions) might be hampered as a result of conditions of ongoing violence. For instance, focus group discussions with listeners in the DRC (Bilali & Vollhardt, 2015, Study 2) suggest that the show might sometimes elicit negative reactions (e.g., hopelessness) because of negative stories of conflict, trauma, or corruption. In these contexts, depictions of negative realities might serve as reminders of ongoing grievances, which in turn might inhibit social change processes. Ongoing violence reduces people's beliefs in their efficacy to exercise control over their own lives (Pearlman, 2013). Uncertainty and fear also increase group polarization (Canetti, Hall, Rapaport, & Wayne, 2013), which could hinder efforts toward increasing empathy for outgroup members.

Disentangling the Mechanisms of Change

As noted earlier in the chapter, the radio dramas have two main goals: (a) They aim to increase awareness (i.e., critical reflection) about the factors that contribute to mass violence and to inoculate people against the influence of conditions that contribute to violence and manipulation by leaders, and (b) they promote critical action through role models to encourage peace-inducing behaviors. Across the studies described earlier, there is no evidence that the radio dramas changed beliefs about the evolution of mass violence (see Table 27.2); however, the intervention influenced a variety of intergroup attitudes, behaviors, and active bystandership (i.e., critical action). Here, we further discuss how these findings shed light on the two mechanisms of change.

Promoting critical reflection. There are three possible explanations for the lack of observed effects on outcomes related to beliefs about the roots and evolution of violence. First, the intervention might have an impact that is not captured by our measures. The items assessing beliefs about evolution of violence (e.g., "Violence is more likely if we obey leaders blindly") were not pre-tested, and they were not previously used in the literature. Therefore, these outcomes might have lower validity than the other measures used in our research. In addition, the fictional drama raises awareness about multiple factors and causes leading to violence. Therefore, the contribution of any single causal factor might be reduced as a result of the program. For instance, if listeners' prior beliefs suggest that obedience toward leaders is the main or the only cause of mass violence, then the intervention should reduce this belief (although obedience toward leaders is one important factor contributing to violence). Thereby, assessing knowledge about the roots and evolution of violence with items that focus on the role of a single factor might not be appropriate to assess the impact of this intervention.

Second, it is possible that the intervention format might not be effective in clearly conveying the evolution of mass violence and the factors that contribute to it. Despite "formative research" conducted by Radio La Benevolencija (i.e., listener groups provided feedback on the programs), we do not have "manipulation check" data to assess whether the intervention effectively conveys such knowledge. In their workshops in Rwanda, Staub and Pearlman lectured on the roots, evolution, and consequences of mass violence. These workshops provided ample opportunity for participants to engage with the new information; interact with other participants and facilitators; and with careful guidance, apply this knowledge to personal and group experiences. This interactive approach has the potential to transform people's beliefs and create what Staub (2011) has called "experiential understanding." However, in the context of fictional dramas, the factors contributing to violence are not explicitly spelled out; rather, the knowledge is embedded in an implicit way in the conflict storyline, developing over several years. The assumption is that listeners will gain an understanding of the evolution of violence by following and engaging with the fictional story. However, even if listeners gain a more complex understanding through their engagement with the fictional story (i.e., experiential understanding through identifying with the characters), "knowledge-test" type items might not be effective to gauge this understanding. Instead, other forms of assessment such as in-depth interviews or behaviors in role-plays might be more appropriate.

Lastly, it is possible that the intervention clearly conveys the evolution of mass violence, but it does not change listeners' beliefs. The goal of critical reflection is somewhat at odds with edutainment programming (i.e., entertaining programs embedding educational material), which aims to produce change in people by influencing them inadvertently through promoting new social norms and role models, rather than by engaging them in critical thinking (Singhal & Rogers, 1999). Edutainment research proposes that such programs are effective if listeners are not aware of their goals and therefore do not resist their persuasion efforts. In contrast to this approach, listeners of the mass media intervention are well aware of the goal of violence prevention and promotion of peaceful intergroup relations (e.g., Bilali & Vollhardt, 2015; Paluck, 2006). If the persuasive content and intent are salient, then people are more likely to show resistance, and the drama might fail to achieve its goals (e.g., Slater & Rouner, 2002).

Promoting critical action through role modeling. Role modeling, the second route of influence of the media intervention, is based on Bandura's social learning theory, as well as on Staub's work emphasizing the importance of active bystanders in the prevention of violence. Encouraging actions that involve moral courage is important to resist and counteract negative social influences (e.g., Staub, 2011, 2015). To disentangle the effect of role modeling from other influences in the radio drama, Bilali et al. (2017, Study 1) created two versions of a prototypical episode of the show in the DRC. In one episode (experimental condition: role modeling) the fictional characters discussed community problems (e.g., corruption, intergroup relations, economic grievances) and planned collective action to address them. A parallel episode used the same stories, except that the fictional characters did not plan actions to address the problems (control condition).

Participants in different communities in the Eastern DRC were exposed to either the role-modeling episode (experimental condition), an episode lacking role modeling (control condition), or did not listen to the show at all. The role-modeling episode increased perceived collective efficacy for change and interpersonal perspective taking. Role modeling also shifted the focus of discussions from grievances to collective efficacy and action for social change. However, listening to the role-modeling episode was also related to more negative intergroup attitudes, such as heightened social distance and stronger agreement that discussions including members of different ethnic groups might aggravate matters. These mixed effects hint at a complex relationship between collective action and intergroup outcomes in the DRC context. They raise questions about whether encouraging collective action and increasing collective efficacy can, under certain circumstances, have unintended consequences for intergroup relations. These results resonate with the debates regarding collective action versus prejudice reduction models as avenues to social change (e.g., Dixon, Levine, Reicher, & Durrheim, 2012). Among members of disadvantaged groups, reducing prejudice and increasing liking of the outgroup seem to also reduce the propensity to engage in collective action benefiting the ingroup (for a review see Dixon et al., 2012). Our research provides evidence on the opposite direction suggesting that encouraging collective action through role modeling might reduce outgroup liking and worsen intergroup attitudes. As part of attempts to generate active bysandership, introducing a positive vision for a shared future of the previously hostile groups might reduce such negative effects (Staub, 2011).

Facilitating Media Effects Through Social Interactions

Interventions targeted at individual-level attitudes, norms, and behaviors might not be as effective as they could be if they ignore community-level influences (Zimmerman, 1995). Media is equipped to target levels beyond the individual, as its effects are likely mediated by discussions among listeners. In the Great Lakes Region, anecdotal evidence suggests that people often come together to listen to the radio either with their families and friends or with other members of the community. Although discussion and dialogue are typically encouraged as they facilitate problem solving and peaceful resolution of conflicts, under certain conditions they might have unintended consequences. For instance, an experimental field study in the Eastern DRC showed that a talk show that encouraged perspective taking and discussions of the drama among groups of listeners following the radio drama *Kumbuka Kesho* led to decreased tolerance and less prosocial behavior toward outgroups, compared to listeners who were not encouraged to discuss the show (Paluck, 2010).

Group discussions might sometimes lead to unintended, counterintuitive effects for several reasons. If discussions focus on past grievances and unhealed wounds resulting from the conflict, they might undermine the intervention goals. For example, focusing on an ingroup's victimization is associated with destructive intergroup attitudes and behaviors (Noor et al., 2012; Vollhardt, 2012). If not conducted appropriately, discussions of intergroup conflict can have a potential for retraumatization. In conflict contexts, discussions might also polarize (Canetti et al., 2013), thus reducing people's belief in their efficacy for social change. If through participation in discussions, individuals targeted by the intervention feel isolated in their opinions, engaging in social change may be perceived as difficult or unrealistic.

In our recent field research in the DRC (Bilali et al., 2017, Study 2), participants listened in groups to one episode of the radio drama and then engaged in unguided discussions for 30 minutes. In discussions, listeners drew a large number of positive lessons from the show, and they found the show to be highly relevant to the problems in their communities. However, a high portion of the discussions focused on grievances (i.e., a focus on "how bad things are"), especially in response to scenes that portrayed conflict and other negative realities. The lack of guidance and goals for discussion might be problematic and can fuel frustration and feelings of disempowerment.

It is also possible that when discussion is delayed, it will have more positive effects. Listening to material that represents conflict between groups may give rise to strong feelings in a society still in the midst of conflict and violence. However, once feelings are more settled, the positive influences of the drama content may become more influential. For instance, the training in community groups in Rwanda described previously showed no immediate positive effects but revealed significant positive effects two months later (Staub et al., 2005).

To facilitate the positive effects of media interventions, Radio La Benevolencija has developed "grassroots" projects, in which community members are trained as conflict resolution agents, using the same conceptual approach as in the media programs (see Staub, 2011, 2014). For instance, in Rwanda, a wide range of individuals were trained. These individuals came from 37 communities that were "strongly impacted by the genocide, and where recovery, in terms of social cohesion, the absence of conflict, and economic activity, was slow ... to notice and address problems between people before they become severe, help resolve conflicts, and foster peaceful relations" (Staub, 2011, p. 381). In an evaluation of the contribution of these grassroots projects on reconciliation, community members and leaders identified the radio drama as having had a substantial influence, and the change agents (i.e., community members trained by Radio La Benevolencija) as having made an important contribution to social cohesion in their communities (Ingelaere, Havugimana, & Ndushabandi, 2009). Such efforts are important to amplify the positive effects of media intervention, and to inhibit potential unintended effects. This approach is also consistent with the initial workshop model designed by Staub and Pearlman, which was highly interactive and included guided discussions as participants engaged with the new information on evolution of violence and its prevention.

Conclusion, Recommendations, and Directions for Future Research

In this chapter, we reviewed the design, development, and research assessing the effectiveness of a mass media intervention to reduce prejudice and promote reconciliation in the Great Lakes Region of Africa. Our goal is to trigger a discussion about the benefits and challenges of using psychological principles to design and implement interventions and policies to reduce prejudice and promote reconciliation in conflict-ridden contexts. Collaborations between scholars and practitioners might prove fruitful for the advancement of theory and practice. These collaborations might contribute to theory and research in at least two ways.

First, our collaborative research highlights the role of the characteristics of conflict settings (e.g., stage of conflict, level of violence or insecurity) in moderating psychological processes and the effects of psychological interventions. While in the post-conflict contexts of Burundi and Rwanda, the intervention had a mostly positive impact on attitudes and behaviors, the results showed mixed effects in the context of ongoing violence in the Eastern DRC. In addition to current conditions in a society, it is also possible that the impact of interventions varies with the degree to which the norms and behaviors disseminated by interventions are in line with or counter to dominant or familiar narratives.

Psychological analysis is important in informing policies and interventions. However, a correct analysis and translation of psychological principles requires an in-depth understanding of the characteristics of the settings (e.g., the nature of group relations, power relations, existing social norms, motivations, historical context, and subjective realities; Fisher, 2007). Future research should more systematically assess how characteristics of conflict settings shape psychological processes and moderate interventions. This knowledge is important to inform theories that bridge different levels of analyses, from the individual to societal processes.

Second, translating psychological principles to interventions provides an opportunity to test and refine theories in the real world by rigorously assessing their impact. Scholars can work with practitioners to isolate and study the specific mechanisms of change of an intervention, either by isolating these processes in a field study or by bringing questions rising from the field to study under controlled conditions. Different studies presented in this chapter assess various mechanisms of change of the mass media intervention, including the influence of raising awareness (i.e., cognitive processes), role modeling, perspective taking, and group discussions. For instance, we found no evidence that the mass media intervention changed beliefs about the roots and factors leading to violence, but instead evidence that the intervention influenced a variety of peace-inducing intergroup attitudes and reported behaviors across contexts.

Practitioners can also benefit greatly from collaborations with scholars. First, scholars can assist practitioners in the state of knowledge in a specific domain to guide interventions. Second, scholars are best positioned to rigorously assess interventions' effectiveness, thereby helping practitioners choose best practices. Third, most interventions include a combination of a variety of activities to maximize the effect on the target population. Even when a program has a positive impact, it is unclear whether one component or a combination of the intervention's elements led to the impact. Scholars can design research programs to disentangle the effects of the different components of these complex programs and interventions. They can assess which ones have a positive impact, and which ones might be working at cross-purposes. In real-world settings, it is likely that a combination of interventions would be most effective; they can identify elements of this combination. Further, they can begin to specify the sequence in which interventions in a post-conflict setting are likely to be most effective (Pearlman & Staub, 2016).

References

Allen, J. G. (2001). *Traumatic relationships and serious mental disorders*. West Sussex: John Wiley & Sons, Ltd.

American Psychiatric Association (1994). *Diagnostic and statistical manual of mental disorders* (4th ed.). Washington, DC: Author.

Bar-Tal, D. (2007). Sociopsychological foundations of intractable conflicts. *American Behavioral Scientist, 50*, 1430–1453. doi: 10.1177/0002764207302462

Bandura, A. (1986). *Social foundations of thought and action: A social cognitive theory*. Englewood Cliffs, NJ: Prentice Hall.

Bilali, R. (2014). Between fiction and reality in post-genocide Rwanda: Reflections on a social-psychological media intervention for social change. *Journal of Social and Political Psychology, 2*. doi: 10.5964/jspp.v2i1.288

Bilali, R., & Vollhardt, J. R. (2013). Priming effects of a reconciliation radio drama on historical perspective-taking in the aftermath of mass violence in Rwanda. *Journal of Experimental Social Psychology, 49*, 144–151. doi: 10.1016/j.jesp.2012.08.01

Bilali, R., & Vollhardt, J. R. (2015). Are mass media interventions promoting peace effective in contexts of ongoing violence? Evidence from eastern Democratic Republic of Congo. *Peace & Conflict. Journal of Peace Psychology, 21*, 604–620.

Bilali, R., Vollhardt, J. R., & Rarick, J. R. D. (2016). Assessing the impact of a media-based intervention to prevent intergroup violence and promote positive intergroup relations in Burundi. *Journal of Community and Applied Social Psychology, 26*, 221–235.

Bilali, R, Vollhardt, R. J., & Rarick, J. (2017). Modeling collective action through media to promote social change and positive intergroup relations in violent conflicts. Journal of Experimental Social Psychology, 68, 200–211. doi: 10.1016/j.jesp.2016.07.005

Blatz, C. W., Schumann, K., & Ross, M. (2009). Government apologies for historical injustices. *Political Psychology, 30*, 219–241.

Brounéus, K. (2010). The trauma of truth telling: Effects of witnessing in the Rwandan Gacaca Courts on psychological health. *Journal of Conflict Resolution, 54*, 408–437.

Canetti, D., Hall, B. J., Rapaport, C., & Wayne, C. (2013). Exposure to political violence and political extremism. A stress-based process. *European Psychologist, 18*, 263–272. doi: 10.1027/1016-9040/a000158

Čehajić, S., Brown, R., & Castano, E. (2008). Forgive and forget? Antecedents and consequences of intergroup forgiveness in Bosnia and Hercegovina. *Political Psychology, 29*, 351–368. doi: 10.1111/j.1467-9221.2008.00634.x

Clark, J. N. (2010). National unity and reconciliation in Rwanda: A flawed approach? *Journal of Contemporary African Studies*, *28*, 137–154. doi: 10.1080/02589001003736793

Dane, A. V., & Schneider, B. H. (1998). Program integrity in primary and early secondary prevention: Are implementation effects out of control? *Clinical Psychology Review*, *18*, 23–45. doi: 10.1016/S0272-7358(97)00043-3

Dixon, J., Levine, M., Reicher, S., & Durrheim, K. (2012). Beyond prejudice: Are negative evaluations the problem and is getting us to like one another more the solution? *Behavioral and Brain Sciences*, *35*, 411–466. doi: 10.1017/S0140525X11002214

Durlak, J. A., & DuPre, E. P. (2008). Implementation matters: A review of research on the influence of implementation on program outcomes and the factors affecting implementation. *American Journal of Community Psychology*, *41*, 327–350. doi: 10.1007/s10464-008-9165-0

Fisher, R. J. (2007). Assessing the contingency model of third-party intervention in successful cases of prenegotiation. *Journal of Peace Research*, *44*, 311–29. doi: 10.1177/0022343307076638

Freire, P. (1973). *Education for critical consciousness*. New York: Seabury.

Hameiri, B., Bar-Tal, D., & Halperin, E. (2014). Challenges for peacemakers: How to overcome socio-psychological barriers. *Policy Insights from the Behavioral and Brain Sciences*, *1*, 164–171.

Henry, P. J. (2008). Student sampling as a theoretical problem. *Psychological Inquiry*, *19*, 114–126.

Hodgkin, M. (2006). Reconciliation in Rwanda: Education, history and the state. *Journal of International Affairs*, *60*, 199–210.

Human Rights Watch. (2012). *World Report 2012: Democratic Republic of Congo*. New York: Human Rights Watch. Retrieved from www.hrw.org/world-report-2012/world-report-2012-democratic-republic-congo

International Commission of Inquiry for Burundi. (2002). *Final report*. Washington, DC: U.S. Institute of Peace.

Kanazayire, C., Licata, L., Melotte, P., Dusingizemungu, J. P., & Azzi, A. E. (2014). Does identification with Rwanda increase reconciliation sentiments between genocide survivors and non-victims? The mediating roles of perceived intergroup similarity and self-esteem during commemorations. *Journal of Social and Political Psychology*, *2*, 489–504.

Kanyangara, P. Rime, B., Philippot, P., & Yzerbyt, V. (2007). Collective rituals, emotional climate, and intergroup perception: Participation in "Gacaca" tribunals and assimilation of the Rwandan genocide. *Journal of Social Issues*, *2*, 387–403.

Kelman, H. C. (1990). Applying a human needs perspective to the practice of conflict resolution: The Israeli-Palestinian case. In J. Burton (Ed.), *Conflict: Human needs theory*. New York: St. Martin's Press.

Lemarchand, R. (2009). *The dynamics of violence in Central Africa*. Philadelphia: University of Pennsylvania Press.

McCann, I. L., & Pearlman, L. A. (1990). Vicarious traumatization: A framework for understanding the psychological effects of working with victims. *Journal of Traumatic Stress*, *3*, 131–149.

Moss, S. M. (2014). Beyond conflict and spoilt identities: How Rwandan leaders justify a single recategorization model for post-conflict reconciliation. *Journal of Social and Political Psychology*, *2*, 435–449. doi: 10.5964/jspp.v2i1.291

Noor, M., Shnabel, N., Halabi, S., & Nadler, A. (2012). When suffering begets suffering: The psychology of competitive victimhood between adversarial groups in violent conflicts. *Personality and Social Psychology Review*, *16*, 351–374. doi: 10.1177/1088868312440048

Paluck, E. L. (2010). Is it better not to talk? Group polarization, extended contact, and perspective-taking in eastern Democratic Republic of Congo. *Personality and Social Psychology Bulletin*, *36*, 1170–1185. doi: 10.1177/0146167210379868

Paluck, E. L. (2009). Reducing intergroup prejudice and conflict using the media: A field experiment in Rwanda. *Journal of Personality and Social Psychology*, *96*, 574–587. doi: 10.1037/a0011989

Paluck, E. L. (2006). The second year of a "new dawn": Year Two evidence for the impact of the Rwandan reconciliation radio drama Musekeweya. *La Benevolenciya Evaluation Report*. Unpublished manuscript.

Paluck, E. L., & Green, D. P. (2009). Deference, dissent, and dispute resolution: An experimental intervention using mass media to change norms and behavior in Rwanda. *American Political Science Review*, *103*, 622–644. doi: 10.1017/S0003055409990128

Pearlman, L. A. (2013). Restoring self in community: Collective approaches to psychological trauma after genocide. *Journal of Social Issues*, *69*, 111–124. doi: 10.1111/josi.12006

Pearlman, L. A., & Saakvitne, K. W. (1995). *Trauma and the therapist: Countertransference and vicarious traumatization in the treatment of incest survivors*. New York: W. W. Norton.

Pearlman, L.A., & Staub, E. (2016). Sequencing trauma recovery and reconciliation interventions in post-conflict settings. In A. Langer & G. K. Brown (Eds.), *Building sustainable peace: Timing and sequencing of post-conflict reconstruction and peacebuilding* (pp. 160–180). Oxford: Oxford University Press.

Prunier, G. (2009). *Africa's world war: Congo, the Rwandan genocide, and the making of a continental catastrophe*. New York: Oxford University Press.

Reyntjens, F. (2009). *The land beyond the mists: Essays on identity and authority in precolonial Congo and Rwanda*. Cambridge: Cambridge University Press.

Rime, B., Kanyangara, P., Yzerbyt, V., & Paez, D. (2011). The impact of Gacaca tribunals in Rwanda: Psychosocial effects of participation in a truth and reconciliation process after a genocide. *European Journal of Social Psychology*, *41*, 695–705. doi: 10.1002/ejsp.822

Rosenbloom, D. J., & Williams, M. B. (1999). *Life after trauma*. New York: Guilford.

Samii, C. (2013). Who wants to forgive and forget? Transitional justice preferences in post-war Burundi. *Journal of Peace Research*, *50*, 219–233.

Shnabel, N., & Nadler, A. (2008). A needs-based model of reconciliation: Satisfying the differential emotional needs of victim and perpetrator as a key to promoting reconciliation. *Journal of Personality and Social Psychology*, *94*, 116–132.

Singhal, A., & Rogers, E. M. (1999). *Entertainment-education: A communication strategy for social change*. Mahwah, NJ: Lawrence Erlbaum.

Slater, M. D., & Rouner, D. (2002). Entertainment-education and elaboration likelihood: Understanding the processing of narrative persuasion. *Communication Theory, 12*, 173–191. doi:10. 1111/j.1468-2885.2002.tb00265.x

Staub, E. (1989). *The roots of evil: The origins of genocide and other group violence.* New York: Cambridge University Press.

Staub, E. (1998). Breaking the cycle of genocidal violence: Healing and reconciliation. In J. Harvey (Ed.), *Perspectives on loss.* Washington, DC: Taylor and Francis.

Staub, E. (2006). Reconciliation after genocide, mass killing, or intractable conflict: Understanding the roots of violence, psychological recovery, and steps toward a general theory. *Political Psychology, 27,* 867–894. doi: 10.1111/j.1467-9221.2006.00541.x

Staub, E. (2011). *Overcoming evil: Genocide, violent conflict and terrorism.* New York: Oxford University Press.

Staub, E. (2014). The challenging road to reconciliation in Rwanda: Societal processes, interventions, and their evaluation. *Journal of Social and Political Psychology, 2,* 505–517. doi: 10.5964/jsppv2i1.294

Staub, E. (2015). *The roots of goodness and resistance to evil: Inclusive caring, moral courage, altruism born of suffering, active bystandership and heroism.* New York: Oxford University Press.

Staub, E., & Pearlman, L. A. (2001). Healing, reconciliation, and forgiving after genocide and other collective violence. In S. J. Helmick & R. L. Petersen (Eds.), *Forgiveness and reconciliation: Religion, public policy and conflict transformation* (pp. 195–217). Radnor, PA: Templeton Foundation Press.

Staub, E., & Pearlman, L. A. (2006). Advancing healing and reconciliation. In L. Barbanel & R. Sternberg (Eds.), *Psychological interventions in times of crisis.* New York: Springer-Verlag.

Staub, E., Pearlman, L. A., Gubin, A., & Hagengimana, A. (2005). Healing, reconciliation, forgiving and the prevention of violence after genocide or mass killing: An intervention and its experimental evaluation in Rwanda. *Journal of Social and Clinical Psychology, 24,* 297–334. doi: 10.1521/jscp.24.3.297.65617

Stevens, G., Eagle, G., Kaminer, D., & Higson-Smith, C. (2013). Continuous traumatic stress: Conceptual conversations in contexts of global conflict, violence and trauma. *Peace and Conflict: Journal of Peace Psychology, 19,* 75–84. doi: 10.1037/a0032484

Tam, T., Hewstone, M., Cairns, E., Tausch, N., Maio, G., & Kenworthy, J. (2007). The impact of intergroup emotions on forgiveness in Northern Ireland. *Group Processes & Intergroup Relations 10,* 119–136. doi: http://dx.doi.org/10.1177/1368430207071345

Uvin, P. (2009). *Life after violence: A people's story of Burundi.* New York: Zed Books.

Vallacher, R. R., Coleman, P. T., Nowak, A., & Bui-Wrzosinska, L. (2010). Rethinking intractable conflict: The perspective of dynamical systems. *American Psychologist, 65,* 262–278. doi: 10.1037/a0019290

Vandeginste, S. (2014). Governing ethnicity after genocide: ethnic amnesia in Rwanda versus ethnic power-sharing in Burundi. *Journal of Eastern African Studies, 8,* 263–277, doi: 10.1080/17531055.2014.891784

Vollhardt, J. R. (2012). Collective victimization. In L. Tropp (Ed.), *The Oxford handbook of intergroup conflict* (pp. 136–157). Oxford: Oxford University Press.

Vollhardt, J. R., & Bilali, R. (2015). The role of inclusive and exclusive victim consciousness in predicting intergroup attitudes: Findings from Rwanda, Burundi, and DRC. *Political Psychology, 36,* 489–506. doi: 10.1111/pops.12174

Zimmerman, M. A. (1995). Psychological empowerment: Issues and illustrations. *American Journal of Community Psychology, 23,* 581–599. doi: 10.1007/BF02506983

28 Identification with All Humanity: The Antithesis of Prejudice, and More

Sam McFarland

Late one night in the winter in 1940, in the small French village of Le Chambon, a shivering Jewish woman knocked on the door of André and Magda Trocmé, the local Lutheran minister and his wife. She was fleeing from the Nazis and desperate for food and shelter. Magda quickly took her in, fed her, and started thinking how to help her. The woman needed false identification papers and a place to hide. Across the next few weeks, Magda and André talked with their parishioners and neighbors, and soon the entire village was providing refuge for fleeing Jews. Some were smuggled to safety in Switzerland. Others were given false identities and hidden on nearby farms. Many were children. Despite a murderous Gestapo raid that killed several members of the community, across the next four desperate years Magda and André led Le Chambon in saving about 3,500 Jews from the Holocaust. When André was arrested and pressed to name all the Jews he had helped, he responded, "We do not know what a Jew is; we only know human beings" (Trocmé, 2007, p. vii).

In the 1980s and 1990s, psychologists conducted several interview studies of those who rescued Jews during the Holocaust, often comparing them to bystanders and Nazi perpetrators. Like the Trocmés, rescuers commonly believed that all human beings belong to one human family. One rescuer, interviewed by Samuel and Pearl Oliner, said it this way, "I had always considered all people regardless of their nationality, ethnic origins or race, religion, and so on, as members of one great family: mankind" (Oliner & Oliner, 1988, p. 157; see also Monroe, 1996).

This volume is about prejudice. But in sharp contrast to prejudice against those of a different race or religion, these rescuers cared deeply for all humanity and risked their own lives to save them. I have studied the structure of generalized prejudice (e.g., McFarland, 2010a), including its negative effects on concern for humanity and human rights (e.g., McFarland & Mathews, 2005). Reading about these rescuers, however, suggested that to help overcome prejudice, a focus is also needed on its opposite, on the sense that, as the rescuer said, we are all "members of one great family."

The Historical Development of Identification with All Humanity

Renaissance historian John Headley (2008) has argued that the concept of "one human family" began in Western civilization in the late fifteenth century with the discoveries of strange peoples in the Americas and in Africa. While many Europeans regarded them as brutes, fit only for enslavement, their discovery also created "the incipient notion of the human race as a single collectivity" (p. 27). That notion has slowly taken root across the centuries that followed. Its growth was expressed in the eighteenth and nineteenth centuries in the struggles to end slavery, in the nineteenth century in the outlawing of abusive child labor and in making education available to all children, and in the early twentieth century in the enfranchisement of women. Also in the early twentieth century, a surge of self-conscious expressions of all humanity as a single group began to appear, as in Gandhi's statement that "All humanity is one undivided and indivisible family."

The term "crimes against humanity" appeared early in the twentieth century and was first used as a legal concept in the Nürnberg trials after World War II (Clapham, 2007). In 1948, when the *Universal Declaration of Human Rights* declared that human rights belong to all human beings, "without distinction of any kind, such as race, color, sex, language, religion, political or other opinion, national or social origin, property, birth or other status" (Article 2), a moral vision of the common humanity of all human beings was affirmed as never before. In the latter half of the twentieth and early twenty-first centuries "crimes against humanity" were slowly incorporated into international law (McFarland, 2011). Likewise, in the late twentieth and early twenty-first centuries, the full humanity of gays, lesbians, and other non-heterosexuals began to be accepted in both public opinion and established law.

Identification with All Humanity as an Individual Difference

While we can track the increasing recognition of the "human" category over time, the extent to which people identify with all of humanity varies, reflecting an important individual difference that merits intensive study. It reflects an absence of prejudice but also refers positively to a sense of belonging to one human family and a proactive concern for all humanity, just as one might have for one's own family. In the sections that follow, I show that feeling identified with humanity (rather than nation, or smaller subgroup) is uniquely associated with prosocial, antiprejudiced behavior. I show that it is conceptually and empirically distinct from other associated individual differences, and uniquely predictive of positive values that are the antithesis of prejudice: an equal respect for all human lives, giving to global charities, and support for human rights. I then conclude by commenting on what might create identification with all humanity, and make suggestions about how we might increase it.

Adler's (1954) concept of *gemeinschaftsgefühl* (social interest, or community feeling) and Maslow's (1954) of self-actualization each envisioned identification with all humanity as a moral perspective that is embraced by psychologically mature persons. But because neither Adler nor Maslow, nor any later researcher, had created a measure of this construct, I decided to do so. With all our focus on negative aspects of prejudice, in the spirit of positive psychology (e.g., Seligman & Csikszentmihalyi, 2000), a strong focus seemed needed on the positive node as well.

To begin this study, we developed the Identification with All Humanity Scale (IWAH).[1] The final scale consists of 9 three-response items in the following form:

1. How much do you identify with (that is, feel a part of, feel love toward, have concern for) each of the following?
   a. People in my community
   b. Americans
   c. All humans everywhere

Responses range from 1 (*not at all*) to 5 (*very much*). The full IWAH is presented in the Appendix. For further details on the development of the IWAH, see McFarland, Webb, and Brown (2012).

The sum of the c. items constitutes the IWAH. The scale has been translated and used in other countries, substituting the country's name for the b. items (e.g., in Poland by Hamer & Gutowski, 2009). Across many samples, alphas for the raw scores are consistently above .85, as they are for identification with community and nation. The three identifications correlate positively, while identification with community and identification with nation correlate more strongly with each other than either does with all humanity. Because our concern is to understand the unique associations with caring about "all humans everywhere," the other identifications are used as statistical controls.

Factor analyses of McFarland et al.'s (2012) first sample (Study 1) and of a sample of more than 3,000 (McFarland et al., 2012, Study 9) found only one eigenvalue greater than 1.0, indicating that the IWAH consists of just one factor. However, Reese, Proch, and Finn (2015) found two correlated factors with German and Luxemburg samples. Their findings mirrored those of Leach and colleagues (2008), whose model of ingroup identification found that identification consisted of two dimensions, defined as *self-definition* (e.g., "To what degree do you think of the following groups as 'family'") and *self-investment* (e.g., "When they are in need, how much do you want to help"). With reference to IWAH, these two factors, while separately identifiable, correlated .55 or higher across Reese et al.'s three samples, indicating a higher-order construct. Because Reese et al.'s results are new, all published studies to the end of 2014 have treated the IWAH as a single dimension.

Across many adult and student samples, participants have averaged almost exactly 3 (*somewhat*) on the IWAH items. Ten percent score 2 (*just a little*) or less, and less than 10% average 4 (*quite a bit*) or higher. The item means for the

---

1 Former graduate students Matthew Webb and Derek Brown made vital contributions to this work.

other two identifications consistently average about half a point higher than the mean of the IWAH items. Fewer than 15% identify as much with all humanity as with their community and nation.

Temporal Stability and Self-Other Perceptions on the IWAH

Two important questions for any new self-report measure are "Is the quality stable over time?" and "Do others who know us well see us as we see ourselves?" On the issue of temporal stability, McFarland et al. (2012, Study 3) conducted a test-retest for the IWAH across 10 weeks for a large adult sample. The Reliable Change Index (Roberts, Caspi, & Moffitt, 2001) indicated that 85% of participants did not change from Time 1 to Time 2.

For self-other consistency, a sample of adults completed the IWAH, while family members and close friends completed it as they thought their sample individual would respond. With scores for two "others" averaged to enhance the reliability of "others" ratings, the self-other correlation was .56 (McFarland et al., 2012, Study 4), comparable to or larger than the self-other correlations for the "big six" personality factors (i.e., the classic Big Five plus a morality factor labeled "honesty-humility") as measured on the same sample by the HEXICO-60 (Ashton & Lee, 2009).

In short, identification with all humanity appears stable for most adults, and others who know us well have a general sense of how much we do or do not identify with all humanity. Similar temporal stabilities and self-other consistencies were found for the other two identifications.

Tests of Convergent and Discriminant Validity

Quite obviously, identification with all humanity should correlate negatively with generalized prejudice (or ethnocentrism; e.g., Altemeyer, 1996) and its major roots, right-wing authoritarianism (RWA; Altemeyer, 1996) and social dominance orientation (SDO; Sidanius & Pratto, 1999). These negative correlations have been found in every sample, typically ranging from −.30 to −.50; those who identify with all of humanity are less likely to be authoritarians and less likely to support social hierarchies that preference some groups over others. Because the identifications with community and nation correlate about .20 with ethnocentrism and authoritarianism, controlling for these identifications by partial correlation indicates that IWAH has a slightly stronger negative association with ethnocentrism or authoritarianism than the raw (zero-order) correlations indicate. However, because the SDO correlates negatively with all identifications, its partial correlation with IWAH is usually about the same as its raw correlation.

We reasoned that the IWAH should correlate positively with dispositional empathy (Davis, 1983), which consists of concern for others and an effort to understand their perspectives. We also proposed that IWAH should correlate positively with post-conventional moral reasoning (Kohlberg, 1969), moral reasoning that relies on abstract ethical principles such as justice rather than on conventional moral norms. Again, these correlations have been found across several samples. The IWAH also correlates positively, as expected, with openness to experience from the Big Five personality factors. Not surprisingly, it correlates negatively with blind patriotism, and in the American context, modestly positively with self-rated political liberalism and preference for the Democratic over the Republican Party.

However, identification with all humanity remains a unique construct, as these correlates altogether explain about half of its variance (see McFarland et al., 2012, Table 3). Further, in regression analyses, the IWAH consistently predicts important dependent measures discussed later and does so beyond the power of ethnocentrism and other correlated constructs.

For an American sample of more than 14,800 (recruited on yourmorals.com), the IWAH correlated substantially with all five moral values on Graham, Haidt, and Nosek's (2009) Moral Foundations Questionnaire (MFQ). The MFQ is derived from Haidt and Joseph's (2004) Moral Foundations Theory, which proposes that human evolution has created in human nature several specific psychological foundations for morality. As examples, the need to care for children became the psychological foundation for the moral value of care (as opposed to harm), whereas the need for group cohesion to ensure group survival became the foundation for the value of ingroup loyalty (as opposed to betrayal). All are inherent in human nature, but their strengths as moral values vary between both societies and individuals. The MFQ assesses individual differences in the strength of five basic values – care, fairness, authority, ingroup loyalty, and purity. For this large sample, as we anticipated, the IWAS correlated positively with care (.42) and fairness (.36), but negatively with authority (−.32), ingroup loyalty (−.30), and purity (−.20). In simultaneous regression, the multiple-R between the five values and the IWAH was .54. Parallel correlations were obtained on a sample of more than 3,600 on the New Zealand Attitudes and Values Study (NZAVS), as well as with social dominance, authoritarianism, and openness.[2] However, for reasons not yet identified, these correlations with the IWAH were all smaller for the NZAVS sample.

We should note that the IWAH does not correlate with any of three measures of the importance of being a moral person, including Aquino and Reed's (2002) Moral Identity Scale, Crandall's (1980) Social Interest Scale, and the Honesty-Morality factor of the Ashton and Lee's (2009) HEXACO-60. Identification with all humanity is something different from thinking of oneself as a moral person or the self-rated importance of being a moral person. The IWAH is also unrelated to

2 I thank Jonathan Haidt and Chris Sibley for making the yourmorals.com and NZAVS data, respectively, available for my analyses.

positive and negative emotionality as measured by Watson, Clark, and Tellegen's (1988) Positive and Negative Affect Scale.

Two Studies of "Known Groups"

One measure of a scale's validity is to test it with "known groups," groups that should score very high. McFarland et al. (2012, Study 6) compared the IWAH scores of key staff and supporters of Human Rights Watch (HRW) and Church World Service (CWS, a Christian international charity) with a general adult sample (McFarland et al., 2012, Study 2 adult sample). Eleven of the 15 HRW and 15 of the 18 CWS participants scored above the 90th percentile of general adult sample, and almost all others scored above the 80th percentile. In a second small study, IWAH scores for seven regional Amnesty International leaders were compared with scores of seven chamber of commerce leaders, matched for age and education, as well as with the same adult sample cited earlier. All Amnesty leaders scored higher than any chamber leader. Also, 42% of Amnesty activists scored above the 99th percentile of the adult sample, and all scored above the 75th percentile. IWAH scores for the chamber leaders did not differ from those of the general adult sample. In short, activists in human rights and humanitarian organizations score high on the IWAH compared to broad population samples or to samples matched for age and education.

The Predictive Validity of the IWAH

What concerns and behaviors should the IWAH predict? Among other things, it should predict

- Support for universal human rights;
- Valuing the lives of ingroup and outgroup members more equally;
- Knowledge of global humanitarian concerns, desire for this global knowledge, and choosing to read about these concerns;
- Giving to international charities; and
- Reasoning logically about both ingroups and outgroups. Logical reasoning should not be distorted in a way that favors one's ingroup or disparages outgroups.

Importantly, the IWAH should predict each of these beyond the power of related constructs.

IWAH and Human Rights Support

To study support for human rights, Melissa Mathews and I (McFarland & Mathews, 2005) developed two measures to assess commitment to human rights. Our Human Rights Choice Questionnaire (HRCQ) contains 10 items in the following form:

On the following items, pairs of issues are presented. Please rate what you see as the relative importance of the two items according to the following scale:

A = Item a is <u>much more important</u> than item b.
B = Item a is <u>somewhat more important</u> than item b.
C = Items a and b are of <u>equal importance</u>.
D = Item b is <u>somewhat more important</u> than item a.
E = Item b is <u>much more important</u> than item a.

1. a. Preventing crimes against humanity around the world.*
    b. Being sure that only the right people immigrate to America.
2. a. Maintaining a strong American military.
    b. Ending child prostitution worldwide.*

    * = the human rights choices

Our Human Rights Scenarios (HRScene) measure describes nine historical and current events and offers respondents choices that range from acting on national self-interest to investing national effort and resources to defend international human rights. A sample item reads as follows:

> In the summer of 1998, representatives from most United Nations countries met in Rome and adopted a treaty to create a permanent International Criminal Court, called the ICC. Now established, this Court is authorized to prosecute suspects, including national leaders, for genocide, crimes against humanity, war crimes, and aggression. While 120 nations voted for the ICC, including all Western European nations, the United States was one of seven to vote against it. Some believe that the Court is urgently needed to deter these horrible crimes and to punish those who commit them. Others fear that American military commanders or officials could be arrested on biased charges, although proponents say that safeguards in the treaty make such arrests very unlikely. But ratifying the treaty will mean that American actions overseas will be subject to a new international law and that a court will be in place to try violators, even Americans, if they commit these crimes.
> The United States is not now a part of the treaty, so Americans cannot now be prosecuted by the Court, even if they commit these crimes. Would you want the Senate to . . .
> A. ratify the treaty, because deterring and prosecuting genocide is the most important thing?
> B. ratify the treaty only if it is changed so that Americans cannot be charged and tried by the ICC?
> C. not ratify the treaty because it might threaten the arrest and trial of Americans by non-Americans?

Other items asked whether the United States should have sent forces to Sudan along with other nations to stop the ethnic cleansing, should tie trade with other countries to their human rights behaviors, and the like.[3]

For one study, a structural model was tested for how authoritarianism, social dominance, ethnocentrism, and identification with all humanity should predict

---

3 The HRCQ and HRScene are available from the author.

commitment to human rights (the factor score of the HRCQ and HRScene). Authoritarianism and social dominance were posited as exogeneous variables, expected to predict ethnocentrism and IWAH, which, in turn, were expected to predict human rights commitment. For separate adult and student samples, these expectations were confirmed: The IWAH strongly and directly predicted human rights commitment, while ethnocentrism did so negatively. The effects of authoritarianism were fully mediated through ethnocentrism and IWAH, and the effects of social dominance were largely so (McFarland, 2010b). The IWAH predicted human rights commitment on these two measures in several later samples, as well (McFarland et al., 2012; McFarland & Hornsby, 2015).

IWAH and the Ethnocentric Valuation of Human Life

Pratto and Glasford (2008) reported subtle measures of the tendency to value the lives of ingroup members more than those of outgroup members. For four sub-measures, individuals had to choose between two policies that pitted (a) the loss of outgroup (Afghani) lives against an economic loss for the ingroup (Americans), (b) the loss of American lives against an economic loss for the outgroup (Afghanis), (c) saving Afghani lives versus American economic gain, or (d) saving American lives versus Afghani economic gain. Pratto and Glasford found, as expected, that participants on average placed greater value on American than Afghani lives. This ethnocentric valuation of human life correlated positively with social dominance orientation and identification with America, but negatively with dispositional empathy.

Clearly, identification with all humanity should predict less ethnocentric valuing of human lives. This is exactly what we found: For separate adult and student samples, the IWAH correlated with the ethnocentric valuation of human life at $-.38$ and $-.49$, respectively. In structural tests for each sample, identification with all humanity directly predicted reduced ethnocentric valuation of human life, while ethnocentrism directly predicted favoring American lives over those of non-Americans. The effects of authoritarianism, social dominance, and dispositional empathy were fully mediated by ethnocentrism and identification with all humanity (McFarland, 2010c).

IWAH and Global Knowledge

Those who identify with all humanity should care about the struggles and sufferings of humanity. If they do, they should attend more than others to events that affect humanity in distant places, even if one's own community and country are not affected. They should, as examples, be more likely to know about recent genocides and human rights abuses, and about efforts to end global suffering. They should express a greater desire for that knowledge and selectively expose themselves to information that creates that knowledge. These hypotheses were tested in three studies.

A multiple-choice Global Knowledge Quiz (GKQ) was updated from that used by McFarland and Mathews (2005). A sample items reads as follows:

1. A major aim of the Millennium Development Project is to
   A. build the tower to replace the World Trade Center destroyed on 9/11.
   B. cut in half the world's worst poverty by 2015. (correct answer)
   C. create democracy in Islamic countries in the Middle East.
   D. develop non-polluting sources of energy as alternatives to oil and coal.

For a student sample, the IWAH and the GKQ correlated .26. In regression analysis, the IWAH, college grades and sex (being male) contributed to predicting global knowledge. College aptitude scores (ACT) and authoritarianism, both of which predicted global knowledge in earlier studies, added no further variance (McFarland et al., 2012, Study 8).

Further, in an unpublished study with adults, an 11-item Desire for Global Knowledge (DGK) scale was developed and tested. One item reads, "It is important to me to understand what is happening elsewhere in the world besides in my own community and nation." A negatively worded item reads, "I can't see why an American would care about events in Africa that don't affect us." This measure had an alpha of .85.

The IWAH correlated .46 with the DGK. In a structural test on an adult sample, the IWAH significantly predicted a desire for global knowledge that, in turn, predicted actual knowledge of global concerns; the effect of the IWAH on global knowledge was fully mediated by the desire for global knowledge. Ethnocentrism negatively predicted the DGK, and its effects on global humanitarian knowledge were also fully mediated by the lack of desire for that knowledge.

These results suggest that individuals who identify with all humanity must selectively expose themselves to more information on global humanitarian issues. To test this hypothesis, a list of 16 articles, supposedly written for a new journal, was presented to large samples of students and adults. Each article contained a title and author and a short teaser on the article's content. Twelve were on varied topics such as finance, sports, and health, but unrelated to global humanitarian concerns. One read:

> *Are Religious People Healthier?*
> *by Jon Mitchell*
> *A number of studies have examined whether religious faith and religious participation make people healthier, mentally and physically. Here's what the studies show.*

The other four were on humanitarian concerns. One read:

> *Can We End Genocide?*
> *by Robert Jost*
> *The twenty genocides of the last century killed over 40 million people. Now, the nations of the United Nations have pledged to end genocide, creating the new Human Rights Council. Will these plans succeed?*

These four were scattered among the 12 other articles.

Participants read all 16 and then selected and ranked the 5 that they most wanted to read. To score selective exposure, 5 points were awarded for selecting a humanitarian article as the first choice, 4 for the second choice, and so on. For adult and student samples, the IWAH correlated .30 and .46 with selecting humanitarian concern articles, respectively. Ethnocentrism, authoritarianism, and social dominance all correlated negatively with selecting these articles. In regression analyses, only the IWAH predicted selecting of the humanitarian articles for both samples (McFarland et al., 2012, Study 9).

In summary, identification with all humanity predicts knowing more about global humanitarian concerns, the desire to know more, and actually choosing to read about humanitarian and human rights issues over other issues. It predicts these beyond the negative effects of ethnocentrism and other correlates.

IWAH and Donating to International Charities

One behavior that identification with all humanity should predict is support for international charities (e.g., UNICEF, Doctors Without Borders). In one study, adult and student samples were used to measure the effects of the IWAH on self-reported charity. For both samples, the IWAH correlated positively with the following:

> "I have given money for an international charity (such as UNICEF, Save the Children)." (5-point scale, "never" to "often")
> "When natural or man-made disasters strike (such as the Asian tsunami, refugee crises in Africa), I give money to aid in relief."
> "I have written letters or e-mails to my senators or congressmen to urge their support for humanitarian relief (such as food aid during famines, providing help for war refugees)."

For the two samples, the IWAH correlated .37 and .36 with the sum of these questions. In regression analysis, the IWAH and dispositional empathy predicted these actions, whereas authoritarianism did not. Ethnocentrism and SDO were not measured in this study (Brown, 2008).

These results are based on self-reports, so the hypothesis that the IWAH predicts giving to humanitarian causes was tested in predictive studies. In three studies, adult participants were offered chances at cash prizes and opportunities to give a portion of their winnings to UNICEF for international humanitarian relief (in two studies, for relief following the 2010 earthquake in Haiti; for the third, for relief following the 2011 earthquake and tsunami in Japan). IWAH scores predicted a willingness to contribute to humanitarian relief for each study, with correlations from .24 to .30. In regression analyses, the IWAH predicted giving in all three studies beyond the negative effects of ethnocentrism or the Big Six personality factors (McFarland et al., 2012, Study 10). Two recent studies have found that the IWAH similarly predicted pledges to Doctors Without Borders for aid for Syrian refugees (McFarland & Hornsby, 2015, Study 1) and for aid in the Ebola outbreak in West Africa (McFarland & Hornsby, 2015, Study 2).

IWAH and Intergroup Forgiveness

Hamer, Penczek, and Bilewicz (2014) have recently studied the effects of national identification and identification with all humanity on the willingness to forgive former enemies of their crimes against one's nation. In separate studies with student and adult samples in Poland, they found that identification with all humanity on the IWAH predicted a greater willingness to forgive both Germans and Russians for their crimes during World War II. In contrast, greater identification with Poland predicted lower willingness to forgive the Germans and Russians.

IWAH and Logical Reasoning About Ingroups and Outgroups

Two lines of previous research have found that prejudice can distort logical reasoning. However, we would expect identification with all humanity to reduce these distortions. If one truly identifies with all humankind, logical reasoning should not be altered by prejudice. This proposition was tested with two logic tests.

Our first test involved syllogistic reasoning. Thistlethwaite (1950) reasoned that in judging the validity of syllogisms (inferences based on deductive reasoning), prejudice would lead individuals to judge valid syllogisms with positive conclusions about outgroups as invalid and to judge invalid syllogisms with negative conclusions about outgroups as valid. As an example, those who are prejudiced against Jewish people should be prone to judge a syllogism with the conclusion "Jews should be encouraged to join Gentile fraternities" as invalid, even if the conclusion logically followed from the premises. Further, they should accept as valid a syllogism with the conclusion "Jewish businessmen tend to stick together and to connive," even if the syllogism is logically invalid. Thistlethwaite found that ethnocentrism did not predict the ability to judge the validity of syllogisms on non-racial matters but did predict logical distortions on prejudice-related syllogisms. Ethnocentrism undermined the ability to judge the syllogisms' validity, leading participants to reject as invalid valid syllogisms with positive conclusions about outgroups, while accepting as valid invalid syllogisms with negative conclusions about outgroups.

We wondered if identification with all humanity might have the opposite effect, leading participants to accept as valid syllogisms that had positive conclusions about outgroups, even if the syllogism is invalid, and to judge as invalid valid syllogisms that had negative conclusions about outgroups.

We presented 64 syllogisms in three simple-to-complex forms, with either valid or invalid conclusions. For example, in a simple syllogism with an invalid conclusion:

      Given: If Pakistanis on the team are not open about their religion, they should have equal playing time.
        Pakistanis on the team are open about their religion.
        Therefore: Pakistanis on the team should not have equal playing time.

Half of the prejudice-related conclusions reflected positive policies and half negative policies toward outgroups. Neutral syllogisms were used to control for logical reasoning ability.

Neither ethnocentrism nor the IWAH predicted accuracy on the neutral syllogisms. Replicating Thisthlethwaite (1950), ethnocentrism predicted logical distortion in the direction of prejudice, with correlations with accuracy from $-.30$ to $-.41$ for the three forms. However, the IWAH did not predict logical distortion; a positive conclusion about an outgroup did not lead those higher on IWAH to accept invalid syllogisms, nor to reject valid syllogisms that had a negative conclusion about an outgroup. In short, ethnocentrism in this study distorted logic in a prejudicial direction, but IWAH did not distort it either toward prejudice or non-prejudice.

Our second test used the Leyens et al. (2000) adaptation of the Wason Task (Wason, 1966). Leyens et al. were interested in testing their theory of infrahumanization, the belief that one's ingroup is seen as more fully human than are outgroups. Specifically, the theory suggests that while both ingroups and outgroups possess primary or animal emotions (e.g., "anger"), only one's ingroup fully possesses secondary, human emotions (e.g., "sympathy").

To test this with subtlety, Leyens et al. adapted the Wason (1966) logic task. On that original task, participants are presented four cards, two with letters showing and two with numbers (e.g., G, F, 5, and 7), and told that there is always a letter on one side of a card and a number on the other. They are then given a conditional statement (e.g., "If there is a G on one side of the card, there is a 5 on the other side") and asked to select the two cards that must be flipped to test the statement. The correct choices are G and 7, but flipping the 5 card is a common error.

Leyens et al. (2000) reasoned that ascribing secondary emotions only to ingroups would seduce participants to make a similar error. They presented participants two cards, one with the name of the ingroup and one with an outgroup, and two with presence or absence of either a secondary or primary emotion (e.g., affection and no affection; hunger and no hunger). As in the Wason task, participants were given a rule, "If this person is (ingroup or outgroup), they possess (primary or secondary emotion)." Participants were asked which cards they would want to turn over to test the rule. They reasoned that for secondary emotions, individuals presented with an ingroup rule would engage in a *matching bias*, interpret group membership as sufficient for the emotion, and erroneously choose to turn over the cards for the ingroup and secondary emotion (e.g., affection), rather than that for the absence of the emotion (e.g., no affection). However, when an outgroup and secondary emotion were presented, respondents should be more prone to interpret the group membership as insufficient for the emotion and be less likely to commit this error. They would be more likely to respond accurately, turning over the name of the outgroup and the absence of the emotion. The researchers found this effect.

We reasoned that if individuals truly identify with all humanity rather than just Americans, they should be less likely to commit this error and should be more able to reason logically on this task when Americans comprise the ingroup. For our study, 32 test items were presented to a large adult sample, with half featuring an American and half an outgroup (e.g., Nigerians). Only secondary emotions (e.g., compassion, empathy) were presented.

The IWAH correlated $-.20$, $p < .01$, with the matching bias for the 16 American items as compared to the 16 outgroup items; participants with higher IWAH scores were less inclined to matching bias on items involving Americans (i.e., better logical reasoning). In regression analysis, only the IWAH and principled moral reasoning contributed to reducing this error; ethnocentrism, authoritarianism, social dominance, and empathy did not. These results suggest that those high on the IWAH are more likely to ascribe human emotions to other groups as well as to Americans.

Who Believes That Identification with All Humanity Is Moral?

As noted earlier, Adler and Maslow regarded identification with all humanity as a moral perspective that fully mature individuals will possess. But do ordinary students share this view? Derek Brown and I examined whether students view identification with all humanity as an expression of high maturity and morality.

A large student sample first completed the IWAH, along with the RWA and SDO. The students were then asked to complete the IWAH a second time "as the **most moral and most mature person you could imagine** [bolded on the questionnaire] would answer."

Fully 86% of the participants believed the most fully mature and most moral person would identify more strongly with humanity than they did themselves. While their own mean response on the IWAH items was almost exactly 3.0, their perception of how a moral and mature person would respond averaged slightly above 4.0. The responses to one item were typical: Just 13% responded that they personally "*very much*" (5 on the response scale) "feel a part of, feel love toward, have concern for all humans everywhere," but 47% believed that a very mature and moral person would "*very much*" do so.

This moral intuition was moderated by both RWA and SDO, which correlated negatively ($-.21$ and $-.20$, $p < .01$ in each case) with the belief that fully mature and moral persons would identify with all humanity. While earlier studies found that RWA and SDO predict reduced identification with all humanity, this study found that they also predict a reduced belief that a mature and moral individual would identify strongly with all humanity. In regression analysis, both RWA and SDO predicted attributing lower IWAH scores to an imagined moral and mature person (McFarland & Brown, 2008).

Still, our students as a group intuited that a fully mature person with the highest morality would identify with all humanity much more than they did themselves. These results indicate a moral intuition such that many, if simply asked, may recognize identifying with all humanity as an important and mature moral value. This moral intuition differs from the moral intuition made popular by Jonathan Haidt (e.g., Haidt, 2001). Whereas Haidt emphasized primitive emotions that drive moral judgments (e.g., the deep feeling that it is wrong to eat one's dead pet), the belief that fully mature and moral persons would identify with all humanity appears logically compelling rather than emotionally driven. Also, Haidt's moral intuitionism emphasizes moral feelings that persons possess and claim, whereas our participants intuited that a fully mature and moral person would possess a morality that they, themselves, did not (McFarland & Brown, 2008).

How Does Identification with All Humanity Develop?

The previous sections show that an identification with all humanity can serve as an antidote to prejudice, and a vital predictor of concern for others (irrespective of race or nationality). Therefore, it is now important to try to understand how identification with all humanity arises. What are its roots in genetics, child-rearing, and religious faith?

The genetic roots of identification with all humanity have not been studied. However, there is evidence that at least two of its precursors, authoritarianism and empathy, as well as ingroup favoritism, are heritable (e.g., Davis, Luce, & Krauss, 1994; Lewis & Bates, 2014). Plausibly, inheriting these dispositions predisposes one to identify more or less with all humanity as an adult.

In an effort to identify, retrospectively, child-rearing practices that induce identification with all humanity, about 200 adults completed the IWAH and 54 items with the stem, "When I was a child, my parents (or caregivers) ..." Every child-rearing practice that seemed potentially relevant was included. The items loaded on seven factors, which we identified as affection and support (e.g., "were very affectionate"), moral and caring ("had concern for suffering people"), intellectual and global ("encouraged me to think about global issues"), punitive ("used physical punishment quite a bit"), religious ("wanted me to be devoutly religious"), patriotic ("were very patriotic"), and spoiling ("were very lenient"). Alas, none of the seven factors correlated at all with the adults' identification with all humanity. We found nothing in parents' child-rearing practices that contributed to identification with all humanity (McFarland, Brown, & Webb, 2013). If parenting values and behaviors contribute to identification with all humanity in adulthood, we have not yet discovered how.

How might religious faith affect identification with all humanity? In a recent unpublished study that I ran, 375 adults completed the IWAH and measures of religiousness (from "nonbeliever" to "very religious"), Christian orthodoxy (whether one believes the main precepts of Christianity), and Christian fundamentalism (the most conservative variant of American Christianity).

While identification with community and America each positively correlated with religiousness, .27 and .21, $p < .01$ in each case, identification with all humanity correlated slightly negatively, $r = -.10$, $p < .05$. Among self-identified Christians, both Christian orthodoxy and fundamentalism correlated positively, .19 to .24, with identification with community and America, but $-.22$ and $-.23$ with the identification with all humanity. In short, religious faith appears to slightly negatively predict identification with all humanity, with Christian orthodoxy and fundamentalism doing so more strongly, but these forms of faith positively predict identification with one's community and nation. McCutcheon et al. (2015) found that those who firmly believe in God identify more strongly with their community and America than do those who firmly disbelieve, but these two groups did not differ significantly in identification with all humanity. In summary, from data collected to date, it appears that Christian faith may enhance identification with community and nation, but not the broader identification with all humanity.

A Test of a Maslovian Model

Maslow would expect that identification with all humanity, as a function of self-actualization, might exist mainly for those who have transcended his well-known lower needs – physiological, safety and security, belonging, and approval. I measured each of these for a large adult sample with brief balanced scales, anticipating that they would correlate negatively with identification with all humanity. Sample items were as follows:

- Physiological concerns (e.g., "I worry that someday I or my family may not be able to get medical care we need");
- Safety concerns (e.g., "I don't worry that much about my personal safety and security," negatively worded item);
- Materialism (e.g., "I want a lot more than I have now (examples: more money, nicer house, expensive car");
- Concern for social approval (e.g., "The approval of my closest group – church, community group, fellow workers, etc. – is very important to me");
- Concern for self-approval (e.g., "I worry about whether or not I am truly a good, moral, and responsible person).

Each measure had adequate reliability. The IWAH correlated $-.19$, $p < .02$, with materialism and $-.20$, with the need for social approval, controlling for the other identifications. All other correlations were less than .10, *ns* (McFarland, 2006). In short, consistent with Maslow's theory, materialism and the need for social approval appear antithetical to, and may reduce, caring for all humanity.

The non-relations with worries about physical safety, security, and personal morality, however, are more consistent with the analysis offered by Boehnke, Schwartz, Stromberg, and Sagiv (1998) than with Maslow's theory. Boehnke et al. found that "micro-worries," worries about oneself and close others, and "macro-worries," worries about the larger world such as "people in the world dying of hunger," are largely distinct rather than negatively correlated.

In summary, we now know very little about the roots of identification with all humanity in heredity, child-rearing, or life experiences. These most likely interact. The heritable qualities of empathy may make one more receptive to educational experiences that lead one to embrace the full human family. Oppositely, the heritable qualities of authoritarianism may make one more receptive to ethno-centric appeals.

Speculating further, substantial intergroup contact may enhance identification with all humanity, but this relationship is likely bidirectional. Binder et al. (2009), using time-lagged correlations, found that prejudiced students sought less contact with minority students, but the contact that did occur reduced prejudice. Similarly, contact with outgroup members may enhance identification with all humanity, but those high on the IWAH likely seek this contact, whereas those low on the IWAH likely avoid it. Understanding how identification with all humanity develops is, to this writer, a most important issue. I hope that others will join me in studying it.

Related Measures

At least six other measures overlap conceptually with the IWAH, and each of these has been shown to predict important humanitarian concerns or behaviors similar to those that would be expected for the IWAH. Schwartz's (1992) measure of universalism, defined in part as "protection of the welfare of *all* people" (p. 10), added unique variance beyond the IWAH in predicting scores on the HRScene (McFarland et al., 2012, Study 6). Nickerson and Louis's (2008) six-item measure of human identity salience (e.g., "How similar do you feel to other human beings?") predicted favorable attitudes toward asylum seekers and opposition to the Australian government's strong anti-asylum policy.

Four measures focus on a sense of global citizenship. The World Values Survey (WVS) Wave 5 (2005–2009) and Wave 6 (2010–2014) single item "I see myself as a World Citizen" positively predicted, in an analysis by McFarland and Hornsby (2015), responses to another WVS item on the willingness to pay more in taxes "to help people in the world's poorest countries." Malsch's (2005) Psychological Sense of Global Community scale (PSGC; e.g., "I feel a sense of connection to people all over the world, even if I don't know them personally"), shortened from 14 to 4 items for the first published study

(Hackett, Omoto, & Matthews, (2015), predicted behavioral involvement in human rights causes. Reysen and Katzarska-Miller's (2013) two-item measure of Global Citizenship Identification (e.g., "I would describe myself as a global citizen") predicted a desire to "dedicate my life to helping others no matter what country they are from." Reese, Proch, and Cohrs's (2013) five-item Global Social Identification scale (e.g., "It is important for me to define myself as part of the world community") predicted a strong sense of injustice about global economic inequality.

Little effort has been made to examine the relations among these measures or their relative power to predict the dependent measures of concern. However, to directly compare the IWAH and full PSGC, McFarland and Hornsby (2015) asked a large adult sample to respond to both measures along with five dependent measures used in earlier IWAH studies. The IWAH and PSGC correlated .72, and both predicted scores on HRCQ, the ethnocentric valuation of human life, the desire for global knowledge, selecting to read humanitarian articles over other articles, and pledging money to Doctors Without Borders for aiding Syrian refugees. However, the shortened four-item PSGC was substantially inferior to the IWAH or to the full PSGC in predicting these outcomes. These five dependent measures yielded a single factor labeled Global Humanitarian Concern (GHC), and both the IWAH and full PSGC contributed to it in regression analysis (McFarland & Hornsby, 2015, Study 1). In short, while the IWAH and PSGC overlap substantially, each possesses unique variance predicting GHC. The added measures of world citizenship did not contribute to GHC beyond the IWAH and PSGC (McFarland & Hornsby, 2015, Study 2). As research on identification with all humanity/global citizenship moves forward, clarifying further the degree to which these six measures are comparable or differ, along with the relative merits of each one, could prove useful.

A Personal Conclusion

I began our studies of identification with all humanity because of my deep abhorrence of genocide and related crimes, profound admiration for the Trocmés and other rescuers, and agreement with Adler and Maslow that "identification with all humanity" reflects a more mature morality than do identifications with smaller ingroups. Further, I do not believe that we humans are fated to categorize our social world only as ingroups and outgroups, or to think ethnocentrically. We are capable of thinking of *all humanity* as our ingroup, even if we do so very little now. My hope is that it will prove useful, for both ethical and scientific reasons, to bring focus to the ideal of identification with all humanity and to offer an operational measure of it. In the end, I want very much to help enlarge our identification with all humanity. But how can we do so?

Can identification with all humanity be taught? Today, in the United States at least, there are almost no public efforts at teaching it. In the 1970s, an American children's television series tried to do so. *Big Blue Marble*, named for its opening photo of the Earth surrounded by black space, featured stories of children from many cultures, encouraged intercultural pen pals, and the like. Its theme song contained the refrain,

> Folks are folks and kids are kids, we share a common name,
> We speak a different way but work and play the same. (Redwine & Paris, 1973)

If there are similar public efforts today, they are being drowned out by the blind patriotism and ingroup loyalty that dominate the public values now taught to children.

So, how do we enlarge identification with all humanity? Perhaps, in addition to resurrecting *Big Blue Marble*, the story of the Trocmés and stories of others like them can inspire this identification. Perhaps, as the moral intuition we found (McFarland & Brown, 2008) suggests, merely presenting the question in a Socratic way of how a moral and mature person would think regarding all humanity might inspire many to realize that it is a moral value they should make their own. In any case, now is the time to direct studies toward how identification with all humanity develops and can be taught. If it can be, our research would suggest that doing so would also enlarge concern for humanity's greatest problems, from crimes against humanity to global hunger.

References

Adler, A. (1954). *Understanding human nature*, W. B. Wolfe (Trans.). Greenwich, CT: Fawcett Publications (Original work published 1927).

Altemeyer, B. (1996). *The authoritarian specter*. Cambridge, MA: Harvard University Press.

Aquino, K. F., & Reed, A., II. (2002). The self-importance of moral identity. *Journal of Personality and Social Psychology*, *83*, 1423–1440. doi: http://dx.doi.org/10.1037/0022-3514.83.6.1423

Ashton, M. C., & Lee, K. (2009). The HEXACO-60: A short measure of the major dimensions of personality. *Journal of Personality Assessment*, *91*, 340–345. doi: http://dx.doi.org/10.1080/00223890902935878

Binder, J., Zagefka, H., Brown, R., Funke, F., Kessler, T., & Mummendey, A. (2009). Does contact reduce prejudice or does prejudice reduce contact? A longitudinal test of the contact hypothesis among majority and minority groups in three European countries. *Journal of Personality and Social Psychology*, *96*, 843–856. doi: http://dx.doi.org/10.1037/a0013470

Boehnke, K., Schwartz, S., Stromberg, C., & Sagiv, L. (1998). The structure and dynamics of worry: Theory, measurement, and cross-national replications. *Journal of Personality*, *66*, 745–782. doi: http://dx.doi.org/10.1111/1467-6494.00031

Brown, D. Z. (2008). *The effects of personal characteristics and religious orientations on identification with all of humanity and humanitarian behaviors*. Unpublished master's thesis. Western Kentucky University. Bowling Green, KY. Available at http://digitalcommons.wku.edu/theses/11

Clapham, A. (2007). *Human rights: A very short introduction*. New York: Oxford University Press.

Crandall, J. E. (1980). Adler's concept of social interest: Theory, measurement, and implications for adjustment. *Journal of Personality and Social Psychology, 39*, 481–495. doi: http://dx.doi.org/10.1037/0022-3514.39.3.481

Davis, M. H. (1983). Measuring individual differences in empathy: Evidence for a multidimensional approach. *Journal of Personality and Social Psychology, 44*, 113–126. doi: 10.1037/0022-3514.44.1.113

Davis, M. H., Luce, C., & Kraus, S. J. (1994). The heritability of characteristics associated with dispositional empathy. *Journal of Personality, 62*, 369–391. doi: http://dx .doi.org/10.1111/j.1467-6494.1994.tb00302.x

Graham, J., Haidt, J., & Nosek, B. A. (2009). Liberals and conservatives rely on different sets of moral foundations. *Journal of Personality and Social Psychology, 96*, 1029–1046. doi: http://dx.doi.org/10.1037/a0015141

Hackett, J. D., Omoto, A. M., & Matthews, M. (2015). Human rights: The role of psychological sense of global community. *Peace and Conflict: Journal of Peace Psychology, 21*, 47–67. http:/dx.doi.org/10.1037/pac0000086

Haidt, J. (2001). The emotional dog and its rational tail: A social intuitionist approach to moral judgment. *Psychological Review, 108*, 814–834. doi: 10.1037/0033-295X.108.4.814

Haidt, J., & Joseph, C. (2004). Intuitive ethics: How innately prepared intuitions generate culturally variable virtues. *Daedalus, 133*(4), 55–66. doi: 10.1162/0011526042365555

Hamer, K., & Gutowski, J. (2009). Social identifications and pro-social activity in Poland. In S. Scuzzarello, C. Kinnvall, & K. R. Monroe (Eds.), *On behalf of others: The psychology of care in a global world* (pp. 163–183). New York: Oxford University Press.

Hamer K., Penczek, M., & Bilewicz, M. (2014, July). *Mutual relationship of national and supranational identifications with forgiveness: Lights and shades of national identification*. Paper presented at the meeting of the International Society of Political Psychology, Rome.

Headley, J. M. (2008). *The Europeanization of the world: On the origins of human rights and democracy*. Princeton, NJ: Princeton University Press.

Kohlberg, L. (1969). Stage and sequence: The cognitive-developmental approach to socialization. In D. Goslin (Ed.), *Handbook of socialization theory and research* (pp. 374–480). Chicago: Rand McNally.

Leach, C., van Zomeren, M., Zebel, S., Vliek, M. W., Pennekamp, S. F., Doosje, B. . . . Spears, R. (2008). Group-level self-definition and self-involvement: A hierarchical (multicomponent) model of in-group identification. *Journal of Personality and Social Psychology, 95*, 144–165. doi: 10.1037/0022-3514.1.144

Lewis, G. J., & Bates, T. C. (2014). Common heritable effects underpin concerns over norm maintenance and in-group favoritism: Evidence from genetic analyses of right-wing authoritarianism and traditionalism. *Journal of Personality, 82*, 297–309. doi: http://dx.doi.org/10.1111/jopy.12055

Leyens, J. P., Paladino, P. M., Rodriguez-Torres, R., Vaes, J., Demoulin, S., Rodriguez-Perez, A., & Gaunt, R. (2000). The emotional side of prejudice: The attribution of secondary emotions to ingroups and outgroups. *Personality and Social Psychology Review, 4*, 186–197. http://dx.doi.org/10.1207/S15327957PSPR0402_06

Malsch, A. M. (2005). *Prosocial behavior beyond borders: Understanding a psychological sense of global community.* Unpublished doctoral dissertation, Claremont Graduate University, Claremont, CA.

Maslow, A. (1954). *Motivation and personality.* New York: Harper & Row.

McCutcheon, L. E., Pope, T. J., Grove, A. R., Bates, J. A., Richman, H., & Aruguete, M. (2015). Religious skepticism and its relationship to attitudes about celebrities, identification with humanity, and need for uniqueness. *North American Journal of Psychology, 17*, 45–58.

McFarland, S. G. (2006, July). *A Test of a Maslovian Model of "Oneness with All Humanity."* Paper presented at the International Society for Political Psychology, Barcelona, Spain.

McFarland, S. G. (2010a). Authoritarianism, social dominance, and other roots of generalized prejudice. *Political Psychology, 31*, 425–449. doi: http://dx.doi.org/10.1111/j.1467-9221.2010.00765.x

McFarland, S. (2010b). Personality and support for universal human rights: A review and test of a structural model. *Journal of Personality, 78*, 1735–1763. doi: http://dx.doi.org/10.1111/j.1467-6494.2010.00668.x

McFarland, S. G. (2010c, July). *Predicting the ethnocentric valuation of human life: Identification with all humanity, generalized prejudice, and other correlates.* Paper presented at the International Society of Political Psychology annual meeting, San Francisco.

McFarland, S. (2011). Presidential address: The slow creation of humanity. *Political Psychology, 32*, 1–20. doi: 10.1111/j.1467-9221.2010.00801.x

McFarland, S., & Brown, D. (2008). Who believes that identification with all humanity is ethical? *Psicologia Politica, 36*, 37–49.

McFarland, S., Brown, D., & Webb, M. (2013). "Identification with all humanity" as a moral concept and psychological construct. *Current Directions in Psychological Science, 22*, 194–198. doi: http://dx.doi.org/10.1177/0963721412471346

McFarland, S., & Hornsby, W. (2015). An analysis of five measures of global human citizenship. *European Journal of Social Psychology, 45*, 806–817. doi: http://ex.doi.org/10.1002/ejsp/2161

McFarland, S., & Mathews, M. (2005). Who cares about human rights? *Political Psychology, 26*, 365–386. doi: http://dx.doi.org/10.1111/j.1467-9221.2005.00422.x

McFarland, S., Webb, M., & Brown, D. (2012). All humanity is my ingroup: A measure and studies of identification with all humanity. *Journal of Personality and Social Psychology, 103*, 830–853. doi: http://dx.doi.org/10.1037/a0028724

Monroe, K. (1996). *The heart of altruism: Perception of a common humanity.* Princeton, NJ: Princeton University Press.

Nickerson, A. M. & Louis, W. R. (2008). Nationality versus humanity? Personality, identity, and norms in relation to attitudes toward asylum seekers. *Journal of Applied Social Psychology, 38*, 796–817. doi: http://dx.doi.org/10.1111/j.1559-1816.2007.00327.x

Oliner, S. P., & Oliner, P. M. (1988). *The altruistic personality: Rescuers of Jews in Nazi Europe.* New York: The Free Press.

Pratto, F., & Glasford, D. E., (2008). Ethnocentrism and the value of a human life. *Journal of Personality and Social Psychology, 95,* 1411–1428. doi: 10.1037/a0012636

Redwine, S., & Paris, N. (1973). *Big Blue Marble original theme song.* Santa Monica, CA.: A & M Records.

Reese, G., Proch, J., & Cohrs, J. C. (2013). Individual differences in responses to global inequality. *Analyses of Social Issues and Public Policy, xx,* 1–22. doi: http://dx .doi.org/10.1111/asap.12032

Reese, G., Proch, J., & Finn, C. (2015). Identity with all humanity: The role of self-definition and self-investment. *European Journal of Social Psychology, 45,* 426–440. doi: 10.1002/ejsp.2102

Reysen, S., & Katzarska-Miller, I. (2013). A model of global citizenship: Antecedents and outcomes. *International Journal of Psychology, 48,* 858–870. doi: http://dx.doi .org/10.1080/00207594.2012.701749

Roberts, B. W., Caspi, A., & Moffitt, T. E. (2001). The kids are alright: Growth and stability in personality development from adolescence to adulthood. *Journal of Personality and Social Psychology, 81,* 670–683. doi: http://dx.doi.org/10.1037/0022-3514.81.4.670

Schwartz, S. H. (1992). Universals in the content of structure and values: Theoretical advances and empirical tests in 20 countries. *Advances in experimental social psychology: Vol. 25.* New York: Academic Press. doi: 10.1016/S0065-2601(08)60281-6

Seligman, M. E. P., & Csikszentmihalyi, M. (2000). Positive psychology: An introduction. *American Psychologist, 55,* 5–14. doi: http://dx.doi.org/10.1037/0003-066X.55.1.5

Sidanius, J., & Pratto, F. (1999). *Social dominance.* New York: Cambridge University Press.

Thistlethwaite, D. (1950). Attitude and structure as factors in the distortion of reasoning. *Journal of Abnormal and Social Psychology, 43,* 442–458. doi: http://dx.doi.org/ 10.1037/h0060661

Trocmé, A. (2007/1971). *Jesus and the nonviolent revolution.* Farmington, PA: Plough Publishing House.

Wason, T. C. (1966). Reasoning. In B. M. Foss (Ed.), *New horizons in psychology* (pp. 135–151). Harmondsworth, UK: Penguin.

Watson, D., Clark, L. A., & Tellegen, A. (1988). Development and validation of brief measures of positive and negative affect: The PANAS scales. *Journal of Personality and Social Psychology, 54,* 1063–1070. doi: http://dx.doi.org/ 10.1037/0022-3514.54.6.1063

Appendix

Identification with All Humanity Scale (IWAH)

1. How close do you feel to each of the following groups?

    1 = not at all close
    2 = not very close
    3 = just a little or somewhat close

4 = pretty close
5 = very close
a. People in my community
b. Americans
c. People all over the world

2. How often do you use the word Awe to refer to the following groups of people?

1 = almost never
2 = rarely
3 = occasionally
4 = often
5 = very often
a. People in my community
b. Americans
c. People all over the world

3. How much would you say you have in common with the following groups?

1 = almost nothing in common
2 = little in common
3 = some in common
4 = quite a bit in common
5 = very much in common
a. People in my community
b. Americans
c. People all over the world

Please answer all remaining questions using the following choices:

1 = not at all
2 = just a little
3 = somewhat
4 = quite a bit
5 = very much

4. Sometimes people think of those who are not a part of their immediate family as a family. To what degree do you think of the following groups of people as family?

a. People in my community
b. Americans
c. All humans everywhere

5. How much do you identify with (that is, feel a part of, feel love toward, have concern for) each of the following?

a. People in my community
b. Americans
c. All humans everywhere

6. How much would you say you care (feel upset, want to help) when bad things happens to

   a. People in my community.
   b. Americans.
   c. People anywhere in the world.

7. How much do you want to be:

   a. a responsible citizen of your community.
   b. a responsible American citizen.
   c. a responsible citizen of the world.

8. How much do you believe in:

   a. being loyal to my community.
   b. being loyal to America.
   c. being loyal to all mankind.

9. When they are in need, how much do you want to help:

   a. people in my community.
   b. Americans.
   c. people all over the world.

29 It's All About Ignorance: Reflections from the Blue-eyed/ Brown-eyed Exercise

Jane Elliott

On Friday, April 5, 1968, I entered my third-grade classroom in Riceville, Iowa, determined to teach my students about the ugliness of prejudice and the discrimination that results from it. I had decided, while watching the news the night before, that the killing of Martin Luther King Jr., who had been one of our "Heroes of the Month" in February, could not go unnoticed by my students. Our lesson plan for the day, since we were involved in studying the Native American unit, was to learn the Sioux Indian prayer that says, "Oh, Great Spirit, keep me from ever judging a man until I have walked a mile in his moccasins." I had decided that I would arrange to have that prayer answered for my students, on this fateful day, by treating them fairly or unfairly, based solely on the color of their eyes. I didn't create this exercise from nothing, you realize; I modeled it on what I learned in the third grade about Adolph Hitler sending people into gas chambers, based, in part, on the color of their eyes. By the end of the day, my students had learned more than I had ever taught them before, and I had learned more than they had.

The first thing I learned was that I didn't know anything about racism, its causes, and/or effects. I had always been taught, by the significant adults in my environment, that discrimination is caused by prejudice, that prejudice is the problem. All you have to do is change people's hearts and behavioral change will follow. I was certain that the same thing would happen with my students; so, after we had said the Pledge of Allegiance to the Flag and had sung "God Bless America," we began to talk about the killing of Martin Luther King Jr. It was obvious that my students weren't internalizing anything that was being said; so I asked them whether they had any idea how it would feel to be treated as many people of color are treated in this country. Of course, they didn't, but they indicated that they'd like to try something that would help them know a little bit more than they knew about that situation.

I told them that skin color and eye color are caused by the same chemical, melanin, and perhaps we could spend the day judging one another by the color in our eyes. They were more than willing to do what I suggested: After all, most of the things that we did in that room were fun, so why shouldn't this be? When all the students were in agreement with the plan, I told them that brown-eyed people were smarter than blue-eyed people and I could prove it to them. Immediately, brown-eyed Debbie,[1] from her desk in the front row, looked up at me through her thick, corrective lenses and demanded, "How come yer the teacher, here, if you've got them blue eyes?" My first thought was, "Why, you little shit!" And my second thought was, "Well, now the fat's in the fire! How do you like being on the receiving end of your own plan?" I immediately justified my being the teacher by claiming that my father had hazel eyes and that gave me the right to be a teacher of children of all kinds, because I could understand people of all kinds.

That was only the beginning of a day of awesome enlightenment. I watched several brown-eyed dyslexic boys, who could neither read nor spell with any degree of accuracy, become readers and spellers in the space of a few minutes. I had, by that time in the year, been trying to teach those kids to spell and read for eight months, with very little success. And now, suddenly, because I changed my expectations of them, told them they had magic eyes, and reinforced their positive behaviors – and, of course, all their behaviors were positive, since they were brown-eyed – they were free to apply everything they had been exposed to in the previous days. Was I hysterical? Was my imagination working overtime?

Not only did my children with learning differences do better on that awful day, the children who until that day had been model students – bright, happy, smart, quick, interested, involved, caring little people – became frightened, timid, dull, disinterested, academically challenged children. They were afraid to speak up because it was obvious that none of their contributions were going to be positively reinforced and, indeed, might be ridiculed by those fellow students who, until they got those great eyes, had been their friends. Those former friends were now malicious, provocative little brown-eyed despots.

My students had never felt any ill will toward people based on the color of their eyes until I told them the lie, and then used every mistake the *Blueys* made to prove the reliability of my claims of their ineptitude. Of course, I also used everything that the *Brownies* accomplished to prove the validity of my claims of their brilliance.[2] I created prejudice where there had never been any previous to that day, and I reinforced it by either damning or praising their behaviors. The more I criticized the Blues, the more miserable they became, and the happier and more cooperative the Browns became. Alarmingly, the more I praised the Browns, the more they exhibited the same discriminatory behaviors that they had witnessed in the significant adults in their environment.

I think that was the most hideous aspect of that horrible day; For the first time in my life, I got to see the way I look to people of color, because, during that 6-hour period, my brown-eyed students exhibited the same behaviors they had seen me exhibit toward the blue-eyed students.

---

1 All names have been changed.
2 *Blueys* and *brownies* are terms commonly used refer to people with blue and brown eyes in the Blue-eyed/Brown-eyed exercise.

Robert Burns (1986), the Scottish poet, said, "O would some power the gift to give us to see ourselves as others see us." I got that opportunity on April 5, 1968, and it literally changed the way I see myself and the world around me.

I went to the teachers' lounge at lunchtime to find someone to whom I could describe what was happening in my classroom. I needed someone to share this agony with and, hopefully, help me resolve what I thought I was seeing in my students. A number of teachers were in the lounge, including the two other third-grade teachers. I tried to describe for them what was going on and when I'd finished my agonizing recounting of the morning's events, one teacher, who was in her early fifties, said to me: "I don't know how you have time to do that extra stuff; it's all I can do to teach reading, writing, and arithmetic." Well, in my estimation, she hadn't really taught reading, writing, and arithmetic yet, so she might as well have done the extra stuff.

As I recall, another teacher, who was in her early sixties and had been molding young minds for more than 30 years, responded to my despair over the killing of Martin Luther King Jr., by saying: "I don't know why you're doing that. I thought it was about time somebody shot that son-of-a-bitch." I waited for someone to contradict her, or at least to show some disapproval of what she had said. Not one teacher even frowned. No one asked her if she realized what she had just said. No one reminded her that she could lose her job for saying something so despicable. Every single one of those teachers either smiled or laughed and nodded. She had expressed their feelings perfectly, and, as the senior member of the group, she had the most right to do so. I went back to my classroom determined that no student would leave my classroom willing to tolerate expressions as ignorant as those that were voiced by those two "educators," and, seemingly, supported by the rest of the teachers in the lounge.

In the middle of the afternoon, we needed to use the pull-down wall map during social studies class; as I pulled down the map, the ring slipped off my finger and the map wrapped around and around itself, with that irritating flapping noise that we all hate. "Well," I said, "I've done it again!" At that point darling Debbie once again let me know exactly what my place was in that room: "Well, whaddaya expect? You've got blue eyes, havencha?" For just an instant, and as God is my judge, I was furious at that child, and then I became furious at myself. I had planned and executed this lesson to teach students not to treat others badly and here I was reacting the same way. And then, blue-eyed Alan, in the back row said, "Aw, Debbie. Her eyes ain't got nuthin to do with it. You know she never has been able to do that right." I didn't chastise him for making such a negative remark about me; I thanked him, because he was defending me, not as his teacher, but as a member of his "race." If my eyes could make me inferior, then his eyes, which were the same as mine, might have the same effect on him, and he had to let everyone know that eye color had nothing to do with the mistake; I was just naturally incompetent in that area, and always had been.

The Lessons I Have Learned

The Brown-eyed/Blue-eyed exercise was the beginning of 40+ years of teaching and learning about prejudice and discrimination. After having done the exercise with people ages 6 to 78, in most of the states of the United States, and several countries, I have come to the following conclusions, among others.

We've got the axiom wrong: Prejudice does not cause discrimination; discrimination causes prejudice. It's a simple scenario: Pick out a group of people on the basis of a physical characteristic over which they have no control; accuse those who are afflicted with that physical characteristic of being inferior; lower your expectations of them, and when they begin to live down to your expectations of them – as they will, since you won't allow them to exceed your expectations – use their incompetency to prove that your expectations were accurate. When they react negatively to your unfair treatment and/or words, blame their negative behavior on their inferiority, which is the result of that physical characteristic. In a very short time, you can convince them, and everyone witnessing this exchange, that you were right about your description of "those people" in the first place.

And, if you sustain the situation long enough, you can create a group of citizens who are so convinced of their own inadequacy that they can be led like lambs to the slaughter. It's even more profound if, once you get them convinced of their vulnerability and need for guidance, you convince the superior group members to contribute some learning or living materials for their use, thereby giving the superior group members the opportunity to remind everyone of how kind, accepting, and even loving the "good guys" are: "We're doing this because we love you, and you really ought to be grateful." It's even more powerful if you throw in some religiosity: "If God didn't want these people to be treated this way, He would have put a stop to it." Or, one of my favorites, "I'm so thankful that God made me White."

I suddenly realized, as a by-product of this exercise, how easy it is to hold onto power, no matter how undeserving you are of having it. All you have to do is appeal to our desires to be part of the power structure, to be accepted by the majority, and to be seen as one of the power players, and we will cooperate with despotic behaviors. I watched students in my third-grade classroom who had been best friends for years go to the dark side to guarantee that they would not be treated as the inferior group members were being treated. I saw the same behaviors in a grown man in an exercise in Kansas City who, when I asked him why he didn't defend one of his blue-eyed female peers, said, "Well, I knew it couldn't last forever, and as long as you're doing it to her, you aren't doing it to me."

Another lesson I've learned, after doing this exercise hundreds of times, is that we don't have a so-called Black problem. You can't blame 100% of the problem on 11% of the population, unless you're willing to admit that that 11% is more powerful than the other 89%. Skin color was not a problem until the 1700s, when Linnaeus began to categorize plants according to physical differences, and ignorant scientists decided that if it made sense to use his methods on plants, it would make equally good sense to categorize humans in the same way (see Linnaeus, 1788). They were wrong, and we are living with their errors to this day. You might say that we are heirs to their errors. The consensus among scientists is that the first modern human beings who evolved on this earth were undoubtedly Black, and every person living on the face of the earth today carries in his or her genetic structure the memory of those first Black females' genetic structure (Walker, Smith, & Smith, 1987). We are all members of the same race, the human race. Believing that there are four or five races on earth is like believing that the sun is a god in a golden chariot who flies across the sky every morning. That latter belief was an ancient Greek myth, and so is the story of several different races a myth.

I found out that you don't have to have people of color in your immediate environment to have racism. The presence of Black people isn't causing the problem. There were no people of color in Riceville, Iowa; yet, when I asked my students, that year and every year that I did the exercise, what they knew about Black people, they knew, and vehemently stated, every negative stereotype that I'd ever heard about Blacks, and some that would never have occurred to me. When I asked them how they knew these things were true, the answer was always the same, "Because my dad said so!" Those kids had never been in the company of a person of color and yet they knew, and were comfortable in repeating, all this garbage. Those innocent children had been systematically and deliberately taught to be racists; they were not born that way, nor were their parents. Their racism was the result of the conditioning that they had been exposed to by the power structure in this society.

I quickly became aware of the fact that the way White women and people of color in this country act is not because of a weakness peculiar to their genes; it's the way human beings react when they are treated unfairly on the basis of a physical characteristic over which they have no control. They aren't acting out because of the way White men feel about them, mind you. I suspect that most White women and people of color are more concerned about how they are going to be impacted by unfair behaviors than they are about others' attitudes toward them in general. The first time I really saw undeniable evidence of this is the day I was invited to speak to a Rotary Club luncheon in a nearby community. At that time, women weren't allowed to join the Rotary; but, since I'd been on the Johnny Carson *Tonight* show, as a result of an article written in the paper about the Blue-eyed/Brown-eyed exercise, I was deemed qualified to address their august group.

The leader of the Rotary Club and I decided we should put the members through the Blue-eyed/Brown-eyed exercise. After all, that Chinese proverb says, "Tell me and I forget. Show me and I remember. Involve me and I understand." Those men didn't understand and they went a little berserk, not because of my prejudice but because of the way I was treating them. That was 46 years ago, and one of the blue-eyed males was still so angry at me when I saw him 20 years later, he would cross the street to avoid meeting me as I walked near the store that my husband and I later owned in that community.

In 1985, I was hired to do the exercise with groups of employees in a major corporation in the western part of the United States. At the end of each exercise, as a culminating activity, I instructed each of the Brown-eyed people, who represented the power group in this exercise, to write three adjectives that described how the Blueys looked to them during the exercise. I instructed the Blueys to do the same thing – to write three adjectives describing how the Browns looked to them during this event.

The words were to be written without consultation among the members of the group. After all had finished writing, first the Browns and then the Blues read their words aloud so that the entire group could see how the participants viewed those who were in the opposite group. The words were utterly astounding. The Browns in that and every group that I've worked with in these 40+ years wrote the same words: distressed, inferior, intimidated, rebellious, docile, withdrawn, stupid, embarrassed, angry, confused, defensive, and frustrated. We then discussed how many of these words are the ones we use to describe women on a day-to-day basis. We had created a stereotype of a group of adult, educated, productive, capable White males and females that was similar in content to commonly held stereotypes of frightened White women and people of color. The Brown-eyed people in the group hadn't come to the workshop with those stereotypes in mind where the Blues were concerned; they were describing the way their fellow employees, half of whom were men, looked as a result of being treated unfairly because of their eye color.

Most of the words they used to describe their peers were those we most often use to describe women. When was the last time you heard a White male described as "docile"? Then I asked the Blues to read their words. They were arrogant, rude, cold, smug, hostile, uncaring, condescending, ignorant, aggressive, and belligerent. I asked the Blues why they used those words to describe their brown-eyed peers and they said, "Because that's the way they looked during this exercise!" Once, again, the writers weren't reacting to attitudes; they were reacting to behaviors. I then asked the people of color in the group if those are the words they use to describe us White folks when we aren't around and they responded with, "Those are some of the nicer ones." Prejudice? No, reactions to behaviors. We agreed that if White people didn't want to be described in those ways, perhaps they'd better change their behaviors toward those who are different from themselves; by making those changes, they might see changes in the way White women and people of color react to them.

Now, I know that I'm going to be castigated for blaming White people for racism. Get over that. I'm not talking about blame, here; I'm talking about responsibility. If we White folks who are so proud of having enough power to create change in this country don't want to be held responsible for the use and misuse of power, all we have to do is share the power, thus making everyone responsible for what happens on our streets and in our classrooms. Can we all take a moment to indulge in a fantasy? Let us imagine that the most powerful family-run businesses in the United States are going to be willing to share some of their power with those who have no power. What prevents that from happening? Is it because of the fear that we White people are now experiencing as we see ourselves losing our numerical majority in the United States? Are we acting in reaction to our dread that once people of color become the numerical majority, they will want to treat us the way we have treated them?

I've learned, while watching the bloviating shouters and spitters and exaggerators on TV, how powerful the media is and how dangerous it is when it is in the wrong hands and being used for the wrong reasons. I think it likely that the media, at the direction of people with unlimited financial resources, is willingly complicit in keeping this fear and these –isms alive, because, after all, fear sells. That, in my opinion, is exactly what's happening. I'm watching the media gin up situations all over the world, in an attempt, it seems to me, to further line the pockets of the owners of the military-industrial complex. Keep the masses frightened while we send their sons and daughters to fight in yet another old White men's war. And, of course, making war and soldiers is so much easier if young men can't get decent jobs and are programmed to be warriors by being encouraged to spend hours playing video games in which killing is routine and the winner of the game is the one who kills the best, the most, and the fastest. Dehumanize young people with what once would have been seen as unacceptable and immoral programming and then accuse them of being bullies and savages.

We aren't born racist. In my view, racism is a learned response and anything you learn, you can unlearn, if you choose to do so. I watched my father, after seeing the first film of the exercise that was made in my classroom, turn from the TV and, with tears in his eyes, say, "I wish somebody'd taught me that when I was nine years old." This was the man who, when I was in high school and would have given my eye teeth to date one of the most handsome and personable boys in school, said, "Stay away from him. His grandmother was a mulatto and that makes him an octoroon and you never know when that will show up in the next generation." "Mulatto?" "Octoroon?" Where did those words come from? My dad, whom I considered the most moral man I'd ever known, learned something from watching my third graders go through that exercise, and he changed his behavior as a result of it. He wasn't born a racist and he wished he'd had the same kind of conditioning that my students were getting. My own children worshipped the ground he walked on; when my daughter brought her Saudi-American baby home and put her in my father's arms, he said, "She's beautiful, Sarah. She's the most beautiful baby I've ever seen." And then there wasn't a dry eye in the house.

My father never spent much time talking about love, but he knew all about justice. I didn't really understand that until I'd done the Blue-eyed/Brown-eyed exercise and had read bell hooks's book *Killing Rage*. We'd all learned the Bible verses telling us that God is love, and that we are to love one another, and I really believed that was the right thing to do. I didn't spend a whole lot of time practicing it, but I believed it, and I also believed that if we all loved one another, we'd have peace on earth. All we had to do was follow the Golden Rule and treat others the way we wanted to be treated. What a power trip all that was! How do we know how all others want to be treated? I'm quite certain that young men and women wouldn't appreciate the treatment I appreciate. When a young man offers to put my luggage in the overhead rack on an airplane, I say, "Thank you very much." I doubt he'd appreciate my doing the same thing for him. And do you really believe that we Christians treat others the way we want to be treated? Do we want to be treated the way people of color and women and members of the LGBTQA are treated? You know better and so do I.

My father wasn't a church-going man, but he taught us that you should never put a stone in another man's path. He refused to "judge a book by its cover" and firmly adhered to the maxim that "A fair thing is a pretty thing and a right wrongs no man." He never treated us in a way that the world would consider lovingly, but neither did he ever treat us unjustly. He seemed to know, without ever saying it, that if you claim to love someone while you're treating them unjustly, they'll never treat you justly and they'll never really love you. However, if you treat others fairly, they are more likely to treat you fairly, and you might end up with a loving society, after all. We'll never have a loving society until we have a just one; bell hooks (1996) says this all so eloquently in *Killing Rage: Ending Racism*, that I hope everyone who reads this chapter will read her book too.

I've learned that those who become incensed at the sight of me putting my "poor little White students through that horrible exercise" have a great deal of difficulty sympathizing with those children of color who go through that kind of thing every day. I'll never forget the woman in the audience in Canada who, after the moderator introduced me and asked for questions from the audience, stood, and asked, "Don't you realize that you could do great psychological damage to those children by treating them that way?" I responded, "How do you feel about children of color who have to endure worse than that kind of abuse, every day?" Her bizarre reply was, as I recall, "That's different; they can take it." It was a moment almost identical to one in Denver, Colorado, where, during the debriefing of the exercise in a major corporation, a White woman turned to the Black woman next to her and said, "This was too harsh. It's never this bad outside of this room." When the Black woman pointed out that she and her children go through this every day, the White woman replied, "That's different. You're used to it. You can take it. We aren't used to being treated this way." Now, there are some diversity specialists who might call that simply responding to having lived a life of White privilege. I call it total insanity and unconscionable, self-imposed ignorance, and I'm utterly flabbergasted by the hypocrisy of calling people of color inferior to White people while expecting them to be stronger, more accepting, and more tolerant than White folks are.

And therein lies the rub. Perhaps what every White person needs to do is to walk in the shoes of a person of color in the United States for a day. Perhaps they would learn to listen more and talk less. Perhaps they would learn to talk *with* people of color, instead of talking at them or to them. Perhaps they'd learn to work with people of color instead of "doing for them." Perhaps they'd never say, as that 70

+-year-old woman in Rochester, Minnesota, said, to a group of vocal Black women, during the debriefing of the exercise, "Why are you people talking about me this way, after all I've done for you? I've tried to help you out, my whole life." She said it to the wrong group and in the wrong setting. But, you see, that's one of the difficulties in always thinking that the right way is the White way, and that we White people have all the answers. In my view, we don't even know the right questions! I wish I had a dime for every time I've heard a White woman say to a person of color, "Just what's it like, being Black?"

And now we come to something that we all ought to be aware of: Stop, for the love of Heaven, saying things like, "I think what we need is a color-blind society." Why must we not see skin color? Is there something wrong with it? Obviously not, since the first modern human beings who evolved on this earth were people of color. Or, how about this one, said to a Black person, "When I see you, I don't see you as Black." Oh, really? If you don't see them as Black, why do you say "Black"? Why don't you say, "I don't see you as orange"? Or green? Or purple? Or, perish the thought, White? And one of my absolute favorites, which is usually said in an attempt to stop affirmative action policies, "Why do we keep talking about differences? Similarities are more important than differences and we're all the same under the skin." I'm 80 years old, and I know that the pimply faced, adolescent boy in the front row at the college lecture is not the same as I am, under the skin. I also suspect that the person who asks that question would probably be the same one who says that for two people to get married, they'd better not be of the same sex.

Practically every time I speak at a corporation or educational facility, someone in the audience expresses the fear that children are being damaged by being treated in this cruel way for a day, that they may be irreparably harmed by this exercise. They say, "Do you ever think about that?" My response to that is as follows: How many of you demanded that your child get those vaccinations as infants, on the off-chance that they might someday be exposed to measles, mumps, diphtheria, smallpox, or polio? Every sensible one of you did, because you didn't want them to contract one of those diseases. This exercise is like those inoculations: It is a shot of the live virus of racism given so that when my former students are exposed to racism, they will recognize it and confront it, instead of letting it disrupt their lives and injure their souls. And let me remind you that there's no "likelihood" of their being exposed to racism (and ageism, and homophobia, and sexism, and ethnocentrism); it is a guarantee that they will be exposed to all the idiocy and ignorance of a society in which, as in the 1700s, we are still treating people unfairly on the basis of physical characteristics over which we have no control, and still being rewarded for doing so.

If I could, I'd invent a shot to be given to all children at birth that would make them immune to their parents' and grandparents' ignorance. I suspect, however, that, instead of giving the shots to the children, I'd administer them to the people who write our laws and our school curriculums. I'd also get my hands on someone in the Christian community who would be willing to stop making the pictures in bibles that make the Baby Jesus look like the Pillsbury Doughboy, and his mother, a Jewess in the Middle East, look like Marilyn Monroe.

In the final analysis, my view is that the problem isn't racism, because there's only one race. It is plain and simple ignorance. And we're all afflicted with it. Perhaps you remember the day Dianne Sawyer interviewed Alice Walker on TV. As I recall, after they'd talked about all the wonderful things that Alice Walker had said and written and done, Dianne Sawyer turned to her and said, "Alice, when I see you, I don't see a Black woman." "Well, Dianne," Alice Walker replied, "That would be pretty impossible." Sawyer, not to be denied her color-blindness, said, "But Alice, I don't see you as Black!" To which Alice Walker reiterated, "But, Dianne, I *am* Black!" At this point, Sawyer reached out, took hold of Alice Walker's forearm, gave it a vigorous shake, and said, "Oh, no!" *Ignorance*! I remember Walter Cronkite saying to three leaders of the Black community, the night after MLK was killed, "When our leader was killed, his widow held us together. Who's going to keep your people in line?" I remember changing the channel in disgust in time to hear Dan Rather saying to several leaders of the Black community, "Don't you think that you Black people should feel sympathy for White people, during this time, since we can't feel the anger that you Blacks do?" I think he used the word, "Negroes," but I've been trying to work that word out of my vocabulary, so I may be misquoting him, there. But the sentiment and insensitivity are the same, regardless of the vocabulary. In my view, these are all examples of ignorance but not necessarily racism.

There is a cure for this ignorance, and it's called "education." I don't mean the kind of schooling that is being provided in most institutions of learning, today. I mean *Education*. The word "educate" comes from the root *duc, duce*, which means lead; the prefix "e-," which means *out*; and the suffix "–ate," which means the *act of*. To educate someone is to be engaged in the act of leading them out of ignorance in every area, but particularly in the areas of empathy, understanding, and acceptance. That is the kind of education that will not show up on the standardized test results, but it is the kind that will make for a more empathetic and accepting society, in the future, for all of us. Rutstein (1993, p. 42) said in his book *Healing Racism in America* that "prejudice is an emotional commitment to ignorance." In my view he was right, and the cure for that ignorance is education.

Some Statements to Consider

So what does all this mean? It means that using the eye-color exercise has provided me with some enlightening experiences that have caused me to draw what I consider logical conclusions. You can argue with my conclusions, but you can't deny my experiences; so here are some statements for you to dispute:

1. *We are not equal.* I am not equal to any of the people I've met in the past 80 years; every one of them can do something I can't do or knows something I don't

know. However, while we aren't equal, we in the United States are guaranteed equitable treatment under the law. I'm not demanding equality; that's an impossible dream. I'm demanding equitable treatment under the law for all of us. And I want it now. Now, some of you will say that in the eyes of God we are all equal. Fine, but while I talk to God constantly, I work constantly with fallible human beings like myself, and we are the ones responsible for guaranteeing equitable treatment for all.

2. *Racism isn't the problem only of the uneducated, the poor, or the lower class.* They aren't the people who write and publish the textbooks, or who run for elective office, or who produce the television shows, or who teach in our schools. And all those entities contribute to the growing level of racism in this country.

3. *Love is not the answer to the problems of the –isms in our society; the answer is justice.* If we claim to love one another but do not treat one another justly, we will not have a loving society, or a just one. However, if we treat one another justly, we may very well find ourselves coming to love one another because we have no reason not to! A Black man at the premiere of the film "Blue Eyed" in Kansas City stood during the discussion following the film and said to the group, "All I want is for Whites to love and respect me." Look at the conundrum we have created with this ignorance: On the one hand, we teach that we must love and show respect for one another while we teach that only White people are truly lovable and deserving of respect. And we send that negative message throughout the media and our educational institutions, in our courts and our city councils, in our real estate associations and our lending institutions, in our libraries and our bookstores, in our country clubs and our fraternal organizations, in our military and maternity wards, in our cathedrals and our country churches. What we do speaks so loudly that it's hard for people of color to hear what we say. And it's even harder for them to believe what we say. But they keep on trying, and I'm damned if I know why.

4. *We don't need a color-blind society – unless there's something wrong with skin color.* What we need is a society that is no longer blinded by color. White people have been, and continue to be, conditioned to the myth of White superiority by the most powerful institutions in our country: the government, the churches, the education system, and the entertainment industry. Those are the agencies that shape our environments, and as long as they are directed by people who see differences as negatives, that's how long we will have racism in this country.

5. *Racism can create mental health problems.* In 1958, racism was identified as a powerful factor contributing to mental illness among children in the United States by the President's Joint Council on Mental Health in Children (Albee, 1958). And they weren't talking about only children of color. All children in a racist society are negatively impacted by racist policies, laws, and behaviors. You see, if you base your worth as a human being – or judge other peoples' worth – on the basis of the amount of a chemical in your, or their, skin, you aren't dealing well with reality and you need to get some therapy. Soon.

6. *White superiority is a myth.* It is a myth that has been foisted on us by about 500 years of conditioning calling itself "education" or, worse, "history," or, even worse, "science."[3]

7. *Racism is not something "out there."* It is not found only in large cities or in the South or where people of color live. Racism is within each of us and it has been

3 Now I realize that some of those who read this material may decide to write me a letter to tell me how wrong I am about all this. Good idea. You do that. But if you're going to be a racist, you're going to have to be very creative when you write that letter, because a good racist will want to give up all the things that people of color have made available for them in the United States. So you'd best write that letter before night since the carbon filament typically used in the lightbulb was invented by a Black man, Lewis Latimer (see Fouché, 2003). Now you're probably thinking that you'll light a candle. No, you won't. People of color had fire before White folks got cold (see James et al., 1989). So you'll wait until morning to compose your correspondence.

Fine, do it in the morning, but don't use an alarm clock to help you to get up on time; people of color had time-measuring devices before White folks realized that time was passing (see Barnett, 1999). Now, when you reach for that piece of paper on which to write your letter . . . Stop! We got paper from the Chinese and the Egyptians, most of whom we have described as being people of color (see Thompson, 1978). No more paper products of any kind for racists. That may make some aspects of your life a little difficult, but you'll find a way to deal with the problem. Now you're thinking that you'll use cloth for a writing surface. Think again. You can't use cotton; we got that from the Egyptians, the Chinese, and the people in India. You can't use silk; we got that from the Chinese. You can't use linen; we got that from the Egyptians. You can't use any woven fabrics because people of color were weaving fabrics while White folks were still looking for a "rabbit skin to wrap their baby bunting in." I'll help you out, here. Go out and find a nice, flat rock. People of color didn't invent rocks. You can scratch your message on a rock (see Harris, 1986, for the origins of writing).

But don't use the alphabet to convey your thoughts; we got our alphabet from the Egyptians and the Phoenicians, still more people of color (see Gardiner, 1916). You must draw pictures to convey your message. If you intend to include any statistics in your letter, you will, of course, express them in Roman numerals, since the numeration system of choice in this country is Arabic. You may, however, use the alphabet and Arabic numerals to address your envelope, since I'm not sure that most US postal workers will be able to decipher zip codes expressed in your "from-Whites-only" materials.

Once you get this rock wrapped and rolled and ready to go, you may be tempted to run out and jump into your automobile to go to the post office. Don't do it. Your car runs on rubber tires and we first got rubber from natives of South America whom we identified as people of color, so of course you'll give up all rubber products (Hosler, Burkett, & Tarkanian, 1999). We may end up having a lot more little racists running around, eh? No problem. You've decided to walk to the post office. Barefooted, I hope, unless you have hand-sewn shoes, since the machine that we use for sewing shoes together mechanically was invented by a Black man, Jan Ernst Matzileger (see Van Sertima, 1983).

Now, when you get your shoes on and start your walk to the post office, you may come to a stop light. Don't stop. The traffic signal was invented by a Black male, Garrett Morgan (see Asante, 2002). You're going to go through that signal and, when you do, some other blue-eyed fool is going to come tearing down the street in his car, run that signal, hit you, and knock you galley-west. They're going to rush you to the hospital where you'll probably need a blood transfusion using stored plasma. Don't take it. A Black man, Dr. Charles Richard Drew, was instrumental in developing that process during the Second World War, so you'll never take a blood transfusion using stored plasma (see Asante, 2002).

Now, all of this may be giving you a headache and you may be tempted to take an aspirin. Resist that temptation, at all costs, for we got aspirin from the Egyptians (Nunn, 2002). You'll just have to learn to live with pain. Perhaps you're one of those people who eat to relieve his or her tension and you're ready to race to the cupboard or pantry for relief. Well, be very careful what you choose to munch on, because the vast majority of grains and other cereal crops came to us from people of color (Diamond, 1998). Now you may be tempted to buttress your belief in White superiority by quoting from the Bible. Please be aware that the basic tenets of every major religion on the face of the earth originated in societies of people of color (Parrinder, 1999). As you can see, a committed racist, and I think all racists should be committed, who lives his or her belief in White superiority may not live very comfortably or for very long, but at least he or she will die happy. Now, about those funeral customs . . .

planted there by a racist society and is being nurtured by those with whom we communicate. Many people from little all-White communities in the midwestern United States, who have never been in the company of people of color, carry the stereotypes of those "others" who are different from themselves with them wherever they go and absolutely refuse to deny their conditioning at the same time that they are denying their racism. The presence of these stereotypes is obvious in the language they use and the behaviors they exhibit when they encounter people of color, or when they read about, think about, hear about, or talk about those who are other than White.

8. *Racism is not a Christian value.* The Vatican released a document in 1988 stating that "Harboring racist thoughts and entertaining racist attitudes is a sin" (Pontifical Commission, 1988, p. 34). Therefore, according to Pope John Paul II, those of you who choose to maintain your Christianity will have to give up your racism. And those who choose to maintain their racism will have to give up their Christianity. I know people in the United States who will give up their Christianity rather than their racism because they have seen proof in this country that racism is stronger than Christianity. If it isn't, why is racism such a strong and enduring force in our "Christian Nation" of the United States? I'm relieved that a pope finally spoke out about this problem, even though it seems to me that his words have been pretty much ignored in the past few years. Now, if we can just get the present pope to address sexism . . .

9. *"Good deeds will not go long unpunished."* If, as a result of reading this chapter, you become even more determined to actively work at reducing racism, sexism, ageism, homophobia, and ethnocentrism, be prepared to suffer "the slings and arrows" of outraged others. You'll soon need a support group, so I'd suggest that you share this material with someone you trust and then organize a 12-step program for Recovering Racists. You think I'm being facetious. Think again. Habits of a lifetime are hard to break, particularly when the society responds positively to perpetuation of those undesirable habits and negatively to any attempted change. Remember this: Some people grow older while others grow up. It's a choice you make. It's time for us to stop raising children and start raising reasoning, responsible adults.

Concluding Comments

Okay, so how do we start those changes? Start with yourself, by going to my website, janeelliott.com, and downloading the learning materials you will find there. Follow the directions on each sheet and then read every book listed in the bibliography. In my view, education is the answer to the whole problem and the fact that you've read this chapter is an indication either that you found it educational or that you are lost on a desert island and this book is the only thing you salvaged out of your luggage. I hope it's the former, instead of the latter.

References

Albee, G. W. (1958). *The task force on mental health* (2nd annual report). Cambridge, MA: Joint Commission on Mental Illness and Health.

Asante, M. K. (2002). *100 greatest African Americans: A biographical encyclopedia.* Amherst, NY: Prometheus Books.

Barnett, J. E. (1999). *Time's pendulum: From sundials to atomic clocks, the fascinating history of timekeeping and how our discoveries changed the world.* Boston: Houghton Mifflin Harcourt.

Burns, R. (1986/1786). To a louse: On seeing one on a lady's bonnet at church. *The Poetical Works of Burns: Cambridge Edition*, 43–44.

Diamond, J. M. (1998). *Guns, germs, and steel: A short history of everybody for the last 13,000 years.* London: Vintage.

Fouché, R. (2003). *Black inventors in the age of segregation: Granville T. Woods, Lewis H. Latimer, & Shelby J. Davidson.* Baltimore: Johns Hopkins University Press.

Gardiner, A. H. (1916). The Egyptian origin of the Semitic alphabet. *The Journal of Egyptian Archaeology, 3*(1), 1–16.

Harris, R. (1986). *The origin of writing.* Lasalle, IL: Open Court.

hooks, b. (1996). *Killing rage: Ending racism.* New York: Henry Holt and Company.

Hosler, D., Burkett, S. L., & Tarkanian, M. J. (1999). Prehistoric polymers: Rubber processing in ancient Mesoamerica. *Science, 284*(5422), 1988–1991.

James, S. R., Dennell, R. W., Gilbert, A. S., Lewis, H. T., Gowlett, J. A. J., Lynch, T. F. . . . James, S. R. (1989). Hominid use of fire in the Lower and Middle Pleistocene: A review of the evidence [and comments and replies]. *Current Anthropology, 30*(1), 1–26.

Linnaeus, C. (1788). *Systema naturae per regna tria naturae secundum classes, ordines, genera, species* (Vol. *1*). Leipzig: Impensis Georg Emanuel Beer.

Nunn, J. F. (2002). *Ancient Egyptian medicine.* Norman: University of Oklahoma Press.

Parrinder, E. G. (1999). *World religions: From ancient history to the present.* New York: Barnes & Noble Books.

Pontifical Commission.(1988). Justitia et Pax: The church and racism: Towards a more fraternal society. Washington, DC: United States Catholic Conference.

Rutstein, N. (1993). *Healing racism in America.* Springfield, MA: Whitcomb Publishing.

Thompson, S. O. (1978). Paper manufacturing and early books. *Annals of the New York Academy of Sciences, 314*(1), 167–176.

Van Sertima, I. (1983). *Blacks in science: Ancient and modern.* Piscataway, NJ: Transaction Publishers.

Walker, A. C., Smith, S. D., & Smith, S. D. (1987). Mitochondrial DNA and human evolution. *Nature, 325*, 1–5.

Index

acculturation, 13, 147, 414, 419–421, 424, 426–428, 430–434, 436–437, 480
affordance management, 7, 24–25, 30, 34, 38
aggression, 37, 94, 102, 109, 122, 127–128, 131, 140, 142, 144, 157, 164, 174, 209, 233, 237, 282, 300–303, 315, 318, 325, 329–330, 334, 337, 339, 354, 417, 478, 573, 638
Allport, 3–4
Ambivalent Racism, 10, 270
Ambivalent Sexism Theory, 11, 295–296, 300, 308, 312, 322
anger, 8, 25, 35, 37, 112–117, 119–126, 128–129, 131–132, 137, 142–143, 182, 356, 487, 490–491, 498, 530, 568, 582, 643, 664
anti-atheist prejudice, 12, 45, 345, 355, 359–362, 365
anti-gay prejudice, 205, 359, 375
anti-immigrant prejudice, 13, 453
Aversive Racism, 10–11, 267, 270, 274, 284

benevolent sexism, 11, 19, 184, 220, 295–296, 298–299, 311–317, 319, 321–324, 326–333, 335, 337–342, 457, 492, 496
Big Data, 6

collective action, 8, 14, 18, 56–58, 60–62, 64, 82, 86, 121–122, 129, 162, 168, 313, 390, 428, 470–471, 474, 480–481, 485–495, 497–499, 617, 623–624
common identity, 8, 74, 78, 85, 89, 104, 281–282
conflict resolution, 9, 16, 125, 598, 625, 628
contact valence, 13, 20
contempt/disgust, 8, 115, 117
criminal justice, 15, 19, 184, 259–260, 494, 542–546, 548–549, 551–553
cultural diversity, 13, 88, 105, 422, 426–429, 433

developmental process, 16
disordered eating, 12, 398, 407
Dual Process Model, 9, 188, 374, 386
dyadic modelling, 11

Electroencephalography, 10, 252
empathy, 9, 16, 56, 97, 119, 121–122, 124, 137, 143, 152, 158, 173, 196–197, 220, 228, 233, 326, 373, 411, 464, 475, 484, 490, 494, 533–535, 540, 619, 622, 635, 639, 641, 644–645, 647, 650, 664
epidemiology, 15, 561, 577
ERP, 96–97, 252, 256–257, 259
ethnocentrism, 43, 52, 66, 91, 94, 105, 178, 202–203, 205, 213, 229, 237, 419, 422, 440–444, 456, 477, 504, 517, 538, 635–636, 638–639, 641–644, 663, 667
evidence-based, 4, 10, 16, 607, 611
Evolutionary Psychology, 21–24
eye-tracking, 96
eyewitness identification, 15, 550, 557–558

false consciousness, 54, 62, 178, 458, 489
fear, 8, 21, 24, 25, 35, 37–38, 56, 82, 113, 115–117, 119, 122–124, 126, 128, 131–132, 135, 137, 140, 142, 164, 194, 206, 213, 229, 264, 269, 271, 299, 309, 335, 348, 354, 371, 398, 415, 418, 440, 446, 452, 494, 496, 502, 515, 583–584, 593, 599, 611, 621, 638, 661, 663
field experiments, 16, 253, 562
Field research, 94
fMRI, 96–97, 250, 252, 255–256, 264–265, 304
Functional Magnetic Resonance Imaging, 10, 250

gender inequality, 11, 299, 304–306, 309, 311–312, 314, 316, 318, 323, 326, 328–329, 331, 333, 337–338, 340, 457, 496
generalized prejudice, 13, 157, 172, 188, 190, 203, 213–215, 218, 364, 386, 438–446, 448–453, 457–458, 632, 635, 651
genetic, 6, 10, 22, 31, 91, 212, 217, 222–238, 645, 650, 659
Go/No-Go Association Task, 10, 249
group status, 8, 13, 20, 211, 265, 281, 336, 473, 522–527

health, 15, 19, 147, 159–160, 182, 259, 276, 305,
    307, 348, 353, 358, 369, 371, 383, 387, 389,
    393, 395, 397–398, 401–403, 409–410, 414,
    494, 559–562, 564–580, 617, 640, 665
health outcomes, 15, 159, 560, 562, 564,
    566–569, 572–573
heritability, 10, 16, 224–235, 237–238, 650
heritability of prejudice, 10, 231, 235
heterosexism, 12, 183, 317, 372, 561, 571
historical paradigms, 4–6
homophobia, 12, 282, 371, 387–389, 483, 663,
    667
hostile sexism, 203, 298, 301, 304, 313, 316–317,
    322–328, 330, 333–335, 337–340, 384
humanitarian, 16, 119, 125, 637, 640–641,
    647–648

Implicit Association Test, 10, 148, 247–248, 260,
    262–265, 274, 290–291, 355, 572
implicit prejudice, 10, 15, 123, 138, 244,
    252–253, 260, 263, 267, 279–280, 291, 439
indirect contact, 13, 466, 475–476, 479
Information Search Model, 14, 519–520, 523,
    526–527, 531, 536
ingroup bias, 8, 11, 72, 82, 88, 90–91, 93–95, 97,
    102–104, 106, 110, 117, 256, 265
Ingroup Projection Model, 8, 66
ingroup prototypicality, 68–69, 78, 82, 89, 109
intergroup conflict, 9, 31, 43, 47, 64–65, 89,
    106–107, 115, 122, 124–125, 220, 348,
    353–355, 390, 415, 459, 469, 472, 474, 476–477,
    479–480, 490, 494, 496, 499, 599, 624
intergroup contact, 9, 12–14, 20, 62–63, 82, 109,
    116, 125, 131–132, 134–135, 147–148, 174,
    206–207, 213, 217, 288, 308, 362, 377–378,
    381, 389, 417, 420, 429, 431–433, 435, 451,
    459, 463–464, 466–468, 472–473, 475–479,
    483, 490–491, 493–498, 509, 514, 520–522,
    527, 529, 531, 533–534, 538–540, 611, 647
Intergroup Emotions Theory, 8, 19, 111
Intergroup Threat Theory, 9, 13, 147, 459
intimate relationships, 11, 284, 298, 302–303,
    312, 322, 326, 328–330, 334, 336, 339

job hiring, 10, 102
justice system, 15, 19, 260, 542–544, 547,
    551–553, 610

legitimizing myths, 9, 200–201

mass media, 16, 393, 397, 608, 616–617, 623,
    625–627, 629
medical, 10, 23, 139, 254, 276, 282, 287,
    292–293, 384, 395, 398–399, 405–406,
    409–410, 578, 646
mental health, 15, 567, 569–571

minimal group, 27, 55, 91, 94, 106, 108–109, 450,
    459, 465
minority groups, 15, 47, 48, 51, 56, 62, 79, 172,
    231, 258, 271, 382, 422, 430, 442, 467–468,
    470–471, 474–475, 479, 482, 498, 536, 552,
    560, 649
Modern Racism, 10, 269, 291
multicultural ideology, 14, 217, 422–424, 432,
    532
Muslim prejudice, 12, 345, 354–356, 362, 425

neuropsychological, 6, 10
Neuroscience, 44, 96, 107, 110, 250, 255,
    259–260, 263–265, 292, 367, 558, 576, 579
nonverbal behaviour, 10

oppression, 3, 7, 11, 19–20, 63, 149, 159–160,
    163, 169, 184, 220, 293, 369, 384, 435, 459,
    559–564, 566–567, 569–572, 614
outgroup hostility, 4, 8, 90, 94, 157

paternalism, 298, 342
peer socialization, 12, 377, 379, 381
perceived discrimination, 15, 54, 63, 160, 420,
    426, 432, 479, 566–567
perceived stereotypicality, 15, 543, 545–553,
    556–557
physical health, 15, 398, 560, 566, 569, 573
political conservatism, 10, 133, 186, 198, 218,
    228, 231–233, 254, 269, 389
political mobilization, 14
political psychology, 95, 599, 605
prejudice reduction, 11, 13–14, 16, 18, 56–57, 64,
    89, 206, 389, 431, 479–481, 483–484,
    486–487, 489–490, 492–495, 499, 514, 516,
    541, 607–608, 624
priming designs, 10

reducing prejudice, 8, 13, 15, 17, 206–207, 362,
    378, 513, 624
reducing sexism, 296, 308–309, 311
relative deprivation, 486
religion, 12, 31, 70, 135, 243, 284, 344–346,
    349–357, 359, 361–363, 366–370, 384, 393,
    439, 500, 514, 632–633, 643, 666
Right-Wing Authoritarianism, 9, 12, 172, 175,
    177, 181, 183, 185, 191, 214, 218, 220, 366,
    456

Self-Categorization Theory, 7, 64, 113
Self-Regulation of Prejudice, 14, 504–505
sexual identity, 12
sexual prejudice, 12, 36, 180, 227, 371–390, 450,
    457
sexual stigma, 12, 372
sexual violence, 11, 300–301, 313, 315